## EUROPE BY TRAIN

KATIE WOOD was born and educated in Edinburgh, where she read Communications then English at university. After a short spell in Public Relations she spotted the gap in the market for a guide on training round Europe on a budget. *Europe by Train* allowed her to combine her two greatest loves, travelling and writing, and the first edition of this now-classic book was published in 1983. Since then she has written some 34 guidebooks on topics ranging from family holidays to the environmental and social impacts of tourism. Her books have been universally praised for their practical, down-to-earth approach and the quality of her research.

A fellow of the Royal Geographical Society, Katie continues to travel widely and write freelance for numerous newspapers and magazines, from the *Wall Street Journal* to *Bella* magazine and is currently the Travel Editor of the *Sunday Post* newspaper.

She lives in Perthshire with her husband and two sons, but remains addicted to 'do it yourself', money-saving travel. Her books encourage thousands of young people each year to stretch their wings and experience the wonders of a world she knows and loves so well.

*[Handwritten notes:]*

Doc note
r conditions,
accomodate,
neds

hw

Phone #s :
- U.S. Consolate
- Disabled traveller agency
  phone # (car rentals, tours)
- train stations (advanced -
  w.c. accommodation notice)
- #/List of banks/BOA

Multiple copies of passports
- Temple - Oviedo phone #s
  to ensure pickup from
  train station

*Also by Katie Wood and published by Robson Books:*

Cheap Sleeps Europe

# EUROPE BY TRAIN

**KATIE WOOD**

### RESEARCHERS
Peter Gibbs
Henrietta McClure

Robson Books

First published by Fontana 1983

This edition first published in Great Britain in 2000 by Robson Books, 10 Blenheim Court, Brewery Road, London N7 9NT

A member of the Chrysalis Group plc

British Library Cataloguing in Publication Data
A catalogue record for this title is available from the British Library

ISBN 1 86105 306 1

Printed by Mackays of Chatham plc, Chatham, Kent

# CONTENTS

Foreword 8
Introduction 10
*Cheap Sleeps Europe* 11
Map of Europe 12-13

**PART ONE: EURORAILING**

**The Advantages of Train Travel** 16

**Travelling Europe by Train: The Options** 19
BIJ – Eurotrain – Wasteels – Rail Europe – Inter-Rail – Eurail – The Europass – Country passes – Special trains – Other services

**Before You Go** 34
Preplanning Crossing the Channel – The Channel Tunnel Connections – The Future Getting to Europe by Plane – 'No-frills' Airlines – Charter Flights – Passports and Visas – Health

**Essential Preparation** 45
What to take – Budgeting – Money – Insurance – Politics – Last-minute reminders

**Train Information** 57
Night travel – Eating – Train splitting – Supplements – Timetables – Public holidays affecting trains – Hazards – Trains in Eastern Europe – Train and bike travel

**Station Information** 66
Pictograms – Reservations – Some helpful tips

**When You're There** 70
Accommodation – Eating – City transport – Communications – Shopping – Tipping – Women travellers – Lone travellers – Gay and lesbian travellers – Disabled travellers

**PART TWO: THE COUNTRIES**

**Austria** 89
Vienna – Southern Austria – Graz – Central Austria – Salzburg – Western Austria – Innsbruck

**Belgium** 115
Ostend – Bruges – Brussels – Southern Belgium – Antwerp – Ghent

**Bosnia-Hercegovina** 137
Sarajevo – Mostar – Medujorde

**Bulgaria** 141
Sofia – Plovdiv – Veliko Tąrnovo – Black Sea Coast

**Croatia** 153
Zagreb – Dalmatian Coast – Dubrovnik – Istrian Peninsula

**The Czech Republic** 161
Brno – České Budéjovice – Pilsen – Prague – Olomouc

**Denmark** 175
Copenhagen – Århus – Odense – Aalborg – Legoland

**Estonia** 191
Tallin

**Finland** 199
Helsinki – Turku – Tampere – Northern Finland – Oulo – Southern Finland – Savonlinna – Imatra

**France** 215
Calais – Rouen – Bayeux – Mont St Michel – Brittany – The Loire Valley – Paris – Alsace and Lorraine – Strasbourg – The Alps – Burgundy – Dijon – Lyon – The Riviera – Nice – Marseille – Provence – Avignon – Arles – Nîmes – Aix-en-Provence – Central/South-West France – Bordeaux – Cerbère

**Germany** 261
Berlin – Potsdam – Dresden – Leipzig – Weimar – Erfurt – Northern Germany – Bremen – Hamburg – Lübeck – Hannover – The Central Belt and the Harz Mountains – The Black Forest – Heidelberg – Freiburg – Tübingen – Stuttgart – The Harz Mountains – The Rhine Valley – Cologne – The Moselle Valley – Frankfurt – Trier – Munich – Augsburg – The Alps and the Romantic Road – Würzburg

**Greece** 313
Northern Greece – The Peloponnese – Athens – The Islands – The Saronic Gulf Islands – The Cyclades – Santorini – The Sporades – North-East Aegean – The Dodecanese – Crete – The Ionian Islands – Corfu

**Hungary** 347
Budapest – The Danube Bend – The Hungarian Plain – Lake Balaton – Western Hungary – South-West Hungary – Pécs

**Ireland** 365
Dublin – South-East Ireland – Cork – South-West Ireland – Limerick – Galway – Connemara – North-West Ireland

**Italy** 397
Northern Italy – Piedmont and Trentino – Lombardy – Milan – Emilia-Romagna – Bologna – The Italian Riviera – Genoa – Veneto – Venice – Verona – Padua – San Marino – Tuscany – Florence – Siena – Pisa – Umbria – Rome – Southern Italy – Naples – Puglia – Sicily – Sardinia

**Latvia** 465
Riga

**Lithuania** 473
Vilnius

**Luxembourg** 481
Luxembourg City – Provincial Luxembourg

**Macedonia** 491
Skopje – Western Macedonia

**Morocco** 499
Tangier – Rabat – Casablanca – Marrakech – Meknes – Fez – Off-the-track places

**The Netherlands** 517
Northern Netherlands – Amsterdam – Outside Amsterdam – The Hague – Rotterdam – Southern, Central and Eastern Netherlands – Haarlem

**Norway**  537
Southern Norway – Stavanger –
Kristiansand – Oslo – Central
Norway: The Sognefjord – Bergen –
Trondheim – Bodø – Northern
Norway: Nordland – North Cape

**Poland**  557
Warsaw – Cracow – Gdańsk – Toruń –
Poznań – Wrocław

**Portugal**  579
Lisbon – Porto and the Costa Verde –
The Costa Prata – The Plains and
Mountains – The Algarve

**Romania**  595
Bucharest – Transylvania – Moldavia
– The Black Sea Coast – Western
Romania

**Russia and Belarus**  611
Moscow – St Petersburg – Elsewhere
in European Russia – Belarus

**Slovakia**  629
Bratislava – Košice

**Slovenia**  637
Ljubljana – Lake Bled – South-West
Slovenia

**Spain**  649
Madrid – San Sebastián – Northern
Spain – Andorra – Barcelona – Valen-
cia – Central Spain: Castile –
Andalusia – Seville – Costa del Sol –
Gibraltar

**Sweden**  683
Stockholm – Malmö – Gotland –
Gothenburg – Lapland

**Switzerland**  701
Zürich – Lucerne – Berne – The
Bernese Oberland – Lausanne – Basel
– Geneva – The Grisons – Ticino –
Liechtenstein

**Turkey**  731
Istanbul – North-West Turkey – The
Aegean Coast – Mediterranean Coast
– Central Anatolia – Ankara – Eastern
Turkey

**The Ukraine**  747
Kiev – Lvov – Odessa – Simferopol,
Yalta and the Crimea

**The United Kingdom**  759
London – Southern England – Bath –
Devon and Cornwall – Oxford –
Stratford – Cambridge – South Wales
– North Wales – Northern England –
Liverpool – York – Scotland: Edin-
burgh – Glasgow – The Highlands –
Northern Ireland

**Yugoslavia**  805
Belgrade – Bar

**Appendices**  809
I    Inter-rail discounts  810
II   British, Irish and continental
     ferries  817
III  Eurail aid offices  818
IV   CIEE offices  822
V    Tourist offices  825
VI   International telephone
     codes  829
VII  Common conversions  830
VIII Basic vocabulary  831

**Index**  833

# FOREWORD

This guide is unique. Sure, there are plenty of other travel books that mention train travel in passing, but no other devotes every page to comprehensive coverage of train and station information as well as details of budget accommodation and sightseeing. This guide stemmed from economy-minded travel all over Europe and is researched and updated each year. It was created because I, like thousands of others, needed such a book and it didn't exist.

*Europe by Train* is now in its 18th year and I hope you will enjoy reading it and benefit from my experiences. It highlights the finds made when travelling around Europe on a tight budget in recent years and explains the different ways of using various rail passes which offer an exceptional opportunity to get around, see the sights, meet new people and broaden your horizons. This guide will help make your trip easy, relaxed and most of all, enjoyable. Bon voyage.

### PRICES AND EXCHANGE RATES
Because these fluctuate, we can only give a rough guide. As a reference, this book uses £1 = $1.60, but this rate (and all prices listed herein) is subject to change. The cost of living in former communist countries is particularly vulnerable to inflation as these countries move further towards a market economy.

### FREE BOOKS FOR THE MOST HELPFUL LETTERS
Please feel free to write in with your comments and suggestions. Obviously, in a book containing the amount of data that this one does, information and prices quickly go out of date. Though I try to update as thoroughly as possible every year, I would appreciate your assistance if you find something that has changed or if you feel a place deserves more detailed treatment. While I enjoy reading about your experiences, please keep your letters brief and concise (2 sides of A4 maximum, preferably typed). Try to give me as much detail as possible (i.e. full address, telephone number and directions), and quote the relevant page numbers from *Europe by Train*. The writers of the 6 best letters of 2000 will each receive a free copy of the updated 2000 guide.

All correspondence should be addressed to me, care of my publishers, at the address in the front of the book.

**ANY POTENTIAL RESEARCHERS OR BUDDING JOURNALISTS OUT THERE?**

Many of you write asking if I need researchers to help me update my guides. I do; however, there are stringent rules that apply.

**RESEARCHER CRITERIA:**

1. You must have travelled very extensively.
2. You must be very interested in travel. I mean maniacally interested, not just keen on going to foreign parts. Are you the type who never misses a travel programme; who immediately turns to the travel sections of newspapers and magazines; who yearns for foreign travel more than anything else?
3. Do you know, or are you prepared to learn, all about the travel industry?
4. Do you write well? You need to be up to A-level English at least, preferably degree level, and be competent in your use of language. You will need to be concise yet interesting. Can you read a tourist booklet and translate it into a couple of sentences? Could you pick out the most salient points? This is what guide-book writing is all about.
5. Can you work to deadlines? Publishing schedules wait for no one, and if a guide isn't on the shelves by the holiday season, forget it. I work to very strict deadlines and I am a hard task mistress! And the fact that you had to stay up half the night to finish your piece should not be obvious to the reader. Could you deliver in time? You will be contractually bound to do so.

If, after reading the requirements, you still feel you have what it takes, please send me a fully typed CV, photo, list of where you've travelled and samples of any published writing or any travel writing to me care of the publishers (address on preceding pages). If you do not comply with these rules, no reply will be sent. Sorry, but each year I'm inundated with enquiries and can only respond to those who have shown that they can follow instructions.

# INTRODUCTION

Congratulations! Well done. You have dipped into this book because you are the sort of person who loves a bargain and hates wasting money. You have a yearning to find out more about that intriguing Continent on your doorstep, you have a spirit of adventure and the capacity to enjoy life to the full. You are a person after my own heart. A sand and sangria holiday, cosseted in a Costa high-rise is clearly not for you, or me.

Rail travel is retro? Not a bit of it. It's fast, efficient, majestic, like riding in a limousine with your baggage close at hand. Recently, I asked a group of Eurorail addicts to describe the experience in a word. Immediately two said 'fun' and three said 'romantic'. Now when was the last time you heard those words used about air or coach travel? It's true, as you glide out of a big station, looking for adventure and whatever comes your way, that subtle and persistent rhythm soon finds a way of lifting your heart. It's an amazingly sociable form of transport that draws you to people and allows you to focus on the ambiance and culture of a country as stations, local characters, and scenery come and go.

Does this book work? Don't take my word for it. *'An absolute godsend'… 'my best travelling companion'… 'our sixth trip using your guide'*, are typical comments from recent letters. As you can see, it's crammed cover to cover with practical advice and tells you 99.9% of everything you need to know for getting about and finding a bed for the night. The remainder, I'm afraid, you'll have to discover for yourself!

If you are still in doubt, sketch out your route and check out the many special deals on offer. See how favourably the cost of Eurorailing compares with other means of travel. See too how astonishingly fast it is becoming. On inter-city routes it's often faster than flying. By the year 2003 London–Brussels will take just two hours, London-Paris 2hr 20mins. Then consider the 'hassle factors' of coach, car and plane. You'll be convinced there's no easier way to go. With big investments underway in many areas for new trains, track and facilities, all this can only get better.

So pack your bags, pack this book, and get your ticket to ride. Go on, turn the page and jump right into the world of opportunities that Eurorailing opens up. You will love it.

Katie Wood
January 2000

# Cheap Sleeps Guide

Every year, the most common question I am asked is how to make finding accommodation easier. From years of experience on the rails of Europe, I can sympathize, and agree that finding a bed is the one drawback of flexible rail travel. Booking too many beds ahead decidedly cramps your style, yet spending a night in a station or park leaves you vulnerable, exhausted the next day, and is far from ideal.

There are enough hostels, pensions and campsites to go around in Europe (supply does keep pace with the demand) – it's just a case of knowing where to go and in which areas to look. This is fine if you have spent the last 10 years doing it, but most Eurorailers need a little guidance. Such was the reasoning behind my *Cheap Sleeps Europe* guide. The first edition came out in 1992 and was an immediate success. The 2000 edition has been revised and complements the updated *Europe by Train*. Every major city and tourist location throughout Europe is covered, especially those areas where readers have had trouble finding a bed. International youth hostels, privately run hostels, pensions, campsites and sleep-ins are all covered. Buying this book will save you shelling out on the *Youth Hostels Handbook* and the *Campsite Directory*, not to mention time and aggravation at Tourist Offices trying to get recommendations and bookings for places to stay.

With a copy of *Europe by Train* and *Cheap Sleeps Europe*, you will have all you need (apart from the *Thomas Cook European Timetable*) to plan your European trip.

Your input and suggestions are, as always, welcome. If an establishment seems to you unworthy of its recommendation, or if you come up with a new find, please drop me a letter (the address is on the opening pages) and share the benefits of your experience with other Eurorailers. The writers of the three best letters of 2000 will each receive a free copy of the updated 2001 guide.

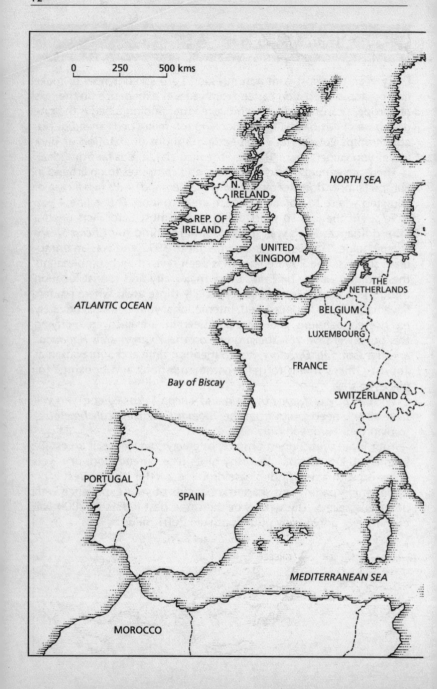

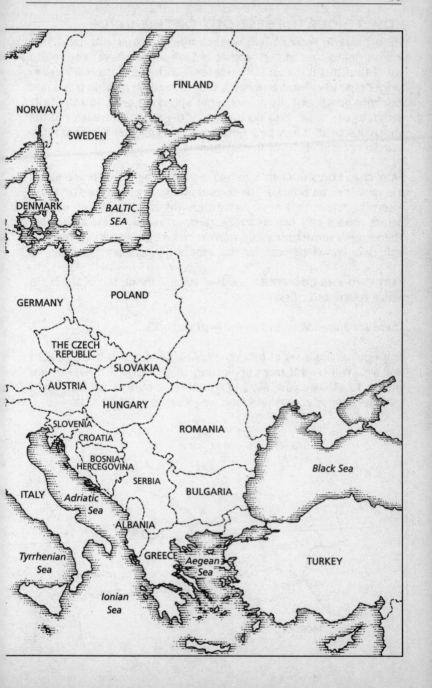

## HOW TO GET THE BEST OUT OF THIS GUIDE

Short break in France? Two weeks touring Austria and Italy? Two month grand tour of the capitals of Europe? Whatever your plans you'll find this book an easy reference aid. For starters it's set in bigger type than most to make it easy to read on moving trains and low light conditions. Its no-nonsense approach gives you the facts without fuss – a working document for the serious traveller, not the armchair tourist. It may be a good idea to keep a pen handy to make margin notes of items of special interest.

**PART ONE: EURORAILING** is in two sections. The first tells you about the various ticket options. The second offers advice and tips on those essential details that need to be thought about or taken care of before you set off – like insurance, passport, what to take and so on. Then there's some handy information on what to expect en route. A little prior knowledge can cut out a lot of unnecessary anxiety.

**PART TWO: THE COUNTRIES** is alphabetical with sub sections on individual towns and cities.

There are appendices and an index at the back.

This book is not a set of inflexible instructions, nor is it anticipated that you will read it from beginning to end. Use it however you choose to achieve your aims of trouble-free budget rail travel and value for money accommodation wherever you decide to go.

# PART ONE

# EURORAILING

## THE ADVANTAGES OF TRAIN TRAVEL

'If God had meant us to fly, he'd never have given us railways.' There's a lot you don't get with modern high speed European rail travel. No checking-in up to two hours ahead, no lost baggage (it stays near you in the rack), no cramped seats or seatbelts, no emergency drills, no turbulence, no diversions due to weather or air traffic controllers' strikes… You can use a train for a one-off trip or you can spend your whole holiday jumping on and off at stations as you please. Is it suitable for everyone? The under 26 market is spoilt rotten with special deals. But anyone of any age, individuals, groups, families, senior travellers, can make tracks around Europe. This book tells you how. Watch for bargains and special offers. Spend a little of that hard-earned cash and make the most of the wonderful experiences that await. Trains are great places for meeting people. Tripping around the highways and byways by Eurorail is exciting, educational, enlightening, enjoyable, entertaining and easy. And, as you may well discover in peak seasons, it's also very popular.

## FREEDOM

I'll bet you've done it. Made a list of the places you'd love to visit in Europe and thought, hey… some day soon I'm going to get there. Well, how about tomorrow? We're not suggesting a bit of planning and forethought isn't vital before you and your backpack leap on to the first Eurostar train to Europe – it is. But one of the greatest attractions of Europe by train is the carefree feeling of freedom you will enjoy. Haven't you ever yearned to be able to wake up one morning in Paris, give the sky the once over and if you don't like the look of things, get on a train to Barcelona?

With a rail pass, this dream becomes a reality. It's entirely up to you where you spend your time, when and how often you move on and which route you choose to get there. Warsaw, Budapest, Helsinki, Athens, Marrakech – it's quite a heady feeling, never really knowing where you will be tomorrow.

## DREAM TICKET

For the independent traveller, go-as-you-please rail passes are the stuff of fantasy. Compared to hitching, driving, or even flying, the advantages are enormous. For starters, you can cover a massive amount of ground relatively quickly, without breaking the bank. You'll usually leave from and arrive at stations right in the middle of cities (for instance, in Venice you step out of the station and right on to the banks of the Grand Canal, the main artery of this incredible city built on water). You'll cut out the frustration of being caught in the inevitable traffic jams on Europe's roads during high seasons. And you'll end up with more time at your chosen destination to relax or sightsee.

If you're worried rail is too restrictive for the route you want to take, rest assured: virtually all major sights can be reached by train, and the few exceptions can be got to by bus or bicycle (you can rent bikes from an increasing number of stations throughout the continent).

Also remember that if you're on a train you can walk about and stretch your legs, go for a meal or a snack and, providing you aren't travelling on a reserved seat, you can plant yourself wherever you want.

## RAIL RENAISSANCE

Every year Europe's main roads become more congested and improvements move at a slow pace, compared to the investments continually being made to the European rail network. In northern Europe, second-class seats today are comparable to the first-class of 20 years ago. Speeds in excess of 120mph are now common in France, Great Britain and Germany, and as the networks are expanded this will become the norm everywhere. As new, simplified routes between cities emerge, you're more likely to find a train to take you direct to your final destination rather than having to change.

All this means letting the train take the strain is now a serious alternative to flying. You can avoid Europe's increasingly congested airports and the air traffic delays that go with this. Wave goodbye also to confusing, time-consuming check-in procedures and hanging around for the compulsory one or two hours in airport lounges.

Compared to flying, the train (assuming you can take a high-speed express and not a local shunt-about) can actually travel faster than a plane on a distance of under 400 miles, allowing for the time it takes to commute to and from airports. It's also becoming a much cheaper alternative to high-price European short hops, especially with the fondness airports have these days for charging departure taxes. Germany's ICE between Frankfurt and Basle is a case in point – it's ten minutes faster and more than £100 cheaper than the plane.

## SPEEDING THINGS UP

Eurostar is at the forefront of the European rail revolution and is making serious inroads into airlines' business. Last year Eurostar carried millions of people between London Waterloo and Paris and Brussels, claiming a bigger market share to those destinations than airlines. There are now around 30 journeys between London Waterloo and mainland Europe every day, while Eurostar's connections with the French, Belgian, Dutch and German railway systems have opened up the whole of Europe to high-speed travel.

From Paris it's easy to reach Eurostar's hub station at Lille and tap into the French Railways' network of high-speed TGVs for all points south and on to Italy and Spain. Change at Brussels for connections to destinations anywhere in Belgium, Holland and Germany.

As prices come down, so do journey times: London–Brussels takes just 2 hours 40 minutes; Paris to Brussels is 1 hour 25 mins; Paris–Lyon is a speedy two hours; London to Cologne is 5 hours 30 mins; London to Amsterdam takes just over six hours. A new TGV high-speed service from Lille to Geneva is expected to be under way this summer, saving two hours on the current nine-hour journey to Switzerland. And by 2007, the British high-speed line from St Pancras will knock a further 40 minutes off journey times to France and Belgium.

## FOR THE RECORD

Almost all European trains are driven by diesel or electric power and are government-owned. The main exceptions are some of the mountain lines in Switzerland and the various privatized sections of what was once British Railways. From an environmentalist's point of view, trains are good news when you bear in mind they consume up to 17 times less energy than aeroplanes and five times less than cars to transport the same volume of people. A train carries more people per square metre than cars can – and with fewer pollution problems.

## WAY TO GO

Why? For starters there's the standard of service. Anyone who has travelled in North America will notice the difference straight away: in general, European trains are faster, more plentiful, more punctual, serving many more destinations. Historically, the European network has not been maintained on a profit-making basis and few countries' networks actually make any money. They are essentially a public service, as the Inter-Rail and Eurail passes demonstrate. For example, though you may pay £159 for an Inter-Rail pass, it can easily save you that much, or more, off the standard point-to-point fares. Having said that, there is more of a trend nowadays for public sector businesses to be more financially accountable, so things may change. In the meantime, this is the age of the train.

## BONJOUR ... HOLA ... DOBRY DEN ... SALUT ...

It's not just about sightseeing. Rail travel is an all-in experience. The informality of the train means that it's almost impossible to make a trip on one of the more popular routes in the summer months and not end up swapping yarns with fellow travellers. On overnight journeys, the intimacy of the train compartment makes it impossible! Whether you're sitting alongside locals or hanging out with fellow backpackers, the social scene can be half the fun of train travel. Don't miss the chance to pick brains for ideas on where to go and what to see – if the person in the seat next to you is from or has just been somewhere you fancy visiting, he's going to have more up-to-date information than even this guide book!

## WELL? WHAT ARE YOU WAITING FOR?

Are you convinced? You ought to be. Without doubt rail is the safest, most relaxing, most fascinating way to discover Europe. So what are you waiting for? This incredibe, diverse place, with its huge differences in people, culture, scenery and climate is waiting for you. Wherever you travel in Europe – even if you have been before – there's always something new to explore. And you can do it all, if you want, at one fell swoop – and even with just one ticket. If you want to broaden your horizons, if you want to experience the richness of life, if you want a taste of adventure... welcome to Europe by Train.

# The Options

The introduction of the Euro currency means rail price structuring throughout Europe is in a state of flux. Most countries will be reviewing their national rail prices during the first quarter of the year, and likewise the main rail pass operators. We have given the most up-to-date prices available at the time of going to print.

There are three basic schemes to choose from: a **BIJ/rover ticket** following a set route, an **Inter-Rail/Eurail pass** (depending on where you live – Inter-Rail tickets may be purchased by residents of Europe, Eurail is available to non-Europeans) or an individual country's **national rail pass**.

If you plan to see a lot of Europe, Inter-Rail/Eurail is the best option as it lets you take in as much as is physically possible in the allotted time. On the other hand, if you want to focus on a certain area – Greece, for example – it may work out cheaper to purchase a BIJ ticket and/or a Greek rail pass. Before handing over any money, sit down and define your objectives. Do you want to:

i) see as many countries as possible, sampling just a little of each and visiting only a few cities;

ii) head for a specific area, taking in some of the sights along the way; or

iii) concentrate on one country, touring it in depth and immersing yourself in the culture?

All three methods are equally enjoyable and great fun in their own way. The choice is yours. Your ticket, whichever method you choose, is non-transferable and non-refundable even if lost or stolen, so keep it close at hand and never let it out of your sight. Ideally, keep your ticket hidden away somewhere separate from your passport and money.

Check your name and other details are correct before you leave the issuing agent's office. A simple mistake such as transposing two letters in your name could lead to your pass being confiscated by an over-zealous conductor, leaving you stranded in the middle of nowhere.

**WHAT ISN'T COVERED?** Not included in the price of your ticket are seat reservations, meals, 'fast train' supplements (such as EuroCity/ InterCity and TGVs), Jetfoil and catamaran supplements (on BIJ tickets), accommodation and port taxes – on certain ferries.

In many cases, these 'extras' are obligatory (e.g. all Spanish expresses require a seat reservation), so check before you set foot on that train or ship. Trains marked with 'EC' or 'IC' at the top of the timetable column require a supplement (usually only £2–£5). Some long-haul ferries require you to book a berth (but this can be avoided by taking a shorter crossing and a connecting train).

If you plan on buying a first-class option, check first that it's going to be worth your while: many trains do not have first-class accommodation.

## BIJ

The BIJ scheme (*Billet International pour Jeunes*) operates under the auspices of the continental railways and offers reduced fares to people under 26. Eurotrain is the largest company in this scheme followed by Wasteels and Rail Europe. Between them these companies offer fares to more than 2,000 destinations throughout Europe, the CIS, Turkey and North Africa, with discounts of up to 40%. Euro-train tickets include ferry crossings to the continent.

BIJ tickets are valid for up to two months (six months for returns to Morocco and Turkey) and allow you to break your journey anywhere along your route. For example, if your final destination is Rome, you could travel out via Paris, Lyon and Turin and return via Florence, Lucerne, Luxembourg and Belgium.

In addition, there are often seven or eight routings to a particular city, so it's possible to go out via one route and return by another. The cost difference between purchasing two singles and a return is usually only £10 to £20, so pick the routes which take in the places you most want to see.

Sample fares for return journeys from London include: Ostend £29, Paris £49, any Netherlands station £59, Basle £88, Rome £140, Madrid £144, Berlin £149, Warsaw £163, Lisbon £164, Prague £192, Vienna £217, Athens £245, Budapest £247, Moscow £263, Stockholm £274.

## TRACKING DOWN RAIL BARGAINS

In the past it was a complicated business to buy a European rail pass. Now though it is wonderfully simple. These London based companies vie with each other to come up with the best fare. It helps to have a reasonably clear idea of where and when you want to travel to narrow down the options before you talk to them. Put them to work for you to find the best deal.

## EUROTRAIN

Eurotrain is the leading UK operator in continental rail travel for the 'under 26' crowd. In addition to BIJ fares (see above), they offer several 'circle route' tickets taking in a variety of cities. The Dutch Explorer, for example, covers London, Amsterdam and Brussels. Other Explorer passes include the Venetian, Eastern, Riviera and Spanish Explorer, all of which are available to under-26s, full-time students holding an ISIC, teachers or academic staff, accompanying spouse and children of eligible persons.

Eurotrain also provides individual rail passes for the following destinations:

- **The Czech Republic:** seven days' unlimited travel on national railways, from £15.50.
- **Czech and Slovak Republics:** seven days' unlimited travel on national rail networks of Czech Republic and Slovakia, from £24.
- **Hungary:** seven days' unlimited travel on national railways, from £23.
- **Poland:** seven, 14 or 21 days' unlimited travel on the national rail network for £21, £38 and £49 respectively.
- **Portugal:** seven, 14 or 21 days' unlimited travel on the national rail network for £35, £59 and £87 respectively.
- **Spain:** Five-day regional pass, for £9.50. Valid on the rail services of RENFE-Cercanias in any one of the three surrounding areas of Madrid, Barcelona or Malaga. Up to four can be bought at a time, so if you need 20 days' unlimited travel in the specified areas, you need to buy four passes.
- **Spanish Explorail:** a national rail pass available for seven (£75), 15 (£90) or 30 days (£119), valid on all RENFE metropolitan and local trains, and available to holders of the ISIC card, under-26 cards, their spouses and children.

For further information, contact their handling agents: Usit CAMPUS (formerly Campus Travel), 52 Grosvenor Gardens, London SW1W 0AG (Tel. 0870 240 1010). In the US, contact the Usit youth travel specialists at the New York Student Center, International AYH Hostel, 895 Amsterdam Avenue (at West 103rd Street), New York NY 10025, Tel. 212 663 5435.

## WASTEELS

Wasteels Travel are the originators of discount rail tickets. Wasteels UK is part of the international Wasteels group, Europe's largest rail operator with more than 200 local offices in 22 countries throughout Europe. Their BIJ scheme operates in the UK under the name Route-26. They act as agents for Italian Railways, offering a variety of Italian passes and travel bargains.

The Kilometric Ticket is valid for two months and allows up to 20 journeys (to a maximum of 3,000 kilometres) throughout Italy. One advantage of this ticket is that it can be used by up to five people, the mileage for each person being deducted from the total allowable. It costs £150 for first class and £88 for second.

Another option is the Italy Rail Card which covers the entire Italian network apart from seat reservations and supplements. Current prices are:

|           | 8 days | 15 days | 21 days | 30 days |
|-----------|--------|---------|---------|---------|
| lst class | £188   | £236    | £274    | £328    |
| 2nd class | £128   | £158    | £186    | £220    |

Wasteels also supply passes for other countries, sell international rail tickets and make reservations. They are agents for Eurostar youth fares. Current specials for under-26s with an ISIC card from London to Paris are from £45 (one way), £59 return, Monday to Thursday, £79 weekends. Amsterdam from £65 and Milan from £117 (train and cross channel ferry). Their special 'mini-tour' tickets combine several major European cities and places of interest.

For more information, contact Wasteels next to platform 2, Victoria Station, London SW1V 1JT (Tel. 020 7834 7066).

## RAIL EUROPE

Rail Europe was formed in 1997 when the French railways SNCF merged with British Rail International. This makes them a leading player in rail travel – including Eurostar – from the UK to the Continent.

As well as **Inter-Rail Passes**, Rail Europe sell **Euro Domino**. These are flexible passes giving you unlimited travel for three to eight days in a one-month period in up to 26 European countries, plus Morocco.

You buy a coupon for each country you wish to visit and you are free to travel on the trains of your choice. Fast train supplements (e.g. TGVs in France and Talgos in Spain) are included and you can opt for second- or first-class travel. The French ticket gives special fares on Eurostar services to Paris. Macedonia is now covered by the scheme. Adult prices for 1999 are as follows. Youth prices are for those under 26 years of age at the start of the pass. Children (aged 4–11) travel at half price. Four, six and seven day passes are also available.

**EURO DOMINO PRICES 2000**

| Country | 3 days | | | 5 days | | | 8 days | | |
| --- | --- | --- | --- | --- | --- | --- | --- | --- | --- |
| | 1st Adult | 2nd Adult | Youth | 1st Adult | 2nd Adult | Youth | 1st Adult | 2nd Adult | Youth |
| ADN/HML | 59 | 46 | 33 | 62 | 49 | 36 | 66 | 53 | 40 |
| Austria | 104 | 68 | 53 | 125 | 84 | 65 | 57 | 108 | 83 |
| Belgium | 53 | 35 | 26 | 63 | 43 | 33 | 79 | 55 | 40 |
| Bulgaria | 40 | 26 | 21 | 53 | 37 | 29 | 73 | 53 | 41 |
| Croatia | 50 | 33 | 25 | 65 | 44 | 33 | 89 | 59 | 45 |
| Czech Republic | 43 | 28 | 21 | 63 | 42 | 32 | 92 | 61 | 48 |
| Denmark | 75 | 50 | 36 | 104 | 69 | 49 | 148 | 96 | 69 |
| Finland | 103 | 69 | 52 | 139 | 92 | 70 | 192 | 128 | 98 |
| France | 152 | 99 | 79 | 205 | 139 | 111 | 284 | 198 | 159 |
| Germany | 169 | 112 | 86 | 199 | 133 | 100 | 243 | 165 | 122 |
| Greece | 59 | 40 | 31 | 79 | 53 | 38 | 108 | 73 | 48 |
| Hungary | 48 | 32 | 24 | 73 | 49 | 36 | 110 | 75 | 54 |
| Ireland | NA | 40 | 36 | NA | 55 | 50 | NA | 79 | 69 |
| Italy | 127 | 87 | 65 | 58 | 106 | 80 | 203 | 133 | 102 |
| Jugoslavia | 42 | 31 | 23 | 50 | 39 | 28 | 61 | 51 | 36 |
| Luxembourg | 18 | 12 | 9 | 22 | 15 | 11 | 28 | 18 | 13 |
| Macedonia | 24 | 16 | 12 | 30 | 20 | 15 | 40 | 26 | 18 |
| Morocco | 31 | 23 | 22 | 47 | 35 | 32 | 71 | 53 | 48 |
| Netherlands | 48 | 32 | 24 | 77 | 51 | 38 | 121 | 79 | 60 |
| Norway | 116 | 89 | 67 | 156 | 122 | 92 | 215 | 172 | 130 |
| Poland | 38 | 29 | 24 | 52 | 40 | 32 | 71 | 55 | 44 |
| Portugal | 59 | 40 | 26 | 79 | 53 | 37 | 109 | 73 | 53 |
| Romania | 44 | 29 | 21 | 68 | 45 | 33 | 104 | 69 | 51 |
| Slovakia | 36 | 24 | 18 | 48 | 32 | 24 | 65 | 44 | 34 |
| Slovenia | 46 | 33 | 24 | 57 | 41 | 31 | 73 | 53 | 41 |
| Spain | 90 | 70 | 52 | 133 | 106 | 80 | 196 | 159 | 122 |
| Sweden | 135 | 102 | 83 | 168 | 129 | 102 | 218 | 168 | 132 |
| Switzerland | 119 | 79 | 59 | 139 | 89 | 69 | 179 | 109 | 89 |
| Turkey | 39 | 29 | 19 | 49 | 39 | 29 | 89 | 49 | 39 |

ADN = Adriatica di Navigazione
HML = Hellenic Mediterranean Lines
These are ferry services between Brindisi and Patras. NB: It is cheaper to buy this pass than the normal return ticket.

For more information contact 08705 848 848. Or find the website (http://www.raileurope.co.uk). Euro Domino Passes are also available from Wasteels. Pass holders qualify for discounts on Eurostar, P&O Ferries, Hoverspeed and Scandinavian Seaways.

## EUROPEAN RAIL LTD

European Rail Limited is an independent travel agency selling only European rail tickets by phone and web site. They can combine special fares from all rail companies and come up with cheap fares for many routes. Real rail experts work here. They are at Tavistock Square, WC1H 9HR, tel. 020 7387 0444, www.europeanrail.com

## DEUTSCHE BAHN

The UK office of German Railways sells every continental ticket available and charge no booking fee. Tickets are sold by phone and posted out first class that day. Tel. 020 7317 0919.

## FREEDOM RAIL

This fledgling company, is another in the new breed of Internet ticket sellers. Visit them at www.freedomrail.co.uk. Here you can view their European route map and order tickets. When payment has been verified, you'll receive your tickets within seven days. They will also e-mail you a personalized itinerary with train times for as many destinations as you like, starting at £20 for three destinations.

## INTER-RAIL

### A BRIEF HISTORY

The Inter-Rail scheme has been around for over 25 years, and has become a traditional rite of passage for young people under the age of 26. By 1991, the programme had been expanded to include a pass allowing those aged over 26 to get in on the act, but the resulting phenomenal success did not please everyone.

At the end of 1992, the French, Italian, Portuguese and Spanish rail authorities complained their trains were more packed than ever, but they were receiving far fewer of the proceeds than their north European counterparts. Such squabbling led to a massive price hike on the youth pass and several countries abandoned the 26+ scheme altogether.

In 1993, trying to get more than a dozen countries to agree on new prices and formats seemed impossible. New zoned passes were introduced for the under-26s (more on this later) whilst others were deleted, and the adult pass seemed once again to be in danger of total disintegration. And yet, by 1994, a greater selection of passes than ever emerged.

The scheme has continued to evolve in the latter half of this decade, and for the under-26s Inter-Rail prices actually fell in 1998. In a major development, the over-26 scheme was extended to cover the same ground as the under-26 pass. This means an Inter-Rail pass will give anyone unlimited travel within 28 countries. Whatever your age, at current prices this is an incredible deal.

### UNDER-26 PASSES

First, there is the all-zone (28 countries) Inter-Rail for those under 26, which sells at £259. It's valid for one month. In addition, there are eight zoned Inter-Rail passes. These can be bought as single or multiple zones, so that you can make up your own itinerary. It means, of course, that you pay only for travel to the places you really want to see. Zoned passes make a lot of sense for those wishing to tour part of Europe in depth and offer more flexibility than the individual country passes, Euro Domino or Euro Youth. The eight Inter-Rail zones are:

A. The Republic of Ireland
B. Sweden, Norway and Finland
C. Denmark, Germany, Switzerland and Austria
D. Poland, the Czech Republic, Slovakia, Hungary and Croatia
E. France, Belgium, The Netherlands and Luxembourg
F. Spain, Portugal and Morocco
G. Italy, Slovenia, Greece, Turkey and boats between Brindisi (Italy) and Patras (Greece).
H. Bulgaria, Romania, Yugoslavia, Bosnia-Hercegovina and Macedonia.

A card for a single zone is valid for 22 days and costs £129. Monthly passes for any two zones will be sold at the fixed price of £169, any three zones at £195 and all zones at £219.

All cards offer unlimited travel during their validity, but normal supplements are payable, except on lightly loaded TGV services.

Countries participating in the all-Europe Inter-Rail youth scheme are: Austria, Belgium, Bulgaria, Croatia, the Czech Republic, Denmark, Finland, France, Germany, Greece, Hungary, the Republic of Ireland, Italy, Luxembourg, Macedonia, Morocco, the Netherlands, Norway, Poland, Portugal, Romania, Slovakia, Slovenia, Spain, Sweden, Switzerland, Turkey and the new 'Yugoslavia'. Also included in the deal is the Brindisi–Patras ferry crossing.

**WHO QUALIFIES?** Anyone living in Europe for six months who is under the age of 26 on the first day the pass becomes valid. It's up to you to decide when the pass will start. If you want to travel for more than one month, buy two or more passes and get the dates to run consecutively.

**BUYING AN INTER-RAIL:** Inter-Rail passes can only be sold through the offices of national railway authorities or their duly appointed agents. In the UK, this means directly from Rail Europe, selected stations or authorized travel agents. Do not buy a pass from someone on the street as the rail authorities carry out rigorous checks; your pass may be confiscated and you could be ejected from the train. If in doubt, check with the rail authority in your country before you buy.

**USING AN INTER-RAIL:** You can purchase a youth Inter-Rail pass up to 2 months in advance, provided you will still be under 26 on the first day of use. Since you can't change the start date, however, it's a good idea not to purchase a ticket until your plans are finalized. Take care when choosing your start date: the pass runs from 12.01am on the first day to midnight on the preceding day of the next month, so a pass starting on 14 February will be valid until midnight on 13 March. Unfortunately, since February has only 28 days (three years out of four, at any rate) you get 28 days of travel rather than 31.

**REDUCTIONS:** An all-Europe Inter-Rail pass in the UK entitles you to discounts of 34% on trains in Britain and Northern Ireland and 50% on most Channel ferry services to the continental ports, although these percentages are subject to change.

Many ferry companies offer reduced rates for Inter-Rail ticket holders. Both Sealink and P&O ferries give 30–50% discounts on most of their services, while B&I and Irish Continental (Rosslare–Cherbourg or Rosslare–Le Havre) offer a 50% reduction. See the individual country sections and Appendix I for further details of ferry discounts.

For full details, check the Guidance Notes on the back of the pass or ask a rail agent for some help.

### OVER-26 PASS

The Inter-Rail 26 pass has been extended to cover the same countries and zones as the under 26 pass. A one zone pass costs £179, two zones costs £235, three zones costs £269 and a 'global' pass covering all zones costs £309.

Countries participating in the all-Europe Inter-Rail youth scheme are: Austria, Belgium, Bulgaria, Croatia, the Czech Republic, Denmark, Finland, France, Germany, Greece, Hungary, the Republic of Ireland, Italy, Luxembourg, Macedonia, Morocco, the Netherlands, Norway, Poland, Portugal, Romania, Slovakia, Slovenia, Spain, Sweden, Switzerland, Turkey and the new 'Yugoslavia'. It also includes the Brindisi–Patras ferry crossing.

**WHO QUALIFIES?** Anyone of any age holding a current passport

(though presumably not under 26) who has been resident in Europe for more than six months on the first day that pass becomes valid.
**BUYING AND USING AN INTER-RAIL 26 PASS:** The rules are the same as for the youth pass. Don't be tempted by cheap imitations because they are bound to be duds; don't book too far ahead as start dates once confirmed cannot be altered; do treat your pass with great care – stolen, lost or disfigured passes will not be replaced.
**REDUCTIONS:** An all-Europe Inter-Rail pass in the UK entitles you to 50% discount on most Channel ferry services to the continental ports, although this percentage is subject to change.

Many ferry companies offer reduced rates for Inter-Rail ticket holders. Both Sealink and P&O ferries give 30–50% discounts on most of their services, while B&I and Irish Continental (Rosslare–Cherbourg or Rosslare–Le Havre) offer a 50% reduction. See the individual country sections and Appendix I for further details of ferry discounts.

For full details ask a rail agent for help.

## EURAIL

### A BRIEF HISTORY

The first Eurail pass issued in 1959 came into existence because Europe had a new and expensive network of intercity trains that needed passengers. Its purpose was to entice potential passengers from the other side of the Atlantic by offering two months of second-class travel on any or all of the member rail systems.

The scheme was expanded to include one- and three-month passes, 15-day passes, 21-day passes, first-class travel, and such fringe benefits as free access to many ferry and steamer connections and free or discounted bus transportation. The Eurail Youthpass, aimed at those under the age of 26, was such a success that Europe developed its own youthpass system, Inter-Rail, followed closely by the country passes.
**WHO QUALIFIES?** The Eurail Passes are available to anyone who resides outside Europe and North Africa or has arrived in Europe no more than six months ago. The Eurail Pass is not valid in Great Britain and Northern Ireland or on cross-Channel ferries.
**PASSES AVAILABLE** The **Eurail Youth Flexipass** is open to anyone under 26 and gives unlimited second-class travel in 17 countries and allows either 10 or 15 days of travel in a two-month period. The **Eurail Youth Consecutive Pass** is also available to under 26s and is valid for 15 days, 21 days, one, two or three months.

The **Eurail Pass** has no age restriction and comes in first-class only; again 15-day, 21-day, one-, two- and three-month Eurail Passes are available. **The Eurail Flexipass** is a first-class version of the Youth Flexipass, without the age restriction, and allows 10 or 15 days of travel in a two-month period.

The **Eurail Saver Pass** is a first-class pass for two or more persons each holding a Saver Pass travelling together and works out about 15% cheaper than a regular Eurail Pass.

Prices for Eurail passes sold in Europe:

| | Eurail Pass | Saver Pass | Eurail Youthpass |
| --- | --- | --- | --- |
| 15 days | $610 | $518 | $427 |
| 21 days | $790 | $672 | $549 |
| 1 month | $980 | $832 | $685 |
| 2 months | $1386 | $1180 | $970 |
| 3 months | $1714 | $1456 | $1189 |
| | Eurail Flexipass | Eurail Saver Flexipass | Eurail Youth Flexipass |
| 10 days in 2 months | $720 | $612 | $504 |
| 15 days in 2 months | $948 | $806 | $659 |

If you were unable to purchase your pass before leaving home, it is possible to buy one in Europe from Rail Europe at 179 Piccadilly London, (tel. 08705 848 848) or from any Eurail Aid office in any participating country, but you must do so within six months of your arrival. Passes purchased in Europe cost 20% more than those purchased outside.

The countries currently participating in the Eurail scheme are: Austria, Belgium, Denmark, Eire, Finland, France, Germany, Greece, Hungary, Italy, Luxembourg, the Netherlands, Norway, Portugal, Spain, Sweden and Switzerland. This is not as wide-ranging as the Inter-Rail card, but many of the countries not covered by the Eurail scheme are in eastern Europe and have their own passes, which can be very cheap.

**FREE TRAVEL UNDER THE EURAIL SCHEME:** Reductions on some of Europe's private railways are also included (many of these are Swiss mountain railways). Children aged between 4 and 11 benefit from a 50% reduction on first-class passes only. Children under four travel free.

**REFUNDS:** Refunds are subject to a 15% surcharge. You can only get a refund from the office at which you bought your pass.

## Other Eurail options:

### THE EUROPASS
The Europass makes sense for those wishing to make an in-depth tour of a few European countries, rather than a whistle-stop tour of

all 17. The five main countries in the scheme are France, Germany, Italy, Spain and Switzerland. You can travel on any five days in a two-month period, visiting any or all of these countries. On payment of a specified supplement, the reach of the pass can be extended to include one or two of the four associate zones, Austria/Hungary, Belgium/Luxembourg/the Netherlands, Portugal and Greece. On payment of a further supplement additional travel days (up to 15) can be added.

**EUROPASS – 1ST CLASS PRICES**

|  | 2 Adults* | Adult |
| --- | --- | --- |
| Any 5 days in 2 months | US$326 | US$384 |
| with 1 associate country | US$384 | US$450 |
| with 2 associate countries | US$422 | US$494 |

*Prices per person based on 2 people travelling together, i.e. 15% partner discount.

### Europass Youth – (under 26) 2nd class

| Any 5 days in 2 months | US$2576 |
| --- | --- |
| with 1 associate country | US$306 |
| with 2 associate countries | US$343 |

Contact Rail Europe at 500 Mamaroneck Harrison, New York NY 10528 (Tel. 914-681 3216).

## COUNTRY PASSES

Many countries offer passes giving you the freedom of their rail network. If you really want to explore a country in depth, this is an excellent way to do so. The obvious disadvantage is that it can cost more to get to the country in question than to purchase an Inter-Rail card.

One option is to buy a BIJ ticket to the first city inside the border of your target country and then use the country's rail pass to get around. Another is to combine a country pass with a cheap flight (see p.40). Another drawback is that most country passes do not cover buses and ferries, whereas BIJ tickets include ferry crossings and Inter-Rail offers reductions on both.

Most country passes offer a more flexible timescale (with tickets valid from four days to one month) and are usually open to anyone, not just those under 26. Some passes are excellent value, but others aren't worth the money. Before committing, find out how extensive is the rail network, how useful the pass will be to you, and what it will cost to get to that country.

For complete details of national rail pass systems and other discounts, see under PASSES AVAILABLE in the relevant sections for each country in Part Two.

**AUSTRIAN RAIL PASS** Valid for three days within a 15-day period, the pass can be extended for up to five extra days. It gives discounts on some boats, bike rental, some private railways, and to children. 2nd-class tickets cost around £65 ($105), and £10 ($16) per extra day. First class is half the price again.

**BALTIC STATES** 7, 14 or 21 days of unlimited 2nd-class travel in Estonia, Latvia and Lithuania for around £25, £35 and £45 respectively.

**BELGIUM** The Tourrail Card is valid for any five days within a month. For adults over 26, the second-class card is 2,200BF. First class costs 3,390BF.

**BENELUX TOURRAIL CARD** Valid in Belgium, the Netherlands and Luxembourg, the card can be used for any five days within a month. For those over 26, the cost is £86; £59 for under 26s. First class is £128.

**BRITRAIL PASS** Since Great Britain is not covered in the Eurail or Inter-Rail scheme, if you are from North America your best option is to purchase a BritRail Pass. This is valid for unlimited travel throughout Great Britain (England, Scotland and Wales), with the notable exception of the London Underground.

Prices for 2000 BritRail Classic Pass (consecutive days travel):

|  | Under 26 | Adult | | Senior (60+) |
|---|---|---|---|---|
|  | Standard (only) | Standard | 1st | Standard (only) |
| 8 days | US$215 | US$265 | US$400 | US$340 |
| 15 days | US$280 | US$400 | US$600 | US$510 |
| 22 days | US$355 | US$505 | US$760 | US$645 |
| 1 month | US$420 | US$600 | US$900 | US$765 |

The BritRail Flexipass allows travel on a certain number of days within a set period. Prices for 2000:

|  | Under 26 | Adult | | Senior (60+) |
|---|---|---|---|---|
|  | Standard (only) | Standard | 1st | 1st (only) |
| 4 days in 2 month | US$185 | US$219 | US$315 | US$300 |
| 8 days in 2 month | US$240 | US$315 | US$459 | US$435 |
| 15 days in 2 months | US$360 | US$515 | US$770 | US$655 |

Anyone buying one adult or Senior Pass can take one accompanying child (5–15).

BritRail passes can only be purchased in North America, where they are available from most reputable travel agents or direct from Rail Europe, Westchester One, 44 South Broadway, White Plains, NY10601 (Tel. 1-888-BRITRAIL).

The London Visitors Travel Card offers unlimited travel within London on London Transport. There are also a number of regional rover passes that can be purchased within the UK. Passes available include Scotland, Ireland or the South East. (See the UK section for further details.)

## London Visitors Travel Card

|  | Adults | Child |
|---|---|---|
| 3 days | US$32 | US$14 |
| 4 days | US$41 | US$16 |
| 7 days | US$63 | US$24 |

**CARTE 12–25** France's under-26 discount railcard is available to anyone aged between 12 and 25 and costs £27. It offers up to 50% reduction on off-peak (blue) and ordinary (white) trains, 50% on TGV's (subject to availability) and 25% at all other times.

**LA CARTE ZOOM – CORSICAN RAILWAYS** This week-long freedom pass means unlimited travel for 290F (around £30). Any of Corsica's train stations sell the tickets, and storage of a bag weighing up to 20kg is free at the station's left luggage department.

**CZECH EXPLORER PASS** Seven days of unlimited travel on national rail services for £15 (2nd class) and £23 (1st class). There's also a separate Seven-day Explorer pass covering the Czech and Slovak Republics, for £23 (2nd class) or £35 (1st class).

**EUROPEAN EAST PASS** Covering only first-class travel on the Austrian, Czech, Hungarian, Polish and Slovakian railway lines, this pass (available only outside these countries) is valid for any five days within a month, and can be extended to up to 10 days. Discounts include 50% on all Donauschiffahrt Wurn and Kock boats between Passau and Linz, 15% on all DDSG-Blue Danube Schiffahrt GmbH boats between Melk, Krems and Vienna, 10% on the Schneeberg and Schafberg cog railways, and on scheduled OBB boats on Lake Wolfgang and Lake Constance, and 40% on bike rental. A five-day pass costs about £115 ($185), with each extra day costing £14 ($23).

**EXPLORAIL PASS – SPANISH RAILWAYS** This pass from youth rail specialist Campus Travel (Tel. 020 7730 3402) is valid throughout

Spain's RENFE network. Under-26s, ISIC card holders and students under 30 (together with their spouses and children) get seven days' unlimited rail travel (though not on high-speed trains) for about £73; 15 days for £88; 30 days for £115.

**FINNRAIL PASS** three, five or ten days of unlimited travel within one month for 600mk, 810mk or 1090mk respectively (second class). Under-26s are eligible for a 25% discount, under-17s travel half-price. First-class passes are also available.

**FERIEN TICKET – GERMAN RAIL** Valid for a week's unlimited travel on local and regional trains in one of 54 zones, the ticket costs £21.50 per person, or from £8 each for up to four people travelling together. An additional week costs half price, and if you combine two or more regions, you pay half price for the other regions. In some zones, public transport is included. The catch is you need a London–Germany Eurostar ticket or other through-train ticket to qualify.

**IRISH PASSES** The **Irish Explorer** ticket offers five out of 15 days' travel within the Republic for Ir£67, and Ir£100 for eight out of 15 days. This also includes suburban trains and the Bus Eireann network. For the whole Irish rail network, including Northern Ireland, there is the **Irish Rover** ticket: Five of 15 days for IR£83. An **Emerald Card** for unlimited train and bus travel for eight days out of 15 costs Ir£115, Ir£200 for 15 days in 30.

**ITALIAN RAIL CARD** Valid for eight, 15, 21 or 30 days in first and second class. Prices in second class are £128 for eight days, £158 for 15, £186 for 21 days and £210 for 30. The **Flexirailcard** is valid for either four days in one month (£88), eight days in one month (£122) or 12 days in one month (£156).

**MOROCCO** The *carte d'abonnement* is valid for unlimited travel for a month on all trains but the fast TNR services. It costs 1,146dh for first class and 767dh for second (which works out at about £5 return per 100 km).

**POLRAIL PASS** Valid on all Polish Railways trains, the pass entitles the holder to a free seat reservation, which can be booked at your departure station, at any rail booking office, or on the train. In the UK you can get it at Wasteels. Current prices are:

| Days | Adult | | Youth (Under 26) | |
| --- | --- | --- | --- | --- |
| | 1st | 2nd | 1st | 2nd |
| 8 days | £76 | £52 | £53 | £36 |
| 15 days | £88 | £60 | £61 | £41 |
| 21 days | £104 | £68 | £72 | £48 |
| 1 month | £128 | £88 | £88 | £69 |

**PORTUGAL**
A tourist pass (Bilhete Turistico) gives one, two or three weeks of unlimited travel for 18,000$, 29,200$ or 41,200$ respectively.

**SCANRAIL PASS** For those intent on exploring the Land of the Midnight Sun, the ScanRail Pass is the way to go. It allows you up to 21 days' unlimited travel on the national rail networks of Denmark (DSB), Finland (VR), Norway (NSB) and Sweden (SJ).

You can also travel free on the following ferries: Scandline's inland ferry services in Denmark; Helsingor (Denmark)–Helsingborg (Sweden); Rodby (Denmark)–Puttgarden (Germany); Trelleborg (Sweden)– Sassnitz (Germany). In addition, you can travel free on NSB buses between Trondheim and Storlien, and buses between Lulea/Boden and Haparanda. Further discounts are available on a wide range of bus and ferry links. For a complete breakdown, see the Norway section or contact Rail Europe or Wasteels. Current prices are:

|  | Under 26 | | Adult | |
|---|---|---|---|---|
|  | 2nd | 1st | 2nd | 1st |
| *ScanRail Flexi* | | | | |
| 5 days in 2 months | £95 | £129 | £125 | £169 |
| 10 days in 2 months | £125 | £174 | £169 | £229 |
| *ScanRail* | | | | |
| 21 days consecutively | £145 | £195 | £195 | £259 |

## SPECIAL TRAINS
If you have the opportunity, there are some trains which are a delight to travel. All are accessible with a first-class rail pass, though the majority have both first- and second-class carriages and are therefore available to Inter-Rail, Eurail Youthpass and BIJ ticket holders (though there may be a supplement). A complete list of these trains is contained in the *Thomas Cook European Rail Timetable*, but our particular favourites are as follows:

| TRAIN NAME | CITIES |
|---|---|
| BLAUER ENZIAN | Dortmund–Cologne–Stuttgart–Munich–Salzburg–Klagenfurt |
| CANALETTO | Zurich–Lugano–Milan–Venice |
| CATALAN TALGO | Barcelona–Port Bou–Avignon–Geneva |
| CISALPIN | Paris–Lausanne–Brig–Milan |
| FRANZ HALS | Amsterdam–Munich |

| KOMET | Hamburg–Zurich |
|---|---|
| HAMLET | Copenhagen–Hamburg |
| LIGURE | Nice–Genoa–Milan |
| NORDPILEN | Stockholm–Boden–Kiruna–Narvik |
| REMBRANDT | Amsterdam–Cologne–Basle–Zürich–Chur |
| ROMULUS | Vienna–Klagenfurt–Venice–Florence–Rome |
| TRANSALPIN | Basle–Zürich–Innsbruck–Salzburg–Vienna |

## OTHER SERVICES

**YOUTH HOSTEL ASSOCIATION:** The Youth Hostel Association offers a variety of excellent-value packages based on combined rail travel and YHA accommodation. The scheme currently operates in 15 different countries including Iceland, Israel, Japan, Australia and New Zealand. For further information write to YHA Travel, Trevelyan House, 8 St. Stephen's Hill, St. Albans, Herts. AL1 2DY (Tel. 01727 855215).

**SENIOR CARDS:** The British Senior Railcard gives a 30% discount on UK fares to those over 60. The Rail Europ Senior Pass, combined with a senior card from another country, will entitle the bearer to 30–50% discounts on first- and second-class cross-border travel between any of the following: Belgium, Croatia, the Czech Republic, Denmark, Finland, France, Germany, Greece, Hungary, Ireland, Italy, Luxembourg, the Netherlands, Norway, Portugal, Slovakia, Slovenia, Spain, Sweden, Switzerland (most lines) and the UK. Information on further discounts can be obtained through Thomas Cook Travel offices or Rail Europe (Tel. 0807 848 848).

# Before You Go

## PREPLANNING

A little time spent now on planning is not only fun, it will also ensure you get the most out of your time abroad. Get hold of a large map of Europe, and start thinking about where you want to go. Once you get down to brass tacks, you'll realize Europe is a lot bigger than it at first may seem – this is where sticking pins into maps at random might come in handy! Start by mapping out a rough itinerary of where you want to visit.

There are three main considerations: the places you'd like to see, how much time you want to spend at each one and the most scenic route to get there. Once this is done, pencil in a route between the cities, checking its feasibility against a timetable. Make sure you use the appropriate timetable for the season you want to travel in (summer services run from mid-May until mid-September). If the schedule you need isn't out yet, try to find a copy of last year's edition rather than using the winter schedule. (See Timetables section in train information chapter).

**TIME ALLOCATION** For those who want to do a whistle-stop tour taking in as many countries as possible, time is crucial. Most cities require a minimum of two days to see everything; this means spending at least one night there. You can maximize your time by sleeping on trains, arriving in cities early (7am) and leaving late (10pm). This saves you time and money, but you could also miss out on some great scenery.

**DESTINATIONS AND ROUTES** Most Eurorailers have a few special places in mind before they set off. By using a timetable and the information in this book, you'll be able to work out the quickest and best routes between destinations. There are often two or three routes to choose from, and one is bound to appeal to you more than another.

**WHEN TO GO** For obvious reasons, most Eurorailers find themselves on the road (or rail) between June and September. Travelling in the high season gives you the advantages of encountering more fellow backpackers, better weather and being sure everything is open. However, prices are higher, the character of a place may be swamped by crowds of tourists, accommodation is harder to find, tourist industry people have less time for you and there are generally more hassles on the trains. For the lucky few who can choose when to travel, I'd recommend spring to early summer.

**TIME DIFFERENCES** Bear in mind the different time zones you will pass through and allow for this when making connections. Timetables usually list departures and arrivals in the local time; the notable exception to this is the former Soviet republics, where all times listed in Russian timetables are Moscow time, regardless of which zone the city is actually in. The table below lists the various time zones for the countries covered in this book:

| COUNTRY | TIME | COUNTRY | TIME | COUNTRY | TIME |
|---------|------|---------|------|---------|------|
| Albania | CET | Greece | EET | Portugal | GMT |
| Austria | CET | Hungary | CET | Romania | EET |
| Belgium | CET | Ireland* | GMT | Russia | MST |
| Belarus | EET | Italy | CET | Slovakia | CET |
| Bosnia-Hercegovina | CET | Latvia | EET | Slovenia | CET |
| | | Liechtenstein | EET | Spain | CET |
| Bulgaria | EET | Lithuania | CET | Sweden | CET |
| Croatia | CET | Luxembourg | CET | Switzerland | CET |
| Czech Rebulic | CET | Macedonia | CET | Turkey | EET |
| Denmark | CET | Malta | CET | Ukraine | EET |
| Estonia | EET | Morocco | GMT | UK | GMT |
| Finland | EET | Netherlands | CET | Yugoslavia | CET |
| France | CET | Norway | CET | | |
| Germany | CET | Poland | CET | | |

GMT is the standard time zone, all others are calculated as follows: CET adds one hour to GMT, EET adds two hours to GMT and MST adds three hours to GMT. From the end of March to the end of September all time zones add 1 hour for Daylight Savings Time except that marked by a *, where Daylight Savings Time continues until the end of October.

**ADVANCE TOURIST INFORMATION** Now you know which countries you want to visit, contact the appropriate Tourist Office in your own country before you leave. They'll be glad to send you booklets and maps to whet your appetite and give you an idea of what to see and, more importantly, what you can afford to miss.

While most offices provide these services for free, there is an unfortunate trend for Tourist Offices to 'pay their way' by charging for literature and their time. An increasing number now operate premium-rate phone lines to handle enquiries and others may ask for a small 'donation' to cover postage costs.

In the meantime, though, most information is free and there's nothing to lose by asking. Remember, though, Tourist Offices are in the business of selling their country, so take claims like 'the most beautiful city in Europe' with a pinch of salt.

**INTERNET RESOURCES** Web-wise readers will know how to search for information. Much is already available – good, bad and indifferent. Sometimes, perhaps surprisingly, it's not always as up-to-date as you may think. Here are a few useful sites to start you off:

| | |
|---|---|
| www.mapquest.com | Local and international maps to street level |
| www.eventsworldwide.com | Every major world event |
| www.towd.com | Guide to 2000 tourist information offices |
| www.city.net | 5000 destinations |
| www.travelocity.com | News, daily events, weather, etc |
| www.fco.gov.uk/travel | Advice on trouble spots |
| www.hotelguide.com | 60,000 posh hotels to B&B worldwide |
| www.hostels.com | Directory of hostels |
| www.xe.net | Currency exchange rates worldwide |

## CROSSING THE CHANNEL

Many Eurorailers start their trip in Britain and use the ports of Dover and Folkestone as their departure point for sailing to France. There are, however, many alternatives to these routes. Not all ferry ports have rail connections, but those without a rail link usually have bus connections run by the ferry operators. These bus services sometimes require an additional reservation and/or fare, so check with the ferry company. Bear in mind that some services are seasonal (e.g. Truckline's Poole to Cherbourg service runs only from May to September).

There are more than a dozen ferry routes between the UK, Ireland and the Continent, many of which have special rail connections (boat trains) with the ferry, allowing you to walk straight off the boat and on to a waiting train. Ostend and Hoek van Holland both have boat train connections to Germany, and Dieppe has one to Paris via northern France.

From Dover, there are frequent services to Calais operated all year round by P&O Stena Line, Sea France, and Hoverspeed. Hoverspeed's Seacat service makes the crossing in under an hour. Hoverspeed operates a fast Catamaran from Dover to Ostend. From Portsmouth you can take P&O to Cherbourg and Le Havre or Brittany Ferries to St Malo and Caen. Brittany Ferries also operate a service between Plymouth and Santander in Spain.

If you're in Ireland, or planning to go there, Irish Ferries run services from Rosslare in Ireland to Cherbourg and Le Havre. Stena Lines operate between Belfast in Northern Ireland and Stranraer in Scotland, though the shortest crossing on the Irish Sea is P&O's super new Jetliner service between Larne and Cairnryan. Although there is no railway station on the Scottish side, there's a fairly decent bus service to nearby Stranraer. Stena Lines also runs services between Fishguard in Wales and Rosslare, and Irish Ferries goes between Pembroke in Wales and Rosslare.

A summary of the main cross-channel and Irish Sea ferries is contained in Appendix II with the approximate journey times and frequency. The introduction of newer, faster ferries on many routes means that operators, times and even ports-of-call are subject to change. It would be wise to double check at the planning stage of your trip.

## THE CHANNEL TUNNEL

The 31-mile rail tunnel under the English Channel links Britain and continental Europe for the first time since the Ice Ages. Work first started back in 1881, but was abandoned for fear of a French military invasion. A century later, an unprecedented trans-European finance consortium was set up, and in 1987 engineers set to work. On 6 May 1994, after years of delay, the Channel Tunnel was opened by Queen Elizabeth and President Mitterrand of France.

There are two services using the tunnel: **Eurostar**, the passenger train; and **Le Shuttle**, which transports car, coach and lorry. Eurostar operates up to 22 trains a day from London Waterloo to and from Paris, and up to 11 to and from Brussels. The Cheriton (nr Folkestone)–Coquelles (nr Calais) vehicle-transporter service Le Shuttle runs four trains every hour, 24 hours a day, 365 days a year. It's only 35 minutes platform to platform.

**EUROSTAR**

This high-speed passenger train has revolutionized travel between Britain and Europe. More than half the people travelling from London to Paris now go by train. In Britain, the main Eurostar terminal is London Waterloo, though on many services you can also join the train at Ashford, Kent. Eurostar focuses on two routes:

- **London Waterloo–Paris Gare du Nord** (three hours). Gare du Nord is close to the centre of Paris. Some services stop at Lille. Trains also stop daily at Calais-Frethun, a few kilometres from Calais.
- **London Waterloo–Lille Europe–Brussels Midi/Zuid** (2 hrs 40 mins). For an extra £10, you can get a connecting train to any other station in Belgium.

As prices come down, so do journey times: London–Brussels takes just 2 hours 40 minutes; Paris to Brussels is 1 hour 25 mins; Paris–Lyon is a speedy two hours; London to Cologne is 5 hours 30 mins; London to Amsterdam takes just over six hours.

## CONNECTIONS

Eurostar connects with the French, Belgian, Dutch and German railway systems.

- **Lille** is the hub of Eurostar travel and a major gateway for France's high-speed TGV rail network. Change here for Lyon, Bordeaux, Nice, Cannes and other destinations. In a major development, a new French TGV high-speed service between Lille and Geneva is expected to get under way this summer, chopping two hours from the current nine-hour journey to Switzerland.
- **Paris** has connections to most French destinations, Switzerland, Italy and Spain, and a new generation of TGV high-speed trains – due out early in the new millennium – is expected to slice intercity travelling times by up to a further 20 per cent.
- From **Brussels**, high-speed Thalys trains go to Antwerp, Rotterdam, Amsterdam and Cologne – making Amsterdam just over six hours from London, and bringing Cologne within 5 hours and 30 minutes of London. Recent upgrading across northern Germany has already shaved London-Berlin trips to 10 hours (a saving of two hours).Thalys trains now also serve Dusseldorf and Dortmund, while by the year 2001, new 206mph InterCity Express trains will reduce Cologne–Frankfurt from a 2 hr 20 mins journey to a short haul of under an hour.

## THE FUTURE

Plans to operate through Eurostar trains from the English Midlands, North of England and Scotland are unlikely to come to fruition.

But by the year 2007, the British high-speed line from St Pancras through Kent is expected to slice a further 40 minutes off journey times to France and Belgium.

**FARES** Fares start at £79 return for rail pass holders. Keep an eye out for special deals such as summer savers, which offer discounts of up to 40%. Typical sample return fares from London include:

- to Amsterdam in Holland from £79 (Eurostar and Thalys)
- to Liege in Belgium from £89 (Eurostar and local service)
- to Cologne in Germany from £89 (Eurostar and Thalys)
- to Interlaken in Switzerland from £153 (Eurostar, TGV and local service)
- to Florence in Italy from £228 (Eurostar and couchette in overnight Paris–Florence sleeper).

**SNOW TRAINS** Eurostar also operates a winter ski service from Waterloo and Ashford to the French Alps. The **day-time** service (weekly, on Saturdays from the end of December to mid-April) is non-stop to Moutiers and Bourg-St-Maurice in eight hours, with fares from £159 return, £105 one way.

There's also an **overnight** service, timed to give skiers an extra couple of days on the pistes. Passengers leave London or Ashford on Friday evening, change at Lille and arrive in the heart of the French Alps first thing Saturday morning. Fares again are around £200 return, £100 one way.

For **reservations**, phone Eurostar (Tel. 08705 848 848) or contact the Rail Europe Travel Centre at 179 Piccadilly, London W1.

**DISNEYLAND PARIS** Eurostar also has regular services between London Waterloo and Disneyland Paris. The trains take three hours and go straight to the gates of the Magic Kingdom. Services run daily through summer and during school holidays, and weekends in the winter. There's a big range of fares, starting at £55 return for children and £79 return for under-26s. To book, tel. 08705 848 848.

## GETTING TO EUROPE BY PLANE

Whether you're flying to Europe from the Americas, Australasia, Ireland or the UK, you want to do it cheaply. The basic rule is: the more you pay, the greater the flexibility; the less you pay, the more restrictions. A little preplanning will save money and buy you extra time on your trip. It is therefore important to choose the right city as your starting point so you can visit the countries not covered by your rail pass either before your pass starts or after it expires; there is no sense in wasting precious days of your pass where you can't use it.

There is no shortage of airlines or different types of tickets (see p. 40), so take your time and do your homework before buying.

## 'NO FRILLS' AIRLINES

In Britain, there's a mini-revolution going on with short hops to Europe. A number of so-called **'no-frills' airlines** are cutting budget air fares to the bone, and the resulting competition can mean big bargains for travellers. Look out for advertisements in the travel sections of the national newspapers or ask your travel agent specifically for details. At the time of going to press offers include, for example:

- **Ryanair** – Various European destinations, including Dublin from £30 one way, Stockholm from £50 one way, Frankfurt (Hahn) from £25 one way; Tel. 0870 333 1238.
- **Go** – British Airways' cut-price venture. Various European routes, including Lisbon, Copenhagen, Milan, Lyon, Zurich and Rome from under £100 return; Tel. 0845 605 4321.
- **Easyjet** – Various destinations, including Barcelona, Geneva, Madrid, and Athens from £70 return; Tel. 0870 6000 000.
- **British Midland** – various special deals on European routes, Belfast from £59 return, Dublin from £69 return and Paris from £69; Tel. 0870 240 7035.

Decide where, when and how much you can afford. Most travel agency services are free and they may help with some new ideas, so use them to the full. You can also try booking direct on the Internet. Contact your local student travel office: this can be a goldmine of information, sometimes with special flights open to everyone, not just students or the under-26s.

Also, for last-minute deals, trawl through teletext, the Internet and newspaper travel sections.

If you don't know where the local student travel office is, consult the listing of CIEE offices in Appendix IV or check with the information office at a nearby college or university.

### TICKET TYPES

Most reduced airfares must be purchased up to 30 days in advance, so try to book as far ahead as possible and talk to as many other travellers as you can to pick up tips. Don't forget to check the smaller or less popular airlines and ticket routings – a good example of this is Icelandair's New York to Frankfurt run via Reykjavik.

### SCHEDULED FLIGHTS

**APEX** Your best chance of big savings with scheduled flights is to book early, or try consolidators, who buy up blocks of seats at special bulk rates and pass on the savings to their customers. They usually advertise in the back of newspapers' travel sections.

For the best bargains, bag an APEX (Advanced Purchase Excursion fare) ticket. A Super-APEX fare is also available on some routings and this allows you even more freedom. Check the small print on any ticket purchase as many allow you to arrive and depart from different cities (and countries), use different airlines for the separate legs of your journey, or even to postpone your return flight – for a small fee of course. Also ask whether your fare has any 'student' or 'youth' discounts, as this may provide further savings.

**STANDBY** During the peak season (June to September), you can expect all the airlines to be fully booked. Unless you reserve well in advance, you could be forced to fly standby – if it's even available. Not all airlines offer standby and your choice of destinations is restricted, as are the number of seats available. Tickets are sold on a 'first come, first served' basis the day of the flight, so it pays to be organized. You stand a better chance of getting a flight midweek rather than at the weekend. Call the airline a few days before you want to leave and check seat availability (don't mention the word 'standby', though, as some agents may become suddenly unhelpful).

The night before the flight, call once more to confirm that there are still open seats. Get to the airport early (6 or 7am) before the ticket counter opens. Once you've bought your ticket, go straight to the gate and get your name on the standby list. Once this is done, it becomes a waiting game that could last all night.

**BUDGET FARES** These are similar to standby tickets, except that you have the security of a confirmed seat reservation. First, call the airline and tell them which week you want to leave and return (if so desired). Seven days or so before the day of your flight, the airline will get back to you with the exact details. This way the airline gets to choose the date and time most convenient for them, not you. Usually the savings aren't much better than a good APEX fare, but if you don't want to risk a standby flight and you're too late to buy an APEX ticket it's worth a shot.

## CHARTER FLIGHTS

If cash is tight and you can't afford flexibility, go for a charter flight. This gives you the luxury of a seat reservation at a lower cost, but will involve backtracking to the airport you arrived at. But beware – some countries will not allow you to use the return half of the ticket if you have left the country during your stay. Greece is notorious for this – a day-trip to Turkey can cost you a full-fare ticket home if you're not careful. We know, it almost happened to one of our researchers! Check with the charter company first and make sure to read the 'owner-participant' contract so you are aware of all the rules.

**PACKAGE HOLIDAYS**

A similar option is to buy a low-cost 'package' holiday to your destination. This gives you a flight and a place to stay while you familiarize yourself with the area and local routines. During the winter, you can find long-stay holidays (e.g. four–six weeks) including a flight and room for as little as £300. This can be a great way to provide yourself with a base from which to explore a country in depth; and if you get low on cash, you have a room until your return flight home. As the flights on package holidays are usually charters, the same restrictions on leaving the country may apply; check it out with the company first.

## PASSPORTS AND VISAS

If you already have a passport, make sure the photo is up to date and actually looks like you. If the picture was taken when you were 16 and you're now 23 and sporting a beard, you will have problems at borders in eastern Europe. If you don't have a passport, make sure to apply a couple of months in advance to allow plenty of time to get any visas you may need.

Try to get all the necessary visas before you leave your home country, as it is often harder to get a visa when you're abroad. There are several reasons for this: the embassy staff may not speak English, they may be unfamiliar with visa procedures for your nationality, or even impose restrictions on you that would not be required at home (e.g. having a certain amount of money). Before you leave, be sure to **double check** with the embassies of all the countries you plan to visit to make sure their entry requirements haven't changed.

**UK RED TAPE** Same-day passport applications can be made in person at the London Passport Office. Applications by mail take from 10 days to a month. Passports are valid for 10 years and application forms can be found in post offices. You will need your birth certificate, a photo ID card, two recent photos and £28. Note that the old British Visitor's Passport which used to be valid for one year has now been withdrawn.

Bulgaria, Romania and Turkey issue visas at the border, usually for a small fee. British nationals also require visas (in advance) for: Belarus, Bosnia-Hercegovina, Russia, the Ukraine and the new Yugoslavia. No visas are required for the Baltic states, eastern Europe or Morocco, but the duration of your stay may well be restricted.

There are a number of agencies that will advise you on visa requirements and application procedures. One of the friendliest is the Passport and Visa Service in London (Tel. 020 7833 2709). Do remember that they are agents and out to make a quick buck or two; it is better to contact the embassy concerned directly.

**IRISH RED TAPE** Passports are valid for 10 years. Applications can be made through the Passport Office or by mail; you will need your birth certificate, a photo ID, two recent photos and £47.

Croatia and Turkey issue visas at the border, usually for a small fee. In addition, Irish Nationals require require visas (in advance) for: Belarus, Bulgaria, Lithuania, Romania, Russia, the Ukraine and the new Yugoslavia.

**AMERICAN RED TAPE** Passport applications can be made at any Passport Office and are valid for 10 years (five years for those under 18). Applications by mail will only be accepted if you live in a remote area or if you have an expired passport and are applying for a replacement. You will need your birth certificate, state driver's licence or ID card and two recent photos. Replacement passports and passports for renewal cost US$55, first-time passport applications cost US$65.

Croatian and Macedonian visas are issued at the border. In addition, Americans require visas (in advance) for: Belarus, Lithuania, Romania, Russia, the Ukraine and the new Yugoslavia.

Contact the Visa Center at 507 Fifth Avenue, Suite 904, New York, NY 10017 (Tel. 212 980 3957) for up-to-the-minute information.

**CANADIAN RED TAPE** Applications can be made at any Passport Office or the Passport Section, Department of Foreign and International Trade, 125 Sussex Drive, Ottawa, ON KIA 0G3. Passports are valid for five years only. You will need your birth certificate or citizenship card, a photo ID, two recent photos and CDN$60 for your application.

Croatian and Macedonian visas are issued at the border. In addition, Canadians require visas (in advance) for: Belarus, Bulgaria, Latvia, Poland, Romania, Russia, the Ukraine and the new Yugoslavia.

**AUSTRALIAN RED TAPE** Passports can be applied for at either a Passport Office or post office and are valid for 10 years (five years for those under 18). You need your birth certificate or nationality papers, a photo ID, two recent photos and Aus$188.

Croatian and Macedonian visas are issued at the border. In addition, Australians require visas (in advance) for: Belarus, Bosnia-Hercegovina, Bulgaria, the Czech Republic, France, Hungary, Latvia, Poland, Romania, Russia, Slovakia, Spain, the Ukraine and the new Yugoslavia.

**NEW ZEALAND RED TAPE** Passport applications can be made at any Passport or Link Office. You need your birth certificate or nationality papers, a photo ID, 2 recent photos and NZ$80.

Croatian visas are issued at the border. In addition, New Zealanders require visas (in advance) for: Belarus, Bosnia-Hercegovina, Bulgaria, Hungary, Latvia, Lithuania, Poland, Romania, Russia, Slovakia, the Ukraine and the new Yugoslavia.

## HEALTH

Before you leave, ask your doctor to refer you to a travel clinic or specialist who can check the current requirements and advisories for the regions you intend to visit. They should also be able to provide you with recommendations about taking care of your health while abroad. A few preventative measures could not only save your trip from disaster, but also save you a packet on doctor's bills or hospital fees. It's not a bad idea to have a dental check up befor you go and if you wear glasses take a spare pair or the prescription. If you need regular medicine take a supply to last you.

Health literature and information including the excellent booklet 'Health Advice for Travellers' is available free in the UK from the Department of Health by telephoning 0800 555 777. Constantly updated info is available on CEEFAX pages 460-464.

- Make sure you get all vaccinations recorded on a **World Health Certificate**, and take it with you to avoid any complications while you're travelling.
- None of the countries covered in this guide imposes any vaccination requirements unless you are arriving from an 'Infected Area'. Unfortunately, the World Health Organisation until 1993 classified the **Ukraine** as an 'Infected Area' because of an outbreak of cholera and diphtheria of epidemic proportions. Though these are now officially under control, the Crimea continues to wage war with cholera and diphtheria is still rife throughout. A diphtheria booster is strongly recommended, and you should be particularly choosy about whom you kiss. Another Ukrainian quirk is their heavy-handed **AIDS** policy. In the past, visitors planning to visit for more than three months, or those returning to the Ukraine after an absence of more than a month, were sometimes asked to have an AIDS test at the border. However, an up-to-date WHO certificate from your home doctor should suffice.
- Those planning a trip to southern **Morocco** or the wilds of eastern **Turkey** are advised to get a typhoid vaccination and some anti-malaria pills. You should also check that your inoculations for tetanus, MMR (mumps, measles and rubella) and polio are up to date – not as a requirement of entry, but as a matter of common sense.
- If you're only travelling in EEA countries (that is, the **EC**, **Austria** and **Scandinavia**) and you're an EEA citizen, go along to your local post office and get form E111. This service is often neglected by travellers of Europe by train, which is surprising as it provides medical cover in EEA countries to the same level that a national of that country enjoys. In theory it takes a few days to obtain, but usually can be granted there and then. Take your

National Insurance number with you. You may, however, have to pay part or all of your treatment and drugs. Keep receipts and claim back the cost from the DSS when you return home.

- Doctors in Europe can be very expensive and often a chemist can give just as good advice – free! To find a **24-hour chemist**, either ask at a police station or go to the nearest chemist's shop and look in the window, as there's often a notice saying where one is open.
- If you've got to carry **prescribed drugs** or **injection needles** for medical reasons, take a prescription or doctor's note about them, as you could otherwise be prevented from carrying the medicine through customs, especially in eastern Europe and Turkey.
- The further south you go the more **mosquitoes** and other undesirables you'll encounter; take some insect repellent and, if you're a scratcher, something to soothe the bites.
- A small pack of **plasters** and a supply of **painkillers** won't go amiss either.
- Don't forget **sun-screen** and **sunglasses**, and try to stay out of the midday sun in places around the Mediterranean.
- Watch out, girls, in eastern Europe it's still difficult to get hold of **tampons** or **sanitary towels**, so take a supply along with you. Also, if you'll need **contraceptives**, take them from home.

**SAFE EATING AND DRINKING** Whether or not you can drink the tap water while travelling depends on where you go and your personal constitution. As a general rule, problems mainly occur in the more remote areas or less developed countries. However, if you have a weak stomach, stick to **bottled water** throughout your trip. Make sure that seals on bottled water are unbroken, or you will probably be getting the local tap water in a recycled bottle. If you plan to camp, carry water **purification tablets** or boil all water before you drink it.

Steer clear of **under-cooked meat**, be careful with **eggs**, and avoid eating **raw, unpeeled fruit or vegetables**. It's not a bad idea to take your own vegetable peeler; alternatively, try to wash fruit and vegetables yourself and be cautious with prepared salads. Take along some **multivitamin** pills to keep body and soul together during those long hauls. Remember to pack **indigestion** and **anti-diarrhoea** tablets, just in case you eat something that doesn't agree with you.

# Essential Preparation

## WHAT TO TAKE

The big danger here is blowing the budget for your once-in-a-lifetime European jaunt on a once-in-a-lifetime shopping opportunity. Think hard about what you need, and what you can carry. Obviously this very much depends on where you're going and at what time of the year: if you're off to Scandinavia in the spring, an extra jumper will certainly come in very useful. However, there are various points to remember, irrespective of where you are going or the time of the year.

Unless you're visiting family or friends in Europe and expect to be met at every station, we strongly advise that you use an **internal-frame backpack**. The advantages are manifold: it immediately makes you recognizable as a member of the Eurorail club and this stimulates conversation and communication which otherwise might not take place. Also – and more importantly – both your hands will be free, allowing you to produce your maps, passport, etc., at the right moment.

Shops specializing in **outdoor equipment** are an invaluable source of information and help. They will, in most cases, give free objective advice on what you really need for your trip and which brand names to look out for to suit your budget.

If you're starting from scratch it'll take about £200 to get together all the basic gear required to camp your way round Europe, but once bought this will see you through future trips and you'd easily spend that much on grotty accommodation in just one Inter-Rail trip.

Names to look out for in the UK are Milletts and the YHA shops and Field & Trek Equipment (catalogue from 3 Waters Way, Brentwood, Essex, CM15 9TB and from many branches of W. H. Smith – it costs a couple of quid). In the US, check out REI stores, which carry just about everything.

**PACKING** Every summer Europe is full of backpackers wishing they hadn't taken so much. Before you set out, put out on the bed everything you want to take with you – then halve it. Before you finally make up your mind, try wearing your rucksack with everything you intend to take in it on a good walk. Remember, you'll be returning with more than you left with in the way of presents and souvenirs, so leave room for them. The golden rule is: travel light –it can make the difference between a relaxing and an exhausting holiday. By the way, it's not a good idea to pack opened or breakable food products with your clothes, unless you want to go round smelling of gorgonzola or salami. A friend of mine packed some of her favourite olive oil. Big mistake! You can't imagine the mess when the bottle broke.

## ESSENTIALS

**THE BACKPACK** This will be your most important single piece of equipment, so make sure it is both comfortable and light. The three most important features you should look out for are: it sits just above your hips and has a support belt for round your waist; the shoulder-straps are well padded and the tension can be adjusted; and (most important of all) that your pack is 'high' rather than 'wide' when packed to capacity. I wish I had a pound for every Eurorailer I've seen creating havoc along narrow train corridors. If they're not pulling the door shut on someone's leg, they're laying out the natives with swinging cameras and boots hanging from the sides.

**CARRY-ON PACK** In 1999 the International Air Transport Association stated that the dimensions for carry-on bags as hand luggage for storage in overhead lockers in aircraft should be no bigger than 115cm: the sum of the height, width and depth combined. This has spurred manufacturers into producing a new generation of compact, lightweight and easily manageable packs. For short trips or combined rail/air journeys these are worth checking out, particularly if you are a frugal packer. The Kipling Server Duffel/Trolley for example, made from tough rubberised nylon has internal and external pockets, wheels and an extractable carrying handle. Unzip the back and it converts into a rucksack. Look out for a useful range by American firm Eagle Creek at camping shops. It includes a backpack that converts to wheeled luggage – an excellent idea, especially for more senior travellers – with a zip-off day pack. It's expensive, but well made.

**DAYPACK** A small daypack is invaluable for carrying maps, guidebook, camera, films, water, food, etc. Some people get a lockable version and use them as a personal safe, carrying all the important gear too bulky to go in moneybelts. You'll find that a daypack used in this way will become your constant companion, and you'll very quickly get used to never letting it out of your sight.

**VALUABLES** Keep a separate note of your ticket and passport numbers. If you do lose your passport, notify the police and get a copy of the report the police make out, then go along to your country's nearest consulate or embassy. A photocopy of both your passport and your birth certificate, kept separately, may help your case.

Another very useful thing to have with you are a couple of passport photos, which can come in handy for impromptu visas, replacement ISICs or passports.

One idea, very popular with the Scandinavians, is to buy a pouch to hang round your neck, inside your shirt or top, with all your tickets in it. Keep your cash separate – in a safe inside pocket, perhaps. Another good idea is a moneybelt. You can pick up one of these in most camping or travel orientated stores.

Put your name and address on the inside of all your luggage.

**SLEEPING BAG** Unless you plan to spend all your time staying with friends or in hotels, you'll need a good bag. Hostels charge for bedding (though many in northern Europe won't allow you to use your own bag, which is very frustrating – but the rule).

At some stage in your travels, it's likely you'll be a deck passenger on an overnight ferry somewhere. And a sleeping bag can double as a pillow on long journeys and overnighters in reclining seats (top tip: consider packing an old pillow case for making your own pillow, whether it's using a sleeping bag or a spare jumper).

If you don't have a sleeping bag and can't borrow one from a friend, go along to your local camping shop and get the best you can afford. When you're shopping around for a bag, price is likely to be your main criterion, as it's not difficult to spend more on your sleeping bag than on your ticket. Size when packed down and weight are worth bearing in mind.

If you're going to northern Europe it's a good investment to go for a good duck-down sleeping bag. Although the initial cost is steep, you get back the value over the years and it's well worth the extra cash. Do not make cutbacks in this: there are few things worse than a cold sleepless night before a hard day's sightseeing. Buying a cheap bag is a classic false economy.

If you're taking a bag and plan to do a lot of camping or sleeping out on southern beaches, then a foam pad is also advisable. Try and get one that is long enough but not too wide (remember those train corridors). Lie down on it in the shop to check it out. Print your name on it as you'll find pads disappear with irritating frequency.

**SHEET SLEEPING BAGS** can be a very useful addition. In very hot weather, it's all you need; in cold weather, it's extra insulation; and a sheet sleeping bag can be used inside or outside your main sleeping bag to protect it from dirt – it's much easier to wash than your main bag. If taking a sheet sleeping bag, ensure it is to YHA standards. Note: At some hostels you may find it compulsory to hire sheets, even if you do have your own.

**COMFORTABLE WALKING SHOES** (already broken in) are essential as you can expect to spend as much time walking as you will on trains. Don't go over the top and wear boots that would look better on Everest than strolling round the Vatican. If you're heading south, a pair of sandals is a necessity to give your feet a chance to breathe. If you don't have any, don't worry: they're cheap in southern Europe.

**CAMPING GEAR** If you're heading for northern Europe and plan to camp a lot, get a sturdy tent with a fly-sheet; however, if you'll be mainly in the south, pick a light one, preferably of nylon. A small Calor gas stove can save you a lot of money, especially in places like Norway where buying a cup of tea or coffee can be expensive. Gas refills are widely available, so don't bother carrying spares. Unless you're camping non-stop for a month, don't carry a lot of food

supplies and camping equipment with you, bu...
Shopping from the local supermarkets makes muc...
Remember to take a torch for those late-night pitches.

**CLOTHES** Obviously it depends on where you're going, w...
planning to do and the time of year. Use your common se... ut
*don't take anything you don't absolutely need* and remember, though
you may look terrific in your white jeans when they're newly washed,
you'll look terrible after you've sat up all night in them on a train.
Specialist travelwear suppliers like Rohan (Telephone 0870 601 2244
for catalogue) can kit you out in comfortable hard wearing easy-care,
lightweight gear. There are some super new hi-tech fabrics on the
market. Good value for money, if you're planning a lot of travelling.

Dark, comfortable clothes that won't show the battering you're
giving them are best. Smart casual gets you more respect than sloppy
casual. Laundries are often expensive, so take a little washing powder or
liquid detergent and wash your own clothes. Washaway tablets from
Boots the chemist are particularly handy.

If you're going anywhere near beaches, take a sarong: they're
praised by travellers for their versatility (skirt, towel, sheet, wrap,
shawl, scarf, cover-up for when entering churches, sun-protector)
Remember, it rains in Europe too. A friend of mine once spent 9 days
camping in Germany. It rained every day!

This check list may help:

- ❏ underwear - three pairs should do if they are fast drying;
- ❏ lightweight trousers - one–two pairs;
- ❏ shirts (long sleeves can be rolled up), T-shirts;
- ❏ shorts or skirt, sarong and a hat;
- ❏ fleece or jumper;
- ❏ rainproof coat or cape;
- ❏ shoes - two pairs - sandals for hot climates;
- ❏ socks and handkerchiefs;
- ❏ swimsuit and lightweight towel;
- ❏ toothbrush, small tube of toothpaste, soap and facecloth, minimum toiletries (decanted into small containers) tiny first aid kit, razor.

**USEFUL** extras include

- ❏ a compact **camera** (one you can afford to lose) and film;
- ❏ a multi-purpose Swiss army-style **penknife**, preferably with a **bottle opener** and **corkscrew** attached;
- ❏ a small **alarm clock** for making sure you catch those early-departures; earplugs and an eye mask may help you sleep;
- ❏ a small **torch** (Maglites are top quality and come tiny enough to fit on a key ring or attach to your penknife);

bungee cord

a lightweight **padlock** and chain or cable – especially for solo travellers. These can come in handy for hostel lockers, dodgy hotel doors, and for securing your backpack to luggage racks (or to other packs). Go for combination padlocks rather than keys;

❑ a **universal sink plug** and length of string for a washing line;

❑ **toilet paper**, and a large plastic bag for items to be washed;

❑ a small **calculator** helps make sense of various currencies;

❑ A CD or mini-disk player is good on longer journeys, only it's not cool to sing along in a crowded carriage;

❑ a **notebook and pen** - get shopkeepers to write down prices if you don't know the language. That way you'll know when you're being ripped off;

❑ A small sewing kit and safety pins - very useful for running repairs;

❑ if it's likely to be cold, thermal underwear keeps you snug and take up little space.

Try to take the absolute minimum. You can always buy extra items along the way. Generally rolled items crease less than folded. Smaller items or ones prone to leak can be put into clear plastic bags. And pack things inside other things - socks in shoes, for example.

With electronic gadgetry becoming micro-sized, you may want to consider taking an electronic notebook, If you do, weigh up the cost of losing it and copy off valuable data first. A mobile phone is becoming an essential accessory.

## BUDGETING

Exactly how much money you have to spend will affect your lifestyle in many ways. I'm making the general assumption that the average traveller of Europe by train is short of cash and won't ever be keen to spend more than necessary on basics such as accommodation and food. There's no shortage of information for those wishing to spend more – other 'budget' guides to Europe you can buy will list hotels for £30 ($54) a night, or restaurants for £20–25 ($36–45) meals. I'm not interested in that. After all, who needs advice on how to spend money in Europe? Also, you experience more of the real country when living like the locals on a budget.

It's a straight fact that £30 ($45) a day in Norway will just about get you a hostel bed and a cafeteria meal; the same £30 in Spain will give you a hotel bed and a restaurant meal, so take into consideration the countries you want to go to and budget accordingly.

On average, for your bed and daily food, you'll need at least £30 ($48) a day for the expensive countries, £20 ($32) a day for the intermediate ones, and £15 ($24) a day for the cheap ones.

- **The most expensive countries are:** Norway, Sweden, Finland, Denmark, Switzerland and Austria.
- **The moderately expensive countries are:** Germany, the United Kingdom, Ireland, the Netherlands, Belgium, Luxembourg, France and Italy.
- **The cheap countries are:** Spain, Greece, Portugal, Turkey, eastern Europe and Morocco.
- **The southern part of Europe** remains much cheaper than the north, but to take full advantage of this cheapness you have to be prepared to accept the local standards of hygiene, cuisine, etc.
- **Eastern Europe** is cheap for food, drink and entertainment, but hotel accommodation is expensive, so hostel or camp – though watch out for escalating camping prices in Hungary and Poland.
- The basic fact of the matter is that **camping** and **hostelling** are cheap all over Europe, and if you are prepared to do this and buy your food in the local shops and markets to make your own picnics, you can travel at very little expense.
- Remember, if you're travelling on your own and you insist on a single bedroom in a cheap hotel, it can double your costs, so **double up** with fellow travellers where at all possible.

## DISCOUNT CARDS

One way to save money in Europe is to take advantage of an expanding network of discount card schemes (offering savings of 10-30% on many items) for those under 26. In Scotland, there's the Young Scot card, in England the Euro Under 26 card, in Belgium the Cultureel Jonger en Passport, in France the Carte Jeune, and so on. The cards cost £6, can be bought from a variety of outlets, and offer literally thousands of discounts on meals, clothes, souvenirs and other goods. The cards can all be interchanged – so you can buy a Scottish card and use it to get discounts in France, for example.

**INTERNATIONAL STUDENT IDENTITY CARD** This offers worldwide **discounts** on venues, flights and accommodation in 88 countries for full time students. It can save you as much as 75% on museums and art galleries, etc., and, in some cases, gives free entry. It also entitles you to up to 30% discount on rail travel (Eurostar included), and on some air fares, discounts on YHA goods and accommodation, as well as reduced entry into some pubs and clubs. There's even a **free 24-hour emergency help line** from anywhere in the world giving advice on where to get hold of English-speaking doctors and lawyers, where to get emergency medicine, and they will also send urgent messages to your family in an emergency. For more details, tel. NUS Services 01625 413200. When purchased in the USA, it also provides you with automatic **accident/sickness insurance** anywhere you travel (outside the US).

ISIC can be purchased through Student Union branches in the UK, student travel offices or from one of these addresses (you need a certificate from your college or university, a photograph and £6):
**UK** ISIC PO Box 36, Glossop, Derbyshire, SK13 8HT or visit CAMPUS (formerly Campus Travel), 52 Grosvenor Gardens, London SW1W 0AG (Tel. 020 7730 3402).
**REP. OF IRELAND** Usit, 19–21 Aston Quay, Dublin 2 (Tel. 01 6798833 or 01 602 1600).
**N. IRELAND** Usit, Fountain Centre, College Street, Belfast (Tel. 01 232 324 073) or University Road, Belfast (Tel. 01 232 241 830).
**USA** CIEE and USIT, New York Student Center, 895 Amsterdam Ave., New York, NY 10025 (Tel. 212 666 4177 or 212 663 5435) or Council Travel, 205 East 42nd Street NY (Tel 212 822 2700).
**CANADA** Travel Cuts, 187 College Street, Toronto M5T 1P7 (Tel. 416 979 2406).
**AUSTRALIA** Australian Student Travel/STA, 208 Swanton Street, Melbourne VIC 3053 (Tel. 3 9639 0599).
**NEW ZEALAND** 10 High Street, Ground Floor (Tel. 9 309 9723), STA Travel, 233 Cuba Street, Wellington (Tel. 385 0561).

For further information contact ISIC on 01620 413200.

## STUDENT TRAVEL OFFICES

Geared specifically to the needs of young budget travellers, visit CAMPUS (formerly Campus Travel), Council (US), CUTS (Canada) as well as STA and WST (worldwide) who are the market leaders. They nearly all sell BIJ, Inter-Rail and Eurail tickets, and the staff will work out the cheapest alternative for you. They also sell ISICs and are usually found in university or college campuses. Note: They offer their services to anyone under 26, not just students.

## THE COUNCIL ON INTERNATIONAL EDUCATIONAL EXCHANGE (CIEE)

The CIEE is a non-profit, membership organization based in the US. Their travel experts, Council Travel, are one of the foremost organizations concerned with budget travel and help travellers of all ages with low-cost travel (air, train, etc.) as well as accommodation problems. In fact, they cover every aspect of your trip from your Student ID card to your airline ticket and reservations. Get hold of their *1999 Student Travel Catalogue* by writing to CIEE, 205 East 42nd Street, New York, NY 10017-5706 (Tel. 212 666 4177or 212 822 2700). They also have offices in other US and European cities (see Appendix

IV). The catalogue provides information study and work abroad. Use the council's ex... ble to get the lowest possible air fares, rail p... packages.

## A USEFUL TIP

Go to your local library and explore the world of travel gra... see what's available. It's amazing what funds are around, but it pays off to do your research well in advance. Try Rotary International (Tel. 01789 765411), Round Table (Tel. 0121 456 4402) or the Chamber of Commerce (Tel. 020 7248 4444).

## MONEY

### THE EURO – A SINGLE CURRENCY THROUGHOUT EUROPE

The European Monetary Union (EMU) will soon profoundly affect your money requirements. It is a scheme to replace the separate currencies of the individual member countries of the European Union with a single currency called the Euro (though Britain and Denmark have opted out of the scheme).

The Euro came into being on 1 January 1999 as an 'electronic' currency. Coins and banknotes will not be issued until 2002. Each member country has had to meet certain financial criteria before being allowed to join the single currency. The following countries have been approved so far: Austria, Belgium, Finland, France, Germany, Ireland, Italy, Luxembourg, the Netherlands, Portugal and Spain. Denmark, Greece and the UK will not be part of this first wave of countries. You may come across goods and services displaying prices in both Euros and local currency. Be aware and check carefully. Payments by credit or debit cards can be made in either Euros or the local currency. Cash purchases can't be made until 2002.

There's a 'Catch 22' situation with money in Europe. It's a big risk to carry around all your cash in ready notes, even in a moneybelt. Weighed against this is the fact that by taking traveller's cheques you face continual queueing, especially in the summer, not to mention the problems trying to find a bank or travel agent to cash them.

**PLASTIC** Credit and debit cards can be useful, providing you keep them for emergencies. They are OK in towns and cities, but you'll be hard-pushed to find a cash dispenser in remote areas, and the risk of losing cards or having them stolen is serious. It goes without saying that you should be very careful indeed and keep cards separate, so that if you are robbed you don't lose them as well.

You are also at the mercy of fluctuating exchange rates. This can work to your benefit in a country with high inflation where the local currency is falling against your home currency – but it works both ways.

...want to pay money into your credit card account before ...ave so that it is in credit and you run less risk of paying interest. It is also becoming increasingly easy to find cashpoints from which you can withdraw cash using Visa/Mastercard (you'll need a PIN number).

Remember, if you use a credit card to buy your traveller's cheques from a bank before leaving home this will be treated as a cash advance and you start paying interest right away. However, if you have a Thomas Cook credit card and buy your cheques from them, you have up to 55 days to settle the bill before paying interest. One advantage of using credit cards to pay for your initial ticket, or any other tickets *en route*, is that there is often some kind of travel insurance built in. Check it out and remember that these 'incentives' vary from card to card and from time to time.

Beware: French credit cards have an electronic chip in them instead of just a magnetic chip, so automatic card-reading machines in France may not accept UK and US cards.

**TRAVELLER'S CHEQUES** If you decide to play safe and take most of your money in traveller's cheques, get them from VISA, Thomas Cook or American Express. Don't find yourself trying to cash an obscure brand of traveller's cheque. When buying your traveller's cheques, always buy some in small denominations as this is more economical on a tight budget. If you offer a £50 cheque and ask for £30 in French francs and £20 in Italian lire, most banks will charge you first to change into francs, then again into lire. It's better to get traveller's cheques in denominations of £10 ($20). Anyone from the USA or a major European country should buy cheques in their own currency – unless you're planning to spend 99% of your time in one country.

**LOCAL CURRENCY** In general, it's a good idea to take some bank notes of the countries you know you'll end up in, especially if there's a chance you will arrive late at night or at the weekend. As a rule, take £25 ($45) cash in four or five currencies in case there's no opportunity to change money on arrival and you have to pay for your room in advance. For more obscure currencies it's best to order cash from your bank at least two weeks in advance. However, banks do not always give the best rate – shop around. It's always worth while taking along a few US dollar notes as a standby as they will be accepted in most countries, particularly in eastern Europe where goods and services may be priced in US dollars.

**PERSONAL CHEQUES/EUROCHEQUES** You can cash a personal cheque of up to £100 or sometimes more in any European bank displaying the EC symbol if you've got a Eurocheque Encashment card and cheque book. Eurocheques are normally written in the local currency (US dollars in parts of eastern Europe) and no commission should be charged when cashing them (it's deducted from your account). Girobank plc no longer runs its Postcheque service.

# BANKING

Banks in all countries open in the morning from Monday to Friday, but beware of public holidays and the siestas in Mediterranean countries (see individual country details for banking hours). In some countries, such as Germany, post offices (which have longer opening hours) will change money for a lower commission rate than banks

## MONEY IN EASTERN EUROPE

'Hard' currency from the West helps strengthen the local stuff; as a result some countries insist on a minimum exchange requirement. This is nearly always more than is strictly necessary, and in some cases you'll have difficulty trying to get rid of it. To discourage black-market dealings, you may have to declare all your hard currency and any valuables. This declaration is normally carried out on the train at the border. If you're thinking of playing the black market you will have to 'forget' to declare some of your hard currency because if, on departure, you cannot account for the missing money or produce the required receipts, you will be in trouble.

## BLACK MARKET

The freeing up of exchange mechanisms is starting to finish off the black market (as in Poland). The authorities in parts of eastern Europe still come down with a heavy hand on those caught in the act – and in some cases this means imprisonment. Hard currency is very much in demand and many private citizens are prepared to pay far more than the official rate to get it. Some people are still prepared to pay high prices for jeans, pocket calculators, etc., though this is becoming less common. In general, never have any dealings with anyone who approaches you in the street; at best, you're likely to get poor rates and, at worst, they could be plain-clothes police or an informer. A final word: tipping is not general practice here, so hang on to your cash.

## MONEY TIPS:

1. Take a money belt or neck pouch.
2. Sending money abroad is expensive, so take ample with you.
3. Banks tend to offer better rates than station, hotel or 24-hour exchange bureaux. A similar rule applies to commission rates.
4. Check commission rates to see if it is a fixed amount per transaction or a percentage. Also beware of places charging commission individually on traveller's cheques. Thomas Cook cheques can be

exchanged with no commission at any Thomas Cook *bureau de change*; the same is generally true of American Express.

5. In some countries, notably in eastern Europe and Italy, ripped or damaged notes may not be taken.

6. If taking your Eurocheque guarantee card or credit card, remember your PIN number; there are many cashpoints in Western Europe where you can get cash advances.

7. If you spot travellers arriving when you are leaving a country, offer your spare currency. It is a useful way of getting rid of that loose change and gets you small change for another country. Be discreet in countries where currency control exists.

8. Remember, you can't change currency in coins, only notes, so get rid of all the shrapnel before you leave each country –you can spend it at the last minute at train stations on snacks or drinks to take on your journey.

## INSURANCE

You are unwise to skimp on insurance cover, but at the same time, don't pay for unnecessary coverage. It depends very much on where you're going, and for how long. If you've a lot of expensive new camping gear and photographic equipment then undoubtedly that too needs to be covered. Shop around for the best deal; call in at your local student travel centre and see what they have to offer. STA Travel (tel. 020 7361 6161) offer a range of policies designed especially for backpackers, with some policies covering lost Inter-Rail tickets. It could be you're already insured through your home policy (your parents' or your own), so check up first. Eurotrain offer a travel insurance scheme. It's worth bearing in mind that train travel is very safe, but your health and your valuables are a different matter. If adventurous activities such as white water rafting and bungy jumping are your scene check the small print for exclusions. As mentioned earlier, some credit card companies include travel insurance if you pay for your ticket with their card.

**AMERICAN AND CANADIAN TRAVELLERS** If your personal policies don't provide adequate cover abroad, check with your travel agent or CIEE office to see what options are available.

## POLITICS

It makes sense to find out something about the local political situation before you travel. Read the newspapers and watch TV. Once there, take advice from reliable sources – local police, consulates, airlines and other travellers. If you are planning on visiting a volatile area, let the local embassy or police know. Avoid provoking controversy. You may have strong political beliefs, but keep quiet about them, especially close to local election times, even if you seem to have a sympathetic audience. Listen and learn from other people's beliefs, and dress and speak with respect for local customs and religions.

General safety rules apply – avoid ghetto areas, stick to well-lit streets and be cautious about accepting offers of help from strangers. Keep an eye out for suspicious packages and don't leave your own luggage lying around unattended. If you are confronted by criminals, terrorists or armed thugs, offer no resistance. Trying to be a hero isn't clever and may prove fatal.

**LAST-MINUTE REMINDERS**

1. Check your passport/visas are valid.
2. Photocopies of these and other documents ( tickets, passes, cards etc.) may be useful – pack a set separately or keep with a friend. Leave a duplicate accessible set at home. A photocopy of your Inter-Rail card is a requirement for some ferries.
3. Make sure your money matters and funds for travelling are sorted out.
4. Check your tickets. Leave a copy of your itinerary behind so friends and family at least have some idea of your plans in case of emergency.
5. Pack your kit and test it out. Make sure your footwear is comfortable. Ruthlessly eliminate those non-essentials.
6. If there's a chance you may want to hire a car (if you're over 21) or do some driving, take your licence and an International Driving Permit, available from the AA or RAC. (You'll need your passport, a passport photo, your driving licence and £4.)
7. Make sure you have adequate and valid insurance cover.
8. Remember to cancel the milk, papers etc!
9. If you want to be sociable, taking along a pack of cards or a travel chess set.
10. Photos of your family or postcards of your home town are always good ice-breakers.
11. Pack a pre-filled water bottle for long thirsty journeys and something to nibble. Not chocolate, it gets all over the place. Dried fruit or biscuits are good. Prices for drinks on trains can be high.
12. Pack this guide and a copy of *Cheap Sleeps Europe 2000*.

## Train Information

### NIGHT TRAVEL

Travelling at night has distinct advantages for the Eurorailer who doesn't mind missing the scenery of a particular area or the fact that night trains invariably take longer to get to their destinations. The advantage of night travel is that you save money on accommodation and at the same time add an extra day to your stay by arriving in the morning, ready to start your tour. Of course, how you spend the night and the amount of sleep you manage to get depends largely on which of the sleeping arrangements you opt for (and how good a sleeper you are). Basically there are five ways of travelling at night:

1. **Sit up all night** in a seat. It's free, but not guaranteed to find you fresh enough for a full day's sightseeing the next day. In this case, a neck air cushion is a good idea, but be careful as guards often get upset if they see your footwear on the seats.

2. **Pull-down seats.** These are great when you can find them, as they're free yet still allow you to stretch out, thus increasing the chances of sleep. Once all six seats are pulled down, they join together to form a massive bed. How much room you end up with depends on how full the compartment was originally; if there are only two or three of you in the compartment, you're home for a good night's free sleep. Reserve one if you can.

3. **Couchettes.** This is a seat by daytime, which at night is converted into a proper full berth. There are six to a compartment in second class and four in first class. There is rarely sex segregation, as the couchettes are nearly always full. For your £10–15 ($16–24) (average cost, but see under individual countries) you get a sheet, blanket and pillow, and there's a bed-light. You can use the washroom next to the toilets for washing. Each couchette has a luggage rack, but it's always wise to take your valuables to bed with you. Standards of couchettes vary enormously as they're run by the individual national rail networks, so that in Germany they're very good, while in Spain and Italy they could be better. Reservations for couchettes are more or less essential in the summer. You are required to book at least five hours before the train leaves the station.

4. **Cabines.** French Railways operate Cabine 8, a compartment (in new air-conditioned coaches) with eight semi-reclined bunks enabling you to stretch out in your own sleeping bag. They are completely free, but as they are very popular you will find it worthwhile reserving ahead.

5. **Sleepers.** Sleeping cars are a great step up in comfort from couchettes, but they're also a lot more expensive. As in Britain, European sleepers come in two classes and offer: a proper bed with all the trimmings, a sink with soap, towels and warm water, an electrical outlet and occasionally your own WC.

Sleepers are operated either by the Wagons-Lits Company (an international concern) or by a subsidiary of the railway. Many of these are developing into combined groups, collectively calling themselves Trans Euro Nuit/Nacht/Notte. The Scandinavian and East European countries operate their own sleepers. The average two- or three-berth sleeper is £20–45 ($32–72) a person, but price is dependent on the distance you're covering.

Very often, your train gets into the station an hour before departure; if you've had a hard day, this is good to know as you can get yourself bedded down earlier. If you take the train right through to its final destination, you can often lie in for another half-hour or so in the morning, once it arrives, before getting ousted. Other tips:

- If the train is packed, it might be worth asking the guard for permission to sleep in first-class. Watch out when the train enters for the yellow stripe along the outside of the carriage, just below roof level; this indicates first-class.

- If you're reserving a couchette or sleeper, try for the top berths as they're roomier, there's more air and they afford you a slightly greater degree of privacy.

- If you're going by sleeper or couchette on an international trip (or even for some internal ones in Italy), the attendant will take your passport, visa and ticket from you so that, in theory anyway, you won't need to be woken up at the border in the middle of the night. Don't worry, they will be returned the next morning.

- When you get into the couchette check for ticketless passengers hiding in the compartment (under the bunks).

- Most night trains do not have a bar or eating facilities on board so if you're the type of person who enjoys a midnight feast or gets thirsty in the night, you had better bring your own supplies along or you'll wake up with an empty stomach and a throat like a vacuum cleaner.

- The best trains for a good night's sleep are those that don't cross international borders (difficult to avoid) or stop every couple of hours at stations *en route*. On these, you'll have customs officials coming in for a nose-around at 3am, or train announcements blaring out all night long (and you can bet it'll be your carriage that stops right beneath the loudspeaker).

- Once you're all in, lock the door and hope you've not landed yourself – as I have so often in the past – with a collection of snorers!

- My advice to insomniacs is to have a heavy meal before the journey, take some ear plugs, and don't hold back on the local vino.

**WARNING:** A few years ago, many travellers on Italian and Spanish trains accepted the 'hospitality' of their fellow travellers in the form of doped orange juice and other drinks, and woke up many hours later to find they had been robbed. Some copycat incidents occurred, but following arrests, this worrying trend seems to be over (but be wary). Thieves have also been known to use a knock-out spray, sprayed through compartment vents, to steal belongings, though such incidents are very rare.

## MAIN NIGHT TRAINS

Below is a list of just some of the many good night trains in Europe. Remember, you can save money by sleeping on these night trains and cover more ground during your vacation.

| | |
|---|---|
| Cologne–Copenhagen | Madrid–Lisbon |
| Amsterdam–Munich | Madrid–Santander |
| Barcelona–Geneva | Malmö–Stockholm |
| Barcelona–Madrid | Milan–Paris |
| Barcelona–Milan | Nice–Geneva |
| Barcelona–Paris | Ostend–Berlin |
| Barcelona–Malaga | Paris–Amsterdam |
| Basle–Hamburg | Paris–Hamburg |
| Belgrade–Thessaloniki | Paris–Munich |
| Brussels–Rome | Paris–Nice |
| Brussels–Munich | Rome–Nice |
| Copenhagen–Hamburg | Vienna–Cologne |
| Hamburg–Munich | Vienna–Frankfurt |
| Heidelberg–Lugano | Vienna–Paris |
| London–Edinburgh | Vienna–Venice |
| Madrid–Algeciras | |

Don't forget it is often preferable to sleep in a good compartment than in a crowded youth hostel. Try pretending you're sound asleep when the train pulls in to stations and you'll raise the chances of being left undisturbed.

## EATING

As a general rule, all Eurocity and most Intercity and long-distance express trains have a separate dining car with set-price meals from £5–15 ($8–24) or a bar/buffet car serving drinks, sandwiches and light snacks. It's a very satisfying experience having a leisurely meal along one of the scenic routes even if you can only afford it once.

But few travellers of Europe by train can afford to indulge in buffet or restaurant meals on the trains because they're never cheap. The majority of the dining services offered on European trains are run by the Wagons-Lits Company. The quality of the food and service varies from country to country though, as it really depends on the staff and hygiene of the host country. Don't be fooled by the mobile minibars that wheel temptingly past you – they are extremely expensive, with coffee costing anything from £1. On top of that, the food and drink is often of very poor quality. Stock up with food from a supermarket before you leave and treat yourself to a good picnic on the train.

Remember: You can't drink the water from the train washrooms anywhere in Europe; buy your drink before you get aboard.

## TRAIN SPLITTING

Trains in Europe undertake some pretty complicated routes and use one another's rolling stock. Consequently, trains on long international journeys often split into various sections at certain points, so it's obviously important to check that you get on the relevant part of the train. The best policy is to ask and make sure you're on the right segment before you settle down. If your coach is going to be shunted about on to another train, find out at which station it's due to happen and at what time. It's all made quite easy by the signs posted on the doors and windows at intervals along the train, e.g.:

| PARIS | CALAIS | MILANO |
| --- | --- | --- |
| (Nord) | VENEZIA | (Centrale) |

This shows that the coach starts at Calais, stops at Paris (Nord) and Milan (Centrale) and terminates in Venice. There will also be a '1' or '2' to tell you the class of the carriage; and often a symbol indicating smoking or non-smoking. Whatever happens, don't get out of a train which is due to split up, and then get back on another car with the intention of walking along to your seat – you could find you're no longer connected to that bit of the train! Just in case you do get separated from your fellow travellers, carry your own money, ticket and passport at all times. This advice is also relevant in case one of you gets mugged – that way you won't lose everything at once.

In some stations, mainly terminals, you'll find the train reversing and going back in the direction you've just come. This is often the case in Switzerland. Don't worry about it, as it's just a standard shunting procedure. This often takes place on the last stop before, or the first after, an international frontier, and is used to reduce the number of carriages or add extra ones. If you have any doubts, ask the ticket inspector as soon as you are on board.

## SUPPLEMENTS

An Inter-Rail or BIJ ticket alone is not sufficient to travel on many of the express trains, or the EuroCity services. If you want to use these trains, you'll have to pay a supplement, which is calculated on the distance you're travelling and the type of express you've chosen (unless you have a regular Eurail). Some countries, notably the Scandinavian ones, do not charge supplements as such, but make seat reservations compulsory on expresses. (Full details are found under the individual country chapters.)

It's often worth inquiring how much the additional first-class supplement is, particularly if you're feeling under the weather and the train's packed. (As a survivor of the Spanish olive oil epidemic of '81 trying to get home, I can vouch for it!)

## TIMETABLES

One of the best timetables is *Thomas Cook's European Timetable*. This is published on the first day of each month. The June to September issues have a full summer schedule and there are summer service forecasts from February to May. The full winter schedule appears in the October to May issues, with forecasts in August and September. Although it seems expensive, the timetable is worth its weight in gold and can save you hours of queueing (particularly at Italian stations). It also has a table of airport city centre links.

- The *Thomas Cook European Timetable* is available from all Thomas Cook travel agents (price £8.99) or direct from Thomas Cook Publishing (Tel. 01733 503571, price £10.50, including UK postage and packing), and also from European rail specialists Rail Europe (08705 848 848).
- In North America, contact The Forsyth Travel Library Inc, 226 Westchester Ave, White Plains, NY 10604 (Tel. 800 367 7948).
- In Australia and New Zealand, write to World Rail, 10 Commerce Street, Auckland.
- Or from any country outside North America, write to Thomas Cook Publishing Office, PO Box 227, Thorpe Wood, Peterborough, PE3 6PU, UK.
- Back issues are available at half price, but be sure to ask for one with the appropriate summer or winter schedules.
- Also worth thinking about is the Thomas Cook *New Rail Map of Europe* which costs £5.95 (or £7.20 by post), published biennially.
- Another good idea is Thomas Cook's excellent *Guide to Greek Island Hopping*. The latest edition is more comprehensive (and longer) than ever, and costs £12.99 (or £14.50 by post).

The best value is the free UIC international timetable on ABC lines, though copies are like gold in most travel agents. Also good to have is the Eurail timetable, free from any Eurail issuing office.

Bear in mind the change from winter to summer schedules: all European rail networks start their summer schedules on the last Sunday in May and the winter schedules on the last Sunday in September, except in Britain. Also check the time zone the country's in and keep an eye out for local and national holidays.

If you want the more detailed national timetable and rail map for a particular country (often hard to find), contact the SBB Timetable Shop, Office 224, Hauptbahnhof, CH-9001 St Gallen, Switzerland, which runs a mail order service, though check first with Thomas Cook Publishing, by sending them a self-addressed envelope and asking for their list.

## INTERNATIONAL TIMETABLE SYMBOLS:

|  |  |
|---|---|
| R | Reservations compulsory |
| } | Trains running on certain days only |
| 1,2 | 1st/2nd class |
| ▄ | Couchette |
| ◆ | Trains subject to special regulations stated in the information notes of the relevant timetable |
| 🛏 | Sleeping car |
| ✗ | Restaurant car |
| 🍴 | Buffet/Cafeteria |
| 🏨 | Frontier border station; customs and passport checks |
| ⚲ | Drinks service and snacks |
| ✗ | Except Sundays and public holidays |
| ①,② | Mondays, Tuesdays, etc. |
| 🚌 | Connection by bus |
| ⛴ | Connection by boat |

## PUBLIC HOLIDAYS AFFECTING TRAINS

At public holiday times, you'll find services are amended, and those trains that are operating will be busier than usual and with more reservations. Check with stations for details and turn up earlier for the train. We list all the relevant holidays under the individual country chapters. In many countries the day, or at least the half-day, preceding an official public holiday is also regarded as a holiday. We give below a calendar of moving holidays for 2000:

| | |
|---|---|
| Ash Wednesday | 8 March |
| Good Friday | 21 April |
| Easter Monday | 24 April |
| Ascension Day | 1 June |
| Whit Monday | 12 May |

**MUSLIM HOLIDAYS:**

| | |
|---|---|
| Ramadan begins | 27 November |
| Id-ul-Fitr | 8 January |
| Id-ul-Adha | 16 March |
| New Year | 6 April |

## HAZARDS

On those long hot runs in southern Europe, where temperatures are high and trains aren't air-conditioned, the temptation is to stick your head out of the window to cool off. Be warned: you may cool off more than you anticipated. An unexpected drop of rain upon your face may just be your worst fear realised that someone's been to the loo further up.

Moreover, don't be reassured by the notices announcing that it's illegal to throw rubbish out of the window. Expect anything, and be on your guard, especially for cans and bottles. Most importantly of all, always keep an eye out for open or unsecured doors; even the safety-conscious DB (Deutsche Bundesbahn) estimates that nearly 225 people were killed in five years by falling from trains.

Always carry your valuables with you when you go to the loo and be extra careful on night trains, as this is where most theft occurs. Often a small padlock securing your bag to a fixed point is enough to deter a thief. The importance of keeping your passport on you at all times cannot be stressed enough. Obtaining an emergency passport involves considerable red tape and can restrict the options on your journey.

## TRAINS IN EASTERN EUROPE

Train travel in eastern Europe has improved immeasurably since the for a while. Station facilities are basic, so don't expect luxuries like showers or permanently staffed Tourist Information booths. To avoid unbelievable anxiety and frustration while travelling in eastern Europe, it's useful to remember the following:

1. Tickets are often only valid for the specific date and class stated on your ticket. To change your date is more trouble than it's worth, so always be sure of the exact date and time you wish to leave before buying your ticket or making a reservation.
2. Queueing is a fact of life, so try to buy tickets and make reservations at odd hours: one of the best times is late at night, since queues begin long before offices open in the morning. Whenever possible, try to buy your ticket/make your reservation from western Europe at the appropriate student office.
3. For all international journeys, tickets and reservations are often obtained through the official government travel agents (listed under each country). Otherwise use the train stations where queues are slightly shorter.
4. Make sure you're in the right queue. There's often one queue for journeys over 100 kilometres, another for reservations, etc. These are not immediately obvious as often there are no signs and it's quite possible to stand for up to an hour in the wrong line.
5. When you reach the front of the queue try and get everything possible done in one go, so you don't have to queue again later: buy your ticket, make your reservation, ask what platform the train leaves from, etc. Write it all down first, in case the assistant doesn't speak English.
6. Try to view the whole exercise as an initiative test, and always be prepared for any eventuality. It's not uncommon to discover that all second-class seats are fully booked so, unless you fancy another hour's wait at the end of the queue, it's best to have considered alternative trains or routes and whether you are prepared to pay the extra. Compared to the West, you'll find train fares are cheaper, but this is changing. It is often worth the extra cost to go first class for the added comfort, space and – sometimes – cleanliness.

## TRAIN AND BIKE TRAVEL

Those wishing to combine a cycling and train holiday will find the situation varies greatly in different countries. In some it is easy to arrange transport for your bike, in others almost impossible. Many railway systems publish leaflets giving details of trains on which cycles can be accommodated, with costs where relevant. You can take your bike free on Sealink Stena Ferries to France and Northern Ireland. For routes to Eire, Holland and on Hoverspeed services, there is a charge. In some countries it is possible to hire bikes.

For advice and details contact the Cyclists' Touring Club, Cotterell

House, 69 Meadrow, Godalming, Surrey, GU7 3HS (Tel. 01483 417217). They publish loads of information including very useful Country Information Sheets and also have many other services, including cycle insurance – but you must be a member to benefit. If you take your cycling seriously it's a bargain at £25, half price for students.

## Station Information

The average station in a major European city will have most of the following facilities:

1. **Ticket desk:** At large stations, tickets for domestic and international trains are usually purchased at different windows, so make sure you're in the right line.
2. **Information office:** Marked with a blue letter 'i'; you can find out times and availability of trains here. If the office is packed, check outside for posted timetables. There are normally separate posters for arrivals (white background) and departures (yellow background) with all fast trains listed in red. Each listing will show the arrival/departure time (in 24-hour format), the train number, name, routing information (point of origin, final destination and important stops) and the track or platform number. In addition, major stations often have computerized information boards showing the arriving and departing trains for the next few hours. Each platform will also have a 'train composition board' showing where each car goes and the class of service it contains.
3. **Left luggage:** Big stations will have a manned depot (usually open from around 5am to midnight) and/or automatic lockers. Check that the depot will be open when your train is due to leave and if not, use a locker. Before you put any money in the slot, make sure your bag fits into the locker.
4. **Lost property office:** Usually open from 9am to 5pm on Mondays to Fridays only. If it's an emergency (e.g. you've lost your backpack or passport), go to the station master's office.
5. **Station master's office:** In theory this official is in charge of the trains, not the passengers. However, since the station master runs the station, this is your best bet in an emergency.
6. **Telephones and post-boxes:** Most stations are equipped with these, and major terminals will have international telephone booths and post offices. In the smaller ones, stamps can usually be bought from machines or newsagents, and international calls placed through the local operator.

7. **Shops and newsagents.**
8. **First aid offices:** Most stations have some sort of first aid station. For those that don't, find the station master's office where they should have a first aid kit at least. In Germany and France, there are special travellers' aid offices called Bahnhofsmission and Bureau d'accueil where multilingual staff will help you if you're ill, lost or generally in distress.
9. **Toilets:** These will vary dramatically in cleanliness and are not always free of charge.
10. **Waiting rooms:** As with toilets, they vary in cleanliness but are obviously useful to Eurorailers. Many close at night, so don't count on sleeping there, though the ones in city terminals are often open 24 hours.
11. **Baths and showers:** Most large stations have these facilities and you can often buy or rent towels, soap and shampoo. The cost is usually around £2 ($3) for a bath or £1.50 ($2.50) for a shower.
12. **Bureau de change:** Unless you are really desperate, these are a bad idea as their exchange rates are usually extortionate. You are better off looking for a cash machine (which most major stations have) and taking money off your credit card.
13. **Tourist Information office:** These offices frequently hand out free maps and guides of the local area and, for a small charge of £1–£2 ($1.50–$3), will book accommodation for you somewhere.

If there are any outstanding features to a particular station (like a good, cheap snack bar), they will be listed under the 'Station Facilities' section of the particular city.

## PICTOGRAMS

The majority of stations are clearly signposted with universal pictograms which overcome the language barrier. Most are extremely straightforward; however, there are some that may cause confusion, and these are explained below:

Meeting Point

Lost and Found

Luggage and baggage storage pictograms can even catch old hands in the wrong line. For example, the signs for self-service luggage-carts and the porter are very similar:

Self-Service Luggage-Cart

Call for Porter

In some stations, you will have enough trouble fighting the porters off without going looking for them, especially in Morocco!

Confusion can also occur between the luggage registration office (for sending luggage through to your next destination) and the left-luggage or baggage check room:

Luggage Registration Office

Baggage Check Room

At both of these offices, you will receive a ticket that must be presented when you pick up your luggage. Make sure you get one before you leave, since it can be almost impossible to retrieve your bag without it.

Automatic lockers may be marked by either a pictogram:

Locker

or a written sign similar to the following:

**CONSIGNE DES BAGGAGES** (French)
**GEPÄCKAUFBEWAHRUNG** (German)
**CONSIGNA DE EQUIPAJES** (Spanish)
**DEPOSITO BAGAGLIO** (Italian)

# RESERVATIONS

Unless you don't mind slouching in the corridor for hours on end, a seat reservation is common sense during the summer months. On many services, reservations are compulsory (marked with an 'R' on the timetable) and you could face a fine for boarding a train without one. For the equivalent of £2–£3 ($3–$5), a seat reservation is worth the effort.

When making a reservation, be sure to tell the clerk exactly what you want. More often than not they won't ask you, so make your wishes clearly known when booking (e.g. if you do not specify non-smoking it will usually be presumed you are a smoker). Try writing down all the details before getting to the counter, bearing in mind:

1. **Class:** Make sure you do not end up in first class unintentionally.
2. **Smoking/non-smoking.**
3. **Which side of the train:** This can make a big difference; for example if you wind up on the north side for a Riviera journey you will miss all the views.
4. **Facing backwards or forwards:** Some people prefer to be looking either in the direction of travel or away from it.
5. **Aisle or window seat:** Window seats often have pull-out tables which can be handy for eating or writing, whereas the aisle seats afford more leg room.

If you choose not to reserve a seat (or for some reason cannot), check at the information office how busy the train will be. In many western European countries, you can make reservations up to two months in advance, while sometimes in eastern Europe you cannot make a reservation until the day of departure. In the latter case, get to the station as soon as the ticket office opens. Requirements regarding reservations are covered in the individual country chapters later on.

When making a reservation, try to get to the office between 9 and 11am or 3 and 5pm during the week. You would be amazed at how many people show up at lunch time on a weekday when all the locals are out in force trying to make their own reservations for the weekend.

If you find yourself on a train without a reserved seat, quickly shoot down the corridors looking for spaces on the reservation boards outside each compartment or on the seats themselves. If this fails, find the conductor or a guard as soon as possible and check to see if any more carriages are being added or if any reservations have been cancelled or are unused.

## SOME HELPFUL TIPS

Always check the name of the station you're dealing with if a city has more than one. Don't assume that a northbound train will leave from the northern station; it doesn't always follow. The following list shows cities with more than one station. A * indicates that a station other than the main one is used for connecting ferry services.

| | | | |
|---|---|---|---|
| ANTWERP | COMO | LIÈGE | PORTSMOUTH |
| ATHENS | DOVER | LISBON | PRAGUE |
| BARCELONA | DUBLIN | LONDON | ROME |
| BASLE | ESSEN | LYON | ROTTERDAM |
| BELFAST | EXETER | MADRID | SAN SEBASTIÁN |
| BELGRADE | FOLKESTONE | MALMÖ | SEVILLE |
| BERLIN | GENEVA | MANCHESTER | STOCKHOLM |
| BILBAO | GLASGOW | MARSEILLE | TILBURY |
| BOULOGNE* | HAMBURG | MILAN | TOURS |
| BRUSSELS | HARWICH* | MUNICH | TURIN |
| BUCHAREST | HELSINGBORG* | NAPLES | VENICE |
| BUDAPEST | HENDAYE | NEWHAVEN* | VIENNA |
| CALAIS* | IRÚN | OPORTO | WARSAW |
| CASABLANCA* | ISTANBUL | PARIS | ZÜRICH |

The city-centre maps on the reverse side of the *Thomas Cook European Rail Map* indicate which cities have more than one mainline station. Also, bear in mind that the distances between stations in these cities can be quite substantial (in London, for example, Paddington and Liverpool Street stations are about eight km apart; in Paris, the Gare de Lyon and Gare St Lazare are about 6.5 km apart). The moral is: don't count on split-second connections, especially between stations.

## When You're There

## ACCOMMODATION

To preserve the advantage of travelling at will, it is advisable not to book too many nights' accommodation or train journeys in advance – if you bother to book any. However, to counteract the negative side-effects of total flexibility, it's a good idea to arrive in major cities as early in the morning as possible in order to find yourself a bed for the night. Get to the tourist accommodation office, which is often located in the station, before noon. However, almost every town has affordable places to stay within a few blocks of the station, so don't

despair if you arrive late at night, as you should be able to find somewhere within walking distance.

As accommodation is the largest potential headache for Eurorailers and I'm limited for space, I'm restricting suggestions to the main
tourist centres. If you plan to travel off the beaten track or arrive late
in peak season, I strongly recommend you buy my *Cheap Sleeps
Europe 2000*. For the price of a tourist board booking, it will save you
a lot of time, trouble and money in the end. It is the only publication
out to contain hundreds of recommendations in all categories with
everything from where to sleep rough in safety to cost of B&Bs.
Remember, those travelling in July and August will end up paying
more for accommodation, as prices often go up with demand.

My suggestions tend to be biased towards hostels and to places
located near stations. There are basically four types of accommodation open to you: cheap hotels; youth or student hostels; camping
and private accommodation. Theoretically, there is a fifth option –
and it will certainly ensure you get round Europe at a phenomenal
rate – to sleep on the trains, not just in couchettes or sleepers which
vary in price from £5 to £40 ($8–64) for a night's sleep, but for free
in normal seats. As we've discussed night travel already and I don't
really recommend you spend your whole trip doing this, we'll
concentrate on the others.

**CHEAP HOTELS/PENSIONS**
If you're travelling with your girlfriend/boyfriend or husband/wife,
don't fancy camping and can't get into private accommodation, this
is your only real alternative if you want to spend the night together.
The advantages are obvious: relative comfort and convenience. If
you're in a city and you haven't long to be there, it's best to try for
one located near the centre, to save on bus journeys and hassles.
The disadvantages are: it's more expensive, and if you're in a really
cheap hotel, you often find a sort of 'skid row' atmosphere. The
hotels I list under each country are the best compromise I could find
between clean, pleasant surroundings and a fair price.

- If there are two or more of you, it's a good idea for one person to
  wait in the Tourist Office queue with all the luggage, while the
  other goes looking for a room. If you all want to go off to hunt
  together, leave your heavy packs in left luggage. You won't
  regret the £1 ($1.50) or so you spend for the extra comfort and
  speed you'll get out of it.
- You invariably find hotels close to the stations; the rooms in these
  places are generally cheap and, of course, very convenient.
- Once you've found a suitable place and have been told the price,
  ask the receptionist again if she has nothing cheaper. Often this

works and you get a cheaper room tucked away near the top.

- The luxury of taking a room with a private bath or shower is bought at a high price, so you do best to use the communal one. Always ask how much a bath or shower costs. If you're travelling in a group it can be cheaper to have a room with a bath than to pay for four showers. In the vast majority of cheap hotels it's not included in the price, and it can come as a nasty shock when you get the bill.
- Unfortunately the British institution of **B&B** is rare in Europe. Breakfast is often extra and rarely does it merit the name or the cost. Anyway, it's far cheaper and more entertaining to find a coffee bar or café where the locals go.
- **Pension**s (guest houses) are often far more attractive and friendly than hotels. A double bed is usually cheaper than two singles.

Remember to check all the following before deciding on a room in a hotel:

- the price of the room, including all taxes;
- whether breakfast is included;
- whether a bath/shower is included;
- whether there is nothing cheaper;
- whether the hotelier would mind if three or four people used a double room;
- and finally, when you must check out the next day, to avoid paying for another night's accommodation.

One easy way to book ahead is to use the London-based **hotel reservation centre** Accommodation Line, which specializes in economy hotels and B&Bs in Italy, Spain, France, Amsterdam, Budapest, Brussels, Dublin, London, Prague and Vienna. This is most definitely not your cheapest option, but if you can afford to splurge, it will take the hassle out of phoning ahead, and also guarantees clean, centrally located and friendly accommodation (with up to triple or quadruple sleeping in some places). Write for a brochure to 1st Floor, 46 Maddox Street, London W1R 9PB (Tel. 020 7409 1343 or Fax 020 7409 2606).

## HOSTELS
**YOUTH HOSTELS:** Youth hostels offer simple basic accommodation for men and women in separate dormitory-style bedrooms, washing and toilet facilities, and a common room.

- Hostels run by the **International Youth Hostel Federation** are good value and an ideal place to meet up with other travellers. They're the next cheapest alternative to camping, ranging from £3 to £20 ($5 to $32) a night, though most are £5–12 ($8–$20).

- You need to be a member of your own country's YHA or that of the country you're in, though often you can buy **temporary membership** on the spot.
- If you're already a member of the YHA, attach a **photo** of yourself to your YHA card to allow you to hostel in Europe.
- Many hostels have their own **communal kitchen**. In this way you can buy food at supermarket prices and cater for yourself for next to no cost at all. Economical meals (including vegetarian options) are laid on at many hostels (we list these under each country).
- Nowadays hostellers are not expected to do domestic **chores**, but any help offered is appreciated.
- At the very least, respect other hostellers' **health** and **hygiene**.
- Even if you bring your own **sleeping bag**, most hostels still insist you hire their sheets – a pain, but nothing you can do about it. Some hostels will accept standard YHA sheet sleeping bags, however.
- The general rule is that you can't stay more than **three nights** at any one hostel, but it is up to the hostel.
- If you've never hostelled before, go round a couple at home so you get to know what it's like. If you're expecting room service or breakfast in bed, forget hostelling.
- Average cost in the UK is around £7 ($12) a night and average meal £2–4 ($3.25–6.50).

**BOOKING AHEAD:** During July and August it's a good idea to book your hostel bed ahead in the major tourist cities. Try phoning ahead, but often they will tell you they are full, even when they aren't.

If you're going to be doing a lot of hostelling in Europe, a useful system is **International Multi-Lingual Booking Cards**: they cost 5p each and allow one or more people to reserve beds and meals. You should be able to buy them at your local hostel or from your country's Youth Hostel Association head office. You post the cards on to the hostel concerned with an International Reply Coupon (60p at post offices). Beds reserved through this scheme are held until 6pm. Scottish Hostels offer a free Fax Ahead reservation service.

Another option is to take advantage of the **International Booking Network** (IBN). Telephone one of the main national access numbers listed below (have your credit card handy) and you can reserve a bed at least for the first night of your trip from home. Some of the more remote hostels are not covered by the IBN, however.

| | |
|---|---|
| AUSTRALIA | 02 9261111 |
| ENGLAND | 01629 581 418 |
| NEW ZEALAND | 09 379 4224 |
| REP. OF IRELAND | 01 830 4555 |

| NORTHERN IRELAND | 01232 324733 |
| SCOTLAND | 01786 891400 |
| UNITED STATES | 0202 783 6161 |

Hostels vary a tremendous amount, though generally the further south you go in Europe, the less strict the rules tend to be and the more basic the accommodation becomes. Some hostels insist on midnight **curfews** and lock you out between 10am and 4pm, while others are far more liberal. If in doubt, it's always a good move to phone ahead from the station and check out if there's space and what rules, if any, apply. Many hostels are open only in the summer.

Good news is that, following a **worldwide inspection** of their hostels the IYHF has implemented an international Assured Standards scheme. Hostels must meet prescribed levels of comfort, cleanliness, security, privacy and welcome, or be struck off the list. Our findings are that this seems more or less to be the case, especially in Scandinavia where you can expect some spectacular hostels.

Be aware of the increasing number of unofficial hostels, especially in southern Europe. Many call themselves '**Student Youth Hostels**' and, though they impose no curfews or sex segregation, the facilities they offer are often very poor and the charges are more than those of official youth hostels.

If you intend to stay in youth hostels frequently, get a full list of all YHA hostels in Europe or buy *Cheap Sleeps Europe 2000*, which lists the best ones, along with other accommodation options.

If you need more hostelling information, the London office of the YHA is: 14 Southampton Street, London WC2E 7HY (Tel. 020 7836 8541). Go along in person. Written or telephone enquiries should be addressed to their head office: Trevelyan House, 8 St Stephen's Hill, St Albans, Herts AL1 2DY (Tel. 01727 855215). Check out the Internet site: http://www.iyhf.org

**STUDENT HOSTELS:** Student hostels are similar to youth hostels, but instead of a YHA card you need an international student ID card. Many student hostels are unused student dorms and only open during university vacations.

**YMCA INTERPOINTS:** YMCA Interpoint is a summer programme running throughout Europe between July and September. Offering cheap accommodation, Interpoints are run by young people for young people and also help with the social needs of young travellers. Leaders organize activities (sightseeing, excursions, parties, etc.) and they are useful, cheap and very friendly places to stay.

They are also good in a crisis, helping out if you lose your passport, etc. Costs vary, but about £6 a night is average. There are Interpoints available in the following cities:

**Denmark** – Copenhagen (2), Odense
**England** – Nottingham, St Leonard's-on-Sea, Dover
**Finland** – Helsinki, Tampere
**France** – Toulouse
**Ireland** – Dublin (2), Newcastle (2)
**Latvia** – Riga
**Netherlands** – Enschede, Utrecht
**Norway** – Bergen, Bodø, Oslo
**Poland** – Gdynia
**Scotland** – Aberdeen
**Slovakia** – Bratislava, Kremnica
**Sweden** – Gothenburg, Stockholm, Sundsvall
**Switzerland** – Geneva, Zürich

To use the centres you need to buy a **YMCA Interpoint Pass**. These are available at any Interpoint and cost about £2. They can also be bought from the YMCA International Co-ordinator.

For further info, including directions from the stations, write to **National Council of YMCAs** in Ireland Ltd, St George's Building, 37–41 High St, Belfast. Most of them are listed in this guide, and all of them are in my book *Cheap Sleeps Europe 2000*.

## CAMPING

If you're keen on the 'great outdoors', camping in conjunction with a rail pass is ideal for you. There's no shortage of scenic sites, and even the major cities of Europe have campgrounds on their outskirts. But as a general rule we advise against it for big cities. The advantages of camping are obvious: it's cheap, if you're on a campsite you have all necessary facilities to hand, and it adds a dash of 'pioneering spirit' to your holiday. Prices on official campsites range from £2 to £6 ($3–10) a tent, and £2 to £7 ($3–11.50) per person.

The **International Camping Carnet** is only useful if you're doing a lot of camping at the various European campgrounds which insist on it, such as those in the state forests of France and Denmark. You can buy the carnet at most sites.

The disadvantages of official camping are: other people, cars, radios, tents all around, queueing for showers, etc. Unofficial camping, however, removes all these problems and can be a memorable experience. Remember to check with the farmer or landowner before pitching tent for the night, and observe strict hygiene.

It's quite feasible to camp throughout your entire trip. A tent, gas stove, utensils, sleeping bag and foam mattress will solve all your accommodation problems at once. Don't skimp too much on equipment, however; a good tent is far and away the most important thing. (For more information, see 'Essential Preparation'.)

### PRIVATE ACCOMMODATION
This is an interesting and, in many ways, preferable alternative to hotels. Price-wise, it's slightly cheaper than hotels, but more expensive than hostels or camping. Individuals arrange through local tourist authorities for tourists to come and stay at their houses for any period of time from a night to the whole summer. It's an excellent way to meet the locals and get a home-from-home atmosphere. It also provides the perfect opportunity to ask all the questions you want about the country, but otherwise could not. Understanding the locals gives you a much better insight into the country, and, for my money, this is the best form of accommodation.

Ask at the Tourist Office and they will arrange the details for you. The only problem is that you may find all the places full in the high season as in many cities there are more prospective guests than recipient hosts.

### ACCOMMODATION – EASTERN EUROPE
Since the collapse of the communist regimes, many of the former tourist-grade hotels have gone beyond the budget traveller's price range, as the authorities take advantage of increased demand. This coupled with the lack of infrastructure has not made your accommodation problems any easier. Your best choice is private accommodation. It is cheaper, gives you a better idea of eastern European life, and can be arranged at Tourist Offices, or negotiated in the street. You will often find women meeting trains to offer their flats or rooms. This is common and perfectly acceptable, but use your own judgement if you are worried about the safety aspects of this. Camping is another good option but, as always, check how far out the site is and check on the public transport situation, especially if you need an early morning connection.

At the official Tourist Offices expect long queues, especially in summer, as demand is increasing faster than bureaucracy is improving. However, some of the old rules take a long time to go; for instance, you may still be told that all the youth hostels were booked up months ahead by large parties. In some places, such as Prague, several unofficial Tourist Offices have sprung up, which should help to relieve demand.

## EATING
Whenever possible sample the local cuisine. Apart from being an extremely enjoyable way of learning about another culture, it's often a lot cheaper and more appetizing than eating more familiar food. If the restaurants are too expensive, don't despair; you'll find nearly

every supermarket has a section devoted to regional specialities where, with a little bit of imagination, you can prepare yourself a veritable feast. Like everything else, a little background knowledge can add greatly to one's enjoyment. Here are the basic rules, accumulated over years of good and bad eating out:

1. Avoid expensive, pretentious-looking restaurants and cafés with no prices displayed.
2. Read the menu first, then add up the cost of your choices and all taxes and service charges before ordering.
3. Go for 'menus of the day' or tourist menus with fixed prices.
4. Serve yourself whenever you can.
5. Don't buy food or drink from vendors on the trains or from stalls in the stations. Buy it in advance from supermarkets.
6. If you've an addiction to something like coffee in the morning, take your supplies with you in the form of a camping stove, a small pan and some instant coffee.
7. When it comes to cheeses, wines, meats, biscuits, etc., buy the local stuff. Imports are always more expensive and it's good to sample the local produce.
8. Use fast-food chains if nothing else is available for cheap, reliable snacks. They're often far better and cheaper than local snack bars, especially in southern Europe where hygiene is often suspect.
9. Be adventurous and try something new. Ask for the house wine: it's always cheaper than listed wines and there's a good chance it's the popular wine of the region.
10. Eat breakfast out when it's optional at your hotel, as it's nearly always cheaper in a local café.
11. Make lunch your main meal of the day. Prepare yourself a big picnic whenever possible. Even when you eat at restaurants, it's at least 15% cheaper than in the evening. Avoid tourist areas, where the prices are always higher; search out university areas, where prices are more reasonable.
12. Look out in the stations for drinking water taps and fill your bottles for free when you get the chance.
13. Vegetarian travellers and others with special dietary requirements might need some advance organization. There are various specialist publications available. Contact The Vegetarian Society, Parkdale, Dunham Road, Altrincham, Cheshire, WA14 4QG (Tel. 0161 928 0793).

Certain foods may be unavailable in some countries. The Maltese use little fresh milk, and foods for young babies are harder to find where prolonged breastfeeding is the norm, e.g. southern Spain.

## CITY TRANSPORT

If you're going to stay in one place for more than a day or so, find out about the cheap travel passes on offer. Some cities offer day passes, others weekly ones and, if your accommodation is out of town, they can save you quite a bit. Many big cities are offering combined public transport and sightseeing passes. Some of these are extremely good value, and get you in free to many museums and other attractions as well as giving you unlimited free rides on all city transport. Ask at tourist offices.

Before rushing off to buy one, however, check on a map for the location of the main sights you're interested in, as in many towns these are all within easy walking distance of one another and you won't need a transport pass. If you're not in a rush, using the buses as opposed to the underground lets you see a bit more of the city – which is worth bearing in mind.

Tickets for the buses and underground can often be bought at tobacco kiosks, or from machines in central locations. Also beware of large on-the-spot fines for non-ticket holders. *Thomas Cook's Railpass Guide* is particularly good on local transport.

## COMMUNICATIONS – TELEPHONE AND MAIL

You will usually find both these facilities at the general post office.

### TELEPHONE

Some countries offer special telephone kiosks for international calls. Find out the international dialling code before you start and remember to drop the leading zero from area codes.

Always try to dial direct as it's much cheaper. Direct dialling codes to and from each country can be found in the basic information for the country or in Appendix VI. Never telephone via the switchboard at hotels or hostels as they invariably add on a lot – sometimes as much as the call itself – for themselves. Throughout Europe it's pretty standard that calls after business hours (7pm–8am) are charged at a cheaper rate. In nearly every country, dialling instructions in either English or pictograms are to be found inside telephone boxes.

A free **BT Chargecard** allows the cost of internationally dialled calls to be transferred to your home bill.

**Mobile Phone** If you are taking one, check reception coverage and use with your service provider before you set off. New generation dual band (GSM900 and GSM1800) mobile phones automatically switch between networks for European use (known as roaming). Call charges are higher than normal and you will probably be paying for incoming calls. Remember to keep your phone secure at all times.

**Telegrams** are expensive and in almost every case you'll find it cheaper making a quick phone call; but if that's impossible, write out your message and hand it to the clerk to avoid spelling mistakes.

**VOICE MAIL** A recommended means of keeping in touch with friends and family is by **Voice Mail**. On subscription you are given your own phone number which can be accessed from anywhere in the world using a personal security code. You can then leave a recorded message for anyone who is following your travels and pick up any messages from them. Travellers' Connections (Tel. 020 7240 3979) offer monthly subscriptions or yearly rates.

## MAIL

Airmail letters from major west European cities to the USA and Britain usually arrive within a week. Those from southern or eastern Europe tend to take longer, and postcards are even worse. Use surface mail (by ship) for posting home any books or clothes you don't fancy carrying around. It's usually very cheap – but very slow.

Trying to collect mail in Europe is more often than not a nerve-racking business. If you've no fixed address, the best method to use (and it's free or costs very little) is **poste restante**. This means your mail is sent to you c/o the main post office in any city or town. Depending on the country's domestic postal system, your mail should be at the *poste restante* office filed under your surname. Just produce your passport or equivalent proof of identity and pick it up. If the clerk says there's nothing for you, get him to check under your first name. In eastern Europe, get the sender to put a '1' after the city's name to ensure it goes to the main post office.

Holders of **American Express** cards or traveller's cheques can get mail sent to AMEX offices to await collection.

**CYBERSPACE** New technology is rapidly improving communication for the traveller. **Internet Cybercafes** are springing up all around Europe (there's a couple of hundred in London alone). Now you can surf the net, catch up on the latest football or cricket results, sort out last minute changes to travel plans, or chat online with friends and family. Before setting off, get yourself set up with a web based e-mail account from one of the free services like Hotmail, Pop-mail, Mail-Start, RocketMail, Yahoo! or Bigfoot. It will take about five minutes to set up and works like an electronic mailbox. All you do is pay the cafe's hourly or half-hourly rate (costs vary between £1to £5 US$1.50–8 per hour), type in your user name and password and then collect your messages or send ones to any other computer connected to the Internet, anywhere in the world. Don't worry about your lack of net knowhow, the staff are there to help. Some places will even feed and water you as part of the deal – like Madrid's Internet Cafe, which will ply you with *tapas* and coffee.

If you're not *au fait* with e-mail or the Internet, go along to a local cyber cafe to familiarize yourself with the system before you leave home. For a global list of Internet cafes, consult the Netcafe Guide, at http://www.netcafeguide.com

While you're at it, http://www.hostels.com/bulletinboard is an excellent source of information on hostelling for budget travellers. You can also post messages on Travel Mate (http://www.travel-wise.com/solo/) with motto Travel Alone But Not Lonely. It helps connect budget travellers with people who don't mind you crashing on their floor if you're desperate.

## SHOPPING

Unlike many other guidebooks, I don't include details on shopping. I take it for granted that most people won't have spare cash to blow in the shops, and if you do, you'll have enough common sense to head for the centre and find the main shopping areas for yourselves.

In general, the student area of a city is cheaper, and for food the large supermarkets are your best bet.

Shopping hours vary from country to country but they're all based round the 8–6 routine, though lunch hours can range from none at all to three hours. As a basic rule, the further south you go, the longer the 'siesta', and you can count on only a half day on Saturday.

## TIPPING

Tipping is anything but an exact science. In western Europe, most restaurants and cafés usually include a service charge and technically one shouldn't feel under pressure to tip over and above that. In practice though, a lot of people, albeit mainly locals, tend to do just that, sometimes even up to an additional 10–15%.

In eastern Europe, the old idea of taking 20 Western cigarettes as a tip is gradually dying out. If you're in an area where it is clear that you are more wealthy than the locals, tip generously but not patron-izingly. In most countries it is standard to leave some loose change for lavatory attendants.

## WOMEN TRAVELLERS

Each year I receive letters from women travellers who have encoun-tered problems when travelling alone. It's a sickening fact of life that women are victims of harassment, verbal at best and physical all too often; so it makes sense to take certain precautions to help avoid problems. The further south and east you get in Europe, the less emancipated women are, and the more men will look on you as a sophisticated Westerner, and easy game.

The single most important thing to do is to **dress appropriately**. In Muslim countries especially, any large area of naked flesh (including arms, lower legs and shoulders) is read as the equivalent of a green light. Even a T-shirt and jeans can be construed as seductive clothing there. A cover-up shawl in light cotton is a good investment. Never mind if other European women don't seem to bother with this.

If you are travelling alone, or could be in a situation where you are with just one or two other women and a lot of men, heed this advice (I have travelled in every continent as a lone woman, and I do understand the problems. These rules are the tip of the iceberg):

- No mini-skirts, no shorts, and always wear a bra. Wear sloppy, loose cotton trousers/skirts and tops. Clothes that don't show your shape are more comfortable for travelling anyway. Save showing off your curves (if you must) for the West, where they will be quietly appreciated, not read as an open invitation.

- On trains, especially on the type with no corridor and with entrance from outside compartment doors, do not necessarily choose an empty compartment. Choose one with other women in it. It might be less private, but empty compartments can soon fill up with men, and then you've no control over the situation. It's a good idea to meet other women travellers anyway.

- Couchettes that are not allocated on a single sex or family basis are another potential headache. Always have a word with your attendant to ensure you're in with a family or other women. Simply do not accept a couchette with a male majority – it's unreasonable to expect you to. You'd be better spending the night sitting up in a public compartment.

- Do not sleep in parks or stations, ever. Women on their own are at great risk if they do this. Who's going to know if anything happens to you? Throw yourself on the mercy of the station master, police, embassy, local church, anywhere, but don't sleep rough. Plan ahead and get into town in time to find a room.

## LONE TRAVELLERS

The thought of travelling alone in Europe is more daunting than the actual experience. Certainly don't worry about being lonely. During a month of travelling your confidence will grow and you'll make many new friends, of many nationalities, quite easily. Staying in youth hostels is an excellent way of meeting people; it is easy to strike up a conversation whilst stringing up a makeshift washing line between bunks! During the summer it is easy to spot other lone travellers on the popular routes, who may wish to have a chat. Another great advantage of going alone is that you have more freedom to go where you want, when you want, with no arguing over the next destination. If you're cautious by nature, try a short trip first.

The main problem of travelling alone is that you have to be even more vigilant with your belongings. Never leave your gear unattended in a public area, not for even an instant. Carry your passport and other important documentation on your person, don't leave them in hotel rooms. Be wary of smiling 'hello my friend' strangers, however plausible and charming. In circumstances even remotely suspicious, trust your instincts and act accordingly. A good policy is to leave an idea of your route with relatives or friends, even if it is only a rough plan. Phone or e-mail home regularly to let people know you're okay, and where you're heading to next.

## TRAVELLING WITH CHILDREN

As every parent knows, travelling with young children is hard work. That said, travelling by train with children does have its benefits. Firstly of course children love trains. Unlike a car where they are strapped in, here they can move about, often have a table to spread out their toys, books or drawings, have your undivided attention and entertain a captive audience of nearby passengers as well. Nursery facilities on some trains are excellent. It pays to check in advance. Mainline French trains have bottle heaters and proper nappy changing rooms. German expresses even have 'crawl areas' for toddlers. When travelling with children you need to plan their needs carefully. Tired little ones are grumpy, so try to arrange your journey around normal activity patterns. Make sure they get enough sleep, don't get bored and eat food that resembles whatever they are used to at home. It's a good idea to give them their own 'identification papers', perhaps in a neck pouch (just like mum's) for once mobile, they have the knack of vanishing when you are scanning the departure board. If a favourite cuddly toy is taken on the journey, treat this with the same importance as a member of the family. On the accommodation front, though more expensive, rooms with en suite facilities are the wisest choice.

## SENIOR TRAVELLERS

Don't be put off if this book seems to concentrate on the needs of youngsters under 26. It's just that they are still learning many of the things that senior travellers take for granted. You have maturity, experience and common sense on your side. Eurorailing is especially suitable for 'empty nesters' who hanker after retracing the adventure trails of their youth or discovering some of the places and treasures they always promised themselves they'd see. So what if you'd rather collapse into bed instead of at the disco, if you think Posh Spice is something to sprinkle on tandori chicken, if you prefer café con leche to piña colada? As long as you are young at heart and reasonably fit you will cope admirably. If in doubt, try a short trip first to test your wings. Senior travellers, while not inclined to waste money, often benefit from allowing a little bit more in the kitty for extra treats – the occasional taxi to your hotel after a long day, a splurge on good food and wine, a room with a view... If you are touring, break the journey into manageable sections. Do not turn a long trip into a test of endurance. Recognize your limitations and be realistic about your expectations. Relaxation and enjoyment should be top of your priorities so build into your schedule the occasional rest day where you stay put, have a lie in, laze about, stroll in the park, take in the local scene, catch up on correspondence and generally unwind. Travelling in late spring or early autumn will give you a far better choice of accommodation and avoid the crowds and baking heat of summer. The older you are, the longer it takes to recover from injury or illness so take your level of fitness into account when you are making plans. Take along any special treats like your favourite tea, for example. You may miss these more than you think. Senior travellers (usually defined as 60 and over) are entitled to many discounts on travel, local transport, entertainment and museums and galleries. But you may have to show proof of age!

## GAY AND LESBIAN TRAVELLERS

The general rule of thumb is the gay scene is further developed and more tolerant in western and particularly northern Europe than in the old Eastern Bloc countries and parts of southern Europe. The major gay cities are universally known and certainly include London, Paris, Amsterdam, Berlin and Madrid, though as one would expect, any large European metropolis is going to have at least some sort of an area where the gay scene is developed.

Be aware of the fact that the age of consent in most cases will be higher than the heterosexual age and that in Romania it is still illegal to practise homosexuality.

A useful contact in the UK is the London Lesbian and Gay Switchboard (Tel. 020 7837 7324), which operates a 24-hour service.

## DISABLED TRAVELLERS

The facilities available for disabled travellers vary widely across Europe, as you would expect. In general, the best facilities are available in the north of Europe and in Italy. However, even the countries with well-advertised facilities are not always up to scratch, relying as they do on the staff to be available to help.

- In the UK, **wheelchairs** can be accommodated on many trains, but to guarantee this it is advisable to contact the station first, to ensure that ramps and a space are available. In France and Germany mainline expresses offer services with station assistance, adapted loos and extra space seating. For other trains, SNCF publishes a booklet with the disabled traveller in mind. Elsewhere you may end up having to fold your wheelchair away.

- There are several important things to consider when travelling by train, the first being the **platform access**. In many places the access to platforms requires steps up to a bridge or down to an underpass. Lifts are often hidden away from sight and can only be operated by a member of staff, with the appropriate key. Another problem, especially at smaller continental stations, is the height of the train compared with the platform. Planning in advance, to ensure staff are available to help, is the only solution here.

- Be familiar with your condition. **Medical terms** are precise and internationally understood, whereas colloquialisms are not always meaningful to foreign medical personnel. The generic name of a medicine can be obtained from a doctor or pharmacist: a particular brand name may not be available, but generic formulae will be.

- Check the **accessibility of sites** with Tourist Information centres. It may be more expensive to join a tour, but the guide may provide a helping hand or know of a more accessible route. Roads may be unpaved and unlit, pavements, if any, uneven and kerbstones steep: the wheelchair user is rarely catered for away from main centres and you should be physically able to cope with the terrain.

- **Attitudes** to disability vary. The disabled may, on one hand, be treated as a normal part of society (which, of course, they are) or they may be closely questioned about their condition. This may seem impertinent but is often only genuine interest in the disabled person's welfare, and, in time, may lead to a greater understanding of the disabled traveller's needs.

- **Bathroom facilities** may be unsuitable for the disabled in southern Europe: toilets are often of the eastern 'squat' type in Turkey and parts of Greece. Ask around – people are very understanding and will always do their best to direct you to Western-style facilities. Hot water may be restricted to certain times of the day and, in time of drought, may be rationed and turned off for intervals. Be flexible: alternatives may turn out better than the original plan. Try to meet obstructive people with charm and, above all, remember: 'Where there's a will, there's a way!'

Good sources of information on accessibility and services are provided by the British, French and Italian national tourist offices, but ask at the others as well – you may be lucky. Any of the disabled pressure groups will also be willing to help, with several of them producing guidebooks – try contacting **RADAR**, 12 City Forum, 250 City Road, London EC1V 8AF (Tel. 020 7250 3222), or **The Society for the Advancement of Travel for the Handicapped**, 347 5th Ave, New York, NY 10016 (Tel. 212/447 7284). Also listen to Radio 4's programmes, such as *Does He Take Sugar?*, which feature field tests of accessibility.

# PART TWO

# THE COUNTRIES

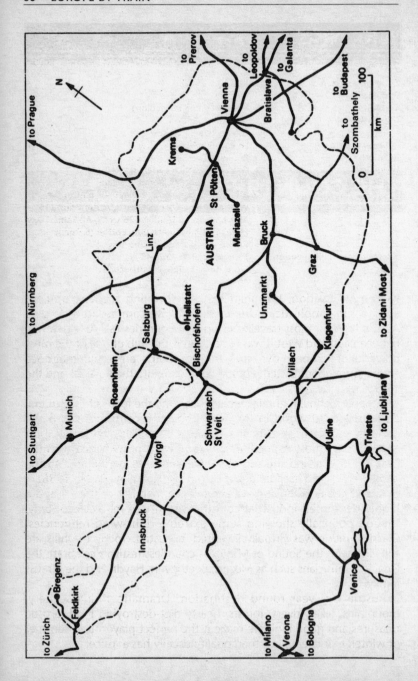

# AUSTRIA (Österreich)

| | |
|---|---|
| Entry requirements | Passport |
| Population | 7.8 million |
| Capital | Vienna (pop.: 1.5 million) |
| Currency | Austrian Schilling |
| | £1 = approx. AS20.50 |
| Political system | Federal Republic |
| Religion | Roman Catholic |
| Language | German (English widely spoken) |
| Public holidays | New Year's Day, Epiphany (6 Jan.), Easter Monday, Labour Day (1 May), Ascension Day, Whit Monday, Corpus Christi, Assumption (15 Aug.), National Holiday (26 Oct.), All Saints' Day (1 Nov.), Immaculate Conception (8 Dec.), Christmas Day and Boxing Day |
| International dialling codes | To Austria: int'l code 43 |
| | From Austria: 00 + country code |

Its central position, turbulent history, stunning scenery, opulent architecture, sophisticated lifestyles and welcoming attitude puts Austria high on most traveller's 'top ten' countries list. As a gateway between East and West it was for centuries the hub of one of the most powerful of European dynasties, the Habsburgs, an empire that once spread throughout Eastern Europe until it ran into the Russians and the Turks.

Imperial Vienna, naturally enough, became the focus of the cultural and intellectual world in the 18th and 19th centuries, when the greatest musicians, artists and thinkers of the day set up shop in *Mitteleuropa's* most happening city. It all went pear-shaped with the First World War and the subsequent collapse of the empire. Austria had barely picked itself up again before the Nazis invaded in 1938.

Austria today is thriving – a progressive member of the EU and a highly developed industrial country with a free market economy, though politically showing some extreme right-wing tendencies. Classical music was virtually invented in Austria. Today the hills are still alive with the Sound of Music, as countless festivals celebrate the legacy of musicians such as Mozart, Beethoven, Haydn and the Strauss family.

Austria is a year round destination. Dramatic alpine scenery, mountains, lakes, rivers, forests, hearty diet-destroying food, artistic treasures and good nightlife make it the perfect playground summer or winter. Not cheap, but then quality usually has a price.

## AUSTRIAN FEDERAL RAILWAYS
### (ÖSTERREICHISCHE BUNDESBAHNEN, ÖBB)

Trains are clean, comfortable, and run on time. The stations are also generally pleasant, but expect big queues in the summer. Most intercities run two hours apart.

EuroCity *(EC)* trains travel on domestic routes as well as cross-border routes and have complementary first and second class reservation, a restaurant car and direct refreshment service. InterCity *(IC)* are regular domestic trains stopping in larger cities and major tourist areas. Refreshments are carried on board. D Züge are expanded trains on EC and IC long distance routes. EuroNight *(EN)* are domestic and international sleeper trains. Local trains can be slow, especially on mountainous routes, so avoid them unless you have plenty of time up your sleeve.

**PASSES AVAILABLE** The Austrian Rail Pass (*Bundes-Netzkarte*) is valid for three days of travel within a 15-day period, on all Austrian Railways routes, and can be extended for up to five extra days. The card gives discounts on Danube ships between Passau and Linz, as well as on Wolfgangsee and Lake Constance. You can get 40% discount on rent-a-bike, 10% discount on the Schafberg and Schneeberg private railways, and children get further discounts. Only available to buy outside Austria itself, 2nd-class tickets cost around £65 ($105) for three days within 15, with an extra £10 ($16) per extended day. First class is half the price again.

Another option is the one-year ticket (*VORTEILScard*), valid on the whole Austrian rail network, including most private railways. Costing AS1,290, it gives half-price travel on any Austrian Railways train, and reductions on bike and car hire.

Eurail and Inter-Rail passes are valid. Austria is in Inter-Rail zone C, along with Germany, Switzerland and Denmark. Euro Domino tickets are also available. For details, see the Inter-Rail section in Part One.

There's also the European East Pass, covering only first-class travel on the Austrian, Czech, Hungarian, Polish and Slovakian railway lines, and available only outside these countries. It is valid for any five days' travel within a one-month period, and can be extended up to 10 days. There are discounts on ships and for bike rental. A five-day pass costs about £126 ($205), with each day of extension costing an extra £14 ($23).

**INTER-RAIL BONUSES** See Appendix I for reductions.

**EURAIL BONUSES**
Puchberg am Schneeberg–Hochschneeberg rack railway: 10% reduction.

St Wolfgang–Schafbergspitze rack railway: 15% reduction.
Steamers on Lake Wolfgang: 20% reduction.

**EURAIL AID OFFICES**
Vienna Westbahnhof Tel. (01) 5800 33598
Salzburg Hauptbahnhof Tel. (0662) 8887 5428
Innsbruck Hauptbahnhof Tel. (0512) 503 5460

**REDUCED FARES**
50% reduction on steamers operated by steamship companies on Lake
  Constance.
50% reduction on steamer day trips operated between Linz and
  Passau or vice versa by Wurm & Köck.
15% reduction on steamer trips operated by DDSG Blue Danube
  Schiffahrt GmbH.

## TRAIN INFORMATION
The Austrian Railways head office is at Elisabethstrasse 9, A-1010 in
Vienna (from Britain, tel. 0043-1-580 00, fax 0043-1-580 025 001).
Information officers have yellow cap bands and are nearly all
multilingual, and most other rail staff speak at least a little English.
Luggage lockers use 10-Schilling pieces. Children under six travel free
on ÖBB. Groups of six or more qualify for reductions (special booking
procedures necessary).

**RESERVATIONS** Are not necessary, but if you want to book ahead, it
costs AS30 and can be done until two hours before your train leaves.

**NIGHT TRAVEL** Night trains are few, simply because the distances are
short. Sleepers and couchettes are clean and comfortable. Reserve
at least five hours beforehand. Couchettes cost from AS200. There
are also compartments with pull-down seats which cost nothing.

**LEFT LUGGAGE** You can leave your luggage at any station in Austria
for AS20 per piece per day. Some stations have luggage lockers;
these cost AS20–AS40 per day and are accessible 24 hours.

**EATING ON TRAINS** There are dining cars on all intercity trains, and
mini-bars on all except local services. But it's an expensive way to
go; picnics are the sensible budget option. If you don't get to a
supermarket before the train leaves, there are well-stocked kiosks at
most stations. Vienna's stations, in particular, have delicatessens open
long hours, including Sundays.

**SCENIC TIPS** If you're leaving Vienna for Salzburg, stop off at the village of Mariazell. It's beautiful. Surrounded by mountains, it was a religious pilgrimage site. Take the cable-car for the view. From Vienna take the train to St Pöten from Westbahnhof, then change to a train for Mariazell.

The main Innsbruck–Zell am See–Salzburg line is one of the most scenic. If you're going from Innsbruck to Italy, take the train to Brennero for spectacular mountainous scenery. If you're heading towards Slovenia, try Vienna–Trieste – this goes via Klagenfurt and Udine. If you're travelling from Innsbruck to Munich or vice versa, try the route via Garmisch – again, the alpine scenery is breathtaking.

Bregenz, on the Bodensee in the west of Austria, is a good place to sail across to Germany. From here you can go to Konstanz over the border (ask about reductions for train pass holders). Also at Bregenz you can take the Pfanderbahn up to the top for a panorama of the Alps and over the Bodensee. The Vorarlberg Tourist Office in Bregenz on Anton-Schneider-Strasse has information on alpine villages and excursions.

Sail the Danube from the German–Austrian border (Passau) to Vienna or from Vienna to Passau. The trip lasts 1½ days, stopping overnight at Linz. Alternatively, there's the Linz–Vienna trip or vice versa. The prettiest part of the journey is from Krems to Melk. The train runs from both Melk and Krems. Further information from DDSG, Reisedienst 2, Handelskai 265. In Passau, go to DDSG-Schiffs-station, Im Ort 14a, Dreiflusseck. Get off the boat and take a look around as often as possible as many of the stopping-off places are well-preserved medieval or Baroque towns.

**BIKES** Nearly every big station in Austria rents out bikes – *Fahrrad am Bahnhof* – though have a look at the traffic before committing yourself. Prices are normally around AS90, but your train ticket should get you half price.

## TOURIST INFORMATION
Austria is very well geared to tourists, and there's always plenty of free information and maps to be had from the Tourist Offices (*Verkehrsverein*) in every large town. They'll also give out the addresses of provincial tourist boards if required.

**ISIC BONUSES** 50% reductions on most art galleries and museums. 10% on Rosen Hotels. For further information, contact Ökista at Türkenstrasse 4–6, Vienna (Tel. 3475260).

**MONEY MATTERS** 1 Austrian Schilling (AS) = 100 groschen (gr).

Banking hours are Mon.–Fri.: 8am–12.30pm and 1.30pm–3pm, Thurs.: to 5.30pm. The main banks in Vienna stay open over lunch. Cash traveller's cheques in large denominations as commission charges are high. You can cash Eurocheques without paying commission if you stay at the Ruthensteiner hostel near the Westbahnhof.

**POST OFFICES** Mon.–Fri.: 8am–12 noon, 2pm–6pm; Sat.: 8am–10am. Stamps can also be bought from Tabak-Trafik shops.

**SHOPS** Mostly have the same hours as post offices, closing on Saturday afternoons. Food shops usually open before 8am, but close for lunch 12.30–3pm.

**MUSEUMS** Often closed Mondays.

**TIPPING** 10–15% is added to bills in restaurants but a tip is also expected – rounding up the bill will do. *Einschliesslich Bedienung* means 'service included'.

## SLEEPING

**HOSTELS** You need an International Youth Hostel Association membership card to stay at any of the hundred or so Austrian youth hostels (*Jugendherbergen*), though guest cards are available. They're usually open around 6am–10pm and charge about AS130–240 for bed and breakfast, from AS65 for just bed, and about AS65–130 for a meal, with an extra charge where cooking facilities are available.

At many hostels breakfast is compulsory; check first. Space allowing, you can stay more than three nights at most hostels unless you're travelling in a large group. If you are, write in advance to the warden to book. Keep in mind that some hostels are open only May–mid-September.

**HOTELS** Hotels are nearly always spotless, but also nearly always wildly expensive, particularly in Vienna and Salzburg. Prices off-season are 20–40% cheaper, and in May, June and September they can also be 15–25% less expensive than in July and August. Expect to pay at least AS430 for a double, and upwards of AS650 in Vienna and other cities. Bear this in mind if you're approached by a hotelier trying to fill his hotel – he may be offering you a bargain. Don't be put off by this approach as it's a buyer's market; ask the price and location and what's included. You're under no obligation.

**PRIVATE HOUSES** (*Privat Zimmer/Zimmer Frei*): Rooms are around AS170 per person and can be an interesting alternative.

**CAMPING** The International Camping Carnet is not obligatory, but it'll often get you preferential treatment. The grounds are generally very good: clean, efficient and well-planned. Austrians are keen campers themselves, so in peak season, pitch as early as you can. Charges are from AS25 per person and AS25 per tent, with Vienna at around AS55 per person and per tent.

## EATING AND NIGHTLIFE

Austrian dishes are simple and hearty, but if you've a sweet tooth, welcome to pastry paradise. You'll usually find pork (*Schwein*) and fish better value than lamb and beef, although *Tafelspitz* (boiled beef) is good and cheap, and with a noodle or dumpling soup makes a filling meal.

Budget-wise, though, the best news is the *Wurst* – Austria's hot sausages are great for a cheap bite on the hoof, and they come fried, boiled, smoked or spicy. Vienna's most famous dish, *Wiener Schnitzel* (fried, breaded veal), is found everywhere and thick goulash soups are great on winter days.

The coffee-and-cakes scene is good news all round, except for the price. *Strudel* is excellent, so too the *Sachertorte,* a wickedly rich dark chocolate cake. But you may well end up eating picnics (cheap supermarkets include Billa, Hofer and Konsum) or from fast-food chains most of the time, since restaurant prices are similar to those in Britain. Try a traditional dish at least once, though; you won't regret it.

Nightlife in Austria ranges from sleepy in alpine areas to lively in the cities. Discos and bars cost big bucks in Austria and anyway they're mostly a bit on the smooth side. Best to head for a wine tavern or beer cellar in the student areas, where prices are generally lower. The east of the country is best for wine.

If you're into opera, Vienna's the place. The season runs from September to June, and while seats are pricey, cheap standby tickets (AS50) can sometimes be had two hours before a performance, if you're prepared to queue. 'Smart casual' dress is acceptable.

## Vienna (Wien) city phone code: 01

This city of sweet surprises reflects the spirit of another era - elegant streets and traffic free boulevards, attractive parks, Baroque and over-the-top art nouveau façades. But an air of slightly faded charm is being replaced with a new vibrancy and masses of style. It is a city of pleasure and indulgence. Relax and soak up the atmosphere. This great capital city of music is where so many famous musicians and composers lived and worked – Strauss, Schubert, Haydn, Mozart, Beethoven, Brahms, Schönberg, Mahler... today their houses are memorials and their music is celebrated in dozens of regular concerts. Alongside this runs a lively pop, rock and folk music scene – hip hop to house, techno to jungle – centred around the Danube Island Festival which in June attracts over two million visitors.

Within the ring of broad streets that replaced the old city walls, Vienna has a picturesque medieval centre, crowned by the steeple of St Stephan's cathedral. Magnificent palaces have become art museums, and there's a popular wine district in the woods on the outskirts of the city.

The capital is divided into 23 districts, radiating from the First District – the 'Ring' in the city centre. Vienna's not actually on the Danube – the river runs through the outskirts – but the Danube canal is part of the city. However, if you're heading for Hungary, sailing on the Danube in Budapest costs a fraction of the price charged in Austria.

Use this book (check out the **Free Vienna** tips below) and do your sums carefully in Vienna. It's a great place, but at a price.

## STATION FACILITIES

There are two main terminals: the Westbahnhof and the Südbahnhof, with trains leaving daily from Westbahnhof at Europaplatz to France, Switzerland and Germany. Trains for Eastern Europe, southern Austria, former Yugoslavian states and Italy leave from Südbahnhof. Trains to Budapest leave from both stations. Trains for Berlin and Prague leave from Franz Josef Bahnhof or Wien Mitte Bahnhof. For further info, telephone 1717.

## TOURIST INFORMATION

The main office is at Kärntnerstrasse 38, behind the Opera (Tel. 5138892), open 9am-7pm, closed Sun. There are also Tourist Offices at Westbahnhof and Südbahnhof. Like all Austrian Tourist Offices, they provide an accommodation-finding service. Pick up the city map, transport map and the *Young Vienna Scene* magazine. The English-language weekly *Austria Today* has up-to-date listings. There is also an information centre for young people at Bellaria-Passage (Tel. 1799), open Mon.–Fri. noon–7pm, Sat. 10am–5pm. Tourist information for all of Austria is available at Margaretenstrasse 1 (Tel. 588660), open Mon.–Fri. 9am–5pm.

The main stations have train information, reservations desks and left-luggage lockers. Südbahnhof and Westbahnhof have post offices and foreign exchange bureaux as well as shower facilities and other commercial concessions.

Trams 6 and 18 connect the South and West stations. To get to the city centre from Südbahnhof take tram D or 5-Bahn 1, 2 or 3 to Südtiroler Platz (1 stop), then U-Bahn 1. From Westbahnhof take Tram 58 or 52, or U-Bahn 3. From Franz Josef, turn left down Althastrasse to Alserbachstrasse, turn left again, and walk to Friedensbrücke, on U-Bahn 4.

## ADDRESSES

**POST OFFICE** Fleischmarkt 19. Open 24 hours.
**AMEX** Kärntnerstrasse 21–23, Mon.–Fri.: 9am–5.30pm, Sat.: 9am–12noon (Tel. 515400-770).U-Bahn Stephansplatz
**UK EMBASSY** Jauresgasse 12 (Tel. 716130)
**IRISH EMBASSY** Landstrasser Hauptstrasse 2, Hilton Centre (Tel. 7154246)
**US EMBASSY** Boltzmanngasse 16 (Tel. 31339)
**CANADIAN EMBASSY**
Laurenzerberg 2 (Tel. 53138-3000)
**AUSTRALIAN EMBASSY** Mattiellistrasse 2–4 (Tel. 5128580)
**NEW ZEALAND** Springsiedlergasse 28 (Tel. 3188505)
**POLICE EMERGENCY** Tel. 133
**MEDICAL EMERGENCY** Tel. 144/141
**ÖKISTA (student travel)** Karlsgasse (Tel. 50243). Can help with accommodation and train tickets.
**EURAIL AID OFFICE** Vienna Westbahnhof, Tel. (01) 5800 33598

## GETTING ABOUT

Go to Karlsplatz U-Bahn station for info on city transport and a leaflet in English called *Exploring Vienna by Train*, which explains ticket details and how to use the system. There are various tram, underground and bus passes on offer, but most of Vienna is easy to see by foot.

Tickets for a single journey within the central zone on buses, trams, U-Bahn and S-Bahn (free with an Inter-Rail pass) cost more from the driver than from vending machines. Strip tickets for four or eight journeys, within one zone, are also available and more than one person can use them by cancelling the appropriate number of strips in the machine. The eight-day Environmental Pass is used like strip tickets, but each strip is valid for one full day. Other options are 24-hour (AS50) or 72-hour (AS130) explorer tickets, and the Vienna Card (AS210), which gets you 72 hours of unlimited city travel along with various entrance reductions and discounts. Late-night theatre or concert-goers can use their tickets to travel anywhere on any line for two hours before and six hours after the start of the performance.

Tickets can also be bought from automatic machines in stations and on some trams, so have AS5 and AS10 coins to hand. Night buses radiate from Schwedenplatz. Forget the city tours, taxis and *Fiakers* (two-horse coaches at AS400 a go), as they'll cripple your budget.

# SEEING

Free leaflets from Tourist Information offices will give you all the history, details, opening times, etc. The obvious starting point is the city's medieval centre; and at its heart **St Stephan's Cathedral** and the square **Stephansplatz** (at the intersection of Graben and Kärntnerstrasse) – it's a good place to sit and watch. But rather than suggesting a sightseeing circuit, and having everyone tramping the same well-worn route, we list the major sights so you can devise your own route using the map. **Use the Vienna Card** (AS210) for discounts ranging from 10-50% off entrance prices at over 30 main attractions as well as at selected cafes, stores, theatres and galleries.

**St Stephan's Cathedral:** Built in the 13th and 14th centuries, it's the most important Gothic building in Austria. Climb the 343 steps of the south steeple (or take the lift up the north steeple, AS50) for a 360 degree view of Vienna, or go down to the catacombs and look at the Habsburgs' innards in the Old Prince's Vault.

**The Hofburg:** The Habsburgs' sprawling winter palace encompasses every architectural style from the 13th to the 20th century. It includes the Spanish Riding School and the new Lippizzaner Museum (you can watch the Lippizaner stallions training in the mornings) and the Burgkapelle, where the Vienna Boys' Choir performs (both are closed for periods in summer). Entrance costs around AS50 (reductions for ISIC holders).

**Schönbrunn Palace:** The Habsburgs' summer palace is at Schönbrunner Schloss-Strasse in the outskirts, south-west from Westbahnhof, U-Bahn 4. The English tours for AS145 are worthwhile. Also see the Gloriette temple, the gardens and the butterfly collection.

**The Belvedere:** Even more impressive than the Hofburg and Schönbrunn, this exquisite Baroque palace and gardens encompass the national gallery of modern art and a museum of medieval art.

**The Kunsthistorisches Museum** (Museum of fine Arts), Maria-Theresien Platz: One of the great art collections and the fourth largest gallery in the world. Superb Egyptian-Oriental collection, world's largest collection of Breughel plus Rubens, Rembrandt, Dürer.

There's also the **KunstHausWien** at Untere Weissgerberstrasse 13, open 10am–7pm daily, housing international art and interesting contemporary exhibitions.

Those are the main sights but, if you've time, take in the **Freud Museum**. Followers of the psychoanalyst can visit his house at Berggasse 19 (AS60), small but well documented.

Of interest to music lovers will be: the **Haydn Museum** at Haydngasse 19; **Mozart Erinnerungsraum**, Domgasse 5; the **Schubert Museum**, Nussdorferstrasse 54; **Schubert Sterbezimmer**, Kettenbrückengasse 6; and **Johann Strauss Museum**, Praterstrasse 54.

At all these addresses, the composers' original houses are still standing. Entrance fees seem to be changing constantly, but municipal museums should be free for all on Friday mornings and national museums offer reductions for all students and ISIC holders. Don't be surprised, though, if the rules change – especially outside the high season. Pick up the leaflet *Museums Wien* from the Tourist Office.

Alternatively, take a picnic to the city's greenbelt, the Wienerwald (**Vienna Woods**), which borders the city on its southern and western sides. Take tram 38 to its terminus at Grinzing, then bus 38a to Kahlenberg. You can also bike there with rent-a-bike firm Pedal Power at Ausstellungersstrasse 3 (Tel. 729 7234). Their various cycle tours start at 10am, cost around AS230 for students, AS280 otherwise.

**FREE VIENNA:** There's very little you don't have to pay for in Vienna. Having said that, soaking up the atmosphere needn't cost a penny. People pay a fortune to be guided through Vienna's streets on tours, but if you put on your hiking boots, you'll cover the same territory for free.

- Walking **the Ring** (once the city walls and now a tree-lined boulevard) will take you past many of the architectural gems and most important places.
- Less strenuous is a stroll in **Stadtpark**, the **Vienna Woods** or Vienna's favourite amusement park, the **Prater**.
- And you can spend a pleasant day simply strolling through the cobbled back streets and exploring the ancient arcades and hidden courtyards.
- Don't forget that entrance to cathedrals and churches is generally free: two not to miss are **Stephansdom**, the old town's hulking Gothic cathedral, and Vienna's finest Baroque church, the **Karlskirche** at Karlsplatz.
- If you're lucky, you can see the **Vienna Boys' Choir** perform for free, in the chapel of the Hofburg on Sunday mornings. (Be there at 8.30am for the chance of free standing space.)

## SLEEPING

Cheap beds are few and far between in the summer, so book in advance if you can. Student hostels don't open till July (making late June a particularly bad time), hotels are ridiculously expensive and the cheap pensions get full quickly. For a full run-down of the best places, get hold of *Cheap Sleeps Europe 2000* or the ISIC accommodation booklet.

There are two main accommodation-finding services in Vienna: the travel agencies at the stations, and the student organization Ökista. If you want to save the commission charge, try phoning yourself. Most hoteliers speak English, or you can try out your phrase-book German.

**HOSTELS** A novel place to sleep is the bell tower of a church at **Türmherberge Don Bosco**, Lechnerstrasse 12 (Tel. 7131494). Take Tram 18 from Westbahnhof or Südbahnhof to the end or U-Bahn 3. Men only. Costs AS75. Don't confuse with hotel Don Bosco. Cheap and basic. No catering, and don't expect a long lie in – the alarm bell is very loud and very close!

**Ruthensteiner**, Robert Hamerlinggasse 24 (Tel. 8934202 and 8932796). Offers 77 beds with all facilities, near Westbahnhof: turn right out of Westbahnhof, right into Mariahilferstrasse, left into Palmgasse and right into Hamerlinggasse. Costs from AS129 for dormitory to AS245 for a single room. Free showers, lockers available.Bike rental. Internet access. 24hr reception. Breakfast available at AS25.

**Jugendherberge**, Myrthengasse 7/Neustiftgasse 85 (Tel. 5236316). One of the best bargains in Vienna, with 241 beds and all facilities. It's modern, clean, central, and each four or six-bed room has an ensuite bathroom.1.00am curfew. AS165. B&B, but you must be an IYHF member. Advance booking is essential. Walkable from Westbahnhof, or U-Bahn 6 to Burggasse, then bus 48a to Neubaugasse, hostel nearby.

**Jugendgasthaus Brigittenau**, Friedrich-Engels Platz 24 (Tel. 33282940). 30 mins from centre. 330 beds, all facilities, 24 hr reception. From AS145. Near the Danube. Must be IYHF member. Tram N from Schwedenplatz (U-Bahn 1 or 4) to Friedrich-Engels Platz.

**PENSIONS Pension Columbia**, Kochgasse 9 (Tel. 4056757), quiet with doubles from AS700, including breakfast. Tram 5 from outside Westbahnhof.

**Pension zur Stadthalle**, Hackengasse 35 (Tel. 9824272). The cheapest singles are from AS470 and the cheapest doubles start from AS660. All prices include breakfast, and they will give a 10% discount if you show this book! Turn left outside Westbahnhof and then left again; Hackengasse is on your right.

**PRIVATE ROOMS Hedwig Gally** has private rooms near the West-bahnhof at Arnsteingasse 25/10 (Tel. 8929073/8931028). Prices start around AS400 for a double, AS500 for a double with shower.

**Irene Hamminger**, Türkenschanzstrasse 34 (Tel. 3450305) offers rooms in a Viennese villa for AS400–500 for two people – 15 minutes from the city centre.

**Frank Heberling** runs an establishment at Siccardsburggasse 42 (Tel. 6040229); phone first. Very friendly, walkable from Südbahnhof.

The city Tourist Offices also arrange private rooms for a small fee.

**CAMPING** All grounds are well out of the city and charge about AS65 per person and AS60 per tent.

**Wien West II**, Hüttelbergstrasse 80 (Tel. 9142314). Get off train at Hütteldorf, then bus 52b. Open April–October.

**Wien West I**, just up the same street (Tel. 9142314). Open mid-July to end of August. But I've had reports of declining standards in Wien West I and II, despite promised improvement.

**Camping Süd** (Tel. 869218), open August, close to the Atzgersdorf-Mauer S-Bahn station. Noisy.

Quite near this site is the **Rodaun-Schwimmbad** site at An der Au 2 (Tel. 884154). Take tram 58 from Westbahnhof to Hietzing, then tram 60 to the end. Hot showers, laundry, supermarket and there is a free swimming pool. Open end March–mid-Nov.

Also ask at the Tourist Office for details of other sites, further out, but worth a try if it's really busy. If you are really desperate, sleep out at the Prater Park, but it's not to be recommended.

## EATING AND NIGHTLIFE

Food, glorious food. The Viennese love hearty and wholesome dishes. You are in a high cholestorol zone here – be warned! Prices are high but, as usual, if you know where to look you can find good food that won't bust your budget.

Cafés, with their pastries and cakes smothered in cream, are a Viennese institution, but they're expensive, so make your visit on a wet afternoon when you can hang around reading the papers, playing cards and generally getting your money's worth. Try Freud's one-time watering hole, **Cafe Landtmann**, still the meeting place of actors, politicians and journalists at 1 Karl Lueger Ring 4, or the popular and lively student haunt **Cafe Stein**, 9 Wahringerstrasse 6.

For picnics, the self-service supermarkets have a good variety of breads, sausages, cheeses, fruits and wines. Vienna's largest market, the **Naschmarkt**, lying from the 4th to the 6th districts, has some interesting food bargains and plenty more besides. Get to it by the underground to Kettenbrückengasse.

**SUGGESTIONS** There's nowhere really cheap to eat in the centre of Vienna, but have a good look at any 'menu of the day' you see. Check out the **Naschmarkt** restaurant chain (there's one on Schwarzenberg Platz). Or try the Hungarian and Turkish restaurants; they're usually good value.

The **Schnell-Imbiss** counters (quick snacks) all over the city serve cheap, filling bites (AS40–80), and of course there's always **McDon-**

**ald's**, one of them very convenient for the Westbahnhof on Mariahilferstrasse heading towards the city, on the left-hand side.

The best area to head for is the 7th district around the **Neustiftgasse**, where you will find the **Phoenixhof** and **Puppenstube** restaurants. You can get a good meal and wine for around AS150 and if these are full there are other places in the vicinity.

The student restaurant **Mensa** is at Universitätsstrasse 7. It's open for lunch and dinner, Mon.–Fri., and there's no problem getting in as long as you look like a student. Prices from around AS50 for a basic meal and is good value for money.

Vegetarians should try **Gasthaus Wrenkh**, Hollergasse 9 (15th district) or at Bauernmarkt 10 (1st district).

Nightlife for the Viennese means opera or theatre. Young people tend to congregate in the coffee houses (*Kaffeehaus* or *Konditorei*) rather than in pubs or discos, but Vienna still has a few surprises up its sleeve.

A good night out can be had at the **Prater** – Vienna's large amusement park on the outskirts of the city. Entrance is free and the rides average AS15–25, although the big wheel, built in 1895 by British engineer Walter Bassett, costs AS30. Open from Easter to October. Take tram 21 or U-Bahn 1, it's reasonably obvious where to get off.

Bars and nightclubs can be sleazy and expensive, so watch out. For techno dance try **U4 Disco**, Schönbrunnerstrasse 222; it's very popular with the young Viennese and it's easy to get to, or look at the latest *Youth Scene*. In general, though, you're better off heading for a wine tavern or beer cellar. These represent best value by far. Try: **Esterhazykeller**, Haarhof, good student crowd with the best prices in town; or subterranean **Zwölf-Apostelkeller**, Sonnenfelsgasse 3, near St Stephan's, so low down from street level, the walls are covered with straw to diminish the dampness. The lowest level is the liveliest. Open Sundays, but closed all July. And for the connoisseur, **Melkerkeller**, Schottengasse 3, run by Benedictine monks, has excellent wine.

Europe's largest bowling alley is in Vienna. It's the **Bowling-Brunswick** at Hauptallee 124 and costs around AS25 a line. Plenty of students congregate here.

For the quintessential Viennese experience, head for the **opera** or **ballet** at the **Staatsoper**, 1 Openring 2, or the **Volksoper**, 9 Wahringerstrasse (for Austrian opera, and AS20 standing-room tickets, arrive at least two hours before performances). The principal venue for **classical music** is the **Musikverein** at 1 Karlsplatz 6, home of the Vienna Philharmonic. Check with Tourist Information for up-to-date programmes, but don't use an agency to buy tickets, as they charge a 30% commission. Tickets are sometimes available on the night. Standing room is available at the opera; queue and tie a scarf around the barrier to reserve your place.

# Southern Austria

If from Vienna you're heading to Italy or the former Yugoslavia, you'll pass through the southern regions of Burgenland, Steiermark and Kärnten.

**Burgenland**, a farming province next to the Hungarian border, is famous for its wines. About 50km south-east of Vienna is the province's capital, **Eisenstadt**, where the composer Josef Haydn is buried. Between late August and early September this turns into a lively place, thanks to its Weinwoche (wine week).

**Steiermark**, or Styria, along the Slovenian border, is the green heart of Austria, covered with mountains, forests, grasslands and vineyards through which the Weinstrasse (wine road) runs. Its capital is **Graz**. The journey between Salzburg and Villach is particularly scenic and if you fancy visiting a typical alpine town you could do worse than choose **Badgastein**. Although expensive, the views over the valley and the powerful waterfall are worth a relaxing few hours.

**Kärnten** (Carinthia) is an attractive region with lakes, wildlife parks and rolling hills. **Klagenfurt** is its capital, with two campsites and a youth hostel in its centre; it's a good base for exploring the surrounding **Naturpark Kreuzbergl**.

# Graz

Fans will be delighted to discover this is Arnold Schwarzenegger's birthplace. Austria's attractive, bustling second city and university campus (50,000 students) is small enough to be explored on foot. Start your rambles at the **Hauptplatz**, which is the main market square. Worth seeing are the 16th-century town hall, the **Landhaus** and the armoury next door, the **Zeughaus**. There are also a couple of decent museums and art galleries. The **Cathedral** dates from the 12th century, and the old royal residence, the **Burg** (now government offices) is worth a look.

## TOURIST INFORMATION

The station has a tourist office, but if you head towards town for 200m, there's a much bigger one at Herrengasse 16 (tel. 807 50) The train station is on the outskirts, so you have to walk or get a short tram ride (no. 6) to and from the central Hauptplatz. If you're staying on consider purchasing a Graz Card for free local travel and discounts.

## SLEEPING AND EATING

You can book **private rooms** through the tourist office, but they're likely to be in the suburbs. The **youth hostel** is more central at Idlhofgasse 74 (Tel. 714876).

There's very little in the way of cheap hotels, but the **Pension Iris**, on Bergmanngasse, is one of the more highly recommended ones.

Best bets for eating are the alleys off the Hauptplatz, and the cafés and bars that line the streets close to the university, east of the Stadtpark.

# Central Austria

South of the Linz–Salzburg line lies an unspoilt region the tourist hordes haven't yet discovered. It's a beautiful area, steeped in tradition, with tiny wooden villages alongside mountain lakes, and alpine scenery of the glossy tourist brochure variety. Added to which, prices are surprisingly low.

From Vienna or Salzburg catch a train to Attnang Puchheim, then take a local train going in the direction of Stainach Irdning, passing through Gmunden, Hallstatt and Obertraun.

**Gmunden** is a lovely town at the northern end of the Traunsee, the largest lake of the region. Tourist Information is at Am Graben 2. Traunsteinstrasse is a good street for accommodation.

The third stop after Bad Goisern is **Hallstatt** – with its backdrop of cliffs and a waterfall, one of the most beautiful of Austria's lakeside hamlets. The village is on the shore opposite the train station: the only way across is by ferry (about AS25). The oldest salt mines in the world (they claim) are here, as well as an incredible graveyard. Walking and sailing are excellent; you can rent a small boat from AS120 an hour. The small youth hostel at Lahn 50 (Tel. 06134 279) is open May–mid-September (excellent facilities), and there's camping at **Campingplatz Häll** (Tel. 06134 329). Tourist information is in the **Prähistorisches Museum** just off Seestrasse; they'll advise on other accommodation, too.

The next stop along at the other end of the lake is Obertraun, site of the **Dachstein Ice Caves**. They're interesting but expensive. There's a **youth hostel** at Winkl 26 (Tel. 06131 360). It opens at 5pm, and is more pleasant than the hostel in Hallstatt; AS100 for B&B. Again, open peak season only.

# Salzburg city phone code: 662

At any time of year Salzburg oozes tourists. But rightly so because surrounded as it is by stunning scenery and built on either side of the Salzach river, the city of Salzburg really has everything going for it. The concentration of onion-domed churches, medieval turrets and ancient spires creates one of the most beautiful skylines in the world. Named after the essential mineral that made its wealth – salt – the fortunes made from that trade are plain to see in the Baroque churches, palaces and squares of this rather sedate city. The prince-archbishops who ruled ancient Salzburg built so many grand churches, palaces, mansions and gardens that the city was dubbed the Rome of the North.

Never mind the fact that both the von Trapp family and old Wolfgang Amadeus himself eventually left the place, Mozart's home town never lets you forget he is Salzburg's most famous son, and the adulation grows stronger year by year. From late July to the end of August, Salzburg becomes the centre of the musical world, when its Summer Festival featuring hundreds of indoor and outdoor performances fills every hotel, hostel and campsite with the thousands who flock to the annual music event.

Such charms, however, have the effect of making Salzburg hideously expensive and geared more to the middle-aged and middle-class. It's a university town, though, so there are a few student hostels and restaurants that are less than half the price of their commercial counterparts.

Salzburg is 3¼ hours from Vienna, two hours from Munich in Germany, 2½ hours from Innsbruck and five hours from Zürich; there are daily trains to Cologne, Hamburg and Copenhagen. The Tourist Information office at the station will help you find a room for AS30. It is to the left side of the building facing you as you come out of passport control.

## STATION FACILITIES

Train information: 7am–8.30pm daily (Tel. 1717) and reservations Mon.–Fri.: 9am–5.30pm, Sat.: 9am–12.30pm.
Tourist information: 8.30am–8pm. (Tel. 871712).

There are all the usual amenities, including 24-hour left-luggage lockers.

## TOURIST INFORMATION AND ADDRESSES

The main Tourist Information offices are at Mozartplatz 5 (Tel. 847568, 88987330) (open all year Mon.–Sat.: 9am–6pm, Sun.: 9am–6pm, summer only) and at the station. There is an **information centre** for young travellers, Jugend-Service-Stelle, at Hubert-Sattler-Gasse 7 (Tel. 80722592) open Mon. and Wed.: 10am–7pm; Tues., Thurs. and Sat.: 10am–4.30pm, and Fri.: 10am–2pm.

**City transport** information and free maps can be obtained from the bus drivers. Single fares are AS20. Most sights are within walking distance of the centre, but its worth considering splashing out on a **Salzburg Card**, which in addition to unlimited public transport gives free admission to most of Salzburg's attractions and discounts to others. A 24-hour card costs AS200, 48 hours AS290 and 72 hours AS380.

**POST OFFICE** Residenzplatz 9, Mon.–Fri.: 7am–7pm, Sat.: 8am–10am or 24-hour service; main railway station.
**AMEX** Mozartplatz 5–7 (Tel. 842501)
**ÖKISTA (Student travel service)** Wolf-Dietrich-Strasse 31 (Tel. 883252), Mon.–Fri.: 9.30am–5.30pm.
**EURAIL AID OFFICE** Salzburg Hauptbahnhof (Tel. 662 8887 5428)

## SEEING

Gone are the days when Salzburg depended on salt; the new gold is tourism. Small wonder, given the impressive Baroque legacy of the prince-archbishops who poured the proceeds of the salt trade into creating the city of their dreams. Their residence, the **Hohensalzburg Fortress**, shouldn't be missed. Take the funicular up the 534m to the fortress, or you can walk; the view from the top over the city is another essential sight. If you're suffering over-exposure to your travelling companion, you might find quite rewarding a quiet hour in the torture section of the **museum** there.

The other four main city sights are the **Residenz** (17th-century archbishops' palace), the **Mirabell Palace**, the **cathedral** and **Mozart's Birthplace** at Getreidegasse 9. On the outskirts are the country estate and water gardens of the Renaissance **Hellbrunn Palace**. Take bus 55 from the station.

If you've had enough of tourists, there are several escape routes: two of them a short bus or train ride away over the border in Bavaria. The first is a trip to Hitler's retreat, the **'Eagle's Nest'**, and the second is a visit to the **salt mines**. Although organized excursions to the salt mines run several times a day from Mirabellplatz, you can do both trips independently. The starting-off point for both trips is Berchtesgaden. You might opt to take the bus as it runs more frequently than the train, and since the journey is quite short the cost is reasonable at around AS45. (Discount with Inter-Rail, free on Eurail.) Once you are at Berchtesgaden, get a bus to the mines, where you can hire protective clothing for around 28DM. Check to see if your bus passes the mine entrance on the way to Berchtesgaden.

For the 'Eagle's Nest' you will need a head for heights, and a local service bus to the entrance road, where you change to special buses for the trip up to the car park. Don't even think about going any further if you suffer from vertigo, for the bus seems to be suspended in mid-air for most of the tortuous journey up the single-track mountain road. You then walk into the middle of the mountain before going up to the eyrie in a brass-panelled lift. Total cost about 20DM. The view is quite spectacular, although you might be just as happy to take a cable car to the top of the Untersberg (1,740m), which will give you fine views of the alpine scenery without the same expense in time and money, but even this is relatively expensive at AS200 return.

Alternatively, take one of the regular *Sound of Music* tours round the locations of this popular musical. Details from Tourist Information.

**FREE SALZBURG:** Tramping the **Mozart** trail – Salzburg's major draw card – is not a budget option (although you can gawk at the outside of the house in which he was born for nothing: Getreide-gasse 9, at the head of the Rathausplatz). But the city's other main attraction – its **architecture** – is as much appreciated from the outside, from where it's free, as from the inside. The city centre seems custom-made for walkers: the network of alleys and passageways can only be explored by foot, and many areas are pedestrianized. Entrance to **cathedrals** and **churches** is generally free, and there are some particularly good examples of Baroque architecture among them. Have a look at the mother of them all, the **Kollegienkirche** in Universitatsplatz – usually crowded with **market** stalls on weekday mornings – and compare with the Romanesque/Gothic 13th century **Franciscan Church** at Sigmund-Haffnergasse. Close by is the **cathedral**, and just off Kapitalplatz is **St Peter's Abbey**, whose **cemetery** and the **monks' caves** cut into the cliffs are definitely worth a look (there's an AS12 charge to visit the catacombs, though). Alter Markt has an **open-air market**, and Salzburg's narrowest house on the north side of the square. **Schloss Mirabell** is a must on any Baroque City tour; the palace now houses public offices, but you can have a look inside, and walk in the Mirabell's **formal gardens** behind.

## SLEEPING

Forget hotels, especially during Easter and the summer arts festivals – prices are sky-high – and try one of the hostels or campsites. Otherwise, private accommodation is the way to go: Tourist Information have a list of options. Tell them what you can afford, then wait and see what they come up with. If all else fails, consider going out to one of the villages on the outskirts. For instance, Maria Plan, a few minutes by train, is quiet, with good connections to the city, and has several pensions to choose from. Refer to *Cheap Sleeps Europe 2000* for more options.

**YOUTH HOSTELS** The **YO-HO International Hostel** at Paracelsusstrasse 9 (Tel. 879649) is only a few blocks away from the station. It is reasonably well kept, but noisy, with a washing machine and drier on-site. Although showers and breakfast are extra, you can choose from Continental, British or American. There is also a cheap restaurant/bar which serves an excellent Wiener Schnitzel. Expect to pay around AS150 for a bed.

The **Jugendgastehaus Salzburg** at Josef-Preis Allee 18 (Tel. 8426700) has 390 beds and all facilities, but fills up quickly so go early or book in advance. It closes 9am–11am and at midnight. Reports on cleanliness vary. Take bus 5 to Justizgebõude then a short walk.

Near the centre of town is the **Jugendherberge Aigen** hostel at Aignerstrasse 34 (Tel. 623248). Buses 5 or 6 and change to 49 at Zentrum. It can get very busy and noisy.

The hostel at Glockengasse 8 (Tel. 876241) can be reached by bus 29; get off at Hofwirtstrasse. Open Apr.–Oct. only.

Three blocks west of the train station is the Haunspergstrasse hostel, at Haunspergstrasse 27 (Tel. 875030). Open July-August only.

**PENSIONS Zum Junger Fuchs,** Linzergasse 54 (Tel. 875496). AS220-400. Very good. Walk from the Staatsbrücke bridge along Linzergasse.

Also try the **Elizabeth** at Vogelweiderstrasse 52 (Tel. 871664). Doubles about AS350–520.

**CAMPING** There are several campsites; most are open May–30 September and prices vary from AS50–75 per person and tent. If visiting the sights near Berchtesgaden, try **Camping Allwegehein** on Untersalzberg mountain (Tel. 08652 2396).

**Camping Gnigl**, Parscherstrasse 4 (Tel. 643060), situated on the side of a football pitch, is convenient and very cheap. It's only AS80 for 2 people sharing a tent with the use of the facilities in the club house free – a bargain, as the showers are possibly the hottest and cleanest you could find. Take bus 29 from Makartplatz.

Another option is **Camping Nordsam**, Samstrasse 22a (Tel. 660494). Take bus 33 from the station and get off by the camping sign. It's a three-minute walk round the corner. A little more expensive at AS100 per person and AS95 per tent, but the location makes it worthwhile.

## EATING AND NIGHTLIFE

There's no shortage of elegant cafés and flash restaurants in which to blow your budget, if you're feeling reckless. But if you're trying to keep a lid on spending, head for the snack bars around **Alter Markt** and **Judengasse**. There's a cheap stand-up *Imbiss* place, with a larger range than most, at Judengasse 10, where Wiener Schnitzel and chips can be had for around AS100. Or check out **Pitterkeller**, Rainerstrasse 6, near the station. The food's not bad and it's cheap by Salzburg standards.

Stock up on picnic food from the open-air market on Thursday mornings by St Andrew's church. And there are two every weekday on **Universitätsplatz** and **Franz-Josef Strasse**.

Outdoor drinking is the thing here, thanks to the excellent tradition of **Beer Gardens**. The good citizens of Salzburg are more orientated towards beer than wine, probably because of their proximity to the German border. Beer cellars invariably offer good value in eating and entertainment, as well as drinking. Try **Augustiner Bräustübl**, Augustinergasse 4 – there are several small stalls in this building – or **Strobl Stüberl**, near the station at Rainerstrasse 11.

For drinking only, the **Stiegl Beer Cellar**, Festungsgasse 10, has a great atmosphere and views over the city to match (but it's closed in winter), the lively **Am Steintor** at Giselakai 17, or the **Students' Centre**, Gstättengasse 16, weekdays 9am–12noon and 1pm–6pm.

# Western Austria

From Liechtenstein, the route through the Arlberg Tunnel to the Vorarlberg Alps is one to stay awake for. Mountain meadows, wooden chalets and dramatic peaks make this a memorable train journey. If you have time to explore, Feldkirch and Bregenz make the best bases.

**Feldkirch** is an old town with many reminders of its Gothic heyday. The Tourist Office is at Herrengasse 12 (Mon.–Fri. 8.30am–12noon, 2pm–6pm, Sat. 9am–12noon). They'll suggest walking tours. There's a youth hostel (Tel. 05522 73181) at Reichsstrasse 111 and a campsite.

**Bregenz**, on the shores of Lake Constance (Bodensee in German), is the capital of the Vorarlberg region. With its medieval old quarter, it is an atmospheric setting for its opera festival from late July to late Aug. The information office is at Bahnhofstrasse 14 (Tel. 433 9110) There's a new youth hostel at Mehreranerstrasse 3-5 (Tel 428 67) and four campsites.

## Innsbruck city phone code: 0512

Set in a ring of snow-capped mountains, Innsbruck – capital of the Tyrol and queen of the Austrian ski scene – is well worth a day or two, even if you're not a winter sports fanatic. It's a pretty city, with its own fair share of Baroque façades, cobblestone courtyards and imperial pomp: under Maximilian I from the late 15th century, Innsbruck was the seat of an empire for 150 years.

### STATION FACILITIES

Train information: daily 7am–9.30pm (Tel. 1717) and reservations daily 8am–7.30pm (Tel. 1700). There's a Tourist Information kiosk and all the usual amenities, including 24-hour left-luggage lockers.

There's a wonderful centre for young travellers at the station (open 9am–10pm). Seize the opportunity to be treated like a human being and make the most of this excellent facility.

For food and provisions, head towards the Maria-Theresienstrasse area, two streets straight ahead from the station.

There are daily trains from Innsbruck to Cologne, Hamburg, Munich (2½ hours), Salzburg (2½ hours), Vienna (5½ hours), Milan, Rome, Venice and Zürich (4 hours).

### TOURIST INFORMATION AND ADDRESSES

The office at the station (open daily 9am–10pm) will find you a room and change your cash. There's another office at Burggraben 3, in the city centre, open daily 8am–7pm.

Most of what you'll want to see is walkable, but you can buy **public transport** day tickets and various multi-journey deals from the Tourist Offices, tobacconists and some hotels. Consider buying an **Innsbruck Card** (24 hours AS230, 48 hours AS300, 72 hours AS370), which gets you free city transport, ascents on the Nordketten, Patscherkofel and Hungerburg cable cars, and entrance to many of the city's main attractions (plus a free drink at the Casino!). The cards are available from Tourist Offices, or Tel. 535630.

**POST OFFICE:** Maximilianstrasse 2 (one block away from the Triumphal Arch)
**AMEX:** Brixnerstrasse 3
**ÖKISTA:** The student travel service is at Josef-Hirnstrasse 7
**EURAIL AID OFFICE** Innsbruck Hauptbahnhof, Tel. (0512) 503 5460

**ALPINE INFORMATION** Since you're in one of the best alpine centres in Europe, you may want to head for the hills. Check up on conditions before setting off at Wilhelm-Greilstrasse 17 (Tel. 5320 175), or, if you prefer an organized hike, contact Tourismusverband at Burggraben 3 (Tel. 59850). Some free hikes are available, in theory, to those staying for three nights or more; persistence at the Tourist Office should get you information on these.

**MOUNTAIN HUT SCHEME** More than 700 huts are in the mountains surrounding Innsbruck. They belong to various local and national alpine associations, and a tour of them, or even just a night in one, is cheap and memorable. Many of the huts have some cooking facilities and some even serve up hot food. Prices range from about AS170 to AS350 for a night. Washing facilities tend to be basic.

Before setting out, make sure you have emergency food supplies, a waterproof and are wearing good climbing boots. The distress call in this neck of the woods is six visible or audible signals spaced evenly over a minute, followed by a minute's break, then the six signals again.

## SEEING

You never lose sight of the Alps in Innsbruck. The main shopping street, Maria-Theresienstrasse, is overlooked by the Nordkette mountains. At one end of the street is the **Triumphal Arch** and at the other, the old Gothic town. Don't miss Innsbruck's famous symbol, the **Golden Roof** – an ornate Gothic balcony built in 1500 from 2,657 gilded copper tiles. There's also a **cathedral**, a **museum** detailing Maximilian's life story, and the **Hofburg** (Imperial Palace).

The **ski jump**, on the hillside above the town, gives a great overview of all this, and there's also a (rather small) **Olympic Museum** to see here. But for a more spectacular panorama, take the cable car up to **Hafelekar** at 2,250m: catch tram 1 to the Hungerburg funicular, then the cable car; but be warned – it is expensive. There are also two other cable car routes.

The 1964 and 1976 Winter Olympics were held at **Igls** near Innsbruck, and you can still see the set-up (bus J from Innsbruck station or tram 6). Enjoy the view, but stay out of the cafés there.

Though rather touristified, the village of **Fulpmes** is a pretty example of an alpine village, and it's in good picnic country. Take tram 1 to Stubaitalbahnhof where the mountain train leaves. An alternative is to take the tram direct from the main station. Buy a hiking map (*Wanderkarte*) and try the rewarding walk from Fulpmes to the **Pfarrachalm** mountain inn.

**FREE INNSBRUCK:** This ancient city is compact, and you can get its measure very easily on foot. In fact, Innsbruck owes much of its picturesque charm to the views of the Alps on the edge of the city – and those are best seen from the streets.

- You can get the **classic postcard view** if you walk up Maria-Theresienstrasse, past the **Anna Column** – if you've packed a camera, take it with you.
- If you stay one night in a hotel in Innsbruck or Igls, you automatically become a member of Club Innsbruck, whose Club Card will get you free **mountain hiking**, unlimited use of skiing and cross-country buses, and reductions on ski passes, cable car rides and at some city attractions (along with a free glass of Sekt at the Casino!).
- There's quite a variety of **markets** to poke around in – get a list from the Tourist Office.
- In season, you can get the full alpine treatment at a free **Tyrolean evening** in front of the **Golden Roof** most Thursday evenings at 8.30pm.

## SLEEPING

The main youth hostel at Reichenauerstrasse 147 is a long way from the town centre, has a 10pm curfew, and is reportedly unfriendly with strict rules. Take bus O or R to Campingplatz or a 30-minute walk. Cost is around AS140 (Tel. 346179).

The **Glockenhaus** Hostel at Weiherburggasse 3 (Tel. 286515) is 10 minutes' walk from the town centre and 20 minutes' from the station, although there is a pick-up service from the station if you arrange in advance; alternatively, use bus K. Beds are limited but they also have a building at Innstrasse 95 (Tel. 286515), where there's dormitory accommodation. Neither of these takes phone reservations, and there have been complaints about them. The owners lay on ski rental and organize skiing, hiking, river rafting and wind surfing excursions. A typical price is AS300 for a double; there are also singles and larger rooms.

Alternatively, try the hostel, **Torsten-Arneus** Schwedenhaus, at 17b Rennweg (Tel. 585814). Open July and August only. Small rooms at AS165 including breakfast. There is also a small hostel at **Sillgasse** 8a, although reports on its cleanliness vary and it is only open peak season. Only five minutes' walk from the station, it charges AS190 for bed, breakfast and shower (Tel. 571311).

The **Pension Tautemann**, at Stamser Feld 5 (Tel. 281572), charges AS450–500 for a double room with shower, en suite WC, and includes breakfast. Very comfortable.

The only campsite is **Kranebitten**, an hour's walk from the station, or bus LK from Bozner Platz.

Avoid eating evening meals in the pensions. The meal may be 'fixed price', but the extras can be expensive.

## EATING AND NIGHTLIFE

Cheapest bets are towards the university area. Try **Gasthaus Gruber**, Innrain 160 (between university and Old Town). **University Mensa** (off Innrain) at Herzog-Siegmund Ufer 15, 2nd floor, offers cheap meals for ISIC holders, lunchtimes only. Good value grub is available in many old town restaurants, on the way from Maria-Theresienstrasse to the Golden Roof – and the places around here are lively in the evening. Across the river on Innstrasse, there are loads of cheap schnitzel joints and ethnic restaurants and grocers.

Picnic fodder can be picked up from the farmer's market in the Markthalle on the corner of Innrain and Marktgraben.

A pleasant, short excursion out of town leads you to **Hall**, 8km down river. Drive up the 1,500m Hinterhornam, then walk on to the Walderalm dairy farm and enjoy the vista of the Inn river valley stretching beneath you as you eat!

## NOTES

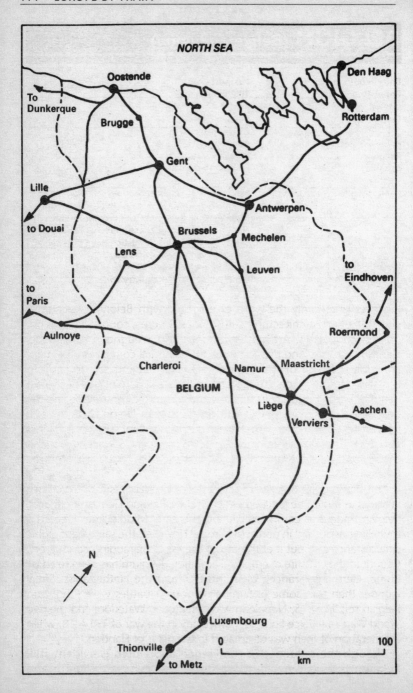

# BELGIUM (Belgie; Belgique)

| | |
|---|---|
| Entry requirements | Passport |
| Population | 10.2 million |
| Capital | Brussels (pop.: 1.2 million) |
| Currency | Belgian Franc |
| | £1 = approx. 60BF |
| Political system | Constitutional Monarchy |
| Religion | Roman Catholic |
| Language | French, Flemish and German (English widely spoken) |
| Public holidays | New Year's Day, Easter Monday (24 Apr.), Labour Day (1 May), Ascension (1 June), Whit Monday (12 June), Flemish Community Day, National Day (21 Jul.), Assumption (15 Aug.), All Saints' Day (1 Nov.), Armistice Day (11 Nov.), King's Birthday, Christmas Day |
| International dialling codes | To Belgium: int'l code 32 |
| | From Belgium: 00 + country code |

Richness is certainly the word to associate with Belgium. A country choc full of art, architecture, culture, gastronomy, sophistication and, oh yes, chocolates. Art masters Rubens and Breughel, Belgian lace, Flemish tapestries and diamonds all put this small country on the map. Now it's the turn of the bureaucrats who, having set up shop in Brussels, are intent on creating powerful new networks. The 'sweet heart' of Europe is today its political and economic centre, housing the headquarters of both NATO and the European Union. Belgium is a beer drinkers' paradise with hundreds of excellent local brews. It is also the birthplace of Tintin and his dog Snowy, the Smurfs (remember them?) and Joseph Merlin, who, back in the mid 1700's invented the roller skate.

Not bad for a country with only 280km between its furthest points. Wedged as it is at the junction between the Latin and Germanic cultures, Belgian trade and commerce during the early Middle Ages created a town life unequalled in northern Europe. However, the same geographic circumstance also put it at the top of the list of marauding conquerors. Caught in the crossfire of empirical ambition, Belgium has been ruled by Rome, Germany, France, Spain, Austria, and the Netherlands. Small wonder then that some of Europe's bloodiest battles were fought on Belgian soil: in 1815, Napoleon was defeated in Waterloo, and the two World Wars saw fierce fighting, particularly in the war of 1914–18, when a generation of men was decimated in the fields of Flanders.

Though the influence of the French and Dutch is evident still, Belgium has not one, but two distinctive cultures: Flemish and

Walloon. The Flemish, who live in the north and west, speak a language closely akin to Dutch, and still demonstrate the hard-working characteristics of their Germanic forebears. The Walloons, on the other hand, speak an old French dialect, and are in every way more like their French neighbours. Tensions between the two persist.

Bruges, Brussels, Antwerp and Ghent are the four main centres of interest. And although Belgium is the second most densely populated country in Europe, it's still possible to find solitude among the forests of Ardennes in the south and on the white sands of the North Sea coast.

## BELGIAN NATIONAL RAILWAYS

**(NATIONALE MAATSCHAPPIJ DER BELGISCHE SPOORWEGEN, NMBS)**
**(SOCIÉTÉ NATIONALE DES CHEMINS DE FER BELGES, SNCB)**
In 1835, Belgium was the first country in continental Europe to build a railway. Today, its rail system is one of Europe's most reliable and extensive. Trains are frequent, fast and go just about everywhere, and fares are low. The fastest services are the Euro-City services and the Inter-City services (!C), and the semi-fast services are 'Inter-regional' (IR numbers). No supplements are charged for any trains running wholly within Belgium, but supplements are payable for travel on certain international trains.

Crossing the country takes only 3½ hours, and trains leave for most internal destinations every hour – good news for Inter-Railers and Eurail pass holders, who can use Brussels as a base from which to explore the rest of the country on day-trips. Brussels to Bruges, for example, takes only an hour.

Meanwhile, new rail connections last year from Brussels have opened up the rail network in the north of Belgium even further. Antwerp, Ghent, Leuven and Mechelen are all under an hour from Brussels, while in the south, Namur and Dinant are within easy reach by rail.

## EUROSTAR AND THALYS

The Channel Tunnel paved the way for the advent of Eurostar, the high-speed passenger train between London Waterloo and Brussels Midi/Zuid. Eurostar operates up to 11 trains a day to and from Brussels, the trip taking just 2 hours and 40 minutes.

If you want to travel by Eurostar, keep an eye out for special deals such as summer savers, which offer discounts of up to 40%. Typical return fares from London cost from £79. Add an extra £10 to the fare, and you can get a connecting train to any other station in Belgium. For **reservations**, phone Eurostar (Tel. 0990 186 186) or contact the Rail Europe Travel Centre at 179 Piccadilly, London W1 (Tel. 08705 848 848).

From **Brussels**, high-speed Thalys trains go to Antwerp,

Rotterdam, Amsterdam and Cologne – making Amsterdam just over six hours from London, and bringing Cologne within 5 hours and 30 minutes of London.

And by the year 2007, the British high-speed line from St Pancras through Kent is expected to slice a further 40 minutes off Eurostar journey times.

**PASSES AVAILABLE** Train travel in Belgium can be a bargain. Three types of ticket give rover travel within Belgium: The **50% Reduction Card** (600BF for one month) allows you to buy an unlimited number of single journey tickets at half the normal price.

The **Tourrail Card** is valid for five days of your own choice within a one-month period. For adults over 26, the second-class card is 2,100BF. First class costs 3,230BF. The **Benelux Tourrail Card**, valid in Belgium, the Netherlands and Luxembourg, works like the Tourrail, and costs 4,400BF or 3,100BF for under 26s. First class is 6,600.

For the under-26s again, there's also the 10-trip **Go Pass** (1,420BF).

The **Pass 9+**, allows 10 single journeys between any two Belgian rail stations, departing after 9am, for 2,100BF 2nd class or 3,230BF 1st class. Up to 10 different people can use the journeys.

**Eurail** is valid on intercity buses as well as trains. The **Inter-Rail** pass has been broken down into zones, so you needn't pay for travel to areas you won't be visiting. A £129 ticket will buy you 22 days in any zone. Belgium is in Zone E, along with France, Luxembourg and the Netherlands. A **Euro Domino** ticket is also available for Belgium. (For details of Euro Domino and the eight Inter-Rail zones, refer to the relevant sections in Part One of this guide.)

**INTER-RAIL BONUSES** See Appendix I.

**EURAIL AID OFFICE** Travel Centre (International services), Gare de Bruxelles-Midi, Tel. (02) 555 2525/555 2555.

## TRAIN INFORMATION

Information officers speak good English, other rail staff speak both Flemish and French. If you're spending any time in Belgium, buy a copy of the official SNCB timetable (*indicateur/spoor-boekje*) from any station. It has an introduction in English and details schedules and supplements. There is also a free pocket-sized booklet giving details of the main services. Failing that, large posters everywhere give departure and arrival information.

**RESERVATIONS** Unnecessary and, anyway, impossible on inland routes. International reservations cost 80BF and can be made up to two months in advance. If you're that highly organized, you can reserve seats on trains for Austria, Denmark, France, Germany, Italy and Switzerland at most large stations, as the SNCB's computer is linked up with these countries.

**NIGHT TRAVEL** Belgium is too small to warrant inland services, but SNCB have couchettes and Wagons-Lits sleepers on international routes. (To save a bit of money, look out for German rolling stock with pull-down seats.)

**LEFT LUGGAGE** Most stations have coin-operated lockers or luggage offices for about 60BF per item per day.

**EATING ON TRAINS** Services on inland trains are few and far between, though some have a mini-bar and others a buffet. On International trains, as always, grub is expensive. Happily, Belgian supermarkets are renowned for great food, so stock up in advance, and don't count on station shops for grazing; there aren't any, except in major cities.

**BIKES** SNCB run a scheme called *Train Vélo* (*Trein Fiets* in Flemish) which allows you to take advantage of Belgium's perfect (i.e. flat) cycling. You can rent a bike from upwards of 170BF per day (with a rail pass) from about 35 stations. Most roads have cycle tracks and they're a great way to explore the countryside. Make sure you ask for a free tour map.

## TOURIST INFORMATION
Every large town has a **Tourist Office**. For the provinces and the country in general, ask at the main office in Brussels. If you've any problems they can't solve, try the **Info-Jeunes** (Info-Jeugd) branches in most large towns.

**ISIC BONUSES** Reductions on rail and bus tickets, 50% off most museums. For further information, contact Connections, 13 rue Marché au Charbon, 1000 Brussels (also a Eurotrain office), or ACOTRA, rue de la Madeleine 51, 1000 Brussels.

**MONEY MATTERS** 1 Belgian franc (BF) = 100 centimes.
Banking hours are Mon.–Fri.: 9am–12noon, 2pm–4pm. Late opening, Friday till 4.30pm. AMEX are the only bank that does not charge high commissions on traveller's cheques. Eurocheques are thus the preferred means of payment. The station exchanges take no commission, but their rate of exchange is about 10% below the official one. The ferries

give a good rate and their commission is considerably less.

**POST OFFICES** Open Mon.–Fri.: 9am–5pm, offices in smaller towns tend to shut for lunch.

**SHOPS AND MUSEUMS** Shops open 10am–6/7pm, Mon.–Sat., with lunch from 12noon–2pm. Bakers and newsagents open early in the morning, and you can usually find a grocer open on Sunday somewhere. Many shops stay open till 9pm. Late night Friday. Museums often shut either on Mondays or Fridays, and some close in the afternoons.

**TIPPING** The Belgians' reputation for keeping their hands outstretched for a tip may be somewhat exaggerated, but there is definitely a tipping culture. Restaurant bills normally include service, but accepted practice is to 'round up'.

## SLEEPING

Both Tourist Information and the Info-Jeunes offices help with accommodation. Even budget hotels are expensive (rock-bottom minimum 1,000BF double) but clean, and continental breakfast is included. In the main, though hostels are your best bet – either the IYHF ones or those run by an organization called Amis de la Nature/Natuurvrienden. There are two IYHF organizations, one for the French region, one for the Flemish. There are a few unofficial ones, as well as student hostels which offer a more relaxed atmosphere. All of these are given in the *Budget Holiday* booklet which you can pick up at any Tourist Information office, or, for a wider range of options, refer to *Cheap Sleeps Europe 2000*.

Note that unmarried couples wanting to share a bed might have problems if they are under 18, as hoteliers can be imprisoned for up to three years under Belgian law for allowing this.

## EATING AND NIGHTLIFE

Don't let those Brussels sprouts put you off – Belgian cuisine can be mouth-wateringly good. As the Belgians themselves would have it, food is French in quality but German in quantity. It's hearty, yes, but also quite pricey. If you're eating out, go for your main meal at lunch time as the best-value fixed menu is not available at night.

Every region has its specialities, but the national dish is mussels and fried potatoes. Locals go mad, too, over Belgium's white gold, w*itloof* (endive). Typical also are *carbonnades flamandes* (beef stewed in beer) and *waterzooi* (chicken and vegetables stewed in sauce).

Make sure you budget for the sweet stuff. G*aufres* (waffles) are famous, pastry and cakes are good, and Belgian pralines (filled chocolates) are to die for, especially the fresh cream-filled white ones from any branch of Leonidas.

If you splurge early on, you can always fall back on the cheapest and most prolific of fast food in Belgium: chips. Thin, delicious and served with big blobs of mayonnaise. There's always a *friterie/frituur* near a station, and they serve kebabs, sausages, etc., too. Failing that, check out the well-stocked supermarkets in even the smallest towns.

And to wash it all down? Wine may be good and cheaper than in the UK, but beer is the pride of Belgium. It brews more than 400 varieties, the strongest of which are produced by monks in the monasteries of Orval, Chimay and Postel. In the cities, it's quite common to find pubs serving up to 50 varieties (La Houblonnière in Brussels boasts 100). A glass of one of the Trappist brews makes a good nightcap, or for those willing to try anything once, knock back some *kriek*, a cherry-flavoured beer.

There is no shortage of theatres, cinemas or discos, and the set-up is very similar to the UK. Don't waste your time looking for cheap seats or student discounts; there aren't any.

## Ostend (Oostende) city phone code: 059

Chances are you will land at Belgium's 'Queen of seaside resorts' if you're coming from England by ferry or Jetfoil. Though the beaches are long and sandy, there's not much else to see. But if you want to stop overnight, the **youth hostel** De Ploate at Langestraat 82 (Tel. 805297) is only five minutes from the docks and station and is very good. It gets full in the summer, though, so try to book in advance. You can get **tourist information** from the office at Monacoplein 2 (Tel. 701199).

## Bruges (Brugge – Flemish; Bruges – French) city phone code: 050

This is Belgium's most visited town – and deservedly so. Stop here, even if you visit nowhere else in Belgium: its ancient ramparts have survived sieges, sackings, occupations and burnings. For 200 years, it was, with Venice, the most important commercial and cultural centre in the western world, and the Counts of Flanders spent fortunes making the guildhalls, palaces and churches as impressive as they could. All this glory came to an end when the harbour silted up in the

15th century and made trade impossible.

In the 19th century, while most of the other Flemish cities threw themselves headfirst into industrialization, Bruges was left behind in its medieval rags. Today, the beautifully preserved centre is more like an open-air museum than a 20th-century city. With carillion chimes, cobbled streets, canals lined by weeping willows and crossed by humpbacked bridges (*brugge* means 'bridge' – the city has more than 80 of them), it's little wonder Bruges – known as the 'Venice of the North' – is considered one of the most appealing cities in all of Europe.

## STATION FACILITIES

The station is on the southern edge of the town, 1½ km from the city centre. If you don't feel like a walk (although it is a pleasant 15-minute stroll through the large park) buses leave every five minutes for the centre; get off at the *Markt* (main square), close to the main Tourist Information. There's train information daily, 6.30am–10.30pm (Tel. 382382, multi-lingual) and all the usual amenities including cycle hire and a post office. The station shuts 1am–4.30am.

There are two trains every hour from Brussels and three every hour from Ghent and the coast. Daily trains to: Amsterdam, Cologne, Vienna, Koblenz, Berlin, Belgrade, London (via Ramsgate), Munich, Salzburg, Basle, Brig, Milan, Paris.

## TOURIST INFORMATION AND ADDRESSES

The Tourist Office at Burg 11 (Tel. 448686) is open Apr.–Sept., Mon.–Fri.: 9.30am–6.30pm, Sat. and Sun.: 10am–12pm, 2pm–6.30pm; Oct.–Mar., Mon.–Fri.: 9.30am–5pm, Sat.: 9.30am–1.15pm and 2–5pm. Closed Sunday. They will sell you a map, give you leaflets and fix up a bed for you. There is an exchange bureau in the building Apr.–Oct., daily except Wednesdays.

The **Youth Information Centre**, JAC, on Kleine Hertsbergerstraat 1 (Tel. 33 98 45), amongst other things, has lists of cheap rooms and eateries. Open Mon. and Wed.: 9am-noon, 1.30pm-8pm; Tues.: 1.30pm-8pm; Fri.: 9am-noon, 1.30pm-6pm; Sat.: 10am-12.30pm.

The **post office** is nearby at Markt 5, open Mon.-Fri.: 9am-6pm, Sat.: 9am-noon.

## SEEING

The **Markt**, Bruges' main square, and nearby **Burg** square form the heart of the city. Lining the Markt are a series of magnificent buildings, including **The Belfry**, built from the 13th to the 15th century. Is it leaning slightly, or is that just the Belgian beer talking? Climb its 366 steps for a good view of the old town and listen out for the **carillon** (47 chiming bells). Two museums next door to each other on the

Dijver are **Gruuthuse** and **Groeninge** (closed at lunchtime, and on Tuesdays in winter). Gruuthuse is devoted to applied arts, housed in a beautiful 15th-century mansion, while Groeninge shows off Flemish painting and contemporary art.

The open top **boat trips** through the maze of canals may seem a rip-off at around 200BF a go (every half hour, daily 10am-6pm), but they're actually quite good value, giving a unique perspective on some of the city's most beautiful spots and fun when it rains as they hand out umbrellas! **Bus fares** are a set fee for any distance, but Bruges is best seen on foot. The Tourist Office can recommend organized **walking tours**, although Bruges is compact enough to explore yourself without fear of missing anything.

Cyclists enjoy a privileged position in Bruges. In over 50 one-way streets they can cycle in both directions! **Hire a bike** at the station (325BF per day) or from de Ketting , Gentpoortstraat 23 (150BF per day), and cycle to **Sluis**, just over the Dutch border. Follow the Bruges–Sluis canal for 15 km to Sluis, where there's a windmill worth seeing. Bruges Tourist Office does a handy little guide of cycling tours.

**FREE BRUGES:**
- Don't miss Michelangelo's marble treasure *Madonna and Child*, in the 13th-century **Church of our Lady** in Marienstraat, next to the Memling Museum.
- There's also Bruges' oldest parish church 300m to the north, **St Saviour's Cathedral**, built 12th–15th century.
- In the **Basilica of the Holy Blood**, on the corner of the **Burg**, there's a relic said to contain the blood of Christ.
- In the unlikely event you're feeling amorous after all that, the **Lake of Love** is worth a walk in the park. Also known as the **Minnewater**, it was once part of Bruges' outer harbour. Adding intrigue to romance, there's a 16th-century lockkeeper's house to visit there.
- Cross the bridge beside Minnewater to the **Begijnhof**, a serene spot off the Wijngaardplein. It's encircled by former almshouses for the widows of fallen Crusaders, though Benedictine nuns live there now, still dressed in the style of the 15th century. You can wander around the interior and the grounds for free or pay a few francs to visit the **museum** in the house next to the gate.

## SLEEPING

Remember that Bruges is very, very popular, hostels fill up quickly in the summer, so get there early or book ahead.

The IYH hostel **Europa** at Baron Ruzettelaan 143 (Tel. 352679) is 15 minutes' walk from the station in the other direction from town. Because it's not so central, there's a better chance of getting a bed.

Curfew is at 11pm. You'll need an IYHF card and 375–470BF for B&B in dorms. There are double rooms and quads, too. Closed Mon.–Sat.: 10am–1pm, Sun.: 10am–5pm, and over Christmas and the New Year. Take bus 2 to Steenbrugge and get off shortly after the canal (the third stop). The driver will point it out.

Some good private hostels are more centrally located. The **Snuffel's Sleep-Inn** at Ezelstraat 47–49 (Tel. 333133) is excellent value, 430BF for B&B in dorms (singles, doubles, triples and quads available). It's basic but comfortable, central and friendly, and there is a good choice of reasonably priced meals with a happy hour in the bar each evening. Get there early as there are only 56 beds.

Try **The Passage**, Dweersstraat 26 (Tel. 340232), from 380BF for dorms (singles and doubles also available), or the quirky **Charlie Rockets** at Hoogstraat 19 (Tel. 330660). **Hotel Lybeer**, Korte Vulderstraat 31 (Tel. 334355), from 700BF. **Bauhaus** at Langestraat 135–137 has 81 beds (Tel. 341093). Cost from 430BF for dorms, or 950BF for a double with B&B. Five minutes from market place, near the windmills.

For camping in style – there's even a restaurant – **Camping St Michiel** at Tillegemstraat 55, St Michiels (Tel. 380891), charges from 110BF per person, 130BF per tent. It's quite a way out: 25 minutes' walk from the Markt, or bus 7 from the station or 't Zand. Change traveller's cheques here free of commission.

## EATING AND NIGHTLIFE

Avoid the Markt and 't Zand, where prices are high. As Bruges is not a university town, there's no specific cheap student area, but you can get by. **The Straffe Hendrik - De Halve Maan** at Walplein 26 is a cosy brewery tap room with its own special tipple from the brewery next door. **Soul Food** at Langestraat 15 does some reasonable vegetarian dishes.

The **Vismarkt** (cross the river from the Burg, then turn left) sells fresh seafood, and cheap supermarkets can be found at Noordzandstraat 4, just off 't Zand, and at 55 Langestraat (the Battard).

Plenty of bars and late-night cafés are dotted around the old town; **Vlissinge** on Blekerstraat claims to be among the oldest in Europe, and **Brugs Beertje** at Kemelstraat 5 offers 300 varieties of beer.

## EXCURSIONS

'Alternative Flanders' can be experienced through one of the good, **cheap bus tours** offered by Quasimodo's. They cover everything including the World War I and II battlefields of **Ypres**, and Flanders and the cemeteries and even do a 'chocolates, waffles and beer tasting' tour, all expertly guided (Tel. 370470 or call at 52 Engelendalelaan, 8310 St-Kruis, or Poortersstraat 47).

# Brussels (Brussel – Flemish; Bruxelles – French)
city phone code: 02

Year 2000 Brussels is a European City of Culture. Visitors are in for a real feast of delights because this city with 1000 years of history is determined to excel. Compact in size, it is eminently walkable and a treasure trail of over ninety or so museums and galleries. Officially bilingual, Brussels is headquarters of the European Union and NATO. With the world's largest number of diplomatic missions and the highest concentration of journalists outside Washington DC it is 'the beating heart of Europe'. But in the narrow streets of its old town, Brussels is as provincial as can be, with beer, waffles and traditional dishes of rabbit and duck being knocked back at tiny restaurants lining cobbled streets.

At its centre is 'the most beautiful square in Europe' – the Grand' Place, a huge market square dating from the 12th century and bordered by the gilded façades of 17th and 18th century guild houses. See it in the daytime and then again when it's floodlit at night.

## STATION FACILITIES

Brussels has three main stations: **Gare du Nord** (near the Botanical Gardens), **Gare du Midi** (serving the south of the city) and **Gare Centrale** (conveniently located for the Grand' Place). There are interconnecting trains between the three stations every 15–20 minutes. For information, call 555 2525.

**Eurostar** trains make use of the Channel Tunnel, linking London's Waterloo station with Gare du Midi in 2 hours and 40 minutes. Trains also leave Brussels daily for Holland, Denmark, Germany, Switzerland, Italy and France. It takes less than three hours to get to Cologne, Paris or Amsterdam from Brussels.

Booths near the Gare du Midi sell food, and there are friteries in the nearby rue de France. You'll find social segregation at the Midi in the form of the Brussels Tavern snack bar complex. Officially, this is for the use of EuroCity or IC passengers only, but in practice you can get in if reasonably dressed. However, prices are roughly double those elsewhere in the station.

For Tourist Information, go to Gare Centrale and walk across Place de l'Europe for three blocks. For information on city transport, head down to the métro station at Gare du Midi.

There's a post office near Gare du Midi (open 24 hours) and at Centrale.

Finally, if you arrive late at night when the Tourist Office is shut, head for the Gare du Nord, as there are several student hostels in this area.

## TOURIST INFORMATION

The best is at Rue de Marché-aux-Herbes, Grasmarkt 63 (Tel. 504 0390). The TIB in the Town Hall on Grand' Place (Tel. 513 8940) is also OK but gets very busy. Hours of both the city's Tourist Offices are, Mar.–Sept.: 9am–6pm daily; Oct.–Nov.: 9am–4pm Mon.-Sat., 10am–2pm Sundays; Dec.–Feb.: 10am–2pm Mon.–Sat., closed

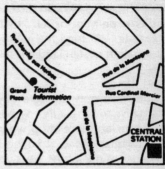

Sunday. They'll help with accommodation and have maps and all the usual handouts.

Other organizations providing help are:

**Acotra World** (Tel. 512 8607). This youth organization provides a free room-finding service. They're open weekdays 10am–5.30pm.

**Info-Jeunes**, rue Marché-aux-Herbes 27 (Tel. 512 3274) is near the Grand' Place and is open Mon.–Fri.: 12am–6pm.

## ADDRESSES

**POST OFFICE** First floor of tall building at Place de la Monnaie; *poste restante* here

**AMEX** 100 Boulevard du Souverain (Tel. 676 2111), open Mon.–Fri.: 9am–5pm, Sat.: 9.30am–noon

**UK EMBASSY** Britannia House, 85 rue d'Arlon (Tel. 287 6211)

**IRISH EMBASSY** 19 rue Luxembourg (Tel. 513 6633)

**US EMBASSY** 27 blvd du Régent (Tel. 513 3830)

**CANADIAN EMBASSY** 2 av. de Tervuren (Tel. 741 0611)

**AUSTRALIAN EMBASSY** 6 rue Guimard (Tel. 286 0500)

**NEW ZEALAND EMBASSY** 47 blvd du Régent (Tel. 512 1040)

**AMBULANCE** Tel. 100

**POLICE** Tel. 101

**24-HOUR CHEMIST** 99 av. Houba (Tel. 479 1818)

**EURAIL AID OFFICE** Travel Centre (International services), Gare de Bruxelles-Midi (Tel. (02) 555 2525/555 2555)

**USIT OFFICE** Connections, 19-21 Rue du Midi, 1000 Brussels (Tel. 550 0100)

## GETTING ABOUT

Tickets costing a flat fare of about 50BF within the city are valid for transfers between métro, bus and tram for one hour. There's also a one-day travel card for 130BF. You can buy a 10-trip pass from métro stations for 340BF. The Visit Brussels passport, sold at the Tourist Office, costs 300BF and includes other tourist discounts. For information on city transport, there are offices under the Place Rogier, Porte de Namur and Gare du Midi, or Tel. 515 2000.

One tip – if using the métro take a map with you: there is limited information posted, and it is hard to understand.

## SEEING

If you have only a single day, a bus tour is the best bet. As an alternative to the luxury coaches and six-language operations that end your tour at a lace shop where the driver gets a back-hander, try **Chatterbus**. Aimed at young Eurorail types, it's run by the former manager of one of the city's youth hostels and takes in all the places you'd want to see – and a few the city authorities would rather you didn't. You'll get a good tour of the city and an honest assessment of the places not worth exploring further. The cost is around 650BF, or 500BF if you stay at one of the youth hostels.

The same group runs **Brussels on Foot** tours during the summer at around 250BF each. If you're in a group, they will arrange off-beat tours such as hijacking a tram, or a beer-tasting night, including beer-flavoured food, and they also have lists of ordinary Brussels residents who are prepared to act as guides for the price of the telephone call to book them.

Book through youth hostels, or call Chatterbus directly (Tel. 673 1835). As Chatterbus is more of an informal service than a profit-making business, you may find it only runs on certain days and at certain times. But it is well worth making the effort to catch one of these tours.

Otherwise (and if you've a bit more time), start exploring at *the* sight of Brussels, the **Grand' Place** – a well-preserved square of Gothic guildhalls and public buildings from the 17th century. Opposite the **Maison du Roi** (the city museum) is the Gothic **Town Hall**, considered Brussels' most elegant building.

The **Musée des Beaux Arts** has a good collection of early Flemish masters, including Rubens, and next door is the **modern art gallery**, whose massive collection is one of the largest in Europe. (Combined admission 150BF; closed Monday).

Brussels' answer to the Eiffel Tower is the **Atomium** (200BF), an immense model of an iron molecule, built to celebrate the 1958 International Exhibition at Heysel. At its foot is **Mini-Europe**, a collection of 350 models of well-known European sights. Entrance is 395BF. Open Mar. 25-Jan. 7. Also in the same area, known as **Bruparck**, there are **an underground water and sauna park**, a **food and entertainment park** called The Village, a **planetarium**, an **IMAX theatre** with a seven-storey-high screen, and a **27-screen cinema** complex. The Belgium Comic Strip

Centre (200BF), rue des sables 20, is a converted Art Nouveau warehouse with 30,000 accessible volumes of comic strips on computer, a comics reading room and stars of course, Hergé's Tintin. (Closed Mondays).

There are several day trips worth making from Brussels: **Leuven**, a medieval university town (20 minutes by train); **Waterloo**, site of the battle, now with museums; and **Bokrijk**, the largest open-air museum in Europe with more than 100 reconstructions of medieval buildings (Apr.–Oct.). Trains from any Brussels station (90 minutes). Note that it is quite a walk from the Waterloo station to the Wellington Museum – and too far to walk to the battlefield. A bus runs in peak season, otherwise take the bus directly to the battlefield from Place Rouppe (between Gare du Midi and Grand' Place) every 30 minutes, all year round.

There is a good amusement park at **Bierges**, a half-hour from Gare du Nord, called **Walibi**. For a more relaxed day trip, head to **Louvian**, thirty minutes away by train; it's a pretty place, littered with ornate houses and excellent coffee shops.

**FREE BRUSSELS:** There are so many free things to do, you may well end up spending nothing at all.

- First and foremost on any city sightseeing list is the bizarre symbol of Brussels, the **Mannekin-Pis** (a small statue of a boy having a pee), behind the town hall on Rue de l'Étuve. There are several stories as to his origin, the main one being that he saved the city by damping down some dynamite – in a natural and effective fashion.
- The **Grand' Place** is a hive of activity day and night. There is a daily **flower market** (Apr.–Nov., closed Mondays) and a **bird market** on Sunday mornings. Between April and August, and during December, 800 coloured **floodlights** illuminate the Town Hall, to the atmospheric accompaniment of 15th century chants.
- In late June/early July, the historic pageant known as the **Ommegang** is preceded by parades through the streets. The processions end with a huge show in the Grand' Place, though you need to book (and pay) for seats in advance (details from the Tourist Office).
- Walk down the **Petite rue des Bouchers**, crowded with tiny restaurants, to the **Galeries St-Hubert**, a network of galleries built in 1847. Designer heaven in every sense – at designer prices.
- The **National Library**, next to the Central Station, has **formal gardens**. From them, there's a great view of the library's ornate **clock**, over the lower archway. Its moving figures are worth a look when it strikes midday.
- Keep walking through the library gardens to **Place Royale**, site of **Coudenberg Palace**, and the town centre during the years of Austrian rule in the 18th century. The view from here over the lower town is worth seeing.

- The **Petit Sablon**, not far from Place Royale, is a small garden lined by 48 statues representing Brussels' medieval guilds. Each of the craftsmen depicted carries an object that reveals his trade.
- The **Musée Instrumental**, located from June 2000 at Place Royale, has the largest collection of musical instruments in the world (over 6,000), some of them dating back to the Bronze Age.
- Behind the Petit Sablon is the **Palais d'Egmont**, where once lived Christina of Sweden, Louis XV and Voltaire. It's now Belgium's Foreign Affairs offices, but the security guards will sometimes let you into its gardens.
- The immense **Palais de Justice** (closed weekends) is quite possibly the ugliest building in Europe. Built on the site of Gallows Hill at the end of Rue de la Régence, this is a building designed to scare.
- **St Michael's Cathedral** at Place St-Gudule is a magnificent mix of Romanesque and modern architecture.
- **Brussels Park** is home to the **Palais Royale**, open for visits from late July to early September.
- The **Palais de la Nation** (in Brussels Park) is the seat of the Belgian Parliament. You can tour the building when the parliament's two houses are resting.
- **The Museum of Art and History** (150BF, but free first Wednesday afternoon of each month, closed Monday) at 10 Parc du Cinquantenaire is a vast array of decorative art, history and periods.
- The **Bois de la Cambre** on the edge of town (south of the Palais de Justice) is a rambling park, popular with local families. Just before it is the **Abbaye de la Cambre**, a 14th-century cloistered church with an 18th-century courtyard and a terraced park. Tram 94 from Sablon or Place Stephanie takes 10 minutes to get there.
- **Antiques market**, Grand Sablon, Saturdays and Sunday mornings. In December, it's a traditional European Christmas Market.
- **Midi Market**, near Gare du Midi, is the North African community's Sunday morning souk, full of exotic goods.
- Old Market (the **Vieux Marché**) in Place du Jeu de Balle is a working-class flea market (daily, 7am-2pm). The earlier you get there, the better.

## SLEEPING

Unless you're prepared to go a long way out of town for the campsites, your choice is limited to hostels or hotels. The good news is there's not much difficulty getting a bed, even in summer. The best area is round the Gare du Nord. If you have any trouble, **Acotra** (see under tourist info) will find a bed for you, or get hold of *Cheap Sleeps Europe 2000* for more options.

**STUDENT HOSTELS** New Sleep Well at rue Damier 23 (Tel. 218 5050) is the best value in the city. It's clean, central (near Gare du Nord, in the direction of Place Rogier), cheap and has a good atmosphere. It makes an effort to be different (the piped background music is all classical!). Dormitory beds cost around 400BF, singles 700BF and doubles 1100BF. Try to reserve ahead as it's popular. In summer, it arranges city tours by local students.

Another student hostel which offers good value is **CHAB's Centre Vincent Van Gogh** at 8 rue Traversière (Tel. 217 0158) close to the Botanique métro station, or 10 minutes' walk from the Gare du Nord. It has 180 beds in dorms – use own sleeping bag – (330BF), 3/4 bedded rooms (460BF), twins (540BF, with private showers and toilets 570BF) and singles (685BF). There's also a sleep-in for 300BF. 10% reduction with ISIC. Although school groups are accepted in low season, the preferred age range in summer is 18–35. Open 7.30am–2am. This hostel also has kitchen, restaurant, laundry and locker facilities. They organize walking tours of Brussels and free, or cheap, music and art events, plus there is an open-air cinema at the nearby Botanique Culture Centre.

**YOUTH HOSTELS** There's a hostel at Heilige Geeststraat 2 (Tel. 511 0436) near the Kappelle Kerk/Église de la Chapelle; head down Keizerslaan from Central Station. It's known as the **Bruegel** and costs from 395BF to 660BF, including breakfast. You'll need an IYHF card.

The **International Accommodation Centre Jacques Brel** is at rue de la Sablonnière 30 (Tel. 218 0187). It has 134 beds and charges between 395BF and 660BF, including breakfast. It is open all year round, but booking is essential. Has a cafeteria, information and TV room; métro Botanique or Madou.

**PENSIONS/HOTELS** There are a few at Avenue Fonsny (opposite Gare du Midi): the Merlo is OK and reasonably priced by Brussels standards. **Hôtel Sabina** at 78 rue du Nord (Tel. 218 2637) and **Hôtel de l'Yser**, 913 rue d'Edinbourg (Tel. 511 7459) are worth investigating. The **Hôtel du Grand Colombier** at rue du Colombier 10 (Tel. 217 9622 or 219 5136) charges around 1,100BF for a double, with shower, including breakfast. The **Sleepwell**, 27 rue de la Blanchisserie (Tel. 218 5050) offers a 10% reduction with ISIC. Refer to *Cheap Sleeps Europe 2000* for other suggestions.

**CAMPING** Try **Beersel**, Steenweg op Ukkel 75 (Tel. 331 0561 or 378 1977), nine km south of the city, or Paul Rosmant, at Warandeberg 52 (Tel. 782 1009). Métro to Kraainem, then bus 30 to Place St Pierre.

Also **Grimbergen** at Veldkanstraat 64 (Tel. 269 2597), open Jan.–Oct., bus G from Gare du Nord to terminus, then walk.

## EATING AND NIGHTLIFE

Eating on the streets is the way to go here. There are plenty of fast-food chains, waffle stalls, and no shortage of cheap restaurants with fixed-price meals. **Rue des Bouchers** may be the heart of Touristville, but it's also full of locals tucking into pyramids of *moules marinières* (400–500BF) and choosing from towers of shellfish on ice.

There's fresh produce at the **open-air market** at Place St-Catherine. **Department stores** offer good food at reasonable prices and the shopping centre, **City 2**, located off Place Rogier (five minutes from Gare du Nord), has several cafés; the one on the top floor does soup and as much salad as you can get on your plate for around 100BF. Open 9am–8.30pm. The **Vietnamese and African** restaurants are also good value and **Le Breton**, 59 rue des Drapiers, offers authentic Belgian food, beer and wines in a studenty atmosphere.

And don't forget the **chocolate**. Brussels is pralines paradise, a mecca for addicts the world over. It's not sold in shops, but in gilded temples to the art of chocolate. And the chox themselves are displayed like jewels in glass cases, and dispensed by supermodels or aristocrats each wearing a single white glove. They're expensive, but just as you wouldn't dream of visiting Egypt without seeing the pyramids, you can't leave Brussels without checking out the chocolate. Try Leonidas at 46 Anspachlaan; Godiva at 22 Grand' Place; Neuhaus at 25-27 Galérie de la Reine; or Planète Chocolat at 57 Rue du Midi.

At night, head for the Gare du Midi – the student quarter. Discos are expensive, but pubs are just as lively. The club scene changes constantly – ask around for what's hot and what's not.

To meet the locals, go to **La Mort Subite** (Sudden Death) at Rue Montagne aux Herbes Potagères. It's a genuine beer hall, where locals share long benches as they knock back white lagers, Trappist brews and raspberry beers. Another locals' haunt is **Bierodrome** at Place Fernand Cocq 21.

**Films** are good value (usually 180BF for students), and the Styx, 72 rue de l'Arbre Bénit, shows revival films with midnight meals, which usually attract an interesting crowd.

# Southern Belgium

The main line to Luxembourg passes through Namur and the **Ardennes**. To explore the area, it's best to base yourself at **Namur**; the regional Tourist Office is at rue Notre Dame 3 (Tel. 081 22 29 98). For information on the city, go to the pavilion next to the station or the **Info-Jeunes** at the belfry in the town (Tel. 081 71 47 40). Namur has one of the friendliest **youth hostels** in Europe at rue Félicien Rops, 8 La Plante (Tel. 081 22 36 88, bus 3 or 4 from the station).

# Antwerp (Antwerpen – Flemish; Anvers – French)
city phone code: 03

Somewhat underrated on the tourist trail, Antwerp, home of artists van Dyck and Rubens, offers good sightseeing, good food, friendly citizens (Dutch and English speaking) and lively nightlife. Its prime location on the river Scheldt made it one of Europe's most powerful cities by the 16th century. Today it is the second largest European port, and for 500 years has been the diamond capital of the world. The diamond district, also known as the Jerusalem of the North, is home to the largest settlement of orthodox Jews in northern Europe. Belgium's second city is compact and pedestrian friendly, with one of the world's most famous zoos located right in the centre, next to Central Station.

## TOURIST INFORMATION

There are two **stations**: Berchem and Central; international trains stop only at Berchem, except those from Amsterdam.

The **Tourist Office** is at Grote Markt 15, open Mon.–Sat.: 9am–6pm; Sun. and holidays: 9am–5pm (Tel 232 0103). The international student travel office is at Connections–Eurotrain, Melkmarkt 23 (Tel. 2253161). Most of the museums are shut on Mondays.

## SEEING

Most **sights** are concentrated in the narrow streets of the old town, the centre of which is the **Grote Markt**. Flanked by the magnificent Renaissance city hall (the **Stadhuis**), the square is bordered by 16th-century guildhouses. To the south is the **Cathedral of Our Lady**, inside which are four Rubens altarpieces. There's more of the master at **Rubens' House**, at Wapper 9, and still more in galleries and churches around the city. There is also **St Charles Borromeo's Church**, the **Plantin-Moretus Museum** of 16th-century printing and **Castle Steen**, the oldest building in Antwerps.

**FREE ANTWERP:**
- The **Royal Museum of Fine Arts** at Leopold de Waelplaats 1-9 (open 10am–4.45pm, closed Monday, free Fridays) houses more than 1,500 paintings by old Flemish masters, including Rubens,

Van Dyck, and Breughel. One of the best galleries in the world.

- **Centraal Station**, the main train station and eclectic monument, was built 100 years ago as a 'railway cathedral'.
- The **Diamond Museum** at Lange Herentalsestraat 31 (open daily, 10am-5pm) hosts cutting and polishing demonstrations on Saturday afternoons. There are a number of other free diamond-cutting exhibitions, and tours of diamond works; ask at the Tourist Office for details.
- On Sunday mornings, there's a famous **bird market** on the Oude Vaartplaats.

## SLEEPING

Don't be taken in by the 'rooms for tourists' advertised in cafés around the station – they're brothels!

Fifteen minutes' walk from Central Station (or five mins on bus 23 to Stuivenberg Hospital) is **Globetrotters' Nest International Hostel**, at Vlagstraat 25 (Tel. 2369928). It costs 400BF for a night in a seven-bed dorm (including breakfast), with sheet hire costing 80BF for the first night only. Double rooms with private lounge and TV are also available for 1100BF, also including breakfast. There are kitchen facilities, free hot showers, a mini market, bikes for rent, and a well-equipped recreation and TV room.

The student hostel **Boomerang** at Volkstraat 49 (Tel. 2384782) is centrally located and reasonably priced, though reports of standards vary. Take bus 23 from Central station to the Museum stop, or tram 8 from Berchem station.

The **New International Youth Hostel** at 256 Provinciestraat (Tel. 2300522) is clean, friendly and near the station, down Pelikaanstraat, 20 minutes to Provinciestraat. The **youth hostel** (IYHF) is at Eric Sasselaan 2 (Tel. 2380273). Tram 2 or bus 27 from Central station, to just after the bridge across the main road.

**Hôtel Florida**, at De Keyserlei 59, is right in front of Central Station (Tel. 2321443) around 1200BF single, 1800BF double.

There is a **campsite** at Vogelzanglaan (Tel. 2385717), bus 17 to the Holiday Inn Crowne Plaza hotel, which is cheap. Another site is located at **St-Annastrand**, on the left bank of the river (Tel. 2196090).

## EATING AND NIGHTLIFE

Herring, eel and *witloof* (endives) are the local specialities, along with fast food standby mussels with chips and mayonnaise. The Prinsstraat area (round the university) has several cafés doing fixed-price menus. **Lenny's** on Hendrik Conscienceplein, is good, and there are several other eating places and bars nearby.

For a quick fix of chocolate, try the Queen of Belgium's favourite stocking-up shop, **Del Rey**, at Appelmanstraat 5.

Antwerp is famous for its 300 **bars** and **nightclubs**. They're easy to find–just follow the noise. The old town is good and lively in the evenings, and round the Grote Markt there's no shortage of bars and restaurants, though they're on the pricey side. Try the trendy student hang-out Oude Waag, Het Elfde Gebod (the Eleventh Commandment) and the ancient De Pelgrom.

Watch out for the gin and beer shops, too. The De Vagant gin shop has an assortment of 350 genevers, the local gins, while the beer shops sell an array of 280 Belgian beers, including the cherry beers, Trappist monk beers and even a green beer called Paranoia.

## Ghent (Gent – Flemish; Gand – French)
city phone code: 09

Of all the Flemish cities, Ghent, with its step-gabled façades, gilded spires and tranquil canals, is the most stately. Best known today for art, flowers and a glut of historic buildings, Ghent in the 14th century was queen of the Flemish cloth industry, and the largest town in western Europe.

Day trippers from Antwerp should get off at **Dampoort station**, which is nearer the centre, but from all other destinations you go on to **St Pieter's station** train information 7am–9pm daily (Tel. 2224444). Reservations have much the same hours and there are all the usual station facilities. Daily trains to: Cologne, Vienna, Koblenz, Berlin, Belgrade, Munich, Salzburg, Basle, Brig, Milan, Brussels, Paris.

From the station, take Tram 1 to the centre, **Korenmarkt. Tourist Information** is at Botermarkt Crypt, Town Hall (Tel. 2665111) 2 Apr.–6 Nov.: Mon.–Sun.: 9.30am–6.30pm; 7 Nov.–14 April: Mon.–Sun.: 9.30am–4.30pm.

All the sights are central and within easy walking distance of one another. The main sights are: the **Cathedral of St Bavo**, containing Van Eyck's *The Mystic Lamb*. Next door is the **Belfry**, 's'**Gravensteen** – the 12th-century **Flemish Counts' Castle** – and the **guild houses** by Graslei.

Until June 2000, Ghent is celebrating the 500th anniversary of the birth of Emperor Charles V. with exhibitions, festivals and special events culminating in a parade and pageant.

The **youth hostel** De Droecke is at Sint-Widostraat 11 (Tel. 233 7050). Alternatively, use pensions or, during holidays, the university halls of residence at Stalhof 6 (Tel. 2647100), just off Overpoortstraat (open 24 hours, all single rooms).

The **university** at Overpoortstraat is also your best bet for eats and nightlife, and has the added advantage of being near the station –

take bus 9, 70, 71 or 90.

There is camping at **Camping Blaarmeersen**, Zuiderlaan 12 (Tel. 221 5399), bus 51, 52 or 53 to the Europaburg, then bus 38, or a 30-minute walk from St Pieter's station.

NOTES:

# BOSNIA-HERCEGOVINA

Before being torn apart by civil war, the towns and cities of this mountainous region of former Yugoslavia were once known for their beauty. Now their names are more familiar as no-go war zones, remembered for chaotic news footage of brutal fighting, war crimes and the (mainly Serbian) efforts at 'ethnic cleansing'.

In March 1992, the population of Bosnia-Hercegovina voted with a 99% majority for independence from Yugoslavia. The Serbs who lived in the region boycotted the referendum. The country was nevertheless officially recognized by both the EC and the USA on 6 April. Belgrade responded with propaganda of a 'Greater Serbia', which helped incite Serb extremists to fight for control, and on 2 May, Sarajevo was placed under siege by Serbian forces. A peace accord was signed in late 1995, and the siege ended on 26 February, 1996.The situation today is still far from settled, the future uncertain. Only those living on the very edge, or with close family ties within the country would consider a visit. Check with the Foreign Office for the latest update.

Though normality is slowly returning, our advice would still be to avoid the area.

**GENERAL INFORMATION** We have abandoned the normal format for this section, since Bosnia-Hercegovina is still in such a state of turmoil that much of the usual intelligence is irrelevant. The information given here represents as clear a picture as we are able to give in the circumstances. Where rail track has been restored, trains are limited. In fact, bus services are more reliable, though roads are in poor condition. Tourist services are meagre, and the country is still considered unsafe by governments around the world. Apart from continuing civil disorder in some areas, the major dangers to travellers are the millions of land mines and unexploded ordnances (UXOs) littering the countryside and still to be cleared. The capital, or what is left of it, is Sarajevo and the political system depends on which town you are in.

**ENTRY REQUIREMENTS** In theory, citizens of Ireland, the USA and the UK do not require a visa to enter Bosnia-Hercegovina; citizens of Australia, Canada and New Zealand do. In practice, it may be a soldier who decides whether or not to let you in.

**POPULATION** The population at the last count was around 4.5 million, though at least two-thirds of that number live as displaced refugees in communities divided along ethnic lines.

**RELIGION** The country used to be comprised of 49% Muslims, 32% Orthodox Serbs and 19% Catholic Croats, but what is left now is anybody's guess.

**LANGUAGE** Bosnian, Serbian and Croatian are spoken (see the language notes under Croatia and Yugoslavia).

**MONEY MATTERS** A new Bosnian currency has recently been introduced – the convertible mark (KM), fixed at a 1:1 exchange rate to the Deutschmark. There are about 3KM to the UK pound and about 1.9 to the US dollar.

**TELEPHONES** Telephones are back up and running: to call Bosnia-Hercegovina, the country code is 387; to phone out of Bosnia-Hercegovina, dial 00 first.

**EMERGENCIES Police**: Tel. 664 211. **Fire**: Tel. 93. **Medical emergency**: Tel. 94.

Shelling from Serb guerrillas camped in the hills during the siege of 1992-1996 left the official capital in rubble. Reconstruction is under way with a vengeance, but Sarajevo's former beauty, shaped by 500 years of Turkish rule, may never be regained. Sarajevo was the only oriental city in Europe, and before the civil war, the Turkish bazaar of Bascarsija was one of the great bazaars of the world (two others being Marrakech and Istanbul). There used to be 73 mosques here and until the four-year siege, the river front had been virtually unchanged since 1914.

## Mostar

Though touristy, this town used to be quite beautiful, with a magnificent 16th-century Turkish bridge stretching across the river Neretva and a well-preserved old town. Several 14th-century mosques and other exquisite architecture have survived in the old Turkish quarter, but the bridge that made Mostar famous was completely destroyed by shelling. The Neretva River is an uneasy borderline in a city that remains divided, with Croats on the west bank, and Muslims on the east side.

## Medujorde

This town is a modern pilgrimage site for Catholics who maintain that visions of the Virgin Mary have been, and are still, seen here. Much of this region is under Croat control (being Catholics, the Croats have struggled to keep the area from being destroyed or desecrated), enabling determined pilgrims to visit.

NOTES

........................................................................................................................

........................................................................................................................

........................................................................................................................

........................................................................................................................

........................................................................................................................

........................................................................................................................

........................................................................................................................

........................................................................................................................

........................................................................................................................

........................................................................................................................

........................................................................................................................

........................................................................................................................

........................................................................................................................

........................................................................................................................

........................................................................................................................

........................................................................................................................

........................................................................................................................

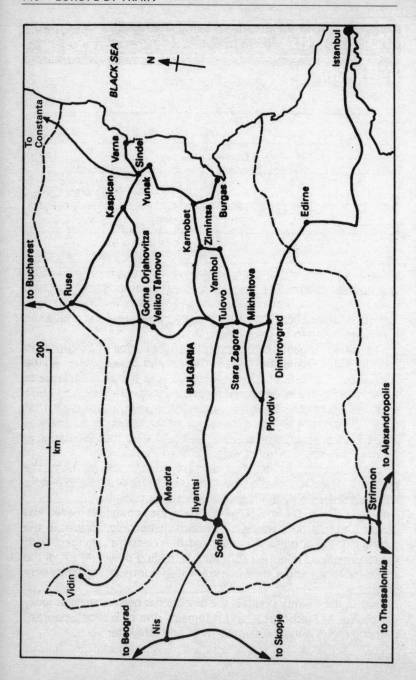

# BULGARIA

| | |
|---|---|
| Entry requirements | Passport and visa |
| Population | 8 million |
| Capital | Sofia (pop.: 1 million) |
| Currency | Leva |
| | £1 = approx. 3000 Leva |
| Political system | Republic |
| Religion | Eastern Orthodox |
| Language | Bulgarian (Russian widely spoken; some German, French and English understood) |
| Public holidays | New Year's Day, Liberation Day (3 Mar.), Easter, Labour Day (1 May), Bulgarian Culture Day (24 May), Christmas Day |
| International dialling codes | To Bulgaria: int'l code 359 |
| | From Bulgaria: 00 + country code |

Bulgaria is a country that's easy on the eye, with much natural beauty and unspoilt charm. The long sandy beaches of its Black Sea coast form a magnet for hordes of Eastern and Western visitors each year. Tourism is centred here and many pleasant inland areas and handsome towns lie waiting to be discovered.

The country's name comes from the Asiatic tribe of Bulgars who conquered the Danubian plains in the 7th and 8th centuries. A little later, their empire flourished in literature and the arts, while trade turned them into a leader in south-eastern Europe. However, it wasn't too long before the Ottomans muscled in with an invasion that brought 500 years of occupation. But luckily Bulgarian culture was preserved thoughout this time, with writers and artists given refuge in their monasteries – many of which survive today.

During the World Wars, after being allied with the Germans, the Bulgarians were occupied by the USSR until 1946, when they became a Socialist People's Republic with a Soviet-style constitution.

In 1989, Todor Zhivkov, Bulgaria's hard-line communist leader, was ousted from position, which led towards democratic reforms. In the summer of 1990, political parties and free elections emerged, with the renamed and reformed communists holding power. Much of the 1990s has been under their control, with reforms taking effect very slowly.

Indeed, the country's path in the nineties has been somewhat rocky – a bit like its landscape – and it remains one of Europe's poorest, suffering high inflation, unemployment and ethnic tensions.

## BULGARIAN STATE RAILWAYS (BDZ)

Bulgarian trains tend to be slow and overcrowded. Sometimes things come together and they run on time, but don't bank on it as this is the exception rather than the rule. There are three types of trains: express (*Ekspresen*), fast (*Brzi*) and slow (*Putnichki*). Avoid the latter at all costs. Unfortunately, BIJ only run as far as Sofia.

Theoretically, you should be able to cross the country to the Black Sea coast and return again late the same day – trains leave Sofia early every morning, arriving at Burgas in the early afternoon. In practice, delays at intermediate stations make this unrealistic. Whenever you get the chance, purchase your ticket at least a day before setting off. Reservations are recommended on most expresses, or arrive at the station early to be certain of a seat. Alternatively, take the overnight sleeper trains. A lot of services between Bulgaria and former Yugoslav states have been suspended due to the civil war. If possible, aim to buy your ticket in other Eastern countries before getting the train, as the fare charged once you're on board the train is higher. Also, as Bulgarian Railways tend to overcharge for international journeys, try to buy a return ticket outside the country.

**PASSES AVAILABLE** The Inter-Rail pass has been broken down into zones, so that you pay only for travel within the area you want to visit. For £129 you can spend 22 days touring a zone. Bulgaria is in Zone H, along with Yugoslavia, Romania and Macedonia. For details of the eight Inter-Rail zones, see the Inter-Rail section in Part One of this guide.

A Euro-Domino ticket is also available for Bulgaria, see Part One -The Options.

## TRAIN INFORMATION

Few staff speak English, so you might find German and French more helpful. Timetables are given in the Cyrillic alphabet (see below), but there is a Latin equivalent shown against international trains. If you're stuck, try: *Ot koi peron zaminava vlaka za… ?* (From which platform does the train to… leave?). Depend on your *Thomas Cook European Timetable* for most of the time.

**RESERVATIONS** Reserve at least one day in advance to be sure of a seat. They're obligatory on international expresses, but are not available on the Sofia–Istanbul leg of the Munich express. They can be made through BalkanTourist or RILA offices. By now, they may be available for foreign travellers at stations, but don't count on it.

**NIGHT TRAVEL** All couchettes and sleepers are operated by the state railways and fall well short of Western standards.

**EATING ON TRAINS** There's either a buffet car or mini-bar on all fast trains.

## TOURIST INFORMATION

BalkanTourist Offices can be found in nearly every large town. However, it is in the process of being broken up into private tourist agencies so expect regional name changes, like *Varnenski bryag* in the Varna region. They will usually speak English and answer all your travel and accommodation questions, as well as give out tourist information. Note also that with recent political upheaval some street names have altered – more than once in some cases. Your best bet is to find information before you go.

Try Independent Travel Line, Sofia House, 19 Conduit St, London W1R 9TD (Tel. 020 7543 5588); they're the non-package holiday part of Balkan Holidays.

**ISIC BONUSES** Cheap entrance charges to many museums and galleries are available with an ISIC card (obtainable from ORBITA Travel, Hristo Botev 48).

**MONEY MATTERS** Banking hours are 8am–12.30 noon and 1pm–3pm, Mon.–Fri. Be sure to keep hold of your exchange receipts. As usual, forget the blackmarketeers as you risk being ripped off.

**SHOPS** Open 8am–5 or 7pm, with a siesta from 1pm to 2pm.

**MUSEUMS** Tend to shut on Mondays, but there's no fixed pattern; opening times also tend to vary.

**LANGUAGE** Similar to the Russian language, Bulgarian is written with the Cyrillic alphabet, with some variations.

It is also well worth noting that in Bulgaria a nod means 'No' (*Ne*), and a horizontal shake means 'Yes' (*Da*), though as contact with the West increases, expect confusion.

| CYRILLIC ALPHABET | | ENGLISH EQUIVALENT | SOUND VALUE | CYRILLIC ALPHABET | | ENGLISH EQUIVALENT | SOUND VALUE |
|---|---|---|---|---|---|---|---|
| А | а | A | for Anglia | П | п | P | for Park |
| Б | б | B | for Bed | Р | р | R | for Road |
| В | в | V | for Vault | С | с | S | for Soft |
| Г | г | G | for Garage | Т | т | T | for Trail |
| Д | д | D | for Day | У | у | Ou | for Cool |
| Е | е | E | for Engine | Ф | ф | F | for Fair |
| Ж | ж | Zh | for Azure | Х | х | H | for Hot |
| З | з | Z | for Zebra | Ц | ц | Ts | for Tsar |
| И | и | I | for In | Ч | ч | Ch | for Cheese |
| Й | й | Y | for Yes | Ш | ш | Sh | for Ship |
| К | к | K | for Kerb | Щ | щ | Sht | for Ashtray |
| Л | л | L | for Lip | Ъ | ъ | U | for Under |
| М | м | M | for Morris | Ь | ь | J | for Yodel |
| Н | н | N | for Nut | Ю | ю | Yu | for You |
| О | о | O | for Austin | Я | я | Ya | for Yard |

**TIPPING** It is good manners to round up your bill, especially in the poorer countries or regions where it is blatantly obvious that as a tourist you have a lot more money than them.

## SLEEPING

Be aware that when dealing with BalkanTourist Offices and its successors, they will always try to fill up their own hotels first. These tend to offer a poor service and be more expensive. Whenever possible, a room in a private home is your best bet, as they're always a lot cheaper and more interesting. If you decide to accept a local's offer of a room, you're still supposed to register this with the police. But there's no real need if you've already got a couple of official stamps on the card you were given at the border. However, be careful here, for you could still face a fine if you cannot account for several nights. As time goes on, this bureaucracy is diminishing and you probably will not be bothered. Between mid-July and mid-September, you should be able to find a cheap bed in one of the ORBITA student hostels. ISIC holders making reservations through ORBITA can get reductions of up to 50%.

There are also 100 or so official campsites which cost about £2 per tent and similar per person. Beware of recent reports, however, which suggest that some campsites are gradually being neglected by the authorities. Don't partake in freelance camping as it's illegal, with a fine if caught. Most accommodation still has to be paid for in hard currency, but this is slowly changing.

## EATING AND NIGHTLIFE

Food is tasty and cheap in Bulgaria. There's a strong Turkish influence on national dishes, with lamb and pork the most common meats. If possible, try *haiduchki kebab* (lamb cooked with onions, white wine and pepper) or one of their fabulous meat and vegetable dishes, slowly cooked in an earthenware pot, known as *gyuvech*. You really can't go wrong with any of the charcoal-roasted meat dishes with fresh salad. Vegetarians should try *shopska* salad, vegetarian versions of *gyuvech*, or one of several aubergine dishes, including *iman bayaldu*. Yoghurt originated from here too, and Bulgarians are addicted to the stuff: the thick sheep's milk type is especially good, but not always available. Ice cream is excellent as well. Upset stomachs are not uncommon in Bulgaria and very few loos supply paper, so bring plenty with you!

For drinks, Bulgarian wine has a very good reputation and can be enjoyed cheaply here. Try any *slivova*, a spirit made from plums, but avoid the native beer as it has little to recommend it.

You should find at least one theatre in most Bulgarian towns – including open-air ones in several cities – where a range of plays, operas and ballet can be seen. The local BalkanTourist Office will provide tickets and also give information on arranged folklore events. Keep your eyes peeled for occasional rock concerts with local bands as well.

## Sofia city phone code: 02

A city of well over a million people, bustling Sofia, the 'greenest city in Europe', has plenty to offer the visitor. For a start, the ski slopes of the Vitosha mountains are only half an hour away, while the city itself retains over 250 historical monuments and landmarks from its Thracian, Roman, Bulgar and Ottoman days. But the splendour of this rich heritage is slightly tainted by the many communist-inspired concrete piles around the city.

### STATION INFORMATION

The train station is one of the most modern and impressive you're ever likely to find, with every facility under the sun. But the down side is that washing and toilet facilities are grim, as are the restaurant and café. It is open 4am–1am, but do be prepared to wait if requiring train information. The BalkanTourist money exchange office is open 8am–9pm. Allow plenty of time for your train as the station has a confusing numbering system for platforms divided into *zapad* (west) and *istok* (east) sections. It has also become apparent that the station attracts vagrants and criminals, so keep hold of your luggage at all times and do not think about sleeping there.

### TOURIST INFORMATION

The BalkanTourist Office at the station (open 8am–10.30pm) is just one of many dotted all over the city, though a very poor example. The main office is on bul Stamboliyski 27 (open 8am–7pm daily); they can organize private rooms, guided tours at good rates, and will provide general information. The branch at Boulevard Vitosha 1 (Tel. 43331) houses the **American Express** office (open Mon.–Fri.: 8am–8pm, Sat.: 8.30am–1.30pm).

   For train information telephone 311111.

## ADDRESSES

**CENTRAL POST OFFICE** Gurko Ulitsa 2, open daily 7am–10.30pm. Also *poste restante* here.

**ORBITA – STUDENT TRAVEL OFFICE** Hristo Botev 48 (Tel. 801506). Will grudgingly find you a room in a student hostel. From pl. Sveta Nedelya walk down Stambolijski and take fifth left. Open daily 9am–12 noon and 1pm–5.30pm, but times unreliable.

**RILA** International Railway Bureau, Gurko Ulitsa 5 (Tel. 870777). All tickets for international journeys, except those wanted for same day's travel, can be bought here. Open Mon.–Fri.: daily 8am–7pm, Sat.: 9am–2pm. Make sure you have your exchange forms with you.

**UK EMBASSY** Vasil Levski Boulevard 38 (Tel. 9801220).

**US EMBASSY** Ulica Suborna 1a (Tel. 980 5241). Americans should register with Consular section of the embassy upon arrival in Bulgaria. Go to Kapitan Andreev 1.

**AUSTRALIA, CANADA, IRELAND, NEW ZEALAND** These countries have no diplomatic presence in Bulgaria. Informally we are told that the UK embassy may help out. Alternatively, try your own embassy in Athens.

**24-HOUR CHEMIST** Alabin Ulitsa 29 (Tel. 879029). Dial 178 for current information.

## GETTING ABOUT

The city buses and trams are reasonably priced and if you plan to use them a lot, one- or five-day cards are available. Tickets can be bought in advance from the special kiosks and grocery stalls, at a flat fare of 10 leva. Don't forget to stamp the tickets in the machines on board. A metro system is under construction; expect changes to bus/tram routes as more sections are opened. If you want a taxi, get your hotel to call the cheaper state-operated firm. The main area worth seeing, however, is easily walked around.

## SEEING

Sofia's two main churches are on Nevski Square: the 20th-century neo-Byzantine **Alexander Nevsky**; and the 6th-century, early Byzantine **St Sophia**. The former, topped with its golden domes, is dedicated to the Russians who fell liberating Bulgaria from the Ottoman Empire. The crypt is wonderful, stuffed full of beautiful icons from all over the country (closed Tues.).

The **National Archaeological Museum**, on Boulevard Stambolijski (closed Mon.), with displays of Roman, Greek, Thracian and Turkish finds, is housed in the former Buyuk mosque. In the former Palace of Justice, at Boulevard Vitosha 2, is the **National History Museum**, which contains national treasures, including Thracian gold and ecclesiastical art plus much more. It's probably the best one to visit, open 10.30am–6pm, Fri. 2pm–6.30pm, closed Mondays.

On September 9th Square is the former royal palace, built during the Ottoman empire. This now houses the **National Ethnological Museum**. The **National Gallery of Painting and Sculpture**, also here, may be relocated to Alexander Nevski Square, open 10am–6pm, closed Mondays.

On Georgi Dimitrov Boulevard, there's the 16th-century **Banya Bashi Mosque**, behind which is the run-down mineral baths building. Both of these have been recently undergoing renovation; the mosque is now reopened, the baths sometime in the future.

**FREE SOFIA:**

- There's an **open-air market** near the station on Georgi Kirkov Ulica, while on Georgi Dimitrov Boulevard is the **Hali** market hall, built in the National Revival style (though supposed 'restoration' has spoilt the inside, and it may still be closed for 're-restoration').

- If you've bought some lunch and want a mellow place to eat it, head for the **City Gardens** down by Dimitrov Mausoleum. Otherwise the **Yuzhen Park** is to the south of the city where the modern **Thirteen Hundred Years Monument** can be found. For a bit of life and soul check out the **street musicians** and **performers** on Boulevard Vitosha.

- The **Boyana Church** is also worth seeing, at the foot of Mount Vitosha, with its restored medieval frescoes. The courtyard of the Sheraton Hotel is home to the 4th-century **St George Rotunda**, Sofia's oldest standing building. Built during the late Roman period, it has been used as both church and mosque. The St George church may be closed for restoration; it's been going on for some time. Situated below street level is the church of **Saint Petka Samardzhiyska**, built in the 14th century in a rather plain style so as not to upset the Ottoman conquerors.

## SLEEPING

For private accommodation use either ORBITA or BalkanTourist on Stambolijski 27 and expect to pay 20000–40000 leva for a double through BalkanTourist, less through ORBITA. Be aware that your host will probably not speak English and don't be alarmed if BalkanTourist give you the keys of the house and there is no one there. If these offices are shut, stay in the station and act 'lost'. You'll soon find locals offering you a place in their house for about 15000 leva per person. Some people have halved the price by *discreetly* paying in hard currency (sterling, dollars, marks, francs). If the trend in Bulgaria follows that in other eastern European countries, expect the cost of accommodation to soar.

**ORBITA Student Hostel**, Boulevard James Bauchar 76 (Tel. 63939) is OK and not too far out from the centre, tram 9.

Worth a try are **Hotel Bulgaria** at Boulevard Russki 4, near the Dimitrov Mausoleum (Tel. 870 191) or **Hotel Slaviya** at Ulica Sofijski Geroi 2 (Tel. 443441), tram 13 from station, about three stops down General Totleben. Be warned – prices are rising rapidly and former bargain hotels suddenly become 4-star ones. These hotels now cost upwards of £25 for a double.

If things call for desperate measures, head down to the **university**, set in a park off Boulevard Lenin (trams 1, 2, 7, 9, 14 and 18, then change to 4 or 10), and ask around for a student to let you share. There are several hostels in the Vitosha National Park. Book via the PIRIN agency at Boulevard Stambolijski 30, who will give you directions.

**Camping Vrana** (Tel. 781213) is on Boulevard Lenin, where you can pitch a tent or rent a bungalow. Bus 313, 213 or 305 from station to Orlow Most and then bus 5. Another site is **Cherniya Kos** (Tel. 571129), at the base of the mountains, which also has bungalows. Take tram 5 from the city to the end of the route, then bus 58 or 59. Both sites open May–Oct.

## EATING AND NIGHTLIFE

Good cheap food is easy to find in Sofia, though prices are rising. Bulgarian specialities can be had at **Koprivshtitsa**, Boulevard Vitosha 3; for Russian food, try **Krim**, Slavyanska 17; and for Indian, **Ramayana** on Hristo Belchev 32. In Sofia's centre there are new 'European' restaurants too, as well as **Forum** and **Havana** which claim to be Cuban. You'll have no problem finding Bulgarian-style fast-food places if you make for Vitosha - Eddy's Tex Mex Diner is the 'in' place. There are also plenty of self-service places if you're really cutting corners.

For the latest on shows and concerts BalkanTourist can provide details, though these tend to be more classical than popular. The National Folk Ensemble put on some good things too.

## EXCURSIONS

If your lungs are feeling the effects of a long smoke-filled train journey to Sofia, then a good hike up to the **Vitosha Mountains National Park** will sort them out. It's a winter ski resort area, eight km from Sofia, and you can get there by taking tram 5 to its last stop, then it's a short uphill walk to the cable car. Alternatively, ask at BalkanTourist for details of the several bus routes up to Vitosha. If you're feeling energetic **Zlatniy Mostove**, the glacial moraine, should provide the necessary challenge.

Another possible excursion from Sofia is to the **Rila Monastery**, 120 km to the south, with its hundreds of medieval icons. BalkanTourist can arrange day trips but they will be costly; alternatively, with some difficulty it is possible to get yourself there, by catching the occasional bus from the Ouchna Koucha terminus, or by taking the train to Kocherinovo station, then bus. If dressed respectfully and carrying your passport, you may spend the night here. **Camping Bor** is within walking distance of Rila. Ask at BalkanTourist or the bus station for the services, and book accommodation in advance.

## Plovdiv city phone code: 032

Plovdiv, the 'cultural capital' of Bulgaria is 2½ hours from Sofia by train and the country's second largest city. Once through the industrialized suburbs, the old town has a great deal worth seeing. From the station bus 1 or 7 will take you to the central square.

For information go to Puldin Tour at Boulevard Balgariya 106 (Tel. 553848) take trolley-bus 102 or 2 from the railway station, to just over the river. Although you can get a map here, they're not very helpful with accommodation, apart from private rooms. Try **Hotel Feniks**, Kapitan Raicho 79 (Tel. 224729) at around 55000 leva per person in a double. Or **Hotel Bulgaria**, Patriarch Evtimii 13 (Tel. 226064). **Camping Trakiya** (Tel. 551360) is the nearest site, four km west, bus 4 or 23.

Food-wise, if you're really cutting costs, there's a **self-service canteen** opposite the railway station and another on Maksim Gorki. Otherwise use the cafés around 19 Noemvri Square or the restaurants in the old town or in the cheaper hotels.

Plovdiv's Roman name of Trimontium refers to the three hills on which the main attractions of the old town are located. The labyrinth of cobbled streets lead you along the path of houses from the National Revival Period and remains of the old fortress wall. There's a restored portion of a **Roman amphitheatre** too, which is now used for theatrical performances. Other **Roman remains** can be seen in the Tsentralen Square and in 19 Noemvri Square where the partial remains of a Roman stadium are on display. The square also hosts the 15th-century **Djoumaya Mosque**. In the old town is the **Ethnographical Museum** as well.

In Saedinenie Square, the **Archaeological Museum** has many ancient relics of Plovdiv. However, a lot of its excellent collection of Thracian gold has been replaced with mock-ups as the originals now lie in the National History Museum in Sofia.

To the south of Plovdiv is the working **Bachkovo Monastery**. Founded in 1083, with early 16th-century structures, the monastery is a straightforward trip on a Smolyan-bound bus from the Rodopi bus terminal.

## Veliąko Ţarnovo city phone code: 062

This stunning ancient city overlooking the Jantra river was Bulgaria's capital until the Ottoman invasion of 1396 and is well worth the trouble to get there. Take the train from Sofia towards Varna and change at Gorna-Orjahovitza. You will arrive at the station, on the southern outskirts, at the foot of the Sveta Gora hill. Take one of the many buses to the city centre.

BalkanTourist is at Vasil Levski 1 (Tel. 21836). Try Motel-camping **Sveta Gora** for tents and chalets, bus 14 from Balkantourist, or bus 15 from the station. In the old town **Hotel Yantra**, at Velohova Zavera Square 1 (Tel. 2 03 91), is a moderate priced hotel or alternatively try **Hotel Etar**, Ivailo 1 or **ORBITA**, Hirsto Botev 15.

**Varosha** and **Tsarevets** are the two main areas of interest. Walk around these to get the best from them, but prepare for tired legs – it is not exactly flat. From BalkanTourist head into Varosha, the former Ottoman town. The **National Revival Museum** is on the site of the Ottoman town hall, or *Konak*, with the **Revolutionary Museum** nearby, in a former Turkish prison. All museums are shut on Mondays.

The ruined fortress of **Tsarevets** – approached by a stone causeway – was once home to a royal palace and cathedral and is almost completely surrounded by the river. Some of the impressive ramparts can be viewed, as well as palace ruins, although archaeological digs are still uncovering more each year. Even if you fail to get excited by a load of old stones, the wonderful views make the uphill struggle well worth the effort.

## Black Sea Coast – Varna and Bourgas

**Varna** and **Bourgas** are the two main cities along the coast, each served by about six trains a day from Sofia. Be warned, due to the increasing popularity of the area, accommodation is extremely difficult to find during the summer, for both Eastern and Western travellers.

Of the two, Varna has more going for it, with an early Christian basilica, Roman ruins and a few reasonable museums. If you get bored with topping up your tan at the beach, visit the museum town, **Nessebur**. This is a UNESCO listed heritage centre, with ruins of over 40 medieval churches.

In Varna there is a former BalkanTourist Office, open all year, opposite the railway station, at Ulitsa Musala 3 (Tel. 225174), open 8.30am–12.30pm and 1pm–6pm. The hotel next to it is worth trying: the **Musala** (Tel. 223925).

The nearest campsite is **Camping Panorama**, which is at the eastern edge of the Golden Sands resort, about 25 km from town. It can be reached by bus 9 or 109 from Varna. There's also camping at **Galata**, bus 17 from Boulevard Botev.

Bourgas has a Primoretz Tourist Office at pl. Garov (Tel. 42727). Ask about accommodation. The cheapest hotel is probably **Primorets** at Liliana Dimitrova 1 (Tel. 44117).

## NOTES

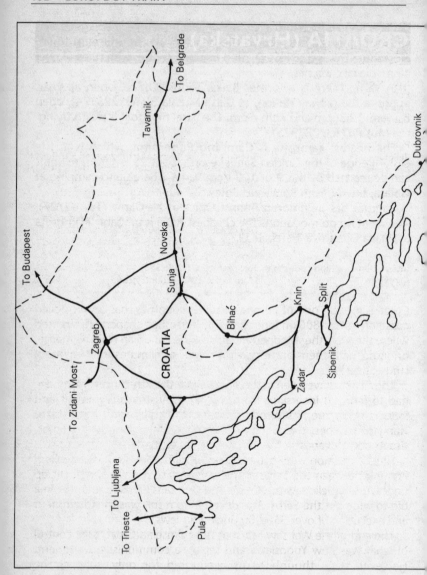

# CROATIA (Hrvatska)

| | |
|---|---|
| Entry requirements | Passport. South Africans require visa. |
| Population | 4.8 million |
| Capital | Zagreb (pop.: 1 million) |
| Currency | Kuna (HKN or Kn) |
| | £1 = approx. 11.7 Kuna |
| Political system | Parliamentary democracy |
| Religions | Roman Catholic, Serbian Orthodox and Muslim |
| Language | Croatian, some English and German in tourist areas, Italian in the north-west |
| Public holidays | New Year's Day , Orthodox Christmas, Easter, Labour Day (1 May), Statehood Day (30 May), National Uprising Day (22 June), Independence Day (5 Aug.), Assumption Day (15 Aug.), All Saints' Day (1 Nov.), Christmas Day and Boxing Day |
| International dialling codes | To Croatia: int'l code 385 |
| | From Croatia: 00 + country code |

Croatia, though one of Europe's smaller countries, has an unspoiled coastline some 1800km long. Roughly horseshoe shaped, it's situated where the Alps, the Mediterranean and the Panonian Plain all merge, bringing with them an appealing range of climates and beautiful landscapes.

The Croats have been settled here since the 7th century and have had to fend off incursions from the Turks, Austrians, Venetians and Italians. After the First World War and the collapse of the Austro-Hungarian empire, the country became part of the 'Kingdom of Serbs, Croats and Slovenes'.

Hitler's invasion during the Second World War brought appalling fighting between the Serbs and Croats. A fascist government set up under Ante Pavelic saw the Croats and Germans working together in a bid to wipe out the Serbs. The devastating result was the internment and execution of over 350,000 (including Jews).

The end of the War saw Marshal Tito (himself a Croat) take control of what was now Yugoslavia and set up a communist government. However, even though Serbs accounted for only 30% of the population, they controlled 80% of all positions of power, which included the police and military. This imbalance in favour of the Serbs saw them given preferential treatment and caused growing resentment among the non-Serbs.

Following Tito's death in 1980 and an increased nationalist drive, Croatia declared its independence in June 1991, along with its neighbour Slovenia. But, with the Serbian minority against the decision and in control of the Yugoslav National Army, tension inevitably erupted into full-scale war.

On 15 January, 1992, Croatia's re-declared independence was recognized by the EC and since 1995 the country has been at peace. Tourism has quickly re-emerged with the Croats making a determined effort to demonstrate their country is safe and welcoming for visitors.

## CROATIAN STATE RAILWAYS

### (HRVASTSKE ZELJEZNICE, HZ)

During the war, railways were hit hard but all lines have now been restored. Several trains a day run between all major towns. Expresses are usually modern, comfortable and no more expensive than the slower local trains.

New high-speed lines are still planned for the routes Rijeka–Budapest and Paris–Istanbul. The latter will end up cutting 600 km off the current route *and* travelling at 220 km/h down the coast of Croatia, through Albania and Greece. The project is being co-ordinated by all the railway boards of Europe.

HZ's main head office is at Mihanoviceva 12, 10000 Zagreb (Tel. 457 7111 or 9830).

**PASSES AVAILABLE** Croatia is in Inter-Rail Zone D along with the Czech and Slovak republics, Hungary and Poland. (For further details of the eight Inter-Rail zones, refer to the Inter-Rail section in part one of this guide).

A Euro Domino ticket is also available, see Part One -The Options.

## TRAIN INFORMATION

Zagreb and Pula should have someone who speaks English, otherwise try German or a bit of Italian in Istria. As usual, a note with the city, train, date and time is usually enough to get you where you want to go regardless of the language barrier.

**RESERVATIONS** Required only on international trains to countries other than Slovenia.

### NIGHT TRAVEL

Only international overnight trains have sleeping accommodation. Most trains drop their first-class cars at the border and carry only second-class couchettes. Normal compartments have pull-down seats and are rarely full during the off season.

### EATING ON TRAINS

There's a trolley service on internal trains while the international trains have the normal range of snack bars and dining cars.

**SCENIC ROUTES** The only scenic route still open is the line from Ogulin to Rijeka, which is worth the time if you are heading for Istria.
**BUSES** The bus lines are extensive and very good while only a little more expensive than the train.

## TOURIST INFORMATION

Croatia was the hub of the tourist industry in the old Yugoslavia, so there's a tourist office of some description in almost every city, usually with someone who speaks a little English. These are still being reorganized into separate offices for national, regional and local affairs, though any office should be able to give you the basics. Most have free maps and inexpensive guides to sights, though they may be less helpful with accommodation.

**ISIC BONUSES** Discounts are given for many sights, so always show your ISIC card before buying tickets.
**MONEY MATTERS** 1 Croatian Kuna (HKN)=100 lipas
Banking hours are generally Mon.–Sat.: 7am–7pm. During the summer some premises in coastal resorts and smaller towns may close for a siesta from 2pm to 5pm. You may also find that some banks will close earlier on a Saturday. People waiting in front of banks will ask if you want to change money. This is generally not a good idea since you won't actually get that much more and you may find yourself stuck with old Yugoslav dinar, which are worthless.
**POST OFFICES** Open Mon.–Sat.: 7am–7pm with the same pattern for siestas and Saturdays as banks and shops. Post offices in tourist areas open on Sundays and remain open until 10pm on weekdays. Stamps can be bought at newsagents', though without an airmail sticker post will go overland.
**SHOPS** Open Mon.–Sat.: 7am–8pm. In the summer a lunch break will not be taken in most towns. During the evening you may find that some premises will open until 9 or 10pm. On Saturday expect some shops to close around mid-afternoon.
**MUSEUMS** Many of these were closed during the war and the exhibits moved to underground storage for safety. Check with the Tourist Offices to see which ones have reopened.
**MEDIA** On the radio, news is broadcast in English five minutes past the hours of 8am, 10am, 2pm, 8pm and midnight.

## SLEEPING

The *Studenski Dom* and youth hostels are good value (open May–Sept.) at around £5 with a 50% price hike in July and August. Private rooms are another option and can be arranged by the Tourist Office for a fee, though they may require a minimum stay. Alternatively, look for *sobe* or

*Zimmer* signs in people's windows. There are also several campsites along the coast, but most cater to auto-caravans and are quite expensive. Camping illegally is strongly discouraged.

## EATING AND NIGHTLIFE

A glut of self-service cafeterias and takeaway shops mean you've got no shortage of cheap places to eat. All towns have some sort of farmers' market with home-grown produce, as well. Between these and local bakeries, delicious picnics can be made for next to nothing. You can also fill that gap with a local favourite: *bureks* (greasy pastry stuffed with cheese or meat). In Istria, Italian dishes are very good and half the price they are in Italy. Plus, anywhere on the Adriatic you'll find great seafood dishes.

Nightlife here has been somewhat subdued. However, the towns at night do offer the sound of cafés bellowing out loud music where younger crowds hang out.

## LANGUAGE

Regardless of what any linguist tells you, Serbo-Croat is not a language but a mix of Serbian and Croatian words. Serbian and Croatian are not only written using two different alphabets (Cyrillic and Latin) but also pronounced differently.

Before arriving I purchased a Serbo-Croat phrase-book. I was met by scowls and worse until someone told me that 80% of what was in the book was actually Serbian. Most people here speak a second language; English is common among the young and German among the old. Here are some basic Croatian phrases to help break the ice:

| | | | |
|---|---|---|---|
| Good morning | *Dobar dan* | one | *jedan* |
| Goodbye | *Do videnja* | two | *dva* |
| Yes | *Da* | three | *tri* |
| No | *Ne* | four | *četiri* |
| Please | *Molim* | five | *pet* |
| Thank you | *Hvala* | six | *šest* |
| Excuse me | *Izvinete* | seven | *sedam* |
| I would like... | *Zelim...* | eight | *osam* |
| Where is... | *Gde...* | nine | *devet* |
| I'm looking for... | *Trazim...* | ten | *deset* |

## Zagreb city phone code: 01

At more than 900 years old, Zagreb was once an important city in the Austro-Hungarian empire. Today, it's not only the country's political capital, but its economic and cultural centre too.

The train station, sited in the middle of the town, has a full range of facilities, including an information office, left luggage, restaurant, and bureau de change.

## TOURIST INFORMATION AND ADDRESSES

**TOURIST OFFICE** Trg Josipa Jelacica 11, open Mon.–Fri.: 8am–8pm; Sat.–Sun.: 9am–6pm (Tel. 481 4054), and Trg NS Zrinjskog 14 (Tel. 481 4051).
**POST OFFICE** Branimirova 4, open Mon.–Sat.: 7am–8pm; with *poste restante* open round the clock
**UK EMBASSY** 121 Vlaska (Tel. 455 5310)
**IRISH EMBASSY** Contact nearest embassy – Zürich, Switzerland
**US EMBASSY** Hebrangova 2 (Tel. 455 5500)
**CANADIAN EMBASSY** Mihanoviceva 1 (Tel. 457 7905)
**AUSTRALIAN EMBASSY** Mihanoviceva 1 (Tel. 457 7433)
**NEW ZEALAND EMBASSY** Contact nearest embassy – Rome, Italy.
**AMEX** c/o Atlas Travel, Zrinjevac 17, open Mon.–Fri.: 8am–7pm; Sat.: 8am–12 noon
**MEDICAL ASSISTANCE** 24-hour pharmacy at 3 Trg Josipa Jelacica
**EMERGENCY NUMBERS** Police 92, Fire Brigade 93, Ambulance 94
**STUDENT TRAVEL OFFICE** Croatian YHA, Savska 5 (Tel. 482 9284)

## SEEING

There are three main divisions within the city: the new town, the lower town and the upper town. The latter is where you should head for to take in **St Stephen's Cathedral**, **St Mark's Church** and the **Croatian National Museum**. To find out which museums are currently open and what's going on in town check with the Tourist Office on Trg Josipa Jelacica. Be sure to ask about the Zagreb Welcome Card too, which offers discounts and free travel on the city's transport network.

## SLEEPING

Zagreb has a distinct lack of budget accommodation. The only **hostel** is at Petrinjska 77, near the train station, and costs about £7–8 (Tel. 484 1261). Alternatively, in the summer, the Centar Turist Biro on Savska cesta 25 may be able to put you up in a student dorm. If you're young, try the **Centre for International Youth Co-operation** (Information and Accommodation section), Dezmanov prolaz 9, 10000 Zagreb (Tel. 278 239). Failing that, try the tourist office on Trg Josipa Jelacica for private rooms. The only campsites are outside of town and this is not a city where you really want to be far from the centre.

## EATING

Picking up the free booklet *Zagreb Gastro* from the tourist office is a good way to start your search for food, as it lists all the best places. Otherwise, head for the area near the cathedral for cheap eats. Here, you'll also find the local fish and farmers' markets. To the north of Trg Josipa Jelacica, on Tkalcicva, a younger crowd hangs out in the bunch of little cafés, though they are expensive by local standards. If you want something to take away, the small shopping arcade off Gajeva houses a variety of stalls and even has a **Hard Rock Café**. But when your sweet tooth kicks in try Croatia's premier chocolate maker, **Kras**.

# Dalmatian Coast

## SPLIT

The regional cultural and economic capital of Dalmatia, Split dates back to Roman times. The local Tourist Information is at Preporoda 12, inside the city walls, while Dalmatiatourist is on the waterfront at the west end of the palace.

**Diocletian's Palace** was built in the 3rd century before going on to become a medieval town – with its apartments becoming houses and its corridors the streets. The palace's basement provides entry to the city and will bring you out in the **Peristyle**, a large courtyard with old Roman columns. On your right-hand side is the impressive **Cathedral** and **Tower**, from which spectacular views can be had, while to the left is the **Temple of Jupiter**. Straight on is the modern glass and steel bank, the interior of which is amazing. Thanks to law, historical artefacts are prevented from being moved, so the bank has had to leave a column, part of a wall and a beautiful mosaic in the middle of its lobby.

While strolling around, look out for the **Archaeological Museum** and markets just outside the east gate. Make sure you don't miss the statue of **Gregorius Nin** either, which was cut in half and buried by the Serbians. Touching the toe is supposed to bring good luck and grant you your heart's desire.

Private rooms are the only real accommodation option in the city, though there are a few campsites in the vicinity. Check with the tourist office (Tel. 342 544) for details on both.

# Dubrovnik

Unfortunately, even its status as a UNESCO world heritage site didn't stop the Serbs from bombing Dubrovnik's beautiful old walled city heavily. Today, much of the city has been rebuilt, with little damage now visible.

A walk along the 2km of **City Walls** will provide a colourful spectacle of the red-roofed city. It will also map out how extensive the damage was, with original dark red tiles next to the brighter replacement ones. Both the **Franciscan** and **Dominican Monasteries** are worth visiting. Check with the Tourist Office on Placa to see if the hostels are open and, if not, have them fix you up with a private room. There is a **youth hostel** at Bana Jelacica 15–17 (Tel. 432 241).

## Istrian Peninsula

### PULA

The ancient town of Pula with its fine collection of Roman ruins, being in Istria, escaped all the fighting. The decidedly Italian flavour of the place stems from the time when it once belonged to Italy and, as such, many of the people speak Italian instead of their native Croatian.

It makes an ideal place to base yourself whilst exploring the region and the island of **Brijuni**. In the summer, concerts and open-air plays are held in its remarkably well-preserved **Roman amphitheatre**. Beneath it lies the **Archaeological Museum**, interesting even though everything is written in Croatian. Be sure to also check out the **Town Hall** and the **Temple of Augustus** which, after being destroyed during World War II, was rebuilt stone by stone.

If you want to stay there's a popular hostel beside a clean pebble beach on Zaljev Valsaline (Tel. 210 003), or try the Tourist Office at Istarska 13 for private rooms.

NOTES:

.................................................................................................

.................................................................................................

.................................................................................................

.................................................................................................

.................................................................................................

.................................................................................................

.................................................................................................

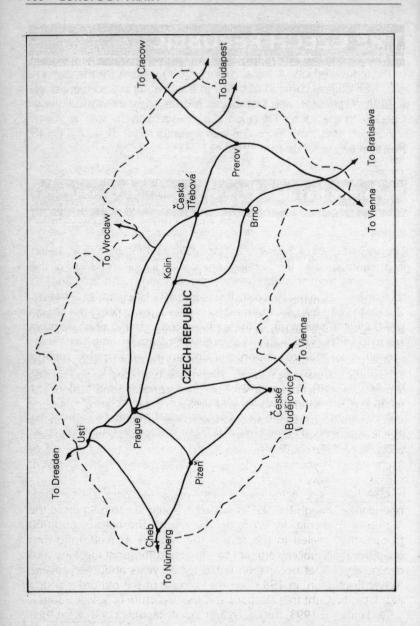

# THE CZECH REPUBLIC

| | |
|---|---|
| Entry requirements | Passport |
| Population | 12 million |
| Capital | Prague (pop.: 1.5 million) |
| Currency | Czech Koruna |
| | £1 = approx. 56.6Kčs |
| Political system | Republic |
| Religion | Catholic and Protestant |
| Language | Czech (some German and English understood) |
| Public holidays | New Year's Day, Day of the Three Wise Men (6 Jan.), Easter Monday, May Day, VE Day (8 May), Pentecostal Monday, Day of Cyril and Methodius (5 July), Death of Jan Hus (6 July), Foundation of Republic Day (28 Oct.), All Souls' Day (1 Nov.), Christmas and Boxing Days |
| International dialling codes | To the Czech Republic: int'l code 42 0 |
| | From the Czech Republic: 00 + country code |

The independent republic of Czechoslovakia first appeared on the scene in 1918 following the break-up of the Austro-Hungarian empire at the end of the First World War. It consisted of Slovakia along with the Czech lands of Bohemia, Moravia and Silesia.

Apart from the Czech and Slovak peoples, the country also included substantial German-speaking minorities which, preceding the Second World War, had attracted the eye of a certain Adolf Hitler. The infamous 1938 Munich Agreement between Britain, France, Germany and Italy saw him given the territories – Czechoslovakia didn't get a look-in on the decision – and, after Poland and Hungary had also taken parts, the whole country quickly fell under the control of the Nazis. Sadly, their five-year occupation also witnessed the murder of most of the country's Jews.

After the war, Czechoslovakia was more or less back to its original boundaries, though the USSR decided it would like to hold on to the region of Ruthenia. In 1968, however, with the help of 600,000 troops, they reeled in the rest of the country as well, following disapproval of Dubček's attempt to combine communist ideology with democracy. Soviet occupation lasted for 21 years until the peaceful 'Velvet Revolution' in 1989 saw the collapse of the old order and, a year later, brought free elections and the departure of Soviet troops.

On January 1 1993, the Czech and Slovak Republics both went their separate ways after Slovakia declared independence. And since then the Czech Republic has come off the better of the two, witnessing a rapid transformation towards a market economy and a considerable influx of foreign investment. Tourism has rocketed too, which is not surprising given that it is home to a wealth of beauty and history and has one of Europe's most stunning cities in its capital, Prague.

## CZECH STATE RAILWAYS (ČSD)

The service is a hot contender for the title of slowest in Europe, but if you're lucky you may find you have no complaints at all. Like Britain, the Czechs have their own 125 – the only trouble is it's 12.5 mph. However, the system is relatively dense and so most places can be reached by rail. Trains are frequent and tickets are sold according to the speed of the train. Don't cut corners here as it's generally recognized that even buses are faster than the expresses. Go for the fastest possible (*Expresní* or *Rychlík*). Unfortunately, these require seat reservations and supplements, and that may mean queues. Generally avoid travel on Friday and Sunday afternoons. Price rises (up to 60% in some cases) in the past few years mean that rail travel is not as cheap as it once was.

**PASSES AVAILABLE** The Inter-Rail pass has been broken down into zones, so that you pay only for travel within the area you want to visit. For £129 you can spend 22 days touring a zone. The Czech Republic is in Zone D, along with Slovakia, Poland, Hungary and Croatia. For details of the eight Inter-Rail zones, see the Inter-Rail section in Part One of this guide. A Euro-Domino ticket is also available – see Part One for details.

The Czech Explorer Pass offers seven consecutive days of unlimited travel on the Czech Republic rail services of CD. 2nd class at £15, 1st, £23. There's also a seven-day Explorer pass covering the Czech and Slovak Republics, priced at £23 for 2nd class, £35 for 1st.

The European Eastpass is also valid.

## TRAIN INFORMATION

Take it for granted that the staff will be friendly but won't speak English at information offices, so have the German vocabulary and/or a pen and paper with your request at the ready. If you still haven't any success, try: *Z kterého nástupiště odjíždí...vlak do...?* (From which platform does the train to...leave?). However, there are generally plenty of timetable boards available, though they can be a bit confusing. Express trains are marked in bold or red letters: Arrival – *Příjezd*, Departure – *Odjezd*. Many of the left-luggage lockers in the main towns are vandalized – it's not that you've got the combination wrong. The left-luggage offices normally cost 5–10Kčs, depending on weight.

**RESERVATIONS** Reserve well in advance to be sure of a seat, as trains are always busy. This is obligatory on some expresses marked with an Ⓡ or *míst*. Use the ARES office located at many stations. If you are going on to Hungary, it is essential to specify which of the routes you are taking and get your ticket from the appropriate counter. The crossing points are Štúrovo and Komárno in Slovakia.

**NIGHT TRAVEL** Sleepers and couchettes are operated by the state railway and run on all long journeys. Avoid sleepers, as they tend to be expensive. On international routes, numerous thefts from couchette compartments have been reported, so beware.

**EATING ON TRAINS** There's either a restaurant car or a buffet on selected fast trains.

**SCENIC TRIPS** Along the Labé river between Lovosice and Děčín; and along the Berounka River south-west of Prague.

## TOURIST INFORMATION

The official state-run agency was Čedok, who now operate as a private travel agency rather than an information office. They suggest tours and book accommodation etc. ISIC holders can get discounts of up to 50% on international tickets bought at their offices. The student travel offices (CKM) are staffed by students and issue ISIC and IYHF cards. They are normally very good.

**MONEY MATTERS** 1 Czech koruna (Kčs) = 100 haléřů (hal).
Banking hours are Mon.–Fri. 9am–5pm with a break at lunchtime. There is no longer any minimum currency exchange and the black market has died down. Avoid the remains of the black market; you will be ripped off, and are likely to be given worthless Polish Zloty, not Koruna. Private exchange offices are now flourishing, permitted under new laws. The best rate is from feeding notes directly into an electronic machine inside the Czech National Bank in Na Prïkopě.

The Czech Republic and Slovakia each have their own individual currencies and it is not possible to use Slovakian money in the Czech Republic (or vice versa).

**POST OFFICES** Open 8am–5pm, at noon on Saturdays.

**SHOPS** Open 9am–6pm on weekdays and close at noon on Saturdays.

**MUSEUMS** Open Tues.–Sun.: 10am–5pm. Generally closed Mondays.

**TIPPING** Round up the price of your meal.

## SLEEPING

Despite the revolution, the accommodation situation has not really improved. This is due to increased demand and lack of infrastructure; however, the situation will improve as new developments are financed. The prices below are likely to be subject to inflation. For advance booking use CKM (address in Prague section,), or the National Federation of Hotels and Restaurants, Senovazne náměstí 23 11201 Prague (Tel. 2414 2676) but allow for a long wait and a booking fee.

Hotels are graded from C (1-star) to deluxe A (5-star). The rare 2-star doubles should cost about 650Kčs per night, though bargains can still be found outside the main towns. Make sure you have agreed beforehand on the cost. In a country where the main language is Czech, the second Russian and the third German, your chances of winning an argument in English are somewhat minimal.

Staying at a private home also works out a lot cheaper than hotels. In Prague, Pragotur is the main official agency for this form of accommodation. New private agencies are coming forward to supplement Pragotur and Čedok. Don't be surprised if you are approached in the station or even on the street by a budding host; take the usual precautions. Advance accommodation can also be arranged from the UK through Czechbook, Japes Mill, Trebrownbridge, Cornwall PL14 3PX (Tel. 01503 240629).

Apart from Čedok offices, it's also possible to find accommodation through the student travel offices (CKM) during July and August. They usually charge around 250Kčs for dorm beds. In Prague avoid the AVE accommodation service in the station as they charge a hefty commission.

Dormitories (*internáty* or *koleje*) are converted into youth hostels (*střediska*), many of which have good two-bedded rooms from only 400–600Kčs per person on an IYHF card, more without.

There has been an increase in the numbers of independent hostels in the main centres. Finding out about these may be a problem, as Čedok and other agencies will direct you to their own hostels. Look in the stations for notices, or ask fellow travellers.

The Czechs are keen campers with over 400 sites in the country, at an average of around 200Kčs.

## EATING AND NIGHTLIFE

Food is generally pretty uninspiring: lots of pork and few salads and veggies. Dinner is eaten early. If you go after 8.30pm you're likely to have very little choice. Specialities include *zeleninová* (a vegetable and cream soup) and any dish made from pork (*vepřové*). For cheap meals, try any of the self-service stand-up restaurants (*automaty*).

A lot of the grade-1 and 2 restaurants have dancing, but apart from this things are very quiet by Western standards. Čedok should be able to help out on what open-air concerts, etc., there might be. The best way to find out what's happening is to ask any young locals. They will probably advise you to head towards a wine bar (*vinárna*) or beer hall (*pivnice*), where most young people meet. Try Budvar, Prazdroj or any other beer you're recommended, for not only is Czech beer among the best in Europe, it's also the cheapest.

# Brno city phone code: 05

Capital of Moravia and a royal city, founded in the 13th century, Brno has quite a lot to offer. It lies on the rail line between Prague and Bratislava.

The new Taxatour Brno information desk in the station, the Tourist Information Centre at Radnicka 8 (Tel. 42 211090), and CKM at Česká 11 (Tel. 213147), are the best bets for accommodation suggestions. The city fills up during the several exhibitions and trade fairs held every year. The summer **student hostels** are at Purkyňova 93 and Kohontova 55; apply to the CKM office. The nearest camping site is the **Obora**, 15 km from Brno (Tel. 791105), not easily reached by public transport. There is another site at Modrice though private accommodation may be your best bet.

The **Špilberk Castle**, founded 1277 and rebuilt in the 18th century, houses the **Municipal Museum** and **Art Gallery**. See the display of torture instruments in the museum. Dominating the city and castle is the **Cathedral of St Peter and St Paul**. Also worth seeing is the **Old Town Hall** and the **Capucin Monastery**, complete with mummified monks on display. Also see the colourful outdoor **cabbage market** (*Zelny Trh*).

# České Budějovice city phone code: 038

Lying in the beautiful region of south Bohemia this town, like Pilsen, is renowned for its beer – Budvar or Budweiser – and its salt trade. It can be reached from Prague by a couple of trains a day, taking around two hours. The more frequent buses from Prague may be a better bet.

Budějovice was founded in 1265 as a Royal Borough, at the strategic meeting point of the Vltava and Malše rivers. The town is centred on the large Zižkova náměstí surrounded by painted Baroque buildings. The **Town Hall**, dating from 1555, was modified in the early 18th century, to give its current frontage. The 72m high **Black Tower**, also on this square, dates from the 16th century, built as a watch tower and belfry for the **St Nicholas Church**. The tower is a good viewpoint, open Tues.–Sun.: 10am–6pm. Close to the Malše river bank are the remains of the original Gothic city defences. The Tourist Office is at Otakara II on the main square (Tel. 59480) and they can arrange accommodation. Try also CKM at Karla IV which has student hostel information. The **Stromovka** campsite (Tel. 38308) is on Na Dlouhé Lávce, open Apr.–Oct, bus 16. The large **Masné Krámy** beer hall is lively and is an ideal place for trying the local beer and to get some basic food. Canoe trips are one of the Czechs' favourite summer pastimes and some of the best trips are in this area. Ask at the Tourist Office.

## Pilsen (Plzeň) city phone code: 019

This is an ugly, uninspiring place and the regional centre of western Bohemia. But to beer fans, Pilsen is something of a pilgrimage as it's the birthplace of Pilsner Urquell beer. And, if that status is not enough, it can go one better again, as it's also the town of the Skoda car.

See the **Burgher's Brewery** (tour at 12.30 Mon.–Fri.), the **Brewing Museum** on Veleslavínova Street (Tues.–Sun.: 10am–6pm). The **Abbey of the Virgin Mary** and **St Bartholomew's Church** are the town's other saving graces.

The Tourist Information Office (MIS) is on Republic 41 (Tel. 703 2750). Čedok are on Sedláčkova 12, close to the town centre, on the corner of Sedláčkova and Prešovská, open Mon.–Fri.: 9am–6pm (shuts for lunch). There's a **youth hostel** at 4, Vejprnická 56 (Tel. 286443), take tram 3. You can also try the **university** for student rooms on Bolevecka. The nearest campsite is **Bílá Hora** (Tel. 534 905) which also lets chalets; take bus 20 or 39 from the centre.

## Prague (Praha) city phone code: 02

'Golden'... 'hundred-spired'... 'the crown of the world'... 'a stone dream'... just some of the beguiling adjectives applied to this splendid city. Once the 14th-century capital of the Holy Roman Empire, Prague today is almost a museum in itself. Its bridges, parks, hills and fascinating array of architectural styles provide an exhibition of sights matched only by a handful of cities in the rest of Europe (London, Paris, Rome). Now flooded by waves of Western tourists each year, Prague demolishes any preconceptions of an Eastern European city. Lying in the centre of Bohemia, it is without doubt one of Europe's gems.

### STATION FACILITIES

There are three main stations in Prague: Praha-Hlavní (Wilsonovo), Masarykovo and Holešovice. The first two are located close to the centre, with the latter to the north, across the Vltava river. Hlavní (Wilsonovo) is used by domestic services and international trains to Germany, Poland, Russia and Hungary; Masarykovo is mainly for domestic services. Holešovice has international trains for Germany, Russia and Hungary. Some trains from Germany call at Holešovice before getting to Hlavní (Wilsonovo). All these stations are served by the metro system, and have the usual facilities, including an influx of exchange offices. The left-luggage facilities at Holešovice are available 24 hours. Take care when setting locker combinations and with left-luggage receipts; theft at stations is common.

## TOURIST INFORMATION

There is a Tourist Information Office in the main concourse at Hlavní (Wilsonovo) station, which hands out basic information. The AVE office, also at the station, will also help out with accommodation, but charges a hefty commission.

Alternatively, from the main station (Praha-Hlavní) or Praha-Masarykovo, walk up Hybernská to the Prague Information Service at Na Příkopě 20 (Tel. 544444) and also Staroměstské 22 (Tel. 223411) and in the Lesser-Town Bridge Towers. They'll give you a free map, *What's On* and general information (open Mon.–Fri.: 9am–7pm, Sat.–Sun.: 9am–6pm).

There are also a considerable number of privately run 'tourist offices' set up around the city. AVE Agency will book accommodation ahead. You can also try the Pragotur room-finding service (see 'Addresses' below). In general be careful: some private agencies have 'i' signs which is a bit misleading as they're only trying to let their own rooms.

## ADDRESSES

**POST OFFICE:** Jindřišská 14, 24-hour service. Also *poste restante* here (closes 1pm on Saturdays). International phone calls from here.

**CKM (THE STUDENT AGENCY)** Na Příkopě 18 (Tel. 2419 7111)

**STUDENT TRAVEL OFFICE** GTS International, Ve Smeck-d, 27 (Tel. 9622 4300)

**FIRST AID** Palackého 5 (Tel. 2242 2520)

**POLYCLINIC FOR FOREIGNERS** Roentgenova (Tel. 5292 2146)

**UK EMBASSY** Thunovská Ulice 14, Malá Strana (Tel. 5732 0355)

**IRISH EMBASSY** No diplomatic representation in the Czech Republic; try the Irish embassy in Vienna or Berlin. In an emergency the UK or any other EU embassy may help.

**US EMBASSY** Tržiště 15, Malá Strana (Tel. 5732 0663)

**CANADIAN EMBASSY** Hradčany, Mickiewiczova 6 (Tel. 2431 1108)
**AUSTRALIAN EMBASSY** Use UK for emergencies, otherwise try own embassy in Vienna
**NEW ZEALAND EMBASSY** As Australia
**PRAGOTUR** Za Pořičskou branou 7 (Tel. 231 1116), Na Příkopě 20 (Tel. 264023), Staroměstskénám. 1 (Tel. 2448 2018)
**TELEPHONES** Can be found at post offices and in most metro and train stations. Phonecards (150, 240, 300, 360, 450 Kčs) are available from post offices and newsagents.

## GETTING ABOUT

The underground is efficient and cheap, and the bus and tram network covers every corner of the city. Buy tickets in advance from news-stands, hotels, machines and tobacconists, and stamp them on the buses. The basic single ticket costs 12Kčs and is valid for 60 mins. Non transfer tickets cost 8Kčs and are valid for four stops on one metro line or for 15 mins on a tram or bus. There are special 'tourist tickets' valid on the metro, trams, buses and the Petřín funicular: buy a one-day pass for 70Kčs, three-days for 180Kčs, one week for 250Kčs and 15 days for 280Kčs. The metro, and most trains, stop at midnight. Punch all single tickets in the yellow machines at the metro entrance, or on the tram or bus. Be warned: the on-the-spot fine for having the wrong ticket is high – 200Kčs – and ignorance of the rules will not be accepted. Forget taxis altogether.

## SEEING

Don't judge the city by its station. I nearly boarded the first train out again on my first visit, but it is in two halves – the platforms ancient, crowded and dirty, and the rest of it like an airport terminal. Had I done so, I'd have missed a city with as much to see and do as Paris. Prague started off as five separate towns, and each merits a visit: the New Town (Nové Město), the 19th-century commercial centre; the Old Town (Staré Město), medieval buildings and fascinating Jewish Quarter; the Lesser Town (Malá Strana), the Baroque area of palaces and churches; Hradčany, the area round Prague Castle; and Vyšehrad, the 9th-century fortress-town opposite the castle.

A good way to get your bearings is to take a boat trip on the Vltava. Leave from Vltava Quay in the New Town and rather than return by boat take metro line B from Palacky Bridge (Most Palackého). Also worth a visit is the **National Technical Museum**, open 9am to 5pm except Mondays. The main hall has a large selection of cars made by Czech manufacturers in the 1920s and 1930s. Beneath, there are guided tours along reconstructed mining galleries.

**NOVÉ MĚSTO** The main sights are **Wenceslas Square**, locally known as *Václavské náměstí*, the main boulevard, the **National Museum** and **Charles Square** (*Karlovo náměstí*), the largest square in Prague, with a park in its centre and the **New Town Hall** on its north side. Also **Dvořák's Museum**, Ke Karlovu 20, is in this vicinity.

**STARÉ MĚSTO** The Old Town dates back to 1120 – and you can feel it. The **Powder Tower**, used to store gunpowder in the 15th century, gives a good view from the top (if it is not covered in scaffolding).

The **Jewish Quarter** houses the oldest synagogue in Europe (1270) and the 15th-century **Jewish Cemetery** with its 12,000 tombstones piled on top of one another. The museum in **Klaus Synagogue** tells of the extermination of Jews in the Second World War. A single combination ticket permits entry into all the exhibits in the Jewish Quarter.

**MALÁ STRANA St Nicholas' Church** is the finest Baroque building in Prague and just north of it is the palace of the Habsburg general, Albrecht Wallenstein.

**HRADČANY Prague Castle** today is the seat of the Czech president, but it used to be the palace of the kings of Bohemia. Try to get on a tour round it; ask for details at the information stand in **St Vitus' Cathedral**. A good view over the city can be had from the adjacent terrace. Also in this 'royal city' is St Vitus' Cathedral itself, which is quite incredible, and is certainly the most detailed Gothic church in central Europe, with amazing stained-glass windows. The National Gallery is in the **Šternberk Palace** in the castle square and has an excellent collection of French Impressionists. The **Strahov Monastery**, west of the castle, houses the **Museum of Czech Literature**.

**VYŠEHRAD** The **Vyšehrad Fortress** has in its grounds the 11th-century Rotunda of St Martin, and in its cemetery Dvořák, Smetana and other Czech 'greats' are buried. If you have a couple of hours to spend, the **zoo** in the north of the city at Trojá (Tel. 841441) is well worth a visit too.

**RIVER VLTAVA** Sightseeing trips on the Vltava leave from the Jiraskuv Most quay and are well worth taking.

**ONE HOUR WALKS** A variety of different guided tours leave from the Astronomical Clock in the Old Town Square, every hour from 2pm–5pm (Tel. 060 701094). Show your copy of *Europe by Train* and you may get them for half-price, which is 120Kčs.

**FREE PRAGUE:** It won't cost a penny to soak up the atmosphere of **Old Town Square**, the centre of medieval Prague. Here you'll find the 1490 Astronomical Clock of the **Old Town Hall** which 'performs' every hour. The **T'yn Church** on the east side of the square is a twin-Gothic-spired church with a Baroque interior and dates from 1365. Connecting the Old Town with the right bank of the Vltava is the beautiful Baroque **Charles Bridge** which has superb views of the castle, the island of Kampa and the River Vltava. Nearby is **Bethlehem Chapel** where the Czech hero John Hus preached.

For a good view over the whole of Prague, take a walk along the observation paths to the orchard-covered slopes of **Petřín Hill**. **Golden Lane**, where the alchemists tried to turn their lead into gold, is another charming walk and don't forget to explore **Malá Strana** where the riches of 17th- and 18th-century merchants have been spent. The **Lesser Town Square** and **Neruda St** are testament to that.

- **National Museum**, Václavské nám. 68 – Free first Mon. of the month.
- **National Gallery of Bohemian Art**, inside Prague Castle – Free first Fri. of the month.
- Visit the gardens of the **Bertrama Mozart Museum**, Mozartova 169.
- **Wallenstein Gardens**, Letenská Street.

## SLEEPING

This is your main headache in Prague. As the number of tourists has increased drastically, the situation has got worse. Pragotur, AVE, CKM, or private agencies or a private arrangement are your best bets for finding a room. Prepare yourself for the inevitable long queues and insist on somewhere central and cheap. They often charge a hefty commission. Private accommodation is cheaper, so ask for this or, better still, the student hostels. Avoid any hostels being plugged at the station, as they tend to be a bit unsavoury. You will probably do best contacting the campsites yourself; and will be pleasantly surprised by the sites' quantity and quality. Get a list from Prague Information Service.

Try the following IYHF hostels: **CKM Junior Hotel**, at Zitna 12 (Tel. 292984) near to Hlávní Nádraží station; **Hotel Beta**, Roskotova 1225 (Tel. 61262158), bus 124, 205 from metro Budějovická line C (good reductions with ISIC); **Hostel Branik**, SOU Vrbova (Tel. 4021682), metro Smichovske nádraží line B; and **Hotel Standart**, Vodni Stavby (Tel. 875258), 10 mins from metro Nádraží. IYHF Hostels in Prague are open 24 hours, expect to pay between 200 and 600Kčs.

Other student hostels can work out slightly cheaper. **Domov Mladeze**, Dykova 20, tram 16 from Náměstí Miru metro or **ESTEC Kolej Strahov**, Vaničkova 5, bus 217 or 143 from metro Dejvická are both good options.

The **Purple House**, at Krásova 25, Žižkov, offers a collection of self-contained apartments, rooms and dorms five minutes' walk from the train station. Clean and highly recommended. For private rooms try

**Věra Hlaváčová**, Na Bálkaně 126/2116 (Tel. 66314166). Take tram 9 from Hlávní Nádraží for the 15-minute ride to Spojovací. Comfortable rooms with kitchen facilities and English-speaking hostess.

Campsites abound around Prague, including **Sokol Trojá** at Trojská 171 (Tel. 8385 0468) and **Džbán**, at Nad Lavkou 3 (Tel. 369 006). Refer to *Cheap Sleeps Europe 2000* for more accommodation options.

## EATING AND NIGHTLIFE

Beer halls (*pivnice*) and wine cellars (*vinárny*) are dotted all over the city. Take advantage of the Czech beer while you can. Popular spots are **U Prince**, Old Town Square, opposite the town hall, good but pricey in a wonderful setting, open daily; **U Fleku**, Křemencova 11, much akin to a Munich beer hall (Germans are supplied free of charge); also, **U Hrocha**, Thunovská 10, Malá Strana. The strongest beer, *Branik*, can be found at **U Supa**, Celetná 22. These are safe bets for cheap food and drink, as are the stand-up snack places. Don't expect a huge menu, but what's there is usually OK. There are plenty of *automaty* – self-service restaurants – in the Wenceslas Square area, which are good and cheap, try the **Staropraška Rychta** or the **Halaligrill**. If it's pizza you're after, head for **Pizzeria Kmotra**, at Vjirchářích 12, Nové Město. Or, for a cheap splurge, head for the **Akademii Restaurant** at Karlova 26. Netheads can get a fix at the **Internet Café**, Stepanska 18 (Tel. 2423 3024). Temporary e-mail facilities can be set up for you.

Cafés and smaller bars are the most likely places to meet Czech students. Try: **Hogo Fogo**, Staromeštska 4, **Lavka**, Novotneho lavka, Staré Město or the **UPM**, 17 Lisopadu, metro Staromeštska **U Malvaze**, Karlova 10, is a big student dive. At night, the places to be are the Old Town Square and Charles Bridge – both have illuminations and street entertainment. Best clubs are **Radhost FX**, Belehradska 120, metro I.P. Pavlova or **Bunkr**, Lodecka 2, Nové Město. For live music head to **Arkadia**, Na Příkopé 22, Nové Město, or **Agaharta Jazz Centrum** on Krakovska, Nové Město. Don't forget to try *Absinthe*, a dangerous green concoction only available in Prague. Its hallucinogenic properties (and vile aftertaste) allegedly have led to several gruesome murders. Try it at your peril.

The citizens of Prague love their ice-cream (*zmrzlina*). One of the best ice-cream places we have found outside Italy is in Prague, on Vodičkova in the shadow of the new town hall. You can join the queue on the pavement to buy one to enjoy in the nearby Charles Square (*Karlovo náměstí*) or queue up inside for a seat in this popular café.

The Prague Spring Festival, from May to June, is a big draw for music, opera and drama lovers, but note that the official programme is printed in September, so misses many last-minute productions. Always ask at the time. Prices vary enormously, with local artists offering the best value. The monthly *What's On* and other guides can be had from PIS, Na Příkopé 20. The Laterna Magiká, Národní 40, is a combination of films, ballet and drama which deserves a mention, but you usually need reservations of up to a month.

**EXCURSIONS** Half an hour away and an easy day trip is the amazing 14th-century castle of **Karlštein** – Bohemia's finest example. Take the train from Smíchovske station – on the metro. (It is being restored so check opening times before you go.) Guided tours last an hour; find out when the next one in your language is as soon as you arrive.

The famous spa of **Karlovy Vary** (Karlsbad) also makes an interesting trip. Trains take about three hours to get there. Čedok is at Tržiště 23.

Another castle of note is **Křivolklát**, medieval seat of Bohemia's kings, located above the Berounka river, a worthwhile sight in its own right. Take the train from Prague-Smíchov, change at Beroun, then on to Křivolklát. The site where St Wenceslas was murdered is in the church complex of Stara Boleslav, to the north of Prague. To get there take the half-hour bus journey from Florenc or Palmovka bus stations in Prague.

## Olomouc city phone code: 068

**Olomouc** is just one of many beautiful historic towns you may consider visiting in the Czech Republic. It became an important city as early as the 11th century, and today is the capital of North Moravia and a tourist's delight. It's on the direct line from Praha-Hlavní, with the journey taking around $3\frac{1}{2}$ hours. From the station, the centre is a 15-minute walk and on several tram routes. Tourist Information, ATIS, is at Horní náměstí (Tel. 551 3385), located in the city central square, providing the usual facilities. Opposite is Čedok, while CKM is at Denisova 4 (Tel. 522 2148). Try these for accommodation suggestions, or in July and August the **Studencentrum**, at Křížkovského 14, may help to find a room. Try **Hostel Envelopa**, at 17 Listopadu 54 (Tel. 522 3841) or the pension **U Domu** close to the cathedral at Domska 4 (Tel. 522 0501). There are no campsites in the town, but half an hour away by train, in Šternberk, there is a Grade A site. Make sure you get precise directions before heading off.

There are plenty of beer halls, wine cellars and restaurants. To meet local students try **Mikulovská vináarna** and **U Trojice** wine cellars, in the city centre.

The town is a protected urban reservation. The main sight is the superb 12th-century **St Wenceslas Cathedral**, with the **Przemysl Castle**, **St Ann's Chapel** and **Chapter Deanery** nearby. The Renaissance **Town Hall** is also worth a look, as are some of the buildings of the university, the second oldest in Czechoslovakia. A trip on bus 11 from the railway station will bring you to the Kopeček hill, with a good view of the town, and site of the 17th-century **Virgin Mary Church** and **Monastery**.

NOTES

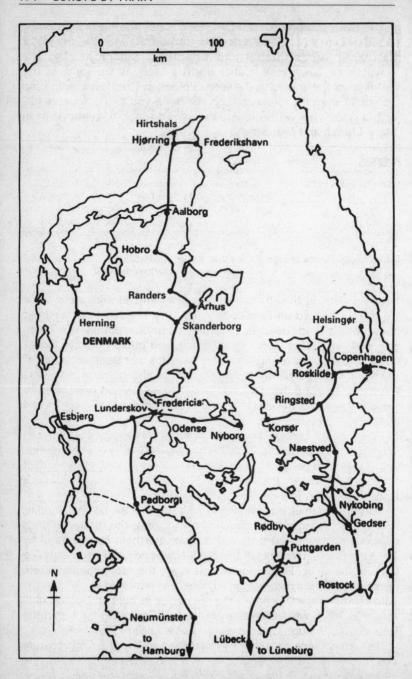

# DENMARK

| | |
|---|---|
| **Entry requirements** | Passport |
| **Population** | 5.2 million |
| **Capital** | Copenhagen (pop.: 1.5 million) |
| **Currency** | Krone |
| | £1 = approx. 11kr |
| **Political system** | Constitutional monarchy |
| **Religion** | Lutheran |
| **Language** | Danish (English widely spoken) |
| **Public holidays 1998** | New Year's Day, Maundy Thursday (20 Apr.), Easter, Great Prayer Day (19 May.), Ascension Day (1 June), Whitsunday (11 June), Whit Monday (12 June), Constitution Day (5 June), Christmas Eve, Christmas Day, Boxing Day, New Year's Eve. |
| **International dialling codes** | To Denmark: int'l code 45 |
| | From Denmark: 00 + country code |

Visitors exploring this smallest of Scandinavian countries are in for a treat. This relaxed and welcoming country has scores of unspoilt islands, white sandy beaches, castles, a countryside dotted with Viking sites and historic yet lively cities. Efficient and budget friendly tourist authorities make travelling here a pleasure. It's true Denmark is one of the world's most expensive countries, but it's also safe and clean, and there's no end of public facilities, free information and help given to smooth the way of travellers – young people are especially well looked after.

At the tip of continental Europe, Denmark is the bridge between Scandinavia proper and the European mainland. It's a land of the sea, with a mainland peninsula (Jutland) and 406 islands. More than 100 of these are inhabited, the largest being Funen and Zealand, where Copenhagen was founded in the 12th century.

Though Denmark is something of a bit player in the Europe of today, it held centre stage in the past. From its shores, the ruthless Vikings pillaged and plundered their way through northern Europe, until by 1033 the Danes ruled England, Ireland, Normandy and also controlled trade in the Baltic. During the Middle Ages, the economy prospered. Denmark became a medieval superpower, and remained so well into the 16th century. In fact, Denmark did not release its hold on Norway until as late as 1814, while the Faroe Islands and Greenland fall within the kingdom still, though Greenland won home rule in 1979.

The acceptance of Luther's Reformation in the late 16th century was followed by a flowering of the arts and sciences. Culturally, the 19th century was Denmark's 'Golden Age'. Today the nation enjoys one of the highest standards of living in Europe.

## GETTING THERE

From Britain, take either the train from London to Copenhagen (26 hours) or one of the Scandinavian Seaways DFDS ferries; look for off-season reductions. There are ferries from Harwich to Esbjerg (20 hours) and Newcastle to Esbjerg (19 hours, summertime only). There's a 50% reduction with an Inter-Rail on Scandinavian Seaways DFDS ships.

## DANISH STATE RAILWAYS

### (DANSKE STATSBANER, DSB)

You'll spend as much time on water as you do on land. As an island nation, Denmark is well served by ferries, with entire trains clamping down on to specially adapted boats connecting the islands with one another. With hourly intercity trains, they've had plenty of practice and have the operation down to a fine art. Passengers are free to get off the train and wander about. There's a great feeling of camaraderie once you're on board – particularly on the Kalundborg–Århus crossing (three hours).

A fixed rail link across the Great Belt strait now operates, linking the main islands and the Jutland peninsula. This new system has ended the Nyborg–Korsør train ferries, and cut an hour from journey times between Copenhagen and the major cities in Fyn and Jylland. In July 2000 the massive 16km road-rail-bridge linking Copenhagen with Malmö in Sweden is due to open. This will complete an unbroken rail link from the Mediterranean to the Arctic.

The rail network is divided into four categories:

1. *Lyntog* (Lightning trains) *L*. Almost as luxurious as EuroCity and used on long hauls, such as Copenhagen to Frederikshavn. DSB IC3 InterCity trains serve all major cities.
2. *InterCity IC*. Equally fast, serving the shorter distances between large towns.
3. *Regionaltoget*. Slower regional trains, connecting the smaller towns with the main network.
4. *S-tog*. Copenhagen's underground, connecting the city with the suburbs.

**PASSES AVAILABLE** The ScanRail pass is the best ticket to go for. There are two types. The best value is the one allowing one month's unlimited travel throughout Denmark, Finland, Norway and Sweden. The other allows a certain number of days' travel within a fixed period. It too is valid on Danish, Norwegian, Swedish and Finnish state railways, and both types of pass allow free or up to half-price travel on inter-Scandinavian ferry and bus routes, with discounts on some inter-island sailings. See Part One of this guide for details.

The NorthStar ticket gives reductions on 2nd-class return travel from Copenhagen to Oslo, Stockholm, Sweden, Gothenburg, Ostersund and Kiruna. Buy the ticket two days prior to departure.

Children under four travel free and those between 4 and 11 go half price. Children with an ordinary children's ticket can take an adult on 2nd class for the price of a child.

Both Eurail and Inter-Rail passes are valid. Denmark is in Inter-Rail Zone C, along with Germany, Austria and Switzerland. A Euro-Domino ticket is also available. For details of both Euro-Domino and the eight Inter-Rail zones, see the Inter-Rail section in Part One.

**INTER-RAIL BONUSES** See Appendix I.

**EURAIL BONUSES** The following services are free:

Ferry crossings Århus to Kalundborg, Knudshoved to Halskov, Nyborg to Korsør, Fynshavn to Bøjden.

Ferry crossings Rødby Faerge to Puttgarden (Germany).

Ferry crossings operated by the Danish and Swedish State Railways between Helsingør and Helsingborg (Sweden).

**EURAIL AID OFFICE** Central Station, Copenhagen (Tel. (33) 150 400 21742)

**REDUCED FARES**

25% reduction on the hydrofoil of the Flyvebadene Company between Copenhagen and Malmö.

50% reduction on the ferries of Stena Line between Frederikshavn and Göteborg (Sweden) / Oslo (Norway).

30% reduction between Hirtshals and Kristiansand/Frederikshavn/Moss (Norway) on the normal fares of the steamship company Color Line.

50% reduction on the normal fares of the Steamship Company DFDS between Esbjerg–Harwich, Copenhagen–Oslo.

50% reduction on the Hjørring–Hirtshals private railroad.

## TRAIN INFORMATION

In Copenhagen's central station, there's an **Inter-Rail Centre** for holders of Inter-Rail, Scanrail, BIJ and Eurail passes (Tel. 3314 0400 ext. 13467). It's very useful for information (throughout the day, there are news bulletins in English, German and French, and tape-recorded tourist information in the same languages, and you can use the lounge, showers, telephone, cooking stove and message board.) Open May–Sept, daily 6.30am–10.30am and 4pm–10pm; also July–Aug., afternoons only.

**Timetables** are posted all over the stations and all staff speak fluent English. If you're spending some time in Denmark, ask for the *Køreplan*, a timetable for all the ferries, trains and buses.

**RESERVATIONS** Are compulsory on any IC or Lyntog train crossing the Great Belt between Sjaelland and Fyn (that is, from Korsør to Nyborg), and most international trains. The cost is 30kr. You can pay on the train, book at the station, or tel. 3315 1515.

**NIGHT TRAVEL** Couchettes/sleepers cost *relatively* less in Scandinavia than elsewhere in northern Europe. A couchette costs around 70kr and a bed in a two-berth sleeper about 175kr. Within Denmark, they operate between Copenhagen and Esbjerg as well as to Struer and Frederikshavn.

**EATING ON TRAINS** There are no dining cars, even if you could afford them, though most trains have kiosks and trolleys selling snacks and drinks. The coffee is reasonably priced, but the sandwiches are as expensive here as they are everywhere else. Think ahead and carry picnic food; otherwise, try to survive till you get aboard the ferries, as they have self-service cafeterias.

On international crossings, brave the locals' feeding frenzy and check out the duty-free shops. Scandinavia's tax systems push up prices on land, so stock up now on cheese, wine, cigarettes and chocolates.

**SCENIC TIPS** There's good coastal scenery between Frederikshavn and Copenhagen. Choose the route via Odense and Fredericia. If you're heading for Stockholm from Copenhagen, the best route is by train to Helsingør (one hour) then via ferry to Helsingborg (free on Inter-Rail).

**BIKES** Do as the Danes do, and get on your bike. Denmark is a cyclist's dream, with few hills, a network of bike paths in the countryside and special lanes in towns and cities.

In Copenhagen, the bikes are free. The city has provided 2,500 free cycles for visitors to use while they sight-see. Just find one of the 125 City Bike parks dotted around the city centre, deposit a 20kr coin, and get pedalling. Careful, though – the City Bike Patrol (apart from hunting down missing bikes and doing maintenance) keeps an eye on cyclists, and stops riders from venturing outside the city limits. Return the cycle to any rack to collect your deposit.

Outside Copenhagen, you can hire a bike in the summer at most of the larger stations for 35–50kr per day, plus a deposit of 100–200kr. Ask at stations for leaflet *Take a Train – Rent a Bike*. Bikes are allowed on most regional, interregional and S trains but not on InterCity or EuroCity trains. A special ticket is required: 110kr.

## TOURIST INFORMATION

The Tourist Offices in Denmark are the best in Europe, particularly for the under-26s. They are friendly and efficient – and if every tourist board were like them, we'd be out of a job!

For news in English, and information about exhibitions and other events in Copenhagen, tune in to Radio Denmark, programme 3 on 93.8 MHz at 8.30am, Mon.–Fri.

**ISIC BONUSES** 50% off some films, theatres and museums. For further information, contact DIS Skindergade 28, Copenhagen.
**MONEY MATTERS** 1 krone (kr) = 100 øre.
Banking hours are Mon., Tues., Wed., Fri.: 9.30am–4pm, Thurs.: 9.30am–6pm. Bank commission varies from 10 to 18kr. There are late-night facilities at Central station and Tivoli park in Copenhagen. Some Tourist Offices may exchange money out of banking hours. Those with credit cards can use cash dispensers labelled *Kontanten*, coloured red and valid for Mastercard and Visa.
**POST OFFICE** Open Mon.–Thurs.: 9am–5pm, Fri.: 9am–7 or 8pm, Sat.: 9am–12 noon, with variations in smaller towns.
**TELEPHONES** Either fully automatic or through the operator if the number starts with letters. Insert 1kr for local calls or 2kr for long distance. You do not get change from 25 øre coins and older machines give no change at all.
**SHOPS** Hours vary from town to town. In general: Mon.–Thurs.: 9 or 10am–6 or 7pm, Fri. to 7 or 8pm, Sat. to 1pm or 2pm (in Copenhagen and other large towns, most city centre shops stay open till 5pm on Saturdays).
**TIPPING** Tips are normally included in most bills but it is customary to add a few more loose coins. Give a krone or two to an attendant in public lavatories.

## SLEEPING
**Youth hostels** require you to register before 9pm and have IYHF membership. The maximum charge is 90kr per night in a dorm or between 160 and 350kr in a private room. In most hostels, breakfast can be had for around 40kr, dinner for 65kr. Outside Copenhagen an 11pm curfew is the norm. Hostelling International Denmark have introduced a national star rating system: 5-star hostels offer the best facilities. Most hostels have four-berth rooms rather than dormitories. Town mission hostels are excellent, clean and cheap. A free booklet listing all of Denmark's hostels and many campsites is available from the Tourist Office.

There are more than 500 **campsites** (Camping Carnet – 30kr – required). An overnight stay will cost between 45 and 60kr.

If you can't get into a hostel and don't want to be bothered with camping, stay in a **private home** (anything but a hotel, as these really are very expensive). Tourist information will put you in touch with a Danish family who'll put you up. This costs 150–250kr and can be organized before you set foot in the country. Any Tourist Office in Denmark can do it, or try their UK agent, the Host and Guest Service, 103 Dawes Road, London, SW6 7DU (Tel. 020 7385 9922).

**'Sleep-Ins'** are also worth investigating. They are temporary hostels providing cheap and central places to sleep in the summer. Check with the Tourist Offices for the current locations.

For further options, refer to *Cheap Sleeps Europe 2000*.

## EATING AND NIGHTLIFE

Food in Denmark is expensive, but don't despair: in a sandwich culture the supermarkets are well-stocked, and you can create your own *smørrebrød* (open sandwiches) happy in the knowledge you're experimenting with Danish cuisine's most famous export.

*Pølser* (hot dog) stands are on most street corners, and to wash them down, there are more than 50 varieties of Danish beers, the best-known being Carlsberg and Tuborg.

No visit to Denmark would be complete without Danish pastries, though they're actually known as *wiener brød* locally. Even if you're not a fan, try the authentic article: in Denmark they're not so sickly as and much more delicious than the anglicized version.

Look out for cafés with signs *Madkurve kan Medbringes* (literally, 'Bring your own food') – you can take your own picnic for the price of a coffee.

All-you-can-eat buffet tables are expensive, but good value.

ISIC gives you 50% off films, theatres, etc., and there's no shortage of pubs or coffee houses in Denmark. In Copenhagen, the tourist service **Use It** has leaflets which give the lowdown on what's on, and they also give out entertainments listings.

# Copenhagen (København)

National capital, major seaport, commercial hub, seat of royalty. This city's impressive credentials belie its easy-going small town feel. Situated on the north-eastern shore of Zealand, it's a well-run, exciting place with an almost Parisian *joie de vivre*. As the largest city in Scandinavia, it's also the cheapest. And the good news doesn't stop there...

Not only are the Danes a socially minded lot, but they are keen Eurorailers themselves. Which for visitors means sympathetic backup and support unmatched in the rest of Europe.

NOTE: Copenhagen phone numbers beginning with '31' will be changing in early 2000. Check new codes by dialling 80 808080.

The YMCA's Inter-point offers advice on what to see and where to go and helps with problems, at Valdemarsgade 15 (Tel. 3131 1574). Open 8am–10.00am and 2.30pm–5.30pm, late June–early August. You can also stay there for 70kr (30kr for breakfast).

The information centre called **Use It**, is open all year, and is sponsored by the city youth organization. It offers countless free or non-profit-making services: free maps, tourist information and advice, a series of leaflets on cheap restaurants and hostels, and free luggage storage. The Use It centre is at Rådhusstraede 13 (Tel. 33 730620), a 10-minute walk from the central station along Tietgensgade, down one side of the Tivoli Gardens, on into Stormgade, then left into Rådhusstraede. There is a restaurant, jazz club, rock/folk club and cinema where you can meet fellow travellers and young Danes. Use It will also find you a bed you can afford, or help you out if you've an emergency or crisis. They're open in summer 9am–7pm and off-season 11am–4pm.

Bear in mind the YMCA/YWCA set-up is a Christian organization and can be quite strict – even in laid-back Copenhagen – so if you're after advice on the hottest places for evening entertainment, etc., go to Use It.

For an off-beat tour of Copenhagen, contact **GuideNet**, Norrebrogade 52 (Tel. 3536 1516). Their young guides will show you 'the' places to eat, drink and be merry, all for around 30kr.

Copenhagen Adventure Tours will take you on an alternative sightseeing trip around the city's canals by 'unsinkable' inter-com equipped kayak (Tel. 40 504006).

These sorts of facilities are unique in Europe: make the most of them (you won't find anything remotely like them further south).

## STATION FACILITIES

The Hovedbanegård (central station) is the terminus for all main-line trains. **Information** is available 8am–10pm (Tel. 3314 1701) and **reservations** 8am–9pm. The station is closed 1.30am–4.30am.

You should be able to get **something to eat** until late evening from the many buffets, snack bars or restaurants, and there's a **supermarket** near the station which is open 8am–midnight. There is also a **foreign exchange**, a **post office** and **left-luggage** locker facilities.

Hovedbanegård is a particularly fine station with many facilities, including the **Inter-Rail Centre** (see Train Information above).

The **platforms** are below ground level. The 'S' trains (suburban electrics) also use the station. Look out for drunks.

It takes 40 minutes from Copenhagen to Malmö, five hours to Gothenburg, 5–7 hours to Hamburg, and six hours to Stockholm.

The nearest **room-finding service** is at Bernstoffsgade 1, but since their commission is 15kr, it is best to go to Use It, who offer the same service for free.

## TOURIST INFORMATION

*Danmarks Turistråd* – Tourist Information – (Tel. 3311 1325) is located at Bernstoffsgade 1, opposite the railway station. Open May 1– mid Sep.: Mon-Sat 9am–8pm, Sun 10am-8pm; Mid Sep.-Apr. 30: Mon.- –Fri.: 9am–4.30pm, Sat.: 9am–1.30pm. They are efficient, friendly and helpful and there are leaflets on everything you could possibly need to know. Be specific and ask for printed information on everything you might need – for instance: camping, walking, other parts of Denmark, etc. Don't forget to pick up their free map and a copy of *Copenhagen This Week* and *Playtime,* Use It's free guide for low budget visitors.

## ADDRESSES

**USE IT** Rådhusstraede 13 (Tel. 33730620 and 33156518). Youth and student organization great for help of all kinds. They'll even hold your mail and find you a bed for the night. Not always over-friendly, but useful!

**POST OFFICE** Tietgensgade 35-39 (behind Central station). *Poste restante* also here. Open 11am–6pm, 10am–1pm on Saturday.

**AMEX** Amagertorv 18 (Tel. 3312 2301)

**UK EMBASSY** Kastelsvej 36-40 (Tel. 3544 5200)

**IRISH EMBASSY** Ostbanegade 21 (Tel. 3142 3233)

**US EMBASSY** Dag Hammarskjölds Allé 24 (Tel. 3555 3144)

**CANADIAN EMBASSY** Kristen Bernikowsgade 1 (Tel. 3312 2299)

**AUSTRALIAN CONSULATE** Strandboulebarvden 122 (Tel. 3929 2077)

**NEW ZEALAND EMBASSY** The NZ ambassador in Brussels (see under Belgium) is accredited to Denmark, or see Australia. UK may also help.

**24-HOUR CHEMIST** Steno Apotek, Vesterbrogade 6C (Tel. 3314 8266)

**EURAIL AID OFFICE** Central Station (Tel. (33) 150 400 21742)

## GETTING ABOUT

The **S-tog** is free with any rail pass. If you haven't got one, the **buses** are a better bet at 11kr a ride. All tickets are interchangeable between buses and trains providing they are used within the hour.

The best bet all round is to invest in a **Copenhagen Card**, which gives unlimited travel by bus and rail in the whole of the metropolitan area and North Zealand. It also gives free admission to more than 60 sights, attractions and museums, and a range of other discounts. If you don't already have a rail pass that gives free or reduced ferry crossings to Sweden, the Copenhagen Card allows a 25–50% reduction. It is valid for one, two or three days and costs 155kr, 255kr and 320kr respectively. Children 5 - 12 pay half price.

For 70kr you can buy a **24hr ticket** valid for unlimited train and bus travel within greater Copenhagen.

The **Copenhagen Zone travel card** is handy as most of Copenhagen's museums and sights lie within the central traffic area. This is part of the broader joint zone fare system that embraces all HT/Copenhagen Transport buses, DSB/State Railways and S-trains in metropolitan Copenhagen and North Zealand, as well as some privately operated railway routes in the area. It is therefore possible to interchange between trains and bus routes on the same ticket. Get a timetable and brochure (in English) from a railway station.

There are also discount cards for **10 journeys** within a specified number of zones. A 10-trip tricket for three zones, for example, costs 105kr. Note that clip cards are stamped face up in automatic machines.

Copenhagen is a cyclist's city so take advantage of **City Bikes**, which provides 2,500 bikes free for communal use. Insert your 20kr coin into one of the 125 racks in the city and pedal away. When you return the bike, you get your money back.

For a ferry to Malmö in Sweden, Pilen (Tel. 3332 1260) usually has the best offers. Bonuses for Inter-Rail may be available. The jetfoil saves you 45 minutes' travelling with an Inter-Rail reduction, otherwise the trip takes 1½ hours.

## SEEING

Copenhagen is designed for walking. Among the network of bustling city centre streets is **Strøget**, the longest pedestrianized thoroughfare in the world. It starts from the northeast corner of the **Radhuspladsen** (square of the City Hall – whose 350ft tower you can climb for 20kr) and cuts through several squares until it reaches the plaza at Kungens Nytorv. There are six well-planned city walking tours which last about two hours (ask Tourist Information or Use It).

Don't forget the free **city bikes** as an alternative to walking. And most of the sights, including the symbol of Copenhagen, the **Little Mermaid**, can be seen during the good 20-45kr **boat trips** round the harbour and canals (there's also a waterbus; buy a 30kr day ticket and jump on and off at each sight). Canal tours leave from Gammel Strand and Nyhavn. **Bus tours** are good but expensive. They leave from City Hall Square, next to the Palace Hotel (from 125kr; discounts with the Copenhagen Card).

The **Copenhagen Card** (see above) gives free admission to more than 60 sights. A comprehensive leaflet provided with the card gives full details of opening times, locations, discounts, and other facilities.

**Tivoli** (the famous amusement park) is in the centre across from the train station. It has, over the years, become increasingly commercial. Entrance 45kr, with rides from 10kr but generally overpriced; a Tour Pass ticket at 178kr allows unlimited rides. Avoid eating here. Open May–mid-Sept., 11am–midnight.

The best view of old Copenhagen can be seen from the top of the **Round Tower** (on Kobmagergade, 15kr), built in 1642, the summit of which is curiously reached by a continuous spiral ramp. Another good view of the town can be had from the unusual tower of **Vor Frelsers Kirke** on Prinsessegade and Torvegade. The spiral staircase is on the *outside* of the church's spire and gets progressively steeper and more uneven. Not recommended in high winds or rain! It costs 20kr to climb it.

Copenhagen has a multitude of museums, the best of which are the **Workers' Museum** (Arbejdermuseet) at Romersgade 22, and for Danish history and the Vikings, the **National Museum (Nationalmuseet)** at Ny Vestergade 10.

Don't miss **Nyhavn**, the rejuvenated 'new port', opposite Kungens Nytorv. It was here Hans Christian Andersen wrote his first fairy tale. Today, its Hanseatic merchants' houses have been restored, there are old sailing boats in the docks, and the whole harbour area is buzzing with open-air bars, cafés and restaurants.

**FREE COPENHAGEN:** If you're on foot, you will not miss **Strøget**, a series of streets throbbing with life. And the city's medieval atmosphere lives on in the **Latin quarter** in the area around the university – host to a multitude of bookshops, *bric-à-brac*, a good selection of cafés and the **Vor Frue Kirke**, Copenhagen's cathedral.

- The walk to the harbour and the **Little Mermaid**, along the **Langelinie** and through the grounds of the **Kastellet** (Citadel), is the best part of the trip, as the statue's nothing special. Look out for the nearby **Gefion Fountain**.

- Worth a look are the **Thorvaldsen's Museum** for the work of Denmark's famous sculptor; the **Frihedsmuseet** (Resistance Museum), tracing the rise of opposition to German occupation during the Second World War; and **Ny Carlsberg Glyptotek**, for ancient and impressionist art (admission is 15kr, but free on ISIC, and on Wed. and Sun.).

- A favourite with thirsty Eurorailers are the tours run by the **Carlsberg** and **Tuborg** breweries – mainly because of the free samples afterwards (but beware of the time limit on your quaffing!). 10am - 4pm (not weekends): take bus 6 or 18, west from City Hall Square. Tuborg tours run at 10am, 12.30pm and 2.30pm: S-tog line A to Svanemøllen or Hellerup, or bus 6, 21, or 23, north from City Hall Square. The Tuborg brewery has also opened the **Eksperimentarium**, an interactive science museum, in an old bottling hall on Tuborg Havnevej 7, entrance fee 75kr.

- 'Alternative' Copenhagen can be experienced at **Christiana** on Prinsessegade. Occupied in 1971 by a group of hippies who enjoyed the liberal Danish attitudes to pot, drinking and nudism, it makes an interesting visit! The veggie café and craft stalls are good, and restaurants, bars and shops are cheaper than in the rest of the town. Avoid taking photographs of the inhabitants to avoid any unpleasantness.

- An alternative to Tivoli is the free entry amusement park of **Bakken**. Take the S-tog to **Klampenborg** (free on Inter-Rail and Eurail) and walk through the park. Open Apr.–end Aug., 12 noon–12 midnight.

- Opposite the Rosenborg Slot (castle and gardens) is the **Botanisk Have**, 25 acres of botanical gardens, with a tropical Palm House. Open daily.

- On a sunny day, the **Bellevue** is a popular draw for locals. It's a beach between Copenhagen and Helsingør – known locally as *Fluepapiret* (fly paper) for its ability to draw bikini-clad blondes and local likely lads. Windsurfing, kite hire, waterbikes.

**EXCURSIONS** The best day trip from Copenhagen is 40 km north to **Frederiksborg Castle** at Hillerød (35 minutes by S-tog, leaving from the main station).

Less than half an hour by train from the capital is the town of **Roskilde**. In the last weekend of every June, it becomes Scandanavia's answer to Glastonbury, with more than 100 international and local bands playing to crowds of upwards of 100,000 rock lovers. Contact the tourist information offices well in advance of the festival each year for details of who is scheduled to play.

## SLEEPING

Hotels in Copenhagen are busy all year round, and with prices starting at 400kr; you are better investigating the city hostels, private house schemes and campsites. If you are organized in advance try the apartment booking agency Citi-Let, at Fortunstrade 4, DK-1065, Copenhagen K (Tel. 3325 2129; Fax. 3391 3077).

**HOSTELS** These are busy in summer, so don't waste time touring round them yourself. Use It will help you find a bed (when their office is shut, they often post up the latest bed situation just outside their office).

The main youth hostel (you'll need an IYHF card), **Bellahøj** at Herbergvejen 8 (Tel. 38 28 9715), is very good and situated in a park in a nice suburb about 15–20 minutes from the city centre. The cost is 85kr. Take bus 2 from the station almost to the end of the route. Security can be a problem, so use the lockers in the basement.

The **Copenhagen Youth Hostel** (IYHF) at Vejlandsallé 200, very clean and modern, is 85kr per night. Book in after 1pm (Tel. 3252 2908). Take bus 13 or train to Valby station, changing to bus 37.

**Vesterbro Ungdomsgård**, Absalonsgzide 8 (Tel. 33 31 2070), is more expensive than the other hostels, due to its good location. Take bus 6 from the station, or a 10-minute walk along Vesterbrogade. Cost: 130kr.

There is a **YMCA** hostel in Copenhagen which costs 70kr. A 15-minute walk from the station to Valdemarsgade 15 (Tel. 3331 1574; open July to mid-Aug.).

**SLEEP-INS** Are another option and can be found in converted ice-rinks or gymnasiums at various changing locations throughout the city. Check *Copenhagen This Week*, Tourist Information, or telephone 3526 5059. Very few restrictions; IYHF cards are not required; co-ed dorms; bring your own sleeping bag. The cost is 80–115kr, including breakfast. Current options include the one at Blegdamsvej 132 (Tel. 3526 5059) and Sleep-In Heaven at 7 Struenseegade (Tel. 3535 4648).

**PRIVATE ACCOMMODATION** Go to any Tourist Office to ask for a room in a private house and expect to pay up to 250kr for a single, 350kr a double. They also take about 15kr commission per person.

**HOTELS** If you have no alternative and want to stay in a hotel, try the **Amager** in Amagerbrogade (Tel. 3254 4008). It's handy to the airport and it's got the oldest lift in Denmark. Funky eh!

You will also find places in the area behind the central station on Helgolandsgade (Absalon Hotel) and Colbjørnsensgade (Ansgar Hotel), but expect to pay anything from 650kr for even the cheapest hotels in the capital.

One worthy exception is the **Cab Inn** hotel, which has small (cabin-like) rooms with the usual hotel comforts (including en suite bathroom, TV, tea and coffee-making facilities) for very good prices. Rooms for four (in bunks) cost 740kr, triples 630kr, doubles 520kr and singles 410kr. All-you-can-eat breakfasts go for 40kr. You'll find it on Danasvej 32-34 in the Frederiksberg area (Tel. 3321 0400).

**CAMPING** There are seven sites costing around 50kr per person with Danish camping pass. The all-year site is at Absalon Camping, 132 Korsdalsvej (Tel. 3641 0600): take the S-tog, line B or H, to Brøndyøster station. Cabins are available for up to five people, but the shop here is expensive.

## EATING AND NIGHTLIFE

This is varied, interesting and there is no shortage of places to choose from. For meals, you can't do much better than the set menus at

Chinese restaurants. To keep you going there are *pølser* (hot dog) stalls, fast-food chains, daily specials (*dagens ret*) and *smørrebrød*. (See the Use It brochure *Where to Eat*.)

Studenterhuset (university refectory), 52 Kobmagergade, charges 17kr for a sandwich. At Pasta Basta, Valkendorfsgade 22, eat as much spaghetti as you can for around 70kr. There are good 'eat-as-much-as-you-can' places, at reasonable prices (typically 40–80kr), for example, Ankara at 8-10 Krystalgade or Husets Cafe at Rådhusstraede 13 (part of Use It). Also try any of the Indian, Italian or Turkish restaurants. For true Danish marine atmosphere, experience a typical herring buffet or smørrebrød (40-80kr) at Nyhavns Faergekro, 5 Nyhavn.

There are hundreds of pubs, clubs and discos. Most start getting lively around midnight and close at 5am. Late night drinking can be expensive with beer at around 25kr a bottle. Base Camp at Building 148, Halvtolv, Holmen is Copenhagen's largest eatery and nightclub, Mantra at Bernstorffsgage 3 offers free breakfasts for those who make it through to dawn. **Nyhavn** (the dock district) provides an interesting nocturnal wander; locals stock up on supermarket beer to drink by the boats. Note it's not advisable for girls to go there alone at night.

The **Use It** house is as good and cheap a place for a drink as any, and Frederiksberggade comes alive at night. Good **jazz** can normally be found on Norregade. For live music listings pick up mags like *Hust*, *Neon Guiden* or *Gaffa* in music stores. Basically though, you really won't need to look hard for nightlife in this city.

## Odense

The island of Funen, wedged between Zealand and Jutland, is known as the Garden of Denmark. It was local boy, fairy tale writer Hans Christian Andersen, who gave it that name. His home town, Odense – one of Denmark's oldest cities – has two museums dedicated to his life and work. You can visit his house (**H.C. Andersens Hus**) at Hans Jensens Straede 37–45 (30kr, no reductions) and there is more memorabilia at **H.C. Andersens Barndomshjem** (childhood home), Munkemollestr. 3–5 (10kr).

**Tourist Information** is in the town hall, south of the station (Tel. 6612 7520), open in summer 9am–7pm, Sun. 11am–7pm. The **Odense Eventyrpas Card** gives free admission to museums, indoor and outdoor pools, and other attractions, as well as allowing free local bus, train and boat rides (50kr for 24 hours, 90kr for 2 days).

**St Canute's** 13th-century **Cathedral** and the **Open-Air Folk Museum** (30kr) are both worth a look. Dedicated Eurorailers will enjoy

Scandinavia's biggest railway museum (30kr) and 'the King's' fans will not miss the Elvis Presley Museum's 1500 items of memorabilia (35kr).

At **Ladby** (20 km north-east of Odense), you can see the coffin ship of a 10th-century Viking chief.

B&B at Pjentehus, Pjentedamsgade 14, has doubles at 280kr, breakfast 30kr. The **youth hostel** is at 121 Kragsbjergvej (Tel. 6613 0425). It has 168 beds, and is on bus route 61 or 62 from the station (cost 80kr). There's a **campsite** at Odensevej 102 (Tel. 6611 4702), bus 1, cost 50kr.

# Århus

Denmark's second city is an important centre of trade with a lively university and fully deserves its reputation as the country's cultural centre. Excellent music and entertainment venues and international festivals have put Århus on the map. At the heart of the town is the 12th-century **Cathedral**, around whose Gothic walls radiates a labyrinth of well preserved medieval, pedestrianized streets lined with cafés and shops. You'll find plenty to see and do.

Worth seeing are **Den Gamle By** (Old Town), a reconstructed 16th-century Jutland village of 75 buildings; the **Prehistoric Museum,** which has the amazing red-headed mummy of the Grauballe bog man; the **Viking Museum** (free); and Queen Margarethe II's summer home, **Marselisborg Castle,** whose rose gardens are open to the public. The new Vadestedet is a popular café promenade along the river.

**Tourist information** is in the Town Hall (Tel. 8940 6700), one block from the station, and is open 9.30am–6pm (shorter hours out of season). There's a small charge to book accommodation.

For free entrance to all the city's museums and sights, along with free sightseeing tours and unlimited bus travel, ask at the tourist office for the **Århus Pass** (88kr one day, 110kr two days, 155kr seven days).

The **student centre** at 84 Niels Juelsgade that helps run the **City Sleep-In** at Havnegade 20 (Tel. 8619 2055). You can do laundry there and rent bikes for 50kr a day. The **IYHA hostel** is Vandrerhjemmet Pavillonen at Marienlundsvej 10 (Tel. 8616 7298); closed 12 noon–4pm. It's good and well situated in a forest, near beaches. Take bus or tram nos 1, 2, 6 or 8 to the terminus, then follow signs.

The **campsite** (Tel. 8627 0207) is four km out at Blommehaven, Ørneredevej, bus 6 or 19 to the door. Own beach, cycle paths.

Your cheapest lunch is at the Matematiske Fakultet (**university**) off Langelandsgade; closed after 1pm and all July. Even better is the **Use It Youth Centre** at 15 Vester Allé. They also give free concerts and plays.

For nightlife, try **Musikcafeen**, Mejlgade 53; **Train**, at Toldbodgade

6 (minimum age 23); or if you're a night owl, head for the **Café Paradis** – it's open to 6am on weekends.

# Aalborg

The 1,000-year-old centre of north Jutland is where you can see the remains of a Viking village and mass grave (at Nørresundby, on the outskirts; take bus 6 from near the tourist office). Aalborg's **Old Town** is well-preserved and spotless, and check out the 15th-century **Monastery of the Holy Ghost**, **Aaborghus Castle** and **dungeons**, **Budolfi Cathedral**, and the baby brother of Tivoli, **Tivoliland**. There is a new **museum** at the Viking site, with many artefacts from the area.

Tourist Information is at Østeragade 8 (Tel. 9812 6022).

All Americans in Aalborg on 4 July should make their way to the Rebild National Park, 30 km south of the city, for the most extensive Independence Day celebrations outside the USA.

The Aalborg Vandrerhjem **hostel** is at Skydebanevej 50 (Tel. 9811 6044) and costs 85kr per night. Two **campsites** are located nearby: Fjordparken (Tel. 9811 6044) and Strandparken (Tel. 9812 7629). Bus 2 or 178 from the centre or railway station.

# Legoland

One of Denmark's most famous exports is Lego, the children's plastic building brick. At **Billund** in mid-Jutland there is a mini-town comprising houses, railway, harbour, boats and cars – all made out of the stuff.

Legoland is open Apr-Oct., with some indoor exhibitions from Easter to mid-Dec. Take the train to Vejle and then bus 912 from the station to Billund (around 40kr each way). Journey takes about an hour.

Legoland opens at 10am and closes at 8pm. A one-day pass is available for 130kr and this includes all rides. Another option is a one-day combined ticket with return coach travel and admission. Reduced entrance fees may be offered later in the day. Call Legoland on 7533 1333 for more information.

There are also aviation and motor vehicle museums close by, open daily 10am–8pm.

Best option is to see Legoland as a day trip, but there is a **campsit e** very near, at Nordmarksvej 2 (Tel. 7533 1521), and a **hostel** at Ellerhammers Allé (Tel. 7533 2777).

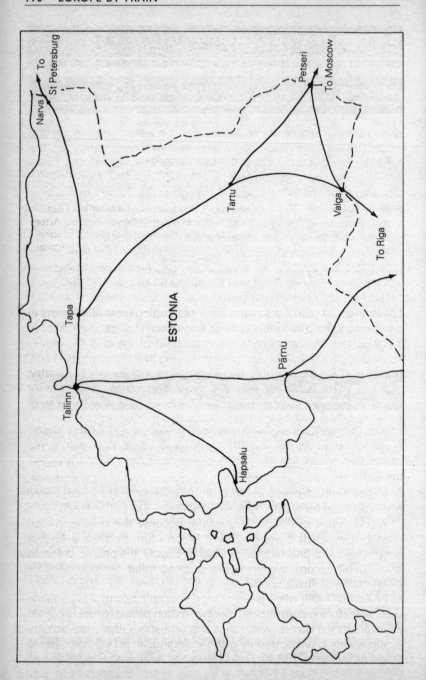

# ESTONIA (Eesti)

| | |
|---|---|
| Entry requirements | Passport. No visa required for citizens of USA, UK, Ireland, Canada, Australia and New Zealand. |
| Population | 1.5 million |
| Capital | Tallinn (pop.: 0.4 million) |
| Currency | Kroon (EEK)<br>£1 = approx. 24.2 kroon |
| Political system | Parliamentary democracy |
| Religion | Protestantism, Lutheranism & Russian Orthodox |
| Language | Estonian, Russian widely spoken (see note on languages), some English and German |
| Public holidays | New Year's Day, Independence Day (24 Feb.), Good Friday, May Day (1 May), Whitsun, Victory Day (23 June), St John's Day (24 June), Restoration of Independence Day (20 Aug.), Christmas Day and Boxing Day |
| International dialling codes | To Estonia: int'l code 372<br>From Estonia: dial 8 + 00 + country code |

For almost 800 years Estonia has been a stomping ground for many of its warmongering neighbours. The first to arrive were the Danes in 1219, who took control of the northern half of the country, closely followed by German Teutonic knights moving into the south. By 1346, however, it was the knights who were in control of the whole country: a position that lasted for over 200 years. This was a good time for many of Estonia's coastal regions, as trade – on its way to Western Europe and the East – expanded and flowed through its ports.

The Swedes were the next invaders to get a piece of the action, but lost their grip on Estonia when they were defeated by Russia in the 18th century. Repressive central government from Moscow, though, left Estonians worse off than before and yearning for independence. This was finally declared in 1918, but the freedom they had waited over 700 years for was to be short-lived.

World War II saw Hitler's Germany become the new uninvited guests, after which it was the Soviet Union's turn to begin a 45-year reign. Under this final regime, in a bid to 'Russify' the people, enforced mass deportations were carried out, coupled with large-scale immigration of Russians.

By August 1989, when pressure for democratic reform was bubbling over, a plea for freedom inspired over two million people to form a human chain across the borders with Latvia and Lithuania. Other mass demonstrations were characterized by patriotic singing, an act that gave rise to the years between 1988-91 being known as The Singing Revolution.

Finally, in August 1991, after so long in the shadows of foreign dictators, Estonia declared itself a sovereign state and was free again.

These days, with a stable economy, as well as standing in line for EU membership, things are looking up for the Baltic state as it continues to build a post-Soviet future. One industry they are keen to exploit is 'green tourism', which is hardly surprising given that some 40% of the country is covered in dense forest. With outdoor attractions such as bird-watching, horse riding and hiking becoming increasingly popular, you'll probably hear plenty of singing but this time it will just be the birds!

## GETTING THERE

Tallink Express ferry services operate several crossings daily between Tallinn and Helsinki (Finland). There is a 30% ISIC discount.

## TRAIN INFORMATION

Someone at Tallinn's station usually speaks English but you'll be hard pressed to find English speakers elsewhere. Most signs are now in Estonian rather than Russian – which still isn't a great help.

**PASSES AVAILABLE** Inter-Rail and Eurail passes are not valid in Estonia. The Baltic States Explorer Pass gives seven, 14 or 21 consecutive days of unlimited 2nd-class rail travel around Estonia, Latvia and Lithuania. Around £25 for seven days; £35 for 14; and £45 for 21 days. Sample journeys might be Riga–Tallinn (seven hours) two trains a day; Vilnius–Riga (6.5 hours) four trains a day.

**RESERVATIONS** Compulsory on international trains. Domestic trains get very busy so it's wise to book one or two days ahead. Pay the extra when first class is available, it won't cost much but is definitely worth it.

**NIGHT TRAVEL** Night trains are slow and not the best place to get a good night's sleep.

**EATING ON THE TRAIN** Sporadic trolley services offer decidedly dodgy looking food, so pack picnic supplies before you leave.

## TOURIST INFORMATION

Most towns will have a tourist office of some sort, though offices in larger cities tend to be better equipped. Don't expect mounds of information, though it's improving. For details of Estonia's green tourism industry contact Kodukant Eco-Tourism Initiative, Saariso EE3482 Jõesuu, Pärnuma. Fax (372 44) 43 779 or e-mail: aivar_r@mv.parnu.ee. Also visit the web sites www.estonia.org and www.tallinn.ee/turismiinfo.

**ISIC BONUSES** Between 20–50% discount on airlines, national buses and ferries to Finland and Sweden. Show your card for *everything*.
**MONEY MATTERS** 1 kroon (EEK) = 100 senti.

Estonian banks are open Mon.–Fri. 9am–4pm. Credit cards are accepted in the more expensive hotels along with some shops and restaurants. Some traveller's cheques, such as American Express, can be cashed in a few of the major banks. The best currencies to exchange are US dollars and Deutschmarks. Currency exchange offices are open Mon.–Sat. 9am–6 or 7pm. Some open Sun.

**SHOPS** In general, open daily 9am–6pm. If no price is marked on an item expect to pay an inflated tourist price. With tourism on the up and up, the prevailing Estonian attitude seems to be that those visiting can afford to pay more than the locals.

**MUSEUMS** Times vary greatly, but many are open 11am–4pm.

**LANGUAGE** Estonian is the national language, but phrase-books are few and far between in bookshops. Russian is widely spoken, along with some English or German. Years of Soviet rule have, however, left a strong anti-Russian sentiment in the country, so bear this in mind before unleashing your repertoire of Russian phrases. People will probably react more warmly with the following Estonian words and phrases:

| | | | |
|---|---|---|---|
| Hello | *Tere* | Thank you | *Tänan* |
| Goodbye | *Head aega* | Excuse me | *Vabandage* |
| Yes | *Jah* | Do you speak | *Kas teie räägite* |
| No | *Ei* | English? | *inglise keelt?* |
| Please | *Palun* | Russian? | *rooski keelt?* |

**TIPPING** As with most Eastern European countries, tipping is very much appreciated. In restaurants where a service charge is included, round up your bill with loose change.

## SLEEPING AND EATING

Since the introduction of a national youth hostel scheme in 1991, there are now 16 hostels charging between £2–5 a night. The home of the Estonian Youth Hostel Association is at Tatari 39, Tallinn (Tel. 6461 455). They'll book accommodation for you but they advise you to reserve – wait for it – a staggering four weeks in advance! In summer, student dorms are a good option as well and will cost around £4–6. Camping is extremely cheap, with sites charging about £2 per person.

Cheap cafés and restaurants abound but don't expect a high level of cuisine. Vegetarians are not well catered for, so rescue comes in the form of vegetable shops and markets, where you can stock up.

# Tallinn

Tallinn's superbly preserved medieval core lies in stark contrast to the ring of Soviet-styled buildings which surround it. Foreign occupation has always been a factor in its history and, as a result, the Danes, Swedes, Russians and Germans have all left their mark on the city. Today, however, with its cobbled streets, rich history and architecture, foreign occupation tends to come from the growing number of tourists it attracts.

## TOURIST INFORMATION

The main Tourist Information Office, indicated by a green 'i', is at Raekoja plats 10 in the centre of the old town (Tel. 6946 946). It has free maps and lists of cafés, restaurants, hotels, B&B, transportation, etc. Pick up a copy of *Tallinn This Week*. There's another office at Tallinn Harbour (Terminal A).

**EMBASSIES** The British Embassy (Tel. 631 3461) and the American Embassy (Tel. 631 2021) are both at Kentmanni 20 while the Canadian Embassy is on Toomkooli 13 (Tel. 631 7978). Irish nationals should contact the Irish embassy in Helsinki; Australians, their embassy in Stockholm; and New Zealanders should use their embassy in Moscow.

## GETTING ABOUT

The city has a good system of buses, trams and trolley buses which run every day from 6am–12 midnight. Tickets can be bought from drivers or at kiosks. If you intend staying a while, consider the 10-day *kümne päeva kaart* available from kiosks for EEK 80 and valid on all public transport. The Tallinn Card is a general discount card for visiting museums and galleries and the free use of public transport - 24hr EEK195, 48hr EEK 270, 72hr EEK 325.

## SEEING

Tallinn's heart, and most of its sights, lie in the quarters of the magnificent medieval **Old Town**: a fact reflected in its current status as a UNESCO World Heritage Site. This in turn is split into an upper and lower town, and surrounded in part by almost two kilometres of medieval ramparts.

At the north end of the **Lower Town** check out the **Great Coast Gate**, a 16th century city gateway, and its accompanying tower, affectionately known as **Fat Margaret**. The tower, originally built to guard the gate, is now home to the **Maritime Museum**. Nearby, on

Pikk, is **Oleviste Church**, one-time proud record holder of the highest spire in Europe. Along here you'll also find some of Tallinn's best medieval houses and guildhalls.

To the south, the cobbled **Town Square** of Raekoja plats is home to Europe's oldest surviving **Town Hall**. Look out for Vana Toomas (Old Thomas) who stands guard over Tallinn sitting atop the roof, he's been there since 1530: it's the weathervane, and long-time symbol of the town.

To reach the **Upper Town** head for **Niguliste Church** and take Lühike jalg to the **Alexander Nevsky Cathedral**. Behind here is **Toompea Castle** – these days home to Estonian parliament – and the 14th century tower **Pikk Hermann**. Another interesting place is the museum housed in the **Kiek-in-de-Kok** tower at the southern end of Komandandi.

**FREE TALLINN:**
- On summer evenings make your way to Raekoja plats which holds traditional Estonian **song and dance**.
- There are also a few markets to nose around in: **Kadaka turg**, 10 minutes from the centre on the junction of Tammsaare and Mustamäe is advertised as 'if you're looking for it, it's probably here', so test them out. It's good for clothes and CDs, pirated of course. Although not actually free, **museums** are the next best thing – very, very cheap! Entry is usually only a few kroons and by flashing your ISIC card you might even get a discount. Try one (or more) of the following:
- **Historical Museum**, Pikk 17
- **City Museum**, Vene 17
- **Natural History Museum**, Lai 29
- **Town Council's Prison Museum**, Raekoja 6

## SLEEPING AND EATING

The Tourist Office have lists of accommodation and campsites but they will probably suggest the agencies **Rasastra** for home or private accommodation **and the Balti Puhkemajad** for hostels. The youth hostel, **The Barn**, well-located in the Old Town at Väike-Karja 1 (Tel. 631 3252) is very popular so advance bookings recommended. There's also **Hostel Akmis**, Parnu Road 162; five minutes from Viru Square by bus nos. 5, 18, 36 or 57, get off at Suusavabrik, hostel 100m on right. For **B&B** try 'UUS 22' in the old town, singles EEK290 (Tel. 6411 464).

For your daily supplies try the supermarket, **Kaubahall**, at Aia 7, or **Tallinna Kaubamaja**, on Gonsiori opposite the Viru Hotel. The **snack bar** at the station is also a good place to fill up very cheaply. For take-out pizza there are 3 **Peetri** places around town on Lai 4, Liivalaia 40, and Pärnu mnt. 22.

Plenty of cafés and bars occupy Raekoja plats. You can get inexpensive meals here and many of them also feature live music and dancing. Most popular clubs are Holywood, Dekoltee and the gay club (or as the locals say, a club for free spirits), Nightman. If you fancy the walk, **Neitsitorn** is a charming old café at the top of Lühike jalg serving mulled wine from wooden casks.

NOTES:

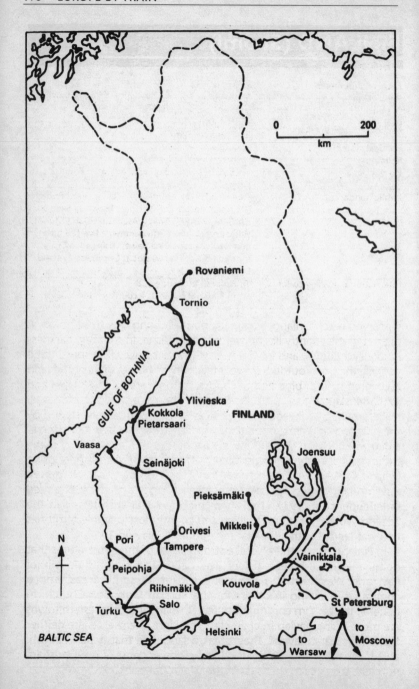

# FINLAND (Suomi)

| | |
|---|---|
| Entry requirements | Passport |
| Population | 5.1 million |
| Capital | Helsinki (pop.: 532,000) |
| Currency | Finnish Markka |
| | £1 = approx. 9 mk |
| Political system | Republic |
| Religions | Lutheran and Orthodox |
| Languages | Finnish, Swedish and Lappish (some English spoken) |
| Public holidays | New Year's Day, Epiphany (6 Jan.), Good Friday (21 Apr.), Easter (21-24 Apr.), May Day Eve (30 Apr.), May Day (1 May), Ascension Day (1 June), Whitsun (11 June), Midsummer's Eve (23 June) and Day (24 June), All Saints' Day (4 Nov.), Independence Day (6 Dec.), Christmas Eve and Day, Boxing Day |
| International dialling codes | To Finland: int'l code 358 |
| | From Finland: 00, 990, + country code |

Once you reach Finland, you really do feel a long way from home. A quarter of the country lies above the Arctic Circle. In summer, darkness hardly ever comes, and in winter, daylight lasts only a few hours. But if you like the great outdoors, you'll feel right at home: 70% of the land is covered by lush pine and birch forests, there are 187,888 lakes and 179,584 islands.

Hemmed in by Sweden and Norway to the north and west, and by the Russian wilderness to the east, Finland is growing in importance as a gateway between Western Europe and Russia and the countries of the Baltic rim. For centuries, Sweden and Russia played political chess, using Finland as the pawn. Sweden held sway for 650 years, and the czars of Russia ruled for another 100 years, before Finland finally proclaimed independence in 1917. There was more conflict with Russia in the Second World War, during which the country lost valuable territories and was landed with large war reparations to pay off.

In Finland today, there's still a strong sense of the two cultures that dominated its turbulent history. The nation is an interesting mix of East and West, with Swedish still spoken in some areas, and a continued following in others for the Russian Orthodox Church. In general, the eastern communities feel Russian, and the western towns are more Scandinavian in character. The Finns themselves are neither Slavic nor Scandinavian. They speak a language that is part Finnish, part Hungarian, and are believed to be descendants of pre-Christian, nomadic tribes from the west of the Ural mountains.

Prices in Finland are 'reasonable by Scandinavian standards': i.e. not cheap for young travellers.

## GETTING THERE

Unless you're going by train and bus round the north of Sweden, your most direct route is to take a ferry from Stockholm to either Turku or Helsinki. It's a beautiful cruise of 10–12 hours and 13–16 hours respectively. The main shipping lines are Silja and Viking. An Inter-Rail or Scanrail gets you a 50% reduction on both lines, while Eurail holders travel free with Silja and get a 50% reduction with Viking. Facilities on both lines are excellent. Cabins are expensive, so get your sleeping bag down on deck somewhere, or, better still, head for the free 'sleep-in'. On the older ships, these have 60 beds, but the excellent new ships on the Silja Lines Turku–Stockholm route have 200 places available on all sailings.

It is well worthwhile taking a day sailing, as the route is very scenic and you pass many small islands on the way, with the ship constantly zigzagging to keep in deep water. Snacks and coffee on the ship are reasonably priced, as are the duty-free goods – reasonable by Scandinavian standards, that is. There are several services each day, with prices varying depending on the crossing. The Helsinki ferries leave at 6pm or 7pm and cost a minimum 120mk (before discounts) on Viking Line, or 220mk (before discounts) on Silja Line. The Turku ferries leave at 8am, 8.30am, 8pm, 8.20pm and 9pm during high season, and cost a minimum of 85mk on Viking Line, and 100mk on Silja Line.

There are also regular ferry crossings between Finland and Germany (32–36 hours) and Tallinn in Estonia (3 hours 30 mins). For travel with a difference contact Mr Rolf Tubenthal in Hamburg (Tel. 4940 3705 2593), who arranges trips on container ships.

## FINNISH STATE RAILWAYS

### (VALTIONRAUTATIET, VR)
#### INFORMATION:
Finnish Railways, Room 286, PO Box 488, Fin-00101, Helsinki (Tel. 358-9-7071) or in the UK, Aeroscope Ltd (Tel. 01608 650 103).

Big, solid and reliable (like the Finns!), the majority of the rolling stock is new, with the fastest (the Pendolino S220 between Helsinki and Turku) travelling up to 200km an hour. There are four types of trains: IC-trains (*IC-juna*), special expresses (*Erikoispikajuna*), regular expresses (*Pikajuna*) and locals (*Henkilöjuna*). Their service extends as far north as Lapland and includes nearly 6,000 km of line.

Finland is one of Europe's gateways to the East, with the Russian border only a short trip from Helsinki. Day trains provide a fascinating route to St Petersburg (from 286mk one way, seat only), Moscow (from 499mk one way, including a berth) and Vyborg (from 218mk one way, seat only). There's also a night train.

**PASSES AVAILABLE** The **Finnrail Pass** entitles you to three, five or ten days of unlimited travel within one month for 600mk, 810mk or 1,090mk respectively (second class). Under-26s are eligible for a 25% discount, under-17s travel half-price. First-class passes are also available.

Group tickets are good for parties of at least three people. For groups of between 3 and 10 people, there's a 20% discount on single tickets (returns are twice the price of a single); for groups of more than 10 people, the discount is 25%.

The **ScanRail Pass** is valid for travel anywhere in Scandinavia and allows 21 days travel for £212, or five days of travel within 15 days for £139. The ticket should be purchased outside Scandinavia, as more restrictions apply if it is bought on arrival. Under-26s are entitled to around 25% discount; a first-class ScanRail Pass is available for a supplement of 30%.

The **Inter-Rail Pass** has been broken down into zones, so you don't have to pay for travel to areas you will not be visiting. For £129 you can tour a single zone for 22 days (over-26s pay £179). Finland is in Zone B, along with Sweden and Norway. **Eurail Passes** are valid, and a **Euro Domino** ticket is also available. (For further details on Euro Domino tickets and the eight Inter-Rail zones, refer to the relevant sections in Part One of this guide.)

**INTER-RAIL BONUSES** See Appendix I, plus free entry to the VR Railway Museum in Hyvinkää, and Narrow Gauge Railway Museum in Jokioinen (Gare Minkio).

**EURAIL BONUSES** Free services:

Buses, particularly those which operate during certain hours of the day as train substitutes.

Ferry crossings operated by Silja Line between Vaasa and Umea.

Note that the service between Vaasa and Sundsvall has been withdrawn.

**EURAIL AID OFFICE** Helsinki Central Station, international services. Tel. 09 707 5703

**REDUCTIONS** 50% reduction on the normal adult rate for the ferry crossing from Helsinki to Travemünde on the Finnjet (bookings earliest seven days before departure).

## TRAIN INFORMATION

Staff speak English at the major stations. Contact the *Neuvonta* at the station if you have problems.

**RESERVATIONS** Obligatory on the IC-trains and special expresses (marked 'EP' in timetable); optional on other trains. Oddly, reserved seats are not marked, making it difficult to tell if a seat is free. Costs are between 20mk and 30mk. On the IC and EP fast trains, and on the Pendolino 220 between Helsinki and Turku, supplements of 25–90mk must be paid.

**NIGHT TRAVEL** There are no couchettes, only reasonably priced sleepers (60–90mk in a 3-berth compartment or 120–180mk in 2-berth. Reductions off peak). During the busy periods (Easter – when fares are higher – and July/August) try to reserve sleepers as far ahead as possible.

## TOURIST INFORMATION

City offices, *Matkailutoimistot*, provide excellent maps and leaflets on their locality. For Finland as a whole, the Finnish Tourist Board, MEK, tel. 4176 9300, www.mek.fi has its base in Helsinki. Museums tend to close on Mon.

**ISIC BONUSES** Student discounts on museums, art galleries and theatres. 50% discount on *Scanhotel* chain between June and mid-August, weekends rest of the year.

**MONEY MATTERS** 1 Finnish markka (mk) = 100 penni (p).
Banking hours are Mon.–Fri.: 9.15am–4.15pm, but vary by locality. Banks give the best rate of exchange. All banks and exchange bureaux close over the midsummer weekend holiday.

**POST OFFICES** Open 9am–5pm, Mon.–Fri. Stamps are also sold at bookshops, newsagents', R-kiosks, hotels and stations. Post boxes are yellow.

**SHOPS** Mon.–Fri.: 9am-5pm or 6pm (with department stores staying open to 8pm summer weekdays). Saturday hours 9am–2pm or 3pm (department stores to 6pm).

**TELEPHONES** Accept 1 and 5mk coins only, returned if no reply. There are also card phones that accept all major credit cards, and variously priced phone cards are sold for use in special booths.

**TIPPING** In Finland, tips are normally given only in fairly smart restaurants.

## SLEEPING

There's no age limit for Finland's 160 **hostels** and you don't need IYHF membership, except in the most expensive category, which often have saunas. However, the international hostelling card will give you a 15mk reduction, as well as a wide range of other discounts in Finland. Hostel charges vary from 60–150mk, though most are around 80mk. Breakfast costs 25–35mk. For further information about youth hostels in Finland, contact Suomen Retkeilymajäjarjestö (SRM, the Finnish Youth Hostel

Association), Yrjönkatu 38 B 15, FIN-00100 Helsinki (Tel. 694 0377).

There are about 350 **campsites**, graded on a star basis with five grades, and varying in price from 25 to 95mk per night (for a family with max. three adults plus children with tents, a caravan or trailer). For more details on hostelling and camping, ask at Tourist Information for the excellent current leaflet *Finland Budget Accommodation*.

**Private accommodation** and small **boarding houses** are also available (85–170mk a night): ask at Tourist Offices. **Summer hotels** are often made out of student dorms, and they're usually clean, modern and reasonably priced. The cheapest you'll get a hotel room for, (double) with breakfast, is 100–160mk per person.

For **hotels**, ask at the Finnish Tourist Office in your own country about the FinnCheque advance booking discount system.

## EATING AND NIGHTLIFE

As with the rest of Finnish culture, the gastronomic influence is a mix of East and West. Scandinavian-style cuisine centres on delicate fish dishes (salted Baltic herring, whitefish, crayfish, salmon – hauled from under thick ice in the winter) and game (reindeer – sometimes dried – and elk). Other dishes are traditionally Russian, with lots of cabbage, pork, mutton, casseroles and stodgy pastries. Rye bread and fruit-filled pancakes are local specialities, and if you're very lucky you'll come across the delicious cloudberries, which grow mainly above the Arctic Circle in the midnight sun. Lingonberries, cranberries and blueberries are plentiful during the summer.

The *baaris*, *grillis*, *krouvis* or *kahvilas* are a mixture of cafés and fast-food chains. They're OK but vary dramatically in quality. The student-run cafés are your best bet.

Nearly all restaurants have set lunch and dinner menus, but you're better advised to starve yourself and look out for a *Voileipäpöytä or Smörgåsbord* (Scandinavian cold table) for a set price, usually available at lunchtime. This often includes hot dishes as well, and you work on the basis of eating as much as you can for a set price.

Heavy tax on **alcohol** means high prices; a pint of beer in a restaurant or bar will set you back 15–30mk. The cheapest outlet is the disturbingly named ALKO chain (there's one in every town), where dangerously strong local brews like Lapin Kulta, Lahden, Olvi, Karjala, and Koff cost 8–9mk a bottle. The rough vodka called *koskenkorva* is extremely popular locally (a litre costs about 145mk). Knock some of this stuff back, and you'll soon know why Finns have a reputation for getting legless.

Despite this, Finns are keen on **dancing** and there's plenty of it on Vappu Night (End of April). This is the students' spring festival – a good excuse for Helsinki's 20,000 students to let rip on a bender after the long winter.

Should you hanker for a birch-leaf rubbing session with the locals, the Finnish **sauna** is for you. The sauna is part of everyday life in Finland – there's one for every three people – and it can be quite a social event. It's cheaper to take a sauna in a group, though do not necessarily expect mixed saunas. They're cheapest at public swimming baths (15–25mk), and most hotels welcome non-residents (30–50mk).

## Helsinki city phone code: 90

Finland's capital since 1812 is one of nine European cities of culture for the year 2000. It is clean, bright and modern. This Western city of manageable size has a Nordic outlook, a dash of eastern mystery and yet is comfortably in tune with high technology. Helsinki is a city of the sea, built on a large peninsula fringed by a scattering of islands. It was founded in 1550 as a market to compete with Tallinn (across the Baltic Sea), but fires have razed most of the traditional wooden buildings, and today's impression is of a city of contrasting architectural styles. The centre is a fascinating mix of Scandinavian, European and Russian architecture – an interesting reminder of Helsinki's geographical location betwixt East and West. Many buildings reflect the Russian imperial style of the 19th century, while solid eastern-looking architecture contrasts with new department stores selling well-designed consumer goods. In some ways, you feel closer to Russia in Helsinki than you do in Budapest.

Your first impression will probably be of the outdoor harbourside market, a daily event in front of the City Hall and President's Palace. The Kauppatori, opposite the tourist office and beside the south harbour, is a lively street fair, with stalls selling flowers, fruit, vegetables, fish fresh off the Baltic Sea trawlers, and handicrafts. Because the city centre grew up round the port and market area, Helsinki is easily negotiated on foot – the port is only 15 minutes' walk from the central train station.

Though the winters can be grim, in the summer, there's almost endless daylight – which seems to be all the excuse Helsinki folk need to go out on a bender. Summer for many Finns appears to mean non-stop partying, punctuated only by back-to-back festivals and outdoor events. Finns are proud of their culture, and the attitude is reflected in the wide variety of entertainment to be had. Among the concert halls and theatres is the Helsinki Opera House – home of the Finnish National Opera. Art is well-represented in a range of galleries, and there are plenty of museums and exhibitions.

## STATION FACILITIES

There are daily trains from Helsinki to Turku, Tampere, Kontiomäki, Oulu, Kemi and Rovaniemi (10-13 hours). If you have a Russian visa, there are also two trains daily to St Petersburg and two to Moscow.

Helsinki Central is one of the world's few architecturally famous stations. It's a classic example of Art Nouveau, designed by Eliel Saarinen.

Train information is available Mon.–Sat: 7am-10pm, Sun.: 9am-10pm (Tel. 0100121, International queries – west Tel. 664849, east Tel. 625216).

The station shuts during the following hours: Mon.–Thurs., Sun.: 1am–5 am,. Fri.–Sat.: 12 midnight–5am.

There are left-luggage lockers on both the lower and upper floors. The small ones on the upper level are too small for packs and cost 10mk. You may get a pack in the larger ones on the lower level.

Hotellikeskus is the accommodation-finding service in a building between the station and the nearby post office, at Asema-aukio 3 (Tel. 171133). They take 10mk commission per find. Summer hours: Mon.–Sat.: 9am–7pm, Sun.: 10am–6pm; off-season: Mon.–Fri.: 9am–5pm. They also have a list of all the IYHF youth hostels in Finland.

## TOURIST INFORMATION

The city **Tourist Office** is near the port, west of the market at Pohjoisesplanadi 19 (Tel. 169 3757). Open May–Sept., Mon.–Fri.: 9am–7pm, Sat.–Sun: 9am–3pm, mid-Sept.–mid-May, Mon.–Fri.: 9am–5pm, Sat.–Sun.: 9am–3pm. They produce very comprehensive leaflets and are incredibly helpful. Pick up a tourist map, *Helsinki This Week*, *Helsinki Guide* and *Helsinki on Foot*,

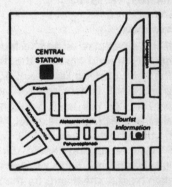

which includes six self-guiding tours. If you're staying for a while, ask them about the city transport passes.

Another possibility is the **Helsinki Card**, valid for either 24 hours at 120mk, 48 hours at 150mk, or 72 hours at 180mk. Not only does it allow you free travel on all public transport (including the Suomenlinna ferry), but it also entitles you to free entry to about 50 museums and other sights.

## ADDRESSES

**FINNISH TOURIST BOARD** Eteläesplanadi 4 (Tel. 41769300) for information on all of Finland. Open Mon.–Fri.: 9am–5pm, Sat.: 9am–1pm during the summer.

**POST OFFICE** Mannerheimintie 11, open Mon.–Fri.: 9am–6pm *Poste restante* is here.
**AMEX** Paivarinnakatu 1 (Tel. 9-818383), open Mon.–Fri.: 9am–1pm, Sat.: 10am–2pm
**UK EMBASSY** Itäinen Puistotie 17 (Tel. 2286 5100)
**IRISH EMBASSY** Erottajankatu 7 (Tel. 646 006)
**US EMBASSY** Itäinen Puistotie 14a (Tel. 171931)
**CANADIAN EMBASSY** Pohjoisesplanadi 25b (Tel. 171141)
**AUSTRALIAN EMBASSY** Use the embassy in Stockholm, or the Honorary Consul in Helsinki, Museokatu 25b (Tel. 44 7233).
**NEW ZEALAND EMBASSY** The NZ ambassador in the Hague, the Netherlands, is accredited to Finland, or use the Australian embassy in Stockholm.
**24-HOUR CHEMIST** Yloipiston Apteekki, Mannerheimintie 96
**STUDENT TRAVEL AGENCY** Travela, Mannerheimintie 5c (Tel. 624 101). Near the train station.
**HELSINKI TODAY** Tel. 058 for information and events in English, 040 for news and weather.
**EURAIL AID OFFICE** Helsinki Central Station, international services. Tel. (09) 707 5703

## SEEING

If it's a wet day or you're fed up with walking, tram 3T does an excellent round trip from the station in a figure-of-eight loop through the heart of Helsinki. It takes 45 minutes, and all the main sights are pointed out. Otherwise, the Tourist Office has the booklet *See Helsinki on Foot*, or will book you on organized walking tours. Another alternative is TandemTaxi (Tel. 40/540 0400), which does guided tours on bikes built for two.

Culture vultures should start at the **National Museum** (Suomen Kansallismuseo) north of Mannerheimintie from the station (15mk), then head to the islands for the **Seurasaari Open-Air Museum**, bus 24 to its terminus, and the **Suomenlinna Fortress Island** (actually six islands, and though still a military garrison, also home to a collection of parks and museums), reached by hourly ferry (20mk return) from the tourist office.

The new, state-of-the-art, contemporary arts museum, **Kiasma**, has a whole range of multi-media installations. Also worth a look is the **Cygnaeus Gallery**, an old villa housing a collection of 19th and 20th-century Finnish paintings and sculpture. Finland is also rightly acclaimed for being a world leader in manufacturing design, and the **Museum of Art and Design** (50mk) at Korkeavuorenkatu 23 brings together all the best the country has to offer.

**FREE HELSINKI:**

- A good starting point is the neoclassical centre of town, around the **Senate Square** (Senaatintori). On the square – one of the most graceful in Europe – stand the **Lutheran Cathedral**, **University** and **Government Palace**, all built in the early 19th century, during the rule of the Russian czars.
- Head from there down towards the sea front to browse round the **Kauppatori**, the colourful daily market. Though it can get very busy with tourists, it's not at all a tourist trap, and you can pick up some interesting examples of Finnish handicrafts from the stalls there. Anywhere around Stockmann's department store is good for window shopping.
- Nearby are the **President's Palace**, the **City Hall** and the **Orthodox Uspenskin Cathedral**, from whose terrace you can get a great view of the island-studded bay.
- The old warehouse district of **Katajanokka**, behind the cathedral, is worth a look. Its 19th-century brick buildings are being transformed into galleries, boutiques and restaurants.
- Stroll with the locals along the **Esplanadi** (behind the cathedral), a promenade buzzing with street life and cafés. On one side are the showrooms of some of the country's top designers, and on the other, the esplanade gardens. On summer afternoons, there is always some form of street entertainment. Between June and August, there's open-air folk dancing and music concerts at the Esplanade band stand.
- The **Nordic Arts Centre** (Pohjoismainen Taidekeskus) is one of the many museums on **Suomenlinna,** though the fortress island is well worth visiting for the parks alone. In the summer, special outdoor events are scheduled regularly – check with Tourist Information for a full list.
- The **Rock** or **Temppelia Ukio Church**, on Lutherinkatu 3, is a Helsinki landmark. Carved into a hill of solid rock, and looking for all the world like something out of *Dr Who*, only its copper dome is visible from the outside.
- There are open-air concerts every Sunday in July at **Kairopuisto park,** an island at Helsinki's south-east corner (very popular with romancing locals). Check with the Tourist Office for a full programme of events.
- For a walk on the wild side, head for the island **Pihlajasaar**, which is pretty much given over to countryside.
- Another island, **Seurasaari,** is a historical park lined with 19th-century houses. It makes for great picnicking, and the small beaches there are popular for swimming (though obviously only at the height of summer).

- **Hietaniemi beach** is popular for partying on warm summer evenings.

## SLEEPING

You'll find the **Hotel Booking Centre** in the west wing of the main station (Tel. 2288 1400). Open Sept. 1–May 31: 9am-5p.m., Mon.–Fri. (closed weekends) and June 1–Aug. 31: 9am–7pm Mon.–Sat. and 10am–6pm Sun. Hotels in Helsinki are often fully booked in summer; hostelling is a better bet.

**HOSTELS** Try the **Olympic Stadium youth and family hostel**, Pohjoinen Stadionintie 3b (Tel. 496071), 50–120mk with IYHF card. Located in the Olympic Stadium complex and reached by tram 3T or 7A from Mannerheimintie, just out of the station.

Eurohostel, at Linnankatu 9, right near the port (Tel. 622 0470) is spotlessly clean and welcoming. It has single and double rooms, and is open all year, price 120–185mk. ISIC reductions.

There's also **Erottajanpuisto**, Uudenmaankatu 9 (Tel. 642 169); **Kongressikoti**, Snellmaninkatu 15a (Tel. 135 6839); **Omapohja**, It. Teatterikuja 3 (Tel. 666 211); and **Union**, Unioninkatu 39a (Tel. 278 3854).

Extra beds in the busy summer months can be found at the **Summer Hostel Academica**, Hietaniemenkatu 14 (Tel. 1311 4334), open June–Aug. Head across Mannerheimintie from the station, and down Arkadiankatu, then Pohjoinen Rautatiekatu to the junction with Hietaniemenkatu. There's also **Kallio Youth Hostel**, Porthaninkatu 2 (Tel. 773 3429), open June 22–Aug. 31; and **Hotelli Satakuntalo**, Lapinrinne 1a (Tel. 695851) has dorm facilities and single rooms.

Refer to *Cheap Sleeps Europe 2000* for more options.

**CAMPING** The nearest campsite is **Rastila** (Tel. 316 551), 13km east of the centre. Take the metro from the station to Östra centrum, then bus 90, 90a, 96 or 98; first stop after the bridge. Open all year, around 25mk per person.

## EATING AND NIGHTLIFE

Apart from the excellent markets (the best is the Kauppatori at Market Square, and the nearby Kauppahalli covered market hall), there are plenty of stalls, fast food places and cafés, so the only problem with eating is the price. For a quick bite on the hoof (almost literally), try smoked reindeer meat from the food stalls in Kauppahalli. The less adventurous have plenty of other choices, including vegetarian snacks, authentic Italian and Vietnamese food, and kebabs. Along the waterfront, if you're lucky, you can get hold of freshly smoked fish sold directly from the boats.

Away from the markets, **Stockmann's** department store has a good basement food hall, and if you're splurging on a restaurant meal, you've the usual choice of Chinese, Indian, etc., or Russian. **Vanhan Kellari**, Mannerheimintie 3, is a good self-service, popular with students. Open till 1am. **Kasvisravintola**, Korkeavuorenkatu 3, has good vegetarian food. Open Mon.–Fri.: 11am-6pm, Sat.–Sun.: 12pm–6pm. Closes 5pm in summer.

At the first signs of summer, you'll see pavement cafés overflowing into the streets – the locals love drinking outdoors, and make the most of their short summer. Serious drinkers take shots of the local firewater, Koskankorva, mixed with fruit juice. The Kallio district, about a kilometre from downtown, is full of typical Finnish pubs and beer gardens. For trendier places, head for Uudenmaankatu, in the city centre. The following drinking dens are worth a try: **Hamlet** at Vilhonkatu 6; **Konig** at Mikonkatu 4; or **Kaarle XII** on Kasarmikatu 40. **KY Exit** at Pohjoinen Rautatiekatu 21 is popular with students. **Zetor** 'the tractor restaurant' at Kaivokatu 10 combines Finnish food, home-made ale, tractors and rock and roll! There is an Irish pub, **Molly Malone's** (Tel. 171 272), which has live Irish music at weekends, or try **O'Malley's**, at Hotel Torni, Yrjonkatu 26. For jazz, try **Storyville**, Museokatu 8.

Also check out the **Pub on wheels** (ask at the Tourist Office for details), which takes pretty much the same route through the centre of town as the 3T tram – only with beer thrown in! If you fancy joining the Finns as they liven up on the dance floor, head for Lady Moon on Kaivokatu 12 or DTM (Don't Tell Mama - a gay and straight crowd) at Annankatu 32. For something a little tamer, **Happy Days**, at Pohjoisesplanadi 2 is a fairly groovy hangout too.

If you're in Helsinki on **May Day** (April 30) or **Midsummer's Eve** (June 25), prepare yourself for a late night, as these holidays are celebrated by staying up all night dancing and drinking. Watch out, too, for the late-summer **Helsinki Festival** – two weeks of concerts, theatre shows and arts events.

There are about 30 **cinemas** in Helsinki. All films are shown in their original languages.

# Turku (Åbo) city phone code: 2

The national capital until 1812, Turku is Finland's oldest city. It's not actually known exactly how old the city is; Turku's age is counted from the oldest document recording its existence – a letter from the Pope in 1229. While Helsinki bears the mark of Russian influence, Turku is clearly more Swedish – in fact, one of the city's two universities still uses Swedish as its chosen language. Built at the mouth of the River Aura, the city today is an important commercial centre with an energetic cultural life.

If you're arriving on the ferry from Sweden, take the train or bus from outside the terminus to the city centre.

## TOURIST INFORMATION

The information office is at Aurakatu 4 (Tel. 2627 444), open Mon.–Fri.: 8.30am–6pm, Sat.–Sun.: 9am–4pm. The office for South-West Finland Tourism is at Lantinen Rantakatu 13 (Tel. 251 7333).

## SEEING

Another Finnish city built on water. You can get an overall feel for the place by following the **riverside walkways** along the banks of the Aura. Along the way are lively summer restaurants, cafés and art galleries. Look out, too, for the **museum ships** in the river. **Suomen Joutsen**, a sailing vessel open to the public, is anchored in the Aura and the museum ship *Sigyn* nearby is also worth a visit. From the Auransilta and Martinsilta Bridges, boats leave on short excursions through the **Turku archipelago** to the neighbouring town of **Naantali**.

Away from the water, the main sights are the 12th-century **castle**, originally a Swedish stronghold, which now houses part of the **Provincial Museum** (entry 30mk) – get off the train at the harbour station to see it and save a 25-minute walk; **Turku Cathedral**, dating from the 13th century; the **Sibelius Museum**, housing many instruments and the composer's personal possessions; and the **Luostarinmäki Museum**, where craftsmen put on live demonstrations of their skills in an old-style street.

## SLEEPING

**HOSTELS** Kaupungin Retkeilymaja (Hostel Turku) at Linnankatu 39 (Tel. 2316578). 128 beds in dorms and small rooms. Take bus 10 or 20 from the station to the Market Square; from here or the ferry terminus take bus 30, getting off at the Martinsilta Bridge. Reception open 3pm to midnight, 60–120mk and 20mk for sheets.

Turisti-Aula (Tel. 231 1973) is central and very good. One block north of Käsityöläiskatu, it costs from 120mk single to 250mk double. **CAMPING** On the island of Ruissalo (Tel. 258 9249), 10km out. Take bus 8 from Market Square. Buses are infrequent, and it's a 20-minute ride. Facilities are good, with a decent restaurant and beach nearby. It also has a sauna.

## EATING

Head straight for the **Market Place** (8am–2pm), where the food's good, as cheap as you can expect to find, and is a sight in itself. There is also an evening market in the summer until 8pm. Just up the road is the **Kauppahalli** (covered market). It's open 8am–5pm and Saturday morning, and is full of delights. You'll find several **pizza** places around town, and the **department stores** have good cafés.The **restaurants** and **coffee houses** along the River Aura walkways are entertaining places to eat and drink on warm summer days.

# Tampere city phone code: 3

Finland's second city is a lake land of scenery and culture. Built on the banks of the Tammerkoski Rapids and on the isthmus between two big lakes, Tampere has another 180 smaller lakes within its city borders. Although an industrial centre, it has plenty going for it to make it worth a visit.

## TOURIST INFORMATION

At Verkatehtaankatu 2. Open June 1–Aug. 31: weekdays 8.30am–8pm, Sat. 8.30am–6pm, Sun. 11.00am–6pm; Sept. 1–May 31: weekdays only, 8.30am–5pm (Tel. 3146 6800).

## SEEING

**Särkänniemi** not only has an **amusement park**, but also an **aquarium**, **dolphinarium**, **planetarium**, children's **zoo** and the **Näsinneula Observation Tower**, which gives a good view of Tampere and its surroundings. The **Sara Hildén** modern art museum is also nearby (open 11am-6pm daily, closed Mon.).

The **Lenin Museum** at Hämeenpuisto 28 (open Mon.–Fri.: 9am-5pm, Sat.–Sun.: 11am–4pm) is possibly unique as the only museum outside Eastern Europe dedicated to the life of V. I. Lenin.

The **cathedral**, built in 1907, is worth a look for its altarpiece and frescoes, as is the **orthodox church** at Tuomiokirkonkatu 27, which, although it is the only neo-Byzantine church in the Nordic countries, has the largest bells in Finland.

## SLEEPING

**HOSTELS Uimahallin Maja Youth and Family Hostel** at Pirkankatu 10–12 (Tel. 222 9460) is central for most of the sights, open all year, and about one km from the railway station. Head down Hämeenkatu and bear right at the end.

The **YWCA** at Tuomiokirkonkatu 12a is close to the station. Open mid-June–late Aug. (Tel. 254 4020).

An alternative is the hostel and summer hotel **Domus**, at Pellervonkatu 9 (Tel. 255 000). Take bus 25 from the station; only open 1 June–31 Aug.

The **Interpoint Hämeenpuisto** at Hämeenpuisto 14 is also fairly central and nearer the station. Head down Hämeenkatu and Hameenpuisto, but only open 15 July–15 Aug. It costs around 40mk.**CAMPING Härmälä** camping has 400 beds in log cabins for 3 to 5 persons, open early May–late Aug. only (Tel. 2651 355 or, in winter, 6138 3210). It also hires out boats. Take bus 1 from outside Tourist Office. There's also Taulaniemi Camping at Taulaniemi, Teisko (Tel. 378 5753). It's 35km out, and open mid-May–mid-Sept only.

# Northern Finland

If you want to sail in the midnight sun and walk in the forests of Europe's remotest northern land, prepare yourself for a minimum of 20 hours' train travel from Helsinki, and buses and ferries which don't always connect as smoothly as one would like. The end goal is a unique experience, but to be honest it's easier to get up to the Arctic tundra through Norway or Sweden.

## Oulu and Rovaniemi

These are the most attractive of the northern towns. The trip from Helsinki to Rovaniemi, just 8km south of the Arctic Circle, isn't too bad – a direct 12-hour train journey – and this takes you to a handy starting point for your Lapland excursions.

The **Tourist Offices** at Oulu and Rovaniemi will supply you with all you need to know and suggest accommodation.

The Rovaniemi **youth hostel**, at Hallituskatu 16 (Tel. 344 644) is good and clean, open all year, and costs 90–120mk. Turn right outside the station and follow the signs. There's also **Matka Borealis** at Asemieskatu 1 (Tel. 342 0130) and **Outa**, Ukkoherrantie 16 (Tel. 312 474).

At Oulu, try any of the following: the **Summer Hostel Otokyla**, Haapanatie 2a (Tel. 530 8413); **Kortteeri**, Vellamontie 12 (Tel. 550 9700); **Oppimestari**, Nahkatehtaankatu 3 (Tel. 884 8527); or **Valkkyla**, Kajaanintie 36 (Tel. 880 311).

# Southern Finland

This outdoor recreation paradise, with its numerous lakes and woods, is one of Europe's last wildernesses. Savonlinna is a good centre at which to base yourself. In this neck of the woods, you really ought to camp to get the feel of the Finnish outback. The Tourist Office can arrange canoes and bikes for you.

## Savonlinna

This is Frontier Land. Yet Savonlinna, six hours from Helsinki, and not far from the Russian border, is a pretty spa town fashionable 150 years ago with the Russian aristocracy. The centre – a cluster of islands linked by bridges – has more charm than any of the other towns in the Lake Region.

Don't wait on the train for the main station at Savonlinna; get off at the stop near the centre, Savonlinna Kauppatori, as you're nearer the **Tourist Office** here. It's at Puistokatu 1 and is open in early June and late Aug. 8am–6pm every day, late June–late Aug. to 10pm every day, and 9am–4pm Mon.–Fri. on other dates (Tel. 517 510).

At the heart of the town, on a small island, is the medieval castle of **Olavinlinna**, with the old wooden houses of **Linnankatu** surrounding it. Take the English guided tour of the castle.

During most of July, the **opera festival** takes place, and it fills up beds at an incredible rate. Tickets are expensive.

Use the **open-air markets** for picnic provisions, and try to stay at the excellent **Malakias youth hostel** at Pihlajavedenkuja 6 (Tel. 533 283), 120-180mk, either a 15-minute walk along Tulliportinkatu and Savonkatu, or bus 2 or 3 from centre. Camp at Savonlinna Camping (Tel. 537 353) at Vuohimäki, 6 km from the centre, take bus 3. It costs from 80mk per tent.

## Imatra

Built next to the Karelian rapids on the Vuoksi river, the small town of Imatra in South Karelia is almost on the Russian border. The **Ukonlinna youth hostel** and **campsite** (Tel. 432 1270) **is** on the sandy shore of a lake in the forest. Despite the three km walk, or bus ride, it is a great place to relax.

# FRANCE

| | |
|---|---|
| Entry requirements | Passport |
| Population | 58.6 million |
| Capital | Paris (pop.: 10 million) |
| Currency | Franc |
| | £1 = approx. 9.8F |
| Political system | Republic |
| Religion | Mainly Roman Catholic |
| Language | French |
| Public holidays | New Year's Day, Easter, Labour Day (1 May), VE Day (8 May), Ascension Day, Whitsun, Bastille Day (14 Jul.), Assumption Day (15 Aug.), All Saints' Day (1 Nov.), Remembrance Day (11 Nov.), Christmas Day |
| International dialling codes | To France: int'l code 33 |
| | From France: 00 + country code |

Year 2000 is a great time to visit France. A year long celebration to mark the millennium is planned with unique festivities combining French *savoir faire* and *joie de vivre*. For example, a 1000 kilometre line of trees, the Méridienne Verte, will be planted along the Paris Meridian from Dunkerque, across the Pyrénées to Barcelona in Spain. On Bastille Day, 14 July, the world's largest picnic will take place along this line extending through 337 towns and villages. 'PeripheRock' will be an enormous free-to-all party encircling Paris on the ring road with music and dancing all night long on 21 June.

France is a wonderful country for rail travel. Eating and sleeping is cheap, getting around is easy, and a long and eventful history has left behind a wealth of attractions and pleasures to experience. Physically, it's a country of great diversity; a nation of ancient villages, walled medieval cities, châteaux-filled valleys, sun-drenched fields of grain and flowers, alpine vistas, and glamorous seaside resorts. And then there's Paris, city of landmarks, and still today one of the most romanticized cities in the world.

Because of the efficient and extensive rail network, you can make as much or as little of France as you want. It's just as possible to explore each region in depth as it is to take an overnight express straight to the Riviera, if time and tanning are of the essence.

France (Gaul) was part of the Roman Empire till the Germanic Franks moved in during the 5th century. Charlemagne was crowned by the Pope on Christmas Day 800, but after his death the French nobles tried to go it alone. More successful than most were the Dukes of Burgundy and Normandy. In 987 the Capetian dynasty began to centralize power, which led to a period of prosperity and trade, and the eventual emergence of Paris as the intellectual centre of Europe in the 13th century.

England's Norman kings held vast estates in France till the Hundred Years' War sent them packing. This further strengthened the French monarchy; a process which continued under the Valois and Bourbon kings, till Louis XIV said it all: *'L'état, c'est moi'* ('I am the state').

Under the Sun King (Louis XIV), literature and the arts flourished, and in the rest of Europe to speak French became the height of sophistication. From this high point things gradually turned sour, and heads began to roll with the revolution in 1789. The First Republic didn't last long; then out of the chaos emerged Napoleon and dictatorship. During the 19th century the French Empire continued to grow, with power changing hands constantly between democracy and dictatorship. The revolution of 1848 brought about the Second Republic, which was followed by a *coup d'état* and the dictatorship of Napoleon III (nephew of the first).

The Third Republic of 1870 survived until the German occupation of France in 1940. After Liberation the Fourth was created, and de Gaulle got the Fifth off the ground in 1958.

## FRENCH NATIONAL RAILWAYS
### (SOCIÉTÉ NATIONALE DES CHEMINS DE FER FRANÇAIS, SNCF)

Arguably Europe's best railway, with the most luxurious carriages travelling at the fastest speeds on the most extensive rail network. On the Sud-Est and Atlantique routes the high-speed TGVs (*trains à grande vitesse*) offer the only convenient services (Paris–Lyon– Marseille–Toulon and Nice), and are well worth the supplement. In general, though, supplements are required only on about 40% of journeys. The high-speed network is being expanded with huge investment, not only within France but to neighbouring countries, and has already included the Channel Tunnel link with England.

The network serves more than 2,500 destinations using four different types of trains: TGV; Eurocity; Corail; and Turbo-train. The non-supplement Corail trains are almost indistinguishable from the Eurocity in comfort and in many cases run at the same speed.

Strasbourg is only four hours away from Paris, with Berne just 4½ hours and Marseille only an incredible four hours. You can get to Lyon, gateway to the Alps, in two hours, Bordeaux is three hours from Paris, and the Spanish border is just over five hours away.

Lille and the Channel Tunnel are connected by the TGV Nord route, the tunnel being under two hours from Paris and Lille just one. There's been a breakthrough too for Eurostar passengers using Lille as a TGV hub. Without having to stop at Paris, passengers coming from London (and Brussels) can go direct from Lille to Brittany, the south-east and and the south-west. This makes the journey time of, for example, London–Bordeaux only seven hours.

Further improvements to the TGV will give more powerful units, which will cut inter-city times by up to an extra 20%, and sleeper services are also in the pipeline. And by the year 2001, the completion of the high-speed line between Valence, Marseille and Montpellier will cut the travel time between Paris and Marseille to just three hours. The next development is the TGV Est route, which by 2005 will bring Strasbourg to within 2 hours 30 minutes of Paris, with onward connections into the heart of Europe. Future projects include the possibility of tilting TGVs, based on the super-fast Italian Pendolino trains, to be used on routes such as the French Riviera lines.

There are two special overnight trains from Calais to the **French Riviera**. Depending on the season they may call at Paris Nord, but no change is required (see Thomas Cook timetable 13). These trains have no seating accommodation, so you will have to go for either a sleeper or a couchette at about £9 extra.

If your main aim is to get to the French Alps from London, consider the Eurostar **Snow Trains**, an eight-hour service laid on to transport skiers from Waterloo to Moutiers and Bourg-St-Maurice (see Part One of this guide for details).

As with most other aspects of French life, the train network is centred on Paris, so if your route is via Paris, generally you're OK, but if you're crossing France from east to west, your impression of SNCF will be somewhat less glowing.

**PASSES AVAILABLE** The **Inter-Rail Pass** has been broken down into zones, so you don't have to pay for travel to areas you will not be visiting. For £129 you can tour a single zone for 22 days (over-26s pay £179). France is in Zone E, along with Luxembourg, Belgium and the Netherlands. **Eurail** passes are valid, and a **Euro Domino** ticket is also available. (For further details on Euro Domino tickets and the eight Inter-Rail zones, refer to the relevant sections in Part One of this guide.)

**BIGE** tickets give a reduction of around 20% on travel within France to students under 26, and the **BIJ** ticket gives discounts of around 20% on trains leaving France for other European destinations, again to under-26s. Contact rail operator Wasteels at Victoria Station, next to platform 2, London SW1V 1JT (Tel. 020 7834 7066).

**CARTE 12-25** This scheme for the under-26s offers up to 50% reductions on TGVs (depending on availability) and up to 50% reductions on off-peak ('blue period') and 25% off tickets during the 'white period'. Valid for one year from the date of the first journey, it costs £28 (270F). The card is valid in first or second class. Similar schemes, called **Carte Enfant** and **Carte Senior**, are available for those under 16 and over 60 respectively. Couples (married or cohabiting) can take advantage of the **Découverte à Deux** tariff for discounts of up to 25%. Ask at SNCF offices.

**THE 'BLUE' AND 'WHITE' TARIFF CALENDAR** (not applicable to TGV's)
The French Railways tariff calendar is colour coded as follows:

'Blue' (off-peak) period: generally 10 am Mon.–12 noon Fri. and 0.01 am Sat.–3pm Sun.

'White' (standard) period: generally 12 noon–12 midnight Fri.and 3pm Sun.–10 am Mon., plus some French public holidays.To help you plan your trip(s), you are supplied with a copy of the tariff calendar when you buy your 12-25 Card.

**WHERE TO BUY YOUR RAILCARD** Take your passport, as proof of your age, and a passport-size photograph to the Rail Europe Travel Centre, 179 Piccadilly, London W1V OBA (Tel. enquiries: 08705 848 848).

**FAMILY TRAINS** 'Family trains' run on 11 long-distance routes, mainly from Paris, but also from Nice and Nantes. Each train has fully-equipped play areas where young children can while away the journey as their parents look on. Special menus are available for family groups and there are even power points for baby's bottle-warmer. There is no additional cost and children under four travel free if they don't occupy a seat. If they do, quarter-price fares are charged – but this only applies to family trains. Provided at least four full-fare-paying passengers, including at least one under 12, are in a group, a whole compartment may be reserved.

**ROVER TICKETS** Those resident outside France and Britain could consider the new BritRail Pass, Eurostar and Euro Domino (details in Part One). There is also a France Railpass for USA residents.

**EURAIL BONUSES** Free: Digne–Nice or vice versa on the Chemins de Fer de la Provence.

P&O Stena offer the following discounts to passengers: 50% reduction on normal fares for the ferry crossings Calais–Dover, Cherbourg–Portsmouth and 30% reduction on the normal fare of the Le Havre/Portsmouth sailing.
Sea France offer a 50% reduction on services between Dover/Calais.

## TRAIN INFORMATION

*Agents d'accueil* ('welcome officers') wear orange caps and armbands and help with travel queries and any problems, e.g. if you've had your backpack stolen. Rather than sit in information offices, they are usually on the platforms and are very approachable. English is spoken by rail staff at most major stations. At the ticket barriers in all French stations you'll see a bright orange machine. Use this to validate your ticket only if you've bought it in France. Otherwise ignore it. But if you have a French-purchased ticket, including *Résa* reservation/supplement cards (see below), you must validate it, or risk a fine.

**RESERVATIONS** Compulsory on Eurostar, Eurocity and TGVs as well as a few of the Rapide trains. On Eurocity services, the reservation charge is included in the supplement you'll have to pay. The supplement depends on distance – between 50F and 75F. Other optional reservations cost about 14F. Reservations can be made up to noon, for trains between 5pm and midnight on that day, and up to 8pm for trains from midnight to 5pm the following day. For trains to or from Paris, give yourself two–three days if possible.

If you are very well prepared, you can reserve up to four months in advance (and on the 12–25 Card, this could get you up to a 60% reduction). Eurocity services can be booked up to one hour before departure. It's a good idea to reserve on international trains and on days before public holidays.

On some services, the reservation ticket is known as *Résa*. Note that on these services you must validate the reservation ticket along with the main ticket.

**NIGHT TRAVEL** Sleeping services are good, but costly. A sleeper or couchette in France costs more than anywhere else in Europe. SNCF offer both 1st- and 2nd-class couchettes with four and six berths respectively. They cost about 80F and must be reserved in advance, not later than 8pm.

French Railways have introduced a brilliant new concept in budget night travel, the **Cabine 8**. This is a 2nd-class air-conditioned coach with compartments containing eight semi-reclined bunks that are completely free of charge to use. If you are contemplating a long-haul overnight journey in France, check to see if Cabine 8 coaches have been added to the train you intend to use (check this in the Thomas Cook timetable, in the French section). In view of their success, it is advisable to reserve your bunk, for the standard seat reservation fee.

Unless you're loaded with cash, avoid the TEN (Trans Euro Nuit) sleepers. Second-class sleepers are either (T3), three beds, or (T2), two beds.

**EATING ON TRAINS** Come prepared if you want to picnic, as surprisingly few stations have delicatessens selling fresh croissants, pâtés and cheeses. Instead, there are good but pricey restaurants and bars. You'd do far better going for a meal (which you can at least be sure will be good), rather than for a snack from the ridiculously priced mini-bar trolleys, from which a coffee, for example, will cost at least 12F.

**SCENIC TIPS** Train journeys anywhere in southern France will not disappoint. The Alps provide a spectacular backdrop on any run. If you just want to breeze through, consider the Paris–Turin route (10 hours) which goes via the 14 km Mont Cenis tunnel. For the best alpine scenery, change at Culoz or Aix-les-Bains, for Chamonix.

Or if you're heading for the coast, we recommend the run from Grenoble to Marseille (five hours), then Marseille–Genoa (be sure to sit on the right-hand side of the train on the Riviera stretch). All this journey along the Côte d'Azur is beautiful.

On the other side of the country, the lines between Clermont-Ferrand and Béziers, and Limoges and Toulouse provide fine upland scenery. The Perpignan–La Tour de Carol is another favourite, as is Valence–Briançon.

**BIKES** With more than 30,000 km of cycling trails in France, sight-seeing by bike is a good option. SNCF runs a Train and Bike (*Train et Vélo*) scheme, with rental from many stations from 50F a day (plus around 1,000F deposit). SNCF has complex rules for taking bikes on trains, but generally avoid rush hours, and remember that in regional areas there will be room only for a couple of bikes. Where trains allow bikes on at no extra cost, the timetable will have a blue cycle symbol on it.

**ADVANCE TICKETS** Tickets to and within France can be purchased in Britain at rail station Travel Centres and at Rail Europe Travel Centre, 179 Piccadilly, London W1V 0BA. Telephone 08705 848 848 for travel information and credit card bookings.

(Note: British Rail International, BR's former European ticket sales operation, has been taken over by SNCF. The French rail company has merged the two to form European rail specialist Rail Europe, which deals with Eurostar, Inter-Rail, Eurail, and French railways bookings. Address and telephone line as above.)

## TOURIST INFORMATION

There are more than 5,000 Tourist Information offices in France. They're called *Syndicats d'Initiative* or *Offices de Tourisme*. Those designated *Accueil de France* will help you out with your travel and accommodation problems, as well as booking a bed for you for a small fee. The French tourist literature is good and generally free. Always ask for a map. If you're touring a whole region in depth and require further information, look up the address and phone number of the Comité Régional de Tourisme, and contact them. You'll also find regional Youth Information Centres in some places. Tourism Offices are open all year, while Tourist Information Centres are open either in the summer or in the winter.

**ISIC BONUSES** Up to 40% reduction on long-distance coach journeys. Discounts on OTU car rental. 50% off all state museums, galleries, and theatres. 50–70F off Crous University accommodation between 1 June and 30 Sept.

**MONEY MATTERS** 1 franc (F) = 100 centimes.

In Paris, banks are open Mon.–Fri.: 9am–4.30pm without a break. Outside the capital, banks are often closed on Mondays, and each day for lunch from 1pm–3pm. More and more banks are now opening on Saturday mornings too. Beware: banks often close early the day before a Bank Holiday.

Shop around before exchanging currency, as banks vary with their commission charges. Not all banks have exchange services, but there are exchange counters at large train stations, airports, some post offices and bureaux de change. If you're arriving on a Sunday night, your best bet is the main station in larger cities, though commission charges average 10F and credit cards and some traveller's cheques are not accepted. French traveller's cheques are much more useful than those in sterling or dollars. Also, if relying on Eurocheques, note that not all banks take them.

**POST OFFICES** Open Mon.–Fri.: 8am–7pm, sometimes with a midday break, and from 8am–12noon on Saturdays. In big cities and at larger railway stations, post offices may be open later in the evenings, or on weekends. In Paris, the post office at 42 rue du Louvre is open 24 hours a day. Stamps can also be purchased from tobacconists, or any café or shop with a red Tabac sign.

**SHOPS** Usually shut around 12 noon–2pm and even until 3 or 4pm in the south. They generally open 9am–7pm and close Mondays. Some food shops, especially bakeries, are open Sun. mornings. Hypermarkets are huge shopping warehouses, including supermarkets and restaurants. They're usually good value. Some of the big names are Casino, Auchan, Carrefour, Leclerc, Attac, Franprix, Champion, Continent. They're usually open Mon.–Sat.: 10am–7pm, or until 10pm on late-opening nights. Some open Sunday mornings.

**MUSEUMS** Follow the same pattern as shops; you'll find many of the state-owned ones closed Tues., with municipal ones shutting Mon.

**TIPPING** Tipping is rife in France. In restaurants, the words service compris or sc on your bill means a tip is included. If you have a coffee or beer on the pavement, always leave some change for the waiter (you need not bother if you stand at the bar or counter).

## SLEEPING

**HOSTELS** Use the facilities offered in the Foyers des Jeunes Travailleurs in all major centres. These student hostels are usually more central and less strict than youth hostels (they don't make a fuss about unmarried couples, etc.).

The Accueil des Jeunes en France (AJF) has numerous hostels throughout France (5,000 beds in Paris alone).

Another organization, Union des Centres de Rencontres Internationales de France (UCRIF), operates 60 hostels throughout France, with 16 in Paris. B&B costs 65F–270F, depending on comfort levels, location and season.

There are about 300 youth hostels (*auberges de jeunesse*) which charge 40–85F per person, with an optional 20F breakfast (in Paris, reckon on about 120F). They can also sometimes sting you for extra 'residence' tax and bedlinen hire. For IYHF hostels, membership is obligatory. You can join up in France either at the head office at 10 rue Notre Dame de Lorette, Paris, or at major hostels. Refer to *Cheap Sleeps Europe 2000* for more options.

**HOTELS** Hotels offer some of the best value in Western Europe – even in Paris. They run on a 1–4-star system with the government fixing prices. These are posted on the back of hotel room doors, so always check you've been quoted the right price. One-stars start at about 100F and are perfectly adequate, so long as you don't expect the luxury of a bath. In France a shower or bath (and often breakfast, too) will almost always cost extra. Try to reduce your costs if you're travelling in a group by getting a third bed put in the room – this'll cost an extra 30% or so and is cheaper than another room.

**CAMPING** Camping should present no problems in France as nearly every major town has at least one site, and there are more than 9,000 nationwide. At some you can rent tents or caravans. They also operate on a 1–4-star system. The International Camping Carnet is advisable at most sites – you can buy it at site offices on the spot.

## EATING AND NIGHTLIFE

Here in France, eating has become an art. Meals are a social occasion: there's no such thing as a hurried snack, and the midday lunch break is at least a 12-till-2 affair, often involving a steady flow of wine. Cafés are for sitting and watching the world go by, not for cheap eating. If you're desperate for a coffee, check the price and size of cup first, make it last and enjoy the atmosphere as long as possible, because that's what you're paying for.

The chain self-service restaurants, such as Flunch, are often cheap and cheerful, but don't expect the best in French cuisine. Vegetarians be warned, some chain restaurants (e.g. Quick) will often refuse to serve beer if you do not order a meat main course!

Wine is cheap and the parks free, so it's far better to get a baguette (about 4–5F) under your arm and head for the corner charcuterie and crémerie, where you can choose from a huge selection of cheeses (*chèvre* is goat). Fortunately, supermarkets are reasonable and of a high standard.

Look out for branches of Prisunic, Monoprix, Uniprix, or Codec.

Eating out in the evening will give you a great insight into the French lifestyle, and the fixed-price menus are always a safe bet, with bread usually included in the price. Try where possible to sample the local dishes. Each region has its own specialities based on local produce.

Typically French dishes include cassoulet from Toulouse (white bean stew with meat or poultry), Alsatian sauerkraut, bouillabaisse from Marseille, beef bourguignon, and steak and fries (bought alone, chips will often come with dollops of mayonnaise). French salads are fabulous, especially in the south, where the Nice version comes with olives, tuna, egg and anchovies.

## Calais

Calais does not have much going for it, but you may find yourself stuck here waiting for a ferry or train. It is some walk into the town; the bus stops running late at night and a taxi is expensive. The youth hostel, the Centre Européen de Séjour, is on av. Maréchal de Lattre de Tassigny (Tel. 03 21 34 70 20). It's set on the beach within walking distance of place d'Arme. Alternatively, try the cheap hotels in town; the Hotel du Beffroi, 8/10 rue Gershell (Tel. 03 21 34 47 51), 150 – 320; Hotel Victoria, 8 rue du Commandant Bonningue (Tel. 03 21 34 38 32) 160 – 300F.

The Tourist Office and accommodation service is at 12 bd Clemenceau (Tel. 03 21 96 62 40).

## Lille

If you're arriving in France via the Channel Tunnel you may find yourself with time to kill in Lille. This is no hardship, as the town is one of the most inviting in the area. The international hub for **Eurostar** services has a historic maze of pedestrianized streets at its centre; ask for a map from the **Tourist Office** at place Rihour (Tel. 03 20 21 94 21). It's easy walking distance of the brand new **Euralille** Eurostar station. There's plenty to see in the Old Town, including the **Grand Palais**, the **Museum des Beaux Arts** (the second most important in France), and a cracking **market** at Wazemmes.

Although Lille has been French for nearly 700 years, it still feels Flemish – not surprising, as it is only just across from Brussels. The Flemish influence is obvious when it comes to food: mussels, chips and beer is the good old standby, but more substantial fare can be had from the many (quite pricey) brasseries and bistros. In fact, Lille has something of a reputation for food, having been voted (along with Paris and Lyon) one of the top three gastronomic destinations in France.

Students make up a quarter of the population, so as you'd expect, there's a sparkling nightlife.

Try to avoid staying overnight, as cheap accommodation is not plentiful (though if you're stuck, try around central Grande-Place). Best bet is to make use of the Tourist Office's free accommodation booking service. There is a **youth hostel** at 12 rue Malpart (Tel. 03 20 57 08 94), and **summer camping** in the village of Bondues, 10 km north of Lille, at Le Ramiers, Bondues (Tel. 03 20 23 13 42).

## EUROSTAR CONNECTIONS

Lille and the Channel Tunnel are linked by the TGV Nord route. With Lille being only an hour from the tunnel, Eurostar passengers have the advantage of using Lille to bypass Paris, and travel directly to Brittany and the south-west. Lille is the gateway to France's high-speed TGV rail network, with connections to Lyon (three hours), Bordeaux (5 hours 15 mins), Nice (eight hours), Nantes (four hours), Marseille (5 hours and 45 mins) and other destinations. The new TGV high-speed service between Lille and Geneva cuts travel between Britain and Switzerland to seven hours.

Further improvements in the pipeline mean that by 2001, the French Riviera will be six hours from London, and when the St Pancras–Channel Tunnel link is completed in 2007, another half hour will be slashed from the journey.

# Rouen

Many Inter-Railers, *en route* to Paris, pass through Normandy without stopping, and that's a real pity. It's a pretty area, with a fascinating history.

Situated on the Seine, Rouen – 'city of a hundred spires' and the capital of upper Normandy – is a beautiful medieval town, perhaps best known for the burning of Joan of Arc.

## TOURIST INFORMATION

At 25 place de la Cathédrale (Tel. 02 32 08 32 40); during summer open Mon.–Sat.: 9am–7pm, Sun.: 9.30am–12.30pm, 2.30pm–6pm; winter, shut Sundays. They will hand out useful leaflets and help you find a cheap room. **Amex** is at 1-3 Place Jacques Leilieur (Tel. 02 32 08 19 20).

## SEEING

There's a fine collection of beautiful half-timbered houses in the **Old Town**, which dates from the 12th century. A circular walking tour (ask at the tourist office) enables you to appreciate the main sites. The cobblestone **Rue du Gros-Horloge**, adjacent to the tourist office, connects the **Old Market Place** to the **cathedral**. The Old Market Place was where Joan of Arc was burnt at the stake in 1431, at the age of 19. It now contains the **Ste Jeanne D'Arc** national monument, a church and a small covered market, all designed by Arretche.

Notre Dame Cathedral dates from the 12th century and is a fine example of Gothic architecture. Rouen has many fine churches; perhaps the most notable is **St Maclou** for its large five-panelled porch. The nearby **St Maclou Cloister** at 184–186 rue Martainville should also not be missed. This tranquil cloister is one of the last examples of a medieval plague cemetery and was used as a charnel house until the 18th century.

## SLEEPING

Cheap rooms are plentiful and many are in the heart of the old city. Tourist Information will assist.

**HOTELS** Near the station at rue de Cordier 32, is the **Hotel Normandya** (tel. 02 32 08 32 44) with singles and doubles at 110–160F. The **Hostellerie du Vieux Logis**, rue de Joyeuse 5 (tel. 02 35 71 55 30) has doubles from around 120F.

The **HOSTEL** is called Centre de Séjour at 118 boulevard de l'Europe (Tel. 02 35 72 06 45), and costs around 80F including breakfast. Take bus 12, direction Diderot, from the railway station. Alternatively, cross the river, turn left and walk along the river bank.

## EATING AND NIGHTLIFE

Seafood, pâté, Rouen duck, calvados (apple brandy) and the traditional Normandy ciders are all recommended. *Galettes* (whole wheat pancakes filled with meat, cheese or vegetables) and *crèpes* are cheap and filling. Most restaurants are good value and offer fixed menus. The many small bars offer cheaper snacks or just a single course, and fast-food burgers are also available. A cheap meal can be had at the **Maison des Jeunes**, 114 av. de Bretagne, close to the Centre de Séjour, and you'll find the greatest concentration of eating establishments in **Place de Vieux-Marché** and the area immediately north of there.

# Bayeux

This small city, with its medieval masterpieces – the cathedral and the world-famous Bayeux Tapestry – deserves at least a few hours' sightseeing. It is also noted for its connections with William the Conqueror.

Tourist Information is on Pont St Jean (Tel. 02 31 51 28 28), and will provide the usual assistance and information. Open 9am–6.30pm, shutting for lunch, and Sundays off season.

## SEEING

**Queen Matilda's Tapestry** (also known as the **Bayeux Tapestry**) is the 70-metre embroidered cloth that illustrates the story of the Norman Conquest of Britain. It is now magnificently displayed in the Cultural Centre on rue de Nesmond. Open May–mid-Sept. 9am–7pm, otherwise closed over lunchtime and with slightly shorter hours; last admission one hour before closure.

The **cathedral** was originally completed in 1077 and is now an impressive mixture of Norman and Gothic architecture. The **Baron-Gérard Museum** has fine displays of old paintings, lace, porcelain and tapestries. A combined ticket for four museums can be obtained. Also worth a look is the **Museum of the Battle of Normandy 1944** in boulevard Fabian Ware. Open 9am–7pm in the summer, the museum recounts the Allied invasion of France June–Aug. 1944 and is near a British military cemetery.

## SLEEPING

**HOSTELS** The Centre d'Accueil Municipal, 21 rue des Marettes (Tel. 02 31 92 08 19), is about 2.5 km from the station; ask at Tourist Information. Auberge de Jeunesse Family Home, centrally located at 39 rue Général de Dais (Tel. 02 31 92 15 22), is a 17th-century labyrinth of rooms with about 130 beds. It's good value at about 100F. Follow the signs from the station.

**CAMPING**

The campsite is at blvd d'Eindhoven (Tel. 02 31 92 08 43), open March–Nov.

# Mont St-Michel

Although not on a direct railway line, the effort of getting to Mont St-Michel will be well rewarded. One of France's most famous sights, the 'marvel of the Western world' is a solitary village and 11th-century abbey perched dramatically on a small island. Linking the mount to the mainland is a causeway that occasionally floods completely at high tide. A tide table is available from the local **Tourist Office**, located at the entrance to the mount (Tel. 02 33 60 14 30). Open Mon.–Sat.: 9am–7pm.

## GETTING THERE
Mont St-Michel is on the boundary between Normandy and Brittany. Take the train from Caen to Rennes and get off at Pontorson. Mont St-Michel is about 16 km away and reached by STN bus, from opposite the station – about seven buses a day during summer. Be warned: this is France's top attraction, so be prepared for hordes of tourists.

## SEEING
The splendid **abbey** dominates the island and is open 9.30am–11.45am and 1.45pm–4.15pm (to 6pm May–Sept., all day during high season), closed on holidays. The guided tour lasts around 45 minutes, at about one-hour intervals. The **Merveille** or 'marvel' is a group of superb early 13th-century buildings and is aptly named. The **village** is a steep labyrinth surrounding the abbey and is itself encased in **ramparts** which have good views of the bay.

## SLEEPING
Mont St-Michel has 15 or so hotels, all expensive. The nearest **hostel** is at the Centre Duguesclin, rue Patten, Pontorson (Tel. 02 33 60 18 65), open June–Sept., 0.8 km from Pontorson station. **Camping** sites are better situated, at Camping du Mont St-Michel (Tel. 02 33 60 09 33), with 350 places. It may get crowded in the summer, but do not be tempted to sleep rough on the causeway or beach, as the tides are unpredictable and dangerous.

# Brittany

You'll curse the rail network if you want to visit this region in depth. Local trains all connect with the main Paris–Brest line rather than other nearby towns. On the new TGV line from Paris, it now takes only just over two hours to Nantes and around two hours to Rennes.

For accommodation and general information on the area, visit the Rennes **Tourist Office** on the Pont de Nemours, Mon.: 2pm–6pm, Tues.–Sat.: 9am–6pm (Tel. 02 99 67 11 11). There is a **campsite** (Tel. 02 99 36 91 22), open April–Oct., and a **youth hostel** at 10–12 Canal St-Martin (Tel. 02 99 33 22 33).

From **Rennes**, it's possible to make a day trip to the impressive walled port of **St Malo**, formerly a pirates' stronghold, and preserved almost intact.

Pushing south, **Nantes** has a majestic 15th-century ducal palace, as well as a very good museum devoted to Breton folklore. There are two **youth hostels** in Nantes, one at 2 place de la Manu (Tel. 02 40 29 29 20) and the other at 9 bd. Vincent Gâche (Tel. 02 40 12 24 00). There is also a **campsite** (Tel. 02 40 74 47 94), open all year.

The historic town of **Concarneau** is also worth a trip. Take the train to Rosporden and then a railway bus (free on Eurail) to Concarneau. Check your timetable first, because the bus doesn't connect with every train.

## The Loire Valley

No stretch of river anywhere can match the Loire for its treasure trove of royal castles, fine furnishings and art. In a valley full of grand châteaux and palaces, perhaps the most impressive are **Chambord** and **Chenonceau.** To do justice to the area would take at least a week. Fortunately for the Eurorailer, most of the celebrated architecture lies between Angers and Blois, a distance of about 129 km. Most of the châteaux are easily accessible, all shutting around 6pm.

Where you base yourself depends on your style. There are campsites everywhere, and youth hostels at Saumur, Tours and Blois. Wherever you end up, go along to the train information desk in the area and pick up one of the local timetables that give details for all the smaller stops.

**BLOIS** Gateway to the Loire Valley. See the **bishops' palace**, the **château**, the **old quarter** – all charmingly set among fine churches, cobblestone lanes and gardens. The campsite **Camping du Lac de Loire** at Blois (tel. 02 54 78 82 05) is good. It's about five km out of town: take a bus or taxi from the station, or the métro to Port Maillot and then the campsite bus. The last bus from Blois leaves at 6.15pm.

**TOURS** For those who prefer a cheap hotel, it's best to base yourself here in this historic city. Tours was once the capital of the kingdom of France. For places to stay, try first around the station, where rooms are plentiful. Try **Mon Hôtel** at 40 rue de la Préfecture (Tel. 02 47 05 67 53) or **Hôtel Comté** behind the station, at 51 rue Auguste Comté (Tel. 02 47 05 53 16).

If you're out of luck, the Tourist Office is just in front of the station at place Maréchal Leclerc (Tel. 02 47 70 37 37). Open Mon.–Sat.: 9am–12.30pm, 2pm–9pm, Sun.: 10am–12.30pm, 4pm–9pm). For a small fee they will fix you up with a room and give free advice on bus tours, etc., to the châteaux. If you can't afford the bus, you can rent bikes at the station for around 85F a day (plus a hefty deposit).

The town itself, like Blois, has a picturesque **old quarter** and a former **bishops' palace** which now hosts the **Musée des Beaux Arts**.

Further down the line, **Saumur** and **Angers** both have very impressive castles perched on high, overlooking the Loire and Maine respectively. If you prefer to stay at this end of château country, the *Syndicat d'Initiative*, opposite the station at Angers, will find you a room for a small charge.

# Paris

Paris is undoubtedly one of the best loved cities of the world. It is everything you've heard and more – art and architecture of a richness, variety and splendour that has to be seen to be believed, culture and cuisine of the impeccable standards. By day and by night Paris effortlessly captivates and charms the hearts of visitors with an air of excitement and romance.

With an excellent public transport system and all the major sights within easy walking distance of each other, the city is easy to explore. And there's a lot to see: tree-lined boulevards, formal squares, cobbled courtyards, pavement bistros, street markets, buskers and mime artists – not to mention famous landmarks like the Eiffel Tower, Notre Dame and the Sacré Coeur.

First let's get the geography sorted. Paris has 20 *arrondissements* (districts) fanning out to the north and south of the Île de la Cité in the River Seine, the island site of the original settlement. The Seine divides the city into the Left Bank (*Rive Gauche*) and Right Bank (*Rive Droite*). Generally speaking, the Left Bank is the trendy, studenty and less expensive area, and the Right Bank is more classy, though both have *chic* galore.

**THE STATIONS** Paris is the hub of France's high-speed rail network. There are five international stations in the city: if you're heading off, make sure you know which station your train leaves from.
1. **Austerlitz** serves southern France, Spain and Portugal.
2. **Est** serves Germany, Switzerland and Austria.
3. **Lyon** serves the south-east of France, Italy and Switzerland. TGVs from here include services to Geneva (3hrs 30 mins), Lausanne (3hrs 45mins), Montpellier (five hours) and Nice (7hrs 15mins).
4. **Nord** serves Belgium, Holland, Scandinavia, Germany, the north

of France, and Britain's ferry entry ports of Calais and Boulogne. Eurostar trains also arrive, via the Channel Tunnel, at Gare du Nord.

5. **St Lazare** serves Britain's entry ports of Dieppe and Le Havre. There is a sixth station, **Gare Montparnasse**, in the south of the city. It serves Brittany and Aquitaine, and runs TGVs (at 186mph) to Bordeaux (three hours), Toulouse (4 hrs 30 mins), Rennes (2 hours), Nante (2hrs 15 mins), Vannes (3hrs 30 mins), Quimper (4hrs 15mins) and Brest (four hours). Use the central train information number and reservations number (see below).

## STATION FACILITIES

Plan well ahead, and use your timetables, as train information queues can be up to two hours long in the summer. At Gare du Nord, reservations for the TGV to Lyons are now made at an automated machine.

SNCF **buses** will get you from one station to another, or **métro** line 5 connects Est, Nord and Austerlitz (From Gare de Lyon, take métro line 1 to Bastille, then change to line 5. From Paris Nord, take line 5 to Austerlitz, Est and Lyon – change to line 1 at Bastille. Gare de Lyon can also be reached by buses 61 and 65 from Austerlitz and bus 65 from Est.) An additional route from Nord to Lyon is to take RER line B to Châtelet Les Halles, then RER line A to Lyon (much faster).

Each station has **left-luggage** lockers, **bars**, **cafés**, **shops**, **toilets**, **washing facilities** and **waiting rooms** – normally open from early morning well into the evening. If you arrive on a train after midnight, you will find a left-luggage locker and a vending machine, but don't expect a bureau de change or Tourist Office to be open.

**Austerlitz** has train **information** daily 7am–10pm (Tel. 00 33 836 353535) – central no. for all SNCF and **reservations** 8am–7pm (Tel. 01 45 65 60 60). Use both these numbers for all stations, it's a central telephone line. The station closes 0.30am–5.30am. For **Est**, train information and reservations are open the same hours as Austerlitz (same telephone numbers), though the station is shut for the slightly shorter time of 1.15am–5.45am. There are **post office** facilities at both these stations (8am–7pm, half day Sat.).

Lyon and Nord, the two big stations in the north of the city, close 1am–4am and 2am–5.45am respectively and there are **post office** facilities at both stations, Mon.–Fri.: 8am–7pm, till noon on Saturday (rue Diderot for Gare de Lyon).

**EURAIL AID OFFICES** Gare de Lyon, Espace Voyages (Tel. 01 53 33 11 67)
Garde de Nord, Bureau Information Espace Grandes Lignes, (Tel. 01 55 31 52 02)
Garde de St Lazare, Service International, (Tel. 01 53 42 27 62)

## TOURIST INFORMATION

The main office of the Paris Convention and Visitors' Bureau is at 127 av. des Champs Elysées (Tel. 01 49 52 53 54) (métro to Charles de Gaulle-Étoile). Open daily (during the summer): 9am–8pm. The English-speaking staff will give you information on Paris and the Île de France. They also run a wide-ranging accommodation-finding service on a commission basis. For recorded Tourist Information on each week's events in English, phone (01) 49 52 53 56. There are also tourist bureaux at all the main railway terminals and the Eiffel Tower.

**ACCUEIL DES JEUNES EN FRANCE (AJF)** This non-profit-making office for the young is at 119 rue St Martin (Tel. 01 42 77 87 80), across from the Pompidou Centre (Beaubourg). Take the métro to Les Halles or Rambuteau. Open Mon.–Sat.: 9am–6pm. They'll find you a bed or a place in a Foyer for 120F and upwards. They also have offices at Gare du Nord (Tel. 01 42 85 86 19), and at 139 boulevard St-Michel (Tel. 01 43 54 95 86), open June and July only. The policy these days seems to be to pay the full accommodation price to AJF when booking, so remember to change money before joining the queue. To get the best rooms, be in the queue by 8am.

**UNION DES CENTRES DE RENCONTRES INTERNATIONALES DE FRANCE (UCRIF)** This centre for young tourists is at 27 rue de Turbigo (Tel. 01 40 26 57 64). It can arrange reservations in most regions of France as well as Paris, and gives advice on travel. There's a restaurant and a hostel too (B&B for 70F-280F, depending on location).

**USIT VOYAGES** 12 Rue Vivienne, 75002 Paris (Tel. 01 42 44 14 00), Mon.–Fri.: 9.30am–6pm, Sat.: 1pm–4.30pm. The youth travel specialists (with English-speaking staff) will help you with all travel requirements, and fix you up with an ISIC (métro: Odéon or Luxembourg).

**FÉDÉRATION UNIE DES AUBERGES DE JEUNESSE (FUAJ)** 27 rue Pajol (Tel. 01 44 89 87 27). The central booking facility for IYHF hostels in Paris, France and also for some European destinations. They can also arrange sightseeing coaches and various other services.

**INTERNATIONAL STUDENT TRAVEL OFFICES** Paris Council Travel, Place de L'Odeon 1 (Tel. 01 44 41 89 89); and CTS France, rue de Carmes 20 (Tel. 01 43 25 00 76).

## ADDRESSES

**POSTE OFFICE AND POSTE RESTANTE** 52 rue du Louvre (Tel. 01 40 28 20 00), open 24 hours a day (métro: Louvre)

**AMEX** 11 rue de Scribe, Mon.–Fri.: 9am–5.30pm, Sat.: 9.30am–5pm (Tel. 01 47 77 77 07) (métro: Opéra). Also 26 Avenue de L'Opéra (Tel. 53 29 40 39), 2 Rue St Eleuthère (Tel. 42 23 93 52), 4 Rue Louis Blériot (Tel. 47 77 71 59) and 38 Avenue de Wagram (Tel. 42275880)

**UK EMBASSY** 35 rue du Faubourg St Honoré (Tel. 01 44 51 31 00).

The British Consulate is at 16 rue d'Anjou (Tel. 01 42 66 38 10) (métro: Concorde or Madeleine), Mon.–Fri.: 9.30am–12.30 and 2.30pm–5pm.

**IRISH EMBASSY** 12 av. Foch, 16e (Tel. 01 44 17 67 00) (métro: Charles de Gaulle-Étoile)

**US EMBASSY** 2 rue St Florentin (Tel. 01 43 12 23 47)

**CANADIAN EMBASSY** 35 av. Montaigne (Tel. 01 44 43 29 00) (métro: Franklin-Roosevelt)

**AUSTRALIAN EMBASSY** 4 rue Jean Rey (Tel. 01 40 59 33 00) (métro: Bir-Hakeim)

**NEW ZEALAND EMBASSY** 7 rue Léonard de Vinci (Tel. 01 45 00 24 11) (métro: Victor Hugo)

**24-HOUR CHEMIST** Pharmacie Dhéry, 84 avenue des Champs-Elysées (Tel. 01 45 62 02 41) (métro: George V), open 24 hours.

**EMERGENCY SERVICES** Ambulance 15; Police 17; Fire 18

**SOS HELPLINES** Doctors: (Tel. 01 47 07 77 77.)

## GETTING ABOUT

The Paris **métro** is one of the world's best underground systems and you're bound to use it at some point to get quickly round this sprawling city. It's cheap and efficient. Trains run from 5am to 12.45am. Lines are numbered but referred to by their final destinations. Buy tickets in *carnets* of 10 for 52F and hold on to them till the end of your journey. The same tickets can also be used on the **buses** – validate them in the machine on the bus, using two if crossing a zone – and central Paris **RER** trains.

**Tourist passes** (known as Paris Visite) are valid on both métro and buses, and available for one, three or five days, over three or four zones. Buy from Tourist Offices, in the main métro and RER stations, SNCF stations and at Paris airports. They cost from 55F for three zones (not including airports).

Crime on the métro, including drug users and dealers, has caused problems for the authorities. Be especially careful late at night. Also beware of buying a ticket at anywhere other than an official booth – you are only asking to be ripped off.

## SEEING

The most famous and most popular sight (six million visitors a year), the **Eiffel Tower**, looks its best floodlit at night. Recent renovations have made great improvements, but it is still expensive to ride the 276m to the top. There are three stages of lifts, getting progressively more expensive the higher you go. It is possible to walk up the first two stages to save on the cost (20F and 42F), but if you use the lifts all the way there is a 59F charge. The queues can be long, even with all lifts in action; and make sure you check you're in the right queue. The view from **Sacré-Coeur** is just as impressive. Go at night on 14 July (National Day), to catch the spectacular hour-long fireworks display.

An alternative view can be had from the **Tour Maine-Montparnasse** (209m) at rue de l'Arrivée. The lift up is said to be the fastest in Europe, and it'll cost you 46F.

If you don't have much of a head for heights, you can always head in the opposite direction ... the **Paris Sewers**, at place de la Résistance 7e, offer an alternative perspective.

**TOURS** The famous *bateaux-mouche* cruises down the Seine are by far the best-value sightseeing option. Try to get on the river in the evening, when all the famous monuments are illuminated.

Leaving from Pont de l'Alma on the Right Bank, 40F will buy you a 1½-hr cruise with recorded commentary. (Don't take one of the over-priced lunch/dinner cruises – they're over 300F and definitely not worth it!)

You can even get boats all the way up the Canal St Martin, taking you through the quiet waters of the lesser-known areas of the city.

**Paris Vision** and **Cityrama** bus tours both have pre-recorded commentary and will give you a pretty comprehensive idea of the city. A two-day pass (135F, discounts available) for the **Paris L'Open Tour** allows you to get on and off as often as you like and stops at most notable sights. It uses double decker buses so the views are great. Shop around, as city tours vary from reasonably priced to extortionate.

**MUSEUMS** All state-owned museums in Paris are shut on Tues. and those owned by the city close on Mon. An ISIC will get you into most places for half price. There are more than 100 interesting museums in the city; pick up a leaflet on them from Tourist Information.

The **Museum and Monument Card**, available from métro stations, Tourist Office and major museums, permits direct entry to 75 museums and monuments in the Paris region. Valid for one day (cost 80F), three consecutive days (cost 160F) or five consecutive days (cost 240F); unlimited visits are permitted and access is immediate, avoiding the often lengthy queues. The card can be bought in advance, but your name and the date must be written on it on your first visit in order to validate it.

- **The Louvre**, métro: Pyramide, Cour Napoléon. Treasures include the Venus de Milo and the *Mona Lisa*. A new section includes the primary arts of Africa, Asia and the Americas. Open 9am–6pm, except Mon. and Wed.: 9am–10pm. On Mon. only certain rooms are open, and many departments close at 5pm or 5.30pm every day. Closed Tues. Entry is 45F, or 26F after 3pm. Under-26s are entitled to a reduction, it's free to those under 18, and it is half price to everyone on Sun. Remember, you must leave your hand luggage at the entrance. Queues are very long on Sat. and Sun.

Love it or hate it, it is impossible to miss the controversial 21m-high **Glass Pyramid** entrance in the courtyard of the Louvre. Designed by I M Pei, it houses the reception area, restaurants and shops, and has greatly expanded gallery and exhibition space.

- Housed in a former railway station, the wonderful **Musée d'Orsay**, exhibits works by the big name Impressionists. It is situated on the Left Bank, near the Tuileries. Closed Mon. Admission 40F, open 10am–6pm, from 9am on Sun. Reduced entry for 18–24-year-olds and ISIC holders. You can spend all day here or in the Louvre.

- **Georges Pompidou Centre**: Open again on January 1st 2000 after extensive refurbishment, the centre is home to just about every modern art form you can think of. Entrance is free, but special exhibitions and the cinema usually incur a charge of anything up to 40F. A special one-day pass is available. The centre (known as the 'Beaubourg') is a good place to meet trendy young Parisians and see interesting exhibitions. Closed Tues., it's open 12 noon–12 midnight; holidays: 10am–10pm.

- For button-pushers, the **Cité des Sciences et de l'Industrie**, at 30 av. Corentin-Cariou, will keep you occupied all day. A combination of science exhibitions, computer games, practical demonstrations and videos are all included in the 50F admission, (35F Saturdays), discount with an ISIC card. The Planetarium is included, but entry to the giant movie theatre is extra. Take buses 150, 152 or 250a.

- **Musée National du Moyen-Âge, Thèmes de Cluny**: 6 place Painléve (corner of blvd St Michel and blvd St Germain). Open 9.15am–5.45pm, closed Tues (30F). Medieval art housed in a 15th-century mansion next to the Roman baths of Paris.

- **Musée de L'homme**: Palais de Chaillot, place du Trocadéro. Open 9.45am–5.15pm (30F). Very good anthropological museum – documentary films are shown daily.

- **Victor Hugo's House** at no. 6, Place des Vosges is now a museum.

- The **Museum of Jewish Art and History**, near the Marais Jewish quarter, highlights the social history of Jews in France.

- The new **Museum of Music**, at the Cité de la Musique at La Villette, follows the history of music from the Renaissance to today.

- At the Rohan Wing of the Louvre is the **Museum of Fashion and Textiles**.

- The **Picasso Museum** houses an exceptional collection of all phases of the artist's work in a sumptuous 17th century mansion.

- Fittingly located in the all-night neon district of Pigalle, the **Paris Museum of Eroticism**, at 72 bld de Clichy (Tel. 01 42 58 28 73) is a seven-storey house full of erotic objects and art from all over the world.

- Some of the more **off-beat** museums can make interesting diversions, among them: the Museum of Forgeries, the Doll Museum, the Perfume Museum, the Police Museum, the Spectacle Museum (which displays the glasses of the stars), the Wines Museum, the Lock Museum (which displays an exhibit that can kill or maim anyone trying to force entry), and a Curiosity Museum (a collection of illusions, based on the adventures of Alice in Wonderland). Ask at the tourist office for details.

**FREE PARIS:** If you're travelling on a shoestring, Paris is good news. This is a city whose character can easily be absorbed from the streets. All the big sights can be seen for nothing; just make sure you've got your walking boots on.

- Strolling along the banks of the **Seine** is one of the most pleasant of Parisian pastimes; the **embankments** are also an ideal place to picnic or sunbathe on a warm day.

- As an introduction to Paris, you can't beat the long walk from the **Arc de Triomphe** on the **Champs Elysées** down through the **Jardin des Tuileries**, via the **Place de la Concorde** and on to the **Louvre**. It takes in many of the most famous sights, and from the Louvre, it's not far to the bridges for **Île de la Cité**, **Notre Dame** and **Île St-Louis**. After a marathon like that, you may well feel justified in splashing out on a river boat trip from opposite Notre Dame (on the Left Bank), up to the **Eiffel Tower**. Top that with an evening in the **Latin Quarter** or **Montmartre**, and you might feel happy to call it a day.

  **THE CHAMPS ELYSÉES** The **Étoile** is the great circle at the western end of the Champs Elysées with 12 avenues radiating out from it, literally a 'star'. In its centre is the massive **Arc de Triomphe**, Napoleon's thank you to his army; note the sculpture of the Marseillaise by Rude. At the other end of the long and elegant Champs Elysées is the **Place de la Concorde**, regarded as the most beautiful square in the world. This is where Louis XVI, Marie-Antoinette and some 1,300 others met their death in the French Revolution.

  **THE LEFT BANK** St Germain-des-Prés, the oldest church in Paris, is surrounded by open-air restaurants and cafés and quiet little streets like **Place Furstemberg** which make a pleasant stroll.

- **Boulevard St-Michel**, the centre of Bohemian student life of the 1960s, still makes an interesting excursion. Sitting in one of the cafés along the Boul' Mich' in the Latin Quarter (so called because the Sorbonne students were lectured to in Latin in the Middle Ages), you're bound to make new friends.

- Also on the Rive Gauche is the beautiful church of **Les Invalides** with its golden dome and the mortal remains of Napoleon. A good view of **Notre Dame Cathedral** can be seen from **Square Renée Viviani**. **THE RIGHT BANK** Opposite the **Louvre** is Richelieu's **Palais Royal** where the Comédie Française is based, and not far from there is the oldest square in Paris, **Place des Vosges**, the beautiful Renaissance square built by Henri IV early in the 17th century.

- The **Sacré-Coeur** is the white dome that dominates all of Paris, built on the hill at **Montmartre**, the artists' quarter that flourished in the late 19th century when many of the Impressionist painters lived and worked there. The artists' quarter is more than the touristy **Place du Tertre**. Stroll along rue Norvins into rue des Saules and check out the **Lapin Agile**, a meeting point for writers and artists and very atmospheric. A climb to the dome of the Sacré-Coeur gives you an 80 km view over Paris, and is cheaper (15F) than climbing the Eiffel Tower. This is a great place to be in the evening, but watch out for pickpockets in this area. Even someone asking the time might be after your watch.

- **Île de la Cité** and **Île St-Louis**: The tiny island where Paris began in pre-Roman times is the Île de la Cité. The oldest bridge in Paris, the **Pont Neuf**, leads you to the statue of Henri IV and on to the **Palais de Justice** (law courts). The **Sainte-Chapelle** is a Gothic church built to house holy relics, dating from 1248. The relics have now been moved to Notre-Dame, but the stained-glass windows here can be viewed.

- **Notre Dame** is only a short walk from here; this 13th-century cathedral is the first church of Paris, where Napoleon was crowned and all national celebrations are staged (the cathedral itself is free to enter, but to climb the towers and visit the crypt costs 50F).

- **Pompidou Centre**: Reopening 1 January 2000,(see above) this eccentric building includes an excellent library with hundreds of daily newspapers, including most English and American ones. Entrance is free, but special exhibitions and the cinema may incur a charge. There's usually plenty of free entertainment in the form of fire-eaters and street artists outside.

  **PARKS** Pick up a copy of the 'green Paris' map at the Convention and Visitors Bureau and explore the infinite variety of styles found in the parks, squares and gardens of the city. They make good picnic venues too.

- The **Bois de Boulogne** is the wood at the western edge of the city with seven lakes, a waterfall, various sports facilities and a campsite. The **Bois de Vincennes** is the wood on the south-eastern edge. There's a zoo, a racetrack and a couple of museums out here too. The two most central parks are the **Jardin des Tuileries** and the **Jardin des Champs Elysées**; the **Luxembourg**, off blvd St Michel, is very picturesque, dotted with statues in a formally laid-out garden in French style. **Parc Monceau** features many follies, grottoes, magnificent specimen trees and rare plants.

## SLEEPING

**Campsites** are not central, and with so much to see in Paris the commuting may waste valuable time. Private accommodation is hardly heard of in Paris, so your choice is between a cheap hotel, a student hostel or a Foyer. Your choice will be dictated not just by your pocket but also by how many you are. Paris really is a city for lovers – it's often virtually the same price for a single or a double bed, so couples are on to a good deal in hotels, whereas singles are better off in a Foyer.

The average night in a hotel double room is anything upwards from 200F, for one star, and a single Foyer stay will be about 100F. Always ask hoteliers if there's nothing cheaper and get as many as possible into a room to bring the cost down. If you have any problems, try the UCRIF/AJF information office at Gare du Nord, but don't try sleeping there or you'll be ejected about 1am, or mugged. Also try the UCRIF/AJF and FUAJ offices listed under Tourist Information.

One easy way to book ahead is to use the London-based hotel reservation centre Accommodation Line, which specializes in small family-run hotels in Paris. This is most definitely not your cheapest option, but if you can afford to splurge, it will take the hassle out of phoning ahead, and also guarantees clean, centrally located and friendly accommodation (with up to triple or quadruple sleeping in some places). You pay in advance in Britain (from £20 per person per night). Write to 1st Floor, 46 Maddox Street, London W1R 9PB or Tel. 020 7409 1343. Refer to *Cheap Sleeps Europe 2000* for more options.

**IYHF HOSTELS** The main **youth hostel** is at 8 blvd Jules Ferry, near place de la République (Tel. 01 43 57 55 60). Take the métro to République. Cost is 110F and they'll help you find an alternative if they're full.

A 411-bed hostel called **Auberge de Jeunesse d'Artagnan** is at 80 rue Vitruve (Tel. 01 40 32 34 56). The nearest métro is Porte de Bagnolet. Open 24 hours.

There is also a temporary hostel, open July–15 Sept.; book through the Jules Ferry hostel.

**HOTELS** The number after the street name (e.g. 7e) refers to the *arrondissement* (district) of the city. Hotels in the 10e *arrondissement* are always within easy walking distance of Gare du Nord and Gare de l'Est. The best districts to concentrate your attention on for cheap hotels and basic B&B-type accommodation are around the Marais (4e), Le Quartier Latin (5e), The Louvre and Les Halles (1e and 2e) and Gare de Lyon (10e).

Try: Sibour Hôtel, 4 rue Sibour, 10e (Tel. 01 46 07 20 74); Adix Hôtel, 30 rue Lucien-Sampaix, 10e (Tel. 01 42 08 19 74); Le Centrale, 6 rue Descartes, 5e (Tel. 01 46 33 57 93); Jeanne d'Arc, 3 rue de Jarente, 4e (Tel. 01 48 87 62 11) and Hôtel des Alliés, 20 rue Berthollet, 5e (Tel. 01 43 31 47 52).

**FOYERS AND STUDENT HOSTELS**
**CIS Léo Lagrange**, 107 rue Martre Clichy (Tel. 46 28 3157, métro: Mairie de Clichy). **Maison des Clubs UNESCO**, 43 rue de la Glacière (Tel. 01 43 36 00 63, métro: Glacière).

**Hôtels des Jeunes (AJF)**, at 3 locations: 11 rue du Fauconnier, 6 rue de Fourcy 4e (métro: St-Paul) and 12 rue des Barres 4e (métro: Pont Marie), (all Tel. 01 42 74 23 45).

**Centres Internationaux de Paris (BVJ)**, has four locations, including 20 rue Jean-Jacques Rousseau 1e (Tel. 01 42 36 88 18, métro: Châtelet or Louvre).

Other independent hostels to try: **Foyer International d'Accueil de Paris**, 30 rue Cabanis (Tel. 01 45 89 89 15, métro: Glacière), the newly refurbished **Auberge International des Jeunes**, 10 rue Trousseau 4e (Tel. 01 47 00 62 00), 95F breakfast included; a **Maison International des Jeunes**, charging 110F for basic B&B, is at 4 rue Titon, métro: Faidherbe-Chaligny or Nation 11e (Tel. 01 43 71 99 21); catering for 18–30-year-olds only, it is open 8am–2am.

The two CISP (**Centre International de Séjour de Paris**) hostels may also be worth a try, but do not get good reports. They are at 6 av. M. Ravel (Tel. 44 75 60 00, métro: Porte de Vincennes) and at 17 blvd Hellerman (Tel. 01 44 16 37 38, métro: Porte d'Italie).

Two Foyers normally for women only: 234 rue de Tolbiac (Tel. 01 44 16 22 22), short stays only allowed during July and Aug., otherwise one month minimum (métro: Tolbiac).
**CAMPING** Camping du **Bois de Boulogne**, allée du Bord de l'Eau (Tel. 01 45 24 30 00). Take the métro to Porte Maillot, then bus 244, then a short walk. Shower facilities are limited and it costs around 70F per night; get there early in summer.
**STUCK IN PARIS WITH NO MONEY FOR A BED?** There are good overnight trains to Salzburg (from Est), Venice (from Lyon) and Copenhagen (from Nord).

## EATING AND NIGHTLIFE
Simple **picnics** have never tasted as good as they do in France, where it's easy to knock up a delicious impromptu feast of baguette, pâté, cheese, fruit and of course, wine. There are **open-air markets** and *boulangeries* (bakers) in every district while the *épiceries* (grocers) stay open till 7.30pm.

There are plenty of **fast-food** chains and **self-service** cafés, though it's often just as cheap to look for a French restaurant that offers a *menu du jour*, and eat real French cuisine – for once at a price you can afford. The areas round rue de la Huchette and rue Mouffetard in the **Latin Quarter** make good hunting ground for reasonably priced restaurants. Around the La Huchette area, though, watch out for the plate throwing – it gets excessive at times. For good, cheap French restaurants, try the street Grégoire de Tours.

If you want a change from French food, there are plenty of alternatives provided by the numerous immigrants from France's ex-colonies. The centre of the **North African** (Algerian, Tunisian, Moroccan, etc.) restaurant area is between rue St Jacques and blvd St Michel; there are also many Greek and Italian restaurants here.

Often the best value set menus are in **Chinese** restaurants. Try the Palais de Chine for especially good value. It's at 31 rue St Jacques, off the blvd St-Germain.

For those wanting to eat at **student restaurants** on their ISIC, call at CROUS, 39 av. Georges Bernano (métro: Port Royal), open Mon.–Fri. 9am–5pm, for a list of all the places you can eat for under 25F in this scheme. CROUS is shut during June and July.

**A few suggestions:** Crêperie St Germain, 27 rue St André des Arts; Chartier, 7 rue du Faubourg-Montmartre – about 65F for three courses and a drink in a very traditional restaurant; Restaurant des Beaux Arts, 11 rue Bonaparte – good cheap set menus; expect a really good set meal with wine from 70F; Country Life vegetarian restaurant, 6 rue Daumou, Mon.–Fri.: 11.30am–2.30pm; Crêperie de la Houff, 9 rue Mouffetard; Au Grain Folic, 24 rue de la Vieuville, Montmartre, 7pm–10pm, small but good vegetarian. Maison Berthillion, 31 rue St-Louis-en-l'Ile, has the city's best ice cream, but expect to queue.

There's an active **theatre, opera** and **cinema** scene – for details of what's on, buy *Pariscope*, or read the local listings in the various English language publications found at tourist offices.

The area along the Seine on the Left Bank is best for affordable **jazz** and **rock** clubs. Le Caveau de la Huchette, 5 rue de la Huchette, is known to all Parisian students as their informal club, but they ask 60F (70F Friday and Saturday,) drinks from 30F, on nights when there's jazz or dancing. For **clubs** try Le Palace on rue du Faubourg-Montmartre. Closed Mon. and Tues. Entrance 120F or free if you eat in the restaurant (130F minimum). Les Bains, on rue du Bourg-l'Abbé, is the ultimate rowdy club in an old Turkish bathhouse. **Live music** is good at Le Gibus, 18 rue du Faubourg; some nights advertised as gay but the crowd is happily mixed (métro: République). Another good jazz club worth trying is New Morning, 10 rue des Petites Écuries (10e). The best thing to do is look around and read the local listings.

The **cafés** at Montparnasse remain a typically Parisian vantage point from which to watch life go by, but watch out for the prices. In August, when many French restaurants are closed, these are often the only places open.

If you were thinking of visiting the **Moulin Rouge** or **Lido**, you might as well forget the rest of your European itinerary; a night out in one of these places will cost you 500F minimum. It's actually more of a spectacle walking round the **Blanche** and **Pigalle** areas, just down from Montmartre, or Montparnasse, but watch out for drug-pushers and pickpockets. For serious red-light seekers, the place is rue St Denis.

Slightly more sedate a time can be had watching the fountains at the **Trocadéro** and admiring the view of the **Eiffel Tower**, or wandering down by the **Seine**; often there are buskers in the area round **place du Vert Galant**. On a fine evening, wandering around the **place de Tertre**, Montmartre, is also a great experience.

If you get your skates on, you can join the three hour Friday night roller rally that takes 5000 exuberant rollerbladers on a 25km route through Paris. It's supervised by 30 nimble gendarmes on skates and leaves pl d'Italie at 9.45pm.

**EXCURSIONS Versailles**, the elaborate palace of Louis XIV, is the main attraction near Paris. Entrance to the palace costs 45F (35F if you're under 25), with an optional, but worthwhile, 25F guided tour of the opera and chapel. Get there early, or you'll be queueing all day instead of viewing. The gardens cost 17F, but go there after seeing inside, as the fountains usually aren't switched on until after 3.30pm. Take RER C5 from St Lazare or Invalides out to Versailles RG. The palace is open Tues.–Sun.: 9.45am–5pm (free to under-18s, half price on ISIC, half price Sun.).

Also within striking distance is the palace of **Fontainebleau** with its beautiful park-forest. Take the train from Gare de Lyon. Open 10am–12.30pm, 2pm–6pm, except Tues. Fill in your Inter-Rail and take it to the ticket office: you'll be given a free ticket for Fontainebleau or Versailles on the suburban railway.

Of course, the most publicized excursion from the French capital now is to see Mickey and his pals at **Disneyland**. Fans of theme parks will love the place, though it is more expensive than its Florida counterpart. Officially, you're not allowed to take in your own food (as Disney makes as much profit on its food outlets as on entrances). Several readers have, however, written in with tales of successfully smuggled-in baguettes. Be discreet and you may save money. You can get there on the RER. Take Route A from Charles de Gaulle-Étoile to Marne la Vallée/Chessy. Journey time, around 45 mins.

Cheaper and more popular with the French themselves is **Parc Asterix**, featuring the indomitable Gaulish village from the series of cartoon books. A day pass costs 160F. A special bus service runs from the Roissy Charles de Gaulle airport RER and bus station 1.

**Chantilly** is an attractive small château, reached by train from Gare du Nord, but it's open only on Sundays and holidays.

**Chartres**, home of the world's most famous Gothic cathedral, is an hour away from Gare Montparnasse.

For a refreshing alternative, take the hour-long train ride to **Epernay** where Moët et Chandon, on av. de Champagne, stump up for a sparkling tour with free samples.

## Alsace and Lorraine

After a history of occupation, the German influence is strongly felt in this region, especially in the cuisine. Local dishes include *choucroute* (sauerkraut with ham and sausage) and *backaoffe* (casserole with lamb, pork, beef and potatoes); wash it all down with some *pression* (local draught lager), and you'll have a meal you won't forget.

## Strasbourg

Best known as the seat of the European parliament, the capital of Alsace is one of France's most attractive cities. There's loads to see and do and in early June there is an **International Music Festival**. The Tourist Office, opposite the train station, will supply you with a map (small charge) and information on the city, as well as help you find a bed for the night. The 'Strasbourg Pass', valid for three days (58F), offers free entry or discounts to selected attractions.

The main **Tourist Office** is at 17 place de la Cathédrale (Tel. 03 88 52 28 28). **Amex** is at 31 place Kleber (Tel. 03 88 21 96 59). Both **youth hostels** are quite far away, so it's best to try somewhere more central like **Hôtel de l'Ill**, 8 rue des Bateliers (Tel. 03 88 36 20 01), or the **Hôtel Suisse**, 2–4 rue de la Râpe (Tel. 03 88 35 22 11). There are several hotels near the station, and the Tourist Office by the station puts up a board with suggestions when closed.

### STATION FACILITIES

Strasbourg has one of the largest stations in France. Train information is available daily 7.30am–9pm (Tel. 03 88 22 50 50) and there's also a Tourist Information office outside the station arrival hall. The reservations desk is open Mon.–Sat.: 8am–8pm and Sun.: 8am–7pm.

There is also a foreign exchange, left-luggage lockers, left-luggage store, showers, cafeteria, restaurant, waiting room and post office. Daily trains to: Luxembourg (two hours), Brussels (four hours), Munich, Stuttgart (2.5 hours), Basle (1.5 hours), Zürich (2.5 hours), Milan, Lyon, Paris (four hours).

From the station, walk down to **Petite France**, full of well-preserved old houses bordering the canal, then wind your way through the covered bridges and narrow medieval streets to the Gothic **Cathedral**. Try to arrive for 12.30pm, when the astronomical clock comes into action, or see the sound and light show in the evenings. You can also climb to the top for an additional few francs. South of the cathedral, the **Le Palais Rohan** contains a fine museum of archaeology, ceramics and paintings. Closed Tues. Boat trips are available around the city; try the early evening, as they're too busy during the day. For **eating**, try the areas around place du Marché aux Cochons de Lait and place du Corbeau. If you like to eat in a crowd, try Pont Saint Martin at 13–15 rue des Moulins (Tel. 03 88 32 45 13) overlooking the river.

**HOSTELS** The youth hostel, René Cassin, at 9 rue de l'Auberge de Jeunesse, Montagne Verte (Tel. 03 88 30 26 46), is about 2½ km from the station on bus 3, 13, 23 from Marché Ste Marguerite to Auberge de Jeunesse. Although IYHF membership is obligatory, it is a good investment as card-holders go free to the city's museums. The hostel is good, with friendly staff, cost 72F for B&B; the campsite costs 40F per person.

The CIARUS hostel is at 7 rue Finkmatt (Tel. 03 88 15 27 88), a well looked after establishment.

There is another hostel at rue des Cavaliers, Parc du Rhin (Tel. 03 88 45 54 20), but this is further out. Take bus 21 from central station to Parc du Rhin; the nearest station is, however, **Kehl** in Germany, a kilometre away. Alternatively, stay at the hostel at Kehl.

Another suggestion, if you arrive when it's very busy, is to travel to **Colmar**, where there are two hostels.

## The Alps

If you can only get to one alpine destination in France, make it **Chamonix**. The mountain railway winds its way through picture-book villages and is an unforgettable experience; sit on the right-hand side for the best view. Another memorable adventure is the cable car to the **Aiguille du Midi**.

The Chamonix Tourist Office at place du Triangle de l'Armite (Tel. 04 50 53 00 24) is open till 7.30pm in summer. They will help you find accommodation (not cheap), or you could try camping; the Tourist Office can supply details of the 18 sites in the area. Four are 15 minutes' walk from the centre. Check out the price of Le Chamoniard chalets or other gîte (cottage) accommodation with the Tourist Office. The **youth hostel** is at Les Pélerins, west of Chamonix (Tel. 04 50 53 14 52). It does dinners and packed lunches, and you can also get discounts on cable cars here. It is about a 40-minute walk from town but only a few hundred metres from the nearest station. Also try the **private hostel**, Chamoniard Volant (Tel. 04 50 53 14 09), friendly and clean; ask for details at the Tourist Office.

If you have only a day and want to head for the hills, ask Tourist Information for the list of *promenades à pied* (**walking tours**). Tell them how long you want to walk and ask for suggestions, as the possibilities are endless. If you take your walking seriously, contact the **Club Alpin Français** on av. Michel Croz (Tel. 04 50 53 16 03) for information on mountain refuges and conditions.

Even if you don't make it up the mountains, you can rub shoulders over a beer with the climbing set in the Nationale, rue Paccard. Local alpine food specialities include smoked sausage, various cheeses and, of course, fondue.

Two other very beautiful spots are Aix-les-Bains and Annecy. **Aix-les-Bains** is a pretty spa town on a deep-blue lake, with good walks in the surrounding hills and around the lakeside. The hostel at Promenade du Sierroz (Tel. 04 79 88 32 88) is very good. Take bus 2 towards Plage-Piscine and the Grand Port if you don't fancy the walk of about three km.

**Annecy** is another picturesque lakeside town. The old town with its narrow streets and fortress is well worth seeing. The campsite, Le Belvédère, is good value and gives a great view of the lake (Tel. 04 50 45 48 30). The hostel is La Grande Jeanne at 16 route du Semnoz (Tel. 04 50 45 33 19). Take bus 1 towards Paradis!

## Burgundy

If wine is what lures you to Burgundy, be sure to visit the **Musée du Vin** in the Hôtel des Ducs de Bourgogne at **Beaune**, and **Maison Patriarche**, rue du Collège, where they even give you a little bottle to take away with you.

Vineyards aside, Burgundy possesses some of the finest abbeys in France, the most spectacular being at **Vézelay**. Though this isn't on the rail, there's a bus from **Avallon**, which is. From Paris or Dijon, change at Laroche-Migennes. You could also visit the ornate monastery and other historic buildings of **Cluny**, which is on the SNCF bus route between Mâcon and Chalon-sur-Saône.

# Dijon

In Celtic times, it was an important stop for tin merchants *en route* from Britain to the Adriatic. In 1000AD the dukes of Burgundy made it their capital. In the 14th and 15th centuries, it was a great centre of science, art and learning. But today, the capital of Burgundy is more widely known than ever before – and all thanks to its mustard. The famous wine-based recipes are not Dijon's only claim to fame, though: a range of other edible specialities like *cassis* (blackcurrant liqueur), spiced bread (*pain d'épices*) and snails has helped create a thriving commercial and industrial centre.

## STATION FACILITIES
Train information and reservations are available Mon.–Sat.: 8am–7.30 p.m and Sun.: 9am–12 noon, 2pm–6.30pm (Tel. 03 80 41 50 50). The station also has all the usual buffets, left-luggage lockers and stores as well as a foreign exchange. It is shut 1am–4am.

Daily trains to: Paris (2½ hours, 1 hour 40 min by TGV), Strasbourg (four hours), Venice, Genoa, Lyon (1½ hours) and Marseille–Nice.

## TOURIST INFORMATION AND ADDRESSES
The main Tourist Office is in place Darcy (Tel. 03 80 44 11 44), five minutes' walk from the station, open daily 9am–12 noon, 2pm–9pm (until 7pm in winter). Room-finding service available.

**POST OFFICE** Place Grangier, Mon.–Fri.: 8am–7pm, Sat. and Sun.: 8am–12 noon

**SOS MÉDECINS** Tel. 03 80 73 55 55 for on-call doctors

**EMERGENCY** Tel. 17 (medical emergency Tel. 15)

**POLICE** Tel. 03 80 76 80 30

**CENTRE INFORMATION JEUNESSE DE BOURGOGNE** 22 rue Audra (Tel. 03 80 244 18 44)

## SEEING AND SLEEPING
Dijon's well-preserved heritage is best seen on foot; ask for the Tourist Office's free brochure on walking tours (recorded commentaries for Walkmans can also be hired here). The former **Ducal Palace** houses an art museum worth seeing, and the streets of the **old town** surrounding it make for interesting strolling. The **Archaeological Museum** exhibits artefacts dating back to the 9th century BC (closed Tues.).

The **youth hostel** at 1 blvd Champollion (Tel. 03 80 72 95 20) is good but a long way from the station. Bus 6 from station to place de la République, change to bus 5, to Épirey. **The Foyer International** d'**Étudiants** at av. Maréchal Leclerc (Tel. 03 80 71 70 00) requires an ISIC and is also quite far out of town. **Hôtel Confort Lamartine**, 12 rue Jules Mercier (Tel. 03 80 30 07 47) has cheapish rooms, or try the **Hôtel Monge**, 20 rue Monge (Tel. 03 80 30 55 41).

The **campsite** is at 3 Bd Chanoine Kir (Tel. 03 80 43 54 72), overlooking the lake. It's clean, and in the summer it fills up early, so phone first. Bus 12, direction Fountain d'Ouche.

Restaurants can be an expensive luxury in Dijon, so buy from the **market** stalls not far from rue de la Liberté. Be sure to sample some of the local produce: the gingerbread made with honey and spices, and eaten with butter or jam, is divine. One of the least expensive **restaurants** is Moulin à Vent at 8 place Françoise-Rude.

For a jar of the famous **mustard**, go to Maille on rue de la Liberté.

# Lyon

France's second city is built at the meeting of the Saône and Rhône rivers, a spectacular location that's made it an important crossroads from the time of Julius Caesar. Impressive Roman ruins are still in evidence. Today, Lyon is a thriving, contemporary cultural and business centre, progressive in outlook and with a well deserved reputation for great food and excellent nightlife.

## STATION FACILITIES

There are two train stations: **Part-Dieu** on the TGV line, and **Perrache**, for other trains. Both stations have the usual facilities: Part-Dieu has no Tourist Office; Perrache's office is towards the métro interchange. Both stations are open long hours, from around 5am to 12 midnight.

Daily trains to Paris (two hours by TGV), Marseille (three hours by TGV), Turin (four hours) and Geneva (two hours).

## TOURIST INFORMATION AND ADDRESSES

Central Tourist Office at place Bellecour (Tel. 04 72 77 69 69), with a smaller branch at the Perrache station. Open Mon.–Fri.: 9am–7pm, Sat.: 9am–6pm, Sun.: 10am–6pm, shorter hours off-season. Also at av. Adolphe Max in the Old Town, during high season.

**STUDENT TRAVEL OFFICE** Council Travel, 35 rue Victor Hugo (Tel. 478 38 78 38) and visit Voyages, 33 rue Victor Hugo (Tel. 04 72 77 81 91).

**POST OFFICE** place Antonin-Poncet, close to the Tourist Office and medical emergency service

**AMEX** 6 rue Childebert, (Tel. 04 78 37 40 69)

**SOS MÉDECINS** (Tel. 04 78 83 51 51)

## SEEING

The city is split neatly into three sections: Vieux Lyon on the Saône side (west); the Presqu'Île, which is the tongue of land between the Saône and Rhône; and the Modern City, on the Rhône side (east).

The **Old Town** is a protected area, with well-preserved Renaissance houses. Between and under these run little alleyways called **Traboules**, originally used for carrying silk around, but exploited by the Resistance in the war. The Gothic **St Jean Cathedral**, on rue St Jean, has an astronomical clock and a treasury, both worth a visit.

The **Croix Rousse** district, to the north of the Presqu'Île, is where the silk and weaving trade was based. Today, the traditional methods have been revived at the **Maison des Canuts**, 10–12 rue d'Ivry. The **Terreaux** quarter, with its lead fountain, and the **Hôtel de Ville** complex are also worth a visit.

To the west of the old town is the **Fourvière Hill**, the site of important Gallo-Roman remains. Get to the hill via the steep streets and steps known as the **Montées**. The **Parc Archéologique de Fourvière** contains an impressive **Roman Amphitheatre**, a smaller **Odéon** and other Roman remains. There is also a museum of finds from the site.

The **Fine Arts Museum**, housed in the 17th/18th-century **Palais St Pierre**, was once a Benedictine abbey. The **Museum of Printing and Banking** is also worth seeing for its analysis of the influence these trades had on Lyon. Probably the most important of the city's museums is the **Musée Historique des Tissus**, which exhibits fabrics and silks from around the world.

## SLEEPING

The **youth hostel** is at 51 rue Roger Salengro (Tel. 04 78 76 39 23), about five km from the city centre. From Perrache station, get bus 53 or 80 or 36 from Part-Dieu to États-Unis Viviani or Viviani Joliot-Curie.

The **campsites** are all about 10 km from the centre; Dardilly at Porte de Lyon is well recommended (Tel. 04 72 17 08 92), 40 minutes on bus 3 from Hôtel de Ville to Parc d'Affaires.

Cheap **hotels** worth trying: **Alexandra**, 49 rue Victor-Hugo (Tel. 04 78 37 75 79); **Hotel d'Ainay**, 14 rue des Remparts d'Ainay (Tel. 04 78 42 43 42); **Hôtel Vaubecour**, 28 rue Vaubecour (Tel. 04 78 37 44 91).

## EATING

While there are many gastronomic delights well beyond the wallet of the budget traveller, there should be no trouble in picking up a reasonably priced meal. Vegetarians can try **Le Pétisson**, 17 rue Pont du Temple. **Le Vivarais**, at 1 place Gailleton, serves local specialities.

# The Riviera (Côte d'Azur)

**EXCURSIONS** **Nice,** unofficial capital of the Côte d'Azur, is busy, bright and breezy. Should you hanker after rubbing shoulders with the rich and famous in **Cannes, Monte Carlo, Juan-les-Pins** and **St Tropez**, a day on the beach can cost you next to nothing. The beautiful people of St Trop have not permitted such vulgar inventions as public trains to spoil their paradise, so you'll have to bus it from St Raphael to get there. Still, if you want an all-over-tan – or to scrutinize other people's – it's the only place to be.

There's a wide choice these days of cheap places to stay, all within easy striking distance of the more glamorous resorts. A good place to base yourself is at the Saint Michel Ment (Tel. 04 93 35 81 23) **campsite** at **Menton**, near the Italian border. A tent for two people costs from 36F a night, depending on season. Look out for bogus lifts from the station to the campsites as we've had reports of drivers taking money and leaving people at the site entrance, knowing it to be full. The **Menton youth hostel** (Tel. 04 93 35 93 14) offers fabulous views over the bay, as well as what is reputed to be the best youth hostel evening meal in France.

For windsurfing, sailing and other water sports, make for **St Raphael**, as prices are cheaper here and there's more likely to be wind than further up the coast.

Another reasonably cheap place to make your base is **Biot**. Look hard for the station between Nice and Cannes, as it's easy to miss. Biot has a particularly good **campsite** opposite the station. Le Logis de la Brague is cheap and close to the beach.

In **Cannes** itself, there is a 16-bed **private youth hostel**, Le Chalit, at 27 av. Gallieni (Tel. 04 93 99 00 28). Try also the **hostel** at 35 av. de Vallauris (Tel. 04 93 99 26 79), 75/85F.

Another good spot is **Villeneuve-Loubet-sur-Mer**, between Antibes and Nice. It is a small, pleasant town with several **campsites**. A friendly and cheap one is the Savoy (Tel. 04 93 20 16 06), which is right on the beach. There is easy access to other resorts via the trains that run frequently along the coast.

A good **campsite** just outside **Toulon** is Camping Beauregard (Tel. 04 94 29 43 48), reached by bus 27 or 9.

# Corsica

The beautiful island of **Corsica** can be reached from either Nice or Marseille. The cheapest fare is on a night ferry travelling fourth class (sleeping on deck) from Nice, Marseille or Toulon, one way. **Bonifacio**, **Ajaccio** (Napoleon's hometown) and **Bastia** are the three most attractive centres on the island.

Be aware that the trip to Corsica can be expensive, as rail passes aren't valid (although Inter-Railers do get a reduction, and Eurotrain has reduced fares from Nice to Corsica; details available from USIT).

However, Corsican Railways have introduced a week-long freedom pass which costs 290F (around £30). The introduction of **La Carte Zoom** means unlimited travel for seven days, which offers the possibility of huge savings on the pricey standard fares (e.g. a return journey between Ajaccio and Bastia normally costs 316FF). Any of Corsica's train stations sell the tickets, and the big bonus for Eurorailers is that you can store your backpack at the station's left luggage for free.

# Monaco

If you hit a cloudy day, go through to sumptuous **Monaco**, put on your best bib and tucker (but try not to lose your shirt) in the famous casino at **Monte Carlo**: you must be able to prove you're 21 or over. The cheapest slot machine is 1F, and minimum bet at roulette 25F. The **palace** is also worth seeing, but is expensive. The **Oceanographic Museum**, where Jacques Cousteau was director for many years, has all things aquatic, including 450 species of fish. Open all year 9.30am–7pm, except during the **Monaco Grand Prix** when it, like everything else in the principality, gives way to the thundering Formula 1 cars.

Those staying overnight should try to get into the **Relais International de Jeunesse** in Cap d'Ail (Tel. 04 93 78 18 58) just outside Monte Carlo. The excellent **Princess Stephanie Youth Centre** (Tel. 337 93 50 75 20) is at 24 av. Prince Pierre, and has an age limit of 26. No advance reservations allowed here; registrations start at 10.30am for the 60 places in mixed rooms.

# Nice

Nice is without doubt the place to make your base on the Riviera; it's cheaper than the more pretentious resorts along the Côte d'Azur, has more facilities suited to the Eurorailer's lifestyle, and is a bright, lively and engaging city. It gets very busy, especially in August; you might have to get up early for a space on the pebbly beach. But you're only a few minutes by train from the less crowded beaches of small resorts like **Villefranche**, **Beaulieu** and **Menton**. Take care at the station, as professional luggage thieves are always on the look-out for tourists.

## STATION FACILITIES

Nice Gare de Ville has an information office open daily 8am–8pm. Reservations can be made Mon.–Sat.: 8am–6.45pm and Sun.: 8am–12 noon, 2pm–6.45pm. There is also a Tourist Information office, foreign exchange bureau, cafés, left-luggage lockers and stores, and showers. The station is shut 0.30am–5.30am.

Daily trains to: Paris, Strasbourg, Genoa, Milan, Rome, Marseille.

## TOURIST INFORMATION AND ADDRESSES

The main office is to your left, coming out of the station, at av. Thiers (Tel. 04 93 87 07 07). Youth Information CIJ, 19 rue Gioffrêdo (Tel. 04 93 80 93 93).

**POST OFFICE** 23 av. Thiers. Daily 8am–7pm

**POSTE RESTANTE** rue des Postes

**AMEX** 11 promenade des Anglais, Mon.–Fri.: 9am–12 noon, 2pm–6pm, Sat.: 9am–12 noon (Tel. 04 93 16 53 53)

**NIGHT CHEMIST** 7 rue Masséna (Tel. 04 93 87 78 94). 7.30pm–8.30am

**SOS MÉDECINS** Tel. 04 93 85 01 01

**SNCM** 3 av. Gustave V (Tel. 04 93 13 66 66), for boats to Corsica

**USIT VOYAGES** 10 rue des Belgiques, 06000 Nice (Tel. 04 93 87 34 96); also Eurotrain office

**EURAIL AID OFFICE** Gare de Nice-Ville, Bureau Information/Reservation, (Tel. 04 92 14 80 00)

## SEEING

At the heart of the old town is Place Massena, with elegant buildings from the Baroque and Belle Epoque eras, and restful gardens skirting a walking zone. The medieval warren of narrow alleys, and open-air flower and fish markets, are a sharp contrast to the commercial, touristy feeling on Nice's famous sea front, where the pebble beach stretching the length of the Bay of Angels is fringed by the palm-lined walkway known as the Promenades des Anglais.

For a view over Nice and the Mediterranean, climb the 90m to the **château**. If you've only an hour or two, spend it walking the length of the Promenade des Anglais. Eating in the cafés is ridiculously expensive, but the people-watching is great. Among the main things to see are: the **Palais Lascaris** at 15 rue Droite (former residence of the Count of Ventimiglia), the **Russian Orthodox Cathedral**, the old **Port** of Nice where the beautiful people park their yachts, the **Matisse Museum** at av. des Arènes with some of the artist's works and personal possessions, and the **Musée National Marc Chagall**, av. du Dr Ménard.

## SLEEPING

Beds are in great demand at any time, but particularly so during the Jazz Parade each July. You need to come early and phone around. Most of the cheap hotels are located around the station area. Refer to *Cheap Sleeps Europe 2000* for more options.

**HOSTELS** The IYHF youth hostel is four km away at route Forestière du Mont Alban (Tel. 04 93 89 23 64), bus 14. **Les Collinettes** is the university accommodation at 3 av. de Robert Schumann (Tel. 04 93 96 99 27) bus 17, girls only. The **Relais International de Jeunesse** (Tel. 04 93 81 27 63), av. Scudéri, is OK, but could mean a long wait to be checked in. **Meublé Let's Go**, 26 blvd Raimbaldi, 2nd floor (Tel. 04 93 87 04 40), five minutes from station,
**HOTELS** Central, clean(ish), and affordable: **Les Orangiers**, 10 bis av. Durante (Tel. 04 93 87 51 41); **d'Orsay**, 18 rue Alsace Lorraine (Tel. 04 93 88 45 02); **Hôtel Antares**, 5 av. Thiers (opp. the station) is reputedly good, or try **Madame Garstandt**, 55b rue Gambett, close by.
**CAMPING** In summer you'll find people camping on the beach, but as it's the only stretch on the Côte d'Azur where camping is tolerated, it is a bit of a bear pit down there. An alternative is the campsites at **Villeneuve-Loubet**, eight km from Nice, and on the rail line to Cannes. They are expensive, but facilities are good. A map of the sites is available from the Tourist Information Centre at Nice train station. If stuck, go to the hostel in Menton.

## EATING AND NIGHTLIFE

Food in Nice is among the best in France. Italy's proximity (30 minutes away) has an obvious influence on the cuisine – in fact, the pizzas in Nice are better than many you'll find in Italy – and there's plenty of fresh seafood from the Mediterranean. The salads named after the city are meals in themselves, piled high as they are with olives, tuna, boiled egg, tomato and anchovies. Sitting in an outside restaurant on one of the pedestrianized streets watching the world go by is one of life's great pleasures, and there is a good choice of set menus at prices under 100F.

Try **Le Félix Fauvre**, 12 av. Félix Fauvre; **Chez Davis**, 1/1b rue Grimaldi; **Chez Nino**, 50 rue Trachel (100 beers).

For self-service, try the **Café de Paris** at one of three locations: 42 rue Pastorelli, rue Masséna or in the Old Town. Another is the **Café Casino**, almost opposite the station. For those cutting corners, there are some good supermarkets in the centre.

Discos and clubs are expensive; a walk down the Promenade des Anglais or in the Old Town is just as entertaining.

# Marseille

This economic and industrial metropolis, major port and centre of higher learning with over 45,000 university students is France's oldest city (dating back to 600 BC). It may not have the charm and finesse of the Riviera resorts but it does have character. Work is underway restoring the city centre, and developing new facilities like the newly renovated 60,000 seat arena used for the World Cup.

## STATION FACILITIES

Marseille St Charles has train information Mon.–Sat.: 9am–7pm but is closed Sun. and holidays (Tel. 08 36 35 35 35). The reservations desk has the same hours. Tourist Information hours are winter: Mon.–Fri.: 10am–1pm, 1.30pm–6pm; summer: 8am–8pm. The station, which closes 1.30am–4.30am, has all the usual amenities you would expect from a busy international station.

Daily trains to: Paris, Strasbourg, Lyon (four hours), Nice (2.5 hours), Milan, Bordeaux, Nantes, Amsterdam, Brussels, Rome, Barcelona.

## TOURIST INFORMATION AND ADDRESSES

At the station, and also at 4 La Canebière near the Old Port (Tel. 04 91 13 89 00), open 9am–7.15pm, 8.30am–8pm during high season. They have an accommodation-finding service.

**YOUTH INFORMATION** 96 La Canebière (Tel. 04 91 24 33 50)
**POST OFFICE** Place de l'Hôtel-des-Postes (metro: Colbert)
**AMEX** 39 La Canebière (Tel. 04 91 13 71 21)
**EURAIL AID OFFICE** Garde de Marseille-St Charles (Tel. 04 95 04 14 08)
**DOCTOR** Tel. 04 91 52 84 85
**SOS MÉDECINS** Tel. 04 91 52 91 52

## SEEING

Known to generations of British and American sailors as 'can-o-beer', Marseille's most famous street is Canebière, leading from the Old Port to the **Réformies church**. This gets quite lively at night, but you're safer walking round here than in the slums of the North African quarter. That said, there is nevertheless a lot to see. The **Musée des Beaux Arts** in the Palais de Longchamps is the city's art gallery. The **Musée des Docks Romains** (Roman docks), 12 place Vivaux, was discovered after a German bomb in 1943 revealed the ancient storage depots complete with giant jars. **St Victor's Abbey**, a fortified church, built between the 11th and 14th centuries, has a **crypté** and **catacombs**. The **Cathédrale St Mairie Majeure** is a 19th-century neo-Byzantine building.

Off the coast, served by a regular boat shuttle service from the Old Port, is the **Château d'If**. This old fortress, once also a prison, is associated with Alexandre Dumas's *The Count of Monte Cristo*. Slightly further from the centre is the park and **Château Borley**, built in the 18th century. The **Basilica of Notre Dame de la Garde**, in Romano-Byzantine style, was built in the 19th century, has a great view over the city and is open 7am–7.30pm, bus 60 from Cours Jean Ballard. For a complete contrast, visit Le Corbusier's 17-storey **Cité Radieuse**, a study in concrete.

## SLEEPING

The two youth hostels are a long way from the centre but are okay once you get there. **Marseille-Bois Luzy** (FUAJ) is at av. de Bois-Luzy (Tel. 04 91 49 06 18), bus 8 from Bourse (near Canebière), and the **Auberge de Bonneveine** (FUAJ) is at 47 av. J. Vidal (Tel. 04 91 73 21 81), métro to St Marguerite Dromel, then bus 47. Beware when looking round for a cheap hotel, especially near the docks – many of them are 'multi-purpose' establishments. Two you might investigate are **Beaulieu Glaris**, pl. Marseillaises 1 (Tel. 04 91 90 70 59) and **Hotel Gambetta**, near the train station at 49 León Gambetta (Tel. 04 91 62 07 88). The Tourist Information Office has a list of B&Bs with singles from 130F.

## EATING AND NIGHTLIFE

The famous French fish stew *bouillabaisse* comes from Marseille, and the locals certainly know how to make it. There's no shortage of restaurants, or cafés; look for the fixed-price menus. The **Tunisian** and **Moroccan** restaurants are cheap, though not always good (and it's not wise for unaccompanied girls to head into the North African quarter at night). **Chez Papa** down by the port does a spectacular **ice-cream** sundae.

There are discos aplenty – just watch out you don't go into too low a dive as, if things get nasty, we've heard the police don't lose too much sleep over the occasional mugged Eurorailer. For tips on where to go, ask at the Tourist Office for their guide *Nocturnes*.

# Provence

Provence's rich countryside has acted like a magnet for artists – and Eurorailers – for years. The best time to go is May or September, as rooms are hard to find in July and August when Aix-en-Provence and Avignon stage their **arts festivals**. If you're going to or from the south or west and have plenty of time, consider breaking your journey at **Valence**. This is a pretty, peaceful town with a good **youth hostel/campsite** called Centre l'Épémière (Tel: 04 75 42 32 00). The centre is good value, with a swimming pool and bar/restaurant, though quite a walk from the station.

# Avignon

Avignon is another of the nine European cities of culture for the year 2000 and is planning dozens of exceptional millennium events. If you're coming from Lyon, consider making a quick diversion by getting off the train half an hour before Avignon, at **Orange,** to have a look at one of the finest Roman theatres in the world.

In Avignon, you'll see the walled city is dominated by the palace of Pope Clement V, who fled here in the 14th century after a fracas with Philip the Fair of France. The **Palais des Papes** is an impressive Gothic fortress; tours in English are available. For a superb view of the River Rhône, visit the **park** above the palace.

The **Tourist Information** office is at 41 cours Jean-Jaurés (Tel. 04 90 82 65 11), open 9am–lpm, 2pm–6pm, Sat.: 9am–1pm, 2pm–5pm, closed Sun. During the **festival** in July the Tourist Office is open Mon.–Sat.: 9am–6pm.

Finding a bed will be your greatest problem in Avignon, but there are **accommodation services** at Place de l'Horloge and at the Tourist Office, which you're advised to use to save yourself hassle.

If you don't mind large dormitories, try the **youth hostel** at **Auberge Bagatelle** (Tel. 04 90 86 30 39), located on the Île de la Barthélasse in the middle of the Rhône. Prices are good and there is a superb view of the palace.

Also try the **YMCA Foyer**, 7 chemin de la Justice (Tel. 04 90 25 46 20), 95F.

Finally, there's a hostel, called the **Squash Club**, at 32 blvd Limbert (Tel. 04 90 85 27 78). From the station, walk around the city walls to the right.

Avignon has several **campsites** near each other on the Île de Barthélasse: **Camping Municipal** (Tel. 04 90 82 63 50), **Camping**

**Bagatelle** (Tel. 04 90 86 30 39), **Parc des Libertés** (Tel. 04 90 85 17 73) and **Camping des Deux Rhônes** (Tel. 04 90 85 49 70). They are all within walking distance of the station, or take the no. 10 bus from near the post office. Last bus runs about 7pm (5pm Sun.).

# Arles

An important centre in Roman and medieval times, with an impressive **Amphitheatre** that has reverted to its function of blood bath, with imported Spanish bulls replacing the gladiators. The **Museum of Christian Art** is well worth a visit, as is the **Roman Theatre** and the **Roman Cemetery**.

**Tourist Information** is on blvd des Lices (Tel. 04 90 18 41 20): they'll supply a ticket for entry to all the museums and monuments, as well as help you out with accommodation if necessary. The **youth hostel** is on av. Maréchal-Foch (Tel. 04 90 96 18 25), a block behind the Tourist Office.

If you want to venture into the **Camargue**, Arles is about the nearest you'll get by rail (they rent out bikes at the station; the going is flat).

# Nîmes

The **Maison Carrée** and the **Amphitheatre** steal the show in an area rich with the best Roman remains in France.

**Tourist Information** is at 6 rue Auguste (Tel. 04 66 67 29 11), open Mon.–Fri.: 8am–7pm, Sat. 9am–noon and 2pm–5pm, Sun.: 10am–noon, and they run a similar system to Arles, giving out a single ticket for entrance to all the monuments (reduction with ISIC). They'll also give you the best route to the **Pont du Gard**, the 2,000-year-old Roman aqueduct (almost intact), and the old Crusaders' port of **Aigues-Mortes**, now well inland because of silting up. Both are worth the trip.

There are also several castles in the area; the best is at **Uzés**, open all year; ask again at Nîmes Tourist Office for the route.

The **hostel** is about three km out at **Chemin de la Cigale** (Tel. 04 66 23 25 04). **Camping** is also a possibility here. Take either bus 6 or 20 – note the last bus is at 8pm.

## Aix-en-Provence

Architecture, elegance, greenery and delightful fountains give Provence's intellectual and cultural centre an air of sophistication that is unusual for a provincial place. Sit in any café and you'll sense an air of self-importance. The birthplace of Cézanne is rather a snobbish city, but it is also breathtakingly beautiful. The **Museum of Tapestries** in the former **Archbishop's Palace** is particularly interesting. Avoid their festivals in June and July, as prices and crowds increase dramatically.

**Tourist Information** is at 2 place du Général de Gaulle (Tel. 04 42 16 11 61). **Amex** is at 15 Cours Mirabeau (Tel. 04 42 26 93 93). For sleeping, try **Hôtel des Arts**, 69 blvd. Carnot (Tel. 04 42 38 11 77) or **Hôtel Paul**, 10 av. Pasteur (Tel. 04 42 23 23 89), which is good value and has rooms for up to four people. The **youth hostel** is at 3 av. Marcel Pagnol (Tel. 04 42 20 15 99). Take bus 8 to Estienne d'Orves or 12 to Vasarely from the place de Gaulle, as it's two km from the station. Look out for the Vasarely building. There's a **student travel office** at 7 Cours Sextins (Tel. 04 42 92 48 48), and at 12 rue Victor Leydet (Tel. 04 42 38 98 92).

# Central / South-West France

The sparsely populated **Auvergne**, **Dordogne** and **Languedoc** regions are not well served by the railways. But if you have the time and patience to tackle the local trains, you will not regret it.

**Carcassonne**, the medieval gem of the Languedoc region, is arguably Europe's best-preserved relic of the Middle Ages, and certainly the most interesting walled city in France. The bonus is that it's on the main line and services are good. After centuries of building and fortifications, Carcassonne was left to rot in the 16th century, and it wasn't till the 19th that restoration began. The **Tourist Office** is on blvd Camille Pelleton; they find rooms and are generally helpful. Arrive early, as Carcassonne is not a well-kept secret and in the summer, rooms get scarce.

The towns of **Clermont-Ferrand** and **Périgueux** are not particularly interesting in themselves, but they make excellent bases from which to explore the lush Auvergne and Dordogne. The **tourist board** at Clermont is at 69 blvd Gergovia, and Périgueux's is in av. de l'Aquitaine. They'll provide details on the surrounding area and how best to reach the places of interest. **Accommodation** should be no problem in either town: most of the cheap hotels are near the stations.

The prehistoric capital of Europe, **Les Eyzies-de-Tayac** – about 40 minutes south-east of Périgueux by train – is worth visiting for its **cave paintings**. The caves are within easy walking distance of the station, as is the **Tourist Information** office (Tel. 05 53 06 97 05). There are plenty of **hotels** to choose from in the village and there's **camping** on the other side of the river.

## Bordeaux

The wine capital of France, Bordeaux is a good place to head for if your money's running out – you could always spend a week or two working on the grape harvest in September. The city is terribly French, and it is worth a short stay for a totally different perspective on the France you will have discovered elsewhere.

### STATION FACILITIES
Train information can be found at Gare St Jean 8am–9pm (Tel. 08 36 35 35 35). The reservations desk has similar hours, but shuts earlier and has a limited service at weekends. The station, shut midnight–5am, has all the usual facilities, including a **post office** and **shower**. Daily trains to: Paris, Lyon, Nantes, Toulouse, Marseille, Nice, Biarritz, Madrid and Lisbon.

### TOURIST INFORMATION AND ADDRESSES
**TOURIST INFORMATION** 12 cours du 30 Juillet (Tel. 05 56 00 66 00), just off the Esplanade des Quinconces
**POST OFFICE** 52 rue Georges Bonnac
**AMEX** 14 cours Intendance (Tel. 05 56 00 63 33)
**MEDICAL EMERGENCY** Tel. 15
**CENTRE INFORMATION JEUNESSE AQUITAINE** 5 rue Duffour-Dubergier (Tel. 05 56 56 00 56). They will help with accommodation. The walk into town takes about 30 minutes.
**STUDENT TRAVEL OFFICE** 284 rue Ste Catherine (Tel. 05 56 33 89 90)

### SEEING
Bordeaux is a good city for walking. Start by strolling along the old waterfront before turning away from the river towards the **Old Stock Exchange**. Behind the 18th-century façades of **Place de la Bourse** is the medieval city; a network of pedestrian streets and the **Cathédrale**

**St Andrée**. Look out for the **Esplanade des Quinconces**, the largest square in France; the **Musée des Beaux Arts**; the **Musée des Arts Décoratifs;** and the smart shopping streets round **Rue Bouffard**. Also worth seeing are the interesting **Museum of the Resistance** and **Museum of Aquitaine**. In the **Esplanade des Quinconces**, there's the **Monument aux Girondins**, erected to commemorate the Deputies of the Revolution.

Daily wine tours, arranged by the Tourist Office, are a good way to get the flavour of the place. The cost is around 160F per person, high season, Sat. only during low season.

## SLEEPING

Finding a bed is no problem, even though many places close in August. The basic **FUAJ youth hostel** is close to the station at 22 Cours Barbey (Tel. 05 56 91 59 51). Head down cours de la Marne, fifth turning on left. There are 247 beds, a bar, kitchen and a great atmosphere. Only open 7am–10am and 6pm–11pm, but backpacks can be left at reception.

There are several cheap **hotels** in the area (ask at the Tourist Office on arrival); these include the **De Famille**, cours Georges-Clemenceau 76 (Tel. 05 56 52 11 28) and the **Dauphin**, rue du Palais-Gallien 82 (Tel. 05 56 52 24 62).

For **camping**, check out Les Gravières at Courréjan, a half-hour bus ride on route B, leaving from the bus station at Quai Richelieu, down by the river. The site is a few minutes' walk from the end stop.

## EATING AND NIGHTLIFE

Predictably enough, the local cuisine makes good use of the regional wines with a variety of dishes using the delicious *bordelaise* sauce. **Set menus** at affordable prices can be found in restaurants on rue des Augustins, place Général Sarrail, and rue du Maréchal-Joffre.

The Sunday-morning market at Quai des Chartrons sells no end of fresh, local produce, and for further stocking up, go to the main **shopping** street, rue Ste Catherine, where there are plenty of good **supermarkets**. There are several eating places in this street, too.

Ask Tourist Information for a *What's On* and try sampling the regional wines at **bistros**. For club life, try **La Factory** at 28 rue Mably, which has three floors of techno and house music, or look around the **Quai de la Paludate**, which is full of clubs. For hot clubbing try **IN n'OUT**, 32–34 rue Cornac (closed Tues. and Wed.).

# Cerbère

If you are heading for Spain along the Mediterranean coast and decide to break your journey for the night at the border, give the station and the beach a miss. Instead walk back along the main road towards France for a few hundred metres and take the footpath up the cliff. Both the scenery and the sleeping potential here are much better.

## NOTES

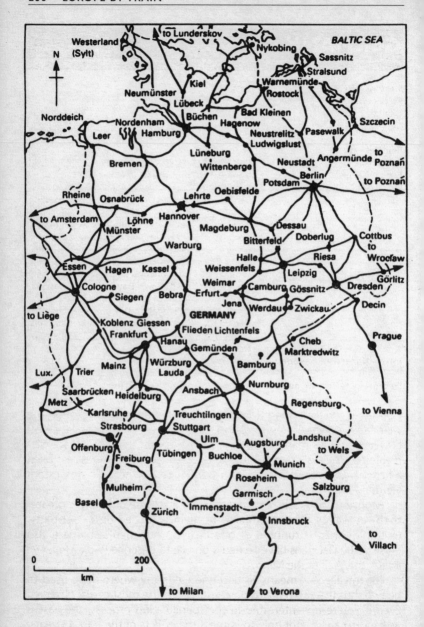

# GERMANY

| | |
|---|---|
| Entry requirements | Passport |
| Population | 81 million |
| Capital | Berlin (pop.: 3.5 million) |
| Currency | Deutschmark |
| | £1 = approx. 3DM |
| Political system | Federal Republic |
| Religions | Protestant and Catholic |
| Language | German (English spoken in major cities) |
| Public holidays | New Year's Day, Epiphany (6 Jan., Bavaria and Baden-Württemberg only), Good Friday, Easter Sunday and Monday, Labour Day (1 May), Ascension Day, Pentecost Sunday and Monday, Corpus Christi Day (in Baden-Württemberg, areas of Bavaria, Hesse, Rhineland-Palatine and North Rhine-Westphalia), Ascension Day (in some areas of Bavaria and in Saarland), Day of Unity (3 Oct.), All Saints' Day (1 Nov., in Bavaria, Baden-Württemberg, Rhineland-Palatine and North Rhine-Westphalia), Day of Prayer and Repentance (in Bavaria observed only in regions with predominantly Protestant pop.), Christmas Day and Boxing Day. |
| International dialling codes: | To Germany: int'l code 49 |
| | From Germany: 00 + country code |
| Emergency telephone numbers | Police 110; ambulance 112; fire service 112 |

Germany is still adjusting to being a unified country, even though the wall came down eleven years ago. Its emergence on that night of 9 November 1989 marked the end of the Eastern Bloc, but 40 years of division took its toll; merging the backward east with the west has been a heavy burden to the new nation (shouldered in the main by western German taxpayers).

Enormous contrasts remain. Nowhere are these differences greater than in salary and standard of living (in eastern Germany, unemployment is running at one in five), but mental barriers also persist. The Germans have coined a phrase to describe it: *die Mauer im Kopf* – the Wall in the Mind.

For travellers, it means visiting one Germany where there used to be two, but the gap remains obvious to even the most casual observer. Even if you're not interested in the reunification process, the east is well worth a visit, not only to witness the effects of the past 45 years, but also to absorb its fascinating history – as exemplified by the beautifully restored city of Dresden. And in the west, despite the continued economic crisis, there's a continued sense of renewal –

especially in Berlin, where a gruesome past is being exorcised as the new capital seizes the chance to reinvent itself.

The Germany of today has been shaped by a historical thirst for expansion and power. Even the medieval merchants of the Hanseatic League – associated with the towns of Lübeck and Hamburg – conspired to control much of northern Europe's wealth. Long after the rest of Europe had formed itself into single nation states, 'Germany' remained in pieces, thanks to its huge number of feuding princedoms, and a lack of natural boundaries.

These divisions came to a head in the Thirty Years' War of 1618–48, when the Catholic south (defending the Habsburg emperors) and the Protestant north (inspired by men such as Luther and the Reformation movement) slugged it out between them. In 1871 Bismarck was the force that created the German nation. Autocratic rule, attempts to conquer an empire, and rapid industrialization led to discontent. This topped by Kaiser Bill's blunderings led to the First World War. After the failure of the liberal Weimar Republic, Hitler started stirring things up again, and we all know what Nazism led to.

The end of the Second World War saw Germany occupied by the Allies. Cold War tensions led to partition. Germany has survived all these trials, and – despite the chaos – is once again at the dawn of a new era.

## GERMAN RAIL

### (DEUTSCHE BAHN, DB)
### 18 Conduit Street, London W1R 9TD (Tel. 020 7317 0919).

DB offer one of the best deals in Europe. They're fast, clean and efficiently run. Unlike Britain and France, where all the main lines radiate from the capital, the Germans have an excellent series of interconnecting cross-country lines, which serve all the principal cities and the smaller towns throughout the country. Various timetables are produced for the different regional areas. Trains range from the fast and flashy InterCity Expresses (ICE), which offer 175 mph travel with an hourly service between Hamburg and Munich, to the less speedy InterCity trains (IC), which require a 6DM supplement (supplements for journeys across a frontier vary). Apart from the speed on the ICEs, other facilities include built-in radios and coat cabinets; the ultimate in comfort for a bit extra. These trains are excellent, but charge a supplement. The InterRegio (IR) trains are nearly as fast as the InterCitys, and connect smaller cities to the IC network (they require a small supplement). EuroCity (EC) trains connect Germany with neighbouring countries. *Schnellzüge* (D) and *Eilzüge* (E) serve the regional areas, and in the cities *Bahnen* or *Nahverkehrszüge* are slow local trains.

**EUROSTAR, THALYS, INTERCITY EXPRESS AND ICT** Eurostar's high-speed service under the English Channel to Brussels (in 2 hours 40 minutes) has onward connections now with the international Thalys express to Aachen and Cologne. Six departures daily from London Waterloo will get you to Germany in under four hours (Tel. 0870 6000 778 or 020 8390 8833). The speedy Eurostar–Thalys link means Cologne is 5 hours 30 mins from London, while upgrading in northern Germany slices two hours from the 12-hour London–Berlin journey.

Dusseldorf and Dortmund will also benefit from Thalys services, while by the year 2001, a new 206mph InterCity Express will have chiselled down the travelling time between Cologne and Frankfurt from 2 hours and 20 mins to less than an hour.

Also new on the tracks are the ICT tilting trains, adapted from Italy's runaway success, the Pendolino. The state-of-the-art ICTs are designed for speed and comfort, with luxurious extras similar to ICE facilities. Expect to pay top dollar for a seat on one of these.

**PASSES AVAILABLE** EuroDomino Pass Germany allows three–eight days' unlimited travel within a month, for the whole of Germany (see Part One of this guide). The ticket is also valid on KD day ships (not hydrofoils) between Cologne and Mainz. The ticket includes all supplements, but not reservations. ICE supplements are included, but charges for extra services on these trains are not included. Reservations cost 5DM and are available up to 15 minutes before departure. Adult second-class tickets cost: three days £129, four days £139, five days £159, six days £169, seven days £179 or eight days £189.

Those under 26 can purchase a three-day pass for £99, four day-pass for £109, five-day pass for £119, six-day or seven-day pass for £129 and an eight-day pass for £139. Cards are available from appointed travel agents, Rail Europe (tel. 0990 848 848), continental booking offices or DB, 18 Conduit Street, London W1R 9TD (Tel. 020 7317 0919). In the United States, write to German Rail, DER Travel Service, 11933 Wilshire Blvd, Los Angeles, LA 90025 (Tel. 310 318 9744).

If you plan on spending a long time in Germany, look out for the **DB Bahn Card**. It's valid for a year and gets you 50% reduction on all rail tickets, although you still have to pay EuroCity and IC supplements. Prices start at £49 for those under 22 or students under 26, and £79 for others. Bahn Cards can be purchased from Rail Europe (tel. 0990 848 848) or DB, 18 Conduit Street, London W1R 9TD (Tel. 020 7317 0919).

DB's Regional Pass no longer exists, but the **Ferien Ticket** provides an alternative. Valid for a week's unlimited travel on local and regional trains in one of 54 zones, the ticket costs £21.50 per person, or from only £8 each for up to four people travelling together. An additional week costs £8 per person, or from £4 each for up to four people travelling together, and if you combine two or more regions, you pay half price for the other regions. In some zones, public transport is included. The catch is you need a London–Germany Eurostar ticket or other through-train ticket to qualify.

Those aged under 26 can buy **Twen Tickets**, which give up to 20% off single and return fares.

For people travelling together throughout Germany a **mini-group ticket** can be purchased. The first adult pays full fare, additional adults pay half price and children quarter price. The maximum group size is 5.5 (each child counts as half). Another special deal is the **Happy Weekend Ticket**, which for a flat fare of £14 per person (maximum five people travelling together) allows a weekend excursion on local trains.

Both **Eurail** and **Inter-Rail** passes are valid. The **Inter-Rail** pass has been broken down into zones, so you don't have to pay for travel to areas you will not be visiting. For £159 you can tour a single zone for 22 days (over-26s pay £229). Germany is in Inter-Rail Zone C, along with Switzerland, Austria and Denmark. For details of the eight Inter-Rail zones, see the Inter-Rail section in Part One of this guide.

### EURAIL BONUSES
**FREE SERVICES** Ferry crossings from Puttgarden and Rødby Faerge (Denmark) between Sassnitz and Trelleborg (Sweden).

Ships operated by the KD German Rhine Line making regular day trips on the Rhine between Cologne and Mainz and the Moselle between Koblenz and Cochem (but not ships making cruises of several days between Basel and Rotterdam or vice versa, or between Trier and Koblenz or vice versa). An extra charge will have to be paid for the use of hydrofoils.

Europabus line 189 – Burgenstrasse (Castle Road) from Mannheim–Heidelberg–Heilbronn–Rothenburg or der Tauber–Ansbach–Nürnberg-am-Main.

Europabus line 190 – *Romantische Strasse* (Romantic Road): Frankfurt/M–Rothenburg or der Tauber–Augsburg–Munich/Filssen.

**REDUCED FARES** 50% reduction on normal fares for TT Line's Travemünde–Trelleborg. Student rate for Finnjet's Travemünde–Helsinki.

35% reductions on some regular Lake Constance steamer services or on Worm and Kock's Passau–Linz line (50%).

25% reduction on the Freiburg–Schauinsland rack railway.

25% reduction on the mountain railroad Garmisch Partenkirchen–Grainau–Zugspitzplatt and on some cable cars in the summit area.

## TRAIN INFORMATION
In 1994 Deutsche Bahn started a customer-care programme with intensive cleaning programmes and recruiting of security and service staff to

improve station standards. One of the main results has been the 'service points' in stations all over Germany. These service points are located in the middle of the station hall and are often open 24 hours a day to answer all sorts of queries. So if you need any help, contact them first for advice.

**Left-luggage** lockers take 1DM and 50 Pfennig pieces.

**RESERVATIONS** Can be made up to 15 minutes before departing, but not after 10pm. They are not included in the price of the supplement: there is a charge of 5DM for reservations purchased at the same time as the ticket and 9DM for those made separately. A supplement for IC/EC will cost 7DM, or 9DM if you buy it on the train.

**NIGHT TRAVEL** Overnight trains operate throughout the year, going as far as Moscow or Rome.

Some German compartments have **pull-down seats** which make excellent free beds. **Couchettes** have six berths whilst tourist-class sleepers (four-berth) cost about 50% more. Three-berth compartments are also available and it's often possible to get one between two out of season, as they're usually under-booked.

DB has extended the special couchette service between Dortmund and Munich known as the **Twen-Nachttramper** (Night Tramper) to include services between Aachen and Copenhagen via Hamburg, and Hamburg to Munich. It allows you to have a couchette for only a small fee and all you need is a sleeping bag or blankets. If you don't have either, you can buy a paper blanket on board for around 8DM from the conductor. You don't have to worry about reservations either, as you can pay the fee on board, although the number of places is limited and the service has proved to be very popular. Look out for extra services being laid on and check with DB before booking couchettes for an overnight journey, in case your route has come into the scheme.

**CityNightLine** is an international sleeper train connecting Germany with Switzerland and Austria. The service runs between Dortmund, Cologne and Vienna; Hamburg and Zürich; Berlin, Dresden and Zürich. Each service has reclining seats, and a variety of sleeper cabins.

A sleeper train, **InterCityNight**, operates between Frankfurt, Cologne Berlin; Hamburg and Munich; Munich and Berlin. Choose between reclining seats or cabins. Reservations are compulsory, and the fare includes breakfast.

Some robberies have been reported on the **Poland–Germany** night trains. Take extra care.

**WOMEN-ONLY SLEEPERS** *Damen Couchettes* are available on all sleeper trains in Germany, and on three international night trains to and from Austria, Belgium and Holland. Prices are the same as for ordinary

couchettes, but berths must be reserved at least two days in advance.
**EATING ON TRAINS** Prices are lower than on British trains, and the quality is higher. So if you've the money, it's worth considering a meal on the ICs. Other trains (except E-trains) have mini-bars, which are pricey. Taking your own picnic food is still the best bet.
**SCENIC ROUTES** The Alps, the Rhine valley, Black Forest, the Romantic road and the Castle trail all provide scenic routes within Germany.

If you've always wanted to go **cruising** down the Rhine, it's best to do it between Koblenz and Rüdesheim or Mainz, as this gives you magnificent views of both sides of the valley. If you're coming from the opposite direction and want to stay with rivers, then head to Giessen from Koblenz.

To see the Black Forest, there are a variety of options. The Romantic and Castle roads are arguably best seen by Europabus, which are nearly always busy and require advance reservations. The Munich–Nürnberg, Heilbronn–Heidelberg train follows more or less the same route as the bus at no extra cost.

For the Alps, try the line to Salzburg or Innsbruck from Munich – both are equally attractive. If you're going to Switzerland, try Freiburg–Basel or Würzburg–Zürich.
**BIKES** Can be hired from around 370 stations throughout Germany from 8DM upwards to anyone with a valid ticket or rail pass. You can either do a circular tour of the region or merely cycle from A to B and return the bike to another station.

## TOURIST INFORMATION

Tourist Offices are usually called *Verkehrsamt* or *Verkehrsverein*. Many towns in eastern Germany have an office, simply described as an 'information office'. There are also *Reisebüros* across the country. Many cities have free pamphlets specially prepared for the under-26s.

**ISIC BONUSES** Museum discount, with varying reductions at some sports centres. For further information, contact Europa Sprach Club, Amalienstrasse 67, Munich 40. There are branches in all main cities. In Berlin also try the Jugend Tourist Office at Alexanderplatz 5, 1026 Berlin.
**MONEY MATTERS** 1 Deutschmark (DM) = 100 Pfennige.
Banking hours vary, but generally are Mon.–Fri.: 9.00am–12.00 noon, 1.30pm–3.30pm; Thurs.: until 6.00pm. Closed Sat. It's also possible to change money at some post offices; they often give a better rate.
**POST OFFICES** Open Mon.–Fri.: 8am–6pm, Sat.: 8am–12 noon.
**SHOPS** Open Mon.–Fri.: 9am–6.30pm; Thurs. until 8.30pm. In smaller towns they shut for lunch, 12 noon–3pm. On Sat. they only open till 2pm, and until 4pm on the first Sat. of each month.
**MUSEUMS** Hours vary depending on locality. Generally in West Tues.–Sun.: 9am–5pm, East 10am–5pm. Check with Tourist Infor-

mation, as many museums are closed on Mondays. Many offer free admission on Sundays.

**TIPPING** Usually included in restaurants, but it is customary to leave loose change up to a maximum of 5%. Always tip lavatory attendants, especially if you plan to return!

## SLEEPING

**Youth hostels** cost 16–25DM a night and there are more than 600 scattered throughout Germany. Tourist Information will have a free map and brochure showing their locations. In Bavaria there is an age limit of 27 in hostels. **Youth guest houses** (*Jugendgasthäuser*) are in nearly all the large towns, but they tend to be stuffed with groups, so always phone first. There's no uniform system of classification for Germany's hostels and hotels, so you'll find they vary dramatically. The accommodation side of Tourist Information, however, is usually very obliging and you need never feel really stuck as in the end they'll fix you up with something in your price range.

Cheap **hotels** can often be found near the stations. In smaller places, look out for signs saying *Zimmer frei* (room to let) or *Gasthof* (inn), and for **private accommodation**, turn to Tourist Information for lists.

With more than 2,000 **campsites** in Germany, you shouldn't find any problems. Again, Tourist Information will have a free map and brochure showing where they are. Facilities are generally very good and prices usually fair.

There is still a problem in **eastern Germany**, due to growing demand and a lack of infrastructure. This is despite the fact that private citizens are now able to offer **B&B**, and formerly East German-only establishments are now available. **Inter hotel** prices have now risen beyond the budget traveller's range – upwards from £80. This leaves the former **Jugendtourist** hostels and campsites, but even here the demand will mean overcrowding. Ask at local Tourist Information offices and *Reisebüro* for suggestions, including **Verband Christlicher Hospize**, which has hostels in Berlin, Leipzig and Weimar. Refer to *Cheap Sleeps Europe 2000* for more options.

## EATING AND NIGHTLIFE

German food is as varied as French – the difference is that the former like to eat more of it. There are countless varieties of beer and *Würst* (sausages), but the cuisine is much more varied than such a dull stereotype would allow. Regional specialities include *Grünkohl mit Pinkel* (green cabbage with bacon sausage) from the north, *Sauerbraten* (braised beef in sour sauce) from the west, and (good for picnics) Westphalian *Pumpernickel* (black bread) or *Vollkornbrot* (bread made of whole unground grains of wheat). Many of the *Würst* look revolting, but don't let that put you off – whether spicy, smoked, hot or cold, they're generally cheap and very tasty. Vegetarians tend not to be well catered for, though most big towns have a few non-meat eateries.

The **food halls** of the large department stores (e.g. Hertie, Kaufhof) are real showpieces, and the quality and quantity of the produce means there's no excuse for not living off picnics and saving your Marks that way. **Fast food** is also available in the major cities, and *Schnell-Imbiss* stalls with *Würste* and beer also crop up. **Alcohol** can be very expensive in Germany, and note too that if you drink at one of the **beer gardens**, it is not unusual to be charged a deposit for your glass – remember to claim it back.

The Germans are keen on large-scale celebrations: some of their **festivals** resemble Wagnerian opera sets, and no expense is spared. If you get a chance to join in, do. As far as **music** goes, the **classics** are always well represented and there's an active **jazz** and **club** scene in all the major cities.

## Berlin phone code: 030, occasionally '9' in front of eastern Berlin numbers

There is no other city – in Europe or elsewhere – like Berlin. Once as elegant and cosmopolitan as Paris and London, it emerged as the seat of Hitler's gruesome Nazism, and was reduced to rubble in the Second World War. Then in August 1961, after mounting tensions between east and west, the infamous Wall was raised, splitting the city in two. When in 1989 Berliners tore the wall down with their bare hands, the collapse of the Eastern Bloc followed, and so began an exciting, chaotic period of reunification.

With a background as dramatic as this, it's no surprise Berlin is a city of fascinating contrasts. Though virtually nothing of the Wall remains (much of it was carried off as souvenirs by Berliners), the two enforced halves retain obvious differences. This was a city at the heart of the Cold War, and that alone makes it worth a visit. But today it's not so much the sights that are worth coming for, as the atmosphere – the world-famous *Berliner Luft*. Berliners are rebuilding – cranes dominate the skyline, and the sound of hammers and pneumatic drills rumbles through the streets. Such enormous changes are restoring Berlin to the vibrant, energetic city of old. Now the capital of the reunited Germany, Berlin is at a new crossroads.

## STATION FACILITIES

The three main stations are Bahnhof Zoo (Zoologischer Garten), Ostbahnhof (formerly Hauptbahnhof) and Lichtenberg. **Bahnhof Zoo** and **Ostbahnhof** currently serve international destinations, and

**Lichtenberg** domestic and eastbound trains, but check your timetable. Lichtenberg can take 40 minutes or more to reach by S-Bahn or even taxi from Zoo, so plan your schedule carefully. Ostbahnhof has been undergoing massive rebuilding of its platforms, so watch your feet. The formerly important border station, **Friedrichstrasse**, has lost its importance. When arriving, use Bahnhof Zoo.

Train information is available on a central number – 19419 – and all stations are open 24 hours. Lichtenberg doesn't have a foreign exchange bureau, but all three stations have post offices, 24-hour left-luggage lockers, shops, toilets and restaurants. There is also a Tourist Office at Bahnhof Zoo station. Luggage lockers also available at Alexanderplatz and Friedrichstrasse S-Bahn stations.

Daily trains from Ostbahnhof to Munich (eight hours direct, seven with changes), Frankfurt (Oder) (one hour), from Lichtenberg to Warsaw (six hours), Dresden (two hours); from Bahnhof Zoo to Cologne (5½ hours), Hamburg (three hours), Frankfurt am Main (five hours), Würzberg (4½ hours) and Hannover (three hours).

## GETTING AROUND

Owing to the split city syndrome, the places you'll want to see are often a fair way from each other, so you'll need to use local transport at some time or other. A variety of tickets covering different parts of the transport network are available, so consider the options carefully. There's a dense network of buses, trams, subways (U-Bahn) and inner-city trains (S-Bahn).

If you're in Berlin for three days, buy the **Berlin and Potsdam Welcome Card** (29DM). Valid for 72 hours, it gives free public transport for one adult and up to three children, and free entry or up to half-price reductions on tours, walks, boat trips, museums, theatres, and other events.

Alternatively, a single ticket covering the whole network for two hours costs 4DM, the *Kurzstrecke* (Short Trip) is valid for three stops on the U-Bahn or S-Bahn or six stops by bus or tram and costs around 3DM. A *Tageskarte* (day ticket) is valid until 3 am the following day and costs 7.50DM (zones AB or BC) or 8.50DM (zones ABC). If you're staying for longer, then the seven-day or month Umweltkarte costs around 40DM or 88DM. All multiple tickets must be obtained from the machines at S-Bahn and U-Bahn stations or from the local transport office in front of Bahnhof Zoo. Individual and multiple tickets must be validated before use, by stamping them in a red machine at the platform entrances to U/S-Bahn stations or at bus stops before boarding.

## TOURIST INFORMATION AND ADDRESSES

**TOURIST OFFICES** On the Budapesterstrasse side of the Europa

Centre (a short walk from Bahnhof Zoo station, opposite the zoo), open Mon.–Sat.: 8am–10.00pm; Sun.: 9am–9pm (Tel. 250025; Fax. 2500 2424), this is the central number for all Berlin Tourist Offices. Accommodation service for 5DM. The free book *Berlin for Young People* is excellent. Among other bits of interesting information, it lists 20 or so cheap pensions. The city magazines *Prinz*, *Tip* and *Zitty* can also be useful.

There's also a Tourist Office at Bahnhof Zoo, open 8am–11pm,and in Tegel Airport's main hall, open 8am–11pm (Tel. 4101 3145).

In the east, there's one at Pariser Platz, at the Brandenburg Gate.

**POST OFFICE** Bahnhof Zoo. Open Mon.–Fri.: 6am–midnight, Sat.–Sun.: 8am–midnight. Also *poste restante* here. Most offices are open 8am–6pm weekdays.

**AMEX** Friedrichstrasse 172 (Tel. 201 7400), Mullerstrasse 176 (Tel. 462 3072) and Bayreuther Strasse 37 (Tel. 2149830), Mon.–Fri.: 9am–5.30pm, Sat.: 9am–12 noon.

**CURRENCY EXCHANGE** Alexanderplatz, Bahnhof Zoo, Friedrichstrasse, Ostbahnhof, also major hotels.

**ARTU REISEBÜRO** Hardenbergstrasse 9. Student Travel office selling BIJ tickets and IUS card. Open Mon., Tue., Thur., Fri.: 10am–6pm, Wed.: 11am–6pm, Sat.: 10am–1pm.

The foreign embassies and consulates will be changing locations over the next few years as they move into a new complex which is still under construction. Check that the office you want is still where it says it is below by contacting the Auswärtiges Amt Dienststelle Berlin, 10992, Postfach 610187, or visit them at Wedersches Markt (tel. 201860; Fax. 2018 6252). This is a general office for foreign service.

**UK EMBASSY** Unter den Linden 32–34 (Tel. 201840; Fax. 2018 4158). Open Mon.–Fri. 9am–noon and 2–4pm

**IRISH CONSULATE** Ernst-Reuter-Platz 10 (Tel. 3480 0822; Fax. 3480 0863). Open Mon.–Fri. 10am–1pm

**US CONSULATE** Neustädtische Kirchstr. 4–5 (Tel. 238 5174; Fax. 238 6290)

**CANADIAN CONSULATE** Friedrichstrasse 95 (Tel. 261 1161; Fax. 262 9206.). Open Mon.–Fri. 8.30am–12.30pm and 1.30pm–5pm

**AUSTRALIAN CONSULATE** Uhlandstrasse 181–3 (Tel. 880 0880; Fax. 8800 8899). Open Mon.–Fri. 9am–noon

**NEW ZEALAND NATIONALS** Contact New Zealand embassy in Bonn, Bundeskanzlerplatz 2-10 (Tel. 228 228 070)

**EURAIL AID OFFICE** Reisezentrum, Zoo (Hardenbergplatz 11) (Tel. 2974 9277)

**EMERGENCY DOCTOR** Tel. 310 031

**EMERGENCY PHARMACIST** Tel. 01 141

# SEEING

At the head of western Berlin's main thoroughfare, the **Kurfürstendamm**, is the massive **Europa Centre**, four floors of pubs, shops, dance floors, boutiques, tourist office and a cinema which shows a useful introductory film on Berlin's history. Berlin's premier department store, **KaDeWe** at Tauenzienstrasse, is well worth a look, if only for its food halls.

In **Tiergarten** park, the 70m victory column, the **Siegessäule**, celebrating Prussian victories in the 1860s and 1870s, can be climbed (2DM) for an impressive view towards the 18th-century **Brandenburg Gate**.

The city zoo, which has more species than any other in the world, costs 12DM, students 10DM. Next to the zoo is the world's most extensive collection of fish and reptiles in the **Aquarium** on Budapesterstrasse (12DM, students 10DM, or combined ticket with zoo, 19DM, students 16DM). The **Olympic Stadium** conjures up images of Jesse Owens and Hitler and is worth the 1DM entrance fee. Take U-Bahn 1.

**Schloss Charlottenburg** lies a few km north-west of Berlin, bus 145 or 204. This 17th-century palace houses several galleries and museums and is the best example of Prussian architecture you'll find around Berlin (closed Mon., entire palace complex Tageskarte 15DM, students 10DM, under 14 free) The **Egyptian Museum** opposite has a fine collection, including the fabulous bust of Queen Nefertiti. The **Dahlem Museum**, near U-Bahn Dahlem-Dorf, is a complex of seven museums (closed Mon.), so you're bound to find something to interest you. The **Bauhaus Museum**, with exhibits of the school's designs (closed Tues.), is at Klingelhöferstrasse.

The photographic story of German 19th- and 20th-century history at the recently renovated **Reichstag** also makes an interesting visit. The Reichstag is fast becoming the city's number one tourist attraction. You can now explore the building and climb inside the new dome for a spectacular panoramic view of the city. The parliament now meets under the 3,000 square meters of vaulted glass. You can listen to the debates of the German Bundestag and have a snack at the restaurant, though it isn't cheap.

Another chilling reminder of the past are the crosses nearby, commemorating those shot trying to go over the wall.

East Berlin's museum complex lies on the Spree canal, just north of the end of Unter den Linden: **Museum Island**, where the main eastern Berlin museums are located. Avoid Mon., when most are shut. General hours 10am–5pm, but various exhibits only certain days. Admission to each museum costs 4DM for adults, 2DM for students, or a combined day pass is 8DM for adults and 4DM for students. Free Sunday. There is also the *Wochenkarte* which is valid for the whole week (adults 25DM; students 12.50DM).

On Museum Island are: the **Pergamon** (stunning collections of

Eastern and Roman artefacts), open Tues.–Sun. 10am–6pm; free first Sun. of month, the **Bodemuseum** with its Egyptian works; and the **Alte Nationalgalerie** with its impressive collection of 19th-century art; open Tues.–Sun. 9am–5pm. The **Alte Museum** has been converted into a special-exhibit museum and it regularly showcases major exhibitions. The museum is open Tues.–Sun. 10am–5pm and it costs around 10DM (students 5DM) depending on the exhibition. Restoration work is being carried out on some of the museums listed above so you may find that they are either partly or totally shut when you are there. Ask at the tourist office for the latest information. The great neo-Renaissance **Berliner Dom**, the former court church of the Hohenzollern family which was severely damaged in an air raid in 1944, has been fully restored and is also on the island and worth a visit. (Entrance 5DM; students 3DM).

The **Märkisches Museum**, which is housed in a beautiful building on the banks of the Spree River at Am Kölnischen Park, traces Berlin's history. There's also a good collection of applied art. Closed Mon./Tues. Entrance is 2DM, 1DM for students.

For a good view over the city, climb the Berlin Radio Mast, **Funktürm**, or the **Fernsehtürm** (TV Tower) at Alexanderplatz (8 DM). There's a not-too-expensive revolving restaurant at the top, and also a bar. Not far away, in the **Grünewald**, is the **Teufelberg**. At 114m high, it is the highest hill between Warsaw and the Netherlands. It is made of an enormous mound of rubble from the ruins of Berlin after the Second World War. It now has a ski and toboggan run, and at the very peak is an American radar station.

## TOURS

The **Spree River** flows through the city and it's possible to take a boat ride on one of the white **excursion boats** (*Weisse Flotte*) from April to Sept. You can get off at various points: the best stop is the **Mecklenburger Dorf**, a reconstruction of a 19th-century German village. Boats leave eight times a day from Treptower Park S-Bahn station. (The commentary is usually given in German only.)

For a cheap tour alternative, take the double-decker '**Bus 100**', which takes in many sights (from the zoo, outside the Europa Centre, or from Alexanderplatz). It's a normal service bus, so there's no commentary – unless you're lucky enough to get the one driver in Berlin who prides himself on giving passengers a guided tour as they go.

Another option is to join a **walking tour**. The Yellow Walking Tour Company meet each morning at 10am outside Bahnhof Zoo. For 10DM you'll get an up-beat, three-hour historical and cultural insider's guide to the city.

**FREE BERLIN:** The number one tourist draw of today is the scant remains of the **wall** (*die Mauer*), where 80 East Germans died trying to escape to the west (the last person was killed less than two months before the wall tumbled in November 1989).

- Cross through the site of the old Checkpoint Charlie to compare the development of the two sides of the city separated for so long. The actual hut is now in the fascinating **Museum of the Wall** (near the checkpoint) on Friedrichstrasse.

- Not far from the main exit of the Ostbahnhof is the **East-Side Gallery** – a kilometre of wall that has been transformed into an open-air art gallery celebrating freedom.

- **Kurfürstendamm** (Ku'damm) pulsates with life late into the night and is the city's preferred promenade and thoroughfare. The famous Berlin institution **Café Kranzler** is found on the junction with Joachimstalerstrasse, but eat elsewhere, as it is expensive.

- The ruined **Kaiserwilhelm Gedüchtniskirche** is unmissable. The square around it is a focal point of the Ku'damm and a popular meeting place (though it can be a bit dodgy at night). The church itself tells the city's story – bombed, partly rebuilt and its ruins preserved as a stark war memorial, it reflects Berlin's mix of old and new.

- The **Tiergarten** is a beautiful park at the centre of reunified Berlin. Its 630 acres have recovered not only from the devastation of the war, but also from being stripped for firewood by freezing Berliners in the bitter winter of 1945–46.

- The 1,390m **Unter den Linden**, at the heart of eastern Berlin, is the most impressive street in the east. From here you can see the **Brandenburg Gate**, spruced up after the Wall came down, and the east's city centre.

- The **Museum für Deutsche Geschichte** in the Arsenal (*Zeughaus*), the oldest building on Unter den Linden, offers an audio-visual history of Germany in English, and there's Hans Eickworth's 1968 bronze Monument to the Border Guards.

- The **Berliner Dom** (cathedral), closed for many years, is close to the east's hideous old parliament building, whose fate is yet to be decided.

- The **Nikolaiviertel** quarter is a cat's cradle of narrow streets and alleys around the **St Nicholas Church**. It is interesting for the reconstructed half-timbered buildings, mullioned windows and the odd quaint corner. **Marienkirche** is Berlin's oldest church, dating from the 13th century, just off Alexanderplatz.

- The **Synagogue** on Oranienburgerstrasse was burnt during the horrors of Kristallnacht in 1938; in recent years it's been undergoing restoration. There's a **Monument to the Victims of Fascism and Militarism** on Unter den Linden and the **Soviet War Memorial** in Treptower Park, which is reached on the S-Bahn.

- The **German-Russian Museum Berlin-Karlshorst**, at Zwieseler Strasse 4, gives a free English guide to the account of German-Russian relations since 1917.
- More forward-looking visitors can gauge just how ambitious Berlin is by visiting the temporary museum and exhibition box on Strasse des 17 Juni at **Potsdamer Platz**, not far from the Brandenburg Gate. A huge red box straddles the construction area – before the war a busy square, and after it the widest expanse of no-man's-land separating the east and west. With the help of modern gadgets and gizmos, the **Infobox** gives a powerful insight into Berlin's history and plans for future development.
- Two of the four sections of **Wall** still standing are just behind the Infobox. Another is outside the **Prince Albert Grounds** along Niederdircherstrasse nearby. The Gestapo, the SS and other Nazi organisations had their headquarters in buildings here. They were destroyed after the war, but in 1987 their foundations were excavated, and an exhibition documenting Nazi atrocities has been staged just behind the wall. The **Topography of Terrors** is at Stresemannstrasse 110 (Tel. 254 5090).

## SLEEPING

Finding a bed isn't easy and during peak periods, Berlin's **budget accommodation** becomes scarce. This is one city where you would be really wise to book ahead; write about two–three weeks in advance to the **Verkehrsamt Berlin** at the Europa Centre, 10787 Berlin 30, stating how much you can pay. Alternatively, try booking flats through **Zeitraum**, who charge from 30DM per day, discounts for students. Open Mon.–Fri.: 10am–1pm and 3pm–7pm at Horstweg 7, 1000 Berlin 19 (Tel. 440 8690). **Mitwohnzentralen's** room-finding service comes highly recommended. Contact them at least a week in advance at Ku'damm Eck, Kurfürstendamm 227–228, Berlin (Tel. 3078 6 6002) and they could find you a room for as little as 40DM. They take a 3DM service fee.

If you aren't organized enough to plan ahead, don't worry; ask at **Tourist Information** for their map of Berlin with all the hotel and hostel listings. For **hotels**, look at the board at Bahnhof Zoo, though they tend to be expensive. You will probably have better luck in the old west Berlin, due to lack of established facilities on the eastern side. But you could try your luck at desk 13 of **Reisebüro** on Alexanderplatz or **Jugendtourist**, which is also situated there.

In response to the huge demand for low-budget accommodation in Berlin, city authorities have established **'The Tent' Bernachtung im Zelt**, another option for backpackers. Ask at the tourist centres.

If you're desperate, the **Bahnhofmission** in the station will help out. Refer to *Cheap Sleeps Europe 2000* for more options.

**HOSTELS Ernst Reuter** (IYHA) at Hermsdorfer Damm 48–50, 13467 Berlin (Tel. 404 1610; Fax. 404 5972) is good, though well out of the town centre, in a leafy suburb, by a lake; around 26DM per night including breakfast, U-Bahn 6 to Tegel then bus 125 (ISIC reductions).

**Jugendgästehaus Berlin** (IYHA) at Kluckstrasse 3, 10785 Berlin (Tel. 261 1097; Fax. 265 0383) is the most central, around 32DM including breakfast. It is clean and comfortable, though institutional, with two bunk beds per room. 10 minutes from Ku'damm by bus 129 or U-Bahn to Kurfürstenstrasse. Being central, it gets very busy, so don't count on getting in unless you book well in advance.

Although it is 20 minutes on the S-Bahn to Nikolassee, try also at **Jugendgastehaus am Wannsee** (IYHA), Badeweg 1, Ecke Kronprinzess-Innenweg 14129 Berlin (Tel. 803 2035; Fax. 803 5908). It is clean, cheap and very modern (32DM per night). Each room has its own shower, breakfast included. To book these hostels contact **DJH Central Booking Service**, Kluckstrasse 3, 10785 Berlin (Tel. 262 3024; Fax. 262 9529).

The **Studentenhotel** is at Meininger Strasse 10, Berlin 62 (Tel. 784 6720; Fax. 788 1523), a way out at Schöneberg. Take bus 146 or U-Bahn 4 to Rathaus Schöneberg; cost for two-bed room 44DM per person. There are also quads for 39DM per person. You can't check in until 2pm but it is possible to leave luggage there. No curfew.

**David's** is a private hostel, centrally located (seven minutes from Zoo). B&B costs 33DM, or you can pay 25DM for bed only (the breakfast buffet is 5DM). There are five four-bed rooms, tea and coffee is free, and there are cooking and clothes washing facilities too. You must phone to reserve a bed, and get directions (Tel. David at 395 7788 or 0177 395 7788).

Another private hostel is **Circus**, at Am Zirkus 2-3 (Tel. 2839 1433; Fax. 2839 1484). Dorms cost 25DM, triples 28DM, doubles 30DM and singles 38DM (breakfast not included).

**PENSIONS** The area round Fasanenstrasse and Uhlandstrasse is your best bet. Also on Carmerstrasse, Grolmannstrasse and Knesebeckstrasse.

Try **Pension Savoy** (Tel. 881 3700) at Meinekestrasse 4; **Pension Knesebeck** (Tel. 312 7255) at Knesebeckstrasse 86; or **Pension Kreuzberg** (Tel. 251 1362) Grossbeernstrasse 64. Also ask at Tourist Information for B&B, now opening up on the eastern side of the city.

**CAMPING** Try the friendly **Camping Kladow** 1 and 11, Krampnitzer Weg 111/117, bus 135, then 135e (Tel. 365 2797).

Or **Zeltplatz Dreilinden**, Kremnik-Ufer (Tel. 805 1201), bus 118. Another is **Kohlhasenbrücke**, Neue Kreisstrasse, U-Bahn Oskar-Helene-Heim, bus 18 (Tel. 805 1737).

Also try the former **Intercamping Krossinsee** site – tram 86 to end, then walk across bridge, and take the third turning on the right.

## EATING AND NIGHTLIFE

Berlin's cultural life is very energetic and there's always plenty happening in the evenings. Festival follows festival and the student community is large and active. *Tip*, the bi-weekly listing of what's on, and *Zitty* are worth buying if you're staying a while. The **cafés** here are an institution. Try **Schlander** on Olivaer Platz or **Café Mohring** on Ku'damn (Berlin's most authentic Art Nouveau coffee house). The **department stores** have good cafeterias and there are plenty of cheap fast-food chains and sausage stands. On Oranienstrasse in Kreuzberg, you'll find many good authentic Turkish restaurants. The cheap University cafeterias are at Kiebitzweg 23 in Dahlem, and Am 17 Juni.

For pubs, clubs and dance floors, head for the area round **Konstanzerstrasse**, **Düsseldorferstrasse**, **Joachimstalerstrasse** and **Lietzenburgerstrasse**; there are literally thousands.

Many of the bars in the former **East Berlin** are north of the river from Friedrichstrasse station. Try the **Kleine Melodic**, Friedrichstrasse 127, for dancing.

For a taste of 1930s Berlin, try **Zum Trichler** on Schiffbauerdamm, only a stone's throw from **the Brecht Ensemble Theatre.** A very atmospheric place to have a drink, as the walls are lined with old photos of Brechtian productions, murals and clocks. There is even a small stage for cabaret performances.

In the **Irish Pub** on Eisenacherstrasse (and also in the Europa Centre) you're guaranteed to meet a fellow Brit; most of the staff speak English. The **Irish Harp** pub, off Olivaer Platz, has great atmosphere, good food and reasonable prices. And in **Leierkasten** on Zossenerstrasse you'll bump into the local students.

**Nollendorfplatz** and **Winterfeldtplatz** are the areas for hardcore clubbers. Check out **E-Werk** (Wilhelmstrasse 43) and **Quasimodo** (Kantstrasse 12). Techno freaks should not miss Berlin's *Love Parade*, usually on the second weekend in July. For happy House, go to **Tacheles** (Orienburgerstrasse 53). Groove, Acid Jazz and Soul seekers head for **Delicious Doughnuts** (Rosethalerstrasse 9).

If you miss a hostel curfew don't despair, as many bars begin to serve breakfast at 2am (**Schwarzes** on Kantstrasse 148 serves food around the clock) and Berlin is literally open all night.

### GAY AND LESBIAN BERLIN

As one of Europe's leading gay and lesbian cities, there's no shortage of clubs, bars and other facilities. First the practicalities: the German word for 'gay' is *Schwul* and 'lesbian' is *Lesben*. Men can get information from the gay info centre Mann-o-Meter, Motzstrasse 5 (Tel. 216 8008) and lesbians can try the Spinnboden-Lesbenarchiv, Anklamerstrasse 38 (Tel. 448 5848). There's also the Schwules

Museum at Mehringdamm 61.

For entertainment, try **Hafen** on Motzstrasse, or the area around the **Nollendorfplatz**. Don't miss **Christopher Street Day Parade** in the last weekend of June.

## Potsdam phone code: 0331

Frederick the Great chose this town in 1744 as his permanent seat, and from then on Potsdam flourished to become one of the main imperial centres of Europe. The city is less than an hour from the centre of Berlin (take S-Bahn line S3), so it makes a good day trip, though there is a lot to see.

Baroque palaces and elaborate pavilions are the highlights of the impressive 600-acre **Sans Souci Park** and surroundings. The **Sans Souci Schloss**, the large **Neues Palais**, **Schloss Charlottenhof**, the **orangerie** and gold-plated **chinese teahouse** are all here. Nearby is the **Sicilian Garden**. Another large park, the **Neuergarten**, on the shores of a lake, includes the **Schloss Cecilienhof**, scene of the Three Powers' agreement to divide Germany. Part of this complex is now an expensive hotel. Most of the palaces are open 9am–5pm, closing at lunchtime; some also closed Mon. and out of season.

Potsdam's centre has been extensively rebuilt, but the Dutch quarter retains its charm and elegance. Just outside the town is the incredible **Einstein Observatory Tower**. Make the effort to see it if you can.

The **Tourist Office** is at Friedrich-Ebert-Strasse 5 (Tel. 275580; Fax. 275 5899), there is also Sanssouci-Information near the old windmill, opposite Schloss Sanssouci (Tel. 969 4200) . Take one of several trams to the city centre from the Potsdam-Stadt station. Ask at Tourist Information for the usual leaflets, maps and accommodation suggestions.

At present the only hostel is shut, with no plans to reopen it. The closest hostel is **Jugendgastehaus am Wannsee** (IYHA), Badeweg 1, Ecke Kronprinzess-Innenweg on the outskirts of Berlin (Tel. 30 803 2035; Fax. 30 803 5908). It is clean, cheap and very modern (32DM per night). Each room has its own shower, breakfast included. To book, contact **DJH Central Booking Service**, Kluckstrasse 3, 10785 Berlin (Tel. 30 262 3024; Fax. 30 262 9529).

There are several **campsites**, but they too are some distance away.

For **eating**, go to **Altes Jagdschloss**, Am Jagdschloss Stern, and have a beer at the **Froschkasten** on Kiezstrasse.

## Dresden phone code: 0351

Less than two hours from Berlin, Dresden is the cultural centre of eastern Germany and, though the old city was devastated by saturation bombing in February 1945, what was left has been carefully restored. The new city is green and well laid out.

## STATION FACILITIES

English is not as widely spoken in the former East Germany as in the west. In Dresden, even at the train information desk, if you ask: 'Do you speak English?' you're quite likely to get: 'No. Only Russian'. There will be at least one English-speaking person on duty; even so, try to get as much information as you can before you leave Berlin.

The **train information desk** and **travel centre** is open Mon.–Fri.: 6.15am–9pm, weekends 7am–9pm. Reservations can be made 5am–10pm; 6pm on Sat. and Sun. There is also an information line, call 19419. There are all the usual shops, **left-luggage facilities** and food outlets, and the station is open 24 hours. The **post office** is near Hauptbahnhof (on Pragerstrasse). The **Eurail Aid Office** is at the Resezentrum/Touristickschalter (Tel. 461 3508).

Through-trains use the elevated platforms on each side, terminating ones the central platforms.

Daily departures to Berlin Lichtenberg ($1\frac{1}{2}$ hours), Leipzig ($1\frac{1}{2}$ hours), Munich (eight hours), Cologne ($7\frac{1}{2}$ hours), Hamburg ($5\frac{1}{2}$ hours), Hannover ($4\frac{1}{2}$ hours), Frankfurt (six hours), Warsaw (0 hours).

There is another main station, **Bahnhof-Neustadt**, and many trains call at both, with eastbound ones tending to use Neustadt only. The facilities here are similar to those at the **Hauptbahnhof**.

## TOURIST INFORMATION

Dresden information centre is at **Pragerstrasse** 10/11 (Tel. 4919 2116) (five minutes from station). Open Mar.–Oct.: Mon.–Sat.: 9am–8pm; Sun.: 9am–12 noon.; Nov.–Feb.: Mon.–Sat.: 9am–6pm. You can change money here (Mon.–Fri. only). The what's on leaflet, *Dresden-Information*, is also available.

There is also a Tourist Information office at **Neustädter Markt** which is open Mon.–Fri.: 9am–6pm; Sat.: 9am–4pm; Sun. 11am–4pm.

Bus and tram tickets have to be bought in advance, though most of the worthwhile sites are walkable from Hauptbahnhof, along pedestrianized Pragerstrasse. The **Dresden Card** (28DM) gives 48 hours of free travel within the city, entrance to 11 museums and discounts other exhibitions and tours by tram, bus and paddle steamer.

**Amex** is at Hoyerzwalderstrasse 20 (Tel. 807030). The booth is open Mon.–Fri. 7.30am–6pm.

## SEEING

From Hauptbahnhof, head down pedestrianized Pragerstrasse, then bear left towards the river, where most of the sights are located. Near to Pragerstrasse is the **Kreuzkirche**, which houses a cross of nails taken from the ruins of Coventry cathedral. At the **Albertinum**, one of Dresden's great museum complexes, you will find the **Grünes Gewolbe** (Green Vault), containing a fabulous collection of the treasures of the Saxon dukes. Opens 10am, closed Thurs.

Further down the Brühlschen Terrasse above the River Elbe, you will pass down the Munzgasse. Down here are the remains of the devastated **Frauenkirche**, still surrounded by rubble, but now being rebuilt. Further along the river is the Catholic **Cathedral** and the immense **Residenzschloss**, the palace of the Saxon electors and dukes. It too is being rebuilt from the ruins, hopefully in time for the city's 800th anniversary in 2006.

Next comes the magnificent **Opera House**, close to which is the old **Augustinerbrücke**, leading to the New Town across the river. This area holds little of interest except a statue of the **Golden Rider**, Augustus the Strong, so named because he fathered 300 children.

Back on this side of the river, close to the opera, is Dresden's pride and joy, the **Zwinger Palace**. It is an incredible piece of Baroque architecture, within which are half of Dresden's impressive museum collection. They are the magnificent **Gemäldegalerie Alter Meister** (closed Mon.); the **Historic Museum of Weapons** (closed Mon.); the **Mathematisch-Physikalischer Salon** (maths and physics, closed Thurs.); and the **Zinnsammlung** and the **Porzellansammlung**, both of which display the famous Dresden porcelain (closed Fri.).

## SLEEPING

Sleeping options are rapidly improving here. There is a 110-bed IYHF riverboat hostel due to open on the Elbe (check with the tourist office) and a number of other new hostels opening their doors.

The established **youth hostels** are: **Hübnerstrasse** 11 (Tel. 471 0667; Fax. 472 8959), a few blocks from the station, down Winckelmannstrasse, then into Schnorrstrasse, which leads into Hübnerstrasse, a possibility at 26DM including breakfast. **Oberloschwitz** (24DM) at Sierksstrasse 33 (Tel. 268 3672; Fax. 268 3672), take tram 5 to Nürnbergerplatz, change to bus 61 or 93, get off two stops after crossing the Elbe. Then it is only a short walk away. **Radebeul** (24DM), Weintraubenstrasse 12 (Tel. 838 2880; Fax. 838 2881). **JGH Dresden** (35-40DM), Maternistrasse 22 (Tel. 492 6290; Fax. 492 6299).

The **campsites** are far flung; ask at the Tourist Information Centre for full details. A series of sites are located to the north, in a wooded area; bus 81 to the terminus, then a 15-minute walk.

The Tourist Office will also find rooms in **private homes** for you.

## EATING

Tourism has pushed prices up, but you can eat cheaply from supermarkets or Imbiss fast food stands on Pragerstrasse. Restaurants in the Am Zwinger complex on Wilsdufferstrasse sometimes offer reasonably-priced meals. Places in the Neustadt, away from the touristy areas, are better value. Also try Am Thor on Hauptstrasse for a drink. The cafés on the cobbled Munzgasse are worth a try, and there's also the university cafeteria on Reichenbachstrasse 1.

## Leipzig phone code: 0341

The second city in eastern Germany, built at the junction of two military roads and trading routes, is only one hour from Dresden, and though it is more a commercial and industrial centre, there are still enough points of interest to make it worth a stop-off. It makes a fascinating contrast to some of the more opulent western towns: bullet holes in walls, crumbling façades of buildings, the old-fashioned feel of the tram service. The atmosphere of World War II damage and post-1945 neglect is still tangible.

Tourist Information is at Richard Wagner Strasse 1 (Tel. 710 4260; Fax. 710 4265), open weekdays: 9am–8pm, Sat.: 9am–4pm, Sun.: 9am–2pm. The room finding service (Tel. 710 4255) is open Mon.–Fri. 9am–6pm, Sat.: 9.30–2pm. There is an Amex office at the airport (Tel. 224 1850) which is open Mon.–Fri. 8am–6pm and 8am–noon at weekends. There's another Amex office at Bergplatz 2 (Tel. 967000) on the 2nd floor of the building just behind the Neus Rathaus. This office is a travel agency and does not exchange money or deal with travellers' cheques. Opening hours are Mon.–Fri. 9.30am–6pm.

## STATION FACILITIES

The Hauptbahnhof is reputedly Europe's largest terminus, with 26 platforms. Many facilities are duplicated, so if one is shut, look around. The **train information** desk is on the platform near track 15, it's open 6am–10pm (Tel. 19419), with reservations during the same hours. The **foreign exchange** is open Mon.–Fri.: 7am–7.30pm, Sat.: 10am–4pm, and there are all the usual shops, **left-luggage lockers** and cafés. The station shuts 11.15pm–4.30am. Leipzig's small S-Bahn system departures are also from here (platforms 6 and 7).

There's a **Eurail Aid Office** in the station, Tel. 968 3378.

Daily departures to Berlin (Lichtenberg) (two hours), Cologne (six hours), Dresden (one hour), Hannover (3½ hours), Frankfurt am Main (4½ hours), Munich (six hours) and Warsaw (0 hours).

## SEEING

Start your sight-seeing in the partly pedestrianized area that begins opposite the station. It is known as the **Ring** promenade. The old, 16th-century **Altes Rathaus** (town hall) now houses the city history museum. The **Nikolaikirche** nearby is also worth a visit.

The composer Bach spent his last 27 creative years working as the *Kantor* (Choirmaster) in **St Thomas's Church** and is buried here. The boys' choir, once conducted by Bach, can be heard on most Fri. evenings and Sat. afternoons. Dating from 1212 and 1496, St Thomas's has recently been restored.

Across the way, the **Johann Sebastian Bach Museum** (4DM, students 2.50DM) chronicles the composer's life. There are two daily tours at 11am and 3pm and there are concerts two or three times a week (15DM).

Bach was not the only musical genius in Leipzig. Mendelssohn conducted the Gewandhaus Orchestra, Europe's oldest, and also financed a monument to Bach. The city also has strong literary connections, with large numbers of book shops and libraries. Goethe set the scene between Faust and the devil in the **Auerbach's Keller** in Madlerpassage, the decorations of which are now based on the book.

**EXCURSION** The small town of **Colditz**, location of the famous castle used as an officers' POW camp in World War II, is nearby. The story of Colditz was made into a film and later a TV series. Much of the castle is inaccessible to the public, but it is worth making the trip even so, and the beer brewed here is excellent.

There are plans to turn the castle into a tourist attraction, which will no doubt lead to a certain amount of disruption in the next few years. Ask at the Tourist Information Centre for details, particularly if you wish to see the cellars and church escape sections, as this must be arranged with the appropriate museum authorities.

## SLEEPING AND EATING

As with the rest of what was East Germany, hotels formerly in the budget area are now well outside it. The **Jugendherberge** hostel is at Volksgartenstrasse 24 (Tel. 245 7011; Fax. 245 7012) – note that it has moved from Käthe-Kollwitz Strasse. Expect to pay around 25DM.

The **Auensee campsite** is at Gustav-Esche-Strasse 5 (Tel. 465 1600)

Take the S-Bahn to Wahren, or tram 10, 11, 28 or 30 from the Hauptbahnhof. Trams 10 and 28 terminate at Wahren, then follow the main road for about 10 minutes. There are also two person bungalows for rent (around 80DM).

Ask the Tourist Offices about **private accommodation**.

There are plenty of reasonably priced **restaurants** and **pubs**, but expect the costs to be approaching western German levels. The best places to eat are near the **Markt**, or at the cheap **self-service restaurants** on Grimmäischestrasse. There is a well-stocked **supermarket** opposite the station's Wintergartenstrasse exit and in the **Horfeu** department store.

## Weimar phone code: 03643

This city is famous for inspiring such creative thinkers, composers and artists as Liszt, Schiller, Goethe, Nietzsche, Herder and Cranach. Last year it was designated Cultural Capital of Europe and much work went into cleaning up the city and renovating buildings and monuments. Now is the time to visit Weimar and explore its narrow streets, alleys and tiny squares.

This town was the site of the first German Republic (the Weimar Republic) which fell in the 1930s, just before Nazism rose to power. On its outskirts lies the notorious Buchenwald concentration camp.

Weimar is only an hour from Leipzig and makes a good day trip from there if you can't spare the time to stay.

### TOURIST INFORMATION

Tourist-Information-Weimar is at Marktstrasse 4 (Tel. 24000; Fax. 240040), open Mon.–Fri.: 9am–7pm; Weekends: 10am–4pm. Take bus 1, 4, 6 or 7 from the station to Goetheplatz and walk to Theaterplatz, then along Schillerstrasse to the Marktplatz. They can arrange bus tickets and accommodation. Also consider the Weimar Card (around 25DM), which gives 72 hours of unlimited bus travel, free entrance to the art museums, and up to 50% off city tours and other attractions. Most of the city's cultural sites are controlled by the Weimar Classics Foundation at Frauentorstrasse 4 (Tel. 5450). They sell a discount card (25DM, students 15DM) which gets you into all the foundation's museums for free.

### SEEING

The **Lucas-Cranach Haus** is the richly decorated Renaissance building in the Marktplatz. Close by is the **Schlossmuseum**, with its collection of German Renaissance works, and the Gothic church, **Herderkirche**. The **Kirms-Krackhow Haus** has displays on the philosopher Herder and poets Schiller and Goethe, among others. There are museums devoted to Schiller and Goethe, and Liszt, also within walking distance. A few new buildings of interest opened last year, including the **Museum of Modernity**.

**EXCURSION** The rococo **Schloss Belvedere**, a former royal summer palace, can be reached by bus from Goetheplatz – ask at the information office for details. The Nazi concentration camp of **Buchenwald** can also be reached by bus, leaving from stop no. 31, near the Hauptbahnhof. Today it is a grim memorial to the more than 56,000 Jews, communists and others killed between 1937 and 1945. An excellent English guidebook is available from the memorial bookshop.

## SLEEPING AND EATING

There are four youth hostels: the **Am Poseckschen Garten**, at Humboldtstrasse 17 (Tel.850792; Fax. 850793), charges 24DM per person for B&B, including linen. It's around 2½ km from the station. The **Germania**, at Carl-August-Allee 13 (Tel. 850490; Fax. 850491), has 121 beds, 24DM. **Maxim Gorki** (24 DM) is at Wilden Graben 12 (Tel. 850750; Fax. 850749). **Am Ettersberg**, Ettersberg-Siedlung (Tel. 421111; Fax. 421112) charges 24DM. All include breakfast.

Ask at Tourist Information for details of **private B&B**.

There is no convenient campsite – the nearest is listed under **Erfurt**, and is some distance from here.

People eat early in Weimar and you'll find places closing from 8pm, and all weekend, so get some supplies in. Try **All Weimar**, Steubenstrasse 27, or the **Elephantkeller** on the Markt. For good, affordable Chinese food, try **Ginkgo**, upstairs on Grüner Markt 4.

## Erfurt phone code: 0361

The capital of the forested and mountainous region of Thuringia is just a short journey from Weimar. Built at the intersection of major trading routes, Erfurt prospered in the Middle Ages as a centre of trade and learning. Now dubbed the City of Flowers, it is worth visiting for its very well-preserved medieval centre alone.

The **Tourist Information** Centre is at Fischmarkt 27 (Tel. 664 000; Fax. 664 0290) near the Rathaus. Open Mon.–Fri.: 9am–7pm, weekends.: 10am–4pm.

Erfurt's skyline is dominated by the twin towers of the Gothic

**Cathedral** and the 13th-century **St Serverus Church**, on the Domberg. The unusual bridge, **Krämerbrücke**, is lined with a collection of restored 14th-century houses. Not far away is the **Anger**, another restored street of Renaissance and Art Nouveau buildings. Erfurt boasts several monastic buildings, including the Gothic **Augustinerkloster**, a 13th-century complex restored after war damage. There is an exhibition here dedicated to **Martin Luther**, who was briefly a monk in Erfurt.

The **youth hostel** is at Hochheimerstrasse 12, about 5 km from the centre. Take line 5 from Hofbahnhof to Hochheimerstrasse (Tel. 562 6705; Fax. 562 6706). Cost per person: 25DM per night. Ask at the Tourist Office for **private accommodation** or for a cheap **hotels** (pretty scarce here). If stuck, try commuting from Weimar, 20 minutes away by train.

For good cheap food try **Suppen-Grün**, the soup bar at Regierungsstrasse 70 (closed Sun.). There's a supermarket in the InterCity Hotel on Willy-Brandt-Platz at the train station.

# Northern Germany

Northern Germany – the area between Schleswig and Bremen – is comparatively unspoilt by tourism. The main centres of interest are **Bremen**, **Hamburg** and **Lübeck**, and if you've time you could take in the little towns of **Hameln** (of Pied Piper fame) and **Celle**.

## Bremen phone code: 0421

The Hanseatic city of Bremen, with its port Bremerhaven, is the oldest seaport in Germany. As a member of the Hanseatic League, the prosperous medieval trading alliance of northern and Baltic towns, it was a major maritime trading power for centuries.

The **Tourist Information** office is right in front of the station, open Mon.–Wed., Fri.: 9.30am–6.30pm; Thurs. and Fri.: 9.30am–8pm; weekends: 9.30am–4pm (Tel. 308 0051; Fax. 308 0030). **Amex** is at Am Wall 138 (Tel. 174600). Open Mon.–Fri. 9am–5.30pm; Sat. 9am–midday.

Tackle Bremen on foot, starting with the old medieval section round the **Marktplatz**, the **Rathaus**, the **Statue of Roland** and **St Peter's** 11th-century **Cathedral** with its cellar full of mummified bodies. The old section of the town called the **Schnooviertel** is particularly attractive, with half-timbered houses and narrow winding streets dating back to the 1500s. Take a stroll down the **Wallanlagen** (Rampart Walk), dominated by its windmill. Have a look in the craft shops in Böttcherstrasse, a narrow pedestrian street.

The **youth hostel** is at Kalkstrasse 6 (Tel. 171369; Fax. 171102), about 20 minutes' walk from the station, or bus 26 or tram 6 from the station to Brill. The charge is around 22DM.

The **campsite** at Am Stadtwaldsee 1 is excellent. (Tel. 212002). Take bus 26 outside station. At Hemmstrasse, change to bus 28, which stops at the campsite. Clean, friendly, with a good cheap restaurant, it's only open Apr.–Oct. and costs 7.50DM per person and 4–8DM per tent.

## Hamburg phone code: 040

Germany's second largest city after Berlin calls itself the Gateway to the World, a name earned well enough during its days as an important medieval Hanseatic trading city. Even today, more than 13,000 ships put in each year to the country's largest sea port – an average of one every 40 minutes. Though an eighth of its total area is covered with docklands, there is more to Hamburg than a busy port. Unlike many of Germany's cities, Hamburg does not lack character or things to see.

### STATION FACILITIES

The train information is open daily, 6am–11pm (Tel. 19419 for schedules) and the reservations desk daily, 5.30am–11pm. There's a 24-hour service point and during normal hours there are all the usual facilites including a post office.

Daily trains to: Copenhagen (five hours), Hannover (1½ hours), Frankfurt (3½ hours), Vienna, Munich (5½ hours), Basel (6½ hours), Zürich, Milan, Bremen (one hour), Düsseldorf (3¾ hours), Cologne (four hours), Brussels, Paris.

The Hamburg metro, particularly around the Hauptbahnhof, is unsavoury at night, so be careful.

### TOURIST INFORMATION AND ADDRESSES

There is a Tourist Information office inside the station (open daily all year round, 7am–11pm, Tel. 3005 1201; Fax. 3005 1333). There's another between piers 4 and 5 (St Pauli Landungsbrücken office) Tel. 3005 1200. Open daily 10am–7pm. There's a third office in the Hanse Viertel mall, open daily 9am–6pm. All three offices can supply you with maps, a fortnightly programme of local events, *Where to Go in Hamburg*, and *The Hamburg Guide*. Ask for *Prinz*, *Muzikszene*, *Tango* or *Oxmox* for entertainment.

There's a separate information office (*Hotelnachweis*) also at the station and they'll find you a bed for a fee.

The Hamburg Card is a good discount option for sightseers. Available from any Tourist Office, it covers the city transport systems, as well as 11 museums. Current prices are 12.50DM for a one-day ticket and 26DM for a three-day ticket. For 10DM, you can get the Hamburg Card Light, which is good for three days but excludes free travel.

Rail pass holders go free on Hamburg's S-Bahn.

**BRITISH CONSULATE** Harvesthuder Weg 8a (Tel./Fax. 448 0320)
**IRISH CONSULATE** Feldbrunnenstrasse 43 (Tel. 4418 6213)
**NEW ZEALAND CONSULATE** Heimhuderstrasse 56 (Tel. 4425 550)
**CANADIAN CONSULATE** ABC Strasse 45 (Tel. 3555 6295)
**U.S. CONSULATE** Alsterufer 27 (Tel. 411710).
**AUSTRALIAN NATIONALS** Contact Bonn or Berlin
**POST OFFICE** on Gr. Burstah 3 (Tel. 40 638 80 or 40 638 20). *Poste restante* and 24-hour telephone service are here also.
**AMEX** Ballindamm 39 (Tel. 309080) and at the airport
**EURAIL AID OFFICE** Hamburg main station (Tel. 39 18 43 13)
**24-HOUR CHEMIST** Central Apotheke, Rodingsmarkt 1 (Tel. 378 6730)
**AMBULANCE** Tel. 112
**POLICE** Opposite train station (Tel. 110)
**STUDENT TRAVEL OFFICE** STA Travel, Rentzelstrasse 16 (Tel. 45 03 84 00)

## SEEING

Tours of the famous port are available. The best leave from Landungsbrücken. **St Michael's**, the 18th-century Baroque brick church, affords a good view from its tower. Listen out for the tower herald playing his trumpet at 10am or 9pm. The lift up the tower costs 4DM.

Of the many museums in Hamburg, the best are: the **Hamburg Art Gallery**; the **Decorative Arts and Crafts Museum**; the **Millers' Veteran Car Museum**; and the **Hamburg History Museum**. Take a day trip to the nearby open-air museums: the **Vierlande Museum** (S-Bahn to Bergedorf) and the **Museum Village** in Volksdorf (U-Bahn). All museums are closed Mon.

## SLEEPING

There are plenty of cheap pensions north of the station along Steindamm and Bremer Reihe, so you shouldn't have any problems. Consider spending 1DM for the Hotelführer list available from the Tourist Office. For cheap hotels – and there are plenty – head for the commercial area or, if you don't mind the noise of squeaking bedsprings, the red-light district.

At 24DM, the **Jugendherberge auf dem Stintfang** Hostel overlooking the harbour is excellent, though the evening meal is poor value. It is at Alfred-Wegener-Weg 5 (Tel. 313488; Fax. 319 1037). Always use the lockers provided, as security has been a problem in recent years. Nearby Landüngsbrücken station is on both S-Bahn (free to Inter-Rail) and U-Bahn.

Less central is the **Horner-Rennbahn** hostel at Rennbahnstrasse 100 (Tel. 651 1671; Fax. 655 6516). Take the U-Bahn to Horner-Rennbahn.

The best of the campsites, **Buchholz**, is at Kielerstrasse 374 (Tel. 540 4532), open summer.

## EATING AND NIGHTLIFE

The **university Mensa** at Schlüterstrasse 7 is your best bet, although seafood and fish restaurants are plentiful and good. Try the ones along Landüngsbrücken, or the Fischerhaus at the St Pauli fish market. Landüngsbrücken, however, has recently become more expensive. Also try near the station.

One thing Hamburg's not short of is nightlife. The famous **Reeperbahn** and **St Pauli** area is one of the liveliest in Europe, with the trendiest clubs, dance floors and bars in the town. The area is also famous for sex shops and porn movie-houses, but this should not put you off. Use your common sense to avoid falling into the tourist rip-off traps: also do not look for beds in the **Palais d'Amour** as it offers more than beds for the night.

Be sure to visit **Die Fabrik** on Barnerstrasse, one of Germany's first and best-known youth centres for music and student hangouts. Also try the laid-back **Templehof** (Hamburger Berg 12), the **Mojo-Club** at 1 Reeperbahn, or Hamburg's oldest jazz venue, **The Cotton Club** at Alter Steinweg 10.

## Lübeck city phone code: 0451

Forty minutes from Hamburg is the attractive old town of Lübeck, former headquarters of the medieval trading group, the Hanseatic League. The Old Town, surrounded by water, is an impressive collection of Gothic brick architecture. Since 1987 Lübeck has been protected as a UNESCO World Heritage Site. You'll see as many Scandinavians as Germans here as this is one of their favourite holiday destinations.

**Tourist Information** is in the station. Open Mon.–Sat.: 10am–6.30pm, Sun.: closed. They charge 4DM for maps and the office is always busy so you'd be better off heading to the office in the Old Town at Breitstrasse 62 (Tel. 122 5413/122 5414; Fax. 122 5419). The maps here are free and staff can help with accommodation although they don't book rooms. The office is open Mon.–Fri.: 9.30am–6pm, Sat.–Sun.: 10am–2pm.

Lübeck is known as the 'City of Seven Spires' because the skyline is dominated by the tips of the city's imposing churches and the cathedral. Bombing was extensive during the war, and you can see the shattered bells at the foot of the former belfry in the **Marienkirche**, where they have lain undisturbed since being blasted from their settings in 1942. For a good view of the city, the lift up the tower of the **Petrikirche** is good value at 3.50DM (reductions for students).

The actual city centre is quite small and it's possible to walk round all the sights: the 13th-century **Rathaus** with its original black glazed tiles, the Romanesque **St Marien Dom**, the **Holsten Gate**, and the old **City Walls** and **Museum**. Lübeck is renowned for its brickwork, so take a close look at the gabled houses, particularly **Buddenbrookhaus**, which Thomas Mann used as the background to his novel *Buddenbrooks*.

There are two **youth hostels**. The **Folke-Bernadotte-Heim** (26DM) is at Am Gertrudenkirchhof 4 (Tel. 33433; Fax. 34540). A second more expensive hostel (29DM) is at Mengstrasse 33 (Tel. 7020399; Fax. 77012).

The good **campsite** at Steinrader Damm 12 (Tel. 893090/892287) is reached by bus 7 or 8 from the station towards Dornbreite. The buses stop near the site entrance. Tourist Information will find other rooms for you, or get hold of a copy of *Cheap Sleeps Europe 2000* for more options.

## Hannover phone code: 0511

North Germany's major rail junction is primarily known as a centre for trade fairs. This year it's hosting the mother of them all – Expo 2000, the world exhibition. When you arrive, ask about special events at the Tourist Office and, if possible, try to arrange accommodation in advance.

ICE trains link Hannover to the southern part of Germany, with Munich 4½ hours away, Frankfurt 2½ hours. **Eurotrain** has an office at Karl-Wiechert-Allee 23 (Tel. 5670). The **Eurail Aid Office** is at the station (Tel. 286 5465).

The **Tourist Information** office is next to the main station at Ernst-August-Platz 2 (Tel. 301420/301421; Fax. 301414). Open weekdays 9am–7pm; Sat. 9.30am–3pm. Ask for the booklet *The Red Thread*, which guides you around the main sights of the city with the help of a red line painted on the pavements. **Amex** is at Georg Strasse 54 (Tel. 363 428).

Worthy of special mention are the 300-year-old **Royal Gardens**, **Baroque Garden**, **Berggarten** and **George Garden**. The gardens are linked to the city by the 1½ km Herrenhausen Avenue, lined by 1,300 lime trees. The gardens are often the venue for music and theatre, and Festivals of Light are often held. Check with Tourist Information for details.

During the summer, there's the Marksmen Festival and the Lake Maschsee Festival. The **flea market** on Hohes Ufer every Sat. is an interesting diversion. The **Kestner Museum**, the **Museum of History** and **Lower Saxony Regional Museum** are also worth a look.

There are three **youth hostels**. One is at Ferdinand-Wilhelm-Fricke-Weg 1 (Tel. 1317674; Fax. 18555), 20 minutes from the station on tram 7 or 3 to Fischerhof. A more expensive youth guest house operates at the same address. A second youth hostel is the **Naturfreundehaus** at Hermann-Bahlsen-Allee 8 (Tel. 691493), 30 minutes from the station by tram 3 or 7 to Spannhagenstrasse. The third hostel is also a **Naturfreundehaus** (Tel. 580537; Fax. 958 5836). It is a fair way out of the centre in Misburg, Am Fahrhorstfelde 50. Take U-Bahn 4 to Misburgerstrasse, then bus 631 to Misburg Waltfriedhof. Go the end of am Fahrhorstfelde and then it's a few metres up a track. The beds fill quickly so reserve.

For good curry, try the **Taj Mahal** on the corner of Schiffgraben at Hinüberstrasse 21. For international snacks, head for the Markthalle. **Hannen Fass** at Knochenhauerstrasse 36 is a nice pub which serves good food.

## The Central Belt and the Harz Mountains

Frankfurt, Düsseldorf and Bonn are all fairly modern industrial centres that offer little reason to break your journey. You would do far better to head for centres like **Marburg**, **Göttingen**, **Hannoversch-Münden**, **Karlshafen**, **Goslar** or the resorts round Münster: **Attendorn**, **Alt-Astenburg** and **Berleburg**. These have far more of the aspects of German life you're probably looking for.

## Baden-Württemberg – the Black Forest

Many travellers consider the south-western region, from Karlsruhe to Basel, to be Germany's most enchanting. The pace of life is slower and the villages and towns dotted round the forests really are as attractive as the tourist brochures make them look. The main towns of this region are Heidelberg, Freiburg, Tübingen, Baden-Baden and Stuttgart. The first three are picturesque old university towns and worth a day or two. Unless you've plenty of time (and money), forget Baden-Baden as it's very expensive. Stuttgart is an interesting industrial city. A day trip from Heidelberg to Freiburg, Donaueschingen and Offenburg is a good 'pushed-for-time' introduction to this area.

## Heidelberg phone code: 06221

Most of Heidelberg's sights can be seen in a day, and are well worth the trip. This is Germany's oldest university town, famous also for magnificent castle ruins, quaint streets, traditional bars and myriad antique shops.

Start your tour (get a bus or taxi as it's a 40-minute walk into town) at the **Marktplatz** and take in the **Heilig-Geist Kirche** and **Haus Zum Ritter**, a Renaissance mansion house, now a hotel and restaurant. The **old university** has an interesting students' jail, *Studentenkarzer*, which was in use from 1778 to 1914. The walls are covered in graffiti. Entrance is only 2DM. From here, cross the Karl-Theodor Bridge or Old Bridge over the River Neckar and take the hour-long **Philosopher's Walk** to the 429m **Heiligenberg**. Apart from a good view of the town, there are reconstructed Roman ruins and the 12th-century **St Stephen's Cloister**.

Back across the river, inside the amazing **Schloss** is the **German Apothecary Museum** with interesting reconstructions of laboratories of the 17th century. You can get up to it by funicular railway from Kornmarkt if you don't fancy the climb.

The **Tourist Information** office, just outside the station, is open Mon.–Sat.: 9am–7pm, Sun.: 10am–6pm, Mar.–Dec., closed Sun. Jan. and Feb. (Tel. 14220; Fax. 142222). They run an accommodation-finding service for a small fee and supply you with leaflets and maps. Ask for *All Around Heidelberg*, *Heidelberg This Week* and the official town map, which includes a picture map and a walking tour of the main sights. Try to get around town by bus and tram.

There is a special **Tourist Ticket** available, 36 hours at 7DM or 11DM depending on the areas travelled. There is also the **Heidelberg Card**, which gets you free entrance to all the main sights, along with free city transportation; ask at the Tourist Office. **Amex** is at Kornmarkt 2 (Tel. 601 816; Fax. 601860), this office only deals with travellers' cheques. The other office at Bruckenkopfstrasse 1-2 (Tel. 45050; Fax. 410333) holds post and is also a travel agency.

**HS Reisebüro**, who do student travel deals, are at Bismarckplatz (Tel. 27151), and the **Eurail Aid Office** is at the train station (Tel. 525 341).

Heidelberg gets its fair share of middle-class, middle-aged tourists, so hotels tend to be expensive. Still, there's a **youth hostel** at Tiergartenstrasse (Tel. 412066; Fax. 402559), on bus routes 33 or 330 with connecting tram at night. The hostel is always very busy so, if possible, fax. your reservation as far in advance as you can.

The **Neckertal campsite** is in Schlierbach (Tel. 802506). You are not allowed to leave the campsite before 8am, so don't pitch your tent there if you have an early start the next morning. Your passport is kept as security. There is a train station nearby, but services are limited to two trains at night, and one in the morning. The **Haide campsite** is between Heidelberg, Ziegelhausen and Kleingemund. Take bus 35 to Orthopädische Klinik, then across the bridge and 10 minutes further along the river (Tel. 06223 2111).

Use the **Mensa** restaurants for meals – there's one off Universitätsplatz and another in Marstallhof. Or you could try a historic student inn. These are dotted all round the city, the most famous including **Roter Ochsen**, Hauptstrasse 217 and **Schnookeloch**, Haspelgasse 8. The **station** restaurant is reasonably priced, providing you pick carefully from the menu. A filling meal with beer can be had for around 18DM. For takeaways and picnic food head for the delicatessens and fast-food outlets on **Hauptstrasse**. There are a few cheap restaurants on **Bergheimer Strasse** which are worth a try.

## Freiburg-im-Breisgau phone code: 0761

The gateway to the southern Black Forest is famous also for its Kaiserstuhl vineyards and sparkling nightlife. It is an attractive place, right on the edge of the romantic Hollental valley. Though the city suffered badly during World War II bombing, it has been fully restored and is today as picturesque as ever. The university is the source of most young Freiburgers' social life, and the summer schools based there make sure things don't grind to a halt outside term-time.

Two blocks down Eisenbahnstrasse from the station is the **Tourist Information** at Rotteckring 14 (Tel. 388 1882; Fax. 388 1887). They can arrange accommodation for you, or if you're staying more than two days, you can get into **private accommodation** (*Privatzimmer*). Also ask for details of the 24-hour, 48-hour and 72-hour tourist passes. These will save you money, especially if you find yourself staying out of the centre.

At the centre of the **Altstadt** (Old Town) is the beautiful medieval cathedral (the **Münster**), plastered with intricate carvings and gargoyles. Climbing the Münster spire is a rewarding and exhilarating experience (cost 2DM). Opposite the cathedral to the south is the 16th-century **Kaufhaus** (merchants' hall), and nearby is the **Rathaus** (town hall) made out of two old patrician houses. Medieval and Baroque art of the Upper Rhine can be seen in the **Augustiner Museum**.

There's a **youth hostel** and a **campsite** in Kartäuserstrasse at 151 and 99 respectively (Tel. 67656; Fax. 60367 and Tel. 35054; Fax. 289212). Take tram 1 from the station to Stadhalle, then take the subway to the left and after about five minutes you'll cross the river and then the canal. The entrance to **Hirzberg Camping** is about 50 metres on the left. The campsite has caravans for rent (from 20DM for one person, 25DM for two, 30DM for up to four people), and tents cost 10DM (for two people) or 15DM for a bigger tent. The campsite also has bikes for rent for 18DM a day. With woods and forests all around, you shouldn't be stuck for a place to pitch your tent, but if things are desperate, see the **Bahnhofmission** at the station.

In the last week of June, Freiburg stages its **Wine Festival**. Baden white wine from here is well worth trying, and Freiburg has many wine bars and cheap (by German standards) **eating** places. Concentrate on the university area: Augustinerplatz and Escholzstrasse (where cheap pasta dishes can be found 6–7.30pm).

# Tübingen phone code: 07071

The University of Tübingen, founded in 1477, still makes use of the town's Renaissance castle (**Schloss Hohentübingen**) and you can only visit it at weekends Apr.–Oct. There is a good view over the old town and the Neckar from its gardens. In the centre there are old gabled houses and a 15th-century church, **Stiftskirche**. In the Neckar on a man-made island is the **Platanenallee**, an avenue of plane trees which makes a good walk. Reach it via the Eberhard bridge. The **Rathaus**, in Marktplatz, dates from 1435 and has an interesting astronomical clock.

The **Tourist Office** is by the main bridge, the Neckarbrücke (Tel. 91360). Hourly trains run to/from Stuttgart and take an hour.

The **youth hostel** is at Gartenstrasse 22/2 (Tel. 23002; Fax. 25061), 10 minutes from the station. There's a **campsite** on the banks of the Neckar (Tel. 43145) at Rappenberghalde 61. The university Mensa restaurant is on the corner of Wilhelmstrasse and Keplerstrasse and is open for lunches and dinners.

## Stuttgart phone code: 0711

The capital of Baden-Württemberg, heavily bombed during World War II, was rebuilt as an industrial centre and today is home to the Porsche factory and Bosch electronics. Despite its rapid modernization, more than half of the city remains woodland, vineyards (it is the largest wine-growing city in Germany) and parks.

### TOURIST INFORMATION

**Tourist centre**: *i-Punkt*, Königstrasse 1a, near the station (Tel. 22280; Fax. 222 8253), open 9.30am–8pm (Sat.: 9.30am–6pm, Sun. and holidays: 11am–6pm, Sun. Nov.–Apr.: 1pm–6pm). In addition to providing details of walking tours and maps, they can help find, and book (no booking fee), budget accommodation.

Also try JIZ (*Jugend-Informationszentrum*) at Hohestrasse 9 (Tel. 293058), specifically for forthcoming events and where the action is. The **Eurail Aid Office** is at the train station (Tel. 2092 2464).

There's a three-day **Stuttgart City Pass**, giving free unlimited use of all public transport, admission to two museums and reductions to other attractions and services. Ask at the tourist office.

**Amex** is at Schillerplatz 4 (Tel. 162 4920; Fax. 162 4922) and there's a branch at Lautenschlagerstrasse 3 (Tel. 187 5100; Fax. 187 5132) as well as at the airport.

### SEEING

The city has the most abundant mineral water springs in western Europe, and the **mineral baths** make a refreshing diversion from the **Schlossgarten**. Alternatively take U14 to Mineralbäder, where **Leuze** mineral baths have both an outdoor swimming pool and a heated indoor pool.

**FREE STUTTGART:** With so many pedestrianized streets, Stuttgart is best seen on foot.

- The big squares **Schlossplatz** and **Schillerplatz** are typical of Stuttgart and are surrounded by most of the major sights.
- The **Schlossgarten** stretches northwards to the River Neckar and here you can enjoy landscaped woods, lakes and a zoo.
- There's an outstanding collection of museums, and the city-owned ones are free of charge. Those especially worth a visit include the imposing extension of the **Staatsgalerie** (built by a British architect) on Konrad-Adenauer Strasse and the **Mercedes Benz Automobile Museum** just outside the main city, open Tues.–Sun.: 9am–5pm. Take S-Bahn 1 to Neckarstadion or bus 56.

## SLEEPING

Should be no problem as *i-Punkt* will help. The **DJH Hostel** at Haussmannstrasse 27 (entrance on the corner of Werastrasse and Kernerstrasse) is central and modern and is only 10 minutes from the station. Take S-Bahn 15 to Eugensplatz (Tel. 241583; Fax. 236 1041). The non-DJH **Jugendgästehaus** at Richard-Wagner-Strasse 2 (Tel. 241132 and 248 9730) has expensive but comfortable single or double rooms. Take U-Bahn 15 to Budenbad.

The **campsite** at Cannstatter Wasen (Tel. 556696 or 561503) is less central, on the banks of the river Neckar. It costs around 9DM per person and per site.

## EATING AND NIGHTLIFE

Wine is varied and excellent here, whilst local culinary specialities include *Maultaschen* – lentils – with Wiener sausages, and hand-made noodles, or roast beef with sauerkraut.

Follow the locals to a nearby *Kneipe* for a popular meeting place and refreshment. They normally fill up very quickly and become quite lively.

Stuttgart has a lively **youth scene** and the many **jazz** clubs are popular. Ask at *i-Punkt*, JIZ or any young resident for the latest details. Not to be missed in summer/early autumn are the variety of **street fairs** and 'happenings'. The **Wine Festival** in late Aug.–Sept. at Schillerplatz and Marktplatz is lively, whilst the **Canstatt Volksfest** in late Sept.–Oct. should not be missed, as it is equalled in scale only by the Munich Oktoberfest.

# The Harz Mountains

If you're looking for medieval charm, go no further. With half-timbered houses, castles, and torture chambers among the 1,600 historical buildings, it's no wonder **Quedlinburg** has been recognized by UNESCO as one of the world's most important cultural treasures. **Tourist Information** is at Markt 2 (Tel. 03946 905622). **Wernigerode** has the famous wooden houses, a fine town hall and a hilltop castle, as well as being the starting point of the Ham narrow-gauge steam railway. There are two hostel-like **guesthouses** with beds for 25DM, telephone 03943 632061 or ask at the tourist office. The **Jugendgästehaus** at Friedrichstrasse 53 is clean and bright with modern facilities. The **Tourist Office** is at Nicolaiplatz 1 (Tel. 03943 633035).

To reach either of these small towns, take a train from Halberstadt. Services connect Halberstadt to Magdeburg and Halle. A few buses a day cross the old border to Bad Harzburg, which has train connections to Hannover and Braunschweig.

A short distance from Bad Harzburg is the old imperial town of **Goslar**, with numerous half-timbered buildings, the **Imperial Palace** and the frescoed **Hall of Homage** in the town hall. **Tourist Information** is at Marktplatz 7. There's a **youth hostel** at Rammelsberger Strasse 25 (Tel. 05321 22240; Fax. 05321 41376).

## The Rhine Valley

The popular image of the Rhine as a romantic cruising vantage point for seeing the vineyards, castles and cliffs of its beautiful river valley is certainly founded on truth. But it is somewhat idealistic, as the Rhine today is still Europe's main commercial waterway, and as such carries its fair share of barges and freight loads. Nevertheless, the section of the river that flows through Germany is considered the most scenic.

Köln–Düsseldorfer lines run boats from Frankfurt to Cologne which give a 50% discount to Inter-Railers and are free to Eurail card holders. The most attractive segment of the journey is from Rüdesheim to Koblenz, or vice versa. **Oberwesel** is a lovely place, but almost closes down on Mon. The youth hostel is fantastic, complete with swimming pool. It's at Auf dem Schönberg (Tel. 06744 93330; Fax. 06774 7446) and costs around 28DM, including breakfast. Phone to book in after 8am. Stop off here on your way from Cologne to Bingen – it's about three hours down the line – and finish your journey by boat.

## Cologne (Köln) phone code: 0221

Cologne is the largest city on the river Rhine. Since Roman times, Cologne has prospered as a centre for trading, and in the Middle Ages it was a member of the powerful Hanseatic trading alliance.

After heavy World War II bombing, it was largely rebuilt, and now straddles both sides of the river. Visitors, though, stay mostly on the left bank. Even if you can afford only a few hours, you should have no problems, as everything is near the station. **Tourist Information** is at Unter Fettenhennen 19 (Tel. 221 3345), **Amex** is at Burgmauerstrasse 14 (Tel. 925 9010). (Post is held here free for four weeks).

As you approach Cologne, the sight of the city's Gothic cathedral (**Kölner Dom**) – with its twin spires soaring more than 500 feet into the sky – will take your breath away. Leaving the station, you'll find yourself in the huge **Domplatz**, a square given over (like most of the old town) to pedestrians, and linking the station to the old Roman city. During the summer, it's a lively meeting place, bustling with sightseers and street entertainers.

The **Cathedral** is right opposite the train station. Started in 1248 to house the remains of the Three Magi, the Cathedral was completed only in 1880; see the 14th-century stained-glass windows, altarpiece and the Shrine of the Magi. In World War II, 90% of Cologne was razed to the ground, but amazingly the cathedral escaped almost intact, and was used at one point to hold prisoners of war. Open 7am–7pm. For an impressive view of the city, climb the 509 steps up the **tower** (half price with ISIC), tower open 9am–4, 5 or 6pm daily, depending on the season.

From Cologne, you can take an hour-long **cruise** on the Rhine for around 12DM. It makes two stops to allow break of journey, so if you wish to visit the **zoo** or take the **cable-car** across the river, this is a relatively cheap and pleasant way to do it. You also get a great view of the *Dom* from the river. If you just want to take the cable-car, the times change daily so either telephone 762006 or visit the Rheinseilbahn terminus near the zoo, for information.

If you're on the scent of **Eau-de-Cologne**, you won't be disappointed. Less than 10 minutes' walk from the cathedral is the house where the 4711 brand was created. It's named after the number of the house where the perfumed water was made – the house was allocated to its makers by the French during the Napoleonic occupation. Though early claims that 4711 worked miracle cures had to be withdrawn, you can still buy it at Number 4711, and splash it on as a refreshing skin tonic (ask at Tourist Information for directions).

Other places of interest are the **Roman-Germanic Museum** exhibiting Cologne's Roman remains, which is right next to the Cathedral, and the **Wallraff-Richartz-Museum/Museum Ludwig** with its impressive collection of German works. (Entrance 10DM). The **Museum of Arts and Crafts** at An der Rechtsschule includes vast collections of arts and crafts from the Middle Ages to the present day. Open Tues.–Sun.: 10am–5pm, until 10pm first Thurs. each month. Admission 5DM. The **Käthe Kollwitz Museum** at Neumarkt 18–24 has sculptures and black and white graphics by the great socialist artist (5DM). Museums are closed on Mon. Students can get half-price admission to all the museums. If you're not a student but plan to visit more than a couple of museums invest in a **Museum pass** (around 20DM) which allows free entry to all museums on two consecutive days.

If you've a sweet tooth, it's worth hunting out the **Stollwerk chocolate factory**, which has a museum and café by the river, along with a climate-controlled cocoa tree plantation. You can watch chocolate being made. Keep an eye out for giveaways!

And if you're in the area during the seventh week before Easter (!), don't panic: the wacky costumes and spontaneous singing are simply the locals' way of celebrating the **Cologne Carnival**. Germans from all over the country converge on Cologne for this fairly surreal street party, and if you're lucky enough to witness it, you're unlikely to ever forget the experience!

**EXCURSION** If you are based in Cologne, **Aachen** is well worth a half-day visit, being 40 minutes away by train. The **Rathaus** and **Cathedral** are of great interest in this former capital of the Holy Roman Empire.
**EUROSTAR** Eurostar's high-speed service under the English Channel to Brussels (in 2 hours 40 minutes) has onward connections now with the international Thalys express to Aachen and Cologne. Six departures daily from London Waterloo will get you to Germany in under four hours, and to Cologne in 5 hours and 30 mins (Tel. 0990 186 186).

## STATION FACILITIES

The **Hauptbahnhof** has an information desk open from dawn till dusk and a 24-hour service point. It has all the usual amenities and is shut 1am–4am. The Eurail Aid Office is open 5.30am–11pm (closing half an hour earlier at weekends), Tel. 19 419.

Daily trains to: Düsseldorf (30 mins, 5 per hour), Hamburg (four hours), Copenhagen (nine hours), Hannover (three hours), Mainz (16¾ hours), Frankfurt -am-Main (2½ hours), Würzburg (3½ hours), Nürnberg (4½ hours), Stuttgart (three hours), Vienna (10 hours), Munich (six hours), Innsbruck, Zürich (six hours), Basel (4½ hours), Paris (5½ hours), Brussels (2½ hours), Rotterdam (three hours), The Hague (three hours), Amsterdam (2½ hours).

## SLEEPING

**HOSTELS** There are two hostels in Cologne which are very good but suffer from the same problem – they fill up fast. The nearest to the main station, and reputedly the best, is at Siegesstrasse 5a (Tel. 814711; Fax. 884425). It's a 20-minute walk across the Rhine, but is only two minutes' walk from the Deutz station and is well sign-posted. Beds from 32DM, breakfast included.

You can also try the other youth hostel at An der Schanze 14 (Tel. 767081; Fax. 761555), which is more luxurious, but further out and more expensive; 39DM. You cannot book by phone, so get there as soon as possible after reception opens at 11am. Take U-Bahn lines 5, 15, 16 or 18 to Boltensternstrasse and then a five-minute walk.

Tourist Information, just opposite the cathedral, will also find rooms from about 35DM upwards.
**CAMPING** There are two campsites at the end of the Rodenkirchen Bridge. **Campingplatz der Stadt Köln** is at Weidenweg (Tel. 831 966). Although facilities are limited, there is a good bar across the

road. Cost is around 7DM per person and 5DM per tent. The site is open from May to late September.

## EATING AND NIGHTLIFE
Salzgasse in the Old Town is where to go for eats, and in the city centre are all the usual excellent department stores with food halls for buying groceries. The square immediately in front of the Cathedral is lively and interesting, often with street musicians performing, and a 'peace wall' to which you can contribute messages. The university cafeteria is at Zulpicherstrasse 70. After dark, head for Hohenzollernring, an area full of good places with live music. For great Jazz, try **Papa Joe's Klimperkasten** at Alter Markt 50, or **Papa Joe's Em Streckstrump** at Buttermarkt 37.

# The Moselle Valley

Mosel (as it is known in Germany) is the less commercial (some say less scenic) cousin of the Rhine, though tourism – along with wine-making – still provides the main income for the region. **Boats** run between Cochem and Koblenz (KD lines with the same reductions as on the Rhine). The **hostel** at Koblenz is very good and overlooks the confluence of the Rhine and Mosel. It's at Koblenz-Ehrenbreitstein on the right bank, bus 7, 8, 9, 10 from the station (Tel. 0261 972 870; Fax. 0261 9728730). The towns to visit are: **Bernkastelkues, Traben-Trarbach** and **Cochem**. You can hire bikes at Cochem. This is the region for wine tasting – ask at the Tourist Information offices for tours of the local cellars.

# Frankfurt-am-Main phone code: 069

Frankfurt is Germany's most important finance and trading centre, a city of large skyscrapers with a major international airport and what is claimed to be Europe's largest railway station. Each year it hosts the world's largest book, musical instrument and consumer goods fairs. It's a large and interesting city but the main sights can be visited in a day.

## STATION FACILITIES
**Frankfurt (Main) Hauptbahnhof** is massive. It simply has everything and the only thing to note is that it shuts 1am–4am (though you can stay overnight if you have a train ticket – not recommended, though).

**Left-luggage** lockers are always available (4DM per piece) and there's a 24-hour **service point**. Call 19419 for timetable information and reservations.

Daily trains to: Hamburg (3½ hours), Hannover (2½ hours), Munich (3½ hours), Cologne (2½ hours), Berlin (5½ hours), Brussels (five hours), Amsterdam (five hours).

## TOURIST INFORMATION AND ADDRESSES

**TOURIST OFFICE** The main Tourist Information Centre, next to the Hauptbahnhof entrance in the main hall, is open Mon.–Fri.: 8am–9pm; weekends: 9am–6pm (Tel. 2123 8849). Another office is at Römerberg 27, open Mon.–Fri.: 9.30am–5.30pm; Sat.–Sun.: 9.30am–4pm (Tel. 2123 8708). There is also an information stand, **City-Info**, at Zeil 94a, in the centre of the commercial district, open Mon.–Fri.: 10am–6pm; Sat.–Sun.: 10am–4pm.

Ask them about the Frankfurt Card, which gives one (10DM) or two days (15DM) of free travel on public transport, and 50% discount for 15 museums, the zoo and other attractions.

**POST OFFICE** On the first floor of the station, open Mon.-Fri.: 6.30am-9pm; Sat.: 8am-6pm; Sun.: 11am-6pm. The main branch is at Zeil 90, inside Hertie's department store; open Mon.–Fri.: 9.30am–8pm, Sat.: 9am–4pm. (Tel. 2111; Fax. 296884).

**AMEX** Kaiserstrasse 8; open Mon.–Fri.: 9.30am–6pm, Sat.: 9.30am–12.30pm (Tel. 2105 111; 24hr hotline (0130) 853100; Fax. 283398). Holds post for four weeks.

**UK CONSULATE** Bockenheimer Landstrasse 42 (Tel. 170 0020; Fax. 729553)

**IRISH NATIONALS** See Berlin

**US CONSULATE** Siesmayerstrasse 21 (Tel. 75350; Fax. 748938)

**CANADIAN NATIONALS** See Berlin

**AUSTRALIAN CONSULATE** Gutleutstrasse 85 (Tel. 273 9090; Fax. 232631)

**NEW ZEALAND NATIONALS** See Bonn

**SOUTH AFRICAN CONSULATE** Ulmenstrasse 37 (Tel. 719 1130)

**EURAIL AID OFFICE** Main train station (Tel. 265 4581)

**24-HOUR MEDICAL SERVICES** Uni-Clinic at Theodor Stern Kaiin Sachsenhausen (Tel. 630 11)

**EMERGENCY PRESCRIPTIONS** Tel. 19292

**STUDENT TRAVEL OFFICE** Campus Travel, Bergerstrasse 73 (Tel. 43 08 9011)

## SEEING

The area around the **Römerberg** is a must-see, with its rebuilt 15th-century **Römer** (city hall), beautiful timber-worked houses and **St**

**Nikolaikirche**. Nearby is the **Dom** (Cathedral), built between the 13th and 15th centuries. The coronation of German Emperors took place here between 1562 and 1792. Among the museums worth a visit are the **Historical Museum**, collections from the Middle Ages to the present day, the **German Film Museum**, about the history and origins of the film industry and the **Goethe-Haus** museum and library, where Goethe was born in 1749. The **Jewish Museum**, **Natural History Museum** and various art museums, particularly the **Städel Museum** on the south bank of the Main River, are also worth a look. Museums generally open Tues.–Sun.: 10am–5pm, Wed.: 10am–8pm, and are often free on Wed.

## SLEEPING AND EATING

The **youth hostel** is at Deutschherrnufer 12 (Tel. 6100150; Fax. 6100 1599). Take tram 16 to Textorstrasse. It is pleasantly situated across the River Main and on the edge of *Sachsenhausen*, the city's liveliest area for entertainment and reasonable eating places. The *Apfelwein* around here is cheap and plentiful. The nearest **campsite** is at An der Sandelmühle 35 in the Heddernheim district. Take U-Bahn 1, 2 or 3. Around 10DM per person and 6DM per tent.

The fruit stalls and shops in the underground mall in front of the station are quite good for stocking up on picnic items. Frankfurters are not a Frankfurt speciality (they are known locally as Wieners!).

## NIGHTLIFE

*MainCity* is a monthly English guide to what's on in town. It costs 5DM and is widely available. Jazz is popular and there are lots of places to enjoy it, including at the **Jazzkeller** (Tel. 288537) at Kleine Bockenheimer Strasse 18a. If you prefer international dance music, then **Brotfabrik** on Bachmannstrasse 2–4 is the place to go. A fashionable gay bar is **Zum Schwejk** at Schäffergasse 20.

## Trier phone code: 0651

Germany's oldest city and one-time capital of the western Roman Empire (with Roman baths, arches and amphitheatre remains to prove it), Trier has many interesting churches and museums, as well as the house where Karl Marx was born. **Tourist Information** is next to the Porta Nigra; ask there for details of the **Trier Card**, which offers admission to seven museums and reduced rates for the theatre, tours and other attractions. A three-day card costs 25DM, including free public transportation (17DM without).

The (IYHF) **youth hostel** is at An der Jugendherberge 4 (Tel. 146 620; Fax. 1466230) and the **campsite** is at Luxemburgerstrasse 81 (Tel. 86921)

There is a good **market** next to the cathedral (and while you are there, take a look at the impressive interior decor). For a good view of the city itself, follow the Römerstrasse up from the north bank of the Mosel to the Madonna statue.

For other cheap **eats** try either of the two **university Mensas** at Universität Schneidershof or at the Tarforst campus. The **Greek restaurant** next to the youth hostel serves good, filling and reasonably-priced meals. For cheap beer and good food, head for the **Löwenbrau Brauerei**, near the amphitheatre. It is off the Gartenfeldstrasse, 100m after the railway bridge. The tree-shaded patio, where food and drink are served, is across the road from the main entrance.

## Munich (München) phone code: 089

This is the tourist mecca of Germany – capital of Bavaria and regarded by some as the most German of all cities. Despite the visiting hordes, Munich is a laid-back sort of place, and given the charm of its parks, the buzz of its beer gardens, and the huge number of things to do and see, it's a place in which you'll want to linger.

Ruled for more than 650 years by the Wittelsbach family, who brought the world-famous art collections and rich architectural heritage to the city, Munich is a city of numerous churches and stately homes. With the Alps as a backdrop, it has one of the most uplifting skylines in Germany – and its cultural life is just as invigorating.

Though the famous Oktoberfest beer bonanzas are the big annual draw – pulling in upwards of six million people who each knock back an average of a litre of beer – festival follows festival all the year round. **Fasching** with its masked carnivals kicks them off in February, ending on Shrove Tuesday; the beer inaugurations follow in March; then comes the summer season of concerts and operas from May to August; the **Oktoberfest** lasts from end Sept. to early Oct.; and the Christmas markets round it all off.

And this doesn't even take into account the countless student-based activities going on round **Schwabing**, Munich's lively Latin quarter.

## STATION FACILITIES

München Hauptbahnhof's **train information** is open daily 6am–11pm (Tel. 19419), travel centre 6am–10.30pm and reservations Mon.–Fri.: 5.20am–11pm, Sat.: 5.10am–10.40pm, Sun.: 6am–10.40pm. There's also a **Tourist Information** (Mon.–Sat.: 8am–10pm, Sun.: 11am–7pm) on site and a foreign exchange desk which is open daily 6am–11pm. There's a full complement of facilities, including a **24-hour café** and waiting room, though the station shuts 1.30am–4.30am.

Daily trains to: Paris (8½ hours), Brussels (eight hours), Zurich (4¼ hours), Milan (7½ hours), Vienna (4½–5½ hours).

## TOURIST INFORMATION

The **Fremdenverkehrsamt** (Tourist Office) is at the front of the Hauptbahnhof, opposite platform 11, and is open daily 8am–10pm (Tel. 2333 0256/71; Fax. 2333 0233). The staff are helpful, fluent in English and will supply you with maps, details of walking tours and pamphlets and find you a room for 5DM. Get the monthly programme of events and the *Young People's Guide to Munich*, which is excellent. There is also a small office just inside the entrance to the Neues Rathaus on Marienplatz (Tel. 2333 0272 or 2333 0273) which has free brochures and cheap city maps.

During the summer, another information service operates at the Hauptbahnhof. It's called **EurAide**, and you'll find it along track 11 in the main hall, June–Sept., 7.30am–noon and 1pm–6pm daily, and same hours in October until the end of the Oktoberfest. The English-speaking staff will help with train and tourist information, and are great at giving tips on the very latest things to see and do. (Tel. 593889; Fax. 550 3965).

Munich's **city transport** system is one of the best in Europe, and also one of the most complicated. There are buses, trams, the U-Bahn and the S-Bahn. (Note: Rail pass holders get free travel on the S-Bahn only.)

Whilst it is tempting and apparently easy to travel free on public transport, you take the risk of an on-the-spot fine of around 65DM if a squad of police operates a random check (which are frequent). Ignorance is no excuse – the police reason that anyone who can work out how to get to their destination can operate the idiot-proof ticket dispensers or obtain a pass! Offenders or those unable to pay are taken to the police station for a statement. It obviously makes sense to have a valid ticket (and don't forget to stamp it in the box marked with an 'E' before you go to the platform or as soon as you get on the bus).

You need only one ticket, even if your journey takes in the tram, bus and underground systems. For further information, pick up leaflets at the underground at Hauptbahnhof, or S-Bahn stations. Weekly passes, day passes and multiple journey tickets are available.

## ADDRESSES

**POST OFFICE** Arnulfstrasse 32. Mon.–Fri.: 8am–8pm; Sat.: 8am–midday. (Tel. 5454 2336). Also *poste restante* here. You can change money but it's cheaper at the Amex office. There's also a post office upstairs at the train station (Tel. 552 2620) but it does not send packages or change money.

**AMEX** At Hotel Bayerischer Hof, Promenadeplatz 6, Mon.–Fri.: 9am–5.30pm, Sat.: 9am–12.30pm (Tel. 290 900; 24hr hotline (0130) 853100), also Kaufinger Strasse 24 (Tel. 228 01387), Mon.–Fri.: 9am–5.30pm, Sat.: 10am–1pm, and at the airport.

**UK CONSULATE** Bürkleinstrasse 10 (Tel. 211090)

**IRISH CONSULATE** Mauerkircherstrasse 1a (Tel. 985723)

**US CONSULATE** Königinstrasse 5 (Tel. 28880)

**CANADIAN CONSULATE** Tal 29 (Tel. 2199 570)

**AUSTRALIAN NATIONALS** Contact the embassy in Berlin

**NEW ZEALAND NATIONALS** Contact the embassy in Bonn, Bundeskanzlerplatz 2-10 (Tel. 228-228 070)

**EMERGENCY DOCTOR** Tel. 55 8661

**EMERGENCY PHARMACY** Tel. 594 475

**EMERGENCY MEDICAL SERVICE** Tel. 551771

**STUDIOSUS-REISEN (STUDENT TRAVEL)** Amalienstrasse 73 (Tel. 500 6000)

## SEEING

To get the city's history in perspective, first stop should be the palace of the Bavarian rulers (the **Residenz**), which houses a spectacular array of riches. Open Tues.–Sat.: 10am–4.30pm, Sun.: till 1pm (4DM).

The **Bavarian National Museum** gives a good introduction to what makes the region different from the rest of Germany, and has the most extensive collection of arts and crafts in the world (closed Mon. but open till 5pm; after 3.30pm they sometimes let you in for free).

The **Deutsches Museum** is a fascinating museum located on an island in the Isar River; it is the largest technical museum in the world (with lots of buttons to push), and has exhibits such as U-boats, a Messerschmitt jet fighter, a planetarium and old locomotives. Entrance 10DM and a visit to the planetarium is 3DM extra (discounts with an ISIC card ). Open daily 9am–5pm.

The **BMW Museum** (part of the factory) offers good guided tours of the factory itself, and the museum is superb and includes a spectacular audio-visual show. It's the last stop on U-Bahn 2 and 3. It's open daily from 9am–5pm. Last entry 4pm. While there, visit the park (take U-Bahn line 3; it's a 10-minute ride), scene of the 1972 Olympic Games, and marvel at the impressive architecture either from ground level or from the top of the Olympia Tower. Entrance to the park is free, around 6DM for the lift up the tower, which is well worth it for the stupendous view, unless the weather is lousy. Don't eat in the restaurant at the top as the prices are exorbitant.

The **Alte Pinakothek** is one of Europe's finest art galleries. Entrance 7.50DM.

As a break from sightseeing, there's **rowing** boats on the lake, or sports enthusiasts might relish a visit to **FC Bayern**, one of Europe's most successful football clubs. Tickets can be bought from Tourist Offices or try your luck with the touts at the ground.

## THE OKTOBERFEST BEER FESTIVAL

Contrary to what its name suggests, the annual Oktoberfest takes place mostly in September, spilling over into the first few days of October. With around six million litres of beer, 400,000 *Bratwurst* sausages, 600,000 spit roast chickens and 24 roasted oxen consumed during each festival, you'd think revellers would be quietly nursing the worst hangovers of their lives after the first day or so. But beer buffs reckon the high-quality beers, all brewed locally and made extra-strong just for the festival, rarely cause headaches.

The tradition came about after the party thrown in 1810 to celebrate the marriage of Crown Prince Ludwig of Bavaria to Princess Therese von Sachsen-Hildburghausen. The locals enjoyed the carousing so much that they decided to hold one every year.

Modern-day revelry is generally contained within seven gigantic brewery tents, surrounded by smaller wine and food tents (run by Munich's best eateries). Each of the large tents can hold up to 10,000 people seated at (or dancing on) wooden trestle tables and benches, all served by waitresses carrying an astonishing eight or nine steins at once. The background to all this is usually a thigh-slapping Bavarian oompah band, its members dressed in traditional lederhosen, frilly shirts and feathered hats. From this description you might not think it, but proceedings can get pretty riotous.

Alongside this spectacle, there's a huge funfair, and a collection of old-fashioned Bavarian entertainment stalls, providing bemused onlookers with a variety of stunts, such as bird-whistling, dancing, ringmastering flea circuses and juggling.

**FREE MUNICH:**
- **Marienplatz**, the attractive pedestrian zone, is at the centre of Munich. The neo-Gothic **Town Hall** is located here (look out for the Glockenspiel show at 11am, noon, 5pm and 9pm May–Oct.; 11am Nov.–Apr.), as is the old town hall (**Altes Rathaus**). On Sunday mornings in summer, a brass band in full Bavarian uniform plays in front of the town hall.
- Just off Marienplatz is the 12th-century church of **St Peter**. If a white disc is out on the platform, climb its tower for a view extending to the Alps (a red disc means you'll just see over Munich).
- Near here is the **Frauenkirche**, with its green onion-topped twin towers; it is the symbol of the city and houses various works of art, tombs and relics as well as the mausoleum of Emperor Ludwig IV (presently closed).

- **St Michael's Church** and the Baroque **Theatiner Church** are also worth a look.
- Eight blocks west of Marienplatz is **Karlsplatz**, the main square of Munich. All the city transport starts from here and **Sonnenstrasse**, a major shopping street, begins. For yet more exciting window shopping, check out **Neuhausenstrasse** and **Kaufingerstrasse**.
- North of the Residenz is the university area (Schwabing) with Leopoldstrasse at its centre. Nothing much goes on in daytime here, but it's a lively place at night.
- To the east of Schwabing lies the **English Garden**, ideal for sunbathing (nude!) and a picnic.
- A great panorama can be had for free by walking up one of the hills in the **Olympic Park** (take U-Bahn line 3; it's a 10-minute ride).

## SLEEPING

Munich is busy all year, particularly during the Oktoberfest, when beds are very scarce. Still, there are plenty of places if you know where to look. Expect to pay about 25–40DM for student accommodation, 17–40DM at youth hostels and up to 70DM in pensions. Try to arrange hostel accommodation ahead of time or turn up early! Ask at Tourist Information for the *Accommodation Guide to Munich*.

The cheapest sleep to be had is at the **Youth Camp** (*Jugendlager am Kapuzinerhölzl,* known as the 'Big Tent') at Frank-Schrank Strasse 8; open end June–early Sept.: 5pm–9am. For a few marks you get an air mattress, blankets and a place in the circus tent, not to mention tea (free) in the mornings and evenings. You won't get turned away, and there is a great 'international' atmosphere; maximum stay is three days only. Take U-Bahn 1 to Rotkreuzplatz, then tram 12 to Botanischer Garten. Take your passport for ID to avoid paying a 50DM deposit for blankets; ask for plenty of these if it is late in the season as it can get chilly.

**YOUTH HOSTELS** You must be under 27 or accompanying a child to use Bavarian youth hostels.

**Wendl-Dietrich Strasse** 20 (Tel. 131156; Fax. 167 8745) is fairly central but large, impersonal, fills up early and is usually full of noisy adolescent school groups. It could be cleaner, and the lockers are dodgy. Security is a bit suspect too. Costs from 25.50DM including breakfast. Take U-Bahn 1 to Rotkreuzplatz.

The other IYHF hostel is at **Miesingstrasse 4** (Tel. 723 6550/723 6560; Fax. 724 2567). This is a much nicer, cleaner hostel and still fairly close to the action. It is south-west of the city in the suburb of Thalkirchen. Take U-Bahn 3 to Thalkirchen and then follow the signs. Beds are 29DM.

There's also one at **Burgweg** (IYHF) 4–6, Pullach (Tel. 7930643 and 7930644; Fax. 793 7922), but this renovated castle is a half-hour journey and also fills up early. There are no lockers (and we've had reports of thefts here) and it has an infuriating token system for showers. The staff, however, are very helpful and it costs from 20DM including shower and breakfast in a small dormitory. Take S-Bahn 7 (free on Inter-Rail) to Pullach, signposted from station. Last train from Munich is 10.40pm and curfew is at 11.30pm.

**Haus International**, Elizabethstrasse 87 (Tel. 120060) is a good private hostel but a bit more expensive, with prices from 40DM per person in a dorm to 58DM for a single. No IYHF card required. There is a disco in the basement and no curfew.

Try **CVJM-YMCA** Jugendgästhaus, Landwehrstrasse 13 (Tel. 552 1410; Fax. 550 4282) near to Hauptbahnhof, Beds in triples from 38DM, singles around 50DM.

If you're stuck for a place to stay try the **Augsburg Youth Hostel**, at Beim Pfaffenkeller 3 (Tel. 0821 33909; Fax. 0821 151149), about 40 minutes away by DB train.

**PENSIONS** Some of the cheapest are located in Schillerstrasse and Landwehrstrasse.

**HOTELS** For a reasonable hotel try the **Helvetia** at Schillerstrasse 6 (Tel. 590 6850; Fax. 5906 8570), on the right as you leave the train station. There are hostel-like dorms (from 20DM per person) where breakfast is extra or you can B&B in doubles from 35DM per person. Single rooms from 55DM. The **Haberstock** next door is a good-value pension.

**CAMPING** One well-equipped campsite is at Zentrallandstrasse 49 (Tel. 723 1707), open mid-March–late Oct. Take U-Bahn 3 to Thalkirchen (Tierpark), then bus 57 to Campingplatz Thalkirchen (or a 20-minute walk). Although central and convenient for the Oktoberfest, it can get very crowded and noisy, with cleanliness suffering as a result. Refer to *Cheap Sleeps Europe 2000* for more options.

## EATING AND NIGHTLIFE

Bavarian cooking is not for the weight-conscious. It's stodgy, the portions are huge, and it's all very, very tasty. Munich's speciality is *Weisswurst*, a sausage made of veal and parsley. You can buy it at any number of stalls and eat it as a quick snack with a beer to keep you going.

The **Viktualienmarkt** is an attractive sight, but it's cheaper to buy your supplies from one of the superb **food halls** of the department stores, Kaufhof, Hertie, Deutscher Supermarkt or the cheaper Pennymarkt and Aldi. The displays and high standards in these places really open your eyes if you've been weaned on dull supermarkets at home.

The **student canteens** (*Mensas*) have cheap lunches at Arcisstrasse 17 or Leopoldstrasse 15, open 11am–2pm, and all over Schwabing you'll find reasonably priced eating places.

If you're desperate, there's also a Wendy **self-service** outside the station. And for cheap and delicious doughnuts and so on, try Strüdel Stube in Orlandostrasse (near the Hofbräuhaus).

A quarter of the world's beer comes from Bavaria, and Munich is at the heart of this huge industry, with a social life that revolves round the beer halls and gardens. These are good places to eat, drink and make new friends. Avoid the touristy Hofbräuhaus as you're unlikely to meet the locals there; try instead the beer gardens in the **English Gardens** below Chinesischer Turm or the studenty **Max Emanuel** brewery (Adalbertstrasse 33).

For a taste of authentic Munich nightlife, **Augustinerkeller** at Arnulfstrasse 52, **Donisl** at Marienplatz, and **Hundskugel** (Munich's oldest pub) at Hotterstrasse 18 are the most representative.

For nightlife, **Schwabing** is the area to head for. **Studiosus Reisen**, Amalienstrasse 73, have tickets for concerts, theatres, etc., with reductions. There's music and dancing at **The Drugstore**, Feilitzschstrasse 12, and the university has occasional 'events' such as **open-air dances** outside term-time, which you can infiltrate if you can pass yourself off as a German student. You could also check out one of Munich's increasing number of **Irish pubs**.

**EXCURSIONS** The concentration camp of **Dachau** lies 22 km north-west of Munich. A visit here will put into perspective the atrocities that were committed during Nazi rule, and will leave an impression that even the opulence of Munich will fail to erase. Built in 1933, the old administration block is now a museum, and a film in English is shown twice a day; check times at Tourist Information. Get there on the S-Bahn line 2, direction Peterhausen (free to Inter-Railers) to Dachau, then buses 720 or 722 to the camp (closed Mon.). Buses are infrequent on Sundays and the alternative is a 45-minute walk.

**Nymphenburg Palace and Park** is Munich's Versailles. Home of the Bavarian kings, situated in a 495-acre park, the palace makes a pleasant day trip. Closed Mon. The surrounding park is free, but entry to the palace is not. If visiting in winter, don't forget to pack your skates because the lake freezes to form a spectacular open-air ice rink.

Europe's largest zoo, **Hellabrunn**, is six km south of the city, and the Benedictine monastery at **Andechs** (buses 951 or 956), serves some of the strongest home brew in Munich.

A good day trip from Munich is to the fairy-tale castle of **Neuschwanstein**, which featured in the famous film *Chitty Chitty Bang Bang*, and was built by 'mad' King Ludwig II. Take the train to Fussen and bus Bf 971 the 5 km to Hohenschwangau. It is then a steep one km walk up to the entrance. The entrance fee includes a rather hurried guided tour.

While on the subject of films, you may wish to spend some time at the **Bavarian Film Studios**, which are near Pullach. Although quite expensive, with the only tour in German, you can walk through the U-boat used for the film *The Boat* and see other sights.

## Augsburg phone code: 0821

This ancient city, just over half an hour up the main line from Munich, is well worth visiting. Founded by the Roman Emperor Augustus in 15 BC, the city developed into a vital medieval trading centre. Today Augsburg is the capital of the region known as Bavarian Swabia and it is Bavaria's third city.

### ADDRESSES

**TOURIST INFORMATION** Bahnhofstrasse 7; open Mon.–Fri.: 9am–6pm; Sat.: 9am–1pm (Tel.502070; Fax. 502 0745). There's also a branch office at Rathausplatz (Tel.502 0724), open Mon.–Fri.: 9am–6pm; Sat.: 10am–4pm, Sun.: 10am–1pm.
**POST OFFICE** Halderstrasse 29, on the left as you face the station.

### SEEING

Augsburg's sights are close together and best seen on foot. Don't be put off by the view from the main station, which is not situated among the city's best attractions. Get yourself instead to the city hall, from where organized walking tours in German and English begin.

With the aid of maps from the tourist office, you can guide your own walks, if you feel so inclined, and a stroll along **Maximilianstrasse** is a good place to start. Its southern end is dominated by the 93m high tower and onion dome of the church of **St Ulrich and Afra**. This dates from the 15th century. Further along, at no. 46, is the **Schaezler-Palais**, the finest example of rococo architecture on offer in Augsburg. It houses the best of the city's art collection. Of particular interest is the finely decorated banqueting hall on the top floor. This is 23m long, the walls are lined with mirrors and it has an impressive ceiling fresco.

The fountains in Augsburg are famous, and three of the most attractive can be seen on Maximilianstrasse: **Herkulesbrunnen**, **Merkurbrunnen** and **Augustusbrunnen**. The latter personifies the four rivers of Augsburg and when you reach it you will be standing in front of the **Rathaus**. This looks impressive from the outside; once inside, proceed to the top floor for the newly refurbished **Goldener Saal** (golden hall), which was ravaged in the last war. The adjoining **Perlachtürm** offers a good view of the entire city from a height of over 70m. From here the **Dom** (cathedral) can be seen. This stands at the northern end of Augsburg's main street. The oldest part of it, the crypt, is said to date back to AD 823. Since then, the cathedral has been greatly expanded. Aside from its appealing architecture it also holds some Romanesque and Gothic frescoes. On Saturday evenings at 6pm, organ recitals are performed in the cathedral.

Augsburg's main attraction, for which it is world-famous, is the **Fuggerei**, the world's oldest social housing scheme. The main entrance is in the Jakoberstrasse, a short walk eastwards from the city hall. It was begun in 1516 by Jakob Fugger, whose family was wealthy and influential. Residence in the Fuggerei has always been reserved for Catholics, poor but hard-working and free of sins. Their annual rent amounts to just 1.72DM (the equivalent of a 'Rhine Guilder'). One of the houses has been restored as a museum in order to depict life as it was there when the Fuggerei was founded.

To see the rest of Augsburg, follow the coloured signs. They trace a leisurely tour of the old town.

**FREE AUGSBURG:**
- See this lovely city on foot. Augsburg has a large network of canals along which to wander, and the town is said to have more bridges than Venice. Parts of the city wall are still intact and are of great historical interest. A plan of the various walking routes is available at the Tourist Office.
- There are no entrance fees for city museums at weekends and public holidays.

## SLEEPING
The youth hostel is at Beim Pfaffenkeller 3 (Tel. 33909; Fax. 151149), near the cathedral, and is reached from the main station by tram 2 to Stadtwerke.

## EATING AND NIGHTLIFE
The cheapest meals are to be found in the traditional Bavarian **Gasthaus**, of which there are many. If you're willing to pay a bit more, a good meal at a reasonable price can be had at **John Bentons**, Maximilianstrasse, just beyond the Perlachtürm.

The best **pubs** are in the old town. Try **Die Kneipe** (The Pub), or the Irish pub, **Fuchsbau**, both on Mittlerer Lech. In good weather, a visit to a **Biergarten** is a must. The best are **Thing**, on Vorderer Lech, and **Zeughaus**, on Zeugplatz.

# The Alps and the Romantic Road

This is the route to take for fairytale castles and medieval churches set among rolling green hills. The scenic stretch from Füssen to the vineyards of Franconia has been dubbed *Romantische Strasse*, and with a surfeit of picturesque towns, it's not surprising this is one of the most loved areas of Germany.

Rail is not the best way to get to those hidden little corners of Bavaria. Better to use the **Europabus 'Romantische Strasse'**. They offer two routes: Füssen to Würzburg, and Munich to Füssen (free to Eurail, EuroDomino and German Rail card holders). Make further enquiries in the Starnberger Bahnhof part of Munich station.

Places of note *en route* are: **Nördlingen**, with its perfectly preserved circular medieval fortifications and 15th-century St George's church; **Dinkelsbühl**, also with a St George's church that is a Gothic masterpiece, *Deutsches Haus* and Old Town Hall; **Rothenburg** – visit the Rathaus, St Jakob's church and the Folterkammer (torture chamber); and **Würzburg**.

# Würzburg phone code: 0931

Surrounded by vineyards, and at the heart of the Franconian wine region, Würzburg is home to the stunning Baroque palace, the **Residenz.** Once the magnificent home of the prince-bishops, it is now the main lure for tourists visiting Würzburg. Open April-Sept.: Tues.–Sun.: 9am–5pm; Oct.–Mar.: 10am–4pm (7DM, less with an ISIC card). On the other side of the river Main is the 13th-century **Marienberg Fortress**, another of the princes' homes. Near the fortress is the **Käppele**, an ornate Baroque church which allows you an excellent view from the top. The **Mainfränkisches Museum** houses sculptures and carvings and is located in the Marienberg Fortress.

## STATION FACILITIES
The Hauptbahnhof has **train information** 7am–9.30pm and a 24-hour **service point** and **luggage lockers** (Tel. 34425). The station itself shuts down after midnight and opens at dawn. All the usual facilities are at hand.

Daily trains to: Nürnberg (one hour), Vienna (6½ hours), Munich (2½ hours), Stuttgart (2½ hours), Mainz (2 hours), Paris, Cologne (3½ hours), Frankfurt-am-Main (1½ hours), Hamburg (3½ hours).

## TOURIST INFORMATION

There's one just in front of the station (open Mon.–Sat.: 10am–8pm; Tel. 37436) which will give you a free map and sell you a hotel list for 0.50DM. They will also find rooms for a fee of 5DM. The main office is in the Palais am Congress Centrum (Tel. 37335), open Mon.–Thurs.: 8.30am–5pm, Fri.: 8.30am–midday. Another office is in the Haus zum Falken (Tel. 37398) on the Marktplatz. There is a 24hr accommodation hotline on 19414.

**STUDENT TRAVEL OFFICE** SRID Reisen, Zwinger 6 (Tel. 52176).
**EUROPABUSES** Buses down the Romantic Road from Würzburg to Rothenburg and Munich depart daily at 10am, and to Frankfurt at 6.45pm.
**POST OFFICE** Bahnhofplatz 2 (Tel. 330).
**AMEX** Haugerpfarrgasse 1 (Tel. 355 699)

## SLEEPING AND EATING

The IYHF **youth hostel** is at Burkarderstrasse 44 (Tel. 42590; Fax. 416862), under 26 only, and costs 25–29DM. The **campsite** is at Mergentheimerstrasse 13b (Tel. 72536). Trams 3 and 5 get you there. The campsite is not signposted, but follow directions to the Würzburg Canoe Club and register in the club restaurant, from whence you will be directed to your pitch.

For cheap **hotels** and **pensions**, ask at the Tourist Office for suggestions. Recommended are **Siegel**, Reisgrubengasse 7 (Tel. 52941) or **Spehnkuch**, Röntgenring 7 (Tel. 54752). Both charge around 90DM for doubles.

Eat at the **university Mensa** in the Studentenhaus at the corner of Mänzstrasse and Jahnstrasse. Open for lunch and dinner on weekdays, during term times only. There are several cheap fast-food places around the centre, and if you have time, try the local white wines.

NOTES:
...............................................................................................................
...............................................................................................................
...............................................................................................................
...............................................................................................................
...............................................................................................................
...............................................................................................................

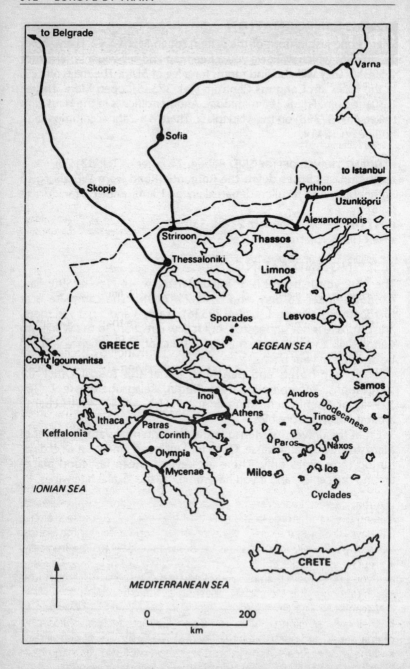

# GREECE

| | |
|---|---|
| Entry requirements | Passport |
| Population | 10.65 million |
| Capital | Athens (pop.: 3.7 million) |
| Currency | Drachma (GDR) |
| | £1 = approx. 520GDR |
| Political system | Parliamentary Democracy |
| Religion | 98% Greek Orthodox |
| Language | Greek (English is the second language) |
| Public holidays | New Year's Day, Epiphany (6 Jan.); Ash Wednesday, First Sunday of Lent, Independence (25 Mar.), Orthodox Good Friday, Greek Easter Sunday , Easter Monday, Labour Day (1 May), Whit Monday, Assumption (15 Aug.), Ochi Day (28 Oct.), Christmas Day, Boxing Day |
| International dialling codes | To Greece: int'l code 30 |
| | From Greece: 00 + country code |
| Time | GMT + 2 (+3 in summer) |
| Emergency telephone numbers | Police 110; ambulance 112; fire service 112 |

It's difficult to have a bad holiday in Greece. More than 15,000 km of coastline and around 2,000 islands means lovers of the sun and sea could spend months exploring, while fans of mythology, archaeology and the arts could devote a lifetime to studying the pre-classical, Hellenic and Byzantine sites of ancient Greece.

It is the sea, too, that provides a way of life for many of the country's inhabitants. Though farming remains important to the Greek economy – famous for products such as olives and olive oil, feta cheese, wine, tobacco, almonds and walnuts – on many of the islands the main occupations are still fishing and harvesting sponge. Shipping is vital: Greece's merchant fleet is the largest in the world.

Tourism, though, has outstripped shipping as the leading light of the economy. Every year, Greece is a magnet to millions of Europeans, causing the summertime population to almost double. Eurorailers, after a few days absorbing the classic sights of Athens, tend to sail for the islands, where the under-30 social scene is the best you're likely to find. Ironically, it's much easier to get to know Germans and Swedes here than Greeks – and you get to know them very well indeed if you share the same nudist beach (although it is technically legal only at three beaches).

Meanwhile, the Greeks themselves consider Western Civilization to be their greatest export. Politics, medicine, law, architecture, philosophy, drama, music and poetry all began here in the birthplace of democracy, and the ancient ideals of the movers and shakers of 300 years ago have been the inspiration for many constitutions around the world.

Greek history begins about 2,500 BC with the Minoan civilization on Crete, a full 1,000 years before the Mycenaeans got it together on the mainland. The classical period reached its peak in 5th-century BC Athens. As independent city-states, Greeks may have shared the same culture, but they were always at each other's throats – until Alexander the Great of Macedon sorted them out and conquered an empire. Greece became part of the Byzantine Empire and was eventually conquered by the Ottomans, who ruled for 400 years.

The formation of the modern Greek state began with the War of Independence in 1821, a process which ended in 1947 with the return of the Dodecanese islands. They still play cricket on Corfu, one of the Ionian islands controlled by the British till 1864. After the Germans left Greece in 1944, civil war broke out and continued for five years until the communists lost.

Relations with the Turks remain as strained as ever (particularly after the Turkish invasion of Cyprus in 1974), and Greece today is still prone to showy acts of bravado against them. Political tensions with Macedonia, meanwhile, are growing, and Greece is digging its heels in with Britain, too, with bespectacled balladeer Nana Mouskouri turned Euro MP, and lobbying for the return of the Elgin Marbles by 2004, when Athens hosts the Olympic Games.

Greece is one of the poorest countries in the EC. But despite that, a huge number of Albanians have sought refuge here, allegedly raising the crime rate and filling up hostels and hotels at the lower end of the market.

## GETTING THERE

Travelling by train is still the cheapest way of getting to Greece, especially since the introduction of a new airport tax. Charter flights offer little in the way of flexibility, although 'bucket shops' in Athens offer cheap flights to those with ISIC cards. The main lines run from north to south, with limited branch lines in central and northern Greece and in the Peloponnese.

There are problems in going by train, not least of which is deciding on your route, especially considering recent events in the former Yugoslavia. One option is by boat from Italy, on the Brindisi to Patras line (free to those with a Eurail pass). It's a 19-hour sailing, and from Patras there are trains every few hours to Athens.

Note that it is now illegal to take into Greece any substance containing codeine. Whilst guards rarely check, you can be prosecuted for it.

**THE BELGRADE–ATHENS RUN** This was a popular route into Greece before the troubles in the former Yugoslavia. For now, it is still best avoided. Our advice is to stick to the Brindisi–Patras ferry, or go by rail through Bucharest and Sofia to Thessaloniki in northern Greece. If you do decide to go via the former Yugoslavia, heed this good advice:

1. Travel out of season, or at least try to avoid mid-July/August.
2. Go for the fastest train possible – it's worth the supplement. Try and get on the through-train from Munich or Vienna, or travel overnight in a couchette/sleeper. (It's advisable here to book in advance.) Sleepers are expensive but couchettes are reasonable.
3. Take along plenty to eat and drink. The trains aren't air-conditioned and you don't know how long a train may stop *en route*.
4. If you get on a train, try to pay for a couchette or sleeper. Have plenty of 'hard' currency on you as dinars are usually refused. Always keep a receipt in case you are asked for extra payment.
5. Look out for Greek or 'Yugoslav' guards trying to extract unwarranted supplements. Waving a Thomas Cook timetable can sometimes scare them off. Otherwise argue and kick up as much of a fuss as possible.

**THE ITALIAN RUN** Trains are crowded and the toilets dirty, but your real problems start at Brindisi, beginning with the 1½ km walk down to the docks. Avoid the rip-off reservation agencies at all costs – during most of the year, you don't need to reserve unless you want a cabin (pricey, but advisable in bad weather). However, to make sure of a seat during the peak months of July and August, advance reservation is recommended. Port taxes are extra.

Before boarding, all passengers must check in at the Shipping Line Office. Passengers who wish to break their voyage at Corfu must declare their intentions when they pay their port taxes.

It can be windy on the Brindisi–Patras ferry, but don't let the cooling breeze kid you into not taking precautions against the sun. Putting a rucksack on sunburnt shoulders rather takes the edge off your holiday enjoyment.

If you are going to Corfu, seriously consider flying from Athens, rather than taking the boat from Brindisi. It can cost as little as £45 and takes only 50 minutes.

## GREEK RAILWAYS

### (ORGANISMOS SIDIRODROMON ELLADOS, OSE)

Greece is a mountainous country and therefore many towns are not connected by rail, although OSE uses a large number of connecting buses and the few local trains there are will seem slow (except by Eastern European standards). The international long-distance trains are flatteringly called 'expresses', although some new trains on the Intercity Athens–Thessaloniki route have cut the travel time from 9 hours to 5¾ hours. Some of these require a small supplement, and Inter-Rail pass holders must pay extra on expresses and Intercities.

Inter-Rail and Eurail passes are valid. Euro Domino tickets are also available (see Part One of this guide). There are some Inter-Rail bonuses in Greece, but always ask for student discounts.

Over recent years a lot of money has been invested in OSE, particularly in northern Greece. Speed, service and efficiency are gradually improving. The Patras–Athens run is earmarked for major investment – and that should come as a relief to many Eurorailers.

## EURAIL BONUSES

**FREE SERVICES** Eurail Pass and Eurail Youthpass travellers can use steamers operated by Hellenic Mediterranean and Adriatica di Navigazione between Patras and Brindisi and vice versa. If you have the choice, opt for the latter. However, between 10 June and 30 Sept., you must pay a high-season surcharge.

## TRAIN INFORMATION

English is spoken by information officers at all major stations. Phone 145 or 147 for up-to-date schedules and prices.

**RESERVATIONS** Are advisable – and free. This is one country where it pays to be organized. Go to an OSE office rather than the station – the staff are more helpful and it's generally less hassle. Book a seat as far in advance as possible for international trains. On Intercity trains and some expresses (ask at station), reservations are obligatory. You can reserve up to a month in advance. On internal routes, reservations are also possible, but you have to do it by post and it's really not worth the hassle. Reservations for the Intercity between Athens and Patras can only be made within the hour prior to departure. Beware – there are no tickets placed on reserved seats so chaos often ensues!

**NIGHT TRAVEL** Couchettes and sleepers are both cheap by northern standards. If you can get one, go for it.

**ROVER TICKETS** The Greek Tourist Card covers second-class travel only and offers 10, 20 or 30 days' unlimited travel for up to five people. Prices range from around 15,000GDR to 92,000GDR These tickets can only be purchased from the OSE Head Office, 1Karolou Street, Athens, or from the international window at Thessaloniki station.

For information on the Freedom Pass (EuroDomino), see Part One.

The Inter-Rail pass has been broken down into zones, therefore you pay only for the places you want to visit. For £159 you can travel for 22 days in one zone. Greece, along with Italy, Turkey and Slovenia, is in Zone G. The pass also covers the ADN/HML ferry service. For details of the Inter-Rail zones, refer to the Inter-Rail section in Part One of this guide.

**FERRIES** Though some charter flights go to the bigger centres, the best way to get to the islands is by sea. Tour agencies in Greece do not always advertise rival lines so it is worthwhile touring all the agencies. In Piraeus, most of the agencies on the waterfront block offer a comprehensive chart of everything sailing that week, and some will also recommend cheap **hotels** in the area.

On the islands, check and re-check: Greek ferry timetables change without notice from day to day, depending on the season and weather conditions. Note that the majority of islands are connected to Piraeus (Athens).

## TOURIST INFORMATION

For information about the country, accommodation and the main sights, see the National Tourist Organisation of Greece, known as EOT in Greece (main office: 2 Amerikis St, Athens. Tel. 331 0437, 331 0561, 331 0562; Fax. 325 2815). For any other information, contact the Tourist Police (Tel. 171). Don't be put off by their name – their role is to help you sort out your problems.

**ISIC BONUSES** Up to 50% off internal flights and ferries, up to 80% reductions on theatres and museums. Olympic will grant reduction only if the internal flight is part of an international journey charged at a standard fare, and not Apex. Consult the nearest Olympic offices or USIT Student Travel Service, at 1-3 Filellinon St, Syntagma Square, 105 57 Athens (Tel. 324 1884; Fax. 323 8447).

**MONEY MATTERS** Banking hours are generally Mon.–Fri.: 8am–2pm (to 1.30pm on Fridays). In major tourist centres, banks open again from 3.30pm–6pm. All banks give more or less the same rate.

You can also change money at the Post Office (ELTA). Trying to change money at weekends other than in large resort hotels can be a non-starter.

**POST OFFICES** Open Mon.–Sat.: 7.30am–2pm. In Athens and other major tourist centres, they're open till 7pm. Stamps can also be bought from kiosks. The price is the same everywhere; it is illegal for anyone to sell stamps for more than their face value.

**SHOPS** Hours can vary wildly. Supermarkets are open Mon.–Fri.: 8am–8pm, Sat.: 8am–3.30pm. Food shops: Mon.–Fri.: 8am–2pm and 5pm–8pm, Sat.: 9am–3.30pm.

**MUSEUMS** Usually open in winter 9am–3.30pm; summer 8am–5pm. They tend to close on Mon. or Tues. EU students get in free, other students get a 50% reduction.

## SLEEPING

**HOSTELS** The **youth hostels** are nothing to get excited about, and currently there are none recognized by the IYHF. However, this situation is expected to change soon. Contact the **Athens International Hostel** in 16 Victor Hugo Street (Tel. (01) 523 4170) for up-to-date news on this.

Another good contact is the **Greek Youth Hostel Organisation** at 4 Dragatsaniou Street, Fl. 7, Athens (Tel. (01) 323 4107; Fax. (01) 323 7590).

Many hostels have an annoying habit of imposing a curfew on guests (sometimes this can be as early as 10pm).

**HOTELS** Graded A, B, C, and D (A is deluxe; D is fourth class – usually pre-war hotels with very basic facilities). For a D-class hotel, expect to pay 4,200-7,200GDR for a single, 5,200-10,200GDR for a double. These rates do not include private shower or breakfast.

Hotel prices should be posted at reception, and on the back of the door in each room. This is the maximum price a hotelier can charge (though taxes are extra). Some pensions and hotels charge 10% extra for short stays or 20% during high summer which is permitted. Off season, you can sometimes bargain to get the price down. More information is available from the **Hellenic Chambers of Hotels**, 24 Stadiou Street, Athens (Tel. (01) 323 7193; Fax. (01) 322 5449).

**CAMPING** The National Tourist Board (2 Amerikis Street, Athens) and the Tourist Guide of Greece (137 Patission Street, Athens) issue a list of official **campsites** and facilities, giving an approximate price. Expect to pay at least 1200GDR per person plus 1000GDR per tent. It is illegal to camp outside the official **campsites**, since there is increasing concern about campers leaving litter, causing fires and destroying the environment.

**THE ISLANDS** Your best bet is to stay in private homes. This can frequently be arranged on the spot, as you'll often be met at the ferry by locals offering rooms to let. **Privately let rooms** (*dhomatia*) are divided into three classes (A down to C); they are usually slightly cheaper than **hotels** and are, in general, spotlessly clean. There's usually a choice on offer (the most expensive room tends to be shown first). Price is not necessarily an indicator of quality, so always ask to see the room before agreeing to take it at the price quoted.

**Camping** is illegal on many islands but nearly everyone is forced to do it at some stage as during July and August all the hotels and private rooms are full. There is some 'legal' camping on licensed campsites and the police sometimes turn a blind eye to people camped in the sand however, they are stepping up action (they can confiscate your passport and you can be fined around 50,000GDR) and the official policy of EOT now is that you can't come to Greece by charter flight without having pre-booked accommodation. If you have to camp illegally, keep the place clean.

## EATING AND NIGHTLIFE

Don't expect to eat as cheaply as you would have a few years ago, as high inflation continues to push up prices. Always check the prices first in small shops and bakeries and make sure you know what you're paying for.

On the islands it's easy to live off bread, cheese and watermelon (*karpouzi*) during the day, and eat out at night. If you need that added luxury of a cup of coffee for breakfast to see you through the day, be sure what you're ordering or you'll end up with sweet Greek coffee instead. An alternative is *café frappé* (iced coffee), which is much more refreshing.

When eating out, you'll often be ushered into the kitchen. Take your time, as this is the local custom of choosing. *Arni* is lamb; *moschari*, veal; *chirino*, pork; *kotopoulo*, chicken. Avoid the fish unless you've got plenty of money or are on the islands, where it's fresh. *Moussaka* is a combination of meat with potato or aubergine, in béchamel sauce. *Dolmades* are minced meat and rice wrapped in vine leaves and are delicious hot or cold. If you're down on your luck, there's always a *souvlaki* stand (meat kebab wrapped in bread) not far away, and at around 350GDR, they're good value.

Don't overdo it with *ouzo* (the local aniseed spirit), or you'll know all about it the next morning. Watch how the locals drink it – you might want to pick up their trick of following it with a water chaser. Give Greek beer a try – the new brew is called Mythos; it's good and generally cheaper than imports, which cost between 500-1,000GDR. For the evening meal, try at least one bottle of the local *retsina* (wine with pine resin) before returning to the *aretsinato* wine.

A service charge is usually included in the bill, but it is polite to leave some small change.

There are numerous local festivals celebrating everything from Easter to wine. The Greeks use any excuse to have one, as they love to let their hair down and dance. Once a bouzouki gets going, anything can happen. Nightclubs are dull and expensive by comparison. Films are shown in their original language, and are always cheaper in the suburbs.

# Northern Greece

Northern Greece is real 'spaghetti western' country. The mountains are rugged and the scenery wild and untamed. The two provinces of this area are Macedonia and Thrace.

If you're entering Greece from Macedonia or Bulgaria, your first main centre will be **Thessaloniki** (also known as **Salonica**). This is Greece's second city and was also the second city of Byzantium, founded in 316 BC. There are some impressive Byzantium churches as well as some interesting Roman remains. Don't be put off by the ugly station as this is an attractive city and the people are very friendly and hospitable. Thessaloniki is cooled by sea breezes and the wide streets have many interesting shops. There is also an excellent copper market and several good beaches near the city with frequent buses and boats to them.

Take a stroll through the old Turkish **Kastra Quarter**, visit the **Archaeological Museum** and the churches of **St George** and **St Demetrius** (the city's patron saint). The Byzantine walls around the city can make an afternoon's walk. The Roman palace of **Galerius** is in Navarino Square.

**Tourist Information** can be obtained from the office at 8 Plateia Aristotelous (Tel. 031 271 888 or 031 222 935), open Mon.–Fri.: 8am–8pm, Sat.: 8.30am–2pm. The **tourist police** at 4 Dodekanissou Street (5th Floor) (Tel. 031 544 162 or 031 554 871) or at the airport (Tel. 031 425 011) can also help you. The **Eurail Aid Office** is the railway station, open 5.30am-1pm, then 2pm-8pm (Tel. 031 519 519). The **Student Travel Office** is Etos Travel at 44 Al Svolon (Tel. 31 263 814). There's an **Amex** at 19 Tsimiski Street (Tel. 031 261521) open Mon.–Fri.: 10am–4pm, Sat.: 9am–2pm. Also at 23 Nikis Avenue, in Memphis Travel, (Tel. 031 222 796).

The **youth hostel** at 44 Alex. Svolou Street (Tel. 031 225 946; Fax. 031 262208) is noisy, basic and quite expensive. Get there on tram 8, 10, 11 or 31 and get off at the Arch of Galerius. Head towards the water and turn left two blocks later onto Alex. Svolou Street. Good **hotels** include the Argo, at 11 Egnatia Street (Tel. 519 770), Acropol (Tel. 536 170) and Averof (Tel. 538840; Fax. 543194). **Camping** is not very convenient, the nearest sites are about 28km away on the average beaches of Perea and Ayia Triadha. Either take bus 72 from Platia Dhikastirion or, in summer, catch the boat from the White Tower

**EXCURSIONS**
- For an impressive day trip from Thessaloniki, head east by bus (nearest train station is Droma) to the port of **Kavala**. This prosperous town has an amazing **old quarter** and a huge medieval **aqueduct** leading from Mount Simbolon. The **Tourist Office** is at the corner of Eleftherias (Tel. 051 222 425 or 051 231 653). Open Mon.–Fri.: 7am–2.30pm. It helps with accommodation and gives out a useful town map.
- Hourly ferry crossings are possible from here to the popular resort island of **Thassos**, mythical home of the Sirens. Here you'll find many rooms for rent. The **Tourist Office** is on the main street, parellel to the seafront.
- There are many good **beaches** on the mainland, but the best are on **Sithonia**, the central prong of the **Halkidiki** peninsula. All are well connected to Thessaloniki by bus. South-east of Thessaloniki is

the self-governing monastic commune of **Mount Athos** (no female has been allowed in for 900 years). If you want to visit, contact the Ministry of Northern Greece in Thessaloniki (ask for Mrs Plessa), at least a month in advance, and be able to give a sound reason for your visit (Room 221, Pl. Dikitirou, Thessaloniki. Tel. 031 26 4321). A letter of recommendation (e.g. from a university) is usually required and this should cite proven religious or scientific interests. Only 10 visitors a day are allowed onto Mount Athos so don't be surprised if you're not one of the lucky few. If you do not have permission, you can always see the monastries by boat (organized boat trips cost around 3,150GDR).

- To see some early Christian art, the nine Byzantine monasteries and nunneries at **Meteora** are breathtaking: 24 perpendicular rocks upon which, 600 years ago, the Byzantine monks built their monasteries. Situated 21 km north of **Kalambaka**, it takes four hours to reach by train from Thessaloniki; change at Larissa. If you are planning to stay in the region, your best bet would be to **camp** at one of the four sites on the national road between Trikala and Kalambaka. There's Kalambaka (Tel. 0432 22309), Philoxonia (Tel. 0432 24466), Theopetra (Tel. 0432 81406) and International (Tel. 0432 22239). There's also Camping Vrahos at Kastráki.

- **Larissa** is a picturesque town with a medieval fortress and an ancient theatre. The Tourist Office is at 18 Koumoundorou Str (Tel. 041 250 919). If you are travelling to Athens from Larissa, stop at Thebes (Thiva), the birthplace of Hercules, whose feats feature in Greek mythology. Nearby is the spring of Agios Theodoras, better known as the **Fountain of Oedipus**.

- North-east from Thessaloniki is **Algaia Eleni**, near Langadas. The best thing to happen here is the ritual of the fire-walkers which takes place annually 21–23 May. The **police station** (Tel. 0321 63333) can give you more details and help find accommodation.

## The Peloponnese

The spectacular **Corinth Canal** separates the Peloponnese plain from Greece's mainland. This region, with its remnants of the ancient Greeks, Turks, Franks and Venetians, is becoming increasingly popular with tourists. Among the most famous sites is Olympia, where the first Olympic Games were staged.

On the main circular line from Patras to Athens lie Kalamata, Tripolis, Argos and Corinth. **Kalamata** is a sprawling town which was devastated by an earthquake in 1986 but it makes a good base. The Kástro, built by the Franks, survived the quake and is one of the most pleasant parts of the town. There is a tourist police post at the station (Tel. 0721 95 555), and a good **campsite**, Maria's Sea and Sun, (Tel. 0721 41060). Take bus 1 east past the other campsites

Near Argos lies the unspoilt town of **Nafplion** with a picturesque Venetian fort in the middle of the neighbouring bay. There are frequent bus connections (the bus station is on Odhos Singrou) to surrounding towns. There is a good **youth hostel** at 15 Argonafton Street (Tel. 0752 246720). A 15-minute walk from the bus stop, it charges about 1000GDR per person per night and a further 900GDR for huge home-cooked dinners. (Closed in winter). Other accommodation is generally overpriced but a good, cheapish **hotel** is the Argolis on Argos Street (Tel. 0752 27721). Singles are normally 4,000GDR but the owners charge students half price.

You can rent bicycles from Riki and Pete, Navarino St (Tel. 0752 24547 or 21407) for 1,000GDR per day. The **Tourist Office** can be found at 25 Martiou but you are better off trying the **Tourist Police** (Tel. 0752 28131) who are to the right at the top of Syngrou.

The new town of **Corinth** has nothing much to recommend it but the old town has a lot hidden away in its quiet corners. The station is in the new town, but buses leave for 'Arhea Korinthos' where you can see columns from the Temple of Apollo and the rostrum from which St Paul preached Christianity to the Corinthians. To catch these sights at their best, visit around 9am, as by lunchtime the coach tours arrive and they become besieged by tourists.

For **tourist information**, Tel. 0741 23282. If you are staying overnight in New Corinth, try **Hotel Acti**, 3 Ethnikis Anistasis St (Tel. 0741 23337) down by the sea, or **camp** at Corinth Beach (Tel. 0741 27967), three km west of town, for 1100GDR per person plus 650GDR per tent. A regular train and bus service connects it to the city station. Three km down the road is the Blue Dolphin site (Tel. 0741 25766), again on the beach. (1,400GDR per person plus from 850GDR per tent).

Just down the line is **Mycenae** (Mikines) which dates back to 3000 BC and was founded by Perseus, the mythical slayer of Medusa. Many of the treasures found here are now in Athens, but you can still see the Gate of the Lions, the royal tombs and the Treasury of Atreus. The small **youth hostel** is at Iphigeneia Street 20 (Tel. 0751 76285). Take the bus to Ancient Corinth and get off at the bottom of the hill. The building is also a restaurant.

Mycenae is served by two **campsites**. Camping Mycenae (Tel. 0751 76121; Fax. 76247) lies in the middle of the town and is a superb camping spot. The owner cooks for the campers and hot showers are included. **Camping** Atticus is a little further out.

Further south is **Epidavros**, whose main attraction is the 4th-century BC amphitheatre in which classical Greek dramas are staged on Fri. and Sat. nights from June through till the last weekend in Aug. Plays are performed in Greek, but by the end of the performance the language ceases to be a barrier. For information about performances, contact the Festival Office, 4 Stadion Str Syntagma, Athens (Tel. 01 322 1459). Tickets can also be purchased before the show at the theatre (Tel. 0753 22026) and cost around 2,000GDR for students (a full-priced ticket is between 4,000 and 6,000GDR).

**Sparta** may have been the seat of a mighty empire in ancient Greece, but the modern town is a big disappointment. But **Mystra**, a short bus ride away, has an impressive display of Byzantine churches, palaces and a castle.

**Patras** is the main town of the Peloponnese, the ferry landing from Brindisi in Italy. There's not much to see, but if you're killing time, look round the **Venetian Castle**, **Archaeological Museum**, **Municipal Theatre** and **Psila Alonia Square**. The busiest and most spectacular time to visit is in July–September, when the summer festival takes place, and drama, dance and music are abundant. The carnival in Feb./March is one of the biggest in the country, with a grand parade through the city centre.

The police station (Tel. 061 451833/061 451893) can help with enquiries and there's also a **Tourist Office** on the waterfront (Tel. 061 622249). There are a few **camping sites** to choose from including Kavouri Camping (Tel. 061 428066), two km north of town (take bus 1 from Agios Dionysios church); further out, eight km east of the town, are two sites, Rio Camping (Tel. 061 991585) and Rio Mare Camping (Tel. 061 992263). Both sites charge 1,200GDR per person. (Take bus 6 to Rion). The **youth hostel** is at 68 Iroon Polytechniou St (just over a kilometre's walk from the ferry terminal); it has no curfew (Tel. 061 427278). Stay here with caution as many women travellers have reported unpleasant incidents in recent years.

There's a **Eurail Aid Office** at the train station, open 8am-8pm in summer and 8am-2pm in winter (Tel. 061 221 311 or 061 273 694), and an **Amex** agency, Albatros Travel, at 48 Othonos Amalias St (Tel. 061 220127). Down the street at No. 14 is an **exchange** office (Tel. 061 622 602).

About five trains a day make the worthwhile seven-hour trip to **Olympia**, site of the first Olympic Games in Ancient Greece. There are many archaeological sites and museums in the city and its surrounding area, not surprisingly since the Temple of Zeus used to hold Pheidias' gold and ivory statue of the God, one of the Seven Wonders of the Ancient World.

The **youth hostel** is at 18 Kondhili Street (Tel. 0624 22580); it's cheap but has an 11.30pm curfew. **Camping Diana** (Tel. 0624 22314) is a shaded site 200m uphill from Praxitelous Kondilia Avenue where you'll find the **Tourist Office** (Tel. 0624 23100). Open 9am–10pm daily in the summer. The **campsite** offers students a 10% discount. There is another **campsite** two km out on the road to Pirgos (Tel. 0624 22745).

## Athens (Athinai) phone code: 01

The 'cradle of Western civilization' can sometimes seem the least civilized capital in Europe, with frenzied traffic, squalid accommodation, suffocating heat, and street after street of ugly concrete blocks. But if 20th-century Athens has nothing much to offer, the ruins of the magnificent ancient civilization at its heart make the crowds, noise and pollution all fade away.

If you're going island-hopping, Athens – or rather Piraeus, its port – is your starting point. Ferries leave from here for the islands (there are upwards of 1,500 to choose from in the Aegean and Ionian seas), and the average fare for a deck passenger on a five-hour voyage is about 5,000GDR.

## STATION FACILITIES

**ATHINAI-LARISSA** There is a full range of facilities here including a Tourist Police office. Left luggage is also available in the daytime only. There are daily trains to Thessaloniki and Istanbul.

**ATHINAI-PELOPONNESE** If you're travelling to the Peloponnese or Patras (for the ferry to Italy) use the Athinai-Peloponnese station, adjacent to the Larissa station (six Patras trains daily).

## TOURIST INFORMATION

The Tourist Police are at 77 Dimitrakopoulou St (Tel. 171; open 24 hours) and there's an information desk in the National Bank of Greece on Syntagma Square (Tel. 32 22545), open Mon.–Fri.: 8am–6.30pm, Sat.: 9am–2pm.

The main **EOT office** is at 2 Amerikis St (Tel. 331 0437, 331 0561 or 331 0562; Fax. 325 2815), open Mon.–Fri.:9am–7pm, Sat.: 10am–2pm. Pick up the free map and leaflets on campsites, hostels, etc., and *This Week in Athens,* which provides information on clubs and sights. They don't operate an accommodation-finding service, but try the Hotel Chamber desk in the National Bank of Greece. A good source for information is the Athenian newspaper which is published in English every month. There is also an office in the East Terminal of the airport (Tel. 961 2722; Fax. 964 1627). The office is on the left before the exit.

## ADDRESSES

**POST OFFICE** 100 Aiolou St, near Omonia Square. Also Syntagma Square. Open Mon.–Fri.: 7.30am–8pm, Sat.: 7.30am–2pm, Sun.: 9am–1pm

**OTE OFFICES** 85 Patission Street or 50 Athinas Street. Open Mon.–Fri.: 7am–9pm, Sat.: 8am–3pm, Sun.: 9am–2pm

**AMEX** 2 Ermou Street, Syntagma Square (above McDonald's), weekdays: 8.30am–4pm, Sat.: 8.30am–1.30pm (Tel. 324 4976/324 4979)

**UK EMBASSY** 1 Ploutarchou (Tel. 723 6211); open Mon.–Fri.: 8.30am–1pm

**US EMBASSY** 91 Vassilissis Sofias Street (Tel. 721 2951; Fax. 645 6282); open Mon.–Fri.: 8.30am–5pm

**CANADIAN EMBASSY** 4 Ioannou Gennadiou St (Tel. 727 3400; Fax. 727 3460)

**AUSTRALIAN EMBASSY** 37 Dimitriou Soutsou St (Tel. 721 3039); open Mon.–Fri.: 8.30am–12.30pm

**NEW ZEALAND CONSULATE-GENERAL** 24 Xenias St (Tel. 771 0112, 777 0686), or contact the Ambassador in Rome (see under Italy).

**ISIC/USIT** 1-3 Filellinon Street, Syntagma Square (Tel. 3230 483 or 324 1884; Fax. 323 8447)

**EUROTRAIN** 11 Nikis Street (Tel. 322 1267; Fax. 322 1531)

**EURAIL AID OFFICE** 1 Karolou Street (Tel. 522 4302) and 17 Filellinon Street, Syntagma Square (Tel. 323 6747 and 323 6273)

**STUDENT TRAVEL OFFICE** 53A Patision Ave and Marni St (Tel. 522 2228)

**LATE-NIGHT CHEMIST** Tel. 107 or 102

**RED CROSS FIRST AID CENTRE** 21, 3 Septemvriou St (Tel. 150 or 552 5555)

**TOURIST POLICE** Tel. 171; English spoken

**POLICE** Tel. 100

**AMBULANCE** Tel. 166

## GETTING ABOUT

Looking at the **taxi** tariffs, they seem a huge bargain, but by the time you've been ripped off, they're not such a hot idea. Make sure the meter is switched on and that the display reads no more than 250GDR (set starting rate) when you first get in – attempts at overcharging tourists are all too common. Do not be fooled by any claim that each person in the cab should pay what's on the meter – it's not true; split the fare. Make a note of the cab number and if in doubt ask for a receipt. Having said that, Greek taxis can be the bargain of Europe. A short hop around the city should cost no more than 600–1500GDR. Rates double between midnight and 5am.

The **public transport** system is not great, but it is easy to use. There are buses (city buses are blue with three digit numbers), trolley-buses and a metro. The cost of a ride on each is 100GDR. There are no travel cards or concessions. Buses and trolley-buses are usually packed, and run 5am–12.30am. You can take a bus out to the nearby beaches from the bus station in the centre of town. Tickets are purchased in advance from kiosks or newsagents': look out for the sign *Isitiria Edho* ('Tickets here'). After midnight, there is only an hourly service.

The metro runs every five minutes between Piraeus and central Athens (20 minutes) from 5am till 12.15am.

## SEEING

Athens reached its zenith around 400 BC when Plato, Socrates and Aristotle were strolling around the Acropolis. It is antiquities like this beautiful site – all clustered round the old town, or **Plaka** district – that make a few days in Athens worthwhile.

Try to get to the **Acropolis** as soon as it opens at 8am, before the hordes swarm up and destroy its atmosphere. The white-stone **Parthenon**, the temple dedicated to the goddess Athena, is held up as the epitome of architectural perfection. See also the **Erechtheion**, the **Temple of Athena Nike** and the **Propylaea**, the gates to the sacred site. The **Acropolis Museum**, with exhibits of the finds – statues, friezes, etc – has recently been refurbishment, and is well worth a visit.

The summer opening hours for sites and museums given below are included with some trepidation as the authorities are notorious for changing the times without notice. To be sure of admission, visit between 9am and noon. Don't count on getting in anywhere on a Monday.

The Acropolis is open daily from 8am–7.30pm in summer and from 8.30am–4.30pm in winter. Entrance is 2000GDR, half price for students. **Pnyx Hill** offers a beautiful view of the Acropolis, and there's a *son et lumière* show here at 9pm each night, which costs around 1,000GDR.

The ancient **Agora**, north of the Acropolis, was the marketplace and still has the remains of the old administrative centre. The **Temple of Hephaistos** is considered the best preserved in Greece. This site is open 8.30am–3pm, Tues.–Sun. It is well worth a visit (1,200GDR admission, 600GDR for students). (There are several entrances to the Agora, including one at the edge of Monastiraki, one on Adrianou Street and one on Thission Square).

The **National Archaeological Museum** at 44 Patission St has the best collection of ancient Greek artefacts in the world: gold death-masks, vessels, jewellery, statues and frescoes. Open Apr.–Oct. Mon.: 12.30pm–7pm, Tues.–Fri.: 8am–7pm, weekends: 8.30am–3pm. Nov.–Mar. Mon.: 11pm–5pm, Tues.–Fri.: 8am–5pm, weekends: 8.30am–3pm. Admission 2,000GDR, student reductions available.

The centre of modern Athens is **Syntagma** (Constitution) **Square**.

Avoid the cafés, which are very expensive. From here take Amalias Avenue towards the **Presidential Palace** and Vasilissis Olgas Avenue for the **Olympic Stadium**.

**FREE ATHENS:** On the budget front, Athens is said to be the least expensive city in Europe. Most of the monuments charge an entrance fee, but there are a few things to see for nothing.

- Syntagma Square is flanked on one side by the **Greek Parliament**, where you can watch the bizarre changing of the guard ceremony. On Sundays at 11.15am, there's a more elaborate ceremony.
- The attractive **National Gardens** are a haven midst the traffic and concrete jungle, and a good resting and picnic spot. Get to it down Amalias Avenue, from Syntagma Square.
- At the far end of the gardens, you'll find **Hadrian's Arch**, built by the Roman emperor. This is where visiting heads of state are officially welcomed.
- The famous **Flea Market** on Ifestou St, adjacent to Monastiraki Square, makes a colourful walk and can produce some good bargains in equipment and leather goods. Beware of pickpockets and bum-pinchers. Closes 2pm Sun.
- For a fantastic view over Athens, an uphill climb to the summit of **Likavitos** is well worth the effort.

**Some words of warning:**

- Athens can become oppressively hot and polluted in the summer, so beware of heat exhaustion and breathing difficulties, especially if you are an asthma sufferer. In an attempt to control the pollution, city-centre traffic bans may be put into effect when the air quality deteriorates below a certain level in hot weather. Public transport can get very crowded at such times; check local weather forecasts or contact tourist information for day-to-day details.
- Though Athens does not have a big crime problem, it has a bad reputation for pickpockets and petty thieves. This is especially bad in the Omnia Square area, so be careful. Be careful, too, about where you choose to stay (see SLEEPING below).
- Women may find Athens a very 'macho' city. Best way to deal with the catcalls and stares is to ignore them, and keep walking. Beware of con artists, and keep them in mind if you bump into anyone who's overly friendly.

## SLEEPING

There are hundreds of places to stay in Athens and unless you're arriving very late on an August night you should be OK. That's not to say that all places are clean, friendly or have even the bare essentials, but most are cheap. Always try to book in advance.

You may find young English-speakers from various hostels (some of which are fairly grotty) joining the trains just before Athens, extolling the virtues of their establishments and handing out leaflets. This is a good way of earning bed and board for those who plan on spending some time in Athens. Take what they say with a pinch of salt, but go and see for yourself nonetheless. Security regarding belongings and valuables is sometimes suspect.

Athens has had a large influx of refugees in recent years, turning certain areas and many of the cheaper hotels and hostels into little more than refugee camps. So check your information carefully, get help from the tourist police, and be prepared to look around.

Basically, the nearer to Syntagma Square, the more you can expect to pay. Head for the Plaka, as it's not only an attractive central place to stay (right underneath the Acropolis) but also one of the cheapest districts. Get hold of a copy of *Cheap Sleeps Europe 2000* for a full range of options.

**HOSTELS** Try **Hostel Aphrodite**, 12 Einardou Street (Tel. 881 0589 or 883 9249; Fax. 881 6574). It has a safe bar and friendly staff (in season, ask for Kevin Banks, who is happy to help with queries, and can book tours and excursions at student prices). It's also on a quiet street within walking distance of the metro (Victoria Square) and both train stations.

**Student's and Traveller's Inn** at 16 Kidathineon Street (Tel. 324 4808; Fax. 321 0065) has an unbeatable location – right in the heart of the Plaka. Doubles from 9,000GDR. There's a courtyard and an Internet café.

At Syntagma Square is **George's Guesthouse** (46 Nikis Street, Tel. 322 6474). It's small and a bit run down, but is a bargain considering its location (around 6,000GDR for a double).

**Tempi Hotel** at 29 Foulou Street (Tel. 321 3175; Fax. 325 4179), in Monistriika, is some way out, but on a nice square and close to a metro. Friendly and family-run.

Also close to the metro and train stations is **Hotel Zorbas** at 10 Glyfordou Street, just off Victoria Square. It's clean and small, with private showers in some rooms.

The **Student Hostel No. 5**, at 75 Damareos St, Pangrati (Tel. 751 9530; Fax. 751 0616) is a bit out of town, but worth the trouble of travelling to. Very clean, well organized and extremely friendly. Trolley-buses 2 and 12. Dorm bed 1,800GDR, roof bed 1,500GDR.

Cheap, friendly and 3 minutes from Larissis Station, **Hotel Phaedra** (Herefondos 16; Tel. 322 7795) in the Plaka is clean and reasonable (9,000GDR for a double).

**Thisseus Inn** on Thisseus 10 (Tel. 324 5960) is centrally located, 3 blocks west of Syntagma; it's cheap but clean. Dorm beds from 2,500GDR.

There's a **hostel** at 1 Agiou Meletiou and the **YWCA** is at 11 Amerikis St (Tel. 362 4291) (women only).

Athens International **youth hostel** is at 16 Victor Hugo Street and is (at time of writing) the only officially IYHF-affiliated hostel in the whole of Greece. However, this area tends to be unsafe these days and is best avoided, especially at night. Tel. 523 4170; Fax 523 4015 for more information.

**CAMPING** The nearest **campsite** is quite far out: 198 Athinon Avenue, Peristeri (Tel. 581 4114); take buses 822 or 823 from Eleftherias Square (Thission underground station).

There is another, better, **campsite**: Voula **Camping**, 3 Alkionidon (Tel. 895 2712). Take bus 118, 122 or 153 from Vass. Olgas Avenue. It's 15 km from Syntagma, but offers a pool, bar, restaurant and beaches.

## EATING AND NIGHTLIFE

There are lots of restaurants and coffee shops in the Plaka district, but it can be expensive. Night clubs run from Plateia Thisseon all the way to Piraeus, but they too are expensive (and foreigners are not always welcome). Better to look away from the touristy areas for a quiet local taverna in which to spend the evening. If you choose to eat out in Athens and if the signs are in English, then more often than not the food is more expensive and touristy.

For great food at good prices in a friendly atmosphere, try **Kouklis** at Tripidon 14, which is an excellent, reasonably priced Greek restaurant. Vegetarians are catered for at **Eden**, 12 Lissiou St, Plaka, which is open every day until midnight and is housed in an historic neoclassical building.

For cheap eats, fill up on shish kebabs (*souvlaki*) and *dolmades* (vine leaves stuffed with meat). There are plenty of cheap supermarkets. Avoid fruit from stalls as it's over-priced and the quality suspect.

The Athens festival takes place during the summer. This includes open-air performances in the Herodus Atticus Odeon. For details contact the box office at 4 Stadhiou Street (Tel. 32 21459). There are often performances in the National Park on summer evenings; ask at the tourist office. For the Athens gay scene, check the listing magazine *Athinorama*.

**EXCURSIONS** Sixty-nine km away is the amazing **Temple of Poseidon** at **Cape Sounion**, a rocky promontory rising 60 m out of the sea. The temple dates back to 440 BC and is dedicated to the God of the Sea. Like the Acropolis, get there as early as possible; buses leave from Mavromateon St every half hour, until 9.30pm (2,500 GDR round trip). Byron carved his name on the temple, but be warned: the Greek authorities will not be amused if today's visitors, famous or otherwise, attempt to do the same.

For **Delphi**, 178 km north-west from Athens, take the local train to Livadhia and take the bus (800GDR) direct from there. Alternatively, take a KTEL bus from 260 Liossion Street: approximately eight buses run a day (2,850GDR). This, the 'navel of the universe', is the site of the Delphic Oracle and was the holiest place in Ancient Greece.

Little is left of the **Temple of Apollo** but there's still a fascinating museum (which houses the famous bronze charioteer), a 400 BC theatre and the stadium where the Pythian Games were held.

The **Tourist Office** is at 44 Pavlou St, close to the bus station in the town hall (Tel. 0265 82900). Open Mon.–Fri.: 7.30am–2.30pm. The friendly staff at the bus station can also point you in the right direction. The **Tourist Police** office (Tel. 82220) and the general police station are at 3 Angelos Syngrou Street, behind the church at the top of Apollonos Street. Open 9am–2pm.

The **campsite** Apollon (Tel. 0265 82750; Fax. 0265 82639) is 1½ km west of Delphi on the Amfissa road. Buses for Patras depart from Kifissoo St.

# The Islands

For many people, Greece *is* the islands. The impact of tourism on some of these idyllic outcrops has been harsh; on others, island life has changed little. But each year, more and more quiet fishing villages are becoming both touristy and cosmopolitan, and while some remote islands probably still have a decade or so to go before they're turned into mini Majorcas, many have only a year or two, and some are there already.

For a remote haven, choose an island which has only a weekly sailing from Piraeus – the fewer the ferries, the fewer the crowds (and the less reliable the service). Another way to find a gem is to ask fellow backpackers. Here are seven things to bear in mind:

1. Buy your ticket from one of the agencies in Piraeus – there is a 20% **surcharge** if you pay on the boat. Some of the Athenian hostels offer what appear to be bargain tickets – beware of hidden port taxes and surcharges. Daily departures include: Chios, Eyina, Crete, Paros, Naxos, Ios, Samos, Kos, Lesvos, Milos, Andros and Tinos in the summer. Many agents act for specific boats and will tell you theirs is the only service; don't accept them at their word. Ask around and compare prices. Take into account that routes taken

and the speed of the boats can vary considerably. Before buying a ticket, establish how many stops there will be *en route* to your island and the estimated time of arrival.

2. Avoid the **southern Aegean islands** in August because they can receive the incredibly strong *meltemi* (northern wind) which can ruin your sunbathing and sightseeing.

3. If you plan on going far afield, go for an **overnight** boat, as it costs no extra to sleep on deck and saves you the price of a night's accommodation.

4. The **Port Police** at Piraeus can be reached on Tel. 422 6000 if there are any problems, and the Directorate of Tourism of Mainland Greece and the Islands is situated in **Zeas Marina** (Tel. 413 5716 or 459 3145).

5. Whichever ferry you disembark from, you will find touts peddling their **accommodation**. Much of it is cheap, but ensure that you know exactly where it is before you agree to anything – it is not uncommon for a 'within walking distance' site to be, in reality, a half-hour bus trip away.

6. Always check **departure** times for your next visit as soon as you arrive on an island. Ferries out here are notoriously unreliable, so work out alternatives and plan for the worst. Keep some spare cash for port taxes.

7. In the summer, you can buy an **inter-island pass**, which allows travel between four islands (Paros, Naxos, Ios and Santorini) for around 12,000GDR – only slightly more expensive than a return to Santorini. Ask at the Piraeus agencies, or at Hostel Aphrodite on 883 9249 or 881 0589.

## The Saronic Gulf Islands

These islands, within four hours of Athens, are among the most crowded and expensive in Greece. But they are beautiful, with ancient temples and monasteries on the mountainsides, and pebbly beaches backed by green hills.

**EYINA (AEGINA)** The closest to Athens, and sailings are from the central harbour at Piraeus (Tel. 45 11311). (For the other islands, sailings are from Zea Marina, close to Piraeus, Tel. 45 27107.) Take the hydrofoils which supplement the steamer services and take only half an hour. The tourist police are on Leonardov Lada St (Tel. 0297 27777) and there's a Tourist Office in the town hall, to the right of the ferry quay (Tel. 0297 25588). Look for bed and food (especially pistachio nuts) around the port in Eyina town and admire the well-preserved Doric **Temple of Aria** and the view from the **Temple of Apollo**. The bay of Agia Marina has the best beaches but is packed with Athenians at weekends.

Eyina is very much a family tourist area, so accommodation is not particularly cheap and fills up quickly. Try the **Hotel Plaza** (Tel. 0297 25600). All the rooms have private bathrooms. Doubles with a sea view for around 12,000GDR. Ask the Tourist Office for more suggestions.

**POROS** Actually two small islands, both packed out in summer and heavily commercialized. It has some good beaches and lush pinewoods. The Tourist Information in the town of Poros (on the waterfront, opposite the ferry docks) will help you find a bed. The Tourist Police are situated on Agiou Nikolaou Street (Tel. 0298 22256), open 24 hours. See the **Monastery of Zoodhohos Piyi** and visit the **archaeological museum** on the waterfront (open Tues.–Sun. 8.30am–3pm; entrance is free). Try to get out to the village of **Trizina**, close to Poros on the mainland. It lies close to the ancient city of the same name and is the legendary birthplace of Theseus.

**HYDRA (IDRA)** All you expect a Greek island to be: narrow winding streets, donkeys (no cars allowed), beaches, blue sea and sky. Only 3½ hours from Piraeus, it is one of the beautiful people's islands. Consequently the prices, especially along the harbour, are crippling. Best avoided in peak season. For a truly memorable view, climb up to the hilltop monastery of **Agia Triada**. The Tourist Police at Navarhou N. Votsi St (Tel. 0298 52205; open 24hr) will find you rooms, which are cheaper on the other side of the town. Alternatively, ask around the fishermen's quarter of Karmini, a kilometre to the west of town.

**SPETSES** A charming island of pines, with **Agii Anargyri** as its best beach. The island is popular with wealthy Athenians and, as a result, it is relatively expensive. The harbour town does have a few cheapish **hotels** (the Star, the Faros and the Dapia) and the Tourist Police on Botsari St (Tel. 0298 73744) will fill you in with any other information you may need.

## The Cyclades

At the hub of the Greek ferry system, these are the most visited of the Aegean islands. And whether your idea of the perfect Greek island centres on whitewashed cliff-top villages and cobbled streets, or wild party nights, you'll find your idyll here among the 211 islands in this group.

If you're visiting in the winter, you may find that many of the tourist amenities are not available, you may also struggle to find cheap accommodation as many establishments close between late Oct. and early April.

**IOS** A popular destination for the young and the restless – those with lots of energy and little money. Here, all-night drinking and rowdy partying is the general rule. The main village is packed full of bars, but during the day try getting your water bottle filled up with locally produced wine from the greengrocers! The beaches to the south of Ios at Manganari are secluded and beautiful. If you don't want to join the crowds sleeping on the beach, try camping at Purple Pig (Tel. 0286 91302). There's an Amex at Acteon Travel Agency, Port Square (Tel. 0286 91343/91009). Accommodation owners are not allowed to approach you so you will not get hassled the minute you arrive on the island. However, the owners do stand in line waiting for you to approach them. How refreshing!

**MYKONOS** The island to experience tourism, not Greece. It's very beautiful, very expensive and very gay. There are nude beaches (the Paradise beach and Super Paradise, mostly gay) and a sophisticated night life, with countless bars, clubs and restaurants. There's also stunning scenery, magnificent beaches, whitewashed houses and windmills.

There are a few reasonably priced hotels: the Philippi at Kaloyera 32 (Tel. 0289 22294), the Apollon on Mavroyenous (Tel. 0289 22223) and Terra Maria (Tel. 0289 24212) at 33 Kalogera Street. Tourist information is available from both the Tourist Office (Tel. 0289 22699), open 9am–9pm, and the Tourist Police (Tel. 0289 22482), on the waterfront. There are three different information offices at the dock which are numbered according to the type of accommodation you're after: 1 for hotels (Tel. 0289 24540); 2 for rooms to let (Tel. 0289 24860) and 3 for camping (Tel. 0289 23567). Paradise Beach Camping (Tel. 0289 22852/0289 22129) is inexpensive and well-appointed and a van arrives to meet all boats as they arrive. The other officially listed campsite is Mykonos Camping (Tel. 0289 25915/0289 22916) which is near Paradise Beach but is smaller, quieter and slightly cheaper. Amex facilities are available at Delia Travel, The Quay (Tel. 0289 22322/24300).

Mykonos is very well connected by ferry – there is at least one ferry a day travelling to Tinos, Paros, Santorini, Ios, Naxos, Andros and Piraeus. If you're travelling to any of these, there are also daily Flying Dolphins (Hydofoils) which take less than half the time but are twice the price. Also, they tend not to stick to their timetables as they are so dependent on the weather conditions. The choice is yours!

There are also boat trips from Mykonos to **Delos**, the ancient religious centre of the Greek world, where you can see the ruins of the Sanctuary of Apollo, the Terrace of Lions and the Sacred Harbour.

**PAROS** A beautiful and very clean island, but very commercialized. It's a popular destination for gay travellers and young people who can't afford to stay on Mykonos. Its beautiful old church, Panagia Ekaton-dapiliani (open 9am–1pm and 5pm–9pm) makes it worth a trip and you can enjoy a fish meal in the attractive fishing village of Naoussa. The beaches are heavenly and there's good windsurfing to be had at Hrysi Akti (Golden Beach) on the south coast. Boats depart, several times a day, to all the major nearby islands. A complete schedule is posted at the Tourist Office in the windmill, by the dock (Tel. 0284 24528), open daily 8am–midnight. You'll find most of the hotels and rooms just off the waterfront in the old town of Parikia. There are five camp sites to choose from but Camping Koula (Tel. 0284 22081) is the most convenient (400m north of the town).

**ANDIPAROS** This small island opposite Paros used to be quiet and unspoilt but now it is fast becoming overrun by tourism, however it still has a way to go before it rivals Paros on the commercial stakes. It is still worth a trip, whether it's to enjoy yet more wonderful beaches or to visit the stalactite caves, which are some of the best in Europe (open 10.30am–4.45pm; entrance 400GDR). There is a frequent ferry service and buses (the only bus service on the island) go directly to the entrance of the cave on the south side every hour from 10.30am to 2.30pm (costs 1,300GDR for a round trip).

Camping Andiparos (Tel. 0284 61221) lies 800m north-west of the town on Agios Yiannis beach, and Hotel Mandalena (Tel. 0284 61206), to the right of the dock, is inexpensive.

**SIFNOS, SIKINOS, SERIFOS, MILOS** The 'dry islands' – **Sifnos** with around 365 churches and chapels, and a gastronomic delicacy of roast kid and olives; **Sikinos**, which has a very good beach; **Serifos**, with iron ore mines and annual August fiesta; and **Milos** – are all relatively tranquil, but their landscape is rather barren. Milos (Plaka) the capital is the discovery site of the Venus de Milo, and houses an archaeological folklore museum.

**ANDROS AND TINOS** The attractive islands of **Andros** and **Tinos** are large enough to allow visitors to spread themselves out. Tinos becomes a sacred island on 15 August, and pilgrims attend celebrations in honour of the Virgin Mary. Her icon at the Church of Evangelistria is said to have miraculous properties. There is no Tourist Office as such, but the tourist agency, Mariner (Tel. 0283 23193), next to the pharmacy, and the Tourist Police (a few mins. out of town on the road to Kionia) can help with any queries.

**NAXOS** In Greek mythology, **Naxos** is the place where Dionysus sprang from the thigh of Zeus. It is large and fertile with a mountainous interior. The Tourist Office can be found across the boat dock on the waterfront (Tel. 0285 25201/24358), open daily 8am–midnight. The Panorama Hotel on Afitritis (Tel. 0285 24404) in the old town is reasonably priced. The Irene Studios (Tel. 0285 23169) by the Galini Restaurant in newer Naxos is a good place to stay and there's a shuttle service from the dock. For camping, try Naxos Camping (Tel. 0285 235 00/23501) off Agios Giorgios Beach or Maragas Camping (Tel. 0285 42552/42599), which is further out but practically on the beach. There's a shuttle bus from the ferry dock or catch a regular bus to Ag. Anna beach.

The bus service for the islands is very good. Try and get to the town of Apiranthos: the folk art and Michael Bardini (Cycladic Art) museums are free in the mornings. Apollon and Ayia Anna have the best beaches.

**KEA** If you do not want to leave the mainland for too long, take a ferry from the port of Lavrio (south-east of Athens) to **Kea**, a journey of only 90 minutes. It is a quiet picturesque island, and its most famous asset is a colossal lion carved into the solid rock during the 6th century **BC** at the port of Korissa.

## Santorini (Thira/Fira)

This most dramatic of Aegean islands was formed 4,000 years ago by a massive volcanic explosion, and beaches like Perissa, with its black volcanic sand, never let you forget you're on a volcano. The boat trip out to the little island of **Nea Kameni**, where the volcano still smoulders, is worth it. The best beaches are Kamari and Monolithos, and for a break from sunbathing, see the ruins from the Minoans, Romans and Venetians.

From the harbour, get to the town of **Fira** (ferries dock at Athinios now) where you can find rooms at reasonable prices. Beware of the hotel touts at Athinios: they will hustle you into a mini van and take you somewhere miles out of town. Beware also of some hoteliers' habit of charging for two nights if you book in before noon. It may be unethical but it's technically legal.

**Guest houses** are operated by the GNTO at the small village of Oia on the north-west coast of the island, site of spectacular sunsets. Try also **Pension Petros** in Thira (Tel. 0286 22573), a great family-run place.

Alternatively, there are **youth hostels** at **Fira** (Tel. 0286 22387), **Oia** (Tel. 0286 71209/292/290) and **Perissa** (Tel. 0286 82182). The **Kontohori** hostel on Agios Eleftherios (Tel. 0286 22722 or 22577) offers a very good deal, but avoid the offer of roof accommodation: it's cold and mosquito-infested. **Perissa Camping** (Tel. 0286 81343) is situated near the beach of the same name, and there is **Santorini Camping** at Fira (Tel. 0286 22944/23203).

The monastery of **Profitis Ilias** on the island's summit houses a great religious celebration each year on 20 July. Visitors are invited to join the islanders in a meal of traditional dry pea soup, followed by energetic folk dancing.

There's an **Amex** agency at X-Ray Kilo, Main Square, Fira (Tel. 0286 22624).

# The Sporades

Sporades means 'the scattered ones': these thickly forested islands are strewn just off the mainland, with fine sandy beaches, translucent waters and dense pine forests. Once the quietest islands in Greece, their fledgling tourist industry has in recent years succumbed to full-blown commercialization, and now their best beaches tend to be very busy in high season.

You approach them by boat from Kimi (port authority: Tel. 0222 22606), Ayios Konstandinos (port authority: Tel. 0235 31920), or Volos (port authority: Tel. 0421 38888), which you reach by bus or train from Athens. To get to Volos, change at Larissa (almost hourly). Before leaving for the islands, you can book accommodation on the mainland at the Hellenic Chamber of Hotels, 24 Stadiou Street, Athens (Tel. 01 323 7193; Fax. 01 322 5449).

**SKIATHOS** The most touristy, with a thumping good nightlife. There's a superb beach at **Koukounaries**, surrounded by pine groves. For a decent night's rest try one of the **pensions** on Evangelistras St in Skiathos town. Many homes advertise **rooms to let** (*dhomatia*) in the summer months and their prices are reasonable. Of the four official **campsites**, Aselinos, Xanemos and Koukounaries (Tel. 0427 49250) are recommended. The Tourist Police office (Tel. 0427 23172) is in a small white building on Papadiamantis Street and the **Amex** agency is on the same street at no. 21 in the Mare Nostrum Holidays travel agency (Tel. 0427 21463 or 21464).

**ALONISSOS** This island may at first impression appear soulless and unattractive. It is, however, one of the more traditional and friendly of the Greek islands. From the port of Patitiri, head for Marpounda or Kokkinokastro, where there's a good pebble beach, and archaeological remains such as the **sunken Byzantine ship** at Ayios Petras. The sea around this island has been declared a Marine Conservation Park, so do not leave rubbish lying around. The local **room-owners' association** (Tel. 0424 65577), located on the waterfront, will help you find accommodation. The official **campsite** is Ikaros **Camping** (Tel. 0424 65258) on Steni Vala Beach.

**SKOPELOS** This stark outcrop may look forbidding as you approach its cliffs from the sea, but the interior of the island is a rather a lush place, with olive groves and plum trees, and thick forests of pine. Also inland lie the ruins of the medieval bishops' palace, and many churches and monasteries. There are good beaches at **Stafilos** and **Agontas**. If you intend to stay in **Skopelos Town**, try to get a room up the hill, as the town sewage discharges into the harbour and can smell awful on a hot day. (There are no campsites on Skopelos). When you've tired of sunbathing, two places worth popping into are the **Folk Art Museum** and the **Photographic Centre of Skopelos**.

**SKYROS** Flat-topped white houses stand on the cliffs and folk crafts still flourish here on the most beautiful and unspoilt island of the Sporades. The long, dark sand beach is wonderful, and there are countless little coves for swimming and scuba diving. Make sure you visit the 1000-yr-old **Monastery of St. George** and the **Castle of Licomidus** from where you can get great views of the town of Skyros below. Try the **campsite** (take bus from ferry to Magazia), or use one of the restaurants for a room. The Tourist Office (Tel. 0222 92789) near the post office offers all the information services you'll need, including help with accommodation, boat trips and buses.

## North-East Aegean

These islands lie very close to Turkey, and yet surprisingly bear few traces of the Ottoman empire. Instead, they nurture their Greekness, and despite burgeoning tourism in some areas, the atmosphere remains firmly traditional. If you don't mind going a bit further out of your way, you will be rewarded with unspoiled villages, quiet beaches and dramatic mountain scenery.

Samos, Lesvos (Lesbos) and Hios are the three most popular, and all are linked by boat services to the islands of the Dodecanese, Cyclades and Crete.

**SAMOS** The birthplace of Pythagoras and the goddess Hera (Juno) is heavily wooded with a rocky coastline and a good beach resort, Kokari. This is a good island stop for travellers on their way to Turkey, with Kusadasi only a couple of hours away, and boats there running daily. The central island area around **Pirigos** and **Mitilini** is rich in archaeological sites and museums. The capital, **Samos Town** (Vathi) has a good archaeological museum (open Tues.–Sun.: 8am–2.30pm; 800GDR; students half price). When you arrive, go for information to Samos Tours at the end of the ferry dock (Tel. 0273 27715) or the Tourist Office further down the waterfront, by Pythagoras Sq. (Tel.

0273 28530/28582; only open in July and Aug.). Accommodation is scarce in the summer months, but try the **Pension Ionia** at Manoli Kalmoiris 5 (Tel. 0273 28782) or the **Pension Avli**, Areos 2 (Tel. 0273 22939).

**LESVOS (LESBOS)** Once home to Aesop of the fables and the 7th century BC poet Sappho, Lesvos is also known as Mitilini after its principal city. It is a mass of olive trees and has some incredible, traditionally designed buildings in its port of Mithimna. The coast of Patraon in the north-west is abundant in archaeological finds and there is a petrified forest at Sigri. To get to Lesvos from Piraeus, there is a daily boat service, and from Salonica a weekly service. The **Tourist Office** at 6 James Aristarchou, Mitilini (Tel. 0251 42511) is very helpful (shuts at 3pm) and the **Tourist Police** office is in Mitilini, behind the customs house (open 8.30am–5.30pm; Tel. 0251 22776). There's also a **Rooms to Let** office one block from the centre of the waterfront. In Mitilini, the domatia owners belong to a cooperative called Sappho Self-Catering Rooms in Mitilini. Most of their accommodation is in the side streets running off Ermou.

**CHIOS (HIOS)** Birthplace of Homer, Chios has an interesting Byzantine monastery, the Nea Moni,and a lively bazaar. Because of its literary connections, the village of **Vrontado**, five km from Chios, holds a 'Homeria' (events of art and literature) every summer. The Tourist Office, 11 Kanari Street (Tel. 0271 44344), can help you find accommodation and fill you in on the details. A ferry connects the island to Turkey and Lesvos once a day, and to Inousses every hour. Contact the port authority (Tel. 0271 22837) or the Tourist Office for more information.

# The Dodecanese

These are the most easterly islands of Greece, the furthest from the mainland and just a few kilometres from Turkey. Despite more than 300 years of Turkish rule, Greek tradition is strong here, but there are also lasting reminders of other occupations through the centuries, including those of the Crusaders and the Italians.

Sailing from Piraeus can take up to 20 hours. Ferries travelling this route have alternately scheduled departures at 1pm every day, stopping at Kos *en route*. It's a long haul, but your efforts are rewarded with superb beaches, mountains, medieval buildings and an air of historical importance unique to these islands. If you are travelling by ferry around these islands, expect cancellations due to rough seas, especially out of season. Kos, Rhodes and Leros all have airports, and with a student discount of 25% on Olympic Airways flights, air travel can become as competitive as the unreliable services by sea.

The two main islands are **Rhodes** and **Kos**, the latter of which is regarded as the birthplace of modern medicine. The Knights of St John captured the islands in the 14th century, and much later they were occupied by the Italians during World War II.

**RHODES** In ancient times, Helios, the sun god was particularly worshipped on the island and today it is fair to say that Rhodes is an island of eternal summer, with no fewer than 300 days of sunshine a year. There's masses to see in Rhodes and you could easily spend a day or two exploring the Old Town alone. There are plenty of interesting museums, including the **Archaeological Museum**, housed in the former Hospital of the Knights, in Museum Square, as well as some fascinating ruins, such as the **Temple of Aphrodite** which dates from the 3rd century BC. The Suleymaniyah Mosque and the Grand Masters' Palace are also worth a visit. The Tourist Police (Tel. 0241 27423) and Tourist Information (Tel.0241 23255) are at Rimini Square near Mandraki, the port area. The EOT at the corner of Makariou Street and Papagou Street (Tel. 0241 23655/23255) will help you with accommodation, bus and boat schedules (they close at 3pm).

The old town has the best cheap places to **sleep**, such as Pension Andreas, Omirou 28D (Tel. 0241 34156) and Hotel Strathis, 60 Omirou Street (Tel. 0241 24357). The **Rodos Youth Hostel**, Ergiou 12 (Tel. 0241 30791) is cheap and cheerful. For **eating**, check out Taverna Mike's if you like seafood. Yiannis, 41 Apellou Street, serves massive portions of hearty fare. The best **bar** in town is Cafe Besara on Sofokleous which also serves light snacks.

If you need hydrofoil, ferry and excursion boat information, look no further than Triton Tours on Plastira St (Tel. 0241 21690/30657). The ferries to Israel stop at Rhodes, but only for a couple of hours. Marmaris in Turkey is a few hours away by boat.

The west coast of Rhodes is incredibly windy and the east coast is where the best beaches are. There is a huge variety of watersports on offer. Take a bus from the east side of Plateia Rimini to **Faliraki Beach**, which is a lovely beach but often crowded with youngish package-holiday makers in the summer. There's a **campsite** near here (Tel. 0241 85 358) and there's another one 64 km down the east coast at Lardos (Tel. 0244 44203/44249). Nightclubs are as plentiful as the bars. Women beware of Rhodes men (*Kanaki*), who are real charmers.

Most shops stay open until well past 9pm, so do your souvenir hunting in the evening. Rhodes is tax-free, so booze is a bargain. There's an **Amex** agency, Rhodos Tours, at 23 Ammochostou St (Tel. 0241 21010).

**Lindos** has archaeological remains and is an extremely picturesque town, but the package-deal customers flock here in summer and prices become astronomical. It can still be very romantic if you are with the right person!

**KOS** The birthplace of Hippocrates is a fascinating island, with great beaches, ancient Roman and medieval monuments, mosques, a Crusader fortress (Tues.–Sun.: 8am–2pm. Admission 850GDR; students half price), and a wonderful atmosphere. At **Paradise Beach**, 50 km south of the capital, you will find clean sands, peace and quiet – except for a nearby Club Med complex. On the south-eastern outskirts are the ruins of Hippocrates' medical school and sanctuary at the Asclepion. Further west, on the coast road, lies the **Petaloudes Valley**, where millions of butterflies gather each summer. If it is nightlife you are after, go to Platia Eleftherias.

For **accommodation** try Pension Alexis, at 9 Irodotou St (Tel. 0242 28798/0242 25594) or Hotel Afendoulis, 1 Evrilpilou Street (Tel. 0242 25321), in Kos Town. **Camping**, though not legal outside the official site, is idyllic. The official campsite, **Kos Camping** (Tel. 0242 23910), is 2.5 km out of town, towards Cape Psalidhi, and is closed during the off-season. The site sends a minibus to meet arriving ferries.

The Tourist Police (Tel. 0242 24444) on the waterfront and the Tourist Offices at Akri Miaouli Street, Hippokratous Street and Vasileos Georgiou Street can help with any queries. There's also an **Amex** at 1 Heroon Polytechniou Square (Tel. 0242 26732/24447).

Kos has good ferry and boat links with the other islands and the mainland, but check with boat operators beforehand, since times are prone to change.

## Crete (Kriti)

The home of Europe's earliest civilization holds an important place in the ancient world. As early as 2000 BC, the Minoans controlled a maritime trading empire from grand palaces decorated with fine art and craftwork. Evidence of this advanced society was uncovered only this century, during excavations at Knossos and Festos. The island is also the legendary birthplace of Zeus and home of the Minotaur.

Crete is divided into four regions, with Heraklion, Hania, Rethymnon, and Ayios Nikolaos as their capitals. There is superb scenery along the route through the Amari Valley down to Ayia Galini, which is flanked to the east by Mount Ida and to the west by Mount Kedros. Around Ierapetra and the Lasithi Plain, the scenery is unusual and dramatic.

And then there are the monasteries of Kera and Arkadi, both with magnificent icons and frescoes, the latter bearing testament to Crete's Venetian period.

There are daily sailings from Piraeus to the ports of both Hania (Tel. 0821 89240) and Heraklion (Tel. 081 226073), both of which take approximately 12 hours. Sailings for Rethymnon leave on Mon., Wed., Fri., Sun. (Tel. 0831 29221).

**Heraklion** (Iraklion) is the main port of Crete with connecting ferries to Piraeus. Apart from the amazing **Archaeological Museum** off Eleftherias Square, where you'll find the Hall of the Minoan frescoes, and the Morosini Fountain, the city has little to recommend it. However, there are some good sites to see from Heraklion.

The ruins of the greatest of the Minoan palaces can be seen at **Knossos**, legendary home of the Minotaur. The ruins are open daily in summer from 8am–8pm, and in winter from 8am–5pm. Admission is 1,500GDR but there is a student discount and they are free on Sunday. To get there take bus 2 which stops along 25 Augoustou Avenue.

The Tourist Office in Heraklion is opposite the Archaeological Museum at 1 Xanthoudhidhou St (Tel. 081 228203/244462), open, Mon.–Fri.: 8am–2.30pm. There's an **Amex** agency, Adamis Tours, at 23 25th August St (Tel. 081 246202).

If staying, try the **youth hostel** at 5 Vironos St, just off 25 Augustou Avenue (Tel. 081 286281/222947) or the newer hostel (Tel. 081 280858) at 24 Handnakos St. **Camping** Iraklion (Tel. 081 286380), west of the city, is strictly run and expensive. The area below Platia Venizelou is the best place to look for rooms.

Further west is **Rethymnon**, which has Venetian and Turkish buildings. There is an excellent and popular **youth hostel** at 41 Tombazi St (Tel. 0831 22848), and the Tourist Office is on El. Venizelou Avenue (Open Mon.–Fri.: 8am–2.30pm;Tel. 0831 29148). **Camping** Arkadia (Tel. 0831 28825) and **Camping** Elizabeth (Tel. 0831 28694) are four km out of town.

**Plakias**, due south of Rethymnon on the south coast of the island, makes a perfect low-budget diversion from the north coast. The rocky inlets disguise a number of idyllic coves, several of which are 'clothes optional'. The hills behind the coastal strip are also full of interesting villages and monasteries. The **youth hostel** has a friendly, laid-back atmosphere, and is a short walk inland – follow the signs (Tel. 0832 32 118 or 0831 22 848).

In **Hania** (Khania), the elegant ex-capital of Crete, the Venetian architecture makes you feel more as if you're in Italy than Greece. The Tourist Office on the first floor of the Megaro Pantheon, 1866 Square, behind the Greek Agricultural Bank, is open 7.30am–2.30pm (Tel. 0821 92624). Try the harbour area for rooms, or Hotel Meltemi (Tel. 0821 92802) next to the fortress. **Camping** Hania is four km west of the city (Tel. 0821 31138).

For the high spot of your trip, walk along the **Samarian Gorge**, the largest in Europe and a nature lover's dream, but in the summer a tourist haven. Take the bus to Xyloskalo, through the Omalos mountains, for this six-hour walk. The walk will end in the small town of Ayia Roumeli, on the southern coast. From here you can get a boat to Loutro or Hora Sfakion, where you can catch a bus back to Hania. Before you set out for this trip, pack refreshments and sensible footwear. You'll need them.

In eastern Crete, **Ayios Nikolaos**, like Malia, is the tourist trap. It's very picturesque but often short of rooms. Enquire at the Tourist Information Office at 21A S. Koundourou Street (Tel. 0841 22357/24165). Or try **Pension** Christodoulakis, 7 Stratigou Koraka Street (Tel. 0841 22 525). The harbour nightlife is the best thing about this town - there are bars and clubs to suit all tastes.

Fifty-two kilometres west, at the village of **Psihros**, is the path that ascends to the Dhiktan Cave (*Dikteon Andron*), the legendary birthplace of Zeus, and venue of cult worship (open daily 10.30am–5pm). At the village you can hire a donkey from the locals if you do not wish to climb up to the cave by foot. There are many other caves of archaeological and historical interest; ask at Tourist Information for more details.

**Sitia**, east of the city, is near the fantastic palm beach of **Vaï**, as seen in the Bounty Bar adverts, which is swamped with tourists during the day (beware: the authorities are very strict on illegal **camping**). The **youth hostel** at 4a Therissou Street (Tel. 0843 22693) can usually squeeze you in. There is no Tourist Office, but the Tourist Police at 31 Therissou Street, open daily 7.30am– 9pm (Tel. 0843 24200) will be able to help.

## The Ionian Islands

These islands off the north-west coast of Greece escaped Turkish invasion, but instead were occupied in turn by the Venetians, the British, the French and the Russians. The legacy of these periods is evident today, with cricket still played in Corfu and Italian widely spoken. Compared to the islands of the Aegean, the Ionian islands are green and fertile, thanks to heavy rains between October and March.

## Corfu island phone code: 0661

If you're taking the ferry from or to Italy, you can break the trip here.

Take the opportunity if you've a day or two to spare, particularly if you can avoid the crush months of July and August. If you are travelling from Patras, possession of an Inter-Rail ticket entitles you to travel deck class, not second class, on the ferry, so the trick is to get on early and find a bench to lay out your sleeping bag.

Corfu doesn't look terribly Greek; in some ways it's more like the French Riviera. The Venetians, French and British have all left their colonial stamp on Corfu, and it's very easy to see in the buildings, food and people. Corfu Town is one of the prettiest of all Greek towns, with several restored and renovated historic buildings and traffic barred from some parts of town.

The town's two castles, one Venetian, one Byzantine, have huge ramparts to explore, and look out too for the British-built neo-classical palace now housing exhibitions and a museum of Asian art. In the old town, the church of Agios Spiridon is worth a look, and for a peek at ancient artefacts found on the island, look into the small archaeological museum.

The festival of Corfu takes place in September and features ballet, concerts, operatic and theatrical offerings. From June until then, the GNTO puts on a season of folk dances and 'sound and light' performances in English, French and Italian at the old fortress to the north-east of the town.

When you disembark from the ferry, you are likely to be met at the port by reps from just about every **hotel** with spare beds. Or you can turn left to the Old Port; the road to the right of the Hotel Constantinopolis is where to start your own search for a cheap bed. Try the **Hotel Europa** (Tel. 39304), in Neo Limin, which charges about 6,000–8,000GDR for a double room, and rents out mopeds for 4,000GDR. Another recommendation is **Hotel Ionian** at 46 Xenofondos Stratigou (Tel. 30268) also near the Old Port. This hotel is slightly nicer and a bit more expensive.

The lively **Pink Palace Hotel** is owned by Dr George and his sister (Tel. 531031). At Agios Gordhios, it's right on the beach and can be reached by bus from the Old Port. It is a backpacker's heaven and there are many activities designed to get even the quietest person to join in, such as the infamous ouzo circle. It charges from 6,500GDR per person, with breakfast, dinner and shower included. You can also do your laundry here.

The **Tourist Police**, 31 Arseniou St (Tel. 30265), will fix you up in a **private home** if they like the look of you. Walk along G. Theotaki Street in the direction of Sanrocco Square, it's on the 4th floor. **Tourist Information** is at the corner of Rizospaston Voulefton Street and Iak. Folila Street, on the 1st floor (Tel. 37520). The office is only open May–Sept. Mon.–Fri.: 7.30am–2.30pm. The **youth hostel** is far out and invariably full. The hostel is about 4½ km north (Tel. 91202), take bus 7 from Plateia San Rocco to Kondokali Beach. The reception is open 8am–12 noon, 5pm–8pm. There is also a **camp site** at Kondokali Beach (Tel. 91202) which is the most convenient of the island's six camping grounds. Follow the directions to the youth hostel above. If you want to stay on the opposite side of the island, there's Camping Vatos, which is cheap, friendly and has full facilities, including bar and restaurant. You can get free minibuses to and from the nearest beach as well as a free minibus service to the early-morning ferries (Tel. 94505).

**Pelekas Beach**, on the west coast, is a favourite of Eurorailers, as is Karousadhes in the north of the island. (Campsites at both). We don't recommend you hire a moped, but if you must, make sure you get a helmet and haggle for the petrol, which is always a rip-off. Moped hire usually costs around 4,000–5,000GDR.

**Paleokastritsa**, on the west coast, has sandy beaches, blue water and stalls selling jewellery. It's a good place to go scuba diving (contact the Baracuda Club or the Tourist Office for details).

Back in Corfu Town, there's an **Amex** agency at 20a Kapodistriou Street (Tel. 30883/32469).

For picnics, the best place to shop is the produce **market** on Odhos Dhessila. Beware of some of the cheap food stalls, as food poisoning seems to be a recurring hazard.

The Old Port area is good for evening **meals**. Try **Restaurant Andronik** (Tel. 38858) at 21 Arseniou St, which serves great food and attracts a multi-ethnic clientele (it was founded by Armenian refugees in 1920). **Faliraki Restaurant** on the corner of Kapodistriou and Arseniou Street is also good. **Yisdhakis** at 20 Solomou Street is an authentic Greek restaurant, and places like the **Kastelo Taverna** opposite the fish market provide simple, cheapish Greek cooking.

In Corfu town, the best **night spots** are on the road heading north out of town. Try Hippodrome, Apocalipsis, Coca and Sax.

- **A word of warning:** there have been reports of local boat owners offering day trips to Albania. Don't be tempted – the uneasy political situation means visiting Albania is not to be recommended. Acts of piracy by Albanians on Corfu resorts and on the nearby islands appear to have petered out, thanks to patrols by Greek navy gunboats.

**PAXI AND ANDIPAXI** The island of **Paxi** and its little neighbour **Andipaxi**, 30 minutes away, are becoming more touristy due to their proximity to Corfu, but these small islands still have a lot of charm. Every day a car ferry leaves Corfu for Paxi, which takes about three hours. Paxi is covered with grape vines and olive trees, and on 15 Aug. there is a festival at the monastery of **Panayia**, carrying on into the evening with dancing in the main square in **Gaios**. The Tourist Police (Tel. 0662 31222) should be able to help you find rooms to stay in. If you decide to camp illegally on the sandy beach at Mogonissi, be tidy and careful; fire can start particularly easily in summer.

**ITHACA** The legendary home of Odysseus, Ithaca is a small mountainous island with many historical caves associated with the hero. Linked daily by boat from Paxi and Corfu, it has a music and drama festival every July and Aug. The main town of **Vathi** has many shops and houses in the middle of a horse-shoe-shaped harbour. Try to find rooms to let by walking up around the back streets of the ferry quay, or enquire at Polyctor Tours in the main square, or see the Tourist Police (Tel. 0674 32205).

**ZAKINTHOS AND KEFALONÍA** The lush, mountainous island to the west of the Peloponnese is **Zakinthos**. It has a rich Roman and Venetian history, though much of the capital has been rebuilt following an earthquake in 1953. Visit the huge beach and clubs at Laganas. Reached by ferry (60 minutes) from Killini, near Patras, or by plane (45 minutes) from Athens, Zakinthos is a mostly unspoilt island, deserving of the title 'Flower of the East'. Visit the neo-Byzantine Museum and the Venetian fortress in Zakinthos Town, and stay at the Hotel Egli on Lombardou Street or contact the Rooms for Rent office on St Lucas Square on the waterfront (Tel. 0695 26809). The English speaking Tourist Police can be reached on 0695 27367.

On Zakinthos, and also the nearby island of **Kefalonía**, the **Marine Turtle Project** is currently taking place. There are free talks and slide shows, during which arrangements to see the beaches can be made. The project organizers are keen to promote wildlife issues here and to generally educate people as to the importance of protecting nature. Check it out if you are in the area.

These last islands have traditionally been much quieter than many of the better known places, though inroads by the British package holiday operators have changed things somewhat. Kefalonía has also become much more popular as a direct result of Louis de Bernieres' bestselling *Captain Corelli's Mandolin* which was set on the island.

A rising crime rate, put down to Albanian refugees (and highlighted by the murder of a retired British couple a few years ago in Kefalonía – two Albanians were arrested), spurred the government to up the numbers in Kefalonía's police force, and to deport all illegal immigrants. Locals, however, and other ex-pats who continue to live there, still say that if peace and tranquillity are what you are looking for, this is the area to come to.

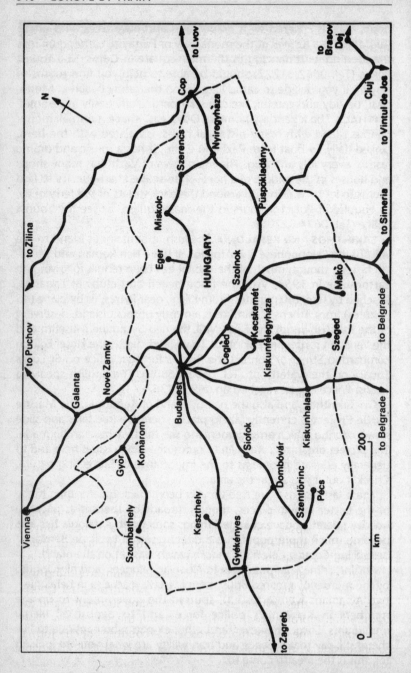

# HUNGARY

| | |
|---|---|
| Entry requirements | Passport. Australians and New Zealanders also require a visa. |
| Population | 10.5 million |
| Capital | Budapest (pop.: 2 million) |
| Currency | Forints |
| | £1 = approx. 401ft |
| Political system | Republic |
| Religions | 65% Catholic, 25% Protestant |
| Language | Hungarian (some German and English understood) |
| Public holidays | New Year's Day, National Day (Revolution Day) (15 Mar.), Easter Monday, Whit Monday, Labour Day (1 May), St Stephen's Day (Constitution Day) (20 Aug.), Remembrance Day (23 Oct.), Christmas Day and Boxing Day |
| International dialling codes | To Hungary: int'l code 36 (+1 for Budapest) |
| | From Hungary: 00 + country code |
| | For long-distance calls within Hungary: 06 + number |
| Emergency telephone numbers | Police 107; ambulance 104; fire service 105, |

Hungary's history is one that has seen many centuries of struggle against foreign domination. After becoming a Roman province in 10 AD, it was overrun by waves of Vandals, Huns, Avars and Franks until the Magyars in the 9th century set up a kingdom and converted the people to Christianity. A few centuries later in 1526 the Turks, who for years had been knocking on Hungary's door, finally entered and ruled for almost 150 years. They were then succeeded by Austria's Hapsburgs.

During the 1840s Hungarian nationalism grew strong and in 1848 culminated in a failed attempt to secure independence from the Habsburgs. However, in a complete turn-around less than 20 years later, the country was partnering Austria as ruler of the Austro-Hungarian empire, which stretched across the greater part of Central Europe.

At the end of the First World War, things came to an end when the empire collapsed and Hungary declared itself a republic. But by 1947 the Communist Party was in power and the country was tied to the Soviet Union, being ruled on Stalinist lines. In 1956 Budapest was the centre of a large and violent anti-communist uprising too, which saw many lives lost before it was quashed by Soviet troops. There was a further revolution in 1989, this time successful, and the country finally broke free from the clutches of the Soviets.

Hungary is one of the more prosperous countries of the former communist bloc, though like many of the others it is still struggling to mix Western commercialism with decades of restrictive politics.

Tourism is the growth industry, with its focus on Budapest followed by Lake Balaton and the Danubian Plain. Fortunately, these areas are the most accessible in a country where travel can be quite slow.

## HUNGARIAN STATE RAILWAYS
### (MAGYAR-ÁLLAMVASUTAK, MÁV)

Trains are slower than in Western Europe, as well as being crowded in summer. There are often long gaps between services, but with patience it's possible to explore nearly all the larger towns and tourist centres on an Inter-Rail ticket. Inter-City followed by *Sebesvonat* expresses are the fastest services. The ultra-slow *Személyvonat* take an age to get anywhere. Bear in mind that the railway network is very centralized and it's always easier to enter or leave Hungary via Budapest. Whenever possible, make your seat reservations (*fielyjegy*) in advance, at the MÁV booking office at Andràssy út 35, Budapest (Mon.–Fri.: 9am–6pm, Tel. 01 322 8049). Keep an eye out for any trains with new carriages, especially the new Inter-City trains, as they are a vast improvement on the old rolling stock.

### INTER-RAIL BONUSES

Free entry to **Metró Museum**, metro station Deák Ferenc tér, Budapest V; **Transport Museum**, Városligeti-Körút 11, Budapest XIV; and **Horse Carriage Museum**, Paràd-fürdö.

**PASSES AVAILABLE** For information on the Euro Domino and Explorer Passes, see Part One of this guide.

The Inter-Rail pass has been broken down into zones, so that you don't have to pay for travel to places you've no intention of visiting. Hungary is in Zone D, along with the Czech Republic, Slovakia, Poland, and Croatia. For £159 you get 22 days' travel in a single zone; over 26s pay £229.

Eurail and the European Eastpass are also both valid, see Part One of the guide for details.

## TRAIN INFORMATION

German has often been the best language to use, but the Germans are not always popular these days. Try English first so as to establish your nationality, rather than letting people think you are German and that you have a lot more money than you actually do have.

**RESERVATIONS (FIELYJEGY)** Compulsory on international express trains and Inter-City trains and, to be sure of a seat, book several days in advance.

**EATING ON TRAINS** All long-distance trains have either a buffet car or mini-bar, but it is cheaper to stock up beforehand in a supermarket.

## TOURIST INFORMATION

All towns have their own local Tourist Information offices (*Idegenforgalmi Hivatal*) in addition to the IBUSZ offices which deal with all aspects of travel and accommodation.

**MONEY MATTERS** 1 Forint = 100 Fillér.
Banking hours are generally Mon.–Thur.: 8.30am–3.30pm and Fri.: 8am–1pm. Although they often close earlier. When changing money you should use only the official exchange offices. Do not change it on the street as you may receive counterfeit money and in any case it is illegal. Foreign exchange brought into the country can be taken out when leaving, as can Hungarian currency up to the value of 50,000Ft. Make sure you keep receipts for any money changed and for any major purchases you have made. Many offices will accept credit cards, traveller's cheques and Eurocheques.

**POST OFFICES** Open Mon.–Fri.: 8am–6pm. The quickest service for phone calls, faxes, telexes and telegrams is the main Post Office or the Telecom Information and Service Office (Budapest V, Petöfi utca 13). Stamps can also be bought from tobacconists (Mon.–Fri.: 8am–8pm and Sat.: 10am–4pm).

**SHOPS** Most shops are open Mon.–Fri.: 10am–6pm with supermarkets and grocery stores generally open from 8am–6pm or to 7pm in larger towns. On Sat.most shops are open 10am–1pm, although in Budapest some shops are open longer. There are also some 24hr shops. Late-night opening on Thurs. is usually till 8pm, with many tobacconists, pastry shops, foodstores and large shopping centres in general also opening on Sun. While the cost of living has increased dramatically for Hungarians, prices are still comparatively low for Western European tourists.

**MUSEUMS** Most open Tues.–Sun.: 10am–6pm (winter 9am–4pm or earlier). Admission is usually free on either Tues. or Wed. Showing your ISIC card will normally get you a discount or even free entry. More information on opening times and exhibitions is available from Tourinform, V. Sütö utca 2, Budapest (Tel. 01 117 9800).

**BICYCLES** Certain stations rent out bicycles throughout the year and MÁV are now encouraging people to take their bike on the train. Help with routes, maps and other matters can be obtained from the Bicycle Touring Association of Hungary (*Magyar Kerélípáros Tírázok Szahŏv*), VI Bajcsy-Zsilinszky üt 31, Budapest . (Tel. 01 332 7177). Ask for the *Cycling Tours in Hungary* booklet published by IBUSZ.

**HIKING** The best areas are in the north, including the woods around Visegrád and Badacsony, north of Budapest; the Matra mountains near Eger; and the Bukk mountains west of Miskolc. There is no network of huts for hikers, and most campsites tend to be located near towns, but youth hostels are a good option as is staying in a farmhouse. Contact Falusi turizmus Centrum at VII Dohány utca 86, Budapest (Tel. 01 321 4396) for information on farmhouse accommodation.

**MEDICAL CARE** First aid is free, but a fee is charged for proper medical treatment, the rate of which depends on the institution concerned. Medical insurance is advisable.

**TIPPING** Leave 10–20% if you have had good service and it is not included on the bill.

## SLEEPING

The local Tourist Offices may fix you up in a **private house** for about 2,000–3,500Ft (up to 5,500Ft in Budapest) for two people per night (plus 30% for the first night). In small towns, look for the sign *Szoba Kiadó* (or *Zimmer frei*) and don't automatically refuse a room if you're approached at a railway station. If you're out of luck, the student travel service Express has several **hostels** and cheap student **hotels**. Beds in a hostel/student hotel start at about 1,500Ft. There's no need to be a member of the IYHF, and it's possible for couples to get a room to themselves. Most hotels, especially the budget ones, are booked up and are expensive, but if you're desperate, one-star hotels both in and out of Budapest start from 3000Ft.

**Camping** is a realistic possibility. There are over 200 authorized sites, officially graded from 1 to 3, depending on the facilities offered, and many are concentrated along the Danube and Lake Balaton. For more detailed information, contact the Hungarian Camping and Caravanning Club at IX Kálvin tér 9, Budapest (Tel. 01 217 7248), where you can get copies of their Hungarian camping guides, canoeing maps of the Danube and general camping advice. Camping in the wild is prohibited but undertaken none the less.

## EATING AND NIGHTLIFE

Hungarian food is excellent by any standards, and it's cheap. Try *pörkölt* (a stew with paprika), *paprikás csirke galuskával* (chicken with a sour cream paprika sauce), *hogybegy* (meat pancakes) or *goulash*. Vegetarians should try *gombafejek rántva* (mushroom coated with breadcrumbs) with *gnocchi*, and *somlói galuska* (sweet dumplings in rum and chocolate sauce) or *rétes* (strudel) to follow. The cheapest places are the self-service restaurants. Choose and collect your food, then pay the cashier. Look out for the tourist menus as they're normally exceptionally good value; if you're really broke and don't mind standing up, try a *bisztró*. Also try the Hungarian spirit, *pálinka*, a clear brandy made from apricots, cherries or other fruits. Hungary has quite a bit of nightlife, particularly in Budapest. There are student discos and open-air concerts as well as nightclubs.

# Budapest phone code: 01

In 1867 Buda, on the west bank of the Danube, became capital of Hungary, though by 1873 it had been joined by Pest on the opposite bank to form Budapest. After suffering heavy bomb damage in World War II, renovation and rebuilding has left the city with some fine buildings and magnificent bridges. There's plenty to see and do here and, because food and transport are still fairly cheap by Western standards, you can rise above your usual humble lifestyle and 'indulge' a little (or a lot). The fact that 20% of the country's population also lives here helps create a very cosmopolitan feel.

## STATION FACILITIES
There are three main stations: Déli (south, Tel. 175 6293) which serves the south-west, Keleti (east, Tel. 113 6835) and Nyugati (west, Tel. 149 0115). For rail information within Hungary call MÁV Central Information (Tel. 322 0856) between 9am and 5pm. If you are stuck, remember *pályaudvar* means station. Expect delays, especially left luggage. Give yourself plenty of time, especially in the evenings. Nyugati has a 24-hour mini market.

## TOURIST INFORMATION
Of the six major tourist agencies operating in Budapest, the best over-all source of information is Tourinform at V, Sütö utca 2 (Tel. 317 9800). Open Mon.–Fri.: 9am–7pm, Sat. and Sun.: 9am–4pm. Here the multi-lingual staff will answer any questions you have and can also sell you a three day 'Budapest Card' for around 3000Ft (there's also a two day card). This gives free travel on all public transport (plus a reduced rate on the airport bus) and free entry to 55 Budapest museums; the Zoo and Botanical Garden; Amusement Park; and the Pálvölgyi and Szemló Caves, also discounts in some restaurants. (You can also purchase the card before you travel from Danube Travel Ltd, 6 Conduit Street, London W1R 9TG (Tel. 020 7724 7577) In the UK, the three day card costs £10). Also pick up a copy of the monthly *Budapest Panorama*, which has a city map and details of special exhibitions.

   IBUSZ has an office at Ferenciek tere 10 (Tel. 318 1120), on the corner of Petöfi Sándor utca and operates an accommodation service. Open Mon.–Fri.: 8.15am–5pm. Cooptourist is in the department store opposite Nyugati Station (Tel. 312 3621). Open Mon.–Fri. 9am–4.30pm.

## ADDRESSES

**MAIN POST OFFICE AND INTERNATIONAL TELEPHONE EXCHANGE**
Petöfi utca 13 (also *poste restante*), open Mon.–Fri.: 8am–6pm, Sat.:
8am–2pm. There are 24-hour post offices sited near Keleti and
Nyugati stations.
**UK EMBASSY** V, Harmincad utca 6 (Tel. 266 2888)
**US EMBASSY** V, Szabadság tér 12 (Tel. 267 4400)
**CANADIAN EMBASSY** XII, Zugligeti utca 51-53 (Tel. 275 1200)
**STUDENT TRAVEL CENTRES** Express, Semmelweis utca 4 (Tel. 317
8845/317 8600). They sell ISIC cards, book student hostels, tours
etc. Branch office at Keleti station (Tel. 342 1772). Also at Szabadság
tér 16 (Tel. 131 7777) and V, Zoltán utca 10 (Tel. 111 9898/111
6418).

## GETTING ABOUT

Public transport is efficient and cheap. A single costs 80ft. Buy tickets
in advance for buses, metro, trolley buses and trams from tobacconists and ticket offices. Validate the tickets on entry. Tram, bus and
metro services run 4.30am–11.10pm, with night services on the
busiest routes. The metro has three lines, transfer at Deák tér. There
is also a one-day travel pass valid for all public transport in Budapest,
for 650ft (or a three-day pass for 1350Ft), which is worth buying if
you plan to make at least eight journeys. Do not be tempted to
dodge paying because of the ease with which you can avoid paying;
fines are up to 3,000ft, and inspectors do not take a day off. Make
sure you validate a new ticket when changing lines.

## SEEING

Buda, set among gentle hills, is a mixture of winding medieval
streets, with superb views over the city and neat suburbs, while Pest
is the centre of commerce and government.

The rebuilt **Royal Palace** – virtually destroyed in 1944 – houses
the **Museum of Contemporary Art** (Wing A), the **Hungarian
National Gallery** (Wings B,C and D) with its superb collection of
Hungarian art and its world-class collection of modern works, the
**Budapest History Museum** (Wing E) and the **National Széchényi
Library** (Wing F). Each has a separate entrance and prices and opening times vary so check before visiting. The Margaret bridge takes
you to **Margaret Island**, in the middle of the Danube. You can get a
bus back if you're shattered.

**St Stephen's Basilica** is the impressive church in Pest beside the
**Parliament**. A walk through the courtyards of this complex with the
sun setting over the Buda hills can be truly memorable.

The **Parliament Library** is the fifth largest book collection in

Europe, with 400,000 volumes. As long as the National Assembly isn't in session, you can take a guided **Parliament Tour** (800ft, students 400ft) around the **Cupola Hall**, **Main Chamber** and **Ornamental Staircase** of this neo-Gothic building. Open Wed.–Sun. from 10am. Two other museums are the **Fine Arts** and the **Hungarian National**. The Fine Arts is in Városliget (the city park), which has rowing boats for hire on the lake, and amusement parks. In the centre of the lake is an island upon which is **Vajdahunyad Castle**.

If you want to cleanse your pores of the grime of train travel, take an authentic Turkish bath. Try the old Ottoman baths of **Kiràly Fürdö** on Föutca 84. Men's sessions (popular with gays) take place on Mon., Wed. and Fri., and women's on Tues., Thurs. and Sat., all 6.30am–6pm. Also try the **Hotel Gellért**, where you can soak away your backpack-induced aches and pains in the thermal waters kept constantly at 38°C.

For excellent views of the city, take the cog railway into the **Buda hills**. Metro to Moszkva tér, then two stops on tram 18 or 56 will get you to the start of the railway – operated almost entirely by children, who do everything but drive the trains on the 11km route through the Buda Forest.

One of the most scenic bus routes is the number 16, which runs between Erzsèbet tér and the castle district, crossing the chain bridge. Tram 2 also has a pretty route, rattling alongside the Danube from the central market to the Parliament building.

**FREE BUDAPEST:** With your camera loaded and finger at the ready, head for the old town of Buda on **Castle Hill**. Here you'll find the **Fishermen's Bastion** (Halaszbastya), noted for its seven turrets symbolising the seven tribes of the Magyars. It also offers superb views of the Buda hills, Margaret Island and bridges over the Danube.

Crowning the hill is the splendidly photogenic **Matthias Church**, where the Hungarian kings were crowned. In summer you can listen to organ recitals on Fridays at 8pm, though if this isn't your thing, check out the **buskers** performing on **Szentháromság tér** (Trinity Square) instead. Loads of fountains and statues are also scattered throughout the area.

Gellért Hill offers magnificent views too, and is home to the 14-metre **Liberation Monument** and the equally enormous **Gellért Statue**.

But if it's a lazy afternoon you're after, cross Margaret Bridge to **Margitsziget** (Margaret Island). With over 10,000 trees to keep you company, it's a great place for a wander or just to crash out. On summer evenings there are often outdoor concerts and plays as well.

The **City Park** (Varosliget) is also great strolling territory, with plenty of façades to suit everyone's architectural tastes.
Floodlighting on summer evenings makes a walk along the Danube well worthwhile too.
There are many other free attractions in the city, so try some of the following:

- **Bible Museum**, IX, Ráday utca 28
- **Church of St Anne**, I, Batthyány tér 8
- **Dorottya Galéria** (Art Gallery), V, Dorottya utca 8
- **Vigadó Galéria** (Art Gallery), V, Vigado tér 2
- **Mühely Galéria** (Art Gallery), 2000 Szentendre, Fö tér 20
- **Museum of Electronics**, VIII, Kazinczy utca 21
- **Nemetzi National Gallery** – free for students
- **Hadvtöténeti Múzeum** (Museum of Military History), I, Tóth Árpád Sétány 40 - Free Sat.
- **Néprajzi Muzeum** (Museum of Ethnography), V, Kossuth Lajos tér 12 - Free Tues.
- **Iparmüvészeti Muzeum** (Museum of Applied Art), IX, Üllöi út 33-37 - Free Tues.
- **György Ráth Museum**, VI, Városligeti fasor 12 - Free Tues.
- **Kiscelli Museum**, III, Kiscelli utca 108 - Free Wed.

## SLEEPING

Budapest gets busy in summer, so don't hang about getting organized on the bed front. Head for the student accommodation office for Hostelling International IYHF at Keleti station or EXPRESS main office at Semmelweis utca 4 (Tel. 317 8600). Often you may meet students advertising this accommodation service on the international trains arriving in Budapest, so you can chat to them and find out what's what! These are good places to stay if you want to meet fellow travellers. For private rooms IBUSZ and Budapest Tourist have desks at the main train stations. Generally speaking, it is safer to go here than with private touts.

For hostels try the fruitily named **Strawberry** at Ráday ut 43–45 (Tel. 218 4766),open July and Aug., or the **Strawberry II** hostel at Kinizsi utca 2–6, which is the student quarter near the university (Tel. 217 3033); the **Donati IYHF Hostel** is close to Battyanyi tér (Tel. 201 1971), only open June to Sept. The **Yellow Submarine** (Tel. 327 283) is close to Nyugati train and metro stations and practically opposite, but so nice, is the **Best Youth Hostel** (Tel. 332 4934). The **Back Pack Guest House** at 33 Takács Menyhért (Tel.185 8946/385 5089) charges around 1300Ft. And there's also a very friendly guest house, **Németh Vali,** one metro stop from the train station at VIII, Osztály u. 20-24 (Tel. 313 8846).

The campsites are rarely full to capacity. and some are very pleasant, particularly those in the Buda Hills. Try **Római Camping** at Szentendrei utca 189 (Tel. 368 6260). Take the metro to Batthyány tér, where you change to the suburban railway, HEV, and get off at Római Fürdö, within sight of the campsite. Costs around 900Ft per person plus 750Ft tent fee but this includes use of nearby pool. **Zugligeti Niche Camping** at Zugligeti utca 101 (Tel. 200 8346) has good facilities and is in a pretty location. Take Bus 158 until the last stop. The site is opposite the chairlift to János-hegy. Open April–Oct. Check availability through Budapest Tourist Office.

Refer to *Cheap Sleeps Europe 2000* for more accommodation options.

## EATING AND NIGHTLIFE

Hungarian cuisine is one of the tastiest in Europe and in Budapest you can eat well at any price. Fixed menus for lunch are common. Look out for places called *bisztrós*, *büfés*, self-services and grills for even lower prices. Even a tourist trap, with gypsy music, wine and three courses, should not be excessive, but exercise your discretion! Try **New York Café**, VII Erzsébet Körút. 9–11, which has amazing *fin-de-siècle* decor, gypsy music and dancing. The carp from Lake Balaton are a speciality here. There are no restrictions on dress and it's possible to get a three-course meal with wine and coffee for a good price. There is a small door charge.

For Hungarian cuisine, the popular **Bohém Tanya**, Paulay Ede utca 6 is worth a try, as is **Alfoldi Kisvendéglo**, V, Kecskeméti utca 4. An Italian restaurant on Museum Kit opposite the National Museum is very good value. For those seeking an alternative to the aggressively carnivorous menus of most eateries, try the **Vegetarium**, a reasonably priced vegetarian restaurant at V, Cukor út 3 or **Ghandi**, V Vigyázó Ferenc utca 4. There are all the usual fast-food outlets dotted round the city.

The meals on the Danube are good, too. Boats leave from below the Duna Hotel at 5.30pm and 8pm and the cruise lasts two–three hours – plenty of time to enjoy the meal knowing it won't break the bank. Wine cellars (*borozó*) often serve good meals, and the Hungarian wines, particularly Tokaji and Egri Bikavér (Bull's Blood), are quite something. Consider coffee and cakes or ice-cream on the terrace by the river at the **Atrium** or **Forum** hotels.

The other 'must' is a visit to the world-famous pastry shop, **Ruszwurm** (Szentháromság 7, opposite the Matthias church), which has its own varieties of cakes and strudels, plus original furnishings and intricate bread sculptures.

The covered central **market** at the Pest end of the Szabadsàg bridge buzzes with life and has some of the best food in the city, including wonderful cheeses and cooked meats. **Skala Csarnok**, just north of Blaha Lujza, is open until 8pm, selling fresh produce and a range of tasty snacks upstairs.

For dancing **E-Play Cyberclub** at VI, Terezkrt 55 offers you techno heaven, or alternatively you can salsa with the best of them at **Franklin Trocadero Café** at V, Szent István körut 15. **Angyal**, at VII Rakoczi utca 51, east of the Astoria metro station, is Budapest's liveliest and most popular gay bar.

Check out the **Express Cocktail Ship**, one of the Danube cruisers, which takes you round Margaret Island. There's rock, dancing and boozing. Times vary depending on the time of year, so make sure you get on the right boat.

There's traditional folk dancing in **Buda Park** and a list of events is published in *Coming Events in Budapest*. For up-to-the-minute information, buy a copy of the *Daily News*, a newspaper published in English and German every day except Sun. and Mon. Apart from reporting national and international news, it carries regular listings of English language films in Budapest and other cultural events and is available from news stands and hotels.

# The Danube Bend

About 24 km north of Budapest, the Danube makes a dramatic sweeping arc and offers you some of the country's most stunning mountain scenery and villages. Much of it is possible to view on a day trip from Budapest; boats leave the capital daily from Vigadó tér dock. Further information is available from **Dunatours** (Tel. 01 131 4533) Bajcsy Zsilinszky utca 17 in Budapest or in Szentendre, Bogdányi utca 1 (Tel. 26 311 311). The journey to Esztergom, the heart of medieval Hungary, takes 1½ hours. Consider taking a single (to Szentendre) and return to Budapest by bus and then suburban train.

**Szentendre**, the 'Town of the Arts', is an old Serbian market town and artists' hangout, with lots of small museums, churches and Baroque houses. The **Margit Kovács Museum** is a superb collection of ceramics inspired by Hungarian folk art; open Tues.–Sun.: 10am–6pm or 4pm in winter.

The main square (Fö tér) is the venue for a summer festival and one of the many **Open-Air Ethnographic Museums** (near Angyal utca, about 5 km from the station) has examples of traditional buildings from all over the country. Try the inns and coffee shops for a taste of the culinary overlap of the many cultures in this town. The tourist office, Tourinform, is at Bumsta Jeno utca 22 (Tel. 26 317965). For accommodation try the **Aradi Panzió** at Aradi utca 4 (Tel. 26 314274) or the **campsite** on Pap Sziget (Tel. 26 310697), open May–Sept. ???

A few kilometres up river, **Visegrad** is right on a bend among the forested mountains. This was a Middle Ages stronghold and has a **Fortress** and **Royal Palace**. The views over the Danube Bend are out of this world, and there's considerable scope for woodland walks. Tourist Information (of a sort) is available from the **Bauer Folk Art** at Fö utca 46, alternatively try Visegrad Tours, by the Sirály Restaurant, who can help with, and book, accommodation. There's a camping site, **Kek Duna Autós Camping** (Tel. 26 398102) by the Danube near the town centre and a less convenient site near Mogyoró-hegy (Tel. 26 398227) which also has bungalows to rent. Both sites are open May–Sept.

**Esztergom** has some of the oldest and best-preserved remains in Hungary – including the first cathedral of the Christian religion. This was the residence of the Magyar kings until the 13th century and has the honour of being the oldest royal town in Hungary. Take in the **Christian Museum** and **Royal Palace** remains, but most of all visit the **Basilica**. You can climb the dome/bell tower to enjoy superb views over the surrounding country and into Slovakia. Note that Esztergom Kertváros is not the main station. Camping is provided at **Gran Camping**, Nagy-Duna Setany (Tel. 033 402513/489563). Open May–Sept. Gran Tours at Széchenyi tér 25 (Tel. 033 417052) can recommend and book private rooms.

# The Hungarian Plain

To the east of the Danube lies the real peasant land of Hungary's dusty central plain. An in-depth exploration of the huge grassland will uncover pockets of rural life virtually unchanged for generations. Trains run through the Plain and the Budapest–Bucharest line stops off at the main settlements like Kecskemét and Szeged. **Kecskemét**, home town of the composer Kodály, has only a small area of old town left. Walk along **Bánk Bán** and János Hoffman streets. The **Town Hall** at Kossuth tér 1 is the most impressive building and also home to Tourinform. The campsite is five km from the station at Sport utca 5 (Tel. 76 329398).

**Szeged**, near the frontier with Serbia and Romania, was completely destroyed by flood in 1879, but the town still has something of its rich past when it was under Turkish and, later, Austrian rule. The **Dóm Tér** (Square) was created in 1920 for the **Votive Church**, and

Hungary's best Serbian Orthodox church is on the north side of the huge square. Also worth seeing are the **Black House – Heroes' Gate** and a performance of the Szeged **Open-Air Theatre Festival** (the town comes alive in late July and Aug. when the festival takes place). The Tourist Office (Szeged Tourist) is at Klauzál tér 7 (Tel. 62 321 800) and there's a Tourinform office at Victor Hugo utca 1 (62 311 711).

During the summer, dormitory beds become available in student hostels. Try **István Apáthy Kollegium**, on Apáthy utca (Tel. 62 455 729) or **Jancsó** on Semmelweis utca 7 (Tel.62 455 041) (beds are also available here at weekends throughout the year), both bookable through EXPRESS at Kigyout 3 (open Mon.-Fri.: 8am–4pm; Tel. 62 481 411). Camping is provided at various sites; try **Napfeny** at Dorozsmai út 2 (Tel. 62 421 800) or **Partfurdo Camping** at Küzép-kikoto Sor (Tel. 62 430 843). Both open May–Sept.

For good cheap south Slav and Hungarian food, try Hagi at Keleman utca 3 in the centre. For the less adventurous, there's Numero Uno Pizza, on Vörösmarty utca. For tasty grilled chicken, head for Jumbo Grill at 4 Mikszáth Kálmán utca.

## Eger phone code: 036

Famed for its red wine *Egri Bikavér* – rather menacingly known as 'Bull's Blood' – Eger is a historic Baroque city lying in the north-east of the country. With its strong 'vino' connection, it's not surprising that an interesting local tour exists involving the 'Election of the Wine-General of the Valley of the Beautiful Lady'. The worthiness of any particular candidate for this post is linked to an ability to drink as much wine as possible. For more information, contact Tourinform, Dobo István tér 2 (Tel. 321807). The **Tourist Motel** at Mekcsey utca 2 (Tel. 429014) is a fairly cheap option. If you're here in the summer, a number of colleges offer cheap accommodation, phone 411 686 for directions and availablility. The Express office, Széchenyi utca 28 (Tel. 427757) can also help with accommodation. **Dobo Istvan Square** is the town centre; just north of this is the **Castle** and the underground casements.

Eger is a good place to base yourself if you fancy delving into the forests and villages of inner Hungary, and there are various campsites, such as **Autós Camping** at Rákdóczi utca 79. Reserve through Eger Tourist, Bajcsy-Zsilinszky utca 9 (Tel. 411724).

East of Eger is **Miskolc**, east of which in turn lies the world-famous wine-producing town of **Tokaj**.

Further south and east of there is the **National Park of Hungary**, where you can see protected animals and beautiful plants, many of which can only be found in this region. There are the bird reservations, which contain one of the largest water-bird feeding and breeding sites in Central Europe.

North-west of Miskolc is **Aggteleki National Park**; and the nearby **Baradla Caves**. The caves are cold but fascinating, with stalactites as long as 45m.

# Lake Balaton

Lake Balaton is Central Europe's largest lake - nearly 80km long and varying in width from 1.5km to 14km - and playground to hordes of Hungarian, Austrian and German holidaymakers. Known as the 'Hungarian Sea', it's surrounded by rolling hills and vineyards interspersed with picturesque old towns.

**Siófok**, on the southern shores, has warm shallow waters and seethes with tourists in the summer. There are eight campsites in this area, the nearest, **Aranypart Nyaralótelep** (Tel. 84 352801), being 200m from the train station. Try **Ifjúsàg Camping** at Siófok-Sosto (Tel. 84 352571). Bicycles can be hired from the train station if you can produce your train ticket.

**Balatonföldvár** is the most scenic of the southern Balaton resorts, with trees coming down close to the lakeside. It's a good centre for watersports and has quite a bit of nightlife. For accommodation try **Hotel Juventus** (IYHF) (Tel. 84 340 313) or there's **Magyar Tenger Camping** located at Kemping utca 6 (Tel. 84 340240).

**Tihany** and **Balatonfüred** are on the northern shore and are quieter and prettier. Tihany has Celtic and Roman ruins and a beautiful yellow **Benedictine Abbey** looking down on the peninsula, where you will find the Club Tihany complex. Organ recitals are held inside the abbey in summer. The **Open-Air Museum** gives a good idea of the Balaton folk traditions and the thatched-roof houses set among the hills add to the charm. The Tourist Office is at Balatontourist, Kossuth Lajos utca 20 in Tihany village (Tel. 87 448519. Open Mon.–Sat.: 8.30am–6.30pm, Sun.: 8.30am–1pm), information is also available fromTihany Tourist at Kossuth utca 11 (Tel. 87 448 481 open daily April–Oct. 9am–7pm).

Balatonfüred is a health spa which tends to attract wealthy Hungarians and Germans. See the **Medicinal Springs**, busy **Harbour** and **Round Church**. The tourist office is Balatontourist, by the pier at Tagore sétány 1 (Tel. 87 342 822) open Mon.-Sat.: 8.30am–6.30pm, Sun.: 8.30am–12 noon (shorter hours in winter). There's also a Tourinform office at Petöfi utca 8 (Tel. 87 342 237). Camping can be found by the water's edge 600m from the train station at **Fured Camping**, Széchenyi utca 24 (Tel. 87 343 823), open Apr.–Oct. It is the biggest site in the country, with a 3,500 capacity. There are several hotels including the **Hotel Uni** at Széchenyi utca 10 (Tel. 87 342239) which has reasonably cheap rooms and the **Hotel Blaha Lujza** at Blaha Lujza utca 4 (Tel. 87 343 094) which used to be the summer house of the 19th century actress and singer Lujza Blaha.

**Keszthely** is at the western end of the lake. There are various things to see: the first European agricultural college, **Georgikon**; the **Helion Library**, with many rare books and antiquities; and the **Balaton Museum**, which gives an account of the natural history and geology of the lake region. There is a good campsite, **Castrum**, at Mora Ferenc utca 48 (Tel. 83 312 120).

Day trips to try in this area are the **Lóczy Cave**, the **Gaspar** and **Jokai** look-out points and wine-tasting at **Badacsony**.

# Western Hungary

Between Budapest and Austria lies **Transdanubia**, which can be overrun with bargain-hunting Austrians. **Györ** is a large industrial city 90 minutes from Budapest by train. The old town has been lovingly preserved. See the **Carmelite Church** and Baroque **Cathedral**. For entertainment, sample the gypsy atmosphere of **Vaskakas Tavern** beneath the castle or the magnificent **Kisfaludy Theatre** at Czuczor Gergely utca. The bustling open-air **market** is at Dunakapu tér. Tourinform is in a pavilion on the corner of Baross utca and Arany János utca (Tel. 96 311771). Rooms in the area are neither plentiful nor cheap. Express at Bajcsy-Zsilinszky út 41 (Tel.96 328 833), open Mon.–Fri.: 8am–4pm, can arrange accommodation during the summer in the **KTMF** student hotel. The **Hotel Szárnyaskerék** at Révai Miklós utca 5 (Tel. 96 314629), by the train station, is one of the cheaper hotels.

Only 60 km from Vienna is **Sopron** – over 700 years old with more than 400 protected buildings. It was the location of the largest Iron Age settlement in Europe and the amber road from the Roman period ran through here. Scores of late Renaissance and Baroque structures are found in the inner city, including **Széchenyi Palace**, the **Dominican Church, Fabricius House**, the **Synagogue** and the **Franz Liszt Museum**. Look out also for the Firewatch Tower and the Gate of Loyalty. The **Sopron Festival** is at the end of June and the start of July with some of it also taking part in the **Ferto Rakos Quarries** 10 km away (between Sopron and Lake Ferto). The Festival Bureau is at

Széchenyi tér 17 and sells tickets for all events. Worthy of a day trip is the **Esterházy Palace Ferto Castle**, the 'Hungarian Versailles' where Joseph Haydn spent some years as court musician. One of his compositions, the *Farewell Symphony*, received its first performance at the palace. The **Music House** was built as a home for him by the Esterházys, and now serves as the **Haydn Memorial Museum**.

The **Lóvér** campsite (Tel: 99 311 715), a couple of kilometres south of town, is accessible by taking bus 12 from Deak tér. When crossing from Sopron to Austria, expect to be surrounded by Austrians returning from shopping expeditions, which can cause delays at customs!

**Köszeg** is a quiet town on the Austrian frontier, famous for holding off the huge Turkish siege of 1532. On **Juristic Tér**, the cobbled main square, is the Gothic **St James Church** with its wonderful frescoes. **Juristic Castle**, where the Turks were beaten back, is now a historical museum (closed Mon.).

## South-West Hungary

Southern Transdanubia has a pleasant mild climate and lovely green hills. **Nagykanizsa** is the major town of the Zala hills which lie in the west; it is also home to many horse shows. Much of the architecture is Baroque and the town is surrounded by forest parkland and a rowing lake. Apart from the **Tomb of Mustafa Pasha** and the **Thury Gyorgy Museum** (open Mon.–Fri. 9am–3pm, entrance about 100Ft), the town is also famous for its beers, especially Dreher. The area is poorly connected by train, so the bus service is the major form of transport to and around neighbouring villages. Information on accommodation can be obtained from Zalatour at Fö utca 13 (Tel. 93 311 185) or the Express office at Déak tér 1 (Tel. 93 314375). The nearest camping site is **Zalatour Camping**, Kemping utca 1 (Tel. 93 319 119), open May–Sept. It also rents out bungalows.

**Szigetvár**, which lies further south, is another place famous for being besieged by the Turks. This story is told in the museum (open 9am–4pm, closed Mon.; entrance 150Ft) in the **Fortress**. Also visit the **Ali Pasha Mosque**, now a church. The Tourist Bureau is located inside the **Oroszlán Hotel** on Zrinyí tér 2 (Tel. 73 310116), open 8.30am–4pm, and will set up accommodation. You can stay in dormitories in the fortress itself (advance booking is advisable because soldiers and school parties are often billeted there).

**Mohács**, in the south-east of the region, is situated on the banks of the Danube and plays host to the **Busojaras Parade** of monstrous figures wearing traditional carved masks, held seven weeks before Easter on the last Sunday of Shrovetide. The great Battle of the Mohács of 1526 made the town famous and a memorial site is open on the battle ground.

## Pécs phone code: 072

The attractive town of Pécs lies four hours from Budapest and 30 km from Mohács. Here you'll find many fantastic churches, such as the Romanesque **cathedral**, the former Turkish mosque of **Gazi Kasim Pasha**, and the enormous **Synagogue**, open daily (except Sat.) from 9am. One of the city's most famous treasures is the painted burial chamber and **Christian Mausoleum** unearthed in I. Istvan tér. A later **Roman Crypt** and graves can be found in Apaca utca, open May–Oct., Tues.–Sun.: 10am–6pm (though opening times are erratic). A walk down Káptalan utca brings you to the **Vasarely Museum**, named after the initiator of 'Op Art', and Zsolnay porcelain museum. There is a **Mining Museum** on Maria utca 9.

Tourinform at Széchenyi tér 9 (Tel. 213 315), open in the summer months Mon.–Fri.: 9am–7pm, weekends 9am–2pm, will arrange accommodation for you and can also exchange money, as can the IBUSZ office next door (closed Sun.). The Express office is situated at Bajcsy-Zsilinszky utca 6 and can organize accommodation in student hostels. To get there, turn right when leaving the train station.

For hotel accommodation **Laterum**, Hajoczy utca 37–39 (Tel. 315 829/252 113) is good, but a long way from the centre and often filled with Nato troops bound for Bosnia. Other options include **Kikelet**, Karolyi M. utca 1 (Tel. 310777) and the central Fönik Hotel (Tel. 311680) at Hunyadi János ut 2. **Hotel-Camping Mandulás** on Angyán Janos utca 2 (Tel. 315981) unsurprisingly offers you hotel and camping accommodation. Get there on bus 34.

The environs of Pécs have much to offer for days out: take bus 35 into the scenic **Mecsek Hills** and climb the 194m **Television Tower**, on Misina Peak, for a stunning view, or try **Abaliget**, 15 km away, which has a stalactite cave and two artificial lakes for rowing and swimming. Less than two hours away is the **Gemenc Forest National Park**, which is the largest and most beautiful wildlife reserve in the country. A flood plain forest, it contains otter, deer, wild boar, white-tailed eagles, black storks and wildcats. For those wishing to stay in this peaceful area, there's a camp site 5km north of the centre, at the junction of route 6 (Tel. 74 312 458; open mid March to mid Nov.). There's also a camping site at Baja: **Sugovica Camping** on Petöfi-Sziget (Tel. 79 321 755), which has swimming, rowing and tennis facilities. Further information from Tolna Tourist in Szekszard (Tel. 74 312 144).

NOTES:

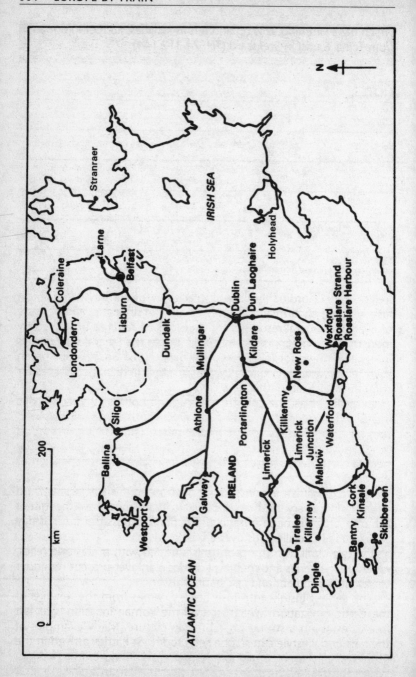

# IRELAND

| | |
|---|---|
| Entry requirements | Passport (not necessary for UK nationals) |
| Population | 3.6 million (1.7 million Northern Ireland) |
| Capital | Dublin (pop.: 1 million) |
| Currency | £1 = approx. 1.2 punts (IR£) |
| Political system | Parliamentary democracy |
| Religion | 94% Roman Catholic, 4% Protestant, 2% Other |
| Languages | English and Irish (Gaelic) |
| Public holidays | New Year's Day, St Patrick's Day (17 Mar.), Good Friday, Easter Monday (24 Apr.), one 'Bank Holiday' in May (1 May), June (5 June), August (7 Aug.) and October (30 Oct.), Christmas Day, Boxing Day. There are also some local holidays. |
| International dialling codes | To Ireland: int'l code 353 |
| | From Ireland: 00 + country code |
| Time | GMT (+1 in summer) |
| Emergency telephone numbers | All emergency services 999 |

Ireland is extraordinarily beautiful, and full of contrasts: the south lush with rolling farmland, the west stark and dramatic, and because of a lack of mineral resources the countryside remains unscarred by industry – and green as green can be. But as the Emerald Isle cashes in on its renown for loveliness, and rival tourist boards turn green themselves with envy, Eurorailers are heading here in their droves for something else altogether.

In recent years, the country has shrugged off its homely, bucolic image. The legend they come to experience these days is summed up in a single Gaelic word: *craic*. It means conviviality, or a good time, and it's found everywhere in an informal country where the people are down-to-earth and sociable. There must be few other places in the world where travellers can get to know the locals quite so easily. The Irish are justifiably proud of their hospitality, and although not every Irishman is a William Yeats, most have the 'gift of the gab' and will need no encouragement to pass the time of day with you – especially if it's over a beer.

On top of all this, the country is studded with prehistoric relics, ruined monasteries and medieval castles – an ever-present reminder of Ireland's turbulent and fascinating history.

The earliest insight into Irish history comes from the remains of the Celtic civilization, which, spared the Roman invasion, was left free to establish a strong pre-Christian culture. Many examples of their art and lifestyle can still be seen today. St Patrick arrived in the 5th century, when he is said to have banished all snakes from Ireland. While the rest of Europe suffered the 'barbarian' invasion that followed the collapse of the Roman Empire, Ireland became a land of saints and scholars – a sanctuary for religious communities that soon became seats of learning.

The Vikings destroyed all this with their plundering in the 8th and 9th centuries, and though they were defeated by Brian Boru in 1014, the inter-tribal warfare that followed his death was the cue for the kings of England to invade. Parliament came under the control of a British minority, who gradually began taking land from the Irish Catholics to give to Protestant settlers from Scotland and England.

After the 1801 Act of Union, Ireland became part of the United Kingdom, but the Potato Famine (1845–48) that followed the widespread blighting of Ireland's staple food and caused a million deaths gave rise to both an increase in Irish nationalism and the mass emigration of a further million people. A number of unsuccessful rebellions occurred, but it was not until the Easter Rising of 1916, when a group of rebels took over most of Dublin and declared an Irish Republic, that the final impetus for independence arrived. Fierce fighting gutted the city, until British troops regained control.

The execution of the rebel leaders sparked the War of Independence that led to the 1921 treaty, removing British forces from all of Ireland, except the six counties that today constitute Northern Ireland. This sparked a new civil war between the anti-treaty (Republican) and the pro-treaty (Free State) forces. In 1937, the remaining 26 counties became fully recognized and independent as Eire.

After the 1998 historic referendum on the conciliation initiative for Northern Ireland (see under United Kingdom), ordinary people on both sides hoped it would be the start of lasting peace.

The country has four provinces: Ulster, Munster, Leinster and Connaught (Northern Ireland is dealt with in the UK chapter). Although trains will get you to all the main centres, the best way to get to grips with Ireland is to hire a bike – even if you don't really know where you are going, you won't regret it when you get there. Head for the local pub, enjoy the *craic*, and ask around for B&B.

## GETTING THERE

Irish Ferries operate from Le Havre to Cork and from Le Havre, Roscoff and Cherbourg to Rosslare (Tel. +44 0990 171717). Brittany Ferries operate from Roscoff and St Malo to Cork (Tel. +44 0990 360 360). Stena operate regular sailings from Britain to Ireland (Tel. 0990 707070). For a little more money you may like to take their new catamaran service from Holyhead which reduces the crossing time to under two hours. Swansea Cork Ferries (Tel. 44 01792 456116 (Swansea); 021 271166 (Cork)) also operate the one route. Eurail pass holders travel free (or get big reductions) on services to Rosslare (normally around IR£70 adult single, IR£265 adult return). Inter-rail-ers get approx. 50% reduction on most routes. Check with the relevant operator or see Campus Travel, 52 Grosvenor Gardens, London SW1 0AG (Tel. 020 7730 3402) for details. If you're not a student, check the prices. Return air fares from London or Cardiff to Dublin can be had for as little as £49.

## IRISH RAILWAYS

### (IARNROD EIREANN, IE)

**ENQUIRIES:** (61) 315 555 Travelling on trains is expensive, but ISIC card-holders with a valid travel-save stamp receive up to 50% off. A **travel-save stamp** costs £8, available from USIT in either London (Campus Travel, 52 Grosvenor Gardens, SW1W 0AG, Tel. 020 7730 3402) or Dublin (Aston Quay, O'Connell Bridge, Tel. 677 8117, 602 1600 or 679 8833), and allows big discounts on trains and provincial buses, half price on all single or return fares on Northern Ireland Railways and similar discounts on car ferries and boats to the Aran Islands. Trains are reasonably fast around the Dublin area and to major towns, but don't expect speeds similar to those on the continent. In many areas (especially in the west), buses are the main form of transport. Irish Rail can also be contacted in Ireland on Tel. (01) 836 6222, or, for both Irish rail and bus information in London, Tel. 020 8686 0994.

**PASSES AVAILABLE** Eurail and Inter-Rail passes are valid in the Republic. The Inter-Rail pass has been broken down into zones. For £159 you get 22 days' travel in a single zone (over-26s pay £229). The Republic of Ireland is Zone A. (For further details on the eight Inter-Rail Zones, and the Freedom (Euro Domino) Passes, see Part One of this guide.)

The **Irish Explorer** ticket offers five out of 15 days' train travel within the Republic for IR£67, and IR£100 for eight out of 15 days. This includes travel on Intercity, suburban trains and Dart. Alternatively, for the whole Irish rail network, including Northern Ireland, there is the **Irish Rover** ticket: five of 15 days for IR£83, and for 15 out of 30 days Ir£98. An **Emerald Card** for unlimited train and bus travel for eight days out of 15 costs IR£115, IR£200 for 15 days in 30.

**INTER-RAIL BONUSES** Discounts of 25–50% are available on all routes to Ireland from the UK and France with Irish Ferries and Stena Line. You must book in advance to receive the discount.

**EURAIL BONUSES** Free ferry crossings on Irish Ferries between Rosslare and Roscoff (15 hours), or Cherbourg (17 hours). An extra charge is made for cabin accommodation. Port taxes are extra and payable in Irish punts (IR£). Again, book in advance. Always check the sailing schedule.

**REDUCED FARES** Bus Eireann offers Eurailpass holders a reduction on the price of their three-day Bus Rambler Ticket (which covers bus services operated by Bus Eireann and Cork, Limerick, Galway and Waterford City buses). The ticket is valid for three days' travel within eight days and costs around IR£26.

## TRAIN INFORMATION

**RESERVATIONS** Not necessary. If you want to make one, you must do so by 5pm on the preceding day.

**NIGHT TRAVEL** There are no night services in Ireland.

**EATING ON TRAINS**

Most long-distance trains have catering facilities ranging from bar service to set meals, but are quite expensive.

**BIKES** Are often the only way to get to the local hostel and see the neighbourhood. Hire costs about IR£8.50 (deposit IR£40) a day from most towns. The fee for taking your bike on a train or bus is around IR£5.

## TOURIST INFORMATION

There are 86 offices scattered throughout Ireland, 28 of which are open year round. They are open Mon.–Fri.: 9am–5pm, Sat.: 9am–1pm. They have a good selection of local and national maps and literature; although these will cost you, the staff are always friendly.

**ISIC BONUSES** With the ISIC you can get a travel-save stamp ticket for IR£7. This entitles you to up to 50% off all one-way journeys, on buses and trains, as well as reductions to some cinemas, theatres and museums.

**MONEY MATTERS** 1 Irish pound (IR£1) or punt = 100 pence (p). Banking hours are usually Mon.–Fri.: 10am–12.30pm and 1.30–3pm, however, in larger towns and cities they stay open until 4pm and often have one night a week where they stay open to 5pm.

The British pound is nearly equal to the Irish pound but is not interchangeable.

**POST OFFICES, SHOPS AND MUSEUMS** Mostly open 9am–5.30pm, Mon.–Sat.(though post offices tend to shut at 1pm on Sat), with late-night opening Thursday or Friday. Some shops stay open as late as midnight and some smaller towns have early closing one day a week. A small number of supermarkets in larger urban areas open on Sun. from 12noon–6pm. Museums vary the most, so check with the nearest Tourist Information Office. In winter, many tourist attractions are either shut or open shorter hours.

## SLEEPING

**HOTELS** are very expensive, so if you don't want to camp, stick to approved Irish Tourist Board bed and breakfast (**B&B**, IR£13–18) or **HOSTELS** (IR£7–10). Most approved premises display the shamrock sign. You can also get hold of useful publications from Tourist Information offices, including the *Irish Farmhouse Association Guide* (IR£3) (Tel. 061 400700) and the *Family Homes of Ireland B&B Guide* (Tel. 091 550 055).

**HOSTELS** For advance information on **youth hostels** contact An Oige, 61 Mountjoy Street, Dublin 7 (Tel. 01 8304555; Fax. 01 830 5808). Youth hostels tend to be situated in the most scenic parts of the country, but are not always near a station. There are 37 registered holiday hostels, confined to IYHF members.

There are also over 150 **independent hostels**. Some allow **camping** in their grounds for considerably less than the price of a room. For a full list, contact Dooey Hostel, Glencolmcille, Donegal (Tel. 073 30130) or the IHH Office, 57 Lower Gardiner Street, Dublin 1 (Tel. 01 836 4710).

**CAMPUS ACCOMMODATION** During the summer, it's often possible to stay in student accommodation on campus. For information, contact MUSA (Marketing University Summer Accommodation), UCC Castlewhite Apartments, University College, Cork. (Tel. 021 902793; Fax. 021 344099).

**CAMPING** Organized **campsites** charge IR£3–10 a tent. There is usually no problem **camping** in fields, provided you ask the owner's permission. Most hostels will let you camp on their land for IR£3-4 per night, which includes the use of kitchen and shower facilities.

## EATING AND NIGHTLIFE

Ireland's renown for its formidable drinking culture has far outstripped its reputation for cooking, and no wonder. Eating out has never been much of a tradition here, perhaps because most of the nightlife is centred on the pubs, and Irish dishes are wholesome but basic and very similar to English fare. They tend to be either heavily meat-based (the stews are always filling, but quality varies) or built round potatoes.

**Pubs** and **cafés** offer a wide variety of traditional dishes, including tripe and *drisin* – white pudding – at reasonable prices, and Irish cooking is often a highlight of a stay in a **guesthouse** or **B&B**, where Irish stew or boiled bacon and cabbage may appear on the menu. *Colcannon* (potatoes fried in butter with onions and cabbage, or sometimes leeks; the traditional Hallowe'en dish) is popular year-round, and can be delicious.

Once you're fed up with stews and potatoes, you'll have to fall back on self-catering. Food is quite expensive, particularly in the more popular tourist areas, and the only way to survive on a tight budget is to supplement food from the excellent **bakeries** and **supermarkets** with the hearty 'pub grub' offered in most bars. Picnics are no hardship, though, as vegetables and breads tend to be fresh, varied and of good quality, and Irish cheeses are very good – the only problem is, with such a huge variety, you're spoiled for choice.

Ask at Tourist Information for their booklet *Special Value Tourist Menu*, which lists many restaurants that provide decent 3-course meals at fixed prices. Some restaurants outside Dublin shut by 9pm, so eat early. Junk food addicts are more than adequately catered for in all cities.

If you're in to sport, make tracks for the local Gaelic football pitch, or catch a game of the ancient Irish sport of hurling.

The best way to sample the nightlife is over a pint of stout while listening to the locals swapping stories. Pubs are the focal point of Irish life and the place to come for good food, great beer – including Guinness, Beamish, and Murphy's – traditional music and a chance to meet the Irish, who are mostly a friendly, warm lot. With a little coaxing, they will be only too happy to let you know the local legends, whether it be fairies, witches, leprechauns or heroes like Prince Cuchulain.

The illicit Irish liquor, *poteen*, is made by many farmers and can be bought if you find the right person. Alternatively, with a lot less effort you can try the Irish whiskeys. Jameson's, Bushmills and Paddy's are the best known, and though they might seem expensive, you'll find the measures are larger than normal. On a cold day, ask for hot whiskey (served with cloves and lemon), or an Irish coffee (with whiskey and cream). Whatever you do, though, don't make the mistake of asking for Scotch!

# Dublin city phone code: 01

In Gaelic, the city's name means Blackpool, but Ireland's capital is the very antithesis of that kitsch resort. Dublin has character. The contrast of the elegant Georgian quarter with the dingy slums only a mile or two away is typical of the division of Irish history. Despite this, Dublin is no longer seen as down at heel. Huge investment has spruced up its streets and image, and today it's a dynamic city that loves to party – a top destination for stag and hen nights, and rivalling Paris, Amsterdam and Barcelona as the most popular destination for a European weekend away.

## STATION FACILITIES
Dublin has two main stations: Connolly (Tel. 836 3333), with northbound trains; and Heuston Station (Tel. 836 5421) for trains to the south and west. The Dublin Area Rapid Transit (DART) serves 27 stations in County Dublin and County Wicklow.

There are all the usual facilities at both stations, including left luggage, which is only available during the day. The night information desk at Connolly Station can be reached Mon.–Fri.: 5pm–9.30pm, Sat.: 7.30am–9.30pm, Sun.: 5pm-10pm, (Tel. 703 1843). At Heuston Station, the night information desk is open Mon.–Fri.: 5pm–10.30pm, Sat.: 7.30am–10.30pm, Sun.: 8am–10.30pm (Tel. 703 1842). Be warned that both stations are quite risky after dark.

For train information, telephone 8366 2222.

## TOURIST INFORMATION AND ADDRESSES

**MAIN OFFICE** In a converted church in Suffolk Street, just off the bottom of Grafton Street (Tel. 1850 230330 (freephone) or 6057700). Will arrange accommodation for a small booking fee and 10% deposit. For phone bookings, call 1800 668668. They also have good maps for sale. Also at Baggot Street Bridge, open daily 8am–10.30pm. Money exchange facilities are provided. You can also telephone the Irish Tourist Board in London on +44 01207 493 3201. The **Temple Bar Information Centre** at 18 Eustace Street (Tel. 671 5717) gives out information on what's on. Pick up a copy of *Temple Bar Guide* and/or *Gay Community News*

**GENERAL POST OFFICE** O'Connell St, open Mon.–Sat.: 8am–8pm, Sun.: 10am–6.30pm (Tel. 705 7000)

**AMEX** 116 Grafton St (Tel. 677 2874), open Mon.–Sat: 9am–5pm, and Dublin Tourism Centre, Suffolk St (Tel. 605 7701)

**STUDENT TRAVEL AGENCY ISIC/USIT** is at 19–21 Aston Quay; open Mon.–Fri.: 9am–6pm, Sat.: 11am–4pm (Tel. 677 8117, 602 1600 or 679 8833). Also a Eurotrain office. Books B&Bs in summer and has its own hostel

**EURAIL AID OFFICE INTERNATIONAL RAIL TRAVEL CENTRE**, 35 Lower Abbey St (Tel. 836 6222), or contact Coras Iompair Eireann at Heuston Station on Tel. 677 1871

**UK EMBASSY** 31/33 Merrion Rd. (Tel. 269 5211)

**US EMBASSY** 42 Elgin Rd, Ballsbridge (Tel. 668 8777 or 668 7122)

**CANADIAN EMBASSY** 65–68 St Stephen's Green (Tel. 478 1988)

**AUSTRALIAN EMBASSY** Fitzwilton House, Wilton Terrace (Tel. 676 1517)

**NEW ZEALAND CONSULATE** 46 Upper Mount St (Tel. 676 2464)

**EMERGENCY TELEPHONE** Tel. 112 or 999

## GETTING ABOUT

You won't need city buses for sightseeing, as it's all easily negotiated by foot ('shanks's mare' as they call it). However, if your accommodation is out of the centre, it might be worth your while to get a bus/train pass (one-day pass IR£5; four-day pass IR£12) from Dublin

Bus in Upper O'Connell Street. This is also the departure point for open-top sightseeing tours; the all-day, hop-on hop-off tickets aren't bad value if you want to survey all the sights but save your feet.

DART (Dublin Area Rapid Transport) is the suburban train line running along the coast from Howth to Bray, fed by a network of buses. It's a good, efficient service, gives amazing coastal views, and at around IR£1.20 a ride is not too expensive (the one- and four-day bus/train passes include travel on DART). It stops around 11pm.

City buses cost up to IR£1.80 and operate 6am–11.30pm. Late-night buses operate until 3am Thurs.–Sat. Catch them at the Bank of Ireland building, IR£2.50, no passes accepted.

Tel. 873 4222/836 6111 or 872 0000 for information on all public transport.

## SEEING

The obvious starting point is **O'Connell Street**, designed in the 18th century to be one of Europe's most elegant boulevards. It was here – at the **General Post Office** – that the Easter uprising of 1916 had its headquarters. Much of the original street was destroyed during the fighting and more still in further warfare in 1922. You can still see the evidence on the pock-marked walls of the Post Office.

O'Connell Street is now more high street than grand promenade, though down the centre a string of statues make it worth a stroll. The statues include Charles Stewart Parnell, who inspired the 19th-century Home Rule movement; Father Theobald Matthew, who championed abstinence from alcohol; trade union leader James Larkin; and, reclining in a pool of water, the goddess of the River Liffey – dubbed by locals the 'floozie in the jacuzzi'.

From O'Connell Street, head across the river for the oldest university in Ireland, **Trinity College**. Founded in 1591 by Elizabeth I, on the site of a confiscated monastery, Trinity produced such men as Oscar Wilde and Thomas Moore. Don't miss one of the oldest parts of the college, the **Old Library**, home to some of the world's most outstanding manuscripts. Pride of place in the 64-metre **Long Room** is reserved for the 8th-century illuminated manuscript, the **Book of Kells**. Admission is IR£3.50 (less for students), and it's open Mon.–Sat.: 9.30am–5.30pm; Sun.: 12pm–5pm. (Closed on Sun. in Oct.–May). A recent addition to Dublin's list of tourist attractions is the college's **'Dublin Experience'** in the arts block. Open daily 10am–5pm, this sophisticated multi-media interpretation of the city's history costs IR£2.75 (IR£2.25 for students). There are also combined tickets (IR£5.50, less for students) which also allow entry to the library.

Oscar Wilde was not the only celebrated writer to emerge from Dublin. The city was full of literary genius, including that of satirist

Jonathan Swift, playwrights Richard Sheridan and George Bernard Shaw, poet W.B. Yeats, Dracula author Bram Stoker and novelist James Joyce. Manuscripts, letters, photographs and other memorabilia from many of these men is on display at the **Dublin Writers Museum** at 18 Parnell Square North, in an 18th-century house on one of Dublin's grandest Georgian squares.

If this whets your appetite for Irish literature, check out the **James Joyce Centre** at 35 North Great George's St, nearby. It's one of many restored Georgian town houses in the street, and was featured in the author's greatest work *Ulysses*. Even if you're not a fan, the house itself – with stucco ceilings by Stapleton – is well worth a look. Joyce at one time lived at Martello Tower (near the nudist beach at Sandycove), now the **Joyce Museum,** focussing on his life and works. Take DART to Sandycove.

Another chance to see how Georgian town houses used to be is on offer at **Newman House**, at 85 and 86 St Stephan's Green (open June–Sept., Tues.–Fri. 12noon–5pm, Sat. 2pm–5pm, Sun. 11am–2pm; otherwise by appointment only). The interior of the houses boast probably the best plaster work in the country, with No 85's ceilings and walls featuring Baroque decorations, and those at No 86 rococo in style. In the mid-19th century, the houses became part of the Catholic University of Ireland (Trinity College was a Protestant university, only used in big numbers by Catholic students in the past 30 years), whose scholars included Patrick Pearse, Eamon de Valera and James Joyce. The **Physics Theatre**, where Joyce attended lectures, is kept as it was in his day.

**Dublin Castle** (Mon.–Fri. 10am–5pm, Sat.–Sun. 2–5pm) is the historic heart of the city. Preceded by a Gaelic ring fort and a Viking fortress, parts of the original 13th-century Norman castle are still standing. The **State Apartments** were built as the residential quarters of the viceregal court and, along with the **Viking Undercroft Fortress** and the **Chapel Royal**, are open to visitors. The 12th-century **St Patrick's Cathedral** on Patrick Street is also worth a look.

Grim, grey and hulking, **Kilmainham Gaol** was a central player in Ireland's struggle for indepence. This is where many of the leaders of rebellions from 1799 until 1916 were detained, and where some died. Now a visitor's centre with guided tours, an audio-visual presentation and an exhibition, it gives an insight not only into the history of nationalism, but also the social conditions of the times. Opening hours are May–Sept: 10am–6pm daily; Oct.–Apr. Mon.–Fri. 1–4pm, Sun.1–6pm; admission: adults IR£2, students IR£1.

Stepping back in time even further is the Dublinia exhibition (on Christ Church Rd, in a hall attached to Christ Church Cathedral), which uses atmospheric multimedia presentations to evoke medieval Dublin. Open daily Apr.–Sept. 10am–5pm; Oct.–Mar.,

Mon.-Sat. 11am–4pm, Sun. 10am–4.30pm. IR£4 includes entrance to **Christ Church Cathedral**, which was founded in 1038. The cathedral's crypt is the oldest structure in Dublin.

A popular way to round off the day is with a few 'free' pints of **Guinness**: go to their brewery – the biggest in Europe, producing more than 2.5 million pints of the black stuff every day – at St James' Gate, watch the film about its production, then sup up. Open Mon.–Sat.: 9.30am–5pm, Sun.: 10am–4.10pm (last admission). Oct.–May: 10am–3.50pm, Mon.–Fri. IR£3, IR£1.50 students.

**FREE DUBLIN:** Dublin is a great place for strolling, with a centre compact enough to explore by foot.

- Check out the architecture: the most elegant individual buildings of Dublin are the **Custom House**, on the north bank of the river Liffey, and the **Bank of Ireland** in College Green. This building once housed the Irish Parliament, and vestiges of its important past remain: see the 18th-century 1,233-piece Waterford crystal chandelier in the original House of Lords, and look in at the main banking hall.
- For a breath of fresh air, head for **St Stephen's Green**, an oasis in the middle of the city. Note the Georgian town houses around the park, and have a look too at the big Georgian squares – Fitzwilliam (the smallest and best-preserved in the city) and Merrion (young Oscar Wilde lived at No 1, Daniel O'Connell at No 58, and W.B. Yeats at Nos 52 and 82). Just off the park, at Earsfort Street, is the new **National Concert Hall**, which features music to suit all tastes.
- At the back of Trinity College university, through the grounds, are the **Dáil** and **Seanad**, the seats of the Irish Parliament on Kildare Street. You cannot visit when Parliament is in session.
- In the same street is the **National Museum** (Free; Tue.–Sat.: 10am–5pm and Sun.: 2–5pm), which is good for historians and has a comprehensive exhibition on the 1916 uprising. There is also a fine collection of Bronze Age, Iron Age and medieval gold objects.The Gallery is getting relocated to opposite the train station and some of the collection has already moved, check with the Tourist Office to find out the latest.
- The **Natural History Museum**, connected to the National Museum, is also free. Opening hours are Tue.–Sat.: 10am–5pm and Sun.: 2–5pm.
- Around the corner, on Merrion Square, is the **National Gallery**, which has an excellent collection of Rembrandts and several rooms devoted to portraits of Irish literary men such as George Bernard Shaw and Brendan Behan. (Closed Mon.).
- The small **Dublin Civic Museum** on William Street South focusses on Dublin's history. (Closed Mon.).

- The **Irish Museum of Modern Art (IMMA)** often has interesting exhibitions. It's close to Kilmainham Gaol at the Royal Hospital. (Closed Mon.).
- **Phoenix Park** is the largest enclosed park in Europe. Its vast grounds host everything from motor racing to rock concerts. There's also the second highest obelisk in the world and one of the world's oldest zoos, famous for breeding lions. Take bus 10 from O'Connell Street. Don't be tempted to pitch your tent here, as the official residence of the President of Ireland is nearby and the police take a dim view of campers in the vicinity. It's also unsafe at night.
- Street life is best sampled in **Grafton Street**, the main shopping artery. Pedestrianized and always bustling with buskers and other pavement artists, this is the modern-day promenade for Dublin's youth. It's here too, at the intersection with Suffolk St, that you'll find the statue of fishmonger **Molly Malone** (known locally as 'the tart with the cart').
- Cross the Liffey via the Halfpenny Bridge (for pedestrians only) to get back to the north side, and **Moore Street**, where modern-day versions of Molly Malone ply their wares from fruit and vegetable barrows. This market street is a good place to stock up on cheap picnic supplies.

## SLEEPING

You can expect to pay IR£25 minimum in a **hotel**, so stick with the student and youth **hostels**. For help, go round to the USIT office, 19 Aston Quay (Tel. 677 8117, 602 1600 or 679 8833), or get hold of *Cheap Sleeps Europe 2000* guide book for a full range of options. Always reserve ahead if possible, especially in the summer and at weekends.

The **ISAACS Hostel**, 2-5 Frenchman's Lane (Tel. 855 6215) is a very central old warehouse and costs from IR£8 a night in a dorm bed. (Be warned, it's noisy). Another hostel near Connolly train station is **Jacobs Inn** at 21 Talbot Place (Tel. 855 5660) which has the luxury of private bathrooms for all rooms; IR£11–15 for dorms. The **Brewery Hostel**, right beside the Guinness Brewery, at 22 and 23 Thomas St, is 10 minutes' walk from the city centre, but if you get a group together, there's a free shuttle service (Tel. 453 8600). All rooms have private bathrooms; IR£10–12 for dorms, for doubles IR£19–22. **Barnacles Temple Bar House** (Tel. 671 6277) is right in heart of Dublin's buzzing entertainment quarter. Price: from IR£10 in dorms, IR£18–20 per person in a doubles All rooms en suite, light breakfast included. **Avalon House** (Tel. 475 0001; Fax. 475 0303) at 55 Aungier Street is another good hostel which has wheelchair access and a cheap cafe. Beds from IR£9.

**YOUTH HOSTELS** 61 Mountjoy St (Tel. 830 1766; Fax. 830 1600) is very good and costs IR£10 a night, including breakfast.

The YWCA at Radcliffe Hall, St John's Rd and Lower Baggot Street (Tel. 662 4463) are also worth checking out, as are the two independent hostels that charge fromIR£9 a night: Cardijin House at 15 Talbot Street (Tel. 878 8618/8788484) and Kinlay House at 2–12 Lord Edward Street (Tel. 679 6644).

**B&BS** Avoid the ones near the station. Instead, try Mrs Gartland at 2 Goldsmith Street (Tel. 830 1857), only five minutes or so from O'Connell Street. Be assured of a warm welcome and a full Irish breakfast at around IR£15 per person.

Finally, if you can't find a **B&B** near the city centre, try Mrs Canavan at 81 Kincora Road, Clontarf (Tel. 833 1007), reached by bus 30 or 44a from the Abbey Street bus station. Clontarf is a pleasant suburb with views out to Dublin Bay, but it's several miles out.

**CAMPSITES** You can pitch a tent for IR£5 at Donabate, just north of the city. Shankill Caravan and camping park (Tel. 282 0011) is open all year round, 16 km south on the N11. Bus 45/45A/84 or the DART to Shankill and costs about IR£6.50 for a tent. There's another site at Camac Valley, Corkagh Park on Naas Road (Tel. 464 0644 ). It's 30 mins out of the city centre by bus (take nos 77/77A/49/65).

## EATING AND NIGHTLIFE

The pub is at the centre of Ireland's social life, and the atmosphere in a good Dublin pub takes some beating. The hot spot these days is the **Temple Bar** area, near the river. It's the city's entertainment quarter – Dublin's Left Bank – a restored network of tiny streets on the south bank of the Liffey, now with a huge variety of eating places, pubs, beer gardens, clubs, galleries, outdoor music and plenty of buskers. You'd be hard-pressed to beat Temple Bar as a general area to spend the evening: go to **Fitzsimons Bar** in East Sussex Street for traditional music and set dancing. Another good venue is **The Norseman**. There's no shortage of trendy eateries round here. Try **Gallagher's Boxty House** at 20 Temple Bar; it serves its namesake (a potato pancake) stuffed with various fillings at reasonable prices.

Elsewhere, there's no end of atmospheric watering holes, and they're all central enough. Off Grafton Street, Duke Street has **Davy Byrne's** (whose gorgonzola cheese sandwiches with mustard were immortalized in Joyce's *Ulysses*), and trendy pub **The Bailey** (once the haunt of the literati). The following places all have something unique, whether it be traditional music, good beer or a great atmosphere – in fact, most have all of them: **O'Donoghue's** and the **Baggot Inn** (a good venue for live rock – Dublin's thriving rock scene has spawned big names like U2, Bob Geldof, Thin Lizzy, Sinead O'Connor and

Hothouse Flowers), both in Baggot Street; **Mulligan's Pub**, Poolbeg Street; **Scruffy Murphy's**, off Mount Street; **An Beal Boacht**, Ranelagh Bridge; **The Long Hall** in South Great George's Street; and **The Brazen Head**, Lower Bridge Street, said to be Dublin's oldest pub.

In the city centre, there's no shortage of fast-food chains and pubs offering excellent-value lunches. Anywhere around the university is your best bet, as restaurants here cater for the student market. **Bewley's** have old-fashioned cafés at 78 Grafton St, 13 South Great George St, 12 Westmoreland St and, north of the Liffey, 40 Mary St, all doing good meals at reasonable prices. Cheaper places to eat include **Flanagan's** at 61 O'Connell St, the **Kylemore Café** in O'Connell, and **Beshoff's** in Westmoreland St. Shop for food in Moore St.

For an organized *ceilidh* or musical pub-crawl, meet at **Oliver St John Gogarty's** (Tel. 671 1822) on the corner of Anglesea Street and Fleet Street at 7.30pm Sat.–Thurs.

Dublin's pubs have played their part in the city's literary life, a fact highlighted by the **Literary Pub Crawl** starting each night around 7.30pm from the Duke pub in Duke Street (check with tourist office for current times). You can join the pilgrimage to the best-known stamping grounds of the Irish literati, where actors perform their works. Get set for a bender, as the trail lasts two and a half hours at the very least.

# South-East Ireland

Counties Wexford, Carlow, Kilkenny, Tipperary and Waterford are the home of Anglo-Norman castles, race-courses, crystal factories, early Christian relics and tributes to the occasional US president who claimed Irish roots.

From Dublin, you might have caught a glimpse of the Wicklow mountains, only 16 km from the capital. A day or two exploring this area from the base towns of **Glendalough** (with its 7th-century monastery) or Wicklow can be rewarding, before crossing the county border south into Wexford.

On the main line south from Dublin is **Enniscorthy,** a small town in the Slaney Valley. It was a rebel stronghold during the 1798 revolt against the British. The castle is now a folk museum and if you hit it in the first week of July, expect a great atmosphere, as the Strawberry Festival livens things up considerably. The town offers excellent angling. Further west, the port of **New Ross** contains **St Mary's Abbey** and the 600-acre forest of the **John F. Kennedy Arboretum Park**, with nature trails, gardens and panoramic views (May–Aug.: 10am–8pm, April and Sept.: 10am–6.30pm, and Oct.–March:

10am–5pm; adults around IR£2.50, student reductions).

The small fishing port of **Wexford** might seem an unlikely venue for an opera festival, yet the annual event has put the old Viking town firmly on the international operatic calendar. For two weeks every October, the festival of opera takes over the town, while traditional music, blues, jazz, poetry readings and other cultural events are staged alongside it, mostly in the more informal settings of bars and pubs. Apart from music, Wexford has one or two other points of interest, including the **Bull Ring** and ruins of the **Selskar Abbey**, which was razed by Oliver Cromwell. If you're interested in finding out more about Wexford's history and its Viking past then visit the **West Gate Heritage Centre** beside the gate and watch the audiovisual display. (IR£1.50). Ask for information on the free guided walking tours at Tourist Information on Crescent Quay (Tel. 23111). There's **camping** at the Ferrybank Camping & Caravan Park (Tel. 053 42987) from Easter to late Sept.

Nearby, at North Sloblands on the Slaney Estuary, is the **Wexford Wildfowl Reserve**, a wintering place for swans, geese, gulls, pintails and other wild birds. The reserve is freely accessible, and open all year.

Four km inland from Wexford is **Ferrycarrig**, home of the **Irish National Heritage Park** (open daily: 10am–7pm (last admission at 5.30pm), March–Nov., admission: IR£4, IR£3.50 for students). Using full-scale models of settlements, homesteads and burial places from the Stone Age through to Norman times, it charts 9,000 years of social change in Ireland.

Take the road into **Carlow County** from Bunclody and turn off at the Tullow road to see the herbaceous **Altamont Gardens** (open Sun. 2pm–6pm, till the end of Oct., Tel. 0503 59302) with its home-made teas.

**Carlow** County is best known for its **Megalithic Field** monuments (dolmen). Particularly noteworthy are the **Haroldstown Portal Tomb** (northeast of Tullow) and the **Browneshill Dolmen** (reputedly the largest in Europe, and dating from 2000 BC). Nearby **Clonmore Castle** was completed in 1180 from the stones of a ruined abbey.

There's a museum at **Tullow** (open every Sun. afternoon and also on Wed. afternoons in the summer) by the Slaney River Bridge. There's another in the town hall at **Carlow Town** (May–Sept.: 11am–5pm, admission IR£1.50), and a castle dating from 1207 (ask permission to visit from the mineral water company who own the site, otherwise view it through the gates).

**Leighlinbridge** is guarded by the ruins of a 12th-century Anglo-Norman castle. **Bagenalstown** was originally modelled on Athens.

For walkers, the **South Leinster Way** is a pleasant section of the proposed round-Ireland walking route, from Wicklow in the north-east, via towpaths along the River Barrow, to **Graignamanagh** in the south. This ancient town, in south-eastern **Kilkenny** County, contains the massive Norman **Duiske Abbey**, fully restored, with a larger-than-life effigy of a Norman knight inside. Guided tours of both the abbey and town can be arranged through the Kilkenny Tourist Office on Rose Inn Street (Tel. 056 51500).

Up the road at **Thomastown** lies the 12th-century Cistercian **Jerpoint Abbey**, well preserved and restored, open mid-June–Sept. (9.30am–6.30pm in summer, otherwise 10-5pm. Closed Tues. Adults IR£2, students IR£1).

The town of **Kells**, just west of Thomastown and surrounded by lush farmland, is the site of the magnificent walled ruins of Kells Priory, founded in 1193. This Kells has nothing to do with the famous illuminated manuscript – the *Book of Kells* comes from the town of the same name in County Meath.

**Kilkenny City** is a beautiful little place, and well worth a stop. It took its name from a monastic settlement established by St Canice. Its peak of some 1,500 years as a centre of civilization came in 1642, when it became a major political capital during Cromwell's reign.

**St Canice's Cathedral** was begun in 1251 (its Round Tower offers a staggering panorama to those who ascend its 167 steps), and this impressive Gothic church has a large collection of sculpted monuments.

**Kilkenny Castle** was started in 1172 and was the home of the powerful Anglo-Norman Butler family. The **Long Gallery** of the building has an interesting collection of family portraits, but the building is perhaps most remarkable for its modern art gallery. (Castle and Gallery open: Apr.–May daily 10.30am–5pm; June–Sept. daily 10am–7pm; Oct.–March Tues.–Sat 10.30am–12.45pm and 2pm–5pm, Sun. 11am–12.45pm and 2–5pm; admission IR£3 adults, IR£2 students (access by guided tour only)) . The park adjoining the castle and the flower garden are kept in superb condition and are a great place to wile away a sunny afternoon. (Entrance is free). Also worth visiting is the **St Francis Abbey** brewery, in the yard of Smith-wick's Brewery. Guided tours are available Mon.–Fri. at 3pm for the brewery - tickets free at the tourist office (June–Sept.). For sporting enthusiasts, a hurling match takes place most summer Sundays, in the city's **Nolan Park**.

The city's annual Arts Week takes place in August. Walking tours of the city depart from the Tourist Office at Shee Alms House, Rose Inn St (Tel. 056 51500), Mon.–Sat. six times a day, Sun. four times, mid March–Oct.; Nov.–Feb. Tues.–Sat. three per day, and cost IR£3.00, students IR£2. They can also fix you up with accommodation.

**Dunmore Cave**, 11km north of Kilkenny, is a natural limestone cavern with impressive stalagmites and stalactites. The discovery of human bones and coins possibly point to a massacre by Vikings in the 10th century.

Over the border in County **Tipperary** is one of Ireland's most famous sights, the **Rock of Cashel**. The medieval ecclesiastical centre is built on the grey outcrop called **St Patrick's Rock**, and the remains of the magnificent cathedral, Romanesque chapel and Round Tower dominate the countryside. A subterranean museum displays items of historical interest; and a full guide service is provided (June–mid-Sept., 9.00am–7.30pm, off-season 9.30am–4.30pm; last admission 45 mins before closing; IR£3.00 adults, IR£1.50 students). There's a handy hostel at 6 John Street (Tel. 062 62330); dorm beds IR£8, doubles IR£20. From Apr. to Sept., there's a tourist office in the town hall on the main street.

Nearby, in the shadow of Cashel's ancient rock , **Bru Boru** has been developed as a major cultural centre for Irish music, drama and tradition.

North-east of Cashel, on the border with Kilkenny, are the **Slieveardagh Hills**, an area strongly connected with the revolutionary 19th-century Young Irelanders movement and the development of a coal-mining industry. The history and geography of the area are the focus of a study weekend in July.

Ahenny, Killamery, Kilree and Kilkieran are the sites of seven ornate early Christian **High Crosses**.

At **Carrick-on-Suir** there's a fine Elizabethan **Manor House** residence of 1568, next to the remains of **Carrick Castle** (open mid-June–Sept.: 9.30am–6.30pm, adults IR£2.50, students IR£1.25).

On the way west to the racecourse at **Clonmel** (one of many in this equine heartland) is the **Tipperary Crystal Works**, a recently established industry that carries on the region's international reputation for hand-cut crystal. Guided tours give visitors the opportunity to view all stages of crystal production.

The **North Munster Way** can be picked up on the banks of the Suir and followed via Clonmel to the borders of County Cork.

Passing through **Tipperary Town** and its racecourse will bring you to the town of **Cahir** and its **Castle**, built on a rocky island in the middle of the river Suir, and containing an audio-visual unit for the whole south-eastern area, and a full guide service; open June–Sept.: 9am–7.30pm, and for the rest of the year 10am–4.30pm (admission IR£2.50 adults, IR£1.25 students).

South and west towards the **Knockmedown Mountains** at the border with County Waterford, the limestone caves of **Mitchelstown** should be visited (open all year, with guide service 10am–6pm, admission IR£2.50, students IR£1.25). Also in the area is the **President Reagan Centre** at **Ballyporeen**, which commemorates the birthplace of the former US President's ancestors, and his visit there in 1984 (open by appointment).

County **Waterford** is best entered via **The Vee**, a switchback route through the Knockmedown mountains, which allows the visitor the best views of the beautiful border area. Nestling in the southern foothills is **Mount Melleray**, a Cistercian monastery.

Going south from here to the cathedral town of **Lismore**, you can see the majestic **castle** perched above the river Blackwater. The castle gardens are open 1.45pm–4.45pm May–Sept., except Sat. The **Lismore Heritage Experience** exhibition (free) is recommended.

Directly east of Lismore is **Dungarvan**, with its substantial Anglo-Norman **castle**, which was sacked during the Cromwellian Wars. Parts of this castle still overlook the town's harbour.

Between Dungarvan and Youghal (in County Cork) is the site of the **Ardmore Monastic settlement**. Legend has it that in the 5th century (30 years before St Patrick arrived in Ireland), St Declan crossed from Wales to set up shop in the stunning surrounds of Ardmore. The site, marked today by an 11th-century round tower in ruined St Declan's Cathedral, overlooks the bay. The area around it is believed to be the oldest parish in Ireland.

**Waterford City**, only an hour away from the ferry port of Rosslare, was founded by the Danes and grew to be Ireland's fifth largest city. Its most famous landmark, **Reginald's Tower**, was built on the waterfront in AD 1003 by the Vikings, to help defend the city. For an insight into the Viking and early Norman history of Waterford, visit the **Waterford Heritage Centre** nearby (July–Aug.: Mon.–Fri. 9am–8.30pm, Sat.–Sun. 9am–5pm;Mar.–June and Sept.–Oct. Mon.–Fri. 10am–5pm, Sat 2–5pm admission IR£1.50, students IR£1; 25% off with walking tour ticket).

**Christ Church Cathedral**, on Cathedral Square, is an ornate building in Renaissance style. Among its relics is the 15th-century tomb of James Rice, decorated rather ghoulishly with a decaying corpse. On the other side of Cathedral Square is the **French Church**, founded by Franciscans in the 13th-century, and later used by Huguenot refugees.

Walking tours of the city leave the Tourist Office (41 Merchant's Quay, Tel. 051 875 788) and end at Reginald's Tower, visiting 10 historic locations *en route*, at 11am and 3pm, Mon.–Sat. (IR£2 per person, information from the Tourist Office).

The city stages a **Festival of Light Music** every year in October. The festival is held in the **Theatre Royal**, part of the newly renovated Georgian building which houses **Waterford City Hall**. A massive glass chandelier is the centrepiece of the council chamber. Waterford is famous world wide for its crystal, and you can witness the entire crystal-making process at the **Waterford Crystal Visitor Centre** at Kilbarry, where there are regular factory tours and a video presentation (in summer, showroom open 8.30am–6pm. Tours between 8.30am–4pm. In winter, showroom open 9am–5pm; tours 9am–3.15pm; IR£3.50, students IR£1.75. Tel. 051 373 311).

If, at the end of a hard day, you fancy a change from medieval castles and early Christian monasteries, you could do worse than follow the N25 north from the coast to **Ballinavough** (near **Lemybrien**), where the collection of antique dolls and toys of Helen Collendar can be viewed 6pm–9pm daily, June–Sept., at her home (admission IR£3.00). If even that sounds too energetic why not stay the night in Waterford (try the **Viking House Hostel** on Coffee House Lane (Tel. 051 853827) or the Waterford Hostel, 70 The Manor (Tel. 051 850163)) and settle into one of the cosy pubs in the Quays for the evening. One of the best places, and Waterford's oldest pub, is T&H Doolan's on George Street.

## Cork (Corcaigh) phone code: 021

Three hours away from Dublin on the main line, Ireland's second largest city is bursting with history and charm. Built on a marsh (*corcaigh*), the so-called 'Venice of Ireland' has a network of bridges spanning the river Lee and her tributaries, but the city's heart is a warren of cobbled lanes on the island itself.

Washington Street is a good place to start your wanderings: see the neo-classical **courthouse**, and further along Western Road is **University College Cork**. North of Western Road is **Fitzgerald's Park**, which houses the **Cork Public Museum** (open Mon.– Sat. 11am–1pm and 2.15pm–6pm, Sun. 3pm–5pm; free, except 75p on Sun.). The park is a perfect setting for a picnic, with beautiful scenery on the banks of the Lee. **St Anne's Church** ('Shandon') in John Redman Street is known as the '4-faced liar'. The views from the tower are excellent and you can try your hand at ringing the bells. (Open Mon.–Sat. 10am–4pm; church tower IR£2.50, students IR£1.25).

In Bishop Street, Gothic **St Finbarr's Cathedral** stands on the site of the saint's original monastic settlement, and boasts a golden angel who, legend has it, will blow its horn to signal the end of the world. Near St Finbarr's, on Barrack Street, is the **Elizabeth Fort**, which dates back to the 16th century. A walk down towards the city's docks brings you to **City Hall**. Enter to see the busts of the two Lord Mayors (Tomas McCurtain and Traolach McSuibhne), who died during the Civil War.

Spruced-up **Paul Street** is a lively pedestrianized thoroughfare lined with restaurants and boutiques, and with plenty of live street theatre in its cobbled square. Many of the big old buildings there have been renovated and turned into trendy eateries and art and craft studios – all well worth a wander.

While you're in the city centre, don't miss Cornmarket Street and the remains of the old **Coal Quay market** at the junction with Castle Street. This used to be a massive open-air market in days long gone, and though it is still busy with various stalls, trade these days is mostly in second-hand goods.

For more traditional stalls, head to the Grand Parade (at the end of St Patrick's Street) and the **English Market**. Here you'll find all the fruit, cheese, vegetables, meat, fish and snacks you could hope for, in a huge covered labyrinth of a market.

In an area known as Sunday's Well, you can visit **Cork City Gaol**, where many republican prisoners were held during the Civil War. It's a very atmospheric place, and the headphone-and-tape tour (IR£3.50; less for students), followed by an audiovisual presentation, is well worth the 25-minute walk from the city centre.

The **Crawford Art Gallery** has an excellent permanent collection with works by famous Irish artists, such as Jack Yeats and Sean Keating (Closed Sun.). Not only is it good, it's also free!

Cork has two breweries: Beamish & Crawford in South Main Street and Murphy's in Lady's Well; it's worth enquiring about brewery tours.

**EXCURSIONS Blarney Castle** (Tel. 021 385252), 10 km down the road from Cork, is a must - as long as you don't suffer from vertigo. It is the site of the famous **Blarney Stone**, where legend says you can gain the 'gift of the gab' by dangling from the battlements to kiss it. Even if you can't pluck up the courage (there's a very nice man on duty to guide you through it), the castle itself is worth the trip, and the gardens which surround it are quite lovely. (Open Mon.–Sat. 9am–6.30 or 7pm, or to sundown in winter. Sun. 9.30pm–5.30pm; entrance IR£3.00, students IR£2).

Fifteen km away by rail is **Cobh** (pronounced 'Cov'), a pretty seaside resort that in the 19th century was the departure point for immigrants – some of whom sailed to their deaths on the liners *Lusitania* and *Titanic*. Information on guided walking tours can be obtained from the Tourist Office (Tel. 021 813301) on Grand Parade (open 9am–7pm in the summer, Sun. 11am–1pm).

A good day trip is to Dundanion castle in **Blackrock** (take the no. 2 bus), from where, in 1669, William Penn sailed for America. Nearby Blackrock castle is a fine setting for a pint and a sandwich.

## SLEEPING

**Hotels** are unbelievably expensive, so head for Western Road, where you will find plenty of bed and breakfasts and the **An Oige youth**

**hostel** at 1 Redclyffe, Western Road (Tel. 543 289). **Sheila's Tourist Hostel** is an independent hostel in Wellington Road (Tel. 505 562, fromIR£7 in dorms). Great facilities, including laundry, bike hire, cafe and sauna. Another good one, though not a patch on Sheila's, is **Isaacs Hostel** at 48 MacCurtain Street (Tel. 508388). The most convenient **camping site** has now closed down but there are two sites about five miles out of town. Try **Bienvenue** (Tel. 312711) near the airport (catch the airport bus) or **Blarney Caravan and Camping Park** (Tel. 385167).

The Tourist Office on Grand Parade (Tel. 273251) will help with accommodation and book rooms in B&Bs. For more options, get hold of a copy of *Cheap Sleeps Europe 2000*.

## EATING AND NIGHTLIFE

Examine menus carefully before ordering, as eating out in Cork can be pricey. The **Lon Wah Chinese** in Oliver Plunket Street does a good value high tea. **The Gingerbread House**, on Paul St, serves great coffee, baguettes and quiche. There are plenty of **fast-food** joints in the city centre for burger addicts and **Paddy Garaboldi's Pizzas** are worth trying (in Carey's Lane).

A good bet are the pubs, where you can fill up on standard pub grub over a good Cork pint of stout (Murphy's rather than Guinness). And pubs are also the place to be for night life in general. The Western Road boasts the **Western Star**, a watering hole for Cork's many international rugby stalwarts. **De Lacy House** (Oliver Plunket Street) offers the best in music and socializing. The **Grand Parade Hotel** (Grand Parade) gives a great choice with its two stages and three dance floors.

The most unusual venue in Cork is **Nancy Speirs Backstage** in Barrack Street, with its excellent architecture. To sample a local *ceilidh,* enquire at the **Aras, Conradh na Gaeilge** at Dyke Parade.

# South-West Ireland

This is an enchanting region of rugged, unspoilt landscapes: mountains, lakes and islands, deserted coves and quaint fishing ports. It is almost impossible to travel through towns and villages here without encountering the myths and legends that haunt the area. Old Celtic crosses, ruined abbeys, castles and ring forts (mystical places where the Celts believed the faerie gods lived) are all here.

Keep on your toes, because this is the land of the banshee (a mythical ghost who forewarns a death in the family with an earsplitting scream), leprechauns (spirits who jealously guard the pot of gold at the end of each rainbow), and tree gods (who will curse you should you harm the tree they are assigned to guard).

The small, attractive fishing village of **Kinsale** (Cionn-tsaile) lies 27 km from Cork. In 1601, the Spanish landed here to help O'Neill against the English, but suffered defeat a year later. Kinsale is Ireland's culinary capital, and there is no shortage of bed and breakfasts here. Dempsey's Hostel on Eastern Road (Tel.021 772124) is a safe bet, failing that, ask at the Tourist Office on Pier Road (Tel. 021 772234). For a great night out with traditional music, head to The Spaniard on the hill.

Three kilometres east of Kinsale, at Summer Cove, is one of the best preserved star forts in Europe. **Charles Fort**, shaped in star formation, was built in the 17th century after the Battle of Kinsale. The clifftop fortress housed British troops until 1920. Open mid-June to mid-September daily 9am–6.30pm; mid-April to mid-June, Tues.–Sat.: 9am–5pm, Sun.: 2pm–5pm.

The town of **Bantry** is a peaceful place famous for its summer regatta and beautiful views of Bantry Bay. For B&B, head to the Bantry Hostel, Bishop Lucey Place, north east of the town centre (Tel. 027 51050) (open mid March–early Nov. Dorm beds for around IR£7). For a good meal, reasonably priced, try Pete's Grill, washed down with a pint and some atmosphere in the Anchor Tavern near the bus stop. The Wolfe Tone in Wolfe Tone Square serves excellent pub grub and there's live music in the summer. The Tourist Office, only open in the summer, is in the main square (Tel. 027 50229).

While you're in this area, **Bantry House**, nearby (open daily 9am–6pm, until 8pm in summer) is a lovely Georgian mansion in Italianate gardens, overlooking Bantry Bay (House and gardens IR£5.50, students IR£4; gardens IR£1.50). Its collection of treasures includes a tapestry made for Marie Antoinette. Next door is the **1796 Bantry French Armada Exhibition Centre**, which focusses on Theobald Wolfe Tone's attempts to instigate an Irish revolution. Pieces on display include weapons and other relics from a ship sunk during France's attempt to invade in 1796 (IR£3, students IR£1.75).

A good day trip from Bantry is to **Glengariff**, where you can walk up to Lady Bantry's View for an excellent view of the countryside and bay for miles around. Alternatively, head to the parks and mountains of **Goughan Burra**, source of the River Lee, for a perfect picnic site.

A third excursion could be made to **Cape Clear Island**. Take the bus to Skibbereen, famous for its international busking festival, and from there travel to Baltimore. From here, a ferry (around IR£8 return) will take you to an island so peaceful and trouble-free there is no need for a Garda (police) station (remember to check the times of the boat back!). *All Gaeilge* (Irish Gaelic) is still the main language of the island, but everyone can also speak English. See the ring of St Ciaran's church and the Holy Well there and visit the Heritage Centre, open daily 2–5.30pm (IR£1.50), then head to the pub, The Night Jar, and chat to the locals. If you want to stay, there's a youth hostel, Cleire Lasmuigh, (Tel. 028 39144/028 39198) at the Island Adventure Centre. There's also B&B on the island and a campsite (Tel. 028 39136) at the south harbour.

The harbour town of **Dingle** is famous for its shops and houses being colour-washed all the hues of the rainbow. The town has several good fish restaurants and there are said to be 52 pubs. Since 1984, the town's most famous resident has been Fungi the bottle-nosed dolphin; you can take a boat trip to see him out in the bay for IR£6, or swim with him in the morning for rather more (IR£10 if you have your own wetsuit, IR£14 if not). (Tel. 066 51188). Dingle **Oceanworld**, opposite the harbour, has 160 species of fish, a walk-through tunnel and touch pool (Tel. 066 52111; IR£4.50' students IR£3.50).

Hiring a bike is a great way to enjoy the scenery, but beware of the potholes! Cycle up the hill, if you are fit, to Connor Pass for some impressive views (but only if the weather is good), or take the Slea Head coastal route to the west. At ancient Dunberg Fort and other Stone Age settlements on the coast, you can enter some of the beehive dwellings. The Tourist Office on Main Street (Tel. 064 41233) can help find accommodation.

## Limerick  phone code: 061

Ireland's third largest city is on the River Shannon, the longest navigable river in Ireland or Britain. A heavily industrialized port with high unemployment in the past, Limerick has struggled to shrug off its unattractive image. But in recent years, there's been a huge change in the city – put down largely to the tax-free area around nearby Shannon airport, which has brought new jobs and economic regeneration. However, the tourist industry is still not big business here and this can come as a welcome surprise after Cork and Dublin.

The city itself has some pretty Georgian houses and other elegant buildings. Examples of the city facelift include **The Granary**, a grain store which was adapted to a warehouse and later a pub and library. Also worth checking out are the **Custom House**, the imposing 13th-century **King John's Castle** (whose battlement walkways and towers give great views on the Shannon and surrounding countryside) and **St Mary's Cathedral**.

The town is famous for its delicate handmade lace, and the Limerick Lace Collection can be seen in the **Convent of The Good Shepherd** in Clare St (open business hours on weekdays only).

To get Limerick in perspective, get yourself down to the Shannon and follow the waterfront walkways for the best views of the city.

The **Tourist Office** is on Arthur's Quay (Tel. 317 522). The **youth hostel** is at 1 Pery Square (Tel./Fax. 314 672) or try Barrington's Lodge & Hostel at George's Quay, beds from IR£8.50 (Tel. 415 222).

For **B&B** try Shannon Grove Guest House, Athlunkard, Killaloe Road (Tel. 345 756; Fax. 343838), run by the friendly Mr and Mrs Marsh. Facilities are excellent for around IR£20 per person. It is easy to reach by bus: take the Shannon Banks Service from the town centre, which runs approximately every 30 minutes, and the stop is near the house. There is storage space for bikes and the house is only a short distance from the start of the walking trail from Limerick to Galway via Gort.

Thirteen kilometres from Limerick City on the main Galway road stands the fully restored medieval **Bunratty Castle**. It houses a superb collection of antique furniture and furnishings. It is open to visitors daily (last admission 4.15pm; around IR£5), and medieval banquets and entertainments are held twice nightly. The **Folk Park** in the grounds of the castle contains farmhouses and cottages, a forge and other features of life at the turn of the century.

One of Ireland's most important archaeological sites is 17km south of Limerick, at **Lough Gur**. Around the lake there are many megalithic remains, including stone circles, dolmens, and graves. The **Stone Age Interpretive Centre** here tells the Lough Gur story with an audio-visual presentation (open May-September 10am–1pm, 2pm–6pm daily).

Just around the coast from Galway, in the North Shannon region, lies the **Burren**, a stark region of unique beauty. Consider a day-trip to visit the spectacular **Cliffs of Moher** (but only if the weather is fine) and the **Aillwee Caves** at Ballyvaughan (closed in winter).

## Galway phone code: 091

The ancient seaport of Galway is a lively, friendly and cosmopolitan city, with a thriving arts scene and great pubs. Founded in the 12th century by Norman traders, it was dominated by the 14 families who gave rise to the city's nickname, the City of Tribes. By the 16th century, Anglo-Norman nobles had all the power, trading extensively with the West Indies, France and Spain – particularly in the wine business. The trading collaboration has left an obvious legacy in the city architecture, best demonstrated by remains such as the Spanish Arch, one of the gateways to the old town.

Today Galway is the fastest growing city in Ireland, and, largely thanks to good road and rail links with Dublin, is a popular destination for the Irish themselves. This makes it an extremely busy place at weekends and during the numerous festivals staged throughout the summer.

It's also a big student city, with about 20 per cent of the population studying either at the university (which majors in Celtic studies and the Irish language) or the Technical College – all of which only adds to the city's trendy, youthful buzz.

## TOURIST INFORMATION AND ADDRESSES

**TOURIST OFFICE** East of the station in Victoria Place, off Eyre Sq., open July–Aug.daily 8.30am–7.45pm; May–June and Sept. daily 8.30am–5.45pm; Oct.–Apr. Mon.–Fri. and Sun. 9am–5.45pm, Sat 9am–12.45pm, (Tel. 563 081); also on Seapoint Promenade, Salthill. Open daily June–Aug.: 9am–8.30pm.

**ACCOMMODATION AND INFORMATION SERVICE** Tel. 562 030

**POST OFFICE** Eglinton St; open Mon.–Sat.: 9am–5.30pm (Tues. opens at 9.30am)

**AMEX** 7 Eyre Square (Tel. 562316)

**STUDENT TRAVEL USIT**, Kinlay House, Eyre Square (Tel. 565 177), opposite the Tourist Office

## SEEING

If you're arriving by train or bus, you'll be dropped off right in the city centre, at Eyre Square, Galway's largest open space in the centre of which is **Kennedy Park** - JFK visited Galway in 1963. The compact city is easily explored from here. The Spanish arch is a kilometre's walk from Eyre Square down Williamsgate Street, which becomes Shop Street, then High Street and finally Quay Street. **Lynch's Castle**, down Shop Street, is named after a mayor who hanged his own son.

The **Church of St Nicholas**, where it is said Columbus prayed before setting out on one of his voyages of discovery, is also in Shop Street. Founded in 1320 by the Normans, this is one of the best examples of a medieval church in Ireland.

If you're around here on Saturday morning, check out the small **market** alongside the church. It's an excellent place to pick up fresh local produce (organic food is big here), a huge variety of cheeses, fresh soda breads and delicious home-made cakes. Further round the church, the market evolves into crafts and second-hand goods.

Next to the **Spanish Arch** (part of a fort built in the 16th century on the quays where Spanish ships unloaded) is the **Galway City**

**Museum**, with exhibits detailing the history of the area, and some interesting photographs of the old fishing village of Claddagh.

The small **Nora Barnacle House Museum**, the former home of James Joyce's wife, is open Mon.–Sat. mid-May to mid-Sept. Entrance is IR£1.

You can stroll along walkways by the banks of the **River Corrib** and see the salmon jump at **Salmon Weir Bridge** in the spawning season.

Across the river is **Claddagh**. Though it was, until 1927, a fishermen's enclave of thatched cottages, it's now remembered only for the Claddagh Ring – worn by Irish people around the world, often as a wedding ring, and showing two clasped hands encircling a heart.

The biggest annual event is the **Galway Arts Festival**, during the last two weeks in July (with a heady mix of music, theatre, poetry and arts), followed – literally – by the **Galway Races**, usually at the beginning of August. Another big occasion, especially for seafood enthusiasts, is the **Galway Oyster Festival** at the end of September. Count on not just masses of the revered shellfish, but plenty of music and other events organised to complement the festival.

In the summer evenings, check out the **Simsa**, a traditional musical presentation in the Irish-speaking theatre on Middle Street.

## SLEEPING, EATING AND NIGHTLIFE

There are plenty of **hostels** and **B&B**s in the centre of town. The **IYHF Hostel** at St Mary's College is open from late June to late August (Tel. 527411). Some of the independent hostels here are excellent value. **Kinlay House** on Merchant's Rd (Tel. 565244) is a lively, modern hostel with a communal area that feels more like a favourite coffee house. Open all year, they charge between IR£7.50 and IR£12 for dorm beds and IR£13–20 for a twin bedded room. **Great Western House** (Tel. 561139) in Frenchville Lane, just off Eyre Square, is right opposite the train and bus station, and even has a sauna. Price per night: IR£7.50–12.50 for dorms and IR£14–16 for twin bedded rooms.

There's also **Lough Corrib Hostel** (tel. 552 688) on Camp St and **Barnacles Quay Street House** (Tel. 568 644) at 10 Quay Street. If these are full up, try **camping** at **Ballyloghane Caravan Park** on Ballyloughane Beach, Renmore (Apr.–Sept.; Tel. 755338/752029); at Barna, Silver Strand Caravan and Camping Park (Tel. 592040) or at Salthill (Tel. 523972/522479). Refer to *Cheap Sleeps Europe 2000* for more options.

If you're hostelling, you can cook in the communal kitchens – there's a good supermarket in the Eyre Square shopping centre: stock up there, because prices elsewhere in the city centre are high. The exception is the small, but excellent market on Saturdays around the Church of St

Nicholas, on Market Street. A booklet called *Special Value Tourist Menu* from the tourist office has the latest tips on good-value meals, and there're plenty of fish 'n' chip shops to keep you going. For Italian and French cuisine, try Brannigan's in Upper Abbeygate Street.

At night time, it's really just a case of following the crowds. **An Pucain** in Forster Street, **Crane's Bar**, William Street, and **Connor's** in Salthill are lively and have traditional music. Also worth a try is the **King's Head** on Shop Street, which serves possibly the smoothest Guinness in Ireland. The bars on Quay Street can be good, too, and there are other lively places over the bridge around Dominick Street.

At the end of July, Galway plays host to Ireland's premier horse racing and trading festival, known as 'the crack'. The town is swollen with Irish expatriates back from Britain, and drinking reaches Olympic proportions. Pubs stay open late and there is much dancing and card-playing.

**EXCURSIONS** The remote and fascinating **Aran Islands** are strung across the mouth of Galway Bay, about 48km offshore. You can reach them by ferry (90 minutes) from Galway pier. Contact Aran Ferries at Galway's tourist information office (Tel. 563081) or Island Ferries (Tel. 091 561767/091 568903).

The three islands are Inishmore, Inishmaan and Inisheer. On all of them, Gaelic is the main tongue, and tradition is ingrained in the lifestyle and folklore, though the massive tourist trade has somewhat diluted the experience. The islands are overrun with huge numbers of visitors in July and August; going between April and October is best, though you shouldn't miss the chance to enjoy the views (weather permitting) during the boat trip at any time of year.

**Inishmore**, the largest at 13km by 3km, has fewer than 1,000 inhabitants, but has been most affected by tourism. It can be visited from Rossaveal all year round, weather permitting (the crossing takes 35 minutes and costs IR£15 return; a connecting bus runs from the Galway Tourist Office).

Life out here is a hard one based on fishing. This is where the famous Aran sweaters come from and where tweed trousers and skirts are woven to keep out the Atlantic winds. You'll find peace and solitude among the spectacular granite mountains.

Visit the prehistoric forts and remains during your hike round these fascinating islands (or you can make the same trip on bicycles hired at the pier). **Dun Aengus**, built on a sheer cliff 60m above the sea, is the most famous of the Iron Age stone forts and one of the better preserved; its walls are 18 ft thick and form a semi-circle around a sheer drop.

The **Aran Heritage Centre** (April to October, 10am–7pm daily) will put it all in perspective for you.

Afterwards, stop off in the pubs of Kilronan (the main village on the island) to hear the Gaelic-speaking jaunting-car drivers.

**Inishmaan**, in the middle, has only around 300 inhabitants, most of whom still rely on farming and fishing. Tourism is not big here, allowing for peaceful exploration on foot of its cliffs, coves and early Christian remains. Do stop for a coffee at **An Cora** (Tel. 099 73010), the small coffeeshop inside the old Irish Cottage at the pier. It also serves food and is a good place to pick up tourist information. (Only open in July and Aug.) If you're in need of something stronger, head for **Padraic Faherty's**, the thatched pub.

**Inisheer** is small and flat, but has particularly nice, sandy beaches. This is a popular place for Irish schoolchildren to be sent during their summer holidays to learn their mother tongue.

There are plenty of B&Bs and camping is IR£3–4 on official sites with water and toilets. The **Aran Tourist Office** can help you find accommodation (Tel. 099 61263) and there are some good hostels, including the **Aran Islands Hostel**, (Tel. 099 61255) at Kilronan and the **Mainistir House Hostel** (Tel. 099 61169) on Inishmore, which charges IR£6.50 a night, breakfast included; the hostel has a van which meets guests at the ferry pier. They are crowded in the summer. On Inisheer there is also an independent hostel called **Bru Radharc Na Mara Hostel** (Tel. 099 75024/099 75087) which charges around IR£7.50 for a dorm bed.

The islands can also be reached from Doolin in County Clare. Doolin Ferries can be contacted on 065 74455.

Neighbouring villages to Galway all have their beauty spots and interesting features. **Doolin**, south of Galway, has great pubs with live music, whilst **Tuam** has many remains that show it to be the 12th-century seat of the kings of Ireland. The nearby **Craggaunowen Centre** features excellent reconstructions of ancient houses, and also preserved here is a Bronze Age currach (roundish boat made of waterproof hides). St Brendan sailed from Dingle peninsula in a similar currach in the 6th-century AD. In 1976, the explorer Tim Severin sailed the Atlantic in a reconstructed currach to prove that Brendan and other Irish missionaries could have made the journey long before Columbus. For the Tourist Office tel. 093 25486. In the summer a steam railway plies the 20-minute route from Tuam to Athenry and connects up with the main Dublin to Galway intercity line.

One kilometre off the main Galway to Limerick Road is **Thoor Ballylee**, the 13th and 14th century tower which the poet W. B. Yeats bought for £35 in 1916. He renovated it and lived here on and off with his family in the twenties. It's open daily (10am–6pm) from Easter to Sept., admission is IR£3, students IR£2.50.

The best way to explore the area is by bicycle. These can be hired from Europa Bicycles, Hunters Building, Earls Island (Tel. 091 563355), or from the Great Western Hostel in Frenchman's Lane.

## Connemara

The bleak and rugged mountain region of Connemara lies north of Galway, between Lough Corrib and the Atlantic. Dominated by the Twelve Bens mountain range, it has a jagged, unspoilt shoreline and several interesting traditional villages where Gaelic is the mother tongue. Connemara needs to be explored by bus or bike, as there are no trains. If you're feeling fit, this is great hiking country. The **Western Way** footpath, which stretches from Oughterard to Leenane through the Maamturks (the other major mountain range), is a great route to appreciate the stunning scenery. If you are coming from Galway, the **youth hostel** at Indreabhan (Inverin) is probably your best starting-point (Tel. 091 593 154).

The **Connemara National Park** runs two-hour accompanied nature trails every Mon., Wed. and Fri. throughout the summer (Tel. 095 41054). The nearby village of **Carraroe** holds summer festivals and is worth a visit, as is **Kylemore Abbey**, a massive old lakeside building with Gothic features. Built in 1864 by Galway MP Mitchell Henry, for his ill wife, the Abbey is these days run by Benedictine nuns as a boarding school, with the Gothic chapel, the hall and other rooms open to visitors (Tel. 095 41146).

The region is also known for the **Connemara ponies** – wild, rugged creatures which can be seen in all their glory during August at the Connemara Pony Show in Clifden. **Ross Abbey**, a ruined Franciscan friary near Headford, has fine views from its tower.

Accommodation can be found at **Lough Corrib Hostel** in Camp Street, Oughterard (Tel. 091 552688; Fax. 091 552666) which charges from IR£7, and is open all year.

## North-West Ireland

Counties Mayo, Sligo and Donegal may lack the warmer climate of the south, but they more than make up for it with their dramatic and beautiful scenery, and prehistoric remains.

**County Mayo** is an unspoilt area of rugged mountains, trout lakes and salmon rivers. **Westport**, in Clew Bay, is worth stopping at to see the beautiful estate of the Marquess of Sligo, three km from the town. **Westport House** is his Georgian mansion, open to the public Apr.–Sept., entry around IR£6.50. You can enjoy the grounds for free. The town is very busy on the last Sunday in July, when thousands of pilgrims climb **Croagh Patrick**, where St Patrick is said to have fasted and prayed. The Tourist Office (Tel. 098 25711) and the post office are in the Mall. For sleeping, try the Club Atlantic on Altamount Street (Tel. 098 26644).

**Sligo** is a county incredibly rich in archaeological sites and atmosphere. All this makes it quite unsurprising that the poet W.B. Yeats took such inspiration from the area, and is commemorated throughout the county. The mountains are the area's big attraction – principally Knocknarea and Benbulben. The imposing hulk of flat-topped **Benbulben** inspired a number of Yeats' poems, and at 1730 ft it is one of the most spectacular mountains in the country. **Knocknarea** is easy to climb and well worth the effort for the view you get from the summit. There is a 24m cairn, rumoured to be that of Maeve of Connacht, a warrior queen. And **Lough Gill** is a great place for quiet walks and communing with nature, while the county's hills are scattered with megalithic tombs.

**Sligo Town**, with a population of only 25,000, is the main centre of north-west Ireland. It's a compact town, though, and very easy to get to know. The Tourist Office at Temple Street (Tel. 071 612010) will give you help and information, and has guided walks at 11am every day during the summer. There's also an info. booth on O'Connell Street in the Quinnsworth arcade. The main sight in the town is the ruined 13th-century Dominican friary, **Sligo Abbey**. Also worth a visit is the **County Museum** (free entry), which has an extensive collection of first editions of Yeats, and the **Yeats Memorial Museum** on Hyde bridge, open in the summer on weekdays 10.30am–1pm and 3pm–5pm.

For accommodation, try the hostel Eden Hill on Pearse Road (Tel. 071 43204) or the White House Hostel on Markievicz Road (Tel. 071 45160/071 42398).

Just outside the town is **Carrowmore Megalithic Cemetery** (open in the summer), which contains tombs dating back to 4000 BC. **Rosses Point**, a holiday resort eight km from Sligo, has nice sandy beaches and bracing Atlantic breezes. Another recommended day trip from Sligo is to walk on the shores of **Lough Gill**, a broad lake with luscious woodland covering the surrounding hills. If you have transport, the northern shore is the most interesting, though you can follow the sign posts to do an entire circuit of the lake.

**County Donegal** is not served by rail, but if you want to do a bit of hitching, the far north-west will provide you with wild and unpolluted terrain. The **Glenveagh National Park**, 22½ km north-west of

Letterkenny, covers an area of 10,000 hectares and has various nature paths and a castle in its grounds. From the visitor's centre, take a bus along the banks of Lough Beagh to the crenellated 19th-century castle and gardens. Climb the steep path behind for views over the lake.

**Letterkenny** itself holds an International Folk Festival in August: information is obtainable from the Tourist Office in Derry Road (Tel. 074 21160).

**Donegal Town** has its own 15th-century castle which is open in the summer months 9.30am–6.30pm (guided tours on the hour). The Donegal Tourist Office on Quay Street (Tel. 073 21148) can help with accommodation, though there is a good hostel in the town at Ball Hill (Tel. 073 21174), as well as Cliff-view Holiday Hostel on Coast Rd (Tel. 073 21684) and Donegal Town Independent Hostel at Doonan (Tel. 073 22805).

West of Donegal is the valley of **Glencolumbkille**, where the village, overlooked by dramatic cliffs on either side, is home to a number of craft shops and a folk museum incorporating restored houses from the 18th and 19th centuries (open Mon.–Sat.).

There is much here for the visitor to admire: **Slieve League**, for instance, near Carrick, has the highest sea cliffs in Europe, where a 630m mountain seemingly falls into the Atlantic. The tweed industry is alive and thriving here. Magee's of Donegal is the main exponent, though for the major centre of the handknits and weaving industry go to **Ardara**, west of Donegal itself. The most breathtaking route to get there is to travel via the **Bluestack** mountains; once in the village itself, you can hire a bicycle from Donal Byrne (ask in the village for directions to his place) and explore the coastal scenery.

NOTES:

# ITALY (Italia)

| | |
|---|---|
| Entry requirements | Passport |
| Population | 57.9 million |
| Capital | Rome (pop.: 3 million) |
| Currency | Lire |
| | £1 = approx. 3,068L |
| Political system | Republic |
| Religion | Roman Catholic |
| Language | Italian (some English spoken in major cities) |
| Public holidays | New Year's Day, Epiphany (6 Jan.), Easter Sunday, Easter Monday, National Day of Liberation (25 Apr.), Labour Day (1 May), Assumption (15 Aug.), All Saints Day (1 Nov.), Immaculate Conception (8 Dec.), Christmas Day, Boxing Day |
| International dialling codes | To Italy: int'l code 39 (note: you must dial the full town codes, including the digit 0, even if you're in the town itself) |
| | From Italy: 00 + country code |
| Time | GMT +1 (+2 in summer) |
| Emergency telephone numbers | Police112; ambulance 113; fire service 115 |

Italy can be the ultimate love-hate relationship. You'll be annoyed and frustrated, but your greatest Inter-Railing stories will probably originate in this exciting and beautiful country, and somewhere along the way you will probably fall in love with it. Relax, slow down, spend some time here soaking up a rich cultural heritage and an even richer appreciation of life ... Italy will grow on you.

Three themes dominate Italy's history: Empire, Church and the Renaissance, all of which have played a major role in shaping Europe as a whole. From the 8th century BC onwards there were Greeks in southern Italy and Sicily, and Etruscans in the north. The Romans conquered an empire that reigned supreme over much of the barbarian world until its downfall in the 5th century AD.

But even as Rome's power faded, the city found a new role as a centre for Christianity. Italy became disunited and power was left in the hands of local kings and dukes. Even the Pope and the Holy Roman Emperor could not agree over who ruled what, and eventually the Pope fled to Avignon in 1303.

The greatest cultural flowering in history came in the 15th century when the Kingdom of Naples and powerful city-states such as Venice and Florence began to take a competitive interest in the arts. The fortunes of glory-seeking princes, merchants and bankers were poured into patronage for the artists and intellectuals whose work gave rise to the Renaissance and soon spread throughout Europe.

Alongside this came the development of humanism – a secular movement that recognized human achievement – which produced artists like Leonardo da Vinci and Michelangelo.

Disunity and rivalry led to outside intervention by Spain, Austria and finally Napoleonic France. This foreign domination created desire for unity, initially under Garibaldi, leading to the unification of Italy in 1870. After the First World War, Mussolini and the Fascists rose to power, which eventually brought about an alliance with Hitler just before the Second World War. A new republic was established with the Italian Constitution in 1948.

Since then, Italy has developed with lightning speed from an agricultural to an industrial country, though the pace of economic change has not been uniform. Even today, the wealthy north is a world away from the south, where poverty continues to be a problem, and from where the notorious mafia crime families wield power over the economy, society and politics. In 1982, they were so feared that the Italian parliament passed an anti-mafia law, which was followed by the biggest mafia trials in history.

Italians today, as they have been for centuries, are fascinated with politics – small wonder in a country that has seen more than 50 administrations since the end of the Second World War. The famous Latin temperament is exercised publicly in animated political discussions from bar rooms and piazzas to government offices. Where else but Italy would there be a parliamentary punch-up over a footballing refereeing decision? And perhaps only in Italy, too – birthplace of Machiavelli, who declared: the end justifies the means – could a judge appointed to clean up the scandal of government corruption be later accused of corruption himself.

Ever since the days of the 18th-century Grand Tour, when wealthy young men were sent to Europe to broaden their outlook, travellers have been bewitched by Italy's art, cities, mountains, islands, lakes, countryside and uninhibited lifestyle. Today, touring here remains a roller-coaster ride through a passionate country with an unbeatable combination of ancient and modern. Add to this distinctive food, excellent wine, and a perfect climate. What more could you want?

## ITALIAN STATE RAILWAYS

### (FERROVIE DELLO STATO, FS)
### NATIONAL TRAIN INFORMATION TEL. 062 28 07 24

The Italian rail network can be one of the best in Europe, but you can still have some pretty wild experiences, especially in the south. In peak season, second class gets incredibly busy on the main lines, so either move early for a seat or, if it is a long trip, reserve. Beware of dishonest passengers who claim your reserved seat as their own.

Ask for proof. If forced to stand in the corridor, try for one of the pull-down seats that are often available.

There are various categories of train in Italy. These include the Locale, Rapido, Express, Fast (Diretto) and very fast (Direttissimo). Intercity, Eurocity and most definitely the Eurostar all usually require a supplement. Pay beforehand at the station as it's twice the price on board. Check your timetable for precise details. Do not forget to stamp your supplement ticket in one of the yellow machines, or your ticket will not be valid. Avoid the 'Diretti' and 'Locali' services for any long-distance travel, as they are agonizingly slow and often prone to delays.

A word of warning: there are still many stories of crime on certain routes, especially on the Bari/Brindisi run and south to Sicily. Common sense should prevail at all times. Keep your valuables well hidden and be careful who you talk to, and what food or drink you accept from them. Be especially alert overnight.

Finally, when catching a train, double check between the main automated departure boards and the yellow 'partenza' sheets, just in case things have been inexplicably changed. Travelling on the FS can be irritating or entertaining, all depending on how you look at it. Either way, it will be unforgettable!

**PASSES AVAILABLE** The **Kilometric** card (no age restrictions) is valid for up to 20 trips or a maximum of 3,000 km travel, and can be used by as many a five different people. Each trip is calculated by multiplying the distance travelled by the number of adults. Valid for two months, this pass can be bought from every large station in Italy as well as from any Compagnia Italiana Turismo (CIT) office, and costs £89 second-class if bought in London or around 210,000L when bought in Italy. In practice, this pass is only worthwhile if you're travelling in a group.

If you are intending to do a lot of travelling it may be worth considering the travel-at-will **Italy Railcard** or **BTLC** ticket (*Biglietto turistico libera circolazione*) which is valid for eight, 15, 21 or 30 days in first and second class. You can buy it in major Italian stations or from CIT (the phone number of the CIT office in Britain is 0891 715151 - calls charged at premium rate) or Wasteels in London before you go (Wasteels Travel is next to Platform 2, Victoria Station, London. Tel. 020 7834 7066; Fax. 020 7630 7628). It is possible to extend the validity of all but the eight-day ticket. Prices in second class are £143 for eight days, £179 for 15, £207 for 21 days and £250 for 30.

The **Flexirailcard** works in the same way as the Railcard, but is valid for either four days in one month (£113), eight days in one month (£157) or 12 days in one month (£202). Tourists can also buy **circular tickets** for journeys of over 1,000 km which start and finish in the same town, or start and finish at any frontier. These work out slightly cheaper than the normal fare but are likely to be of limited appeal, as you are not allowed to go through the same town twice and every break of journey has to be endorsed.

The **cartaverde** is available to those aged between 12 and 26. If you're planning to be in Italy some time then it is a good investment. It is valid for a year and costs around 40,000L. It gives 20% discounts on all state train fares. For those over 60, there is also the **carta d'argento** (silver card) which costs the same as the cartaverde and gives the same discounts.

**Day return** tickets for journeys over 50 km have a 15% discount, as do **three-day return** tickets for journeys over 250 km.

Both **Eurail** and **Inter-Rail** are valid. The Inter-Rail pass has been broken down into zones, so that you pay only for travel within the area you want to visit. For £159 you can spend 22 days touring a zone. Italy is in Zone G, along with Greece, Turkey and Slovenia (the Zone G pass also includes the ADN/HML ferry). For details of the eight Inter-Rail zones and Freedom (EuroDomino) passes, see Part One of this guide.

## EURAIL BONUSES
### FREE SERVICES

Eurail Pass and Eurail Youthpass travellers can use steamers operated by the Adriatica di Navigazione and Hellenic Mediterranean Lines between Brindisi and Patras and vice versa. Between mid-June and end of Sept., they must pay a high-season surcharge. During July and August, advance reservation, which costs about 5,000L, is recommended. Special accommodation and port taxes are extra.

Before boarding, all passengers should check in early at the shipping line office at the pier. Passengers who wish to break their voyage at Corfu must declare their intention of 'stop over' upon delivery of the ticket. Holders of tickets for Corfu (as final port of destination) cannot continue their voyage to Patras.

In Brindisi, beware of signs announcing 'Inter-Railers Sailing to Greece This Way' – these will take you to agencies which have recently been ripping off innocent Inter-Railers with £30 'reservation' fees. Go straight to the shipping offices in the harbour, where you will be charged a port tax of around £6 (with an extra £3.50 if you stop off at Corfu).

Adriatica are less strict about deck passengers staying on deck than Hellenic. You will need your boarding card stamped by the police before embarking.

Eurailers travel free on the Civitavecchia–Golfo Aranci (Sardinia) and Villa San Giovanni–Messina (Sicily) routes.

Note, rail travel in Italy is inexpensive so it is probably not worth your while buying a railcard (Eurail/Inter-Rail) if you are only planning to travel in the country.

## TRAIN INFORMATION

Information officers generally speak English, but are sometimes less than helpful as they get fed up with the long queues in the summer, so try to use your Thomas Cook timetable whenever possible. Many stations have Digiplan machines that issue free computerised print-outs of train times and possible routes to your chosen destination.

**RESERVATIONS** Are optional on all non-supplement trains. It's a good idea to book on runs between major cities, as the trains are always crowded. It's possible to reserve a seat for the entire journey from London to Italy.

**LEFT LUGGAGE (BAGAGLI)** Many Italian stations seem to count a rucksack with bedroll and sleeping bag attached as three items, and charge accordingly. It's approx. 5,000L per item for 12 hours.

**NIGHT TRAVEL** This is a good move in Italy where prices are low and distances often long. You can get a couchette from Paris to Rome or vice versa for a 41,000L supplement. (The one way adult fare is 192,000L). They are either first-class four-berth or second-class six-berth. When reserving, ask for 'Finestrino' or 'Superiore' as these are the top bunks which offer the most room and privacy. If you're asked to give up your passport for the night, don't worry as this is standard practice. Many Italian trains (*espresso*) also have pull-down seats. Avoid seats next to the corridor as theft is rife, especially in the south. Do not take moneybelts off under any circumstances.

**EATING ON TRAINS** There are mini-bars on all major trains, but if you're on a tight budget stick to picnics, as prices can be very high.

**SCENIC TIPS** Some of Europe's most spectacular alpine scenery can be seen on the Berne–Brig–Milan and the Zürich–Lugano–Milan runs. Innsbruck–Bolzano–Verona and Vienna–Venice also offer some fine mountain views.

One of the most popular routes is from Nice down to Pisa, as there's a lot more than just the Mediterranean coast to feast your eyes on (the train passes most of the Riviera beaches). Make sure you sit on the coastal side, though. Anywhere around the Bay of Naples has excellent coastal views, particularly along the private narrow-gauge line to Sorrento.

If you're arriving at Brindisi, there are three very different routes to choose from: along the southern coast to Catania in Sicily; up the Adriatic coast to Rimini; or over the mountains to Naples. Another beautiful run is Sulmona to Isernia, part of the excellent electrified line from Rome to Pescara.

The short journey from Monfalcone to Trieste also affords wonderful panoramic views, as does the journey from Venice to Ljubljana in Slovenia.

**BIKES** Scooters and bikes can sometimes be hired from local Tourist Offices.

## TOURIST INFORMATION

Before you set off to Italy, it's worth writing to the State Tourist Office (ENIT - Ente Nazionale Italiano di Turismo) at 1 Prince's Street, London W1R 8AY, or Italian Government Travel Office, 630 Fifth Ave., 1565, New York, NY 10111, asking them to send you their excellent free *Travellers' Handbook* which is updated annually and contains the latest information. ENIT is the national tourist office and has an office in Rome. In provincial capitals, there are Ente Provinciale per il Turismo (EPT) offices. City Tourist Board offices (Azienda Autonoma di Soggiorno e Turismo (AAST)) can also be found in many towns. In smaller places look out for Pro Loco offices. The Azienda di Promozione Turismo (APT) offices can be quite good but if you want help with accommodation they will only recommend establishments which have paid to be on their books. Private agencies are springing up everywhere. A word of warning – they operate on a commission basis so don't expect to get impartial or complete information.

**ISIC BONUSES** 20–50% discounts on sea travel. For further information, contact CTS Viaggi per la Gioventù, Via Nazionale 172, Rome. Discounts on Museum entry. Show card wherever you go, you never know where it might give you a discount.

**MONEY MATTERS** The unit of currency is the lira, for which there are notes for everything between 1,000 and 100,000. There are also 50, 100, 200 and 500L coins. Banking hours are Mon.–Fri.: 8.30am–1.30pm and 3pm–4pm. Some exchange agencies (*cambio*) give a better rate; you will have to shop around. In general, a bank like Credito Italiano is better. The *gettone* (Italian phone token used as currency) is used as the equivalent of 200L. Cash point machines are widely available, so get your cirrus symbol working for you.

**POST OFFICES** Open 8am–6.30pm Mon.–Sat., smaller towns either have no service on a Sat. or close at midday. Stamps are also sold at tobacconists' (*Tabacchi*).

**SHOPS** Open 8.30/9am–12.30/1pm and 3.30/4pm–7/8pm, except in northern Italy, where the lunch break is shorter and shops close earlier. Most stores take a half day on Mon., generally opening at about 4pm. Many shops in tourist centres stay open all day. Supermarkets, e.g. CRAI and ESSELUNGA, can be difficult to find in town centres, so if you see one, stock up.

**MUSEUMS** Opening hours are generally 9am–1 or 2pm. Many museums are shut on Sun. afternoons, Mon. and public holidays. A number of churches shut between 12 noon and 3pm. NB. Most churches, especially the major cathedrals, will not admit people wearing shorts or with uncovered shoulders (or girls with short skirts), so dress sensibly and with respect. Museum cards have been discontinued, though a pass is still available for Rome. Any UK citizen under 18 can get into state museums free.

**CRIME** Small-time crime is prevalent in the major cities and in the south of the country. Crowded streets or markets and packed tourist sights are favourite spots for criminals. Minimize the risk of losing your valuables by being discreet: don't flaunt valuable belongings. Gypsies, refugees or hustlers sometimes approach using a piece of cardboard or newspaper to distract your attention while their accomplices relieve you of your possessions: be alert.

## SLEEPING

There's no shortage of hostels, hotels and pensions in Italy to choose from. Each has its own fixed charges, mostly 15,000–40,000L, as worked out by the provincial tourist boards. Always check behind the door to see if it includes IVA (Italian VAT), breakfast and a shower, as these are often extra.

There about 60 **youth hostels** scattered throughout Italy (open for IYHF members only), as well as numerous student hostels in all the main towns (open to everyone). Many Italian hostels do not accept phone reservations. For further information on youth hostels in Italy contact Associazione Italiana Alberghi per la Gioventu (AIG), Via Cavour 44, 00184 Rome (Tel. 06 4871152; Fax. 06 488 0492). Expect to pay between 18,000-30,000L.

Hostels are not automatically your best bet, as many operate a curfew (usually about 11.30pm) and shut during the siesta. We've found inexpensive **hotels** are more reliable in their cleanliness and flexibility. Look for the signs *Pensione, Albergo, Locanda and Soggiorno*. Females also have the option of staying at the local **Casa Famiglia**, which are run by nuns and offer a bed for about 25,000L. Wherever you stay, don't be afraid to give up your passport when you check in as this is standard practice.

One easy way to book ahead is to use the London-based hotel reservation centre Accommodation Line, which specializes in economy hotels and B&B in Italy. This is most definitely not your cheapest option, but if you can afford to splurge, it will take the hassle out of phoning ahead, and also guarantees clean, centrally located and friendly accommodation (with up to triple or quadruple sleeping in some places). Write to 1st Floor, 46 Maddox Street, London W1R 9PB or Tel. 020 7409 1343.

**Camping** represents another alternative. Prices range from 9,000 to 18,000L. Lists of camping sites are usually available at the tourist offices. Freelance camping is illegal, though the authorities may turn a blind eye in the off season.

For the full low-down on sleeping options in Italy, get hold of a copy of *Cheap Sleeps Europe 2000*.

## EATING AND NIGHTLIFE

Italy represents one of the best deals in Europe for good-value eating. The pizza stalls give you a cheap and tasty lunch, and in the evening, especially in Rome, you're spoilt for choice. Some places bump up the bill if you choose to sit outside to eat your meal, so check first. Always check the bill. Watch the *pane e coperto* – the bread and cover charge. It ranges from 1,000 to 3,000L. Also check whether the bill includes service (*servizio compreso*). Even if a service charge is included (usually 10 to 15%), it is polite to give an extra tip if service has been good.

Snacks and afternoon coffees can be a bad idea: they inevitably end up costing as much as a meal. Expect to pay 20,000–40,000L for a full meal with wine in a trattoria, and 18,000–25,000L for the *menu turistico*. Fast food abounds in the usual outlets.

In general, breakfast at a hotel or pension isn't worth it, as all you're likely to get is a cup of coffee and a roll (which are normally cheaper at the local bar). If you can do without breakfast, go straight to the nearest supermarket or local market, though these – along with public toilets – are scarce in Italian city centres. You may be forced into a café – with high prices and an old crone outside the toilet demanding money. To avoid this, be organized, and check your picnic supplies whenever you come across a market. In the evening *rosticcerie*, *trattorie*, *tavole calde* and *osterie* represent the best value. Cheap restaurants can be found and the standard of cooking can be high, even on a fixed-price menu.

Finding vegetarian food should not be too difficult, but just in case, contact the Vegetarian Society in Altrincham before you go.

After the evening meal most Italians wander round to a few cafés and bars, soaking up the local colour and chatting to friends and neighbours. The dancing and nightclub scene is not startling, but there are a few flash – and expensive – places in the main cities. Musical and cultural events are thick on the ground in places like Rome, Florence and Milan. Pick up the *What's On* from the local Tourist Office of whichever centre you're in, and make good use of your ISIC card.

Note: phone numbers in Italy seem to be constantly changing. Over the past few years, the prefixes (codes), including the zero, have been incorporated into the number. So whether you're calling from the same town/city or from another one you dial the whole number. E.g. Rome's code was 06, now it is part of the number. To cause even more confusion, all numbers are due to change again this year - the initial zero will be replaced by a 4 (3 for mobiles). For more information, ask at the local tourist office.

# Northern Italy

Venice and Florence are the jewels of the North, and Milan and Turin are the industrial powerhouses. It is here where the money's made, and to a large extent this is where it stays. Parts of the north are heavily industrialized, and prices tend to be higher, but there are too many interesting towns in this area simply to head south without first exploring this region.

## Piemont and Trentino – Alto Adige

**Piemonte**, bordering France and Switzerland in the north-west of Italy, is almost encircled by dramatic mountain scenery. It is one of the country's wealthiest regions, with its capital, **Turin** (Torino) centre of the car industry and producing more than 85 per cent of Italy's cars, and Olivetti being another big corporation putting the city on the map.

Turin, on the main line to Rome, Florence, Naples and Paris, is more of a stopping-off place than a tourist centre, though there are lots of museums to keep you busy if you do decide to stay a day or two. The **sixteenth-century quarter** is attractive enough to merit a visit, as is the former **Royal Palace**, which is open for guided tours only; Tues.–Sun.: 9am–1pm and 2–6pm. The gardens were designed by Louis le Notre, who designed the gardens at Versailles. Entry is free. The **Palazzo Madama** is an impressive building with its richly decorated façade. The **Egyptian Museum** (open Tues.–Sat.; 8.30am–10pm; Sun. 8.30am–8pm; admission 12,000L (under 18 and over 60 free)) and the **Galleria Sabauda** (open Tues.–Sat.; 9am–2pm; Thurs. 9am–7pm; Sun. 10am–10pm; admission 8,000L (under 18 and over 60 free)) in the Palace of the Academy of Sciences, Piazza Castello are two of the best museums in town. The artifacts in the Egypt Museum are almost as extensive as the ones in the British Museum. The Galleria, on the third and fourth floors, has masterpieces from the House of Savoy and important Dutch and Flemish paintings. Climb the 164m

**Mole Antonelliana** for a panoramic view over the city and on to the distant Alps (daily 9am–7pm, closed Mon.). Do check that it is open first as it has been shut while the **National Museum of Cinema** was being installed, and for general restoration work. The Tourist Office is at P. Castello 165 (Tel. 011 535181//011 535901) and there is a smaller office at Porta Nuova station (Tel. 011 531327), open Mon.–Sat.: 9am–7pm. Amex is at the airport (Tel. 567 6697).

**FREE TURIN:**
- A must is the famous fake in the **Chapel of the Holy Shroud**, housed in a casket behind the apse of the **Duomo**. The cathedral is closed on Mon. and Sun. afternoons.
- The **Medieval Village** in the Parco del Valentino makes an interesting diversion.

If you want to stay, try **the IYHF Ostello Torino**, Via Alba 1 (Tel. 011 660 2939; Fax. 011 660 4445), across the river from the park: take bus 52 to the third stop over the river.

The campsite is much further out at **Campeggio Villa Rey**, Strand Val. S. Martino 27 (Tel. 011 819 0128); open March–Nov.

The pink-coloured **Dolomites** and the proximity to Austria and Switzerland make **Alto Adige** feel like a totally different country. In fact, the region was part of Austria right up until 1919.

**Bolzano** (Bolzen) is on the main line from Munich and still feels more Austrian than Italian in character. This is the capital of the Südtirol/Alto Adige area and German is still spoken here. The town is built on the Brenner Pass, an important alpine passageway used and fought over since medieval times. Tourist Information is at Piazza Walther 8 (Tel. 0471 307000), where the **Gothic Cathedral** stands. This Tourist Office gives excellent lists of accommodation information and can also direct you to the best walks and hikes in the area. It is open Mon.–Fri.: 9am–6.30pm; Sat.: 9am–12.30pm. There is another Tourist Office on Piazza Parrocchia 11, which is open Mon.–Fri.: 9am–12noon, 2pm–5pm. (Tel. 0471 993808).

The **Museo Dell'alto Adige** has a rare collection of wooden sculptures and paintings and the village of **Gries**, across the River Talvera, makes a lovely walk. There is a **campsite** at Moosbauer, Via San Maurizio 83 (Tel. 0471 918492; Fax. 0471 204894). Take bus no. 10 A/B from the station (last one is at 8.30pm) and get out at the hospital. Then it's one km down San Maurizio.

**Brunico**, half an hour from the Austrian frontier, still feels like a part of Austria. The dominating Tyrolean **Castle of Bishop Bruno** was built in 1251. Walk for half an hour to the **Plan Di Coroes** for an incredible alpine view.

Another Roman town on the Brenner route is **Trento**, half an hour from Bolzano on the line to Verona. Walk down **via Belenzani**, which is lined with Renaissance and Venetian palaces. The **Cattedrale di San Vigilio** is an impressive building and the museum next door, the **Museo Diocesano**, has some interesting sacred paintings and other ecclesiastical items (open Mon.–Sat. 9.30am–12.30pm and 2.30–5.45pm; 5000L, students 1000L (this includes access to the archaeological excavations beneath the cathedral)). Have a look also at the church of **San Francesco Saverio** and the bishops' house, **Il Castello Di Buon Consiglio** (the Castle of Good Counsel). Trento's Tourist Office, Azienda Autonoma, is in Via Alfieri 4 (Tel. 0461 983880) and is open Mon.–Sat.: 9am–6pm; Sun.: 9am–1pm. For info. on biking, skiing or hiking, contact the APT office at V. Romagnosi 3 (Tel. 0461 839000). The **hostel** is the best place to stay while you're here. It charges from 20,000L per person, including breakfast, and is situated on Via Manzoni 17 (Tel./Fax. 0461 234567).

The mountains near Trento are good for day trips. The Tourist Office in **Vaneze**, halfway up **Monte Bondone** (Tel. 0461 947128) can help you with accommodation, if you decide to stay here.

## Lombardy

Lombardy is the prosperous commercial and industrial centre of Italy, yet it also has rich farmlands. It stretches from the Swiss border to the plains of the Po valley, taking in Como, on Lake Como, Bergamo, Mantua (Mantova) and the main city, Milan.

**Como**, at the southwestern tip of Lake Como, is an ancient silk-producing city. Half an hour from Milan by train, it attracts masses of tourists lured by the beauty of the alp-encircled lake. Head for the **Piazza del Duomo** to see the old **Pretorian Palace** called Il Broletto (1215). Next to this is the **Palazzo del Comune** and the Renaissance Gothic **Duomo**. The church of **San Fedele** is reached by taking Via Vittorio Emanuele. Tourist Information is near the ferry dock at Piazza Cavour 16 (Tel. 031 262091), and at the station in Via Venini (Tel. 031 267214). The offices will arrange accommodation for you.

An excellent way to get to know this area is by taking a water bus up the lake, stopping at all the small villages *en route* (avoid the set tours as they are expensive and not good value).

The IYHF hostel is the **Villa Olmo**, on Via Bellinzona 2. Open March–Nov., it is situated one km from the station and charges around 16,000L for a dorm bed and breakfast (Tel./Fax. 031 573800). Try to stay at **Menaggio** on the lakeside. The hostel there,

'La Primula', Via Quattro Novembre 86 (Tel./Fax. 0344 32356) is open Mar.–Nov., overlooks the lake and offers a superb three-course evening meal with wine, reasonably priced, with no curfew or restriction on drink.

Bergamo is divided in two: the lower city, built under the Fascists in the 1920s; and the upper city (Cittá Alta), a medieval settlement reached by funicular from Viale Vittorio Emanuele II. Apart from the Palazzo dell'Accademia Carrara, forget the modern city centre. Once you've taken the funicular up, head for the Piazza Vecchia where the Palazzo della Ragione stands. Opposite this is the Palazzo Nuovo. Via Rocca takes you to a park which has a medieval lookout post from where the view over the Bergamasque valleys is excellent. Tourist Information is on Vicolo Aquila Nera 2 (Tel. 035 232730/035 242226) and is open 9am–12.30pm and 2.50pm–7.30pm daily. The IYHF hostel Bergamo (Tel. 035 361724/035 343038) is on Via Galileo Ferraris 1. Open all year.

The Gonzaga family ruled Mantua (Mantova) for 400 years. One of the legacies of those days of the Renaissance courts is the sumptuous palace (Palazzo Ducale) on Piazza Sordello. There are more than 500 rooms, including the miniature suite specially constructed to house the court dwarfs. It also houses some superb examples of Renaissance art. It's 12,000L or free on ISIC, closed Mon. and Sun. afternoons in winter. Opposite the palace is the medieval Cathedral, which is impressive enough, but pales into insignificance beside the beautiful Church of Sant'Andrea. The Palazzo del Tè in the south of the city was the Gonzagas' summer home (closed Mon. Entrance is 12,000L; students 5,000L). If you're here in the summer, the Jazz Festival at the end of July is not to be missed. There's a street parade and a range of concerts. If chamber music is more your thing, try to visit in April or May when the town hosts a chamber music series. Tourist information is at Piazza A. Mantegna 6 (Tel. 0376 328253); watch out for their 12–3pm siestas.

# Milan (Milano)

As the rich man of Italy, Milan has all the glitz and glamour you would expect of a centre of the fashion world. This is the place to spot supermodels and here you will *never* feel overdressed. Most Eurorailers don't get off at Milan, but while it is not exactly Venice in the sightseeing stakes, the city is an ancient art centre and its museums display a wide range of important collections. Added to which, there are more things going on in the evenings here than anywhere else in Italy. Do be warned though that in August the city practically closes down completely as the Milanese head to the coast for their summer hols.

## STATION FACILITIES

There are five stations in Milan: Centrale, Genova, Vittoria, Nord and Garibaldi. Unless you are taking local trains, you will only use Centrale. Some consider the Centrale station to be one of the most impressive in Europe, if only for its sheer size. Since a fire in 1983, the whole station has had a facelift, making it even more spectacular. It is a thoroughly modern station with full facilities. There is a useful supermarket here, which also has a snackbar attached, downstairs and to the right (with the trains behind you), which is open 5.30am to midnight. Left luggage 5,000L for 12 hours, open 24hr. Take care at night and avoid the main entrance area, which is often frequented by drug pushers.

For train enquiries telephone 0267 5001.

## TOURIST INFORMATION AND ADDRESSES

**APT** Via Marconi 1 (Tel. 02 7252 4300), open Mon.–Fri.: 8.30am–8pm; Sat.: 9am–1pm and 2–7pm; Sun.: 9am–1pm and 2–5pm. To the right as you face the Duomo in the Palazzo di Turismo. They will supply you with a free map of the city, marking the metro and main train/bus lines. Another useful free map gives locations of all the hotels and pensions in the centre. Get the free guides *Milano:Where, When, How* and *Milano Mese*, which gives information on activities and clubs.They do not reserve rooms but they will phone to check availability. Expect to queue a long time before you are served. There's also an office on the 2nd floor of Centrale station (Tel. 02 7252 4370/02 7252 4360).

**POST OFFICE** Piazza Cordusio 4 (near the Duomo); also *poste restante*. Open Mon.–Fri.: 8.30am–7.30pm, Sat: 8.30am–1pm. There are two post offices at Centrale station

**AMEX** Via Brera 3, beyond the Piazza della Scala (Tel. 02 7200 3693). Mon.–Thu.: 9am–5.30pm. Friday closes at 5pm.

**UK CONSULATE** Via San Paolo 7 (Tel. 02 72 3001; emergencies Tel. 033 5810 6857)

**US CONSULATE** Via Principe Amedeo 2/10 (Tel. 02 2903 5141)

**CANADIAN CONSULATE** Via Vittore Pisani 19 (Tel. 02 67581; emergencies Tel. 0 6758 3994)

**AUSTRALIAN CONSULATE** Via Borgogna 2 (Tel. 02 777041)

**NEW ZEALAND CONSULATE** Via d'Arezzo 6 (Tel. 02 4801 2544)

**EURAIL AID OFFICE** Centrale Station

**24-HOUR CHEMIST** Centrale station (Tel. 02 669 0735/02 669 0935)

**STUDENT TRAVEL OFFICE** CTS, Via S. Antonio 2 (Tel. 02 5830 4121)

## SEEING

For those of you sightseeing for a day, invest in a one-day tourist ticket costing around 5,000L for unlimited travel on buses, trams and the underground. Tickets are available from the Duomo underground station and the Central FS and Cordorna underground stations. You can also buy a book of ten tickets for 14,000L. Otherwise, single fare tickets cost 1,500L and must be purchased in advance, they can be bought from tobacconists, bars and metro station newsagents.

The centre of Milan is the Piazza del Duomo, where you'll find the **Cathedral** (*Duomo*), the third largest church in Europe. This is where Versace's funeral took place in 1997. Ascend to the roof for the view (stairs 6,000L; lift 8,000L). Remember to dress modestly.

The **Museo del Duomo** is on the right as you face the Duomo (open Tues.–Sun. 9.30am–12.30pm and 3–6pm. Admission 8,000L).

The famous opera house, **La Scala**, with its perfect acoustics, has been the scene of many a Verdi premiere, and there's a museum there showing costumes, manuscripts and other operatic memorabilia. It's north of the Duomo, through the gallery, on Piazza della Scala (open 9am–12noon, 2pm–5.30pm, entrance 6,000L).

In 1995, Leonardo's masterpiece, *Last Supper*, was restored, however it still looks worse for wear after centuries of damage from floods and bombing. To see for yourself, go to the convent next to **Santa Maria delle Grazie** (warning: they charge 12,000L to see it unless you are under 18). The **Museum of Science and Technology**, Via S. Vittore 21, is worth visiting to see the complete aircraft and ships as well as working models of Leonardo's inventions. Open all day except Mon., entrance costs 10,000L.

The **Brera Palace** and **Art Gallery** on Via Brera is Milan's finest gallery. Housed in the palace is a varied collection of Italian art and a library of books and manuscripts (open Tues.–Sat.: 9am–9.45pm; Sun. 9am–12.45pm and 2.30–7.45pm; closed Mon., entrance costs 8,000L, or is free to EU residents under the age of 18; wheelchair access). The **Poldi-Pezzoli Museum** is a private collection with some rare sculptures and tapestries (closed Mon., open Apr.–Sept. Tues.–Fri.: 9.30am–12.30pm and 2.30–6pm; Sat.: 9.30am–12.30pm and 2.30–7.30pm; Sun.: 9.30am–12.30pm; Oct.–Mar. Tues.–Fri.: 9.30am–12.30pm and 2.30–6pm; Sat.: 9.30am–12.30pm and 2.30–7.30pm; Sun.: 9.30am–12.30pm and 2.30–6pm. Entrance 10, 000L), Via Manzoni 12.

**FREE MILAN:**

- The **Museum of Antique Art** is housed in **Sforza Castle** (closed Mon., entrance is free). It can be reached by underground from Centrale station. Among its collection is Michelangelo's *Rondanini Pietá*, his last, unfinished work. Enter from Corte Ducale, Piazza Castello.

- Behind the castle is the **Sempione Park**.
- Fans of medieval architecture should not miss **Sant'Ambrogio Basilia**, which houses religious treasures, including a jewel-studded altar and mosaics from the 5th century.
- On the **feast day of St Ambrose**, 7 December, the church is the centre of a lively festival, with the streets around it crammed with market stalls.
- Close to Piazza del Duomo is the church of **San Satiro** – another must for anyone interested in architecture and the Renaissance style.
- The **Cathedral** (*Duomo*) at Piazza del Duomo is well worth seeing, even if you don't fancy climbing the 158 steps to the view from its roof (for which there's a charge).
- At the central crossroads in the **Gallerie del Duomo** (just north of the Duomo, on Piazza della Scala) is a little hole in the floor. If you place your heel in it and spin around it is meant to bring you luck for the coming year!
- Milan's style centre is the clutch of streets beyond the Duomo. At the boutiques on **Via Monte Napoleone**, **Via Manzoni**, **Via della Spiga** and **Via Sant'Andrea**, you can ogle at the best efforts of the fashion world, but prices are so ludicrous you'll only be window shopping.
- For something a little more affordable, check out the **open-air market** on Viale Papiniano on Tuesday and Saturday mornings.

## SLEEPING

There are plenty of suitable places just north or west of the station, you shouldn't have a problem finding somewhere to stay except during an international trade fair, when lodgings of any sort are difficult to come by. Accommodation is on the expensive side, if you manage to find a single room in a half-decent place for under 52,000L you've done well. The Tourist Office will help you out if you've hit a fluke blackspot, or refer to *Cheap Sleeps Europe 2000*.

The **Piero Rotta** youth hostel, Via Martino Bassi 2 (Tel. 02 3926 7095), open 7am–9pm, 4pm–12.30am, is half an hour away by metro (Line 1, direction Molino Dorino, get off at QT8) and allows three days' stay maximum. Dorm bed and breakfast costs 24,000L including sheets and shower. IYHF card-holders only. You can only check in between 4pm and 11pm and you must leave by 9am the following morning. It is clean, efficient and unfriendly.

Single women under 25 may want to try the nun-run **Protezione della Giovane** at Corso Garibaldi 123. Beds from 38,000L. Tel. 02 2900 0164.

Affordable places near the station include **Albergo Salerno**, Via Vitruvio 18 (Tel. 02 204 6870), which charges around 50,000L for a single; 80,000L for a double. The **Italia** on the same street at no. 44 charges about the same but the rooms are not as nice (Tel. 02 669 3826).

The **Hotel Nuovo** (Tel. 02 8646 0542) at Piazza Beccaria 6 is in a great central location, near the Corso Vittorio Emanuele II. Doubles for around 85,000L. Also try the **Hotel San Tommaso** at Via Tunisia 6 (Tel./Fax. 02 2951 4747). Doubles around 92,000L. Slightly cheaper is the **Hotel San Marco**, at 25 Via Piccinni (Tel. 02 204 9536/02 2951 6414).

For **camping**, head for **Campeggio Autodromo di Monza** (Tel. 039 387771); open Apr.–Sept.; take a train to Monza (11 minutes) from Centrale station and catch a bus. It's full of motor-racing buffs due to the nearby track.

## EATING AND NIGHTLIFE

The secret of Milanese cooking is that they use butter (not olive oil, as they do elsewhere in Italy). Try some local dishes, and see if you can discern the difference – though, with the amount of money knocking about Milan, locals tend to eat out a lot, so restaurants are more expensive here than elsewhere. If you want to go up-market without paying up-market prices, try **Pane e Farina** at Via Pantano 6 (Tel. 02 869 3274).

**Street markets** are scattered throughout the city and generally open Tue., Thurs. and Sat., providing all the ingredients for picnics. The station area is not good for restaurants, so take the metro to the centre. For a cheap meal near the centre, try the **Spizzico Pizza Bars**. There are plenty of cheap places in the Via Marghera area.

**Flash** in Via Bergamini (near the Duomo) serves good-value sandwiches and pizzas. Students at the Université degli Studi di Milano recommend the pizza place opposite their University main entrance on Piazza Sant'Alessandro (good pizza at good prices, nearest metro stop is Missori).

Ice-cream lovers should head for Milan's most famous *gelateria*: **Viel Gelati** on Via Lucia Beltrami, open Thurs.–Tues. until 2am. A cheaper alternative is **Viel** on Via Marconi 3E, next to the Tourist Office.

For a good night out in the Navigli district take the metro (Green line) to Sant'Ambrogio. This area is full of pubs, bars and jazz music. For an interesting evening and a closer look at Milan's transvestite community, try **Scimmie**, a jazz fusion club, at Via Ascanio Sforza 49. **Elefante** is one of Milan's gay clubs. For pubs try **Giamaica** at Via Brera and for rock/disco try **Rainbow** and **Grandi Magazzini**, both of which feature live music.

# Emilia-Romagna

This is the region from the lower Po valley to the Apennine mountains north of Tuscany. Its name derives from the Roman Road, Via Emilia, built in 187 BC from Rimini on the Adriatic Sea to Piacenza on the upper Po River. Emilia Romagna has the richest cuisine in Italy: it is here that tortellini, tagliatelle, Bolognese sauce, Parma ham and Parmesan cheese originated.

Built on the Emilian Way, **Parma** is known for its architectural and gastronomic delights. The old town centre is **Piazza Garibaldi**, with the **Town Hall**, **Clock Tower** and **Governor's Palace**. The **Duomo** is Romanesque and on its cupola is Correggio's *Assumption of the Virgin Mary*, while the striking red marble **Baptistery** is another famous feature. The **Historical Pharmacy of St John** (in Piazza di San Giovanni) features some early decorative work of Parmigianino. In contrast, the **Madonna della Steccata** (just off Piazza Garibaldi) has the painter's last work for his home town: he was imprisoned twice for failing to meet the deadline for completion of the frescoes.

The **Palazzo della Pilotta** has been restored since its Second World War bombing to become the city's museum and the **National Gallery** reviews the school established by Correggio as well as the medieval-Renaissance Italian works.

**Tourist Information** (*Azienda Promozione Turistica*) is available at Via Melloni 1b (Tel. 0521 234735/0521 218889) and a **youth hostel** at 5 Parco Cittadella (Tel. 0521 961434: it's advisable to phone in advance). The only **campsite** near Parma is in the same location as the hostel. Like the hostel, it allows only three days' maximum stay and both are open Apr.–Oct.

**Ferrara** was once an independent duchy ruled by the dukes of Este, in whose courts flowered some of the most gifted philosophers, artists and writers of the Renaissance period. The **Castello Estense** fortress, surrounded by a moat and complete with dungeons and a chapel, is open to the public. The **Palazzo Schifanola**, in Via Scandiana, is where the dukes went for amusement; it's now a museum; the archaeological museum is in the Renaissance **Palazzo di Ludovico Il Moro,** currently undergoing restoration. The town's **Cathedral** stands opposite the **Palazzo Comunale**. Today the town is an agricultural and industrial centre.

**Camp** at **Campeggio Comunale Estense** on Via Gramicia (Tel. 0532 752396), open Easter–Oct. Take bus 11. The **Tourist Office** is at Castello Estense 21, inside the central castle.

In the 5th-century, the Byzantine Empire made its western capital at **Ravenna**. The town was also the birthplace of Christian iconography. The high spot of Ravenna is a visit to the 6th-century **Church of Sant'Apollinare in Classe** (bus 4 or 44 from the station). Back in town, **San Vitale Basilica**, the octagonal church, contains some mosaics, but the **Tomb of Galla Placidia** has the best in Ravenna. The poet Dante is buried in the grounds of the **Church of San Francesco**.

Ravenna is a well-heeled town with a higher calibre of tourist! The **Tourist Office** at Via Salara 8 (Tel. 0544 35404) will supply maps, information and help with accommodation. There is also video information round the corner on Via S. Vitale.

There's a youth hostel, **Dante**, on Via Aurelio Nicolodi 12 (Tel. 0544 421164), open April–Oct. It's good, 20,000L for dorm bed and breakfast, and reached by bus 1–11. Cheap hotels include the **Albergo Al Giaciglio** at Via Rocco Brancaleone 42 (Tel. 0544 39403).(Singles from 35,000L; doubles 55,000L), and the **Ravenna** at Via Marconcelli 12 (Tel. 0544 212204), near the station.

For **camping**, head to **Marina di Ravenna** in Via delle Nazioni, or further along the coast to **Camping Classe** out at the Lido di Dante, which is extremely friendly and serves cheap food. Be warned, the mosquitoes are vicious, the campsites are not cheap (though most include tennis courts and swimming facilities) and transport to and from the town is difficult because bus services are poor.

Near the hostel is the Coop Supermarket and **Chiosca Piodina Romangnola** which serves *piodina*, kind of grilled, open-top sandwiches. The student refectory is at 8 Via Oberdan but arrive as early as 11.45am. If you want a quick meal, try **Free Flow Bizantino** next to the main fruit and veg. market, in Piazza Andrea Costa.

# Bologna

Important crossroads for rail and road, one of the oldest university towns in Europe, a Renaissance city of culture and learning, birthplace of Bolognese sauce (where would students the world over be without it?), and today as red as Moscow was. This is where some Eurorailers met a tragic death in 1980 when the station was bombed. It has since been rebuilt on the northern edge of Bologna. Trains run to Florence, Venice, Rome, Vienna, Sicily and other destinations.

## TOURIST INFORMATION AND ADDRESSES

Apart from the one at the station, there are offices at Piazza

Maggiore 6 and Via Marconi 45 (Tel. 051 239660). General siesta-time is 12.30pm–3.30pm. They'll help out on accommodation (they book rooms for free) as well as providing the usual services.

**POST OFFICE** Piazza Minghetti, Mon.–Fri.: 8.15am–6.30pm, Sat.: 8.15am–12.20pm. (Tel. 051 260932)

**STUDENT TRAVEL OFFICE** CTS, Largo Respighi 21F (Tel. 051 261802)

**24-HOUR CHEMIST** Tel. 192. Late-night chemists are also at the train station and at Piazza Maggiore 6

**AMEX** Via Indipendenza 12 (Tel. 051 238411)

## SEEING

It is worth coming here just to enjoy the porticoes which line all the main streets of the city. The main street is **Via Rizzoli**. At one end is the pedestrianized **Piazza Ravesnana**, where the Garisenda and Asinelli towers can be admired, or climbed. At the other end is the **Piazza Maggiore**, which on Sun. becomes the site of puppet theatre shows. You can't miss the **Basilica of St Petronius** – it's huge. Seven churches join into another conglomeration at the **Basilica Santo Stefano**. The courtyard behind one of the churches has the **Basin of Pilate** where Pontius Pilate is said to have washed his hands when symbolically absolving himself of responsibility for Christ's death.

## SLEEPING, EATING AND NIGHTLIFE

The scope isn't huge in Bologna for budget beds, especially since the **youth hostels** are about six km from the city at San Sisto, Via Viadagola 14 (Tel. 051 519202). To get there take bus 20 or 93 from Via de' Mille or Via Irnerio (the main road running parallel to the train station on the right). This hostel charges 18,000L for bed and breakfast. The second IYHF hostel further up the road, **Le Torri San Sisto 2**, at number 5 (Tel./Fax. 051 501810), is a bit more expensive at 20,000L; both are open late Jan.–mid Dec.

Some alternatives are **Apollo** (Tel. 051 223955), Via Drapperie 5 (off Via Rizzoli), where single rooms cost 55,000L and doubles 95,000L; **Garisenda**, Galleria del Leone 1 (Tel. 051 224369); or **Albergo Panorama**, Via Livraghi 1, off Via Ugo Bassi, (Tel. 051 221802; Fax. 051 266360). On the 4th floor, great views; friendly management; incredibly clean. Doubles around 98,000L.

If you are arriving late, check outside the station's Tourist Office, where they post up-to-the-minute accommodation vacancies after hours.

In contrast, finding a great place to eat is a doddle: the cooking everywhere is terrific and cheap, and it's almost unheard of to have a bad meal. Vegetarians should head for **Centro Naturista Bolognese** in Via degli Albani 6 or **Ristorante Clorofilla** on Strada Maggiore and though there is a university refectory, this is one place it'd be a shame to use, as there are so many family-run *trattorie*. For a variety of restaurants near the station, bear left across the main road and enter the courtyard there.

In the evening the young crowd hang out around **Piazza Maggiore**. To reach the Piazza from the station, take the bus if you are short of time, as it is about a mile to walk. Bologna's city council encourages **open-air raves**, where entrance is either free or very cheap. The summer arts festival, **Bologna Sogna**, involves everyone taking to the hills for all-night revelry. For information on what's happening, look out for posters advertising events, especially around the university quarter.

## Liguria (The Italian Riviera)

Known as the Italian Riviera, this narrow coastal strip stretches east from the French Côte d'Azur to the hills of Tuscany. It's a lot less flashy than the French Riviera, and cheaper too. **Genoa** is the main town, though it's one of Italy's most important ports rather than a typical sunseeker's hangout (see below).

There's a good and picturesque rail line serving the Riviera, starting at Marseille in France, passing through the border at Ventimiglia and going on to Bordighera, San Remo, Albenga and Genoa.

Rather than staying on the Côte d'Azur, you may wish to stop on the Italian side of the border at **Ventimiglia**. Worth checking out are the **Hotel XX Settembre**, Via Roma 16 (Tel. 0184 351 222) or the **Hotel Regina**, Corso Genova 39. There's a nice campsite, **Camping Roma**, at Via Peglia 5 (Tel. 0184 239009; Fax. 0184 239035), which has a bar and market nearby. Open Apr.–Sept. The **Tourist Office** is at Via Cavour 61 (Tel. 0184 351183).

**Bordighera** is an attractive resort which prides itself on its abundant palm trees (the town supplies the Vatican with fronds for Palm Sunday). It was a favourite among European royals in the 19th century. The oldest part of the town is on the hill, and below is the new town. Prices here tend to be high, so (although the police aren't keen on this practice) try sleeping on the beach and avoid restaurants without fixed menus. In late July and August, the town presents the Salone Internazionale Umorismo, a comedy festival, with performances in the Palazzo del Parco. Ask at the Tourist Office, Via Roberto 1, for more information (Tel. 0184 262322).

The Italian Riviera's largest resort is **San Remo**, but unless you've money to burn in the casino, stick to the beach. There are plenty of pizzerias and cafés, but this resort is one of the most commercialized and is not recommended too highly. If you do decide to stay, the Tourist Office at Largo Nuvoloni 1 (Tel. 0184 571571) can help you find accommodation. At the end of every February there is a song festival important enough to have attracted guests like David Bowie and the Spice Girls!

One of the best beaches in the area is at **Alassio**. The old town used to be the haunt of the wealthy British. Check out the wall signed by a host of celebrities. Off the sand, tennis, golf and skiing are favourite pastimes. Just off this stretch of the coast you'll find the island of **Gallinara**, which was once a haven for monks. For further information, the Tourist Office is on Viale Gibbi 26 (Tel. 0182 647027).

At **Albenga** you can visit the **Roman Naval Museum** and see the remains of a Roman ship sunk in the 1st century BC. Today Albenga is a market town and is more down to earth than many of the surrounding resorts, though it boasts a wealth of cathedrals and churches that outline its artistic, architectural and historical development over the centuries.

Two **campsites** lie to the west of Albenga: **Camping Delfino** (Tel. 0182 51998), which is open all year round, and **Camping Sant'Anna** (Tel. 0182 640702), closed Nov.–Mar.

# Genoa (Genova)

Genoa, birthplace of Christopher Columbus and the city where Marco Polo was kept a prisoner of war in 1298, is the largest port of northern Italy. It became an artistic centre in the 16th and 17th centuries, when Flemish masters, including Rubens and Van Dyck, came to paint the portraits of the town's wealthy merchants. Their palaces can still be seen in the Renaissance upper town. There's also a medieval harbour quarter, and the **Circonvallazione a Monte**, a boulevard which winds its way in and out of the hills.

## STATION FACILITIES

Genoa has two stations: the Porta Principe (main station) and Brignole. Trains bound for the north use Principe, trains heading south use Brignole. Through-trains stop at both, except for those going northwest (Milan–Nice) – they use only Principe. There are trains connecting the two stations regularly. Train information, (Tel. 010 2741) from 7am–11pm. Left-luggage 6am–10pm, 5,000L for 12 hours.

Daily trains to Frankfurt, Milan (1½ hours), Venice (4½ hours), Turin (two hours), Bologna (three hours), Florence (4½ hours), Rome (5½ hours), Naples and Nice (three hours).

## TOURIST INFORMATION AND ADDRESSES

**APT** on Porto Antico, Palazzina S. Maria, to the left of the aquarium. (Tel. 010 24871; open daily 9am–6.30pm). There is a branch office at Via Roma 11 (Tel. 010 576791); open Mon.–Fri.: 8am–1.15pm and 2pm–6.30pm, Sat.: 8am–1.30pm. There is also an office at Principe station (Tel. 010 246 2633). **Informagiovani** in Palazzo Ducale (open Tues.–Fri. 10am–1pm and 3–6pm) has great maps and information on events and what to do in the city.

**POST OFFICE** Piazza Dante 4, Via Rela 8. Open Mon.–Sat. 8.10am–7.40pm

**UK CONSULATE** P. della Vittoria 15 (Tel. 010 553 1516)

**US CONSULATE** Via Dante 2 (Tel. 010 584492; on the 3rd floor)

**24-HOUR CHEMIST** Dial 192

## SEEING

Genoa's a confusing city so make sure you have a detailed city map - if you haven't already got one, your first port of call should be Informegiovanni, see Information above. Via Balbi, running east from the main station, is a fine example of Old Genoa and is also the site of the **Palazzo Reale Fine Art Gallery**. In the historical centre of the city, visit the **Duomo San Lorenzo**, off Piazza Matteot.

There are 17 museums and galleries, but **Galleria di Palazzo Bianco** and **Galleria di Palazzo Rosso**, both on Via Garibaldi, are the cream of the crop. The former contains a superb Flemish collection and the latter displays works by many famous masters such as Tintoretto, Caravaggio and Van Dyck. (Both galleries are open Tues. and Thurs.–Fri.: 9am–1pm; Wed. and Sat.: 9am–7pm; Sun.: 10am–6pm. Entry to one costs 6,000L, to both 10,000L. Free on Sun.). Other cultural sites worth a visit are the gallery and frescoes of **Palazzo Cataldi** and the antiquities in **Palazzo Doria Tursi**. The **Museo d'Arte Orientale 'E.Chiossone'** houses a wonderful collection of Japanese and Chinese paintings and artefacts, including 1,000 engraved Japanese sabres (open Tues. and Thurs.–Sun.: 9am–1pm; 6,000L).

Around the east of the harbour, the Via San Lorenzo leads past the **Cathedral** of the same name into Piazza de' Ferrari. Beyond this square Via Dante leads past the main post office to Piazza Dante and the site of **Christopher Columbus's childhood home**. Further north, along Via Antonio Gramsci, is the poverty-stricken district of **Pré**, which is worth a visit – but not after dark! Near the port, the **Aquarium** is the biggest in Europe.

## SLEEPING, EATING AND NIGHTLIFE

The **campsites** are unpleasant; you're better off heading down the coast to the towns of Riviera di Levante if you want to camp. Otherwise, the **International Youth hostel Genova** in Via Costanzi 120 (Tel./Fax. 010 242 2457) charges from 22,000L per night for bed and breakfast and is situated three km from the station. Take bus 40 from P. Delba Nunziata. Good facilities and helpful staff. To stay here you must be a member but don't panic if you're not as you can buy membership on site.

Alternatively, try the **Pensione Mirella**, Via Gropallo 4/4 (Tel. 010 839 3722), which charges around 70,000L for doubles. Ask at the tourist offices for more options.

Regional specialities are *cima genovese* (stuffed cold veal) and *pandolce* (orange-flavoured cake). There are scores of pizzerias and restaurants, and the prices all seem very much on a level, but we recommend **Emma's Trattoria** in Piazza de Serraglio.

## Veneto

This region encompasses the north-eastern Po valley from the Dolomites to the coastal resorts. It is the site of the city many consider to be the most beautiful in the world: Venice. Close by are the art towns of Padua, Verona and Treviso, and Lake Garda is a stretch of azure water in the foothills of the Alps nearby. Trains from Verona stop at Peschiera and Desenzano, and there are numerous campsites in both towns.

## Venice (Venezia)

The first sight of Venice, as you leave the train station, is enough to take your breath away. Nothing you could ever read could quite prepare you for the impact of being deposited bang in the middle of a setting no other city in the world can rival. Your first view from the top of the station steps will be of boatmen poling their way up the palace-lined Grand Canal: with the sun glinting off reflections on the water, it's the best introduction to Venice you could possibly have.

The city is built on 118 islets connected by 400 bridges, with 150 canals winding their way through the maze. There are no cars, only boats. Venice in the summer is choked with crowds and prices are hugely inflated, but even if you can't avoid peak season, it is all worth it, because this is one city you'll never forget.

It was here that Casanova, the world's most famous lover, lived and partied – and was denounced as a spy. In 1755, he was imprisoned in the attics of the Ducal Palace, but the following year managed to escape to Paris, where he continued to indulge a bottomless appetite for food and women, before being pardoned and returning to Venice 20 years later.

Venice's palaces and multitude of churches reflect its glorious past when, as an independent city-state, it ruled over most of the Mediterranean. During the Renaissance, Venice was the trading port with the Middle East, and became the centre of European commerce. The doges (the city rulers) were wealthy enough not only to build sumptuous residences and dozens of churches, but also to commission large-scale works of art from the Venetian school – the likes of Titian and Tintoretto – and patronize the sciences too. Their 1,000-year independence came to an end in 1797 when Napoleon gave Venice to the Austrians. When Italy was united, Venice joined, and its popularity as a tourist trap of the 20th century has brought it new wealth, much of which is used to prevent the entire city sinking and being lost for ever.

## STATION FACILITIES

The main station is called Santa Lucia. It is a very busy station with full amenities including showers and left luggage, though allow extra time to queue! (Tel. 041 78 51 11).

Some trains stop only at Venezia-Mestre on the mainland, so check. To reach Venezia-Santa Lucia from Mestre, there are both trains and buses. The station is situated at the west end of the town, right on the Grand Canal. It's possible to go everywhere by foot, but it's more fun to take the *vaporetti* (waterbuses) from outside the station. Nos 1 and 34 take you down the Grand Canal to San Marco Square. No. 2, which is the faster, limited-stop service, takes you to San Marco and Lido following the Giudecca canal route.

Trains run regularly to Padua (½ hour), Milan (three hours), Florence (three hours), Bologna (two hours) and Rome (four–five hours).

## TOURIST INFORMATION

The Tourist Office in the station (Tel. 041 719078) handles accommodation and gives out free maps (not very good). It's always very busy so your best bet is to head for the central Tourist Office (APT) near San Marco Square on Palazzeto Selva (Tel. 041 522 6356). However, they will not help with accommodation. In high season, there's also an office in the Lido at Gran Viale 6a.

The student Tourist Office (CTS) is at Dorsoduro 3252 (Tel. 041 520 5660); they'll help you out with accommodation and student travel.

It's advisable to fix up accommodation before you arrive as the queues in the tourist offices are terrible. All APT offices are outlets for the useful youth discount card, called the Rolling Venice Card, (*carta giovane*). The card costs around 5,000L and gives discounts at hotels, museums, restaurants and on the three-day waterbus pass, see below, to those aged 14–29.

## ADDRESSES

**POST OFFICE** Salizzada Fondego dei Tedeschi, near the eastern side of the Rialto Bridge. Telephone office here also. Mon.–Sat.: 8.15am –7pm. Also at San Marco Square, opposite the basilica

**AMEX** 1471 San Marco. Mon.–Fri.: 9am–5.30pm, Sat.: 9am–12.30pm

**UK CONSULATE** Dorsoduro 1051 (Tel. 041 522 7207)

**EURAIL AID OFFICE** Santa Lucia station (Tel. 041 715 555)

**EMERGENCIES** Tel. 113

**FIRST AID** Tel. 118

**STUDENT TRAVEL OFFICE** CTS, Dorso Duro Ca'Foscari 3252 (Tel. 041 520 5660)

## GETTING ABOUT

Gondolas look beautiful, but at 120,000L plus an hour it's not surprising few Eurorailers use them. Walking and waterbus are the only budget options (water taxis are expensive). The waterbuses cover all Venice. A trip on bus 1 or 82 is good, as it takes in quite a few sights down the Grand Canal. They run frequently and fares are around the 5,000L mark. A 24-hour pass (*biglietto turistico 24 ore*) costs 15,000L. A three-day pass is also available at 30,000L (20,000L if you have a Rolling Venice Card). Remember to validate your ticket, failure to do so or travelling without a ticket can result in a hefty fine. There are also a few buses, but their routes are restricted.

## SEEING

No wonder Venice's famous son Marco Polo was so good at exploring – Venice is the easiest place in Europe in which to get lost. There are so many winding back-streets and alleys, unexpected quiet squares and little hump-back bridges that you really can't do without a map. Highly recommended tools for getting about in Venice include the red storti-Edizioni Foligrat *Mestre-Venezia* map and the English–Italian magazine *Un Ospite di Venezia (A Guest in Venice)*, which gives up-to-date information on exhibitions, special events and *vaporetto* timetables.

Venice is divided into six main districts, and each district (or *sestiere*) can have duplicate street names, so be sure to *which* district your required street belongs. Streets do not possess individual numbers, but a *sestiere* number, which can go up to 6,000, but not in any obvious logical pattern.

The following are some of the most unmissable sights (reduced rates apply to those under 18 and those over 60, unless stated otherwise):

- **St Mark's Square (Piazza San Marco)**: Venice revolves round this incredible piazza. **St Mark's Basilica** and the **Doges' Palace** are here, as are the **Law Courts**, the beautiful **Moors' Clock Tower** and the **Old Library**, now an archaeological museum. Follow the sign posts to walk here from the station.
- **St Mark's Basilica**: This amazing Byzantine church is a riot of gold, marble and mosaic. (Women: bring a shawl to cover your shoulders and arms; men: wear long trousers to be let in.) It was originally the chapel for the doges, and became the city cathedral in 1807. Do not miss the Bronze Horses or the Scala d'Oro. Climb up the basilica for a grand view.
- **Doges' Palace (Palazzo Ducale)**: This pink-and-white fairytale palace was the home of the Venetian government and the rulers of the republic. Admission 17,000L, reduced rate 10,000L (includes entrance to the Museo Correr and other sites). The connecting bridge between the palace and the prison is known as the **Bridge of Sighs**. You can book to go on a Secret Itineraries Tour, through the palace, over the bridge and through the prison. Call 041 522 4951, reservations essential. The tours are only in Italian and cost 10,000L, reduced price 6,000L.
- Take the lift up the **Campanile** (8,000L) for a view you'll never forget. Remember your map and you can study the city and islands laid out below you.
- **The Academy of Fine Art (Galleria dell'Accademia)** has the best of the Venetian school's work: Canaletto, Tintoretto, Bellini, Veronese, etc. Closed Mon. Entrance costs 13,000L and there are no ISIC reductions. Tel. 041 522 2247.
- **Basilica dei Frari**: After St Mark's, this is Venice's most prized church. It houses two Titians and a Bellini. Next to it is the **Scuola di San Rocco**, with a collection of 56 Tintorettos on biblical themes. Entrance costs 8,000L (6,000L for reductions).
- **School of St George**: Beyond St Mark's Square at Calle dei Furlani, this beautiful museum offers a frieze of paintings by Carpaccio, and is usually much quieter than the other museums. Entrance costs 7,000L (reduced rate 5,000L). Closed Monday.
- **Guggenheim Gallery**: A modern art gallery with an excellent, **extensive choice of Surrealist works. Open Sun.–Mon. and**

Wed.–Fri.: 11am–6pm; Sat.: 6–9pm; closed Tues. Admission 12,000L, ISIC or rolling Venice card 8,000L.

**FREE VENICE:** The citizens of Venice charge quite steeply for admission to their greatest treasures, but the good news is that art, history, beauty and atmosphere are part of the very fabric of this city. The two most famous landmarks, **St Mark's Square** and the **Rialto Bridge** over the Grand Canal, are two prime examples.

- The **Rialto Bridge** can be reached via Salizzada San Giovanni Crisostomo. The view from it down the Grand Canal, especially at dawn and sunset, is postcard perfect.
- Cross the Rialto Bridge to get to the famous waterside **Rialto Market**. Tues.–Sat. mornings are best; by early afternoon, things are winding down, and on Mondays there's no fish market. With a huge variety of stalls selling fresh produce, this is the best place to stock up on picnic provisions.
- Remember, the **churches** generally charge no admission, and they're often full of works of art by Italian masters. Three well worth visiting are: **St Mark's Basilica** (an absolute must); **Santi Giovanni e Paolo** (also called San Zanipolo), a huge Dominican church where 25 doges are buried; **Santa Maria dei Miracoli**, on Campo dei Miracoli (off Calle Castelli).
- A few streets away from the 'sights' is the quieter, less touristy western side of Venice. It's a great place to go to escape the hordes and just sit in a square or by a canal watching a gondola go by.

**FESTIVALS** During the first two weeks of Feb., see Venice's famous Masked Carnival, and on the third Sat. of July, there's the **Festa del Redentore** (including an hour-long firework show). If you are in Venice in the last week of Aug. and the first week of Sept., make the most of the International Film Festival and stay around for the **Regata Storica** – a pageant of beautiful boats down the Grand Canal on the first Sun. in Sept.

**EXCURSIONS** Just east of Venice lies the **Lido**, the beach resort of the rich and famous. Also worth a trip are the islands of **Murano** (ferry 12 from Fondamente Nove), where Venetian glass is blown (but buy it in Venice itself as prices on Murano are even more inflated); **Burano**, a colourful little fishing island; and **Torcello** with its Byzantine cathedral.

## SLEEPING

Accommodation in Venice is no more expensive now than in Rome or Paris. The area near the station is as good as anywhere to look. Watch out for hotel guides offering 'cheap' rooms at the station: some are not as good a bargain as they seem. If all else fails, take the train to Mestre, eight minutes away, and base yourself there where bed and food are cheaper. It is illegal to sleep in railway stations in Italy and you are likely to have a hose trained on you and end up soaked if you try it.

In high summer, seriously consider travelling to Padua for accommodation. It's only 30 minutes by train from Santa Lucia station and there is a regular service. Accommodation is much cheaper there, even in the summer, but you are strongly advised to book (and arrive) well in advance, as there can be an unwillingness to hold cheap rooms until your time of arrival if demand is high. Refer to *Cheap Sleeps Europe 2000* for further options.

**HOSTELS** The **youth hostel** is on the island of Giudecca at Fondamenta Zitelle 86 (Tel. 041 523 8211; Fax. 041 523 5689); take the waterbuses 5 and 84 from the landing stage along from the Piazza San Marco. Open Feb.–Dec., no phone bookings. Reception is closed between 9.30am and 1pm (11pm curfew). Expect to pay 27,000L for bed and breakfast.

Also out here are a few **pensions** and a religious hostel (women only), **Istituto Canossiane**, Ponte Piccolo 428 (Tel. 041 522 2157); curfew 10.30pm. To get there, take waterbus 5 to Sant'Eufemia, and walk to your left when you get off. Reception opens at 4pm and it's around 20,000L each for a dorm bed.

More expensive is the **Istituto Ciliota** at San Marco 2976 (Tel. 041 520 4888), which caters for women and married couples only. To get there take *vaporetto* 2 to San Samuele. A double room costs in the region of 70,000L. **Domus Civica** (ACISJF), at San Polo 3082, (Tel. 041 721103/041 524 0416) between the Basilica dei Frari and P. Roma, is a church-affiliated hostel. Good facilities, doubles from 70,000L. Rolling Venice or ISIC cards give 20% reductions. Curfew 11.30pm. Reserve ahead. Only open mid-June–Sept.

**CAMPSITES** Head for the Jesolo Peninsula and the Litorale del Cavallino, where there are lots of beach campsites. Take *vaporetto* 14 from near San Marco to Punta Sabbioni. **Camping Miramare** (Tel. 041 966 150), open Feb.–Nov., is neat and clean and offers four-person cabins for 58,000L to those without tents. **Marina di Venezia** (Tel. 041 530 0955), Via Montello 6 at Punta Sabbioni is another good one. Open April–Sept.

There is also an expensive year-round site at Fusina in Via Moranzani (Tel. 041 547 0055), which you can get to by waterbus in summer (no.16) or road bus no.13 from the railway bridge near Mestre station, though reports differ as to cleanliness. It costs

10,500L per person and 7,500L per tent. Don't forget mosquito repellent. Call ahead.

**Camping Rialto** at Via Orlanda, Mestre, is open May–Sept. There are also two sites out by the airport but they are expensive and not particularly nice.

**HOTELS AND PENSIONS** If you are travelling alone, find a partner quick, or head for a hostel, as a single room will cripple you financially. There are many cheap pensions in the Lista di Spagna near the station. **Albergo Adua**, at 233a Cannaregio (Tel. 041 716184) has doubles from 75,000L, and more rooms in a building nearby.

**Locanda Ca' Foscari**, Dorsoduro 3887 1B (Tel. 041 710401; Fax. 041 710817) is clean and reasonably priced, on Calle della Frescarda near the university..

Near the Mestre station, at Via Parini 4, there are lots of affordable places. A friendly welcome and attractive rooms are offered at **Col di Lana** (signposted from just outside Mestre station). The one-star **Albergo Giovannina** at Via Dante 113 (Tel. 041 926396) has doubles from 90,000L.

## EATING AND NIGHTLIFE

The golden rule here is: the fewer tourists, the cheaper it will be. So, unless you're feeling particularly flush, don't have a coffee in St Mark's Square, head off the beaten track. Also be wary of grabbing a cuppa or sandwich just outside the stations as the stalls tend to pump up their prices, don't get tempted by the inviting aromas – food and drink a few minutes further on is half the price.

Use Rialto Market at the foot of the Rialto bridge in the mornings, and in the evenings there are a few street stalls selling fruit and veg. in the main pedestrian streets at night, including near Campo SS. Lunardo, towards the Santa Lucia train station. Look out for the many tiny delicatessens selling huge varieties of cheeses, hams, salamis, breads and olives. In many of these, you can get sandwiches to order (though they're likely to be just a few slices of ham or cheese slapped inside a bread roll). In supermarkets, there's often a deli counter, and these are good places to get hold of some of the local specialities, such as meat-, cheese- and rice-filled pastries, and *tramezzini* – triangular breads stuffed with all sorts.

There are quite a few fixed-price menus, but although the tourist menus might be easiest on your moneybelt, they're not really good value. Your best chance of a good deal is around the university area in Dorsoduro. Try **Da Silvio** at Crosera San Pantalon 3817 which is a good-value trattoria/pizzeria.

The city seems to go to bed incredibly early and after midnight there is a distinct lack of places to go. Your best bet is to head to the area around Fondamenta della Misericordia in Cannaregio, near the Ghetto or to studenty Dorsoduro. Keep your eyes open for bars and clubs, keep your ear to the ground and keep your money/passport well hidden!

# Verona

Rich in art treasures and Roman remains, Verona is an important farming and business centre, and thousands of music-lovers flock here in the summer for the open-air opera season. But Verona's main claim to fame is as a city for lovers – thanks to Shakespeare, who chose this romantic collection of palaces, churches, gardens and vineyards as the setting for *Romeo and Juliet*.

Midway on the line from Milan to Venice, Verona is a popular destination with Eurorailers who make their base here and travel to Padua and Venice for day trips. From the station, it's a 15-minute walk to the centre of Verona, or take bus 1, 11, 12, 13, 72 or 73 (1,500L per ride, or 4,000L for a day ticket) to the **Piazza Bra**, where the incredibly preserved pink marble **Roman Amphitheatre** should be your first port of call. This is where the opera festival is staged every July and August. There are seats for 22,000, and prices start at about 30,000L, but it's an experience you won't easily forget. A daytime visit to the amphitheatre costs 6,000L or 4,000L for students. Closes mid-afternoon on performance days.

An **Amex** agency is at Corso Porta Nuova 11 (Tel. 045 800 9040). **Tourist information** is at Via Leoncino 61 (Tel. 045 806 8680). The **Veronese Merchants' Palaces** are located in the same square (Piazza della Erbe), and the adjoining **Piazza dei Signori** contains the **Tombs of the Scaligeri**, Verona's medieval enemies. Their house was the **Castelvecchio**, and this fine medieval building (which has been reconstructed after it was destroyed in WWII) is now a showpiece painting and sculpture museum, open Tues.–Sun.: 8am–6pm. Admission is 6,000L (Free the first Sun. of each month). The Romanesque church of **San Zeno Maggiore** is well worth seeing, so is the **Duomo** with its Romanesque doors and Titian's *Assumption*

Juliet's house, **Casa di Giulietta**, is at Via Cappello 23 (6,000L or 4,000L students); it's interesting more because you can see the interior of an old merchant's house rather than for any mythical association with Juliet. You can visit her tomb at the **Museum of Fresco** at Via del Pontiere 5 (5000L, 2,000L students).

**FREE VERONA:**

- You can see **Juliet's balcony** from the cobbled courtyard of her house, *Casa di Giulietta,* at Via Cappello 23, for free (you must pay to get inside the house itself, though). The walls of the entrance archway make amusing reading: they're covered in declarations of teen love, and there's more of the same in books put out to encourage people to 'write a letter to Juliet' rather than add graffiti to the walls. There's a bronze statue of the ill-fated teenager in the courtyard – if you can elbow aside the hordes of over-excited youths, rubbing the breast of Juliet's statue is meant to bring you luck!

- Romeo's house, **Casa di Romeo**, was the home of the famous Montecchi family, on which Shakespeare based his Montagues. It's situated around the corner from P. dei Signori, on Via Arche Scaligeri.

- On Corso Cavour, near Castelvecchio, is the **Arco dei Gavi**, a first-century Roman arch. From here, there's a great view of **Ponte Scaligero**, the bridge that shoots out from the old castle. The 14th-century bridge was blown up by the Germans in 1945, and later rebuilt from the rubble.

  **Note:** Verona's most important churches now charge admission fees (10,000L (students 8,000L) will buy a ticket valid for entry to all of them).

## SLEEPING

The **Ostello Verona hostel** at Salita Fontana del Ferro 15 (Tel. 045 590360) is three km from the station, just across the Ponte Pietra, behind the Teatro Romano; it's inexpensive and well run. Take bus 73 from the station to Piazza Isolo and follow the signs. Or women can try the **Casa della Giovane**, Via Pigna 7 (Tel. 045 596880), who charge from 22,000L for a dorm bed. Advance bookings taken. Curfew 11pm. The **Albergo Castello**, Corso Cavour 43 (Tel. 045 800 4403), offers singles for 90,000L and doubles for 120,000L, with bathrooms. The charming **Locanda Catullo**, at Via Catullo 1 (Tel. 045 800 2786), has doubles from 80,000L. Three nights minimum stay.

Camping is available next to the youth hostel (see above). It costs around 8,000L per person. Call the youth hostel if you want more details (Tel. 045 590360).

## EATING AND NIGHTLIFE

There's a **market** in Piazza delle Erbe, with fruit and veg stalls, and numerous sidewalk eateries lining the sunny side of the square. For cheap set menus, try **Trattoria alla Canna** at Via Scrimiari 5, **Osteria al Cristo** at Piazzetta Pescheria 6, or **Trattoria da Mario**, at Stradone Porta

Palio. Wash the meal down with the local Soave or Valpolicella wine. The noisiest bar in town is **Pub Andy and Miki**, opposite the Ponte di Castelvecchio – so tiny, its trendy patrons spill out into the street.

# Padua (Padova)

Rapid and heavy industrialization has scarred this famous 13th-century university town, but its extraordinary art treasures mean it is worth at least a day's visit. Padua also makes a good base from which to make day trips – accommodation here is much cheaper than Venice, and most of the region's attractions are within easy reach (Venice is only about 30 minutes away by train).

## TOURIST INFORMATION

Pick up maps, hotel listings (no reservations made) and a copy of *Padova Today* and *Where Shall We Go Tonight?* from **Tourist Information** (Tel. 049 875 2077) in the train station (open Mon.–Sat.: 9am–7pm, Sun.: 9am–12.30pm). You can also exchange money here. There is normally only one person working here, so don't be surprised if it shuts at odd times. There is another office at Riviera Mugnai 8, which shuts at 6pm, and yet another at the entrance to the **Museo Civico Eremitani** (same entrance for the Scrovegni chapel) where you can get maps, arrange hotels and change money (open Tues.–Sun.: 9am–7pm).

There's an **Amex** agency at Via Risorgimento 20 (Tel. 049 666133).

A useful item to invest in if you're on a cultural mission in the city is the *Biglietto Unico*, a collective ticket for Padua's museums and monuments. They cost in the region of 15,000L (students 10,000L) and are valid for a whole year. Buy them from the entrance to individual monuments and museums or at the tourist offices.

## SEEING

*The* sight of Padua is the **Cappella degli Scrovegni**, Giotto's masterpiece of medieval art. The chapel is covered from floor to ceiling with incredible frescoes illustrating the life of Jesus, Mary and the story of the Passion in 38 panels. The frescoes are considered to be the world's greatest works of figurative art. Joined to the chapel is the **Museo Civico**, which houses art treasures including work by Giotto and Bellini. Both the chapel and museum are open daily Feb.–Oct. 9am–7pm; Nov.–Jan. 9am–6pm. The museum is closed on Mon. Admission is 10,000L; 7,000L for students.

Further up Corso Garibaldi, on the Via Roma, is the university where Galileo taught physics. The poet Dante also came here. If you visit nothing else in the building of **Palazzo del Bo**, visit the anatomy theatre; this breathtaking construction is the oldest in the world. The **Palazzo della Ragione** (Hall of Justice), next door, keeps a magnificent 14th-century wooden horse and some beautiful frescoes. Entrance is 9,000L (students 7,000L) and it is open Tues.–Sun.: 9am–7pm.

**FREE PADUA:**

- Next door to the Capella degli Scrovegni is the **Chiesa Degli Eremitani**, where there are more magnificent frescoes, this time by the young Mantegna. Have a good look at the carved wooden ceiling. The building is open 8.15am–12 noon, daily.
- The **Scuola Sant'Antonio** contains four Titians also dedicated to St Anthony, who is the patron saint of Padua.
- **Il Santo** (the Basilica di San Antonio) on Piazza del Santo is dedicated to St Anthony (patron saint of lost things), and holds his remains. It has thus become a revered site of pilgrimage.
- Donatello's **Monumento al Gattamelata** (The Calico Cat) is a much-admired bronze statue in the centre of Piazza del Santo.

## SLEEPING

Try the busy, clean and friendly **IYHF Ostello della Città di Padova** at Via Aleardi 30 (Tel. 049 875 2219; Fax. 049 654210). Get there on bus 3 or 8 from the station. Somewhat further out, but worth the hike, is another youth hostel in a **renovated medieval castle**. It's at Porta Legnano in Montagnana (Tel. 0429 81076; Fax. 049 807 0266). Take a local train to Monselice and change for Montagnana. Buy your tickets from the booth here, or at any tobacconist's instead of on the bus.

The nearest **campsite** is in Montegrotto Terme, Via Roma 123 (Tel.049 793400/049 793332), an upmarket site which offers a swimming pool and thermal baths. Take bus M or catch the train to Montegrotto Terme. Open March to Nov.

## EATING

There's an excellent **market**, the Salone, near the university, or try one of the **Mensas** which appear, and rotate, all over the town during the school year. The best one is at 122 Via San Francesco (Tel. 049 660903). They'll be able to give you info. on locations and hours of other mensas. **La Mappe**, Via Matteotti 17, serves decent self-service fare.

# San Marino

On the slopes of Monte Titano, 23 km south-west of Rimini, you enter foreign territory. San Marino is the world's smallest republic (only 61 sq. km). It's also the oldest, having preserved its independence since the 4th century, despite the best efforts of scheming princes and popes. Napoleon was so impressed by its democratic constitution he offered to enlarge the Republic. The offer was turned down – San Marino has never sought to expand but has been regarded as a place of sanctuary ever since it was founded (according to legend) by St Marinus, a Dalmatian stone-cutter fleeing religious persecution. Garibaldi followed in his footsteps, and also once sought sanctuary there.

This unaccountably famous 'toy town' is tacky, full of tourist rip-offs and milks its unique position for all it's worth. You no longer have to wave your passport on the border but you'll probably send postcards with the specially issued San Marino postage stamps (valued by collectors). Beware of getting too much San Marinese currency in your change – it has only souvenir value in the rest of Italy and the lira is valid here anyway.

## GETTING THERE

There are no direct trains, so take the train to Rimini and bus the remaining 23 km. Take the cable car from Borgo Maggiore at the foot of Monte Titano to San Marino (the capital). There are also direct, hourly buses from Rimini train station to the centre of San Marino. (4,000L).

## TOURIST INFORMATION

The Tourist Office in the city of San Marino is on Palazzo del Turismo at Contrada Omagnano 20 (Tel. 0549 882998).

## SLEEPING AND EATING

Make this a day trip rather than an overnight stay, because even the cheapest hotels are extremely expensive and there's no youth hostel. You may find yourself paying over the odds for food, but duty-free drink goes some way to easing the sting.

## SIGHTS

In San Marino city, the **Palazzo del Governo** on the old town's main square – Piazza della Libertà – is a splendid neo-Gothic affair. In front of it is the **Freedom Statue** of San Marino. Just off the square is the neo-classical **Basilica San Marino**. From the Basilica take the road south-east to the three peaks of Monte Titano with their three (rebuilt) medieval tower fortresses. If you've time, have a quick look in either the Garibaldi museum, the stamp and coin museum, the Museum of Weaponry or the intriguingly named Museum of the Incredible but True. In late July there's a medieval festival which consists of all the usual pageantry: dressing up, eating, drinking and being merry. There are parades and musicians and jugglers entertain the crowds. Not to be missed if you're in the area! The National Day of the Republic is celebrated on 3 September with a crossbow competition.

Outside the city, on the border, the medieval village of **Verucchio** has a fortress, the Rocca Malatesta – once the stronghold of Rimini tyrants. There's also a small Archaeology Museum with ceramics dating from 1400 BC. **San Leo**, also a border town, has a particularly fine castle built by the Dukes of Urbino and containing a small picture gallery.

# Tuscany

Tuscany, the birthplace of the Renaissance, is home to some of the finest old cities in the world. Siena and Pisa are medieval, while Florence, the capital, was the centre of the artistic and cultural revolution of the 14th–16th centuries. This is Italy's wealthiest region in every way. The countryside is beautiful, without the south's poverty or the north's heavy industry, there are mountains and coastal beaches, and trains serve even the smallest towns.

# Florence (Firenze)

This is where the Renaissance began, nurtured by the powerful Medici family, and embodied in the work of the artists and thinkers who lived there, including Leonardo, Botticelli, Michelangelo, Galileo and Machiavelli. The legacy lives on in today's Florence, and even the gypsy beggars who prey on tourists in summer can't take away from the centuries of elegance that make the city a place of pilgrimage for art lovers the world over. There are enough churches, galleries, palaces and museums to interest everyone, but there aren't enough beds, so come early to avoid joining the throngs of August station-sleepers who wake to find they've lost more than a good night's sleep – if they haven't been arrested first.

## STATION FACILITIES

Florence Santa Maria Novella station is well-equipped. However, beware of pickpockets and the rates in the foreign exchange office. Left-luggage 5,000L for your rucksack for up to 12 hours. Closed 1.30am–4.15am.

Daily trains within Italy to Venice, Pisa, Rome, Naples, Turin, Bologna and Milan. Daily trains internationally to Geneva, Zürich, Munich, Vienna and Paris.

## TOURIST INFORMATION

There are two Tourist Offices at the station. The best is ITA which is at the end of the bus station to the left as you leave the train station. It also deals with accommodation (commission charged) and is very helpful. The other is Turistica. There is another ITA office at 17 Chiasso dei Baroncelli, just off Piazza della Signoria.

The city Tourist Office (Tel. 055 290833) is at Via Cavour 1r, north of the Duomo. They give out maps of the city and a useful 1/3/5-day guide, but they do not book rooms. Open Mon.–Sat.: 8.15am–7.15pm, Sun.: 8.15am–1.45pm. Expect long queues. at all the offices. If you are desperate you can get a town map from McDonald's in the station.

## ADDRESSES

**POST OFFICE** Via Pellicceria in a very impressive building. Also *poste restante*. Open Mon.–Fri.: 8.15am–7pm; Sat.: 8.15am–12.30pm

**PUBLIC TELEPHONE OFFICE** is at 21r Via Cavour (from Piazza del Duomo towards Piazza San Marco). Here you can telephone and pay a cashier after your call

**BANK** San Paulo (inside station). Open Mon.–Fri.: 8.25am–12noon and 2.40pm–4.10pm, Sat.: 8.25am–11.55am

**AMEX** Via Dante Alighieri 22r (Tel. 055 50981), Mon.–Fri.: 9am–5.30pm, Sat.: 9am–12.30pm

**UK CONSULATE** Palazzo Castelbarco, Lungarno Corsini 2 (Tel. 055 284133)

**US CONSULATE** Lungarno Vespucci 38 (Tel. 055 239 8276)

**EURAIL AID OFFICE** Santa Maria Novella Station (Tel. 055 235 2595)

**STUDENT TRAVEL** CTS, Via Ginori 25 (Tel. 055 289570). Take a number as you enter. Open Mon.–Fri.: 9am–1pm and 2.30pm–6pm; Sat. 9am–noon. There's another student travel service (STS) at 18r Via Zanetti (Tel. 055 284183)

**24-HOUR CHEMIST** At the station by track 16 (Tel. 055 289435) or Via Calzaiuoli 7r (Tel. 055 289490)

**TOURIST MEDICAL OFFICE** 59 Via Lorenzo il Magnifico (Tel. 055 475411)

**FIRST AID** Tel. 055 474891
**POLICE** Via Zara 2 (Tel. 055 49771) or Emergency Tel. 112
**GENERAL EMERGENCIES** Tel. 113

## SEEING

Soaking up the atmosphere is as important in this city as rushing around the historic sites. Try to restrict your visits to museums and galleries to first thing in the morning, to avoid the crowds. Pollution levels can be high in the summer heat, so if you are an asthma sufferer, take precautions. Check at the Tourist Office for details and advice. Cars are banned from the city centre in the day.

The multicolour cathedral with the huge dome is the **Duomo**. The dome, which gives merciful shade in summer, was hailed as the wonder of the 15th century, but the façade of the cathedral is only 19th-century. Climb the 463 steps inside the dome to the **Lantern** for an unrivalled view over Florence (8,500L; open 9am–6.50pm). The 82 metre-high **campanile** next to the dome was Giotto's idea (8,500L; open 9am–5.30pm). Again, great views from the top and slightly fewer steps, a mere 414!

There's a glut of sheer genius in the **Uffizi**, one of the world's largest and most famous art galleries. You'll never get around it all in one visit, so try to pace yourself over a couple of days and don't miss Leonardo or, best of all, *The Birth of Venus* by Botticelli. It's closed on Mondays and Sundays. Entrance is currently 12,000L. Either be prepared to queue for ages or buy an advance ticket on your credit card (Tel. 050 471960 or 055 294883 – there's a handling fee of 2,400L). Some tourist offices also sell them but again it's a question of queuing.

Across the River Arno from the Uffizi is the **Palazzo Pitti**, home to the Medici family during the 16th century. Now it is home to seven museums. (All the museums are open daily 9am–2pm; closed on the 1st, 3rd and 5th Mon. and the 2nd and 4th Sun. of each month). Raphaels, Rubens and Titians are all on show in the **Palatine Gallery**, and you can wander around the **Royal Apartments** and **Museum of Gems** on its ground floor. The **Costume Gallery** and the **Porcelain Museum** display more of the Medicis' possessions. The **Carriage Museum** can probably be skipped out but the **Galleria d'Arte Moderne** has interesting works from the early 19th Century. You could spend a few hours in the Gallery alone!

The **Giardino di Bobolini** (palace gardens) are as rewarding as the museum and are open 9am–7.30pm. Photographers, you can get that famous skyline view of the city from here.

The medieval **Bargello Palace** holds the **National Museum**, an important sculpture collection (open 9am–2pm, closed

Mon.12,000L). If, like thousands of others, you came to Florence to see Michelangelo's *David*, you'll find him in the **Galleria dell'Accademia** on Via Ricasoli (admission 12,000L). The massive **Palazzo Vecchio** was once a Medici residence and contains the sumptuous Hall of the Five Hundred. It's at **Piazza della Signoria** (open Mon.–Wed. and Fri.–Sat.: 9am–7pm, Sun: 8am–1pm).

The other palace you ought to see is the **Medici-Riccardi** on Via Cavour (open 9am–12.45pm, 3pm–6.45pm, closed some Wednesdays and Sunday afternoons). The tiny chapel on the first floor contains Gozzoli's frescoes *The Procession of the Magi* and the Medici Museum downstairs is open 9am–1pm on Sun.

Most of the Medicis are buried in the **Medici Chapels** at San Lorenzo church (closed Mon. and Sun.), and the **Laurentian Library** is considered to be Michelangelo's architectural masterpiece. **San Marco** (admission 8,000L) is worth seeing for the monks' cells which Fra Angelico painted his unique shade of blue as an aid to monastic contemplation. The **Brancacci Chapel of Santa Maria del Carmine** has some beautiful Masaccio frescoes. Brunelleschi's harmonious architectural gem, the **Cappella dei Pazzi**, can be seen in the cloister of Santa Croce church.

**FREE FLORENCE:**

- First stop should be the amazing cathedral, the **Duomo**. Entrance is free, though it costs 8,000L to climb into its dome.
- The **Baptistery** alongside the Duomo is beautiful and well worth a look (open Mon.–Sat.: 1.30am–6pm and Sun.: 9am–12.30pm).
- The **Ponte Vecchio**, crossing the river Arno, was the only bridge to survive the war intact, when the Germans blew up all the others but were rushed by New Zealand troops before they could destroy it. It dates back to 1345 and is now the preserve of upmarket jewellers and goldsmiths, and promenading young locals out to see and be seen.
- The church of **Orsanmichele** on Via Calzaiuoli is an interesting combination of church (ground floor) and wheat granary (first floor). Inside, note the tabernacle by Orcagna, and on the outside, the statues in the niches are by the leading sculptors of the day, including Donatello, Verrocchio and Ghiberti.
- The Medici's Renaissance parish church was **San Lorenzo**, on Piazza San Lorenzo. Brunelleschi designed the old sacristy, and Donatello crafted two pulpits.
- **San Lorenzo Market** surrounds the church with stalls selling all sorts, including the leather specialities of the region.
- **Santa Maria Novella** is a huge building on Piazza Santa Maria Novella. It's filled with famous paintings, frescoes, and a Giotto

crucifix.
- There's more of Giotto in the church of **Santa Croce**, along with monumental tombs to Michelangelo, Machiavelli and Galileo, among others.
- Poets Elizabeth Barrett and Robert Browning lived in the **Casa Guidi**, on the tiny Piazza San Felice. You can visit the house, number 8, by appointment only (Tel. 055 284393).
- Brunelleschi's church of **Santo Spirito** has many fine paintings, and there's an **open-air market** in the square every morning (except Sunday). On the second Sunday of every month, there's a popular outdoor **crafts fair**.

## SLEEPING

Finding somewhere to stay in Florence can be a nightmare, finding somewhere which won't break the bank is even harder. Everywhere is expensive and, to add insult to injury, breakfast is rarely included in the price. If you do decide to stay in Florence, and you should if at all possible, try to book ahead – postal booking is recommended for all accommodation and is essential during peak season. Get hold of *Cheap Sleeps Europe 2000* for the full guide to accommodation options.

**HOSTELS** The highly recommended **youth hostel** is at 2/4 Viale Augusto Righi (Tel. 055 601451; Fax. 055 610300) with 322 beds, but it's for IYHF members only. Rock-bottom price (around 25,000L a night with breakfast), amiable staff, no reservations. Take bus 17b from the station.

The **Istituto Gould**, Via dei Serragli 49 (Tel. 055 212576), is an excellent and popular hostel. No check-in/out on Sat. pm or Sun. No curfew. Singles to rooms sleeping five. (Advance postal booking recommended). **Pio X-Artigianelli** is another hostel at Via dei Serragli 106 (Tel./Fax. 055 225044). It's near the Pitti Palace. Try to get there early.

**Ostello Santa Monaca**, Via Santa Monaca 6 (Tel. 055 268338; Fax. 055 280185), is a private hostel near the centre, bus 11 or a 15-minute walk from the station. It is shut 1pm–3pm, but you can reserve a place and leave your luggage at other times and register properly 4pm–11.30pm.

Women and families can try the convent **Suore Oblate dello Spirito Santo**, Via Nazionale 8 (Tel. 055 239 8202), open July–mid-Oct.

**PENSIONS** If you come up with nothing within five minutes of the station, drop off your pack, as the other pensions are a good walk away. From the station, turn left, then try places along Via Nazionale,

Via Fiume, Via Faenza, Via 28 Aprile, Via Guelfa and Via Cavour.

Via Faenza 56 contains six separate pensions which are all in the budget catergory and worth having a look at.

**Pensione Mary** is clean, bright and friendly. A double costs 110,000L. Rooms sleeping four available. It's at Piazza Indipendenza 5 (top floor) – turn left down Via Nazionale from station. Show this book to get a free breakfast or 10% reduction on a double room! There's no curfew. (Tel. and Fax. 055 496310).

Affordable places near the Duomo include **Albergo Firenze**, 4 Piazzadei Donati (Tel. 055 214203; Fax. 055 212370). Doubles from 80,000L, breakfast included.

CAMPSITES **Italiani e Stranieri** at Viale Michelangelo 80 (Tel. 055 681 1977) is a site open Apr.–Oct., but get in early or the best pitches will have gone. It has good views of Florence and kitchen facilities, and charges around 10,000L per person and 9,000L per tent. Take bus 13 from the station.

**Camping Camerata** is next to the HI youth hostel (Tel. 055 600315) on the 17b bus route. They charge 9,000L per person and from 8,000L per tent.

Six km out of town, there is a municipal site at Villa Farvard which provides free shelter and showers. Take buses 14a, b or c from the station and stop at Rocco Teddabla. Open 7am–10pm. The Panoramico, Via Peramound, outside Fiesole (Tel. 055 599069), is another recommended campsite north of the city. Take bus 7 from the station to Fiesole then walk up the hill to the campsite.

## EATING AND NIGHTLIFE

Florence has by far the best *gelati* (ice cream) in Italy. And **Vivoli**, on Via dell'Isola delle Stinche (off Via degli Anguillara near Santa Croce), is held by many to produce the world's best. If you can stand your ground in the throng (Italians, on the whole, have not yet mastered the art of orderly queueing), you can sample a tiny pot for 2,500L, but less prestigious versions are better value at numerous ice cream parlours around the city – and you're less likely to get an elbow in the face.

For a taste of simple Florentine food, try **Ottavino**, a small bar that is the established meeting place of the market workers: it's at Via dell'Ariento and is open until 1.30pm. If you've really reached rock bottom, **Casa San Francesco** on Piazza Sant'Annunziata (diagonally opposite Chiesa di Sant'Annunziata), run by monks, does a full lunch for a good price.

The **university Mensas** are on Via dei Servi 52 and 66–68, but these are closed from mid-July to Aug. The **self-service restaurant** at Piazza della Stazione 25 does a really cheap meal; another favourite is **Trattoria ZaZa** at Piazza Mercato Centrale 26. A busy but good place is **Trattoria il Constadino**, Via Palazzuolo 69/71. There are lots of good, affordable places to eat near the station and in the university quarter. Vegetarians should try **Ristorante Il Vegetariano** at 30 Via delle Ruote. Either eat in or have your meal in the garden of this self-service restaurant.

For picnic food, the **Mercato Centrale**, near San Lorenzo, is your best bet; open Mon.–Sat.: 7am–2pm.

On balmy summer nights groups of students and travellers congregate at the Duomo and Piazzale Michelangelo. The **Maggio Musicale Fiorentino** festival is held in May at the Teatro Comunale. And on 24 June, after the parade in 16th-century costume and the *calcio* (football) match of the afternoon, there are fireworks on Piazzale Michelangelo.

## Siena

While Florence is Renaissance, Siena is medieval. According to legend, Siena was founded by the sons of Remus. Its heyday came in the Middle Ages, when the city became a free republic. Siena was heralded as one of the most sophisticated cities in Europe, with powerful merchants wielding control over the wool industry, and the wealth to build an extraordinary cathedral and the most remarkable medieval square in Italy. This success inevitably led to rivalry with Florence however, Siena did not succumb to her neighbour. It was the Black Death in 1348, which wiped out more than two-thirds of the population. In less than five months, that brought Siena's power and prosperity to a sorry end. The city has never really recovered, and the Gothic centre with its steep cobbled streets and palaces has been left undisturbed by development of any kind.

It's 1½ hours from Florence, and there are trains daily passing through Empoli and Poggibonsi. (Trains from Rome go via Chiusi, and you have to change at these stops unless you're taking a direct train.) Call the info. booth at the station for train details 0577 280115. Buses are the best way to travel to Siena, there are direct services to/from Florence and other cities, however they do drop you outside the historic centre at Piazza Gramsci; walk the rest.

There's no **tourist information** at the train station – you need to get to the office at Piazza del Campo 56 (Tel. 0577 280551), open Mon.–Sat.: 8.50am–7pm; reduced hours in winter. There's also a small APT booth near Piazza San Domenico.

The heart of the city is the **Piazza del Campo**, where the Palio (an inter-district horse-race) is held as part of the 2 July and 16 Aug. celebrations, with costume parades and all-night dances following on.

The Gothic **Town Hall** (*Palazzo Comunale*) and the bell tower **Torre del Mangia** in the piazza are well worth a visit. The **Museo Civico** in the Palazzo Comunale houses an exhibition of Sienese art, including frescoes by Pietro and Ambrogio Lorenzetti: *Allegories of Good and Bad Government and their Effect on Town and Country*. Admission to the museum is 8,000L, and it costs 7,000L for the tower.

The **Chigi Saracini Palace** is a music academy, but on request they'll show you round the Renaissance apartments and gallery of Tuscan paintings. Further along is **Piazza Salimbeni** with its four palaces.

**FREE SIENA:** Siena's riches can be appreciated without visiting a single museum. You can get the measure of the place simply by lounging in the sun in the laid-back Piazza del Campo, exploring the dark, narrow lanes on the hills (on the way looking into all the palace courtyards and churches), and paying a visit to the cathedral.

- The striking black and white **Cathedral** is in the **Piazza del Duomo** (bus 1: tickets at station or a 45-minute walk). It is an incredible mix of Romanesque and Gothic, with sgraffito marble paving on 56 different floor panels.
- **San Domenico** church contains the head of Saint Catherine of Siena, along with portraits and frescoes of her. Catherine is the Saint credited with persuading Pope Gregory XI to return from Avignon to Rome. **Casa Sanctuario di Santa Caterina**, the house where she lived as a Dominican nun, is nearby, on Via Santa Caterina (the entrance is on Via Benincasa).
- The busiest and most colourful time to visit the city is on 2 July or 16 August, when *Il Palio* takes place. This is a night-long celebration and torchlit procession in medieval costume. The central event is a traditional horse-race around Piazza del Campo at 7pm. Standing room for the race is free, but arrive early, and remember to book accommodation in advance for this period.

## SLEEPING

Cheap rooms are a bit of a problem here, try **Locanda Garibaldi**, Via G. Dupre 18 (Tel. 0577 284204), doubles from 80,000L. There is a **hostel** at Via Fiorentina 89 (Tel. 0577 52212), a 20-minute bus ride on no. 15 from the station. Beds from about 25,000L, including breakfast. **Casa del Pellegrino** (Tel. 0577 44177) is at Via Camporegio, behind San Domenico.

The nearest **camping** ground is at Siena Colleverde, Strada di Scacciapensieri 47 (Tel. 0577 280044). The site is well maintained and secure, and is open Mar.–Nov. To get there, take bus 8 or 10 from Piazza Gramsci.

For more suggestions, ask at the Tourist Office or visit the Cooperativa Hotels Promotion booth on Via Curtatone, opposite San Domenico (Tel. 0577 288084). The staff there will fix you up with a hotel room.

## EATING AND NIGHTLIFE

Pastries are the local speciality – try *panforte* or *ricciarelli* at any of the Nannini bars or pastry shops in the city. The **university Mensa** is on Via Sant'Agata (closed Aug.), and there's no shortage of good trattorie. Pub **Barone Rosso** on Via dei Termini 9 (Tel. 0577 286686) has live music and sells Guinness, and is open 8pm–3am every night.

# Pisa

Millions come here just to see the Leaning Tower, but Pisa is a lovely town in its own right, with quite a collection of medieval masterpieces. Pisa, built on the Ligurian sea – which has since retreated – was an important port under the Greeks, Etruscans and Romans, and from the 11th–13th centuries was one of the most influential maritime powers of the Mediterranean. There is a Tourist Office in Piazza del Duomo, site of the famous Torre Pendente, but you are better off using the one to the left of the station as you leave.

## SEEING

Bus 1 from the station takes you straight to the **Piazza del Duomo** (also called the Field of Miracles) – with its unusual architectural hat-trick of tower, cathedral and baptistry, it is considered one of the marvels of Italy. The astronomer and physicist Galileo was born in Pisa, and is said to have conducted his experiments from the top of the **Leaning Tower**. It's been ten years since you could actually climb the tower, unless of course you're Tony Blair who did just that last year, but engineers are working feverishly to halt the subsidence, and there are even hopes it may reopen to the public in the not too distant future.

Beside the tower are the **Cathedral** (open Mon.–Sat.: 10am–7.45pm Sun.: 1pm–7.45pm) and the **Baptistry**. Nearby is **Campo Santo**, a beautiful cemetery built by the Crusaders. The **Museo Nazionale di San Matteo**, near Piazza Mazzini, houses important works by many 15th-century artists. Open Tues.–Sat.: 9am–7pm, Sun.: 9am–1pm.

The city's big traditional event is the **Gioto del Ponte**, held on 27 June, when there are festivities in medieval costumes. Other celebrations, regattas and art events occur during the summer.

**FREE PISA:**

- It costs nothing to see the Leaning Tower, as the structure itself is off-limits, and you can view it only from behind wire fencing. Though the Field of Miracles is fenced off, there's no entrance charged to the area itself. However, you do have to pay to enter each of the individual buildings.

- It also costs nothing to wander around the many souvenir stalls in the area, unless of course you're tempted! They all sell the same T-shirts, yes you've guessed, with the famous tower on; the same aprons with different types of pasta or Italian cheese on and the same 'marble' (plaster of Paris) statues of various gods/goddesses in different sizes.

## SLEEPING

Lodgings are difficult if you arrive late. Try **Hotel Galileo**, Via Santa Maria 12 (Tel. 050 40621), down Via San Lorenzo, or the women's hostel, **Casa della Giovane**, Via F. Corridoni (Tel. 050 43061). The latter is a 10-minute walk (turn right from the station) and offers women bed and breakfast for around 25,000L. The **Ostello per la Gioventu** at 15 Via Pietra Santina (Tel. 050 890622) is a private hostel. Beds 22,000L; doors are shut 9am–6pm. Take bus 3 from the station.

The campsite **Torre Pendente** is at Viale delle Cascine 86 (Tel. 050 560665). Take the number 4 bus from Stazione Centrale or follow the signs from Pl. Manin – go past the Cathedral and Baptistery and out through the old walls. Then turn right, then left. Prices are about 10,000L per person and 5,000L per tent. There are two other sites, both by the sea and about 10km from Pisa: **Camping Internazionale** (Tel. 050 36553) in Marina di Pisa and **Camping Mare e Sole** (Tel. 050 32757) in Calambrone. Bungalows available.

## EATING

Next to the Torre Pendente campsite is a **supermarket** where you can stock up on food and drink at reasonable prices. Also haggle at the open-air produce market in Piazza della Vettovaglie. The **university Mensa** on Via Martiri offers good food at cheap prices and is open 12–2.30pm daily, and on weekdays for evening meals 7–9pm. Stay away from eateries near the Leaning Tower – best prices are in the studenty places around **Piazza Cavalieri** and **Piazza Dante**.

## Umbria

Umbria is almost as famous as Tuscany for its rolling, wooded countryside, rivers, valleys and hill towns packed with Renaissance and medieval art treasures. The main difference is that Umbria's attractions are slightly off the beaten track, and that means even the charms of the most visited towns have not yet been erased by tourism.

## PERUGIA

The capital of Umbria is a medieval hill town about 1½ hours from Florence. It's fairly industrialized nowadays and can feel claustrophobic. However, there are some big attractions including the **Cathedral**, **National Gallery of Umbria**, **National Archaeological Museum** and the **Arch of Augustus**.

Tourist Offices can be found at Via Mazzini 21 (Tel. 075 573 6828), at Corso Vannucci 2 (Tel. 075 572 9047) and at Pl. IV Novembre (Tel. 075 572 5341/075 5723327).

The **Collegio del Cambio** at the Palazzo dei Priori has frescoes painted by Raphael and his teacher, Perugino. The opening hours are Mon.–Sat.: 9am–12.30pm and 2.30pm–5.30pm; Sun: 9am–12.30pm. Entry is 5,000L. Next door is the **Galleria Nationale dell'Umbria**, which has a rich collection of paintings. It is open 9am–7pm, and entrance is 10,000L.

The annual jazz festival takes place from late June to early July. Contact the Tourist Office.

There are many cheap **pensions** and **guest houses** in the city, which charge between 35,000L and 50,000L for a single room and from 55,000L for a double. Try **Albergo Anna** at 48 Via dei Prior (Tel. 075 5736304).

Two minutes from the **Cathedral** is the **youth hostel** (non-HI), on Via Bontempi 13 (Tel. 075 572 2880), which charges about 18,000L per person. The **campsite** is 5km out of town at 11 Rocolo, Colle della Trinità. Get there on bus 36 from the station. Open in the summer months only. Expect to pay about 8,000L per person, plus 6,000L per tent. Free use of swimming pool.

If you're after sun and swimming, Perugia is well linked by rail and bus to **Lake Trasimeno** (where you will find superior campsites).

## ASSISI

This medieval hill town is a major centre of pilgrimage, famous for its associations with St Francis. The many monasteries and other historical buildings in the city and its environs are testimony of its importance.

Tragically, Assisi was badly hit by the 1997 earthquake that caused severe damage throughout central Italy. Many historical monuments were devastated, including the Upper Basilica (see below), which may still be closed for repair.

Despite the crowds and the commercialism, Assisi still manages to retain some charm and is worth a day's excursion.

St Francis's tomb lies in a crypt at the **Basilica di San Francesco**, where two churches have been built one above the other. Open daily, except for Sun. mornings. The Upper Basilica is adorned by Giotto's frescoes illustrating the life of the saint (but they could be the work of an imitator).

Also worth a visit are the **Cathedral of St Rufino** and the **Basilica of St Chiara**, where the body of St Claire is preserved in the crypt.

Outside the city walls is a Franciscan shrine in **San Damiano**, built on the spot where St Francis heard the voice of Christ and wrote his *Canticle of the Creatures*.

For a good view over to Perugia, visit the fort/castle. Or, on the northern outskirts of Assisi is the cathedral **Rocca Maggiore**, where you can climb up for a superb view over the town and valley.

On the opposite side of the town in a suburb five km away is the basilica of **Santa Maria degli Angeli**, which contains the Porziuncula: the nucleus of the first Franciscan monastery and the Cappella del Transito where St Francis died.

In the centre of Assisi is the 1,000-year-old **Temple of Minerva**, behind which is the Roman Forum. The **Tourist Office** is opposite the temple on the Piazza del Comune (Tel. 075 812534), open 9am–1pm, 3.30pm–6.30pm. Ask here for addresses of private homes and religious institutions that offer accommodation.

A **hostel** and **campground** are situated one km from Assisi at Fontemaggio (Tel. 075 813636). The hostel charges 24,000L for a bed, the campsite 8,000L per person and 6,000L per tent. Take the bus from the station to Piazza Matteotti.

The IYHF **Ostello della Pace** in Via di Valecchie is 1.5 km away from the train station (a 10-minute walk from Piazza San Pietro). Open Mar.–Dec., it charges 23,000L for bed and breakfast (Tel./Fax. 075 816767).

# Rome (Roma)

Rome is three entities in one huge, sprawling city. Ancient Rome is the one most people come to see, with the incredible ruins of the capital of the Roman Empire heading any Essential Sightseeing list. Next is Vatican City, the world centre of the Catholic Church, home to the Pope and one of the most beautiful churches in the world. The third face of Rome is the least-loved – the modern, dirty, bustling metropolis.

You'll find the Romans proud, arrogant and conceited, but you'll look back with affection on the overwhelming beauty and dimensions of St Peter's, the atmosphere in the Colosseum, and the Trevi

Fountain when it's floodlit and buzzing with people. Everything is on a massive scale, solid and 'eternal'.

The main station is Roma Termini, which has comprehensive facilities. There are daily trains within Italy to Pisa, Genoa, Milan, Venice, Florence, Bologna, Ancona, Naples, Brindisi and Sicily. Daily international trains to Nice, Innsbruck, Munich, Brussels, Vienna, Basle and Paris. Trains running from the north of Italy to the south and vice versa stop at Tributina station, so you don't have to come into the centre.

Keep a close eye on purses and wallets, even if in handbags or waist pouches, as pickpockets are very good at their job.

## TOURIST INFORMATION

Before leaving the station, go to the Tourist Office at the end of **platform 3** and pick up a map of the city. Apart from the office at the station, there's one very near the station at **Via Parigi** 5 (Tel. 06 4889 9255/06 4889 9253), open Mon.–Sat.: 8.15am–7pm. Queues are slightly shorter. To get there, leave the station by the main doors and head towards the large fountain in Piazza della Repubblica. Once past this, take the small road at the first turning on the right.

There is another information centre called **Enjoy Rome** (Tel. 06 445 1843), which is on Via Varese 39 just past the junction with Via Milazzo. It is a great meeting point for backpackers, can give you all the information you may need about Rome, and provides a free map and free luggage storage for customers. It has information about short-term apartments and other types of accommodation, walking, cycling and bus tours and emergency aid. The centre is open Mon.–Fri.: 8.30am–2pm, 3.30pm–6pm, and Sat.: 8.30am–2pm.

The information service **Let's Go Italy 2000** is on Via Calatafimi 15, open daily from 9.30am to 6pm. The staff speak seven languages and they can provide you with free maps of Florence, Rome and Venice as well as information on night life, trains, accommodation, city tours, theatres, museums, restaurants and trips out of town. They can save you money and time; show this book to get a 10–20% discount on accommodation. To get there, come out of the station and turn left along Via Marsala; Via Calatafimi is fourth right.

Generally, shops and churches are open 9am–1pm, 4pm–8pm. Museums generally close about 1pm or 2pm and all day Mon. Romans take their holidays in August, and you'll find many restaurants shut.

## ADDRESSES

**POST OFFICE** Piazza San Silvestro 19, open Mon.–Fri.: 9am–6pm for *poste restante*, Sat.: 8am–2pm, telephones 8am–12 midnight. Also large branch office at 30 Via delleTerme di Diocleziano, next to Termini station

**AMEX** Piazza di Spagna 38; open Mon.–Fri.: 9am–6pm, Sat.: 9am–12.30pm (Tel. 06 67641 for lost/stolen cards and/or cheques issued in the US; otherwise Tel. 06 72281) and Largo Caduti Di el Alamein 9 (Tel. 06 7228 0308)

**EURAIL AID OFFICE** Stazione Termini

**YOUTH TRAVEL SERVICE** CTS, Via Genova 16 (Tel. 06 462 0431/06 446791). They help out on accommodation, issue ISICs, etc. Also a Eurotrain office

**24 HOUR PHARMACY** Farmacia Internazionale, P. Barberini 49 (Tel. 06 482 5456). There's also a 24-hour 'drugstore' in the underground area of Termini Station. For a list of late-opening pharmacies in central Rome phone 06 1921

**INTERNATIONAL MEDICAL CENTRE** Via Giovanni Amendola 7, 2nd floor, Tel. 06 488 2371

**AMERICAN HOSPITAL (ENGLISH SPOKEN)** Tel. 06 225 3333

**POLICE** Tel. 113

**AMBULANCE** Tel. 118 or 06 5510

**UK EMBASSY** Via XX Settembre 80a (Tel. 06 482 5441)

**US EMBASSY** Via Vittorio Veneto 121 (Tel. 06 46741)

**CANADIAN EMBASSY** Via Zara 30 (Tel. 06 445981)

**AUSTRALIAN EMBASSY** Via Alessandria 215 (Tel. 06 852721)

**NEW ZEALAND EMBASSY** Via Zara 28 (Tel. 06 441 7171)

## GETTING ABOUT

Avoid taxis – they are expensive. The buses are cheap and the underground continues to expand. Bus tickets (1,500L) are valid for an hour and a quarter, and you may use the bus or tramway with the same ticket provided you do not exceed the time limit. Cancel the ticket in the machine as you board (board at either the front or the back but not in the middle). Buses run 5.30am–12 midnight.

Buy tickets from Tabac shops, newsagents or the stations (look out for the ATAC sign). There are three kinds of tickets: BIT – normal ticket; BIG – one-day ticket (6,000L) and BIS – one-week ticket (24,000L). You can buy a route map from the bus kiosk at the station (9,000L), which shows all major sites and streets.

Bicycles and especially scooters are the favoured mode of transport for thousands of Romans, and most of them seem to have a death wish. If you fancy your chances alongside some of Europe's most maniacal motorists, stands throughout the city rent out bikes and scooters, especially along the Via del Corso, or try I Bike Rome (Via Veneto 156, Tel. 06 322 5240). Rates for bicycles are generally from 15,000–18,000L a day. For scooters, expect to pay from 40,000–100,000L a day. Our advice: don't consider bikes or scooters unless you're well insured.

## SEEING

Though the three faces of Rome are not strictly geographically distinct, we've tried to group them as such, to help you plan your day's route. Ideally, you need four–five days here, but the prices and the pace of the city may put you off staying so long. Be on your guard constantly for pickpockets, including young children begging, and watch out particularly for the motorized thieves who cruise about on mopeds and whip handbags off shoulders and wallets from pockets. A common ploy is for children or hustlers to distract you by thrusting cardboard notices in your face while an accomplice swiftly lifts your valuables.

**ANCIENT ROME** Imperial Rome is clustered south of the Piazza Venezia, the modern city centre. The main sight here is **The Colosseum** (free for lower levels, 10,000L for upper). Check the opening times when you arrive, as they can vary greatly from day to day. This huge arena seated 55,000 Romans whose idea of sporting entertainment was to watch Christians being eaten by starving lions, or gladiators fighting it out to the bitter end.

The **Roman Forum** was the commercial, religious and civic centre of ancient Rome. Look out for the three **Triumphal Arches**, the **House of the Vestal Virgins** and the six temples. Here also is the **Curia** (Senate House), the **Basilica Aemilia** and the **Rostra** - the speaker's platform which was erected in 44 BC by Caesar. Enter by Via dei Fori Imperiali which leads straight onto the Via Sacra, the city's oldest street which cut through the heart of Republican Rome.

Opposite is the **Imperial Forum**, including **Trajan's Forum** with its famous column, and the **Basilica of St Maxentius**, the ancient law court and exchange. The **Mamertine Prison**, just off Via dei Fori Imperiali, is where Nero kept St Peter.

**Palatine Hill** (Monte Palatino) is where Nero, Mark Antony and other famous historical figures were based. Many ancient structures were incorporated into the **Palazzo Farnese** when it was built in the 16th century. See the frescoes on the **House of Augustus**, the remains of the **Palace of the Flavians** and the **Palace of Septimius Severus**.

On the **Appian Way**, the ancient Roman road to Brindisi, you'll find the **Baths of Caracalla** (near Piazzale Numa Pompilio; entrance 8,000L), and the **Catacombs of St Sebastian**. There are five tiers of burial chambers and many Christian saints and martyrs here, at 110 Via Appia Antica (admission 8,000L). Remember to buy two tickets, if travelling by bus, as there is nowhere to buy them at the catacombs. Bus 218 from Piazza San Giovanni.

The **National Museum of Rome** (opposite Termini station, open

9am–2pm, Sun. closes at 1pm and closed Mon.) has the best collection of artefacts from the Roman Empire, though many of these have been moved across the square to the reopened 19th-century **Palazzo Massimo**. At Piazza dei Cinquecento 68, Palazzo Massimo has four floors of artefacts from six centuries of Roman history. On display are statuary, sculptures, mosaics, frescoes, coins, jewellery and pottery. Opening hours are Tues.–Sat.: 9am–10pm; Sun. 9am–8pm. Closed Mon. (Tel. 06 4890 3500). 12,000L entry; free last Sun. of month. **Castel Sant'Angelo** (Hadrian's Mausoleum) was the Pope's fortress to flee to in times of danger. Now it's a museum of weapons, art and relics (Lungotevere Castello), open 9am–7pm, closed Tue. (admission 8,000L). Look out also for the **Theatre of Marcellus**, the **Pyramid of Caius Cestius** on Piazza San Paolo and the remains of four ancient **Roman Temples** in Largo Argentina. All the Roman remains that don't close on Monday tend to close on Tuesday.

**FREE ANCIENT ROME:**
- **The Pantheon** is the best preserved of all the sites of ancient Rome. It was started in 27 BC and, having been a temple to the gods for over 600 years, became a Christian church in the 7th century. The kings of Italy and the artist Raphael are buried here. It's at Piazza della Rotonda. Opening times are 9am–6.30pm Mon.–Sat., and 9am–1pm Sun. Mass on Sun. is 9.45am–11.15am.
- **The Colosseum** is free to enter on the lower levels.
- Wander around the **Roman Forum** at your leisure.

**PAPAL ROME** The independent state of the **Vatican City**, home to the Pope, is the spiritual centre for 630 million Roman Catholics throughout the world. The Vatican has its own stamps, printing press, currency, radio station, newspaper and railway, all contained within one sq. mile. The Pope himself has held all judicial, legislative and executive powers here since the 1929 Lateran Treaty but he must remain neutral in all Rome's municipal affairs and in Italian politics.

There's a Pilgrim Tourist Information Office at Piazza San Pietro, near the basilica.

The 17th-century **St Peter's Square** leads up to **St Peter's Basilica**, the church whose dome can be seen all over Rome. Inside are works by Raphael, Michelangelo, Bernini and Bramante. (Cover your legs and shoulders if you want to get in.) For the full impact of this church, come at 8am and climb the stairs to the top of the dome for a breathtaking view (5,000L on foot, 6,000L if you take the lift). The basilica itself is open 7am–7pm in summer.

The **Vatican Museums**, which include such treasures as Michelangelo's **Sistine Chapel**, the **Raphael Rooms**, the **Graeco-Roman Museums** and the **Vatican Library** are located north of St Peter's on Viale Vaticano. It costs about 10,000L on ISIC, 16,000L without, but it's well worth it. They are open 8.45am–1pm (last entry 45 minutes before closing) Mon.–Sat. and the last Sun. of every month, when admission is free for everyone. Note that only an ISIC card is accepted as proof of student status. Not even your passport will do!

Outside the Vatican, the most important churches are **St John Lateran**, with the **Holy Stairs** and **Santa Maria Maggiore**. The former is the church of the popes; the stairs are believed to be those from the palace of Pontius Pilate which Christ ascended during his Passion. You can only climb them if you're officially worshipping, and then only on your knees. The church is south-east of the Colosseum at Piazza San Giovanni in Laterno. The latter has a 5th-century church, the *campanile* is the tallest in Rome and there are some interesting mosaics (Via Liberiana). It's four blocks to the left of Termini.

### FREE VATICAN CITY:
- The Pope's in charge here, the Swiss Guards keep order, and you can currently see them both in action on Wednesdays at 11am (check with the tourist offices for any changes), when thousands come for **an audience with Pope John Paul II**. These ceremonies are sometimes in St Peter's Square, sometimes in a nearby hall, and in the summer are often in the Pope's summer residence, Castel Gandolfo, south of Rome. For tickets, ask at the Prefettura della Casa Pontificia (through the bronze door in the right-hand colonnade) on Monday or Tuesday mornings.
- You can also get a glimpse of the Pope on **Sundays at noon**, when he blesses the crowd from a window of the Vatican Palace.
- There is no charge to enter **St Peter's Basilica**.
- A volunteer group gives **guided tours** of the basilica in English, around 10am and 3pm. Ask at the desk in the portico.
- The **Vatican Grottoes** are in the area of the original basilica, and contain the tombs of many popes. Entrance is among the piers at the crossing.
- The **Vatican Museums** are free on the last Sunday of every month. Get there first thing; the queues are horrendous.

**MODERN ROME** Elegant squares are one of Rome's most appealing features. One of the most beautiful was designed by Michelangelo: **Piazza del Campidoglio** is considered to be the political heart of the city. There are three palaces around it. One is the **Senatorial Office**, one is the **Capitoline Museum** of antique sculptures

(10,000L or 5,000L with ISIC, open Tues.–Sat.: 9am–5pm, Sun.: 9am–1.30pm), and the third is the **Conservatorio**, which has large chunks of hands, toes and heads from Roman statues.

The **Piazza Navona** is a Bernini work, as is **Piazza Barberini**. The **Villa Borghese**, in the north, is the most splendid of Rome's parks. The zoo (open 8am–6pm, late night Thurs.–Sat. Admission 8,000L) and three art galleries are out here. The **National Gallery of Modern Art** on the Viale delle Belle Arti houses the biggest collection of Italian art from the 19th century to the present day. Entrance is around 10,000L and opening times are 9am–7pm Tues.–Sun., 9am–2pm holidays.

**FREE MODERN ROME:**

- The famous **Spanish Steps (Piazza di Spagna)** and the Barcaccia fountain at the bottom attracts a young crowd, day and night, and is one of the most animated scenes in the city.
- In a city of fountains, the **Trevi Fountain**, off Via del Corso, is the most beautiful – and the most crowded. Along with the Spanish Steps, this is *the* place to see and be seen. The Baroque fountain is now floodlit, making it a favourite hang-out at night. Legend has it that if you toss a coin into the water you will return to Rome.
- Next to the Trevi fountain is the **Basilica Santa Maria**, which is as beautiful as the more renowned tourist attractions and far less crowded.
- The **Monument to Vittorio Emanuél II**, in the Piazza Venezia, is the huge white marble 'wedding cake' at the southern end of Via del Corso. It was built in 1911 to celebrate Italy's unification.
- The **Capitoline Museum** offers free access on the last Sun. of each month. Get there early to miss the worst of the queueing.
- There are many street **markets** for those in the mood for browsing. **Via Sannio** plays host to a new and secondhand clothing market, whilst that of the **Porta Portese** is a curio heaven every Sunday morning. Arrive about 8.30am for the best viewing and remember to watch your wallet.

**EXCURSIONS** Mussolini's 1940s quarter of Rome – the EUR – has an amusement park (**Luna Park**) and the **Museum of Roman Civilisation** (entrance 5,000L), which reconstructs ancient Rome as it was under Constantine.

The nearest beach is **Ostia Lido**. It's not one of Italy's best (the sea is very dirty) but it's only 29 km away (metro Line B to Magliana then train to Ostia).

The ancient ruined city of **Ostia Antica** is only a further five km away and can be reached by the same train or by bus no. 4, which leaves Ostia-Lido every 15 minutes. The excavated Roman ruins beside the river Tiber have been preserved by centuries of river mud. This was the capital's purpose-built ship-building harbour and sea port, with temples, trade union headquarters, stadiums, taverns, warehouses, shops and gardens all in an amazing state of preservation. The ruins are accessible 9am–7pm (until 4.30pm in winter), admission around 8,000L. During the summer classic plays are staged in the Roman theatre.

A good **campsite** is situated three km from the ruins at Capitol Campground, Via dei Castelfusono (Tel. 06 565 0621). Free swimming pool and tennis court facilities. To get there take bus 5 from Ostia-Lido central.

East of Rome is the Renaissance Cardinals' Palace, **Villa d'Este** at Tivoli. The gardens are the main attraction here. Take metro line B to Rebbiba and then the blue Cotral bus (6,000L return). If you bus it, you could also take in the sumptuous **Villa Adrian** (admission 8,000L; closed Mon.).

## SLEEPING

Beds are never really a problem, even in July and August, as there are literally hundreds of **pensions**, *locande* and *alloggi*. There are plenty of cheap places beside the station and the prices there are the cheapest in town. For help with finding a place, use either CTS (see addresses), the student help office or the Tourist Offices. Or refer to *Cheap Sleeps Europe 2000* for a full range of options.

**HOSTELS** The IYHF **youth hostel** is at Viale delle Olimpiadi 61 (Tel. 06 323 6267; Fax. 06 324 2613); it is six km out and reports on it are good (costs around 25,000L per night). To get there take the subway to Ottaviano and then bus 32.

Far more crowded are the dorms at the **Pensione Ottaviano**, Via Ottaviano 6 (Tel. 06 39737253 or 06 3973 8138) near Piazza del Risorgimento (Dorm beds 29,000L). Another recommended place is **Pensione Lachea**, Via San Martino della Battaglia 11 (Tel. 06 495 7256). Here doubles cost from 62,000L and triples from 82,000L a night. Advance reservations and deposits are necessary. **Hotel Pensione Dolomiti** is in the same building (Tel. 06 491058) and has singles from 48,000L; doubles 62,000L.

**NEAR THE STATION Pensione Pava** is at Via Pave 14 (Tel. 06 487 3360). At Via Milazzo 20, you'll find **Hotel Galli** (Tel. 06 446 8501) with rooms from 50,000L (single).

To the left of the station is a very Roman working-class neighbourhood, full of colour and life. Via Principe Amedeo has a collection of good pensions; all ask about 50,000L–70,000L a person. They include **Cortorillo** (Tel. 06 488 0954; Fax. 06 481 7613), **Contilia**, **Govoni** and **di Rienzo** (Tel. 06 446 7131), which are all very acceptable. Also try **Hotel Kennedy**, Via Filippo Turati (Tel. 06 446 5373; Fax. 06 446 5417). North of the station is the excellent **Pensione Fawlty Towers** at Via Magenta 39 (Tel./Fax. 06 445 0374 or Tel. 06 445 4802). Doubles from 82,000L. Also highly recommended is the **Backpackers** at 9 Via Solferino which has strict, but reasonable rules: check-in after 3pm, curfew at 11pm and chuck out at 11am. From Termini station exit in the opposite direction from McDonalds. Cross the road and turn left and continue till the crossroads. Via Solferino is directly on the left. There is another hostel, **M&J's Place**, in the same building.

Our advice is not to sleep out in Rome, and avoid at all costs flaking out in the park outside the station or at Villa Borghese. Each summer muggings get more numerous and the gypsies who hang out in this area should be watched like hawks.

**HALLS OF RESIDENCE** There are three university halls of residence, opened by the IYHF from the end of July to the end of September. They are at Via Cesare de Lollis 20 (take bus 492 from the Termini station); CIVIS, seven km from the station at Viale del Ministero degli Affari Esteri 6 (take subway A to Ottaviano, then bus 32); and at Via D. De Dominicis 13 (subway A to Colli Albani, then bus 409). All charge from around 25,000L for bed and breakfast.

**CAMPSITES** None of the several sites around Rome are near the centre. **Flaminio**, at Via Flaminia (Tel. 06 333 1431 or 06 333 2604), is the nearest, open Mar.–Oct. To get there take the underground from Piazza Flaminio and request the stop for the camping site called Due Ponti, or take the 225 tram (from Station Termini take bus 910) to the end station, Piazza Mancini, followed by bus 200 to the site. Or Metro A to Flaminio then bus 202/3/45. The cost is from 13,000L per person,9,000L per tent, and the campsite has free pool and shower facilities. Single and double tents are available for hire at the campsite, and there is a bar, shop and restaurant on site.

**Camping Roma** is on Via Aurelia 8B1 (Tel. 06 6641 8147 or 06 662 8863). Take bus 38 from the train station to Piazza Fiume, then bus 490 to Piazza Irnerio, where you change to bus 246.

**Seven Hills**, Via Cassia 1216 (Tel. 06 3036 2751/06 3033 10826; Fax. 06 3033 10039). 8km north of Rome. Take bus 907 to Via Cassia. Good amenities: swimming pool, disco, supermarket, bar and restaurant. Shuttle service to the Vatican. Around 13,000L per person and 8,000L per tent. Bungalows also available. Open late March to late Oct.

For **Camping Nomentano**, Via della Cesarina, take bus 36 from outside Termini station to Piazza Sempione, then bus 330 to Via Nomentana. Check with Tourist Information for new sites.

## EATING AND NIGHTLIFE

You can eat a good, filling meal in Rome for about 20,000L. Go for the *menu turistico*, which is good value and typically offers good pasta and pizza dishes. **Formula 1**, Via degli Equi 13 does nice pizza washed down with the house red for around 17,000L. The fixed-price menus are reasonable. **La 'Reatina'** trattoria and pizzeria offers good value traditional Italian food at Via San Martino della Battaglia 17.

The area on the right-hand side of the station as you leave is good for tourist menus. The **Osteria da Salvatore** at Via Castelfidardo 39c has cheap set meals. **Trattoria da Bruno e Romana** offers good, traditional, wholesome food at Via Varese 29. For a self-service restaurant, try the one at **Piazza Cinquecento** 47 near the station and others in this area. If you're after a romantic meal, try **Pulcino Ballerino** at Via degli Equi 66/68. Great food, great atmosphere. For vegetarian dishes, try **L'Albero del Pane**, Dei Bianchi Vecchi 39, a health food store selling organic foods. Open 9am–1.30pm, 5pm–8pm.

In the city centre, there are numerous snack bars selling pizza by the piece, pastries and other tasty snacks. If you fancy a picnic in the vicinity of the Trevi fountain, check out **L'Antico Forno** on the corner right opposite the fountain (Via delle Muratte 8). It's a grocery store cum delicatessen, and the price of food and drink there is very reasonable. Open daily 7am–9pm.

For a more extensive choice of picnic food, head for the main **market** in Piazza Vittorio Emanuele, about five minutes east of Termini. In **Piazzale Flaminio**, near the campsite of the same name, is a *rosticcerie* which sells cheap chicken and pizza.

Giolitti's are reputed to have the best **ice-cream** in Rome. They're near the Pantheon at Via Ufficio del Vicario 40.

Avoid the dance floors – they are extravagantly expensive – but **Piper** is reputed to be the biggest and best in Rome. **Saint Louis**, Via del Cardello 13a is a modern club, known for its serious quality jazz. The best gay club is **L'Alibi** at Via di Monte Testaccio 44. Clubs come and go so check that the one you're going to exists before going in search of it. Ask at the tourist office, better still, find out from other travellers/locals over a drink in a pub.Try the **Julius Caesar Pub** at Via Castelfidardo 49 for a good mix of locals and US/British. Another popular watering hole is The Druid's Den at Via San Martino Ai Monti 28. This Irish pub has **Guinness** on tap

If **opera** is more your cup of tea, take in the outdoor performances in the Roman Baths of Caracalla. Buy tickets from the Teatro dell'Opera.

# Southern Italy

In the old geographical 'boot' analogy of Italy, **Campania** is the ankle, **Basilicata** the arch, **Puglia** the heel (the departure point for the Brindisi ferry to Greece) and **Calabria** the toe.

**Campania** is full of interest. Apart from the colourful chaos of Naples, there's the smouldering volcano of Vesuvius, the archaeological remains of Pompeii, Herculaneum and Paestum, the romantic towns of Sorrento, Amalfi and Positano and the islands off the coast of Naples: Capri, Ischia and Procida. In August, avoid Agropoli, Catellabate and San Marco, all south of Naples, as these places are packed with holidaying Italians.

# Naples (Napoli)

If you've come down from the north, you'll feel you're in a different country. Naples is a crazy city: overcrowded, dirty, smelly and alive. It has the worst traffic you can imagine, with pollution to match, but no tour of Italy is complete without a stop here. The main streets are choked with car horns and lunatic Vespa riders, while the backstreets are right out of the Middle Ages – tiny, cobbled alleys where children kick footballs.

Naples' vital statistics are little short of unbelievable. It has the highest birth rate in Italy; a population density 15 times the national average; unemployment nearing 30%; the slowest traffic in the country – 10mph; only 26 per cent of the province connected to a proper sewage system; and a shocking record of crimes against the environment.

Add to this one further fact: Naples is the crime capital of Italy, so watch your belongings. The city has its own way of getting things done (much of it involving corruption, for the power of the local mafia – the Camorra – is legendary), which the visitor will find unfathomable. You may also find that many of the sights are wholly or partly under restoration or have strange opening times. Change your money before coming to Naples because banks here have a very high commission. Do not expect northern standards of hygiene; until 1973 Naples had no sewers at all. Women travelling alone or with other females will almost certainly be harassed. Either go to the city in a mixed group or consider giving Naples a miss. Despite all this, Naples is a vibrant and exciting city.

There is another side to Naples. Away from the claustrophobic medieval centre, the countryside is all lemon and orange groves, scenic coastal roads and numerous seaside delights.

## TRAIN INFORMATION

Napoli Centrale is the main station, and the one most used by Euro-railers. It has full facilities (including digiplan machines), but the mass of concrete is hard on the eyes if you have just arrived on an overnight service. Beware of pickpockets, junkies, beggars pretending they need money for the train fare home, mangy dogs and persistent approaches from private taxi drivers.

There are daily trains to Rome, Florence, Bologna, Genoa, Milan, Sicily, Venice and Brindisi.

Trains from Rome, and those going on to Sicily, invariably use the central station. The Rome–Bari trains stop at both stations, Piazza Garibaldi and Centrale. There's a connecting elevator between them.

Trains to Sorrento, Pompeii and Herculaneum on the privately run Circumvesuviana railway leave from Stazione Centrale.

## TOURIST INFORMATION AND ADDRESSES

There's a helpful Tourist Office (EPT) at the Centrale train station (Tel. 081 268779; Fax. 081 206666) but you will have to wait ages. Pick up a map and get them to call hotels and ferry companies for you. The main office is at Piazza Martiri 58 (Tel. 081 405311). There are other offices at the airport, at Piazza Plebiscito and Palazzo Reale. The AAST office (081 552 3328) is in Piazza del Gesù, near Piazza Dante.

**POST OFFICE** Piazza Matteotti, open Mon.–Fri.: 8.15am–7.30pm, Sat: 8.35am–12noon (Tel. 081 551 1456). Also outside Station Centrale

**AMEX** Every Tour, Piazza Municipio 5, Via Terzo Bosso Catene 1 (Tel. 081 551 8564)

**EURAIL AID OFFICE** Station Centrale (Tel.081 554 3188)

**UK CONSULATE** Via Francesco Crispi 122 (Tel. 081 663511)

**US CONSULATE** Piazza della Repubblica (Tel. 081 583 8111; in emergencies Tel. 0337 945083)

**24-HOUR CHEMIST** At the Station Centrale

**STUDENT TRAVEL OFFICE** CTS via Mezzocannone 25 (Tel. 081 552 7960)

**TOURIST POLICE** Via Medina 75 (Tel. 081 794 1111)

**AMBULANCE** Tel. 081 752 0696

## SEEING

The city's transport system has some useful passes. You can buy 1½ hour passes for 1,500L and they are valid on all buses, trams and funiculars, but not on the subway. A whole day pass costs 5,000L. All tickets are available from convenience stores.

Naples may have none of the famous sights of Rome, Florence or Venice, but it still has much to offer. If you visited Pompeii or Herculaneum and were disappointed to find none of the artefacts – or bodies – there, visit the **National Archaeological Museum** on Piazza del Museo (close to the Piazza Cavour metro station). Here you'll find one of the best Graeco–Roman collections in the world, as well as the frescoes and jewellery from Herculaneum and the Borgia collection of Etruscan art. Open Mon. and Wed.–Sat.: 10am–10pm, Sun.: 8am–8pm, 12,000L admission.

In nearby Via Duomo, tucked away from the main street, is the **San Gennaro Cathedral**, where every year St Gennaro's coagulated blood apparently turns to liquid. (Legend has it that if the blood fails to liquefy on festival days disaster will strike the city.) You can tour the crypt every day 9am–12noon and 4.30pm–7pm.

Off a small side street to the east of the churches of Santa Chiara and San Domenico Maggiore (see FREE NAPLES) is the chapel of **San Severo**, which charges a small admission fee (6000L or 2,000L students). It's open Mon. and Wed.–Sat.: 10am–5pm; Tues. and Sun.: 10am–1.30pm). Inside are some brilliant sculptures, including a veiled Christ hewn out of a single block of marble, so realistic you feel you are looking at the body through a veil.

The opera house, **Teatro San Carlo** (a source of much Neapolitan pride), and the **Galleria Umberto I**, a 19th-century shopping arcade, are near the **Castel Nuovo** on Piazza Municipio. The castle was built in the late 13th century for Charles I of Anjou; it is open daily.

The museums are no less breathtaking. The **Capodimonte Museum** which overlooks the city from its highest hill at **Volmero** costs 8,000L to see. It was the view from here that inspired the saying 'See Naples and die'.

**FREE NAPLES:**
- The church of **Gesù Nuovo** in Piazza Gesù Nuovo (opposite the Tourist Office) may look like a prison on the outside, but inside is a feast of the Baroque.
- Not far away are the medieval churches of **Santa Chiara** and **San Domenico Maggiore**. The latter contains a painting that spoke to St Thomas Aquinas.
- In July there are a series of free concerts, called Luglio Musicale a Capodimonte, outside the Capodimonte Palace.

## SLEEPING
The **Mergellina** youth hostel is excellent and is at Salita della Grotta

a Piedigrotta 23 (Tel. 081 761 2346); Fax. 081 761 2391); it imposes a three-day maximum stay policy during July and August. 24,000L. Go to the Mergellina stop on the underground.

For a clean, friendly and cheap **pension** head for **Pensione Mancini** (Tel. 081 553 6731) at Via Mancini 33 on the second floor. Only five mins walk from the train station. Dorms cost 28,000L, singles 40,000L and doubles 65,000L, breakfast included.

**Hotels** have a reputation for changing their rates once you are in. Get a clear agreement before you move into your room, but if there are still problems, phone EPT (Tel. 081 405311). **Hotel Imperia** (Tel. 081 459347) is a friendly hotel located in the heart of old Naples at Piazza Luigi Maraglia 386; it's inexpensive, too. Try **Hotel Eden**, Corso Novara 9, near the station (Tel. 081 285344). Another suggestion is **Hotel Ginevra** at Via Genova 116, near the station (Tel. 081 554 1757) which gives 10% off to holders of this guide.

You can camp on the edge of the volcano crater at **Camping Solfatara** (Tel. 081 526 7413), open Apr.–Nov. Take bus 152 directly there or a local train from Piazza Garibaldi station to Pozzuoli and then walk 850m, mostly uphill. The municipal **Cittè di Napoli** campsite is within the Mostra d'Oltremare complex. Take the train to Campi Flegrei and walk. It costs around 9,000L each but you are better off going to the nearby small coastal towns.

## EATING AND NIGHTLIFE

Naples created the pizza, so it is just the place to find out just how far from the original the fast food variety really is. There are hundreds of cheap pizza places, but the best is **Trianon**, Via Pietro Colletta 46 (off Via Tribunali). If you're flush, try one of the seafood restaurants down by the port in the Santa Lucia district. **Renzo e Lucia** on Via Tito Angelini 31133 do good baked fish and **Caffè Osteria** at Via Miroballo 14 gives good value for money.

Neapolitan coffee (*caffè lungo*) is best with plenty of sugar and a cake. *Sfogliatelle* is the speciality cake of the region. Try **Pintauro** at 275 Via Ranoy Toledo. Chips and sandwiches are readily available around the Piazza Garibaldi.

The **university Mensa** is on Via Mezzocanone. Try the vegetarian-Indian **Restaurant Campania**, Gapala-Corso Vittorio Emanuele, open 8am–12 midnight daily except Monday. **Trattoria Avellinese**, Via Silvio Spaventa 31–35 (off Piazza Garibaldi), does great seafood at reasonable prices.

There are plenty of shady bars and rip-off joints down by the port. You'll find your evening strolls being interrupted by people trying to sell you anything from cabbage-leaf Marlboros to watches made from bottle lids. Nightlife doesn't take off until around midnight, after the public transport systems shut, although taxis are affordable. The popular area is around Piazza Amedeo, where there are plenty of bars and restaurants. Nightclubs are expensive and cost around 25,000L with a free drink thrown in.

**EXCURSIONS** The **Phlegrian Fields** (*campi flegri*), on the peninsula west of Naples, have some active volcanoes you can visit.

Further east, **Mount Vesuvius** hasn't erupted since 1944, but it could go at any time, so take the chair lift to the crater at your peril! If you do, make sure it's a clear day, and go early.

Both **Herculaneum** and **Pompeii** were destroyed by a Vesuvian eruption in AD 79. Pompeii was covered with ashes, Herculaneum with mud. Both offer a unique insight into Roman Imperial life; you can see houses and baths preserved from that age. Entrance charges are around 14,000L from 9am until an hour before sunset.

If you wish to stay in Pompeii, there is a good **campsite** by the Villa dei Misteri station. Camping Zeus (Tel. 081 861 5320; Fax. 081 850 8778) is convenient, cheap, friendly and open all year round, and no tent is necessary (8,000L per person).

The private **Circumvesuviana Line**, from Stazione Vesuviana – 1st floor underground at Central station – serves this area, including Herculaneum and Pompeii, and runs on to Sorrento. Inter-Rail passes are not valid. It takes approximately 15 minutes from Naples to Herculaneum (get off at the Ercolano stop) and 45 minutes to Pompeii (make sure you get off the train at the Pompeii Scavi stop). You can also get to Pompeii on the main Naples–Salerno line from Napoli Piazza Garibaldi (free with Inter-Rail ticket).

Visiting the **islands** in the Gulf is easy. Take the ferry from the port, or the hydrofoil from Mergellina.

**Capri**, home to the mythical Sirens, is the most touristy of the islands and very expensive, but the beach at Marina Piccola is the best in the area and the Blue Grotto is unmissable.

The Italians favour **Ischia**, a volcanic island famed for its thermal springs and mud baths.

The town of **Caserta**, 45 minutes by train from Naples, has a superb Bourbon palace, **Palazzo Reale**, known as *petit Versailles*.

South of Naples lies the beautiful **Amalfi Coast**. It is an area of mountains, limestone rock and beaches. There are many small towns dotted along the coast, so the best way to take it all in is by hiring a scooter.

**Amalfi** is a pleasant seaside town with a magnificent Moorish-style cathedral. It once rivalled Genoa and Venice for control of the Mediterranean. The Tourist Office is at Corso delle Repubbliche Marinare 27 (Tel. 089 871107).

Since Amalfi can become quite crowded, it's better to stay at other small towns, like **Atrani**, about a 10-minute walk away. Here you can stay by the beach at A'Scalinatella, Piazza Umberto 12 (Tel. 089 871492). It is inexpensive and the you get a course at a local restaurant thrown in.

Make sure you visit the spectacular cliffside town of **Ravello** and the **Emerald Grotto**, about four km from Amalfi, in the bay of Corica dei Marini.

If you're heading for Sicily, you can stop off at **Salerno** (famous during the Middle Ages for its school of medicine) and catch a bus (it takes about an hour) to **Paestum**, where you'll find ancient Greek temples, better than many in Greece, and some impressive tomb paintings. There are a number of campsites and hotels strewn along the sandy shoreline.

# Puglia

**Bari** and **Brindisi** are stopping-off places for those on their way to Greece. Neither offers much in the way of culture but you may need to use their facilities before you head for nicer scenery. Both have had an influx of immigrants and refugees due to the recent troubles across the Adriatic Sea.

**BARI** In an attempt to attract the young tourist, Bari has introduced a 'Stopover in Bari' scheme whereby people under the age of 30 can enjoy free camping, buses, information centres, museums, cheap meals, luggage storage and free bikes. The offer lasts from the end of June until September, and all the information you'll need about the stopover is available from the booth near the station.

Another part of the scheme is a package that puts you up in a **private home** for two nights at a very cheap rate. For more information, contact the main office at Via Nicolai 47 (Tel. 080 5214538; Fax. 080 521 1822, open 8.30am–8.30pm daily). There is also a 24-hour telephone hotline (Tel. 080 577 2349 ).

To get to the free **campsite**, take bus 5 to Pineta San Francesco park. Staff at the campsite are friendly and helpful, and if you get there early you can borrow a tent.

Good pensions include **Pensione Fiorini** at Via Imbriani 69 (Tel. 080 554 0788). There are a few dorm beds and doubles cost 60,000L. Also try **Pensione Giulia** at Via Crisanzio 12 (Tel. 080 521 8271)

There's an **Amex** agency at Corso di Tullio 36-40 (Tel. 080 5210 022) and a **Eurail Aid Office** at Bari Central Station (Tel. 080 732003 or 080 521 2202) – note that it's closed for three hours between 1pm and 4pm, and on Sundays.

**Ferries** depart for Corfu and Patras, but it's best to book your voyage in advance and to get to the station at least two hours early to pay your tax.

**BRINDISI** This town is worse than Bari, so arrive in the afternoon in time for the regular evening ferry service to Corfu and Patras. We have had reports from travellers that they have found Brindisi extremely hostile so be especially careful. Make sure you have both currencies before boarding, but avoid changing money here. Most of the ferry lines offer discounts to the under-27s and ISIC card holders. Eurail and Inter-Rail pass holders are given free passage on deck on Adriatica Lines (preferable option) and Hellenic Mediterranean Lines, but in the summer months everyone travelling deck class, except for InterRail holders,must pay a supplementary fee of around 20,000L (more if travelling in better class accommodation), there is also 12,000L port tax and 5,000L reservation fee to pay.

Check the schedules carefully if travelling in winter, as not all the boats operate. The boat offices are as follows: **Adriatica Lines**, Viale Regina Margherita 13 (Tel. 0831 523 825); **Hellenic Mediterranean Lines**, Corso Garibaldi 8 (Tel. 0831 528531).

The Tourist Office is EPT, on Viale Regina Margherita, at the dock to the left of the station Marittima (Tel. 0831 523072). Opening hours are Mon.–Fri.: 8am–1.30pm and Tues.: 3–6.30pm.

Pizzeria L'Angoletto, Via Pergola 3, near the fishing port, does great traditional pizzas and pasta. You can stock up for the ferry journey at the open-air produce market on Via Fornari, off Piazza Vittoria, and at the Sidis supermarket near the port.

# Sicily

Sicily is an interesting place to visit despite – or perhaps because of – its reputation as the home of the Cosa Nostra (the Mafia). Because of its strategic position it has been in the hands of just about every empire there ever was, and the legacy of their civilizations has left Sicily a virtual treasure trove.

The backdrop to all this is the hulking great Mount Etna, at 3,232 metres one of the world's biggest active volcanoes. It has erupted 135 times since records began. Sicily is also home to two other actives volcanoes – Stromboli and Vulcano.

## GETTING THERE
The journey from Naples to the largest and most heavily populated island in the Mediterranean takes about eight hours. The standard

crossing is from **Villa San Giovanni** to **Messina** on the train-ferry. In summer the Rome–Sicily run gets crowded, so reserve a seat if you can. Ignore the ferries from Naples to Catania, Siracusa and Palermo. If you're on Inter-Rail you have to pay to get over. Once you're there you'll have to use the railway as your main sightseeing medium, though the buses are reasonably punctual and usually air-conditioned.

**THE EAST COAST** The port of **Messina**, situated on the strait of the same name, was founded by the Greeks. It has been rebuilt twice this century, once after the 1908 earthquake and again after the bombing of the World War II. Consequently, there's not much to see, but if you've time to kill waiting for a ferry, take in the following sights: the largest **Astronomical Mechanical Clock** in the world in the **Norman Cathedral**, and the church of the **Annunciation of the Catalans**. The Tourist Office is on Via Calabria Isolato 301 (Tel. 090 69022).

Half an hour from Messina is **Taormina**, a resort popular with middle-aged Italians and famous for the outstanding remains of its 3rd century BC theatre. The **Greek Theatre** looks out over the live volcano Mount Etna, which makes this setting for Greek drama suitably dramatic. The **Palazzo Corvaja**, the Sicilian parliament house, is in Piazza Vittorio Emanuele and the beach of **Mazzaro** can be reached by funicular.

**Catania** hasn't been swamped by Mount Etna since 1693, but in 1992 the mountain engulfed nearby villages and the countryside with lava. Its 18th-century cathedral is on the beautiful Piazza del Dumo. The cuisine in Catania is highly praised and fresh fish is a particular speciality. For **pensions**, try Pensione Rubens at 196 Via Etnea (Tel. 095 3170 73). There is a campsite, Eucalypto Campeggio at Via San Francesco La Rena (Tel. 095 591 014). There is a **youth hostel** in Nicolosi at Via della Quercia 7 (Tel. 095 7914686).

**Siracusa** was once as important as Rome or Athens and there are plenty of archaeological sites to back this up. The **Archaeological Museum** is at Piazza del Duomo and the ruined Temple of Apollo is on Ortigia Island. The **Greek Theatre** is considered the best of its kind in the world. Opposite is an altar that was used for public sacrifices; a short walk takes you to the **Roman Amphitheatre** built into the rock.

**THE SOUTH COAST** The hillside town of **Agrigento** is the site of the **Valley of Temples**, a collection of ancient columns and temples. Agrigento has frequent train services to other parts of Sicily. The main town is eight km from the sea, where there is a beach resort called San Leone. The AAST **Tourist Office** is on Via Cesare Battisti (Tel. 0922 20454), the main office is on Via Empedocle (Tel. 0922 20391).

**PALERMO** The capital of Sicily is a heady mixture of Arabic and Western influences, with architecture to match its history.

**Tourist Information** is available at Piazza Castelnuova 34 (Tel. 091 605 8111), open Mon.–Fri.: 8.30am–2pm and 3–6pm, Sat. 8am–2pm. There's also a small office at the train station. For a guide to what's on, pick up a copy of *Un Mese a Palermo*, the arts and entertainment guide. There's an **Amex** agency at 38/40 Via Emerico Amari (Tel. 091 587144), and a **Eurail Aid Office** at the train station (Tel. 091 616 4808).

A **late-night pharmacy**, Lo Casio, can be found in Via Roma 1 near the train station (Tel. 091 616 2117).

**FREE PALERMO:**

- Arabic origins can be seen in the **Palace of the Normans** (especially the **Palatine Chapel Mosaics**). Open Mon.–Fri.: 9am–12noon and 3pm–5pm, Sat.: 9am–12noon and Sun.: 9am–10am and 12noon–1pm, unless the Sicilian Parliament is in session.
- Don't miss the church **La Martorana**, again built in the Norman period but with Byzantine mosaics.
- Eight kilometres away in Monreale is the **Norman Cathedral** with its extraordinary medieval mosaics (admission free; open 8am–12noon and 3.30pm–6pm) and next door the **Benedictine Cloister**.
- Stroll through the historic **Vucciria Market** in the old part of Palermo. You could be forgiven for thinking you were in an Arab souk.

Try round the harbour for cheap rooms, or near the station. **Albergo Rosalia Conca d'Oro**, Via Santa Rosalia 7 (Tel. 091 616 4543), singles for 38,000L, doubles for 53,000L. Or if you prefer to camp, take bus 628 from the Politeama Theatre to Sferracavallo, 13 km north-west of town, where there are two **campsites: Trinacria** on Via Barcarello (Tel. 091 530590) and the cheaper **Ulivo**, Via Pegaso (Tel. 091 533021).

Palermo's nightlife is at **Mondello** (which also has a fine beach), but for good eating try the **Da Pino**, Via dello Spezio 6, on Piazza Sturzo, open Mon.–Sat.: 12noon–3.30pm and 8pm–11pm. Local specialities include stuffed swordfish, octopus, fried chickpea sandwiches, pasta with sardines, and spaghetti with broccoli. Watch out also for bread balls stuffed with rice or meat, and pastries filled with watermelon jelly.

# Sardinia (Sardegna)

Midway between Italy and North Africa is the mountainous, untamed island of Sardinia. Though the west is mainly cultivated, the east is wild and almost completely untouched. The Sardinians have a strong independent streak; the region was granted autonomous status in 1948. There are few large towns and only a few real roads, so be prepared to rough it a bit if you're camping, though camping is still by far the best form of accommodation on the island and the scenery is beautiful.

## GETTING THERE

From Italy there are ferries to Cagliari (the capital), Arbatax and Olbia (on the east coast), and Porto Torres (the northern tip). The best **overnight** crossing is with the Tirrenia Line from Civitavecchia (an hour north of Rome) to Olbia. It costs about 50,000L for deck class, takes about seven hours, and reservations are advisable. The Tirrenia office in Civitavecchia is at Stazione Marittima (Tel. 0766 20332/0766 21703). Genoa to Olbia and Porto Torres is also a good choice.

For a **daytime** crossing, the state railways ferry from Civitavecchia to Golfo Aranci is the cheapest (more expensive at the weekend). The crossing takes about nine hours and there are four crossings a day. Golfo Aranci is a short train ride from Olbia.

## GENERAL INFORMATION

The rail network connects the northern and western coasts, but is limited elsewhere. Services are slow and a bit unpredictable, but it's better than hitching. Good cheap pensions are thin on the ground and hotels are expensive. In the north, youth hostels are your best bet – they're cheap and usually on the beach. But you can't beat camping. There are several official sites, but the best fun is to set up your own.

Avoid the restaurants and go for *pizzerie*, *tavole calde* or *rosticcerie*. Fish and seafood are cheap on the coast (cook them yourself), and the markets provide ample picnic food. The local wine is Vernaccia.

There's an Amex agency in Olbia at Corso Umberto 139 (Tel. 0789 24327). The Tourist Office is at Via Catello Piro 1 (Tel. 0789 21453).

**THE EAST COAST** South from Olbia is the most unspoilt region of Sardinia. There are miles of beautiful quiet beaches. **Nuoro** and **Arbatax** are the sites of archaeological remains. To get to this area, you'll need to take the train from Macomer or Cagliari. The coast around **Santa Maria Navarrese** is good for beaches.

North of Olbia is **Costa Smeralda** (Emerald Coast), the 'millionaires' playground'. This is the most commercialized part of the island. **Porto Cervo** is picturesque, chic, and has some of the most expensive land in Italy. The **Golfo di Orosei** is one hour away from Olbia and there is a campsite Cala Ginepro with the best beach in Sardinia.

**Arazachena** has some very good beaches.

It's also worth taking a scenic bus ride from Olbia along the dramatic rocky coastline with its many picturesque bays to **Santa Teresa di Gallura** on the northernmost tip of Sardinia. This little fishing village has a ferry link to Bonifacio in southern Corsica. The Tourist Office can be found at Piazza Vittorio Emanuele 24 (Tel. 0789 754127).

**THE WEST COAST** The capital of Sardinia is **Cagliari**. Concentrate on the medieval centre, the **Castello**, near the harbour. The **Cathedral** is here and not far away is the **Roman Amphitheatre**. The **National Archaeological Museum** is famous for its collection of bronzes from the prehistoric Nuraghe civilization. Don't miss the flea market at Bastione di San Remy on Sun. mornings and try to coincide your visit with the July–Sept. arts festival, when plays are put on in the amphitheatre.

Tourist Information is at Piazza Matteotti 9 (Tel. 070 669255). There's also a branch office at the port. For cheap beds and meals try the streets between Corso Vittorio Emanuele and Via Roma. The nearest campsite is at Quartu Sant' Elena (Tel. 070 803107), a 45-minute bus journey east along the coast; bungalows are also available.

**Sassari**, Sardinia's second city, has an interesting old town which centres on the **Cathedral**. The **Sardinian National Museum** is here and Tourist Information is at Viale Umberto 72 (Tel. 079 231331). This is your best base for exploring north-west Sardinia, and you'll find cheap rooms and meals along Corso Vittorio Emanuele.

An hour from here is one of the prettiest towns on the island, **Alghero**. It's more Spanish than Italian, as for many years it was a Catalan colony. There is an IYHF Hostel at Via Zara 1, open all year round (Tel. 079 930 353 or 079 93 00 15; Fax. 079 930 353). From here take a boat out to **Capo Caccia** and the Neptune Grotto, a series of underground caves. The Tourist Office can be found at Piazza Portaterra 9 (Tel. 079 979054).

NOTES:

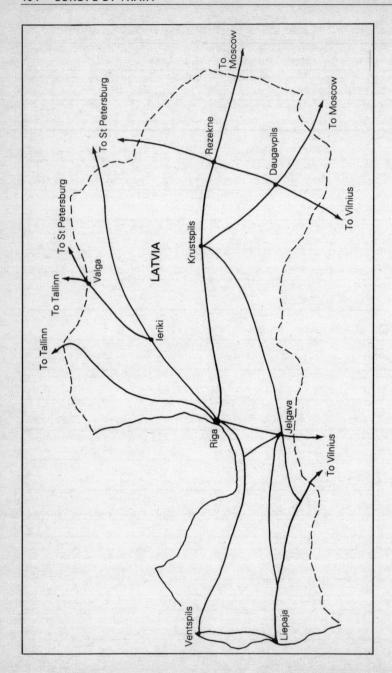

# LATVIA (Latvija)

| | |
|---|---|
| Entry requirements | Passport. Canadians, Australians and New Zealanders require visas. |
| Population | 2.65 million |
| Capital | Riga (pop.: 0.82 million) |
| Currency | Lats (Ls) |
| | £1 = approx. 0.94Ls |
| Political system | Parliamentary democracy |
| Religion | Lutheran, Russian Orthodox and Catholic |
| Language | Latvian, Russian widely spoken (see note on languages), some English and German |
| Public holidays | New Year's Day, Good Friday, Easter, Labour Day (1 May), Midsummer's Day (23 June), St John's Day (24 June), Martin's Day (5 Sept.), Veterans' Day (11 Nov.), Independence Day (18 Nov.), Christmas Day and Boxing Day, New Year's Eve |
| International dialling codes | To Latvia: 00 + int'l code 371 |
| | From Latvia: 007 + country code |
| Time | GMT +2 (+3 in summer) |
| Emergency telephone numbers | Police 02; ambulance 03; fire service 01 |

In many ways Latvian history has mirrored that of its Baltic neighbour Estonia. As in Estonia, when German crusading knights arrived on the scene in the early 13th century it was the start of a long period of foreign domination.

After the knights founded the city of Riga in 1204 it developed into a flourishing member of the medieval Hanseatic League – a powerful association of trading cities. As a result, it wasn't long before Latvia was attracting the beady eyes of other empire-hungry countries and by the start of this century Poland, Sweden and Russia had all grabbed control of it at one time or another.

Independence was declared in 1918 and secured two years later after battles – with Estonia's help – against Russian and German forces. But during World War II the country came under the cosh of the Soviet Union, followed by Nazi Germany, and was again back to square one. Hitler's occupation also had tragic consequences as 90% of Latvia's Jewish population perished in the concentration camp at Salaspils near Riga.

By the end of the war Latvia was beneath the iron fist of the Soviet Union. Stalin's aim was to make the population more like 'Soviets' and to do this he carried out mass deportations – replacing Latvians with Russians. Coupled with the effects of the Jewish holocaust, Latvia's native population subsequently dropped to 50%.

During the late 1980s a renewed drive for liberty was underway and protests were taking place on everything, from political to environmental issues. In August 1991, following the failed Soviet coup against Gorbachev, Latvia took the opportunity offered by the disarray and announced its independence to the world – albeit a little sooner than expected.

Today, the country is still struggling to steer itself along the rocky road to capitalism. Standards of living are low, as are production levels, and both EU and NATO membership seem to be a long way away. Dismantling the legacies of a Soviet era is a difficult uphill task and one it seems that has no shortcuts.

## TRAIN INFORMATION

For information on train schedules contact Latvian Railways, 3 Gogola iela, Riga (Tel.723 3113).There should be some English speakers at Riga station (Tel. 723 3095) but you will probably have to use your ingenuity outside the capital. Alternatively, visit Latvian Railways website at www.ldz.lv/english/services/p_trans.html. Information signs at the station have mostly been changed to Latvian from Russian, though you may still see both.

**PASSES AVAILABLE** Inter-Rail and Eurail passes are not valid in Latvia. The Baltic States Explorer Pass is usually available for 7, 14, or 21 days  and gives unlimited 2nd-class travel within Latvia, Lithuania and Estonia. However at the moment it is not being sold as the line between Estonia and Lithuania is out of action (being repaired). Before you travel, check with Campus Travel (Tel. 020 7938 2188) to see what's the latest. Travelling by train in Latvia is so cheap you may be better off just paying for the journeys you do.

**RESERVATIONS** Obligatory on international trains and definitely recommended on all other routes, as trains tend to be packed. Upgrading to first class won't cost much and is worth taking when it's available.

**NIGHT TRAVEL** Being such a small country means there is no need for an overnight domestic service. International trains do have overnight facilities but don't expect to get much beauty sleep on them.

**INTERNAL TRAVEL** Buses offer a faster and more reliable service than trains, which makes them the best way to see the country.

## TOURIST INFORMATION

Unfortunately, there is a distinct lack of information offices throughout Latvia. Some are marked by a green letter 'i' so keep your eyes peeled. The capital, Riga, has an office at its airport (Tel. 720 7800) and there's also an information bureau in the centre at Skārņu iela 22 (Tel. 722 1731). However this office is due to move to the Blackhead House soon. The cities of Valmiera, Daugavpils and Césis have offices too. There are also two helpful telephone information services 7222 222 and 8008 008.

**ISIC BONUSES** As with most Eastern European countries, your ISIC card will usually get you discounts, but knowing when or where is hard to say. Flash it whenever you get the opportunity.

**TELEPHONING** For any of the new telephones you'll need a card which you can buy from kiosks or post offices. Old phones will be token operated.

**MONEY MATTERS** 1 Lat (Ls)=100 santīmi

In general, banks are open Mon.–Fri.: 10am–4pm or later. In Riga credit cards are accepted in more expensive shops and restaurants and some travellers' cheques (such as American Express) can be cashed in major banks. Outside the capital you will probably struggle, so it is safer to bring cash, preferably US dollars or Deutschmarks in low denomination notes.

**SHOPS** Open in general Mon.–Fri.: 8/10am–6/8pm (often shut for lunch 2pm–3pm), on Sat. they usually close at 5pm. Prices for tourists remain fairly cheap, despite recent increases. In some instances, you may end up paying a price two to three times higher than the locals pay.

**MUSEUMS** Generally open 10am–6pm, though times vary.

**WEATHER** June and July are the best months to visit, as the wind dies down and the sea is warm.

**LANGUAGE** Latvian is the national language, but only half the population are native and use it as their first language. This has led to strong nationalist sentiments and your efforts to master a few phrases will endear you to the locals. Here are some useful ones to help out a little:

| Hello | *Sveiki* | Thank you | *Paldies* |
|-------|----------|-----------|-----------|
| Goodbye | *Ata* | Excuse me | *Atvainojiet* |
| Yes | *Ja* | Do you speak | *Vas jus runajet* |
| No | *Ne* | English? | *anliski?* |
| Please | *Ludzu* | Russian? | *krievski?* |

**TIPPING** Leave up to 10% if you feel you have had good service.

## SLEEPING AND EATING

In summer, universities open their dormitories to travellers, charging from £4.50 per person. Information on Youth Hostels is available on 755 1271.

Food-wise the staple diet is fish and dairy products. Try the local fish dish *Riga Tel'noe*, deep-fried fillets stuffed with a mushroom and anchovy filling. Soups (*zupa*) should provide you with a good fill as well. You won't have a problem getting your daily picnic rations together as bakeries and vegetable markets are pretty well stocked.

## Riga phone code: 2 (except tel. nos with 7 digits)

Riga was founded in 1201 by Bishop Albert von Buxhoevden of Bremen who came on a crusade to convert the local tribes to Christianity. Next year there will be big celebrations to mark the 800th anniversary. Riga took a pounding in the two World Wars and today, although no longer in the grip of Soviet rule, is still an industrial and technological showpiece of the former empire days. Notable reminders of the pre-war days do remain, however, and help create a picture of Riga when it was known as the 'Paris of the Baltic'.

## TOURIST INFORMATION

The Tourist Information Bureau is at Skārņu iela 22 (Tel. 722 1731) and has a friendly English-speaking staff. But, really, all you need to get your hands on is a copy of the excellent city guide, *Riga in Your Pocket*. It's widely available from kiosks and hotel foyers or the Tourist Office, and will only set you back 50 santīmi. Tip 94 in the train station can help with accommodation (Tel. 232 884).

**UK EMBASSY** 5 Alunāna iela (Tel. 733 8126)
**US EMBASSY** Raiņa bulvari 7 (Tel. 721 0005)
**CANADIAN EMBASSY** Doma Laukums 4 (Tel. 722 6315 or 783 0141)
**POST OFFICE** Central PO, Brīvības bulvāris 19. Open 24 hours.
**HOSPITAL** ARS clinic, Skolas 5. Tel. 720 1001/720 1007 or 720 1006. Has English-speaking doctors.
**PHARMACY** Brīvības 74, Tel. 293 514. Open 8am–9pm, or ring bell when closed
**STUDENT TRAVEL OFFICE** SIF, 19 Raina Blvd, office 248 (Tel. 228320)

## SEEING

The **Old Town**, stretching along the bank of the Daugava river, is where you should make for to see the city's main attractions. Through the snaking streets head for its heart at Cathedral Square, flanked by a string of cafés and restaurants. Here you can't fail to notice the imposing 700-year-old **Dome Cathedral**. It's the Baltic's largest place of worship, but if that's not impressive enough, it's also got the fourth largest organ in the world, with 6,768 pipes. It's a superb building reflecting a number of different architectural styles.

The Gothic **St Peter's Church** on Skārņu iela is another dominating structure. Its tower, once made from wood and the highest in Europe, offers a breathtaking panorama over the rooftops of Vecriga.

Other notable attractions include the **Powder Tower**, the city's last remaining 18th century bastion; the **Swedish Gate**, built in 1698 and part of the old town's fortifications; and the churches of **St Jekab's** and **St John's**.

Look out too for **Riga Castle** on Pils laukums. It's home to the Latvian president and houses the **Museum of Foreign Art**, open Tue.–Sun. 11am–5pm. The **Museum of Decorative and Applied Art** at Skārrņu iela 10/20 also exhibits tapestries, sculptures, ceramic and glass works. It's open Tue.–Sun.: 10am–5pm.

**FREE RIGA:** A good way not to trouble your pocket too much is to shop for lunch supplies and head for one of the parks just west of the river in the new town. **Vērmane Park** has an open-air auditorium where free musical performances are held, ranging from classical to traditional folk. Check *Riga in Your Pocket* for details.

- The new town also has some great examples of Jugenstil (Art Nouveau) architecture; savour the best along Elizabetes and Alberta iela.
- Up by the train station, Riga's bustling **market** takes place in five huge wartime Zeppelin hangars. It's a great place to have a rummage and ideal for picking up your fruit and veg. Other free attractions include:
- **Occupation Museum of Latvia**, Strēlnieku laukums 1. Closed Saturday and Monday. Describes Latvia under Hitler and the Soviets.
- **Freedom Monument** at Brīvības piemineklis. Built in the 1930s to commemorate Latvian independence and symbolically guarded by two soldiers. In the 1980s and early 1990s the park and the monument became focal points in the Latvians' renewed struggle for independence from the Soviet fold.
- Nearby, in Bastejkalns, are five red stone slabs which lie as **Memorials to the Victims of 20 January 1991**, who were killed here when the Interior Ministry was stormed by Soviet troops.

## SLEEPING, EATING AND NIGHTLIFE

For student dormitories, the **Riga Technical University Hostel** has double and triple rooms for 4Ls per person and is at Azenes 22a, Tel. 203395 or 613843. Otherwise try the dorms at Basteja bulv. 10 (Tel. 721 6221). Information on youth hostels is available from Laimdotas 2a (Tel. 755 1271).

The **Tûrists**, Slokas iela 1 (Tel. 761 9090; Fax 786 0008), is a big Soviet-style hotel with clean and reasonably priced rooms (around 22–40Ls for a double). The **Saulite Hotel**, near the station at Merķeļa 12 (Tel. 722 4546 or 722 8219), is slightly cheaper with bright and comfortable renovated rooms. Prices for single-to-quadruple accommodation cost between 5 and 20Ls.

Details of private rooms can be had at Patricija, Elizabetes 22–26 (Tel. 728 4868) and at the Information Bureau on Skārņu iela (Tel.

Tel. 722 1731 or 722 1731; Fax. 722 7680)

**Bars** and **cafés** are the best places to head for if you want cheap meals. Definitely worth trying is **Andalūzijas Suns** (The Andalusian Dog) at Elizabetes 83/85, a café named after a Dali and Buñuel film with large artistically served portions at reasonable prices. They also cater for vegetarians and if you suddenly get the urge to send an e-mail, you can do that here as well. **Anre** at Aspazijas bulvaris 30 also serves inexpensive meals and decent cakes. Fast food junkies will be pleased to know there are plenty of outlets around the city.

If you want to treat yourself, try **Ice Queen** at Ģertrūdes 20 it's the best ice-cream in the city.

There are lots of decent nightclubs to try, don't be surprised to find that many have strip shows and other 'adult' entertainment acts. **Bimini** at Caka 67–69 is popular with foreigners and has European DJs and **Monte Kristo** at Merķeļa iela 8 stays open 24hrs. **Pepsiforum** is near McDonalds in the centre but the hippest place to be seen is **Vernisaj** which has live music and two dance floors, one of which gyrates rather strangely. Ask for directions at the tourist office and check in *Riga in Your Pocket* for the latest.

Riga has the only permanent **circus** in the Baltics (shut from June to Sept.). It makes a good evening out with its out-of-the-ordinary acts, where else can you see performing pigs? It's at Merķeļa iela 4 (Tel. 722 0272 or 721 3279).

**EXCURSIONS** One of the highlights of any trip to Latvia is the superb 18th century **Rundale Palace** 80 km south-west of Riga.

**Salaspils**, the site of one of Hitler's concentration camps, lies just over 20 km from Riga. Take the train to Darzini and walk to the monumental statues, a memorial to more than 100,000 Jews who perished here.

**Sigulda**, in the breathtaking Gauja valley, 50 km north-east of Riga, is the main centre of the **Gauja National Park**. Explore its woods, caves, lakes and several castles. For accommodation, try the reasonably cheap **Senleja Hotel** at Turaidas 4 (Tel. 972162), but be warned, it is a long way from the railway station.

NOTES:
........................................................................................................................
........................................................................................................................
........................................................................................................................
........................................................................................................................
........................................................................................................................

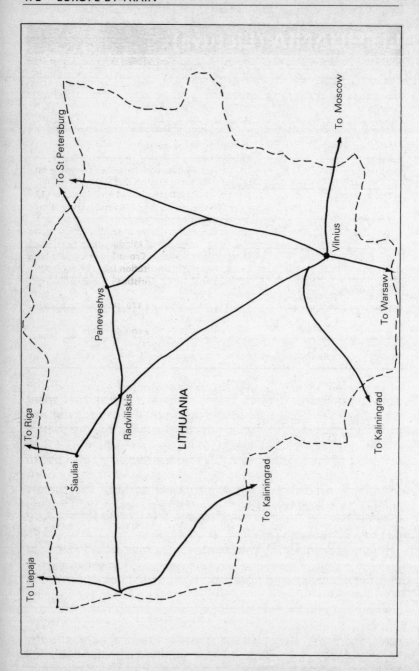

# LITHUANIA (Lietuva)

| | |
|---|---|
| Entry requirements | Passport. New Zealanders also require a visa. |
| Population | 3.7 million |
| Capital | Vilnius (pop.: 0.6 million) |
| Currency | Litas (Lt) |
| | £1 = approx. 6.4Lt |
| Political system | Parliamentary democracy |
| Religion | Catholic |
| Language | Lithuanian, Russian widely spoken (see note on languages), some English and German |
| Public holidays | New Year's Day, Defenders of Freedom Day (13 Jan.), Independence Day (16 Feb.), Restoration of Lithuania's Independence (11 Mar.), Easter, Labour Day (1 May), Day of Mourning and Hope (14 June), Crowning of Mindaugas (6 July), Black Ribbon Day (23 Aug.), Crowning of Vytautas the Great (8 Sept.), Constitution Day (25 Oct.), All Saints Day (1 Nov.), Christmas Day and Boxing Day |
| International dialling codes | To Lithuania: int'l code 370, then the local code, omitting the 82 |
| | From Lithuania: 8+10 + country code |
| Time | GMT + 2 (+3 in summer) |
| Emergency telephone numbers | Police 02; ambulance 03; fire service 01 |

Unlike its Baltic neighbours, Lithuania managed to fend off the constant attacks of German Teutonic knights. In fact, they spent almost 200 years doing so, suitably aided by the dense forest and marshlands that cover the land. By 1410, the threat was over, with a crushing defeat over the knights.

During this time Lithuania had also been staging its own rise to power. The decline of Russia in the 14th century left the door open to foreign invaders and, looking for new territory, they boldly entered. With Belarus and a part of northern Ukraine brought into the clutches of its empire, Lithuania became one of the most powerful states in eastern Europe.

After two centuries of relative peace, war broke out with Russia in the 17th century. Poland and Lithuania, who had formed an alliance back in 1386, combined forces and seized control of Moscow for a short time. But Russia soon retaliated and, in addition to regaining control, also won the prize scalp of Lithuania itself.

Loss of independence continued up until the end of World War I, when it was won back by nationalists. In identical fashion to the other Baltic States, however, it was a position that only lasted until Soviet occupation in 1939.

The next few years brought tragic consequences as Hitler's Nazis arrived and executed 200,000 Jews in death camps. At the end of the war, the return of the Red Army didn't improve matters too much either, as some 250,000 Lithuanians suffered enforced deportation.

In the late 1980s Lithuania was on a serious political path to freedom with the recognition of parties other than communists. On 11 March, 1990, they were miles ahead of the other Baltics and declared their independence, though with such a strong reliance on the USSR, many considered them doomed to failure. However, with the breakdown of the Soviet Union the following year, Lithuania was given a better chance to succeed.

Reform is still biting hard but there are encouraging signs for the future with foreign investment increasing and the privatization of some large-scale industries.

## TRAIN INFORMATION

The rail network is fairly extensive but all but one of the old narrow-gauge lines are now closed, and this means that there are many dead-end routes. It also means that there are gaps in the system and some of the major towns have no rail link. Be warned as well that many maps of the country still mark on lines which are now defunct.

**RESERVATIONS** Trains are usually very crowded so make sure you reserve a seat; for international trains it's mandatory. The Reservation Bureau at Vilnius station (Tel. 822 623927) is open daily: 6am–midnight.

Pay the small extra and upgrade to first class, which is a lot less cramped. *Coupe* compartments (which seat four) or the expensive *SV-deluxe* compartments are more comfortable.

**PASSES AVAILABLE** Inter-Rail and Eurail passes are not valid in Lithuania. For under 26s, ISIC-holders and academic staff the Baltic States Explorer Pass is usually available for a period of seven, 14, or 21 days, however, at the moment they are not for sale as the line between Estonia and Lithuania is out of action (being repaired). In any case, to make these passes cost-effective you really need to use them a lot so you're probably better off buying individual tickets for each journey you make. Before you travel, check with Campus Travel (Tel. 020 7938 2188) to find out what's the latest.

**NIGHT TRAVEL** The only internal night train runs between Vilnius and Klaipeda and is excruciatingly slow. There are also night trains bound for international destinations. They're not great for sleeping on or worth the money.

**EATING ON TRAINS** Pay a visit to the supermaket before travelling as there is no food available on trains. If you're lucky, you may get a decent trolley service on trains from Poland.

**BUS INFORMATION** Many towns and villages are not on the rail network so bus travel is a popular way of getting around the country. Take an express bus for distant destinations. The Vilnius bus station is at Sody 22, next to the railway station (Tel. 822 262482).

## TOURIST INFORMATION

Most places will have a Tourist Office but your greatest source of information are the *In Your Pocket* series of guides which cover everything you need to know on the main cities and their surrounding areas. They are available for Vilnius, Klaipėda and Kaunas and can be bought from newsstands and Tourist Offices for around 4Lt.

**ISIC BONUSES** Show your card whenever you get the opportunity – you never know where the next discount is coming from.

**MONEY MATTERS** 1 Litas (Lt) = 100 centu

Banks are normally open Mon.–Fri.:8am–4pm (some stay open to 7pm), and Sat.: 9am–1pm. Credit cards are accepted in the more expensive shops, restaurants and hotels. Although credit cards and travellers' cheques are steadily gaining acceptance they are still limited in use, so bring cash, preferably US dollars or Deutschmarks. Don't be tempted to pay in foreign currencies either, it's illegal and a definite way to get ripped off!

**SHOPS** Generally hours are Mon.–Fri.: 9am–8pm (food stores tend to open earlier) with lunch at 2pm–3pm. Weekends open 10am–4pm.

**MUSEUMS** Hours vary a lot but usually open 11am–4pm. Most are closed on Mon. and often on another day as well.

**LANGUAGE** In Vilnius you should bump into some English speakers but outside the capital you will struggle – as always, ingenuity is your best policy. Strong Polish ties and a long Russian occupation have inevitably produced a nation of Russian and Polish speakers. Although Lithuanian is the national language it's in danger of dying out, even with 81% of the population native to the country.

| | | | |
|---|---|---|---|
| Hello | *Labas* | Thank you | *Ačiū* |
| Goodbye | *Viso gero* | Excuse me | *Atsiprašau* |
| Yes | *Taip* | Do you speak | *Ar kalbate* |
| No | *Ne* | English? | *angliškai?* |
| Please | *Prašau* | Russian? | *rusiškai?* |

**TIPPING** A tip of up to 10% is normal if you think you've had good service. It is expected at hotels, restaurants, in cloakrooms and in taxis.

## SLEEPING AND EATING

Lithuania has eight youth hostels offering beds for about 25–40Lt per night. Guest cards are usually available for those who are not IYHF members. Contact the head office at Filaretu 17, Vilnius (Tel./Fax. 822 262660) for details. Private rooms are also a good option for budget accommodation and can be booked through *Litinterp* agencies in most towns. There are campsites around too, but they tend to be a long distance from towns.

For your daily sustenance, you should be able to find cheap cafés and restaurants. The *In Your Pocket* guides are ideal for unbiased recommendations. Don't forget bakeries and local farmers' markets are a good source of picnic supplies as well. National dishes include *cepelinai* (meat-stuffed potato dumplings), *kugelis* (a rich potato pie), and a range of dishes made with wild mushrooms.

# Vilnius phone code: 822

Neatly bisected by the River Neris, Vilnius' sights fall mainly into its southern half and in particular the Old Town. With its churches and synagogues, ancient fortifications, courtyards and narrow cobbled streets, it's a real delight to wander through. Add to this an architectural recipe of Gothic, Renaissance, Baroque and classical styles and its hardly surprising that Vilnius holds the status of a UNESCO World Heritage Site.

## TOURIST INFORMATION

The city's main Tourist Information Office is at Gedimino 14 (Tel. 616867), open Mon–Fri.: 9am–5pm, and Sat.: 10am–3pm. Here you can get your hands on the excellent official city guide *Vilnius in Your Pocket*, or you can buy it from hotel foyers and newspaper kiosks. There's also an office at Pilies 42 as well (Tel. 620762) open Mon.–Fri.: 9am–7pm and Sat.: 12 noon–6pm, and at Vilniaus 22 (Tel. 629660) open Mon.–Fri. 9am–6pm.

In the arrival hall at the airport, there is the **In Your Pocket Information Centre** (Tel. 8299 99721) which sells maps and guides and books accommodation and car rental. Open Mon.–Sat.: 9.30am–3.30pm.

**STUDENT AND YOUTH TRAVEL** J. Basanaviciaus g. 30 (Tel. 650145)
**PHARMACY** Gedimino 27, Vilnius (Tel. 610135). Open 24 hours but offers only essentials at night.
**STATION FACILITIES** The station's new Tourist Information Office is

open 9am–7pm. There's also a 24-hour left-luggage facility and a currency exchange office in the waiting hall. However, you may want to consider exchanging your money in the centre as there have been occasional muggings here.

**TRANSPORT** You'll get overcharged in taxis so take the bus – you can buy a ticket from the driver or at news stands. To get to the centre take trolley bus 2, 5 or 7 from the stop diagonally opposite the train station.

## SEEING

There are a whole host of churches, monasteries and convents in Vilnius, though many have suffered the ravages of wars, fires and general neglect. The rather squat and cumbersome-looking Catholic cathedral, **Arkikatedra Bazilika**, on Cathedral Square dates from 1387 and was reconstructed in 1777 in neo-classical style. Behind the cathedral you can take a path up to **Castle Hill** where all that remains is the **Gediminas Tower**. From here there's an excellent view of the city's mosaic of steeples and rooftops. The road that leads east round the foot of the hill goes to the **Museum of Applied Arts (Taikqmosios Dailes Muzejus)** (Open Tues.–Sat. 12noon–5pm) home to an exhibit of Lithuanian tapestries, jewellery and ceramics.

Probably the country's most outstanding example of late Gothic architecture is **Peter and Paul's Church** at Antakalnio 1, with its simple white façade standing in stark contrast to its breathtaking interior.

The **Medininkai Gate** – the only city gate to have survived intact – stands at the end of the attractive street, Aušros Vartu, providing an entrance to the old town. Another key road is Pilies gatve which leads you to the stunning 16th century Gothic **St Ann's Church**.

Also check out the state **Jewish Museum** at Pylimo 4 (Tel. 620730). Open Mon.–Thurs. 9am–5pm, Fri. till 4pm. The **Lithuanian National Museum (Lietuvos Nacionalinis Muziejus)** runs through the history of Lithuanian people from the Stone Age to 1940 (the display on the achievements of the Lithuanian Republic during the inter-war period is particularly worth seeing). You can find it at Arsenalo 1. Open Wed.–Sun.: 10am–5pm (Tel. 629426).

**FREE VILNIUS:** Discovering the **architectural surprises** that hide within the narrow twisting streets of the old town is probably the lightest activity on your pocket, especially with free entry to most churches.

- In the north-western end of town Zappa fans – yes, that's right, **Frank Zappa** fans – can pay homage to him at his very own 4m **statue** at Kalinausko 1. He was a cult figure here, in case you were wondering!
- It's worth trying some of the **markets** too, for a real taste of local life. The nearest to the train station is at Halès Turgavietè on the corner of Pylimo and Bazilijonų open sunrise until lunchtime,

closed Monday.
- For a pleasant change of pace, take a river-side stroll to **Vingio Parkas** – the city's main park – which also has a huge open-air theatre for festivals. Other options include:
- **Lithuanian Art Museum**, Didžioji 4 – Free Wed.
- **Vilnius University**. Dating back 400 years, it is one of the oldest in Eastern Europe. Has some charming courtyards and arcades.

## SLEEPING AND EATING

There's a full range of recommended accommodation in *Vilnius in Your Pocket*, including budget options. For B&B in the heart of the old town try the **Litinterp** at Bernardinų 7–2 (Tel. 223850 or 223291; Fax. 223559) which has singles for 70–110Lt and doubles for 120–150Lt. Otherwise the comfortable youth hostel **Filaretai** is at Filaretu 17 (Tel. 254627; Fax. 220149). It's on the International Booking Network (IBN) which means you can reserve it from any other IYHF Hostel in the world. First night 35Lt, with a 4Lt discount for additional nights.

Plenty of little cafés line the walk into town from the station and you should be able to find one that meets your budget and standard of cleanliness. New cafés and bars are opening up all the time so again *Vilnius in Your Pocket* is your most valuable and up-to-date source.

Popular bars include **Betmenas** (Batman) at Gedimino 32 and **Angaras** at Jasinskio 14, which is totally hip and full of students. It has a cybercafé and regular live music. If you're missing your pie 'n'mash and pint of ale head to **Prie Parlamento** at Gedimino 46, which is a re-creation of an English pub. Other good nightspots include **Indigo** (females get in free and there's a male striptease on Wed. night) and **Ultra** which plays techno music and serves cheap drinks, ask at the Tourist Office for directions.

NOTES:
.................................................................................................
.................................................................................................
.................................................................................................
.................................................................................................
.................................................................................................
.................................................................................................

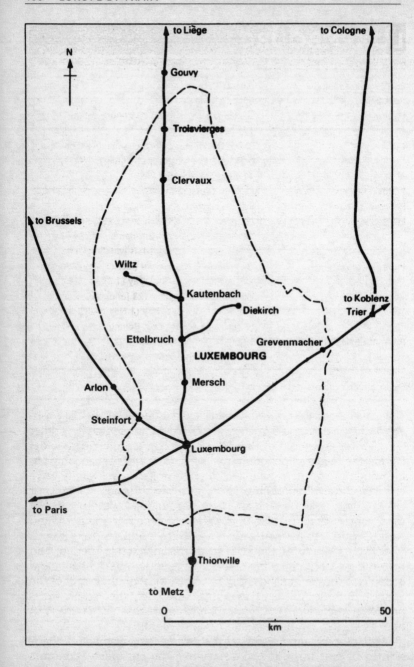

# LUXEMBOURG

| | |
|---|---|
| Entry requirements | Passport |
| Population | 0.42 million |
| Capital | Luxembourg City (pop.: 85,000, agglom. 125,000) |
| Currency | Luxembourg Franc (interchangeable with Belgian Franc but not in Belgium) £1 = approx. 64LUF |
| Political system | Constitutional monarchy |
| Religion | Roman Catholic |
| Language | Officially Letzeburgesch (the people's language), although French and German are spoken by almost everyone. English is widely spoken |
| Public holidays | New Year's Day, Carnival (late Feb, two days), Easter Monday, Labour Day (1 May), Ascension, Whitsun, National Day (23 June), Assumption (15 Aug.), All Saints Day (1 Nov.), All Souls Day (2 Nov.), Christmas Day, Boxing Day |
| International dialling codes | To Luxembourg: int'l code 352 From Luxembourg: 00 + country code |
| Time | GMT +1 (+2 in summer) |
| Emergency telephone numbers | All emergency services 112 |

Tiny Luxembourg, a powerful financial and political centre, has probably more bankers and Eurocrats per square kilometre than any other country in the world. But then, it's only 82km long by 58km wide! During the medieval period, it was three times the size, encompassing much of southern Belgium, and four of its royal family were elected as Holy Roman Emperors. These were turbulent times for Luxembourg, a landlocked small fry surrounded by the big fish of the European empire-building fraternity – Belgium to the north and west, Germany to the east and France to the south.

Over the centuries, it's been invaded, annexed, besieged, and battered. In 1443 Philip the Good of Burgundy seized the city and added it to the Netherlands. It then passed through the hands of the Spanish and the Austrian Habsburgs, and finally the French. Independence came in 1815 and despite being overrun by Germany in both World Wars, it has managed to survive intact.

Perhaps it was survival instinct that influenced Luxembourg's decision to be first through the door when the European Economic Community was born. That early commitment has paid off, with

Luxembourg an important centre at the heart of the European Union, and home to some of the western world's most powerful institutions.

Today, international banking, trade and heavy industry, coupled with low unemployment and a declining birthrate, have delivered a very high standard of living.

The backdrop to all this prosperity is what's been described as the 'green heart of Europe' - a scenic land of wooded valleys and hilltop fortresses that makes ideal camping and hiking country.

## LUXEMBOURG NATIONAL RAILWAYS

**(Société Nationale des Chemins de Fer Luxembourgeois, CFL)**
This is the smallest national rail network in the world – it takes only two hours to cross the whole country – but there are 64 stations, so the train can take you to almost anywhere and there are no supplements to worry about. CFL also run many bus services on which Inter-Rail passes are valid. One example is the service to Echternach in the east of the country.

## TRAIN INFORMATION

For information on international trains, go to the Railway Information Office in Gare Centrale, where English is spoken. If there's a queue, or it's a simple question, look for the information officers wearing yellow capbands.

**PASSES AVAILABLE** **Short-distance** tickets are valid for one hour over a distance of 10km. They cost 40LUF (you can also buy a book of 10 of these tickets for 320LUF). Much better value are the **Network** tickets (160LUF) giving an unlimited number of journeys for second-class travel on all lines of the Luxembourg railway and bus system. Once you stamp them they are valid until 8am the following morning. You can get a book of five network tickets for 640LUF.

If you are taking a bicycle, a 40LUF supplement has to be paid.

Another type of ticket useful for those without an Inter-Rail ticket is the **Benelux Tourail Card**. This pass entitles the holder to five days' unlimited travel in one month in Belgium, the Netherlands and Luxembourg. Prices are: adults £82 and under 26 (junior) £56 (first class adult fare is £120). A second person can travel for half the adult price (not available to under 26s or if purchased in Belgium or Luxembourg). This pass can be bought in the USA, the UK (contact USIT/Campus Travel, tel. 020 7730 3402 or Wasteels, tel. 020 7834 7066) and from train stations in Belgium and Luxembourg. Strangely, you can not buy the Benelux Tourail Card in the Netherlands.

The **Inter-Rail** pass has been broken down into zones, so you don't have to pay for travel to areas you won't be visiting. For £159 you can spend 22 days in a single zone. Luxembourg is in Zone E, along with France, Belgium and the Netherlands. (For further details of the eight Inter-Rail zones, refer to the Inter-Rail section in Part One of this guide.)

For information on the Freedom Pass (Euro Domino) and Eurail, see Part One of this guide.

**RESERVATIONS** It's not possible to reserve on internal trains, and on internationals it's optional, but must be done 24 hours in advance as the train will probably be starting in another country.

## TOURIST INFORMATION

If you require information before you arrive in the country, contact the Office National du Tourisme headquarters, PO Box 1001, L-1010, Luxembourg City (Tel. 4282 8210; Fax. 4282 8238). On arrival, the National Tourist Office is in the main station (Tel. 42 82 82 20) and open 9am–12 noon and 2pm–6.30pm daily. From July till mid-Sept., opening hours are extended to 7pm. Otherwise, there are local offices (*Syndicats d'Initiative*) scattered throughout the country. Most open at 9am and shut at 6pm with an hour-long lunch break but this varies greatly.

If you're spending at least a day here, consider buying the very good value **Luxembourg Card**, which grants free admission to many of the Grand Duchy's attractions. It also gives free travel on all national trains and buses throughout the entire country, and gets 30% reductions on Luxembourg City's tourist train, coach sightseeing trips and certain pleasure boat cruises. There are one, two or three day cards which cost 300LUF (about £4.75), 500LUF (about £8) and 700LUF (about £11) respectively. For a family card covering up to five people, double the prices. The cards are available from tourist offices, the railway and bus stations, youth hostels, hotels and campsites.

**ISIC BONUSES** Some museums and galleries are half price but ISIC and U26 are not widely recognized.

**MONEY MATTERS** 1 Luxembourg Franc (LUF) = 100 centimes.
There are at least 220 different banks from around the world based in Luxembourg. Banking hours are Mon.–Fri.: 9am–12 noon and 1.30pm–4pm, though some banks are open earlier, longer or do not close for lunch; some are open on Sat. mornings. The Luxembourg Franc is interchangeable with the Belgian Franc, but you're best to change them before leaving the country.

**POST OFFICES** Open Mon.–Fri.: 9am–5.30pm (except in Luxembourg City). Station branch opens 6am–8pm. It's possible to cash and pay by Eurocheques in all offices.

**SHOPS AND MUSEUMS**
These vary in their times of opening. Tues.–Fri.: 9am–12 noon and 1pm–6pm seems to be the general rule. All shops are closed on Mon. mornings, and some museums are shut all day.
**TIPPING** Tipping is as relaxed here as in much of Europe. Leave around 10%, or perhaps only your change, but only if you have had good service.

## SLEEPING HERE

There are 14 **youth hostels**, charging between 370LUF and 750LUF per night with breakfast included. Note that from December to February, all hostels except Luxembourg City, Larochette and Wiltz are open only for groups of 10 or more, and reservations for those must be made at least 24 hours in advance.

Pick up the tourist board's excellent free guide on accommodation at the main office next to the station. This lists prices and facilities for all Luxembourg's **hotels** and **pensions**. If you're thinking about **camping**, ask for the free folder giving all the **campsites** and prices. There are a large number of **campsites** all over the country. Expect to pay from 110LUF per tent plus a further 50–200LUF per person. Refer to *Cheap Sleeps Europe 2000* for a full range of options.

## EATING AND NIGHTLIFE

Food here has a strong French flavour. Specialities include Ardennes ham, which you can pick up at supermarkets and butchers' in towns; venison dishes, river trout, Eifel bread and pastries.

There are good wines from vineyards along the river Ahr and the Moselle, but better known are the beers, locally distilled spirits, and mineral waters (from which many of the beers are brewed).

The locals are a fairly cultured bunch, with a good round each year of international festivals, operas, concerts, ballets and theatre. Check up with the Tourist Offices for what's happening in the week ahead, or contact the venues direct: Luxembourg municipal theatre (Tel. 4796 2711), Esch-sur-Alzette municipal theatre (Tel. 540916), Capucins theatre (Tel. 4796 2433). There's also a high-profile national philharmonic orchestra, which puts on regular concerts throughout the year (Tel. 22 99 01-205/201/203).

# Luxembourg City

Perched on a high plateau overlooking cliffs and the valleys of the Petrusse and Alzette rivers, this 1,000-year-old city has one of the most dramatic settings of any in Europe. Around the edge of the plateau is the **Chemin de la Corniche** and **Bld Roosevelt**, which offers spectacular views over the city. Just below the promenade are the **Casemates**, 23km of underground passages, hewn from solid rock, from the times when this area was a fortress (Tel. 226753). To explore them, enter from Place de la Constitution or from the Beck fortress, but check the opening times and remember to show your IYHF membership card for reduced admission (full price around 75LUF).

For those with a little bit of cash to spare and a head for heights, the Compagnie Aéronautique in Junglinster offers an original way to see the city by hot air balloon. Tel. 789075 for further details.

In the western suburbs is the **European Centre**. Luxembourg is one of the most 'European' of continental cities, and home to a number of powerful agencies, among them the European Court of Justice, the European Investment Bank, the European Court of Auditors, the General Secretariat of the European Parliament and the Nuclear Safety Administration.

**FREE LUXEMBOURG CITY:**
- Wander around the old quarters and see the remains of the old fortifications, the historical importance of which UNESCO has acknowledged by adding them to their list of World Heritage sites.
- In the old town is the **Cathedral of Notre Dame**, noteworthy for its Baroque organ gallery and crypt containing the tomb of the 14th-century king of Bohemia, John the Blind.
- Nearby is the **National Museum** (closed Mon., Sat. mornings and Sun. lunchtimes), with a selection of historical and natural artefacts, and a very good collection of 15th-19th century art.
- At the other end of the scale there is a *bric-à-brac* **market** on the **Place d'Armes** on the second and fourth Saturday of each month.
- Also in the **Place d'Armes** during the summer, **open-air concerts** are held several nights a week, with brass and military bands, jazz bands, folklore groups, etc, performing from the band stand.
- The main annual event in the city is the **Schoberfouer**, an amusement fair and market which arrives on the penultimate Sunday in August and lasts into the first week in September.
- The Catholic **Octave Festival** is held in late April and early May.

## STATION FACILITIES

Luxembourg City Gare Centrale has all the facilities you would expect from a modern and wealthy capital. You'll like the little conveyor belts that assist you with your baggage up the stairs! Tourist Information is now in the station and there are electronic information boards all over the city.

## TOURIST INFORMATION AND ADDRESSES

The City Information centre is in the City Hall at place d'Armes (Tel. 222809), open Apr.–Oct., Mon.–Sat.: 9am–7pm, Sun.: 10am–6pm. Pick up an *Agenda Touristique* which lists everything that's going on. Also get a leaflet on the self-guided City Walks (Wenzelwalks) which come with a free map and are designed to take you around the principal attractions in 100 minutes.

**POST OFFICE** Place de la Gare 38, Mon.–Sat.: 6am–8pm. *Poste restante* till 8pm. Also downtown at Rue Aldringen 25, open 7am–7pm.

**STUDENT TRAVEL TEJ,** Voyage Sotours, place du Théâtre 15 on the corner of Rue Beaumont (Tel. 461514), open Mon.–Fri.: 9am–6pm, Sat.: 9am–12pm

**EURAIL AID OFFICE** Railway station (Tel. 492424)

**CHEMIST** Pharmacie du Mortier, avenue de la Gare, open Mon.–Fri.: 8am–6.15pm, and there is a little LCD display outside which lists others or Tel. 112 in an emergency

**UK EMBASSY** Boulevard Roosevelt 14 (Tel. 229864)

**US EMBASSY** Boulevard Emmanuel Servais 22 (Tel. 460123)

**CANADIAN CONSULATE** 24-26 Avenue de la Liberte (Tel. 402420)

**AMEX** 34 avenue de la Porte Neuve (Tel: 228555)

**BUS INFORMATION** A one-trip ticket costs 40LUF (10 one-trip tickets for 320LUF), all-day tickets cost 160LUF; they are available from the driver, as are the better value five-trip books for 640LUF, which several people can use. The sales office is at Luxembourg station, open daily 6am–8pm (Tel. 49 904990).

## SLEEPING

Stay close to the station for cheap **hotels**. Directly opposite the station, rue Joseph Junck is a safe bet, as is rue de la Liberté. Doubles average about 1,700LUF in this area. Try **Le Parisien** (Tel. 492397; Fax. 402092) at Rue Sainte Zithe or the **Brasserie/Auberge le Papillon**, 9 Rue Origer (Tel. 494490).

The **youth hostel** is good, located right in the historic part of the city. The scenery on the bus ride is worth the 10-minute trip. It is sometimes full of adolescent groups and there is a 9am eviction. Take bus 9 from the station. The fare is around 40LUF and it will cost the same again for your rucksack. You can walk through town to it in half an hour. The address is rue du Fort Olizy 2 (Tel. 226889 or 221920; Fax. 223360) and dorm beds cost 415-750LUF per night, including breakfast (non-members pay a nightly supplement of about 110LUF). There are also some doubles.

Kockelscheuer **Camping**, route de Bettembourg 22 (Tel. 471815), is quite a way from the station so it is better to take bus 2. Open from Easter till October.

## EATING AND NIGHTLIFE

Food here isn't terribly cheap, so use the supermarkets and bakeries near the station. The latter offer good sandwiches, but also try the delicious *pâté au Riesling*. Look out for the restaurants which offer a *menu du jour*. These meals are the best buy of the day and prices range between 300 and 450LUF. Try **As Arcadas** at 29 Rue Joseph Junck, near the station, which serves excellent bargain two-course lunches for under 300LUF. Generally, the Italian and Chinese restaurants are the cheapest in town.

In the evenings, head to **Place d'Armes**. People generally congregate here, the eateries are lively, and there are often free concerts in the square. There are also fast-food restaurants in this part of town. Pizza Hut has outlets at place d'Armes and at rue Origer; both are open until midnight.

Nightlife is low-key. However, young people tend to congregate in **Grund** down in the gorge below the city centre, a trendy area full of bars and cafés. There is a spectacular glass **Lift** which makes the descent down the wall of the gorge. The views are stunning, day or night, and the lift – big enough to take bikes – operates till 3am, so you can stay out late and return safely to the city centre above. Get further information and a special leaflet from the Tourist Office.

Also available from Tourist Information are the events guide *La Semaine à Luxembourg* and *Vade-Mecum*, the cultural diary. It lists all theatres, concerts, films, galleries and museums.

## Provincial Luxembourg

The medieval town of **Echternach** lies on the banks of the river Sauer (Sûre). It took a real pounding in World War II (Germany is across the river), but has been well restored and the **Town Hall** is an excellent example of this. The **Benedictine Basilica** has some impressive frescoes and stained-glass windows, and the buried remains of St Benedict.

The Tourist Office is at Porte St Willibrod (Tel. 720230), open 9am–12 noon and 2pm–5pm.

Echternach has a big International Music Festival in May and June (student tickets cost 300LUF and are available from the Tourist Office) and the dancing procession of St Willibrod takes place on Whit Tuesday.

Buses are the easiest method of getting from Luxembourg City to Echternach (every half hour between 8am and 6pm) and they are free to Inter-Rail pass holders. There are 12 daily, taking just over an hour to travel the distance.

There's a **youth hostel** (355–635LUF) at rue André Duchscher 9 (Tel. 720158; Fax. 728735 ) or try **Hotel Le Petit Poète**, Place du Marché 13 (Tel. 720072): doubles from about 1,800LUF.

The cheapest of the town's two **campsites**, Camp Officiel, is 500m from the bus station in rue de Diekirch (Tel. 720272). It charges around 120LUF per person, 120LUF per site and is open Mar.–Oct.

Luxembourg has the most dense network of marked paths in the world. National routes are marked by yellow signs. The YHA maintains the walking routes and maps are available from the YHA at place d'Armes 18 (Tel. 225588) and cost 180LUF. Just a few minutes north of Echternach is a small wedge of hiker's paradise: **Little Switzerland**. This is a beautiful section of the Ardennes, and a walk through the steep gorges and forests makes an exhilarating hour or so. In the northernmost part of the Ardennes is **Trois Vierges**, the heart of hiking country. There is an IYHF Hostel at 24–26 rue de la Gare (Tel. 98018; Fax. 979624).

The Clerve Valley leads to **Clervaux**, about an hour north of Luxembourg City. The 11th-century castles of **Bourscheid** and **Clervaux** are set in fairytale surroundings. There are permanent exhibitions in medieval **Clervaux Castle**, including Edward Steichen's *Family of Man* collection, and concerts are held regularly within the castle (for details, tel. 990570 or 990564). The **Tourist Office** at Clervaux (open 9.45am–11.45am; 2pm–6pm on Sundays) is next to the castle (Tel. 920072). The official campsite at 33 Klatzewe costs 150LUF per person (Tel. 920042), open Apr. to mid-Nov.

Just north of Luxembourg City, at the entrance to the Valley of the Seven Castles, lies **Mersch** with its prehistoric caves and the remains of a Roman villa and a feudal castle. Maps and information are available from the Tourist Office at the town hall (Tel. 35023), closed 11.30am–1.30pm.

Further north lies **Diekirch**, home of a festival on the third Sunday of July, and three **Camping** grounds. Bicycles can be rented at Camping de la Sûre (Tel. 809425) where maps and information are also available. The **Tourist Office** is at 1, Esplanade (Tel. 803023).

**Vianden**, though not directly linked to Luxembourg City by rail or bus, is worth a visit; travel via Echternach. Here you'll find cobbled streets and a magnificent **castle**, admission 130LUF (open daily 10am–6pm (closes at 4pm in winter)), which puts on regular concerts and exhibitions (Tel. 834108 or 849291). This was the cradle of the Grand-Ducal dynasty and dates back to the 9th century. If you're in the area in mid-November, ask about the **St Martin's Fire** celebrations. The ancient custom marks the end of the harvest and the payment of the levy to the feudal lord. Massive bonfires are lit and locals parade through the streets by the light of flaming torches.

The **Tourist Office** is in Victor Hugo's former house (Tel. 84257, open Apr.–Oct. 9.30am–6pm;closed 12 noon–2pm).

A chairlift (*télésiège*) operates from rue du Sanatorium and costs around 160LUF return (summer 9.30am–6.30pm; winter 10am–6pm), and there's a great open-air swimming pool with impressive views over the castle. The **Doll and Toy Museum** (Tel. 84591), open Easter–Oct., features a display of more than 500 dolls dating from 1860.

The **youth hostel** is over the bridge from the train station at Montée du Château 3 (Tel. 84177; Fax. 849427; open Apr.–Oct.). You'll also be able to find cheap **hotels** along this road. Three **campsites** are situated on the edge of the river Oúr: Op dem Deich (Tel. 834375; open Easter–Sept.), Du Moulin and De l'Oúr.

**Wiltz** borders on a valley, and is divided into two parts with a **castle** situated in the High Town. An international open-air festival in July takes place in the amphitheatre in the castle yard and a Battle of the Bulge museum is housed in the castle. A walk through the town leads along a path of stone crosses which remember the plague. The **youth hostel** is at 6 rue de la Montagne (Tel. 958039; Fax. 959440) and has kitchen facilities. There's a camping site, **Camping Kaul**, near the station on Rue Simon Jos (Tel. 950079). Open May to Oct.

On the main line from Luxembourg to Paris, on the western side of the country, is the village of **Bascharage**. Here you can get guided visits to the **Bofferding Brewery**, with a free drink of beer (admission around 120LUF; Tel. 509011-21), or to gem-cutting workshops (Tel. 509032). Telephone in advance to book.

En route to France, stop off at **Esch-sur-Alzette** on the French border. Luxembourg's second city is only 20km away from Luxembourg City with a direct rail link. It is a good place for shopping at reasonable prices and houses the **National Museum of the Resistance**. The **Tourist Office** can be found at the town hall, office 8 (Tel. 547383-246, open Mon.–Fri.: 7.30am–12 noon, 1.30pm–5pm), and **camping** is available at the Gaalgebierg site (Tel. 541069).

NOTES:
........................................................................................................................

........................................................................................................................

........................................................................................................................

........................................................................................................................

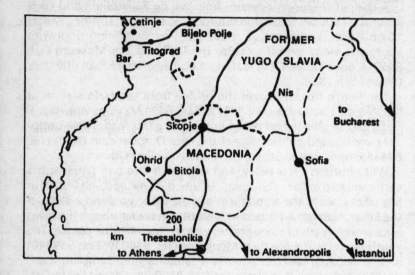

# REPUBLIC OF MACEDONIA

| Entry requirements | Passport (UK only). USA, Canada, Australia and New Zealand nationals require a visa. |
|---|---|
| Population | 2.1 million |
| Capital | Skopje (pop.: 600,000) |
| Currency | Denar (MKD) |
| | £1= approx. 93.5MKD |
| Political system | Parliamentary democracy |
| Religion | Orthodox, Muslim, Roman Catholic |
| Language | Macedonian (some French, English and German spoken) |
| Public holidays | New Year (1 Jan.), Othodox Christmas (6 and 7 Jan.), Old New Year (14 Jan.), Easter, Labour Day (1 May), Sts Cyrilus and Methodius (24 May), Ilinden (2 Aug.), Republic Day (8 Sept.), Partisan Day (11 Oct.), 25 and 26 Dec. |
| International dialling codes | To Macedonia: int'l code 389 |
| | From Macedonia: 99 + country code number or 00 + country code |
| Emergency telephone numbers | Police 92; ambulance 94; fire service 93 |

Though Macedonia managed to ease its way out of the former Yugoslavia with relatively little trouble, the road for one of the newest republics in Europe remains rocky. A poor country in the southern part of the Balkan peninsula, it suffered a great deal under sanctions imposed by the UN, and trade blockades by Greece. And though free now of Serbian rule, ethnic tensions are deeply felt in a nation of Slavs, Albanians, Turks, Serbs and Bulgars. The political situation in general in this part of Europe continues to be potentially unstable, but since Macedonia is on the main line between western Europe and Greece, you might want to consider a brief stop – but be sure to make your outbound train reservations before arriving. Check on current local conditions before travelling.

The Slavs settled here in the 7th century and enjoyed 200 years of peace. Later they fell under alternating periods of rule by the Byzantine and Bulgarian Empires. At the end of the 10th and the beginning of the 11th century (969–1018), a vast empire of the Macedonian Slavs emerged – the Empire of Tsar Samuil – with its capital in Ohrid. When that empire was defeated by Byzantium in the 11th century, Macedonia became a pawn to be passed between Bulgaria, Byzantium and Serbia. This unsettled period came to an end in the 14th century when the Balkan peninsula was added to the Ottoman Turk empire. It remained under Turkish rule for 500 years until the end of the 19th century when Russia defeated Turkey. Macedonia briefly reverted to Bulgarian control, but Western powers forced Bulgaria to return it.

The struggle for control of Macedonia has continued throughout this century, and its territory has been chipped away by Greece, Albania and Bulgaria to where it is today half the size it once was. Eventually, Macedonia was incorporated into Yugoslavia, but a referendum on 8 September 1991 resulted in a 95% vote for independence. For once, Belgrade permitted a former republic to withdraw from the federation without bloodshed.

However, when EU recognition finally came in June 1992 it was granted on condition that the country temporarily use the name Former Yugoslav Republic of Macedonia. This proviso was added at the insistence of the Greeks, whose concern was for their adjoining region of the same name in northern Greece. Greece, however, lifted its blockade over the issue in 1995. For the sake of convenience we continue to use the name 'Macedonia' throughout this section. This does not imply that we either agree or disagree with any interested parties over disputed territory in either Greece or the former Yugoslavia.

Despite such an agitated past, much of Macedonia's cultural heritage has remained intact. Historic monuments abound, with churches, monasteries, mosques, and archaeological sites fairly accessible, and old books, religious icons, national folklore and traditional arts and crafts among the treasures.

## TRAIN INFORMATION
### (Railway Station, Skopje: Tel. 91 234 255)
Obtaining information on the trains can be nigh on impossible unless you're in Skopje where there are English speaking staff at Feroturist Travel Agency (upstairs at the station), who will help with train informaion, sell international tickets and book sleepers to Belgrade. Elsewhere you will have to rely on your ingenuity. The arrivals/departure boards (as well as timetables and everything else for that matter) are in Cyrillic so you would be wise to try to learn the alphabet, failing that, get someone to write down the relevant towns for you (note, Thessaloniki is Solun in Macedonian). Macedonian Railways operates more than 900km of lines, of which a third are electrified. The main north–south line is from Belgrade to Thessaloniki, via Skopje. Express trains run three times a day from Belgrade to Skopje (via Nis). There are also international lines from Vienna, Budapest (via Belgrade) and Istanbul (via Sofia) to Skopje. If you are travelling through Yugoslavia you need a visa and in the present political climate you are unlikely to get one. Unfortunately, there are no direct trains between Macedonia and Bulgaria (you have to change in Yugoslavia). Major investment is currently being made into improving rail links between Varna (Bulgaria) on the Black Sea, and Durres (Albania) on the Adriatic. Domestic services tend to be terminally slow.

**RESERVATIONS** Required on all international trains passing through Macedonia.

**PASSES AVAILABLE** For information on the Euro Domino and Eurotrain Explorer Passes, see 'Eurorailing: the options' in Part One of this guide.

The Inter-Rail pass has been broken down into zones. Macedonia is in Zone H, along with Bulgaria, Romania and Yugoslavia. For £159 you get 22 days' travel in a single zone (£229 for over-26s). Refer to Part One of this guide for further details. Eurail is not valid in Macedonia.

**NIGHT TRAVEL** There are usually both couchettes and sleepers on the international trains passing through Macedonia.

**EATING ON TRAINS** When travelling on local trains you would be well advised to bring your own supplies of food and drink. On international trains you can expect the normal range of services.

**BUSES** These are frequently the only way to get around in Macedonia and are relatively cheap (Intercity Bus Station, Skopje: Tel. 91 236 234).

**SCENIC ROUTES** The only route here worthy of note is the line down to Bitola, which places you within striking distance of Lake Ohrid.

## TOURIST INFORMATION

The bigger cities have travel agents and Tourist Offices. Before travelling to Macedonia we strongly recommend you write to the Macedonian Embassy at 10 Harcourt House, 19a Cavendish Square, London W1M 8DT (Tel. 020 7499 5152) to check on any recent developments (There is no Macedonian tourist office in the UK but the Embassy can help with any enquiries).

**POLICE** Tel. 92

**EMERGENCY MEDICAL ASSISTANCE** Tel. 94

**FIRE BRIGADE** Tel. 93

**ISIC BONUSES** Discounts are given on admission to some museums and sights (most admission fees are reasonable). Your best bet is to show your ISIC card whenever buying tickets.

**MONEY** 1 denar (MKD) = 100 deni

Although the currency is the Macedonian denar, we recommend that you carry a supply of Deutschmarks as an extra safeguard. Credit cards are not widely accepted. Banking hours can be any time between 7am and 7pm weekdays, 7am-1pm Saturday.

**POST OFFICES** Generally open Mon.–Sat.: 7am–3pm. Stamps can also be purchased at various newsagents and hotels, though be sure to get an airmail sticker or your post may take months to reach its destination.

**STREET NAMES** Warning: Names of streets have been changed but the old signs may remain.

**TIPPING** Tipping is not expected, but loose change may be given away.

## SLEEPING

**Hotels** here are very expensive, and there are only 90 of them, but there are plenty of cheap **pensions**. Currently, the only **hostels** are in Ohrid (open summer only) and Skopje. Write to the Macedonian Youth Hostel Association for up-to-date information on hostels in Macedonia: PO Box 499, Prolet 25, 91000 Skopje. (Tel. 91 239947; Fax. 91 235029).

There are **student dorms** (*Studentski Dom*) and **campsites** in both these cities and other major towns scattered across the country. The cheapest option is usually a **private room**. You can pick up lists at Tourist Offices.

## EATING

Macedonian cuisine is a mixture of oriental and European influences with the local specialities being grilled meat kebabs, fish dishes, rice casseroles, bean stews, stuffed pastries and thick soups. In Ohrid they have innumerable ways of cooking trout from the lake and it is worth the effort to try some. Macedonia is big on farming, so you should be able to piece together good picnics from local markets and tasty snacks from street stalls. There are also bland, self-service worker cafeterias in the cities.

# Skopje phone code : 091

On the banks of the River Vardar in the heart of the Balkans, Skopje has always played an important part in this area's history. The Romans were aware of its strategic position and under them Skopje (Scupi) became a thriving city. In turn it was inhabited by the Slavs, Byzantines, Bulgarians, Normans, Serbs and Turks. The city is no stranger to disaster. Floods, fires and earthquakes have wreaked havoc through the centuries – the earthquake of 1963 wiped out most of the city – yet the capital's skyline is one of ancient terracotta tiles, Turkish Bath domes, mosques and minarets. Skopje has two distinct personalities: the old town and the modern new town. The modern sector, already falling apart from lack of repair, is garish and has nothing of interest. (Unless you're into ugly buildings, in which case take a look at the post office building and the building next to it). The old town, however, has much to recommend it.

## SEEING

From the railway station, make your way north-west until you come to Koco Racin, then cross the river. When you come to Bulevar Goce

Delcev, turn left and you will pass the 15th-century **Turkish Baths** on your right just before the Tourist Information centre.

A left turn here takes you to the **Kamen Most** (Turkish stone bridge) and over into the new city and the huge, refurbished shopping centre.

To the right of the Tourist Centre is the church of **Sveti Spas** with some excellent 18th- and 19th-century icons, and the **Mustafa Pasha mosque** where you can climb the minaret for a good view of the old city (100MKD). Across the street is a park with the ruins of **Fort Kale** (10th–12th centuries).

Of the several museums, the best of are the **City Art Gallery** (closed Mon.) near the Turkish Bridge and the **Museum of Macedonia**, which is past the mosque behind an old inn. Nearby is the local vegetable market.

Skopje's old Oriental bazar district is the largest of its kind in Europe. You can happily spend an hour or two here soaking up the atmosphere and looking at the handicrafts, many of which you can see being made.

## SLEEPING AND EATING

There is an **IYHF Associate Hostel** at Prolet 25 (Tel. 114849; Fax. 235029) which costs 550–1350MKD per person including breakfast, and is 500m. from the station. From April to October you can **camp** at Autocamp (Tel. 228246) for around 180MKD per person and tent. You can also hire a basic camping caravan for around 400MKD per person. Alternatively, the Tourist Office (Tel. 116854) will fix you up with a **private room** from around 1000MKD.

Foodwise, your best bet is to wander round the old town. There are a variety of dingy-looking restaurants here which are quite good and frequented by the locals. In the area of Stara Charshiya (Old Bazaar), there are plenty of street stalls and there's a big vegetable market at the north end. If you have a weak stomach, head for the self-service restaurant in the new town just south of the Turkish bridge.

# Western Macedonia

**OHRID** is a popular holiday resort and although it is not on the rail lines, it is definitely worth a visit; you'll have to take the train to Bitola and catch a bus from there. Given the number of historical and cultural monuments here, it's not surprising the town has been made a UNESCO world heritage site.

The city, on the shore of Lake Ohrid, is protected by a medieval wall.

Near the north entrance are two churches worth seeing: **Sveti Kilment** and **Sveti Sofija**. From the churches, walk west until you come to the old **roman amphitheatre**, then continue on to the citadel. Follow the walls of the **citadel** for beautiful views of the area, then head south to the nearby **basilica** and check out the mosaics in its ruins.

Keep walking south and you will pass the ruins of another church and come to a cliff overlooking the lake. At the bottom there are some nice beaches.

From spring to early autumn, the Tourist Office makes sure there is always one festival or another going on in order to lure the throngs. Biljana Tourist Office is at Partizanska 3 in front of the bus station (Tel. 096 22494; Fax. 096 24114). There is also Automoto Sojuz (Tel. 096 22338), another tourist office, on Galičica at Lazo Trpkoski on the east side of town.

There is a hostel (the HI **Mladost Hostel**) about 1½ km to the west of town on the lakeside (Tel. 096 21626). A bed in a dorm will cost around 250MKD, including breakfast. Even if all the beds are full, you can pitch a tent in ther grounds for about 100MKD per person, 150MKD per tent. The hostel is open from April to mid October. Take the Struga bus and ask for mladost. There's also a hotel, the **Mladinski Centar-Hotel Magnus** (Tel. 096 21671), right next to the hostel which costs around 700MKD per person in a two or three-bed room. The price includes three meals a day. You'll get a discount with a hostel card but be warned, in the height of summer you stand zilch chance of getting a bed - unless you book well in advance. Alternatively, have the Tourist Office set you up in a private room.

**BITOLA** Underrated by most guidebooks, Bitola is something of a well-kept secret. While other visitors simply pass through on their way to Ohrid, you could do worse than stay around for a night or two to get the feel of this interesting little town with a definite Turkish flavour. Bitola during the summer is a good place to unwind. If you're pushed for time, at least try to do some exploring while waiting for the connection to Ohrid.

On the south side of town are the pre-Christian ruins of **Heraclea**. The Roman ruins are still being excavated and there is also an early Christian palace and a small museum on the site. On Marshal Tito Square are the 16th-century **Bezistan Bazaar**, the **Mosa Pijade Art Gallery** (in an old mosque) and the **clock tower**. Near the Bezistan is the atmospheric **Stara Charshiya**, or bazaar district, and the city's **market**.

Other than **hotels**, your only chance of a place to sleep is to ask at the Tourist Office for a **private room**. Although officially they can't fix you up, they should be able to point you in the right direction. Alternatively, ask at Dona Tours at Gyuro Gyakovich 47; they organize rooms for around 16DM a night.

NOTES:

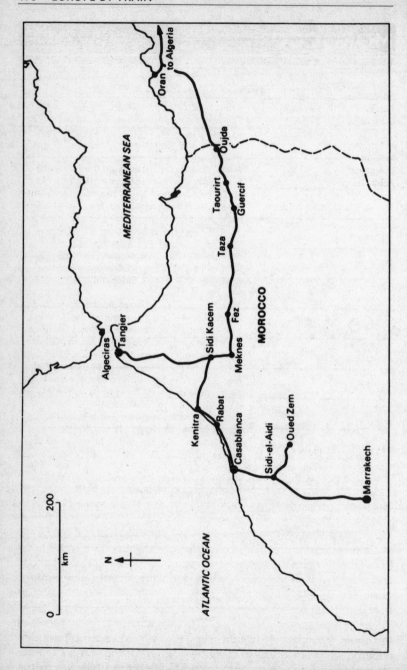

# MOROCCO

| | |
|---|---|
| Entry requirements | Passport |
| Population | 30.5 million |
| Capital | Rabat-Sale (pop.: 1.3 million) |
| Currency | Dirham (dh) = 100 centimes |
| | £1 = approx. 16dh |
| Political system | Constitutional monarchy |
| Religion | Islam |
| Language | Arabic, French and Spanish (in tourist towns) |
| Public holidays | New Year's Day, Independence Manifesto (11 Jan.), Throne Day (3 Mar. – the most important national holiday in Morocco), May Day (1 May), National Day (23 May), Young People's Day (9 July), Feast of the Throne (30 July), Allegiance of Wadi-Eddahab (14 Aug.), Anniversary of the King's and People's Revolution (20 Aug.), The King's Birthday (21 Aug.),Anniversary of the Green March (6 Nov.), Independence Day (18 Nov.). |
| | There are four movable religious festivals: Aid El-Fitr (this year 6 and 7 Jan. and 26 and 27 Dec.), Aid Al-Adha (this year 14 and 15 Mar.), Muslim New Year (this year 3 Apr.) and Aid Al-Mawlid (13 &14 June). Ramadan, Islam's holy month, takes place for 4 weeks, this year starting 28 Nov. It is not a public holiday, but many eating places will be closed during the day, as Ramadan is a time of fasting for Muslims. |
| | Note: Each of the religious holidays, and Ramadan too, is calculated according to the Islamic lunar calendar, and so fall about 10 days earlier each year. |
| International dialling codes | To Morocco: int'l code 212 |
| | From Morocco: 00 + country code |
| Time | GMT (GMT +1 in summer) |
| Emergency telephone numbers | Police 19; ambulance 15; fire service 15 |

Morocco may be only an hour's ferry ride from Spain across the Straits of Gibraltar, but in tradition, culture and landscape, it's a world away from Europe – and the further south you travel, the more alien, exotic and exciting it is. In Marrakech, for example, the vibrant colours, smells, tastes and baking hot sun leave you in no doubt you're on the African continent in an Arab land.

The rail network has been vastly improved and travelling around the country is relatively trouble-free. However, Morocco is a Muslim country, and women should cover up when travelling in more remote areas. With landscape ranging from Mediterranean beaches to the

Sahara desert, four spectacular mountain ranges, fortified villages, medieval towns and the four imperial cities of Rabat, Meknes, Fez and Marrakesh, Morocco will make a tremendous impression. It is a place everyone 'doing Europe' should make every effort to experience.

Most of Morocco was a French protectorate between 1912 and 1956, except for the north, which was Spanish. Morocco's claims to the Western Sahara remain a subject of heated contention. The country is largely unaffected by the dangerous political events in neighbouring Algeria – travel there is definitely not recommended!

## GETTING THERE

There are various ferries from Spain to Tangier (2½ hours) and the Spanish enclave of Ceuta (1½ hours), with the Algeciras–Ceuta crossing being the shortest and cheapest, but as it's not on the railway it might be easier to use the Algeciras–Tangier route. It costs about 3,200 pesetas. Make sure to get your passport stamped by the passport control below deck. The Ceuta ferry is cheaper (2,000ptas). Avoid dealing in drugs and be careful not to be used as a courier. Border guards do not look kindly on anyone caught in possession.

To get from Ceuta to Tetouan or Tangier, walk from Ceuta port to town centre, then catch a bus (100ptas) to the border. Then take another bus (or share a *petit-taxi*) to Tetouan or Tangier. Buses (CTM) are very cheap and quite comfortable. Tetouan–Sidi Lyam-ani by bus is a beautiful run and you can connect from there for trains to Casablanca.

## MOROCCAN RAILWAYS

### (OFFICE NATIONAL DES CHEMINS DE FER, ONCF)

Recently there has been a big improvement in Moroccan trains, although they still do not run as frequently as you might wish. There are three classes on the trains: first, second and *économique*. It is well worth paying the supplement of around £2 to travel in an air-conditioned carriage. The rail network runs north from Marrakech to Casablanca and Rabat, then splits at Sidi Kacem, one line going north to Tangier, the other to Fez and on to Algeria.

The Trans-Maghreb Express, which travels from Casablanca through Meknes, Fez and the fringes of the Atlas mountains to terminate near the border with Algeria, is a laid-back, but beautiful route to travel on if you are intending to pass through, rather than stay in, Morocco. At present, the connecting service to Algeria is suspended, but in any case, remember it is definitely *not* recommended to visit Algeria at the moment.

Some of the major cities, including Agadir and Tetouan, are not served by rail but the ONCF provide bus connections.

**PASSES AVAILABLE** The **Inter-Rail** card is valid here. **Eurail** is not. Your Inter-Rail or BIJ ticket entitles you to use the second-class facilities. The Inter-Rail pass has been broken down into zones, so you do not have to pay for travel to areas other than those you intend to visit. For £159 you can tour a single zone for 22 days (over-26s pay £229). Morocco is in Zone F, along with Spain and Portugal. (For further details of the eight Inter-Rail zones, and the **Freedom Pass/Euro Domino**, refer to the relevant sections in Part One of this guide.)

The *carte d'abonnement* is valid for unlimited travel for a month on all trains but the fast TNR services. It costs around 1,146dh for first class and 767dh for second (which works out at about £5 return per 100 km).

Train travel in Morocco is very cheap, for example, the fare from Tangier to Rabat is approximately £5.50 (2nd class) and the fare from Casablanca to Marrakech is less than £5.

## TRAIN INFORMATION

You'll find the odd official who speaks pidgin English, but generally you'll have to resort to French, which is the official second language, or Spanish. Information: Tel. ONCF 07 774747; Fax. 07 774480.

**RESERVATIONS** Not compulsory, but a good idea if you're on a long haul in peak season.

**NIGHT TRAVEL** Sleeping cars are first class only and come in singles or doubles. They're fairly expensive, so unless you're feeling particularly delicate, try and schedule your travelling for daytime. Second-class cars are often crowded at night.

**COUCHETTES** In the summer, on the Tangier–Marrakesh and the Tangier–Fez–Oujda trains, you can buy couchettes for 50dh. The extra outlay can be worth it for the sake of security – these carriages are locked and guarded.

## TOURIST INFORMATION

Most towns have both a Tourist Office and a *Syndicat d'Initiative*. The Tourist Office should be your first port of call, as they have information and will help find a bed if necessary. When you're organized, make your way back to the *Syndicat d'Initiative,* which will have leaflets on local sights, etc.

A word of warning – unofficial guides (mostly young boys) will pester you offering their dubious services. Fool them into thinking you're Finnish – that usually puts them off! Hustlers are another problem – they'll approach you in the medina (Arab quarter) and souk (market), being incredibly friendly and conversant in a dozen languages. Ignore and avoid them. In an effort to crack down on the nuisance, Moroccan authorities have established police tourist brigades at hustling blackspots; these have proved effective at the ports and train station at Tangier, and at the marketplace in Marrakesh. Finally, when you're at the sights, don't feel obliged to accept the custodian's offer of a guided tour or feel it necessary to give him a tip, as he is already paid by the government. If you do want a guide, opt for an official one. You can hire them from Tourist Offices and hotels; expect to pay about 120–130dh (plus tip) for half a day.

If you wear contact lenses, bear in mind that it can be very dusty, and you may be more comfortable wearing glasses.

**MONEY MATTERS** 1 dirham (dh) = 100 centimes.
Banking hours are Mon.–Thurs.: 8.30am–11.30am, 2.30am–4.30am (during Ramadan 9.30am–2am), Fri.: 8.30–11.15 and 3–4.30pm. Banks charge no commission and have the same rate of exchange everywhere. Buy dirhams in advance if arriving outside banking hours. Keep your receipts, as you will probably be asked to produce them when changing dirhams back, and remember to use banks – the rate on the boat back to Spain is a rip-off. Note that it is forbidden to import or export dirhams, and illegal to change money in the streets.
**POST OFFICES** Open Mon.–Fri.: 8.30am–11.45am, 2.30pm–6.30pm.
**SHOPS** Open Mon.–Sat.: 8.30am–12 noon, 2pm–6.30pm. Haggle like mad wherever you go in the markets (*souks*), even when you see the *prix fixe* sign. Haggling is a way of life here and unless you manage to get the price down by at least 50%, you are a failure. As a general rule, a fair price is about 25% of the first price suggested. Never make any kind of offer, however low, unless you are seriously interested in buying. Decide in your mind what you are genuinely willing to pay and do not exceed that figure just to relieve the pressure.

Check with the *Syndicats d'Initiative* for opening times of individual museums and other sights. Many museums and some monuments are closed on Tues.
**BUSES** More frequent and cheaper than trains, though less comfortable. If you are trying to board a bus at an intermediate stop between its point of departure and its destination, be warned – you will find it difficult to get a space and you could be waiting at your stop for longer than you expected. There is an official baggage charge of about 6dh per pack. Information from the main company, CTM, at 23 rue Leon l'Africain, Casablanca. (Tel 02 448127/312061).
**TIPPING** Waiters in restaurants will appreciate tips, up to 10% if not already included in the bill. Consider tipping a tour guide or someone who has put themselves out for you 5–10dh. Do not allow yourself to be pressurised into parting with your money if they have not really done anything for you – for example, showing you where a hotel is when it's only a few metres away!
**SLEEPING**

Morocco is a country where it pays to be tough. You can live off next to nothing if you don't mind roughing it a bit. **Camping** and **youth hostelling** (*Auberges de Jeunesse*) are very cheap, as little as 20dh a night under canvas or 20–60dh in a hostel, but you're not guaranteed central locations or first-class conditions. For more information on the hostels, contact the head office of the Royal Moroccan Federation of Youth Hostels, Parc de la Ligue Arabe, BP 15988, Casablanca (Tel. 02 470952; Fax. 02 227677). The medina **hotels/pensions** offer the most central and colourful locations and are usually cheaper than the places in the new areas of town.

**Hotels** are graded from 1 to 5 stars and there are fixed maximum prices for each category. You usually pay by the room, so doubling up with friends can bring the unit cost of a room down. The cheapest hotel rooms cost somewhere between 90 and 160dh for a double room, with extra for shower and breakfast. If you find the water is hot at any time, seize the chance for a shower while you can, as the plumbing here is decidedly erratic. Always carry your own loo paper.

If you're planning on spending time hiking in the mountains, there are a series of **refuges** that cost from around 15-50dh per night per person. For a full list of mountain refuges (or any of the other options above), contact the Moroccan National Tourist Office at 205 Regent Street, London W1R 7DE (Tel. 020 7437 0073). Refer to *Cheap Sleeps Europe 2000* for further options.

## EATING AND NIGHTLIFE

If you've an iron stomach, take full advantage of it in Morocco by eating in the souks and from kebab stands. Most decent restaurants offer a good selection of Moroccan dishes. Try *harira*, a rich soup of chicken, macaroni and spices, followed by *touajen* (lamb or chicken stew) or *couscous*, Morocco's most famous dish (semolina, usually topped with lamb, fish or chicken). Try the *djaja maamra* – steamed and stuffed chicken with couscous, almonds and raisins. If you like something sweet to end with, ask for *kab el ghzal* (almond pastries) and mint tea. Often it is difficult in the more remote places to find meals during the day, so eat well at night.

Don't take chances with tap water; drink only bottled spring water, which you have to ask for by brand name. You can trust Sidi Ali, Imouzzer or Sidi Harazem brands. There is little alcohol in this country, although beer is relatively easy to find, especially in towns. The local Stork beer is palatable and there is also Flag beer, expect to pay around 15–20dh for them in bars.

## EATING OR DRINKING WITH MOROCCANS

- Being offered mint tea is a sign of hospitality, and offence may be taken if you refuse.
- If you are invited to share in a family meal, you should use water from the ewer, or water jug, to first wash your hands.
- Do not begin the meal until the master of the house has said the *bismillah* in praise of God.
- Eat only with your right hand. Moroccans eat using their fingers rather than cutlery.
- Taste everything, but don't feel you have to finish everything.
- Avoid drinking, eating and smoking in public in the daytime during Ramadan.

The local *Syndicat d'Initiative* will let you know where the nearest belly-dancer performs and what's happening on the music and dancing scene. Smoking *kif* (hashish) is widespread, but any tourists making a purchase risk unpleasant hassle and demands of fines/bribes at the hands of police – real or bogus.

## Tangier phone code: 09

Tangier isn't the best introduction to Morocco, but if you're on a day trip from Spain, it'll show you some of the exotic differences between Europe and Africa. Be on your guard for hustlers and pickpockets. Also, don't be conned by the official tourist guides who approach you at the port, tell you that Moroccan time is two hours behind Spanish time, and then take you on a tour of the 'sites', which invariably means a trip to their relation's carpet shop. Many readers feel the best advice is to head straight for the station and take the first train out. This is primarily because of the excessive amount of hassle one experiences here, but reports from Tangier signal an improvement in the situation, with special police 'tourist brigades' cracking down on hustling in the port area and round the train station.

The train station (**Gare du Port**) is right below the ferry terminal in the city. Most trains leave from this stop, as well as from the **Gare de Ville**, which is 300m beyond the port gate.

If you are leaving the country from here, remember to turn up early for the boat as you will end up having to queue for passport control, customs and – finally – the boat itself. To buy a discounted ferry ticket to Algeciras you must produce a photocopy of your Inter-Rail Pass (the Café Terminal across from the main station will do one cheaply).

## TOURIST INFORMATION AND ADDRESSES

**TOURIST INFORMATION** is at 29 boulevard Pasteur, open Mon.–Fri.: 8am–2pm in summer (Tel. 938239 or 932996)
**POST OFFICE** Blvd Mohammed V 33 (open Mon.–Sat. 8.30am–12.15pm and 2.30–6.45pm)
**AMEX** Voyages Schwartz, 54 Boulevard Pasteur (Tel. 933459/933471)
**ALL NIGHT CHEMIST** Tel. 932619
**EUROTRAIN OFFICE** 112 av. d'Espagne (Tel. 935540)
**TRAIN INFORMATION** Railway station, Place de la Marche Verte (Tel. 934570/931152)
**BUS STATION AND TAXIS** Sahat Al Jamia Al Arabia (Tel. 94 66 82)

## SEEING

Visit the 17th-century **Dar el-Makhzen** (Sultan's Palace), which is now a museum containing a fine collection of Moroccan art, carpets, jewellery and weapons. (Closed Tues.; entrance 12dh).

**FREE TANGIER:**
- The **mountain** – occupied by the villas of the rich and famous – makes a pleasant walk. The main market place, **Grand Socco**, connects the medina and the new town.
- Climb the **Kasbah**, to the highest point, for views over the city and across to the Straits of Gibraltar. Catch a glimpse of mosaic courtyards and fountains at mosque entrances – but remember, it is illegal for non-Muslims to enter a mosque.
- The **American Legation Museum** is in a lovely old house in the Medina. It has some interesting exhibits and is a reminder that Morocco was the first country in the world to recognise US independence. Entrance is free, knock to get in.
- The **beaches** and **nightlife** are both good, though single girls are in for a hard time from the locals.

## SLEEPING

In the medina, the av. Mokhtar Ahardan is where to look for cheap **hotels** (and also **restaurants**). Accommodation may be a problem during July and August, with some of the unclassified places doubling their prices. So for cheap accommodation in high season, use only officially classified establishments. The **Pension Palace** (Tel. 936128) is at 2 av. Mokhtar Ahardan and costs about 80dh per person (hot water extra). The **Olid** at no. 12 (Tel. 931210) charges about the same. Other budget accommodation possibilities are the **youth hostel** at 8 rue El-Antaki (Tel. 946127; beds around 28dh), or the **Magellan**, 16 rue Magellan (Tel: 372319; doubles 100dh).

Seven kilometres out of town and in sight of the Rock of Gibraltar lies the **camping** site Tingis. It is situated east of the city on the Malabata Rd. To get there take bus 15 from the Grand Socco, then walk along the Doubonah Rd and turn right, or along the rue de la Vieille Montagne. There is another site, Camping Miramonte, close to the beach but it's rather run down. Take bus 12 or 21 to reach it.

## Rabat phone code: 07

From Tangier to the capital of Morocco – Rabat – is about five hours on the main line. This is a clean, organized and structured city edged by the Atlantic Ocean. It has numerous parks and gardens, and most of the town is new and affluent by Moroccan standards. There is a kasbah in the old town but the medina lacks atmosphere and you feel you're back in Europe a lot of the time. Rabat's souks have a good reputation for beautiful rugs and embroidery.

## TRAIN INFORMATION
The Rabat Ville Station is centrally located on Ave Mohammad V, don't be tempted to get out at Rabat Agdal.

## TOURIST INFORMATION AND ADDRESSES
**TOURIST INFORMATION** The main Tourist Office is on Rue al-Abtal to the west of the city (Tel. 681531). Far more convenient is the branch office in the centre at 22 Ave d'Alger (Tel. 730562). The Tourist Centre (*Syndicat d'Initiative*) is at rue Patrice Lumumba (Tel. 723272), which is nearer the station and is open 8.30am–6.30pm every day in season.
**POST OFFICE** Av. Mohammed V; open Mon.–Fri.: 8am–12 noon; 2pm–6.45pm, Sat.: 8.30am–12 noon; open 24hrs for telephoning. The *poste restante* section is across the road from the main building
**BANK** Banque Al Maghrib, av. Mohammed V (Tel.763009)
**AMEX** In Rabat Hilton (Tel. 772151). Take bus for Agdal.
**UK EMBASSY** 17 boulevard de Tour Hassan (Tel. 720905)
**US EMBASSY** 2 avenue de Marrakech (Tel. 762265)
**CANADIAN EMBASSY** 13 rue Jaafar Assadik, Agdal (Tel. 672880)
**POLICE** Rue Seekamo (Tel. 19)

## SEEING
The **Kasbah of the Oudaia Fortress** has a beautiful garden, a Moorish café and the **Museum of Moroccan Arts**: carpets, musical instruments, furniture, etc.(entrance 10dh). The **Tour Hassan** minaret in the 12th-century mosque and the **Mausoleum of Mohammed V**

are close to each other. Access to holy places is usually forbidden to non-Muslims, but this is one of only a few in the country where non-Muslims are allowed. Dress appropriately so as not to cause offence.

A one km walk away is the **Chellah**, an Arab necropolis built in the Old Roman section of Rabat called **Sala Colonia**. The gardens here are ideal for a picnic. The **Royal Palace** is on the other side of the city, and worth a look, though it dates back to only the 1950s. The museum of Archaeology, on Rue al-Brihi, has some impressive exhibits, it costs 10dh and is closed on Tues.

## SLEEPING, EATING AND NIGHTLIFE

You'll do best to book your rooms in advance, especially in July, since it can become vastly overcrowded. The **youth hostel** on 43 Rue Marassa, Bab El Had (Tel. 725769) is conveniently sited just outside the medina walls and standards are good. A dorm bed costs 28–35dh. For hotels, stick to the area around the train station where you will find plenty of cheap places. **Hotel Splendid** at 8 rue Ghazza (Tel. 723283) has a nice interior courtyard, or try **Hotel Central** at 2 Zankat al-Basra (Tel. 767356 or 722131). Doubles 100dh, hot showers extra. There are some cheap places to stay in the medina, try **Hotel France** at 46 Rue Souk Semara (doubles from 50dh) or **Des Voyageurs** (Tel. 723720) at 8 Souk Semarine, near Bab Djedid, which is very popular and cheap but there are no showers.

For **camping**, try Camping de la Plage (Tel. 782368) which is across the river. There are other sites south of Rabat on the beaches, however the nearest is about 25km away.

The medina is the place for cheap eats. Souika Street, the main road through the area, is full of lively *foundouks* (traditional cafes) and shops. There are plenty of stalls and restaurants, with the **Restaurant Bahia** on blvd Hassan II offering good food at budget prices. It's located to your right as you approach the medina from av. Mohammed V. If you want to brave a nightclub, investigate the Sahat Melilya and Temara Beach areas.

## Casablanca (Dar Beida) phone code: 02

Despite the best efforts of Humphrey Bogart's international man of mystery (Rick, in the movie *Casablanca*), the city the movie was named after remains the least attractive for Eurorailers. With over three million inhabitants and a busy port, Casablanca is a crowded, modern and somewhat squalid city. Take the train to the port station for the medina and beaches, but be careful taking photographs, as this is a sensitive military area.

Casablanca does have some character, however, and among its sights are the neo-Moorish public buildings round the **Place des Nations Unies** and the **Makhama** (regional courts). A must to visit is the modern **Hassan II Mosque**, the world's largest, which has room for 80,000 worshippers and a 200m minaret. Access to mosques and holy places is usually forbidden to non-Muslims, but this is one of only a few in the country where non-Muslims are allowed. Dress appropriately so as not to cause offence. There are guided tours daily (except on Fri.) at 9am, 10am, 11am and 2pm (2.30pm in summer). They cost around 100dh.

The souk here is famous for its leather work and Mediouna carpets.

On a branch line a few kilometres north of Casablanca is the beach resort of **Mohammedia**.

## TOURIST INFORMATION AND ADDRESSES

**TOURIST INFORMATION** The Tourist Offices at ONCF, (*Syndicat d'Initiative*) 98 boulevard Mohammed V (Tel. 221524 or 279533), and at 55 rue Omar Slaoui (Tel. 271177), can provide good maps and events listings for night owls.

**TRAIN INFORMATION** Casa Port (Tel. 223011/271837). The 55-minute journey south to Casablanca from Rabat involves the best trains in Morocco, but if you're going further south, make sure you have supplies with you as the buffets are awful. If you can afford it, pay the supplement from second to first class (if you're travelling in peak season).

**POLICE/FIRST AID** Boulevard Brahim Roudani (Tel. 19)

**ALL NIGHT CHEMIST** Place Mohammed V (Tel. 269491)

**BUS STATION AND TAXIS** 23 rue Mohammed Kamal (Tel. 268061-67)

**BANK** Al Maghrib Bank, Boulevard de Paris (Tel. 224110)

**AMEX** 112 Ave Prince Moulay Abdellah (Tel. 222946)

## SLEEPING

Try the friendly, well-maintained and nicely sited **youth hostel** at 6 place Admiral Philbert (Tel. 220551; Fax. 227677), which charges from 35dh per person including breakfast. To get there, turn right from the station, turning up the first small flight of steps on the left. There is a **campsite**, Camping Oasis, at Ave Jean Mermoz (Tel. 253367), 8km out on the P8 road.

## Marrakech phone code: 04

This ochre city on the edge of the Sahara desert is all you'd expect Morocco to be. The palm tree-fringed capital of southern Morocco is heavy with vibrant markets with snake-charmers, fortune-tellers and acrobats, remains from ancient dynasties and incredible midday temperatures of up to 40°C (August maximum).

On arrival get hold of a *petit-taxi* (regular ones cost double) and haggle to fix a price for a ride to the Jamaa el Fna, the square to which all roads in Marrakesh lead. Or you can save 15dh or so and take a 3 or 6 bus from outside the station. You'll be dropped off in the city's main square and from there it's no problem finding a cheap hotel bed. The walk takes about 25 minutes.

## TOURIST INFORMATION AND ADDRESSES

**TOURIST OFFICE** Place Abdel Moumen Ben Ali (Tel. 431088 or 448889). English spoken. Ask for a map and a list of accommodation (it doesn't list the real cheapies). Open Mon.–Sat.: 8.30am–12 noon, 2.30pm–6.30pm. Don't bother making the 1½ km trek here unless you're desperate for them to book a hotel for you. Also, there is a tourist centre at 176 av. Mohammed V (tel. 432097 or 434797).

**POST OFFICE** Place du 16 Novembre, off av. Mohammed V; open Mon.–Fri.: 8.30am–12.15pm and 2.30pm–6.45pm

**AMEX** c/o Voyages Schwartz, 1 rue Mauritania, 2nd floor (Tel. 436600 or 433022); open Mon.–Fri.: 8.30am–12 noon, 3pm–6.30pm

**CHEMIST** Place de la Liberté. Open till 10pm. There is an all-night chemist at rue Khalid Ben Oualid (Tel. 430415).

**BUS STATION** Bab Doukkala (Tel. 433933). Buses to the beach leave from here, but travel at a relaxed pace.

**BICYCLES** Hire mountain bikes from Lune Car, III rue de Yugoslavie (Tel. 447743 or 434369)

## SEEING

The old theological school, **Medersa Ben Youssef**, has some fine marble, mosaics and wood-carvings, and the pale green minaret of the **Koutoubia Mosque** is Morocco's best example. The **Bahia Palace** is 19th-century and the **Palace el Badii** is 16th-century. The **Saadian Tombs** contain the remains of various sultans (admission 10dh; open daily from around 9am till noon and 2.30–6pm (closed Fri. morning) – go in the late afternoon if possible).

The annual National Festival of Popular Art is held in the Badii palace during June. Evening shows (tickets cost about 100dh) of authentic, visual performance span the whole spectrum of Moroccan music. In July, the famous Fantasia is worth coming to see – Berber horsemen charge outside the ramparts in a dramatic and spectacular fashion.

**FREE MARRAKECH:**

- The **Jamaa el Fna** (Assembly of the Dead) square is the showpiece of Marrakech and the hub of life in the city. In daytime it's a busy colourful market and at night the street artists arrive. Be particularly careful of your valuables here.
- The **medina** is colourful and lively and there are various photogenic **markets**, like the ones for spices, musical instruments, dyed wool and Berber carpets. Marrakesh is big on leatherwork, and you can also see shoemakers sewing slippers in the ancient tradition. Hustlers and other pests are notorious in this area, though recent police efforts (with special 'tourist brigades' set up to protect visitors from the nuisance) have cleaned up the marketplace considerably.
- Also go and see the **camel souk** (traditional trading station) which takes place every Thursday.

## SLEEPING, EATING AND NIGHTLIFE

Try the area around the station for cheap eats and sleeps. This quarter is abundant in French-style restaurants and also contains most of the city's bars. The **Hotel de la Jeunesse** at 56 Derb Sidi Banloukate (Tel. 443631) is one of the best budget hostels on this street, charging 90dh for a double room and 100dh for a triple, including cold showers.

Try the **Café Restaurant Marocain** at place Jamaa el Fna nearby, open 8am–11pm. Rue Bani Marin, just off from here, houses good food venues like **Mik Mak** on place Foucauld, which has an excellent *pâtisserie*. Make sure you sample mint tea at least once! **Café Restaurant Oriental** at 33 rue Bah Agnaou (off the Jamaa el Fna) does good menus at reasonable prices.

Another good area for cheap hotels and restaurants is Dejemaa el Fna. **Hotel Farouk**, 66 av. Hassan (Tel. 445913) is clean and modern and convenient for the station. Or try **CTM Hostel** (Tel. 442325) on Place Djemaa El Fna; they have doubles from about 100dh and singles from 80dh.

The **youth hostel** (Tel. 447713) is good by Moroccan standards and is five minutes' walk from the station on rue el Jahed. (IYHF cards are compulsory.) The hostel closes 9am–2pm and after 10pm. At the moment, there is no convenient campsite but one is due to open soon on the P24 Route de Casablanca (16km out of town). Check with the tourist offices for the latest

## Meknes phone code: 05

On the line to Fez and the Algerian border, 4½ hours from Tangier, lies the imperial city of Meknes. From the station, turn left for the medina, hotels and the old town.

## TOURIST INFORMATION AND ADDRESSES

**TOURIST INFORMATION** is at Place Administrative (Tel. 524426) and is open Mon.–Fri.: 8am–2pm; Sat.: 8.30am–12 noon, 3pm–6pm. English is spoken, and some literature is available. Another Tourist Centre can be found at Esplanade de la Foire (Tel. 520191).
**EMERGENCY CHEMIST** Hotel de Ville (Tel. 522664)
**BANK** Bank Al Maghrib, Avenue Mohammed V (Tel. 521012/521051)
**TRAIN INFORMATION** Rue Amir Abdelkader (Tel. 52 06 89/522763)

## SEEING

**Place Mansour**, the pavilion where the Merinid Sultan Moulay Ismail received ambassadors, is up here. There are **underground caves** where the Sultan's slaves were kept, which can be viewed if you ask the guards nicely. The elaborate tomb of **Moulay Ismail** is further up on the right. The mosque in which the tomb is located is one of only a few in the country to admit non-Muslims. Dress appropriately so as not to cause offence.

The 19th-century **Dar Jamai Palace**, at the back of place el Hedim, is now a museum which houses an excellent display of Middle Atlas carpets, particularly the bold geometric designs of the Beni Mguild tribe. The **Dar El-Kebira** (Great Palace) was once the largest in the world. The theological school **Medersa Bou Inania** is the elaborate building in the medina. Entry is 10dh and there is a good view from here.

**FREE MEKNES:**
* The souk here makes yet another dazzling photo opportunity, with stalls specializing in carved wood, mosaics, and metallic animals inlaid with silver thread.

## SLEEPING, EATING AND NIGHTLIFE

Around place el Hedim there are quite a few cheap **hotels**, but if you don't fancy these, the best alternative is **camping**. One of the best sites, and arguably the best one in the whole country, is Camping Agdal which is a 20 min. walk south from place el Hedim (Tel. 555396).

The **youth hostel** at Boulevard Okba Ben Nafi (Tel. 524698) is well-maintained but slightly out of the way. Get there on bus 15. (Dorm beds from 26dh.)

For food, rue Dar Smen and av. de Roumazine are the best ideas. **Free-Time Fast Food** is at 27 av. Hassan II. Moroccan-style nightlife is not hard to find in Meknes.

## Fez (Fes) phone code: 05

The oldest imperial city in Morocco is today considered her cultural and intellectual centre. The huge medina here is unmatched elsewhere in North Africa. You could easily spend days absorbing the colours, smells, filth and constant arguments! The souks here in Morocco's craftwork capital are particularly spectacular, with pottery in hues of Fez blue, gleaming copper trays and good leather work.

## TOURIST INFORMATION AND ADDRESSES

**TOURIST INFORMATION** Place de la Résistance, Immeuble Benani (at the end of av. Hassan II) (Tel. 623460 or 626297); open Mon.–Fri.: 8.30am–12 noon, 2.30pm–6.30pm. Also at place Mohammed V (Tel. 624769).
**POST OFFICE** av. Mohammed V (corner of av. Hassan); open Mon.–Fri.: 8.30am–12 noon, 2.30pm–6.30pm
**BUS STATION** CTM, Av. Mohammed V (Tel. 622041) with buses to Rabat, Casablanca, Marrakech, Meknes and Tangier. Private buses from Gare Routière in Bab Bou Jeloud.
**24-HOUR CHEMIST** Av. Abdelkrim El Khattabi (Tel. 623380)

## SEEING

Expect to get lost in Fez: the **Medina** is so sprawling and unstructured it's inevitable. There is a map in the medina to help you out, but it is not well detailed. You will inevitably be pestered by unofficial guides, so be careful. The majority of them hang out in Bab Bou Jeloud (the location of the Tourist Office). If you accept an offer, haggle him down to about 10dh and emphasize that you wish to go sightseeing, not shopping (he will receive a commission on any goods you buy, and you will end up paying more). Official guides are available at the **hotels** or Tourist Offices for about 130dh per half day and are identified by their traditional costume and badge. Watch out also for pickpockets.

Before entering the medina, check out the **Dar Batha Palace**, which houses the **Museum of Moroccan Arts** at place du Batha (open 8.30am–12noon and 2.30pm–6.30pm, closed Tues.; admission 10dh) and features local artisan traditions; the pottery rooms are outstanding.

The medina is the site of the **El Qaraouiyin Mosque**, built in the ninth century, and the **Koranic University**, which claims to be the oldest in the world, along with the theological schools of **Attarine** and **Bou Inania**.

**FREE FEZ:**
- There are countless **souks** in the **medina** to look at, but only ferret out the tannery if you've got an iron stomach: the vast vats of coloured dyes are intriguing, but the smell is not.
- Climb uphill out of the city centre where you will still find working pit ponies.
- If you come at dusk, you can have a wonderful view and soak up the atmosphere as you hear the calls to prayer.

## SLEEPING, EATING AND NIGHTLIFE

The **youth hostel** on 18 rue Abdesslam Serghrini (Tel. 624085) is good value (40dh with breakfast) and, by Fez standards, very clean and comfortable, with space on the roof if the dormitory is full. Reach it by walking six blocks down from the Tourist Office along boulevard Chefchaouni, turn left to the street below and look for signs. It is about five km from the station. The hostel has a kitchen, so you could buy food and cook it yourself (watch the meat).

Round Bab Bou Jeloud you'll find a few cheap (and fairly basic) **hotels** with doubles from 95dh. Other cheap non-classified hotels are found in the new town, around the area of av. Mohammed V. **The Hotel Renaissance** at 47 rue Abdelkrim el-Khattabi (Tel. 622193), near the av. Mohammed V, charges 70dh for a single room, but has no showers. The **Hôtel du Commerce** (Tel. 622231) in place des Alaouites in Fes-el-Jdid is very clean and charges 65dh for a single room and an extra 10dh for showers.

For **camping**, try Camping Diament Vert (Tel. 608367) at Ain Chkeff which is 6km south of the centre, off the road to Ifrane. There's also Camping International (Tel. 731430; Fax. 731554) on the Sefrou Road. This is a good site, set in large gardens and has a swimming pool, tennis courts, restaurants and bars.

**Bab Bou Jeloud** and the **medina** are the cheap eating districts. The place Mohammed V also boasts plentiful eating places, but is more expensive. Sample the local delicacy of *bisteela* (pigeon, vegetables and nuts, covered in sweet pastry).

An evening stroll in the **old Jewish quarter** is more rewarding than the formal entertainments you'll find. In late May, Fez hosts a Festival of World Sacred Music. Ask at the tourist offices about the **Son et Lumière** shows which are held in Mar., Apr., Oct. and Nov.

## Off-the-Track Places

Many of Morocco's best places are not on the railway, so buses are the only answer.

- **Tetouan**, 1½ hours away from Tangier, is a relatively unspoilt town with a fascinating medina – eat there and try round place Hassan II and av. Mohammed V for rooms. The Tourist Office (Tel. 961916) is situated on the latter at no. 30; open Mon.–Fri.: 8am–noon and 2.30–6.30pm. There is a municipal campsite at Martil Beach (10km away).

- **Asni** in the **Rif** mountain region is 48 km from Marrakech and buses leave each morning from Bab Doukkala and Bab Errob coach stations. It's more fun to share a taxi with several others and a full load should mean your share of the fare comes to about 20dh.

- **Essaouira** is a Berber town on the south-west coast, with a distinctly Portuguese feel to it (it was built by the Portuguese). If you're fed up with travelling and need a break before the long haul back home, sleep here free on the beaches (although never do this if you're alone, and especially not if you're a woman alone). This is a good place to take stock of a very un-European culture and lifestyle. Excellent windsurfing and surfing. Take a leisurely walk up to the 18th-century Moorish fortress (the **skala**) at sunset. The Tourist Office is on Porte Portugaise. Don't miss the souk here: the specialities are jewellery, marquetry, weaving, brassware and embroidery.

- **Agadir**, rebuilt after an earthquake in 1960, is now a modern beach resort populated by package holiday tourists. The Tourist Office is at 'A' Building, place du Prince Heritier Sidi Mohamed (Tel. 846378 or 841367) and can help you with accommodation. There is also an office at av. Mohammed V (Tel. 840307). The Railway Terminus is at route des Orangiers and the bus station is on blvd. Mohammed Cheikh Saadi. There is an International Campsite at blvd. Mohammed V (Tel. 846683). There's an Amex agency at Avenue Des F.A.R. (Tel. 840188).

- Way out at **Mesuga** you are definitely in the Sahara, site of the mountains of sand that were the setting for *Lawrence of Arabia*.

NOTES:
...........................................................................................................................

...........................................................................................................................

...........................................................................................................................

...........................................................................................................................

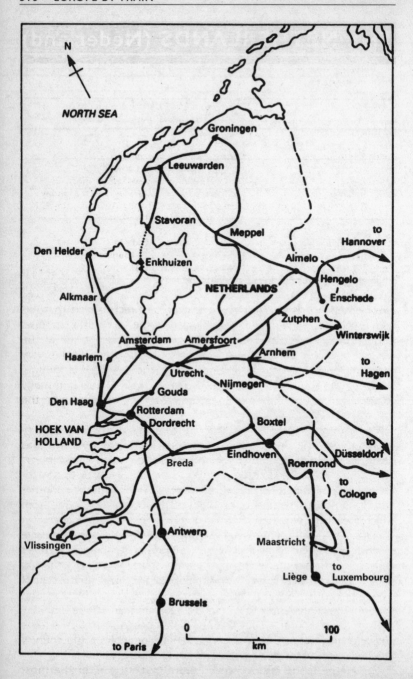

# THE NETHERLANDS (Nederland)

| | |
|---|---|
| Entry requirements | Passport |
| Population | 15.7 million |
| Capital | Amsterdam is the capital; the seat of government is The Hague (pop.: 0.6 million) |
| Currency | Guilder (Florin) (f) |
| | £1 = approx. f3.5 |
| Political system | Constitutional monarchy |
| Religion | Protestant and Roman Catholic |
| Language | Dutch (English widely spoken in cities) |
| Public holidays | New Year's Day, Good Friday, Easter Monday, Queen's Birthday (30 Apr.), Ascension Day (21 May), Whit Monday, Christmas Day and Boxing Day |
| International dialling codes | To Netherlands: int'l code 31 |
| | From Netherlands: 00 + country code |
| Time | GMT +1 (+2 in summer) |
| Emergency telephone numbers | All emergencies 112 |

The Netherlands is an astonishing feat of land reclamation that has seen much of it left with a uniquely flat landscape – a cyclist's paradise.

Windmills, clogs and Edam cheese are a source of pride in the western provinces of North and South Holland, while the north is very different, with a strong regional identity and separate language. However, the south, where people are more like the French in many respects, brings perhaps the most exciting new dimension to the landscape – hills!

The Netherlands as a unified state didn't begin until the 16th century when, under the Burgundians and the Habsburgs, Holland was politically linked to Belgium and Flanders. However, the Spanish rulers fighting for the Catholic cause started to levy heavy taxes to pay for their army, which naturally didn't go down too well with the country's Protestant north. The upshot of it all was the Eighty Years' War, from which the Dutch emerged in 1648, clutching their independence.

During the 17th century, the Dutch 'Golden Age' made massive contributions to European civilization. The likes of Rembrandt, Vermeer and de Hooch led the world in art, while others were busy making huge leaps in science. It was also a time of 'tulip-mania' with the start of a boom, or rather, a bloom in the tulip industry. And as if all that wasn't enough, they doled out a few lessons on seafaring and trade too.

From the start of the 18th century, Dutch power started to decline and after the Napoleonic Wars and French domination, the country gradually developed into a parliamentary democracy.

The Netherlands' history and culture make it one of the most civilized countries in Europe and with an excellent rail service and bicycle-friendly terrain, its a joy to get to know.

## NETHERLANDS RAILWAYS
### (NEDERLANDSE SPOORWEGEN, NS)
Arguably, rail service in Europe doesn't get any better than Netherlands Railways. So trouble-free and efficient are they that by 2005, they will have doubled the number of passengers they transport (or so they hope). Short distances between cities and a frequent inter-city service, at least once an hour, mean you can even see most of the country while based in a single city. A word of warning though: avoid the 'stop-trains', as they do just that at every station before connecting to the main inter-city network. Also note that some trains split to arrive at different destinations, so make sure you're in the right half of the train. The only supplements payable are for Euro-City trains. Apart from a serious accident at Hoofddorp in 1992, NS has a superb safety record.
**EURAIL BONUSES** 30% reduction with Stena Line between Harwich and Hook of Holland.

## TRAIN INFORMATION
You'll have no worries with language as nearly everyone speaks English. Pick-up the *Travelling by Rail in Holland* booklet from the information office, which has a useful map and frequency times.

**PASSES AVAILABLE** Eurail and Inter-Rail passes and Europass and Flex-ipass are all valid. The Netherlands is in Inter-Rail Zone E, along with France, Belgium and Luxembourg. (For further details of the eight Inter-Rail zones, refer to the Inter-Rail section in Part One of this guide.)

The one-day Rover Ticket gives unlimited second-class rail travel throughout the country for £28 (first class £42). During July and August, the excellent value Summer Tour Rover ticket also provides couples travelling together with three days unlimited travel within a period of 10 days. It costs £45 second class (which covers you both). If you are travelling alone you can buy this pass for £34.

The Euro Domino Pass for the Netherlands allows unlimited travel for between three–eight days. A three day ticket costs £59 first class, £39 second class, a five day ticket costs £99 first class and £59 second class and an eight day ticket costs £149 first class and £99 second class. For further details see Part One of this guide.

The Holland Rail Pass allows unlimited travel for any three or five days. A three day ticket costs £57 first class, £38 second class and a five day ticket costs £84 first class, £57 second class. Under 26s are charged £31 for three days travel (£46 1st class) and £46 for 5 days

(£68 for 1st class). An added advantage of this pass is that a second person can travel for half price.

If you are travelling as a group, consider the Multi Rover ticket, which gives two-six passengers a day's unlimited rail travel. It costs £44 for two passengers (£67 1st class) and £72 for a group of six (£111 1st class). A Benelux Tourail Card which gives you unlimited travel throughout Belgium, the Netherlands and Luxembourg can be used for any five days in a month. Prices are: adults £82 (when two adults travel together the second adult can buy the card for half price), under 26 (junior) £56 (first class adult fare is £120, again, a second adult can buy the pass for half price). Note, when two juniors travel together there is not a 50% reduction on the second ticket; each ticket costs £56. You can buy this pass from train stations in Belgium and Luxembourg but, strangely, not in the Netherlands. Purchase the card before you go from USIT/Campus Travel: tel. 020 7730 3402; Wasteels, tel. 020 7834 7066) or from Holland Rail.

For more information on any of these rail passes, telephone Holland Rail in the UK on 01962 773646 or fax. them on 01962 773625.

You can also buy a one day ticket which gives unlimited 1st/2nd class travel (after 9am) and costs around f105/70.

Travellers under 26 get a 25% discount off train travel in and from the country.

**RESERVATIONS** Reservations are only possible on international services outside the Benelux countries, but must be made at a Dutch station. It is also necessary to reserve a seat when travelling on Thalys.

**NIGHT TRAVEL** Couchettes and sleepers are only available on international routes. You can get a quick kip on the hourly all-night service between Utrecht, Amsterdam, The Hague and Rotterdam.

**EATING ON TRAINS** Inter-cities have the usual trolley refreshments while Euro-City trains have restaurant cars.

**SCENIC TIPS** From March to May, a trip between Amsterdam and Leiden via Haarlem will provide you with a fabulous journey through the best of the flowering bulbfields.

**TAXIS** *Treintaxis* are available at most stations, and for a fee of f8 will take you anywhere within the city region. You can also order them to come and pick you up. Amsterdam, The Hague and Rotterdam do not offer this service as they all have their own comprehensive public transport system.

**BIKES** If you want to experience the Dutch way of travel, you can hire a bike at most stations for about f10 per day plus a deposit. Show your train ticket and you'll get it even cheaper. Beware though, before deciding on a marathon expedition: you'll need to return your bike to the same station. Also make sure it's securely locked when not in use as about 20% of bikes are stolen each year.

## TOURIST INFORMATION (VVV)

Throughout the Netherlands you can find tourist offices in every town and village. They produce plenty of information about the area and can book accommodation for you, usually for a small fee. Those who plan to do a spot of cycling can also get a cycle map here, but it's not always free. Many VVV offices have telephone numbers prefixed by 0900. These numbers are charged at premium rate (about f0.50–1 per min. from within the Netherlands). They are answered by recorded messages in Dutch. If you wait for the message to end, someone will then answer the call. Try the Netherlands Board of Tourism in London (Tel. 020 7931 0661 or 0891 717 7777 premium charge line) for maps as well. If you're going to be visiting a lot of museums a *Museum Card*, available from any tourist office, is an excellent investment. It costs about f55 or f25 for under 25s, and entitles you to free or massively-reduced entry to all state museums for a year.

**ISIC BONUSES** Selected museums offer up to 50% reduction.
**MONEY MATTERS** 1 guilder (NLG) (florin) (f) = 100 cents (c).
Banking hours are Mon.–Fri.: 9am–4 or 5pm. There are also GWK exchange offices in 35 railway stations which provide good rates and service. Open Mon.–Fri.: 8am–8pm and Sun.: 10am–4pm. Some VVV tourist offices also exchange money. Stay away from 'store-front-style' exchange shops which can charge as much as 9% commission.
**POST OFFICES** Open Mon.–Fri.: 8.30am–5pm and, in major towns, 8.30am–noon on Sat.
**SHOPS** Generally, Mon.–Fri.: 9am–6pm and Sat.: 9am–5pm. Late night opening till 9pm on Thurs. and Fri.
**MUSEUMS** Opening times are pretty much the same everywhere: Tues.–Sat.: 10am–5pm, Sun.: 1 or 2pm–5pm. Closed on Mon.
**TIPPING** Leave up to 10% if you've had good service.

## SLEEPING

The cost of a bed in one of the Netherlands' 52 IYHF youth hostels varies between f22 and f40 for members, including breakfast. Non-members pay an extra f5. If you don't have your own bedding you may also be charged a f6.50 fee for sheets. Ask at a VVV office for a list of hostels or contact the head office in Amsterdam: Nederlandse Jeugdherberg Centrale, Prof Tulpstraat 2, 1018 HA Amsterdam (Tel. 020 551 3155; Fax. 020 639 0199). Student hostels are also a good bet in summer and are fairly lax if you look like a student. For those who prefer to camp under the stars there are plenty of good sites to chose from. Prices vary widely but if you budget for f20 per person per night, you should be OK. Again, VVV will provide a list. From Apr.–Oct. you can also spend up to three nights in one of the hikers' cabins.

They cost no more than f58 per night for up to four people. The price includes electricty and gas. For more information, contact Stichting Trekkershutten Nederland Ruigeweg 49, 1752 HC Sint Maartensbrug (Fax. 224 563 318).

Hotel accommodation is graded on a star basis, normally with breakfast included in the price. A 1-star single room will probably set you back a minimum of f58. For a small commission you can also book private rooms through the local tourist office. Most are quite relaxed and good value but check how far they are from the centre.

Expect seasonal price increases during the busy high season and reserve your accommodation as early as possible. Amsterdam is particularly busy, so this can't be stressed enough. You can book hotels (no deposit required) in writing, by telephone or fax at the Nederlands Reservation Centre, Postbus 404, 2260 AK Leidschendam (Tel. 070 320 2500; Fax. 070 320 2611).

## EATING AND NIGHTLIFE

As you'd expect, chips and mayonnaise are readily available. For a healthier lunch option though, follow the example of the Dutch who tend to favour *koffietafel* (sandwich and coffee). And with dozens of different cheeses around, there's no excuse for sticking to Edam or Gouda. Of the numerous regional specialities to savour, one of the best is *nieuwe haring* (salted herring). Bought from street stalls and eaten raw, it's surprisingly tender and savoury. Keep an eye out too for the vegetarian Israeli delicacy *falafel*, which also makes an excellent nourishing snack. For your main meal, you can eat your fill at any of the restaurants offering the 'tourist menu'. Value-wise, these meals are hard to beat, so if you like what's on the menu, don't waste your time looking elsewhere. A little more exotic is a *rijsttafel* from one of the many Indonesian restaurants, but not recommended for those with small appetites.

In larger cities there are bars and nightclubs galore (entry for clubs is around f10–f20). At cinemas English films are subtitled into Dutch so you can still watch them with ease. Prices usually start at about f25.

## The Northern Netherlands

This region encompasses the provinces of Friesland, Groningen and North Holland, with the latter including the towns of Alkmaar and Amsterdam. With much of the region reclaimed from the sea, the naturally flat landscape provides ideal cycling territory.

**Friesland** with its lakes, wildlife and bird sanctuaries retains a strong regional identity. Their own language, *Frysk*, is spoken only here and sounds more like 'Double Dutch' to the rest of the country. The provincial capital, Leeuwarden, famous for being the birthplace of World War I spy Mata Hari, is also a birdwatchers' paradise. See the **Fries Museum**, **Oldhove Tower** and **Princessehof Museum of Ceramics**.

On the other side of the Zuider Zee are **Zaandam**, the 'living museum': a reconstructed village of mills and old houses; **Alkmaar** (40 minutes from Amsterdam), famous for its cheese market on Friday mornings (10am–12 noon) from mid-April to mid-September; and **Hoorn**, with its crafts and folklore market.

## Amsterdam phone code: 020

Amsterdam could easily be described as a 'Tale of Two Cities': on one side it's quiet and graceful, with endless canals, narrow houses and tiny winding streets, while on the other it's a city living life in the fast lane, with fast food, loud music and, most famously, seedy sex and drugs. There are so many things to experience here that it is pretty much essential to see it during any comprehensive European tour.

### TOURIST INFORMATION
Amsterdam's main VVV Tourist Office is opposite Centraal Station at Stationsplein 10: daily 9am–5pm. There's also a smaller one inside the station on platform 2: Mon.–Sat.: 8am–8pm, Sun.: 8.30am–4.30pm. Other offices are at Leidsestraat 106, Mon.–Sat.: 9am–7pm and Sun.: 9am–5pm, and Stadionplein, Mon.–Sat.: 9am–5pm. For telephone information, call 0990 400 4040 (f1 per minute). The line is open weekdays from 9am–5pm.

For the latest lowdown on what's happening and where, buy a copy of *What's On in Amsterdam*, priced f4. Similarly, ask for a copy of *Use It*, a student-orientated listings guide. You can also purchase tickets here for public transport and excursions, plus low-priced maps and guides. The Amsterdam Culture and Leisure Pass is also a good investment at around f35. It contains 31 vouchers which give discounts on canal boats, free entry or big discounts to several museums (including the Van Gogh Museum and the Rijksmuseum) and discounts in some restaurants. VVV organize city walks which leave from the Historisch Museum, Kalverstraat 92, Tues.–Fri. and Sun. 11am. You need to book on the tour two days in advance, contact one of the offices for more information.

### ADDRESSES
**POST OFFICE** Singel 250, Mon.–Fri.: 9am–6pm (8pm on Thurs.), Sat.: 10am–1.30pm

**AMEX** Damrak 66 (Tel. 504 8504), Mon.–Fri.: 9am–5pm, Sat.: 9am–12 noon

**MONEY EXCHANGE** GWK office in Centraal Station and American Express at Damrak 66

**UK CONSULATE** 44 Koningslaan (Tel. 676 4343)

**US CONSULATE** 19 Museumplein (Tel. 575 5309 or 664 5661)

**MEDICAL HELP** Kruispost, Oudezijds Voorburgwal 129 (Tel. 624 9031). The Central Doctors Service deals with medical, dental and pharmaceutical emergencies 24hr a day, call 0900 503 2042

**CHEMISTS** Generally open 8.30am–5pm. No 24hr-chemists. When closed a sign will direct you to the nearest late-night one

**GAY AND LESBIAN SERVICES** COC Rozenstraat 14 (Tel. 626 3087 or 623 1192); open Wed.–Sat.: 1pm–5pm or telephone the Gay switchboard on 623 6565 daily 10am–10pm. The Amsterdam Pride parade is in the first week of Aug.

**NBBS** Rokin 38, near Dam Square and Utrechtsestraat 48. Sells Eurotrain tickets.

**STUDENT TRAVEL OFFICE** Kilroy Travels, Singel 413–415 (Tel. 524 5100)

**POLICE** Elandsgracht 117 (Tel. 559 9111 or emergency 112)

## GETTING ABOUT

Telephone information 7am–midnight: 0900 92 92

Free maps of the city's bus, tram and underground network, plus a useful *Tourist Guide*, are available at the GVB office in front of Centraal Station. Open Mon.–Fri.: 7am–7pm, Sat. and Sun.: 8am–7pm. If you're going to make a few journeys during the day, invest in a day ticket costing f10. For those staying longer, you can buy the good value two-, three- and four-day passes, priced f15, f19 and f23 respectively. The **Circle Tram** (No. 20), introduced in 1997, stops at all the important attractions and operates every day from 9am–6pm. Tickets for this cost the same as day passes and are valid on all transport services, not just the Circle Tram Line.

The nationwide **Strippenkaarts** (literally a strip of tickets) are valid on all public transport as well. Buy them at the station, GVB offices, selected tobacconists and post offices. If you need to, tickets can be bought from bus and tram drivers but are more expensive. If you decide on the latter, board from the front. At all other times, however, board trams from the rear and get your ticket stamped by the conductor or at the stamping machine. Note, unstamped tickets are invalid. Bus inspectors are extremely vigilant, especially in Amsterdam in the summer, and it is not uncommon for up to six inspectors to board a single vehicle at each exit. Ticketless passengers are liable to a f70 on-the-spot fine plus the cost of a ticket. Playing the naïve tourist will not help you.

## STATION FACILITIES

The 24-hr **Centraal Station** has a complete range of facilities, including a round-the-clock waiting room for passengers catching night trains.

There are daily trains to Hamburg (six hours), Düsseldorf (2½ hours), The Hague (55 minutes), Brussels (three hours), Paris (six hours) and London (either via Brussels and Eurostar (six hours) or Hook of Holland boat train). Internal trains run approximately every 15 minutes.

## SEEING

Amsterdam's four main canals (Singel, Herengracht, Keizersgracht and Prinsengracht) flow past the main sights, so it's no surprise that a canal boat trip is your best introduction to the city – and it gives your feet a chance to rest! Take your trip during the day, as prices rise dramatically for candlelit night cruises. Bookings can be made at any city Tourist Office, with a circular day cruise costing you around f23. There's also a Museum Boat which combines a canal trip and a museum visit. It departs every 30 mins. and stops near 17 museums. The ticket costs around f23 and gives 50% reduction on the museum entry fee.

**Dam Square** is the heart of the city and lies at the end of **Damrak**, the main shopping street – now tidied up and refurbished. East of here is the old city centre of **Walletjes**, though part of it (Oudezijds Achterburgwal, Oude Zijds Voorburgwal and their surroundings) is perhaps better known as the sex streets of Europe at night (and even during the day).

To the west of the square is **Westerkerk**, which offers a good view from its tower. Behind it at Prinsengracht 263 is **Anne Frank's House** (admission f10), where she famously recorded her diary whilst hiding from the Nazis. There's an Anti-Semitic Exhibition downstairs too. Open Mon.–Sat.: 9am–5pm and Sun.: 10am–5pm; until 7pm June–Aug.

The art buff is well at home in Amsterdam. The **Rijksmuseum** at Stadhouderskade 42 ranks as one of the world's greatest art museums and heads the list of the city's 71 museums. It's got plenty of Rembrandts and other Dutch masters, such as Hals and Vermeer. It's open daily 10am–5pm and entry costs f15. The **Stedelijk Museum** at Paulus Potterstraat 13 (admission f9; open daily, 11am–7pm), also has a diverse modern art collection, including a lot of paintings by the Russian artist Malevich; and the **Van Gogh Museum** (admission f12.50), just along the street has, well, Van Goghs! **Rembrandt's House** at Jodenbreestraat 4–6 (admission f7.50), contains some 250 of his etchings and drawings.

The **Royal Palace** on Dam Square was once known as the 'Eighth Wonder of the World', due to it being supported by 13,659 bits of wood. Entrance around f7, but opening times can vary (generally in summer it's daily 12.30pm–5pm). Next door is the gothic **Nieuwe Kerk** (admission f3), though there's nothing new about this place as it dates from around 1500. Just behind it and a little younger (dating from 1650) is a 'tasting house', **The Three Bottles** (*De Drie Fleschjes*). Bols and Hoppe liqueurs are recommended (in small quantities). While on the subject of booze, you can tour the **Heineken Brewery** at Stadhouderskade 78, Mon.–Fri. at 9.30am and 11am (with extra tours June–Sept. at 1pm and 2.30pm, and on Sat. in July and Aug.). Entrance is only f2.

Also worth seeing are the **Amstelkring** at Oude Zijds Voorburgwal 40, a preserved 17th-century house where repressed Catholics used to hide; the **Maritime Museum** at Kattenburgenplein 1, which is very interesting and has few tourists (though a bit pricey at f12.50); and the **Film Museum** in Vondelpark, open every day with filmshows between 7–10pm.

Amsterdam is the world's diamond centre and if you want to see how a piece of rough glass stone is transformed into a girl's best friend, contact the VVV offices for information on diamond-cutting tours.

The Dutch love to cycle. If you fancy a pedal too, there are several places in the city where you can rent bicycles, although **Rent-a-Bike** at Pieter Jacobszdwarfsstraat 11 is the most convenient. They charge f10 a day, plus a deposit of f200 with ID. This can be extended to the canals as well by hiring a canal bike from four moorings in the city centre. A 2-seater will cost f18 per hour, with a deposit returned when you 'park' the bike at any of the mooring points. You can also pick up bikes at Utrechtsedwarsstraat 105, Sint Nicolaasstraat 16 and Keizersgracht 181. **Yellow Bike** at Nieuwezijds Kolk 29 organizes bike tours throughout Amsterdam from April until Oct. For further details call 620 6940. Be aware of bike thieves and people who throw bikes into the canals!

**FESTIVALS** Throughout June, the **Holland Festival** attracts quality artists from around the world for a programme of dance, opera, music, theatre and film. Tickets are available through the Netherlands Reservation Centre (Tel. 070 419 5544), AUB Ticket Shop at Leidseplein 26 (Tel. 621 1211) open Mon.–Sat. 10am–6pm (until 9pm on Thurs.) or VVV Offices.

In July and August the **Robeco Summer Concerts** at Concertgebouw offer international vocal groups, ensembles and orchestras. The **Drum Rhythm Festival** in July features music from the world of rock and jazz.

**FREE AMSTERDAM:** Let's face it, nobody visits Amsterdam without a wander through the streets of the red-light district – the most obvious free activity for those who want to *observe*. Don't be tempted to take photos though, as budding David Baileys may find their cameras rapidly gurgling to the bottom of the canal!

Away from the streets of sin, there's also plenty to offer the gratis-seeking traveller – 28 different markets for a start. The **Albert Cuyp market**, on Albert Cuypstraat, is probably the biggest and best (Mon.–Sat.: 9.30am–5pm) while the **flea market** at Waterlooplein (Mon.–Sat.: 9am–5pm) is also worth a visit.

- For artists and street performers the best place to head for is Dam Square.
- After a hard night's partying the city's parks are great places to crash out. While canal-side walks are a pleasant way to see some of Amsterdam's architecture. **Herengracht** passes the 17th-century merchants' houses, while **Jordaan** is another district worth a wander – a Bohemian working-class quarter.
- If you're about on the Queen's birthday on 30 April you'll experience one of the most festive days of the year – the whole city centre turns into a stage for street theatre and musicians, along with more markets than you can handle. Other free things to sample include:
- **Open-air music and theatre** performances held daily during the summer at Vondelpark and Amsterdamse Bos.
- A **ferry** journey around the harbour leaving from pier 7 behind Centraal Station roughly every 10 minutes throughout the day.
- **Informatiecentrum de Zuiderkerk**, Zuiderkerkof 72. A 17th-century church with an exhibition of past and future Amsterdam.
- **Museum Harbour**, moored opposite 189 Prins Hendrikkade. An assortment of old Dutch ships.
- **Garden of Vrije Universiteit**, Van de Boechorstraat 8. With flowers, herbs, bonsai and much more.
- Display of lace fans at **Het Kantenuis**, Kalverstraat 124.
- Chess Exhibition at the **Max Euwe Centrum**, Max Euweplein 39a. Open Tues.–Fri. and first Sat. of month: 10.30am–4pm.
- **Geelvinck-Hinlopen House**, Herengracht 518. An exhibition of 18th and 19th-century rooms and antiques. Thurs.–Sat.: 12 noon–5pm.

**DRUGS SCENE** Contrary to what you might think, possession of any amount of drugs is technically illegal. In reality, however, the police only seem to be interested in prosecuting the street pushers. If you do intend to dabble with 'the herb', stick to the coffee shops where you can partake with little fear of prosecution. Special 'cake' and 'tea' can also be tried here. Avoid hard drugs at all costs and ignore any street pushers. The law is tightening up.

## SLEEPING

Amsterdam ranks just behind London, Paris and Rome when it comes to Europe's most popular cities, so it gets extremely busy in summer. Unless you reserve in advance (most private hostels and youth hostels don't accept advance bookings) you could find yourself stuck for a roof over your head. Peak season, hotels will be booked solid, though there is a chance of a bed in one of the hostels or a campsite pitch. On arrival at Amsterdam Centraal, also be prepared for hassle from hoteliers pushing their rooms out of season. The easiest way to book accommodation is through the VVV offices for a small charge. The *Netherlands Reservation Centre* in The Hague (Tel. 070 419 5544) will book rooms too, but they won't necessarily be budget.

**HOTELS** The **Hotel Beursstraat** (Tel. 626 3701; Fax. 690 9012) is in a good central location just five minutes from Centraal station. It's clean and secure,doubles cost from f80 (breakfast is extra).

The **International Budget Hotel** at Leidsegracht 76 (Tel. 624 2784; fax. 626 1839) is in a nice location on a small canal in the centre of the city. It's very popular and has dormitory accommodation for f48. Reservations are recommended. Another good option is the **Hotel Belga** (Tel. 624 9080; Fax. 623 6862) at Hartenstraat 8 in the old centre. Singles from f90, doubles f130

**HOSTELS** You should find a bed in one of the following:

**Vondelpark** IYHF hostel, Zandpad 5 (Tel. 589 8999; Fax. 589 8955). At its busiest in July and August you'll need proof of membership. Beds in dorms for around f34–40. Get there by tram 1, 2 or 5 from station to Leidseplein, then a five-minute walk. Written reservations only. Almost immediately opposite is the **Flying Pig Vondelpark** (Tel. 400 4187) at Vossiusstraat 46. Dorm beds around f28.

**Stadsdoelen** IYHF hostel, Kloveniersburgwal 97 (Tel. 624 6832; Fax. 639 1035). Dorms from f26 (f5 extra for non-members). A more central option with good value food served in restaurant. Tram 4, 9, 16, 24 or 25 to Muntplein or underground to Nieuwmarkt.

**Flying Pig Downtown**, Nieuwendijk 100 (Tel. 421 0583; fax. 421 0802). First right to the end after Victoria Hotel on Damrak. Not far from the station, no curfew and free lockers but breakfast a little on the stingy side.

The city's cheapest hostels are the two Christian establishments charging f25 for bed and breakfast. The **Shelter** is in the red-light district at Barndesteeg 21 (Tel. 625 3230; Fax. 623 2282) – approach the hostel from the Damrak side rather than from Nieuwmarkt. The **Eben Haezer** is at Bloemstraat 179 (Tel: 624 4717; Fax. 627 6137) which can be reached by tram 13 or 17 to Marnixstraat.

**PRIVATE ACCOMMODATION** VVV offices will fix you up for about f55 per person and a f5 commission charge.

**CAMPSITES** The best and most convenient site is **Vliegenbos** at Meeuwenlaan 138 (Tel. 636 8855), across the water from the train station. Take bus 32 or 36 from the station or use the free ferry then walk 20 mins. Bungalows to rent. Open Apr.–Sept., book ahead. Also try **Zeeburg** at Zuider-ljdijk 20 (Tel. 694 4430) which charges around f7 per person per night and f3.50 for a tent. There are plenty of backpackers here along with regular live music. Open all year. Buses 22, 37 and night bus 170 will take you there from Centraal Station.

**Gaasper** at Loosrechtdreef 7 (Tel. 696 7326) costs f6.25 per person and f6.50 for a tent. This site is a bit more geared to families.

Refer to *Cheap Sleeps Europe 2000* for more accommodation options.

## EATING AND NIGHTLIFE

There are cafés galore near Dam Square, round the red-light district and Leidseplein, along with a huge variety of ethnic restaurants. Go for the day's menu for the best value. Recommended restaurants are: **De Keuken Van 1870** at Spuistraat 4; **Egg Cream** at Sint Jacobsstraat 19, open 11am–8pm, and **Haesje Claes** at Spuistraat 275. For Indonesian *rijsttafel*, the restaurants around Damrak are more expensive, so head for Binnen Bantammerstraat, south-east of Centraal station or **Sukasari** on Damstraat. Also worth checking out is the **Great Rijsttafel** at Mandarin Rokin 26. For a bit of toilet humour and some fun, the **Café Chris** at Bloemstraat 42 is your place, as its loo can be flushed only from the bar! **Gary's Muffins** sells great snacks, not surprisingly, muffins and also bagels and stays open to 3 or 4am. There are two outlets, one at Prinsengracht 454, near Leidseplein, the other near Koningsplein on Reguliersdwarsstraat.

Vegetarians have plenty of choices too; try **Bolhoed** at Prinsengracht 60–62, near Anne Frank's House (open 12 noon–10pm) and **Harvest** in Govert Flinkstraat 251 (open 5.30pm–9.30pm Tues. to Sat.) which also caters for special dietary requirements if ordered in advance.

If you're only looking to fill a gap, buy some deep-fried *poffertjes* (mini-doughnuts) from street stalls or pastries from **BLOM** on Nieuwendijk 117–119. There are several good street markets to buy picnic supplies from as well.

There are loads of 'smoking' coffee shops to choose from. **La Tertulia**, on the corner of Prinsengracht and Oude looiersstraat, is popular with backpackers. Some of the most famous include **The Bulldog** at Leidseplein 15 and **Grasshopper** at Oudebrugsteeg 16. For the best dope, go to the **Greenhouse** at Tolstraat 4 (take tram 4).

The lively **Mulligan's** on Amstel 100, near Rembrandtplein, is definitely the pick of Amsterdam's Irish pubs, where you can down a pint or three of Guinness and gorge yourself on Irish stew. Also try **Tara**, Rokin 89 for live music and **Hoppe** at Spui 18.

For the young and hip, **Melkweg** at Lijnbaansgracht 234a (general admission f10–50, plus f4.50 membership on door, closed Mon.) offers live music and disco. In fact, if you're ready to boogie, there are loads of nightclubs in the city. **De Kroeg** at Lijnbaansgracht 16 is worth checking out, whilst **Paradiso** at Weteringschans 6 and **Roxy** at Singel 465 are two of the trendiest clubs and cost f10–50 entry, plus f4.50 membership on door. Also try **Mazzo** at Rozengracht 114 or **Dansen bij Jansen**, a popular student nightclub (student ID required) at Handboogstaat 11 (entrance f5 at weekends, half price during the week).

Most cinemas are located around Leidseplein and Rembrandtsplein. Try **Desmet** at Plantage Middenlaan 4a for art films.

## Outside Amsterdam

**LEIDEN** Half an hour south-west of Amsterdam, Leiden is great for a day trip. Descartes first published his *Discourses* here and its university is still considered the Netherlands' finest. Tourist Information is at Stationsplein 210 (Tel. 0900 222 2333), open weekdays: 9am–5.30pm; Sat.: 10am–4pm.

See the **Old Town;** the **Botanical Museum** (one of Europe's oldest, founded in 1587); and the **Rijksmuseum van Oudheden** (National Antiquities). Both these are on Rapenburg. To have a nose around a windmill, go to the **Museum de Valk** (Falcon), Binnenvestgracht 1, open Tues.–Sat:. 10am–5pm, Sun.: 1pm–5pm. f5 entrance. You can get a great view of the town from the **Burcht**, the 12th-century citadel in the centre. Canal cruises are available in the summer, ask at the Tourist Office.

If you want to stay try **Pension Witte Singel**, Witte Singel 80 (Tel. 071 512 4592), doubles around f90. There is also a popular hostel at Lange Scheistraat 9, **Lits-Jumeaux Youth Hostel** (Tel. 071 512 8457). Loud music and dope, dorm beds f25. The nearest HI hostel is almost an hour away at Langevelderlaan 45 (Tel. 0252 372920). Get there on bus 60. For eating check out **Augustinus** at Rapenburg 24 or **LaBota** on Herensteeg 9. There's a Eurotrain office inside the main train station.

Just north of Leiden, the world-famous **Keukenhof** flower show takes place in the world's biggest garden between mid-March and mid-May. Entrance costs f17.50, or f24 including the bus to take you there. For more information, phone 0252 465555

**WASSENAAR** On the coast 10km from Leiden with a campsite and theme park.

## The Hague (Den Haag) phone code: 070

As the seat of the Netherlands government and home of the Royal family, The Hague has more than its fair share of grand buildings. Some of its finest are the **Binnenhof**, home of the Dutch parliament, and the International Court of Justice housed in the **Peace Palace**. There are also more than 20 excellent museums, some nice parks and a huge annual Jazz festival.

### STATION FACILITIES

There are two stations in The Hague: Hollands Spoor handles trains to Amsterdam and Rotterdam, while Centraal Station deals with those to Utrecht and short inter-city and suburban lines. International trains leave from both stations and each has a full range of facilities. The supermarket at Centraal Station near the Tourist Office is especially handy.

Daily trains to Amsterdam (55 minutes), Rotterdam (30 minutes), Antwerp (1½ hours), Brussels (2½ hours), Paris (six hours) and Cologne (3½ hours).

Tram 1 connects the two stations – or take a train!

### TOURIST INFORMATION

Turn right outside Centraal Station for the Tourist Office at Koningin Julianaplein 30. Open Mon.–Fri.: 8.30am–5.30pm, Sat.: 10am–5pm; July and Aug. also Sun.: 11am–3pm. (Tel. 0900 340 3505; Fax. 346 2412 (for hotel reservations)). There's another office near the beach at Gevers Deynootweg 1134, Scheveningen, which is open Mon.–Sat.: 9am–5.30pm (7pm in high season). Both will sell you a city map and guide for f4.

### ADDRESSES

**POST OFFICE** Kerkplein; open Mon.–Fri.: 8.30am–6.30pm, Thurs.: till 8.30pm, Sat.: 9am–4pm
**AMEX** At Centraal Station (Tel. 370 1210)
**UK EMBASSY** Lange Voorhout 10 (Tel. 427 0427)
**US EMBASSY** Call Amsterdam Consulate (Tel. 310 9209)
**CANADIAN EMBASSY** Sophialaan 7 (Tel. 311 1600)
**AUSTRALIAN EMBASSY** Carnegielaan 4 (Tel. 310 8200)
**MEDICAL HELP** Tel. 346 9669 (night)
**NBBS EUROTRAIN** Schoolstraat 24 (Tel. 346 5819)
**POLICE** Tel. 322 2222 or 112 for emergency
**TOURIST ASSISTANCE SERVICE (TAS)** Zoutmanstraat 44 (Tel. 310 3274), helps tourists who have had accidents or been victims of crime

## SEEING

The **Binnenhof** – the centre of political life in the Netherlands – is a complex of buildings with the **Ridderzaal**, or Knight's Hall, dominating its centre. Open Mon.–Sat.: 10am–4pm, with guided tours at f5–6.

Other attractions include the **Mauritshuis Gallery**, Korle Vijverberg 8, with 16 Rembrandts in its superb collection of Dutch art (open Tues.–Sat.: 10am–5pm, Sun.: 11am–5pm, admission f12.50); the **Gemeente Museum** (Hague Municipal Museum), Stadhouderslaan 41, home to a collection of musical instruments and Mondrian's major works (open Tues.–Sun.: 11am–5pm, admission f10); and the **Gevangenpoort** (Prison Gate) **Museum**, Buitenhof 33, a morbid torture chamber full of medieval instruments (but not the musical ones!) to set your hair on end (open Tues.–Fri.: 10am–5pm, Sat. and Sun.: 1pm–5pm: f6 for guided tour).

Only one of the three royal palaces is open to the public, the **Lange Voorhout Palace Museum**, which displays temporary art exhibitions. There is a two-hour **Royal Tour**, organized by the Tourist office, which passes the two other palaces. The tour leaves from the VVV office in Centraal Station at 1pm between May and Aug. (It costs about f27).

The **Mesdag Panorama**, Zeestraat 65, is a popular and fascinating place to visit, with one of the world's largest cylinder-shaped paintings. Open Mon.–Sat: 10am–5pm, Sun.: 12 noon–5pm; entrance f6.

Just outside the city and built to a tiny 1/25th scale, is the miniature town of **Madurodam**. It has everything from trains to houses and street lamps – and better still, everything works. It is on the expensive side at f19.50. Open 9am–5pm, or until 8pm in April–June, and 10pm in July–Aug. Tram 1, 7 or 9, or bus 22 will take you there.

The town of **Delft**, is just 10 minutes from The Hague. Famous for its pottery, you can see it being made at the **Porceleyne Fles**, Rotterdamseweg 196.

If you fancy a bit of cycling, bicycles can be rented at various venues, though most outlets will want f100–200 deposit. The Garage du Nord at Keijerstraat 27, Scheveningen charges f10 a day, but needs an identity card as deposit.

**FREE (THE) HAGUE:** The Hague is the 'greenest' of Holland's cities, so pack some sarnies and take advantage of this 'picnic city'. Try the **Haagse Bos**, **Westbroekpark** or **Clingendael Park** – the latter also has a Japanese Garden and is open from mid-May–mid-June.

• There are numerous **markets** in the city too: for books and antiques head for Lange Voorhout (Mon. and Thurs.), or for a more general one, Markthof (daily except Sun.).

• Around the end of June, **Parkpop** – the world's largest free pop festival– takes place in Zuiderpark (check with VVV for details).

- The lively **beach** resort nearby at Scheveningen is ideal too, if you want to take a dip or top up your tan. In fact, throughout summer there's plenty happening here and it needn't cost you a thing. Check with the VVV for up-coming firework displays or musical, cultural and sporting events. Around mid-July there's a three-day Scheveningen **music festival** with street parades and musical performances and a great party atmosphere.

## SLEEPING

Beds in The Hague tend to be on the expensive side but there are some reasonable but rather seedy hotels near Hollands Spoor. Try **Aristo** on Stationsweg 164–166. The HI **youth hostel** at Scheepmakerstraat 27 (Tel. 315 7888; Fax. 315 7877) is very good and costs from f33 per night. Failing this, try the **Marion Hostel** at Havenkade 3 (Tel. 350 5050) or the **Scheveningen Hostel** at Gevers Deynootweg 2 (Tel. 354 7003) Alternatively, **Pension Jodi** is at Van Aerssenstraat 194–196 with beds from f40 excluding breakfast. Camping is a great option too, especially **Ockenburgh** at Winjndaelerweg 25 (Tel. 325 2364) where you can pitch near the beach (bus 4 from Centraal Station or bus 26 from Hollands Spoor).

## EATING AND NIGHTLIFE

At night, lively **Scheveningen** is your best bet for cheap eats and bars, or try the streets of Denneweg in The Hague centre. You can get your groceries at the market at Markthof, near Binnenhof, or from the **V&D** supermarket on Grote Markt Straat. When it comes to the usual fastfood outlets like McDonald's and Burger King, you're spoilt for choice, but far healthier and more filling is the inexpensive Italian fare served at **Broodjeszaak Panini** at Gortstraat 16. Vegetarians can try **Ramakiën** at Laan van Meerdervoort 542. **'T Goude Hooft** at Groenmarkt 13 has a traditional Dutch interior and does inexpensive three-course meals.

For those who like a bit of jazz, the Hague plays host to the **North Sea Jazz Festival** in mid-July.

# Rotterdam phone code: 10

Rotterdam, the country's second city after Amsterdam, is where you'll find Europe's largest port. What's more, were it not for a Nazi air raid in 1940, it would still be the capital's architectural rival. Rebuilding after the war has left Rotterdam a bustling, attractive and modern city.

## TOURIST INFORMATION

**MAIN TOURIST OFFICE** VVV, Coolsingel 67, on the corner of Stadhuisplein (Tel. 0900 403 4065). Open Mon.–Sat.: 9.30am–6pm, (until 9pm on Fri.) and also Sun.: noon–5pm from April–Sept.

## SEEING, STAYING, EATING & NIGHTLIFE

The best way to view Rotterdam is, without doubt, from the 180m **Euromast** at Parhaven 20 (Open daily 10am–5/7pm, until 10.30pm Tues.–Sat. in summer; entrance f15). A bit closer to ground (or water even?), you can take a boat tour (f15) round its massive **port**, or for a bit of exercise, stroll along some of its 48 km on foot. The **Boymans Van Beuningen Museum** on Mathenesserlaan (entry f7.50; closed Mon.) is an outstanding modern art museum, while the **Schiel Shielandshuis Museum** at Korte Hoogstraat 31 has an interesting exhibition on the Blitz (admission f7.50; closed Mon.). Also worth a look is the **Maritime Museum** at Leuvehaven (entry f6).

One part of Rotterdam that came through the war virtually unscathed was **Delfshaven**, from where, in 1620, the Pilgrim Fathers set sail for America. In light of its tourist potential, much of the harbour and buildings are being restored.

The city's HI **youth hostel** is at Rochussenstraat 107–9 (Tel. 436 5763; Fax. 436 5569) and charges about f32. Take tram 4 to Saftleuenstraat or Uto. There's also a **Sleep-In** at Mauritsweg 29, near the station (Tel. 414 3256), open mid-June to mid-Aug.; check-in after 4pm. For **camping**, there's a site at Kanaalweg 84 (Tel. 415 3440); take bus 33 or be prepared for a 40 min. walk from the station.

**Bagatelle** is a good hotel near the station (Tel. 467 6348), Provenierssingel 26. Take the Centraal station's rear exit, turn right, and it is about five minutes' walk. Prices range from about f40 for singles to f70 for doubles. Also check out the reasonably priced **Hotel Astoria** at Plienweg 203–205 (Tel. 485 6834).

You can stock up on well-priced food at the large plaza across the square from the main station, which sells groceries and meals. Or there's a huge market (one of the biggest in Holland) on Binnennrotte every Saturday and Tuesday. If you are staying in Rotterdam and want a good night out, try **Ristorante Michelangelo** on the main square.

For entertainment, check out what's on at the **Ahoy**, one of the country's biggest music venues. **Jazzcafé Dizzy** at 's-Gravendijkwal 127 has regular live music, and every Sun. there's live jazz (free) at **Doelencafé**, Schouwburgplein 52.

**EXCURSIONS** Close to Rotterdam, **Kinderdijk** is home to The Netherlands' greatest concentration of working windmills. There are 19 in all, and on Saturday afternoons in July and August you can see them all at work.

A 25-minute train ride from Rotterdam will take you to the small town of **Gouda**. Its famous cheese market is held in the central square on Thursday mornings (10am–12pm) late June–mid-August.

## The Southern, Central and Eastern Netherlands

The southern Netherlands, bordered by Belgium, has some great places worth seeing, including the splendid historic town of **Breda** and the reconstructed medieval town of **Middelburg**, with its miniature town of 'Walcheren' on a 1/20th scale.

**Limburg,** the south-eastern province nestling between Germany and Belgium, is home to historic **Maastricht**, the city of the EU Treaty, nine castles and 193km network of man-made tunnels. If you're coming from Belgium make sure you don't get off the train too early at the first of Maastricht's stations.

**Utrecht** with its medieval city centre and 13th-century cathedral also has the largest shopping centre in the country, Hoogcatharijne. The railway museum in the old station has some steam locomotives, but also check out the **Music Box Museum** and the **Religious History Museum** in Het Catharine convent.

**Arnhem** was badly bombed in 1944 (as seen in *A Bridge Too Far*), but luckily, the 12th-century **Doorwerth Castle** outside the town managed to survive. The main reason people stay here, however, is because of its proximity to the isolated wilderness of **Hoge Veluwe National Park** (open daily 8am–sunset; f7 admission). The **Kroller-Muller Museum**, which boasts 278 works by Van Gogh and some Picassos, is also worth a visit. Open Tues.–Sun.: 10am–5pm; free once you're in the park.

## Haarlem phone code: 023

Haarlem, with its nearby resort of Zandvoort, is one of Holland's most historic and well preserved cities, and just fifteen minutes west of Amsterdam. Its Tourist Office is next to the station at Stationsplein 1 (Tel. 0900 616 1600) and will sell you a map and guide.

### SEEING
The historical heart of the town is Grote Markt, location of the **Renaissance Meat Market**, **Town Hall** and **St Bavo's Cathedral**,

where Dutch artist Frans Hals is buried. You can see some of his work, along with that of other Dutch and Flemish masters, in the **Frans Hals Museum** at Groot Heiligland 62. There's a comprehensive modern art collection here too. Open Mon.–Sat.: 11am–5pm, Sun.: 1–5pm; entrance f8.50.

For even more art, the country's oldest museum, the **Teylers Museum** at 16 Spaarne, has a collection of drawings by Michelangelo and Raphael, open Tues.–Sat.: 10am–5pm, Sun.: noon–5pm.

The **Corrie Ten Boom Museum**, at 19 Barteljorisstraat, is devoted to the life and works of a family who in World War II saved the lives of countless people by hiding them from the Nazis. It is open Mon.–Sat.: 10am–4.30pm.

## SLEEPING AND EATING

The **youth hostel** is ten minutes out of town at Jan Gijzenpad 3 (Tel. 537 3793; Fax. 5371176). Take bus 2 from the station. Open Mar.–Oct.

**De Liede** at Liewegje 17 (Tel. 533 2360) is the nearest campsite. It's open all year round and offers excellent facilities including: a canteen, showers and laundry. Take bus 2 to Zoete Inval, from there it's a short walk. In the summer, there are lots of sites near Zandvoort. If campings's not your thing, the VVV can book you into a private home for around f34, but there's a f10 fee as well.

The fast-food freak will be pleased to know there is a **McDonald's** on Grote Houtstraat 75, whilst the vegetarian is taken care of at the **Eko Eel Café** in Zijlstraat 39, which is open until 9.30pm. For reasonably priced Mexican food try **Alfonso's** at Oude Groenmarkt 8, or the cheap Italian **Piccolo Restaurant** at Rivier Vismarkt 1.

**ZANDVOORT** Miles of sandy dunes and beach welcome you here, as does its coveted Blue Flag, awarded by the European Environmental Organisation for safety and cleanliness. The resort has its own VVV at Schoolplein 1 (Tel. 23 571 7947). For accommodation ask at the Tourist Office.

NOTES:

..................................................................................................................

..................................................................................................................

..................................................................................................................

..................................................................................................................

..................................................................................................................

..................................................................................................................

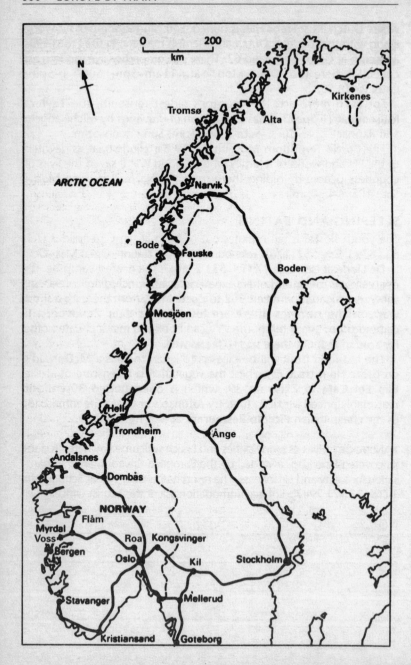

# NORWAY (Norge)

| | |
|---|---|
| Entry requirements | Passport |
| Population | 4.5 million |
| Capital | Oslo (pop.: 0.5 million) |
| Currency | Krone (NOK or kr) |
| | £1 = approx. 12.12.87kr |
| Political system | Constitutional monarchy |
| Religion | Lutheran |
| Language | Norwegian (English widely spoken) |
| Public holidays | New Year's Day, Maundy Thursday, Good Friday, Easter Monday, Labour Day (1 May), Ascension Day, Constitution Day (17 May), Whit Monday, Christmas Day and Boxing Day |
| International dialling codes | To Norway: int'l code 47 |
| | From Norway: 095 + country code |
| Emergency telephone numbers | Police 112; ambulance 113; fire service 110 |

Norway is a stunning and dramatic country packed full of forests, lakes, rivers and mountains. But its most famous features are the fjords – spectacular narrow sea inlets – which run along the west coast and extend up to the most northern reaches of the continent: the best-known is Sognefjord which runs inland for 160km. With roughly a quarter of the country also shivering inside the Arctic Circle, it's no surprise that it has Europe's lowest population density too.

Historically, it's the notorious Vikings that hog the limelight. Between the 8th and 11th centuries these fierce sea warriors sailed west wreaking havoc and settling across many parts of Europe: actions which brought increased standards of living and economic benefits to the whole of Norway. This period also saw Norway unified for the first time under the supreme leader, Harald Fairhair.

With the onset of the plague in 1349, more than half of the population was wiped out. This was followed by 400 years of Danish rule, after which it was the Swedes' turn to take control. In 1905 they both peacefully parted company, which left Norway standing on its own two feet again. Around this time Grieg, Ibsen and Munch were also all busy becoming three of the country's most celebrated figures.

These days, Norway still revels in a high standard of living thanks largely to the discovery of North Sea oil and gas in 1969. Environmentally, though, debates rage on the threat of high levels of acid rain on the countryside (a lot of it from the UK), while the unpopular traditions of whaling and sealing continue to make the headlines from time to time.

Norway provides a feast of magnificent landscapes to savour and is the perfect choice for lovers of the great outdoors.

## NORWEGIAN STATE RAILWAYS
### (NORGES STATSBANER, NSB)

The Norwegians have one of the cleanest and most efficient railway systems in Europe and even though a majority of the trains are pretty slow, they pass through some of the most spectacular scenery. The fastest and most comfortable trains are the *Ekspresstog* (Et, expresses). They run between all the major cities and stop only at main stations, while the *Regionaltog* (Rt, IC) run to and from Oslo and the towns in the surrounding area, and the local trains (Lt) stop at every station. High-speed trains (ICE) run to Göteborg and Skien – supplements are payable. A supplement is also payable on the Myrdal to Flåm line between 1 May and 30 Sept.

**PASSES AVAILABLE** Eurail and Inter-Rail passes are both valid. Norway is in Inter-Rail Zone B, along with Sweden and Finland. For £159 you can tour a single zone for 22 days (over 26s pay £229). Further details of the eight Inter-Rail zones, are available in the Inter-Rail section in Part One of this guide.

For information on the Euro Domino, see pp. 23–24.

The Norway Rail Pass is similar to the Euro Domino Pass but it can only be bought outside Europe and in Norway. The pass is valid for unlimited rail travel in Norway (except for on the airport trains) on any three, four or five days within one month. Reservation fees and supplements still need to be paid. The pass costs: for three days 1100kr; for four days 1364kr and for five days 1540kr. The prices quoted are for 2nd class travel. 1st class prices are approx. 33% more

The ScanRail pass is valid for travel by train (and a few ferries) in Norway, Denmark, Sweden and Finland. The different types of ticket are as follows:

Consecutive 21 days

| Class | 1st | 2nd |
|---|---|---|
| Adult | £282 | £212 |
| Youth (12–25 years) | £212 | £160 |

ScanRail Flexi tickets are available at the following prices:

| | 5 days within 15 days | 10 days within 1 month |
|---|---|---|
| Class | 1st/2nd | 1st/2nd |
| Adult | £185/£139 | £249/£187 |
| Youth (12–25 years) | £139/£105 | £187/£141 |

**INTER-RAIL BONUSES** See Appendix 1

**EURAIL BONUSES**

| | |
|---|---|
| Hirtshals–Kristiansand | 30% |
| Oslo–Copenhagen | 20% |
| Larvik–Frederikshavn/Skagen (Denmark) | 30% |
| Moss–Hirtshals/Frederikshavn (Denmark) | 30% |

**SCANRAIL AND SCANRAIL FLEXI PRINCIPAL BONUSES**

| | |
|---|---|
| Oslo–Frederikshavn (Stena) | 50% |
| Kristiansand–Hirtshals (Color Line) | 50% |
| Oslo–Copenhagen (DFDS) | 50% |
| Larvik–Frederikshavn (Peter Wessel) | 50% |
| Bodø–Fauske–Narvik–Tromsø–Alta–Kirkenes (A/S TIRB-Rutene, FFR, Saltens Bilruter A/S) | 50% |
| Narvik–Harstad–Sortland (Ofotens Bilruter) | 50% |
| Narvik–Sortland–Solvaer (Nordtrafikk A/S) | 50% |
| Narvik–Harstad–Andenes–Solvaer–Leknes (Lofoten Trafikklag A/S) | 50% |
| Fauske–Harstad (Harstad og Oppland Bilruter A/S) | 50% |
| Mosjøen–Sandnessjøen (Helgeland Trafikkselskab A/S) | 50% |
| Grong–Brønnøysund (A/S Torghatten Trafikkelskab) | 50% |
| Andalsnes–Kristiansund (A/S Alesund Bilruter) | 50% |
| Andalsnes–Molde (Veøy Billag A/S) | 50% |
| Oppdal–Kristiansund (Mørelinjen A/S) | 50% |
| Gjerstad–Risør–Tvedestrand (Risør og Tvedestrand Bilruter A/S) | 50% |
| Neslandsvatn–Kragerø (Drangedal Bilruter A/S) | 50% |
| Sortland–Andenes (Andøy Trafikklag A/S, Nordtrafikk A/S) | 50% |
| Ulsvåg–Skutig (Stoklands Bilruter) | 50% |
| Stavanger–Bergen (Flaggruten) | 50% |
| Boat runs in the Hardangerfjord (Snoggbatane) | 25% |

Free travel on NSB Trondheim–Storlien v.v. bus service and many
  others (or 50% discount) but note that supplements are still payable
on certain fast trains

**Accommodation discounts at:**
The Best Western chain of 160 hotels in Scandinavia

**Free or reduced entry to the Railway Museums in:**

| | |
|---|---|
| Gävle (Sweden) | Free |
| Hamar (Norway) | Free |
| Hyvinkaa (Finland) | Free |
| Odense (Denmark) | 50% |

Plus 20% off the price of an Oslo Card

**EURO DOMINO BONUS** 50% off the Scandinavian Seaways route
between Oslo and Copenhagen, the ferry ticket must be bought

directly from the ferry company.

## TRAIN INFORMATION

No problems here as everyone speaks good English. NSB also publish an excellent free series of leaflets giving maps and descriptions of their main tourist routes.

**RESERVATIONS** Domestic reservations (20kr) are compulsory on all major routes, so check first. They should be made in advance. You may get a discount for more than one domestic reservation at a time. If you're travelling to Copenhagen, you're advised to reserve 36 hours in advance and 48 hours at weekends. International seat reservations cost 20kr. Reserved seats are not always marked, so don't be surprised if you get moved on, just when you thought it was safe to get comfortable. On the other hand, don't be too surprised to find someone already sitting in a seat you have reserved in advance. Be polite, and remember: if you reserved the seat, you have the right to it.

**NIGHT TRAVEL** Second-class sleepers with three berths costs about 100kr; with two berths 265kr. Prices are per person. Standards are high – video and snacks are available – and 100kr buys you an excellent hearty breakfast.

**EATING ON TRAINS** Expresses between Oslo and Bergen have dining cars, and if you have a lot of money to blow, the food is excellent, as is the scenery. All other express trains have buffets which serve hot meals as well as snacks, while *Regionaltogs* have a trolley service.

**SCENIC TIPS** There are more scenic routes in Norway than anywhere else in Scandinavia, and possibly even Europe. The jewel of them all is the Bergen–Oslo run. Two other excellent ones are Flåm–Sognefjord and Dombås–Åndalsnes. Be sure to get hold of the free NSB leaflets, which give good descriptions of the various lines.

## TOURIST INFORMATION

There's a Tourist Office (*turistinformason*) at every major town and in most villages in Norway. They help to find accommodation if necessary and have a good supply of local information leaflets. Extended hours always operate from the beginning of June to end of Aug. Norway's one of the most health-conscious of all European countries, and at weekends you'll find, depending on the season, the ski slopes, forest tracks and waterways well used by the 'great outdoors' fanatics. For detailed information on hiking and mountaineering, contact DNT, PO Box 7, Sentrum, N-0101, Oslo (Tel. 2282 2800).

**ISIC BONUSES** 50% discounts on museums, theatres and some coastal steamers. Also 30% reductions on some bus services and a discount at Oslo Youth Hostel. For further information, contact KILROY Travels, Nedre Slottsgate 23, 0157 Oslo (2310 2310).

**MONEY MATTERS** 1 Norwegian krone (NOK or kr) = 100 øre.
Banking hours are Mon.–Fri.: 8.15am–3pm (3.30pm in winter). Some stay open till 5pm on Thurs.

**POST OFFICES AND SHOPS** Opening hours are generally Mon.–Fri.: 8am–4/5pm and Sat. 9am–1pm. Shops open until 6 or 8pm on Thurs.

**MUSEUMS** Vary throughout Norway, but the general pattern is 10am–6pm (May to Sept.) or until 4pm in winter.

## EATING AND NIGHTLIFE

Norway is one country you're bound to lose weight in; it's not that the food is bad, or that you'll be press-ganged into spending all day out hiking in the fjords – it's just that food is so expensive here that you'll rarely be able to afford the luxury of a full stomach. This is the problem in Norway; it's quite easy to spend 225kr a day just feeding yourself with average-quality meals. (That said, it is now much on a par with places like Venice or Florence, and at least the quality is excellent here.) Avoid expensive meat dishes and turn instead to fish, and try to copy the locals: eat a full breakfast of *smørbrødbord* (a huge open sandwich, heaped with a variety of garnishes), have a snack at lunch (bought from a market/shop) and aim for a *koldtbord* (cold table) meal in the evening, where you can eat as much as you like, or a fixed-price menu. If you're planning on self-catering a lot in Norway (and you should), bring some basic supplies with you from home. Vegetarians are in for a hard time, but for vegans the problem is even greater: when Norwegians are not consuming meat and fish, they are attacking the fantastic selection of dairy products on offer.

The Norwegians have a reputation for being quite a serious lot, and to an extent that's fair comment – though catch them after a few drinks at night and you'd never believe it. They're very culture-conscious, and much effort is made to preserve the folk songs and dances of their forebears – the displays of these you may encounter are not put on purely as commercial stunts for the tourists.

## TIPPING

Leave up to 10% if you feel the service has been good, but not if it has already been included in the bill.

## SLEEPING

Norwegian law allows you to camp for free anywhere you want for two nights, provided you keep 150m from all buildings and fences, and do not litter or vandalize the area. If you are camping while you are in this country, remember to bring your own supply of camping gas since it is not freely available in Norway. There are hundreds of official sites, most of which are listed by the Norges Automobil-Forbund (NAF) (Tel. 2234 1400), whose Oslo office is at Storgaten.

Check out Den Norske Turistforening (DNT, the Norwegian Mountain Touring Association) for unusual accommodation. They sell maps and keep many attractive mountain huts (*hytter*) all over the country. Expect to pay about 150kr per night, with a 50kr surcharge to non-members. Huts are open from the end of June to the beginning of September. To find out more, visit the office at Roald Amundsengate 28 in Oslo or contact DNT at PO Box 7, Sentrum, N-0101, Oslo (Tel. 2282 2800).

There are just under 100 youth hostels in the country and standards vary, as do prices (80–180kr). Only a few are open all of the year round. It is strongly advised that you ring ahead to reserve a hostel bed, as demand is high. Norway's hostelling organization is Norske Vandrerhjem. For more information, contact the head office at Dronningens gate 26, 0154 Oslo (Tel. 2313 9300; Fax. 2313 9350).

Alternatively, try booking a private room through the Tourist Office; it is reasonable to pay I50–200kr for a single and 250–350kr for a double room.

Those looking for some real luxury and who have a little more money can buy a Scan Hotel Pass for around 90kr (available at hotels). This entitles you to a 15–50% discount off room rates (including a very good breakfast) usually in 3/4-star hotels. Some nationwide hotel chains, such as Rainbow and Rica, offer good summer and weekend deals. Even with the reduction or deal, staying in a hotel will be expensive, but it may be that you have more funds available than the average traveller and want to see Scandinavia in some style!

# Southern Norway

If you've arrived in Norway at Stavanger, it'll take you about eight hours to get to Oslo by train or around seven to Bergen by ferry.

## Stavanger

Stavanger, the fourth largest city in Norway, is the hub of North Sea oil exploration and home to some interesting sights. The information office (Tel. 5185 9200) is at Roskildetorget 1 (open Mon.–Fri.: 9am–5pm, Sat. 9am–2pm).

The cobbled streets of the **Gamle Stavanger** (Old Stavanger) are lined with gas lamps and the whole area is full of 18th-century wooden houses said to be the best preserved in Europe. The medieval cathedral, **Stavanger Domkirke**, is located in the colourful **Market Place**, which will give you a feel for what Norway was once like. At the inner harbour, see the **Fish Market** and pick up a free *Stavanger Guide* from the nearby information kiosk (open in summer only). They also sell the *Stavanger Card* which is good for discounts on museums and city buses. Both the **Maritime** and **Canning Museums** (open daily, 11am–3pm) are worth a look if you're into boats or fishing.

For a cheap tour of Stavanger, take yellow bus no. 10 on its circular route round the city. Make sure to get off at Gosen and climb the **Ullandhaug Tower** for a good view of the city (free).

**Pulpit Rock** is a 600m cliff rising above the Lyse Fjord. Skip the sightseeing boats and take the cheaper local ferry to Lysebotn. During the summer you can hike up the backside of the cliff in about two hours. Take the ferry to Tau, where a connecting bus will drop you at the trail. If you want to spend the night here, the **Mosvangen youth hostel** (Tel. 5187 2900; Fax. 5187 0630) and **Mosvangen Camping** (open late May to early Sept.) are both about three km south of town, you can catch bus 93 or 130. The cheapest place in town is the **YMCA hostel** (Tel. 5153 2888), open July and the first week of August. There's also a summer hostel, Preikestolen, (Tel. 9453 1111) within walking distance of Pulpit Rock.

For eating, try the **youth hostel**, which offers three meals a day, the **Thai restaurant** on Nedre Strandgate near the harbour, which does cheap lunches, or fill up on a pizza buffet at the **Dickens pub** on the harbour.

## Kristiansand

Surrounded by beautiful countryside, Kristiansand is located between Oslo and Stavanger and near some great beaches. There are ferries to Hirtshals in Denmark – this is the only glimpse of Norway many ferry passengers will get.

**Christiansholm Fortress** dates back to the 17th century and offers a great view of the sea. On your way back to the train station, take in the **Town Square** and **Cathedral**. About a 20-minute walk north of the station is the massive **Ravnedalen Park** and there is a **Zoo** to the north-east of town.

The Tourist Office is at Dronningensgate 2 (Tel. 3812 1314). The **youth hostel** (Tel. 3802 8310; Fax. 3802 7505) is at Skansen 8, about a 10 min. walk from the fortress (open all year). Dorm beds for around 160kr, singles and doubles also available. There's a campsite, **Roligheden Camping**, about three km east of town near the beach (Tel. 3809 6722).

# Oslo

Oslo, the oldest of the Scandinavian capitals, lies at the head of a 97 km fjord on Norway's south-eastern coast. The acres of forests, hills and unspoilt countryside outside the city limits are used at every opportunity by the Oslo folk, to pursue their many outdoor activities. The town itself has no distinctive style and you have to look below the surface for its real attractions: the museums and parks.

## STATION FACILITIES

Oslo (Central) offers a full range of station facilities. Luggage may be left free at the Inter-Rail Centre, otherwise you can pay to use the 24-hour storage lockers. The centre is open 7am–10pm mid-June until Sept. It also offers showers, telephones and information, including maps. All Eurorailers welcome.

## TOURIST INFORMATION

There's a good Tourist Office in Central Station, but the main office is at Vestbaneplassen 1 (Tel. 2283 0050; open daily in summer 9am–7pm; weekdays in winter 9am–4pm), where you can also pick up info. on the rest of the country. Both are extremely helpful and provide various free brochures including the *Oslo Guide*, *Oslo This Week* and ferry and bus timetables. **Use It**, the youth information office, is at Møllergata 3 (Tel. 2241 5132). Very helpful staff who will book cheap accommodation for you and give general info., including what's on in town.

## ADDRESSES

**POST OFFICE** Dronningensgate 15; open Mon.–Fri.: 8am–6pm, Sat.:10am–3pm

**AMEX** c/o Winge Travel, Karl Johansgate 33 (Tel. 2298 3735), open Mon.–Fri.: 9am–5pm, Sat.: 10am–3pm. There's another office at Fridtjof Nansens plass 6

**STUDENT TRAVEL AND NORWEGIAN YOUTH HOSTEL ASSOCIATION** Norske Vandrerhjem, Dronningensgate 26 (Tel. 2313 9300), open Mon.–Fri.: 8.15am–3.15pm

**DEN NORSKE TURISTFORENING (NORWEGIAN MOUNTAIN TOURING ASSOCIATION)** Stortingsgaten 28 (Tel. 2282 2800). If you've come to Norway to climb or camp, call in for leaflets on mountain huts, etc. Open weekdays: 10am–4pm, Thurs. till 6pm

**UK EMBASSY** Thomas Heftyesgate 8 (Tel. 2255 2400)

**US EMBASSY** Drammensveien 18 (Tel. 2244 8550)

**CANADIAN EMBASSY** Wergelandveien 7 (Tel. 2246 6955)

**AUSTRALIAN CONSULATE** Jerbanetorget 2 (Tel. 2241 4433) or contact UK embassy

**24-HOUR CHEMIST** Jernbanetorgets Apotek, opposite Central station

## GETTING ABOUT

City transport includes buses, trams, undergrounds, ferries and local trains (free on Inter-Rail). Pick up the transit map at the station or Tourist Information. The Oslo Card (150kr for one day, 220kr for two and 250kr for three) is good value and gives free transport and entry to most of the sights; a student card gets reductions on most things too.

## SEEING

The Norwegian artist **Edvard Munch** has his **museum** in the east of the city at Tøyengata 53. It's a particularly fine gallery, housing thousands of his Expressionist works. Open daily 10am–6pm in season, 50kr.

From Rådhus Gate down near the harbour, you can enter **Akershus Castle**, built by King Haakon V around 1300, then rebuilt in Renaissance style by Christian IV. It's open Mon.–Sat.: 10am–4pm and Sun.: 12.30pm–4pm, 20kr (May–Sept.); and in the grounds of the castle is the **Norwegian Resistance Museum** describing the Nazi occupation of Norway. The **Vigeland Museum**, Noblesgate 32, shows the work and the background of the Norwegian artist Gustav Vigeland. Take bus 20, or tram 12, 15 to get there. Entrance is 30kr.

The ferry from the Rådhus over to the peninsula of **Bygdøy** takes you to five very interesting places:

1. The incredible **Norsk Folkemuseum**, with 150 wooden buildings filled with material artefacts recreating Norway's past. These include Ibsen's study, houses from Lapland and museums of domestic furniture, clothes and implements. On Sun. there's often folk music and dancing.
2. The **Viking Ship House**: three preserved Viking longboats from AD 800–900.
3. **Kon-Tiki Museum**, showing the balsa-wood rafts used by the explorer Thor Heyerdahl on his voyages.
4. The **Norwegian Maritime Museum**.
5. The **Fràm Museum**: the ship used in the polar expeditions of the 19th and early 20th centuries.

**FREE OSLO:**
- The **Vigeland Sculpture Park** is one of Norway's finest and 1,750 sculptures dotted round it have been termed everything from 'obscene' to 'serene'. Take bus 20, or tram 12, 15 to get there.
- The **Changing of the Guard** takes place at the **Royal Palace**, Drammensveien 1, every day at 1.30pm. The palace is closed to the public but the **Palace Park**, with its various statues, can be seen for free.
- You can also visit the **Rådhus** (town hall) down by the harbour. This *avant-garde* 1950s structure was decorated by contemporary Norwegian artists.
  There's also a **flea market** during the summer on Vestkanttorget.
  Try any of the following as well:
- **National Gallery**, Universitetsgaten 13. Norway's principal art collection.
- **Museet for Samtidskunst** (Contemporary Art Museum), Bankplassen 4.
- **Zoological Museum**, Sars' gate 1.
- **Tollmuseum** (Customs Museum), Tollbugaten 1A.
- **Stortinget** (Parliament Building), Karl Johans gate 22.
- **Museum of Paleontology**, Sars' gate 1
- **Norwegian Museum of Architecture**, Kongens gate 4.
- **Botanical Gardens and Museum**, Sars' gate 1.
- **Oslo Cathedral**, the stained glass windows are by Vigeland.

## SLEEPING

Oslo's not easy on Eurorailers. Forget hotels completely and concentrate on the few hostels and campsites, or settle for private accommodation. You can get a single room in a private house for 150–200kr, or a double for 250–350kr, and you must stay at least two nights. The accommodation service at either of the Tourist Offices can provide lists of accommodation; there is a 20kr booking fee per person. Use It (see Information) also books rooms, there's no minimum stay and no booking fee.

**HOSTELS** The three youth hostels in Oslo are very good, clean, efficient, and with plenty of facilities, but they could hardly be called central. **Haraldsheim** is at Haraldsheimveien 4 (Tel. 2222 2965; Fax. 2222 1025) with dorm beds from 155kr, including breakfast. Reservations strongly recommended. It's open all year and is at the bottom of the hill from Sinsen tram terminus (tram 10 or 11). The **Holtekilen hostel** is a school outside of summer, and lies 10km west of the centre at Michelets vei 55 (Tel. 6751 8040; Fax. 6759 1230). Converted classrooms provide 10-bed dorms for 160kr including breakfast, non-members 25kr extra. Double rooms are available for a bit extra if the thought of a school classroom brings you out in a cold sweat. Open from mid–May to mid–August. Take bus 161 to Kveldsroveien or a local train to Stabekk station and then follow the footbridge. The third hostel is also open in summer only, June–mid-Aug. The **LBM – Ekeberg Hostel** at Kongeveien 82 is about 8km out of town. Take tram 18 or 19 to Holtet. (Tel. 2274 1890; Fax. 2274 7505)

The cheapest place in town is the YMCA hostel **KFUM Sleep In** at Møllergata 1 (Tel. 2220 8397). For around 100kr a night, from July to mid August, it provides sleeping accommodation and kitchen facilities. Reception is open 8am–11am and 5pm–12 midnight, though it is advisable to book in advance. There is also a church-run hostel, the **Oslo Vineyard**, at Lillogata 5 (Tel. 2215 2099; Fax. 2215 0499). Similar to the YMCA. Take tram 12 or 17 to Grefsenveien.

**CAMPING** The campsites are **Bogstad Camping** at Ankerveien 117 (Tel. 2251 0800) (bus 32) and the **Ekeberg** site at Ekebergveien 65 (Tel. 2219 8568) which is more central but only open June to late Aug. (bus 24 from Central station). Showers are hot and free, but shared with the adjacent football pitches.

Campsites in Oslo cost around 70kr per tent and 45kr per person. You can camp for free in any of the wooded areas north of the city provided you stay away from public areas.

## EATING AND NIGHTLIFE

Here more than anywhere else in Europe, you'll find prices sky-high. Don't attempt restaurants or stopping off for a coffee and cake. Eat like the Norwegians: a hearty breakfast and big dinner and expect to average about 120kr for a full meal. There are fast-food chains – **Wimpy** and **Kaffistovas** – which can help eke out the finances, and **Kveldsmat** on Universitetsgata, off Karl Johansgate, is cheap. Vegetarians should venture to **Vegeta Vertshus** at Munkedamsveien 3b, which has a self-service buffet. Small main meals cost about 75kr but go for the slightly more expensive ones which include dessert, a drink and coffee.

For entertainment listings, check out *Natt & Dag*, available free from cafés, bars and shops.

**EXCURSIONS** Skiers should find the world's oldest **Ski Museum** interesting. It's located inside the take-off point of the huge Holmenkollen ski jump. Exhibits here trace the history of the sport and produce evidence that it dates as far back as about 500 BC. Take the Holmenkollen railway from its underground station and walk about 10 minutes from the station.

**Ekeberg Park** gives a great view over Oslo from its hills, where Stone Age carvings from 1000 BC have been found.

# Central Norway: The Sognefjord

The train journey from Oslo to Bergen is an absolute must. The scenery is incredible and during the course of this six-hour journey, you'll pass through fjords, glaciers, tundra, mountains, lakes, plateaux and gorges. Should you choose to break this journey and savour its delights slowly, stop off at **Geilo**, a ski centre, which is half way between Oslo and Bergen. In the summer, there are some lovely hiking routes in the area. There's a hostel near the station (Tel. 3209 0300; Fax. 3209 1896). You could also get out further down the tracks at **Myrdal** and take the other line for the 19 km and 900m journey down to the pretty village of **Flåm**, on the Aurlandsfjord. Please note that a charge of around 50kr is now payable on board the train by all travellers with any form of rail pass.

Should you decide to stay, **Flåm Hostel**, across the river from the station, is reasonable, and there's **camping** next door (Tel. 5763 2121) (though if you don't camp independently here, you never will). The campsite has good facilities, but showers are extra. Expect to pay around 50kr per tent. The Tourist Office is right next to the train station (Tel. 5763 2106) and is open from June to mid-August 8.30am–8.30pm.

From Flåm you can tackle the fjords. A popular trip (and it won't take you out of your way from Bergen) is to take the ferry from Flåm to **Gudvangen**. This two-hour tour takes you past the spectacular scenery of the **Nærøyfjord** and calls at some isolated settlements *en route* whose sole means of communication is the ferry. From Gudvangen take the bus to Voss, where you're back on the Bergen line again.

Another trip worth taking is from Flåm to **Voss**, which is 70 minutes east of Bergen on the Oslo rail line. It costs around 100kr with Inter-Rail and includes bus and ferry connections. There is a commentary in English on both the train section (from Flåm to Myrdal) and the ferry. The bus ride is particularly spectacular as you cross the roof of Norway via the steep road and many hairpin bends. If you stop off in Voss there is a very good **folk museum** including a restored farm which dates back to the 17th century. The Tourist Office can be found in Tinghose (Tel. 5651 0051), about five minutes from the station. For the **youth hostel**, turn right at the station and walk along the lakeside (Tel. 5651 2017; Fax. 5651 0837).

# Bergen city

Bergen was the first capital of Norway throughout the 13th century. These days it is Norway's second largest city and is considered to be the most attractive city in the country with its colourful harbour, red-roofed houses and spruce trees nestling under imposing Mount Fløyen. This was the northernmost city in the Hanseatic League and the **Hanseatic Museum** – a reconstruction of a 16th-century merchant's house – makes an interesting visit. This is in the quarter called **Bryggen**, and in the old timber houses today weavers and craftsmen carry on their trade. Take a guided tour when visiting **Rosenkrantz Tower** and **King Haakon's Hall**; it makes the visit all the more interesting. Also take the funicular up Mount Fløyen and see the view: a return ticket costs 40kr and the cable car operates every half hour from the early morning to 11pm, or midnight in summer. There's good hiking to be had at the top and the trails are well marked. You can walk back down to the city in about 45 mins. If you're feeling more energetic, you could follow the trail to the top of Mt Ulriken (a good three hour walk) and take the cable car down from there and a bus back to Bergen.

On the edge of **Lille Lungengardsvatnet Park** are the **Bergen Art Museum**, with its collection of 18th and 19th century Norwegian art, and the **Rasmus Meyer's Collections**, an art gallery with many works by native artist Edvard Munch. Both are open daily to 5 or 6pm (combined admission fee of 35kr for adults). The **Gamle Bergen** (old town) with its traditional timbered buildings makes a pleasant walk. The Romanesque church of St Mary's is considered Norway's most beautiful church. Tourist Information has details on the May–June **International Festival** held here and also about trips to the fjords and the stunning 'Norway in a Nutshell' round-trip for around 490kr.

Consider investing in a **Bergen Card** which gives free bus travel, free parking, free funicular rides and either reduced price or free entry to most museums. The 24-hour pass costs 130kr and the 48-hour pass 200kr. Buy them at the Tourist Office or from local hotels.

## TOURIST INFORMATION AND ADDRESSES

Tourist Information is at Vågsallmenningen 1 (by the old town) (Tel. 5532 1480), open 8.30am–9pm in the summer (shuts at 4pm in winter). They change money, book you into private houses and supply maps and the *Bergen Guide*. For information on hiking or mountain hut rental, contact the DNT office at Tverrgaten 4 (Tel. 5532 2230).

**POST OFFICE** Smästrandgate; open 8am–6pm, Sat. 9am–3pm.

**24-HOUR CHEMIST** Casualty at Vestre Strømkai 19 (Tel. 5532 1120).

(A chemist at the bus station stays open until midnight.)
**STUDENT TRAVEL** Universreiser a/s Parkveien 1 (Tel. 5554 5000). 25% reductions on fare to Newcastle.

**BUSES** A quick journey, which combines historical interest with beautiful countryside, is to **Troldhaugen**, Nordas Lake, the home and burial place of composer Edvard Grieg. You can join a tour and visit his home and the museum dedicated to him and his work. Get there by taking any bus to the Hopsbroen stop; they depart about every 15 minutes. During the festival period (June to Oct.), recitals take place in the modern concert hall on Wednesday and weekend evenings. Tickets (which include transport) can be obtained from the Tourist Office.

## SLEEPING, EATING AND NIGHTLIFE

If you are dumping rucksacks, note that left luggage may be cheaper than the lockers. For accommodation, the Tourist Office charges 20kr commission per person. Rooms in private homes cost from 180kr for a single, 290kr for a double.

The youth hostel **Montana** is nearly always full (Bergen is very touristy), so call first. It's in a good position, halfway up Mount Ulriken. It costs around 140kr, including breakfast. It's on bus route 4 at Johan Blyttsveien 30 (Tel. 5520 8070; Fax. 5520 8075). Apply directly or at the Tourist Office.

There's a **YMCA Interpoint hostel** (Tel. 5531 7252; Fax. 5531 3577) at Nedre Korskirkealm 4, open from mid-June to early September, costing 100kr, 10 minutes' walk from the station.

Bergen's main camping site, **Bergenshallens Camping** (Tel. 5527 0180), is a 10-minute journey from the city centre at 24 Vilh, Bjerknesvei; take bus 90. It is only open in the summer and is very busy, so if you want the fresh outdoors, check with the Tourist Office first to find out if room is available.

Another campsite to try is **Bergen Camping Park** at Haukås i Åsane on road E39 (Tel. 5524 8808). You can either bring a tent or use one of the camping huts.

The **Polar Bear Bar** in Ole Bulls Plass 9–11, just around the corner from the taxi central, offers the cheapest menu outside the fast-food chains. Vegetarians are catered for at **Den Gode Klode**, at Fosswinklegate 18. Open 11.30am–7pm. At night there is music until the small hours. **Café Opera**, at Engen 24, is a little more expensive for food, but its atmosphere is more conducive, with live bands and art exhibitions making up the surroundings. Foreign newspapers and board games are available on request from the counter. Open 11am–1am, Fri. and Sat. until 3am.

On the whole, though, the food and nightlife news is not too good. All you'll be able to afford are picnics and some of the fairly boring café-type places. Try **Peppe's Pizza** in Bryggen's, Finne-gården 2a and **Fellini**, on Tverrgate, for Italian dishes. The restaurant in the **Fantoft Sommerhotel** is decent and offers a 20% student discount (bus 14 or 15) and **Hulen** is a club run by the town's university students in an old air-raid shelter beneath Nygaardsparken. Location is at 47 Olav Ryesvei, and opening times are Wed./Thurs.: 8pm–1am, Fri./Sat.: 9pm–3am. Gays should go to **Café Fincken**, Nygårdsgaten 2a.

If all this travelling is making you want to crash out at the movies, there is no problem with language, as all films are shown in their original language with Norwegian subtitles.

# Trondheim

Founded in 997 by the Viking king, and now saint, Olav Tryggvason, Trondheim is the historical capital of Norway. Many of the buildings in the small centre date from the 18th century but this town is not stuck in a time warp. It has developed to become an important centre for technology, research and business enterprises as well as boasting the second largest university in the country. Pick up a map and the free *Trondheim Guide* at the station or the Tourist Office.

## TOURIST INFORMATION AND ADDRESSES
The Tourist Office at Munkgata 18 is bang in the centre of town on the corner of the main square, open 8.30am–late in the summer (Tel. 7392 9400). They also rent out bikes if you fancy exerting yourself a bit.

From late June to August there's an **Inter-Rail Centre** at Elgesetergate 1 (Tel. 7389 9538) which offers basic bed and breakfast accommodation (for about 100kr), cooking facilities, seat reservations, and a frequent day and night service to Bodø, Oslo, and Stockholm.

**POST OFFICE** Dronningens gate 10; open Mon.–Fri.: 8am–5pm, Sat. 9am–1pm
**CHEMIST** St Olav Vaklapotek, Kjøpmanrlsgate 65 (Tel. 7352 3122); open daily 8.30am–12 midnight (from 10am on Sun.)

## SEEING
The sights of the city are the medieval **Nidaros Cathedral** (the largest medieval building in Scandinavia), erected over the grave of St Olav and host to the Norwegian Crown Jewels, now on public display (in summer, see them weekdays 9.30am–12.30pm; Sun.: 1–4pm. Rest of

year, open Fri. noon–2pm) (in summer, you can also climb the cathedral tower (5kr)), the 12th-century **Archbishops' Palace** and the interesting **Ringve Museum of Music History**, the **Kristiansten Fortress** and the old town bridge, from where the view of the wharf row is excellent.

The **Tyholt Tower** is also worth visiting. From this rotating 80m tower you can view all Trondheim and the Trondheimsfjord.

## SLEEPING, EATING AND NIGHTLIFE

The **youth hostel** is at Weidemannsvei 41 (Tel. 7353 0490; Fax. 7353 5288). If you want to camp, the nearest campsite is 10 km out at **Sandmoen Camping** (Tel.7388 6135). A No. 44 bus will take you there from the bus station. With a Eurail ticket you can travel for free on the NSB buses in the direction of Stjordal or Storlien. This is excellent if you want to stay at the **Vikhammer Camping**, 15 km north of Trondheim (Tel. 7397 6164) or **Storsand Camping**, 17 km north of Trondheim (Tel. 7397 6360).

The majority of restaurants in Trondheim are situated around the area of Kjopmannsgate, and fast-food venues gather around Olav Tryggvasons gate. **Pizzakjelleren** at Fjordgata 7 challenges the famished traveller to eat as much as possible for around 65kr, and is open until 4am. For the more health conscious, there's a small health-food shop, **Hardangerfrukt**, on the same street at no. 62.

# Bodø

It's 11½ hours from Trondheim to Bodø, but the scenery and the comfortable trains make it feel a lot less. The bus ride from Bodø to Narvik joins up the northern part of the Norwegian railway system and is a fabulous experience. 50% discount on fare with Inter-Rail and Nordturist card. From 2 June to 10 July, the sun never sets here. If you hit a particularly good spell of weather, walk up **Mount Ronvik**, taking your camera with you. This is the coastal area that you should be in if you want to see the Northern Lights (Aurora Borealis) between November and February, although this does depend upon meteorological conditions.

The 1956 **Cathedral** is about the only noteworthy building in the town, but you don't come here for the towns. Head instead for **Salstraumen**, where every six hours millions of gallons of water squeeze through a tiny passage between two fjords, making a spectacular sight. Buses sometimes run to coincide with the tides – ask for the timetable at Tourist Information. There is a reduction with Inter-Rail.

**Mo-I-Rana**, 3½ hours before Bodø, is located on a magnificent fjord. The **youth hostel** (Tel. 7515 0963; Fax. 7515 1530) is open May–Sept.

## SLEEPING

Bodø's Tourist Office is at Sjøgata 21, five mins. walk from the bus station, open Mon.–Fri.: 9am–9pm and on the weekend at 10am–8pm in season (Tel. 7552 6000). They can book private accommodation for you and rent bikes.

There is a very basic **youth hostel** above the station on the third floor which costs about 150kr a night for a dorm bed, doubles also available (Tel./Fax. 7552 1122). For camping, take bus No.12 to **Bodøsjøen Camping** (Tel. 7556 3680), three km south-east of Bodø.

# Northern Norway: Nordland

If you are wanting to visit the **Lofoten Islands**, travel from Bodø by Nordland Express and change at Narvik. The journey is expensive, and does not include an overnight stay in Svolvacr. Narvik also has a separate rail link – the Ofoten Line – which runs the 43 km to the border and on to Sweden. It is a particularly scenic journey. For many years it was the world's most northerly border and today it is still the most northerly electrified line and carries about half the total goods transported by Norwegian Railways, mainly about 20 million tons of Swedish iron ore.

When in **Narvik**, Tourist Information can be found in the main street in Kongensgate 66 (Tel. 7694 3309, open in summer Mon.–Sat.: 9am–7pm, Sun.: 2–7pm; in winter Mon.–Fri.: 9am–4pm). Note that the exchange rate offered here is not that good, but you can book private rooms for a fee.

The **youth hostel** (Tel. 7694 2598; Fax. 7694 2999), which is open from June–Aug., is situated beside the harbour at Havnegate 3 (turn left from the Tourist Office and walk down Kongensgate for 10 minutes). Reservations are recommended.

You can get cheap showers and a sauna at the **Seamen's Mission**, near the harbour in town. It is open 4pm–10pm and has a pool table, as well as cheap coffee and snacks.

From June to August you can take a 15-minute cable car ride in the *Gondolbaner* for magnificent views of the area and, at night, the midnight sun. The service runs from 10am to midnight or later, depending on weather conditions, and costs around 60kr. If you are intending to take the early morning train out of Narvik, bear in mind that the station closes from 10.30pm to 5am.

# North Cape (Nordkapp)

The superbly scenic bus journey from Narvik to North Cape is certainly a worthwhile detour off the rail system – the land of the midnight sun and the most northerly point of Europe. This trip necessitates at least two overnight stops, but the reward is breathtaking scenery over all of its 739 km length. The most popular expedition starts with the midday bus from Narvik, arriving at Alta 11¼ hours later. The feeling of complete isolation is quickly apparent – apart from the abundant wildlife, that is: from June-Oct., Nordkapp is the pastureland for around 5,000 reindeer.

There is a convenient **youth hostel** in Alta at Midtbakken 52 (Tel./Fax. 7843 4409), but in common with most hostels this far north, it does not open until mid-June (closes late Aug.).

There are also four campsites with cabins to rent. **Alta Strand Camping and Apartments** (Tel./Fax. 7843 4022) is the best-equipped site, or try **Alta River Camping** at Øvre Alta (Tel. 7843 4353), about five km out of town. On current timings, the North Cape bus continues on its way the following morning at 7.35am, arriving at Europe's northernmost point at 1pm. The **North Cape Hall** is worth a visit, even if just to sip a coffee overlooking the Arctic Ocean. For those wanting to stay longer, there is a **youth hostel** (Tel. 7847 3377) at Honningsvåg and cabins to rent (expensive).

The adventurous might consider joining up with the coastal voyage or continuing to Kirkenes on the Russian border. Otherwise, the return bus to Alta departs at 2.55pm, arriving back in Alta at 7.55pm, for an overnight stop. The journey continues to Narvik at 9am the following morning. Check your *Thomas Cook European Timetable* for the most up-to-date schedule.

NB: There is a reduction over this route with Inter-Rail or Nordturist. This does not apply to the Honningsvåg to North Cape section or to the ferry crossings.

NOTES:

...............................................................................................................................

...............................................................................................................................

...............................................................................................................................

...............................................................................................................................

...............................................................................................................................

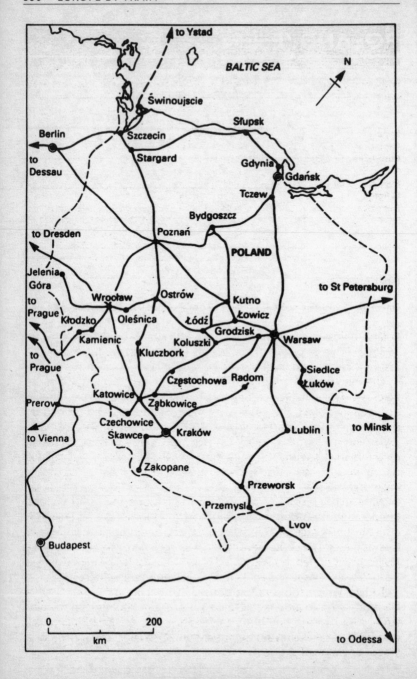

# POLAND (Polska)

| | |
|---|---|
| Entry requirements | Passport. UK, US and Irish nationals do not need a visa for stays up to 90 days. Canadians, Australians and New Zealanders should apply for visas in advance. |
| Population | 38.6 million |
| Capital | Warsaw (pop.: 1.7 million) |
| Currency | Złoty |
| | £1 = approx 6.8zl |
| Political system | Republic |
| Religion | Roman Catholic |
| Language | Polish (German, English and Russian spoken) |
| Public holidays | New Year's Day (1 Jan.), Easter, Labour Day (1 May), Constitution Day (3 May), Corpus Christi , Ascension Day (15 Aug.), All Saints' Day (1 Nov.), Independence Day (11 Nov.), Christmas Day and Boxing Day |
| International dialling | To Poland: int'l code 48 |
| | From Poland: 00 + country code |
| Emergency telephone numbers | Police 997; ambulance 999; fire service 998 |

Poland holds a unique place in the history of Eastern Europe as, in 1985, after years of toil by the Solidarity trade union, it became the first of the countries to throw off the cloak of communism.

This long struggle for independence reflects the strong spirit of the Poles, who have had to endure a rather large serving of invasion and occupation. In fact, the country has been conquered and divided up dozens of times – starting in the 10th century with the eastward expansion of Germanic tribes. On two occasions it even disappeared off the map altogether; firstly, in 1795, when the country was divided up between Russia, Austria and Prussia; and secondly, after Hitler's invasion in 1939.

With such a history of foreign domination and the rising political temperature it no doubt caused, it's hardly surprising that Poland is also the birthplace of Gabriel Fahrenheit, inventor of the mercury thermometer. The composer Chopin was born here too, though while his body lies buried in his adopted home of Paris, his heart will always be in Warsaw – as it was actually removed and buried there!

Today, while still suffering the harsh economic effects of a transformation to a market economy, the outlook for Poland remains strong. And with a rich historical heritage, some 23 national parks, hundreds of lakes and numerous mountain chains, it's worthy of a visit at any time of the year.

## POLISH STATE RAILWAYS
### (POLSKIE KOLEJE PAŃSTWOWE, PKP)

Polish trains are now faster and less busy than they once were, but best of all, they're still reasonably cheap. But whenever possible avoid the *Osobowe* and *Pośpieszne* categories and go for the *Ekspresowe* (expresses). To ensure a seat it's also worth paying the small additional fare for an upgrade to first class. All the large cities have their own commuter trains, called *pociągi elektryczne,* which are more crowded than normal.

Sadly, at present there is a high risk of robbery at main rail stations and on all international train services, so keep all valuables out of sight. Similarly, while on board trains watch out for organized gangs of thieves (Warsaw station is a particular black-spot). The tactic seems to be that one member of the group distracts the tourist while accomplices make off with any accessible luggage.

**PASSES AVAILABLE** The Inter-Rail pass is broken down into zones, so that you pay only for travel within the area you want to visit. Poland is in Zone D, along with the Czech Republic, Hungary, Slovakia and Croatia. For details of the eight Inter-Rail zones, see the Inter-Rail section in Part One of this guide.

Euro Domino tickets are also available (see pp. 23-24).

Eurail is not valid in Poland.

Don't be tempted into buying a Polrail Pass unless you plan on spending plenty of time going around in circles – they are not cost-effective. But those of you who do have a pass can use it on all trains where reservations are mandatory and you also get free seat reservations (bookable at station of departure, any reservation office, or on the train). The pass for under-26s costs £36 (or £54 for first class) for eight days, £42 (£62) for 15 days and £49 (£73) for 21 days (monthly passes are also available). Over-26s pay £52/£58/£70 2nd class and £75/£85/£102 1st class. Polrail Passes can be bought in the UK from Polorbis, 82 Mortimer Street, London W1N 8HN (Tel. 020 7636 2217) or from Bogdan Travel, 5 The Broadway, Gunnersbury Lane, London (Tel. 020 8992 8866).

The European Eastpass is also valid, see Part One of guide for details.

## TRAIN INFORMATION

Unfortunately, officials don't speak a lot of English, so scribble down the name of your destination and the time your train leaves. When in the south and west try a little German, or French if you're in the north. If you're really stuck, try and get your tongue around this phrase: *Z'którego peronu odjeżdża pociąg do...?* (From which platform does the train to... leave?)

**RESERVATIONS** Trains are regularly packed full so you'll need to reserve if you want to guarantee a seat. This should be done at least a day in advance (several days for the Warsaw–Cracow–Zakopane run) and can be done up to sixty days in advance, ninety days for return trips. For international trains you'll have to use the Orbis agency or brave the queues at the international windows (marked *Polres*) – they deal with seat reservations (*miejscówka*) which are compulsory on express and international trains.

**NIGHT TRAVEL** If you're not travelling first class – where the seats recline right back – don't expect high standards. Reserve well in advance at Orbis, Polres and travel agents, especially for couchettes, which are always cheaper than paying for a night's accommodation. However, you may find some couchettes can only be booked shortly before departure. If you're going to Slovakia or the Czech Republic you'll probably be told couchettes are the only seats available – so you'll have no alternative other than to reserve one. Some international journeys to former Eastern Bloc countries are still cheap. However, try to get a carriage supplied by a western country such as Austria.

**EATING ON TRAINS** On all long-haul journeys in Poland, you'll find either a WARS restaurant or buffet car, but some international trains have only minimal facilities.

## TOURIST INFORMATION

There are *Informacja Turystyczna* (IT) offices in every major town. If you plan to stay for a while, it's worth buying *A Guide for Young Tourists* from any Ruch kiosks in Poland.

**MONEY MATTERS** 1 złoty (zl) = 100 groszy (g)

A new currency was introduced in 1995 and old notes have ceased to be legal. Banking hours are usually Mon.–Fri.: 7.30am–5pm and Sat.:7.30am–1pm. You can also exchange money at Orbis, at travel agents and post offices, hotels, and hundreds of KANTOR kiosks (*bureaux de change*), which may give marginally better rates.Don't be tempted to exchange money on the black market as you're bound to be swindled in some way and may well be given counterfeit notes. Keep your exchange receipts, as they may be checked when you leave. You aren't allowed to take złotys out of the country, but you can change back unused money.

**POST OFFICES** Open Mon.–Fri.: 8am–8pm, in smaller places they may shut at 4pm. Getting mail sent on is more trouble than it's worth (allow at least 3 weeks). Most embassies will keep your letters for at least 2 weeks.

**SHOPS** For food, 7 or 8am–6 or 7pm and half a day on Saturday, delicatessens and supermarkets usually stay open longer, others 10 or 11am–6 or 7pm. For opening times of museums, etc., check with

the local IT office. Most are open on Sunday but closed on Monday.
TIPPING 10–15% is standard in restaurants. Taxi drivers usually
include a mark-up in the fare they charge.

## SLEEPING

If you're under 35 and travelling during the summer months, Almatur,
the student travel organization, can help find inexpensive university
dorms. However, you will need student accommodation vouchers
which are available from Almatur offices, or Polorbis (see Appendix V
for address). Fix up accommodation in advance, otherwise you might
have a problem – if you haven't, then get there as early as possible in
the day but you're not assured of a bed.

If you've no luck with the ISHs, try the Polish Youth Hostel
Federation (PTSM). Officially, most require an IYHF card, but it's not
always essential. The good news is that they're very cheap; the bad
news is that some can be like overcrowded prisons. There are a huge
number of hostels (schroniska młodzieżowe) in Poland, all of which are
spartan even by Western YH standards. The head office of the PTSM is
at ul. Chocimska 28, Warsaw (Tel. 022 498354 or 022 498128). The
office is open Mon.–Fri.: 8am–3.30pm.

The more money you're willing to spend, the fewer your problems
are likely to be. PTTK is an organization that runs cheap hotels called
Domy Turysty; you can find out about these from the local IT office, but
don't build your hopes up as they are nearly always full. Standard
Polish hotels are not too expensive.

Private rooms can be arranged through an organisation called Biuro
Zakwaterowania – rooms that you may be offered on the street can be good
value, but obviously there is a risk and they may be a long way out of town.

Finally, if you're getting desperate, try the long queue at the Orbis
office; they might have a spare bed in one of their hotels, if you're
prepared to pay the high prices asked.

There are over 500 campsites in Poland which are classified into
three categories. Category 1 sites are the best and these usually have a
restaurant, category 3 sites are the most basic. Prices vary according to
the category and location. Expect to pay around 18zl. per person.
Some sites have bungalows available for hire, a bed in one will be
around 25zl. Most sites are open from May to Sept. Ask for details
and location at the local Tourist Information.

## EATING AND NIGHTLIFE

You can eat well and cheaply in Poland and the cuisine reflects a mix of
influences, including Russian, Geramn and Turkish. The food is generally
rather heavy and portions are large so you won't go hungry. Pork, fish or
poultry will normally be the best bet. With improved economic climes,

new restaurants are appearing almost daily. You can get a good meal (but not a gastronomic delight) at the top hotels and restaurants. Expect to pay around 28–35zl for a three-course meal. Avoid station restaurants completely, with the exception of Warsaw (and that's only if you're stuck).

**Milk bars** or *bar mleczny* are the cheapest places to eat. These self-service cafeterias sell mainly vegetarian dishes. Most of the fare is made from dairy products, hence the name. It's quite an experience eating in one - it feels very communist. The food is basic and cheap - lunch will only set you back a pound or two.

The freeing up of society has led to a developing nightlife scene, revolving around *kawiarnie* (cafés) and *winiarnie* (bars) and in some places student clubs. Polish vodka is, of course, an internationally renowned tipple and the beer is cheap and excellent.

Being a strongly Catholic country, morals can be strict, so it is not always the best place to advertise open homosexuality, however, there is an English-speaking gay/lesbian information line (based in Warsaw) on Tel. 022 628 5222, but it only operates between 6pm and 9pm on Tues. and Wed. (for women) and between 4–10pm on Fri. (for men).

## THINGS TO BRING AND BUY

Food is fairly cheap and plentiful, so don't stock up on consumables before arriving, unless, of course there is something you really can't live without. Good news for some is that alcohol (but not spirits) and cigarettes are cheaper here than in most European cities due to Poland's status as a 'developing country' – and with it special concessions from Western manufacturers. Make sure you've got enough photographic film before you arrive too, as, although it might be readily available, it's expensive and often past its expiry date.

Poland is rich in handicrafts and as you travel the countryside you're bound to see many bargains – from tapestries and rugs to pottery and woodwork. Note that you can only take goods up to a total of US$200 out of the country duty-free. Some notable exceptions are crystal (80% duty!) and any pre-World War II books or artwork. As a budget traveller you may think these restrictions will not apply to you, but think again: rampant inflation has left many Poles in a position where they have to sell prized family possessions for hard currency. However, don't be tempted to buy Russian military paraphernalia, as it may be confiscated if you're travelling on to other Eastern European countries (problems with border officials are very possible). If you must have that furry hat or grey trench coat, post it home!

Goods that can be bought cheaply are lace, hand-painted silks, wooden toys, handmade utensils and amber necklaces. If you can't make it out to the countryside, there are outlets in the major cities: the Cepelia shops sell arts and crafts; Desa sells artwork by professional

Polish artists; and Jubiler stores sell jewellery. Imports and flashy souvenirs can be purchased at the Baltona and Pewex shops, which only take hard currency, and while more expensive, are still quite cheap by Western standards.

# Warsaw (Warszawa) phone code: 022

Warsaw suffered heavy bombing in World War 11, with over 85% of the buildings being destroyed and 700,000 of the population perishing (over half of the city's prewar population). Luckily for the tourists, the Poles recreated the splendour of the city by building replicas of the original 19th-century structures. This coupled with the city's splendid parks and palaces is what now makes Warsaw so beautiful. However, you can never escape the fact that in 1943, Hitler ordered that no stone of Warsaw should be left standing - an act echoed by the holocaust reminders dotted all round the centre.

## TOURIST INFORMATION

The Warsaw information office is located at pl. Zamkowy 1/13 (Tel. 635 1881), open Mon.–Fri. 9am–6pm, Sat. 10am–6pm, Sun. 11am–6pm. The main Orbis office is at ulica Bracka 16 (Tel. 827 4516), open Mon.–Fri.: 8am–7pm, Sat.: 9am–2pm. The Orbis branch at Marszałkowska 142 sells international train tickets and changes traveller's cheques.

## ADDRESSES

**MAIN POST OFFICE** Świętokrzyska 31/33

**AMEX** Orbis, Marszałkowska 142

**ALMATUR (POLISH STUDENT TRAVEL)** At the university on ulica Kopernika 23 (Tel. 826 2639 or 826 3512); open Mon.–Fri.: 9am–6pm (4.30pm Sept.–June), Sat.: 10am–2pm

**OUR ROOTS (JEWISH INFORMATION AND TOURIST BUREAU)** ulica Twarda 6 (Tel. 620 0566); open 9am–5pm. Sells English publication describing walks of particular historical interest.

**UK EMBASSY** Al. Róz 1 (Tel. 628 1001)

**IRISH EMBASSY** ulica Humanska 10 (Tel. 496655)

**US EMBASSY** ulica Ujazdowskie 29/31 (Tel. 628 3041)

**CANADIAN CONSULAR OFFICE** ulica Matejki 1/5 (Tel. 629 8051)

**AUSTRALIAN EMBASSY** ulica Estońska 35 (Tel. 617 6081)

**NEW ZEALAND** ul. Migdałowa 4 (Tel. 645 1407)

**FIRST AID** ul. Hoża 56 (Tel. 999 or 628 2424)

## STATION FACILITIES

Warsaw has three stations, but the only one you're likely to use consistently is the new Centralna, which also houses a Wasteels office. Domestic train information is available on 620 4512, while international is on 620 5010. To reduce any opportunity for thieves, always keep valuables out of sight.

## GETTING ABOUT

Bus and tram tickets (25p) can be bought at kiosks marked Ruch (*bilety tramwajowe* and *bilety autobusowe*), which also sell one-day (around 80p) and one-week passes (£3). Avoid queues by purchasing beforehand as many as you think you'll use – your ISIC card may get a discount as well. Hotels also sell bus, tram and metro tickets. Don't forget to punch your ticket – there's a machine at either end of buses and trams – as you'll risk a fine if you're caught (Poland is known for its plain-clothed ticket inspectors). A week's pass only needs to be stamped on the initial journey. Note: buses marked with letters are 'expresses' and will cost twice the price of normal buses; after 11pm all fares are doubled; and you have to pay extra for your baggage.

## SEEING

The main sights of Warsaw are concentrated between the **Stare Miasto** (old town) and **Łazienki Park**. Standing at the centre of the old town is **Rynek Starego Miasta**, a beautiful market square flanked with rebuilt Baroque houses; while a block to the south is **St John's Cathedral** – the main focus of Warsaw's deeply religious Catholics. Warsaw's oldest monument, the **Sigismund III Vasa Column** (1644), lies in Zamkowy Square and adjoins the **Royal Castle**, which dates back to the 14th century and is now a museum (open Mon. and Sun.: 11am–5pm, Tues.–Sat. 10am–5pm). Castle tours are obligatory but they are usually in Polish only. Entry is free on Sun. Nearby is the tin-roofed Baroque **Palace**.

Under the Nazis, Warsaw's Jewish population was wiped out and the **Pawiak Prison** – where 35,000 were executed and 65,000 detained – is now a museum. Obviously, there are many sites connected with this period: the **Historical Museum**, on the market square, plays a captured Nazi film showing the systematic destruction of this city; the **Jewish Historical Institute** at Tliomackie ulica 5 looks at what happened in the famous Warsaw ghetto; and the **Mausoleum to Struggle and Martyrdom** on the Al Amoni is housed in the former Gestapo HQ and prison. For more information on what to see, visit the **Our Roots** bureau (see Addresses above).

The **Wilanów Palace and Park** was a 17th-century summer house for one of Poland's kings. The restored palace can be visited, along with the **Museum of the Polish Poster**, in the palace grounds: the palace is closed Tues., the museum shuts Mon. and you reach them by bus 180 from ulica Marszałkowska.

**FREE WARSAW:** The graceful **Łazienki Park**, is one of many open spaces in the city where you can enjoy a stroll. Here, you'll also find miniature lakes, monuments and **Łazienki Palace** (entrance not free) – built for the last Polish king in the 18th century. On the park's southern edge is a **monument to Chopin** where on Sunday afternoons you can hear Chopin recitals.

- **Markets** remain a good way to see ordinary life as well. The daily market on ulica Targowa, Bazar Różokiego, can be dangerous for tourists, but the Sunday flea market in Stadion Moczytlo, ulica Goczewska, is worth a look. The huge Saturday **bazaar** in the Praga district (Stadion 10-lecia) is interesting too, and close to **Praski Park**. The following museums are also free on one day of the week:
- **National Museum** (Muzeum Narodowy), Al. Jerozolimskie 3. Free Thurs. (Closed Mon.)
- **Military Museum** (Muzeum Wojska Polskiego), Al. Jerozolimskie 3. Free Fri.
- **Historical Museum** (Muzeum Historyczny Miasta Warszawy), Rynek Starego Miasta 28. Free Sun.

## SLEEPING

Finding a place to sleep in Warsaw can be a nightmare. The student hostels (open July–Aug.) change location annually so you'll need to go to the Almatur office (see above) to get current details.

There are a few youth hostels which are cheap but rule-ridden and fairly depressing. A selection are located at: Karolkowa 53a (Tel. 632 8829; Fax. 632 9746), take tram 22 or 24; Smolna 30 (Tel./Fax. 827 8952), tram 25; and ulica Międzyparkowa 4 (Tel. 831 1766), tram 2, 6 or 18; bus 174 from the train station, or 175 from the airport. Plan on arriving before 9am to be in with a chance at any of the above hostels. PTTK at ulica Marszałkowska 124 will give you a list of their *Domy Turysty*.

There are some affordable hotels to try including the **Harenda**, Krakowskie Przedmieście 4/6 (Tel. 826 0071; Fax. 826 2625) which is located centrally, near the university campus. A double room costs around £42 per night (excluding breakfast) and the **Saski**, another central hotel, at pl. Bankowy 1 (Tel. 620 4611; Fax. 620 1115), which is slightly cheaper.

Almatur offices will provide a list of campsites. Try **Majawa** at Boh. Bitwy Warszawskiej 1920r. 15/17 (Tel. 233748) which is a good budget option. There are bungalows here as well. The site is south of the bus station. Take bus 154.

There are a few agencies which are worth contacting if you're looking for a private room. Try Syrena, ulica Krucza 17 (Tel. 628 7540 or 629 0537). Alternatively, Informacia Noclegowa is a telephone service which directs people to hotels according to their budget: call them on 641 5366 or 831 0464. Refer to *Cheap Sleeps Europe 2000* for more accommodation options.

## EATING AND NIGHTLIFE

If you've had a hard time finding accommodation, make up for it by eating out in style. Food here is cheap enough to let you eat in all the best restaurants and still think you've had a bargain. The **university cafeteria** on the campus at ulica Krakowskie Przedmieście is ideal for small budgets and don't forget there are always plenty of milk bars around too. Some restaurants worth trying are: **Le Petit Trianon**, ulica Piwna 40/42; **Restauracja Polska**, ulica Nowy Świat 21, is the best Polish restaurant; **Restauracja Bliss** (for Chinese food) ulica Boczna 3; or **Pizzeria Bambola** at ulica Puławska and ulica Wspólna. The fast-food junkie is also well served throughout the city. **Blikle Café** on Nowy Świat 33 is the oldest cake shop in the city - open since 1869, and is also described (by some) as the best cake shop in Europe – see what you think.

Social life in Warsaw revolves around the *kawiarnie* and *winiarnie*. You won't have a problem finding good ones, but the **Fukierowska** wine-cellar at Rynek Starego Miasta 27 (old town market square) is Poland's best and dates back to 1590. Also look up **Pod Herbami** on ulica Piwna and **Zanzi Bar** at ulica Wierzbowa 9/11. Above all, keep your eyes and ears open, as new bars, restaurants and clubs are opening regularly and the 'in' place changes frequently.

If you feel like dancing, **Hybrydy**, ulica Złota 7/9, is a lively student club and **Tam Tam**, ulica Foksal 18, is a hip venue with an African feel. Or perhaps take in a film – the cinema is cheap, and **Bajka**, ulica Marszałkowska 136/138, shows Polish films with English or French subtitles. Another good cinema is **Foksal** on ulica Foksal. For tickets to the opera, concerts or theatre, make your way to **ZASP** on ulica Jerozolimskie (Tel. 621 9454).

Although Warsaw is a fairly conservative city, the gay scene is improving all the time. Good clubs to check out include the men-only **Fantom**, on ulica Bracka. It's dark and dingy but has character. A good general place is **Paradise** disco/bar at the **'Skra'** centre on the corner of ulica Wawelska and Żwirki i Wigury (Thurs.–Sat. nights). **Planeta** at ulica Fort Wola 22 has a gay night on Sun. but it is far out from the centre. For more options, call the Pink Service on 825 3911.

Regular festivals and events in Warsaw include the International Book Fair in May, Summer Jazz days in late June, the Jazz Jamboree in Oct., the biennial Film Festival and the five-yearly Chopin Piano Competition (both taking place this year). Ask at Tourist Office for more details.

## Cracow (Kraków) phone code: 012

The former capital of Cracow in the south – an ancient city of Polish kings and culture – has retained a marvellous mixture of Gothic, Renaissance and Baroque façades. It holds a unique position too, as the only city in Poland to survive the war largely unscathed – a fact that helps the city breathe a strong medieval air and makes it a must to see. This year of all years is the time to visit as the city is one of the European Cultural Capitals of the Year. The Tourist Office will be able to tell you about special events.

### TOURIST INFORMATION

The main tourist office is run by **Wawel Tourist**. It's close to the train station at ulica Pawia 8 (Tel.422 6091; Fax. 422 0471). The office is open mid-Apr.–mid-Oct. Mon.–Fri.: 8am–6pm, Sat.: 10am–midday; mid-Oct.–mid-Apr. Mon.–Fri.:8am–4pm, Sat. 10am–midday and has all the information you could wish to know. Pick up *Kraków: What, Where and When* for latest info. on what's happening in the city as well as a city map. There is also a handful of commercially-run tourist offices, and more springing up, including **Dexter**, Rynek Główny 1/3 (Tel. 421 7706 or 421 3051), open Mon.–Fri.: 9am–6pm and Sat./Sun.: 9am–1pm, and the **Jordan Bureau** at ulica Floriańska 37, both of which are helpful. For concert tickets and information about other cultural events, visit the **Centrum Informacji Kulturalnej** (Cultural Information Centre) at ulica św Jana 2 (Tel. 421 7787; Fax. 421 7731).

### ADDRESSES

**MAIN POST OFFICE** ulica Wielopole 2
**ORBIS** In the main square at Rynek Główny 41 (Tel. 422 4035)
**AMEX** At Orbis
**ALMATUR** Rynek Główny 7/8 (Tel. 422 6708)
**US CONSULATE** ulica Stolarska 9 (Tel. 421 6767)
**PHARMACY** For information on hospitals and 24hr chemists Tel. 422 0511. In an emergency, call 999.

### STATION INFORMATION

Make sure you get off at the main station, Kraków Główny, a 10-minute walk from the centre, and not one of the suburban stations.

Train Information: Tel. 422 2248 or 933; for international services Tel. 422 5654. The bus station is opposite. When using trams, punch your ticket to avoid risking a heavy fine.

## SEEING

The old town (**Stare Miasto**) is the place to head for to see the sights. At its heart is the huge central market square, **Rynek Główny** – the largest medieval market square in Europe. Here you'll find the Renaissance mercantile **Cloth Hall**, which houses the **Gallery of 19th Century Polish Painting**, part of the **National Museum**, upstairs.

16th-century **Wawel Castle** dominates the river Vistula and encloses a **Cathedral**, overseen for many years by Karol Wojtyła (Pope John Paul II). The 15th-century **Collegium Maius** on św Anny is the oldest building of the famous **Jagiellonian University** – one of the oldest in Eastern Europe – and is well worth a visit. There are about 30 museums to choose from so you won't get bored in Cracow. Opening hours are prone to change and many are free on certain days so it's a good idea to pick up a guidebook from the Tourist Office.

**FREE CRACOW:**

- A look in some of the city's churches and synagogues is a good way to 'see for free'. The **Stara Synagoga**, at Szeroka 40, lies in the old Jewish quarter of **Kazimierz** and is Poland's oldest synagogue; while on Rynek Główny you'll find the **Cathedral**, where the bugler plays an unfinished daily warning from the spire – a reminder of the days when Mongol hordes surrounded the city.
- In the old town there are plenty of **street traders**, along with a good mix of **architectural styles** to sample. The **Planty** gardens surround the whole of the old town too, so if you fancy treading some grass, this is the place for you.
- At the north end of Floriańska is **St Florian's Gate** (the original city gateway) and remains of the city's defensive wall.
- During summer the **State Chambers**, **Treasury** and **Oriental Collection** in **Wawel Castle** are free on Wed. (free on Sat. during Winter).
- **Czartoryski Museum**, ulica św Jana 19. Free Sun.

## SLEEPING

With Cracow increasingly becoming a more popular destination, finding somewhere to spend the night can be a bit tricky. To arrange accommodation, the Waweltur office (next to the Tourist Office) at ulica Pawia 6 (Tel. 4221921) is a good place to start. Alternatively, any of the tourist offices will help you a book a room or you could always risk it and accept one of the rooms offered to you at the station.

Establish the exact location and price (be prepared to haggle) and take a look at the room before formally agreeing.

There are a few official **youth hostels**: The one at ulica Oleandry 4 (Tel. 633 8822; Fax. 633 8920) has been highly praised by previous travellers (take tram 15 or 18 from the train station). Otherwise try, Kościuszki 88 (Tel. 422 1951) or Express (non-HI) at ulica Wrocławska 91 (Tel. 633 8862) which has no curfew and is not closed during the day.

For hotel accommodation, **Pollera** at ulica Szpitalna 30 (Tel. 422 1044; Fax. 422 1128) has been highly recommended as well and is only five minutes from the station. Also try **Europejski** near the train station at ulica Lubicz 5 (Tel. 423 2510; Fax. 423 2529).

For camping try **Camping Krak** on ulica Radzikowskiego 99 (Tel. 637 2122), open mid-May to mid-September. Take buses 118, 173, 208,218 and 223 or tram 4, 8 or 40.

## EATING AND NIGHTLIFE

Street stalls are often the best place to eat, though few restaurants will stretch your budget. Try **Staropolska**, ulica Sienna 4 (Tel. 422 5821); **Balaton**, ulica Grodzka for good Hungarian food or **Jadlodajnia Stanisław** at ulica Mikolajska 16 for a popular haunt with the locals. For Chinese, **Shanghai Restauracja Chinska** on ul. Szymanowskiego (near Cloth Market) is popular and reasonably priced.

Due to being a student city, Cracow has better nightlife than much of Poland. Try the student club **Pod Jaszczurami** (Tel. 422 0902) at Rynek Główny 8 or **Rotunda**, ulica Oleandry 1 (Tel. 633 3538), which stays open to 5am at weekends.

**EXCURSIONS** The town of **Oswięcim** is under two hours away – though it's better known as **Auschwitz**, location of the largest concentration camp in Hitler's 'Final Solution'. It's a museum these days, providing a harrowing impression of life and death in the camps. Entry is free, though you can watch a special spine-chilling film showing the camp just after liberation for 3zl. (The English language version costs 15zl to view). An all-inclusive coach trip from Cracow costs around £10. **Birkenau**, 10 mins away, is another huge camp which is connected to Auschwitz by a shuttle bus in the summer.

The salt mine at **Wieliczka** is an amazing complex of underground chambers and includes the **Chapel of the Blessed Kings**, intricately carved from salt. A guided tour takes two hours, so try to get there early to be finished by lunchtime. Open daily: 8am–6pm.

In deeply Catholic Poland, **Częstochowa** is home to the most important religious site. **Jasna Góra Monastery** is the destination for pilgrims from all over the world, who come to see the **Black Madonna**, an icon which is said to have cried during a 17th-century Swedish siege.

The Tourist Office is at Aleje NMP 65 (Tel. 034 241360) and the Orbis Office is at NMP 40/42. For accommodation, there is a **youth hostel** at ulica Jasnogórska 84 (Tel. 034 243121), and the basic, but cheap **campsite** is at ulica Oleńki 30 (Tel. 034 247495).

South of Cracow is the beautiful **Tatra National Park**, with lofty 1,800m mountains of granite and limestone.

**ZAKOPANE** This is the largest town in the Tatra area and makes an ideal base from which to explore the surroundings. The bus from Cracow to Zakopane is a good idea as it's only a couple of dollars and is more scenic than the train.

A funicular railway runs to the top of **Mount Gubalowka** (1,116m) and a cable car up **Mount Kasprowy Wierch** (1,953m). A great six-hour hike to the top of **Mount Giewont** (1,878m) will reward you with a magnificent view from each peak.

**Morskie Oko**, about 40 minutes from Zakopane by bus, is a beautiful mountain lake well worth the trip.

The Tourist Office is at ulica Kosciuszki 7 and the PTTK at ulica Krupówki 37 will give you information on mountain shelters. The **youth hostel** is at ulica Nowotarska 45 (Tel. 206 6203). For camping, try **Pod Krokiwa**, ulica Żeromskiego (Tel. 201 2256), opposite the foot of the ski jump.

## Gdańsk phone code: 058

Famous as the birth-place of the Solidarity movement, the port of Gdańsk lies on the Baltic coast in north-eastern Poland. It's got plenty to offer the Eurorailer, with an historic old town dating from the medieval Hanseatic League – a time when the city was known as Danzig.

## TOURIST INFORMATION AND ADDRESSES

**TOURIST INFORMATION CENTRE** ulica Heweliusza 27 (Tel. 301 4355), open Mon.–Fri. 9am–4pm. There's also the helpful, privately run Agencja Informacji Turystycznej at ulica Długa 45, open daily 9am–6pm (Tel. 301 9327)

**PTTK OFFICE** In the Upland Gate (Tel. 301 6096)

**ORBIS** Hotel Heweliusz, ulica Heweliusza 22 (Tel. 301 5631); open Mon.–Fri.: 9am–5pm and Sat.:10am–2pm. Pick up a copy of *Welcome to Gdańsk* and *Gdańsk, Gdynia, Sopot: What, Where, When*

**POST OFFICE** ulica Długa 23/28
**AMEX** At Orbis (see above)
**ALMATUR** Długa Targ 11/13 (Tel. 301 2931); open Mon.–Fri.:
9am–5pm and Sat.: 10am–2pm
**TRAINS** Gdańsk Główny is 10 minutes from the centre. Train infor-
mation: Tel. 301 1112.

## SEEING

The large market square, **Długa Targ**, is the main focus of the city.
Here, you can take a look at the imposing Gothic **Town Hall** – which
contains a very interesting **Historical Museum** (closed Mon.) – from
whose tower you can get a great bird's-eye view. Meanwhile, a walk
along ulica Mariacka will offer you some grand façades of 17th-century
burghers' houses.

To the old town's north are the former Lenin Shipyards – **Stocznia
Gdańsk** (Gdańsk Shipyards) – home of Solidarity. An open-topped
boat tour starts at the Mołtawa canal, and there's a monument to
workers killed during the rising of 1970.

Gdańsk was where World War 11 started on 1 Sept. 1939.
**Westerplatte**, at the entrance to the harbour, is the exact point where
the fighting began when *Schleswig-Holstein*, the German battleship,
began bombing Polish territory. Now there's a small museum
commemorating the spot and a huge monument in memory of those
who perished; the ruined army barracks and guardhouse have been
left in their damaged state. Get there on bus 106 from the train
station, bus 158 from the centre or on one of the tour boats which
depart from the Green Gate. Ask at the Tourist Office for more info.

Hordes of beachgoers occupy Gdańsk during the summer. If you
fancy risking some bathing in heavily polluted waters; try **Stogi Beach**
(tram 9), which is also a popular windsurfing destination. East of
Gdańsk is the beautiful Mazurian lakeland. Take the train via Olsztyn.

## SLEEPING

The Biuro Zakwaterowań at ulica Elżbietańska 10 (Tel. 301 9371) and
at ulica Heweliusza 8 will help you find a room, so will either of the
tourist offices. Almatur (Tel. 301 2931) manages student hostels and
dormitories. Try getting a bed in the student lodgings on ulica
Wyspiańskiego at nos. five (Tel. 341 0955), 7 (Tel. 341 4985) or 9 (Tel.
341 1536). For **hostels**, the most central one is at ulica Walowa 21
(Tel./Fax. 301 2313), five minutes from the station; closed 10am–5pm.
Be aware of the fact that dormitories are mixed.

**Hotel Jantar** is bang in the middle of the old town on Długi Targ 19
(Tel. 301 9532; Fax. 301 3529). Its good location means it gets busy,
so book or arrive early if possible.

For camping try **Gdańsk-Jelitkowo**, ulica Jelitkowska 23 (Tel. 553 2731). Cheap bungalows available. Trams 2, 4 or 6 from the main train station to the last stop, then a short walk.

Half an hour away in the seaside town of Gdynia is a **youth hostel** at ulica Morska 108C (Tel./Fax. 627 0005), open all year. There are also two campsites at ulica Bosmańska 58 (Tel. 625 1919) and at Szyprów 26 (Tel. 624 80 04).

## EATING AND NIGHTLIFE

The best place to 'lap' up some food is at the milk bars, but if you want to 'splash' out on excellent sea food, try **Pod łososiem**, ulica Szeroka 52/3 (Tel. 301 7652) or **Retman**, ulica Stagiewna 1 (Tel. 301 92 48). For great live jazz, check out the Jazz Club at Długa Targ 39/40 or for all-night disco, go to **Kazamaty**, ulica Doki 1off ulica Wołowa.

**EXCURSIONS** One of the most awesome military fortifications in Europe lies on the banks of the River Vistula (Wisła) in **Malbork** – its sheer scale is best appreciated from the opposite bank of the Wisla (where it's most photogenic). The construction of **Marienburg**, 'the fortress of Mary', was begun by the Teutonic Knights in 1274 after they were driven out of Palestine. In 1309, it became their European HQ and powerbase, and lasted as such until 1457 when the Grand Master was forced to flee to Königsberg. Since 1997 it has been on the UNESCO World Heritage List. During May–Sept. the castle is open Tues.–Sun.: 9am–5pm; Oct.–April., Tues.–Sun.: 9am–2.30pm. You have to go round in an organized tour (available in English) which lasts 2½ hours. Arrive at least three hours before closing time. Malbork is about 45 minutes south of Gdańsk on the main line to Warsaw.

# Toruń phone code: 056

The historic city of Toruń is best known as the birthplace of Polish astronomer Nicolaus Copernicus: a fact that seems to overshadow its rich medieval heyday, which saw it become one of the top Hanseatic trading cities. With the Polish Partitions and subsequently Prussian and German control, the town's economy plunged into sharp decline. When the Treaty of Versailles was signed in 1919, Toruń (or Thorn, as it was then called) was able to join the recently formed Polish state as part of the 'Polish corridor'. Today, Toruń's strong hold on its rich history is reflected in a whole host of architectural styles providing a backdrop to the bustle of a university city.

## TOURIST INFORMATION

The PTTK office is at ulica Fosa Staromiejska 6 (Tel. 621 04222, open Mon. and Sat.: 9am–4pm, Tues.–Fri.: 9am–6pm, in summer Sun.: 9am–1pm) and provides a good source of information. At ulica Piekary 37/39 you'll find the official Tourist Office (Tel. 621 0931; closed Sun. from Sept.–Apr.). Orbis is at ulica Żeglarska 31 (Tel. 26130 or 21714) and Almatur is at ulica Gagarina 21 (Tel. 20470), near the university.

## STATION FACILITIES

Most trains stop at Toruń Główny (main station), about three km from the centre, across the River Vistula (Wisła). Buses 22 and 27 maintain a frequent service between the station and placa Rapackiego. Toruń Miasto is much closer to the centre.

## SEEING

In addition to the **Town Hall**, make sure you take in the **Medieval Walls** and several excellent red-brick churches including **St Mary's Church** on the north-west corner of the town square, and **St John's Church** on ulica Żeglarska. Near St John's on ulica Kopernika is the house where Copernicus was born, now a museum (open Tues.–Sat.: 10am–4pm). The city has six museums and opening times are posted at the town hall, which itself contains the **Town Museum** (open Tues.–Sun.: 10am–4pm).

## SLEEPING

For an affordable hotel in the town centre, five minutes' walk off Rynek Staromiejski, try the **Pod Orlem** at ulica Mostowa 17 (Tel. 25024); and the **Polonia** at placa Teatralny 5 (Tel. 23028). Student residences at the university are available during the summer, check with IT or Almatur for details. The PTTK *Dom Turysty* at ulica Legionów 24 (Tel. 23855) is quite far from the centre. The **IYHF hostel** is at ulica Swięty Józefa 20, 2km north-west of the centre (Tel. 654 4580). Take bus 11 and get there early as there are only 30 beds. **Camping Tramp** at ulica Kujawska 14 (Tel. 654 7187; open May–Sept.) is only a short walk from the main train station; bungalows available. There's also a building with cheap rooms on site.

## EATING

Gingerbread is the local speciality and is widely available in the old town. Ulica Szeroka has a good selection of cafés with outside seating. For reasonably priced restaurant meals try: the **Polonia** hotel (see above) and for Hungarian and Polish food, try **Hungaria** at ulica Prosta 19. Good quality cheap food is also available at the restaurant of the **Zajazd Staropolski** hotel at ulica Żeglarska 10.

# Poznań phone code: 061

During the 15th and 16th centuries, Poznań flourished as an important link in several trade routes, a position, however, that was to decline over the next 200 years. With German unification in 1871 an attempt was made to 'Germanize' the city, but resistance established it as a centre of Polish nationalism. A successful revolution by the local Poles in 1918 ensured Poznań's incorporation in the reconstituted Polish state. Today it is a city with much to offer the tourist: there's a peaceful cathedral quarter, a bustling, attractive centre and lots of cafés to stop in and just watch the world go by.

## TOURIST INFORMATION

The helpful, well-informed staff at the IT Office at Stary Rynek 59 (Tel. 852 6156) provide a good range of material on the city and surrounding area. Open Mon.–Fri.: 9am–5pm; Sat 9am–1pm. In the main hall of the central station, there's a 24-hr Glob-Tour (Tel. 866 0667). Orbis have offices at placa Wolności 3 (Tel. 852 4011) (which sells international train tickets), al Karola Marcinkowskiego 21 and ulica Święty Wojciech 33. New tourist offices are appearing all the time and there's now a City Information Centre inside the Empik store at ulica Ratajczaka 44.

## ADDRESSES

**POST OFFICE** The main office is on ulica Kosciuszki 77
**ALMATUR** al Aleksandra Fredry 7 (Tel. 852 0344)
**PTTK OFFICE** Stary Rynek 90 (Tel. 852 1839)

## STATION FACILITIES

Poznań Główny is about 15–20 minutes' walk from the Stary Rynek at the heart of the old town. Trams 5 and 21 connect the station to the city centre.

## SEEING

The city's most important public buildings can be found at the centre of the impressive **Main Square** (Stary Rynek). Here, lines of gabled houses surround its pride of place: the **Town Hall** (now containing the **Museum of the History of Poznań**) – local legend also has it that two rams saved the city from burning down and at noon you can catch the clock's figure-play re-enacting the event. The **Weighing House** lies to the rear of the town hall too.

A 15-minute walk across the River Warta will lead you to the red-brick buildings of the old ecclesiastical quarter.

The imposing castles of **Rogalin** and **Kórnik** (11 and 23 km from Poznań respectively) are easily reached by bus.

## SLEEPING

The town plays host to many international trade fairs, so inevitably hotels are expensive. Location-wise, you cannot better the PTTK *Dom Turysty* at Stary Rynek 91 (Tel. 852 8893).

Private rooms are a good option: available from the Biuro Zakwaterowania at ulica Glogowska 16 (Tel. 866 5163 or 866 3560) across from Poznań Główny (the staff do not speak English); or from Glob-Tour (Tel. 866 0667) at the station.

The most convenient of the city's **IYHF hostels** is at ulica Berwińskiego 2/3 (Tel. 866 4040); much further out in the suburb of Strzeszyn is the clean and modern hostel on ulica Biskupińska 27 (Tel./Fax.822 1063).

The nearest campsite is the Maltańska (Tel. 87 6155) which is about 2km east of the centre. To get there take tram 8 from the train station.

## EATING AND NIGHTLIFE

Poznań produces two good-quality beers, Lech and Ratusz, which make a nice change from the ubiquitous Tatra Pils. If you're having problems finding suitable pubs or clubs, ask at the Tourist Office, or failing that, at the **Odnowa**, the biggest of the student clubs, at ul Święty Wojciech 80/82.

## Wrocław phone code: 071

The principal city of Poland's Lower Silesia area: Breslau (Wrocław 's former name) became one of the leading cities of Prussia by the early 20th century. However, in the aftermath of the Second World War it became part of Poland and was re-named Wrocław – though many Silesians still use the Germanic name. The city suffered terribly during the latter period of World War II, with three-quarters of it being damaged, including around 400 monuments ruined. Today, rebuilding and restoration, along with 100 bridges, various parks and gardens and the life that a university town brings, make Wrocław well worth a visit.

## TOURIST INFORMATION AND ADDRESSES

Tourist Information is at ulica Rynek 14 (Tel. 44 3111); open Mon.–Fri.: 9am–5pm; Sat. 10am–2pm. Orbis has an office at Rynek 29 (Tel. 343 2665), open Mon.–Fri.: 9am–5pm; Sat. 9am–1pm. PTTK is at Rynek-Ratusz 11/12 (Tel. 343 8331) and Almatur at ulica Kościuszki 34 (Tel.

344 3003) There's a post office near the train station at Małachowskiego 1, while smaller offices operate in front of Wrocław Główny and at Rynek 32.

## STATION FACILITIES

You're most likely to arrive at the main station, Wrocław Główny, about 10–15 minutes' walk from the Rynek. Wrocław Nadodrze receives trains from Łodz. Tram 0 or 1 will take you to the centre.

## SEEING

The 14th-century **Town Hall** with its astronomical clock dominates **Market Square** (Rynek), and ranks as one of Poland's most impressive public buildings. It also houses the **Town Museum**, which is worth a look (if only to see the interior of the town hall). Many of the medieval houses around here have benefited greatly from the town's conservation programme.

Not far from Rynek is the university area: with the ecclesiastical quarter over the River Oder on Ostrów Tumski. For particularly fine views of the latter take a walk along the banks of the Oder. The **National Museum**, near the river at Powstancöw Warszawy 5, is renowned for its collection of medieval stone sculptures and Silesian wood carvings. One of Wrocław's top tourist attractions, the **Racławice Panorama** (open daily May–Sept. 9am–5pm; Oct.–Apr 10am–3.30pm), lies on ulica Purkyniego. The panoramic painting (120m long and 15m high) outlines the Russians' 1794 defeat by the people's militia, led by the national hero Tadeusz Kościuszko. Down near the river, the Prussian King Frederick the Great had a residence at the **Spaetgens Palace**, which is also worth a look.

To reach the **Sudeten** mountains from Wrocław head south towards the Czech border.

## SLEEPING

The IYHF hostel is in the area behind Wrocław Główny at ulica Hugona Kołłataja 20 (Tel. 343 8856), cheap but there's a 10am–5pm lockout and a 10pm curfew. Ulica Piłsudskiego, opposite Wrocław Główny, has several affordable hotels: the **Piast 1**, no. 98 (Tel. 343 0033; Fax. 343 7893); the **Polonia**, no. 56 (Tel. 343 1021; Fax. 447310); the **Grand**, no.100/102 (Tel. 343 6071; Fax. 343 3986); and at no. 88 the **Europejski** (Tel. 343 1071; Fax. 443433). If you want private accommodation, it can be arranged at the Biuro Usług Turystycznych at ulica Piłsudskiego 98.

There's a good **campsite** near the Olympic Stadium at al Ignacego Paderewskiego 35 (Tel. 484651). Get there on trams 16 and 17, which run along ulica Adama Mickiewicza: the stadium is off to the left.

## EATING AND NIGHTLIFE

**Miś**, close to the university at Kuźnicza 48, is a good, popular milk bar. But for cheap, substantial meals try the **Medalion** at ulica Swidnicka 26, opposite St Dorothy's Church. A popular place with tourists is the **Piwnica 'Pod Złotym Psem'** at Rynek 41. The atmosphere in this restaurant/pub is lively to say the least and it is still fairly cheap. For good Italian food try **La Scala** at Rynek 38. The **Pałacyk**, at ulica Tadeusza Kościuszki 34, is the main student club; and the **Rura** at ulica Lazienna 4 offers live music nightly (blues and, especially, jazz).

NOTES

..................................................................................................................

..................................................................................................................

..................................................................................................................

..................................................................................................................

..................................................................................................................

..................................................................................................................

..................................................................................................................

..................................................................................................................

..................................................................................................................

..................................................................................................................

..................................................................................................................

..................................................................................................................

..................................................................................................................

..................................................................................................................

..................................................................................................................

..................................................................................................................

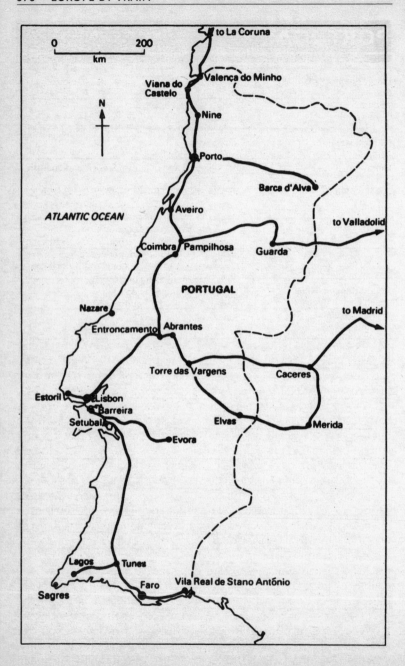

# PORTUGAL

| | |
|---|---|
| Entry requirements | Passport |
| Population | 10 million |
| Capital | Lisbon (pop.: 1.5 million) |
| Currency | Escudo ($) |
| | £1 = approx 318$ |
| Political system | Republic |
| Religion | Roman Catholic |
| Language | Portuguese (some English, French and Spanish spoken) |
| Public holidays | New Year's Day, Shrove Tuesday, Good Friday, Liberty Day (25 April), Labour Day (1 May), Corpus Christi, Feast of the Assumption (15 Aug.), National Day (10 June), Feast of the Assumption (15 Aug.), Republic Day (5 Oct.), All Saints' Day (1 Nov.), Independence Day (1 Dec.), Feast of the Immaculate Conception (8 Dec.), Christmas Day and Boxing Day |
| International dialling | To Portugal: int'l code 351 |
| | From Portugal: 07 + country code |
| All emergencies | 115 |

The Phoenicians, Greeks and Romans all left their mark on Portugal, just as they did with the rest of the Iberian peninsula. By 1143, the country was recognised as a separate nation, though it didn't get to see the back of the occupying North African Moors until they were defeated in 1249.

During the 'Age of Discovery' in the 15th century, explorers such as Vasco da Gama quickly increased Portugal's overseas empire with the discovery of the African coast, India, China and Brazil. After that it wasn't long until they had the biggest empire in the world. But, like all good things, Portugal's glory gradually came to an end, as Spanish conflict and rivalry with other European powers brought about her decline.

The biggest shake-up in the country's history came when the great earthquake of 1755 tumbled Lisbon and tragically took 60,000 lives. A little later, in 1807, this was followed by Napoleon's invasion, an event which saw the royal family up sticks and scarper off to Brazil to escape the risk of death.

After a spell as a military dictatorship, the 1974 revolution gave the country a liberal constitution and since 1986 it has been a member of the European Community. The 1990s were a difficult time for the country which was hit hard by recession, high unemployment and a backwardness in agriculture and education. However, Expo '98 attracted millions of tourists to what is a beautiful and diverse country. Whether Portugal will be able to adjust smoothly to European monetary union this year remains to be seen.

Because of the recent poor economic climes, Portugal continues to be one of Europe's most affordable countries, and for the budget traveller it's a chance to indulge in some good food, good wine and of course plenty of sun to top it all off.

## PORTUGUESE RAILWAYS

### (CAMINHOS DE FERRO PORTUGUÊSES, CP)

The British originally built the Portuguese network with a wide gauge for extra comfort. Much of the 3,600 km network is electrified, but you will also find some of the more remote inland lines are narrow-gauge and steam-hauled. Seat reservations are essential on all international and *rápido (intercidade)* trains. Alfa is a special *intercidade* service which operates between some of the northern cities and makes fewer stops. Reservations essential. The fastest of the non-supplement trains are the *Interregionals*. Next down the list are the slow *Regionals* and *Suburbanos*. Away from the Lisbon area, services can be very slow, so you might feel justified in paying the extra supplements for the intercity *rápidos*; this works out at about 25% above the normal tariff. The standard has improved in recent years, though. It is essential to buy your ticket before you travel, either at the station or from a travel agency, otherwise you will be faced with a substantial fine.

**PASSES AVAILABLE** Eurail and Inter-Rail are both valid. Portugal is in Inter-Rail Zone F, along with Spain and Morocco. (For further details of the eight Inter-Rail zones, refer to the Inter-Rail section in Part One of this guide.)

A Euro Domino ticket is also available in Portugal, see pp. 23-24 for details.

CP issue a more expensive Tourist Pass (*Bilhete Turistico*) which entitles the holder to one, two or three weeks of unlimited travel for approximately 18,000$, 29,200$ or 41,200$ respectively.

Rail Cheque is available in four different values and can be used in one name or a company's name and has no time limit. It gives a reduction of 10% and can be used for purchasing tickets and many other railway services. It comes in values of 40,000$, 100,000$ and 150,000$.

The Portugese Railpass is available from USIT/Campus Travel (Tel. 020 7730 3402) and allows one, two or three weeks' 1st or 2nd class travel for those with ISIC cards and under 26s. Seven days costs £36 (£68 1st class); 14 days costs £59 (£108 1st class) and 21 days costs £88 (£153 1st class).

An International Youth Ticket (BIJ) is available to anyone under 26 and gives discounts on international travel in 26 countries. These can be bought from travel agencies and Portugese Railways International.

Rail Europe Senior cards (Cartao RES) are available to anyone over 60. The card entitles the holder to 30% off the price of international tickets in 20 European countries. Any supplements must be paid in full. A Senior Citizens Card, for those over 65, gives a 50% reduction on all but suburban trains between 6.30am–9.30am and 5pm–8pm except on Sat., Sun. and holidays. Proof of age is required. These passes can be bought in the UK from Wasteels (Tel. 020 7834 7066).

For more information on any of the passes, contact CP in Lisbon on 01 888 4025; Fax. 01 886 7555.

## TRAIN INFORMATION

English is spoken by most information staff. Always check the timetabling of trains with the posters on station walls, as printed timetables cannot always be relied upon to be accurate.

**RESERVATIONS** Seats must be reserved in advance on all international and express trains and also on certain other trains. On other trains, reservations are optional. For international and express trains, reservations are free of charge providing they are made the day before departure; on other trains, reservations are fairly cheap. In general trains are crowded, so it's best to reserve seats in advance.

**SUPPLEMENTS** Eurail Pass holders need to pay a supplement to travel on express trains. Some *rápido* trains carry a saloon observation car which requires a supplement to travel in it. Before you buy your ticket, ask first about the train you are taking. It is worth paying the small supplement on the Lisbon–Porto line.

**NIGHT TRAVEL** There are couchettes on the Sud Expresso (Lisbon–Paris) and the Lusitania Expresso (Lisbon–Madrid). Sleepers run from Lisbon to Hendaye and on the Lusitania Expresso.

**EATING ON TRAINS** All trains except the *regionals* have bars or mini-bars, and some of the *rápidos* have dining cars.

**SCENIC TIPS** As with Spain, you may have enough problems getting where you want to go without worrying about scenic routes; however, the run from Valença in the north down to Lisbon is one of the best Portugal has to offer. Also try the line from Porto along the Douro valley and its branch lines, such as the one to Braganza.

**TIME DIFFERENCE** Portugal is on GMT, which means it is one hour *behind* Spain.

## TOURIST INFORMATION

Is provided by the government-run Postos do Turismo. They have offices all over the country and stalls at major stations.

**ISIC BONUSES** The main perk here is admission to the cheap student restaurants on your ISIC. In addition about 1,200 places – clubs, theatres and so on – also offer discounts. For further information, contact Turismo Social e Juvenil, Turicoop (1st floor), Rua Pascual do Melo, Lisbon.

**MONEY MATTERS** 1 escudo ($) = 100 centavos.

1,000 escudos is known as a *conto*. Banking hours are Mon.–Fri.: 8.30am–3pm. There are late-night exchange facilities at major tourist resorts.

**POST OFFICES AND SHOPS** Open Mon.–Sat: 9am–1pm, 3pm–5 or 7pm (closed Sat. pm).

**MUSEUMS** Open 10am–5pm, although some close for lunch and most are closed all day Mon.

**TIPPING** High tips are not common. Round up your bill to the next highest unit in restaurants and give porters a small note. Add 10% to the meter fare for taxis.

## SLEEPING

The government-run Tourist Board controls all the accommodation within Portugal and will book you a room if required. Hotels are graded from 2–5 stars, boarding houses (*estalagem, albergaria, pensão*), 1–4. By law, prices should be shown at reception and behind the door of each room. Staying in a hotel is not as cheap as you might expect; a double room in a three-star hotel costs about 12,500$ a night. Breakfast is usually included. If it's off season, try to bargain with the hotel owner – the displayed prices are the maximum they can charge, not the actual price.

A student hostel tends to be more expensive than a cheap *pensão*. There are 21 youth hostels (*pousadas de juventude*) in Portugal; all require IYHF cards, most impose a midnight curfew, and prices range from 1,400 to 3,200$. For more information or to book (small charge), contact Movijovem - Agencia de Turismo Jovem, Cooperativa de Interesse Público e Resposabilidade Lda, Av Duque d'Avila 137, 1050 Lisbon (Tel. 01 313 8820; Fax. 01 353 5982 or 01 352 1466).

Camping is another possibility: sites are generally close to towns; cheap, but may be quite basic except in the Algarve, where you have to have a Camping Carnet and things are quite plush.

We recommend cheap hotels and boarding houses. They're normally near the stations, and as prices are unaffected by location, it's not really worth shopping around.

## EATING AND NIGHTLIFE

Food is cheap in Portugal and eating out is a relatively inexpensive affair (1,000–1,500$), except in the Algarve, where prices are marked up for the tourists. In most restaurants the locals will often eat standing at the counter rather than sitting down. Go for fish dishes, especially chowders if you get the chance: they're invariably cheaper and tastier than meat dishes. National specialities include *linguado delícia* (sole cooked with banana). If you don't like fish, pork represents the best value among the meat dishes. Vegetarians will have to cope largely with omelettes and salads. A bottle of wine is often thrown in for the price of the meal; if not, ask for the local plonk (*vinho da casa*). The port is excellent, especially the fruity white port, but, rather surprisingly, it's not drunk a lot in Portugal. The other wines are excellent too.

If you're living on the beaches and need a meat 'booster', keep your eyes skinned for the mobile shops which serve cheap steak sandwiches (*pregos*). Taverns tend to be very basic, but go down well with the local lads.

Bull fighting in Portugal is not as gory as it is in Spain – they're not allowed to kill the bull – but it's still a national obsession. Of the two types of Portuguese bullfight, the *tourada à antiga* is perhaps the more spectacular. Here the bullfighter is dressed in 18th-century costume and fights from a horse.

Clubs and bars are at their best in Lisbon, though by northern European standards many of the clubs are pretty tame and you'll do better heading for a bar which has *fados* (melancholic Portuguese ballads) on the bill. There are no licensing hours in Portugal, so things can often drag right through the night till dawn.

## Lisbon (Lisboa) phone code: 01

Rebuilt after a devastating earthquake in 1755 – only the old Moorish quarter of Alfama escaped destruction – Portugal's capital has developed into a pleasant cosmopolitan city with several places of great interest. In 1994 it became the European City of Culture while in 1998 it was host to the last Expo World Fair of the millennium. These landmarks saw the completion of massive urban renewal projects, resulting in the transformation of the city's flagging industrial area into an attractive waterfront. A plentiful supply of beds and cheap meals, along with a lively nightlife, also add to Lisbon's appeal.

### STATION FACILITIES

International trains and northern and eastern trains use Santa Apolónia station. Trains to the south and south-east leave from Barreiro station, linked to Santa Apolónia by a ferry across the Tagus (free on Inter-Rail); trains to Sintra and the west use Rossio, and trains for Estoril and Cascais use Cais do Sodre Station.

There are daily trains to Porto, Madrid, Irún, Paris.

## TOURIST INFORMATION

The main Tourist Office (Tel. 346 6307 or 346 3314) is in Palácio da Foz on Praça dos Restauradores, open Mon.–Sat.: 9am–8pm, Sun.: 10am–6pm. Pick up a free map and a copy of *Agenda Cultural* which lists all the events. There's also a Municipal Tourist Office across the square at Rua Jardim do Regedor 50 (Tel. 343 3672; open 9am–6pm.). Buy a Lisboa Card here which gives unlimited travel on nearly all of the city's transport and free admission to 25 museums and places of interest. It costs 1,700$ for 24 hours, 2,800$ for 48 hours or 3,600$ for 72 hours.

## ADDRESSES

**POST OFFICE (CORREIOS DE PORTUGAL)** Praça do Comércio, open Mon.–Fri.: 8.30am–6.30pm, or Praça dos Restauradores 58, open Mon.–Fri.: 8am–10pm, Sat. and Sun.: 9am–6pm

**AMEX** Top Tours, Avenida Duque de Loulé 108 (Tel. 315 5885)

**UK EMBASSY** Rua de São Bernardo 33 (Tel. 392 4000; Fax. 392 4186)

**IRISH EMBASSY** Rua da Imprensa à Estrêla 1(4 (Tel. 392 9490; Fax. 397 7363)

**US EMBASSY** Avenida dôs Forças Armada 5 (Tel. 727 3300; Fax. 727 2354)

**CANADIAN EMBASSY** Avenida da Liberdade 144, 4th fl. (Tel. 347 4892; Fax. 347 6466)

**BRITISH HOSPITAL** 49 Rua Saraiva de Carvalho (Tel. 395 5067)

**EUROTRAIN** Rua C. C. Branco 20 (Tel. 352 5986)

**STUDENT TRAVEL** Tagus Youth Student Travel, Rua Camilo Castelo Branco 22 (Tel. 352 5986)

**24-HOUR CHEMIST** British Hospital, Rua Saraiva de Carvalho 49 (Tel. 395 5067) or call 118

## GETTING ABOUT

It's best to get your tram or bus ticket from a Carris kiosk rather than on the vehicle, where it costs 150$. There are passes valid on buses, trams and funiculars from one day only, at around 430$, up to seven days at around 2,265$. Buy them from Carris booths in the main stations, open 8am–8pm. The metro system is limited, but a fast way of getting around; tickets cost 70$. If you're travelling in a group, taxis can work out cheaper than in other European capitals. Consider buying the Lisboa Card, see Tourist Information above.

## SEEING

**St George's Castle**, the fortress on the hill, has dominated Lisbon in one form or another for 1,500 years. Its gardens of peacocks and flamingos make a good vantage point for looking over the city. Near the centre is the **Sé** (cathedral), worth a look for its ambulatory and burial chapel. A good view of Lisbon is obtained by taking the **Ascensor de Santa Justa** up the ornate tower created by Eiffel (admission 150$).

On the outskirts of the city are quite a few sights worth visiting. Go to the **Belém** quarter (tram 15 or buses 14 or 43 from Figueira Square), get off at the **Museu Nacional dos Coches**, and head for the **Hieronymite Monastery** (Mosteiro dos Jerónimos, Tues.–Sun.: 10am–5pm). Here Vasco da Gama is buried, as are various Portuguese kings. The affluent merchants in the spice trade put up most of the money for this beautiful place which was built in the early 16th century. Also in this district is the **Tower of Belém** (400$ or 200$ with ISIC; closed Mon.), one of Lisbon's landmarks, an elegant mixture of Gothic and Renaissance architecture.

The huge **Oceanarium**, the largest in Europe, was built especially for Expo '98. It's well worth a visit. Take the metro to Oriente station.

As far as museums go, the **Gulbenkian Arts and Culture Centre**, Av. de Berna 45 (closed Mon.), the **Museu Nacional de Arte Antiga**, Rua das Janelas Verdes 95, and the **Folk Art Museum**, Av. Marginal, Belém, are the best.

**FREE LISBON:** The **Alfama** district is one of Europe's most colourful, especially in the morning when the fish market's on, or Fridays (washday) when the narrow streets are hung with locals' shirts and undies. But it's pointless our suggesting a route round as it's so sprawling you're bound to get lost, so just wander through at your own pace, and if you happen to pass the church of **São Miguel** or **Largo do Salvador 22** (16th century mansion house) pop in for a look. The area is enclosed roughly by the banks of the Tagus, the castle, the church of St Vincent-outside-the-Walls and the cathedral.

- There's also a **flea market** (Fiera da Ladra) in the Campo de Santa Clara on Tuesday and Saturday. But, if you want to hit the parks for a picnic or indeed, more strolling, **Jardim Botanico, São Pedro de Alcantara**, or **Jardim da Estrêla** are all worthy candidates.
- **Sé** (Cathedral) - free entry excluding the cloisters.
- **Mosteiro dos Jerónimos** (Hieronymite Monastery of Jerónimos) – free on Sun.
- Art galleries at **Centro Cultural de Belém**
- **Museu do Chiadu**, R. Serpa Pinto 4
- **Museu da Fundação Calouste Gulbenkian** - free on Sun.
- **St George's Castle**

## SLEEPING

An average double in a pension is about 5,000–9,000$ per room (singles cost about 3,500–6,000$). There are plenty of cheap places in Lisbon – not everywhere is clean and quiet, but the ones listed are about as close as you'll get. If these don't come up lucky, try yourself round Rua da Alegria, Rua dos Correiros, Rua Augusta and Praça da Figueira. Lisbon's **youth hostel** is at Rua Andrade Corvo 46 (Tel. 353 2696; Fax. 353 7541); it's cheap and a 20-minute walk from the centre, but next to Picoas metro. Reserve if possible. There's also a beachside hostel in Oeiras, 12km from the centre, **pousada da juventude de Catalazete** (Tel./ Fax. 443 0638). Take the train from Cais do Sodre to Oeiras.

As regards budget hotels, **Pensão Beira Minho**, Pr. Figueira 6, 2nd floor (Tel. 346 1846) has cheap rooms, as does **Pensão Pembra** at Avenida da Liberdade 11 (Tel. 342 5010). **Pensão Ninho de Aguias**, Costa do Castelo 74 (Tel. 886 7008) is of very high quality with doubles starting from 7,500$ including breakfast, reservations essential; and **Pensão Arco da Bandeira**, Rua dos Sapateiros 226 (Tel. 342 3478) is also recommended.

As far as camping goes, there are plenty of sites – and free beach camping close by – but the recommended site, and the only one actually in the centre, is the **Parque Municipal de Campismo** (Tel. 760 2061; Fax. 760 7474) (bus 43 from Praça da Figueira).

## EATING AND NIGHTLIFE

The best district is between the port and the Praça da Figueira. Lisbon is no longer as cheap as it used to be, so choose your district carefully. Try Rua dos Correiros (near Terreiro do Pão). Use the **Mercado da Ribeira** outside the Cais do Sodré for picnic food, and watch out you don't get stuck on Sundays, especially in July, when many places close. Fish is generally good value, but don't eat the bread and savouries put out on the tables unless you're prepared to pay the extortionate prices that are often asked for them. **Restaurante Trevo de Madelena** and **Restaurante Central** on Rua da Madalena are both inexpensive. Alternatively, try the highly recommended **Restaurante João do Grão**, at Rua dos Correiros 222. The area near the youth hostel is quite good for eating places, and the cheapest part of town is around the Barrio Alto and in the sidestreets off the rua Misericórdia.

Nightlife starts late and can get pretty lively. The authentic Portuguese folk music, the *fado*, is performed in several restaurants and cafés. Don't go till around midnight, unless you're happy to share your evenings with coach parties from package tours. **O Senhor Vinho**, Rua do Meio à Lapa 18 (Tel. 397 2681), and the **Adega do Ribatejo**, Rua Diario de Noticias 23, Barrio Alto, offer authentic *fados*, but not for under 3,000$. Taxi drivers can be a good source of information on the location of an authentic *fado*. Lively nightlife can be found in the Barrio Alto especially around Rua Diário das Notícias. The gay nightlife centres around here, with several good mixed gay/straight bars and dance spots – try **Frágil** on Rua da Atalaia or **Harry's Bar** on Rua São Pedro de Alcantara.

Port, the national drink, can be sampled at the **Port Wine Institute**, Rua São Pedro de Alcantara 45, Mon.–Fri.: 10am–11.30pm; Sat.: 11am–10.30pm. In the summer the **Lisbon Amusement Park** gives you somewhere to spend time before heading for the bars or cafés later on. The fair goes on till 1am and can be reached by the underground (station: Entre-Campos).

## EXCURSIONS
**Sintra** One of Portugal's oldest towns – and a favourite of Lord Byron's – lies 30 km north-west of Lisbon. The summer residence of the royal family was here and the **Pena Palace** and **Park**, originally set up by a mad Bavarian prince, are well worth the day trip (closed Mondays). The **Moorish Castle** is a must with its fantastic views. The park has more than 400 kinds of trees and many rare plants. Also out here is the 16th-century monastery of **Santa Cruz de Capuchos** and **Monserrate Park**. From June to September the Sintra Festival attracts large numbers of music, opera and ballet enthusiasts and the piano concerts are incredibly popular. Tourist Information is at Praça da República (Tel. 923 1157 or 923 3919).

From Sintra you can catch a bus to **Cabo da Roca**, Europe's most westerly point, with a memorable view from the lighthouse. No. 403 departs to Cascais every 90 minutes and stops at Cabo da Roca. Get off at the Azoia turn-off and walk the last couple of kilometres.

**ESTORIL** For a day's activity (or non-activity) on the beach, head here, a jet-set resort 26 km west of the city, or to **Cascais**, three km further on. The journey to Cabo da Roca is shorter from here than from Sintra. If you want to stop off but can't afford the hotel prices, head a few kilometres back towards Lisbon and get off the train at **Oeiras**. Here you can enjoy a fine beach and an excellent modern, cheap and friendly IYHF hostel just a stone's throw away. It is at Catalazete, Estrada Marginal (Tel./Fax. 443 0638). It's quite small (less than 100 beds) and fills up quickly, so don't lose time in booking your place.

**QUELUZ** A further option is to make for this town 13 km north-west of Lisbon, where the rococo **Palace** used to entertain VIPs of the Portuguese government. It's stuffed full of antiques and can be reached by train from Rossio station.

# Porto and the Costa Verde

Approaching Portugal from the north, two places worth stopping off at are Viana do Castelo and Porto.

**VIANA DO CASTELO** 1½ hours north of Porto, this pretty little fishing resort has a vantage point for views over the whole region including the **Basilica of Santa Luzia**. You can take the funicular up or, better still, walk up the twisting road past the pine and eucalyptus trees till you reach the top. Back down in the town, look out for reminders of the Renaissance in the buildings of the **Praça da República** and the church of **São Domingos**. If you're here in the third week of August, you'll catch the festival: bullfights, processions, fireworks, dancing, etc. The **Municipal Museum** has a collection of the ceramics Portugal is famous for. Rooms aren't a problem: try the streets off Avenida dos Combatentes, or camp at Cabedelo beach.

**PORTO** The country's second largest city is a centre of industry and commerce and is very much a mixture of old and new. Tourist Information is at Rua Clube dos Fenianos 25 (Tel. 02 205 2740; open weekdays: 9am–7pm; closes at 5.30pm in the off-season). Climb the **Igrejados Clerigos** church tower, then visit one of the 20 or so **Port Houses** for a free tour and tasting, but avoid buying any in the port houses' own shops as you will probably find it cheaper in town. Much of this region is unspoilt, as most Eurorailers head for either Lisbon or the overrated Algarve. If you plan to stay in Porto in June make sure you have made reservations as this is the month of the big festival, Festa de São João. Other annual festivals include the Grand Night of Fado in Sept. and the International Celtic Music Festival in March. Again, fix up your accommodation well in advance.

The **youth hostel** at Rua Paulo de Gama 551 (Tel. 02 6177257; Fax. 02 617 7247) is open 24hrs a day. Take bus 35 from Loios (near Praça da Liberdade) or bus 1 from opposite São Bento station. Reservations essential. The **campsite** is at Rua Monte dos Burgos (Tel. 02 812616); bus 6 from Praça da Liberdade. There's also **Camping Moinho de Vento** (Tel. 02 713 5948) about 12km from Porto at Praia da Madalena. Get there on bus 57 from opposite São Bento station.

A day trip to **Regua** in the Douro valley is possible from Porto. This is one of Europe's most scenic routes.

# The Costa Prata

Portugal's Costa Prata or 'Silver Coast' is home to many places worthy of your time. **Óbidos** is a little medieval village, 11 km from the sea, with a preserved **Castle**, old **Town Walls** and the two churches of **Santa Maria** and the **Misericórdia**. Tourist Information is on Rua Direita (Tel. 062 959231).

**COIMBRA** Capital of Portugal in the 12th and 13th century, this city is also the site of the country's very first university and is second only to Lisbon in terms of historical and cultural importance. Set among the beautiful forests and woods of the Beira Litoral region, it's also less than 2½ hours from the capital. Get off at Coimbra-A station, walk two blocks east for the *turismo* in Largo da Portagem. It's open Mon.–Fri.: 9am–7pm, Sat and Sun.: 9am–1pm and 2.30–5.30pm; shorter opening hours in winter (Tel. 039 828686 or 039 833019). Pick up a free map and ask the staff to help fix you up with accommodation.

The **University** is the best sight of the town. The **Old Library** (*Biblioteca*), the **Chapel** and the **Museum** are all impressive (knock on the door to be let in) and the **Ceremonial Hall** is decorated with some fine *azulejos* (ceramic tiles). The **Machado Museum** nearby is a former episcopal palace, and today houses many of Portugal's artistic treasures.

The town's **Cathedral** is 12th-century, as is the Cistercian convent, **Mosteiro de Celas**. On the other side of the bridge is a reconstructed village of all the famous buildings in Portugal, miniature-size: **Portugal dos Pequeninos**.

For cheap beds, look out for *dormidas* round the station: Rua da Sota and the streets around should produce something. The **youth hostel** at Rua Henriques Sêco 14 (Tel. 039 922955; Fax. 039 981790) is recommended. Take bus 7, 29 or 46 from Coimbra-A to Liceu José Falcão. The **campsite** at Praça 25 de Abril (Tel. 039 701497) costs about 250$ per person plus 175$ per tent. Take bus 1 or 5.

For meals, try **O Funchal** on Rua das Azeiteiras, while vegetarians should make for **Flor de Coimbra**, Rua do Poco 5, where you'll be hard pressed to finish what you're given. Much cheaper food than in Lisbon. *Fado* can be found, along with several bars, on Travessa da Rua Nova – the **Diligência Bar** is recommended.

**NAZARE** This unspoilt resort, five km away, sees traditional Portugal happily living alongside tourism (take the bus from Valado on the

Lisbon Coimbra line). There is a nice beach and a funicular (around 100$) to the old town.

## The Plains (Pláncies) and Mountains (Montanhas)

Off the beaten track between Spain and the Tagus, this area is the hinterland of Portugal – a welcome escape from all your fellow tourists.

**EVORA** This is the principal town, three hours from Lisbon. See the **Roman Temple of Diana**, the Capela de Ossos (chapel) containing the bones of 5,000 monks, the **Sé** (cathedral) and the **Museu d'Evora** (free on ISIC). The Tourist Office is at Praça Giraldo 73 (Tel. 066 22671) – look for cheap pensions off this street. All-year **Camping** can be found on the Alcáçovas Road (around 500$ per person and 400$ per tent), outside town (Tel. 066 25190; Fax. 066 29830). Food is cheaper than in Lisbon. **Restaurante Fasca**, on Rua da Raimundo, serves good regional specialities.

## The Algarve

Picturesque fishing villages, lined by mile after mile of white sandy beaches once made the famous southern region of the Algarve one of Europe's prize secrets. But since the early 1970s, that image has been replaced by the dreaded package holiday. Small villages now resemble overgrown building sites, invaded by an army of British holidaymakers. The only real offering it has are the excellent but crowded beaches, where, if lucky, you might be able to scramble a small patch of sand to yourself. Saying that, if you do come out of season or manage to avoid all the busy package resorts, including **Quarteira**, **Vilamoura**, **Monte Gordo** and (especially) **Albufeira**, the area does have appeal. The local cuisine is superb ( a lot of fish and seafood delicacies), while the regional wines are very cheap.

The Algarve is well connected by rail from Lisbon and the north, and the region's main line runs across from Lagos, through Faro, to Vila Real de Santo António in the east.

### SLEEPING
Finding an inexpensive base in the Algarve is next to impossible during the peak summer months from June to August. Look out for *casas*

*particulares* (private accommodation) or else consider sleeping on the beach. If you're around Lagos, an alternative for Inter-Railers is **Novastar** (Tel. 082 342049) which offers beds from around 1,200$. They have a mixture of dorms, six-, four- and two-bedded rooms and camping. Call them at Silves and they'll pick you up.

If you've really set your heart on spending a few days in the Algarve then you ought to consider arriving out of season. March and April are good months, when the weather is mild with temperatures occasionally straying into the low twenties (°C). Cheap accommodation is also relatively plentiful in towns like Faro and Lagos. The weather can become quite windy after September, so bear this in mind before packing too much suntan lotion later on in the year.

**LAGOA** Between Albufeira and Lagos this small town makes a great base. There is a complex specially designed for young travellers, which offers the major service of sending transport to meet all local trains in the small towns. It is open from the end of May to the beginning of October. It is a self-contained unit with a choice of three restaurants/snack bars, and a disco with parties most nights. Accommodation is in dormitories or tents. Also there is a shuttle bus all day to its own beach, which gives access to other, more secluded beaches. It is very popular among Eurorailers because of the cosmopolitan atmosphere.

**LAGOS** Dating from the time of the Celts, Lagos still offers you quite a bit of its colourful past. These include the scattered remains of the **Medieval Walls** and the magnificent church of **Santo António**, on Rua Silva Lopes, which contains some of Portugal's finest gilt carvings. The **Regional Museum** next door has an interesting, if rather disjointed, collection of artefacts telling the town's history.

The Tourist Office is on Largo Marquês de Pombal (Tel. 082 763031). Accommodation is more expensive than elsewhere but there is a wide choice, and many private rooms. The **youth hostel** is at Rua Lancerote de Freitas 50 (Tel./Fax. 082 761970).

**FARO** The capital of the Algarve deserves at least a day trip. Its jumbled streets spread out from a small **Marina** just along from the railway station. Faro has an empty old **Cathedral** just opposite the **Bishop's Palace**. Nearby is an **Archaeological Museum**, the better of a couple of modest museums in town. Try to get to the **Carmelite Church** at Largo do Carmo, near the main post office, as the church has a spectacular gilt interior, and a bizarre **Chapel of Bones** behind it. The chapel was built by an over-zealous bishop in the last century using the skulls and bones of over l,200 monks.

Faro is your best bet for accommodation in the Algarve if you insist on arriving mid-summer. Room prices are over-inflated but you may find something away from the smart shopping centre part of town – aimed very much at the British tourist with lots of cash. Try the **Pensão Residêncial Oceano** on Rua Ivens 21 (Tel. 089 823349). The Tourist Office, open daily 9.30am–7pm in the summer, is on Rua da Misericórdia (Tel. 089 803604), but don't expect much help in finding cheap accommodation. There is a small **youth hostel** with beds at $1,300, on Rua da PSP (Tel. 089 826521; Fax. 89 801413).

**SAGRES** A popular backpackers' destination with some top beaches. It is best reached by the frequent buses from Lagos. Private rooms are widely advertised; expect to pay 3,500$–5,500$ for a single or double. Open-air **camping** is illegal so head to the site just out of town off the Vila do Bispo road (Tel. 082 624351; Fax. 082 64445) The main street, Praça da República, is the centre of nightlife and has good cheap restaurants. The Tourist Office (Tel. 082 624873) is on Rua Comandante Matosa, near Praça da República.

For a total contrast, head inland for a day and escape the masses. There are lots of little villages to explore and the countryside is beautiful. You'll need to take the bus or hire a bike since the railway sticks rigidly to the coast. If you're heading east into Spain, **Vila Real de Santo António** sits right on the border and is a pleasant little town for a few hours' stop. Even if you're not heading onward through Spain, day trips from Vila Real across to **Ayamonte** take 15 minutes by ferry  and customs formalities are minimal. Once in Ayamonte, you can catch a bus to Huelva, where you join up with the Spanish rail network again.

NOTES
.................................................................................................
.................................................................................................
.................................................................................................
.................................................................................................
.................................................................................................
.................................................................................................
.................................................................................................
.................................................................................................
.................................................................................................

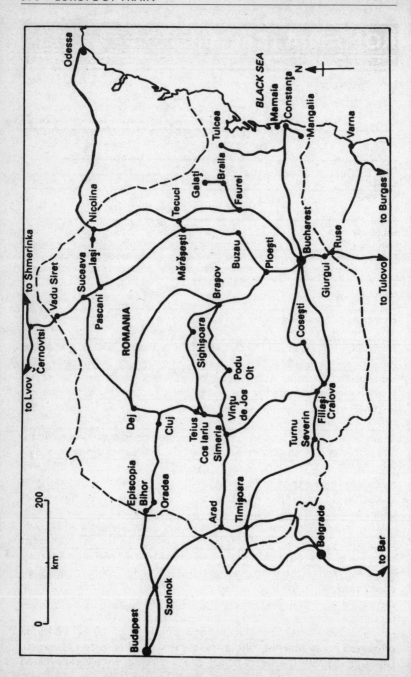

# ROMANIA (România)

| | |
|---|---|
| Entry requirements | Americans with valid passports can travel for 30 days in Romania without a visa, all other western foreigners need a passport and a visa, which should be bought in advance, as there can be problems buying one at the border. Keep hold of your 'exit card', if you lose it you will face problems leaving and have to pay a fine. |
| Population | 22.8 million |
| Capital | Bucharest (2.1 million) |
| Currency | Leu (L) |
| | £1 = approx. 28,565 leu |
| Political system | Republic |
| Religion | Romanian Orthodox |
| Language | Romanian (a little French and German spoken) |
| Public holidays | New Year's Day and 2 Jan., Easter Monday, National Unity Day (1 Dec.), Christmas Day and Boxing Day |
| International dialling | To Romania: int'l code 40 |
| | From Romania: 00 + country code |
| Emergency telephone numbers | Police 955; ambulance 961; fire service 981 |

Pierced by a huge arc of the Carpathian Mountains, Romania also dips into the Black Sea to the east and is bounded by the mighty River Danube to the south. This diverse landscape, with its large variety of wildlife, helps promote the country as an attractive tourist destination – something the Romanians are keen to encourage and develop after the violent revolution of December 1989.

Since becoming a Roman province, the area has played host to Asian, Slavonic and Turkish tribes which have all contributed to the country's population mix – including many gypsies. But the origin of Romania itself didn't begin until 1859 when Moldavia in the east was united with Wallachia in the south – and the name 'Romania' adopted three years later.

After World War I and the collapse of the Austro-Hungarian Empire, the country's territory and population doubled to include, amongst others, the area of Transylvania home to the legend of Count Dracula. But these gains were short-lived and not even the 'Count' connection could prevent them from being snatched out of their hands again during World War II. By 1946 Romania had also become a communist republic, though a year later it had recovered Transylvania.

From 1965 until the December revolution of 1989, Romania remained firmly Stalinist, under the leadership of Nicolae Ceauşescu. During the 1980s the secret police, the Securitate, were widely feared and brutally enforced his regime, which saw widespread destruction of rural villages and historic Bucharest. In short, this period saw the country become one of the most repressive in Eastern Europe, tottering on the brink of bankruptcy.

Up until 1996, Romania was still being run by the communists under the name of the National Salvation Front. But since then the Democratic Convention party has been elected to power and promised an age of reform.

Though travelling the country is still a gruelling experience and likely to test your patience to the full, Romania, with its genuinely warm people, can offer great rewards at the end of it all.

## ROMANIAN RAILWAYS
### (CĂILE FERATE ROMÂNE, CFR)

In recent years Romania has improved its services considerably in response to increased demand. Most trains are still dirty and overcrowded by Western standards, so imagine what they were like before. To travel at reasonable speed and comfort on any of the *Inter-city* (IC) *rapide* (fast) and *accelerate* (semi-fast) trains you will have to pay a supplement. To avoid this, you have to travel on the local *tren de persoane* trains – a fate worse than death. In other words: pay the supplement. Never rely on split-second connections – there are often delays, sometimes running into hours. The Budapest–Bucharest run is a notorious example.

**PASSES AVAILABLE** Romania is in Inter-Rail Zone H, along with Bulgaria, Yugoslavia and Macedonia. For information on the Euro Domino ticket, see pp. 23-24. Eurail Passes are not valid in Romania.

## TRAIN INFORMATION

English is not widely spoken, so be prepared with a French back-up (German can also be useful, especially in the north of the country). If all else fails, try: *De la ce peron pleaca trenul spre...?* (From which platform does the train to … leave?)

Romania has train connections to most neighbouring Eastern European countries, via Budapest, Vienna, Prague and Munich.

**RESERVATIONS** Compulsory on all trains except the *tren de persoane*. The best strategy is to reserve your place out as soon as you arrive, especially on crowded routes, such as Bucharest–Constanţa. Reserve your exit seat before entering the country – queues are horrendous.

**NIGHT TRAVEL** Couchettes and sleepers hardly come up to Western standards and need to be booked well in advance, particularly on the Bucharest–Budapest run. Kick up a fuss if officials demand additional

'reservations' once you're aboard. Rates vary according to distance.
**EATING ON TRAINS** There are restaurants on many long-distance fast trains and buffets on shorter-distance fast trains.

## TOURIST INFORMATION

ONT is the national tourist organization. They have offices in all large towns which give out information and help in finding a room. Lots of private travel agencies have recently opened up across the country, although they mainly arrange package holidays for Romanians some will help to arrange accommodation and local sightseeing tours.

**ISIC BONUSES** Reductions for all international rail travel in Eastern Europe. Also museum entrances reduced with an IUS card. Theoretically, both cards entitle the holder to 50% off at campsites, however, it really depends on the mood of the person on reception – flash your card anyway. For further information, contact CTT, Strada Medeleev 7, Bucharest (Tel. 614 4200).

Inter-Rail bonuses on offer include free entry to the railway museum at Gara de Nord, Bucharest.

**MONEY MATTERS** 1 leu (L) (plural, lei) = 100 bani (not used).Banking hours are usually Mon.–Fri.: 9am–12 noon, 1pm–3pm, Sat.: 9am–12 noon, however they often shut earlier. At present the leu seems to have stabilized after undergoing a long period of high inflation. The black market that once paid over the official rate now offers little profit. Cigarettes, especially Kent or Marlboro, are an alternative informal means of exchange and are useful for tipping. There is also a good black market for coffee. Extra hard currency is useful.

**POST OFFICES, SHOPS AND MUSEUMS** All vary their times of opening, depending on the district. Most keep to the 9–5 routine six days a week. In Bucharest, some shops open on Sun. mornings. Some food shops are open 8am–8pm. Most museums and castles are shut on Mon., some are also closed on Tues. Small museums, particularly those in villages, are prone to shut throughout the winter. Check at the local Tourist Office.

**TIPPING** It is really up to you how much you want to give. Restaurant prices often include a 10% service charge, but waiters will often rush to help Westerners on the assumption that you have hard currency and will leave them a hefty tip as well. Bring a few packs of cigarettes for tipping (Kent, or BT from Bulgaria).

## SLEEPING

Since privatisation, hotels are now charging more realistic rates and privately-owned hotels (opposed to state-owned but rented out to managers) are springing up all the time, especially in the larger towns. Rooms in private homes are becoming less hard to find but very few tourist offices will arrange such accommodation for you. There are a few hostels (*căminul de studenţi*) which are run by the student travel service, CTF, and give preference to large groups when they open during July and August. If you're lucky and make the effort to get to the hostel direct, you will find it inexpensive, although prices have recently shot up. Many Eurorailers choose to camp and although the facilities are usually nothing to write home about (and are often pretty disgusting), there are plenty of sites, many of which have bungalows to rent. Although it is forbidden to just set up camp in the cities and in the Danube Delta, it's OK elsewhere. However, if someone warns you that there might be problems in the area you've chosen, believe them. You can definitely camp where you like in the mountains but be warned, it does get extremely cold at night, even in summer. There is also a network of mountain huts (*cabanas*). You can spend the night in one without reserving beforehand. For information, contact the local tourist office.

You can pay for all accommodation in lei but bear in mind the landlady/hotel manager would much prefer hard currency. Keep hold of your receipts when you change money as these must often be produced: you may have great difficulty if you have changed unofficially.

## EATING AND NIGHTLIFE

Eating is more expensive than elsewhere in Eastern Europe and the food is generally of low quality, as is the beer. Supermarkets usually have reasonably full shelves, but with little choice or variety. You will do well if you happen to like jam, which is colossally oversupplied – unfortunately, this isn't always true of bread to spread it on. Romania's nightlife is not up to Hungary's standards, but after a few glasses of *ţuică*, the local plum spirit, you'll never know the difference. Almost all restaurants take lei, so if the waiter claims only dollars are accepted, he's most likely out to rip you off. Avoid restaurants without menus, since prices will fluctuate wildly.

## THINGS TO BRING AND BUY

Luxury items are scarce or expensive in Romania, so try to bring whatever you may need. If you must have your morning coffee, bring a jar of instant with you, as coffee is almost a myth here and is sold only in the hard currency shops of luxury hotels. In fact, bring two jars and use one to barter with other Eurorailers at campsites or hotels. For those planning on camping or hiking, bring in as much pre-prepared and tinned food as you can carry. Chocolate is almost non-existent and expensive when you can find it, and film is in short supply and of poor quality.

The people here are generally very poor and this is reflected in what you will find for sale. Colourfully embroidered women's blouses are plentiful and cheap in the countryside, as are the small carved wooden flutes which you will see everywhere. There is also a wide variety of woodcrafts, ranging from toys to bowls and kitchen stuffs. Romarta shops carry pottery, glassware and clothing at reasonable prices, and accept lei.

## Bucharest (Bucureşti) phone code: 01

Bucharest was once known as the 'Little Paris of Eastern Europe' and laid claim to some wonderful parks and charming architectural delights. Under Ceauşescu this all changed as he had most of the historical parts of the city bulldozed away. The French flavour of the city seemed lost for ever under the foundations of Ceauşescu's House of the People and other hideous communist buildings. However, now things are beginning to look brighter and the city is beginning to be restored to its former glory. The grand buildings are being rebuild and new shops, bars and clubs are opening up all the time, transforming what was a pretty drab city into a lively and exciting place to visit. Bucharest still has a long way to go before it becomes a popular tourist destination but if you're only here for a few days then you won't be disappointed – even if the train journey there is not one of the most efficient or comfortable!

### STATION FACILITIES
There are five train stations, Gara de Nord, Băneasa, Obor, Basarab and Progresu. Gara de Nord is the biggest and most depressing station and is used most by Eurorailers. Left luggage is opposite platforms 4 and 5. Beware of beggars and conmen here: you can expect to be hassled both by them and by the station police.

There are daily trains to Athens, Cluj, Belgrade, Berlin, Basle, Budapest, Munich, Paris, London, Prague, Sofia, Warsaw, Vienna and Zürich.

### TOURIST INFORMATION
There's a Tourist Office in the station but the main one is ONT at Blvd Magheru 7 (take tram 87 from the station to Piaţa Romana), open Mon.–Fri.: 8am–8pm (info only until 5pm), Sat. 8am–3pm and Sun.: 8am–1pm. Pick up a copy of *Bucureşti: What, Where, When,* which contains listings of all weekend events. You can also get maps at the hotel desks **Bucureşti,** Calea Victoriei 63-81 and **Intercontinental,** Bulevardul Balcescu 4.

CTT, the youth tourist service that deals with groups (the whole of

Romanian tourism centres on groups), is at Strada Medeleev 7 (Tel. 614 4200). The main CFR/TAROM office is at Domniţa Anastasia (Tel. 614 5528), open Mon.–Fri.: 8am–7pm, Sat.: 8am–12 noon.

## ADDRESSES

**POST OFFICE** The main post office is at Calea Victoriei 37 and the poste restante is just off Calea Victoriei at Strada Malei Millo 10, open 7.30am–8pm Mon.–Fri., 7.30am–2pm Sat.

**UK EMBASSY** Strada Jules Michelet 24 (Tel. 312 0303 or 615 3571; Fax. 312 0229)

**US EMBASSY** Strada Tudor Arghezi 7 (Tel. 210 4042 or 312 4040; Fax. 210 0395)

**CANADIAN EMBASSY** Strada Nicolae Iorga 36 (Tel. 222 9845; Fax. 312 0366)

**IRISH, AUSTRALIAN AND NZ CITIZENS** Contact the UK embassy

**EMERGENCY MEDICAL TREATMENT** Spital Clinic de Urgenta, Calea Floreasca 8 (Tel. 679 4310)

**EMERGENCY CHEMIST** Blvd Magheru 18 (Tel. 659 6115). Also at Gara de Nord.

## GETTING ABOUT

Buses, trolley-buses and trams are cheap, and tickets can be bought from all kiosks. Taxis are a bargain too. The heart of a metro system has now been built with three lines (M1, M2, M3) completed. This merely adds to the chaos, as some roads have been closed and many tram routes have been cancelled. There is a flat fare of two 50 lei coins – kiosks at the stations give change. Beware of pickpockets, especially on buses which are chronically overcrowded. If you have the time, and the energy, this city is perhaps best explored on foot – certainly it will prove less frustrating.

## SEEING

Modern Bucharest is hard on the eye, so ignore the new and concentrate on the old. The name Bucharest was given to this town in 1459 by none other than Dracula, a local lad, known here as Vlad the Impaler. By far the most pleasant day's sightseeing is spent out in **Herăstrău park** where you'll find the **Village Museum**. This collection of nearly 300 full-scale displays of peasant houses, farm buildings and churches gathered from all over the country is open 9am–8pm (closed Mon.). The park itself is well-maintained and there's a boating lake, go-cart track, cafés and bars – perfect on a summer's day!

As far as museums go, out of the 40 or so to choose from, the **National History Museum** at Calea Victoriei 12 is recommended (closed Mon.); as is the **Romanian Peasant Museum**, Şos. Kiseleff 3, winner of the 'European Museum of the Year 1995' (open Tues.–Sun.: 10am–6pm); and the **Jewish History Museum**, Strada Mămulari 3. The **National Art Museum**, housed in the former **Royal Palace**, is open for exhibitions only (current lack of sponsorship following serious damage in 1989 prevents it from fully re-opening). **The Museum of Art Collections**, at 111 Calea Victoriei (the early nineteenth-century Ghica Palace), contains an interesting mass of items, including paintings, sculptures, icons and other antiques, which were 'donated to' (confiscated by) the State. Temporary exhibitions are also put on here. Opening hours are Wed.–Sun.: 10am–6pm. Nearby, at the same end of the street are two other museums, the **Ceramics and Glass Museum** at no. 107 (this building is the former Ştirbey Palace) and the **Music of Music** at no. 141 (not that interesting unless you're a particular fan of the composer George Enescu).

**FREE BUCHAREST:** Parks are one of Bucharest's main assets, with the best being **Herăstrău**, the **Student Park** on Lacul Tei, and the central **Cişmigiu Park** - the city's oldest. These are great meeting places and the areas to head for to meet young Romanians.

- However, for an insight into recent turbulent history, visit the **TV station** (bus 131 from Piaţa Aviatoriler) and observe the bullet-ridden buildings where the opposing factions of the 1989 revolution battled for control of the media.
- On Bulevardul Unirii you can gawk at the **Palace of Parliament**, the world's third largest building – after the Pentagon and Potala. **Calea Victoriei** (Avenue of Victory) is an attractive street flanked by some wonderful embassies.
- On Şos Kiseleff stands Bucharest's version of the Arc de Triomphe, (the **Arcul de Triumf**) originally built in 1877 to mark the country's independence from Turkey. Who said the city no longer had a French flavour? (Even the metro stop is called Charles de Gaulle.)
- If you're in the mood for a bit of a rummage, there's a bustling **market** at Piaţa Unirii where Romania's gypsies sell their wares.
- **National Art Museum**, Calea Victoriei 51–53 - free Wed.
- **Museum of Art Collections**, Calea Victoriei 111 – free Wed.
- Admission to most churches and monastries is free. Those of particular note include the oldest church in Bucharest, which dates from 1546, on Str Iuliu Maniu near the ruins of Vlad Dracula's **Cutea Veche** (Old Court), **Stravropoleos Church** (1724) and the **Patriarchal Cathedral** (1658). There are lots of little Orthodox churches hidden away and you're bound to come across some. Have a look inside if they're open.

## SLEEPING

The ONT office (see above) will give you a list of addresses of private homes (if you phone ahead (614 0759) and ask for *Relatia Anglia* you may find someone who will actually fix up the accommodation for you), expect to pay around US$15 for a double room in town. Also try Peter Express (Tel. 659 5761) on Blvd Magheru 32–36. The staff will book singles/doubles fromUS$15/23. You may be approached directly at the station, which will usually be cheaper. Alternatively, there's the excellent, modern youth hostel, **Villa Helga**, at Strada Salcimilor 2 (Tel. 610 2214), which has cable TV and free use of a washing machine. Take bus 79, 86 or 133 from Gara de Nord to Piaţa Gemini. The **YMCA** is at 33 Str Silvestru (Tel. 210 0909; Fax. 665 7046). Get there on bus 123 or 133 from Gara de Nord. For a bed in a student hostel, go to ONT or CTT and ask them for addresses, as these change yearly.

Get a list of hotels from ONT and if you're told they're all full, ignore it and go along to the hotels regardless and ask at reception. There are quite a few affordable places near the Gara de Nord, which charge about US$10–15 single, and US$18–25 for a double. Try **Hotel Dunărea**, Calea Grivilei 140 (Tel./Fax. 222 9820); **Hotel Bucegi**, Strada Witing 2 (Tel. 637 5225); **Hotel Cerna**, Bulevardul D. Golescu 29 (Tel. 637 4087; Fax. 311 0721).

**Camping Băneasa** at present is not advisable as it is home to Somali refugees. There are other sites but they are out of the city in the villages of Buftea and Snagov. Ask at the Tourist Office for directions.

## EATING AND NIGHTLIFE

The kebab and burger bars and the street stalls are the cheapest places to grab a bite at lunchtime. For quick, self-service snacks you could also try the self-service restaurants at the **Dorobanţi** or **Lido** hotels. In the evenings, it is also a good idea to check out the menus in the cheaper hotels, but bear in mind that many smaller hotels stop serving at 8.30pm. **Bistro food** is becoming more popular, these places serve steak and salads and a daily choice of home-cooked food (much like good old pub grub). Try **Bistro Atheneu**, Str Episcopiei 3 – friendly and cheap with good food. For a pizza joint, **Casa Veche** at 15–17 Str Enescu, west of Blvd Magheru serves huge pizzas with a choice of 40 toppings. The house wine is good and there's a nice terrace. **Horoscop Pizzeria** at Bulevardul Cantemir 2 can also be recommended. The originally named **Tandoori** is a great Indian restaurant at Strada Budai Deleanu 4. Traditional Romanian cuisine can be found at **Hanul Manuc** at Strada Iuliu Maniu 62, a bar/restaurant in an attractive setting. Next to the History Museum at Strada Stavropoleos 5 is **Caru cu Bere**, which does some fine meals, has a good selection of beers and offers authentic gypsy music.

There are lots of bars to try, including at least one Irish bar, the **Dubliners Irish Pub**, at B-dul N. Titulescu 18. If you fancy a game of pool, visit **Club Champion** on Şos. Kiseleff. There's also ten-pin bowling, the club stays open 24hrs a day, seven days a week. The best Jazz bar is **Green Hours** at Calea Victoriei 120.

Many restaurants have live acts in the evenings, generally either gypsy music or old pop songs. For something a bit more exciting, go clubbing. Clubs are opening up all the time so check with ONT (or ask some students) where the hip place is at the moment. You could try **Atlantic**, Str Acadamiei 35 or **Martin Club**, B-dul Iancu de Hunedoara 61. The university **Students' Club** is also an option on Saturdays where you can meet young Romanians, an impressive number of whom speak English. It's on Calea Plevnei 61 (metro: Eroiler) and you need your ISIC/IUS. If you are a student and have the advance approval of the Institute of Architecture, you can gain entrance to their **Club-A** on Strada Academiei 2–4 (near the Intercontinental Hotel). The club is popular with the locals and the entertainment varies from disco and jazz to theatre and film. The Institute is near the club. Rock concerts are not generally advertised, ask at the Students' Club or at Club-A. If you'd rather take in a film, there are loads of cinemas to choose from – just check the film has sub-titles and hasn't been dubbed!

**EXCURSIONS** Well worth a day trip is **Snagov**, 40 km to the north. The lake here is a great place for swimming and boating during the summer. Take a boat to the island in the middle of the lake, to visit the 16th-century monastery where the notorious Vlad the Impaler (Dracula to some) has his final resting place. No women are permitted to enter the monastery.

# Transylvania

Transylvania plays host to Romania's most scenic region, but people probably associate it more with the home of the notorious Count Dracula. However, these days the area seems to have been sucked dry of its vampires, though you'll still have an interesting and rewarding time discovering the Transylvanian Alps and the small peasant villages with their rich, active folklore. The best towns to base yourself in are Braşov or Sighişoara.

## BRAŞOV
This town is about 2½ hours from Bucharest, on the edge of the

Carpathian mountains, set among the Transylvanian Alps. It saw heavy fighting in the revolution of December 1989 and many buildings, especially on Piața Teatrului, are pock-marked by bullets with the exception of the Communist Party building, which remained oddly unscathed. The central square, Piața Sfatului, with its attractive baroque buildings and little cafés, is one of the nicest in the country. The 14th century Gothic **Black Church** and the former Council House (1420), now the **Historical Museum** (closed Mon.) are both in the square. Brașov is well-worth a visit but the main attractions in the area are outside the town.

Information on excursions is available from the Tourist Office behind the lobby of the Hotel Carpati, close to Parc Central (Tel. 068 141196). A 'must' see is the Gothic **Castle of Bran**, supposedly Dracula's summer house, which can be reached on one of the frequent buses leaving from Livada Pitesi. Open Tues.–Sun.: 9am–5pm. A visit to the summer residence of King Carl at **Siria Castle** is also recommended for its wonderful interior decoration and furnishings. To get a good view of Brașov and the area, take the Tampa **cable car** (open daily in summer to 8pm, closed Mon. in winter). If you're feeling more energetic you could hike to the top, you should be able to do it in under an hour.

CTT in Strasma Armata Roșie will hand you this year's list of student hostels (bus 4 from station). Or you could try the accommodation service EXO at Strada Postavarului 6 (Tel. 068 144591). The **Dîrste Campsite** (Tel. 068 259080) is 7km away and reachable on bus 3 or 6 to the Saturn terminus and then bus 17 or 21.

**THE FAGĂRAS MOUNTAINS** of the Carpathian range make a great place for hiking amongst the 1,800m peaks and 70 lakes. **Gara Sereş Olt** on the main line from Brașov is a good place to start. There are mountain huts (*cabanas*) spread throughout the region high up on the slopes. Get a map ahead of time in Brașov and reserve *cabana* beds through the Tourist Office there. Make sure to bring a lot of food and a good pair of shoes.

### SIGHIȘOARA

A 2½-hour journey from Brașov, this beautiful medieval town is as yet unspoilt by tourism. This is an ideal spot to break the long haul from Bucharest to Budapest (nearly 14 hours) and it offers more in the way of sights than Brașov .

The **Old Walled Town** is well preserved and among its sights are the **Clock Tower**, the **Town Museum** (closed Mon.), the **Guild Towers** and the **Bergkirche**, a church with good views over the town. The **Church of the Monastery** off the clock tower square is the town's oldest building and not far from here is Dracula's father's house.

The Tourist Office is at no. 10 Strada 1 Decembrie and is open Mon.–Fri.: 9am–5pm, Sat.: 9am–2pm. Get a map and town guide here. During July and August, **Bobby's Hostel** is open at Strada Tache Ionescu 18 (Tel. 065 772232). Alternatively you can camp on the hilltop overlooking the station at **Dealul Garii** (Tel. 065 771046). To meet the locals and have a drink, try **Crama** at Str. Morii 17. There are lots of places to eat in town, especially pizza  restaurants. You can also dine in Dracula's former house in the citadel, **Restaurantul Cetatea**.

## Moldavia

With its small rural villages and beautiful mountain monasteries of northern Bucovina, Moldavia offers you unspoilt lifestyle, where locals still wear national costume. You won't hear a lot of English here either (if any) so brush up on your ingenuity skills. The trains are pitifully slow and you have to change to the smaller lines at Cluj – ask in Bucharest for times and routes.

### SUCEAVA
This is the capital of Moldavia and the best starting-point for a tour of the monasteries. The **Folk Art Museum** is a worthwhile visit. It's in the 16th-century Princely Inn at Strada Ciprian Porumbescu 5, and, in an hour or so, fills you in on the culture of the people that surround you.

The Bucovina Turism office is at Piața 22 Decembrie, though the more helpful Bucovina Estur lies across the square – if not here they may have moved to Strada Ciprian Porumbescu – and can arrange monastery tours.

**THE MONASTERIES Voronet** is the most famous and ancient of the monasteries, dating back to 1488. It's known as the 'Sistine Chapel of the East', owing to its amazing frescoes and unique shade of blue. *The Last Judgement* is the most amazing fresco in Moldavia, showing a whole panoply of figures and scenes from the Bible.

**Humor**, a nearby village, has a monastery obviously built by misogynists (the devil is portrayed as a woman in the frescoes) and from here you can set off for **Sucevița Monastery**. This one is absolutely covered in fascinating frescoes inside and out, from portraits of Plato to the *Arabian Nights*. There is also a small museum here. The actual village of Sucevița has got to be the most charming in Romania. There is a wonderful view over the monastery from the hill opposite and you can camp at the bottom of the hill.

To experience religious life, visit the **Putna Monastery**, where you will rub shoulders with chanting monks. There is no shortage of accommodation here, with a large hotel, campsite and bungalows.

# The Black Sea Coast

Dominated by resorts and huge hotels, Romania's Black Sea coast stretches 246 km from the Danube delta on the Russian frontier to the Bulgarian border in the south.

CONSTANȚA A curious mixture of Roman, Greek and Eastern Byzantine (there's even a mosque and minaret here). See the remains of the **Roman Docks** with its huge piece of preserved mosaic, the **Archaeological Museum** and the **Romanian Naval Museum**. Outside the Archaeological Museum is a statue of the poet **Ovid** who was exiled to Constanța in AD 8.

Part of the beach is sheltered by a tree-and-hedge wind-break; however, you may find that Constanța gets busier than the other resorts in summer, so use your rail ticket to the full and head off for somewhere smaller down the line.

ONT, Blvd Tomis 78, can arrange private accommodation. For hotels, try the **Continental**, further up Bulevardul Tomis. Camping is at Mamaia. Take trolley-bus 150 from the station, and it is a two-minute walk to the site, situated by the sea and usually very crowded in summer.

The resorts of Mamaia, Efone Nord, Efone Sud, Neptun, Saturn and Mangalia are all good places to soak up the sun in more isolated surroundings.

TULCEA The gateway to the unique Danube delta where nature lovers can take a boat trip to see the wildlife; over 300 species of birds, 60 species of fish and well over 1,000 species of plants are to be found in the shelter of this protected area. The **Biosphere Reserve Administration** (ARBDD), at Str Tabarei 32 (Tel. 040 550950) (if it's not there, look near the bus station as the office is supposed to be moving into new premises soon) can give advice and you can enquire here about excursions. (There's no official Tourist Office but the main hotels will be able to help with tourist information.)

**Hotel Egreta** (Tel. 040 517103; Fax. 040 517105) at Strada Păcii 1 is the cheaper of the two high-rise hotels but the cheapest hotel on Strada Păcii (at no. 20) is the **Hotel Europolis** (Tel. 040 512 443), where doubles cost around US$30. For more budget-balancing, the **Han Trei Stele** is at Strada Carpati 16 (Tel. 040 516764). There are also a few floating hotels which you could try. A cheap option is the one belonging to **Navitur** (Tel. 040 518894; Fax. 040 518953). The Navitur offices are opposite the Delta Hotel at Str. Isaccei 4.

# Western Romania

Known as the **The Banat** when it formed part of the great Habsburg Empire, this predominantly flat area is dominated by the three cities of Timişoara, Oradea and Arad. All trains from Hungary and Yugoslavia travelling to Romania pass through here.

### TIMIŞOARA

The city which played such an important role in the revolution of 1989 is an interesting one whose architecture reflects its population of Hungarians and Serbs (now deported). The Hungarian people of western Romania led the fight against Ceauşescu and so it is no surprise that the December 1989 revolution started here and made the city world famous. The impressive **Dicasterial Palace** on Strada Ceahlău is an indication of the great opulence of the old Habsburg rulers. Two trains a day go to Belgrade, and there is a Yugoslav consulate here if you need to apply for a visa (Strada Remus 4, Mon.–Thurs., 9am till noon).

Around the picturesque square, **Piaţa Unirii**, is a Baroque **Catholic Cathedral** and a **Serbian Cathedral**, as well as the **Museum of Fine Arts**. The **Ethnographic Museum** at Sir. Popa Şapcă is in the remains of the old Magyar fort around which the city grew.

Take a walk along the **Bega Canal** through a whole series of parks and visit the **Thermal Baths** on Blvd Vasile Parvan. For a bit of fun go to the **Puppet Theatre** at Piaţa Furtuna.

The old Tourist Office at Strada Piatra Craiului 3 has been privatised and is now an exchange bureau. For tourist information, visit the Agenţie de Turism Banatul (Tel. 056 198862) at Str 1 May 2. At 6 Blvd Republicii is the Cardinal office which books and sells international tickets (Tel. 056 191911). Neither agency will help find accommodation in private rooms..

The cheapest place to stay is the **campground** in the Padurea Forest (tram 1 from the station), where there are also bungalows. It's open from June to mid-Sept.

**ARAD** This is dominated by a huge star-shaped 18th-century **Citadel**, around which the river Mureş flows through a park. The **History Museum** (closed Mon.) is housed in the **Palace of Culture** on Piaţa George Ionescu and has displays on the complex history of the whole area. The Philharmonic Orchestra is also located here.

Bulevard Republicii is the main street and here you will find the former Tourist Office at no. 76, just across from the neoclassical **Town**

**Hall**. Since privatization, it has become the Agenţie Zarandul. It still sells a few maps but for tourist information you'd be better off asking at the larger hotels; try the **Hotel Astoria** on the same street at no. 89.

For accommodation, there are some good new private hotels but none of these fall into the budget category. There are two **motels** within reach of the city, try the one on the Nadlac Road (about seven km from town) or the one further out at Vinga (20 km away; Tel. 057 460026) on the way to Timişoara. Alternatively, head for the **Subcetate** campsite (Tel. 057 285256); follow the river south of the citadel about a kilometre from the bridge near the Park Hotel or take bus 25, 26 or 27. There's also a smaller site, **Camping Voinicul** (Tel. 057 266652) on Strada Digului (take tram 5, 7 or 13 to Strada Voinicilor).

There are a whole series of fairs and gatherings in the villages around Arad well worth day visits, especially the Kiss Fair in **Hălmagiu** in March, as well as festivals in **Pincota** (February), **Birsa** (April), **Sintana** (May) and **Avram Iancu** (June). Ask at the Tourist Office for exact dates.

**ORADEA** This is a common stopping-off point on journeys from Budapest to Bucharest, although it probably does not warrant any more than a day's visit. Oradea has its own **Citadel** and the largest Baroque **Catholic Cathedral** in Romania. Nearby is the grand **Bishop's Palace**, which was based on the Belvedere Palace in Vienna and is now a large **Museum** (open Tues., Thur. and Sat.: 10am–3pm; and Wed., Fri. and Sun.: 10am–6pm) which has displays on the history and people of the Crişana region.

Tourist Information can be got from the Agenţie de Turism Crişul (Tel. 059 130737) at Str Libertăţii 8 (open weekdays 9am–4pm), and the CFR Railway office is at Calea Republicii 2 (open Mon.–Fri.: 7am–7pm).

Cheap places to stay are hard to come by, so you should try the **campground** eight km south-east of Oradea at Băile 1 Mai (bus 15), near the famous thermal baths, or else contact CTT at Stada Vulcan 11.

There are many fascinating caves in the area; try to visit the **Vadu Crisului Cave** (take a slow train east from Oradea), which has tours 9am–6pm each day.

NOTES

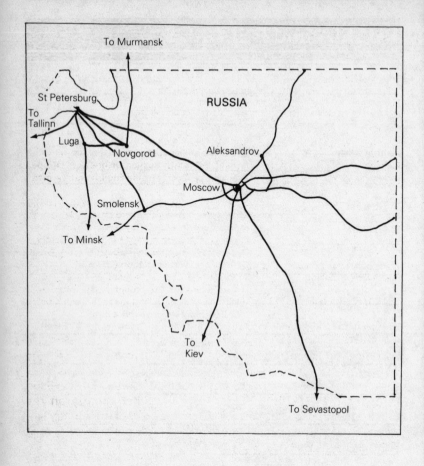

# RUSSIA and BELARUS

| | |
|---|---|
| Entry requirements | All foreigners need a passport and a visa bought in advance (£20). |
| Population | Approx. 147 million |
| Capital | Moscow (pop.: 9 million) |
| Currency | Rouble |
| | £1 = approx 42.6 roubles |
| Political system | Federation of Republics |
| Religion | Several, but mostly Russian Orthodox in Europe. |
| Language | Russian and dialects (some English and German spoken) |
| Public holidays | New Year's Day, Orthodox Christmas (6/7 Jan.), Defenders of the Motherland Day (23 Feb.), International Women's Day (8 Mar.), Good Friday, Easter, Labour Day (1 & 2 May), Victory Day (9 May), Independence Day (12 Jun.), Great October Socialist Revolution (7 Nov.) |
| International dialling | To Russia: int'l code + 7 + number |
| | From Moscow: 8 + 10 + country code. International calls may be easiest made through a post office or (more expensively) a hotel. |
| Emergency telephone numbers | Police 02; ambulance 03; fire service 01 |

Split between Europe and Asia by the Ural Mountains, Russia's huge expanse occupies three-quarters of the Former Soviet Union. Its sheer size is further underlined by the fact that only a quarter of it lies within Europe and even this is bigger than any other country on the Continent. European Russia is also where the heart of the country lies, with 80% of the population here, along with the principal cities of St Petersburg and Moscow.

The first Russian state began as Kievan Rus back in the 9th century and developed into an important and prosperous area of trade. However, Mongols overran the lands two centuries later and it wasn't until the end of the 15th century that they were eventually seen off by Ivan III. Shortly afterwards, another Ivan, this time known as 'the Terrible', became the first of Russia's rulers to call himself 'Tsar'.

More recently, following the Bolshevik Revolution led by Lenin in 1917, Russia donned its cloak of communism for the first time and five years later gave birth to the Union of Soviet Socialist Republics (USSR). This saw Lenin, Stalin *et al.* export Russian domination to the neighbouring states and gradually turn the Soviet Union into a superpower and arch-enemy of the West. However, this decade has witnessed monumental changes, with the fraying seams of the Soviet Union eventually falling apart in 1991.

Not surprisingly, this is a country facing a mountain of challenges. Its road to capitalism has not been easy and coupled with continued question marks over President Boris Yeltsin's health, political instability, rampant crime and the aggression being shown towards Chechnya in the south, travellers should realize that Russia is not your run-of-the-mill tourist destination. However, with patience and persistence and the understanding that a trip to the country will be an experience and a half, Russia has a huge amount to offer.

Lying on the direct route to Poland is the republic of Belarus, formerly called Belorussia or White Russia. If your confidence has been boosted by a trip to Russia, then a stop here could be right up your street!

## GETTING THERE

You can enter Russia from Poland, Estonia, Latvia or Finland; any journey involving a border crossing will be at an inflated price. It is important to remember that Belarus, though lacking in charm as a tourist destination, is *en route* to many of the places you will want to visit and a Belorussian visa *may* therefore be required. The situation is unclear: you might not need a visa for Belarus if the train only passes through *en route* to Russia, but if you are stopping off in the Baltics – so that your destination is not, immediately, Russia itself – then you will need one, and many people have been hauled off trains in the small hours for precisely this reason. Check before leaving home whether a full Russian visa will be sufficient to get you through.

Full visa services, including invitation and registration, are operated by the American-run Traveller's Guest House in Moscow (Bolshaya Pereyaslavskaya ulitsa 50, floor 10, Tel. and Fax 095 971 4059, e-mail tgh@glas.apc.org) and the St Petersburg International Hostel (3rd Sovetskaya ulitsa 28, St Petersburg, Tel. 812 329 8018, Fax 812 329 8019, e-mail ryh@ryh.spb.su): a month's visa costs from £20 ($32). (Increasingly, reputable hotels and other agencies are now contactable by e-mail as it's often the most reliable method of communication.) If you are travelling independently, you must remember to register your visa with OVIR (the Department of Visas and Registration) within three working days of your arrival in Russia. In St Petersburg, the main OVIR office is at Saltykova-Shchedrina ulitsa 4 (Tel. 812 278 2481).

## RUSSIAN STATE RAILWAYS

You could be forgiven for expecting Russian train standards to be rather low. But for the most part, this isn't the case, since as a foreign tourist you will only be given a choice of the best types of train accommodation. The distances involved make overnight trains particularly viable as a mode of transport, the more so since they save you the ordeal of attempting to find a hotel that night.

You'll get a sense of the magnitude of the Russian train system if you travel between St Petersburg and Moscow. Every night, at least a dozen trains make the journey each way, most of them consisting of around 20 carriages – all of them full. Russia's railways carry more people than any other country's and the first rule of Russian train travel is to buy your ticket in advance.

Foreign tourists are usually put on a *skoryy poezd* (fast train, although frankly it isn't), or an *express* (which is faster). You have the choice between soft (*myagkiy*) or hard (*zhyostkiy*) class accommodation, with soft (two upholstered berths in a compartment) being equivalent to first class, and hard (four plastic berths) equivalent to second class. It's worth remembering that on overnight trains you may be obliged to pay a small supplement for your bedding, so don't spend all of your currency before boarding a train west. On many services you will be provided free of charge with tea or coffee by the attendant, called a *provodnik* (male) or *provodnitsa* (female), and hot and cold water is usually available.

Russians and non-Russians both use roubles to buy train tickets, but prices for non-Russians are about 20% higher. The hostels in St Petersburg and Moscow will order tickets for you for around a £3 ($5) handling charge, which saves a lot of wasted energy and at least guarantees you the end product.

Bear in mind that you are unlikely to be allowed to purchase a ticket out of any former Soviet republic (not counting the Baltics) using local currency and be prepared for the fact that the cost of leaving Russia will not be in line with the cost of living in the country. Stories abound of Eurorailers being charged extortionate sums of money to go home, and in this respect the hostel services represent something of a lifeline.

All travellers crossing into Russia by train must be prepared for a lengthy wait at the border whilst all the train's wheels are changed to fit the wider Russian tracks.

One final word of warning: crossing your legs in the 'American' manner (one foot balanced on the other leg) is considered the height of bad manners. You could find yourself emptying a compartment of sensitive Russians by forgetting this peculiar fact.

**PASSES AVAILABLE** Russia is not yet linked into any international schemes. For cheap rail travel, contact the Traveller's Guest House in Moscow or the Sindbad Travel Agency at the International Hostel in St Petersburg (addresses as above).

**TRAIN INFORMATION** Some officials speak English and some German, although they may be loath to do so.

**RESERVATIONS** When buying a ticket you will be given a reservation as a matter of course. It's advisable to buy your ticket well in advance. You won't be allowed to buy one on the train or to board without one. The tried and tested method of slipping an attendant a few dollars has been known to work, but unless you're in trouble it's not advisable. 'Scalpers' are often to be seen in stations selling train tickets at an inflated rate: if you've been too late to get a place on a train, it may be worthwhile taking them up.

**NIGHT TRAVEL** Most journeys you are likely to take in Russia are long enough to justify an overnight trip and all long-haul trains are designed with this in mind. Compartments have two or four berths which convert into beds. Sleeping compartments are mixed sex, and when women want to get changed, men are expected to go and loiter in the corridor.

**EATING ON TRAINS** All long-distance trains have (usually crowded) buffet cars.

**SCENIC TIPS** If you're travelling by day, the journey from St Petersburg to northern towns like Petrozavodsk across the Kola peninsula passes through beautiful tundra scenery.

## TOURIST INFORMATION

Russian tourism has yet to gear itself towards the independent traveller, and in St Petersburg and Moscow you may find that the maps provided by the hostels are the best tourist information you're likely to find in English. For an intensive guide to the whole country, the *Lonely Planet Guide to Russia* is recommended.

**VISAS** The Russian visa system is notorious as an example of rampant red tape. While visa requirements are dropping all over the world, Russia's remain strong, and any ideas of attempting to enter the country without one should be forgotten.

If you're prebooking a holiday through Intourist, then they'll handle most of the visa application process for you, but it's also possible to do it yourself. In England, this can be done by contacting the Russian Embassy, 15 Kensington Palace Gardens, London W8 4QS (Tel. 020 7229 8027). (Some overseas Russian embassies – those in Poland and the Baltics, for example – are less strict in their requirements.) You will need a passport valid for at least a month beyond your return date, three passport photos, a completed application form including your entry and exit dates and your itinerary, proof of accommodation and a fee, varying upwards from a base of £20 ($32) (depending on where you get your visa and how quickly you need it). The system is speeding up, but you should still allow at least a month.

Officially, you cannot visit a town which is not on your visa, but these days the Russian police tend to have more important things to worry about and almost certainly the worst that can happen is that you will be sent back to a town which is on your visa.

If you know somebody in Russia who can invite you and is prepared to put up with the mindblowingly obstructive bureaucracy, ask your nearest Russian embassy for invitation application forms and send one to your friend, who must fill it out and take it to the local OVIR (Russian visa) office for approval. A confirmation of approval will be sent to you, making you eligible for a visa.

Alternatively, the Traveller's Guest House in Moscow and the International Hostel in St Petersburg operate a speedy visa service which can help you obtain a visa in as little as 48 hours (for a small fee). Fax them on 095 280 7686 or 812 329 8019 respectively, giving all personal details (including passport information) and the dates you want to stay there, and they will sort out the red tape for you. Moreover, they won't necessarily hold you to stay for all the nights you have 'booked', leaving you free to move around Russia and choose your own accommodation.

Those who only want a brief taste of Russia can take the trip offered by the Finnish IYHF in Helsinki, which visits St Petersburg but is not subject to such stringent restrictions.

**MONEY MATTERS** On 1 January 1998, the rouble was redenominated, which effectively saw three zeros wiped off its value.

There are officially three exchange rates in Russia:

1. The *bank rate* is what you will get when exchanging hard currency or traveller's cheques in a bank, and is by far the best. There are exchange facilities in most cities. You may have to show your passport, visa and customs declaration form when changing money.
2. The *commercial rate* is used to calculate the price of hard-currency goods (an increasing number of Russian shops sell desirable goods for hard currency only – souvenirs, for example) and credit card purchases. It's increasingly possible to buy for roubles with a credit card in Russia, but it's hard even to calculate how much you'll lose on the transaction.
3. The *official rate* is the extremely poor one Intourist uses to calculate the cost of accommodation and so on.

There's no longer any need to change money on the black market: it's illegal, unprofitable and potentially unsafe. If you're still tempted, bear in mind that Russians are likely to have notes from the old USSR, from the various styles of currency issued by the Russian Republic and possibly from other ex-Soviet republics as well. They come in all colours and sizes and are written in Cyrillic script. If you don't feel confident you can tell which are legal, you shouldn't feel confident that you can change money on the street without being cheated. Keep exchange receipts: you may be asked to show them when you leave the country and in any case without them you will be unable to reconvert roubles to hard currency.

**POST OFFICES** Main post offices are open Mon.–Fri.: 8am–8pm. Outward post usually takes two weeks or so to reach its destination. It helps to start the address of international mail with the country name in Cyrillic: England is **Англия**. All postal services are charged in roubles. *Poste restante* facilities exist but are something of a national joke.

**SHOPS** Shopping in Russia, particularly for food, is an experience you may well be glad to leave behind. The idea is that you find the product that you want and its price, then go to a till and pay for it, at which point you will be given a ticket to take to another counter where it can be exchanged for the goods. You will truly learn the value of body language in Russia. Shops don't openly advertise themselves and it takes a bit of investigation to find them. There are shortages, certainly, but goods are available: half the problem is knowing where to look for things. *Beryozkas*, or hard currency shops, are dependable for life's little necessities like toiletries (and, indeed, food) if you despair of finding them anywhere else.

**LANGUAGE** Russian is written in the Cyrillic alphabet and it will help to familiarize yourself with it; that way you can at least make an educated guess as to what words mean (the word for 'restaurant', for example, reads like *pectopah* – in fact it's pronounced *restoran*). It was invented by a monk (named Cyril) who used a printing set from Greece and then represented some additional sounds by re-using some of the letters backwards. It will also be invaluable on Russia's metro systems.

(The Cyrillic alphabet is reproduced in the **Bulgaria** chapter.)

**TIPPING** It is really up to you how much you want to give, if anything. Restaurant prices often include a 10% service charge and more shouldn't be needed, but staff will expect a further tip as well.

## SLEEPING

Intourist will happily book you into a hotel, but the absolute *minimum* you will pay is £35 ($56) for a single. They offer campsite chalets at lower prices, but these tend to be inaccessible and, in St Petersburg's case, reputedly dangerous. Thus youth hostels have been nothing short of a godsend to budget travellers, charging £8–£15 ($13–$24): well worth it for the security they provide in a very unfamiliar world. Reservations from abroad should be made at least three weeks in advance, bookings made in Russia are accepted not more than two weeks in advance. There is no age restriction at Russian hostels.

Private accommodation is beginning to catch on in Russia and both Moscow and St Petersburg have agencies which will fix you up with a room, either in a self-contained apartment or with a Russian family – an experience you will never forget. The cost varies tremendously and you can usually choose to stay either half- or full-board. In some stations or hotel lobbies you may see a woman at a desk with a stack of postcards with addresses on them. If so, chances are you've found a private accommodation network. For a (negotiable) fee you can stay in the home of Russian citizens supplementing their income. The service isn't aimed at foreigners – few are even aware of it – so if you don't speak Russian, get ready to use body language

Russia is a very poor country, and many hotel owners, upon realizing your nationality, will request a hugely inflated sum in hard currency. Remember, they're accustomed to think of Western travellers as being extremely wealthy. The price you pay will depend on your haggling skills and obviously it helps immeasurably to be able to speak Russian. The same is true in university dorms, where room is often available if you can talk your way in. It would be unethical to advocate bribery, but Russia is a country in which the barter system is alive and well, so slipping somebody a few dollars isn't quite so illicit as it might seem.

## EATING AND NIGHTLIFE

Purchasing everyday food involves undergoing the Russian shopping experience (see above). In cities you may well find yourself snacking your way through the day on a diet of pastry creations (perfectly safe, provided they have no meat in) sold on the street by people trying, like every other Russian, to supplement their inadequate income. Food is available, but be prepared to queue, and go equipped with at least a little vocabulary.

Similarly, Russian restaurants are an experience: suffice to say that the 'customer is always right' ethic has yet to work its way this far east. Don't expect to be able to eat a meal in a hurry, as staff obviously feel that diners need time for digestion between courses – about two hours seems to be just enough. If you want fast food, go to McDonald's. In both Moscow and St Petersburg there are all sorts of restaurants, including pizzerias, Indian, French and Chinese. Hard currency restaurants are more likely to have English-speaking staff, and consequently they cost more.

Nightlife of the pub and club variety is somewhat limited, most young Russians being more inclined to sit at home with a few friends and a good supply of black market *pivo* (beer). The Russians have worked hard to get their reputation as a nation of alcoholics – there are reports of them taking beer supplies home in fully filled condoms when they can't find anything else. Should you find yourself knocking back the vodka in Russian company, remember the all-important phrase *Za Vashe Zdarovye* (spoken with gusto). It means 'Cheers!'

What discos there are usually take place in hotels. A better option is to visit the ballet or opera: at the Bolshoi or Kirov you may have to haggle with touts for tickets, but at smaller venues you can pay a minimal amount for a uniquely rewarding experience and if you're lucky you may find a free buffet included in the price. Try not to look too scruffy.

Russia can be a dodgy place for open displays of homosexuality, which only recently became legal and is still frowned on by many citizens.

# Moscow (MOCKBA) phone code: 095

The headquarters of the former Soviet Union and capital of Russia: Moscow is one of those places you could easily form a love/hate relationship with. On the one hand it's grey, bleak and lacking any sort of buzz, while on the other it's friendly, filled with colourful churches and offers more than enough to keep you fascinated for weeks. The heart of the city undoubtedly beats at the Kremlin, flanked by Red Square and the Moscow river, from which most of the centrally placed attractions can easily be reached.

## STATION FACILITIES
Moscow has eight train stations with rail links to every part of the USSR. Coming from London, Berlin or Warsaw you will arrive at Belarus station (*Belorussky Vokzal*); from St Petersburg, Finland or Estonia, Leningrad Station (*Leningradsky Vokzal*). Most trains from the Baltic States arrive at Riga station and trains from Prague and Budapest terminate at Kiev station (*Kievsky Vokzal*). Trains going to Kiev also depart from this station. Pavelets and Kursk stations serve other parts of the Ukraine. Most of these stations have lockers, left-luggage facilities, cafeterias and national rail information.

St Petersburg, Kiev and the Baltics are all comfortable overnight trips. Direct trains run to Warsaw, Berlin, Prague, Vienna, Budapest, Belgrade, Bucharest, Sofia and even Paris and London (50 hours).

**BUYING TICKETS** You will need to buy your tickets not at the station but at the Central Train Agency, ulitsa Griboeda 6 (metro: Chistie Prudy), or, for international trains, at Intourtrains, Petrovtrason 15 (metro: Okhotny Ryad).

## GETTING AROUND
All of Moscow's stations are linked by the metro, a stunningly efficient and frequently bewildering creation spanning 130 stations. Cards or tickets for use on the metro can be purchased at the stations. Unless you speak Russian, be prepared for a confusing time, as signs are in Cyrillic letters only. The *Let's Go* guide to Russia includes an English map. A recorded voice on the train will tell you which station you are approaching, but it probably won't sound like you imagined it.

Furthermore, stations where lines cross can have as many as four names. And as if all that wasn't enough, many of the station names have changed completely due to post-communist name-purging. A map is therefore very useful; use it constantly and count the number of stations you pass. You'll get the hang of it eventually and in the meantime you can admire the architecture of Moscow's metro stations: it's worth traversing the Koltsevaya (Circle) line just to see the elaborate archways and chandeliers.

## TOURIST INFORMATION AND ADDRESSES

Intourist's information desk is at ulitsa Mokhovaya 13 (Tel. 292 1278), but the only thing they're liable to be able to help you with is entertainment information, an expensive bed or English-language tours of the city. Try their information line (203 6962) which operates between 9am–6pm, though their limited English prevents them from being as helpful as they might. Your best bet is to start at the Traveller's Guest House, where information, maps, etc. are available.

**UK EMBASSY** Naberzhnaya Sofiyskaya 14 (Tel. 956 7200)

**IRISH EMBASSY** Grokholsky Pereulok 5 (Tel. 288 4101)

**US EMBASSY** Novinsky Bulvar 19–23 (Tel. 252 2451)

**CANADIAN EMBASSY** Starokonyushenny Pereulok 23 (Tel. 956 6666)

**AUSTRALIAN EMBASSY** Kropotkinsky Pereulok 13 (Tel. 956 6070)

**AMEX** Sadovaya-Kudrinskaya ulitsa 21a (Tel. 755 9000). Open Mon.–Fri.: 9am–5pm, Sat.: 9am–1pm

**CURRENCY EXCHANGE** Facilities at all banks and major hotels; the Vneshekonombank on Tverskaya ulitsa is recommended

**POST OFFICE** ulitsa Tverskaya 7, not far from the Kremlin, is the main international post office; metro (Okhotny Ryad)

**24 HR PHARMACY** Leningradsky pr. 74 or Multifarma, Tursitskaya ulitsa 27 (Tel. 948 4601)

## SEEING

The **Kremlin**, probably the most famous building or group of buildings in Russia, is bang in the middle of Moscow (metro: Okhotny Ryad, connected by an underpass). Tourists enter through the Kutafia Tower Gate, on the side nearest to the metro. Certain parts of the Kremlin are very much off-limits, but there's a lot to be seen: tourists are shepherded around **Cathedral Square** and other Russian oddities by soldiers with whistles. The cost is minimal and even half price with student ID.

Next to it, on the eastern side, is **Red Square** (*Krasnaya Ploshchad*, which actually means 'Beautiful Square'), dominated by the fairy-tale **St Basil's Cathedral**, once described as 'a box of crystallized fruits'. For a few roubles, pop in and take a look around its labyrinthine interior.

Upstream from the Kremlin is the **Lenin Stadium**, where the 1980 Olympics took place.

The excellent and diverse **Pushkin Museum of Fine Arts** is at ulitsa Volkhona 12, two blocks from metro Krouotkinskaya, though it has recently been closed for renovations (check to see whether it has re-opened). Of particular interest is the 'Trophy Art' which was seized from the Nazis in 1945 and includes many European masterpieces. Across the street is the Moskva outdoor swimming pool, where Russians are to be seen bathing at almost any time of year, regardless of the weather.

Don't be surprised to find that a dual pricing policy is in operation in Russia, whereby foreign visitors are charged substantially more than Russians for admission.

**FREE MOSCOW:**

- Set back against the walls of the Kremlin is the **Lenin Mausoleum**, where you can undergo the surreal experience of seeing Lenin's embalmed body – which looks remarkably like a waxwork. Behind it are the ashes of dozens of communist heroes, including Stalin, Brezhnev and Yuri Gagarin, to name a few. Opposite on the other side of Red Square is the **GUM** department store, a symbol of capitalism's rise in Russia and home to some big Western 'designer' names.

- Also worth seeing is the **Lenin Museum** at Ploshchad Revolyutsii 2, a little way to the north-east. It houses a vast collection of memorabilia about the man himself and will help you realize the full impact he had on Russia and the world (currently closed for repair, so check before visiting).

- Even though the future of the **Arbat** (metro: Arbat) is uncertain it remains a hive of industry in the city. It's a pedestrianized precinct which has long been a haven for free expression, but recently the street artists who populated it have disappeared (supposedly short term).

- For one of the best views of Moscow, head up to the **Lenin Hills**, or if a market is more up your street there's one at Tsvetnoy Bulvar, next to the Old Circus. At **Izmaylovsky Park** (metro: Izmaylovsky), not only can you enjoy a pleasant stroll, but at the weekend you can also visit its enormous market too – arrive towards the end of Sunday afternoon to pick up some bargains.

- Moscow has some great churches, monasteries and synagogues that offer wonderful interiors and are generally free to enter (or at worst, extremely cheap). Check out the **Novodevichy Monastyr** and **Smolensk Cathedral** (metro: Sportivnaya); **Donskov Monastery**, off Shabolovskaya; and the **Moscow Choral Synagogue**, Bolshoy Spasoglinischchevsky per. 10.

The following are both free at present as well.
- **Muzey Gogolya**, Nikitsky bul. 7
- **Museum of the Great Fatherland War**, inside **Park Pobedy** (metro: Kutuzovskaya)

## SLEEPING

Intourist will offer you a range of expensive accommodation from around £45 ($73), without breakfast. They also offer campsite accommodation, starting at £10 ($16) for a tent site.

There are a couple of guesthouses aimed at the budget traveller. The American-run **Traveller's Guest House**, ulitsa Bolshaya Pereyaslavskaya 50, floor 10 (Tel./Fax. 971 4059) is perhaps the best known. It's not easy to find: take the metro to Prospekt Mira, turn left, and take a right turn after about 400m: if you're heading towards four chimney stacks, you're going in the right direction. Turn left on Pereyaslavskaya, and the building – which hardly advertises itself – is on your right. Rates are £10–£27 ($17–$45) per night for dorms or doubles. There's a second guesthouse/hostel on the 7th floor of pr. Vernadskogo 88, korpus 1 (Tel. 437 9997). It's about 30mins. from the centre by metro (Yugo-Zapadnaya). It's only a small B&B hostel but it has good service. The **Prakash Guesthouse**, ulitsa Profsoyznaya 83 (Tel./Fax. 334 2598 or Tel. 334 8201), near the Belyaova metro stop, is another good option with singles from £18 ($30).

Independent Russian hotels, upon realizing your nationality, may charge as much as Intourist would, but by all means try your luck. It's impossible to recommend specific places since so much depends upon luck and timing.

For private rooms you'll find women advertising outside train stations or, alternatively, head for the lobby of the Gostinitsa Centralnaya, next door to Pizza Hut on ulitsa Tverskaya, where you may find a woman with a load of postcards offering accommodation with Moscow residents. In these cases a grasp of the Russian language will help you considerably, and a few dollars will get you a night that may provide a unique experience within easy reach of the city centre.

If you feel this is too risky, try Russian Bear Travel Services, on Prospekt Andropov 35 (Tel. 114 4223), who can arrange dorm-style accommodation in apartments around the city from £5 ($8.50) upwards. There's also the Moscow Bed & Breakfast agency, phone or fax. them on 457 3508.

## EATING

Moscow has a wide variety of eateries representing a surprising diversity of nationalities and catering for almost every taste. In Moscow, as in any other Russian city, a diet of pastry, popcorn and ice-cream is quite possible to get by on and is sold cheaply for roubles all over the place. Even cheaper are the acceptable cafeterias on the top floor of the GUM store. Avoid the steaming heaps of (whole) fish that go for about 7p a pile unless you are extremely strong of stomach. Some hotels reputedly still offer all-you-can-eat buffets for roubles: a bargain beyond belief. Try your luck at the **Hotel Intourist** (opposite the Kremlin) or the nearby **Moscow Bombay**, complete with English menu at Glinishchevsky per. 3. Finally, Pushkinskaya Ploshchad, a lively and youthful part of town, is the home of Moscow's first and most famous **McDonald's**. Much as you might scorn the endless queues of people anxious for a Big Mac, you'll be surprised how good one tastes after a week or so of trying to buy Russian food. **Pizza Hut** is round the corner. Expect to pay £8–£15 ($13–25) for a meal.

For nightlife there are now a lot of clubs and discos, and more opening all the time, but unfortunately, not too many that we would particularly recommend. If you really need to hit the dance floor, try the studenty **Master** at ulica Parlobskaya 6. The **Chance** club in Dom Kultury Serp I Molot (metro 7: Ploshchad Ilicha) is supposed to have a mixed gay and straight clientele too. The live music scene is very good, there are always gigs going on at various venues in the city and you may be able to catch an international group/act live as many include Moscow on their world tours. For listings, check in the *Moscow Times* and *Moscow Tribune* (written in English). To satisfy your cultural appetite, remember that Moscow also has some excellent theatres, orchestras, ballets, operas etc., with tickets often priced very reasonably.

## St Petersburg (САНКТ-ПЕТЕРСБЧРГ )
phone code: 812

St Petersburg, formerly Leningrad, is Russia's cultural capital and in many ways provides your best introduction to the country. Considered to be Russia's most European and cosmopolitan city, its wonderful buildings and canals produce an image that wouldn't immediately spring to mind when thinking of a former Soviet bloc city. Packed full to the brim with history along with a Westernized accommodation system, enjoy the city while you can, as the rest of the country will no doubt feel very different.

Warning: Don't drink the water in St Petersburg. It is infested with the giardia parasite which causes diarrhoea. Even brushing your teeth in the tap water may infect you. Always use bottled water.

## STATION FACILITIES

St Petersburg has four main stations. Moscow station (*Moskovsky Vokzal*) at Ploshchad Vosstaniya, just off Nevsky Prospekt, at Naberezhnaya Kanala Griboedova, handles trains to Moscow and most of Russia; Warsaw station (*Varshavsky Vokzal*), at Naberezhnaya Obvodnogo Kanal 118, handles trains to and from Eastern Europe and the Baltics; and Vitebsk station (*Vitebsky Vokzal*) at Zagordnoy Prospekt 52, covers Belarus and most of the Ukraine. These three are all south of the Neva river. Finland station (*Findlandsky Vokzal*) on Ploshchad Lenina, handles trains to and from Scandinavia.

Direct international services to and from St Petersburg include the Baltic capitals, Helsinki (two trains a day, journey time seven hours), Warsaw and Berlin. Domestic lines cover much of European Russia and the Ukraine.

Moscow station has the best facilities, including a full range of restaurants, shops, a left-luggage store and lockers. The others all have lockers and travel information.

**BUYING TICKETS** Foreigners are supposed to buy their tickets at the central ticket office on Nevsky Prospekt, but Moscow station has an Intourist window on the second floor which should be able to help. The International Youth Hostel will buy tickets on your behalf for a £3 ($5) fee.

## GETTING AROUND

St Petersburg's metro is less extensive than Moscow's, but equally efficient and no less confusing. Many trains have outer doors which prevent you seeing the station as you arrive; and although each station is announced upon arrival, the recorded message also states the next one, which is confusing if you're listening for one name. As in Moscow, count the stations and carry a map at all times.

## TOURIST INFORMATION AND ADDRESSES

Tourist Information in the conventional sense may prove to be a problem, but this might be alleviated by a planned new Tourist Office, scheduled to open on Nevsky Prospekt, just opposite the Grand Hotel Europe. If not, try OST-WESTContact Service, at ulitsa Mayakovskovo 7–27 (Tel. 279 7045), who can provide plenty of free information on all aspects of the city. Intourist's office is at Isaakievskaya Ploshchad 11, opposite the Astoria Hotel. Note that hotel service bureaux can advise on travel, entertainment, etc., even if you're not staying at the hotel in question.

The **International Youth Hostel** gives out a useful map which includes a suggested city tour and there's a helpful travel agency downstairs, **Sindbad Travel** (Tel. 327 8384; Fax. 329 8019).

Pick up a copy of the Friday edition of *The St Petersburg Times* and a copy of the monthly *Pulse*, both are free and have good listings.

**POST OFFICE** Pochmatskaya ulitsa 9, two blocks south-west of St Isaac's Cathedral. International calls can be made here

**AMEX** Conducted through the Grand Hotel Europe, ulitsa Mikhailovskaya 1/7 (off Nevsky Prospekt) (Tel. 329 6060)

**CURRENCY EXCHANGE** All major hotels. The only bank open at weekends is opposite the Grand Hotel Europe. There are exchange offices dealing in many European currencies all along Nevsky Prospekt

**CANADIAN CONSULATE** Malodetskoselsky prospekt 32 (Tel. 325 8448)

**UK CONSULATE** Pl. Proletarskoy Diktatury 5 (Tel. 325 6036)

**US CONSULATE** ulitsa Furshtadskaya 15 (Tel. 271 6455 or 275 1701)

**MEDICAL EMERGENCY** Clinic Complex at Moskovskiy pr. 22 is open Mon.–Fri.: 9am–9pm, Sat.: 9am–3pm. The 24hr emergency phone number is 316 6272.

## SEEING

Nevsky Prospekt, St Petersburg's main street, is very much the city centre and most of the main sights are located here. However, the **Hermitage**, one of the world's greatest art galleries, lies a little to the north-east, near the river. It's open 10.30am–6pm every day except Mon. (entry for non-Russians is around £6 ($10); free for students). You could take days to explore it properly, but among its highlights are the Egyptian and Prehistoric collections and the stunning range of European art, including works by Picasso, Van Gogh and Rembrandt. The famous **Winter Palace**, a huge green and gold building halfway between garish and beautiful, is only one part of the Hermitage. In front of the Winter Palace is the **Alexander Column**, dominating one of the world's largest squares. Slightly overshadowed by Palace Square is **Arts Square** (*Ploshchad Iskusstv*), near the 5-star Grand Hotel Europe (a book in itself).

The magnificent **St Isaac's Cathedral**, offers one of the best views in St Petersburg. You can pay (around 25 roubles) to climb to its colonnade (closed Wed.), and for a further 15 roubles you can enter the spectacularly lavish interior.

Across the River Neva is **Basil's Island**, once the city centre, and **Peter and Paul's Fortress** on Zayachy Island: which was for many years a political prison – Dostoevsky and Trotsky both served time there. Open 11am–5pm every day except Wed. The bridges over the river are raised at night: don't get stranded.

For the evenings, you can get theatre tickets from 42 Nevsky Prospekt for a few pounds.

**FREE ST PETERSBURG:**

- The city has a number of architectural masterpieces to see, which have rather gruesome connections. One is the **Church of the Resurrection**, also known as the Church of Spilt Blood. Dedicated to Tsar Alexander II, killed by a terrorist bomb here in 1881, this domed building is modelled on St Basil's in Moscow. Around the corner is **Mikhailovsky Castle**, built for Paul I, who was strangled here by conspirators in 1801.
- On a lighter note, near St Isaac's Cathedral there are two celebrated photo opportunities: the **Admiralty Building**, with the sailing ship spire on its roof; and **Decembrists' Square**, with the statue of the bronze horseman dedicated to Peter the Great.
- Also on Nevsky Prospekt you'll find a **market**, the **Kazan Cathedral** (opposite the Dom Knigi bookshop), the **Catherine the Great Monument** and **Anichkov Bridge**, with its four 'horse tamer' statues.
- St Petersburg also boasts more parkland than any other Russian city, with the **Summer Gardens**, next to the **Field of Mars** (a monument to the dead of the 1917 Revolution) particularly worth a visit.
- **Hermitage**, Dvortsovaya nab. 34 - free for students otherwise it's around 60 roubles (£6/$10).
- **Museum of Theatre and Music** (Muzey Teatralnovo I Muzykalnovo Iskusstva), pl. Ostrovskovo 6 - free for students.

## SLEEPING

Although St Petersburg is better suited to budget travel than other Russian cities, it's still no easy matter to find a bed. Intourist's cheapest double will set you back around £50 ($81), while their campsite, **Gigno Motel Camping**, is notoriously dangerous.

However, the excellent accommodation booking service, OST–WEST, at ulitsa Mayakovskogo 7–27 (Tel. 279 7045) will be able to help – the staff can fix you up with B&B accommodation or find you a hotel bed. The helpful accommodation agency St Petersburg Bed & Breakfast can be called on 219 4116 and there's also HOFA which is geared to finding budget accommodation, contact them on 275 1992.

The **International Hostel** that opened in St Petersburg in 1992 represented a real watershed in Russian accommodation: run by an American, it was the first hostel in the former Soviet Union and it is hoped that many others will follow. Located on 3rd Sovetskaya ulitsa 28 (Tel. 329 8018, Fax 329 8019, e-mail ryh@ryh.spb.su), it costs £10 ($16) for members (otherwise it's £11 or $17) per night, plus a reservation fee if you use them for visa support (see **Visas**, above). It seems expensive, but it is a superb and friendly hostel and provides the kind of reassurance essential to culture-shocked travellers new to

Russia. (It also has the finest showers in the country.) To get there, turn right from Ploshchad Vosstaniya metro station (or Moscow station) on to Nevsky Prospekt, heading away from the city centre, then turn left on to Suvorovskyi Prospekt and right on to 3rd Sovetskaya ulitsa at the second traffic lights after the Phillips Store. The Sindbad travel agency based at the hostel advertises itself as being able to arrange a variety of local and national excursions.

The **Holiday Hostel** (Tel./Fax. 542 7364) at ulitsa Mikhailova 1, Vyborg Side, south of Finland station next door to the noisy prison (!), charges the same prices as the International Hostel and there's a pleasant roof-top café with great views. Other hostels you could try include **Petrovskiy Hostel** at Baltiyskaya ulitsa 26 (Tel. 252 5381) or **Herzen University Hostel** at Kazanskaya ulitsa 6 (Tel. 314 7472), near the Kazan Cathedral, off Nevskiy prospekt.

University dorms require a lot of haggling and probably a little bribery to get into, but again may be worth a try; Plekanova 6 is the best situated, and Grazhdansky Prospekt 28 (metro: Grazhdansky Prospekt) is the more promising. Be prepared to pay in hard currency if you do have any luck.

## EATING

Street food is available in abundance in St Petersburg, with dozens of stalls along the main streets selling the usual array of pastry and ice-cream: which includes a branch of **Baskin & Robbins** on Nevsky Prospekt 79. In the dingy-looking cafeterias that line Nevsky Prospekt below street level, you can get a coffee for the equivalent of a few pence.

Worth a look are **Kafe** on Karavan ulitsa, right off Nevsky Prospekt; **Chicken Grill Café**, on Prospekt Provishcheniya 84 (metro Gradzhinsky Prospekt); and, for the homesick, there is an English pub restaurant on Nevsky Prospekt.

The **Winter Garden** restaurant in the Astoria still has a rouble menu – this will almost certainly be the only time you'll ever eat a three-course meal with caviar in a 4-star hotel for under £10 ($17). Along similar lines, the **Restaurant Metropol** kept its grand decor as a watering hole for Party officials, and is now very reasonably priced (ulitsa Sadovaya 22). As in Moscow, keep your eyes peeled as new restaurants open and old ones close down on a daily basis.

## Elsewhere in European Russia

Stepping outside of Moscow and St Petersburg in Russia places you firmly off the beaten track. Entering a town that isn't listed on your visa is technically illegal, though the continued slackening of restrictions means you're unlikely to find yourself in trouble for going a little out of the way.

From St Petersburg, north-western Russia can be considered a straightforward, easy trip (by Russian standards). **Novgorod** and **Pskov**, two of Russia's oldest cities, are situated about 250 km south of St Petersburg. Heading north, you enter the tundra: **Murmansk**, on the White Sea, is the world's largest city inside the Arctic Circle, where the sun doesn't rise in December. The Kola peninsula is a region of unparalleled forest scenery.

Within reach of Moscow is the **Golden Ring**, a circle of towns which existed long before the capital. Intourist have been plying these towns for tourism for many years, and with good reason: the old Russian architecture can't be rivalled anywhere else in the country. Suzdal, Vladimir, Yaroslavl and Rostov-Veliky can all be reached from Moscow's Yaroslavl station.

# Belarus

Being hauled off an overnight train and forced to fork out on a one-day transit visa doesn't really do a lot for your first impressions of Belarus – you can't buy a visa in advance unless you have a letter of introduction from contacts within the country. It's a rather dull place with nothing much to attract the tourist.

Following the Chernobyl disaster in 1986, Belarus was left badly affected when 70% of the fallout landed within its borders.

**Minsk** is where some travellers choose to break their long journey from Poland to Moscow: it's not beautiful, but it is lively. Half this city's population was wiped out during World War II. Almost every building has been erected in the past 50 years, but unfortunately for the budget traveller this doesn't include any hostels, so you'll have to pay official hotel rates.

Also in Belarus is the important border town of **Brest**. If you have a chance, the huge fortress there, built to resist Napoleon and used against Hitler, is worth taking the time to investigate.

NOTES

.................................................................................................................................

.................................................................................................................................

.................................................................................................................................

.................................................................................................................................

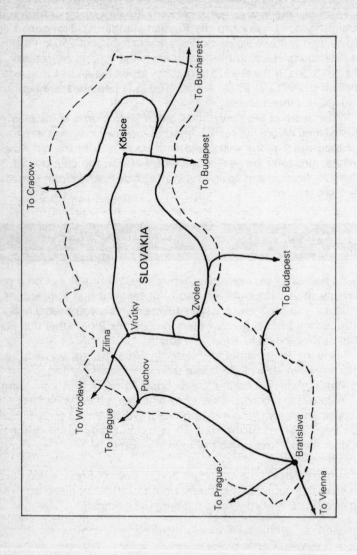

# SLOVAKIA

| | |
|---|---|
| Entry requirements | Passport. US and EC nationals do not need a visa for stays up to 90 days. Canadians, Australians and New Zealanders need visas, available either in advance or at the border. |
| Population | 5.5 million (86% Slovaks; 11% Hungarians; 1.5% Roma and 1% Czechs) |
| Capital | Bratislava (pop.: 0.4 million) |
| Currency | Slovak koruna (Sk)<br>£1 = approx. 67.5Sk |
| Political system | Republic |
| Religion | Roman Catholic |
| Language | Slovak and Czech (some German and English spoken) |
| Public holidays | Establishment of Slovak Republic (1 Jan.), Epiphany (6 Jan.), Easter Friday and Monday, Labour Day (1 May), St Cyril and Methodis Day (5 July), SNP Day (29 Aug.), Constitution Day (1 Sept.), Our Lady of Sorrows Day (15 Sept.), All Saints' Day (1 Nov.), Christmas Eve, Christmas Day and Boxing Day |
| International dialling | To Slovakia: from UK 00 + int'l code 421; from USA and Canada 011 + int'l code 421; from Australia and New Zealand 0011 + int'l code 421<br>From Slovakia: 00 + country code |
| Emergency telephone numbers | Police 158; ambulance 155; fire service 150 |

With the split of Czechoslovakia in 1993, the modern Czech and Slovak Republics were formed. However, the separation effectively left the Slovaks with the raw end of the deal, as the Czechs romped away with the majority of the country's industry and premier tourist sites. Naturally, this has left the Slovaks eager to assert their own identity and place themselves in the market as a serious destination for travellers.

The marriage of the two countries originally took place when the Czech and Slovak lands of the Austro-Hungarian Empire were joined by political union in 1918 to form Czechoslovakia. But, like so many other countries, World War II brought change, and during 1939 the supposedly 'independent state' of Slovakia emerged as a 'puppet' government, with the Germans pulling all the strings.

After the war Czechoslovakia was again 'one', though now the Iron Curtain had been drawn over it and they were to enter the traumas of the communist era. There was a brief respite, though, when an attempt was made to combine communist ideology with democracy in 1968 – but this was quickly quashed as Soviet tanks returned things to normal.

The Velvet Revolution of 1989 and its peaceful protests eventually saw the collapse of the old order and, with nationalism growing strong, the Slovak Republic declared full independence on 1 January 1993.

Although the Slovaks are still struggling with their new way of life and standards of living trail behind that of its former partner, the country has plenty going for it. For a start, with its unspoilt forests and mountains, including the High Tatras – the second highest mountain range in Europe – the country makes an ideal destination for the hiker, the skier and the somewhat curiously termed 'cyclo-tourist' (cyclist).

## SLOVAK STATE RAILWAYS
### (ŽELEZNICE SLOVENSKEJ REPUBLIKY (ŽSR))
The train system in Slovakia is less developed than in the Czech Republic and there are fewer routes available due to the mountainous terrain. However, there are some beautiful journeys to be made by rail: explore the High Tatras on an electric train, or the Low Tatras on the Brezno–Margecany run, following the Hailec and Hron rivers. The Banská Bystrica–Diviaky line is also very scenic.

ŽSR run two types of train, the local train which stops everywhere (osobný vlak) and the direct (rýchlik), which only stops at the larger places en route. Train travel is very cheap and tickets on the local train cost about half the price of direct train tickets. Inter-city (IC) and Euro-city (EC) are the fastest and these require a supplement to be paid (pay the supplement before you board as it's more expensive when purchased on the train). Tickets for domestic journeys can be bought from the station, either on the day of travel or before. Fast trains have first-class compartments and a ticket to travel in one costs 50% more than in standard accommodation. It may be advisable to upgrade if you plan to travel on a busy route at a peak time as it should guarantee you get a seat. Most stations have a left luggage office (around 20Sk) and/or lockers (5Sk).

**PASSES AVAILABLE** Slovakia is in Inter-Rail Zone D, along with the Czech Republic, Poland, Hungary, and Croatia. To tour a single zone for 22 days costs £159. (For further details of the eight Inter-Rail zones, refer to the Inter-Rail section in Part One of this guide.)

For information on the Euro Domino ticket and the Central Europe Pass, see the relevant sections in Part One of this guide.

There is also a Czech Republic/Slovakia Explorer Pass available to holders of an ISIC card and under 26s. They are valid for seven consecutive days and give unlimited travel on the national railways of the two countries. It is priced at £58 for 1st class travel and £38 for 2nd class travel. Supplements, seat reservations, couchettes and sleepers still have to be paid. These passes can be bought from

USIT/Campus Travel. (Campus Travel, 52 Grosvenor Gardens, London SW1W OAG (Tel. 020 7730 3402). Eurail Passes are not valid.

## TRAIN INFORMATION

When reading timetables, bear in mind that the Slovak for Arrival is *Prichod*, while Departure is *Odchod* (abbreviated to *prich.* and *odch.*). *Chodi* (running on) or *nechodi* (not running on) plus either a number or a symbol, 1–6 = Mon.–Sat., two hammers indicate a weekday and a cross represents Sunday, will tell you when the train departs/arrives.

**RESERVATIONS** Trains are busy so try to reserve well ahead of time to be sure of a seat. This is obligatory on some faster trains marked with an **r** or *míst.* If travelling on to Hungary it is essential to specify the route you wish to take, the main crossing points being Štúrovo and Komárom.

**NIGHT TRAVEL** Sleepers (*lehatkovy vozeň*) and couchettes are available on all long journeys. Sleepers are reasonably priced but should be booked as far in advance as possible and at least six hours before departure. In recent years numerous thefts have been reported from couchettes on international journeys, so beware.

**EATING ON TRAINS** There is either a restaurant car or buffet on selected fast trains.

## TOURIST INFORMATION

Throughout the country the official tourist agency is SATUR, though within the capital the Bratislava Information Service (BIS) provides general info and can be used for arranging accommodation. The student travel agency continues, for the time being, to operate as CKM.

**MONEY MATTERS** 1 Slovak koruna (Sk) = 100 hellars (hal).
Banking hours are Mon.–Fri.: 8am–3pm. There is no minimum currency exchange and the black market has died down.

**POST OFFICES** Open Mon.–Fri.: 8am–5pm, closed Sat. afternoons.

**SHOPS** Typically 9am–5/6pm, shutting at noon on Saturdays except in large towns. Smaller shops often close for lunch and very few shops are open on Sun.

**MUSEUMS/GALLERIES** Open Tues.–Sun.: 8/9am–4/5pm. Generally closed Mon. in the summer. Some museums change their opening days in the winter when they are open Mon.–Fri. and closed at the weekends. Tickets are usually under 40Sk and normally around 20Sk.

## SLEEPING

As with the Czech Republic, the accommodation situation, although improving, is still not too good. Demand continues to outstrip supply;

beds can be expensive (although they are generally cheaper than those in the Czech Republic); and lack of infrastructure poses problems. There are some HI-affiliated hostels but they vary tremendously in standard – some are primarily used by local workers and are quite unused to foreigners coming to stay although they will accommodate you if there is space. Likewise, campsites (*autokemping*) vary in quality, though there are plenty of them. Many also have bungalows to rent but these are often block-booked by school groups. Most sites are open from Apr./May to Sept. with few staying open all year. In Bratislava, the university lets out student rooms in July and Aug. However, your best bet is to stay in one of the new privately-owned pensions or in a private room.

## Bratislava phone code: 07

With Slovakia's independence in 1993, Bratislava was transformed into the country's capital. This level of responsibility, however, is nothing new to the city, as for three centuries it was also the headquarters of the Hungarian Kingdom (and where their monarchs were crowned). But while it fails to get swamped with tourists the way its opposite number, Prague, does, it still has over 400 buildings of historical interest to help whet your cultural appetite.

### TOURIST INFORMATION
The Bratislava Information Service (BIS) is at Klobučnícka 2 (Tel. 533 3715; open Mon.–Fri.: 8am–4.30pm (to 7pm in summer); Sat.: 8am–1pm), where you can book accommodation, get a copy of the *Kam v Bratislave* ('Where to Go') publication, and buy a map of the city – they also speak some English. There's another smaller BIS at the train station. The SATUR office at Jesenského 5–9 can be used for booking accommodation as well, while the student agency is at Hviezdoslavovo námestie 16.

### ADDRESSES
**UK EMBASSY** Panská 16 (Tel. 531 9632)
**US EMBASSY** Hviedoslavovo námestie 4 (Tel. 533 3338)
**CANADIAN CONSULATE** Kolárska 4 (Tel. 361277)
**AMEX** C/O Tatratour, Mánesovo nám 3 (Tel. 317965)
**POST OFFICE** The main post office is at námestie SNP 35
**STUDENT TRAVEL OFFICE** CKM 2000, Obchodu 21 (Tel. 5273 1024)
**24-HR PHARMACY** námestie SNP 20
**MEDICAL EMERGENCIES** Go to Mýtná 5

## SEEING

Towering over the city is the 13th-century **Bratislava Castle**. After being burnt down in 1811 and suffering damage during the war, it is now restored and houses the Slovak parliament and the **History Museum**. The nearby **St Martin's Cathedral**, with a distinctive golden crown on its tower, dates from the 14th century and is the resting place of several Austro-Hungarian kings and queens. The **City Museum**, inside the 15th-century **Old Town Hall**, has an interesting torture hall as well. Near the Danube, at Vajanského nábr, lies the **Slovak National Museum**, with collections of geological and natural history. Also worth a visit are: the **Town Gallery**, in the Mirbachov Palace at Franiškánske námestie, which displays 17th–19th-century art; the **Museum of Arms and Fortification** in St Michael's Tower, the only remaining medieval tower in the city; and the nearby **Pharmacy Museum** and palaces where the likes of Mozart and Liszt played their early concerts. For a spectacular view of the city and its surroundings, hop on a bus to Železnà Studničká and take a chair-lift through the forest to the summit of Kamzik.

**FREE BRATISLAVA:**
* Amble along the banks of the Danube to the ultra-modern **SNP Bridge** spanning the river below the castle (although you have to pay for the lift, there's a cracking panorama from the café at the top). Alternatively, one of the best places to see the bridge is from the **Sad Janka Král' Park** (where there's a funfair) on the opposite side of the river.
* Be sure to take in the great view from the castle as well, and if you want a picnic or just to take some time out, the **Grasselkovich Gardens** behind it are ideal.
* In addition to checking out the city's **Cathedral**, also pop along to the following:
* Art Nouveau **Little Blue Church** at Bezručova.
* **Corpus Christi Chapel** on Panská.

## SLEEPING

Try BIS, SATUR or the student agency CKM (see above for addresses) for accommodation suggestions. For a small fee, these offices can also book centrally located private rooms. Alternatively, check out the posters at the station for details of private rooms and hostels. The **Bernolák** hostel at Bernolákova 3 (Tel. 397723) is highly recommended. Take tram 3 to get there. Otherwise, there's a **YMCA Interpoint hostel** at Karpatská 2 (Tel. 398005). Walk from the station to Malinovskeho Street, turn left and it's five minutes from here.

For **camping**, take tram 2 or 4 to the last stop at Zlaté Piesky (Tel.

257018), where there are two lakeside sites (neither of which are particularly pleasant), which also offer bungalows for rent all year round. (Tent camping is only available May–Sept.).

## FOOD, DRINK AND NIGHTLIFE

For food, try the wine bars or beer halls. The largest beer hall in Central Europe is reputedly **Stará Sladovňa**, at Cintorinska 32. The wine bar **Velki Frantiskani** at Františkánská 10 is in an old cellar and offers good local food with occasional folk music. The local Slovak wine is worth a try. For cheap fast-food and drink, try **Gurmian** at Poštova Str. in the city centre. Good pizzas can be found at **Umag Pizzeria**, on the corner of nám Slobody and Žilinská. There are two excellent bars which have live jazz some nights of the week, **17's Bar** at Hviezdoslavovo nám 17 and **Aligator** at Laurinská 7. For a less sedate evening, go to **Charlie's Pub** at Spitálska 4 which has dancing and loud pop music. If it's a club you're after, check out **Galéria Duna** at Radlinského 11 – rock bands often perform here – or, for somewhere slightly different, **U-Club** which is in a nuclear bunker underneath the Hrad.

**EXCURSIONS** Take a boat trip to the ruined 9th century **Devin Castle**: once an impressive fortress of the Holy Roman Empire. During the summer they run from Osobne pristavisko. Trips are also available to Vienna and Budapest.

# Košice phone code: 095

Slovakia's second biggest town of Košice also acts as the administrative hub of the Republic. Historically it dates back to the 13th century when it was an important centre within the Hungarian state. Today, the Hungarian connection still survives, represented by a strong community which helps create a lively cosmopolitan feel.

The AiCES tourist office is at Hlavná 8 (Tel. 622 6938). Open Mon.–Fri.: 9am–5pm, Sat.: 9am–1pm. Ask for information on private rooms and campsites. The CKM Slovakia, Hlavná 82, provides details of student accommodation. There are a few two-star hotels, but these tend to be fairly busy. The youth hostel, **Domov mládeže**, (Tel. 642 9052) is on the western side of town at Medická 2. The Satur office is in Hotel Slovan at Hlavná 1 (Tel. 622 3122). Go there to reserve sleepers and couchettes and buy international train and bus tickets.

The dominating centrepiece of the old town is **St Elizabeth's Cathedral**, the country's biggest church and arguably its finest example of Gothic architecture. Nearby stands **St Michael's Chapel** and the **Urban Tower**, decorated with old tombstones. In the courtyard of the intriguingly named **Executioner's Bastion** – once part of the city's defences – lies the **Rakoci Palace**, now a technical museum. Also worth a visit is the **Miklus Prison**, now a museum.

If you're feeling peckish, try one of the huge sandwiches made by **Bageteria** at nám Slobody 40/74. **Bakchus** at Hlavná 8 also does good cheap food.

**EXCURSIONS** To get to the **High Tatra** mountains, take the train to the industrial town of Poprad-Tatry and then a local service up into the hills. Trains go to Stary Smokovec and Tatranska Lomnica, where there is a campsite.

NOTES
..................................................................................................................
..................................................................................................................
..................................................................................................................
..................................................................................................................
..................................................................................................................
..................................................................................................................
..................................................................................................................
..................................................................................................................
..................................................................................................................
..................................................................................................................
..................................................................................................................
..................................................................................................................
..................................................................................................................
..................................................................................................................
..................................................................................................................

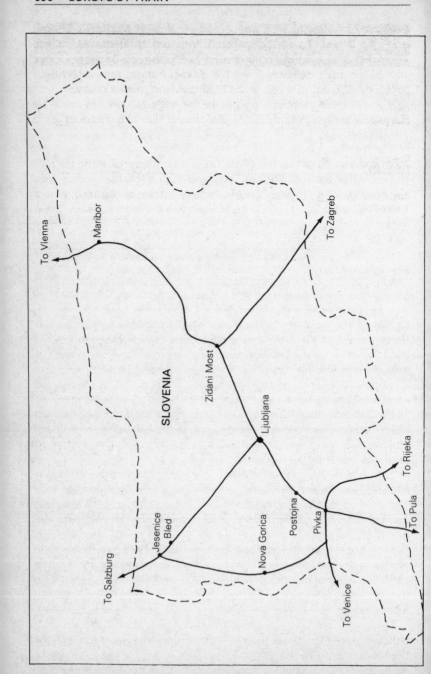

# SLOVENIA

| | |
|---|---|
| Entry requirements | Passport |
| Population | 2.2 million |
| Capital | Ljubljana (pop.: 0.3 million) |
| Currency | Tolar (SIT) |
| | £1 = approx 305SIT |
| Political system | Parliamentary republic |
| Religion | Roman Catholic |
| Language | Slovenian (some English, German and Italian understood) |
| Public holidays | New Year's Day and 2 Jan., Prešeren Day (8 Feb.), Easter Sunday and Monday, Day of Uprising (27 Apr.), Labour Day (1 and 2 May), Whit Sunday, National Day (25 June), Assumption Day (Aug. 15), Reformation Day (31 Oct.), All Saints' Day (1 Nov.), Christmas Day and Boxing Day |
| International dialling | To Slovenia: 00 + int'l code 386 |
| | From Slovenia: 00 + country code |
| Emergency telephone numbers | Police 113; ambulance 112; fire service 112 |

Out of all the republics to break away from Yugoslavia, Slovenia has been the pick of the crop, flourishing under its new independence – though being the most westernized of the republics to begin with, it enjoyed a significant head start. With its beautiful, varied landscape and rich history, the country has the feel of a scaled-down version of Austria or Italy and at a bargain price too!

The Slovenes have been in the region since the 6th century, with history seeing them come under the cosh of the Germans, the Romans and the Habsburgs who, from the 13th century, ruled almost right up until World War I.

Between the World Wars, the country formed part of the 'Kingdom of Serbs, Croats and Slovenes', after which it was incorporated into Tito's communist Yugoslavia. In 1947 the Italian Istrian peninsula was also added and so Slovenia was able to paddle in the waters of the Adriatic.

After becoming the first Yugoslav republic to hold free democratic elections in 1990, the communist era came to an end when Slovenia voted in favour of independence. This was declared on 25 June 1991, though it was followed by 10 days of fierce clashes with the Yugoslav federal army.

The hospitable Slovenes provide a warm welcome to tourists and, although eager to attract the wealthier visitor, they still cater well for the more financially-challenged!

## SLOVENIAN RAILWAYS
### (SLOVENSKA ŽELEZNICE, SŽ)

Slovenian trains are mostly old Yugoslav State Railway stock, though better quality than what you would find in other Eastern European countries. There are modern, electric and air-conditioned expresses between Ljubljana and Pula or Zagreb. Wherever possible stick to these between cities unless you really want to see every little town in the country. Steam trains run between Jesenice–Tomlin, via the Soča valley, Bled and Bohinjska Bistrica, departing every Thurs. from mid-June–mid-Sept. To arrange to go on this line, contact Slovenijatourist at Slovenska 58.

**PASSES AVAILABLE** Slovenia is in Inter-Rail Zone G, geographically the largest of the eight zones, along with Italy, Greece and Turkey (which includes the ferry service between Brindisi and Patras). For further information, see the Inter-Rail section in Part One of this guide.

A Euro Domino pass for Slovenia is quite cheap, but hardly worth the effort as the rail network is not that extensive.

## TRAIN INFORMATION

The *potsniki* (slow trains) stop at every single station and are best avoided. For express services, see the *IC* or *ZV* ('green train') entries on the timetable. You will usually find an English-speaking tourist official in larger towns and tourist areas like Ljubljana and Postonja; otherwise German and Italian will get you by. If not, write down the city, train and time you want and pass it over the counter. In smaller towns there are no information offices, so keep a map and timetable handy. These are usually available free from the information office at Ljubljana station. On timetables, *odhod* or *odhodi vlakov* means 'departures' and *prihod* or *prihodi vlakov* means 'arrivals'. If you don't have time to buy a ticket, you can get one on the train for an extra 200SIT.

The main train routes into Slovenia from Austria are from Vienna to Maribor and Salzburg to Jesenice. If you don't have a rail pass it's cheaper to buy a domestic ticket from either of these Slovene stations to Ljubljana than to buy an international ticket fron Austria to Ljubljana. There are two trains a day between Munich and Ljubljana via Salzburg. Trains from Ljubljana also go to Trieste, Budapest and Zagreb.

**RESERVATIONS** Only necessary on the international expresses, but it is wise to make both inward and outward reservations before entering Slovenia to avoid the inevitable language problem. A reservation costs 160SIT.

**SUPPLEMENTS** Only on EuroCity trains. (258SIT supplement on the *Mimara* (EuroCity) train which travels by day between Munich and Ljubljana.)

**NIGHT TRAVEL** The country is too small to need sleeping facilities, but international expresses have berths and/or couchettes. Trains between Munich and Zagreb, which stop at Ljubljana, have pull-down seats. The *Lisinski* Express runs overnight between Ljubljana and Munich and sleeping carriages are available.

**EATING ON TRAINS** EuroCity trains have German-run dining cars, while the night trains usually have snack or trolley services. Food and drink are expensive, so you'd be better off bringing some sarnies.

**SCENIC TIPS** The best route is the line between Jesenice and Nova Gorica through the Julian Alps. The line from Ljubljana to Zagreb is also worthwhile and follows the Sava river along its gorge. Sit on the right on the way to Zagreb and the left on the way back.

## TOURIST INFORMATION

All major cities and tourist areas have information offices and many have English-speaking staff too. They provide leaflets and maps of sights.

**ISIC BONUSES** A lot of sights and museums give discounts to students, so before buying a ticket, make sure you ask or show your ISIC card.

**MONEY MATTERS** 1 SIT = 100 stotins.

The only unit of currency is the tolar (SIT) which is linked to the Deutschmark. As a result, exchange rates hardly fluctuate. You may find some hotels and other accommodation places still quoting in Deutschmarks (abbreviated to DEM) but it is not as common as it used to be.

Banking hours are generally Mon.–Fri.: 8am–4/5pm. (some banks are closed for lunch from 12 noon–2 or 3pm) and Sat.: 8am–12 noon. Many tourist agencies will change money and are often open longer hours. Cash will usually receive a better rate than travellers' cheques, and the Deutschmark is the preferred foreign currency. There is no black market but exchange rates do vary. Banks charge the least commission (some don't charge commission at all). Tourist offices, hotels, exchange bureaux and travel agencies charge varying rates.

**POST OFFICES** Open Mon.–Fri.: 7am–6pm (Sat. 7am–1pm). The main office in most towns stays open to 8pm. Stamps can also be bought at newsagents. While the postal service is quite good, be aware that letters without an airmail sticker will be sent overland. Post should be addressed to you at Poste Restante, 61101 Ljubljana, which goes to the main office on Slovenska Cesta 32.

**SHOPS** Open Mon.–Fri.: 7.30/8am–7pm (outside Ljubljana shops may close for lunch 12 noon–2 or 3pm), Sat. 8am–1pm).

## SLEEPING

Accommodation in Slovenia is clean and good quality though a little on the expensive side. There are not many cheap hotels but B&B

accommodation in guesthouses or private houses is easy to find. Look for signs for *penzion*, *gostišče* or *sobe* (rooms) or ask the tourist offices and travel agencies to book you a private room. Note that although this kind of accommodation is fairly cheap, many places charge up to an additional 50% for stays of less than three nights. Student dormitories (*Studenski Dom*) are available in the summer, as are youth hostels, though there are only a few official ones. Your best bet might be camping – there are lots of good sites all over the country and many have bungalows and caravans which you can rent if you don't fancy sleeping under canvas. (Bear in mind that camping 'rough' is illegal.) Staying in farmhouses is also popular although it is not a particularly cheap option. Bookings can be made through ABC Farm & Countryside Holidays (Tel. 061 576 127) at Ulica Jožeta Jame 16 in Ljubljana or at Brnik airport (Tel. 064 261 684). If you want to arrange a farmhouse stay from Britain, contact Slovenija Pursuits, 14 Hay Street, Steeple Morden, Royston, Herts SG8 OPE (Tel. 01763 852 646).

## EATING

The food here has a decidedly German flavour to it (lots of schnitzels (*zrezek*) and dumplings (*njoki*, potato ones; *štruklji*, cheese ones)). Most of the restaurants are fairly expensive, but there are also lots of pizzerias and affordable bistros. If you wander round the smaller streets you're bound to find a cheap eatery or two. Ask for the tourist menu whenever possible – it's the best value. Pubs/inns (*gostilna* or *gostišče*) are the best places to sample local fare. Soup features heavily on all menus and is usually pretty good and filling (look for *juha*; *goveja juha* is a beef broth, if it is followed on the menu by *z* something it means it has something with it (usually noodles)). Other popular, cheap dishes include deep-fried cheese with horseradish sauce *(ocvrti sir)*, different forms of sausages (*klobase*) and *zlikrofi* (ravioli filled with potato, bacon and onion). If you've got a sweet tooth, be sure to try a *gibanica* for dessert (pastry filled with poppy seeds, walnuts, apple, sultanas and cheese, topped with cream, delicious!). For picnics, takeaway stalls and farmers' markets are the places to head for. If your cash reserves are getting pretty low, go for a *burek* (a greasy pastry filled with cheese or meat), which is cheap and filling. The local wine is very drinkable, especially the dry, rich, red *Teran* (not advisable to order in restaurants as it can be very expensive). Whites include the *Renski Rizling* and the *Laski Rizling*. There are lots of different fruit brandies to try. *Slivovka* is made from plums and *Pleterska Hruška*, made from pears, is arguably the best. The local beer (*pivo*) is cheap and excellent; *Laško Zlatorog* is probably the best, although Ljubljana-brewed *Union* is just as popular. If you prefer a dark beer, ask for *temno pivo* or try the bottled *Črni Baron* (Black Baron).

# Ljubljana phone code: 061

## STATION FACILITIES

Both the bus and train station are on the north side of town. There's a Tourist Information Office inside the train station which will exchange money, at competitive rates. The 24hr left-luggage office is on the platform beside another *bureau de change*; it costs 50SIT per bag with a compulsory passport check. Train information is available on 311851.

## TOURIST INFORMATION AND ADDRESSES

The Tourist Office is located in the Old Town at Mačkova ulica 1 (in the Kresija building), near the Triple Bridge (Tel. 133 0111). Open Mon.–Fri.: 8am–7pm, Sat.: 9am–5pm. Pick up a free copy of the useful *Ljubljana Where?* The Cultural Information Centre next to Francoske Revolucije 7 can give information about the city's museums, galleries and exhibitions. Slovenijatourist, Slovenska cesta 58, sells international train tickets (one-third off the price for under 26s). If you plan to go hiking, visit the main office of the Alpine Association at Dvoržakova ulica 9 (Tel. 134 3022).

Many of the street names have been changed, so if you can't find a particular street, enquire at the main Tourist Office.

**POST OFFICE** PTT, Slovenska cesta 32; open Mon.–Fri.: 7am–8pm; Sat. 7am–1pm

**AMEX** c/o Atlas Ambassador, Trubarjeva cesta 50 (Tel. 133 2024); open Mon.–Fri.: 8am–4pm; Sat.: 8am–12 noon. (It will hold mail but doesn't cash travellers' cheques).

**AUSTRALIAN EMBASSY** Trg Republike 3 (12th floor), 61000 Ljubljana (Tel. 125 4252)

**UK EMBASSY** Trg Republike 3, 61000 Ljubljana (Tel. 125 7191)

**US EMBASSY** Pražakova 4, 61000 Ljubljana (Tel. 301485; open 9am–midday Mon., Wed. and Fri.)

**CANADIAN EMBASSY** Miklošičeva cesta 19, 61000 Ljubljana (Tel. 130 3570)

**STUDENT TRAVEL OFFICE** Erazem, Trubarjeva 7 (Tel. 133 1076)

**MEDICAL CENTRE** Zaloška cesta 7 (Tel. 133 6236). The emergency unit is open 24hrs

## SEEING

Most of Ljubljana can be seen in a day, but its charm is such that it quickly seduces you and you'll want to stay longer. The city is primarily industrial-based with the most picturesque spots lying in the **Old Town** along the banks of the Ljubljanica, a tributary of the Sava. To get there take a right out of the train station and walk down to Slovenska cesta (formerly Titova cesta) where you go left. This is the main street of the new city and is where you'll find the post office. A left turn before the post office takes you onto pedestrianized Čopova ulica where there are some nice cafés and shops. This street opens out into Prešeren Trg. On the left is the beautiful pink 17th century **Franciscan Church** and an impressive statue of one of Ljubljana's most famous sons, the poet **Prešeren**. This square is surrounded by lovely Art Noveau buildings and to the south of it flows the river which is spanned by the **Triple Bridge**. On the other side of the river you'll find the Tourist Information Centre. If you head east from here you come to the twin-towered **Cathedral of Saint Nicholas** which contains some interesting frescoes. Near the Cathedral is one of the best places to change money in town. Just queue up at the kiosk and wait your turn.

Nearby there's a **general market** on Vodnikov Trg which is worth a visit – handy for fruit and veg too (haggle like mad!) (closed on Sun.). Also have a look at the colonnade along the riverside (you can't miss it) which was designed by Plečnik (perhaps the city's most famous son who is responsible for much of the architecture in Ljubljana and Slovenia as a whole). From here you can take a street that leads up the hill to the city's most prominent landmark, its **Castle** (or *grad*). Although it's not that interesting, make sure you climb the clocktower for a superb view over Ljubljana (300SIT).

If you come back down from the castle on the other path you can either return to the Old Town by going along Reper ulica or, for a longer walk, by continuing along ulica na Grad and turning right past the **Church of St Florian**, and either right again into Gornji trg or straight along Rožna ulica onto Karlovška cesta which takes you past the **Church of St James** (worth a look in), before crossing back over the river and turning right on to Gosposka ulica. To the left is **Križanke**, the former 17th-century monastery complex which was restored by Plečnik and it is now a major venue for gigs and concerts. The annual summer festival also takes place here. Just near here, on Trg Francoske Revolucije, is the **Ilirija Column** which was put up to recognize Napoleon's attempt to create an Illyrian fiefdom, with Ljubljana as its centre. On the other side of Gosposka ulica is the **Municipal Museum** (open Tues.–Sat., 9am–7pm; Sun. 2pm–6pm. Entrance is 500SIT; 300 for students). The **Ursuline Church of the Holy Trinity** on Slovenska cesta is just past the university and a left through the park. It dates from 1726 and has a fabulous altar by Robba. Other museums and galleries (all closed Mon.) worthy of a visit include the **National Museum** on Muzejska ulica, the **Museum of Modern Art** at Cankarjeva ulica 15 and the **National Gallery** at Cankarjeva ulica 20.

**FREE LJUBLJANA:** There are a few things to do that won't trouble your pocket too much.

- If you fancy a picnic or some leisurely walking, head for **Tivoli Park** to the north-west of the city where you'll also find **Tivoli Castle**. Nearby, the wooded **Roznik Hills** are good for a scenic ramble too.
- From the middle of July until September the **International Summer Festival** in Križanke provides music, dance and theatre (only some of the shows/events are free). You can also enjoy live jazz performances in **Jazz Club Gajo** at Beethovnova 8. Open Mon.–Fri. 10am–2am, Sat. and Sun.: 6pm–midnight.
- Don't forget the **Francickanska cerkev** (Franciscan Church) and **Uršulinska cerkev** (Ursuline Church) are both free as well. So is the **Orthodox Church of Sts Cyril and Methodius** (open Tues.–Sat., 3pm–6pm; go up Cankerjeva cesta and turn right onto Prešernova cesta) the modern frescos are worth a visit and you can get to Tivoli Park easily from here.
- On the south side of the river, not far from the Cathedral, in Mestni trg there is the impressive town hall to see with its Gothic courtyard. In front of it is the Baroque **Robba Fountain** which was modelled on the one in Rome.
- For a great view of the city, go to the top of the Art Deco skyscraper, **Nebotičnik**, on Slovenska cesta. There's a café there which serves excellent ice cream.

## SLEEPING

Student hostels are available in summer. Try **Dijaški Dom Tabor** (Tel. 321 067) which is centrally located opposite the Park Hotel.on Vidovdanska ulica 7. Expect to pay around 3000SIT for a single or 2400SIT for a bed in a double or treble. Breakfast is included. A cheaper hostel can be found out of the centre in the Bežigrad district: **Dijaški Dom Bežigrad** (Tel. 342 867) at Kardeljeva Ploščad 28. Expect to pay around 1200SIT per person in a shared room. Also check with the Tourist Office for a list of private rooms or try **Camping Ježica** at the north end of Dunajska cesta on the edge of town (Tel. 168 3912) which is open all year; take bus 6 or 8.

## EATING, DRINKING AND NIGHTLIFE

There's no problem eating cheaply, which is good news for your pocket. What's more, there's plenty of choice too, including the great *burek* stand outside the train station, the self-service restaurants in the New Town, and the small eateries scattered throughout the Old Town. New restaurants are springing up all the time and there are lots of trendy places to eat and drink. For good traditional food try **Kolovrat** at Metodov trg 14, opposite the Cathedral; for pizza you can't beat

**Romeo** at Stari Trg 6, though some prefer the pizzas at **Dvor** which is on the other side of the river. Great pasta can be had at **Fortunat**, Eipprova 1a. There are also a few Chinese and Indian restaurants but they are all on the expensive side. The best Chinese is at **Zlati Pav** at Zarnikova ulica 3. If you're after a burger, there's a McDonald's on Čopova ulica and a **Dairy Queen** on Slovenska cesta.

There are lots of excellent watering holes in town. If you're craving a Guiness, go to **Holidays' Pub** on Slovenska cesta. Other places to try include **Sax Pub**, by the river on Eipprova; **Orto Bar** on the corner of Bolgarska and Grabloviceva, east of the station, which has live-rock evenings; **KUD**, Karunova 4, is a little way out but it's trendy and popular with students and there's often live music or performing arts being staged, and **Flex**, a cellar bar off Slovenska cesta which stays open till the wee hours.

If you fancy a boogie, try **K4** at Keršinikova 4 (one gay night each week) which plays alternative music, for more mainstream sounds, go to **Klub Manhattan** in the Tivoli Recreation Centre in Tivoli Park or **Eldorado** at Nazorjeva ulica 4.

**EXCURSIONS** For an excellent day trip visit **Postojna Caves**. You can get there by train or bus but the bus drops you nearer the caves. Entrance costs 2000SIT (1000SIT with ISIC) and includes a ride on a little train and a multi-lingual tour which lasts a couple of hours. If you enjoy a 'natural wonder' it's well worth the money – the formations here rank second only to Carlsbad Caverns in the USA. Take a jumper as it gets quite cold inside (10°C) or hire a cloak for 200SIT or so. Note, no photography allowed.

Nearby is **Predjamski Grad**: a restored castle built against a cave in the cliff. Admission is 500 SIT (students 250 SIT), which also includes access to the cave. You can either walk the seven km from Postojna or catch a bus from the bus depot and ask the bus driver to let you off at the *Grad*. It's a signposted 10-minute walk along dirt roads from there. Buses run every hour and as you come round the bend, first sight of the castle brings a chorus of clicking cameras.

# Lake Bled phone code: 064

Approximately 56 km from Ljubljana, Bled lies at the foot of the Julian Alps close to the Austrian border. Hourly buses run there (a 90-minute journey) from the capital or take a train to Lesce, 5km outside and then a 10-minute bus trip. There's also a branchline train station (Bled Jezero) near the lake, not far from the campsite.

Although a spa resort, it has not lost any of its character or charm and remains popular all year. The **Castle** and **Museum** (400SIT admission) on the hill overlooking the lake offer some spectacular views of the beautiful island. You can also take a gondola trip which will let you spend about half-an-hour on the island for around 1000–1500SIT per person. If you're feeling a little more energetic, find a couple of fellow Eurorailers and rent a rowing boat for about the same price.

The **tourist office** is next to the Park Hotel at Cesta Svobode 15, (Tel. 741 122) and is open Apr.–Oct., Mon.–Sat.: 8am–7pm, Sun.: 10am–6pm. During the winter the hours are Mon.–Sat.: 9am–5pm and 12noon–4pm on Sun. Pick up a *Bled Tourist Information* booklet here (in English).

The **youth hostel** at Grajska cesta 17 (Tel. 745251; Fax. 745250) is open year round and is conveniently located next to the bus station. Prices are around 1900SIT per dorm bed. Breakfast is extra. The hostel and its surroundings are excellent, but there are only 56 beds, so book ahead to avoid disappointment.

**Camping Zaka** (summers only, Tel. 741117) on the west side of the lake (the side nearest the train station) is in a great location and has good facilities, including a beach, tennis courts and a supermarket. It fills up quickly so phone ahead if possible and have a contingency plan.

## Lake Bohinj phone code: 064

Bohinj is 28 km south-west of Bled. The bus journey there passes through stunning scenery, but nothing can prepare you for the beauty of the lake which is surrounded by high mountains. In a way it is a wilder, less developed version of Bled. Bohinj is the name of the whole valley and the small town a few kilometres to the east of the lake is called Bohinjska Bistrica. Ribčev Lav is the little settlement on the lakeside which has everything you could need on the one road; a friendly **tourist office**, post office, supermarket, restaurant, bus stop, disco and travel agency which can fix up sports activities in the area, such as kayaking and rafting down the Sava.

If you cross the little stone bridge from the village you come to the **Church of John the Baptist** which has incredible frescoes dating back to the 15th century. This is one of the nicest churches you'll ever come across.

The walking in the area is superb and the paths are well marked, for a challenging hike you could tackle Mt Triglav. Alternatively, take the

**cable car** up Mt Vogel (around 1000SIT return) – in the winter this is a great place to ski. The views are spectacular and there are cafés at the top. Mid-Sept. is a special time to be in Bohinj – it is when the farmers bring the cattle down from the high pasture. You can watch the cows process down the mountainside and then join in the festivities of the *Kravji Bal* (cow dance). This involves some serious drinking!

If you want to stay in Bohinj there is the large campsite, **Zlaterog**, (Tel. 723 441) on the west edge of the lake which is open fron May to Sept. Alternatively, the tourist office can fix you up with a private room.

## South-West Slovenia

**NOVA GORICA** This town offers nothing to the tourist, it just happens to be on the end of the scenic line from Jesenice. Our advice is to keep going south to Koper.

**KOPER** Slovenia's main port and, as such, a very industrialized city. However, the place is something of a hidden gem. Only 16 km south of Trieste, the town was Italian before World War II and has a very 'old world' feel to it in places.

From the train station **Muda Gate** provides entrance to the **Old Town**. Past the bridge fountain, head left to Cevljarska ulica, which will lead you to the town centre. Here is the **Town Tower**, the 15th century **Cathedral**, **Palace**, **Loggia** and the **Rotunda** all a legacy of Italian presence. A ramble through the twisting streets will uncover a variety of interesting buildings, shops and eateries.

Unfortunately, cheap places to stay just do not exist. However, in the summer months there is an HI-affiliated **hostel** in the Old Town at Cankarjeva ulica 5 (Tel. 066 391150; Fax. 066 391150). Alternatively, ask at either **Slovenijatourist** or **Kompas** for private rooms and insist on staying in the old city, as rooms here are cheaper and more interesting.

NOTES

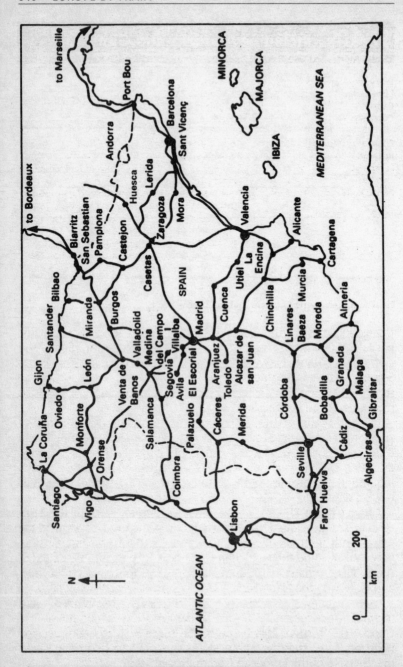

# SPAIN (including Andorra and Gibraltar)

| | |
|---|---|
| Entry requirements | Passport. |
| Population | 39.1 million |
| Capital | Madrid (pop.: 3.2 million) |
| Currency | Peseta (ptas) |
| | £1 = approx. 264ptas |
| Political system | Constitutional monarchy |
| Religion | Roman Catholic |
| Language | Spanish, Basque, Catalan, Galician and Valencian (some English spoken) |
| Public holidays | New Year's Day (1 Jan.), Epiphany (6 Jan.), Good Friday, Easter Monday, May Day (1 May), Corpus Christi (early or mid-June), 25 July, Feast of the Assumption (15 Aug.), National Day (12 Oct.), All Saints' Day (1 Nov.), Constitution Day (6 Dec.), Feast of the Immaculate Conception (8 Dec.), Christmas Day. |
| International dialling | To Spain: int'l code 34 + 9 |
| | From Spain: 07 + country code |
| Emergency telephone numbers | All emergencies 091 |

Occupying most of the Iberian Peninsula, Spain serves you not just paella and tapas, but also a wide variety of landscapes, traditions and culture. This diversity, which sees five different languages spoken – Spanish, Catalan, Basque, Galician and Valencian – stems from the separate kingdoms that covered it during a long period of Christian reconquest from the Muslims.

In the middle of the 15th century, the most powerful of the kingdoms united when Ferdinand of Aragon married Isabella of Castile – and started what was to be a significant 100 years of Spanish history. By 1492 they had unified the whole of the country; the Spanish Inquisition had been introduced; and a certain Christopher Columbus was on his way to discovering the New World.

Charles I and Philip II continued the couple's work in the 16th century, and developed its empire into one of the most powerful in the world, with the majority of Central and Southern America, parts of Italy, Portugal and the Netherlands all under its belt. But the defeat of the Spanish Armada in 1588 saw the country's fortunes begin to sink and, following the Napoleonic Wars, it eventually lost its colonies.

More recently, the first half of this century gave rise to a left-wing republic which culminated in the Civil War of 1936–39 and the start of Franco's dictatorship. After his death in 1975, King Juan Carlos became head of state, steering Spain along the road to democracy and membership of the European Community in 1986.

Today, Spain basks in the scorching trade of its tourist industry, offering the more popular stereotyped images of moorish architecture and flamenco, along with a portion of not-so-popular crowded, concreted coasts.

## SPANISH NATIONAL RAILWAYS
### (RED NACIONAL DE LOS FERROCARRILES ESPAÑOLES, RENFE)

The last few years have seen significant investment to produce improvements on RENFE, and this is still going on. The trains are now clean, punctual and reasonably priced. Unfortunately, supplements are required on all fast trains and the system of supplements is rather confusing. You often have to change trains at the Spanish border, so don't go for a sleeper from France unless you're travelling on a *Talgo*, which adjusts its wheels to the broader gauge. Check carefully in the timetable to see if you will have to change. The AVE high-speed service is about the best in the country, it links Madrid and Seville in only two and a half hours (RENFE are so confident of the AVE trains' efficiency, they even offer money back if their arrive more than five mins late). The *Automotor* trains which cover the medium-haul routes at semi-fast speeds are both comfortable and air-conditioned, and are a better bet than non-air-conditioned expresses. It's safe to say that all non-supplement trains are pretty slow and crowded, but they'll get you there in the end. The *Tranvías* and *Correos* (locals) crawl along and are only for the stalwart. Some routes are now impossible without supplements being paid, Algeciras–Madrid being an example. The RENFE computer is linked to the Rail Europe Travel Shop at London Piccadilly, so you can book ahead from the UK, either at 179 Piccadilly or through appointed travel agents.

**NON-RENFE LINES** A few lines in Spain are not run by RENFE and do not accept rail passes. They are the narrow-gauge lines from Hendaye to Gijón, Gijón to Ferrol, Palma to Inca, Valencia to Gandia and Barcelona to Montserrat.

**PASSES AVAILABLE** Europass, Eurail and Inter-Rail passes are all valid. Spain is in Inter-Rail Zone F, along with Portugal and Morocco. For further details of the Inter-Rail zones, refer to Part One of the guide. Note that Inter-Rail users have to pay a supplement on Talgo and InterCity services and full fare on the high-speed AVE service between Madrid and Seville.

Information on the Euro Domino is also available on p. 23.

The Explorerail pass provides unlimited 2nd-class travel on long-distance trains, excluding International, AVE, Talgo 200, Euromed and suburban trains for seven, 15 or 30 days on the RENFE network. Respective prices are £73, £88 and £115.

In such a highly developed, tourist-led country as Spain there are also, unsurprisingly, an enormous range of rover tickets and discounts. These include 'blue days', 'red days' and the *Chequetrén*, which is available for families or individuals and gives a discount of 15% if you spend enough pesetas.

RENFE operates a discount for all standard fares on about 300 days per year called 'blue days' (*días azules*) when you can expect a 25% or so reduction. The number of these days varies according to the time of year. On the other hand, a 'red day' or public holiday means you'll have to pay 10% more for your ticket.

There's a straight 10% reduction for individuals taking return journeys of more than 100 km, which is applicable to all types of train and all classes.

Travellers under 26 or those with an ISIC card can buy BIJ tickets which allow 20–40% off regular second-class fares within Europe. For more information, contact Westeels in London on 020 7834 7066 or fax. 020 7630 7628.

The RENFE Tourist Card also gives unlimited travel on all long distance services – excluding high speed services – for three to 10 days within a two month period. Prices start at around 18,000ptas for three days and rise to about 46,000ptas for 10 days.

## TRAIN INFORMATION

English is not always spoken, so it pays to have a Spanish back-up prepared. Expect long queues. Due to ETA terrorist attacks, left-luggage facilities at Spanish stations are sometimes withdrawn, or subject to security checks such as X-ray examination. There are normally alternative non-official facilities though; usually in the form of some little fellow posted by the station door or in the nearest café who'll guard your luggage for the same hours at the same fee. If in doubt, ask at the station.

**RESERVATIONS** If you can face the queues it's always advisable to reserve a seat in Spain. Unfortunately, if you decide not to reserve there's no way of telling if someone else has, as reserved seats are not always indicated. On many occasions you settle down in an apparently empty compartment, only to be thrown out just when you thought you were safe. *Reservations are obligatory on all expresses.* The charge to reserve a seat on long-distance trains is 500ptas.

**NIGHT TRAVEL** Spanish couchettes sleep six and are sometimes very old and dirty – you might be better off sleeping on the floor. Sleepers are cheap, however, so all's not lost. The long-distance night train is called the *estrella*. For luxury night travel, the *Trenhotel* (trainhotel) offers sleeping compartments with their own shower and WC. A supplement is payable and advance reservation is essential.

**SCENIC TIPS** Entering from France, the most scenic route is from Toulouse over the Pyrenees, arriving at Barcelona, although if you return to France by this route you can expect to be searched thoroughly, especially if travelling from Barcelona. The main line from here on to Madrid takes in much that is typically Spanish without you having to go out of your way.

If it's mountains you're after, then it's best to head towards the north-west (León–Tuy) or the south (Córdoba–Málaga, Granada–Almería).

## TOURIST INFORMATION

The government-run tourist office has branches in all major towns and at many stations. They have an excellent collection of free handouts on all the regions of Spain. In addition, there are local city tourist offices which supply maps and more detailed information.

**ISIC BONUSES** Reduced entrance to the Prado and Bellas Aries museums. For further information, contact Viajes TIVE, Fernando el Católico 88, Madrid (Tel. 91 543 7412; Fax. 91 544 0062).

**MONEY MATTERS** 1 peseta (pta) = 100 centimos (c).
Banking hours are generally Mon.–Fri.: 8.30/9am–1.30 or 2pm, Sat.: 8.30am–1pm. From June–Sept. banks may be closed on Saturdays. Shop about, as there's no set rate of exchange, and commission rates are high. The La Caixa bank rate is very poor.

**POST OFFICES** Open Mon.–Sat: 8.30/9am–2pm and often later in larger cities (generally open till 8.30pm in provincial capitals). *Lista de correos = poste restante.*

**SHOPS** Open Mon.–Sat.: 9am–2pm, 4.30/5pm–7.30/8pm. Most shops open on Sat. but some close at 2pm and don't reopen. Department stores in large provincial capitals may keep open longer and do not shut during the day.

**MUSEUMS** Vary considerably; most open 10am and shut again for lunch 12.30/1pm, opening again at 4pm till 7pm.

**TIPPING** Tipping is said to be on the way out as most restaurants now include a service charge: however, if you want favourable treatment when you next come, round up to the next highest unit of currency above this. Otherwise add 5–10%. Give a small note to porters and attendants. It's common practice to go into a bar or café to use the WC – leave a tip on the bar if there isn't an attendant.

Note: since 1998 Spanish telephone numbers no longer have a regional code. The old codes are now an integral part of the number.

As a result, all Spanish phone numbers are nine digits long, without area codes.

## SLEEPING

Every large town in Spain has a Brujula office to help find rooms for a small fee. In addition the Tourist Information office issues lists to help freelancers. You shouldn't have any problems as there's always plenty of cheap accommodation around the stations, all of which is inspected and graded by the government. By law, prices must be shown behind the door of each room, and of late, hoteliers seem to be obeying the law. During the summer it's legal for prices to be increased by about 15%, so don't get too excited until you've worked it out.

Hotels are nearly always charged by the room, not per person. *Pensiones* and *Hostales* are officially graded (Hs = *hostal*, HsR = *hostal residencia*, P = *pensión*, CH = *casa de huéspedes* and, cheapest of all, F = *fonda*). Always check to see if breakfast is included in the price; don't assume the management will tell you. Hot showers are another extra which can cost up to 400ptas. In popular towns or resorts expect to pay at least 3,250ptas for a room.

If you think you're being done, the mere mention of *libro de reclamaciones* (complaints book) or *factora* (receipt) should sort out your problems. One of our researchers tried this out in a few establishments and found that the heavy-handed management backed off instantly.

To use any of Spain's 181 youth hostels, you'll need an IYHF card (which you can buy from virtually all hostels for around 1900ptas). Between 800–2,000ptas a night, they are amongst the cheapest accommodation you're likely to find. There is no upper age limit but priority is given to those under 26. To reserve a bed in a hostel, contact the hostel directly. The head office of Red Española de Albergues Juveniles (REAJ) is in Madrid and can be contacted at: Calle de José Ortega y Gasset 71, Madrid 28006 (Tel. 91 347 7700; fax. 91 401 8160).

If you're thinking about camping, you can get information, a map and a *Guía de Camping* (campsite guide) from most tourist offices. There are more than 800 camping sites in Spain and prices start at about 500ptas per person and per tent. Some sites are open all year but many close from Oct. to Easter. Sleeping on the beaches is another alternative, but don't make it too obvious or you'll attract trouble from the police or worse.

## EATING AND NIGHTLIFE

Spain offers some of the most affordable restaurants in Europe. Give your stomach a chance to adapt to the excess olive oil, and don't have too much seafood to start with. Once you've adapted to local conditions, there's an endless variety of regional specialities to sample, all at reasonable prices. Go for the tourist or house menu where possible, as it's usually a safe bet and works out a lot cheaper than ordering individual dishes. Expect to pay anything from 800 to 1,800ptas for your evening meal and remember that the Spaniards don't eat until at least 9pm–10pm. If there's no fixed tourist menu, ask if they do *combinados* – an all-in feast on one plate which often includes something to drink as well. For those low in funds, try *tapas* – delicious and varied titbits available at most bars – but be warned that these are not usually free. The 'Pan and Company' chain in large cities does good *bocadillos* (sandwiches). Local wine is cheap at about 250ptas a bottle, and is a much better buy than beer, though it's often rough and tastes like weak sherry. Spanish cider is excellent. Wine cellars and bars are cheaper and have more local colour than the discos, which make their living by fleecing tourists at the resorts.

The bullfighting season runs from March to October and is recommended only for the bloodthirsty. Anyone who wants to see one, but is put off by the violence, should head for Portugal, where it is illegal to kill the bull.

## Madrid

Bang in the centre of Spain, the capital, Madrid, is not one of the prettiest you'll come across and is definitely not to everyone's liking. Even so, in 1992 it was the Cultural Capital of Europe. The old town has charm, and with the Prado Museum, Madrid has one of the world's leading art galleries. It's also got a nightlife that ranks among Europe's best, and there are those that would argue it's worth a visit just for this alone. But in general the sprawling concrete districts and lack of major sights tend to see people move on to Toledo or Seville instead.

### STATION FACILITIES

Madrid has three stations: Chamartín, serving the north-east, France and eastern Spain; Atocha, serving Portugal and the south of Spain; and Norte (also called Principe Pio), handling what's left. Some trains, e.g. the Paris–Algeciras express, pass through more than one of them. There are interconnecting trains every 20 minutes, and also an underground service. Atocha station is a tourist attraction in itself: a 19th-century iron and glass palace which includes a tropical garden, cafés, bars, a restaurant and a venue for exhibitions!

Because of bomb scares, a system by which the left-luggage lockers could only be used after your kit had been X-rayed was brought in in

1995. If this is in force again it's tough luck at Chamartín, but at Atocha head for some of the bars behind the station (round Calle de Rafael de Riego), and deposit your rucksack for a few hundred ptas.

Don't be surprised if in addition to your rail ticket you get given a Metro-style ticket. This is used to pass through barriers to get to platforms.

There's a tourist information office at Chamartín along with a currency exchange. Trains occasionally may be diverted from Atocha to Chamartín due to railway works – check locally.

Daily trains to Bilbao, Paris, Zaragoza, Barcelona, Valencia, Alicante, Granada, Córdoba, Seville, Lisbon.

## TOURIST INFORMATION

The main regional Tourist Office (Tel. 91 541 2325) is at C. Princesa 1, Torre de España and there's another one at Duque de Medinaceli 2 (Tel. 91 4294951). Both are open Mon.–Fri.: 9am–7pm, Sat.: 9.30am–1.30pm. The municipal (city) office is located at Plaza Mayor 3 (Tel. 91 588 1636), open Mon.–Sat.: 10am–2pm. Pick up a free map and information leaflets here including a very good list of pensions. There is also a special student information office at the Puerta del Sol metro station.

## ADDRESSES

**POST OFFICE** Palácio de Comunicaciones, Plaza de Cibeles; open Mon.–Fri.: 8am–10pm and Sat.: 8.30am–8.30pm, Sun.: 9.30am–1.30pm. *Poste restante* and telegraphs here.

**AMEX** Plaza de las Cortes 2 (Tel. 91 572 0303 or 91 322 5500); open Mon.–Fri.: 9am–5.30pm, Sat.: 9am–12 noon

**UK EMBASSY** Calle Fernando el Santo 16 (Tel. 91 319 0200; Fax. 91 308 1033)

**IRISH EMBASSY** Po. Castellana 46 (Tel. 91 576 3500 or 91 435 1677)

**US EMBASSY** Calle Serrano 75 (Tel. 91 587 2200; Fax. 91 587 2303)

**CANADIAN EMBASSY** Calle Núñez de Balboa 35 (Tel. 91 431 4300; Fax. 91 435 7488)

**AUSTRALIAN EMBASSY** Santa Engracia 120 (Tel. 91 579 0428; Fax. 91 442 5362)

**NEW ZEALAND EMBASSY** Plaza de la Lealtad 2, 3rd floor (Tel. 91 523 0226; Fax.91 523 0171)

**EUROAID OFFICES** Oficina de Viajes RENFE, Alcala 44 (Tel. 91 531

4707) or Oficina Atencion al Viajero at Chamartin station (Tel. 91 314 0829)

**STUDENT TRAVEL OFFICE** Tive, C/Fernando Catolico 88 (Tel. 91 543 7412; Fax. 91 544 0062)

**MEDICAL EMERGENCY** Telephone 061. The Anglo-American Medical Unit is at Calle del Conde de Aranda 1 (Tel. 91 435 1823)

## GETTING ABOUT

For price and speed, the metro is the best means of getting about. It runs till 1.30am and has ten lines connecting Madrid's 164 stations: the *Let's Go* guide to Spain includes a metro map. Buy tickets from machines at stations, individually (130ptas) or in 10s (670ptas), or from kiosks or *estancos* (tobacco shops). Hang on to your ticket till you've finished the journey. Buses are pretty efficient; microbuses are the more luxurious versions of the same theme and both cost the same as the metro.

## SEEING

The **Prado Museum** is the reason why thousands of art-lovers descend on this city each summer. There are over 3,000 masterpieces here, mainly collected by the Spanish royal family in the 17th and 18th centuries. The old Spanish masters (El Greco, Goya, etc.) are well represented, and there's a fair number of Flemish works collected by the Habsburg kings of the 16th century. There's such a glut of genius here, you'll need to pay two or three visits at least. The entrance is reasonable at 500ptas (half price for students). (see **FREE MADRID**). Near the exit is a shop selling very reasonably priced reproductions, postcards and books. The Prado is open daily (except Mon.), Tues.–Sat.: 9am–7pm, Sun.: 9am–2pm. Your ticket to the Prado also admits you to the **Casón del Buen Retiro**, near Retiro Park. Also well worth visiting is the **Reina Sofia Museum** of 20th-century art. Go here to see Picasso's famous painting *Guernica*. Open Mon. and Wed.–Sat.: 10am–9pm, Sun.: 10am–2.30pm, entry 500ptas (students half price) (see **FREE MADRID**).

The **Royal Palace** is the only other 'must' in Madrid. A 45-minute guided tour will take you through the various apartments and the Royal Armoury, which is considered one of the world's best collections of medieval weapons. The palace gardens, especially the **Campo del Moro**, are particularly fine and make good venues for regal picnic lunches. The palace is open except during royal visits, Apr.–Sept. Mon.–Sat.: 9am–6pm, Sun.: 9am–3pm; Oct.–Mar. Mon.–Sat.: 9.30am–5pm, Sun.: 9am–2pm. Entrance costs 950ptas, but with a reduction for ISIC holders (see **FREE MADRID**).

The **Botanic Gardens**, near the Prado Museum, is also a nice place to have a quiet picnic. Entrance costs 200ptas and the gardens are open daily from 10am–8pm.

**FREE MADRID:**
- If you like parks, you're in the right place as they're Madrid's speciality: very busy and especially colourful on Sundays. The **Retiro Park** in the city centre is huge and, apart from its rowing lake, theatre, fountains and statues, the **Crystal Palace** of the Bourbon kings is here too. North-west of the palace is another park 10 times the scale of the Retiro, the **Casa de Campo**, which young Spaniards tend to patronize at weekends.
- On Sunday mornings there's a **flea market** (the Rastro) off the southern corner of Plaza Mayor, where gypsies often congregate and put on street shows.
- **Old Madrid** lies between **Puerta del Sol** (known as the centre of Spain) and the Crystal Palace; notice the descriptive pictures above the street signs to help the illiterate 17th-century locals. These narrow winding streets are the most colourful and interesting in Madrid. Check out the following too:
- **Centro de Arte Reina Sofia**, C. Santa Isabel 52 – Free Sat. pm and all day Sun.
- **Museo de America**, Av. Reyes Católicos 6 – Free Sun. and during holidays.
- **Museo del Prado**, Pl. Canovas del Castillo – Free Sat.: 2.30–7pm and all day Sun.
- **Museo Lázaro Galdiano**, C. Serrano 122 – Free Sun.
- **Museo Romantico**, C. San Mateo 13 – Free Sun.
- **Museo Sorolla**, Po. General Martinez Campos – Free Sun.
- **National Archaeological Museum**, C. Serrano 13 – Free Sat.
- **Naval Museum**, C. Montalban 2 – Free.
- **Royal Academy of Fine Arts of San Fernando**, C. Acalà 13 – Free on weekends.
- **Royal Palace** – Free on Wednesdays for EC passport holders.

## SLEEPING

Cheap beds aren't a problem here, especially in summer when people tend to escape the high temperatures of the city. The Tourist Offices will advise you on accommodation, but won't arrange it for you. Brujula, a private placing agency with branches at Torre de Madrid and Plaza España, will do this for a small fee, but you must visit in person. In fact, you shouldn't need their help as there are hundreds of suitable places, many near the centrally located Atocha station, in streets like Calle Toledo. Recommended is the **Hostal Córdoba** at 21 pts. Santa Maria de la Cabeza (Tel. 91 527 3189); around 1,500ptas for a single room with shower. Just off the peaceful Plaza Santa Ana (right in the epicentre of the tapas bar scene) is the spotlessly clean and comfortable **Hostal Regional** (Calle Principe 18, Tel. 91 522 3373). The beautiful old building also contains another hotel, but the Regional is hard to beat. Safe, too, though short on toilets!

If you're really cutting corners and don't mind other people's nocturnal 'goings-on', or the odd bed-bug, the area south of Puerta del Sol will produce some very inexpensive (from 1,200ptas upwards) *casas de huéspedes*. The **university** lets out rooms to those wanting to stay five or more days, and the best **youth hostel** to stay in is at Calle Santa Cruz de Marcenado 28 (Tel. 91 547 4532; Fax. 91 548 1196). Get there on bus 1, 61 and Circular or on the metro (Argüelles). You need IYHF membership, and a dorm bed and breakfast costs 1000ptas (for over 26s the cost is 1400ptas).

The street with more cheap beds than anywhere else is Gran Vía in central Madrid. **Hostal Alcázar-Regis**, on the 5th floor of no. 61 (Tel. 91 547 9317), is good value for what you get; **La Costa Verde** (9th floor) is cheaper, and **Buenos Aires** (Tel. 91 542 0102) on the 2nd floor has singles for around 2,500ptas and doubles for 4,000ptas.

Ask at the tourist office for the camping leaflet and don't risk the parks unless you're desperate. **Camping Osuna** (Tel. 91 741 0510) near the airport is a reasonable site. Take metro no. 5 to Canillejas (the end of the line), and from there it's very close. It costs around 650ptas per person and per tent. Refer to *Cheap Sleeps Europe 2000* for more accommodation options.

## EATING AND NIGHTLIFE

*Tapas* (tasty snacks served in infinite varieties to accompany your drink) are at their best in Madrid. The locals spend between 6pm and 10pm on the *tapas* circuit in either Pasaje de Matheu or the area round Plaza Mayor. Mussels, mushrooms, omelettes and filled rolls are some of the savouries with which to bridge the gap till dinner, washed down with sangría or wine. The main meal of the day is eaten at lunchtime (2pm–4pm) and dinner, around 10pm, is quite a light affair.

Argüelles, on the metro, is the city's main student quarter. Make for this area to eat cheaply and meet the university students. The bars along Calle de la Princesa are a safe bet to make friends, and back in the centre Calle Echegaray and Ventura de la Vega, off Calle San Jerónimo, also have cheap restaurants. **Restaurant Copatisán**, Calle del Barco 16–18, is very cheap and very good. Closed Aug. For a good paella try **Restaurant El Parque**, Fernando el Católico 78.

The taverns in the alleys off the Plaza Mayor are good starting-places for your evening's pub crawl, Madrid-style. Continue the evening in the *salas de fiesta* (nightclubs), winding up around 3am–4am or later. The Spanish love to party and there are clubs to suit all tastes. Most open around 10pm but some don't bother to open until 3 or 4am (like **Goa After Club** (metro: Grand Via)). For a chic and elegant place try **Archy's** at Calle Marqués de Riscal 11 (open Thurs.–Sat. 11pm–morning); for reggae, check out **Big Bamboo** at Calle Barquillo 42 (opens 10pm Tues.–Sat. and shuts 6/7am). Another cool place (very cool) is **Angels of Xenon** at Calle Atocha 38 (popular with gays), 1200ptas entry which includes a drink (open Fri. and Sat.: midnight–7am).

The list of current events in the *Guía del Ocio* is all you need. Avoid the heavily advertised flamenco shows, as they're incredibly commercial and plastic, and ask about for the best clubs, gigs etc., in the bars along the Aurrera in the Argüelles quarter.

**EXCURSIONS** Forty-eight kilometres from the Norte or Atocha stations is the huge granite monastery-palace complex of **San Lorenzo del Escorial** which King Philip II had built to commemorate his victory over France in the Battle of St. Quentin (1577) and as a mausoleum for his father, King Carlos 1. The building took over 20 years to complete and is very strange to look at, even ugly. It looks more like a high-security prison than a palace. The guided tours take you round the museums, library, church, art gallery and royal apartments for around 1000ptas. Open 10am–6pm (Apr.–Sept. till 7pm; free Wed. for EC citizens).

A few kilometres further on is the **Valle de Los Caidos** – a memorial to those who died in the Civil War, and where Franco is buried in a huge underground basilica complex.

Or, if you just want to cool off, stay in the train to Cercedilla and take the branch line up into the Sierra de Guadarrama mountains.

**ARANJUEZ** If you are *en route* south to Córdoba or Seville, it is worth a stop-off here to see the **Royal Palace**, the **Sailor's House**, the **Prince's Garden** and the **Farmer's House**. The campsite here, **Soto del Castillo** (Tel. 91 891 1395), will entice you to stay a while as it's about the best one in Spain.

## San Sebastián (Donostia)

The jewel in the crown of the Basque resorts, San Sebastián is traditionally one of Spain's major holiday destinations, and it's not hard to see why, given the striking location and superb beaches. It's also a good place to nicely break up a run from Paris to Madrid.

## TOURIST INFORMATION AND ADDRESSES

**TOURIST OFFICES** Calle Fueros 1, and Calle Reina Regente (ground floor, Victoria Eugenia Theatre; Tel. 943 481166; Fax. 943 481172); open Oct.–May, Mon.–Fri.: 9am–2pm, 3.30pm–7pm, Sat.: 8am–8pm; Jun.–Sept., Mon.–Sat.: 8am–8pm, Sun.: 10am–1pm
**POST OFFICE** Calle Urdaneta 9 (Tel. 943 464914)
**FIRST AID** *Cruz Roja* (Red Cross), Calle Matías 7 (Tel. 943 222222)
**MEDICAL SERVICES** Casa de Socorro, Bengoetxea 4 (Tel. 943 440633)
**EMERGENCY** phone 088

## SEEING

The **San Telmo Museum**, in a 16th-century Renaissance monastery on Plaza Ignacio Zuloaga, will fill you in on the differences between the Basques and the Spanish or French (free; open Tues.–Sat.); or visit the **Aquarium** down on the port to see the collection of sea creatures. The **Fish Market** is well worth a visit, as is **Plaza de la Constitución Square**, a former bullring. You can rent a boat and go over to the beach island of **Santa Clara** (there is also a half-hourly ferry in summer), or else just laze about on the beaches of **Zuriolla**, **La Concha** and **Ondarreta**. On the coast is the living sculpture *Comb of the Wind* by Eduardo Chillida.

## SLEEPING

During the summer, cheap beds are hard to find. Try the excellent **campsite** on the Carretera de Monte Igueldo (about eight km from the station – take bus 16 from Alameda de Boulevard; Tel. 943 214502) or the **youth hostel**, **La Sirena** (Tel. 943 310268; Fax. 943 214090). The best pension deal is at **Pensión La Perla**, Loyola 10 (Tel. 943 428123). Another cheapie is **Pensión San Martín** at Calle San Martín 10 (Tel. 943 428714) with singles from 3,000ptas. It's also possible to sleep on the beach, but more risky.

## EATING AND NIGHTLIFE

It's not easy to cut corners in San Sebastián for two reasons: first, there are hardly any places with tourist menus in the Eurorailer's budget range; and secondly, the food is so good you won't feel like living off bread, cheese and fruit. This is one Spanish town where the food is consistently good and, of course, the fish dishes are excellent. The city actually has a Gastronomic Academy, and the exclusive and chauvinistic male-only dining clubs frequently sponsor eating contests. There are several bars and restaurants in the central square, Plaza de la Constitución, but watch the prices here.

For pre-dinner *tapas*, or *pinchos* as they're known locally, try the bars along Calle Fermin Calbertón and, for dancing, **Bataplan** (on La Concha) and **Beartzana** (in Plaza Easo) are meant to be pretty hot. There are festivals all summer, the most interesting being the Basque folklore one, the jazz festival (July) and the international film festival (September). Ask at Tourist Information for details.

## Northern Spain

Running from the foot of the Pyrenees almost to Portugal, this region is one of Spain's lesser visited areas. But its beauty, which lies in its lush forests, good beaches and historic towns, make it well worth discovering. A cooler climate (although still hot) also brings welcome relief to the furnace of the south.

Since Franco's death the Basque region of northern Spain has seen increasing terrorist activity by the ETA (Basque Liberation Front) and in 1996 the first tourist casualties were recorded. However, at present there is not too much cause for concern.

**PAMPLONA** The picturesque old town is well worth a visit for the Festival de San Fermín (*San Fermines*) (7–14 July), better known as the Running of the Bulls. A favourite of Hemingway, the festival is a week-long spectacle of singing, dancing and, most of all, drinking. It is arguably the best street party in Europe: the whole town is bedecked in red and white and in fiesta mood.

The actual bull run begins at 8am when a group of bulls pursues crowds of people to the bull-ring. Although it may be tempting to prove your machismo and run with the bulls, bear in mind that it is dangerous (because of the crowd of runners as much as the bulls) and, in the event of injury, your insurance cover will probably be invalid. Anyway, the best part of the fiesta is the exuberant nightlife around Plaza del Castillo and Calle Navarrería.

If you can tear yourself away from the festivities, the **Museu de Navarre** has some excellent murals. The **Cathedral**, with its beautiful Gothic cloisters, and the **Citadel** are also worth a look.

Tourist information is at Calle Duque de Ahumada 3 (Tel. 948 220741; Fax. 948 211462), open Mon.–Fri.: 10am–5pm; Sat.: 10am–2pm. They will help with accommodation, but you will have to be extremely fortunate or resourceful to find a bed during the fiesta. Try **Fonda La Montañesa**, Calle San Gregorio (Tel. 948 224380), which has dorm beds for around 1,500ptas per person (during *San Fermines* the price rises to about 4,200ptas). **Casa Huéspedes Santa Cecilia**, Calle Navarrería 17 (Tel. 948 222230), has doubles for around

4,000ptas. During the festivities a dorm bed will set you back around 4,000ptas; **Fonda La Union** (Tel. 948 221319) on Calle San Nicolás also has dorm beds which normally cost around 2,000ptas (5,000ptas plus during *San Fermines*).

The nearest campsite is **Camping Ezcaba** (Tel. 948 331665) with excellent facilities and a free swimming pool, seven km away but with bus connections. It's open June–Oct. Does not accept reservations.

If you're out of luck, do not be tempted to sleep rough in the unsafe Plaza del Castillo, but head for the other side of the bull-ring to a park. Showers are available at Calle Eslava 9, open Tues.–Sun.: 7.30am–9.30pm and are widely used by bedless travellers.

**SANTANDER** The port of Santander is wedged between the Basque and Galician regions in the province of Cantabria. This part of northern Spain is mountainous with a rugged coastline, and contains some of the world's best prehistoric cave art in the **Altamira Caves**.

The beaches at Santander are the main reason to stop off, particularly the ones at **El Sardinero**, **Comillas** and **Liencres**. The area by the harbour is the 'new town' and this is where the restaurants and bars are located.

Tourist information is at Jardines de Pereda, open daily: 9am–2pm, 4pm–9pm (Tel. 942 362054 or 942 216120). There are plenty of cheap *hostales* or campsites outside the town.

An interesting excursion from Santander is inland to the picturesque village of **Medina de Pomar** with its fascinating monastery (open 10am–1.30pm) and collection of churches.

**SANTIAGO DE COMPOSTELA** This is the main town in the beautiful province of Galicia, though if you really wanted to explore the dramatic Atlantic coastline you'd be better staying at La Coruña, on the main line to Madrid. Santiago was a popular place of pilgrimage in the Middle Ages for up to two million Christians a year who made the journey here to see where the Apostle St James is buried, and today the pilgrimage journey is still followed by hundreds of walkers and cyclists. This year it is one of the nine cities which have been labelled a European City of Culture and a programme of cultural events, including theatre, music, cinema and television, will be taking place throughout the year. For further information, call 981 582525; fax. 981 557246 or enquire at the tourist office.

The **Cathedral** dominates the town, but it's difficult to isolate other main sights as the whole inner town is a national monument, and deserving of it. The cathedral was started in the 11th century but encompasses many architectural styles. The student quarter lies between the cathedral and the university and this is the best area to head for at night.

The Tourist Office is at Rúa del Villar 43, open Mon.–Fri.:

10am–2pm, 4pm–7pm, Sat.: 11am–2pm (Tel. 981 584 400), and they have a list of the pensions with their prices posted up, but once you're at Turismo you're already in Santiago's main hostel street. Try **Hospedaje Santa Cruz** at no. 42, or **Pensión Lens** at no. 73; where you will get a double for 3,000ptas. The only time you may have trouble is during the annual festival of St James (18–31 July) or around religious feast days when pilgrims flock into the town. **Casa Manoló** near St Benedict's church is the best cheap place to eat.

# Andorra

Nestling between France and Spain in the Pyrenees, Andorra is a small autonomous principality of 65,000 people. Founded in 784 by Charlemagne, it's under the joint suzerainty of the Bishop of Urgel (Spain) and the French President. The official language is Catalan and both French francs and Spanish pesetas are used. Coming from France, Andorra can be reached by train from Toulouse to L'Hospitalet-Près-l'Andorre and then by bus or from Perpignan to La Tour de Carol and then by bus as well. Coming from Barcelona there are buses three times a day. Whichever way you come, it's a dramatic road journey round hairpin bends to the Andorran capital **Andorra la Vella**. The buses don't connect with all the trains, so check the timetable first.

The scenery on the way to La Tour de Carol is fairly dramatic and, once inside Andorra, the mountains are equally spectacular, making for a few days' good hiking.

The Tourist Information office is at Carrer Dr Villanova (Tel. 376 820214; Fax. 376 825823). They'll provide you with maps and accommodation lists. There are no IYHF hostels in Andorra, but finding a room in a *Residencia* should be no problem. Check the Official Price List for hotels: prices start at around 1,700ptas. The owner will take your passport for registration with the police.

Because of Andorra's duty-free status, Andorra la Vella is extremely commercialized, resembling a Spanish costa resort. One consequence of this is that you can pick up extremely cheap duty-frees, for example, a litre of Polish vodka for £3.50! Goods tend to be priced in pesetas, but you can pay in either francs or pesetas and when changing money you can get your cash in whichever currency you want. This can be handy if you are visiting only France or only Spain.

The main sight in Andorra la Vella is the 16th-century **Casa de la Vall**, the seat of the Andorran government. The visit is free with an official guide, but you may need to reserve a place (Tel. 376 829129).

Aside from Andorra la Vella there are a number of small, less commercialized towns in Andorra which could be used as a base for exploring the countryside. The National Festival is on the first weekend in August.

## Barcelona

Located on the north-eastern coast of the Iberian Peninsula, Barcelona is Spain's second largest city and the proud capital of Cataluña. A vibrant, bustling atmosphere occupies the whole city, though none more so than in its old Gothic quarter (or Barrio Gótico). On the streets, you'll hear the regionally spoken Catalan, a language that descends from the French *langue d'oc* rather than Spanish.

As host to the Olympics in 1992, Barcelona carried out huge ancillary projects to make itself a great centre for urban tourism. This topped off with some fine Mediterranean beaches make the city a 'must' to see.

### STATION FACILITIES

Barcelona's main station, Sants, handles most major trains; some also stop at the smaller Paseo de Gracia station nearer the city centre (there are connecting trains every 20 minutes).

Daily trains to: Paris, Geneva, Valencia, Zaragoza, Madrid, Irún, Sevilla, Milan, Montpellier.

For train information, telephone 93 4900202.

### TOURIST INFORMATION AND ADDRESSES

**TOURIST OFFICE** The Centre d'Informació Turisme de Barcelona (Tel. 93 304 3135) is underground at Placa de Catalunya; open daily 9am–9pm. Ask them for their list of budget accommodation, along with your map and leaflets. There are other offices at the train station, in the EU passenger arrivals hall at the airport and at Pl. Sant Jaume. There's also a free info. line: 93 304 3134 or 906 301282 and a general info. line (in English): 1010 (you have to pay for this number).

**POST OFFICE** Plaza d'Antoni López, open Mon.–Sat.: 8.30am–9pm. Stamps from the basement.

**AMEX** Paseig de Gracia 101, open Mon.–Fri.: 9.30am–6pm, Sat.: 10am–12 noon (Tel. 900 994426; 24hr. Tel. 91 572 0303; Fax. 93 415 3700). It charges no commission to change travellers' cheques

**UK CONSULATE** Edificio Torre de Barcelona, Avenida Diagonal 477, 13th floor (Tel. 93 419 9044; Fax. 93 405 2411)

**US CONSULATE** Paseo Reina Elisenda 23 (Tel. 93 280 2227; Fax. 93 205 5206)

**CANADIAN CONSULATE** Paseig de Gracia 77, 3rd floor (Tel. 93 215 0704; Fax. 93 487 9117)

**AUSTRALIAN CONSULATE** Gran Vía Carlos III, 98, 3rd floor (Tel. 93 330 9464; Fax. 93 411 0904)

**NEW ZEALAND CONSULATE** Travesera de Gracia, 64, 4th floor (Tel. 93 209 0399; Fax. 93 202 0890)

**STUDENT TRAVEL OFFICE** Unlimited Student Travel, Calle Rocafort 116–122 (Tel. 93 483 8378)

**EMERGENCY** Telephone 092, 062 or 091

## GETTING AROUND

Although walking is the best way to see Barcelona, there is good public transport by bus and metro. Plaza de Catalunya is the main terminus. Bus and metro rides cost around l40ptas, but you can save money by buying a multi-ticket at metro entrances. A T–1 card for 775ptas allows 10 trips by bus and metro, whilst a T–2 card for 750ptas allows 10 trips on the metro only. The T-DIA card is good for a day's unlimited travel on the metro and bus, it costs 575ptas.

## SEEING

Head for the **Barrio Gótico**, the oldest part of the city, and look out for the **Great Royal Palace** in Plaza del Rey, the **Catedral de Santa Eulalia** and the **Diputación Provincial** (council buildings).

The incredible and unmissable cathedral of **Templo Expiatorio de la Sagrada Familia** is the work of the Catalan architect Gaudí; however, his death before construction was completed threw a spanner in the works, as he didn't leave any plans. Work is now proceeding, however. Open daily 9am–8pm in high season, 9am–6pm or 7pm in quieter months, with an admission charge of 800ptas.

The 'town' of **Poble Espanyol** is worth seeing, as it shows all the different regional styles of architecture in Spain, although it is a bit 'touristy'. It has a souvenir bazaar, several restaurants (not great) and a few discos. Open Mon.: 9am–8pm, Tues.–Thurs.: 9am–2am, Fri.–Sat. 9am–4am, Sun.: 9am–midnight, 500ptas, 1000ptas at night. Take the funicular up the hill, and admire the view over the port and city. For even more dramatic views take the tram up to **Tibidabo**, north of the city. There are also good views from the Palau Nacional and Mirador de L'Alcade (near Parc d'Attractions).

The **Picasso Museum** is at Calle de Montcada 15 (open Tues.–Sat.: 10am–8pm, Sun.: 10am–3pm, entrance 600ptas, students half price) and has lots of his works from the early sketches to his final masterpieces.

There are numerous other museums and art galleries – some of the more interesting ones are: the **Barcelona Football Club Museum** at their ground (Oct.–Mar., Mon.–Sat.: 10am–6.30pm, Sun.: 10am–2pm); **Gaudi's House** at Ctra del Carmel 23 in Parc Guell (Sun.–Fri.: 10am–2pm, 4pm–7pm); and, if you aren't too disapproving of bloodsports, the **Bullfighting Museum** at Gran Vía de los Cortes Catalanes 749 (May–Sept., Mon.–Sat.: 10.30am–2pm, 4pm–7pm, Sun.: 10.30am–1pm). Check with Tourist Information for a full list.

**FREE BARCELONA:** The city has a wealth of free things to do. Its hub is **Las Ramblas**, a collection of streets that start at the port and run to the city centre at Plaça de Catalunya. For sheer entertainment value you can't beat it – the vibrant atmosphere and **street performers** make it the Piccadilly Circus of Barcelona. The **Barrio Gótico** (Gothic Quarter) with its 14th- and 15th-century façades has to be seen as well. South of here is **Montjuic Park**, home to the **Olympic Stadium** – the buildings originally erected here for the 1929 International Exhibition were refurbished specially for the Olympics. **Guell Park** is definitely worth some time too, as is **Citadel Park**. And if you're sick of parks there's always the **beach**. Check out the following too:

- **Museu Arqueològic**, Parc de Montjuïc – Free Sun.
- **Basilica of Santa Maria del Mar**, Carrer de Montcada.
- **Museu Nacional d'Arte de Catalunya**, Parc de Montjuïc – first Thurs. of month.
- **Catedral de Barcelona**, Plaça de la Seu.
- **Adjuntament** (Town Hall), Plaça de Sant Jaume. Pop in to see the courtyard.
  The following museums are all free on the first Sun. of each month:
- **Museu Picasso**, C. Montcada 15-19.
- **Museu Marès**, Plaça Sant Iu 5-6.
- **Museu d'Història de la Ciutat**, Plaça del Rei.

## SLEEPING

The **youth hostel** on Passeig Pujades 29 (Tel. 93 300 3104) charges around 1,500ptas. Reception is closed 10am–5pm but you can leave luggage and reserve a bed after 3pm. It has only 68 beds and gets very crowded, so get there as soon after 8am as possible; its big drawback is the midnight curfew. There are also **youth hostels** at Passeig Mare de Déu del Coil 41–51 (Tel. 93 210 5151; Fax. 93 210 0798) and Numancia 149–151 (Tel. 93 410 2309; Fax. 93 419 6268). The **university** at Calle Mestre Nicolau 14 (Tel. 93 412 4073) offers both sexes bed and breakfast for around 1000ptas.

Your best bet for cheap *casas* and hostels is in Las Ramblas. **Hostal Fernando**, Calle Ferran 31 (Tel. 93 301 7993), is cheap and friendly (dorms and doubles), as is **Hostal Europa**, in an alley off Ramblas

(Boquería 18, Tel. 93 318 7620). Ask for a room with a balcony. Another cheap option is **Hostal Levante** at Baixada Sant Miguel 2 (Tel. 93 317 9565; Fax. 93 317 0526), just off Plaça de Sant Miguel (doubles around 4,000ptas). Also try the friendly **Pension Alamar** (Tel. 93 302 5012) on Comtessa de Sobradiel (singles 1800ptas, doubles 3600ptas; all rooms have balconies).

Although it can be quite rowdy, the **Kabul Young Budget Hotel** is cheap and central at Plaza Reial 17 (Tel. 93 318 5190; Fax. 93 301 4034). Mixed dormitories and free (but cold) showers. There is no curfew or lock-out and it costs only l,500ptas or so. Although you get breakfast and can buy sandwiches at the bar, you are better eating around the Plaça de Sant Jaume.

For camping, there are quite a few sites but they are all a few kilometres out of town. **El Toro Bravo** (Tel. 93 637 3462) is open year round; nearby is the **La Ballena Alegre** site (Tel. 93 658 0504; open mid-Feb.–mid-Dec.). Take bus L95 and L94 (summer only) from Pl. Catalunya or Pl. Espanya. Another one to try is **Filipinas** (Tel. 93 658 2895) which is near the other two sites. Get there on bus L95.(Open all year).

## EATING AND NIGHTLIFE

The Catalans eat late. Dinner time averages 9pm–11pm. There are plenty of places offering *menu del día* in Barrio Gótico, and if you get a chance to sample the regional speciality, Catalan stew, *escudella i cam d'olla*, do so. **Casa José**, Pl. San José: Oriol 10, is the cheapest, though not friendliest, feed in Barcelona. **Pollo Rico**, at calle Sant Pau 31, is a good budget option too, with a decent meal for less than 700ptas. If you're feeling extravagant, go to Barceloneta, the area of colourful winding streets down by the port, and savour the fresh seafood concoctions in **Casa Costa** on Juicio. Vegetarians should head for **Restaurante Bio Centre** on Calle Pintor Fortuny 24, open Mon.–Sat. 9am–5pm.

If you've money to blow, go to the nightclubs and discos like **Georgia**, Pelayo 58, or **El Cordobés** on Ramblas Capuchinos. The **Cafe de l'Opera** at Ramblas 74 is the trendiest café if you've got the cash to spare, but for our money strolling through the Ramblas, stopping at a few cafés *en route*, is as good value as anything.

It gets quite lively at the top of the Montjuic on summer evenings, but if that's too sedate for you, head down to El Barrio Chino (near the docks). By Spanish standards some of the shows down there are pretty hot stuff, but bear in mind that this is the red-light area and can be rather sleazy. Be careful with your valuables.

Gays and lesbians should visit the specialist Complices bookshop at Calle Cervantes 2 (metro: Liceu) for a map of venues. Open Mon.–Fri.: 10am–8pm; Sat.: 12 noon–8pm.

**EXCURSIONS** If you're in desperate need to escape from the stifling heat of the city, it's not far to the good but crowded beaches of the **Costa Brava** and the **Costa Dorada**. **Lloret de Mar** is infested with package tourists, but pretty, while **S'Agaró** is the St Tropez of the Costa Brava. Stay at **San Feliú de Guixols** and travel in the three km to S'Agaró to save yourself a fortune. Buses run to these and other, closer resorts from Estación del Nord at Ali-bey 80, near metro Arc de Triomf, or from Vergara 5, Barcelona. The bus company is Sarfa.

**MONTSERRAT** The town, 61 km from Barcelona, is reached by Catalan Railways (from Plaza de España – about £6 with Inter-Rail discount). Set among the mountain peaks, there is a Benedictine monastery, a Gothic basilica and a nice collection of early paintings by Juan Miró and Picasso. It's a good day trip away from town.

**TARRAGONA** On the Costa Dorada about 100 km south of Barcelona is the rather touristy town of Tarragona. The culture vultures may wish to stop off here and visit the ruins of the provincial Roman capital of Hispania. If you are coming from Barcelona, sit on the right-hand side of the train for a visual extravaganza!

You can pick up leaflets with lots of useful info at Tourist Information, C. Major 39 (Tel. 977 245203), open Mon.–Fri.: 9.30am–8.30pm, Sat.: 9.30am–2pm, 4pm–8.30pm, Sun.: 10am–2pm. Rambla Nova is the main street in Tarragona, and along this long, tree-lined avenue you will find an information kiosk and the post office, as well as countless places offering cheap food.

The **Archaeological Museum** has a fascinating collection of mosaics and is one of the most important in Spain. It is part of the **Cyclopean Walls**, which run for about one km along the highest part of town, starting at the end of Rambla Vella, which runs parallel to Rambla Nova. The wall, which varies in height from 3.5 to 12 m, was built around 600 BC. Also visit the **Roman Amphitheatre** and the 13th-century **Cathedral** in the old town.

The **youth hostel** is at Avenida President Companys s/n (Tel. 977 240195; Fax. 977 243134). It normally has 90 beds, but in July and August the number miraculously jumps to 190. Reserve in the summer. There are also a number of cheap hotels south of the Rambla Nova and a few campsites a few kilometres east of the town. Take bus 9 from the Plaza Imperial Tarraco.

**PORT BOU** Just across the border from France and nestling beside the Mediterranean, Port Bou is a delightful spot for the travel-weary Eurorailer. Relax and bask in a bit of sun for a day or two. The vast railway station is out of all proportion to its surroundings but it is only a short walk to hotels and the rather pebbly beach.

Tourist Information at the harbour is open throughout the day Mon.–Sat., but only in the mornings on Sun.

Although there is no youth hostel and the locals don't like you sleeping on the beach, the **Hôtel Juventas** is highly recommended at around 4,000ptas for a double with washbasin and shower next door. It is at Avenue de Barcelona 2. There isn't really much to do in Port Bou but lie on the beach and watch the skinny-dippers. There are plenty of good cafés, but, although the seafood is good value, the prices are not all that cheap.

# Valencia

If you're thinking of taking some time away from Europe's rail lines and making a detour to the Balearic islands of Majorca, Menorca or Ibiza, Valencia seems to be a logical stop-off point. But actually, there's not a great deal to get excited about here, although it is the point of departure for steamers to the islands.

## TOURIST INFORMATION AND ADDRESSES

**MUNICIPAL TOURIST OFFICE** Plaza del Ayuntamiento 1 (Tel. 96 351 0417; for information in English call 010). Open weekdays: 8.30am–2.15pm and 4.15–6.15pm, Sat.: 9.15am–12.45pm
**REGIONAL TOURIST OFFICE** Estación del Nord, Calle Xàtiva 24 (Tel. 96 352 8573)
**POST OFFICE** Plaza del Ayuntamiento 24
**AMEX** Duna Viajes, Calle Cirilo Amorós 88 (Tel. 96 374 1562; Fax. 96 334 5700). No commission charged on Amex travellers' cheques
**US CONSULATE** Calle de la Paz 6 (Tel. 96 351 6973; Fax. 96 352 9565); open Mon.–Fri.: 10am–1pm

## STATION FACILITIES

Valencia Término has daily trains to: Barcelona, Alicante, Córdoba, Madrid, Sevilla. It also has automatic luggage lockers and a helpful information office.
 24-hour telephone information line: 96 352 0202

**FERRIES TO THE BALEARIC ISLANDS** Transmediterránea, Avenida Manuel Solo Ingeniero 15 or ask at any travel agency (there are several around the main plaza).

## SEEING

The **Palace of the Marqués de dos Aguas** is about the most interesting building around. It's 18th-century rococo and contains about the best collection of Spanish pottery in Spain (closed

2pm–4pm for siesta, closed Sunday pm and all day Monday).

The **Gothic Cathedral** is also worth a look. Climb its tower for a view over the city and visit the museum, which claims to hold the Holy Grail; open Mon.–Sat.: 10am–12.30pm, 4.30–6pm; 250ptas.

Apart from these, the **Museo Provincial de Bellas Artes** is the only other place really worth visiting, with works by Goya amongst others. Free entry, open Tues.–Sat.: 10am–2pm, 4pm–7.30pm, Sun.: 10am–2pm, closed Mon.

The best beaches are further south at **Benidorm** and **Alicante**, but there are closer ones on the Costa del Azahar accessible by bus.

## SLEEPING, EATING AND NIGHTLIFE

The **youth hostel** is at Avenida del Puerto 69 (Tel. 96 361 7459) on bus route 19. Open July–mid. Sept. Round the Plaza del Mercado are plenty of grotty *casas* and *fondas* with beds around 1,200ptas. **Hospedería del Pilar** is very cheap, at Plaza del Mercado 19 (Tel. 96 391 6600; doubles from 3,000ptas).

The Barrio del Carmen is the area both for cheap eating and for nightlife. Rice dishes are the Valencian speciality, but you often have to watch the prices. There are lots of spit 'n' sawdust bars in this area which vary from colourful and 'ethnic' to grimy and revolting.

# Central Spain

About two hours from Madrid lie two towns which should ideally be included on any Spanish itinerary: **Avila** and **Segovia**.

**ÁVILA** Famous because of Saint Teresa, this town has some of Europe's best-preserved medieval battlements, dating from the 11th century, and other buildings from this same period.

Tourist Information is at Plaza de la Catedral 4 (Tel. 920 211387), open Mon.–Fri.: 10am–2pm, 4pm–7pm, Sat.: from 9.30am, Sun.: 9.30am–2pm, 4.30am–8.30pm. There's no problem finding cheap rooms. However, only make for the summer **youth hostel**, Av. de Juventud (Tel./Fax. 920 221716), if you're desperate: it's far from the centre in a fairly unpleasant area and has very limited space.

**SEGOVIA** This has a **Roman Aqueduct** predating Christ, a 14th-century **Alcázar** (palace) (rebuilt in the 19th century), and dozens of churches in different architectural styles.

The Tourist Office is at Plaza Mayor 10 (Tel. 921 460334), open Mon.–Fri.: 10am–2pm, 5pm–8pm, Sat.: 9.30am–2pm, 4.30am–8.30pm,

Sun.: from 11am, and there are plenty of cheap rooms nearby. Try **Pension Aragón**, Plaza Mayor 4 (Tel. 921 460914) which has doubles for under 3,000ptas.

## Other towns well worth a detour

**TOLEDO** For an intensive spectacle of 2,000 years of Spanish history and culture in one or two days, make for Toledo. From the Roman circus, through Moorish and Visigothic mosques and synagogues to Renaissance buildings reminiscent of the Spanish Inquisition, every architectural style is represented and wonderfully preserved. It's interesting to note that Toledo was one of the world's few centres of Arab, Jewish and Christian coexistence. It's possible to make Toledo a day trip from Madrid (it takes 1½ hours) but you'll kill yourself trying to see all the sights in just one afternoon.

Perched up on the high town are buildings such as the **Mosque of the Christ of the Light** (10th century), the **Synagogue of Santa Maria la Blanca**, the incredible medieval **Cathedral**; and dominating the violet-coloured sky is the **Alcázar** which once housed El Cid. El Greco lived in Toledo, and his **House and Museum** can be seen. Many of the sights take a long siesta and don't reopen till 4pm – one that doesn't is the **Museum of Santa Cruz**.

There are many more things to see: go along to Turismo, just outside the Puerta Nueva de Bisagra, and pick up your glossy leaflets and map. The office is open weekdays 9am–6pm (until 7pm in summer, 9am–7pm on Sat., 9am–3pm Sun.).

From the station (at the foot of the hill) take the bus marked Santa Barbara to the centre. For accommodation, if you're looking to do some camping, head for the **El Greco** site (Tel. 925 220090), 1½ km out of town on the N401 road.

Tourist Information will suggest pensions, of which perhaps **Pension Descalzos**, Calle de los Descalzos 30 (Tel. 925 222888 or 925 230702), is the best. **Fonda Lumbreras**, Calle de Juan Labrador 9 (Tel. 925 221571) is another good bet. The **youth hostel** is in a castle 10 minutes' walk from the station and town centre. It's at Castillo de San Servando (Tel. 925 224554) and is beautiful inside with a super pool, though slightly more expensive than a normal Spanish hostel (closed mid-Aug.–mid-Sept. and over Easter and Christmas; no reservations accepted).

Shop around for your meals and eat at the fixed-price menu places near the central Plaza de Zocodover if possible. This is where it all happens in Toledo, especially at night.

**SALAMANCA** Further down the line from Ávila is Spain's oldest university town, Salamanca. The main reason for going there is to see Spain's most beautiful square, the **Plaza Mayor**, built by Philip V in the 18th century. From the station take bus 1 to the centre of the town where Tourist Information is at Casa de la Conchas, Mon.–Fri.: 9am–2pm and 5–8pm; weekends: 10am–7pm. The Municipal office is at Plaza Major 14, open Mon.–Sat.: 9.30am–2pm and 4.30–6.30pm, Sun.: 10am–2pm and 4.30–6.30pm.

An afternoon should be long enough to take in the main sights: the square, university, **Old and New Cathedrals**, and **House of Shells**, but if you come in term-time you might want to stay a night for the active student nightlife.

Look for a room round the Plaza Mayor and Calle Meléndez, which are also the main areas for cheap food.

**BURGOS** Most Madrid–Paris runs go through this old 10th century capital of Castile. Franco was declared military commander here in 1936 and none other than El Cid is buried here. It's the **Cathedral** that you should head for, as the rest of the town has nothing spectacular in it. Entrance around 400ptas (students half price) which gives access to the sacristy, museum and Capilla Mayor (stained-glass dome).

Tourist Information is at Plaza de Alonso Martínez 7 (Tel. 947 203125); open Mon.–Fri.: 9am–2pm, 5pm–7pm, weekends and holidays.: 10am–2pm and 5–8pm.

The **youth hostel** is at Avenida General Vigón (Tel. 947 238539; Fax. 947 220362; closes mid-Aug.) or try **Hostal Hidalgo** at Calle Almirante Bonifaz 14 (Tel. 947 203481; doubles 3,500ptas).

The nearest **campsite** is large and well equipped, but a 3km bus ride from the centre. It's at Fuentes Blacas (Tel. 947 486016) and costs 600ptas per tent and per person.

A short walk away is the Carthusian monastery, **Cartuja de Miraflores**, which is open Mon.–Sat.: 10.15am–3pm, 4pm–6pm, Sun. and holidays: 11.30am–12.30pm, 1pm–3pm, 4pm–6pm and has some ornate tombs (including those of King Juan II of Castlle, Queen Isabel of Portugal and their son, Don Alfonso). Entrance is free.

**VALLADOLID** Just over an hour from Burgos is the university city of Valladolid. If you take a break here, visit the 16th-century house of Miguel de Cervantes, who wrote *Don Quixote*, off the Calle Miguel Iscar, the **Cathedral**, the cloisters of the 16th century **S.Gregorio College** and the **University**.

Tourist Information is at 3 Plaza de Zorrilla (Tel. 983 351801).

**CUENCA** If you're heading for Valencia and the Costa del Azahar, and fancy a short break in the five-hour journey from Madrid, take an hour or more off at Cuenca, about halfway up the line. Walk round the old town, starting at the **Plaza Mayor**, and take in the **City Hall**, the **Cathedral** and the incredible 14th-century **Hanging Houses** on the banks of the Hutecar River.

The Tourist Office is at Calle González Palencia 2 (Tel. 969 178800); open daily: 9am–2pm (no English spoken). A better bet might be the Municipal Tourist Office at Plaza Mayor (Tel. 969 232119); helpful with lots of brochures and maps. Open daily: 9.30am–2pm, 4–6pm.

**Pensión Central** (Tel. 969 211511) at Calle Alonso Chirino 9 is good for a cheap bed. More expensive but with great views is **Posada de San José** (Tel. 969 211300; Fax. 969 230365) at Calle Julián Romero 4, near the cathedral. This is an excellent place to stay and needs to be booked well in advance (a couple of weeks).

## Andalusia (Andalucía)

This is the region where you see Spain at its most beautiful. Incredibly scenic towns mingle in the intense heat with the larger cities of Seville, Granada and Córdoba. A fusion of real flamenco and bullfighting with Moorish palaces and hilltop villages also go towards making this a wonderful area to visit.

**GRANADA** Bus 3, 4, 5, 6, 9 or 11 will take you from the station to the city centre. The Tourist Office is at Calle Mariana Pineda (inside the monument Corral del Carbón) (Tel. 958 221022); open Mon.–Sat.:9.30am–1pm, 4pm–7pm, Sun.: 10am–2pm. There's another at Plaza Mariana Pineda 10; closed on Sundays and Saturday pm. The post office on Puerta Real is open 8.30am–2pm, 4pm–8.30pm, closed Saturday pm and Sunday. AMEX is at Calle Reyes Católicos 31 (Tel. 958 224512).

Once you've found accommodation and disposed of your baggage, visit the huge Arabic fortress on the hill dominating the city: the **Alhambra**. It's one of the world's best-preserved Moorish palaces. The **Alcazaba** (the fortress) and **Watch Tower** go back to the 9th century, and you should visit the **Generalife**, the summer house of the sultans, the 14th-century palace, and see the incredible mosaics and examples of Muslim art. If you want to see the whole lot – fortress, Generalife, royal palace, as well as the remaining grounds – then go early in the day to get its full atmosphere and to be allowed in – in summer, entry is limited to 8400 visitors per day. The Alhambra is open Mon.–Sat.: 9am–8pm, Sun.: 9am–6pm, price 775ptas, but if you are here on a Tuesday, Thursday or Saturday, do head up there in the evening when the whole inside is lit up from 10pm until midnight (same price).

Opposite the Alhambra is **Albayzín**, the hilltop Arab quarter with its crowded, winding streets, and on the other hilltop is the gypsy quarter of **Sacromonte**.

Down in the town take in the Renaissance **Cathedral** (350ptas) and **Royal Chapel**, with its elaborate tombs. Culture fans may be interested in the **Huerta de San Vicente**, the house museum of Federico García Lorca, in Calle Arabial: open 10am–2pm and 5pm–8pm and with free entry on Sundays and public holidays.

The **youth hostel** is the best deal in Granada, although it's a little way out at Calle Ramón y Cajal 2 (Tel. 958 284306; Fax. 958 285285); bus 10 or a 30-minute walk from the station. Other hostels abound near the station in Calle San Juan de Dios. For pensions, try round the station on Avenida Andaluces, or the road up to the Alhambra, Cuesta de Gomérez. **Hostal Residencia Britz**, Cuesta de Gomérez 1 (Tel. 958 223652), is excellent, and the **Sierra Nevada** campsite at Av. Madrid 107 (Tel. 958 150062) is OK; take bus line 3 or 10.

Round Cetti Meriem is the place for cheap meals. **La Riviera** at no. 5 starts meals around 1,000ptas and has a good selection, including vegetarian options. **Las Girasoles** on Calle San Juan de Dios 24 is also excellent value. Depending on your taste, you can try the Tourist Office-recommended 'gypsy flamenco' at **Sacromonte** or head instead for the bars in the centre. As far as serious nightlife is concerned, save your pesetas and go for a nocturnal stroll up by the Alhambra instead. The old Arab quarter, Albayzín, has atmosphere and most bars serve cheap food, but you should watch your valuables at all times.

**CÓRDOBA** This was the 8th-century capital of Moorish Spain, though in many ways it looks as if it's had its heyday. Include it in your itinerary to see the Roman and Moorish remains.

The main area to concentrate on is the **Judería** (old Jewish quarter) with its maze of narrow, twisting streets. Here you will find the **Mezquita**, built in the 8th century; it was the largest mosque in the world before the Christians made it into a cathedral in the 13th century. The structure has an incredible array of decorated arches and pillars, and if you climb the tower you'll see how big the mosque must have been, as the cathedral fits into its original centre. During the summer it is open Mon.–Sat.: 10am–7pm, Sun.: 2–7pm and in winter Mon.–Sat.: 10am–5.30pm, Sun.:2–5.30pm. Entry is 800ptas (free during mass, Mon.–Fri.: 8.30–10am, Sun.: 9.30am–1.30pm) and the ticket also allows entry to the **Museo Diocesano de Bellas Artes** on Calle Torrijos, which is housed in an impressive 17th-century palace and contains the work of local artists from the 13th–18th centuries.

The **Alcázar**, the palace of the Catholic monarchs, is at its best floodlit at night. It's on the banks of the Río Guadalquivir and the Moorish gardens, towers and fountains make it an interesting place to take in. If you do want to go in, it's open Tues.–Sat.: 10am–2pm and 6pm–8pm (last entry is at 7.30pm), Sun.: 9.30am–3pm; . Free entry on Fridays, otherwise 425ptas. The illuminated gardens are open 8pm–midnight.

The municipal Tourist Office at Plaza de Judá Leví 3 (off Manriques) is open Mon.–Sat.: 8.30am–2.30pm, Sun.: 9am–2pm (Tel. 957 200277). The Junta de Andalucía tourist office is at Calle de Torrijos 10 (Tel. 957 47 1235) There's a post office at Cruz Conde 15, open Mon.–Fri.: 8.30am–2pm, 4pm–8.30pm, Sat.: 9.30am–2pm.

The IYHF hostel is **Residencia Juvenil Córdoba** at Plaza de Judá Leví (Tel. 957 290166; Fax. 957 290500) and charges around 1,500ptas for bed and breakfast. It is a sparkling new building with marble floors, in the heart of the Judería. Highly recommended. The biggest selection of cheap pensions are on Calle Rey Heredia and off the Plaza de las Tendillas. Check out the **Hotel/Hostal Maestre**, Calle Romero Barros 16 (for reservations, Tel. 957 472410; Tel./Fax. 957 475395). The hostel has doubles from 4,000ptas and the hotel's doubles cost from 5,000ptas (all hotel rooms have private bath and some have TV).

The **Municipal campside** (Tel. 957 282165) is on Av. Brillante. Take bus 10 from Av. Cervantes near the station. There's a public pool; 580ptas per person and per tent.

Tourist menus are found most easily in the old quarter and for *tapas* and bar crawls, try the Jewish quarter (round the Mezquita). Flamenco here is among the best in Spain, but avoid the expensive private shows: the bar on Calle La Luna is a good place to see students gathering; to sing, play the guitar and dance flamenco.

**RONDA** The main line from Córdoba to Algeciras passes through this delightful town impressively perched on a gorge. See the **Casa del Rey Moro** and the **Renaissance Palace**. Also take a look at the 18th-century bridge spanning the deep gorge beneath the town, as well as the former Moorish fortress and baths, and the cathedral.

For a room, try around the Tourist Information office at Plaza de España. Open Mon.–Fri.: 9am–2pm, 4pm–7pm, closed Saturday afternoon and Sunday (Tel. 95 287 1272). There is plenty of budget accommodation.

**ALGECIRAS** The Tourist Office at Juan de la Cierva is open Mon.–Fri.: 9am–2pm, Sat.: 10am–1pm (Tel. 956 572636). Hostels are cheap and plentiful, so accommodation shouldn't be too much of a problem. You may prefer to stay here rather than in more expensive Gibraltar.

If you are using Algeciras as the departure point for a trip to **Morocco**, buy your ticket from the first office selling ferry tickets to Tangier or Ceuta. Although there are a number of operators on this route, they all charge roughly the same and are quite expensive. It's no cheaper to buy at the ferry terminal than at any of the offices in town (Eurail holders are entitled to 20% off the price of the ticket). A cheaper crossing is to Ceuta for around 1,950ptas single, which also avoids Tangier, though if you do take this trip remember to *get your passport stamped* during the voyage.

The town itself is rather unremarkable and down at heel, but does have good views of Gibraltar, which you can reach from here by bus for around 250ptas (buses depart every 30mins and take 45mins).

Avoid the overnight Paris–Irún–Algeciras train (particularly on Thursday and Friday nights) as it is very overcrowded and full of Arab immigrant workers returning to North Africa. Consequently the return route will be just as busy. The guard has a permanent escort of two armed security guards – which says it all!

# Seville (Sevilla)

Disappointed with Madrid? Well, you'll be delighted with the typical Spanish flavour of Seville: formerly home to Expo '92. It's colourful and lively, with plenty of sights and cheap beds – oh, and of course, it's very, very hot. In fact, during the summer you'll be hard pressed not to succumb to the shade of the parks for a little siesta in the afternoon. Seville is also host to two massive festivals each year, the Semana Santa, a week before Easter, and the April Feria, the last week of the month.

## TOURIST INFORMATION AND ADDRESSES

**TOURIST OFFICE** Avenida de la Constitución 21b (Tel. 95 422 1404; Fax. 95 422 9753); open Mon.–Sat.: 9am–7pm, Sun.: 10am–2pm. This office is always very busy so you may want to try one of the quieter branch offices: Paseo de las Delicias 9 (open weekdays: 8.30am–6.30pm) or at Calle de Arjona (open weekdays: 9am–8.45pm and weekend mornings).

**POST OFFICE** Avenida de la Constitución 32, open Mon.–Fri.: 8.30am–8.30pm, Sat.: 9.30am–2pm

**AMEX** c/o Hotel Inglaterra, Plaza Nueva 7 (Tel. 95 421 1617), Mon.–Fri.: 9.30am–1.30pm and 4.30pm–7.30pm, Sat.: 10am–1pm. Changes cash and travellers' cheques without commission

**UK CONSULATE** Plaza Nueva 8B (Tel. 95 422 8875; Fax. 95 421 0323)

**MEDICAL ASSISTANCE** Ambulatorio Esperanza Macarena (Tel. 95 442 0105)

## SEEING

The **Cathedral** and **Alcázar** complex should be your first stops. The cathedral, the third largest in the world, is built on the site of a former mosque, and the Moorish tower, **La Giralda**, is a leftover from this period. Also included is **Columbus's Tomb**; joint admission to the cathedral and tomb costs 700ptas (200ptas students).

Leave the cathedral at Puerta de los Naranjos, cross the plaza to Puerta Oriente and you'll come to the 14th-century Alcázar palace with its combination of Moorish and Gothic architecture (600ptas, free with ISIC; audio guide 450ptas).

**Plaza de España** and the nearby parks offer romantic settings for an evening stroll, and you can hire out boats at reasonable rates and row round the Spanish Square taking it all in.

Behind the cathedral is the picturesque old Jewish quarter of **Santa Cruz**. There are guided tours, but you're better off wandering around by yourself.

## SLEEPING

Concentrate your efforts on finding a cheap pension (there's no convenient campsite or central youth hostel). Down from the Plaza de Armas station or in the Santa Cruz area are your best bets, especially around Calle Mateos Gago. Rooms start from about 2,500ptas single. Try to get fixed up early, as Seville's popular with Inter-Railers and Spaniards alike.

Of the many hostels in town, try **Hostel Lis** at Calle Escarpin 10 (Tel. 95 421 3088) and **Hostel Paris** at Calle San Pedro Martir 14 (Tel. 95 422 9861 or Tel./Fax. 95 421 9645). A good street to head for is also Calle San Eloy, with the **Hostal La Gloria** at no. 58 (Tel. 95 422 2673) among the best.

The out-of-town **youth hostel** is at Calle Issac Peral 2 (Tel. 95 461 3150; Fax. 95 461 3158). Take bus 34 from opposite Hotel Alfonso XIII to the last but one stop. Before you head there, check that it's open with the Tourist Office as it has been closed for renovations.

**Camping Sevilla** (Tel. 95 451 4379) is 12 km out of town, near the airport. Take bus 70 from Prado de San Sebastián. Sleeping rough in the parks is a dicey proposition as you have not only the police to contend with, but also the local rats.

## EATING AND NIGHTLIFE

Prices in Seville tend to be over the top, but there are plenty of central places with fixed tourist menus, and some few fast-food joints. Again, the area round the Plaza de Armas station isn't bad, and you can eat from about 1000ptas, but some of these places aren't too fussy about hygiene.

The Barrio Triana is a good place to make for to try the local *tapas,* though some bars seem a bit hostile to women coming in on their own.

**Casa Manolo** at San Jorge 16 in the Barrio Triana is cheap and lively. But best value is **El Diamante**, Constitución 10, where an all-you-can-eat buffet costs under 1,000ptas. Speciality dishes can be found everywhere but are especially good at **Mesón La Barca** at Calle Santander 6.

Going to a flamenco is *the* thing to do in Seville. There is no shortage of venues, and by and large they're good value. Avoid the heavily advertised ones and try to make your drinks last as long as possible, as they're (surprise, surprise) overpriced. **Los Gallos** at Plaza Santa Cruz 11 charge about 3,200ptas for entrance, including your first drink. This is a bit on the expensive side, but the entertainment here is excellent. It's popular so arrive early to get a good seat.

**Bull fights** in Seville are said to be some of the best in Spain. If you're tempted, the season runs from Easter to Oct. and fights are usually at 6pm on Sun. During the Feria de Abril, and the weeks before it, there are daily fights. The bull-ring is on Paseo de Cristóbal Colón. Tickets cost from 3,000ptas.

If you fancy an evening at the fair, the **Isla Magica** theme park stays open until 1am during the summer season. A one-day pass will set you back about 3,200ptas.

**EXCURSIONS** The sherry capital of **Jerez de la Frontera** is about two hours from Seville. If you're in this region in the first week of May go down for the fiesta. There are free guided tours and liberal samplings at the bodegas of Sandeman, Gonzalez Byass and others.

**Cádiz**, another 50 minutes away, hasn't much to commend it unless you're after a heavy nightlife scene. However if you're here in early May this year, the town is hosting the ISTA Regatta between 4th and 7th. There will be street pageantry and celebrations to welcome the sailors of the Tall Ships Race, which is expected to be the largest ever international race of square-rigged ships and other vessels.

If you are going on to Portugal, take the train to Huelva, then a 15-minute walk to the bus station for the bus to the ferry at Ayamonte.

## Costa del Sol

The butt of many a joke about package deals to Torremolinos, Spain's Costa del Sol lives up to every bit of its image as an exploited cement-heap of a coastline. In fact, it's difficult to realize you're in Spain, with the food and nightlife plastic and often vulgar. At its best (or worst) in July and August, those in the market for picking up a tan, mingling with Europeans, roughing it on the beach, and all for a low price, need go no further.

**MÁLAGA** Don't stay in Málaga too long: not just because you run a higher risk of getting mugged here than anywhere else in Spain, but because the resorts are often crowded, and it's advisable to make for one and get established first, then head back for a day trip to see this city's sights.

Tourist Information in Málaga is at Pasaje de Chinitas 4 (Tel. 95 221 3445), open in summer, weekdays: 9am–7pm, Sat.and Sun.: 9am–1pm; in winter, Mon.–Fri.: 9am–2pm, Sat.: 9am–1pm. The Municipal Tourist Office is at Av. Cervantes 1 (Tel. 95 260 4410; Fax. 95 221 4120). If you feel you're being followed from the station, turn round and take a good look, then stick to major streets. The instances of Eurorailers being followed from the station to Tourist Information and being mugged *en route* are amazingly high. Whatever happens, don't even think about sleeping out at Málaga station. We realize you'll probably know plenty of people who have and have come out unscathed, but we also know scores who've had their rucksacks actually cut off their backs and been threatened at knife-point to hand over their valuables. Honestly, it's not worth the risk.

The British Consulate is at Edificio Duquesa, Duquesa de Parcent 8 (Tel. 95 221 7571; Fax. 95 222 1130), in case anything nasty does happen.

Tourist Information will give you a leaflet on Málaga's sights. Take in the **Alcazaba** Moorish palace and **Gibralfaro Castle** if you can. El Corte Inglés, the big department store, is useful to stock up in. Usually its toiletries, etc., are cheaper than at the resorts, and its cafeterias are worth a visit too. If you must stay, try **Hostal Residencia Chinitas**, Pasaje Chinitas 2 (Tel. 95 221 4683), doubles from 3,500ptas.

**THE RESORTS** The coastal towns to the east of Málaga are less exploited, but the beaches aren't so good. In places like **Castell de Ferro** and **Torrenueva** you'll avoid the package tourists, but will find the facilities basic. It's easier coming down from Granada to get to the eastern resorts and use the bus for the last lap.

West of Málaga, the electric train runs as far as **Fuengirola**, stopping at Torremolinos, Benalmadena and Los Boliches *en route*. This train is free on Inter-Rail, but to get on to Marbella or further west, you have to resort to buses.

**Torremolinos** is the most commercialized centre. Look for rooms in hostels leading down to the beach. As far as eating and nightlife goes, you'd have a job actually to miss the tourist menus, bars and discos, so there's no problem there. Tourist Information (Tel. 95 237 1159) is on Plaza Pablo Ruiz Picasso (open daily 9am–2pm). If this doesn't appeal, move on to other resorts till you find a suitable one.

**Marbella** is slightly more 'up market', so prices can be higher here. There's a good **youth hostel** here on Calle Trapiche 2 (Tel. 95 277

1491; Fax. 95 286 3227) with dorm beds from 1,000ptas. A tent outside costs around 800ptas per person. As for pensions, try **Aduar** at Calle Aduar 7, (Tel. 95 277 3578) with singles from 1,800ptas and doubles from 2,800ptas.

**Fuengirola** is a good compromise between the two resorts listed above. With its six km of beaches and many cheap beds and restaurants, it's an attractive proposition to the footsore Eurorailer.

## Gibraltar

Gibraltar, one of Britain's few remaining colonies, stands as a gateway to the Mediterranean. Its position as a melting-pot of culture – Mediterranean, British and Arabic – means it's an interesting place to prepare for a trip to North Africa or, indeed, to recover from the culture shock so often experienced in Morocco. Better known as 'The Rock', it has been in the hands of the British since 1704, though, while it still remains dependent on Britain, the largely self-governed colony has a strong desire to become more self-sufficient.

Diplomatic relations with Spain are often strained, so when approaching Gibraltar be prepared for frustrating delays when crossing the border. The easiest way of getting there is by bus from Algeciras to La Linea (around 250ptas). Then simply stroll across the border, which is only a stone's throw from the bus station.

Tourist Information Centres are easy to find. The main one is at Duke of Kent House, Cathedral Square (Tel. 74950).

If the urge takes you, pop into Marks and Spencer, Tesco and Safeway and pick up some of those things you've been missing from home (Marmite, soft loo roll, Pringles etc). Also stock up on cheap cigarettes and alcohol before you leave – prices here are the lowest in Europe (Gibralter is duty free). Spanish pesetas are accepted everywhere, but the pound (sterling) is preferred currency.

A ferry runs to/from **Morocco** on Mondays, Wednesdays and Fridays (£30 return). Check the timetable, as it changes frequently.

### SEEING

Despite being only six km long, Gibraltar has a lot to offer. Visit the **Upper Nature Reserve**; the view from the top, with Africa in the distance, is truly spectacular. Here you can see the famous **Barbary Apes** (local legend has it that if they ever leave, then British rule will also end on the Rock). The nature reserve is also home to **St Michael's Cave**, an immense grotto which has played host to concerts and gala shows in the past. The **Upper Galleries** can also be visited. Excavated by the British during the Great Siege of 1779–83, they provided an impregnable line of artillery within the actual north face of the Rock. An exhibition called *Gibraltar: A City under Siege* can be found on the descent from the Upper Rock (it includes 18th-century graffiti). Also worth a visit is the **Tower of Homage**, sole survivor of a huge Moorish castle now buried beneath housing estates. It's open to the public and also doubles as the local prison!

A general Rock Tour, including the above sites and more, can be arranged with local taxi drivers for around £10 per person, or you can walk and pay entrance fees at each individual site (which works out cheaper). Another option is the excellent cable car to the top of the Rock (£5 return; the cable car ticket gives free entry to St Michael's Cave and the Apes' Den).

The town of Gibraltar, with its narrow, winding streets, is charming in itself. Visit the museum, built within the walls of an ancient Moorish bath house (£2.00; open Mon.–Fri.). Relax under the shade of pine trees in the beautiful Alameda Botanical Gardens. If all else fails, go for a swim off one of Gibraltar's five beaches.

## SLEEPING

The one drawback with Gibraltar is the high price of accommodation. There are a couple of affordable places, the cheapest being the **Toc H Hostel** (Tel. 73431) on Line Wall Road (the south end) which has dorm beds from £5. The **Emile Gibraltar Youth Hostel** (Tel. 51106), on the same road, charges from £10 for a dorm bed and breakfast. Next best is the **Queen's Hotel**, 1 Boyd Street (Tel. 74000; Fax. 40030): singles from £20, doubles from £30 (ask about youth and student discounts). Most travellers stay in La Linea, across the border in Spain. (If you are intent on staying in Gibraltar, try sleeping on the beaches – but be sure to hide from the police as this is frowned upon by the authorities.)

## NOTES

..............................................................................................................................

..............................................................................................................................

..............................................................................................................................

..............................................................................................................................

..............................................................................................................................

..............................................................................................................................

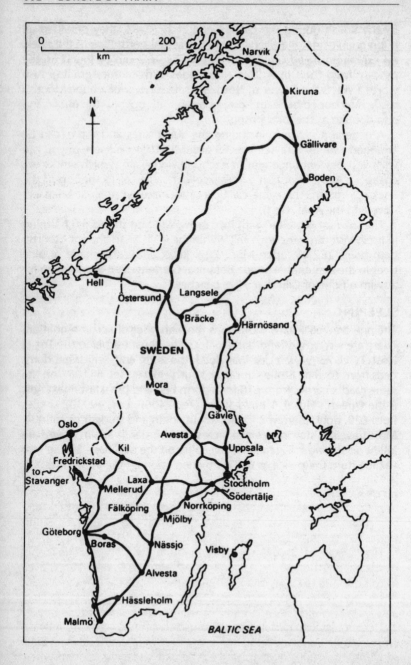

# SWEDEN (Sverige)

| | |
|---|---|
| Entry requirements | Passport |
| Population | 8.9 million |
| Capital | Stockholm (pop.: 1.6 million) |
| Currency | Krona |
| | £1 = approx 13.6kr |
| Political system | Constitutional monarchy |
| Religion | Lutheran |
| Language | Swedish (English widely spoken) |
| Public holidays | New Year's Day, Epiphany (6 Jan.), Good Friday, Easter Monday, Labour Day (1 May), Ascension Day, Whit Monday, Friday afternoon/Saturday closest to 21 June (Midsummer's Eve and Day) , All Saints' Day (31 Oct.), Christmas Eve, Christmas Day and Boxing Day |
| International dialling | To Sweden: int' l code 46 |
| | From Sweden: 009 + country code |
| Emergency telephone numbers | All emergencies 112 |

More than twice the size of Britain and with a fraction of its population, Sweden offers a wide variety of landscapes, climates, cultures and traditions: ranging from the Sami people of mountainous Lapland in the north, to the mild climate, castles and flat, rural setting of the south. But obviously the biggest extreme in the land of the 'Volvo' comes between the permanent daylight of summer and the long dark days of winter.

Having been inhabited since 6000 BC, Swedish Vikings in the 9th and 10th centuries decided to branch out and pushed eastwards across the Baltic Sea. They founded the principality of Novgorod – a seedling that was to grow into Russia – and went on to enjoy a prosperous period of trade. But the German merchants of the Hanseatic League were keeping a close eye on things and soon wanted to get a piece of the action. In fact by the end of the 14th century they had more than a piece – they had a complete monopoly on Baltic trade.

The Union of Kalmar in 1397 united Sweden, Norway and Denmark, but the Swedes gained little from this as Denmark took over as top dog. In 1523, after a national uprising, the Danes were finally driven out of the country by Gustav Vasa, who was later elected king and ended Sweden's economic dependency on the Hanseatic League.

The country reached its peak in the 17th century, winning a Baltic empire under Gustavus Adolphus, though defending this saw war after war until the 1800s. Not surprisingly, it was widely welcomed when the Swedes declared themselves neutral in the 19th century.

These days Sweden has one of the world's highest standards of living and to the tourist this equates to it being one of the most expensive countries in Europe. However, since joining the EU in 1995, they have been making an effort to bring prices more in line with the rest of Europe – though the budget traveller needn't get too excited.

## GETTING THERE

The main routes from the UK are London–Brussels by Eurostar and up through Germany, or from Harwich to the Hook of Holland, then up. This takes about 22–25 hours to reach Stockholm.

By sea there are sailings five times a week from Harwich to Gothenburg and twice a week from Newcastle to Gothenburg in high season. Also, another ferry from Harwich to Esbjerg in Denmark connects up to a through-train to Copenhagen, and a line operates from Newcastle to Esbjerg. These routes are all operated by Scandinavian Seaways.

## SWEDISH STATE RAILWAYS
### (STATENS JÄRNVAGÄR, SJ)

Swedish trains are efficient, clean and comfortable. They are very rarely late and run frequent services (every hour or so) to most of the major cities. The journey from Stockholm to Malmö takes only six hours, and to Narvik in the far north of Norway 20 hours. The long-distance InterCity and InterRegio trains are the fastest, followed by the trains which are used on local routes. The local trains are not as slow as in some countries, but still stop at every station. Modern fast trains (the X-2000s) travel up to 200 kph, and the trains have audio channels in seats and outlets for computers! From Stockholm to Gothenburg takes under three hours, and from Stockholm to Malmö less than five. There are supplements on these and on City Express trains, but see 'Reservations'. Ask at stations for a free copy of SJ Tågtider timetables. Although SJ covers all the major lines, there are many other train operators in Sweden which have there own trains, routes, prices and regulations. For example, on SJ trains you have to arrange to bring your bicycle on board beforehand, whereas on Länstrafik you can just turn up and put your bike on. In summer, there are many special train routes geared for the tourist, the most impressive one is taken by the Inlandsbanan which runs from Mora to Gällivare. It's an incredibly slow journey (19 hrs) but very scenic. Note that travel on the Inlandsbanan from Mora to Östersund and Gällivare is included in the under 26s, but not the over 26s, Inter-Rail pass.

**PASSES AVAILABLE** Eurail and Inter-Rail passes are both valid. Sweden is in Inter-Rail Zone B, along with Norway and Finland. For further details of the Inter-Rail zones, refer to the Inter-Rail section in Part One of this guide.

A Euro Domino ticket is also available, see p. 23 for details.

The Swedish Rail Pass, which now includes all supplements for X-2000 trains, covers all of the country and costs £143 for three days' rail travel within a week, £177 for five days out of 14, £216 for seven consecutive days and £273 for 14 consecutive days.

The popular ScanRail Pass is valid for 21 days in Sweden, Denmark, Norway and Finland and provides unlimited rail travel and discounted ferry services within Scandinavia. For details see Part One of the guide.

People under 26 can always get a 30% discount.

## INTER-RAIL FERRY BONUSES

|  | FROM | TO | REDUCTION % |
|---|---|---|---|
| Stena Line | Göteborg | Frederikshavn | 50% (1) |
| Silja Line | Stockholm | Helsinki | 50% (1) |
| Silja Line | Stockholm | Turku | 50% (2) |
| Silja Line | Vaasa | Umeå | 50% |
| TT-Line | Trelleborg | Lübeck/Travemünde | 50% |
| Viking Line | Stockholm | Helsinki | 50% |
| Viking Line | Stockholm | Turku | 50% |

(1) Reservations are compulsory on sailings. Accommodation charges must be paid in full.

(2) Applicable to four-berth tourist cabin accommodation only.

## EURAIL BONUSES

**FREE SERVICES** Steamer service of the Silja Line between Stockholm and Aland Islands–Turku. (Full fare is charged for cabin space and reservation is compulsory between Sweden and Helsinki.)

Ferry crossings operated by the Swedish and Danish State Railways between Helsingborg and Helsingør (Denmark).

Ferry crossing from Trelleborg to Sassnitz (Germany).

## REDUCED FARES

50% Ferry crossings operated by Stena Line between Gothenburg and Frederikshavn (Denmark).

25% reduction for Eurailpass holders on the hydrofoil of the Scandlines Flyvebädene between Malmö and Copenhagen.

50% reduction on normal fares for the ferry crossing Trelleborg–Travemünde (Germany) on the TT-Line.

50% reduction on the full fare of the TR-Line for the ferry crossing Trelleborg–Rostock.

## TRAIN INFORMATION

No problems here, as everyone speaks perfect English and queues are never too long. For train information, telephone 020 75 75 75.

**RESERVATIONS** Compulsory at a cost of 30–100kr. Tickets bought at stations in Sweden automatically include a reservation. On all trains apart from X-2000 services, for which advance purchase is essential, you can board without tickets or reservations and buy them from the conductor, although you still have to pay the charge on the train.

**NIGHT TRAVEL** This is relatively cheap in Sweden at about 95kr for a couchette and about 175kr for a second-class sleeper.

**EATING ON TRAINS** All long-distance expresses have a bistro or dining car.

**CINEMA COACH** On the night train Luleå–Stockholm is the cinema coach, with a film saloon and bistro. Films change regularly and cost about 60kr entry. Check before you pay the supplement that the films are in a language you can understand.

**SCENIC TIPS** Any line north of Stockholm is of interest, particularly from Östersund onwards, either to Trondheim in Norway or to Kiruna in the far north.

**BIKES** Bikes go as luggage as Swedish trains have no guard's vans. This means that your bike may not travel on the same train, so to be sure it arrives with you, send it three days in advance. Cost per bike is 130kr.

## TOURIST INFORMATION

Every Swedish county has a Tourist Board in addition to the local Tourist Information Offices called *Turistbyrå*. They are very helpful and always have a good selection of maps and brochures.

**ISIC BONUSES** Concessions in museums, theatres and cinemas and 20% off tours and day trips to historic places. For further information, contact KILROY Travels, Kungsgatan 4, Box 7144, Stockholm (Tel. 08 234515).

**MONEY MATTERS** 1 krona (kr) = 100 öre.
Banking hours are Mon.–Fri.: 9.30am–3pm. Bank charges are high for traveller's cheques (approximately 50kr) so it makes sense to cash large denominations. Forex offices, found in the major cities, will change traveller's cheques at a much cheaper commission rate, however, and are worth looking out for. Credit cards are widely accepted in Sweden.

**SHOPS** Most shops are open 9.30am–6pm on weekdays and until 2pm or 3pm on Saturdays. In some larger towns department stores stay open until 8pm or 10pm with some opening Sundays 12 noon until 4pm.

**POST OFFICES** Main city post offices open Mon.–Fri.: 8/8.30am–6/6.30pm; close around 4pm on Sat. Smaller post offices often have shorter hours and may well close at lunch time on Sat..

The *poste restante* service is free in Sweden and stamps are sold at newsagents' as well as post offices.

**MUSEUMS** Normally open from around 10am–5pm.

## SLEEPING

Pick up free lists of hotels and campsites at all regional and local Tourist Offices; many also have a room-finding service called *Rumsförmedling*. They charge a small commission and can find you a room in a private house or in a hotel. In smaller towns and villages look for the sign *Rum* (the Swedish equivalent of B&B, except there's no breakfast). At about 200kr for a single, this represents as good value as you're likely to get – apart from private rooms, which can be booked at local Tourist Offices for around 100–150kr per person, plus a one-off booking fee of 30–50kr. In Stockholm, Malmö and Gothenburg, 350–450kr will get you a package deal which includes bed, breakfast and the city's discount card.

Youth hostels are great and cost between 80–175kr per night; add another 40kr to this if you're not a member. For more information, contact Svenska Turistföreningen (STF), Stureplan 4, PO Box 25, 10120, Stockholm (Tel. 08 463 2100; Fax. 08 678 1958)

Camping's no problem thanks to the Allmansrätt law which allows anyone to camp on unfenced land for one night only. Please be careful about fire though. Tourist Information will direct you to suitable places. If you prefer your comforts, most towns have campsites with excellent facilities costing about 80–150kr per tent (cheaper off season), but these require a Swedish Camping Pass (50kr) obtainable at any site (you can get hold of a free Camping Pass by writing to Svirges Campingvärdars Riksförbund, Box 255, 45117 Uddevalla (Fax. 0522 642 430)). Apply at least one month in advance. Many campsites also have cabins to rent out. These are generally well equipped and cost around 250–375kr for one which sleeps four. If possible, phone ahead to book one as they are very popular.

## EATING AND NIGHTLIFE

Eating out is incredibly expensive in Sweden even at fast-food joints like McDonald's. Always check to see if there's a tourist menu or a cheap set meal (*dagens rätt*) for 50–65kr (note, lunch is served between 11am–2pm). More often than not, you'll be eating from supermarkets, which is no bad thing as the quality and choice are excellent. Most of the regional specialities, such as smoked reindeer meat from Lapland, are expensive and confined to the best restaurants. *Smörgåsbord* is cheaper here than in Norway if you feel like a Scandinavian splash-out.

Nightlife is what you make it in Sweden and there's no shortage of things to do. Alcohol and tobacco are expensive and controlled by the government, but there's not much the authorities can do during the midsummer festival when everyone lets rip with non-stop dancing and drinking, particularly in the north.

# Stockholm phone code: 08

Sitting upon 14 islands, Stockholm is praised as the most beautiful city in Sweden and has all the qualities you'd expect of the country's capital – tidy, well laid-out, socially minded and efficiently run. In 1998 it held the status of Cultural Capital of Europe: a celebrated landmark that saw major renovations and a sprucing up of the city in preparation for it. The local environment has benefited too, with a scheme that has made its waterways clean and safe for swimming. From some of these outlets you've also got the opportunity to sail around the 24,000 islands – or at least a selection of them – that make up the nearby archipelago.

You'll be hard pressed to make out on a tight budget here, as even supermarket food is expensive, but you'll get by if you follow our suggestions and use your common sense.

## STATION FACILITIES
Stockholm Central is well equipped with all the facilities you might expect, including Tourist Information, and there's a 24-hour train information line: Tel. 020 757575. If you don't have 5kr for the station toilet, there's a free (grotty) one next door.

Frequent trains to Malmö, Copenhagen, Gothenburg, Oslo and all Sweden.

## TOURIST INFORMATION
Apart from at the station, there's an office in the centre on the ground floor of Sweden House (*Sverigehuset*), Kungsträdgården, opposite the department store NK (Tel. 789 2495; at weekends 789 2490). It's open weekdays: 8am–6pm; weekends 9am–5pm (daily to 3pm in winter). Pick up maps and *Stockholm This Week* before visiting the Swedish Institute on the first floor, which has useful factsheets on Sweden, and where everyone involved seems incredibly helpful.

## ADDRESSES
**POST OFFICE** Vasagatan 28–34; open Mon.–Fri.: 8am–6.30pm, Sat.:

10am–2pm. Also at the central station; open 7am–10pm, Sat. and Sun.: 10am–7pm. There's another large post office at Drottninggatan 53 (closed Sun.).

**AMEX** Birger Jarlsgatan 1 (Tel. 679 7880); open Mon.–Fri.: 9am–5pm, Sat.: 10am–1pm

**UK EMBASSY** Skarpögatan 6–8 (Tel. 671 9000)

**US EMBASSY** Strandvägen 101 (Tel. 783 5300)

**IRISH EMBASSY** Östermalmsgatan 97 (Tel. 661 8005)

**CANADIAN EMBASSY** Tegelbacken 4, 7th floor (Tel. 453 3000)

**AUSTRALIAN EMBASSY** Block 5, Sergels Torg 12 (Tel. 613 2900)

**NEW ZEALAND EMBASSY** Sture Plan 2 (Tel. 611 2625)

**24-HOUR CHEMIST** Apoteke Scheele, Klarabergsgatan 64 (Tel. 454 8100).

**MEDICAL EMERGENCIES** At night, the duty doctor can be contacted on 463 9100

**STUDENT TRAVEL OFFICE** Kilroy Travels, Kungsgatan 4 (Tel. 234515)

## GETTING ABOUT

The underground and buses are good and charge by the zone, with individual journeys costing 14kr (plus 7kr per additional zone). Three-day transit passes cost 120kr, less for children and seniors (including free entry to Gröna Lund and the Kaknäs Tower (Kaknästornet) and reduced admission to Skansen); 24-hour passes cost 60kr. Buy these at Tourist Information or at stalls in the underground.

The Stockholm Card (*Stockholmskortet*), also known as the 'Key to Stockholm', is available for 199kr for 24 hours, 398kr for 48 hours and 498kr for 72 hours. A children's pass (age 7–17) can be bought in conjunction with an adult pass for 49kr for 24 hours (maximum two child cards per adult card). It gives free travel on buses, the underground, suburban trains, museum entrances, many of the sights and a one-hour sightseeing trip by boat. It also gives you a discount on a boat excursion to Drottningholm Palace. The card can be bought from Tourist Offices, information centres, most camping sites and youth hostels.

The banks also hand out free city maps and if nature calls, the best toilets are in the department stores such as NK. Look out for the underground station at Kungsträdgården – it is like a long art gallery of decorated walls.

## SEEING

Close to Stockholm's centre lie the islands of Gamla Stan, Skeppsholmen and Djurgården where the vast majority of sights are located. **Gamla Stan**, or the Old Town, dates back to the mid-13th century. The narrow medieval streets are full of trendy shops and restaurants, nightclubs and studios. The 18th-century **Royal Palace** is in Gamla Stan and has parts of it open to the public until about 4pm daily, except Mon.

The **Museum of Modern Art** is in the centre of **Skeppsholmen** which is home to a superb collection including the likes of Dali, Matisse and Picasso. Opening times are Tues.–Thurs.: 11am–7pm, Fri.–Sun. 11am–6pm; entrance is 60kr. On the northern tip of this island is the **Museum of Far Eastern Antiquities** which displays a good collection of Easterm antiquities (entrance 40kr). Also on Skeppsholmen is the **National Museum** (Tues. and Thurs. 10/11am–8pm, Wed. and Fri.–Sun. 11/11am–5pm). To the east is **Djurgården**, an island almost entirely devoted to recreation. There are two park areas separated by water, which freezes in winter providing a natural ice rink for the locals. Take the ferry over from Slussen or Nybroplan, or walk from Strandvägen. This is where the 17th-century warship *Vasa* is on view. This flagship of the Swedish navy only lasted 10 minutes on her maiden voyage before sinking into oblivion, till she was rediscovered in 1956 and brought up. She's in a remarkable state of preservation and is well worth the 50kr fee (students 35kr).

If you're into ships and naval history, the **Museum Ships** at Sjöhistoriska Museet will be of interest. Here you can see an ice-breaker, lightship and medieval ship.

Stockholm's open-air museum, **Skansen**, is definitely one of Europe's best. It's called 'Sweden in miniature' with good reason, as an afternoon spent here will fill you in on Swedish folklore, architecture and history more than a week touring the country would. There are over 150 buildings of authentic Swedish design, demonstrations of folk dancing, craftsmen at work, a zoo, an aquarium and lots more. Open daily; May: 9am–8pm; June–Aug.: 9am–10pm; Sept.–Oct.: 9am–5pm; Nov.–Dec.: 9am–6pm. Entrance costs 60kr from May–Aug. (it's cheaper at other times). Not far from here is also the favourite family attraction of **Gröna Lund Tivoli** amusement park. A day ticket costs around 200kr and gives unlimited rides.

The only dance museum in the world is at **Folkets Hus**, Barnhusgatan 12/14, while for gay and lesbian visitors, the centre at Sveavägen 59 (Tel. 736 0215) (T-bana: Rådmansgatan) has a bookstore, café, restaurant and nightly disco.

**FREE STOCKHOLM:** The city offers a number of things to keep the gratis-seeking traveller busy for a while. Worth checking out is the **changing of the guard** which takes place outside the Royal Palace (Mon.–Sat.: 12.15 noon, Sun.: 1.15pm).
* You can also take one of the free guided tours of Sweden's

**Parliament**, on Helgeandsholmen – available in July and August, leaving from the rear of the building Mon.–Fri.: 12.30 noon and 2pm.

- The **Swedish House of Culture** (Kulturhuset) at Sergelstorg is a good example of the country's social-mindedness too. In summer, exhibitions of art and crafts are always on offer as well as free 'creative activities' for anyone who wants to participate. If you're feeling inspired, pop in and model or paint your masterpiece: there's a library and access to foreign newspapers as well.
- **Strandvägen** on Ostermalm is a pleasant waterfront to stroll along, while walks along the city's many other waterways are generally a nice way to spend some time too.
- Cool off by **swimming** in one of the city's many designated bathing areas
- For picnics or just general laziness, the parkland on **Djurgården** is a top choice
- There's a popular **beach** on the small island of Långholmen
- Enjoy the carnival atmosphere of the 10-day **Stockholm Water Festival**, in mid-August

## SLEEPING

Hotellcentralen (Tel. 789 2425 or 791 8666) at the central station will give you a map and list of hostels and hotels or find you a bed for a fee of 40kr per room, 15kr fee for a hostel bed. The International Youth Centre will also help out if you're really stuck. You'd do well to make use of these services, especially in peak season, as beds (especially cheap ones) are thin on the ground, though in July many Swedes head south, leaving a bit of space in the city. Hotellcentralen also has special deals, such as the Stockholm Package which costs around 400kr and includes a hotel room, breakfast and a free Stockholm Card. Ask for more details and about other current offers.

The most memorable place to stay in Stockholm is definitely on board the **af Chapman**. This youth hostel is a 19th-century sailing ship, fully rigged and decked out, and moored opposite the Gamla Stan; it costs around 130kr for a 'berth' in an eight-bed cabin for IYHF members; non-members pay a supplement of 40kr. You need to pre-book or turn up early – 9am at the latest – to stand a chance; call 463 2266 or 679 5017; Fax. 611 7155. There's also a large **youth hostel** beside the ship (same contact numbers and same prices as the ship).

For hostels, try one of the following: **Gustav af Klint** at Stadsgårdskajen 153 (Tel. 640 4077) which is a floating hostel, tends to be rather noisy (dorm beds and four- to two-berth cabins); **STF Backpackers' Inn**, Banérgaten 56 (Tel. 660 7515; open late June–mid-Aug.); **City Backpackers**, Barnhusgatan 16 (Tel. 206920; great hostel near the train station, complete with sauna) or **Columbus Hotell-Vandrarhem**, in a former brewery at Tjähovsg. 11 (Tel. 644 1717).

For affordable hotels and pensions, try **Gustav Vasa**, Västmannagatan 61 (Tel. 343801) or **Tre smü rum**, Högbergsgatan 81 (Tel. 641 2371). Pleasant, small (six rooms) hotel in the centre of Södermalm. Out of the five city campsites, the nearest ones are **Ängby Camping** on Lake Mälaren (Tel. 370420) on underground 17 or 18, and **Bredäng Camping** (Tel. 977071) on subway 13 or 15 to Bredäng station. Refer to *Cheap Sleeps Europe 2000* for more accommodation options.

## EATING AND NIGHTLIFE

Face the fact, you're going to have to spend twice as much as you would in southern Europe to eat out here. Picnics are the answer, in conjunction with bar meals (*bars* are basic self-service restaurants here). In conventional restaurants look out for *dagens rätt* (today's special) for a slightly cheaper lunch or snack. Buy in supplies at **Östermalms Saluhall** or **Hötorgshallen**, the two big indoor markets. The central supermarkets also do a good line in groceries and the prices are cheaper than in the indoor markets.

While *smörgåsbord* are filling and tasty, they also tend to be pricey; however, if you arrive in Stockholm Central after a long train journey, treat yourself to the excellent *stora frukost* (eat-as-much-as-you-like breakfast) which will keep you going all day for around 75kr.

For inexpensive and popular Swedish cuisine check out **Markurells**, Vasagatan 26, Norrmalm or **Slingerbulten**, Stora Nygatan 24, Gamla Stan. For cheap Indian food, try the **Maharajah** at 20 Stora Nygatan. If you're cutting all corners and don't mind plastic atmospheres and fast food, there are a number of outlets to choose from. There are several **McDonald's** beside the Kulturhuset. In the evening the south side of Stockholm tends to be the best area to head for.

There are plenty of pubs and clubs in Gamla Stan, Götgatan and the area around Medborgarplatsen, with bands, from 50kr–60kr entrance. For cheaper entertainment, go over to Skansen or Gröna Lund where there's usually dancing, etc. Check with *Stockholm This Week* for current events. The music pub **Historia** and **Café Opera**, both on Kungsträdgården, are good places to meet young Stockholmers. The former resembles the bar in the TV series *Cheers*. At midnight the chairs/tables are cleared for a disco to begin. Entry is free before 11pm.

## EXCURSIONS

**UPPSALA** The old university town is 45 minutes away by train. On a day trip here you can see the medieval **Cathedral**, 16th-century **Castle**, the oldest **University** in Sweden, **Pre-Viking Burial Mounds**

and the **Upplands Museum**, which details the city's history and customs. Tourist Information is at Fyris Torg 8 (Tel. 018 274800).
**DROTTNINGHOLM PALACE** An alternative excursion is to the residence of the royal family. Built in the 17th century, it lies eight km west of the capital on the island of Lovön. It's all very pretty: Chinese pavilion, unusual 200-year-old theatre, etc. To get there, either head for Klara Mälarstrand (near city hall) and take the steamer, or take the underground to Brommaplan and then change to Mälaröbuses.
**VIEW OF THE ISLANDS** To see at least some of Stockholm's islands in the archipelago, take a bus out to the TV tower at **Kaknästornet**. This 152m tower is reputed to have the fastest lift in Europe, but the view is worth it once your stomach has settled down. There is also a cafeteria and restaurant with prices which are not as extortionate as you will find in similar towers in other countries.

## Malmö phone code: 040

Malmö is Sweden's third largest city and lies within the endless fields and sandy beaches of the country's southern area of Skåne. It's easily reached by hydrofoil from Copenhagen (late this year when the Öresund bridge is completed, the trip to Copenhagen will be even quicker), or by train from Stockholm or Gothenburg, and makes a pleasant stop-off.

### TOURIST INFORMATION
Tourist Information is inside the station. The staff are extremely helpful and can sell you the Malmö Card (*Malmökartet*), which costs 150kr for 24 hours, 275kr for 48 hours and 400kr for 72 hours, and gives free bus transport, free parking, free entry to museums and other attractions, 50% off day trips to Copenhagen by hydrofoil, 50% discounts on sightseeing bus tours and special offers in restaurants and discounts at certain shops. One card is valid for one adult and up to two children (aged 16 and under). (The card can also be bought at hotels and campsites). Pick up the *Malmö This Month* guide, which is free and widely available, for details of events going on.

### SEEING
The train station is handily placed just north of the **Gamla Stan** (old town), the area to concentrate upon. The **Stortorg** is a massive market square, built in the 16th century, and the centre of things. Look for the **Rådhus** (town hall) on one side of the square; it is worth the tour inside. Don't miss the **Lilla Torg**, an idyllic square of medieval houses

and cobblestones off the Stortorg, and full of stalls and buskers in the summer months. Take a look at the **St Petri Kyrka**, a Gothic church behind the Rådhus.

The **Malmöhus** is Malmö's castle, once a prison, with Lord Bothwell, Mary Queen of Scots' last husband, on its guest books. You can visit the royal apartments and marvel at the collection of portraits and fine furniture. Also in the castle complex are several museums, including the **Museum of Natural History**, the **Town Museum** and the **Museum of Art**. There is also an aquarium. One entry ticket (around 40kr) allows access to everything in the complex as well as entry to the other city museums for the rest of the day.

There is a good **beach** south of the Slottspark, further on from the castle.

## SLEEPING

The best of Malmö's two official hostels is **City Youth Hostel**, Västergatan 9 (Tel. 235640). If you can't get in here try the other, 5km out at Backavagen 18 (Tel. 82220; Fax. 510659). Bus route 21A. Alternatively, there's a **KFUM** summer hostel at Betaniaplän 4 (Tel. 76930).

However, camping is your cheapest bet in Malmö, as in much of Sweden; bus 82 from Centralplan or 12B or 12G from Gustav Adolfs Torg will take you to **Sibbarp Camping** at Strandgatan 101 (Tel. 342650 or 155165).

**EXCURSION** Fifteen minutes away is the pleasant university town of **Lund**, which has a magnificent cathedral and an interesting outdoor museum (Kulturen), with demonstration crafts and old houses.

# Gotland

The country's largest island, Gotland, is a popular summer destination for Swedes and is best known for its medieval remains (more than 100 medieval churches), prehistoric sites and connections with the Hanseatic League. Take the ferry from Oskarshamn or Nynäshamn to **Visby**, the major town on Gotland. Destination Gotland is the ferry operator; to find out ferry times and purchase tickets in Stockholm, visit Gotland City at Kungsgatan 57 (Tel. 08 236170) or ask at the local tourist offices for connection times and details: fares are more expensive at weekends, with a one-way ticket costing 190kr as opposed to 145kr on weekdays (35% discount for students). The Tourist Office in Visby is in Burmeister House on Donnersplats (Tel. 0498 201700 or 0498 247065).

Visby is an attractive town with interesting buildings; UNESCO has recognized its importance by making it a World Heritage-listed town. While you are here, check out the **Old City Walls**, the cobbled **Medieval Port**, the Viking remains in the **Gotlands Fornsal Museum** and the **St Maria Cathedral**. The real reason to come to Gotland, however, is to visit the unspoilt countryside. Bicycles can be rented at several places around the ferry terminal and Tourist Office. The going rate starts from around 65kr per day or 325kr per week, or you can rent a moped for about 250kr per day.

The high point of the island's calendar is medieval week, traditionally the first or second week in August.

# Gothenburg (Göteborg) phone code: 031

Gothenburg is Sweden's second largest city, and one of its most attractive. Home to the largest harbour in Scandinavia, it has a distinct British feel to it which gives rise to it being known as 'Little London'. The city is big on parks, museums and canals and, considering it's only about four hours from Stockholm, makes an interesting alternative route down the country's west coast to Copenhagen.

## STATION FACILITIES

Göteborg Central has train information available 7am–10pm daily (Tel. 020 757575). Here you'll also find left-luggage, a supermarket, post office and *bureau de change*. Daily trains leave for Oslo, Stockholm, Malmö, Copenhagen and northern Sweden.

From Göteborg harbour, there are ferry services to Denmark, Germany, England and Holland.

## GETTING ABOUT

You can either buy a 24-hour pass for the excellent bus and tram system for around 45kr, or invest in the Gothenburg Card (*Göteborgskortet*), which gives you free public transport (buses, trams and archipelago boat trips), free or half-price museum entrance, free entry to the Liseberg amusement park and a free boat trip to Elfsborg Fortress. There are also special offers for shopping, special events, entertainment, restaurants and sights. It costs 95kr for 24 hours (50kr for children under 17). The card can be bought at Gothenburg Tourist Offices, the Central Station, Pressbyrån kiosks, hotels, youth hostels and camping sites.

## TOURIST INFORMATION

Apart from the information kiosk at Östra Nordstan, the shopping centre next to the Central station, the main Tourist Office is at Kungsportsplatsen 2 (Tel. 100740), open daily June–Apr.: 9am–6pm (8pm late June–early Aug.) and at other times: 9am–5pm (closed Sat. pm and Sun.). Both offer free maps and an accommodation service (60kr fee for private rooms and 30kr fee for hotel rooms). Prices start from around 200kr for singles, with doubles around 325kr; their hotels are about twice the price.

## SEEING

The centre of Gothenburg is very modern, but if you head off to **Haga**, the old district of wooden houses and coffee shops, you'll see a different side of the city. Of the many parks worth visiting, try to take in the **Botanical Gardens**, **Slottskogen**, with its zoo, lakes and birds, and **Liseberg Leisure Park**, which has everything from discos to fun fairs. The Spaceport, at 83m, is the main feature of the funfair and not to be missed (free entry with the Gothenburg Card; you still have to pay for the rides). The **Art Centre** on Götaplatsen is an interesting place with work by some of the European and Nordic masters, such as Picasso and Rubens, and a good display of photos. For the nautically minded, the **Maritime Museum** (*Sjöfartsmuseet*) has ships from Viking times to the present day, including the submarine *Nordkaparen*.

The **Kronhuset** is the oldest building in the city. The neo-classical **Cathedral** is also worth visiting. The **Feskekörka**, a 19th-century building filled with fish stalls and vendors, is situated by the moat close to Huitfeldtsplatsen. The 7am auction in the fish market is worth getting up for.

## SLEEPING

There are lots of good youth hostels to choose from. Try the **Dalagärda Vandrarhem** (Tel. 557152 or 553981; Fax. 553982 ) on Lillhagsparken 15, Hisings-Backa, where B&B is from 150kr in 2–8 bed rooms. In high season, there are also beds available for 110kr in a large sleeping hall. The hostel is four km from the centre and can be reached by bus. The **Masthuggsterrassens Vandrarhjem** (Tel. 424820; Fax. 424821) is down by the ferry terminal with dorms from 130kr, take tram 3, 4 or 9. **Villa Solhem** (Tel. 918863) in Landvetter is in an attractive location near a lake, about 15 km from the city. There are regular buses to the centre and to the airport. There is also the **Kvibergs** hostel at Kvibergsvägen 5 (Tel. 435055; Fax.432650), which is housed in an old barracks building. Dorm beds start from 110kr per night, single rooms from 200kr. five-bed cabins can also be rented which cost from 500kr per night. Get there on tram 6 or 7. If you fancy a night or two on a ship, the hostel, **M/S Seaside**, is about 300m from the station, along Packhuskajen (Tel. 105970; Fax. 132369), with a price of 180kr for a cabin bed; around 100kr for a dorm bed.

**Kärralund** (Tel. 840200) is the most central campsite and is reached by tram 5 to Welandergatan, though it is rather pricey. Bungalows also available. There are other sites at Askim, 12km from the centre. To get there, catch the Blå Express from the bus terminal.

## EATING AND NIGHTLIFE

Along Kungsportsavenyn (the main boulevard) are restaurants of all kinds and descriptions (from Chinese to Scottish), and alongside them are the increasingly popular fast-food chains. Fish and seafood are naturally in abundance in Gothenburg and often the *dagens rätt* will include a local fish dish. For cheap food you can't beat the student canteen, **Kåren**, at Götabergsgatan 17, while **Solrosen**, Kaponjärgatan 4a, offers excellent value vegetarian meals. Also strongly recommended is the **Figaro** bar/restaurant in the Stora Teatern at the Kungsportsavenyn. For picnic food, the markets on Kungstorget are best.

At night, a lot of the young locals seem to gather round Kungsportsavenyn to cast an eye over the visiting talent; otherwise, you're most likely to meet the resident students in the bar at the **students' union**, Kärhuskällaren, which is near Götaplatsen. Behind the market on Kungstorget is **Ölhallen**, an authentic Swedish pub, and there are quite a few disco and jazz clubs, though their entrance fees put most of them safely out of the average Eurorailer's reach.

# Lapland

It's easier to go up into Lapland from Sweden than from Norway, so take the opportunity while you can. Trains run right up to **Riksgränsen**, just before the border, and **Narvik** in Norway. From Stockholm to the border is a straight 24 hours, though the conditions on the trains don't make this seem as much of an ordeal as it sounds, and the scenery once you're around Gällivare or Kiruna is breathtaking.

Once you're up there, there's an inland line from Gällivare down through Jokkmokk and Arvidsjaur to Östersund.

It's legal to camp on unfenced land for one night, so you can go it alone in a big way, especially out of season. Make sure you leave the place tidy afterwards, though, and treat the plants with respect! Unless you've skin like leather, take with you mosquito repellent of some sort as they're out in force up there. The Svenska Turistföreningen,

Stureplan 4, Box 25,10120, Stockholm, are the people to write to for information on mountain tourist stations and huts, and suggested hiking routes.

To get the most out of a trip to Lapland, plan and book ahead as much as possible. Don't just wander aimlessly on to the train in Stockholm with no food or proper walking boots and expect to pick up relevant supplies once you're there, and don't go with fantasies in your head of great wilderness adventures with Lapps, reindeer and huskies. It's a bit like that, but in reality the towns are a bit grey and morose, and the Lapps (they call themselves *Sami*) are pretty sick of wide-eyed tourists pointing and gawping at them from June to September. If you do go, make sure you have the right equipment with you. Good preparation will ensure you get the most out of this stunning area.

**GÄLLIVARE** This strategic mining town is at the junction of the main line to Narvik and inland line to Jokkmokk. If you've time to kill here waiting for connections, go to the nearby iron mines at **Malmberget** and take the tour round (mid-June–mid-Aug.: Mon.–Fri. 10am–2pm; around 170kr; tours organized by the tourist office). You can also visit a copper mine (June–Aug.: Mon.–Fri. 2pm; around 150kr; again, tours arranged by the tourist office). You could also visit the museum at **Vasara** where there are skis dating back before the time of Christ. Apart from the **Ettore Church** and the largest log cabin in the world, that's about it here.

The Tourist Office is near the station at Storgatan 16, and is open mid-June–mid-Aug.: daily 9am–8pm and the rest of the year 9am–4pm. They'll give you details on how to get up to the **Stora Sjöfallet National Park** and the surrounding mountains. If you're staying, ask about the private accommodation here. The **youth hostel**, at Andra Sidan (Tel. 0970 14380; Fax. 0970 16586), is five minutes from the station. There's also a small private hostel (Tel. 0970 12534) near the river and a campsite.

If you're travelling up to Kiruna and beyond, consider returning via Narvik and Fauske in Norway. (A bus connects the two and Fauske is on the Bodø line.) If, on the other hand, you are heading down to **Luleå**, take some time out to visit the excellent **Museum of Lapp Culture**. In addition to being free of charge, you can also get cassettes to wander around with, explaining the exhibits as you go along. The **youth hostel**, at Örniksvägen (Tel. 0920 252325; Fax. 0920 252419), is open all year round; take bus 6 from Luleå.

**KIRUNA** The city itself is fairly unattractive, so use Kiruna as a base for the surrounding countryside. Tourist Information is at Lars Janssonsgatan 17 (Tel. 0980 18880), open in summer: 9am–8pm weekdays and 9am–6pm weekends; at other times: Mon.–Fri.: 9am–4pm.

There's a youth hostel called **STF Vandrarhem Kiruna**, at Bergmastaregaten 7 (Tel./Fax. 0980 17195). Open all year. Other cheap accommodation includes the **Yellow House** (Tel. 0980 13750), Hantverkaregatan 25.

There is also a campsite about 1½ km from the station, **Rådhusbyn Ripan** (Tel. 0980 63000), which has expensive cabins. The Tourist Information will get you into private houses for 200–350kr, plus a booking fee.

In the summer, there are tours of Kiruna's underground iron ore mines for around 95kr, arranged by Kiruna Guidetur. Their office is near the Tourist Office on Vänortsgatan 4.

If you are going on from Kiruna to Narvik, the north side of the train is the one to sit on to see the most spectacular scenery.

**JOKKMOKK** The **Ajtte Museum**, at Kyrkogatan 3, has special displays on Lapp history and culture and is well worth a visit. You'll find Tourist Information at Stortorget 4 (Tel. 0971 12140), where you can get 'Polar Certificates' to prove you've crossed the Arctic Circle (well, your Mum'll like it).

The **Gamla Kyrka** (old church) is the other main sight. There's an **IYHF hostel** at Åsgatan 30 (Tel./Fax. 0971 55977) and an official campsite, **Notuddens**, about 3 km from the centre.

**ARVIDSJAUR** The **Lapp Village** in the town of Arvidsjaur is still used today by Lapps visiting the town for festivals and gatherings. Tourist Information is at Garvaregatan 4, open 9am–8pm daily in the summer, and they'll arrange private accommodation for you. The **campsite** at Järnvägsgatan 111 (Tel. 0960 13420) does huts as well as tent sites, and opposite the station is the **Central Hotel** at Järnvägsgatan 63 (Tel. 0960 10098). The **youth hostel**, Lappugglans Turistviste, (private) is at Västra Skolgatan 9 (Tel. 0960 12413), 300m from the station.

NOTES
.................................................................................................
.................................................................................................
.................................................................................................
.................................................................................................
.................................................................................................
.................................................................................................

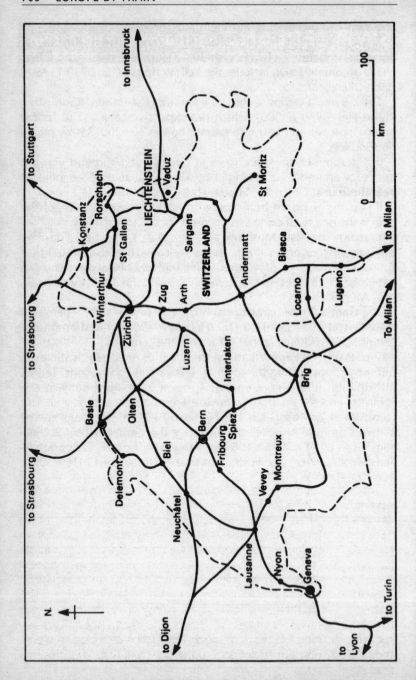

# SWITZERLAND, including Liechtenstein

| | |
|---|---|
| Entry requirements | Passport |
| Population | 7.2 million |
| Capital | Bern (pop.: 0.43 million) |
| Currency | Swiss Franc (SFr) |
| | £1 = approx 2.54 SFr |
| Political system | Federal republic |
| Religion | Roman Catholic and Protestant |
| Language | Swiss-German, French, Italian and Romansch |
| | (English widely spoken) |
| Public holidays | New Year's Day, Good Friday, Easter Monday, |
| | Ascension Day, Whit Monday, Swiss National |
| | Day (1 Aug.), Christmas Day and Boxing Day. |
| | Some cantons also observe 2 Jan., Labour Day |
| | (1 May), Corpus Christi and All Saints' Day |
| International dialling | To Switzerland: int'l code 41 |
| | From Switzerland: 00 + country code |
| Emergency telephone numbers | Police 117; ambulance 144; fire service 118 |

Switzerland is one of the most beautiful and mountainous countries in Europe, though its postcard good looks don't come cheap as it's also one of the most expensive to visit. The small landlocked country in the heart of the Continent is a major focus of tourism, offering urban sophistication, a wealth of historic landmarks and, of course, the magnificent Alps: traditionally home to the sounds of yodels and tinkling cowbells.

Curiously, the Swiss are rather obsessed by punctuality and cleanliness but where these traits originate from is open to debate. Their penchant to produce flashy watches and cuckoo clocks possibly makes them good time-keepers, while cleanliness is perhaps a characteristic that has been passed down ever since the Romans swept up after the Celts.

Today the country is a confederation of 23 cantons (and three sub-cantons), with its roots stretching back to 1291 when the first three cantons formed an alliance against the Habsburgs. By the start of the 16th century it had grown into a feared military superpower, but since Napoleon's invasion the country has taken a stand of neutrality (though in recent years this has been called in to question following allegations of Swiss bankers accepting gold and money from the Nazis in World War II).

Switzerland is one of Europe's top tourist destinations and provides few problems to the traveller. There are plenty of sights and activities to keep you busy, an impressive train service and English is widely spoken. Spending too much money is likely to be your biggest worry, though following our advice and suggestions will help keep this to a reasonable level.

## SWISS FEDERAL RAILWAYS
### (SCHWEIZERISCHE BUNDESBAHNEN, SBB)
### (CHEMINS DE FER FÉDÉRAUX, CFF)
### (FERROVIE FEDERALI SVIZZERE, FFS)

Swiss federal railways and various private railway companies combine to give one of the most extensive and efficient services in Europe. There are even plans (called Rail 2000) to improve services with new lines and half-hourly services, with fast new trains to rise to the challenge. The private outfits tend to serve the resort areas, except for the two largest. Most notable is the Bern–Lötschberg–Simplon line (BLS), Europe's largest private operation, which runs in friendly rivalry with the federal railway. International and intercity trains are federal-run, and intercity or express trains run hourly between all the main centres, while inland expresses run at least every other hour.

There is a supplement on only two inland routes: the Bernina express and the Glacier express. From Chur to Tirano or vice versa it is about £7 each way and from Zermatt to St Moritz or vice versa it is about £9 each way, including seat reservation. A useful spin-off is the free maps and leaflets given out to lure custom.

**PASSES AVAILABLE** Eurail, Europass and Inter-Rail are all valid. Switzerland is in Inter-Rail Zone C, along with Germany, Austria and Denmark. For details of the eight Inter-Rail zones, see the Inter-Rail section in Part One of this guide. Note, Eurail passes are not valid on private lines.

A Euro Domino ticket is also available, see p. 23 for details.

There are a number of rover tickets available in Switzerland, but the most useful is the Swiss Pass. It is available for four days, eight days, 15 days, 21 days or one month (prices: £98, £136, £162, £187, £213 in second class) and gives free travel on state railways, steamers, post buses, town buses and trams plus reductions on private lines. If there are two or more adults (max. five) travelling together on all journeys they can save 15% off each Swiss Pass. This takes the prices down to £83 for four days, £116 for eight, £137 for 15, £159 for 21 days and £181 for a month.

The Swiss Flexi Pass is valid for 3–9 days within a month and costs £94 for three days, £111 for four days, £128 for five days, £145 for six days, £157 for seven days, £170 for eight days and £183 for nine days in second class. New for this year is the Saver Programme Swiss Flexi Pass which gives a 15% discount on each Swiss Flexi Pass if there are two or more adults (max. five) travelling together on all of their journeys (this brings the 2nd class prices down to £80, £94, £109, £123, £134, £145, £156 for 3–9 days respectively). During the summer a number of regional tickets are also available. They are valid for seven or 15 days. With the latter the holder gets five days of free travel plus 10 days of half-price travel. Prices vary widely, depending on the region and class and length of ticket.

If you intend to stay mainly in one place and/or use many private lines, consider the Swiss Card, which gives free travel from the border to a destination and back plus reductions on other journeys. It's £64 second class for a month.

The Favourite Peaks of Switzerland pass has been introduced this year, for £52 the pass holder is entitled to three journeys on any of the following mountain railways: Schilthorn, Titlis, Klein Matterhorn, Brienzer Rothorn, Rochers de Naye, Corvatsch and Säntis.

There are no student discounts on any trains.

**INTER-RAIL BONUSES** On most private railways of Switzerland, Inter-Rail will bring you a 50% reduction, so always ask first (see Appendix I). One that doesn't is Furka Oberalp.

## EURAIL AND EUROPASS BONUSES

### FREE SERVICES
Regular steamer services on the lakes of Geneva, Lucerne, Thun, Brienz, Zürich, Neuchâtel, Biel, Murten, on the Rhine from Schaffhausen to Kreuzlingen and on the Aare from Biel/Bienne to Solothurn.

### REDUCED FARES
35% reduction on steamer services on Lake Constance between Romanshorn and Friedrichshafen and between Rorschach and Lindau.

50% reduction on the Bürgenstock funicular.

35% reduction to the top of Mount Pilatus near Lucerne, by funicular from Alpnachstad, as well as by cable car from Kriens.

35% reduction on entrance fee to the Transport Museum Lucerne, the biggest of its kind in Europe.

25% discount on Jungfrau Region and Rigi railways.

## TRAIN INFORMATION

National Rail Information is available on Tel. 157 2222. English is widely spoken throughout Switzerland and most Swiss timetables have an English section. If you have no luck finding anywhere to stay, look out for the travel-aid men with red, white and yellow armbands. You can store luggage at the stations, either at the counter (around 5SFr per piece) or in the lockers (2–5SFr per locker for 24hrs).

**RESERVATIONS** Must be made for the Glacier express and the Bernina express. Otherwise it's probably only worthwhile reserving if you are going to Italy, where overcrowding can be a problem, or if you hit a particularly busy weekend. Seats/couchettes can be booked up to two months ahead.

**NIGHT TRAVEL** Wagons-Lits run sleepers on all international routes at their standard rates and couchettes are also available. Sleepers can be booked up to three months in advance. SBB have no services on any inland runs.

**EATING ON TRAINS** Most stations are fairly well provided for, which is just as well as even the mini-bars are very expensive. If you've money to burn, the self-service buffet is much better value than the dining cars. Believe it or not, McDonald's have coaches on certain trains between Basel and Geneva, so it's now possible to have a Big Mac, should you feel the urge.

**SCENIC TIPS** To get to grips with Switzerland's many scenic rail routes would take at least a month and involve paying out vast amounts for private lines. Swiss Pass or Swiss Card holders get round this problem, but most Eurorailers have to be content with main-line runs. The possibilities are fortunately endless, without even leaving the main lines:

From Zürich take the train to Chur, then the narrow-gauge Rhaetian Railway to Tikano – Europe's highest line at 2,220m as well as one of the most spectacular. At Chur an alternative is to head towards Zermatt. This line passes over the Oberalp (2,000m) and through the Furka tunnel, but it gives no reduction to Inter-Railers.

Lucerne offers the greatest possibilities; foremost among them is the main line to Milan through the 14½ km Gotthard tunnel which took 2,500 men over seven years to construct in the 1880s. If this isn't spectacular enough, take the branch line to Locarno where you change trains for Domodossola in Italy. This line is a real favourite, passing through some incredible gorges. For the best view, sit on the left-hand side.

Also from Lucerne, the line to Interlaken is equally awe-inspiring. If you haven't seen enough and don't mind paying out, take the private line up to Kleine Scheidegg where, after you change trains, the line goes under the Eiger and on to the Jungfraujoch, Europe's highest station at 3,400m. Private lines also take you up to Mounts Rigi, Pilatus and Titlis from Lucerne.

Bern makes an alternative base for any of these trips, but if, like most Eurorailers, you're in a hurry, the main line to Milan via Brig will not be a disappointment. At Brig, if you've spare cash why not head for Zermatt, and take the cogwheel train up to Gornergrat and see the Matterhorn from close up. Approaching from the west, the train follows Lake Geneva as far as Lausanne, where the line splits to enter Bern or Brig – either route is beautiful.

The Martigny to Le Châtelard (and on to Chamonix) route is another classic. Sit on the left-hand side for the best view.

**BIKES** Can be hired at most SBB stations and some private ones; the cost is approximately 24SFr a day for a basic six-gear model. Racing and mountain bikes are also available. Bikes can be taken on normal/InterCity trains (around 6/12SFr per day) but not on EuroCity (EC) trains.

## TOURIST INFORMATION

Every town has its own well-organized Tourist Offices, usually situated near the station. They keep a good selection of maps and leaflets, as well as running a room-finding service. Ask for the Swiss Holiday Card map: this shows the rail network of the country. If you're planning to visit lots of museums, it might be worthwhile investing in the Swiss Museum Passport which is valid for 180 museums. It costs around 30SFr for a month. English tourist information is available on Tel. 157 5014.

**ISIC BONUSES** There's a variety of reductions on internal fares and in some museums. For further information, contact SSR Leonhard-strasse 10, Zürich, or SSTE, 3 rue Vignier, Geneva.

**MONEY MATTERS** 1 franc (SFr) = 100 centimes (c).

Banking hours are Mon.–Fri.: 8.30am–4.30pm (often closed 12 noon–2pm). Many stations have exchanges which stay open seven days a week. Switzerland is a good place to change money as few banks charge a commission and rates are generally favourable.

**POST OFFICES** Open Mon.–Fri.: 7.30am–6.30pm (often closed 12 noon–1.45pm), Sat.: 7.30am–11am. Longer hours in some cities.

**SHOPS** Open Mon.–Fri: 8.00am–6.30pm, and Saturdays until mid-afternoon. Many shops shut for lunch 12 noon–1.30pm and are often closed Mon. morning and Wed. afternoon, particularly in small towns. Some towns have late opening on Thurs.

**TIPPING** Service is generally included in restaurants and cafés, but if it has been good then round up bills to the nearest 5 or 10 SFr – but don't leave money on the table. Taxis usually include a tip in the charge – if not, give 15%. Give porters and WC attendants 0.5–1 SFr.

**EMAIL** You can now send emails from nearly all public telephones for only 1.50SFr per message (as long as they have no more than 240 characters).

## SLEEPING

Availability and price are the main problems you're likely to face in Switzerland. During the summer, the tourist resorts are packed and then there's always that unexpected conference in town. To avoid paying through the nose for somewhere to stay, arrive as early in the day as possible and start looking right away.

Tourist Offices keep lists of hotels and hostels in the area, and some will find you a room if required for a small charge. Hotels tend to be expensive with singles costing from around 40SFr (doubles start from around 80SFr but you should expect to pay 115SFr on average), so think twice before committing yourself. 'Hotel Garni' means a B&B without a restaurant (also look for *Zimmer frei* signs). Staying in these is a slightly better bet but they are still expensive. Even a dormitory bed in a student hostel can set you back 30SFr or more. Youth hostels often provide the only answer; there are 70 official Swiss Youth Hostels, most of which are very clean and have excellent facilities. IYHF cards are required and you can expect to pay 20–40SFr for a bed (and usually breakfast). For more information about youth hostels in Switzerland, contact Schweizer Jugendherbergen, Schaffhauserstrasse 14, Postfach 161, CH 8042 Zürich (Tel.01 3601414; Fax. 01 3601460; you can also make email bookings: bookingoffice@ youthhostel.ch).

Swiss campsites are among the best in Europe and at only 7–12SFr per person, plus 8–12SFr per tent, you can't go wrong. If you're forced to the hills to sleep out, remember it can get bitterly cold in Switzerland at night, even during the summer. Also bear in mind that some hotels in the mountains have cheaper annexes with dorm beds (*Massenlager* or *dortoir*) and there are Alpine huts which you can stay in. Ask at the local Tourist Office for more information.

Free accommodation is listed in a small brochure, *Schlafplätze für Unkomplizierte*, available for a small fee from the Vereinigung Ferien und Freizeit, Wasserwerkstrasse 17, CH-8035 Zürich.

You can stay in the hay (!) in over 300 farms between May and Oct. (sleeping bag required), Don't just doss down in the first barn you come to, visit the local Tourist Office and ask which farms in the area are participating in this scheme.

If you do decide to stay in a hotel or guesthouse, always ask the management for a Guest Card which entitles the holder to discounts on public transport and at local attractions.

## EATING AND NIGHTLIFE

Although Switzerland used to be *very* expensive, prices have not risen so fast here as in other parts of Europe. Budget travellers will find it a bit of a struggle to eat out, though. A lot of the regional specialities can be bought from supermarkets (try Co-op or Migros) and prices are certainly not as bad as in Scandinavia. Alpine areas have a good selection of cheeses and cold meats ideal for picnics.

The cheapest restaurants (*Gemeindestube*) don't serve alcohol, so if you want a glass of wine with your meal you'll have to check out the fixed-price menus. Look out for *Rösti* (a filling potato dish from the German area) or *Berner Platte* (a mixture of ham, bacon, and sausage with potatoes and green beans or pickled cabbage). If you can get a group together it's worth going for a fondue. Be aware that if you eat bread put out on the table you will be charged for it – as you will for water.

The Swiss don't exactly specialize in budget entertainment; as a result, most young people take to the bars. From spring through to autumn there are plenty of local folk festivals going on in the mountains, and on 1 August the sky is set alight by fireworks commemorating the founding of the Swiss Confederation.

## Zürich phone code: 01

Zürich is Switzerland's largest city and one of Europe's most expensive. Home to the country's biggest concentration of banks, it also offers streets paved with gold – well, actually, all the gold is beneath them: when walking along the average pavement you're striding over the vaults of the world's gold reserves. However, it doesn't really merit more than a day trip, even considering its picturesque old town.

### STATION FACILITIES
Situated in northern Switzerland, not far from the German border, Zürich handles trains to an impressive number of destinations in Switzerland, France, Germany, Belgium, the Netherlands, Hungary, Austria, Slovenia and Italy from its immaculately kept and well-equipped main station (Hauptbahnhof). Female travellers have reported spending a comfortable night in the waiting room here (you need a valid ticket), although I wouldn't officially recommend this option. Train information: Tel. 157 2222.

### TOURIST INFORMATION
The main office is in the train station's main hall. It's open Mon.–Fri.: 8.30am–7/8.30pm, weekends: 8.30/9am–6.30pm (Tel. 211 4000). There are leaflets on everything here and a free accommodation service (Tel. 215 4040). Pick up a copy of *Zürich News* and *Zürich Next* which list what's on in the city. They charge for maps so get a free one in town (try at one of the main banks).

The headquarters of Switzerland Tourism (288 1111) is at Tödistrasse 7, and has information on the whole of Switzerland.

Though the Swiss Student Reception Service is mainly a travel agent, it does also have information on Switzerland. It's at Leonhardstrasse 10 (Tel. 242 3000 or 297 1111) and issues ISIC cards.

## ADDRESSES

**AMEX** Uraniastrasse 14, open Mon.–Fri.: 8.30am–6pm, Sat.: 9am–1pm (Tel. 228 7777; Fax. 228 7700; emergency telephone 0800 550100)

**POST OFFICE** Kasernenstrasse 95/97, open Mon.–Fri.: 7.30am–8pm, Sat. 8am–4pm

**BRITISH CONSULATE** Minervaststrasse 117 (Tel.383 6560; Fax. 383 6561) open Mon.–Fri.: 9am–12 noon

**US CONSULATE** Dufourstrasse 101 (Tel. 422 2566) open Mon.–Fri.: 10am–1pm

**MEDICAL EMERGENCIES** Tel. 261 6100

**FIRST AID** Tel. 361 6161

## SEEING

Getting around Zürich is simple on the modern transport net of buses, trams and S-bahns. Multiple-strip tickets are sold from automated ticket machines, but your best bet is the day card for 7.20SFr, which allows unlimited travel on all forms of transport for 24 hours. If you want to explore the town on bicycle, Globus Department store on Theatreplatz and at Bahnhof Enge lend them out free daily in May–Oct. (from 7.30am–9.30pm). A deposit is required, either your passport or ID card plus 20SFr.

East of the Limmat River is **Old Zürich** with its 16th- and 17th-century guild houses (now restaurants and trendy shops) and nearby are the town's two medieval churches: **Fraumünster** on the left bank and **Grossmünster**, the austere Protestant cathedral, on the right. Walking tours of the old town are conducted daily, taking two hours and costing either around 20 or 30SFr depending which tour you opt for (either the 'Stroll through the Old Town' or the standard tour of the major sites). You can also choose to do the tour of the sites with a cable car and boat ride; this tour takes 2½ hours and costs around 40SFr. Last year saw the introduction of the **Zürich Trolley Experience**, a two-hour tour of the city in an old style bus (29SFr). For more information about any of the tours and the times they go, ask at the Tourist Office.

The **Zoo** in the Zürichberg woods and **Botanic Gardens** at Zollikerstrasse are wonderful picnic spots on good days, and on bad the **Rietberg** in the Wessendonck Villa at Gablerstrasse is excellent, with one of the best collections of non-European art in Europe. Open daily (except Monday) 10am–5pm.

There are all sorts of boat trips on Lake Zürich lasting 1½–4 hours, which Inter-Railers get concessions on, or there's the trip down the River Limmat, which takes you through old Zürich.

**FREE ZÜRICH:**

- **Bahnhofstrasse** is considered by some to be 'the most beautiful shopping street in the world'. However, coupled with prices well out of the reach of the budget traveller, it obviously makes ideal window shopping territory. It runs down from the station to the lake, where you can partake in safe, clean swimming and sunbathing.
- For the chocoholic, the **Lindt & Sprüngli Chocolate Factory** on Seestrasse 204 in Kilchberg has a museum and film and offers free samples. It is open Wed.–Fri.: 10am–12 noon and 1–4pm. Phone ahead on 716 2233
- If coffee's your weakness, visit the **Johann Jacobs Museum: Collection on the Cultural History of Coffee**, Seefeldquai 17, where you can learn all you could possibly wish to know about the coffee bean, see all sorts of coffee pots from around the world and enjoy an excellent cup or two of er, coffee (goes well with a Lindt chocolate!). Open Fri.–Sat. 2–5pm, Sun. 10am–5pm. Take tram 2 or 4 to Feldeggstrasse.
- A nice view over the old town is available by climbing to **Lindenhof** just up from the Fraumünster, where you'll also find some of Zürich's **Roman remains**.
- Not far from the university, in the **Fluntern Cemetery**, lies the grave of author **James Joyce**.
- Check out the markets at **Helvetiaplatz**, **Milkbuckstrasse** and **Bürkliplatz**.
- **Swiss National Museum**, behind the train station at Museumstr. 2
- **Kunsthaus Zurich** (Art Gallery) Heimpl. 1 – Free Sun.

## SLEEPING

It's probably best to forget hotels and keep it as basic as you can. The **campsite** on the Zürichsee is very good (train to Wollishofen, then 10-minute walk) and works out as your cheapest option (10SFr for a tent and around 7SFr per person). It's at Seestrasse 559 (Tel. 482 1612; open May to Sept.).

The **youth hostel** is big and not strictly run. It's at Mutschellenstrasse 114 (Tel. 482 3544; Fax. 4801727) and is reached by tram 6 or 7 to Morgental (no curfew; reception closes 12 noon–1pm). Dorm beds 30SFr. There is a handy supermarket opposite the hostel, which is cheaper than those in town.

For cheap pensions and one-star hotels, try the following: **Foyer Hottingen**, Hottingerstrasse 31 (Tel. 261 9315), run by nuns and only for women or married couples; **St George's**, Weberstrasse 11 (Tel. 251 1144); **Justinusheim**, Freudenberg Strasse 146 (Tel. 361 3806; Fax. 362 2982). These start from 40SFr for singles, 85SFr upwards for doubles (breakfast included). The cheapest place of all is probably the

**City Backpacker Hostel** (also known as Hotel Biber) at Niederdorfstrasse 5 (Tel. 251 9015; Fax. 251 9024), which charges 30SFr in dormitories (also has singles and doubles).

## EATING AND NIGHTLIFE
Round the station is as good as anywhere for cheap places, or use one of the many central **Migros** cafeterias. **Jelmoli**, the department store on Bahnhofstrasse, does good meals – the best value is the all-you-can-eat breakfast for around 14SFr. There's enough there to keep you sustained till dinner. The **Mensa** at Rämistrasse 71 and 101 does cheap meals for students (shut during the summer), and there are a few beer halls where you can pick up *Würst* snacks for not too much.

The bars, discos and clubs are all around Niederdorfstrasse. There are also a substantial number of gay bars in the city – one of the most popular is **Emilio's Bagpiper Bar**, Zähringerstrasse 11.

**EXCURSIONS** From the Hauptbahnhof, take the train for about an hour to **Schaffhausen**, then a further 20 minutes to **Stein am Rhein**. This beautiful little place with its half-timbered houses and wonderful location can also be reached by boat from Schaffhausen quay. Inter-Railers get concessions and you can take the boat as far as **Konstanz**.

Enquire at the Hauptbahnhof about the private mountain trains (Inter-Railers: always check whether you can get half price on the line you've chosen) and strongly consider the chance to get up to an alpine village, away from the bourgeois bustle of Zürich.

# Lucerne (Luzern) phone code: 041

Lucerne is the pick of Switzerland's cities, so if you're only going to stop once in the country, make sure it's here. Set on Lake Lucerne with the Alps as a backdrop, it's magnificently preserved and has everything you always associated with Switzerland. It's 1½ hours from Bern and only 50 minutes from Zürich.

## TOURIST INFORMATION AND ADDRESSES
The Tourist Office is a block from the station at Frankenstrasse 1, open Mon.–Fri.: 8.30am–6pm, Sat.: 9am–5pm; Sun.: 9am–1pm (Tel. 410 7171). Pick up the free city guide and ask about the Visitor's Card which gives discounts at museums, bars, car rental and more. When closed, use the room-finding service at the station.

**POST OFFICE** Bahnhofstrasse, open Mon.–Fri.: 7.30am–6.30pm, Sat.: 8.00am–11am
**AMEX** Schweizerhofquai 4, open Mon.–Fri.: 8.30am–6pm, Sat.: 8.30am–12 noon (Tel. 410 0077; money exchange closes at 5pm during the week)

## SEEING

The **Swiss Transport Museum** (16SFr) might not be top of your list of priorities, but it is actually quite interesting, and gives a discount to Inter-Railers. It's at the end of the park *en route* to the campsite (bus 2 from the station). On Furrengasse check out the small but interesting **Picasso Museum** (Am Rhyn-Haus) too. The **Richard Wagner Museum** in the suburb of **Tribschen** shows the house where he worked and lived, and some of his possessions. You can get there by catching bus 6 or 8, or take the boat from in front of the station (Inter-Rail concession).

The **Glacier Garden** is a beautiful rocky area formed during the Ice Age, while the **Bourbaki-Panorama** (a huge 360° painting of the Franco-Prussian War),is at Löwenplatz and well worth a visit. For a superb view of the town and its surroundings, climb the westernmost tower on the old city wall (closed in winter). But if you want a view from a high vantage point, the cable car up **Mount Pilatus** (2,132m) gives a third off for Eurailers: take the bus to Kriens.

From mid-Aug. to mid-Sept. Lucerne hosts an **International Festival of Music**. Sometimes it celebrates classical music and at other times folk or contemporary music. For further information contact either the Tourist Office or Internationale Musikfestwochen Luzern, Postfach/Hirschmattstrasse 13, CH-6002 Luzern (Tel. 210 3562; Fax. 210 7784). Tickets range in price from 20–230SFr.

If you're feeling adventurous 'Outventure' (Tel. 611 1441) offers many outdoor activities including **bungee jumping** and **tandem paragliding**. You can book these activities from your hostel (pick up service) or telephone the company at the above number. Check that you are properly insured before trying any of these 'sports'.

**FREE LUCERNE:**
- Virtually destroyed by fire in 1993, the reconstructed 14th-century wooden bridge **Kapellbrücke**, is the symbol of the town. Spanning the river Reuss, the roofed structure displays 120 paintings depicting the town's history – though today these are also reconstructions of the original 16th–18th century paintings. The adjoining **Water Tower** served as a lookout tower, prison and archive store.
- Also worth seeing is the beautiful old **Town Hall** on Kornmarkt,

and the old painted houses on **Weinmarkt**. The **Spreuerbrücke** is another covered bridge, this time with paintings on the 'Dance of Death'.

- You can also take a walk up the Löwenstrasse to view the beautiful **Löwendenkmal**, a superb rock sculpture of a dying lion, carved to commemorate the Swiss Guards who died protecting the French king and queen.
- **Jesuitenkirche** (Jesuit Church), off Bahnhofstrasse. Make sure you see its superbly decorated interior.
- Look out for **riverside markets** on Saturday mornings.

## SLEEPING

If you're really intent on a pension or hotel, use the Tourist Office or the station's accommodation service and clearly state your price range.

The youth hostel **Am Rotsee** at Sedelstrasse 12 (Tel. 420 8800; Fax. 420 5616) has over 200 beds and is very reasonable at about 30SFr (35SFr non-members). It's not central and closes 9am–2pm. Bus 18 to the Gopplismoos stop in Friedental, then a two-minute walk or the more frequent bus 1 to Schlossberg, then a 10-minute walk, will get you there. Try to arrive early, as we've had reports of one hour queueing, even at 5pm; the wise arrive early, leave their form and IYHF card in the box provided and return before 10pm. There is also a **'Backpackers'** hostel at Alpenquai 42 (Tel. 360 0420; Fax. 360 0204) which charges from 25SFr for a bed in a shared room and has no curfew.

For hotel accommodation, try the **Tourist Hotel**, St Karliquai 12 (Tel. 410 2474), dorms 31–36SFr with ISIC reductions (doubles around 140SFr), or **Hotel Alpha** (Tel. 240 4280; Fax. 240 9131), at the corner of Pilatusstrasse and Zähringerstrasse 24 (singles from 60SFr, doubles from 95SFr). Also try **Schlüssel**, Franziskanerplatz 12 (Tel. 210 1061), well located for the old town but on the expensive side, around 120SFr for a double. The central **Hotel Linde** (Tel. 410 3193) at Metzgerrainle 3, has doubles for around 90SFr without breakfast (only between Apr. and Oct.) but you're unable to check-in on a Sun.

There are a few **campsites** to choose from but the one we recommend is **Camp Lido** which is excellent: its situation couldn't be improved – near the beach and the lake – and to get to it you can walk through the park. It's at Lidostrasse 8 (Tel. 370 2146) near the Transport Museum and costs 8SFr per person and from 3SFr per tent. Open mid-Mar. to Oct. If it is full, try **Camping Horw** (Tel. 340 3558) which is quiet and by a lake. Take bus 20 to Horw Rank.

## EATING AND NIGHTLIFE

In general, both tend to cater for moneyed European tourists, but if you walk the length of Hertensteinstrasse, you should come up with some suitable pub or restaurant, even if it's just **Migros** at no. 44, or a fast-food place. The **Mr Pickwick Pub** next to the station has also been recommended. If you're after picnic food, underneath the railway station is a good but pricey supermarket – open at odd hours and on Sundays. A new night club has opened up next to the Astoria Hotel and plays techno music at the weekends, whether it will be popular remains to be seen but it may be worth checking out anyway.

Apart from the **International Music Festival** (mid-August–early September), Lucerne is exceptionally sedate. A pub with a collection of Eurorailers determined to make merry will probably be your high spot, unless your budget is elastic.

**EXCURSIONS** The steamer cruises down the **Vierwaldstättersee** (Lake Lucerne to us) are well worth it. Inter-Railers go half price, and you leave from the quay near the station (ask Tourist Information for details of the alternatives).

The huge glowering mountain dominating Lucerne is **Mount Pilatus** (2,100 m). To get up there, you'd do best to take the boat from Lucerne to **Alpnachstad** and then travel up on the steepest cogwheel railway in the world. Return by cable car to **Kriens**, then bus 1 back to Lucerne. It's well worth the effort, and really is an experience you won't forget, assuming you manage to avoid the mid-afternoon crowds and can afford the fare of around 80SFr (reductions with Eurail and Inter-Rail passes).

## Berne (Bern) phone code: 031

Even though it's the capital of Switzerland, there's not much here to interest you for more than a day. Indeed, would anyone consider the birthplace of Einstein's Theory of Relativity to be anything other than a little bit *boring*? It's pretty but not spectacular, and once you've seen the **Clock Tower** (daily guided tours of the interior at 4.30pm), **Bear Pit** complete with bears, **Gothic Cathedral** and **Bernese Historical Museum**, you've more or less done the rounds – unless you collect Swiss stamps and want to visit the vast **Postal Museum**. The city map from the Tourist Office covers a walking tour which will take in all the sights. If you want to cycle round the streets, you can rent a bike for free from TAST Bern. Go to LOEB department store or Casinoplatz from 7.30am to pick one up (deposit of 20SFr required as well as your passport or ID card). The bikes have to be returned by 9.30pm.

## STATION FACILITIES

Train information: Tel. 157 2222. Tourist Information, left-luggage lockers, baths and showers available. Daily trains to Brussels, Basel, Milan, Zürich, Lausanne, Geneva.

## TOURIST INFORMATION AND ADDRESSES

The main Tourist Office is the one at the station. When they close, they leave information on accommodation posted up outside, and there's a free phone to make reservations. Open daily.: 9am–8.30pm (Tel. 328 1212; Fax. 3121233). There's also a new Tourist Office next to the Bärengraben (bear pit), open daily: 9am–5pm (June–Sept.) and 10am–4pm (Mar.–May and Oct.). For general information, tel. 111.

**POST OFFICE** Schanzenpost 1, next to the train station, open Mon.–Fri.: 7.30am–6.30pm, Sat.: 7.30am–11am
**AMEX** Kehrli and Öhler, Bubenbergplatz 19 (Tel. 311 0022), open Mon.–Fri.: 8.30am–12 noon, 1.30pm–5.30pm, Sat.: 9am–12 noon
**UK EMBASSY** Thunstrasse 50 (Tel. 352 5021)
**IRISH EMBASSY** Kirchenfeldstrasse 68 (Tel. 352 1442)
**US EMBASSY** Jubiläumstrasse 93 (Tel. 357 7011)
**CANADIAN EMBASSY** Kirchenfeldstrasse 88 (Tel. 352 6381)
**AUSTRALIAN EMBASSY** Alpenstrasse 29 (Tel. 351 0143)
**STUDENT TRAVEL OFFICE** SSR Reisen, Falkenplatz 9 (Tel. 302 0312) or Rathausgasse 64. Both open weekdays: 10am–6pm, Sat.: 10am–1pm
**PHARMACY/DOCTOR** Tel. 311 2211
**HOSPITAL** The university hospital is on Fribourgstrasse (Tel. 632 2111)

## SLEEPING

Definitely avoid hotels here and stick to the youth hostel or campsite. The **hostel** is at Weihergasse 4 (Tel. 311 6316; Fax. 312 5240), near the Houses of Parliament. It closes 9.30am–3pm in summer and is run quite strictly, costing around 25SFr for a dorm bed including breakfast.

**Camping Eichholz** is down by the river (Tel. 961 2602), a bit out of the city. Tram 9 to Eichholz. The site is open from mid-Apr. to the end of Sept. Also try the year-round **Camping Kappelenbrücke** (Tel. 901 1007). Take the Hinterkappelen postbus to Eymatt.

For a central pension, try **Hotel Bahnhof-Süd**, Bumplizstrasse 189 (Tel. 992 5111), charging from around 60SFr for a bed in a shared room, or **Landhaus Hotel**, Altenbergstrasse 4/6 (Tel. 331 4166; Fax. 332 6904) with dorm beds from 30SFr and doubles for around 120SFr. Breakfast is extra. Use of kitchen and Internet facilities. Take bus 12 to Bärengraben and walk down to the Aare on the left.

## EATING AND NIGHTLIFE

For picnic food there are shops in Marktgasse and Zeughausgasse near the station, or there are always **Migros** for cheap meals. About the only nightspot you can afford, or would find remotely lively, is the **Kornhauskeller** at Kornhausplatz 18. It may bust your budget to eat there, but go for the local beer. The only regular gay club is **Ursus** at Junkerstrasse 1.

### EXCURSIONS :

**FRIBOURG** The best day trip you can take is to the ancient town of **Fribourg**, only 20 minutes away. The river that runs through it, the Sarine, is commonly regarded as the boundary line between the French- and German-speaking sections of Switzerland. Visit the **Église des Cordeliers** with its original St Anthony altarpiece, and take in the view from the bridges that span the river. Most of the sights are on rue de Morat: the church mentioned above, the **Cathedral**, the 16th-century **Town Hall** and the **Museum of Art and History**.

# The Bernese Oberland

**INTERLAKEN** From a Eurorailer's point of view, unless you're stopping off to ski or climb, the stunning beauty of the region is about all there is to really see.

**Balmers Gasthaus**, Hauptstrasse 23–25 in the village of Matten (Tel. 033 822 1961; Fax. 033 823 3361) is great value: under 20SFr in dorms and tents, around 58SFr in doubles with breakfast. Great facilities (including CNN, MTV, email facilities, cellar bar, laundry facilities, free sleds and 20% off ski hire) and always full of Americans. Contrast the quieter **youth hostel** further out in Bonigen-Interlaken, at Aarenweg 21 (Tel. 033 822 4353; Fax. 033 823 2058), take bus 1 from the station. Most hostels do reasonably priced food.

Only an hour from Bern, Interlaken is a good base for heading off into the Bernese Oberland. Inter-Railers get a 50% reduction on the private railways that take you there.

If you've decided that, now you're this far, you want to spend a bit of time here, consider buying the **Bernese Oberland Regional Pass** from this area's private railways board. For 200SFr (160SFr with Swisspass) you get five days' unlimited travel out of 15 on most trains, cable cars and 'gondolas' and the remaining 10 days' travel at half price. It's a lot of money, though, especially when you consider that you can get discounted travel on your Inter-Rail and 25% off travel with Eurail and Swisspass.

Try **Hüsi's Pub** for a good place to meet people from around the world.

Tourist Information is at Höheweig 37 in the **Metropole Hotel** (Tel. 033 822 2121), as well as at Westbahnhof; and for rooms, look at the bulletin board at Westbahnhof listing the hotel rooms as well as *Zimmer frei* (private rooms). Ask for their free regional budget accommodation guide, which is published separately from their normal hotel lists.

**GRINDELWALD** This is *the* destination for serious climbers (though **Lauterbrunnen** is equally beautiful if you're not a climber). What with the **North Face of the Eiger**, the **Jungfrau** and the **Monch**, you won't know where to begin.

There are hourly trains here from Interlaken, though Inter-Rail is only valid on the route to **Jungfraujoch**, the highest railway station in Europe at 3,454m. If you get this far, don't leave till you've taken the cable car to **Männlichen**, **Wengen** and from Grindelwald up to **Pfingstegg**. From Pfingstegg, walk to **Stieregg**. More than likely, this will be the high spot of your travels in this spectacular country.

**Kleine Scheidegg** and Jungfraujoch are also in this area and accessible with the help of an extortionately priced mountain railway. If you're staying, try the fantastic youth hostel **Die Weid** at Terrassenweg (Tel. 033 853 1009; Fax. 033 853 5029), or if it's full, the **Mountain Hostel** (Tel. 033 853 3900; Fax. 033 853 4730) at the Grund station, next to the river, or camp.

**ZERMATT** If this has whetted your appetite, you might as well carry on to the **Matterhorn**. Your best base for excursions here is Zermatt, which you reach by private railway from **Brig** or **Visp** (Inter-Railers half price). Tourist Information is to the right of the station. They'll fix you up with maps, hiking suggestions and a bed.

**Hotel Bahnhof** (Tel. 027 967 2406; Fax. 027 967 7216), opposite the station, is good and has dorms as well as rooms (dorm beds from 28SFr; doubles around 75SFr). The **youth hostel** (Tel. 027 967 2320; Fax. 027 967 5306) is at Winkelmatten, a 15-minute walk from the station, with wonderful views of the Matterhorn. Beds are quite expensive at around 40SFr in dorms, but it does include breakfast, dinner and showers and is cheaper if you stay more than one night. Curfew is at 10pm, but can be flexible – check first!

# Lausanne phone code: 021

You can see the French Alps from Lausanne, home of Switzerland's most spectacular Gothic building: its **Early Gothic Cathedral**. It's in the old medieval quarter, which is the most interesting part of the town (as the rest is very modern) and here you'll also find the **Hôtel de Ville** and the **Château Sainte Marie**, formerly the Bishop's Palace and now the seat of government for the canton.

The funicular to **Duchy** will take you down to the busy port which looks over to Lake Geneva and the Alps. Of the museums, try to take in **Collection de l'Art Brut** in the Château de Beaulieu, where there are interesting exhibits by psychologically disturbed people, criminals and recluses.

## TOURIST INFORMATION AND ADDRESSES

**TOURIST OFFICE** In the main hall of the train station (Tel. 617 7373 or 613 7321), open Apr.–Sept. daily: 9am–8pm; Oct.–Mar. daily: 9am–7pm. They'll kit you out with maps, etc., and arrange accommodation. Ask for the free *Lausanne Official Guide* and enquire about the Lausanne Card, which is valid for 48 hrs and gives discounts in some shops and restaurants and free local public transport (costs 15SFr).

**POST OFFICE** 43 bis avenue de la Gare, open Mon.–Fri.: 7.30am–12 noon, 1.30pm–6.30pm (closed Sat. pm)

**AMEX** 14 avenue mon Repos (Tel. 310 1900; Fax. 310 1919), open for travel services Mon.–Fri.: 8.30am–5.30pm; financial office open Mon.–Fri.: 8.30am–12.45pm and 2–5.30pm

**24-HOUR PHARMACY** Dial 111 to find out which pharmacy is open all night as they rotate

**24-HOUR MEDICAL SERVICE** Tel. 314 1111

## SLEEPING

The **Jeunotel youth hostel** at 1 Chemin du Bois-de-Vaux 36 (Tel. 626 0222; Fax. 626 0226) charges around 28SFr for a dorm bed, including breakfast (singles and doubles also available). Bus 2 to Bois-de-Vaux, then follow the signs.

The campsite is by the lake, **Camping de Vidy-Lausanne** (Tel. 624 2031; Fax. 624 4160) at 3 chemin du Camping, and has tents, caravans and bungalows for hire (open May–Sept.). It is highly recommended. Take bus 1 to Maladière or bus 2 to Bois-de-Vaux.

## EATING AND NIGHTLIFE

Food shouldn't be a problem. There are plenty of grocers' and bakers' shops to buy from, and no shortage of affordable restaurants, but watch out down in Duchy – many restaurants are overpriced, as are many of the small Swiss cafés. **Restaurant Manora** in place St François is a good self-service restaurant worth a visit. There are a few good supermarkets, open seven days a week, at the bottom of avenue d'Ouchy.

If you're staying at the campsite, consider taking a wander into the nearby park and eating at the café bar next to the tennis courts. Although the menu is somewhat restricted, they do an excellent range of pizzas at reasonable prices and both the staff and the customers are young and friendly. If you've just come off a train after a long journey and can't wait for food, **McDonald's** is facing the main entrance to the station. But watch the traffic, as the trolley-bus terminal is here and these vehicles are noise-free as well as pollution-free.

There's no unique nightlife here except in the festival and fête in late June, when the town offers plenty to do at night.

## Basel (Basle) phone code: 061

Basel is Switzerland's second city and cultural capital. Its medieval centre is well worth seeing, but is unfortunately missed by many travellers. Considering its location at the crossroads of France, Germany and Switzerland, you can also take the train from here to just about anywhere in Europe.

### STATION FACILITIES
As Basel is the border, the French effectively share the station with the Swiss. You'll find information for both SNCF and SBB at the station. French trains stop at the west end of the station. Train information: SBB 6am–9pm (Tel. 157 2222); SNCF 7.30am–7pm (Tel. 156 1056).

### TOURIST INFORMATION AND ADDRESSES
As well as one at the station, there's a Tourist Office at Schifflände 5, open Mon.–Fri.: 8.30am–6pm, Sat.: 10am–4pm (Tel. 268 6868; Fax. 268 6870).

**POST OFFICE** Rüdeng 1, open Mon.–Fri.: 7.30am–6pm; Sat.: 8am–12.30pm. There's also a post office on the right as you exit the station
**AMEX** c/o Reise Müller, Steinenvorstadt 33, open Mon.–Fri.: 9am–6.30pm and Sat. 10am–4pm (Tel. 281 3380)

### SEEING
It's the museums in Basel that hog the limelight. If you're tired of trudging round museums and galleries, just take in the two bare essentials: the **Fine Arts Museum** and the **Kirschgarten Museum**,

housed in an old patrician mansion at Elisabethenstrasse 27.

As for the town itself, the 12th-century **Münster** (cathedral) is surrounded by medieval houses and stands in an attractive square. The **Town Hall** is on Market Square, and there are still markets held here today; **Three Countries' Corner** is the spot where the Swiss, French and German borders all meet.

## SLEEPING

The large and rather institutional **youth hostel** is at St Alban-Kirchrain 10 (Tel. 272 0572; Fax. 272 0833). It's clean, friendly and has double rooms and dorms at 28SFr per night including breakfast; a three-course supper costs 12SFr. Curfew midnight. Reserve if possible. Take tram 1 one stop, then tram 3 to second stop.

As far as hotels go, try the following, but insist on their cheapest rooms: **Hotel Stadthof**, Gerbergasse 84 (Tel. 261 8711); **Badischer Hof**, Riehenring 109 (Tel. 692 4144). These one-star hotels have single rooms (without bath or breakfast) starting from around 62SFr. Cheaper hotels are a short journey over the French border in Mulhouse and the surrounding towns and villages.

**Camp Waldhort** (Tel. 711 6429) is six km from the train station at Heideweg 16, Reinach. Take tram 11 to Landhof then follow the signs. Open Mar.–Oct.

## EATING AND NIGHTLIFE

You shouldn't have many problems finding shops and cafés to feed yourself from; there are plenty of alternatives. **Zum Goldenen Sternen**, the oldest pub in Switzerland, at St Albanrheinweg 70, is good for a drink, but watch the food prices.

*This Week in Basel* will fill you in on events, and if you're there around Shrove Tuesday/Ash Wednesday, you should catch some local festivities.

# Geneva (Genève) phone code: 022

Arguably the most international of all European cities, Geneva's rich and well-cared-for air is home to dozens of multinational organizations and peace-negotiating bodies such as the Red Cross and United Nations. It's also a good destination to break up a long haul like Paris–Rome.

## STATION FACILITIES

Genève Cornavin station has train information and reservations (Tel. 157 2222), left-luggage lockers, foreign exchange facilities and Tourist

Information, and the next building is a post office.

Daily trains to: Lausanne, Basel, Bern, Zürich, Montreux, Interlaken, Milan, Rome, Nice, Barcelona, Lyon, Paris.

## TOURIST INFORMATION AND ADDRESSES

The station office operates all year round, but the main office is at rue du Mont-Blanc 3 (Tel. 909 7000; Fax. 929 7011).

**POST OFFICE** rue du Mont-Blanc 18, open Mon.–Fri.: 7.30am–6pm, Sat.: 8–11am

**AMEX** rue du Mont-Blanc 7, open Mon.–Fri.: 8.30am–6pm (in winter closes at 5.30pm), Sat.: 9am–12 noon (Tel. 731 7600; Fax. 732 7211)

**STUDENT TRAVEL AGENCY** SSR is at 3 rue Vignier (Tel. 329 9734; closed Sat.)

**UK CONSULATE** 37–39 rue de Vermont (Tel. 918 2400; Fax. 918 2322)

**US CONSULATE** rue de Pré-Bois (Tel. 798 1605; recorded emergency information 798 1615)

**CANADIAN CONSULATE** rue du pré-de-Bichette 1 (Tel. 919 9200; Fax. 734 7919 )

**AUSTRALIAN CONSULATE** 56–58 rue de Moillebeau (Tel. 918 2900; Fax. 733 5664)

**NEW ZEALAND CONSULATE** 28a chemin du Petit-Saconnex (Tel. 734 9530; Fax. 734 3062)

**MEDICAL HELP** Hôpital Cantonal, rue Micheli-du-Crest 24 (Tel. 372 3311)

## SEEING

The best museums are the **Petit Palais** (Impressionist paintings), **Institut et Musée Voltaire**, 25 rue des Délices (Voltaire's house), and the **Palais des Nations** on avenue de la Paix. Don't miss the **International Red Cross and Red Crescent Museum** at 17 avenue de la Paix. Closed Tues.; open 10am–5pm.

Geneva is the watchmaking capital of the world, so hide your Japanese digital and wander round the superb **Clock Museum**, 15 rue de Malagnou (closed Mon.). Boat trips on Lake Geneva (Lac Léman) are pleasant, but compare prices first. If you want to explore the city by bicycle, Genev'roule, just behind the train station on place de Montbrillant 17, lends bikes out for free (you must leave a 50Sfr deposit and show them either your passport or ID card).

**FREE GENEVA:**
- Most of the things to see in Geneva are free and can be taken in on the one main walk. Starting from the station, walk down **Rue du**

Mont Blanc till you're at the lake, then turn right on **Quai des Bergues**, cross the river on the **Font de L'Île** to the **Place Belair**, then head on to the **Place Neuve** down **Rue de la Corraterie**. Once here, enter the park – good picnic territory – which contains the university and the famous **Reformation Monument**. Inside the university library is also the little **Jean-Jacques Rousseau Museum**.

* The **Vieille Ville** is the old cobblestoned quarter round the **Cathédrale St Pierre**, where Calvin once preached. While on **Rue Hôtel-de-Ville** you can see the **Town Hall** where the Geneva Convention was signed and some 17th-century houses built by Italian religious refugees.

* However, sun-worshippers should head for **Nyon**, on the way to Lausanne, which has a good lakeside **beach**. Also check out the following free attractions:

* **Maison Tavel** (Town Museum), rue Puits-St-Pierre 6

* **Musée d'Art et d'Histoire**, rue Charles Galland 2

* **Cabinet des Estampes** (collection of drawings and prints), Promenade du Pin

## SLEEPING

Summer in Geneva makes affordable beds scarce, so arrive early and immediately aim at getting fixed up. Ask the Tourist Information for their list of foyers, dormitories, etc., and phone around.

The large **youth hostel** is at 28–30 rue Rothschild (Tel. 732 6260; Fax. 738 3987, 10 minutes from Cornavin station via rue de Lausanne) and a dorm bed costs around 25SFr including breakfast (doubles available for around 70SFr). Reception closes 10am–5pm (to 4pm in summer). **Home St Pierre**, at Cour St Pierre 4, by the cathedral, is a great place. It takes only women and is deservedly popular (Tel. 310 3707; Fax. 310 1727); doubles cost 60SFr and dorm accommodation is around 25SFr. Breakfast is extra but well worth paying for.

In July to Sept. student accommodation becomes available. Try **Cité Universitaire**, ave Miremont 46 (Tel. 839 2211; Fax. 839 2223). Excellent facilities including restaurant, disco, TV room, tennis courts, Internet access. Dorm beds for only 18SFr; doubles around 55SFr. Breakfast extra. Lockout 10am–6pm, curfew 11pm. Take bus 3 from the train station (Cornavin) to the last stop at Champel.

Expect to pay from 50SFr per person in budget hotels. Ask for the free *Info Jeunes* brochure, which is brilliantly comprehensive and lists all the budget hotels. Alternatively, as is often the case with Swiss border towns, you could opt to stay in France (at Bellegarde), which is much cheaper.

For camping, try the lakeside **Pointe-à-la-Bise** (Tel. 752 1296), seven km out of town on bus route E.

## EATING AND NIGHTLIFE

Geneva definitely aims its tourism at the well-heeled, but there are some **Migros** and budget restaurants dotted around. A picnic down by the lake is your cheapest and most memorable option, but if it's wet, try the restaurant opposite the station on 17 place Montbrillant, or **Le Zofage**, the university's place at rue des Voisins, with cheap filling *plats du jour*.

Tourist Information will tell you what's on. Geneva actually has the most swinging nightlife in Switzerland, but then that's not hard. But before you get excited, I'm afraid there's probably nothing much you can afford, so content yourself in place Molard or head for a lively bar like **Mr Pickwick's Pub**, 80 rue Lausanne. For live jazz, go to **Au Chat Noir** at rue Vautier 13. If you enjoy the late club scene, try **XS** at 21 Grand Rue, or **Le Tube** at 3 rue de la Université, which caters for mixed gay and straight clientele.

## The Grisons (Graubünden)

The canton of Grisons runs from the source of the Rhine east to the River Inn and on to Austria. This is an area where you'll hear the language of Romansch spoken along with Swiss-German. Its cultural and administrative centre is Chur, and the region also includes flashy resorts such as St Moritz. The trains are narrow-gauge, but Inter-Rails are valid. Take the **Chur–St Moritz** line (two hours), even if you don't get off at the other end, as the scenery is quite beautiful. Accommodation shouldn't be a problem as the canton boasts 28,000 dormitory beds within a 7,000 sq.km area.

**CHUR** Walk through the old-town streets with their medieval houses and pass through the old gate to the **Cathedral**, with its pre-Christian sacrificial stone. The **Hof** (Bishop's Palace) next door is still in use, so don't nose about too much. The pub in there (the **Hofkellerei**) is a good watering-hole, but a bit touristy in summer.

Tourist Information is at Grabenstrasse 5 (Tel. 081 252 1818; Fax. 252 9076). The youth hostel closed down a while back but there is talk of a new hostel opening. Camp Au (Tel. 081 284 2283) by the sports centre charges around 14SFr for one person to stay in a tent. The Tourist Office will be able to help with other accommodation.

**ST MORITZ** The actual town's nothing special and apart from the **Engadiner Museum** *en route* to the famed healing waters of the **Mauritius Springs**, which reconstructs life of days long ago, there's not much else to see. But people don't come here to sightsee; they come to ski or climb. The large general Information Centre, Kurundverkehrsverein, on Via Maistra 12, is open May–June and Nov. Mon.–Fri.: 8am–12 noon, 2pm–6pm; July–mid-Sept. and mid-Dec.–mid-Apr. Mon.–Sat.: 9am–6pm (Tel. 081 837 3333; Fax. 081 837 3377). The office makes free hotel reservations.

If your time's short, do just two things: take the cable car up the 2,400m **Muottas Muragl** and walk the path along the **Sils Lake**. If you're going up to altitude, take some warm clothing – best are several relatively thin layers which you can put on as necessary.

If you're staying, try your best to get into the **youth hostel** at Via Surpunt 60 in St Moritz Bad (Tel. 081 833 3969; Fax. 081 833 8046). It's beautiful – and cheap by Swiss standards (a bus runs between St Moritz Bad and St Moritz Dorf, a distance of about two km). There's **camping** at Olympiaschanze (Tel. 081 833 4090) just beyond St Moritz Bad (open June–late Sept.). Forget hotels; unless you're flush with cash, you're outclassed here, I'm afraid.

If you're in the money, then for around 200SFr you can have a piloted ride down the Olympic Bobsleigh run. Contact the Tourist Office for more information. If you're not feeling so wealthy, you can rent a wooden sled for around 10SFr a day and go on the specially modified track down the Albula valley to Bergün and then return by RHB train (around 30SFr for a day ticket).

If you're heading for Italy, take the train in the direction of **Tirano** on the Italian border (1½ hours), as the scenery around here and on the Passo del Bernina is incredible. Get off at every station and make a day of it, if you've time, as this is the highest line in Europe without cogs or cables.

# Ticino

Known as the 'Swiss Riviera', the region of Ticino is bordered by Italy and, unsurprisingly, offers the 'best of both worlds': the sun, language and ambience of the Italians and the scenery, tidiness and efficiency of the Swiss. Its main attractions are the centres of Lugano and Locarno, along with the area round the lakes of Lugano and Maggiore, which offer superb camping, swimming and walking, away from the crowds.

**LUGANO** An exceptionally pretty town of sunny piazzas, palm trees and the dominating Monte San Salvatore. It's on **Lake Lugano** and lies on the Zürich–Milan main line. Stroll through the little winding streets on the hill at **San Lorenzo** for a view over the town, stopping off at **Santa Maria Degli Angioli** to admire the 16th-century frescoes. Walk down to the lake to the Palazzo Civico where the Tourist Office is (Tel. 091 921 4664; Fax. 091 922 7653). They're open April–Oct. Mon.–Fri.: 9am–6.30pm, Sat.: 9am–12.30pm and 1.30pm–5pm, Sun.: 10am–noon and 2–4pm; Nov.–Mar. Mon.–Fri.: 9am–12.30pm and 1.30–5pm. They'll give you maps, lists of the local mountain huts, and arrange accommodation (fee charged). Free two-hour guided walks around the town leave from the Tourist Office at 9.45am every Monday between Apr. and Oct.

During summer, the **Villa Favorita** houses a fine collection of European and American paintings from the 19th and 20th centuries. From the Paradiso quarter, it's a 10-minute ride on the funicular up **Monte San Salvatore**, with a great view over the Alps and lakes. The funicular from Cassarate up to **Monte Bré** on the other side of the town is another scenic excursion. The **Museum of Extra-European Cultures**, on Via Cortivo 324, has displays from Oceania, Indonesia and Africa. Open Tues.–Sun.: 10am–5pm.

There's a **youth hostel** in Lugano-Crocifisso at 13 via Cantonale, of an exceptionally high standard (Tel. 091 966 2728; Fax. 091 968 2363). For hotels, try the **Montarina** which has rooms from 45–65SFr per person and cheaper dormitory accommodation (around 20SFr). It's at Via Montarina 1 (Tel. 091 966 7272; Fax. 091 966 1213).

There are plenty of markets and food shops offering Swiss-quality Italian food, plus the ubiquitous **Migros** at Via Pretorio. **Commercio** on Via Ariosto do great pizzas, or visit the **Gabbani** *charcuterie* just off Piazza Cioccaro for gigantic salami. There are a couple of nice pubs in Piazza Grande, **Tango** and **Argentino**, and for dancing, try **Prince** on Via Stauffacher 1 or **No Ties** on Via Cantonale. In the evening there are often concerts down by the lake but nightlife here is fairly sedate in general.

**LOCARNO** From Lugano it's about half an hour to Ticino's capital, **Bellinzona**, and from there another half-hour will take you into Locarno, the best place to base yourself for trips round **Lake Maggiore**. To explore this region you'll need to resort to buses; ask for details at the Tourist Office in Largo Zorzi–Piazza Grande. One of the buses from Locarno station goes through Ascona and Brissago and crosses the Italian border at Madonna di Ponte. Get off at Brissago and make for the island, where there's a beautiful botanical garden.

Back in Locarno itself there's a **Museum of Modern Art** in the Pinacoteca Casa Rusca, with the works of Jean Arp and Filippo Franzoni on permanent display. Funiculars take you up to see the town's landmark, the **Madonna of the Rock** (*Madonna del Sasso*). Try **Pensione Città Vecchia**, 13 via Toretta (Tel./Fax. 091 751 4554) for inexpensive and well-located accommodation. The **youth hostel** at

Via Varenna 18 (Tel. 091 756 1500; Fax. 091 756 1501) charges around 32SFr. The hostel is nice and modern with good facilities. During peak season, reserve at least one month in advance.

The private Centrovalli railway from Locarno to Domodossola on the Milan–Brig line is well worth re-routing for. The left-hand side offers the best views of the fantastic scenery.

## NOTES

# Liechtenstein

| | |
|---|---|
| Entry requirements | Passport |
| Population | 31,200 |
| Capital | Vaduz (pop.: 5,100) |
| Currency | Swiss Franc |
| | £1 = approx. 2.54SFr |
| Political system | Constitutional monarchy |
| Religion | Predominantly Roman Catholic |
| Language | German, English and French widely spoken |
| Public Holidays | New Year's Day, 6 Jan., Shrove Tuesday, Good Friday, Easter Monday, May Day (1 May), Ascension Day, Whit Monday, Corpus Christi, 15 Aug., 8 Sept., 8 Dec., Christmas Day and Boxing Day |
| International dialling codes | To Liechtenstein: int'l code 41 +number |
| | From Liechtenstein: 00 + country code |
| Emergency telephone numbers | Police 117; ambulance 144; fire service 118 |

Nestling between Switzerland and Austria, Liechtenstein has enjoyed independent sovereign status since the early 1800s. But even though it uses the Swiss franc it still retains a separate identity, which makes it worth a stop. All travel documents valid for Switzerland are also valid here and the only border regulations are on the Austrian side. Liechtenstein is an extremely prosperous country – which means expensive for the traveller. The country is tiny, 25km by 6km, so although it's worth a visit you probably won't choose to stay more than a day or two – any more would break the bank. The country is divided into two distinct political regions, upper and lower, and three geographical regions: the northern lowlands, the Tirolean Alps and the Rhine valley. Politically, the people are quite conservative (women here didn't get the right to vote in national elections until 1984).

## TRANSPORT

The railway plays a subsidiary role in the country, as it passes through only a part of it and has only two stops. However, the Postbus network is well developed. The best way to enter the principality is by Postbus from either Buchs or Sargans in Switzerland. Services are frequent and the journey times are 30 minutes and 15 minutes respectively. Bus prices are very reasonable: a monthly pass costs 20SFr (10SFr for students), a weekly pass 10SFr (students 5SFr) and few individual journeys cost more than a few francs.

## TELEPHONE CODE

The code for the whole country is 075.

## SEEING

The capital, **Vaduz**, is the seat of government and the home of the Prince of Liechtenstein and his family. Tourist Information is centrally located at Städtle 37 (Tel. 232 1443; Fax. 392 1618) and they will provide information and maps on the whole principality and help you with accommodation. Be sure to pick up a copy of the helpful *Tourist Guide*. You can also get your passport stamped here just to prove you've been (2SFr).

Liechtenstein is a philatelist's dream and the **Postage Stamp Museum** in the centre of Vaduz has many rare stamps both of Liechtenstein and other countries. It has free admission and is open Apr.–Oct. daily: 10am–12 noon and 1.30pm–5.00pm. There's also a place where you can get a Liechtenstein stamp printed with your own name on it! The post office is next door.

The **Liechtenstein State Art Collection** at Städtle 37 is worth a visit for its fine interchanging exhibitions from the collections of the Princes of Liechtenstein as well as from other private and public collections. Open 10am–12 noon and 1.30pm–5.30pm daily (closes at 5pm in winter). Admission 5SFr, or 3SFr to ISIC holders. A new art museum is being built and is due to open this year, ask at the Tourist Office. The **Liechtenstein National Museum** is at Städtle 43, and has the expected displays of archaeological finds, local folklore, history and a good collection of weapons. It has been shut for several years but is due to open again this year. The **Ski-Museum** on Bangarten 10 (open weekdays: 2–6pm; entry 5SFr) is also quite interesting if you have time.

There is good hiking throughout Liechtenstein; many of the Alpine routes and organized tours start at **Malbun**. Another town worth visiting is **Triesenberg**: see the **Walser Museum** with its historical collection on the local Walser community.

**Balzers** is also interesting, notably for Gutenberg castle (unfortunately you can't go in) and its varied churches.

## SLEEPING AND EATING

The **youth hostel** here is one of the friendliest we have come across; it's at Untere Rüttigasse 6 in Schaan (Tel. 232 5022; Fax. 232 5856) and is modern and clean. IYHF membership required. Take the Postbus to the stop Hotel Mühle.

**Camping Mittagspitze** (Tel.392 2686) is on the road to Sargans, between Triesen and Balzers – beautiful site, open all year. The slightly cheaper **Camping Bendern** (Tel. 373 1211) is on the 50/51 bus line. Both sites are excellent and very tranquil. If all else fails, Tourist Information may find you a room in a private house and many inns have rooms, although both these options are more expensive.

Eating out is expensive even by Swiss standards – which is quite scary! Your best bet is to put together a picnic at the **Denner** supermarket on Aulestrasse, or to look out for restaurants offering 'lunch specials'; try to fill up at lunch, as prices are higher for dinner. You should be able to find something decent to scrape by on for under 20SFr. **Azzurro**, near the supermarket, sells big pizzas for around 10SFr. If you fancy trying the local speciality, it's a sort of small cheese dumpling called *Kasknopfle*, and the local wines are worth sampling too.

## NOTES

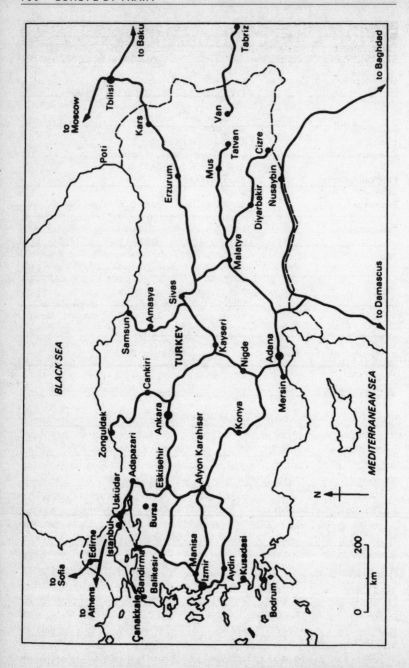

# TURKEY (Türkíiye)

| | |
|---|---|
| Entry requirements | Passport. Travellers have to buy a visa on entry, £10 for UK subjects, US$45 for US citizens. Payment must be in hard currency notes – coins not accepted. |
| Population | 63.5 million |
| Capital | Ankara (pop.: 4 million) |
| Currency | Lira (TL) £1 = approx. 827,850TL |
| Political system | Republic |
| Religion | Muslim |
| Language | Turkish (German, some English and French spoken in large cities) |
| Public holidays | New Year's Day, Sugar Holiday (9 Jan.), Day of the Hajj (16 Mar.), Kurban Bayrami (Festival of the Sacrifice; 17 Mar.), Independence Day (23 Apr.), Atatürk Commemoration Day (19 May), Birth of The Prophet (15 June), Victory Day (30 Aug.), Republic Day (29 Oct.), Ramadan (one month starting 28 Nov.), Kadir Gecesi (Eve of Power; eve of the 28th day of Ramadan). Some of the festivals change date each year (religious festivals are dependent on the lunar calendar). The dates given are for 2000 |
| International dialling | To Turkey: int'l code 90 From Turkey: 00 + country code |
| Emergency telephone numbers | Police 155; ambulance 112; fire service 110 |

Lying between the Mediterranean and the Black Sea, Turkey only has a toe in Europe, as 97% of it lies firmly in Asia. The country has long been home to a mix of Islamic and Western cultures which today provides a fascinating 'Turkish delight' of history and culture far removed from a traipse through the rest of Europe. This stretches back 13 successive civilizations, with some of the best preserved remains found on the west and south coasts.

Turkey began as a nation after the Ottoman Turks – who had spent years chipping away at the Christian Byzantine empire – conquered Constantinople in 1453 and renamed it Istanbul. From then on there was no looking back as the vast Ottoman Empire was created out of Byzantium's ruins. It reached its peak under Süleyman the Magnificent (1520–63) with the Turks controlling Anatolia, the Arabian peninsula, Egypt, North Africa and the Balkans. But things slowly began to turn sour from the 17th century onwards as the powerful empire began to lose its territories.

Following World War I, Turkey was reborn out of the subsequent collapse of the Ottoman Empire. Its leader Kemal Ataturk became a national hero as he dragged the country by the scruff of the neck towards Westernization. As Turkey modernized, many centuries-old traditions were overthrown and the capital was moved from Istanbul to Ankara.

These days the country is a very rewarding destination, with a deserved reputation for warm hospitality. It's also right up the street of the budget traveller, with everything from accommodation to food at a very reasonable price. Women travelling alone are no worse off than anywhere else in southern Europe either, though eastern Turkey may prove more difficult and, with occasional unrest here, it would be advisable for everyone to contact the Turkish embassy for up-to-date details before embarking on a visit.

Be particularly careful with your passport and travel documents – keep a photocopy in a safe place – as many travellers (particularly British Asians) have reported their passports stolen in recent years. There is a flourishing trade in British passports and some people will resort to desperate measures to get their hands on one. Don't accept a drink from strangers as there have been cases of drugs being injected into them – when the traveller wakes up invariably their pack and passport have gone. Basically, if you use your common sense you should be OK.

Also as a word of warning, steer well clear of anything likely to be remotely connected with drugs. In particular, don't carry any loose tablets, even aspirin, and, if you do have medicines with you, carry a copy of the prescription if possible and the original container.

## TURKISH STATE RAILWAYS

**(TURKIYE CUMHURIYETI DEVLET DEMIRYOLLARI ISLETMESI, TCDD)**
Since the whole of Turkey joined the Inter-Rail scheme in 1990 ('European Turkey' joined in 1985) there has been a general improvement in services. However, you can still expect the journey from northern Greece to Istanbul to take more than a day and the trip from Athens to take up to 40 hours. If you are coming direct from central Europe *remember that you must have a transit visa for Bulgaria* – unless you travel through Serbia and change at Thessaloniki in northern Greece, in which case you'll need a transit visa for Yugoslavia. If you decide to travel through Bulgaria, get your transit visa before you leave home.

Railway services in Turkey are slow. Students can get a 10–20% discount on train fares. Apart from the lines in European Turkey and the Haydarpaşa–Ankara run, you are well advised to use the buses. These are fast, cheap and often modern Mercedes–Benz vehicles. Free drinks *en route* are often included. For a rough guide to the main services, consult *Thomas Cook's Overseas Timetable*.

For short journeys, use a *Dolmus* – these are communal taxis which run on set routes. Stop them by waving. Outside the cities they are usually beat-up Ford Transit or VW vans. Very cheap.

**PASSES AVAILABLE** Turkey is in Inter-Rail Zone G, along with Italy, Greece and Slovenia. Your Inter-Rail pass also covers the ferry service between Brindisi and Patras. For further details, see the Inter-Rail section in Part One of this guide.

A Euro Domino ticket is also available (see p. 23 for further information).

Eurail is not valid in Turkey.

## TRAIN INFORMATION

English is spoken by the information staff in big cities, while German is more useful elsewhere throughout Turkey.

**RESERVATIONS** It's always advisable to reserve between Istanbul and Ankara, particularly if you want a couchette or to travel first class.
**NIGHT TRAVEL** Generally, this is the best way of travelling in Turkey. There are first- and second-class couchettes to choose from.
**EATING ON TRAINS** Always be prepared with your own drinks. All expresses should have a mini-bar or buffet.

## TOURIST INFORMATION

There are Tourist Offices in all the major cities.

**ISIC BONUSES** 50% off museums, cinemas, concerts, and 10–20% off rail tickets within Turkey. For further information, contact the nearest Turkish tourism and information office and ask for the *Youth Travel Guide*.
NB: Some places will not accept student cards as there are so many Turkish fakes.
**MONEY MATTERS** Banking hours are Mon.–Fri.: 8.30am–12noon, 1.30pm–5pm. 24-hour exchange facilities are thin on the ground and there are none at the stations. There is a small exchange office at Istanbul station, if you can find it, at the opposite end of the platform from the station entrance. It is open at weekends and has an average exchange rate.

Inflation is a way of life in Turkey, so bear this in mind when looking at prices. Remember to spend all of your lire before leaving the country as you will find it difficult, if not downright impossible, to exchange – particularly in Greece. It is possible to convert lire back to a foreign currency before leaving Turkey if the original exchange slips are produced, proving it was legally exchanged. Make sure you have sufficient sterling to pay for your visa at the border; US dollars and Deutschmarks are grudgingly accepted.

**POST OFFICES** Open Mon.–Fri.: 8.30am–12noon, 1pm–5.30pm. Major post offices stay open till midnight, Mon.–Sat. and 9am–7pm, Sun. Many post offices have exchange facilities; compare the rate to the banks.

**SHOPS** Open Mon.–Sat.: 9/9.30am–1pm, 2pm–6/7pm, Sun.: closed. Food shops open earlier (6/7am) and close late (7/8pm)

**MUSEUMS** All museums shut on Mondays, except for the Topkapi Palace which shuts on Tuesdays. Entry usually costs around $2.

**MOSQUES** A note to non-Moslems – when visiting a mosque, footwear is removed and normally left on a rack or occasionally with an attendant outside. Women especially should dress modestly. At the better-known mosques, overalls are provided for those deemed unsuitably dressed.

**TIPPING** Leave 5–10% in restaurants (15% in an expensive restaurant or if you have had exceptional service); 10–15% for barbers, hairdressers and Turkish-bath attendants. Round up taxi fares.

## SLEEPING

There's no problem finding cheap accommodation in Turkey, but we can't guarantee you'll be happy with the standards of cleanliness. Basically, the hotels registered with the Tourist Board are called *touristic* and are graded *de luxe*, or 1–5 stars. Also there are plenty with no grades at all, many of which are dirty but safe enough. In general, though, discretion is the better part of valour when it comes to a shady set-up. Expect to pay from $20 upwards for a half-decent double (more in Istanbul). Always check the room first and be prepared to bargain if the price seems too high. This tends to be the norm along the Bosphorus, but you can get a reduction with an ISIC card in some places off season. Unmarried couples may have difficulty sharing a room in some parts of Turkey, especially in more rural places or conservative regions, such as along the Black Sea coast and in the southeast.

There are a few *pansiyons* in Turkey and they can be the best places to stay, but there still aren't too many of them. Student dormitories are another option and from mid-July to the second week in September there are about 50 youth hostels in Turkey organized by Yurtkur, the student accommodation organization; most of them allow you to stay if you have a student card, but it's best to have an IYHF to be on the safe side.

Campsites are growing in number but are still a bit primitive in their facilities. Some hotels and pensions will also let you camp in their grounds and use their toilets and bathrooms for a small fee.

## EATING AND NIGHTLIFE

Turkish cuisine is among the best in Europe for sheer good value. The variety of dishes is staggering and, as often as not, you're invited into the kitchen to choose your own. (If you don't like the look of things while you're in, now's your chance to skip out with a suitable excuse.) Turkish specialities include *dolmas* (just about anything stuffed with rice) and anything called *şiş* (like *şişkebab*) done on a spit. *Kadin budu* is a concoction of fried rice and meatballs and, literally translated, means 'woman's thigh' (we don't quite see the analogy). Then how about *kadin gobegi* (woman's navel) for dessert? The wine's not bad and the grape brandy, *raki*, is hot stuff. Expect to pay around $10-$20 for a full meal including wine, though you can eat for a lot less. For a snack, try *lahmacun*, a type of pizza. *Never drink the tap water, especially in Istanbul and Izmir.*

The Turks are big folk-dancers and you should be able to catch each region's favourite without too many problems. The Turkish coffee houses (*Kahve*) are great meeting places, although male only, and, of course, there's always the Turkish bath. This is one way to treat yourself – the pale imitation offered in Western Europe is no comparison. Go and see a belly dancer if there's one advertised, even though they're terribly commercialized these days, but avoid the discos and clubs; although the major cities and resorts are improving, most are still poor Western imitations.

Despite the fact that you will regularly see pairs of males walking along hand in hand, don't be fooled – Islamic law and local custom forbid homosexuality and you could find yourself getting a distinctly cold shoulder if you are too openly gay. However, in the major cities and resorts you will generally be able to find a few gay bars and clubs. Lambda Istanbul is a Turkish gay and lesbian organization. You can find out more about them at  www.qrd.org/qrd/www/world/europe/turkey which has links to a 'Gay Turkey' guide.

## Istanbul city phone code: 0212 (Taksim, Sultanahmet etc.), 0216 (Asian side)

With one foot in Europe and the other in Asia, Istanbul offers you a unique and fascinating city of incredible mosques, bustling bazaars and outstanding legacies of Roman, Byzantine and Ottoman Empires. If you're going to Turkey this is *the* destination as there's so much to catch the eye and imagination – though be prepared to expect dirty and rough areas as well (women on their own should take extra care). If you've had ulcers getting here by train you'll be greatly rewarded, not least by the unforgettable early morning call to prayer floating amongst the minarets.

## STATION FACILITIES

Sirkeci (Tel. 527 0050 or 527 0051) is the main station of Istanbul; from here leave the trains bound for Sofia, Belgrade, Athens and the West. Haydapaşa (Tel. 336 0475 and 336 2063) is the city's other station, on the opposite shore of the Bosphorus; services to Asia, Ankara, Anatolia, Iran, Syria and Baghdad leave from here.

Facilities at both stations tend to close down at night and there is no bath/shower at either station. Sirkeci station has Tourist Information, exchange facilities and left-luggage. Although this is only a trolley on the platform, it is fairly safe as there are many attendants about. Many nearby hotels offer left-luggage facilities, but satisfy yourself on their security before committing your luggage.

## TOURIST INFORMATION AND ADDRESSES

**TOURIST OFFICES** Divan Yolu Caddesi 3, Sultanahmet (Tel./Fax. 518 1802; open daily 9am–5pm); entrance of Hilton hotel on Cumhuriyet Caddesi (Tel. 233 0592); Karaköy harbour terminal; Atatürk Airport; Sirkeci train station

**POST OFFICE** The main branch is at 25 Büyük Postane Sokak (2 blocks from Sirkeci station). 24-hour currency exchange. There are more than 100 post offices in town

**AMEX** Türk Express, 91 Cumhuriyet Caddesi, 2nd floor, open Mon.–Fri.: 9am–6pm (Tel. 230 1515)

**TOURIST POLICE** Across from St Sophia at beginning of Yerebatan Caddesi, open 9am–8pm (24hr hotline Tel. 527 4503 or 528 5369; Fax. 512 7676)

**UK CONSULATE** 34 North Meşrutiyet Caddesi 5 Tepebaşi (Tel. 293 7540; Fax. 245 4989)

**US CONSULATE** 104–108 Meşrutiyet Caddesi 5 Tepebaşi (Tel. 251 3602; Fax. 251 3218)

**AUSTRALIAN CONSULATE** 58 Tepecik Yolu Uzeri (Tel. 257 7050 or 257 7051; Fax. 257 7054)

**CANADIAN CONSULATE** 107/3 Büyükdere Caddesi (Tel. 272 5174; Fax. 272 3427)

**IRISH** 26a Cumhuriyet Cad, Elmadağ (246 6025)

**NEW ZEALAND CITIZENS** Contact the Ankara Embassy, 24/1 Kiz Kulesi Sok (Tel. 312/ 467 9054) or, in Istanbul. the Maya Akar Center, 24th floor, Büyükdere Caddesi 100/102 (Tel. 275 2989; Fax. 275 5008)

**STUDENT TRAVEL** 7-Tur Travel Shop, Gümüşsuyu Caddesi. Student cards and travel.

**MEDICAL HELP** International Hospital, Istanbul Cad 82, Yeşilköy (Tel. 663 3000); American Hospital, Admiral Bristol Hastanesi, 20 Güzel-bahçe Sok, Nişantaşi (Tel. 231 4050)

## GETTING ABOUT

There are cheap buses which leave from Taksim Square. The communal taxis are also good value. They have routes between the main quarters, though if you specify, you should get dropped off where you ask. Most taxis now have meters, but check, and if there isn't one then agree a price before you start your journey. Even if there is a meter check that the driver turns it on to avoid later difficulties. Frequent suburban trains run along the main line from Sirkeci. Inter-Rail is valid.

## SEEING

Basically, Istanbul divides into two main areas which are further subdivided into several small districts. The European part of the city is divided by the **Golden Horn**, and the European and Asian parts are separated by the **Bosphorus Strait**. The vast majority of sights are on the southern bank of the Golden Horn.

**Old Stamboul** is the old walled city across the Golden Horn and it looks like something out of the Fry's *Turkish Delight* advert. For the best panoramic view of the old town, climb the **Galata tower** ($1.50; it's a nightclub in the evenings). The mosques and palaces are wonderful examples, as good as you'll find anywhere, especially **Aya Sofia (Hagia Sofia)**, which was built as a church (the Church of the Holy Wisdom) in AD 532 by Emperor Justinian. For a thousand years it was the largest church, and grandest building, in the world. It was turned into a mosque by Mehmet the Conqueror after the Turks captured the city in 1453. Representational art and images were removed and minarets added. In 1932 Atatürk had it turned into a museum. Today the museum is open Tues.–Sun.:9.30am–4.30pm, and the gallery, which contains Byzantine mosaics and the famous **sweating pillar** believed to have healing powers, Tues.–Sun.: 9.30–11.30am and 1–4pm. Admission is around $5 (reduced rates for students).

Nearby you can catch a glimpse of underground Istanbul at **Yerebatan Sarayi** (Sunken Palace), a vast man-made cavern built in the 6th century for water storage should the city be besieged (open daily 9am–5.30pm; entrance $2).

The palace of the Ottoman Sultans, **Topkapi Sarayi**, is today a complex of museums (entrance around $5); have a look in the **Treasury** and the **Harem** (hourly tours leave every 30 mins.: $2; open Sun., Mon. and Wed.–Sat.) with more than 400 rooms. There's enough here to interest you for hours. Down the hill from the Palace is another museum complex which houses the **Archaeological Museum**, the **Museum of the Ancient Orient** and the **Tiled Pavilion**. A single ticket will get you into all three museums ($3; students $2; open Tues.–Sun.: 9am–4.30pm), although one of them will more than likely be closed.

For a break from the hot dirty city, take a cruise down the Bosphorus. Boats leave Galata Bridge on three-hour round cruises between Europe and Asia. They are cheap, great fun and highly recommended. You can also get five-hour trips which stop off in Asia for four hours' sightseeing (fare about $10). Boats leaving from the palace end of the quay allow you to visit four small islands, the Princes' Islands. There's usually a round trip every half-hour.

The 'modern' city is on the north side of the Galata bridge and includes Istanbul's underground – the Tunel – with only two stations. Also on this side of the Golden Horn is the 19th-century **Dolhambaçe Palace**.

**FREE ISTANBUL:**
- Outside of daily prayer times you can go into any mosque in Istanbul as long as you dress modestly and take off your shoes before entering. The most famous and impressive is the **Blue Mosque** dating from the 17th century. It's an amazing feat of engineering, built to bend with the force of earthquakes – something which has been called into action 20 times already. The interior is decked out in stunning blue Iznik tiles – from which it gets its name – while outside is the **tomb of Sultan Ahmet**, for whom the mosque is built.
- For a change of pace, head for the nearby **Hippodrome**, an ancient park where Byzantine emperors used to hang out and watch chariot races. Here you'll also find an **Egyptian obelisk**, with a history stretching back to 1500 BC.
- However, no visit to Istanbul is complete without a trip to the bustling **Grand Bazaar** (or Kapalıçarşi) which is a great place to wander round. Specializing in leather and carpets, though there's a lot more besides, it's colourful, entertaining and home to more than 4,000 shops. Look out too for the **Sahaflar Çarsisi**, a used book market opposite the university, and the **Egyptian Bazaar** or **Spice Bazaar** in Eminönü.
- Also check out the city's 6km of Byzantine **Land Walls** to the east of the city, built to protect the peninsula from invaders.
- The following mosques are also worth taking in:
- The 16th-century **Süleymaniy Camii** and **tomb**, near the university
- **Kariye Camii**, with its superb frecoes and mosaics, to the west of

the city
- **Yavuz Selim Camii**, Yavuz Selim Caddesi
- **Fatih Camii**, Islambol Caddesi

## SLEEPING

As long as you're not expecting Scandinavian-style cleanliness, you'll cope fine in Istanbul. Beds are cheap and plentiful, and as prices vary little between districts, aim for the most central or convenient. Round the station is OK, but a bit on the noisy side. The central Sultanahmet quarter is near the sights and about the best place to head for. Although we concentrate on the Sultanahmet quarter, you may also find cheap places in the Aksaray area and on the Haydarpaşa side of the Bosphorus.

The IYHF **Yücelt Hostel**, is in the Sultanahmet district at 6 Caferiye Sok (Tel. 513 6150/6151; Fax. 512 7628) and is clean, though somewhat crowded. Dorms cost from $7 and there are doubles with toilet for $18 (breakfast extra), while the friendly staff will help with onward travel arrangements. Alternatively, **The Orient Youth Hostel**, with its 94 beds, is only a 10-minute walk from the station at Yeni Akbiyik Caddesi 13, Sultanahmet (Tel. 517 9493; Fax. 518 3894). Dorm beds from $8 (breakfast included). As well as offering Internet access, they also have a bar where you can see belly-dancing; a terrace café; TV and video; and an information office – plus there's no curfew. Around the corner at 3 Terblylk Sok is the **Sultan Turist Otel** (Tel. 516 9260; Fax. 517 1626), with dorms at $8 and singles and doubles at $17–$25.

Also worth checking out is **Hotel Side/Pension Side** at 20 Utangaç Sok (Tel./Fax. 517 6590) and **Hanedan**, Akbiyik Caddesi, Adliye Sok 3 (Tel. 516 4869; Fax. 517 4524; doubles from $25). **Hostel Merih** at Alemdar Caddesi 20 has been reported to be good for women travellers.

There are several campsites, but **Camping Florya** is excellent, with its own stretch of beach and a cheap restaurant/bar. Take the local train to Florya and prepare for a half-hour walk. Refer to *Cheaps Sleeps Europe 2000* for more accommodation options.

Don't try sleeping rough in Istanbul, it's not worth the risk; there are too many stories of muggings and rape. Don't bother with the black market here either, as police informers are out in abundance, especially in summer, and manage to make a good living out of turning in mugs who accept their offers. The same goes for drugs.

## EATING AND NIGHTLIFE

You'll be pleasantly surprised on both scores here. It's possible to eat exceptionally well for next to nothing, whether you eat from the street stalls or at top restaurants. Fish and seafood are particularly good: go down to the Galata bridge where there are dozens of seafood restaurants, or eat from the pavement fish-grilling stalls. If you've saved sufficient by getting into cheap accommodation, treat yourself to a proper Bosphorus meal of *meze* (mixed starters) and fresh fish. You'll have no trouble finding plenty of suitable places to eat at. The area behind the station (Eminonu) is a good one. Our only particular recommendation is the **Murat Restaurant** on Ordu Caddesi, Aksaray, which does reasonable menus at good prices, next to the Hacibozan Ogullari Baklavaci.

Don't bother with the fabricated Westernized nightlife of discos and nightclubs. To get a taste of real Istanbul, eat late and wander along Meşrutiyet Caddesi and sample the music in the little cafés. Sultanahmet Square will also be lively but can get pretty seedy late-on. There are a few pubs in the area, however, where you'll meet up with other Eurorailers and hitchers. One in particular worth a visit is the **Pudding Shop**, on Divan Yolu Caddesi (off the Sultanahmet), which is one of Europe's classic meeting places, like Harry's Bar in Venice.

The Istanbul Festival from mid-June to mid-July is no longer so classically minded and now features lots of jazz, folk and rock acts. Ask at Tourist Information for details. If you're after belly dancing, head for the Galatasaray district and Istiklasl Caddesi; or if you've promised yourself an authentic Turkish bath, ask at Tourist Information for their recommendations. **Cağaloglu Hamami** at Yerebatan Cad in Cağaloglu is excellent – the full works for $35 (men's section open daily 7am–10pm; women's section 8am–8pm).

# North-West Turkey

**BURSA** The original capital of the Ottoman Empire and subsequently home to some great monuments from this period. Its popularity is also due to its proximity to the sea and the best-known Turkish ski resort **Uludag**. You can get to Bursa by taking a ferry from Istanbul to Yalova and then a bus.

While in Bursa see the **Great Mosque**, **Green Mosque** and **Green Tomb**. Nearby are two interesting museums, the **Ethnographic Museum** and the **Turkish and Islamic Art Museum** (closed Mon.; entrance free to ISIC holders).

Tourist Information is in the centre of town near the covered market. For accommodation, try the **Özen Sükran Otel**, 39 Inönü Caddesi (Tel. 224 221 5453) or **Otel Deniz** (Tel 224 222 9238) at Tahtakale Caddesi 19 (doubles from $15). Alternatively, camp on top of Uludag at **Millipark Camping** (take the cable car).

**ÇANAKKALE** Scene of the World War I Dardanelles campaign and the Trojan campaign. The bus from Bursa takes about 5½ hours. (costs around $8.50). In Çanakkale itself there is a museum with archaeological artefacts from **Troy,** and a **Castle** with its First World War artillery and damage. A minesweeper in the park around the castle is now a monument to Atatürk, who was the Turkish commander during the Dardanelles campaign.

The helpful Tourist Office is next to the harbour – the staff will help you find a room, give you free maps and bus and ferry information. The best place to look for hotels is around the town centre. Çanakkale comes to life every August with the Troy festival.

Across the Dardanelles from Çanakkale lies the scene of the bloody campaign, and **Gallipoli** (Gelibolu) itself. You can take a ferry across to **Eceabat** and then hire a taxi to look around the battlefield, where the **ANZACS** (Australia and New Zealand Army Corps) suffered horrendous losses at Anzac Cove in Churchill's ill-fated campaign. The whole peninsula is a vast war memorial and all cemeteries are well signposted and maintained. Full details from the Tourist Office.

Thirty-two kilometres south is **Troy (Truva)**. There are many buses from the bus station to Troy. The ruins of nine separate cities are not that interesting in themselves, but with a bit of background knowledge and some imagination they are evocative, especially with the wooden horse replica.

## Aegean Coast

**KUŞADASI** This is a good base to explore the fascinating Greek and Roman site of Ephesus. To get to Kuşadasi, either take a train to Izmir and then a two-hour bus ride or take the ferry straight from Istanbul. The small fortified **Pigeon Island** is about the only thing worth a visit in Kuşadasi. The Tourist Office is in the port and is very helpful. There are many cheap sea-front hotels and pensions here, the best area being around Aslander Caddesi.

The real reason for coming here is **Ephesus**, a huge 2,000-acre site chock full of classical ruins, which can become incredibly hot during summer. To reach the site take a dolmus to Selçuk and ask to get off at Ephesus. It is best to look around yourself as tours can be very pricy. See the **Grand Theatre**, the **Temple of Hadrian** and the **Fountain of Trajan**, just to name a few. The site is open each day 8.30am–5.30pm (to 7pm in summer) and admission is about $5 (free with ISIC and reduced rate for senior citizens).

Three-and-a-half hours east by bus are the amazing white cliffs and thermal pools of **Pamukkale** (unfortunately, they have been fenced off and there is no longer any public bathing – you can however have a dip in the warm water of the **sacred fountain** (the spring's source) at the Pamukkale Motel. The pool is open 8am–8pm and admission is around $4 for 2 hours). Above the thermal pools, at the top of the cliffs are the extensive ruins of the ancient city of **Hierapolis**. The **Grand Theatre** is particularly impressive but have a wander round as there is much to see, including the remains of the **Temple of Apollo** which dates from the 3rd century.

Other classical ruins along the Aegean coast are **Bodrum Halicarnassus** and **Bergama Pergamon**, which are well worth a visit.

Ferries link a number of ports to the nearby Greek islands. Although fares are quite steep, this is a way of avoiding the sometimes nightmarish Athens–Istanbul run. Ferry services include Cesme–Chios, Kuşadasi–Samos, Bodrum–Kos, Marmaris–Rhodes and Ayvalik–Lesvos.

## Mediterranean Coast

There are a wealth of beautiful beaches and resorts along this coastline, which is a good place to unwind and relax, though bear in mind that thousands of other tourists will be there with the same objective. The train runs down to **Mersin**, in the eastern part of the coast, which is a bustling place and is best passed through. The Tourist Office is at the harbour, near where Turkish Maritime Lines run a service to Turkish-controlled **Northern Cyprus** (ferry takes eight hrs to Gazimagusa (Famagusta) and costs around $42.50 return, students $38.50). If you go to northern Cyprus, get the immigration authorities to stamp a separate sheet of paper rather than your passport because you may not be allowed entry back into Greece if they see you have been to the Turkish-controlled area of Cyprus.

Small beach towns run along the coast west of Mersin. **Kocahasanli** can be reached by bus and is a large campground right on the beach, a beautiful place. Also try the town of **Korykos**, with its two scenic castles, one on an island offshore, and beaches. There is no shortage of pensions or campsites here.

## Central Anatolia

Central Anatolia is a desolate plateau region of 'frying-pan' temperatures. It's also home to the capital of modern Turkey, Ankara, and the old capital of the Seljuk Turks, Konya.

**KONYA** Once capital of the Seljuks, Konya is an important Turkish centre of Islam and still a big focus of pilgrimage. It was here that the famous Order of the Whirling Dervishes started. See the **Monastery** and **Tomb of Mevlana**, the founder of the Dervishes, the **Archaeological Museum** and the **Market**.

Atatürk clamped down on the whirling and it was only in 1954 that it was allowed to be openly performed again, but this time as a folk dance to entertain tourists and only in the week leading up to Mevlana's death on 17 Dec. If you are here in May or during that week in Dec. you can see the whirling for yourself.

The Tourist Office is on Mevlana Caddesi (Tel. (332) 351 1074; Fax. (332) 350 6461). For accommodation try the **Otel Çesme** at Akifpaşa Sok 35 (Tel. (332) 351 2426), or **Otel Tur**, on Esarizade Sok (Tel. (332) 351 9825).

## Ankara phone code: 312

In 1923 the small, unimportant town of Ankara was thrust into the role of capital of the new Turkish Republic. Since then it hasn't looked back, becoming a sprawling metropolis which is now Turkey's largest city.

## TOURIST INFORMATION

The main Tourist Office is at 121 Gazi Mustafa Kemal Bulvari (Tel. 488 7007 or 231 5572). Open daily.: 9am–6.50pm. Ask for a map and the useful *Ankara Guide*. The Tourist Office at the airport is open 24hrs.

## ADDRESSES

**POST OFFICE** Atatürk Bulvari, open 24 hours with 24-hour currency exchange

**AMEX** Koc Bank, 58 Atatürk Bulvari; open Mon.–Fri.: 9am–4pm

**STUDENT TRAVEL** Emek Işhani, Kat. 11 no.1109, Kizilay (Tel. 118 1326)

**UK EMBASSY** 46a Şehit Ersan Caddesi (Tel. 468 6230; Fax. 468 3214)

**US EMBASSY** Atatürk Bulvari 110 (Tel. 468 6110; Fax. 467 0019)

**CANADIAN EMBASSY** 75 Nenehatun Caddesi (Tel. 436 1275/3178; Fax. 446 4437)

**AUSTRALIAN EMBASSY** 83 Nenehatun Caddesi (Tel. 446 1180; Fax. 446 1188)

**MEDICAL HELP** Hacettepe University Hospital, Hasircilar Caddesi (Tel. 310 3545)

## STATION FACILITIES

Railway station on Hippodron Caddesi. Overnight services from Istanbul, also connections east.

## SEEING

Being such a sprawling city, a map is an excellent investment. The bus network is extensive – buy tickets in advance from street kiosks. **Ulus** is the old section of town where many of the sights are, including the citadel and the Museum of Anatolian Civilizations. The **Citadel** is itself a small walled city with winding lanes, a great place to wander. The **Bazaar** and a **Mosque** are also within the citadel's walls. The **Museum of Anatolian Civilizations** is a world-class museum with exhibits from the huge number of cultures which grew up in this cradle of civilisation (open Tues.–Sun.: 8.30am–5.15pm, admission $2.50, reductions for student card holders) and is situated in a restored covered bazaar.

The other main sight of Ankara is the huge **Mausoleum of Atatürk**, the national hero, in a large park. It is a monument to the man whose adopted name means literally 'Father of the Turks'. There is also a museum of his life and personal effects, open Tues.–Sun.: 9am–12 noon and 1.30–5pm (4pm in winter); Mon.: 1.30–5pm; entrance is free. Also check out the **Ethnographic Museum** and the **Temple of Augustus**.

## SLEEPING

Ask the Tourist Office for a list of hotels. Most of the cheap places to stay are in Ulus. There's dormitory accommodation in summer at 15 Neyzen Tevfik Sok, Maltepe (Tel. 232 2954/2955) and women can try the dorms at 61 Karanfil Sok (Tel. 419 3715 or 419 3067). Alternatively, try the **Hotel Kale**, Anafartalar Caddesi 13, Alataş Sok (Tel. 311 3393 or 310 3521), the **Otel Bulduk**, Sanayi Caddesi 26 (Tel. 310 4915) or the **Otel Ertan**, 70 Selanik Caddesi (Tel. 418 4084 or 425 1506).

If you want to **camp** head for the **D.S.I Kampi Campground** on Bayindir Baraji (Tel. 372 2731) a short ride by dolmus (taxi). Refer to *Cheap Sleeps Europe 2000* for more accommodation options.

## EATING AND NIGHTLIFE

Ulus does not have that great a selection of restaurants; try along the Çankiri Caddesi. The bazaar is always a good place to explore. To meet some Turkish students, try the **Café Melodi** on Atatürk Bulvari.

# Eastern Turkey

Eastern Turkey contains some of the country's most stunning landscapes, including the beautiful mountains around **Lake Van** (its largest lake. However, occasional fighting with Kurdish populations means you will need to keep a check on the latest developments before travelling. The Armenian border should be avoided due to the current political climate between Turkey and Armenia.

**VAN** The city is five km from the largest lake in Turkey. Outside is the imposing **Citadel** and **Ancient City** on the **Rock of Van**, once the capital of the Urartian empire. There is also a small archaeological museum. The Tourist Office is at 127 Cumhuriyet Caddesi.

Other places to visit around the lake are the **Armenian Church** on the island of **Akdamar** or the scenic mountains around the town of **Hakkari**. The ferry across Lake Van takes about four hours.

NOTES

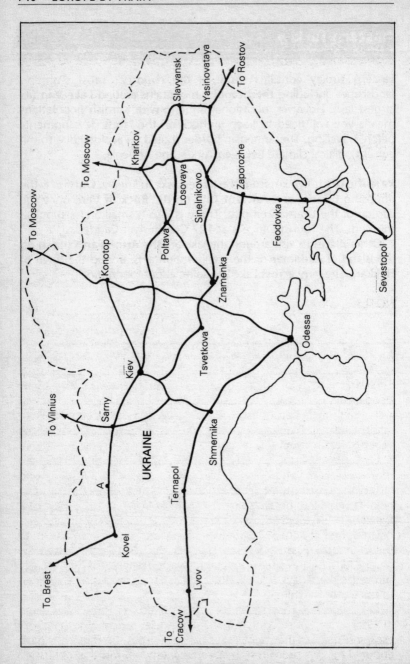

# THE UKRAINE

| | |
|---|---|
| Entry requirements | Passport and visa. All foreign nationals need a full passport and a visa, which should be bought in advance (£20-60) as there have been problems buying them at the border |
| Population | 52 million |
| Capital | Kiev (pop.: 2.6 million) |
| Currency | Ukrainian hryvna<br>£1 = approx 8.2 hryvna |
| Political system | Republic |
| Religion | Russian and Ukrainian Autocephalous Orthodox; also Ukrainian Catholic |
| Language | Ukrainian, Russian; little English, some German spoken |
| Public holidays | New Year's Day, Orthodox Christmas (7 Jan.), International Women's Day (8 Mar.), Orthodox Easter, Labour Day (1 and 2 May), Victory Day (9 May), Independence Day (24 Aug.), Liberation Day (28 Oct.). |
| International dialling | To Ukraine: int'l code 380<br>From Ukraine: 810 country code number. International calls may be easiest made through a post office or (more expensively) a hotel. |
| Emergency telephone numbers | Police 02; ambulance 03; fire service 01 |

The Ukraine has a lot to offer the traveller, but having said that, many people don't know anything about it, so here's a quick run-down: Yalta is a thriving beach resort, Odessa a diverse and fascinating port, and the beautiful capital Kiev was in the 9th century the capital of the very first Russian state.

Over the years the Ukrainians have been invaded and ruled by a motley crew of Mongols, Tartars, Turks, Poles, Hungarians and Lithuanians. Eventually, like so many of its Eastern European neighbours, it also became part of the Soviet Union in 1922. However, the country's nationalist movement always remained strong and was given added impetus following the appalling response by Russia to the Chernobyl disaster. This saw the Kiev May Day Parades given the go-ahead, two days after the explosion, when fallout was over the city (however, these days, you'll be pleased to know, risk of contamination to the visitor is minimal).

On 1 December 1991, the Ukraine declared its independence and in 1996 a new constitution replaced the Soviet system. But there's no escaping the fact that since breaking away from the fold, they have endured massive problems: the poor economy mirrors that of Russia's and you should be aware when visiting that it is not a well-organized country. Even more than in Russia, you will find that the locals expect all Westerners to be wealthy; try not to take the attempts of Ukrainians to milk this wealth as malicious. People in this poor country are understandably out for themselves.

Although the cholera and diphtheria epidemics of the 1980s are now under control, it would still be wise to check your injections; a diphtheria booster is strongly recommended – beware of the water too. You will also need to take your own toilet paper everywhere.

If you go to the Ukraine, you'll be in for an adventure and, as long as you're prepared beforehand, a visit will reward you (one way or the other) with a lifetime of memories.

## UKRAINIAN STATE RAILWAYS

Ukrainian trains are similar to Russian ones and most of what is written in the chapter on Russia applies here. This includes the cautionary note on getting out of the country again: you won't purchase a ticket west for anything other than hard currency, and although coupons may get you a ticket to a border town, the price for crossing the border will still be in dollars. Moreover, there are no hostels in the Ukraine which sell rail tickets. If you can't speak Russian, you'll have to write down all your train details on a piece of paper and present it to a station cashier with a pleading grin. If you're the type of person who needs a lifeline when going to a new country, postpone your visit until such time as the Ukraine sorts itself out.

The Ukraine is not in Inter-Rail or any other international rail scheme.

## TRAIN INFORMATION

All information given in the Russia chapter applies here. Distances within the Ukraine are large, and many overnight trips are possible. Be prepared for a delay at the border as the track gauge changes.

## TOURIST INFORMATION

As in Russia, there's no Westernized system of tourist information. *The Lonely Planet Guide* covers most Ukrainian places of interest, complete with maps, but don't expect accommodation tips: the situation is such that no guidebook can help you there. For general information dial 09 (it will help enormously if you speak Russian). If you want information on the Ukraine before you leave home, contact Bob Sopel Ukrainian Travel (Tel. 0161 652 5050), 27 Henshaw Street, Oldham OL1 1NH. They can arrange accommodation and book train tickets for you.

**VISAS** The Ukraine started issuing its own visas in 1994, and the cost is now between £20–60. Theoretically, visa restrictions are less stringent than in Russia, and the application form does not require a strict itinerary or proof of accommodation. You should be able to buy a visa on the border, but in practice this isn't always the case: buy one in advance if you can, and take a photocopy as well as the original. Once in the Ukraine you should register your arrival, either automatically when checking in at a hotel or by going to the local office of OVIR, the government ministry dealing with foreigners.

A cautionary tale: in the course of updating this guide, our researcher, equipped with a full Ukrainian visa, gained entry to the country with no problem. However, while changing money in Kiev, his passport was examined and suddenly he found himself under arrest; he was escorted to the train station, put on a train by an armed guard, held for several hours at customs and eventually kicked out into Hungary, somewhat disillusioned by the experience. The only explanation he was given was that his visa was invalid, yet the Ukrainian Embassy in London claimed there was nothing wrong with it. Unquestionably, this was just bad luck; but the story serves as a reminder that in a changing country the left hand often doesn't know what the right hand is doing: it's easy to get caught up in bureaucracy.

And after that charming tale, the UK address for visa applications is the Embassy of the Ukraine, Consular Department, 78 Kensington Park Road, London W11 2PL (Tel. 0900 188 7749 or 020 7243 8923; Fax. 020 7792 1708).

**MONEY MATTERS** Ukrainian coupons, peculiar beasts resembling monopoly money, were introduced in 1993 though rapidly went into free fall, so in 1996 a new currency appeared, the hryvna whivh is sub divided into 100 Kopiyky. You can exchange most Western hard currencies in banks and hotel lobbies, however sterling is not popular in some regions (the US dollar is the most widely accepted currency by all banks and exchange bureaux). As in Russia, hang on to exchange receipts: you may be asked to show them when you leave the country and coupons cannot be reconverted to hard currency without them (though even with them it's an arduous task). The advice on black-market money changing is that it's not only illegal but also unnecessary and you risk being cheated; it isn't worth it. Traveller's cheques are not currently accepted in the Ukraine.

**POST OFFICES** Main post offices are open Mon.–Fri.: 8am–8pm. Many have long-distance phones. The Ukrainian postal system is even worse than its Russian counterpart.

**SHOPS** Shopping can be a complicated business: you have to go to the cashier's desk, point out what you want and buy a voucher for it. You then take the voucher and exchange it for your purchases. Hard currency shops here are called *kashtan*. Good buys include pottery and, should you have an unusually large amount of extra space in your backpack, rugs.

**LANGUAGE** Like Russian, Ukrainian is written in Cyrillic, and the two languages are very similar. Ukrainian has two extra letters which look like small 'i's, both neutral vowel sounds. Eighty per cent of words are similar to Russian, though the ones that aren't include 'yes', 'no', 'goodbye', 'thank you', 'good' and 'hotel' (*gotel*). Russian is spoken everywhere.

## SLEEPING

If you're hoping for a trip with no worries about accommodation, either book through Bob Sopel Ukrainian Travel (see Tourist Information) or Intourist or forget it. Intourist, the state commission for foreign tourism in the Soviet Union, is still officially the agency all Western visitors are supposed to go through, but their prices are so extreme as to be prohibitive. The Ukraine doesn't yet have Russia's slowly evolving hostel network, and the problems Westerners face in Russian hotels are possibly worse here. Ask in Russian how much a bed is in a Kiev hotel and you may hear a price in the region of $3; give away your nationality and you will probably find it increased tenfold. One word of warning for tall travellers; Ukrainians tend to be short and the beds are built to fit!

Hotels run by the Central Council for Tourism and Excursions (CCTE), a domestic tourist agency, will probably charge you around $30 a night per person, and if you can live with that, they have a hotel in most major Ukrainian cities. Many other hotels are not officially open to foreigners and it is impossible to recommend individual ones because of their variability. Try your luck: haggle, look pleading and destitute, and you may get a bargain.

Because of this unpredictability, you may want to seek out locals offering accommodation – many stand outside hotels looking for potential customers. They will charge far less than a hotel, but obviously you have no guarantee of quality, or, for that matter, safety. Use your discretion.

## EATING

The Ukraine suffers the same food shortages as Russia, and has the same profusion of people selling pastries and cakes on street corners. The black market also thrives here. As regards restaurants, the fare is wholesome, if bleak, and the service as erratic as in Russia. Hard-currency restaurants exist throughout the Ukraine, providing a guarantee of assistance (Ukrainian menus aren't easily translated) at a cost. Ukrainians also share the Russian taste for vodka, even if most of it does taste like nail varnish remover.

# Kiev (КИЇВ ) phone code: 044

The third largest city of the former Soviet Union, Kiev was founded in the 5th century on the banks of the Dniepr River. After becoming the 'mother of Russian cities' in the 9th century, the 10th century also saw it become the original centre of the Orthodox Christian faith. Today Kiev has developed into a city with a lot going for it: not least its historic buildings and lively atmosphere. When you're starting to weigh up whether the hassles of travelling in the Ukraine are really worth it, an afternoon spent lazing on the hills overlooking the river makes everything seem worthwhile again. As it continues in its new role as the Ukraine's capital, the city – as does the country – still suffers from the effects of a raging economic crisis.

Most of the sights are located on the Dniepr's hilly west bank. Kiev's main street, Ulitsa Kreshchatik, runs along a valley towards the river, starting in the middle of town and ending at a five km stretch of parkland. Outlying Kiev isn't quite so picturesque: away from the old city, which dates back at least as far as the 9th century, the rest of the town is drab, concrete and evidently communist-built.

# Lvov (ПЪВЁЕ) phone code: 0322

Lvov is the principal city of western Ukraine and although badly polluted, its pleasant hilly setting, wonderful historic heart and diverse architecture all make for a worthy visit and not just a mere stopping-off point on the way to Kiev. It's a city more Central European than Russian, with Ukrainian nationalism at its strongest.

## STATION FACILITIES
Lvov is the first city you'll reach if you're coming to the Ukraine from southern Poland. You'll also pass through it if entering from Slovakia or Hungary *en route* to Kiev. International trains run from Lvov to Budapest, Bratislava, Prague, Vienna, Belgrade, Bucharest, Sofia and Vilnius. Within the former Soviet Union, they run to Moscow, Kiev, Ternopol, Vinnitsa, Rovno, Chernovtsy and Simferopol (a station you'll visit if you're heading for Yalta). Lvov railway station is three km west of the centre, at the end of Ulitsa Vokzalnaya. There's no metro in Lvov, but trams 1 and 9 connect the station to Russkaya Ulitsa in the city centre.

## TOURIST INFORMATION AND ADDRESSES

The Intourist Service Bureau is at the Hotel Intourist, Prospekt Shevchenko 1. It's open 9am–12 noon and 1pm–7pm. Also head for the travel office in the Hotel George at Ploshchad Mickiewicza 1 (Tel. 725952) who have maps and plenty of info on the city. The Dom Knigi bookshop on Ploshchad Mitsvekicha should sell tourist maps too.

**POST OFFICE** Vulitsya Slovatskovo 1

**CURRENCY EXCHANGE** Vulitsya Hnatyuka, right off Prospekt Svobodi. Bank at Hotel Dneistr, by Ivan Franka Park.

## SEEING

Lvov fans out from Ploshchad Rynok, the heart of the old city. Its main street, **Prospekt Lenina**, is to the west of the Rynok and has been an important centre for Ukrainian nationalism over the years: the parkland in the middle being a prime spot for impromptu speech-making. **Ploshchad Rynok** was the centre of Lvov life for 500 years from the 14th century. It is home to the **Lvov History Museum** (open 10am–6pm, closed Wed.) and is surrounded by houses with a variety of interesting façades. Amongst Lvov's many churches are **St George's Cathedral**, the former headquarters of the Uniate Church, and the three-domed **Assumption Church** on Podvalnaya Ulitsa. If you're culturally saturated, walk up **Castle Hill** (*Zamkovaya Gora*) for the views, or lie in **Ivan Franka Park** to the west of the city.

## SLEEPING AND EATING

CCTE use the **Hotel Turist** on Vulitsya Engelsa 103 (Tel. 351065); take tram no. 2 from Russkaya Ulitsa. Phone before turning up: the hotel is primarily for groups and may be full. Alternatively, the **Hotel George** on Ploshchad Mickiewicza 1 (Tel. 725952) may be worth a try or **Hotel Karpaty**, Vulitaya Kleparivska 30. The **campsite** is seven km from town on the Kiev road. Check with the Tourist Office that it is still there/open before making the journey.

Two recommended eateries are **Mediviya** at Vulitaya Krakivska 17 and **Lisova Pisnya** on Vulitaya Sichovykh Striltsiv 5, but things change quickly in the restaurant business in this part of the world.

## Odessa (ОДЕССА) phone code: 0482

Odessa, on the Black Sea, the Ukraine's largest port, is a thriving, partying holiday centre. It's also a capital, though not of any country or region, but of black market activity. May to Sept. are the best months to try out some of its beautiful beaches, after which you can

June–Sept. at 1.30pm every Wed. and Fri. The fare is £7.50. Telephone 028 9045 8484 for more information.

There's a **youth hostel** in the city centre at 22 Donegal Road (Tel. 028 9031 5435; Fax. 028 9043 9699). Beds around £10; no kitchen facilities. Also try Arnie's Backpackers (Tel. 028 9024 2867) at 63 Fitzwilliam Street. It's small so reserve or get there early (kitchen facilities). A look around the university area should turn up a pleasant B&B, but it'll cost you twice the price of a hostel bed.

A worthy detour is the **Ulster Folk and Transport Museum** at Cultra Manor, Holywood, 10 km from Belfast. There are reconstructions of 19th-century life from farms to craft centres.

No visit to Northern Ireland would be complete without a trip to the magnificent **Giant's Causeway**, 40,000 columns of basalt wrapped in Celtic legend. The **Causeway Visitors Centre** at Causeway Head is open daily 10am–7pm (earlier closing off-season). The **Whitepark Bay Youth Hostel** (Tel. 028 2073 1745; Fax. 028 2073 2034) in Ballycastle is not too far away, and is situated next to **St Gobhan's Church** – the smallest in Ireland at 4 ft x 6 ft. There is also the **Ballycastle Backpackers** at 4 North Street, near the water front (Tel. 028 2076 3612). Whilst you're there, contemplate a visit to the nearby **Bushmills** at 2 Distillery Road. Established in 1608, its the Oldest (legal) Whiskey distillery and is open for tours (Tel. 028 2073 3218). The **visitor centre** has many creative uses for the liquid gold.

A particularly scenic excursion can be taken throughout the area on the 'Bushmills Bus'. An open-topped affair, it runs five times a day between July and Aug., from Coleraine to the Giant's Causeway via Portstewart, Portrush, Portballintrae and Bushmills. The journey can be broken *en route*.

**LONDONDERRY** (or just **DERRY**), is one of Northern Ireland's most attractive towns and just 2 hours from Belfast. Tourist information is at 44 Foyle Street (Tel. 028 7126 7284). The **Old City Walls** date back to the early 17th century and offer you great views while walking the 1.5 km circuit. The **Guildhall** in Shipquay Place is a neo-Gothic building with stained-glass windows depicting the city's history. The 17th-century Protestant **Cathedral** is noted for its stained glass displaying scenes of the 1688/89 siege. To hear traditional Irish music and to enjoy a pint or two, try one of the pubs on Waterloo Street: **Dungloe Bar**, **Gweedore Bar** or **Peadar O'Donnell's**.

If you're planning to link up with the Republic of Ireland's rail network rather than heading back to Belfast, **Fermanagh**, the province's lakeland, is well worth a bus detour. These leave from Waterloo Place in Londonderry, and tend to go via **Omagh**, where you can break your journey by visiting the **Ulster-American Folk Park** and the nearby **History Park**.

In **Enniskillen**, visit the **Castle Museum** and the tiny **Cathedral**. Stop for a pint at **Blake's of the Hollow**: it's genuinely as old as the hills and you'll not be disappointed. Explore the lakes; even from the land the views can be beautiful. Exit Enniskillen via the Shore Road for Belleek – it's worth hitching to stop off at **Tully Castle**, **Church Hill**; or the **Cliffs of Magho**. From Belleek it's only 40 km to Sligo (Republic of Ireland), where you can rejoin the rail network.

NOTES

.................................................................................................................................

.................................................................................................................................

.................................................................................................................................

.................................................................................................................................

.................................................................................................................................

.................................................................................................................................

.................................................................................................................................

.................................................................................................................................

.................................................................................................................................

.................................................................................................................................

.................................................................................................................................

.................................................................................................................................

.................................................................................................................................

.................................................................................................................................

.................................................................................................................................

.................................................................................................................................

.................................................................................................................................

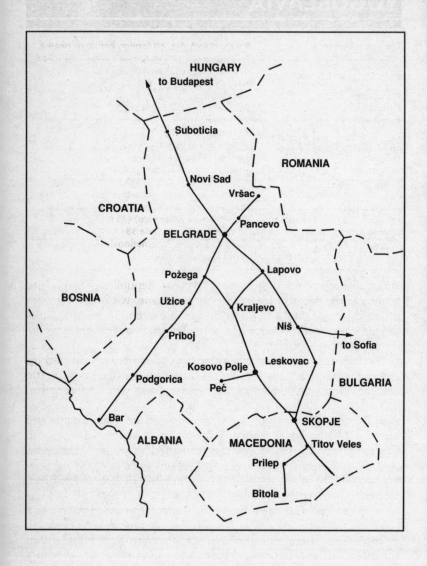

# YUGOSLAVIA

| | |
|---|---|
| Entry requirements | Passport and visa. All foreign nationals need a full passport and a visa, which must be obtained in advance (free of charge at Yugoslav consulates). |
| Population | 11 million |
| Capital | Belgrade (pop.: 1.1 million) |
| Currency | New Dinar |
| | £1 = approx. 18DIN |
| Political system | Federation of two Republics |
| Religion | Serbian Orthodox |
| Language | Serbian, some German spoken |
| Public Holidays | New Year's Day, Orthodox Christmas (7 Jan.), Labour Day (1 May), Constitution Day (27 April), Independence Day (Serbia) (7 Jul.), Independence Day (Montenegro) (13 Jul.) |
| International dialling | To Yugoslavia: int'l code 381 |
| | From Yugoslavia: International calls are usually made from post offices |

Yugoslavia is split not only between the two Republics of Serbia and Montenegro, but also by its diverse landscape, with the low-lying plains of the Danube to the north and extremely mountainous terrain to the south providing a pathway (albeit a rocky one) to the waters of the Adriatic.

Throughout most of the Middle Ages the area was divided up between the rival empires of the Austrian Habsburgs and the Ottoman Turks, though by 1878 Serbia, along with Montenegro, had achieved full independence.

At the end of World War 1, they both joined Slovenia, Croatia and Bosnia-Hercegovina to form the 'Kingdom of Serbs, Slovenes and Croats', which by 1929 had been renamed Yugoslavia. However, World War II brought a split as some regions allied with the occupying Nazis whilst others, under the communist leadership of Josip Tito, fought a fierce struggle against them.

In 1945, with Germany defeated, Tito reformed Yugoslavia as a communist federal republic which he continued ruling until his death in 1980. The federation proved unable to survive after him and in the 1990s fell apart as one republic after another broke away in a series of bloody civil wars.

Gradually all that remained was the rump of Serbia and Montenegro, who shunned all responsibility for the actions of the former government and declared themselves a new Yugoslav federation.

Today, while its devastated economy continues to suffer from the effects of civil war, there is more hope, with a tourist industry slowly emerging after years in the wilderness – though with continuing unrest in the Serbian province of Kosovo, travel here is not advised at present.

## YUGOSLAVIAN RAILWAYS

### (JUGOSLOVENSKE ZELEZNICE) (JZ)

There are adequate services along the main line from Hungary down through Belgrade and on to Macedonia or Bulgaria, and a scenic main branch line from Belgrade to the coast at Bar. International trains are reasonable, although slow and often very crowded, while local trains can be pretty dire. Reservations are needed for international services – make them at the departure station as early as you can.

**PASSES AVAILABLE** Yugoslavia is in Inter-Rail zone H, along with Bulgaria, Romania and Macedonia. Eurail is not valid.

## TOURIST INFORMATION

There's no general system of tourist information. The *Lonely Planet Guide to Eastern Europe* gives reasonable coverage, and there are municipal tourist offices in the main cities, as well as commercial travel agencies.

**VISAS** There are Yugoslav consulates in the Eastern European capitals of Bucharest, Budapest, Prague, Sofia and Warsaw, as well as in the USA, Canada, Australia and the UK, all of which should issue visas on the spot. You are unlikely to be able to enter the country without one, and will probably not be able to get one in Slovenia, Croatia or Macedonia. Note well: Serbian border guards have become quite used to hauling protesting backpackers off international trains and sending them straight back where they came from.

**MONEY MATTERS** Throughout the nineties Yugoslavia has been dogged by inflation and hyperinflation which has produced devaluations of the dinar. This means that the 'new' or 'novi' dinar is still distrusted by a lot of people and you will usually be able to use Deutschmarks. Still, changing money is relatively easy: you can do it at any bank, hotel or travel agency and the rate if you change on the street is unlikely to be any better.

**POST OFFICES** Main post offices are open Mon.–Fri.: 8am–7pm; Sat.: 8am–3pm. Many have long-distance phones. The high rate of inflation means that stamp denominations may not always keep up, so it may be easier to have your postcards franked over the counter.

**SHOPS** Shops keep similar hours to post offices. There are no particular shortages or specialities to watch out for, although you should bring all your film with you.

## LANGUAGE

Serbian is almost always written in Cyrillic, so you'll benefit from spending an hour or two studying the Cyrillic alphabet – see the Bulgaria section.

## SLEEPING

Budget hotels are scarce, and prices are often set in Deutschmarks or US dollars. Your best bet may be to camp or to plan on a long overnight train journey – you should be able to reserve a couchette from Belgrade, but do it early.

## EATING

Serbian food has a Balkan feel to it, tending towards hot, spicy dishes such as grilled kebabs. The cheapest sustenance is a *burek*, a pie filled with cheese, meat or potato often available from street stalls. Beer is cheap but not very exciting. Coffee is served Turkish style: sweet, strong, and tarlike.

## Belgrade code: 0322

Capital of Serbia and Yugoslavia, Belgrade was fortunate to escape damage during the wars of the 1990s. While it doesn't claim to be Europe's most attractive or inspirational city, it's still a worthwhile hub and will easily satisfy a day or so of your time.

## STATION FACILITIES

The main station is on Savski trg, with the main bus station next door. There are frequent trains to Budapest (six hours), two trains a day to Vienna (11 hours), two a day to Thessaloniki and Athens (22 hours) and the Balkan Express to Sofia (nine hours) and Istanbul (26 hours). There is 24-hour left-luggage (you'll need to show your passport) and a currency exchange, although check first at the JIK Bank just outside to see if they're giving a better rate. There is a post office on the south side of the station with a telephone centre for long-distance calls. The other thing to do when you get here is to reserve your seat or couchette for the journey out.

Trains to Bucharest (nine hours) go from the smaller Beograd-Dunav station.

## TOURIST INFORMATION AND ADDRESSES

The city tourist organization has its main office in the underpass on the corner of Kneza Mihaila and Terzije, and opens Mon.–Fri.:

9am–8pm, Sat.: 9am–4pm.
**POST OFFICE** Next to the main station, at Takovska 2 or at Zmaj
Jovina 17

## SEEING

At the heart of Belgrade is the old fortress of **Kalmedan Citadel**.
Surrounded by parkland, it offers great views of the Danube and also
houses a **Zoo**, **Military Museum** and **Natural History Museum**.
Next to the citadel, **Stari Grad**, the oldest part of the city, is also
home to the good **Ethnographic Museum**, which has detailed
explanations in English. A pleasant place to picnic is on **Ada Cigan-
lija**, an island park in the Sava River.

## SLEEPING AND EATING

Budget accommodation in Belgrade is pretty thin at the moment.
Hotels are generally state-owned and charge an exorbitant fixed rate
of around 85DM for a single, 150DM for a double. A short walk from
the station is **Beograd** at Balkanska 52 (Tel. 645 178), which has
rooms with baths and showers. Otherwise try the youth hostel,
about three miles out: the **Pionirski Grad 'SRC'** sports centre at
Kneza Viseslava 27 (Tel. 542 166), take tram 23 or 53. Hostel charges
are approximately 35DM.

The nearest **campsite** is five miles south-west of the city centre at
Kneza Viseslava 17 (Tel.: 555 127), take tram 23 or 53.

A lot of the restaurants tend to be pretentious, but you could try
the **Grmeč** at Makedonska 33, or the **Brod Restoran 'Sent Andreja'**
at Kej Oslobooenja bb for some Chinese and vegetarian food. There
are plenty of fast-food counters and *burek* stands, but make sure the
prices are clearly marked.

# Bar

Although it's an eight-hour journey from Belgrade, the trip to Bar is
worth it, just for the scenic view from the window. It's also the only
practical way for Eurorailers to visit Yugoslavia's other republic,
**Montenegro**. While the town itself is not overly interesting, it's still
one of Yugoslavia's few seaside resorts and gets fairly crowded in the
holiday season. There's a daily ferry to Bari in Italy too. Most hotel
prices are fixed by the government, tend to be expensive, and there
is no youth hostel, although you might be able to get a room from
one of the tourist agencies at the ferry terminal.

# APPENDICES

# Appendix I

## INTER-RAIL DISCOUNTS

## SEA OPERATORS (UK and Ireland)

| | | |
|---|---|---|
| Hoverspeed (Sea Cat) | Dover–Ostend | 50% |
| Hoverspeed | Dover–HoverportCalais | 50% |
| Hoverspeed (Sea Cat) | Folkestone–Boulogne | 50% |
| Irish Ferries | Holyhead–Dublin | 50% |
| Irish Ferries | Rosslare–Pembroke | 50% |
| Irish Ferries | Rosslare–Roscoff | 50% (1) (3) |
| Irish Ferries | Rosslare–Cherbourg | 50% (1) (3) |
| P&O Stena | Dover–Calais | 50% |
| P&O (European Ferries) | Portsmouth–Cherbourg | 30% |
| P&O (European Ferries) | Portsmouth-Le Havre | 30% |
| Scandinavian Seaways | Harwich–Esbjerg | 50% (2) |
| Sea France | Dover-Calais | 50% |
| Stena Line | Harwick–Hoek van Holland | 30% (3) |
| Stena Line | Fishguard–Rosslare (Ship) | 50% |
| Stena Line | Fishguard–Rosslare (Lynx) | 25% |
| Stena Line | Holyhead–Dun Laoghaire (HSS) | 50% |
| Stena Line | Stranraer–Belfast (Ship or HSS) | 50% |

1. Reduction valid on the day of sailing for a single foot-passenger fare.
2. Discount applicable on cabins and couchettes only.
3. Reservations are compulsory on sailings. Accommodation charges must be paid in full. For Scandinavian Seaways, tickets must be purchased in Britain.

EUROSTAR
Inter-Rail Zone A or E Cardholders travel at the Passholder rate.

# AUSTRIA (Zone C)

| | | |
|---|---|---|
| Wolfgangseeschiffahrt | | 20% |
| Zahnradbahn Schneeberg | | 10% |
| Zahnradbahn Schafberg | | 15% |
| DDSG Blue Danube Schiffart GmbH | Melk-Wien | 20% |
| DDSG Blue Danube Schiffart GmbH | Krems-Wien | 20% |
| Donauschiffahrt Wurm & Köck | Linz-Passau | 50% |
| Cycle hire at 130 stations | | 40% |

# DENMARK (Zone C)

| | | |
|---|---|---|
| Scandlines Flyvebadene (Hydrofoil) | Copenhagen–Malmö | 25% |
| Hjørring Privatbaner (HP) | Hjørring–Hirtshals | 50% |
| Scandinavian Seaways | Copenhagen–Oslo | 50% (4) |
| Skagensbanen (SB) | Fredrikshavn–Skagen | 50% |
| Lollandsbanen | Nykobing F. Nakskov | 50% |
| Odderbanen | Arhus–Odder | 50% |

(4) Applicable for economy cabin accommodation only.

# FINLAND (Zone B)

| | | |
|---|---|---|
| Silja Line: | Helsinki–Rostock | Special fare |
| | Helsinki/Turku–Stockholm | 50% |

# FRANCE (Zone E)

| | | |
|---|---|---|
| Chemins de Fer de la Corse | All lines | 50% |
| Chemins de Fer de la Provence | Nice–Digne | 50% |
| SNMC-M: | Marseille–Ajaccio (in 2nd class) | 30% |
| | Marseille–Propriano | 30% |
| | Nice–Calvi | 30% |
| | Toulon–Bastia | 30% |

# NORWAY (Zone B)

| | | |
|---|---|---|
| Color Line | Oslo/Kristiansand-Hirtshals | 50% |
| Color Line | Moss/Larvik–Frederikshavn | 50% |
| Flaggruten | Bergen– Stavanger | 50% |
| Fylkesbaatanei I Sogn og Fjordane | Express and fjord ferries | 50% |
| HSD Hardanger Sunnhordalandske Dampskibsselskap | Express ferries | 25% |
| Norway Bussexpress | Bodø-Fauske | 50% |
| | Fauske-Svolvær/Harstad/Narvik | 50% |
| | Narvik-Tromsø | 50% |
| | Tromsø-Alta | 50% |
| | Alta-Kirkenes | 50% |
| | Otta-Stryn/Måløy/Ålesund | 50% |
| | Ålesund-Trondheim | 50% |
| | Ålesund-Molde-Kristiansund | 50% |
| | Gol-Sogndal/Førde | 50% |
| | Bergen-Nordfjord/Stryn/Ålesund | 50% |
| | Bergen-Stryn-Otta-Tromdheim | 50% |
| | Bergen-Sogndal-Fagernes-Lillehammer | 50% |
| Andøy Traffiklag/Nordtrafikk | Sortland-Ardenes | 50% |
| Ofotens Bilruter | Kiruna-Nordkapp | 50% |
| | Nordkap-Narvik | 50% |
| | Narvik-Sortland/Harstad | 50% |

# SPAIN (Zone F)

Compagnie de Navegación Trasmediterranea:

| | | |
|---|---|---|
| | Barcelona–Palma/Ibiza/Mahón | 30% |
| | Valencia–Palma/Ibiza | 30% |
| | Almería–Mellila | 30% |
| | Málaga–Mellila | 30% |
| | Cádiz–Canaries | 30% |
| | Algeciras–Tangier/Ceuta | 30% |

Ferrocarrils de la Generalitat de Catalunya (FGC):

| | | |
|---|---|---|
| | Barcelona-Sabadell/Terrasa | 50% |
| | Barcelona-Manresa/Igualada | 50% |
| | Ribes de Fresser-Nuria | 50% |
| | Monserrat Funicular | 50% |

# SWEDEN (Zone B)

| | | |
|---|---|---|
| Stena Line | Göteborg–Frederikshavn | 50% (3) |
| Silja Line | Stockholm–Helsinki | 50% (3) |
| Silja Line | Stockholm–Turku | 50% (4) |
| Silja Line | Vaasa–Umeå | 50% |
| TT-Line | Trelleborg–Lübeck/Travemünde | 50% |
| Viking Line | Stockholm–Helsinki | 50% |
| Viking Line | Stockholm–Turku | 50% |

# SWITZERLAND

All these companies give a 50% reduction:

| | |
|---|---|
| AB | Appenzellerbahn |
| AL | Aigle–Leysin |
| AOMC | Aigle–Ollon–Monthey–Champréy |
| ASD | Aigle–Sepey–Les Diablerets |
| BAM | Bière–Apples–Morges |
| BB | Burgenstockbahn |
| BOW | Oberdorf–Weissenstein |
| BrS | Brienzersee |
| BSG | Lac de Bienne |
| BTI | Blei–Tauffelen-Ins |
| BVB | Bex–Villars–Bretaye |
| BVZ | Brig–Visp–Zermatt |
| CEV | Chemins de Fer du Veveysans |
| CJ | Chemins de Fer du Jura |
| CMN | Chemins de Fer des Montagnes-Neuchâteloises |
| EBT | Emmental–Burgdorf–Thun |
| FB | Forchbahn |
| GBS | Gurbetal–Bern–Schwarzenburg |
| GFM | Chemins de Fer Fribourgeois (including bus routes) |
| GGB | Gornergratbahn |
| LAF | Adliswil–Felsenegg |
| LAS | Les Avants–Sonloup |
| LEB | Lausanne–Echallens–Bercher |
| LLB | Leuk–Leukerbad |
| LLPR | Lenzerheide–Parpaner Rothorn |
| LSE | Luzern–Stans–Engelberg |
| LSM | Stockalp–Melchsee–Frutt |
| MC | Martigny–Châtelard |
| MTGN | Montreux–Glion-Rochers de Naye |

# SWITZERLAND (continued)

| | |
|---|---|
| MO | Martigny–Orsières (including bus routes) |
| NStCM | Nyon–Sant Cergue–Morez |
| OeBB | Oensingen–Balsthal |
| PBr | Pont–Brassus |
| RBS | Regional Verkehr Bern–Solothurn |
| RVO | Regional Oberaargau |
| RVT | Regional du Val de Travers |
| SBN | Beatenberg–Niederhorn |
| SGV | Vierwaldstättersee |
| SMB | Solothurn–Moutier |
| SMtS | St Imiet–Mont Soleil |
| SNB | Solothurn–Niederbipp |
| STB | Sensetalbahn |
| STI | SteffisburgThun–Interlaken (including bus routes) |
| SZU | Sihital-Zürich–UetlibergBahn |
| TB | Trogenerbahn |
| TBB | Thunersee–Beatenberg |
| Ths | Thunersee |
| URh | Untersee and Rhein |
| VCP | Vevey-Mont Pèlerin |
| VHB | Vereinigte Huttwil Bahnen |
| WB | Waldenburgerbahn |
| WSB | Wynental-und Suhrentalbahn |
| YSteC | Yverdon–Ste Croix |
| ZSG | Zürichsee |

Details of discounts are compiled according to information provided by the operators concerned. However, this information may be subject to change without notice.

# TRANSPORT MUSEUMS

The following transport museums offer free or reduced admittance to holders of Inter-Rail cards:

| | |
|---|---|
| Belgium | Railway Museum, Gare de Bruxelles, Nord station |
| Denmark | Railway Museum, Jernbanemuseum, Odense |
| France | French Railway Museum, 2 rue Alfred de Glehn, Mulhouse |
| Finland | Railway Museum, Hyvinkaa |
| | Narrow Gauge Railway Museum, Jokioinen (Minkio station) |
| Greece | Railway Museum, 4 Siokou Street, Athens |
| Hungary | Transport Museum, Varosligeti, Korut II, Budapest XIV |
| | Metro Museum, Metro Station Deák Ferenc tér, Budapest |
| | Horse Carrige Museum, Paradfürdo |
| Norway | Railway Museum, Hamar |
| Portugal | Railway Museum, Santarem station |
| Romania | Railway Museum, Bucharest Nord station |
| Spain | Railway Museum, Paseo de las Delicias, 61 Madrid |
| Sweden | Jarnvagsmuset, Museum of Transport, Raisgaten 1, Gavle |

The following museums offer reduced price admittance to holders of Inter-Rail cards:

France       **Grevin Museum of Waxworks, 10 blvd Montmartre, 75009 Paris**
**Historial de Touraine, Château royal, 25 av. André Malraux, 37000 Tours.**
**Musee Grévin de la Provence, Place des Centuries, 13300 Salon-de-Provence.**
**Les évocations en cire, 87 rue de la Grotte, 65100 Lourdes.**
**Musee Grévin, 3 rue Mazarin, 64500 Saint Jean de Luz.**
**Parc France Miniature, 25 route du Mesnil, 78990 Elancourt.**

## INTER-RAIL CENTRES

**COPENHAGEN** A special Inter-Rail centre is open from June–mid-Sept., 6.30 a.m.–10pm, at Copenhagen central station (*Hovedbanegard*) and provides information, refreshments, left luggage and showers. Overnight sleeping is not allowed.

**TRONDHEIM** An Inter-Rail centre is also available at Elgesetergate 1, Trondheim. The centre provides a lounge, showers, toilets, left luggage, information, a train reservation service and cooking facilities, and sells beverages. The centre is open 1 July–25 Aug., 7am–10.30pm daily. Overnight sleeping is not allowed.

### ADDITIONAL FACILITIES

**GERMANY** – Special Bed and Breakfast rates (including welcome drink and town map) for Inter-railers are available at the Youth Hostels at: Jugengästehaus, Miesingtrasse 4, 81379 München and Hotel Einhorn Paul-Heyse-Strasse 10, 80336 München.

**GREECE** – Discount of 15–57% on bed and breakfast rate in Category A or B hotels in Athens; must be paid in advance and booked through Etos travel, 53A Patision Street, 10433 Athens (Tel. +30 1 522 6138, Fax +30 1 522 3720). Discount of 25% on bed and breakfast rate at the Hotel Xenia, Portarias (Tel. +30 421 28645, Fax +30 421 3651); can only be booked within five days of arrival; includes bus or taxi transfer from/to Volos station. Discount of 25% on Greek island cruise Aegina-Poros-Hydra (lunch provided).

**YUGOSLAVIA** – Discount of 20% on accommodation at: the Beograd Hotel, 50 Balkanska Street, Belgrade and the Zeleznicar Hotel, 3 Gravila Principa, Vrnjacka Banja.

## IMPORTANT INFORMATION

1. Replacement cards cannot be issued under any circumstances. You are advised to take out insurance to cover you in the event of the loss or theft of your Inter-Rail card.

2. Inter-Rail card holders must pay the usual reservation fees for seats, couchettes and sleeping berths.
3. Supplements are payable on some fast and high-speed trains, e.g. the French TGV and German ICE trains and all high-speed or inter-city services in Spain.

# Appendix II

## BRITISH, IRISH AND CONTINENTAL FERRIES

## 1. English Channel

| From | To | Operator | Type | Time hours | Average frequency |
|------|-----|----------|------|-----------|-------------------|
| Dover | Calais | Hoverspeed | Hovercraft | 35min | 6–14 daily |
| Dover | Calais | Hoverspeed | Seacat | 50min | 6–14 daily |
| Dover | Ostend | Hoverspeed | Seacat | 2 | 5–7 daily |
| Dover | Calais | P&O Stena | Ship | 1¼ | 30-35 daily |
| Dover | Calais | SeaFrance | Ship | 1½ | 15 daily |
| Folkestone | Boulogne | Hoverspeed | Seacat | 55mins | 4 daily |
| Folkestone | Calais | Eurotunnel | Tunnel | 35mins | 3–4 per hour |
| Newhaven | Dieppe | Hoverspeed | Fast Ferry | 2 | 2–3 daily |
| Plymouth | Roscoff | Brittany Ferries | Ship | 6 | 1–3 daily (summer) |
| Plymouth | Santander | Brittany Ferries | Ship | 24 | 2 weekly |
| Poole | Cherbourg | Brittany Ferries | Ship | 4¼ | 1–2 daily |
| Poole | St Malo | Condor Ferries | Catamaran | 5¼ | 1 daily |
| Portsmouth | St Malo | Brittany Ferries | Ship | 8¾ | 1 daily |
| Portsmouth | Caen | Brittany Ferries | Ship | 6 | 2–3 daily |
| Portsmouth | Le Havre | P&O | Ship | 5¾ | 3 daily |
| Portsmouth | Cherbourg | P&O | Ship | 4¾ | 5–7 daily |
| Portsmouth | Bilbao | P&O | Ship | 29–35 | 2 weekly |
| Weymouth | St Malo | Condor Ferries | Catamaran | 29–35 | 1 daily |

## 2. North Sea

| From | To | Operator | Type | Time hours | Average frequency |
|------|-----|----------|------|-----------|-------------------|
| Harwich | Esbjerg | Scandinavian Seaways | Ship | 22 | 3–4 weekly |
| Harwich | Hk of Hol. | Stena HSS | Catamaran | 4 | 2 daily |
| Harwich | Hamburg | Scandinavian Seaways | Ship | 19 | 3–4 weekly |
| Hull | Rotterdam | P&O North Sea Ferries | Ship | 13½ | 1 daily |
| Hull | Zeebrugge | P&O North Sea Ferries | Ship | 14½ | 1 daily |
| Newcastle | Amsterdam | Scandinavian Seaways | Ship | 14 | 3–4 weekly |
| Newcastle | Göteborg | Scandinavian Seaways | Ship | 18–26 | 2 weekly |
| Newcastle | Hamburg | Scandinavian Seaways | Ship | 23 | 2 weekly |

| Newcastle | Göteborg | Scandinavian Seaways | Ship | 18–26 | 2 weekly |
| Newcastle | Strav/Berg | Fiord Line | Ship | 3¾ | 2–3 weekly |

# 3. Ireland

| From | To | Operator | Type | Time hours | Average frequency |
|------|-----|----------|------|------------|-------------------|
| Cairnryan | Larne | P&O | Ship | 2¼ | 3 daily |
| Cairnryan | Larne | P&O | Fast Ferry | 1 | 3-6 daily |
| Fishguard | Rosslare | Stena | Lynx | 1¾ | 2–4 daily |
| Fishguard | Rosslare | Stena | Ship | 3 ½ | 2 daily |
| Holyhead | Dublin | Irish Ferries | Ship | 3½ | 2 daily |
| Holyhead | Dublin | Irish Ferries | Fast Ferry | 2 | 4 daily |
| Holyhead | Dublin | Stena Line | Ship | 3½ | 2 daily |
| Holyhead | Dun Laoighaire | Stena HSS | Catamaran | 1¾ | 4–5 daily |
| Liverpool | Dublin | IOM Stm Pkt | Fast Ferry | 3¾ | 1–2 daily |
| Liverpool | Dublin | Merchant Ferries | | 7–8 | 1–2 daily |
| Pembroke | Rosslare | Irish Ferries | Ship | 4 | 2 daily |
| Rosslare | Roscoff | Irish Ferries | Ship | 21 | 1–3 weekly |
| Rosslare | Cherbourg | Irish Ferries | Ship | 18 | 1–3 weekly |
| Swansea | Cork | S-C Ferries | Ship | 10 | 1 daily |
| Stranraer | Belfast | Seacat | Catamaran | 1½ | 4–5 daily |
| Stranraer | Belfast | Stena | HSS | 1¾ | 4–5 daily |
| Stranraer | Belfast | Stena | Ship | 3¼ | 2–8 daily |

# Appendix III

## EURAIL AID OFFICES

### AUSTRIA
BB. Wien Westbahnhöf, Europaplatz 1, A-1150, Vienna
BB, Salzburg Hauptbahnhöf, Südtiroler Platz 1, A-5020, Salzburg
BB, Innsbruck Hauptbahhöf, Südtiroler Platz 7, A-6020, Innsbruck

### BELGIUM
Société Nationale des Chemins de Fer Belges, Travel Center, Service

International, Gare de Bruxelles-Midi, B-1070 Brussels

**DENMARK**
DSB Travel Office, Central Station, Banegärdspladsen, DK-1570,
  Copenhagen

**FINLAND**
VR Ltd, Passenger Traffic, International Service, Central Station, SF-
  00100, Helsinki

**FRANCE**
Société Nationale des Chemins de Fer Français, Guichets
  Internationaux, Galerie de Fresques (or Bureaux Informations-
  Réservations), Gare de Paris-Lyon, F-75012 Paris
Société Nationale des Chemins de Fer Français, Service International,
  Gare de Paris-St Lazare, F-75008 Paris
Société Nationale des Chemins de Fer Français, Bureaux
  Informations-Reservations, Gare de Paris-Nord, F-75010 Paris
Société Nationale des Chemins de Fer Français, Bureau SNCF d'Orly
  Sud, Orly-Aéroport, F-94543
Société Nationale des Chemins de Fer Français, Bureau SNCF de
  Roissy, Terminal 1, Aéroport Charles de Gaulle, F-95712
Société Nationale des Chemins de Fer Français, Terminal 2, F-95716,
  Roissy Aéroport Charles de Gaulle
Société Nationale des Chemins de Fer Français, Guichets Billets
  Internationaux, Gare de Marseille-St-Charles, F-13232 Marseille
Société Nationale des Chemins de Fer Français, Gare de Nice-Ville,
  F-06000 Nice

**GERMANY**
Deutsche Bahn AG, Fahrkartenausgabe, Hauptbahnhof, D-6000
  Frankfurt am Main
Deutsche Bahn AG, Kurfurstenanlage 75, D-69115 Heidelberg
Deutschec Bahn AG, Bahnhofplatz 2, Schalter 19/20, D-80335 Munich
Deutsche Bahn AG, Trankgasse 11, D-50667 Cologne
Deutsche Bahn AG, Arnulf-Klett-Platz 2, D-70173 Stuttgart
Deutsche Bahn AG, Hachmannplatz 10, D-20099 Hamburg
Deutsche Bahn AG, Zoologischer Garten, Hardenbergplatz 11,
  D-10623 Berlin
Deutsche Bahn AG, Am Hauptbahnhof, D-01008 Dresden
Deutsche Bahn AG, Ernst-August-Platz 1, D-30159 Hannover
Deutsche Bahn AG, Georgiring 14, D-04103 Leipzig

## GREECE

Chemins de Fer Helléniques, Bureau des Voyages et du Tourisme
no. 2, 1 rue Karolou, GR-10437, Athens
Chemins de Fer Helléniques, Bureau des Voyages et du Tourisme
no. 7, 17 rue Filellinon - Place de Syntagma, GR-10557, Athens
Chemins de Fer Helléniques, Gare Centrale des Voyageurs, Thessaloniki
Chemins de Fer Helléniques, Gare Centrale des Voyageurs, Patras

## HUNGARY

Chemins de Fer de l'Etat Hongrois (MAV), Menetjegyiroda
Kundendienstburo, Andrassy Ut 35, H-1061, Budapest V

## IRELAND

CIE, International Rail Ticket Sales Office, 35 Lower Abbey Street,
Dublin 1

## ITALY

Ferrovie Italiane dello Stato, Stazione Santa Maria Novella, Ufficio
Informazioni, Florence
Ferrovie Italiane dello Stato, Stazione Centrale, Milan
Ferrovie Italiane dello Stato, Stazione Santa Lucia, Venice
Ferrovie Italiane dello Stato, Stazione Termini, Rome
Ferrovie Italiane dello Stato, Stazione Centrale, Naples
Ferrovie Italiane dello Stato, Stazione Centrale, Bari
Ferrovie Italiane dello Stato, Stazione Centrale, Palermo

## LUXEMBOURG

Société Nationale des Chemins de Fer Luxembourgeois, Bureau des
Renseignements, Gare de Luxembourg, Luxembourg

## NETHERLANDS

N.S. Nederlandse Spoorwegen, Bureau NSR 3-32-2, Laan van
Puntenburg 100, Utrecht (in the hall of Utrecht central station)
N.S. International Ticket Office, Amsterdam Central Station, Amsterdam
N.S. Ticket Office, Amsterdam Schipol Airport, Amsterdam

## NORWAY

NSB, Billettekspedisjionen, Oslo Sentralstasjon, N-0048 Oslo

## PORTUGAL

Companhia dos Caminhos de Ferro Portugueses, Bilheteira
Internacional, Estação de Santa Apolania, Av. Infante D. Henrique,
P-1100 Lisbon

Companhia dos Caminhos de Ferro Portugueses, Estação de S.
  Bento, Praça Almeida Garret, P-4000 Porto
Companhia dos Caminos de Ferro Portugueses, Estação de Camino
  de Ferro, Largo de Estação , P-8000, Faro

**SPAIN**
RENFE, Officina de Viajes, Alcala 44, Madrid
RENFE, Madrid-Barajas, International Airport, Madrid
RENFE, Estacion Madrid-Charmartin, Madrid
RENFE, Estación Central de Barcelona Sants, Barcelona
RENFE, Avda. Marques de Argentera s/n, Estacion de Barcelona
  Franca, Barcelona
RENFE, Calle Zaragoza 29, Seville
RENFE, Taquillas Largo Recorrido, Station Valencia Nord

**SWEDEN**
Swedish State Railways, Stockholm Central Station, S-105-50,
  Stockholm

**SWITZERLAND**
SBB, Reisebüro, Hauptbahnhof, CH-4051, Basel
SBB, Auskunftsbüro, Hauptbahnhof, CH-3000, Bern
CFFS, Gare de Genève, CH-1201, Geneva
CFFS, Bureau des Renseignements CFF, Geneva Airport, CH-1215,
  Geneva
SBB, Auskunftsbüro, Bahnhof, CH-6002, Lucerne
SBB, Auskunftsbüro, Hauptbahnhof, CH-8021, Zürich
SBB, Auskunftsbüro Zürich Flughafen, CH-8058, Zürich
BLS, Lötschbergbahn, Bahnhof Interlaken West, CH-3800 Interlaken

**UNITED KINGDOM**
Rail Europe Ltd, 179 Piccadilly, London W1V 0BA
Rail Europe Ltd, 10 Leake Street, London SE1 7NN

# Appendix IV

## CIEE OFFICES

## USA

### ARIZONA

130 East University Drive
Suite E
Tempe, AZ 85281
Tel. (602) 966 3544

### CALIFORNIA

2486 Channing Way
Berkeley, CA 94704
Tel. (510) 848 8604

931 Westwood Blvd
Los Angeles, CA 90024
Tel. (310) 208 3551

953 Garnet Avenue
San Diego, CA 92109
Tel. (619) 270 6401

530 Bush Street
Ground Floor
San Fransisco CA 94108
Tel. (415) 421 3473

### COLORADO

900 Auraria Parkway
Tivoli Building, Suite 203
Denver, CO 80204
Tel. (303) 571 0630

### DISTRICT OF COLUMBIA

3301 M Street NW
2nd Floor
Washington, DC 20007
Tel. (202) 337 6464

### FLORIDA

One Datran Center
Suite 220
9100 South Dadeland Blvd
Miami, FL 33156
Tel. (305) 670 9261

### GEORGIA

Emory Village
1561 North Decatur Road
Atlanta, GA 30307
Tel. (404) 377 9997

### ILLINOIS

1160 North State Street
2nd Floor, Chicago IL 60610
Tel. (312) 951 0585

### LOUISIANA

Danna Student Center
6363 St Charles Avenue
New Orleans, LA 70118
Tel. (504) 866 1767

### MASSACHUSETTS

12 Elliot Street
2nd floor
Cambridge/Harvard MA 02138
Tel. (617) 497 1497

84 Massachusetts Ave
Cambridge, MA 02139
Tel. (617) 225 2555

### NORTH CAROLINA

137 E. Franklin Street
Chapel Hill, NC 27514
Tel. (919) 942 2334

## NEW YORK

205 East 42nd Street
New York, NY 10017
Tel. (212) 822 2700
e-mail info@cieee.org;
http://www.ciee.org

895 Amsterdam Avenue
New York, NY 10025
Tel. (212) 666 4177

## PENNSYLVANIA

3606a Chestnut Street
Philadelphia, PA 19104
Tel. (215) 382 0343

118 Meyran Avenue
Pittsburgh, PA 15213
Tel. (412) 683 1881

## RHODE ISLAND

220 Thayer Street
Providence, RI 02906
Tel. (401) 331 5810

## TEXAS

6715 Hillcrest
Dallas, TX 75205
Tel. (214) 363 9941

## UTAH

1310 East 200 South
Salt Lake City, UT 84102
Tel. (801) 582 5840

## WASHINGTON

1314 N.E. 43rd Street
Suite 210
Seattle WA 98105
Tel. (202) 632 2448

# EUROPE

## AUSTRIA

Schreyvogelgasse 3
A-1010 Vienna
Tel. (43) 1 533 3589 0

## DENMARK

Frederiksholms Kanal 2
Copenhagen 1220
Tel. (45) 33 15 0077

## FINLAND

Kaivokatu 10D,
00100 10 Helsinki
Tel. (385) 0 651 528

## FRANCE

12 rue Victor Leydet
Aix-en-Provence, 13100
Tel. (33) 4 42 38 58 82

1 Place de l'Odeon
Paris, 75006
Tel. (33) 1 44 41 89 89

35 rue Victor Hugo
Lyon, 69002
Tel. (33) 4 78 38 78 38

## GERMANY

Hagenauerstrasse 1
Berlin, 10435
Tel. (49) 30 443 9392

64 Graf Adolf Strasse
Düsseldorf D-40212
Tel. (49) 211 363 030

Adalbertstrasse 32
Munich, D-80799
Tel. (49) 89 395 022

## IRELAND

19-21 Aston Quay
Dublin 2
Tel. (353) 1 6021600

## GREECE

30 Nikis Street
105-57 Athens
Tel. (30) 1  322 0503

## ITALY

Via Locatelli 5
Milan 20124
Tel. (39) 2 6671 3119

Via Mezzocannone 87/119
Naples 80134
Tel. (39) 81 552 0947

Piazza dell'Esquilino 10/Z
Rome 00185
Tel. (39) 6 487 0870

## NETHERLANDS

Rokin 24
1012KS Amsterdam
Tel. (31) 20 626 6876

## NORWAY

Dronningensgate 26
Oslo N-0154
Tel. (47) 2 242 1410

## POLAND

Ul. Kopernika 15
Warsaw 00359
Tel. (48) 22 262 356

## PORTUGAL

Rua General Farinha Beimo 2/4
1150 Lisboa
Tel. (351) 1 353 83 08

## RUSSIA

10th Floor
50 Bolshaya Pereyaslavskaya
Moscow 129041
Tel. (7) 095 931 5952

## SPAIN

Placa CIVICA 6 BIS
Villaterra 08193 Cerdanola
Barcelona
Tel. (349) 3586 4034

## SWEDEN

Burgrevegatan 1
G(teberg, Box 144
401 22
Tel. (46) 31 80 54 00

## SWITZERLAND

Universitaetstrasse 33
Zurich CH-8006
Tel. (41) 1 251 6000

## TURKEY

Halarskargazi Cad. 111/2
Istanbul 34400
Tel. (90) 212 247 8174

## UK

28a Poland Street
London W1V 3DB
Tel. 020 7437 7767/020 7287
3337

# Appendix V

## TOURIST OFFICES

On the following pages are Tourist Offices listings for countries covered in *Europe by Train*. Where we have been unable to locate functioning offices the address of the country's embassy has been included instead. These include: Belarus, Bosnia-Hercegovina, Estonia, Latvia, Lithuania, Macedonia, the Ukraine and the new Yugoslavia

Note, that 0891 numbers are charged at premium rate, which is generally 50p per minute.

**UK OFFICES**
ANDORRA, 63 Westover Road, London SW18 (020 8874 4806 am only)
AUSTRIA, 14 Cork Street, London W1X 1PF (020 7629 0461)
BELARUS, 6 Kensington Court, London W8 5DL (020 7937 3288)
BELGIUM, 29 Princes Street, London W1 (020 7867 0311 or
   0891 887799)
BOSNIA-HERCEGOVINA, Embassy, 320 Regent Street, London W1R 5AB
   (020 7255 3758)
BULGARIA, 186-188 Queens Gate, London SW7 5HL (020 7584 9400)
   or Balkan Holidays, Sofia House, 19 Conduit Street, London W1R 9TD
   (020 7543 5566)
CROATIA, 162-164 Fulham Palace Rd, London W6 9ER (020 8563 7979)
CZECH REPUBLIC, 95 Great Portland Street, London W1N 5RA
   (020 7291 9920 or 0891 171266)
DENMARK, 55 Sloane Street, London SW1X 9SR (020 7259 5959)
ESTONIA, 16 Hyde Park Gate, London SW7 5DG (020 7589 3428)
FINLAND, 3rd floor, 30–35 Pall Mall, London SW1 Y5LP
   (020 7839 4048)
FRANCE, 178 Piccadilly, London W1 (0891 244123)
GERMANY, GNTO, PO Box 2695, London W1A 3TN (020 7317 0908)
GREECE, 4 Conduit Street, London W1 (020 7734 5997)
HUNGARY, c/o Commercial Section, Hungarian Embassy, 46 Eaton
   Place, London SW1 X8AL (020 7823 1032)
IRELAND, 150 New Bond Street, London W1 (020 7493 3201)
ITALY, 1 Princes Street, London W1 (020 7408 1254)
LATVIA, Embassy, 45 Nottingham Place, London W1M 3FE
   (020 7312 0040)
LITHUANIA, 84 Gloucester Place, London W1H 3HN (020 7486 6402)
LUXEMBOURG, 122 Regent St, London W1R 5TE (020 7434 2800)
MACEDONIA, Embassy, 10 Harcourt House, 19A Cavendish Sq.,
   London W1M 9AD (020 7499 5152)

MALTA, 207 College House, Wrights Lane, London W1V 0PP
(020 7292 4900)
MONACO, 50 Upper Brook Street, London W1 (020 7352 9962)
MOROCCO, 205 Regent Street,. London W1 (020 7437 0073)
THE NETHERLANDS, 18 Buckingham Gate, London SW1
(0906 8717777)
NORWAY, Charles House, 5th Floor, 5 Lower Regent Street,
London SW1Y 4LR (020 7839 6255)
POLAND, 1st floor, 310–312 Regent St, London W1 (020 7580 8811),
or Polorbis Travel, 82 Mortimer St, London W1 (020 7637 4971)
PORTUGAL, 22/25a Sackville Street, London W1 (020 7494 1441)
ROMANIA, 83a Marylebone High St, London W1M 3DE
(020 7224 3692)
RUSSIA, Embassy, Kennedy House, 115 Hammersmith Road, London
W14 0QH (020 7603 1000); e-mail info@intourus.demm.co.uk
SLOVAKIA, 16 Frognal Parade, Finchley Road, London NW3 5HG
(020 7794 3263/4)
SLOVENIA, 49 Conduit Street, London W1R 9FB (020 7287 5476)
SPAIN, 22–23 Manchester Square, London W1M 5AP (020 7486 8077)
SWEDEN, 11 Montague Place, London W1H 2AL (020 7870 5600)
SWITZERLAND, Swiss Centre, Swiss Court, London W1V 5EE (020 7437
4577)
TURKEY, 170–173 Piccadilly, London W1 (020 7355 4207 or
020 7629 7771)
UKRAINE, Embassy, Consular Department, 78 Kensington Park Road,
London W11 2PL (Tel. 020 7243 8923)
YUGOSLAVIA, Embassy, 5 Lexham Gardens, London W8 5JJ
(020 7370 6105)

## US OFFICES
AUSTRIA, PO Box 1142, 500 Fifth Ave., 20th Floor, NY, NY 10108-1142
(212 9446880); 11601 Wilshire Blvd., LA, CA 90025 (913 477 3332)
BELARUS, Embassy, 1619 New Hampshire Ave., NW, Washington D.C.
20009 (202 986 1606)
BELGIUM, 780 Third Ave., Suite 1501, NY, NY 10017-7076
(212 758 8130)
BOSNIA-HERCEGOVINA, Embassy, 1707 L. St. NW, Washington 20036
(202 833 3612)
BULGARIA, c/o Balkan Holidays, 411 East 42nd Street. NY, NY 10017
(212 822 5900)
DENMARK, PO Box 4649, Grand Central Station, NY, NY 10163-4649
(212 885 9700)
ESTONIA, Embassy, 2131 Massachusetts Ave. NW, Washington D.C.
20008 (202 588 0101)

FINLAND, see Denmark.

FRANCE, 444 Madison Ave., 16th floor, NY, NY 10022 (212 838 7855);
645 North Michigan Ave., Chicago, IL 60611 (312 337 6301);
9401 Wilshire Blvd., Beverly Hills, CA 90212 (213 271 6665)

GERMANY, 122 E42nd St., 52nd Floor, NY, NY 10168-0072 (212 661
7200); 444 Flower Street, Suite 2230, LA, CA 90017 (213 688 7332)

GREECE, Olympic Tower, 645 Fifth Ave., NY, NY 10022 (212 421 5777);
168 North Michigan Avenue, Chicago, IL 60611 (312 782 084);
611 West Sixth Street, Suite 2198, LA, CA 90017 (213 626 6696)

HUNGARY, 1 Parker Plaza, 1104 Fort Lee, NJ 07024 (201 592 8585) or
150 E 58th St, 33rd fl, New York, NY 10155 (212 355 0240)

IRELAND, 345 Park Ave., NY, NY 10154 (800 223 6470)

ITALY, 630 Fifth Avenue, Suite 1565, NY, NY 10111 (212 245 4822);
500 North Michigan Avenue, Suite 1046, Chicago, IL 60611
(312 644 0990); 360 Post Street, Suite 801, San Francisco, CA 94108
(415 392 5266)

LATVIA, Embassy, 4325 17th St. NW, Washington D.C. 20011
(202 726 8213)

LITHUANIA, Embassy, 2622 16th St. NW, Washington D.C. 20009
(202 234 5860)

LUXEMBOURG, 17 Beekman Place, NY, NY 10022 (212 935 8888)

MACEDONIA, Embassy, 3050 K St. NW, 210, Washington D.C. 20007
(202 337 3063)

MOROCCO, 20 East 46th Street, NY, NY 10017 (212 557 2520)

NETHERLANDS, 355 Lexington Avenue, 21st Floor, NY, NY 10020
(212 370 7367); 225 North Michigan Avenue, Suite 326, Chicago,
IL 60601 (312 819 0300); 9 New Montgomery Street, Suite 305,
San Francisco, CA 94105 (415 543 6772)

NORWAY, see Denmark.

POLAND, 275 Madison Avenue, Suite 1711, NY, NY 10016
(212 338 9412);
333 North Michigan Avenue, Suite 228, Chicago, IL 60601
(312 236 9031)

PORTUGAL, 590 Fifth Avenue, NY, NY 10036-4704 (212 354 4403)

ROMANIA, 342 Madison Avenue, Suite 210, NY, NY 10173
(212 697 6971)

RUSSIA, 8 Third Avenue, Suite 3101, New York, NY 10002
(212 758 1162)

SLOVENIA, 345E, 12th Street, NY, NY 10003-0072 (212 358 9024)

SPAIN, 666 Fifth Avenue, NY, NY 10022 (212 265 8822);
845 North Michigan Avenue, Chicago, IL 60611 (312 944 215);
1 Hallidie Plaza, San Francisco, CA 94102 (415 346 8100)

SWEDEN, see Denmark.

SWITZERLAND, 608 Fifth Avenue, NY, NY 10020 (212 757 5944);

250 Stockton Street, San Francisco, CA 94108 (415 362 2260)
TURKEY, 821 United Nations Plaza, NY, NY 10017 (212 687 2194)
UKRAINE, Embassy, 3350 M St. NW, Washington D.C. 20007
(202 333 0606)
UNITED KINGDOM, 551 Fifth Ave., Suite 701, NY, NY 10176
(800 462 2748 or 212 986 2200); John Hancock Center, Suite 3320,
875 North Michigan Avenue, Chichago, IL 60611 (312 787 0490);
Plaza of the Americas, North Tower, Suite 750, Dallas, TX 75201
(312 623 8196); 612 South Flower Street, LA, CA 90017
(213 623 8196)
YUGOSLAVIA, Embassy, 2410 California St. NW, Washington D.C.
20008 (202 462 6566)

**AUSTRALIA OFFICES**
AUSTRIA, 36 Carringtlon Street, 1st Floor, Sydney, NSW 2000
(02 299 3621)
DENMARK, 60 Market Square, Melbourne, Victoria 3001 (03 62 33 63)
FINLAND, see Denmark.
FRANCE, 25 Bligh St., Sydney, NSW 2000 (02 9231 5244)
GERMANY, c/o Lufthansa House, 143 Macquarie Street, Sydney,
NSW 2000 (02 9267 8148)
GREECE, 51 Pitt Street, Sydney, NSW 2000 (02 9241 1663)
IRELAND, 5th Level, 36 Carrington St., Sydney, NSW 2000
(02 299 6177)
MOROCCO, c/o Moroccan Consulate, 11 West Street North, Sydney,
NSW 2000 (02 957 6717)
THE NETHERLANDS, 5 Elizabeth Street, 6th Floor, Sydney, NSW 2060
(02 9922 4999)
NORWAY, see Denmark.
SPAIN, 203 Castlereagh Street, Suite 21a, Sydney, NSW 2000
(02 9264 7966)
SWEDEN, see Denmark.
SWITZERLAND, 203233 New South Head Road, Edgecliffe, Sydney,
NSW 2027 (02 326 1799)
UNITED KINGDOM, 210 Clarence Street, 4th Floor, Sydney, NSW 2000
(02 9267 4555)

If any of the above offices have moved, or if you discover a new one
that isn't listed, please help your fellow eurorailers and send us a
postcard with the appropriate details to the address on page 4.

# Appendix VI

## INTERNATIONAL COUNTRY CODES

The following is a list of the telephone country codes for the different countries covered in this book:

**EUROPE:**

| Country | Code | Country | Code |
| --- | --- | --- | --- |
| Austria | 43 | Macedonia | 389 |
| Belarus | 7 | Morocco | 212 |
| Belgium | 32 | Netherlands | 31 |
| Bosnia | 387 | Norway | 47 |
| Bulgaria | 359 | Poland | 48 |
| Croatia | 385 | Portugal | 351 |
| Czech Republic | 420 | Romania | 40 |
| Denmark | 45 | Slovakia | 421 |
| Estonia | 372 | Slovenia | 386 |
| Finland | 358 | Spain | 349 |
| France | 33 | Sweden | 46 |
| Germany | 49 | Switzerland | 41 |
| Greece | 30 | Turkey | 90 |
| Hungary | 36 | UK | 44 |
| Ireland | 353 | Ukraine | 380 |
| Italy | 39 (+'0' of town code) | Yugoslavia | 381 |
| Latvia | 371 | Russia | 7 |
| Liechtenstein | 41 75 | | |
| Lithuania | 370 | | |
| Luxembourg | 352 | | |

**OUTSIDE EUROPE:**

| Country | Code | Country | Code |
| --- | --- | --- | --- |
| Australia | 61 | New Zealand | 64 |
| Canada | 1 | USA | 1 |

## PLACING AN INTERNATIONAL CALL

When you want to call another country, you must first dial the international access code for the country you're in. These access codes are listed at the start of each country in the information section. Once you have dialled the access code, then dial the country code for the country you want to call and the phone number. For example:

to call France from the UK; dial 00+33+number.

# Appendix VII

## COMMON CONVERSIONS

### LENGTH

1 inch = 2.54 centimetres
1 foot = 0.305 metre
1 mile = 1.609 kilometre

1 centimetre = 0.39 inch
1 metre = 3.281 feet
1 kilometre = 0.621 mile

### VOLUME

1 cubic foot = 0.028 cubic metre
1 gallon (UK) = 4.546 litres
1 gallon (US) =3.785 litres

1 cubic metre = 35.315 cubic feet
1 litre = 0.22 gallon (UK)
1 litre = 0.264 gallon (US)

### WEIGHT

1 pound = 0.454 kilogram
1 ounce = 28.35 grammes

1 kilogram = 2.205 pounds
1 gram = 0.036 ounce

### SPEED

1 mph = 1.609 kilometre/hour

1 kilometre/hour = 0.621 mph

### TEMPERATURE

Zero°C =32°F
25°C = 77°F
50°C = 122°F
75°C=167°F
100°C =212°F

### DATES

UK/European format: dd/mm/yy
American format: mm/dd/yy

dd=day mm=month yy =year

### TIMES

In the 24-hour clock times after noon are as follows;
1 p.m. = 13.00; 2 p.m. = 14.00; 3 p.m. = 15.00; etc., until midnight, which is
00.00.

# Appendix VIII

## BASIC VOCABULARY

Although it is sometimes possible to get by in English, especially in Germany, Scandinavia and the Low Countries, often it's not. German can often be used in Eastern Europe. We've kept it pretty simple, as theres no point getting too involved in a language you don't know the basics of. If you want a bit more you'll find any number of cheap pocket-sized phrasebooks in most bookshops.

| ENGLISH | CZECH | DANISH | DUTCH |
|---|---|---|---|
| Yes | Ano | Ja | Ja |
| No | Ne | Nej | Nee |
| Please | Prosim | Vaer sa venlig | Alsatublieft |
| Thank you | Děkuji | Tak | Dank u |
| Good morning | Dobry den | Godmorgen | Goedemorgen |
| Goodbye | Na shledanou | Farvel | Tot ziens |
| Where is/are...? | Kde je/jsou...? | Hvor er...? | Waar is/zijn...? |
| Excuse me | Prominte | Undskyld | Pardon |
| How much? | Kolik to stojf? | Hvor meget? | Hoeveel? |
| Can I have...? | Chtela bych... | Kan jeg fa... | Hag ik ... hebben |
| I don't understand | Nerozumim | Jeg forstaar ikke | Ik begrijp het niet |
| Do you speak English? | Mluvite anglicky? | Taler De engelsk? | Spreekt u Engels? |
| My name is... | Jmenjui se... | Mit navn er... | Mijt naam is... |

| ENGLISH | FINNISH | FRENCH | GERMAN |
|---|---|---|---|
| Yes | Kyllä | Oui | Ja |
| No | Ei | Non | Nein |
| Please | Olkaa hyvä | S'il vous plaît | Bitte |
| Thank you | Kiitos | Merci | Danke |
| Good morning | Hyvää huomenta | Bonjour | Guten Morgen |
| Goodbye | Nakemiin | Au revoir | Auf Wiedersehen |
| Where is/are...? | Missa on/ovat...? | Ou se trouve/ trouvent...? | Wo ist/sind...? |
| Excuse me | Anteeksi | Excusez-moi | Entschuldigen Sie! |
| How much? | Kuinka paljon? | Combien? | Wieviel? |
| Can I have...? | Voinko saada... | Je voudrais... | Kann ich ...haben? |
| I don't understand | En ymmärrä | Je ne comprends pas | Ich verstehe nicht |
| Do you speak English? | Puhutteko englantia? | Parlez-vous anglais? | Sprechen Sie Englisch? |
| My name is... | Nimeni on... | Je m'appelle... | Ich heisse... |

| ENGLISH | HUNGARIAN | ITALIAN | NORWEGIAN |
|---|---|---|---|
| Yes | Igen | Sì | Ja |
| No | Nem | No | Nei |
| Please | Kerem | Per favore | Var så god |
| Thank you | Köszönöm | Grazie | Takk |
| Good morning | Jo reggelt | Buongiorno | God morgen |
| Goodbye | Viszontlatasra | Ciao | Ha det godt |
| Where is/are...? | Hol van/ vannak...? | Dov'è/Dove sono...? | Hvor er...? |
| Excuse me | Elnezest | Mi scusi | Unnskyld |
| How much? | Mennyi/Mennyit? | Quanto? | Hvor mye? |
| Can I have...? | Kaphatok... | Posso avere... | Kan jeg fa... |
| I don't understand | Nem ertem | Non capisco | Jeg forstar ikke |
| Do you speak English? | Beszel angolul? | Parla inglese? | Snakker Du engelsk? |
| My name is... | Nevem vagyok... | Mi chiamo... | Mitt navn er... |

| ENGLISH | PORTUGUESE | SERBO-CROAT | SPANISH |
|---|---|---|---|
| Yes | Sim | Da | Sí |
| No | Não | Ne | No |
| Please | Faz favor | Molim | Por favor |
| Thank you | Obrigado | Hvala | Gracias |
| Good morning | Bom dia | Dobro jutro | Buenos días |
| Goodbye | Adeus | Zbogom | Adiós |
| Where is/are...? | Onde esta/ estão...? | Gde je/su...? | Donde esta/estan...? |
| Excuse me | Desculpe | Izvinite | Pardones |
| How much? | Quanto? | Koliko? | Cuanto? |
| Can I have...? | Pode dar-me... | Mogu li dobiti... | Puede darme... |
| I don't understand | Não compreendo | Ne razumen | No comprendo |
| Do you speak English? | Fala ingles | Govorite li engleski? | Habla usted inglés? |
| My name is... | O meu nome e... | Ja se Zovem... | Me llamo... |

| ENGLISH | SWEDISH | TURKISH |
|---|---|---|
| Yes | Ja | Evet |
| No | Nej | Hayir |
| Please | Varsagod | Lütfen |
| Thank you | Tack | Teşekkür ederim |
| Good morning | God morgon | Gunaydin |
| Goodbye | Adjo | Gule gule/Allaha ismarladik |
| Where is/are...? | Var ar...? | Nerede/Neredeler...? |
| Excuse me | Forlat | Affedersiniz |
| How much? | Hyr mycket? | Ne kadar? |
| Can I have...? | Kan jag fa... | ...rica edebilir miyim |
| I don't understand | Jag forstar inte | Anlamiyorum |
| Do you speak English? | Talar Ni engelska? | Ingilzce Biliyor musunuz? |
| My name is... | Mitt namn ar... | Adim... dir |

# Index

## A

Aalborg 189
Åbo see Turku
accommodation
  camping 75-76
  Cheap Sleeps Europe 11
  hostels 72-75
  hotels 71-2
  private 76
  YMCA Interpoints 74-75
  youth hostels 72-75
  see also camping
Agadir 514
Agrigento 459
air travel to Europe 39-42
Aix-en-Provence 255
Aix-les-Bains 235
Alassio 417
Albenga 417
Algaia Eleni 321
Algarve 590-92
Algeciras 657-76
Alghero 433
Alkmaar 522
Alonissos 336
Alps:
  French 242-3
  German 310
Alsace and Lorraine 241-2
Alta 554
Amalfi 456-7
American travellers:
  insurance 56
  passports and visas 43
Amsterdam 522-29
Anatolia, Central 742-43

Andalusia (Andalucía) 673-78
Andiparos 334
Andipaxi 344-45
Andorra 663-64
  see also Spain
Andros 334
Ankara 743-44
Antwerp (Anvers) 131-33
APEX flights 40-41
Arad 607-8
Aran Islands 390-91
Aranjuez 659
Ardennes 130-31
Århus 188-89
Arles 254
Arnhem 534
Arvidsjaur 699
Asni 514
Assisi 441-42
Athens 324-30
Athos, Mount 321
Augsburg 308-09
Auschwitz see Oswięcim
Australian travellers: passports and visas 43
Austria 89-112
  Bregenz 92, 108
  Burgenland 102
  Central 103
  Danube river trips 92
  Feldkirch 108
  Gmunden 103
  Graz 102
  Hallstatt 103
  Innsbruck 109-112
  Kärnten (Carinthia) 102
  Mariazell 92

rail pass 30, 90
  railways (öBB) 90-91
  Salzburg 104-08
  Southern 102
  Steiermark 102
  Vienna (Wien) 94-102
  Western 108
Avignon 253-54
Ávila 670
Ayios Nikolaos 342

## B

backpacks 46-47
Baden-Württemberg 289
Bagenalstown 378
Balaton, Lake 359-60
Balatonföldvár 359
Balatonfüred 359
Ballinavough 382
Baltic States rail pass 30, 466, 474
banks 55-56
Bantry 385
Bar 808
Baradla Caves 359
Barcelona 664-69
Bari 457-58
Bascharage 489
Basel (Basle) 718-19
Bath 776-77
Bayeux 226
Belarus 611-12, 627
  Brest 627
  Minsk 627
  see also Russia
Belfast 800-801
Belgium 115-34
  Antwerp (Anvers) 131-33

Ardennes 130-33
Bruges (Brugge) 120-23
Brussels (Bruxelles) 124-30
Ghent (Gent; Gand) 133-34
Namur 130-31
Ostend (Oostende) 120
railways (NMBS; SNCF) 116-18
Southern 130-31
Tourrail cards 30, 117
Benelux Tourrail cards 30, 117, 482
Bergama Pergamon 742
Bergamo 408
Berlin 268-77
Berne (Bern) 713-15
Bernese Oberland 715-16
bicycles see cycling
Bierges 121
BIJ (Billet International pour Jeunes) scheme 20-21, 29
Biot 247
Birkenau 568
Bitola 496
Black Forest 289-90
black market 55
Black Sea coast:
  Bulgaria 150-51
  Romania 606
'Blauer Enzian' train 33
Bled, Lake 644-45
Blois 228
Bodø 552-53
Bodrum Halicarnassus 742
Bohinj, Lake 645-46
Bologna 414-16
Bolzano (Bolzen) 406

Bordeaux 256-57
Bordighera 416
Bosnia-Hercegovina 137-39
  Medujorde 138-39
  Mostar 138
  Sarajevo 137-38
Bourgas 150-51
Brašov 603-04
Bratislava 632-34
Brecon Beacons 785
Breda 534
Bregenz 92, 108
Bremen 284-85
Breslau see Wrocław
Brest (Belarus) 627
Brighton 775
Brijuni 153
Brindisi 458
Britrail passes 30-31
Brittany 227-28
Brno 165
Bruges (Brugge) 120-23
Brunico 406
Brussels (Bruxelles) 124-30
Bucharest (Bucureşti) 599-603
Budapest 351-56
budgeting 50-51
Bulgaria 141-51
  Black Sea Coast 150-51
  Bourgas 150-51
  Plovdiv 149-50
  railways (BDZ) 142-43
  Sofia 145-49
  Varna 150-51
  Veliako Tarnovo 150
Burgenland 102
Burgos 672
Burgundy 243-45
Bursa 740
Buxton 788

## C

Cabines 58
Cádiz 678
Caernarfon 786
Cagliari 461, 462
Cahir 380
Calais 223
Cambridge 782-84
Campania 452
camping 75-76
  gear 48-49
Canadian travellers:
  insurance 56
  passports and visas 43
Çanakkale 741
'Canaletto' train 33
Cannes 247
Canterbury 774
Cape Sounion 329-30
Capri 456
Carcassonne 255
Cardiff 784
Carlow, Town 378
Carrick-on-Suir 380
Carte Zoom – Corsican Railways 31
Casablanca (Dar Beida) 507-08
Caserta 456
Cashel 380
'Catalan Talgo' train 33
Catania 459
Cerbère 258
České Budéjovice 165-66
Chamonix 242-43
Channel Tunnel 37-38
Chantilly 241
Charles Fort 365
charter flights 41
Chartres 241
Cheap Sleeps Europe 11
chemists 45
Chichester 774

children travelling with 82
Chios (Hios) 338
Chur 722
CIEE see Council on International Educational Exchange
'Cisalpin' train 33
city transport 78
Clermont-Ferrand 255-56
Clervaux 488
Clonmel 380
clothing 48, 49
women alone 81
Cobh 589
Coimbra 589
Cologne (Köln) 295-98
Como 407-08
Concarneau 228
Connemara 392
Constanţa 606
conversions 830
Conwy 786
Copenhagen (København) 180-87
Córdoba 674-75
Corfu 342-44
Corinth 322
Cork 382-84
Cornwall 779
Corsica 31, 248
Costa del Sol 678-80
Costa Prata 589-90
couchettes 58
Council on International Educational Exchange (CIEE) 52-53 offices 822-24
country passes 29-33
Cracow (Kraków) 566-69
credit cards 53-54
Crete 340-42

Crimea, The 754-56
Croatia 153-59
Dalmatian Coast 158
Dubrovnik 158-59
Istrian Peninsula 159
Pula 159
railways (HZ) 154-55
Split 158
Zagreb 156-58
Cuenca 672-73
cybercafés 79-80
Cyclades, The 332-35
cycling 65-66, 178, 519, 705
Cyprus, northern 742
Cyrillic alphabet 143
Czech Explorere Passes 31, 162
Czech Republic 161-73
Brno 165
České Budějovice 165-66
Olomouc 172-73
Pilsen (Plzeň) 166
Prague (Praha) 1 66-72
railways (ČSD) 162-63
Czêstochowa 568-69

**C**

Dalmatian Coast 158
Danube 356-57
river trips 92
Dar Beida see Casablanca
daypacks 47
Delphi 330
Denmark 175-89
Aalborg 189
Århus 188-89
Copenhagen (København) 180-87
Legoland 189

Odense 187-88
railways (DSB) 176-78
Deutsche Bahn 24
Devon 778-79
Diekirch 488
Dijon 244-45
Dingle 386
Dinkelsbühl 310
disabled travellers 83-85
discount cards 51-52
Disneyland, Paris 39, 240
doctors 44
Dodecanese, The 338-40
Donegal, County 393-94
Donostia see San Sebastián
Dover 774
Dresden 278-80
Drottningholm Palace 693
Dublin 370-77
Dubrovnik 158-59
Dungarvan 381

**E**

Eastern Europe:
accommodation 76
money exchange 55
trains 64-65
Echternach 487-88
Edinburgh 791-96
Eger 358-59
Emilia Romagna 413-14
England Channel crossings 36-37
Enniscorthy 377
Enniskillen 802
Ephesus 741-42
Epidavros 323

Erfurt 283-84
Esch-sur-Alzette 489
Essaouira 514
Esterházy Palace Ferto
    Castle 361
Estonia (Eesti) 191-96
    railways 192
    Tallinn 194-96
Estoril 587
Esztergom 357
Eurail:
    aid offices 818-21
    passes 19-20, 27-29,
    400-01
Euro currency 53
Euro Domino passes 23-
    24, 263
Eurocheques 54-55
Europass 28-29
European East Passes 31
European Rail Ltd 24
Eurostar 17-18, 37-39,
    116, 262-63
Eurotrain 21-22
Evora 590
exchange rate 8
Exeter 778
Explorail Passes –
    Spanish Railways
    31-32
Eyina (Aegina) 331-32

F

Fağaŕas Mountains 604
Faro 591-92
Feldkirch 108
Ferien Tickets – German
    Rail 32
Fermanagh 801
Ferrara 413
Ferries 817-18
    English Channel 36-
    37, 817
    Scanrail passes 33,

176-77, 201
Ferrycarrig 378
Fez (Fes) 512-13
Finland (Suomi)
    199-213
    Helsinki 204-09
    Imatra 213
    Northern 212
    Oulu 212
    railways (VR) 200-02
    Rovaniemi 212
    Savonlinna 213
    Tampere 211-12
    Turku (Åbo) 209-11
Finnrail Passes 32, 201
Fira 335-36
Florence (Firenze)
    431-37
flying to Europe 39-42
Fontainebleau 240
food 76-77
    on trains 60-61
    safety precautions 45
    vegetarian 77
Fort William 799
France 215-58
    Aix-en-Provence 255
    Alps 242-43
    Alsace and Lorraine
    241-42
    Arles 254
    Avignon 253-54
    Bayeux 226
    Blois 228
    Bordeaux 256-57
    Brittany 227-28
    Burgundy 243-45
    Calais 223
    Carte 12-25 passes 31,
    217
    Central/South-West
    255-58
    Cerbère 258
    Corsica 248
    Corsican rail pass 31

Dijon 244-45
Lille 223-24
Loire Valley 228-29
Lyon 245-46
Marseille 251-52
Monaco 248
Mont St-Michel
    226-27
Nice 247, 249-51
Nîmes 254
Paris 229-41
Provence 253-55
railways (SNCF)
    216-20
Rennes 227-28
The Riviera (Côte
    d'Azur) 247-51
Rouen 241-42
Strasbourg 241-42
tourist information
    220
Tours 228-300
Frankfurt-am-Main 298-
    300
'Franz Hals' train 33
Freedom rail 33
Freiburg-im-Breisgau
    291-92
Fribourg 715
Friesland 521-22
Fuengirola 680

G

Gallipoli (Gelibolu) 741
Gällivare 698
Galway 387-92
Gand see Ghent
gay and lesbian
    travellers 83
Gdańsk 569-71
Geneva (Genève)
    719-22
Genoa (Genova) 416,
    417-19

Germany 261-311
  Alps 310
  Augsburg 308-09
  Baden-Württemberg
    289
  Berlin 268-90
  Black Forest
    289-90
  Central 289-94
  Cologne (Köln)
    295-98
  Deutsche Bahn 24,
    262
  Dresden 278-80
  Erfurt 283-84
  Ferien Tickets 32, 263-
    64
  Frankfurt-am-Main
    298-300
  Freiburg-im-Breisgau
    291-92
  Hamburg 285-87
  Hannover 288-89
  Harz Mountains 289,
    294-95
  Heidelberg 290-91
  Leipzig 280-82
  Lübeck city 287-88
  Munich (München)
    301-08
  Northern 284-89
  Potsdam 277
  railways (DB) 262-66
  Rhine Valley 295-98
  Romantic Road
    (Romantische Strasse)
    301
  Stuttgart 293-94
  tourist information
    266-67
  Trier 300-01
  Tübingen 292
  Weimar 282-83
Ghent (Gent; Gand)
  133-34

Giant's Causeway 801
Gibraltar 680-81
  see also Spain
Glasgow 796-98
Glencolumbkille 394
Glendalough 377
Glengariff 385
Gmunden 103
Goslar 295
Gothenburg
  (Göteborg) 695-97
Gotland 694-95
Gouda 534
Graignamanagh 379
Granada 673-74
Graz 102
Greece 313-45
  Athens 324-30
  Corfu 342-44
  Crete 340-42
  Cyclades 332-35
  Dodecanese 338-40
  Ionian Islands 342
  islands 330-45
  North-East Aegean
    337-38
  Northern 319-21
  The Peloponnese
    321-24
  railways (OSE) 315-17
  Santorini 335-36
  Saronic Gulf Islands
    331-32
  Sporades 336-37
  Thessaloniki 318-21
  tourist information
    317
Grindelwald 716
Grisons (Graubünden)
  722-23
Györ 360

**H**

Haarlem 534-35

Hague, The (Den
  Haag) 530-32
Hallstatt 103
Hamburg 285-87
'Hamlet' train 34
Hania (Khania) 341
Hannover 288-89
Harz Mountains 289,
  294-95
hazards 64
health 44-45
  disabled travellers
    83-85
Heidelberg 290-91
Helsinki 204-09
Heraklion (Iraklion) 341
Herculaneum 456
Hoorn 522
hostels 72-75
hotels 71-72
Humor 605
Hungary 347-63
  Budapest 351-56
  Danube 356-57
  Eger 358-59
  Hungarian Plain
    357-58
  Lake Balaton 359-60
  Pécs 344-45
  National Parks 358-
    59, 362
  Pécs 362-63
  railways (MÁV) 348
  South-West 361-62
  tourist information
    349-50
  Western 360-61
Hydra (Idra) 332

**I**

Imatra 213
Innsbruck 109-12
insurance 56
Interlaken 715-16

International Camping
  Carnet 75
International Student
  Identity Cards (ISIC)
  51-52
International Timetable
  Symbols 63
Internet:
  cybercafés 79-80
  information 36
Inter-Rail/Eurail passes
  19-20, 24-27, 482-
  83
  discounts 810-16
Inverness 798
Iona 722
Ionian Islands 342
Ios 333
Iraklion see Heraklion
Ireland 365-94
  Connemara 392
  Cork 382-84
  Dublin 370-77
  Galway 387-92
  Limerick 386-87
  North-West 392-94
  passes 32, 367
  passports and visas 43
  railways (IE) 367-68
  South-East 377-82
  South-West 384-86
  tourist information
  368-70
Ischia 456
Istanbul 735-40
Istrian Peninsula 159
Italy 397-462
  Alto-Adige 406-07
  Bologna 414-16
  Emilia-Romagna
  413-14
  Florence (Firenze)
  413-37
  Genoa (Genova) 416,
  417-19

Liguria 416-17
Lombardy 407-08
Milan (Milano)
  408-12
Naples (Napoli)
  452-57
Northern 405-16
Padua (Padova)
  428-29
Piedmont (Piemonte)
  405
Pisa 439-40
Puglia 457-58
rail cards 32, 399-400
railways (FS) 398-402
Rome (Roma) 442-51
San Marino 430-31
Sardinia (Sardegna)
  460-62
Sicily 458-60
Siena 437-39
Southern 452-58
tourist information
  402
Turin (Torino) 405-06
Tuscany 431-40
Umbria 440-42
Veneto 419
Venice 419-26
Verona 426-28
Ithaca 345

J

Jerez de la Frontera
  678
Jokkmokk 699

K

Kalamata 321-22
Kärnten (Carinthia) 102
Kavala 320
Kea 335
Kecskemét 357
Kefalonía 345

Kells 379
Keszthely 360
Kiev 751
Kilkenny City 379
Kinderdijk 533-34
Kinsale 385
Kiruna 698-99
Knockmedown
  Mountains 380-81
Knossos 341
Koblenz 256, 285
København see
  Copenhagen
Kocahasanli 742
Köln see Cologne
'Komet' train 34
Konya 743
Koper 646
Korykos 742
Kos 340
Košice 634-35
Köszeg 361
Kraków see Cracow
Kristiansand 543-44
Kuşadasi 741-42
Kyle of Lochalsh 799

L

Lagoa 591
Lagos 591
Land's End 779
Lapland 697-99
  Arvidsjaur 699
  Gällivare 698
  Jokkmokk 699
  Kiruna 698-99
Larissa 321
Latvia (Latvija) 465-70
  railways 466
  Riga 468-70
  Salaspils 470
  Sigulda 470
  tourist information
  466-67

Lausanne 716-18
Leeuwarden 522
Legoland 189
Leiden 592
Leighlinbridge 378
Leipzig 280-82
lesbian and gay
    travellers 83
Lesvos (Lesbos) 338
Letterkenny 394
Leuven 121
Liechtenstein 726-28
  Triesenberg 727
  Vaduz 727
  see also switzerland
'Ligure' train 34
Liguria 416-17
Lille 223-24
Limburg 534
Limerick 386-87
Lisbon (Lisboa) 583-87
Lismore 381
Lithuania (Lietuva)
    473-78
  railways 474-75
  tourist information
    475
  Vilnius 476-78
Liverpool 788-90
Ljubljana 641-44
Llanberis 786-87
Llangollen 787
Locarno 724-25
Lofoten Islands 553
Loire Valley 228-29
Lombardy 407-08
London 765-73
  Visitors' Travel Card
    31, 767-68
Londonderry 801
Lübeck city 287-88
Lucerne (Luzern)
    710-13
Lugano 723-24
Luxembourg 481-89

Bascharage 489
Clervaux 488
Diekirch 488
Echternach 487-88
Esch-sur-Alzette 489
Little Switzerland 488
Mersch 488
railways (CFL) 482-83
tourist information
    483
Trois Vierges 488
Vianden 488-89
Wiltz 489
Lvov 751-52
Lyon 245-46

## M

Maastricht 534
Macedonia 491-96
  Bitola 496
  Ohrid 495-96
  railways 492-93
  Skopje 494-95
  tourist information
    493
  Western 495-96
Machynlleth 787
Madrid 654-59
mail 79
Málaga 679
Malbork 571
Mallaig 799
Malmö 693-94
Mantua (Mantova) 408
Marbella 679-80
Mariazell 92
Marrakech 508-10
Marseille 251-52
Matlock 787
Mecsek Hills 362
medical insurance
    44-45
Medujorde 138-39
Meknes 510-11

Menton 247
Mersch 488
Mersin 742
Messina 459
Mesuga 514
Meteora 321
metric conversions 830
Middelburg 534
Milan (Milano) 408-12
Milos 334
Minsk 627
Miskolc 358
Mohács 361-62
Moldavia 605
Monaco 248
money:
  black market 55
  credit cards 53-54
  currency 54
  Eastern Europe
    exchange 55
  Eurocheques 54-55
  Euros 53
  exchange rate 8
  traveller's cheques 54
Mont St-Michel 226-27
Montenegro 808
Montserrat 668
Morocco 499-514
  Agadir 514
  Asni 514
  carte d'abonnement
    32, 501
  Casablanca (Dar
    Beida) 507-08
  Essaouira 514
  Fez (Fes) 512-13
  Marrakech 508-10
  Meknes 510-11
  Mesuga 514
  Rabat 506-07
  railways (ONCF)
    500-501
  Tangier 504-506
  Tetouan 514

tourist information
501-502
vaccinations 44
Moscow 618-22
mosquitoes 45
Mostar 138
Mull, Isle of 799
Munich (München)
301-08
Murmansk 627
Mycenae 322
Mykonos 333

## N

Nafplion 322
Nagykanizsa 361
Namur 130-31
Nantes 228
Naples (Napoli) 452-57
Naxos 334-35
Nazaré 589-90
Netherlands, The
(Nederland) 517-35
Amsterdam 522-29
Arnhem 534
Breda 534
Friesland 521-22
Gouda 534
Haarlem 534-35
The Hague (Den
Haag) 530-32
Kinderdijk 533-34
Leiden 489-490
Limburg 534
Maastricht 534
Middelburg 534
Northern 521-22
railways (NS) 418-19
Rotterdam 532-34
tourist information
520
Utrecht 534
Wassenaar 529
Zandvoort 535

New Ross 377-78
New Zealand travellers:
passports and visas 43
Nice 247, 249-51
night travel 57-60
Nîmes 254
Nördlingen 310
'Nordpilen' train 34
North Cape
(Nordkapp) 554
Northern Ireland
799-802
Norway 537-54
Alta 554
Bergen 549-551
Bodø 552-53
Central 548-53
Kristiansand 543-44
Lofoten Islands 553
Narvik 553
North Cape
(Nordkapp) 554
Northern 553-54
Oslo 544-48
railways (NSB) 538-40
Sognefjord 548
Southern 542-48
Stavanger 542-43
tourist information
540
Trondhaugen 550
Trondheim 551-52
Nova Gorica 646
Novgorod 627

## O

Oban 799
Óbidos 589
Odense 187-88
Ohrid 495-96
Olomouc 172-73
Olympia 323-24
Oradea 608
Orkney Islands 799

Oslo 544-48
Ostend (Oostende)
120
Oswięcim (Auschwitz)
568
Oulu 212
over-26 passes 26-27
Oxford 779-81

## P

package holiday flights
42
Padua (Padova) 428-29
Paestum 457
Palermo 460
Pamplona 661-62
Paris 229-41
Parma 413
Paros 333-34
passports 42-43
Patras 323
Paxi 344-45
Peak District 787-88
Pécs 362-63
Pembroke 786
pensions 71-72
Penzance 779
Périgueux 255-56
Perugia 441
Piedmont (Piemonte)
405
Pilsen (Plzeň) 166
Pisa 439-40
Plakias 341
planning:
packing 45-50
routes 34-36
Plovdiv 149-50
Plymouth 779
Poland 557-76
Birkenau 568
Cracow (Kraków)
566-69
Częstochowa 568-69

Gdańsk 569-71
Malbork 571
Oswięcim (Auschwitz)
  568
Polrail passes 32, 558
Poznań 573-74
railways (PKP) 558-59
Tatra National Park
  569
Toruń 571-72
tourist information
  559
Warsaw (Warszawa)
  562-66
Wieliczka 568
Wrocław (Breslau)
  574-76
Zakopane 569
politics 56-57
Pompeii 456
Poros 332
Porto 588
Portsmouth 775-76
Portugal 579-92
  The Algarve 590-92
  Coimbra 589
  Costa Prata 589-90
  Estoril 587
  Evora 590
  Faro 591-92
  Lagoa 591
  Lagos 591
  Lisbon (Lisboa)
    583-87
  Nazaré 589-90
  Óbidos 589
  Porto 588
  Queluz 587
  rail passes 33, 580-81
  railways (CP) 580-81
  Régua 588
  Sagres 592
  Sintra 587
  tourist information
    581

Viana do Castelo 588
Potsdam 277
Poznań 573-74
Prague (Praha) 166-72
Provence 253-55
Pskov 627
public holidays 64
Puglia 457-58
Pula 159

## Q

Quedlingburg 294
Queluz 587

## R

Rabat 506-07
Rail Europe 22-23
Ravenna 414
Régua 588
'Rembrandt' train 34
Rennes 227-28
reservations, 69
Rethymnon 341
Rhine Valley 295-98
Rhodes 339-40
Rhondda Heritage Park
  785
Riga 468-70
Riviera (Côte d'Azur)
  247-51
Romania 595-608
  Arad 607-08
  Black Sea coast 606
  Brašov 603-04
  Bucharest (Bucuresťi)
    599-603
  Contanţa 606
  Fağaŗas Mountains
    604
  Humor 605
  Moldavia 605
  Oradea 608
  railways (CFR) 596-97
  Sighişoara 604-05

Snagov 603
Suceava 605
Timišoara 607
tourist information
  597
Transylvania 603-05
Tulcea 606
western 607-08
Rome (Roma) 442-51
'Romulus' train 34
Rothenburg 310
Rotterdam 532-34
Rouen 224-25
Rovaniemi 212
Russia 611-27
  Moscow 618-22
  Murmansk 627
  Novgorod 627
  Pskov 627
  railways 612-14
  St Petersburg 622-26
  tourist information
    614
  visas 614-15
  see also Belarus

## S

Sagres 592
Salamanca 672
Salaspils 470
Salerno 457
Salzburg 104-08
Samarian Gorge
  341-42
Samos 337-38
San Marino 430-31
San Remo 416-17
San Sebastián
  (Donostia) 659-61
Santander 662
Santiago de
  Compostela 662-63
Santorini 335-36
Sarajevo 137-38

Sardinai (Sardegno) 460-62
Sassari 462
Savonlinna 213
ScanRail passes 33, 176-77, 201, 538, 685
Scilly Isles 779
Scotland 791-99
Segovia 670-71
Senior rail passes 34
senior travellers 82-83
Serifos 334
Seville (Sevilla) 676-78
sexual harassment 81-82
shopping 80
Shuttle, Le 37
Sicily 458-60
Siena 437-39
Sifnos 334
Sighișoara 604-05
Sigulda 470
Sikinos 334
Simferopol 754-56
Sintra 587
Siófok 359
Siracusa 459
Sithonia 320
Sitia 342
Skiathos 336
skiing train services 39, 217
Skopelos 337
Skopje 494-95
Skye, Isle of 799
Skyros 337
sleepers 58-59
sleeping bags 47-48
Sligo, County 393
Slovakia 629-35
  Bratislava 632-34
  Košice 634-35
  railways (ŽSR) 630-31
  tourist information 631

Slovenia 637-46
  Bled, Lake 644-45
  Bohinj, Lake 645-46
  Koper 646
  Ljubljana 641-44
  Nova Gorica 646
  railways (SŽ) 638-39
  South-West 646
  tourist information 639
Snagov 603
snow trains 39, 217
Snowdonia National Park 786-87
Sofia 145-49
Sognefjord 548
Sopron 360-61
Sorrento 424
Spain 649-80
  Algeciras 675-76
  Andalusia (Andalucia) 673-78
  Aranjuez 659
  Ávila 670
  Barcelona 664-69
  Burgos 672
  Cádiz 678
  Central 670-71
  Córdoba 674-75
  Costa del Sol 678-80
  Cuenca 672-73
  Explorail passes 31-32, 650
  Granada 673-74
  Jerez da la Frontera 678
  Madrid 654-59
  Málaga 679
  Montserrat 668
  Northern 661-63
  Pamplona 661-62
  railways (RENFE) 650-52
  Salamanca 672
  San Sebastián

  (Donostia) 659-61
  Santander 662
  Santiago de Compostela 662-63
  Segovia 670-71
  Sevilla (Sevilla) 676-78
  Tarragona 668-69
  Toledo 671
  tourist information 652
  Valencia 669-70
  Valladolid 672
  see also Andorra; Gibraltar
Sparta 323
Spetses 332
Split 158
St Malo 228
St Moritz 722-23
St Petersburg 622-26
St Raphael 247
stations 70
  facilities 66-68
Stavanger 542-43
Steiermark 102
Stein am Rhein 710
Stockholm 241-42
Stratford-upon-Avon 781-82
student hostels 74
Sstudent Travel Offices 52
Stuttgart 293-94
Suceava 605
Suomi see Finland
Sweden (Sverige) 683-99
  Drottningholm Palace 693
  Gothenburg (Göteborg) 695-97
  Gotland 694-95
  Lapland 697-99
  Malmö 693-94

railways (SJ) 684-86
Stockholm 688-93
tourist information 686
Uppsala 692-93
Switzerland 701-25
Basel (Basle) 718-19
Berne (Bern) 713-15
Bernese Oberland 715-16
Chur 722
Fribourg 715
Geneva (Genève) 719-22
Grindelwald 716
The Grisons (Graubünden) 722-23
Interlaken 715-16
Lausanne 716-18
Locarno 724-25
Lucerne (Luzern) 710-13
Lugano 723-24
railways (SBB, CFF, FFS) 702-04
St Moritz 722-23
Ticino 723-25
tourist information 705
Zermatt 716
Zürich 707-10
see also Liechtenstein
symbols 63, 67-68
Szeged 357-58
Szentendre 356
Szigetvár 361

**T**

Tallinn 194-96
Tampere 211-12
Tangier 504-06
Taormina 459
Tarragona 668-69

Tatra National Park 569
telegrams 79
telephones 66, 78-79
  international codes 829
Tenby 786
Tetouan 514
Thassos 320
Thessaloniki 318-21
Thira 335-36
Thomastown 379
Ticino 723-72
Tihany 359
time differences 35-36
timetables 62-63
Timişoara 607
Tinos 334
Tipperary, County 380
tipping 80
Tokaj 358
Toledo 671
Torremolinos 679
Toruń 571-72
Toulon 247
tourist information 36, 67
  disabled 85
  offices 825-28
  see also countries
Tours 228-29
trains:
  advantages 16-19
  eating 60-61
  Eurostar 17-18
  hazards 64
  night travel 57-60
  railpasses 19-33
  reservations 69
  splitting 61
  supplements 61-62
'Transalpin' train 34
Transdanubia 360-61
Transylvania 603-05
travel grants 53
traveller's cheques 54

travelling alone 81-82
travelling with children 82
Trento 407
Trier 300-301
Triesenberg 727
Trois Vierges 488
Troldhaugen 550
Trondheim 551-52
Tübingen 292
Tulcea 606
Tullow 378
Turin (Torino) 405-406
Turkey (Türkíiye) 731-45
  Aegean Coast 741-42
  Ankara 734-44
  Bergama Pergamon 742
  Bodrum Halicarnassus 742
  Bursa 740
  Çanakkale 741
  Central Anatolia 742-43
  Cyprus northern 742
  Eastern 745
  Ephesus 741-42
  Istanbul 735-40
  Konya 743
  Kuşadasi 741-42
  Mediterranean Coast 742
  Mersin 742
  North-West 740-41
  railways (TCDD) 732-33
  tourist information 733
  vaccinations 44
  Van 745
Turku (Åbo) 209-211
Tuscany 431-40

## U

Ukraine 747-56
  The Crimea 754-56
  health 44
  Kiev 751
  Lvov 751-52
  Odessa 752-54
  railways 748
  Simferopol 754-56
  tourist information 748
  visas 748-49
  Yalta 754-56
  see also Russia
Umbria 440-42
under-26 passes 25-26
United Kingdom
  759-802
  Bath 776-77
  Brighton 775
  Cambridge 782-84
  Canterbury 774
  Cardiff 784
  Chichester 774
  Cornwall 779
  Devon 778-79
  Dover 774
  Edinburgh 791-96
  Exeter 778
  Glasgow 796-98
  Highlands 798
  London 765-73
  Londonderry 801
  Northern Ireland 799-
    802
  Oxford 779-781
  POeak district 787-88
  Penzance 779
  Plymouth 779
  Portsmouth 775-76
  railways 760-62
  Salisbury 776
  Scotland 791-99
  Stratford-upon-Avon
    781-82
  tourist information
    762
  Wales 784-87
  Winchester 774-75
  York 790-91
Uppsala 692-93
Utrecht 534

## V

vaccinations 44
Vaduz 727
Valencia 669-70
Valladolid 672
valuables 47, 50
Van 745
Varna 150-51
vegetarian food 77
Veliako Tarnovo 150
Veneto 419
Venice 419-26
Ventimiglia 416
Verona 426-28
Versailles 240
Viana do Castelo 588
Vianden 488-89
Vienna (Wien) 94-102
Villeneuve-Loubet-sur-
  Mer 247
Vilnius 476-78
visas 42-43
  Russia 614-15
  Ukraine 748-49
  Yugoslavia 806
Visegrad 357
vocabulary 831-32
voice mail 79

## W

Wales 784-87
Warsaw (Warszawa)
  562-66
Wassenaar 529
Wasteels Travel 22
water, drinking 45

Morocco 503
  Russia 622
Waterford 381-82
Westport 392-93
wheelchairs 84
Weimar 282-83
Wernigerode 294
Wexford 378
Wick 799
Wieliczka 568
Wien see Vienna
Wiltz 489
Winchester 701
women travelling alone
  80-81
World Health
  Certificates 44-45
Wrocław (Breslau)
  574-76
Würzburg 310-11

## Y

Yalta 754-56
YMCA Interpoints
  74-75
York 790-91
youth hostels 805-08
Youth Hostel
  Association (YHA) 34
Yugoslavia 805-808
  Bar 808
  Belgrade 807-808
  Montenegro 808
  railways (JZ) 806
  visas 806

## Z

Zaandam 522
Zagreb 156-58
Zakinthos 345
Zakopane 569
Zandvoort 535
Zermatt 716
Zürich 707-10